Essentials of

Abnormal Psychology

Second Edition

Benjamin Kleinmuntz

University of Illinois at Chicago Circle

HARPER & ROW, PUBLISHERS
SAN FRANCISCO

Cambridge   London
Hagerstown   Mexico City
New York   São Paulo
Philadelphia   Sydney

1817

Sponsoring Editor: Bhagan Narine
Project Editor: Carol Pritchard-Martinez
Production Coordinator: Marian Hartsough
Designer: Victoria Philp
Photo Researchers: Roberta Spieckerman,
                          Audrey Ross, and
                          Myra Schachne
Cover Designer: Dare Porter
Compositor: York Graphic Services, Inc.
Printer & Binder: Halliday Lithograph
Body and Display Typeface: Palatino

Essentials of Abnormal Psychology, Second Edition

Library of Congress Cataloging
   in Publication Data

Kleinmuntz, Benjamin.
   Essentials of abnormal psychology.

   Includes bibliographical references and indexes.
   1. Psychology, Pathological.   2. Psychotherapy.
I. Gambill, Lionel, joint author.   II. Title.
RC454.K58   1980   157   79-21540
ISBN 0-06-043711-1

Photocredits

p. xiv Burk Uzzle, © 1970 Magnum
   37   Barbara Runnette
   74   © Peeter Vilms, Jeroboam, Inc.
  105   Culver
  106   *Middle* Culver
  112   Hugh Rogers, Monkmeyer
  126   Cary Wolinsky, Stock, Boston
  132   Frank Siteman, Stock, Boston
  184   *left* © Peeter Vilms, Jeroboam, Inc.
  184   *right* Owen Franken, Stock, Boston
  191   Frank Siteman, Stock, Boston
  203   Charles Gateword, Stock, Boston
  204   © Greg Gaar/Icon
  224   © Karen R. Preuss, Jeroboam, Inc.
  229   National Institute of Mental Health/Nilo Olin, TSB
  231   *left* Michael E. Bry, Sausalito
  231   *right* © Hap Stewart, Jeroboam, Inc.
  238   Keystone Press Agency
  249   Larry Burrows, TIME-LIFE Picture Agency. © Time, Inc.
  250   © Eileen Christelow, Jeroboam, Inc.
  258   Alinari/Editorial Photocolor Archives
  259   Alinari/Editorial Photocolor Archives
  264   WTOP-TV Eyewitness News, a United Press International Photo.
  320   © Robert Foothorap, Jeroboam, Inc.
  321   Associated Press Laser Photos, Wide World Photo Agency
  352   Associated Press Photo, Wide World Photo Agency
  358   Keystone Press Agency
  375   GNUM Photo Library, N.Y./Lyon
  426   Anna Kaufman Moon, Stock, Boston
  433   Frank Siteman, Stock, Boston
  437   © Karen R. Preuss, Jeroboam, Inc.
  439   Cary Wolinsky, Stock, Boston
  450   © Ed Buryn, Jeroboam, Inc.
  507   Lester Sloan, Newsweek
  511   Courtesy of A. Bandura
  512   Lew Merrim, Monkmeyer
  538   Reproduced by permission of the University Museum, University of Pennsylvania
  540   Alinari/Editorial Photocolor Archives
  542   The New York Public Library Picture Collection
  543   *upper* The Bettman Archive
  544   The New York Public Library Picture Collection
  545   The Bettman Archive
  564   Courtesy National Institute of Health, Jerry Hecht photo
  565   © Michelle Vignes/ICON

In dedicating this edition of the book to the memory of my parents and oldest brother, I am acknowledging a debt of gratitude to three loving souls who took a keen and curious interest in the strange writing activities of the baby in the family.

To

Nathan Kleinmuntz (1892–1978)

Anna Kleinmuntz (1896–1978)

and my big brother
Julius Kleinmuntz (1920–1979)

Contents

Preface

This revision of an already successful book grew out of the same fascination with the subject that motivated me to write the original. That book has had a widespread and enthusiastic audience, and one of the gratifications of authorship has been to hear from teachers and students eager to make communication a two-way process. They have been generous with their suggestions, objections, and criticisms, and they will find themselves well represented in these pages. Our treatment of the subject is much the stronger for their contributions.

Many of the differences between this and the earlier edition reflect changes in the subject itself. Rapid progress has been made in the last six years in several areas of empirical investigation— for example, origins of aggression, causes of depression, etiology of schizophrenia, and intended and side effects of psychoactive substances—and we have incorporated much of the new information and many of the new concepts throughout the book. Another important change is the new classification proposed in the forthcoming third edition of the *Diagnostic and Statistical Manual of Mental Disorders* (DSM III). Classification continues to be a lively issue among clinicians, and we have in many instances included both the DSM-II and DSM-III categories, as well as arguments on all sides of the debate, on the theory that the differences of opinion that help make abnormal psychology exciting for us also interest and involve the students who use this book.

This edition contains two completely new chapters, one on Aggression and Violence and one on Mental Retardation. New material has also been added on behavioral assessment, observational learning, biofeedback, aging, sexual dysfunctions, sex therapy, and disorders associated with brain damage. The discussion of divergent sexual patterns has been updated to reflect changing concepts and new information. Even more material than in the First Edition is drawn from related disciplines, especially anthropology, linguistics, and neuropsychology. Coverage of the therapies has been expanded, and each of the four major models governing treatment methods is now discussed in a separate chapter.

Other changes—subtle in some instances, obvious in others—have emerged from a deepening or expansion of interests expressed in the First Edition. Some of these interests are of a type commonly called "philosophical"; that is, they are concerns over how individual scientists see their work and their subject matter and what they do with their data. Such concerns underlie the effort throughout Chapter 2 to call the reader's attention to the nature of the often hidden assumptions and premises behind any attempt to call someone's behavior abnormal, and our effort to point out elsewhere that to assess, label, or change another person's behavior is a political act.

They also underlie the attention paid herein to the role of society in disordered behavior and to the ways in which anxiety, stress, and alienation are related to living in a highly technological society. One of the goals has been to present the study of abnormal behavior, not as a *fait accompli,* but as an ongoing, often turbulent, and incomplete process attended by varying degrees of insight and blindness, nonsense and brilliance. We have tried not to skip over or gloss over any of that give-and-take, on the theory that a scientific textbook ought to help sensitize its readers to the differences between good and bad work in science.

For whatever success I have had in communicating my excitement for the subject matter and

in strengthening the book, I am indebted to the many reviewers retained by the publishers. In particular, I would like to thank Richard Leavy of St. Mary's College, and Alan Glaros and R. Douglas Whitman of Wayne State University for their input on this revision. In addition, the creative writing and rewriting talents of Lionel Gambill were especially important in shaping the new manuscript, and I thank him for his invaluable and sensitive assistance.

Benjamin Kleinmuntz

Essentials of

Abnormal Psychology

1 The Nature of Psychopathology

1. What Is Abnormal Psychology and Why Is It Interesting?

2. Defining Abnormality

Ways of Seeing Abnormality Normality and abnormality are elusive concepts. Deciding whether a person's behavior in a given situation is abnormal may involve serious philosophical, practical, semantic, ethical, and, in many cases, political issues. We believe it would be a mistake for anyone to attempt to diagnose or treat psychopathology without an awareness of those issues. We therefore begin our study by attempting, in Chapter 1, to examine the larger context in which abnormal psychology exists. Then, in Chapter 2, we confront and hopefully clarify some of the more important issues.

3. Classification

4. Psychodiagnosis

Labels and Categories In any science observed data must be organized in a meaningful way, not only to make it easier for us to understand the relationships between events, but also to make the collection of data more systematic. In Chapter 3 we discuss the system (and its revision) cur-

rently used to classify abnormal behavior. The obvious logical next step is to apply the classification system to individual cases. That process is called psychodiagnosis, and we shall discuss it in Chapter 4.

5. Biological Determinants of Behavior Disorders

6. Motivational and Sociocultural Determinants of Behavior Disorders

Causes of Behavior Disorders Western science usually assumes a cause-and-effect relationship between events and therefore invests much of its energy in asking why. When psychologists studying abnormal behavior ask why, they are inquiring into what they call *etiology*—a term borrowed from medicine. It is also a convention of Western science to treat biological facts as if they were separate, or different, from psychological ones. Without implying any endorsement of mind–body dualism, we have adopted that scheme for convenience. We shall discuss biological determinants of behavior disorders in Chapter 5; motivational and sociocultural determinants in Chapter 6.

1 What Is Abnormal Psychology and Why Is It Interesting?

Abnormal psychology seeks to describe the how and the why of people's unusual reactions—how some people break with reality, how communication fails, how violence erupts, why individual needs sometimes collide with social demands or cultural taboos, how sexual expression and enjoyment become blocked, and how we keep ourselves from getting what we want.

Despite some popular misconceptions, abnormal behavior is not limited to the strange actions of an unbalanced few. We have all seen it in others, and we have all, to some degree, experienced it in ourselves. Anxiety and depression are common experiences, although psychotic depression is not so common. Similarly, self-defeating or self-destructive behavior is widespread, although the results are catastrophic only for relatively few. Even hallucinations are part of each person's life, in the form of dreams, which are not only universal but perhaps even necessary. Part of the fascination of abnormal psychology is that many of the unusual reactions it studies are the responses many of us make to the problems of daily living.

Thus the answer to the second question of our chapter title is, in part, that abnormal behavior is often unusual and yet not always so odd that people cannot relate it to their own lives. In studying abnormal psychology, we shall often be looking at the unexpected, the offbeat, the behavior that betrays the presence of something other than the humdrum and the routine. Sometimes that behavior is funny; sometimes it is

tragic. A great deal of human suffering falls within the scope of our subject. Furthermore, like events on a stage, much of abnormal behavior is heightened—"bigger than life"—so it is not surprising that psychopathology is a popular subject for plays and films, or that psychotherapy sometimes borrows from the theater, as it has in such enactment techniques as psychodrama and the role-plays of Gestalt therapy.

But this is only one side of abnormal behavior. Much of it is really commonplace—habits or blocks that keep us stuck, replaying a losing game, or shrinking from the risks, real or imaginary, of going after what we want, or reacting to people in ways that stop communication instead of encouraging it. Yet this behavior too is interesting, not only because examining it gives us new insights into material so familiar we seldom notice it, but also because we are looking at behavior that can make the difference between a satisfying and an empty life.

Preliminary Definitions

What determines whether behavior is normal or abnormal? To attempt a serious and useful answer to that question, one has to look at changing values, perceptions, and insights. Society is changing, norms are changing, and scientific models are changing. Some people sum it up as a change in consciousness. In Chapter 2 we shall examine the problems and pitfalls of defining abnormality. We shall also try to show why it is not possible to spell out a set of basic principles of abnormal psychology on which all psychologists agree. In the meantime we shall try to give some tentative, working definitions.

Deviance and Pathology

Deviance and *abnormality* are statistical concepts in that they both refer to departures from the average or norm. *Pathology*, on the other hand, refers to a harmful or undesirable departure. All departures from the norm, including nonpathological ones, are properly called deviant or abnormal. For example, a person may be unusually intelligent, and hence abnormal relative to the general population, but that high intelligence is not considered pathological.

The term pathology, which comes from medicine, refers to any undesirable modification of function or change for the worse in the structure of an organ or body system. The modification need not be *quantitatively* deviant; that is, the change does not necessarily imply the presence of a greater or lesser amount of something. It could be a *qualitative* change in the sense that some factor is present—for example, blood in cerebral spinal fluid—that in itself is pathological, probably signifying hemorrhaging in a portion of the central nervous system.

Our use of these terms does, however, reflect the prevalent practice of referring to them interchangeably. We follow this procedure as a matter of convenience.

We note also that many people tend to place negative value judgments on behavior labeled deviant or abnormal. Psychologists have repeatedly tried to find neutral, nonjudgmental language, but each new term has acted like a euphemism: it has eventually taken on the connotations of the word it replaced. "Mentally ill" was a term coined to try to humanize treatment but, like "sick," it is no longer neutral. To be effective, new approaches will have to reach beyond language.

We shall define psychopathology tentatively as any behavior of a person that is detrimental to that person's health, growth, or functioning.

Behavior

Behavior is any response made by an individual. The responses of greatest interest to psychopathology include such everyday observable acts as walking, talking, playing, laughing, and blushing; such physiological measures as brain waves, heartbeat, blood pressure, and pulse; and such inferred states as feelings, drives, and emotions, as well as conscious and unconscious processes.

These are the raw data of the clinician, although some are more readily available than others: it is easier to observe someone's gaits and gestures than it is to obtain an account of how that person feels at any given time. This does not mean, however, that the behavior pathologist should forego collecting data about drive and feeling states; rather, it suggests a need for greater ingenuity in observing and interpreting certain human responses. In some instances, clinicians may even have to create conditions in which they can exercise control over the unfolding of the behavior in question; where they cannot manipulate these conditions, they must measure as many potentially influencing surrounding variables as possible (see Chapter 4).

Some psychologists (Watson, 1913) have insisted that the definition of behavior be limited to what can be objectively observed and measured. Thus thoughts, sensations, feelings, consciousness, and all other "mental" events would be excluded. Since Watson, many psychologists have tended toward a less rigid and more inclusive definition, and they have also tended increasingly to think of "mental" events as quite tangible phenomena that sometimes *can* be observed by a skillful scientist and can even, in a sense, be measured (for example, with electroencephalographs and polygraphs).

Fact and Fiction About Mental Illness

Fiction	*Fact*
Abnormal people are very different, and therefore attract immediate attention to themselves.	With occasional exceptions, the mentally ill are indistinguishable from the rest of us. In many respects also there is no sharp dividing line between abnormal and normal individuals; rather there is a continuum of behaviors, the maladaptive manifestations of the mentally ill being more extreme, less appropriate, and less adaptive exaggerations of normal reactions.
Mental illness is untreatable.	This misinformation follows logically from the idea that anomalous behavior is qualitatively different from normal. While it is true that in many instances only partial recovery is attained, progress in treatment methods generally has increased the likelihood of remission considerably from what it was in the 1940s, 1950s, and 1960s (Brill, 1966).
Mental health can be preserved by avoiding morbid thoughts.	Self-help books often stress this "power of positive thinking" approach to mental health. This approach overlooks the fact that many personality disorders are a consequence of a life-long pattern of faulty learning. Furthermore, much mental illness may be the *result* of repressing, denying, or in some other way avoiding unacceptable thoughts, feelings, wishes, fantasies, or fears. Although there may be some value in positive programming (use of hypnosis, imaging, or repeated affirmations to encourage a positive self-image and positive expectations), attempts to hide, cover up, or banish unwanted content from one's consciousness are a form of lying to oneself and therefore more likely to perpetuate than to cure behavior pathology.
Mental illness is transmitted genetically.	The facts on this matter are far from conclusive. The evidence gathered to date does indicate that hereditary factors may predispose persons to some disorders, especially among the psychoses; although the actual illness may be precipitated by environmental stress. Many more disorders are traceable, however, to nongenetic sources.

Fact and Fiction About Mental Illness, *Continued*

Fiction	*Fact*
Masturbation causes insanity.	In terms of any statistical criterion of abnormality, masturbation is normal; however, guilt and anxiety are often associated with the act as a result of cultural conditioning.
When people are recovering from a mental illness, it is best not to discuss the treatments they had.	There is nothing more disconcerting to former mental patients than to be ignored or, perhaps even worse, to be treated as an oddity. One should show the same concern and use the same discretion in inquiring about their experience and present condition as one would with a person who is recovering from physical illness.
Therapists explain the origin of the patient's troubles; and once the patient understands this, he or she recovers.	This is not true. In more cases than they might care to admit, specialists do not know the origin of the problem. But even if they did, simply explaining them may not be helpful since more than just an intellectual grasp of one's problems is generally needed. Emotional understanding and acceptance are every bit as essential. In some cases it is equally important to try to change habits and behavior.
Many hospitalized patients try to commit suicide.	The problem of suicide prevention is a serious one with many depressed persons, as well as with drug and alcohol addicts. But only a negligible group of other mentally ill patients threaten or attempt to kill themselves.
Mental health specialists try to teach self-control to their patients.	This implies that psychologists teach and that patients need emotional control in order to become well. Psychotherapy does not consist of lessons in the ordinary sense; rather it is a restructuring of habits and coping mechanisms. Furthermore emotional self-control is neither a symptom nor a cure for recovery of mental health because overcontrol is as common in behavior pathology as loss of self-control.

Is "Mental Illness" a Disease?

For some time contemporary psychologists have been debating the issue of whether behavioral deviations are an illness in the sense that we consider a physical disorder as a disease, or whether they are merely disturbances in interpersonal competence. George Albee (1969), former president of the American Psychological Association and a longtime critic of the "sickness" or "disease" model of mental illness, addresses himself to this question in a paper in which he examines this model and concludes that its application permits mental-health experts to diagnose an individual as sick even though he is functioning well as a member of society. Consequently Albee proposes an alternative model that emphasizes the importance of social-developmental explanations. This model, in turn, carries important implications for the nature of institutions to be developed for behavior change and for the kind of manpower used to deliver care. Specifically with the social-developmental model state hospitals and public clinics would be replaced by social intervention centers largely staffed by less highly trained and more available specialists than psychologists and psychiatrists.

In sharp contrast to Albee's position, David Ausubel (1961) holds that personality disorder is a disease. After examining several propositions in favor of discarding the concept of mental illness, he concluded that, among other reasons, there is no inherent contradiction in regarding mental symptoms as *both* expressions of problems of living *and* manifestations of illness. Along the way to his conclusion he pointed out that a symptom need not necessarily reflect a physical lesion in order to qualify as a manifestation of disease and that it is both unnecessary and potentially dangerous to discard the concept of mental illness just so that clinical psychology can escape from the professional domination of psychiatry.

Experience

While Watson was defining psychology as the science of behavior, Husserl (1913) was attempting to define it as a science of *experience*. Experience is whatever is impinging on a person's consciousness moment by moment. These words, as you read them, are part of your experience at this moment. The concepts of behavior and experience overlap to some extent, but some psychologists prefer to keep both terms, on the grounds that two behaviors that may appear identical to an observer can involve totally different feelings, motives, meanings, and values for the person being observed.

Incidence and Prevalence of Behavior Pathology

How widespread is behavior pathology? The lack of agreement among psychologists about what constitutes abnormality makes any broad, general answer to this question virtually impossible. Furthermore we cannot dismiss that lack of agreement as mere "semantics." Most of us know individuals who would be considered "well adjusted" by some behaviorists and "alienated" by some humanists, as well as individuals who would be considered "self-actualized" by some humanists and "poorly adjusted" by some behaviorists. Similar disagreements could be found between psychoanalysts and behaviorists and between psychoanalysts and humanists, but the word "some" should qualify each assertion.

Despite these limitations some rough but meaningful estimates are possible. Mortality statistics are available for deaths associated with alcoholism and drug addiction, as well as for suicides. Data are also available on the number of people treated for psychological problems in mental hospitals and by psychotherapists in private practice, by private physicians, and by industrial dispensaries. From this information it is possible, for disorders whose diagnosis is reasonably well standardized, to determine the *treated incidence* rate and the *treated prevalence* rate. The treated incidence rate is usually given as the number of *new cases* of a specific disorder per 1000 population recorded during a given year. The treated prevalence rate is usually the number of *cases under treatment* per 1000 population during a given year.

In most parts of the world variations in diagnostic, record-keeping, and case-finding practices make it difficult to obtain reliable incidence and prevalence data. An outstanding exception to this rule is Monroe County, New York, which maintains a psychiatric case register in which all patient-care episodes are recorded. Using information on schizophrenia from that register, combined with U.S. census data and expected population changes, Morton Kramer (1976), former Director of Biometry and Epidemiology of the National Institute of Mental Health's Alcohol, Drug Abuse, and Mental Health Administration, estimated the incidence and prevalence of schizophrenia for the United States in 1970 and computed projected estimates of the incidence and prevalence of schizophrenia in the United States for 1985.

For 1970 the psychiatric case register for Monroe County showed a treated incidence rate of 0.72 (485 new cases) and a treated prevalence rate of 4.78 (3319 cases). The probability of a person born in 1970 "experiencing during his lifetime at least one admission to a psychiatric facility with a diagnosis of schizophrenia" was 6.92 percent.

On the basis of actual 1970 and estimated 1985 census data for the United States, Kramer obtained the following estimates:

1970 treated incidence of schizophrenia
147,139 new cases

1970 treated prevalence of schizophrenia
974,972 cases

1985 treated incidence of schizophrenia
185,649 new cases

1985 treated prevalence of schizophrenia
1,247,806 cases

The percent increase in the incidence of schizophrenia exceeds the percent increase in the population because the ages in which the incidence of schizophrenia is highest are also the ages in which the expected increase in population is highest (15–24, 25–34, and 35–44 years). Schizophrenia is, of course, only one behavior disorder. Furthermore, the true incidence and prevalence rates are almost certainly higher than the treated rates. A similar relationship holds for mortality rates and the true prevalence of the disorders involved. According to the National Center for Health Statistics, mortality data for 1974 included the following:

25,683 deaths due to suicide

1,174 deaths due to drug dependence

18,900 deaths due to alcoholism

Abnormal Psychology and Other Disciplines

Abnormal psychology is the branch of psychology that studies behavior variously defined as deviant, pathological, maladaptive, unfulfilling, self-destructive, self-defeating, or unhealthy. It draws heavily on the resources of several other branches of psychology, as well as several disciplines outside psychology that also study human behavior.

Psychology

From other branches of psychology, abnormal psychology obtains some of the following kinds of information.

Psychology of Perception. Sensory deprivation experiments provide information about *illusions* and *hallucinations*, two phenomena prominent in some disorders (see Chapter 12).

Comparative Psychology. Experiments by Harlow and his associates (Harlow, 1959; 1962; Harlow et al., 1971; Harlow and Zimmerman, 1959), showing that monkeys deprived of contact with a mother grow up abnormally, suggest some possible explanations for similar abnormalities in humans (see Chapter 6).

Developmental Psychology. Some insight into aggressive behavior can be gained from such studies as a survey of child rearing practices and attitudes of more than three hundred mothers (Sears et al., 1957). These researchers noted that punishing aggression in a child produced hostility that eventually led to an outbreak of aggression at some other time and place (see Chapter 17, and Mussen et al., 1979).

Social Psychology. Some light is shed by social psychologists on the role of social and cultural factors in diminishing or precipitating abnormal behavior. See, for example, the discussion in Chapter 17 of the famous Milgram study of obedience to authority (1963), in which subjects, under instructions from the experimenter, repeatedly pressed a button they believed was delivering a painful and dangerous shock to another subject.

Cultural Anthropology

Psychology and cultural anthropology are complementary sciences. Whereas psychology studies the behavior of people in one culture, cultural anthropology uses field study and the comparative method to examine the many forms culture takes. It studies the different mores, folkways, and cosmologies that form the context for individual behavior. Insights gained from anthropology can serve as a check against the tendency to treat culturally learned behavior as if it were universal or biologically determined. For example, Freud believed that all children go through a *latency* period beginning at age 5 or 6 and ending with the onset of puberty, and that their sexual feelings and interests are diminished during that period. But anthropological studies of children in the Trobriand Islands (Malinowski, 1955) showed that children there have no latency period; hence we can infer that the latency period as Freud described it is a product of culture, and not of biology.

In a similar vein, much of what is ordinarily taken for granted because it is everywhere in one's own culture may be meaningless in another culture. Anthropologist Dorothy Lee (1959) explains, for example, that in the Lovedu culture of South Africa in the 1930s the individual was perceived as "unique, noncomparable, nonmeasurable. . . . There was no average against which an individual was assessed, no competitive standard of success. . . . Compensation, reward, payment, punishment, as we know them, were absent in this culture." All of the features Lee cites as absent in the Lovedu culture seem so central to ours that it is hard to imagine what kind of interaction takes place among Lovedu people. Western societies, especially ours, tend to treat competition, reward, and punishment as if they were basic elements in human life. Not only do we need a new set of basic premises to examine the Lovedu; we are forced to recognize that even in this country it *might* be possible for people to grow up and function in society without ever being rewarded, punished, or placed in a competitive situation.

Sociology

Sociology, the study of groups and institutions, also contributes to the understanding of abnormal behavior. A prime interest of sociology is the structure of the family unit as the matrix within which behavior pathology occurs. Its other areas of focus include the role of urbanization in the development of psychopathology and the roles of social isolation and disorganization in the development of behavior disorders. Sociologists have made a particularly important contribution here by demonstrating in several studies that the incidence of serious mental disorder is greater among lower than among upper socioeconomic groups. We shall have more to say about these interrelationships later in the book (Chapters 6 and 12).

Genetics

Work in the field of genetics, particularly behavior genetics, has thrown new light on the relative importance of heredity in transmitting psychological traits from one generation to the next. Most relevant among the early studies in this field have been those on selective breeding, of which Robert C. Tryon's study (1942) is a good illustration. Tryon selected 142 rats "tested" for intelligence by being run in a complex maze and subsequently divided them into "bright" and "dull" groups on the basis of errors made during these tests. By inbreeding generations of "brights" with "brights" and "dulls" with "dulls," he showed that after eight generations separate colonies of "bright" and "dull" rats had been bred. Clearly, his study indicates that heredity and "maze brightness" are interrelated and that, at least in rats, such psychological traits can be transmitted genetically.

More recently, extensive "twin studies" have shown that principles of genetic transmission can be applied to the inheritance of behavioral disorders. Especially suggestive have been early studies by Kallmann (1946, 1953, 1956, 1959) and

more recent studies by Gottesman and Shields (1972) demonstrating that a schizophrenic person's identical twin is more likely to be similarly disturbed than his or her other relatives, close or distant. Similar findings were also reported in more recent studies by Rosenthal (1970). In general, many of these studies show that the incidence of this disorder is higher among close than among distant relatives, but as we indicate in Chapter 12, definitive conclusions on this matter are not yet possible.

Mathematics and Statistics

From mathematics and statistics, behavior pathologists have borrowed the language of measurement. This language permits precise descriptions of traits and their interrelationships and suggests elegant methodology for the design of experiments. The vocabulary of numbers also permits more subtle determinations of events than such terms as "large," "small," "very," or "slightly."

Biology and Medicine

Biology and medicine, which touch on many topics in behavior pathology, since human beings are biological organisms, deal with humans-as-animals. The psychophysiological disorders (Chapter 8) illustrate the intersection of abnormal behavior with biology. Investigation into such disorders as ulcers, asthma, genitourinary disorders, and vascular changes requires familiarity with such subspecialties of biology and medicine as neuroanatomy, biochemistry, and physiology.

Mental Health Professionals

Most of the professionals who provide mental health services (therapy in particular) are either psychiatrists, clinical psychologists, or psychiatric social workers.

Psychiatrists are physicians whose specialized training has been in a mental hygiene setting. Their training consists of medical school, including one year of internship in general medicine, followed by a three-year residency in psychiatry. They are then eligible to practice psychiatry. Psychiatrists are the only therapists legally permitted to prescribe drugs and to use physical treatment methods such as electroshock and psychosurgery.

Clinical psychologists hold a Ph.D. in psychology and have specialized in courses in diagnosing and treating abnormality. Like others taking graduate degrees in psychology, clinical psychologists are exposed to the core courses in psychology; but in addition, they take courses in psychopathology, psychodynamics, and psychotherapy. Clinical psychologists also spend two or three years in applied internship activities in mental health settings. In this regard their training is similar to that of the psychiatrist. The clinical psychologist is especially well trained in psychological testing, research methodology, and statistical design, and thus has greater expertise in conducting research than the psychiatrist or the psychiatric social worker.

Psychiatric social workers take a master's degree in social work and are thoroughly trained in assessing the patient's social adjustment. Their prime responsibilities are to obtain the social history from the patient and the patient's relatives, investigate home conditions, and advise the patient on difficulties encountered in the home or community. Like the other mental health professionals, psychiatric social workers were trained in a mental health setting and conduct individual and group psychotherapy.

Other personnel concerned with mental illness include *psychiatric nurses*, who are registered nurses with additional training in psychology and psychiatry, *psychiatric aides*, who help care for patients in the hospital; and *community mental health workers*, who are given special field training to provide health and welfare services primarily for the disadvantaged. The latter workers include people drawn from groups inhabiting the particular locales and neighborhoods where community mental health centers have been established. In Chapter 25 we will have more to say about the settings in which they help.

Summary

Abnormal psychology is the study of people's unusual and self-defeating reactions. Deciding what constitutes normal behavior is a difficult problem complicated by changes in cultural values and scientific concepts and by divergent views of the proper relationships between the individual and society.

Behavior pathology is widespread in the United States, and at least one disorder, schizophrenia, is likely to increase as the bulge in population growth moves into the age range in which its incidence is greatest.

Besides drawing its basic concepts and methods from its parent science, general psychology, abnormal psychology applies information and ideas from other disciplines, such as anthropology, sociology, behavior genetics, and biology.

Mental health professionals are usually either psychiatrists, clinical psychologists, or psychiatric social workers.

Terms and Concepts to Master

Abnormality

Behavior

Behavior pathology

Clinical psychologist

Deviance

Experience

Incidence

Pathology

Prevalence

Psychiatric social worker

Psychiatrist

Psychotherapy

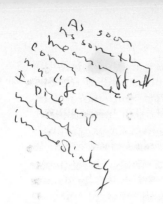

As soon as something commanding [?] in life [?] dries up immediately in me [?]

2 Defining Abnormality

On what basis do we call behavior abnormal? In the past both laypeople and clinicians have often tended to define abnormality in terms of deviation from some supposedly normal standard of behavior. Unfortunately, such standards generally rest on unquestioned and—usually—unexamined assumptions. In this chapter we shall question some of those assumptions.

Changing Attitudes Toward "Normality"

Calling behavior pathological because it differs from a "normal" standard of behavior gets us into several logical difficulties. Two of these difficulties (we shall consider others later in this chapter) are as follows:

1. We must then believe either (a) that this "normal" behavior is the only "sane" or "healthy" or "adaptive" behavior *in some absolute sense* for all humans in all cultures at all times, or (b) that there are many "normal" standards of behavior and that the only "sane" or "healthy" or "adaptive" behavior is conformity to whatever is usual among most of the people one is in contact with at a given time. Thus, for example, conformity to standard X would be pathological in culture Y.

2. Since the standards chosen are inevitably social or statistical norms, trying to use those standards to distinguish normal from abnormal behavior puts us in the position of pretending that our culture is homogeneous and unchanging when in fact it is heterogeneous and changing rapidly.

Not only is our culture becoming more changeable and diverse, "normality" as an ideal is no longer as revered as it once was, either by behavioral scientists or by people in general. In fact, it has acquired something of a bad name, and this in itself puts it on shaky ground as a criterion. We shall begin our exploration of the problem of defining abnormality by looking at some of the trends of recent years that have undermined the traditional notion of normality.

Alienation

By definition the traditional concept of normality identifies health with societal norms. But what if behavior pathology were identified with those norms? What if the socialization process—the process by which a child learns to be a member of his or her society—were the point at which the individual acquires maladaptive patterns of behavior? In essence this is what many existentialist philosophers are saying. In their view the corporate state and the corporate society function in ways that are incompatible with a belief in the uniqueness and worth of the individual. They argue that the socialization process, instead of helping children expand their awareness, numbs that awareness, hypnotizes them, and stifles their authenticity. The result is individuals who are dehumanized and alienated—alienated from

to our

[handwritten margin notes: "David— Alienated from me! I felt alienated yourself, who you from me. I weren't understanding David— don't lose yourself="]

their bodies, from their feelings, from nature, and from other human beings. The existentialist viewpoint is argued eloquently by Scottish psychiatrist R. D. Laing, who tells us (1967, p. 28):

> The condition of alienation, of being asleep, of being unconscious, of being out of one's mind, is the condition of the normal man.
>
> Society highly values its normal men. It educates children to lose themselves and to become absurd, and thus to be normal.
>
> Normal men have killed perhaps 100,000,000 of their fellow normal men in the last fifty years.

Jules Henry, an anthropologist and psychiatrist, says that society has met our survival needs at a high cost to us (1963, p. 12):

> from this primitive necessity has emerged the central problem of the human species, the fact that inner needs have scarcely been considered. . . . the orientation of man toward survival, to the exclusion of other considerations, has made society a grim place to live in, and for the most part human society has been a place where, though man has survived physically he has died emotionally.
>
> This is another reason why, although culture is "for" man, it is also "against" him.

[handwritten: "survival"]

[handwritten: "if its such an instinct — then why has it become such a central problem?"]

Relativity of Perception *[handwritten: problem]*

One of the most difficult ideas for most people to grasp is that perception is influenced by learning. Intuitively, I may be convinced that I am simply describing my sensations when I say that I am looking at a bookcase that contains several telephone directories, some textbooks, and an assortment of paperbacks. But what if I had never seen a bookcase, or a phone directory, or a book of any kind? Obviously, I have learned to assign certain meanings to what I see. And for all practical purposes, the assignment of meaning and the sensory input are simultaneous. Linguist Benjamin Lee Whorf contended that even our way of perceiving time and space is controlled by as-

sumptions about reality that are built into our native language. This viewpoint, called the Linguistic Relativity Hypothesis (or, more commonly, the Whorfian Hypothesis), holds that our grammar, for example, reflects our culture's model of reality and conditions us to see nature in terms of that model. Thus a person whose native language does not require that verbs have subjects has no trouble believing that events can happen without being done by some person or agent. In contrast, our grammar forces us to invent an agent, as in the statement, "It is raining." How reliably can we observe abnormality if the cultural values by which we judge abnormality also control the observation process?

Consensus Nature of Reality

Some people believe that "reality" is a consensus reality, that we allow ourselves to see what is defined by common consent as being there. According to this view, the socialization process conditions us to see some events and to block out others (for example, hallucinations or auras around people). Anthropologist Carlos Castaneda (1972, 1973a & b, 1974, 1978) has presented that viewpoint in his popular Don Juan books, in which he claims that under instruction from a Yaqui Indian sorcerer he was able to experience a different reality (by being socialized within a different consensus). We can, of course, dismiss Castaneda's adventures as either fiction or hallucination, but events that contradict our present models are well documented. For example, the feet of firewalkers in Sri Lanka show no signs of burns after a walk across a bed of coals whose temperature, measured with an optical pyrometer, is 1328°F, a temperature higher than the melting point of aluminum (Grosvenor and Grosvenor, 1966). To the uncritical believer this is magic, and to the uncritical skeptic it is trickery. But a more likely explanation is simply that it is a part of reality that present models do not take into account. Other "paranormal" or seemingly paranormal phenomena have been recorded. The lesson for anyone attempting a definition of abnormality is that neither normality nor reality is quite as clearcut as it seems.

Limiting Effects of Scientific Models

Models guide thought and observation in science just as they do in everyday life. In fact the scientist's main task is to find out how well a model fits observable events, and when the fit is not good enough, to formulate a model that has a better fit. When the Ptolemaic model of the solar system was formulated, it fit well enough to guide observation until the methods of observation were refined to the point at which the data no longer fit. The model then was reformulated in a more complex and cumbersome way to improve the fit. At some point the simpler, more elegant Copernican model became irresistible. But the crucial period was that interval during which the Ptolemaic model was coming apart at the seams. It still guided the observations of most scientists and *prevented* many of them from recognizing or even seeing the data that did not fit. In the eyes of those scientists the Copernican model was unscientific rubbish. But to Galileo, who was already interested in the Copernican model, the events that failed to fit the Ptolemaic model were glaring and obvious.

Science historian T. S. Kuhn has written extensively about the role of scientific models in a fascinating book called *The Structure of Scientific Revolutions* (1970). Kuhn believes that scientific models (or paradigms, to use his term) make research possible by making observation selective: we only study what the model points to. He also believes that models at first *prevent* us from seeing what he calls the anomalies—anomalies are the events that do not fit the model—and that this process continues until the anomaly has forced so many adjustments to the model that scientists are compelled to notice its existence.

Kuhn draws an analogy to a psychological experiment (Bruner and Postman, 1949) that tested people's ability to detect anomalous playing cards, such as a red six of spades and a black four of hearts, when the entire deck of cards was flashed, one after another, for fixed time intervals. As long as the exposure time was brief, subjects correctly identified all the normal cards but also identified the anomalous ones as normal. (The red six of spades was identified simply as a six of spades.) Increasing the exposure time resulted in increasing hesitation and confusion, as well as comments that there was something wrong with the card, until the anomaly was recognized. But some subjects could not adjust their categories enough to identify the anomalies, even when the exposure time was increased.

Kuhn's work is rich in implications: How we perceive reality (in this case, normality) is largely a function of a set of tacit assumptions embodied in our models of reality. By their nature, those models prevent us from seeing the world whole—or, in the case of anomalies, seeing it accurately. We should therefore be especially wary of taking any concept of normality (or reality) as an absolute.

Some Possible Criteria of Abnormality

Determining whether a certain pattern of behavior is normal or abnormal remains a necessary and important part of our responses to people who need help. Without it we have no way to decide who will be treated, what treatment will be used, or whether hospitalization is necessary; we could not even select a homogeneous study sample. Both research and therapy would be stalled.

We have already outlined the ways in which rapid social change increases the need for caution in defining abnormality. As we examine the various criteria of abnormality, we shall see that even in a stable and homogeneous society the definition of abnormality would be a complex task with uncertain results.

Two Examples of Scientific Anomaly

A major obstacle to understanding the nature of scientific revolutions is that once a revolution has occurred, the anomalies that contributed to it are no longer seen as anomalies. Kuhn (1970) points out that after a scientific revolution "the anomalous has become the expected." For example, it is difficult today to understand why Galileo's contemporaries so rigidly refused to look through his telescope at the moons of Jupiter. We can guess, however, that the phenomenon of a planet having planets was so totally weird in the context of their picture of reality (the Ptolemaic model) that it must have seemed like black magic. Today we have a model that treats such phenomena as normal, and we view them as if they had always been normal.

Several phenomena that are still anomalies in the context of our own models have been studied in recent years by physicists Russell Targ and Harold Puthoff, at Stanford Research Institute. We shall describe two of these phenomena, which involve modes of communication that are unconventional and, as yet, unexplained. Targ and Puthoff believe explanations are possible that are not wholly inconsistent with modern physics.

In the earlier experiment (Targ and Puthoff, 1974) a subject (the receiver) was asked to guess whether another person (the sender) was being visually stimulated with 10-second bursts of strobe light. Each session consisted of twelve trials of either no stimulus, a 6-flash-per-second burst, or a 16-flash-per-second burst, in a sequence determined by entries in a random-number table. The subject was seated in a visually opaque, acoustically and electrically shielded double-walled steel room, the sender in another room 7 meters away.

Subjects' conscious guesses were no better than chance. The anomaly is what appeared on the subjects' EEG (electroencephalogram) traces recorded during the trials:

The receiver's alpha activity (9–11 Hz) showed a significant reduction in average power (−24 percent, $p < 0.04$) and peak power (−28 percent, $p < 0.03$) during 16-Hz flash stimuli as compared with periods of no-flash stimulus.

Averaged EEG traces from one subject for the three conditions are shown below:

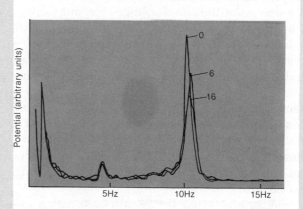

Occipital EEG spectra, O 20 Hz, for one subject (H.H.) acting as receiver, showing amplitude changes in the 9 H Hz band as a function of strobe frequency. Three cases: 0, 6, and 16 f.p.s. (12 trial averages).

The later series of experiments (Puthoff and Targ, 1976) investigated various subjects' "remote viewing" ability—their ability to describe what was being seen by an experimenter in a remote location unknown to the subject. During each session one experimenter remained in the laboratory with the subject while the other experimenter obtained randomly selected travel orders and drove to the chosen site. While the remote experimenter was at the site, the subject made drawings of what he or she believed the remote experimenter was seeing and taped a description of the site. The tape and drawings were locked in a safe before the remote experimenter's return. All three then drove to the site. (This was considered a learning situation, and immediate feedback was therefore considered desirable.)

The sites and the subjects' responses were later blind-matched, first by an SRI research analyst and later by a panel of five additional SRI scientists; none of the judges was associated with the project. Chance would be expected to produce five correct matches in the first series; 24 correct matches were obtained. Each subsequent series yielded similar results.

Even more anomalous results emerged from a series of four trials testing one subject's ability to describe the site before it had been selected. The protocol was as follows: at 10:00 a.m. the outbound experimenter would leave with a package of ten sealed envelopes obtained from a larger pool randomized daily and not in the experimenters' possession. He would drive continuously in the local area until 10:30 and then use a random number generator to generate a digit from 0 to 9. He would count down that number of envelopes, open the one selected, and drive to the site named therein, remaining there from 10:45 to 11:00. He then returned to the laboratory, showing the travel orders to a security guard on his arrival.

Meanwhile, at 10:10 the subject would begin to describe the remote location, completing her description by 10:25, five minutes before the remote experimenter opened the sealed envelope. All four descriptions were blind-matched without error by three judges. A photograph of one of the sites and a portion of the corresponding description are reproduced below:

Subject saw a ''black iron triangle that Hal had somehow walked into'' and heard a ''squeak, squeak, about once a second.''

Source: Targ, R., and Puthoff, H. Information transmission under conditions of sensory shielding. *Nature,* 1974, 252, 602–607. Puthoff, H., and Targ, R. A perceptual channel for information transfer over kilometer distances: historical perspective and recent research. *Proceedings of the Institute of Electrical and Electronic Engineers,* 1976, 64, 329–354.

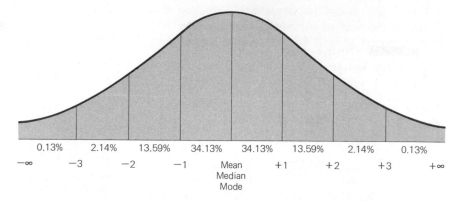

Figure 2.1
The normal curve of probability and some of its statistical properties.

| 0.13% | 2.14% | 13.59% | 34.13% | 34.13% | 13.59% | 2.14% | 0.13% |

| $-\infty$ | -3 | -2 | -1 | Mean Median Mode | $+1$ | $+2$ | $+3$ | $+\infty$ |

Statistical Criteria

Normality, in statistical terms, is what is usual or average. Abnormality, by this definition, is whatever falls outside the usual or average. This definition has a certain appeal since it requires no value judgments about behavior. To establish whether a characteristic is normal or abnormal, the psychologist simply counts cases, stipulates the normal range, and classifies accordingly.

The only assumption necessary for this definition is that the behavior in question distribute itself symmetrically along the familiar *normal*, or bell-shaped, curve (Figure 2.1).

Most biological and psychological traits—height, intelligence, speed of finger tapping, emotional reactivity—distribute themselves normally in the general population. The number of people who vary from the average decreases as we move away from the middle of the curve.

The real advantage of using the normal curve is that its mathematical properties are well known. Especially important for the behavior pathologist are the following considerations.

1. The middle of the distribution is marked by the measure of central tendency, which is called the *arithmetic mean* or *average*. In a perfectly symmetrical distribution this value is equivalent to other measures of centrality, the median (middle score of the distribution) and mode (most frequent score).

2. The shape of the curve changes from convex to concave at the points ± 1 ("plus or minus one") *standard deviation* from the mean. The standard deviation is a measure of variability indicating departures from the mean.

3. Approximately 68 percent of the scores fall within ± 1 standard deviation from the mean; that is, most scores are within one standard deviation left (low score) or right (high score) of the mean. The farther the score from the mean, the smaller the number of individuals having that score.

These properties of the symmetrical curve, especially the areas that define proportions of cases falling within their bounds, permit all sorts of descriptions of normally distributed data because these proportions apply to *all* normal curves.

Suppose, for example, we had a personality test designed to provide an index of a person's self-image: the higher the score, the more positive the self-image. If your score were 115 and the mean score for a large group of people were 100 with a standard deviation of 15, then your score would be $+1$ standard deviation from the mean.

If we add the number of scores that fall between -3 and $+1$ standard deviations, we see that about 84 percent of the scores were lower than 115. A score of 150 ($+2$ standard deviations) would be higher than about 97 percent of the scores.

If we want to define abnormality in terms of this distribution of scores, we simply draw arbitrary cutoff points, say at ± 2 standard deviations, and call all persons abnormal whose scores do not fall within these bounds. Anyone with a score of less than 70 or greater than 130 would be abnormal.

Using statistical criteria of abnormality has several drawbacks. First, the statistical definition lacks content and simply characterizes individuals in relation to a point on a continuum. For example, it equates high incidence in a population with normality. But suppose a population had a high incidence of head-banging, sadism, or sexual problems. Would these behaviors therefore be normal? This is a thorny issue. One could argue that such behaviors would have to be defined as desirable within the frame of reference of that population's values. But then genocide would have to be defined as desirable in terms of Nazi Germany's values. Furthermore, a culture's concept of *desirable* behavior does not always match *actual* behavior in that society. We shall argue, therefore, that some behaviors are *not* normal even when they have a high incidence.

How would this affect our hypothetical self-image index? A person scoring very high would, by the statistical criterion, be abnormal. Yet the idea of having an abnormally positive self-image is meaningless, like having abnormally good sense or abnormally pleasing orgasms.

Statistical criteria, therefore, should not remain content-free, and anyone applying them should be concerned not only with what is usual but also with what is desirable. A similar point is made by Buss (1966), who points out that statistical interpretations of abnormality are often *unidirectional* (average and high IQs are considered

normal, while below average IQs are considered abnormal or subnormal); at other times they are *bidirectional* (for example, low and high blood pressures are abnormal), thus creating confusion about the application of statistical criteria.

Another drawback of statistical criteria is that lines on a continuum are drawn arbitrarily, and persons falling on one side are then called normal while the others are called abnormal.

Still another drawback is that shifts in definitions due to changing times, different cultural standards, or even variations in the law from one locale to the next are not taken into account by arbitrarily drawn cutoffs.

Cultural or Social Criteria

Abnormality cannot be judged outside the societal context because it is within it that standards of behavioral normality are defined: how one should behave in school or church, when to cry and when to laugh, what to wear on various occasions, what behavior is appropriate under which circumstances. In short, society prescribes certain standards of normality, and one is judged abnormal to the degree that he or she is unable or unwilling to adhere to these standards.

One disadvantage of cultural norms is that society's prescriptions may be faulty or undesirable. The Nazi culture preached racial supremacy and followed a deliberate plan of genocide. Did conformity to that cultural norm constitute normality? Similarly, in many criminal subcultures, it is the nonconformist rather than the conformist whose behavior is the more desirable.

A second disadvantage is that for certain groups, whose history and experience have been radically different from those of the majority, the application of cultural norms is inappropriate. For example, black people in America have found it necessary for their own survival to develop a profound distrust of whites and of their country. To protect themselves from serious physical and psychological injury, they have had to develop

Price M. Cobbs, coauthor of Black Rage.

(Courtesy Price M. Cobbs)

what some black psychiatrists have aptly called *cultural paranoia* (Grier and Cobbs, 1968). This form of distrust has become the *black norm* of appropriate behavior within a hostile environment. Thus, as Grier and Cobbs point out, this cultural paranoia is "no more pathological than the compulsive manner in which a diver checks his equipment before a dive or a pilot his parachute" (p. 178).

Black psychiatrist Frantz Fanon (1967, p. 17) has observed that "the black man has two dimensions. One with his fellows, the other with the white man." The effects of these dimensions have been observed in a psychological testing situation where it was shown that blacks control their hostile feelings toward white testers, and it was argued that this inhibition may contribute to an impairment of their performance (Katz et al., 1964).

One of the common pitfalls encountered in the use of cultural criteria is *ethnocentrism*, the fallacy of treating a culturally induced pattern of behavior as if it were a universal, or biologically determined pattern, reflecting some law of nature. Sex mores are an obvious example of the kind of cultural norm that often disguises itself as a biological fact. Another example, one that has drawn increasing attention in recent years, is sex-role typing. Psychologist Sandra Bem has investigated the effects of what she calls "America's sex-role ideology," and her conclusions raise further doubts about the usefulness of judging abnormality by cultural criteria (Bem, 1971). For example, she describes a study (Broverman et al., 1970) in which 79 clinically trained psychologists, psychiatrists, and social workers (many of whom were women) regarded a woman as "healthier and more mature if she is more submissive, less independent, less adventurous, more easily influenced, less aggressive, less competitive, more excitable in minor crises, more susceptible to hurt feelings, more conceited about her appearance, less objective, and more antagonistic toward math and science." These same terms were used by the same clinicians to describe an "unhealthy, immature man or an unhealthy, immature adult (sex unspecified)."

Applying these cultural criteria, we could only call a woman a normal woman if we called her an abnormal person. One of the values of this study is that it shows the double bind a woman is caught in: fear of failure is matched by fear of success, since to succeed as a person is to fail as a woman.

Another study (Bem, 1975a) suggests that androgynous (not strongly sex-typed) individuals of both sexes are better able to adapt their behav-

"...adjustment" was for a long time ...dered a criterion of mental health, ...t only among clinicians, but also among educators. Chancellor Robert Maynard Hutchins (1977) of the University of Chicago had this to say on the subject in his farewell address to the students, February 2, 1951:

The whole doctrine that we must adjust ourselves to our environment, which I take to be the prevailing doctrine of American education, seems to me radically erroneous. Our mission here on earth is to change our environment, not to adjust ourselves to it. If we become maladjusted in the process, so much the worse for the environment.

...ior to the needs of the situation, whereas strongly sex-typed individuals persist in their sex-typed behavior even when it is inappropriate to the task. Again the application of cultural criteria would put the clinician in a bind: if strong sex-typing is called normal, then competence and flexibility in these tasks must be called abnormal.

Cultural definitions of abnormality present another problem, as anthropologist Anthony F. C. Wallace (1969, p. 83) points out:

There is no question that any social attitude which interprets a given behavior or experience as symptomatic of a generalized incompetence is a powerful creator of shame, and thus anxiety, in those who experience or behave in the "symptomatic" way. One may expect, then, that whenever a culture defines a given item of behavior as a symptom of general incompetence, the individual so behaving will suffer from shame, which elicits anxiety. This anxiety will further tend to decrease his competence, thus precipitating a reciprocal interaction between "incompetent" behaviors and anxiety.

In other words, a social stigma is associated with cultural definitions of abnormality that creates the very same anxiety and abnormality that it labels; that is, it becomes a self-fulfilling prophecy. We return to this topic in Chapter 3, where we consider some of the criticisms directed at classifying behavioral abnormalities.

Personal Distress

Most people diagnosed as abnormal by clinicians are also hurting subjectively. They generally experience interpersonal problems, many physical aches and pains—insomnia, nausea, loss of appetite, headaches, and sometimes paralysis—and such emotional symptoms as fear of failure, worry, hypochondria, depression, and agitation.

This criterion is useful only to the extent that people are aware of their distress and are able to express it. Unfortunately, the most severely disordered individuals are the least likely to express subjective pain. The euphoric psychotic patient and the schizophrenic with tenuous reality contact are classic examples, but most of us have known people who were obviously hurting but who stoutly denied that anything was wrong.

Legal Criteria

Forensic or legal definitions of abnormality are by far the most unsatisfactory. From a legal standpoint a defendant is judged *insane* if the defendant's reasoning can be shown in a court of law to have been so impaired as to prevent the defendant's knowing what he/she was doing or distinguishing between right and wrong.

This definition has its roots in the McNaghten murder trial in England in 1843. Daniel McNaghten committed a murder because he was told what to do by the "voice of God." At the trial McNaghten was acquitted by reason of insanity in that he suffered "such a defective reason . . . as not to know the nature and quality of the act that he was doing or if he did know it that he did not know he was doing what was wrong."

In some parts of the United States, *irresistible impulse* is accepted as a criterion of legal insanity. This definition holds a person responsible for his or her actions only if that person was free to behave in some other way at the time of the offense. Thus if a man finds his wife and another man embracing and, in a fit of jealous rage, kills his wife or her lover, he can be acquitted on the grounds that his self-control was impaired and he gave in to an irresistible impulse.

In 1954 the United States Court of Appeals, in the case of *Durham v. The United States*, ruled that an accused is not criminally responsible for an act if it was the product of "mental disease or mental defect." A later elaboration of this ruling includes a statement indicating that an act is the product of disorder if it would not have occurred except for the disease or defect.

The irresistible impulse and mental disease rulings were a vast improvement over the McNaghten rule in that they introduced concepts of behavior pathology into the judicial system. Nevertheless, application of these criteria still depends too heavily on legal descriptions of abnormality.

Another drawback of using forensic criteria is that mental health specialists, when called upon to testify in legal cases, are required to judge whether the accused was suffering from behavior pathology *at the time* of the commission of the crime. In this regard, one psychologist commented as follows (Maher, 1966, p. 212):

> *This involves inferring a patient's clinical condition in the past from evidence . . . in his behavior now. Even where two or more clinicians might agree that the patient is now behaving pathologically, there is still latitude for them to differ about his presumed condition at the time of the crime.*

Miscellaneous Criteria

Society also uses several other standards for judging abnormality. Some of these focus on the unusualness of the behavior in question, and others are related to the research needs of mental health professionals.

Bizarreness. Reactions that show extreme deviations from recognized norms are called bizarre. This term, usually reserved to describe the more unusual, outlandish, or irrational behavior of some mentally ill persons, is essentially an application of the statistical criterion and includes the grimacing and grotesque gestures and actions of some patients as they react to their delusions, illusions, and hallucinations. These behaviors are easily identified and are seen only in severely disturbed individuals.

Inability to Cope. Most people pride themselves on their ability to manage their own affairs and to cope with the complexities of contemporary living. Although the community-at-large tolerates minor inabilities to manage or cope, it prescribes custodial care for members it considers "incompetent," assigns them guardians, or commits them to mental hospitals.

Researchers' Definitions. In an early article on definitions of mental illness frequently used by researchers in selecting study samples, some of the following criteria of abnormality were listed (Scott, 1958):

1. Exposure to psychiatric treatment
2. Social maladjustment
3. Psychiatric diagnosis
4. Objective testing

Among these the most frequently used definition of mental illness is *exposure to psychiatric treatment*. In terms of it, one is considered abnormal simply because one receives psychiatric care. This definition, however, is inadequate, for it excludes many people who, for one reason or another, are potentially diagnosable as abnormal but are not seen by mental health professionals. Moreover, as Szasz (1960) has shown in his classic treatise "The Myth of Mental Illness," people are often committed to mental hospitals, and hence receive psychiatric care, for the convenience of society rather than because of an inherent illness. Another objection is the circular reasoning involved: a person is treated because of being abnormal and is abnormal because of having been treated.

The second research criterion, *social maladjustment*, requires that we judge an individual normal or abnormal on the basis of social consensus. Although this may be a more adequate criterion than exposure to treatment, its shortcoming is that there is considerable disagreement among various segments of the public about what constitutes good or poor adjustment.

Psychiatric diagnosis as a criterion of abnormality has several flaws; we shall mention three. First, mental health specialists do not always agree on diagnoses. Second, as with psychiatric treatment, only a limited number of persons from among the sick population are diagnosed. Third, although professionals decide who is to be hospitalized, the individual's family and community decide who is to be diagnosed. In this sense, psychiatric diagnosis shares the shortcomings of the previous two criteria of abnormality.

The last research definition of abnormality, *objective testing*, is open to many of the same criticisms: answers to test items, and their scoring, reflect conformity to society's norms and mirror the test constructor's ideas of normal behavior. Furthermore, testing also depends on reaching a potentially diagnosable population that may not choose to make itself available.

Psychological Health as a Yardstick for Gauging Illness

Because treating sickness has been one of the chief uses for psychological insights, psychologists have often had little to say about health, except by implication. Some clinicians have complained that this emphasis on sickness has given us a distorted picture of human nature and prevented us from seeing the whole person. A few of these clinicians (Jahoda, 1958; Maslow, 1970; Shoben, 1957) have tried to complete the picture by studying and defining healthy behavior. The absence of such a definition, they felt, had too often led people to assume that health is merely the absence of sickness or of symptoms and to regard every unique response as a sign of pathological deviation.

The late Abraham H. Maslow attempted, during his later years, to describe such a "psychology of health" (1968). While not rejecting what he called the usual Freudian picture, Maslow felt that Freud had supplied only the "sick half" of psychology. He believed that the "healthy half" would offer people more possibilities for improving their lives, an approach he thought would be more fruitful than asking "how to get *unsick*."

Maslow rejected cultural criteria of abnormality on the grounds that the culture could be evil and destructive. He also criticized the use of popularity and adjustment as criteria of normality (1968, pp. 7–8):

Perhaps it is better for a youngster to be unpopular with the neighboring snobs or with the local country club set. Adjusted to what? To a bad culture? To a dominating parent? What shall we think of a well-adjusted slave? A well-adjusted prisoner?

Maslow believed that people could be creative even in their everyday activities, but conceded that few are, and felt that those who do actualize their potential "are often treated badly by their fellows." He also believed that most people in our society are *not* psychologically healthy, and that "personality problems" do not necessarily imply sickness (1968, p. 8):

Personality problems may sometimes be loud protests against the crushing of one's psychological bones, of one's true inner nature. What is sick then is not to protest while this crime is being committed. And I am sorry to report my impression that most people do not protest under such treatment. They take it and pay years later, in neurotic and psychosomatic symptoms of various kinds.

Maslow's statement describes part of the humanistic model. Compare it with the view of a psychologist who considers self-actualization an elitist concept, an ideal out of the reach of most (Buss, 1966, p. 3):

If it is a requirement of mental health, then very few persons are mentally healthy. Most segments of society lead a routine life, hemmed in by the petty details and drudgery of everyday existence. Realizing one's potential requires . . . the motivation and means to break out of . . . the habits and trivial demands of day-to-day living. Few people possess these attributes . . . yet the majority who do not . . . are not maladjusted.

Maslow and Buss quite obviously do not see the same meanings in the events they observe, nor do they describe those events in the same language. It would be fair to say that the majority Buss sees as "not maladjusted" is seen as not

psychologically healthy by Maslow and as "alienated" by Laing (see p. 12). The belief that people who grow up in a modern industrial society are likely to be alienated from themselves and from nature seems to follow from the humanistic model, but psychologists operating out of a different perceptual framework do not see it that way. This is an example of models in conflict, or "paradigm clash," as Kuhn calls it. Such conflicts, as part of the scientific process, are both necessary and healthy.

Critical Comment

Each of the foregoing ways of defining abnormality has advantages and disadvantages. Statistical and cultural criteria have the appearance of scientific rigor because they make it possible to compare an individual against easily defined norms. Unfortunately, that rigor is more apparent than real. In the first place these criteria require the use of discrete categories to describe a continuum. The cutoff points must therefore be located arbitrarily, and that arbitrariness is easily forgotten. What happens then is that the discreteness of the categories, which is only an abstraction, is treated *as if* it existed in nature, which it does not. This is the fallacy of reification, or regarding something abstract as real.

In the second place cultural norms and prescriptions for normal behavior vary from time to time and from place to place, even within one culture. Consequently, behavior that might be viewed as seriously disordered at one time and place may be viewed as part of the normal range of variation at another time and place. In a changing world the ground may be shifting so rapidly that the behavioral scientist is constantly trying to compare an individual to an already outdated norm.

Finally, with the exception of cultural anthropologists, most behavioral scientists have grown up in the culture within which they do research (or in a similar one). Their perceptions are not likely to be totally free of the influence of those same cultural norms.

Personal distress as a criterion of abnormality has the advantage of focusing on the individual's subjective experience. Seemingly, the individual is in a better position than anyone else to know whether he or she is hurting. Unfortunately, as we pointed out earlier, the more seriously people are disturbed, the less likely they are to recognize that condition and seek help. Furthermore, some people are unable to communicate their distress. An autistic child who has not learned to talk is not likely to communicate distress but nevertheless needs help immediately.

Legal criteria are the least satisfactory. They depend heavily on the correct interpretation of terms foreign to mental health specialists. Their usefulness, even in court, can be questioned, and they are virtually meaningless elsewhere.

Bizarre behavior is one of the most extreme reactions to personal distress and hence can only be used as a criterion in a small percentage of cases. Failure to cope is also a relatively unusual reaction. Many sorely troubled people do not show bizarre behavior and do not fail to cope. These criteria may reflect society's unwillingness to tolerate unusualness or incompetence.

Exposure to psychiatric treatment, social maladjustment, psychiatric diagnosis, and objective testing are unsatisfactory criteria because they rely too heavily on societal prescriptions.

Defining abnormality as a failure to actualize one's potential gets us out of the trap of being forced, almost by default, to call the emotionally flat person healthy. (This is, however, a matter of degree, and emotional flatness is traditionally viewed as a symptom of abnormality.) It also allows for a broader spectrum of normality and a more exciting view of therapy. Its primary disadvantage is that it calls for a radical departure from many of our traditional ways of thinking. Many people feel helpless to actualize their potential; they are not likely to do so without first undergoing some drastic change of consciousness, or "deconditioning." Even the concept of self-actualization may seem inaccessible to those who are not ready to believe they have a health-seeking inner nature to fulfill.

Clearly no existing criterion of abnormality is adequate in itself. An eclectic approach, combining two or more criteria, may sometimes have to do, but not all possible combinations are workable. For example, cultural and self-actualization criteria may collide. In actual practice a clinician generally applies different concepts of abnormality in different circumstances. Sometimes these concepts are compatible with each other; sometimes they are not. Until psychology acquires a generally accepted model, many clinicians will have to rely on a combination of training and intuition. When that model *is* finally articulated, many of its elements will already be understood implicitly by some clinicians.

What does this lack of certainty mean in terms of research and treatment? One of the common misconceptions about science is that it is a stronghold of certainty. Actually even the so-called hard sciences do quite well with a great deal less than absolute certainty. Anyone familiar with the current state of theoretical physics can attest to that fact; physicists deal with a great deal of uncertainty but are not greatly handicapped in solving puzzles or in providing the kind of knowledge that nourishes technology.

Certainly, abnormal psychology is not as exact as the physical or natural sciences, and may never be. Its subject matter is people, and people are difficult to study. Aside from the difficulty of doing controlled laboratory experiments with human subjects, any attempt by one person to study another is bound to be influenced by what has been aptly called their "shared humanity" (Kaplan, 1964).

Does this mean that behavior pathologists can say nothing with a measure of confidence? We hope not. But it does mean they cannot exercise the degree of control possible in some other sciences. They may not always be able to predict or control the behavior of an individual human. (Neither, apparently, can a physicist predict the behavior of an individual atom.) Nevertheless, their training and experience with people enhance the precision of their observations and temper their biases.

In view of the drawbacks of the criteria discussed in this chapter, we shall continue to define psychopathology as any behavior of a person that is detrimental to that person's health, growth, or functioning.

Summary

Traditional definitions of abnormality as deviation from a presumed normal standard of behavior are based on social values. Those values are not being taken for granted to the extent they once were, and even the idea of scientific objectivity has given way to a recognition that what science sees is largely a function of scientific models, which always fail to fit some of the phenomena that might be observed.

Statistical criteria of abnormality, as long as they are content-free, treat deviation in either direction as undesirable, but some unusual behavior, such as extremely high intelligence, is desirable. Cultural criteria are subject to the criticism that a culture may have undesirable norms, as the Nazi culture did. Personal distress may be a useful criterion when a person's problems are mild, but those who are most troubled are least aware that they are troubled. Psychological health as a standard (instead of normality) avoids the tendency to make mediocrity the ideal, but requires a change in perception that may be beyond many people. For these reasons we continue to define abnormal behavior as behavior that interferes with one's health, growth, or functioning.

Terms and Concepts to Master

Alienation	Irresistible impulse
Androgyny	McNaghten rule
Anomaly	Model
Black norm	Normal curve
Cultural paranoia	Psychological health
Ethnocentrism	Sex-role typing

3 Classification

Classification—the systematic ordering of objects, events, and organisms into categories—serves an important scientific function, for it arranges information according to a scheme of resemblances and relationships. The members of a class need resemble one another only with respect to the common quality, dimension, or purpose on which the categorization is based. Animals, featherless bipeds, odd numbers, and nonferrous metals are all examples of classes.

The nomenclature, or label, given a class is its identifier, a useful aid to communication. The best-known classification system is the one used in biology, developed by Carolus Linnaeus, an eighteenth-century Swedish naturalist. Linnaeus identified each organism according to its kingdom, phylum, class, order, family, genus, and species.

Taxonomic systems (systems of classification) encourage setting up categories in which mere membership renders highly probable the possession of attributes other than those defined by the class; for example, any member of the class of objects defined by the properties of high strength, susceptibility to corrosion, and capacity to be strongly magnetized can also be assumed to be a conductor of electricity and will probably have other properties of iron and steel (Wilson, 1952). In psychopathology as well, classification according to behavior symptoms carries important implications. For example, we can assume that individuals diagnosed as schizophrenic will manifest certain thinking and emotional disturb- ances, will display other symptoms of psychosis that further differentiate them from neurotics, and will benefit from special treatments appropriate to their disorder. In other words, classification, or nosology, has predictive value.

Classification of abnormal behavior dates back to the Greek physician Hippocrates, who categorized mental diseases according to three classes: *phrenesis*, or frenzy; *mania*, or uncontrolled activity; and *melancholia*, or sadness. He also recognized cases that would correspond to present-day diagnosis of *phobia, hypochondriasis, hysteria,* and the *obsessive–compulsive disorders.* Since the time of Hippocrates many categorization schemes have been created in the attempt to gain additional understanding of mental disease.[1]

The Current System

Contemporary psychiatric nomenclature has its roots, at least in part, in the works of German psychiatrist Emil Kraepelin (1855–1926), who studied thousands of case histories of mental illness in arriving at his categories (Kraepelin, 1926). Kraepelin attributed every disorder to one of four origins, none of which included the possi-

---

[1] Excellent reviews of these classification systems can be found in Menninger's *The Vital Balance* (1963), Eron's *The Classification of Behavior Disorders* (1966), and Zilboorg and Henry's *A History of Medical Psychology* (1941).

bility of psychological causation: metabolic disturbances, endocrine difficulties, brain disease, or heredity. Although Kraepelin assumed that the outcome of behavior pathology was predeter-

mined—that is, patients either naturally recover or inevitably deteriorate—his categories were so comprehensive that, with minor modifications, they remain the basis for the current and forth-

---

The Scientific Method at Work

Science is distinguishable from common sense mainly by method. While both scientists and their lay counterparts begin by observing selecting parts of their subject, seeking its description (what it is like) and explanation (why it is the way it is), only the scientists are duty-bound to reject authority as a basis for truth and are compelled to repeat and test their own and others' findings in a carefully constructed experiment. Here is an example of the distinction as it might occur in testing the therapeutic effectiveness of the drug, Panacea, among hospitalized and mentally distressed patients.

One could proceed to test the drug's effectiveness by consulting authoritative sources, by careful observation of one or more distressed patients before and after they received Panacea, or by way of experiment. Scientists do not necessarily reject the first two options but, compared to their lay counterparts, they would certainly also resort to the experiment.

In the experiment they would first take observations of the behaviors of a specially selected group of target patients. These observations would be made on carefully constructed rating scales that permit quantification of the findings. They would then assign patients to an *experimental* group that is given the drug and a *control group*, similar to or *matched* with the experimental group in most respects (sex, educational level, age, length of hospitalization, severity of mental distress), that is given a *placebo* (an innocuous substance indistinguishable from the one being tested). The placebo group serves as a control in that the experimenter must now demonstrate that the drug Panacea results in greater improvement than treatment with the placebo. Of course neither the experimenter nor the patients must know who is receiving what. This is known as the "double-blind" design and controls for the possibility that scientists may communicate, albeit unwillingly and subtly, to the patient the results that they think should occur. It also controls for the possibility that the patients, if they knew whether they were receiving the placebo or the real thing, might behave accordingly.

Over a period of time, perhaps two or three weeks or longer, the scientist and assistants would record the behavioral changes of the patients, if any. Then, after allowing some time for a follow-up period, they would analyze their rating-scale results to determine whether the experimental group's mental distress improved significantly over that of the control group. If there were improvement only in the experimental group, then the drug may have treatment possibilities. If both groups' behavior improved, then the change may be due to the suggestion that is induced by receiving drug treatment. Occasionally a third matched control group is used—one that receives neither the drug nor the placebo—to rule out the effects on behavior of drug administration. Finally, regardless of the outcome of this experiment, scientists would replicate this study in order to learn whether their findings occurred by chance.

coming official classification systems of the American Psychiatric Association.

This classification scheme, the complete version of which can be found in the *Diagnostic and Statistical Manual of Mental Disorders* (or DSM II, APA, 1968; and DSM III, APA, 1980), is based on the medical illness model (more commonly called the *medical model*). Individuals display behavioral *symptoms*, such as depression or delusions of persecution; these symptoms cluster in a pattern to form *syndromes*, or *diseases*, and anyone exhibiting a syndrome or disease is placed in a diagnostic category; these categories are presented in Table 3.1.

Presumably this psychodiagnosis carries implications about *etiology* (origins), *treatment*, and *prognosis* (course and probable outcome). Unfortunately, the state of present knowledge in behavior pathology does not always permit comprehensive statements about cause or probable outcome, nor do the diagnostic labels necessarily indicate different treatments. As suggested below, these are among the reasons for criticism of classification and formal diagnosis in abnormal psychology.

Criticisms of Diagnostic Classification

Classification in behavior pathology has been criticized on grounds of artificiality, uselessness, unreliability, and misdirectedness. Most of the critics have rejected it for these reasons.

Artificiality, Reification, Self-fulfilling Prophecy

Several critics have objected to present psychiatric categories and labels on the grounds that (a) such abstractions often correspond poorly with the actual experience of individual patients; that (b) clinicians are led by such diagnoses to make assumptions—especially certain medical-model assumptions—that alter their perceptions of, and their behavior toward, individual patients

in counterproductive ways; and that (c) as a consequence the patients themselves tend to act out the part in which they have been cast and thereby appear to confirm the clinician's expectations. We shall briefly summarize the arguments of three of these critics.

Thomas Szasz, a psychiatrist who over the years has been among the most articulate critics of the medical model of behavior pathology, and whom we have already encountered, says about psychiatric categories (1966, pp. 125–127):

However, if we create categories, rather than discover them, how can we be certain that we have got the right things in the right classes?

. . . All discussion of the problem of classification in psychiatry rests on the fundamental premise: that there exists in nature abnormal mental conditions or forms of behavior, that it is scientifically worthwhile and morally meritorious to place persons suffering from these conditions, or displaying such behavior, into appropriately named categories.

And, once so categorized, according to Szasz (1970), the person is publicly stigmatized as dangerous and psychotic and treated differently from healthy people.

Erving Goffman, a sociologist, worked for a year as an assistant physical therapist in a large mental hospital. That experience formed the basis for a book (Goffman, 1961) in which he took issue with some of the prevailing ideas about the mentally ill. Like Szasz, Goffman saw a self-fulfilling prophecy at work, in this case through the assignment of troublesome patients to "bad" wards. Such patients were often not allowed to have recreational equipment, and at night even their clothes might be taken away. In such an impoverished environment the patient had few devices for expressing hostility against the institution:

And the more inadequate this equipment is to convey rejection of the hospital, the more the act

Table 3.1
Partial List of Disorders (DSM III Draft)

Organic Mental
  Senile and Presenile
  Substance-Induced
Drug Use
  Alcohol
  Barbiturate
  Amphetamine
  Hallucinogen
  Cannabis
  Tobacco
Schizophrenic
  Disorganized (Hebephrenic)
  Catatonic
  Paranoid
  Schizo-affective
  Undifferentiated
Paranoid
  Paranoia
  Shared Paranoid *(folie à deux)*
  Paranoid State
Somatoform
  Somatization
  Conversion
  Psychoalgia
Dissociative
  Psychogenic Amnesia
  Psychogenic Fugue
  Multiple Personality
  Depersonalization
Personality
  Paranoid
  Introverted
  Schizotypal
  Histrionic
  Narcissistic
  Antisocial
  Borderline

  Avoidant
  Dependent
  Compulsive
  Passive-Aggressive
Affective
  Episodic
  Manic
  Major Depressive
    Single Episode
    Recurrent
  Bipolar Affective
  Chronic Affective
  Atypical Affective
Anxiety
  Phobic
    Agoraphobia
    Social
    Simple
  Panic
  Obsessive Compulsive
  Generalized Anxiety
Factitions
  With Psychological Symptoms
  Chronic Factitions
  Other Factitions
Psychosexual
  Gender Identity
    Transsexualism
  Paraphilias
    Fetishism
    Transvestism
    Zoophilia
    Pedophilia
    Exhibitionism
    Voyeurism
    Sexual Masochism
    Sexual Sadism

Psychosexual Dysfunctions
  Inhibited Sexual Desire
  Inhibited Sexual Excitement
  Inhibited Female Orgasm
  Inhibited Male Orgasm
  Premature Ejaculation
  Functional Dyspareunia
  Functional Vaginismus
Childhood or Adolescence
  Mental Retardation
  Pervasive Developmental
    Infantile Autism
    Atypical Childhood Psychosis
  Specific Developmental
    Reading
    Arithmatical
    Language
    Articulation
    Enuresis
    Encopresis
  Attention Deficit
    With Hyperactivity
    Without Hyperactivity
  Conduct
  Anxiety
  Eating
  Speech
  Stereotype Movement
Reactive
  Post-Traumatic
  Adjustment
Impulse Control
  Pathological Gambling
  Kleptomania
  Pyromania
  Intermittent Explosive
  Isolated Explosive

Source: Adapted from APA (1980), Diagnostic and statistical manual of mental disorders, third edition.

appears as a psychotic symptom, and the more likely it is that management feels justified in assigning the patient to a bad ward. When a patient finds himself in seclusion, naked and without visible means of expression, he may have to rely on tearing up his mattress, if he can, or writing with feces on the wall—actions management takes to be in keeping with the kind of person who warrants seclusion.

R. D. Laing, a psychiatrist best known for his radical approach to treating schizophrenia, also objects to the implications and consequences of adopting the medical model. He believes that a disease or condition called schizophrenia can only legitimately be called a hypothesis (a theory or notion about the world and about the way people behave), and that to call it a fact is "unequivocally false," an error of "incautious extrapolation" (Laing, 1967). Laing quotes Kraepelin's account of his clinical examination of a patient, pointing out that it is assumed without question that the psychiatrist is ipso facto sane, and that since the psychiatrist and patient are out of contact, something must be wrong with the patient. The patient's behavior, presented out of the context of her own experience, seems bizarre. Yet if Kraepelin's behavior were presented out of the context of *his* experience, it too would seem odd. (He stands in front of the patient with arms outstretched, forces bread out of her hand, and sticks a needle in her forehead.)

Laing repeatedly makes the point that too little attention is paid to the experience of the patient; that is, the attempt is seldom made to look at the patient's behavior from the patient's standpoint. Laing feels this is a direct consequence of the assumption that the patient's behavioral symptoms are merely the result of pathology in the individual.

Laing also believes that the treatment given a patient is adversely affected by the label:

The label is a social fact and the social fact a political event. This political event, occurring in the civic order of society, imposes definitions and consequences on the labeled person. . . . The person labeled is inaugurated not only into a role, but into a career of patient. . . . More completely, more radically than anywhere else in society, he is invalidated as a human being.

Unreliability

The foregoing criticisms deal mostly with the consequences, usefulness, and validity of formal diagnosis. Classification, however, has been most frequently criticized for its unreliability or for its lack of consistency and stability.

Experienced behavior pathologists often differ among themselves in diagnostic formulations, even when these formulations are based on the same symptom information (Chance, 1963; Gauron and Dickinson, 1966; Schwartz and Errera, 1963). A study conducted in two state hospitals by Schmidt and Fonda (1956) exemplifies this type of unreliability. In this study a pair of psychiatrists, using the official diagnostic categories prevalent at that time (APA, 1952), independently diagnosed each of 426 patients. Agreement for the pair was high for organic psychoses and some psychotic categories (for example, involutional melancholia and schizophrenia) but was below fifty percent in many categories.[2]

The more specific the diagnostic categories to be differentiated (for example, schizophrenic versus affective disorders), the less reliable the diagnosis, and, conversely, the larger or more inclusive the diagnostic categories (for example, organic versus psychotic disorders), the more reliable the diagnosis. These results are summarized in Table 3.2.

The unreliability of psychiatric diagnosis has also been demonstrated in two other types of studies. In one of these types, observers at the same hospital are presented with essentially identical data on two occasions and arrive at a different diagnosis each time (Beck, 1962; Wilson and Meyer, 1962); in the other type, it is usually shown that when diagnosticians rediagnose patients after a long time, the second diagnosis does not agree with the first.

These and similar studies demonstrating un-

---

[2] Involutional melancholia is depression that occurs during the later periods of life (see Chapter 14).

The Costly Consequences of Labeling

The issue of whether or not to label human behavior is far from settled. Here are some of the salient arguments that have been offered for its abandonment.

According to one of the longtime critics of labeling, Theodore Sarbin (1967), the question is what criteria should be used to deprive people of their liberty, their civil rights, and their capacity for self-determination. Basically that becomes a problem of how free and open a society we want. This decision, Sarbin holds, is prerequisite to establishing criteria for identifying people who should not be free, for in a truly free and democratic society we cannot relegate some people to a juridically established status of confinement and restraint on the basis of labels.

Labeling should be dropped on other grounds also, according to a statement by Ullmann and Krasner (1975, pp. 35–36), who have consistently opposed its use. In the first place, they argue, its main benefit seems to be to create the illusion that a problem has been solved. A way of dealing with socially abrasive behavior is provided, particularly behavior that is not foreseen and covered by formal rules. Second, once the behavior is labeled, even if it is an illogical or unscientific one, both the labeler and the labeled are comforted: an explanation is given, and a person with a disease is not responsible for contracting the illness and is excused from a number of social obligations.

Furthermore, Ullmann and Krasner point out, there are longer lasting effects of labeling that may be detrimental to the individual and to society. The person is stigmatized and may be treated with caution, concern, or avoidance by others both in work and in interpersonal relationships. In addition this consequence may contribute to the learning of behavior that makes future adjustment more difficult. Society loses because it no longer has the services of a gainfully employed and well-functioning individual, and it is saddled with a costly mental health industry that requires support of its personnel, buildings, bureaucracy, and so on. Besides, Ullmann and Krasner argue, society also loses because some unexpected, disturbing, and seemingly incomprehensible behavior may be socially valuable.

reliability have been widely criticized (Beck, 1962; Buss, 1966; Kreitman, 1961; Ward, et al., 1962) on the following grounds:

First, many of the studies used clinicians of varying diagnostic experience as classifiers.

Second, even when these clinicians were of roughly equivalent experience and background, they were often untrained, or trained to proceed differently in the same study.

Third, in the information provided them, they received extraneous information as well as unequal amounts of information on various patients.

Fourth, clinicians were repeatedly permitted to converse with one another and to compare notes; their reports therefore were based on consensual rather than independent judgments.

And, finally, no precautions were taken in these studies to ascertain that the participating clinicians agreed on the meanings of the diagnostic classes used. When these and other variables are controlled, as they have been in numerous studies (Kreitman et al., 1961; Sandifer et al., 1964; Wilson and Meyer, 1962), some of the unreliabilities vanish.

Wrong Focus

Some investigators, however, do not quarrel with the reliability of classification; rather they criticize the focus or targets of diagnosis and contend that labeling is not as essential as assessing a person's interaction with society. This argument has been forcefully stated by Robert Carson (1969) in his *Interaction Concepts of Personality*. In making this point, he discards the medical model entirely, a repudiation that we believe unnecessary (pp. 220–224):

Disorders of behavior . . . are unrelated to physical pathology . . . [they are] . . . learned patterns of relating to the social environment. . . . I regard these classifications of behavior [such as schizophrenia and obsessional neurosis] as being very nearly meaningless when used in anything but a purely descriptive way. . . .

In Defense of Classification

While granting that current diagnostic nomenclature has numerous inherent problems, and that its users do not always agree in their diagnostic formulations, its defenders have nevertheless argued for its retention on several grounds.

Practical Usefulness

Diagnosis is still used in many settings because it is useful for making many important decisions about patients. For example, diagnosis is used in the legal determination of insanity, in ward and treatment assignments in hospitals, as a screening device in the military and industry, and in the compilation of census figures and statistical data upon which considerable hospital and community planning is based (Caveny et al., 1955, pp. 367–380; Zigler and Phillips, 1961).

Scientific Value

Diagnosis can also be defended on its scientific merits, as Hans Eysenck (1960a) argues in his *Handbook of Abnormal Psychology* (p. 1):

Before we can reasonably be asked to look for the cause of a particular dysfunction or disorder, we must have isolated, however crudely, the dysfunction or disorder in question, and we must be able to recognize it and differentiate it from other syndromes.

And Brendan Maher (1970), who defends diagnosis as a "prerequisite for a systematic search for determinants" and as a "starting point for research, not the terminal point in describing a patient," also emphasizes its potential scientific use in his *Introduction to Research in Psychopathology* (p. 33):

Even though we have seen that descriptive diagnosis may be criticized as misleading when it is allowed to substitute for etiological diagnosis, we should note that it serves an important purpose in the early study of natural phenomena. Before we can begin to search effectively for the origins of a specific pattern of events, we must have established a reasonably good definition of the pattern and have been assured that it tends to recur with some internal regularity.

Practical and Scientific Merits

By far the most cogent defense of diagnosis for its practical and scientific values has been that of Paul Meehl (1959), the distinguished University of Minnesota psychologist, who believes there is a place for the concept of disease entities in ab-

Table 3.2

Agreement Percentage Among Two Psychiatrists Classifying Patients into General and Specific Categories

General Diagnosis	Percent	Specific Diagnosis	Percent
Organic	92	Acute brain syndrome	68
		Chronic brain syndrome	80
		Mental deficiency	42
Psychotic	80	Involutional	57
		Affective	35
		Schizophrenic	51
Characterological	71	Neurosis	16
		Personality pattern	8
		Personality trait	6
		Sociopathic	58

Source: After Schmidt, H. O., and Fonda, C. The reliability of psychiatric diagnosis. Journal of Abnormal and Social Psychology, *1956, 52, 262–267.*

normal psychology. Meehl believes that Kraepelin was not as mistaken as some contemporary psychologists seem to think, that there is much truth contained in the Kraepelinian system, and that the practical implications associated with diagnostic labels are great. Even the most antinosological clinician, according to Meehl, often worries about whether a patient would be labeled "obsessional" or "schizophrenic."

Meehl's fundamental argument for the utility of formal diagnosis is summed up in this statement (p. 103):

There is a sufficient amount of etiological and prognostic homogeneity among patients belonging to a given diagnostic group, so that the assignment of a patient to his group has probability implications which it is clinically unsound to ignore.

He then counters three commonly advanced objections to psychiatric classifications: that they are unreliable, that they pigeonhole people, and that diagnostic labels do not tell us anything about what is wrong with the patient. Against the

first of these objections he argues that some psychiatrists' inability to spot certain abnormalities such as schizophrenia is not good evidence against the existence of this condition as a clinical entity. Concerning pigeonholing he responds that although some old-fashioned diagnosticians use diagnostic labels as a substitute for understanding, psychologists cannot afford to decide the merits of a conceptual scheme on the grounds that people use it wrongly. And regarding what diagnostic labels tell us, he states that there is no contradiction between classifying a patient and attempting concurrently to understand that patient's motivations and defenses.

Critical Comment

The view of psychiatric diagnosis expressed in this book, as reflected in the repeated reference to DSM II and DSM III categories, is close to that of Meehl. We believe that the answer to classification difficulties lies not in rejecting such schemes, but in improving the procedures for arriving at diagnoses. The principal rationale of this view is that although psychiatric diagnosis may not be completely valid and reliable at present, it is still the most satisfactory method available for organizing and communicating descriptive information for practical and research purposes. To abandon the present system without a usable replacement would be to stall the very process that generates change.

We agree with the critics in urging that clinicians be sensitive to the patient's dilemma. We also join them in decrying the dehumanizing treatment sometimes given patients to whom diagnostic labels have been attached, in particular the withholding of any means of expression, described by Goffman, and the denial of the patient's autonomy, cited by Laing. The real need, it seems to us, is not for nosology to disappear but for clinicians to be trained so that they will be more aware of the patient as a human being and more interested, perhaps, in what the patient may be trying to say.

In the meantime, rather than condemning nosology, we believe that clinicians should become masters of it, while simultaneously improving the taxonomic systems on which it is based. This involves, in addition to sharpening psychodiagnostic skills and tools (observation, interview, objective tests; see Chapter 4), applying quantitative methods to record the observations on which classifications of behavior pathology are based.

Summary

Classification is an important scientific procedure. It consists of arranging information into categories. The current psychiatric classifications—which began with Hippocrates' three categories of phrenesis, mania, and melancholia—are based also on Kraepelin's work of the 1920s.

Paul E. Meehl, distinguished University of Minnesota clinical psychologist.

(Courtesy Paul E. Meehl)

Current criticisms of diagnostic labeling are directed at its alleged lack of usefulness, validity, and reliability, and at some of its perceptual and behavioral consequences. In this book diagnosis is defended on grounds of its usefulness in research and treatment.

Terms and Concepts to Master

Affect	Nosology
Classification	Self-fulfilling prophecy
Etiology	

4   Psychodiagnosis

We shall now examine the methods clinicians use to search for signs and cues from which inferences can be made about abnormal behavior. Their three main psychodiagnostic tools are observation, interviews, and psychological tests (Table 4.1); each has its particular strengths and shortcomings, as we shall see.

Observation

Basic to all scientific study—physical, biological, and psychological—is observation of the subject under investigation. In psychodiagnosis, however, the complex interaction between observer and subject introduces many difficulties that do not exist in other sciences. For one thing the subjects observed are often aware of being studied, and may feel called upon to behave in prescribed ways;[1] for another, psychologists are as human as their subjects, and imbue them with their own feelings, needs, or wishes, which may distort the results. Nonetheless, psychologists must be content to make observations under these less-than-optimal circumstances; and they must, whenever possible, correct for the distortions that arise.

Naturalistic and Controlled Observations

Observations are usually either *naturalistic* or *controlled*. Natural observation is observing the actions of organisms in their familiar and indigenous surroundings. This is especially useful for viewing ongoing behavior in all its complexity with minimal interference. The clinicians who visit the homes of patients to study family patterns (for example, at dinner or at play) are using this method; and although their presence may modify their subjects' behavior, the clinicians nevertheless have the advantage of obtaining firsthand impressions of them in their everyday environment.

Observations can be *naturalistic*, however, without being made at the subject's home base. For example, during the diagnostic interview, the observer may note the client's behavior, general appearance, and demeanor while they are talking. The observations are naturalistic in that the diagnostician does not manipulate the environment or the client in any way to produce these reactions, but simply lets things happen unrestrictedly in the office or hospital ward. This is the more common form of naturalistic observation in psychodiagnosis. Naturalistic observations are difficult to obtain without numerous hardware aids and rating scales to improve the precision of data collection and recordings.

Controlled observations usually occur in the laboratory, where psychologists can modify surroundings according to their needs.

---

[1] This is sometimes called the "guinea pig" effect, or "role selection"; subjects ask themselves the question, "What kind of person should I be as I do these tasks?" (Webb et al., 1966, p. 16).

The major distinction between the two conditions, although it is not always sharp, is that in naturalistic settings psychologists wait for behavior to unfold; in controlled settings they create circumstances and systematically introduce variables that elicit responses. The controls may consist of special arrangements of furniture and toys in a playroom, or they may involve systematically varying numerous aspects of a situation (for example, amount of stress, noise level, number of persons). In either case, the psychologist strives to control conditions so that they are standard and replicable.

The Interview

Interviewing adds language to observation. If we want to know how people feel, what they experience, how much they remember, and what their emotions and motives are, we can ask them. Unfortunately, however, human interactions are not always that straightforward. By its very nature, the desired information is private; people either cannot or will not readily disclose it. Often they are not aware of their inner thoughts and motives, but more often they intentionally hold back, disown, deny, and distort.

Consequently, the diagnostician must use great skill in obtaining information. Among the many types of interviews available, the *intake* and *mental status interviews* are the most popular.

Intake Interview

The intake interview, as the name suggests, is the initial contact between interviewer and respondent in the clinic or hospital. For the interviewee the intake interview is often an ordeal. Feelings are likely to be near the surface ready to erupt. More often than not, the decision to seek help, or being forced to seek help, has made the interviewee ill at ease, self-conscious, and defensive. He or she may have misgivings about that deci-

Table 4.1
Sources of Information for Psychodiagnosis

Source	Information Yield
Observations	
Naturalistic	Assess reactions to everyday situations; scars, tremors, needle marks; expressive behaviors and ratings of any of these behaviors.
Controlled	Obtain reactions to rigged stimuli, information about specific behaviors under contrived conditions, and ratings by others who remember the subject.
Interviews	
Intake	Establish relationship with patient; assess motivation for participating in treatment; impart information about agency; set expectations; collect basic life data.
Mental Status	Assess mental preoccupations; observe attitude, appearance, and behavior; observe mood fluctuations and speech.
Psychological Tests	
Personality	On self-report inventories, collect responses about personal habits, unusual beliefs, or fantasies; on projective techniques, obtain responses to unstructured situations and assess needs and inner states.
Intelligence	Ascertain IQ level; determine extent of mental deficit, if any; test for central nervous system involvement.

The Computer as Intake Interviewer

A computer-assisted psychiatric assessment unit is currently functioning as part of the admissions procedure at a mental hospital in Salt Lake City (Johnson and Williams, 1975). The system works somewhat as follows: Patients enter the hospital and are greeted by a receptionist who opens for each a computer file by entering basic identifying information into the system. Patients are then introduced to another person whose interview is designed to determine their ability to complete a computerized self-report testing battery. If, as is generally the case, the patient is able to do so, the computer administers a mental status interview and submits a DSM II diagnosis and narrative report to a professional.

The computer next administers several standard self-report personality tests and an intelligence test. As each test is completed, the computer analyzes the responses and prints a narrative report. This report is submitted to a staff that subsequently meets and works out an optimal treatment plan for the patient.

The computer system seems to be well received by patients and staff alike. Its main advantages are that (1) the hospital's intake capacity and efficiency have improved considerably (more patients processed in less time), (2) the system collects standardized clinical data on all patients instead of the prior haphazard and random bits of information, and (3) as a result of ongoing monitoring during the patient's stay at the hospital, the system provides constant measures of patient progress.

sion, and may entertain any of several common misconceptions about what is expected. This is not surprising, since the interview is an unfamiliar experience to most people; and because it is the initial session, the interviewer is a stranger. Some people find it difficult enough to confide in members of their own family; to reveal their innermost secrets to strangers can be much more difficult. The interviewer must understand this and make proper adjustments, for he or she is responsible for setting the tone and carrying most of the burden during this initial contact (see Figure 4.1).

Beyond the first goal of the intake interview, which is to establish a relationship with the patient, the clinician must assess motivation for treatment. Since the groundwork is to be laid for possible further contact, the clinician usually imparts preliminary information about the nature of the institution, fees to be charged, and the extent to which the patient's expectations can be met by the clinician's agency. If the agency is inappropriate, other community resources can be discussed and recommended.[2]

The intake interview, which is usually kept quite brief, also includes gathering identifying information (name, age, education, and so on), assessing the nature of the problem, and superficially exploring other matters that will be pursued more thoroughly in the mental status interview.

Mental Status Interview

The mental status interview, usually conducted in the hospital, is a depth study taken at the

---

[2] A discussion of the various available mental health resources is presented in Chapter 25.

earliest possible time after the intake interview; its purpose, as the name implies, is to assess mental preoccupations and behavior pathology. It probes more deeply than the intake and consists of inquiries about suicidal thoughts, voices, relationships with others in the family, and sexual behavior, to name just a few sensitive areas it touches. Considerable skill is needed to get this information without causing the patient discomfort; and generally it has been found that a gentle manner and a permissive atmosphere are more productive than inquisitorial questioning in hostile or businesslike surroundings.

Table 4.2 lists the six categories in which the interviewer collects information. The clinician is urged (Wells and Reusch, 1945; Menninger, 1952) to use as many direct quotations as possible in reporting the interview and to refrain, at least at this stage of psychodiagnosis, from extrapolating beyond his or her observations.

The first of these categories—*general appearance, attitude,* and *behavior*—consists of information about the respondent's physical stature and bearing, style of dress, unusual mannerisms and actions, and attitude and demeanor during the interview. The most obvious kind of deviation

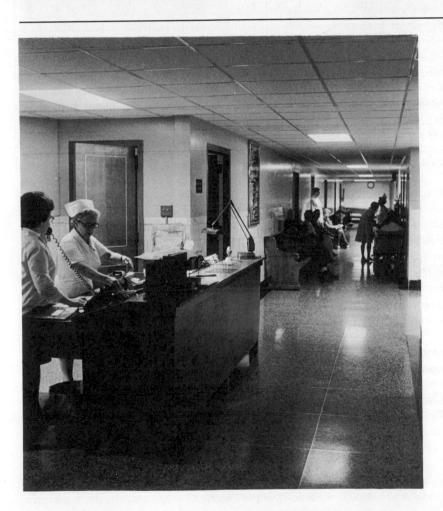

Figure 4.1
This hospital ward scene is typical of those to which many prospective patients are subjected before the intake interview. The strange surroundings and the often long wait can be an ordeal and may cause some misgivings about the decision to seek psychiatric consultation.

Table 4.2
Excerpts from a Mental Status Interview of a 29-Year-Old Male

Category	Example of Report
General appearance, attitude, and behavior	He is friendly and cooperative. Has made no complaints about ward restrictions. He smiles in a somewhat exaggerated and grotesque manner.
Discourse	He answers in a deep, loud voice, speaking in a slow, precise, and somewhat condescending manner. His responses are relevant but vague.
Mood and affective fluctuations	His facial expressions, although not totally inappropriate, are poorly correlated with subject of discourse or events in his environment.
Sensorium and intellect	The patient's orientation for place, person, and time is normal. His remote and recent memory also are normal. Two brief intelligence measures indicate about average intelligence.
Mental content and specific preoccupations	He readily discusses what he calls his "nervous trouble." He complains of "bad thoughts" and a "conspiracy." He reports hearing voices saying, "Hello, Bill, you're a dirty dog."
Insight	The patient readily accepts the idea that he should be in the hospital. He feels that hospitalization will help him get rid of these "bad" thoughts. He is not in the least defensive about admitting to auditory and visual hallucinations or to the idea that everyone on earth is his enemy.

Source: Reproduced with permission from B. Kleinmuntz. Personality measurement: an introduction. *Huntington, N.Y.: Krieger, 1975, p. 159.*

that could occur, for example, is illustrated by the antisocial personality,[3] who may sink into the chair, throw legs and feet up on the interviewer's desk, and say, "What's up, doc?" If the interview is conducted in the hospital, the clinician makes a special effort to collect information from hospital aides and nurses about the patient's general behavior in the ward.

The second category consists of the respondent's manner of speaking, or *discourse*. There are many qualitative and quantitative speech anomalies among people, and each of these anomalies has its particular diagnostic significance. The following excerpt, which illustrates the circumstantial speech of some manic psychotics (see Chapter 14), is an example of how some patients never quite get to the point:

Dr.: *What brings you here?*
Pa.: *I can tell you what does; but telling you and bringing you are one and the same. Get what I mean? One and the same thing because this is a hospital, and I tell you they brought me to a hospital, and it is nothing more or less than just that; and it brings all of us to our destinies.*

The third category is the patient's *emotional*, or *affective, tone*. Is the patient happy or dejected? Does he or she show emotion that corresponds to the topic of discussion? How stable is the patient's mood during the interview? For example, some people with a diagnosis of hebephrenic

---

[3] See Chapter 16 for a description of the antisocial personality.

schizophrenia (see Chapter 12) have such widely fluctuating emotions that during a single interview they may display extreme mirth, followed moments later by sadness, and then by uproarious laughter.

Evaluating *sensorium*—the fourth category—consists of establishing whether the patient knows where he is, that he realizes he is a patient in a clinic or hospital, and that he is not confused about the season or the year during which all this is happening. This is also the part of the interview in which, if time does not permit lengthier intelligence tests such as we describe later, the interviewer makes some assessment of *intelligence*. Typically, the interviewer gives the patient several brief arithmetic problems (for example, subtract 7 from 100 and continue until told to stop); the interviewer may ask about the meanings of several words taken from a standard vocabulary list; or may try three or four items from a test of abstract reasoning (for example, in what way are a table and chair alike? a poem and a statue?).

The fifth category is the patient's *mental content*. More than most areas of probing, this may touch upon sensitive material. To illustrate, we present an excerpt from an interview with a paranoid 35-year-old male who had tried to kill his mother-in-law:

Dr.: *You say that you've done nothing unusual, yet the police brought you here last night.*

Pa.: *I tried to use the telephone in my own house, and my mother-in-law tried to stop me.*

Dr.: *What do you mean?*

Pa.: *I tried to register my invention. You see, I have information that someone is trying to steal my ideas.*

Dr.: *So you tried to call the patent office?*

Pa.: *No, I tried to call the president. This is too important, and I'd rather not trust some flunky or clerk with this information.*

Dr.: *How often have you called the president?*

Pa.: *A couple of times.*

Dr.: *What kind of invention do you have?*

Pa.: *(He produces a long document that had been rolled up and tucked inside his jacket). It's a plan to restore vision to the blind.*

Dr.: *Do you want to tell me more?*

Pa.: *I don't know, can I trust you?*

Dr.: *I should tell you that I must share this information with other hospital personnel.*

Pa.: *OK, here is how it works. The antenna on the top of the skull fits into the splice of the optic nerve by means of the mathematical formula that you see here. . . .*

The last category of information obtained during the mental status interview contains an estimate of the patient's *insight* into his or her disorder. That is to say, the interviewer attempts to learn whether the respondent understands the extent of the disorder and why he or she is at the clinic or hospital. Paradoxically, as we indicated earlier, the more severe the mental disorder is, the less likely the patient is to appreciate the fact of being ill.

Evaluation of the Interview

Three main sources of errors in interviewing contribute to its unreliability as a psychodiagnostic tool: errors arising from the complexity of the *interview process*, those occurring because of the fears and anxieties of the *interviewee*, and those arising from the *interviewer* (Table 4.3).

Interview Process Errors. As indicated in Table 4.3, these errors arise because of the complexity of the two-person interaction that defines the interview. Furthermore, these errors are random in the sense that they are chance variations that do not produce inaccuracies in one particular direction. For example, a respondent may not feel up to par on a particular day and therefore may present a distorted sample of behavior. Had the person been interviewed a day later, his or her behavior might have been considerably different. Similarly, the interviewer may be preoccupied on

Table 4.3
Sources of Error in the Interview

Error Source	Description	Resolution
Interview process	Results from the complex interaction of interviewer, interviewee, and setting; usually results in random, rather than directional, error	Conduct as many interviews as feasible with the same respondents
Interviewee	Results from fears and anxieties; misinformation; role expectations	Carefully structure the interview situation and anticipate expectations
Interviewer	Results from idiosyncrasies of various interviewers; recording errors; making inferences beyond obtained data; poor training; theoretical biases; inexperience	Standardize interviewer strategies and intensive training; establish a uniform system for collecting data

Source: Reproduced with permission from B. Kleinmuntz. Personality measurement: an introduction. *Huntington, N.Y.: Krieger, 1975, p. 169.*

a particular day and therefore may present atypical behavior. If a combination of these influences is operating at any particular time, communication between interviewer and respondent is impaired.

Interviewee Errors. These errors may arise, as we indicated in our discussion of the intake interview, because of the interviewee's anxieties in a new situation or misgivings about seeking help. A skillful interviewer can use these apprehensions to advantage and enlist cooperation by means of them; but if they are neglected, they may disrupt the interview. Moreover, the interviewee's role expectations may interfere with communication. Consider, for example, the person who has read or heard that psychologists and psychiatrists like to hear about dreams because these are important clues in revealing personality. Now he finds himself in a situation in which he is expected to talk about dreams, but unfortunately he has no dreams to relate. How he adapts to that situation may have little to do with the way he typically behaves. Therefore the interviewer obtains a picture of behavior in a situation of considerable stress and anxiety rather than one that reflects true personality.

Interviewer Errors. These errors come about because the interviewer is not a reliable observer or recording instrument. First, because of his unique background or mental set, he may not see or hear exactly what has occurred; or if he does observe accurately, his notes may amplify, minimize, omit, or round out responses. These recording errors may be made either before or after the interview ends.

A second kind of interviewer error occurs because of the inexperience of some psychodiagnosticians. For example, untrained and inexperienced interviewers who do not know how to motivate others to talk freely do not obtain much information.

One common error of this sort comes about when an interviewer permits the interview to deteriorate into a hail-fellow relationship. This atmosphere does not encourage the interviewee to divulge his thoughts and problems; instead he may think that he should not bother his newly found friend with his troubles.

Then there is the interviewer who inadvertently discourages further discussion by a comment such as, "Well, I guess we beat that subject to death"; or who, on hearing anything about a favorite topic—be it golf, life insurance, or sex—probes into it prematurely, relentlessly, and irrelevantly. Roy Schafer (1954, p. 21), in an excellent chapter on interviewing, discusses this voyeuristic, or "peeping Tom," tendency of some diagnosticians.

Finally, in another interviewer error, aptly called the "pathology bias" by some (Daily, 1960), the diagnostician sees symptoms and defense mechanisms in everyone (or interprets as pathological any response that is unusual or unique). In this regard one psychologist who advocates a positive approach to mental health has said, "There is abundant empirical knowledge concerning the . . . anxious and the neurotic . . . there is little information and even less conceptual clarity about the nature of psychological normality" (Shoben, 1957, p. 183).

The Validity of Interviews. So far, we have described the types of errors that commonly occur during the interview and noted that these errors contribute to the interview's unreliability. Most criticisms of the interview, however, have focused on its lack of validity—that is, its tendency not to yield the information that is useful for psychodiagnosis and personality assessment. Two studies of interviewing in another context are particularly relevant to this issue; one showed that the interview added no new information to test scores and high school achievement in predicting college success (Sarbin, 1943); the other showed that ratings obtained from interview information were of little practical use in predicting the success of graduate students in a clinical psychology program (Kelly and Fiske, 1951).

If the interview is so deficient in reliability and validity, why is it the method of choice for so many professionals? Evidently the interview has uses that are not affected by its inadequacy as a predictive tool. In the clinic or hospital the interviewer acquires firsthand information about the interviewee's appearance, voice, and mannerisms, as well as other impressions and clues that can be obtained only from person-to-person contact. But perhaps more importantly, the interviewer, by a show of interest in another human being, is recognizing the interviewee as a person, and not just another number.

Psychological Testing

Psychological tests, referred to as "one of the great success stories of modern psychology" (Holtzman, 1971, p. 546), add another dimension to clinical assessment. By means of them psychologists obtain a more complete picture of personality than they can from observations and interviews alone, and since the tests are more quantifiable, the psychologist is better able to compare scores among respondents. In addition, psychological tests permit evaluation of intelligence and brain damage; but, as we also indicate, they are not without their problems.

Most psychologists would probably agree with the following definition of a psychological test: *a standardized instrument or systematic procedure designed to obtain an objective measure of a sample of behavior.*

This definition includes terms that require further explanation. For example, the term *standardized,* as intended above, refers to the construction of uniform test items and writing instructions to assure identical administration and scoring. Optimally, test constructors take precautions to control all variation except that which their tests or procedures intend to measure. Thus standardization is analogous to experimental control. The test constructor, like the experimenter, controls the conditions under which observations are made so that findings will be replicable.

What does it mean to *sample behavior*? It means that for practical reasons the tester must be satisfied with just a portion of behavior rather than the entire domain of relevant responses. These samples may consist of physical acts such as those observed on certain performance tests, or, as is more common in personality testing, they may be self-descriptive reports.[4] A prime requisite of this sample, in either case, is that it be representative of the behavior in question so that inferences can be made about the larger domain from which it was drawn. Thus a brief test of a one-semester mathematics course should contain portions that fairly represent all facets of the subject matter covered that semester. In personality assessment, however, matters are not always that straightforward. Personality tests usually consist of questions about wishes, memories, beliefs, attitudes, or symptoms, and the problem for the test constructor is to select items that will reflect internal states and personality.

And, finally, a test is *objective* if its administration, scoring, and interpretation remain independent of the judgment of the tester. This means that two testers viewing the same set of responses will arrive at identical scores and interpretations.[5]

Of the large number of tests in existence, three types are particularly important for abnormal psychology: personality, intelligence, and intellectual impairment tests.

Personality Testing

There are two major types of personality tests: *self-report inventories* and *projective techniques*. The first consists of self-descriptive statements with which respondents either agree or disagree; pro-

jective techniques, in sharp contrast, confront respondents with unstructured test stimuli to which they are asked to make imaginative responses.

Self-report Inventories

The first self-report test, developed during World War I, was constructed in response to General Pershing's observation of the "prevalence of mental disorders" in the United States military forces. He suggested that screening methods be devised to eliminate unfit draftees. Two psychologists, Woodworth and Poffenberger, who at the time were investigating the question of emotional fitness for warfare, responded with the creation of the pioneer Woodworth *Personal Data Sheet* (Woodworth, 1920).

This self-report test replaced the then prevalent procedure of interviewing each soldier individually. Since several hundred thousand recruits were being processed at that time, a large saving in time and money resulted. Before long, the paper-and-pencil version of psychiatric screening caught on. Now each recruit could be "interviewed" by asking him such standard questions as, "Do you blush easily?", "Are you sometimes afraid of the dark?", and similar items (Table 4.4).

The Woodworth *Personal Data Sheet* was developed by collecting items of information from available psychiatric textbooks and casting them in a suitable test format. In addition the test constructors gleaned items from case histories and hospital records of psychiatric patients. A total of 116 Yes-or-No items was included, and a recruit's score consisted of the number of symptoms that he admitted to having (out of 116). Recruits who reported many symptoms were detained for further questioning.

Although Woodworth's test picked up an impressive number of maladjusted recruits, its construction, in retrospect, was naive. There were minimal safeguards against test faking, and the number and format of the items were unsatisfac-

---

[4] Performance tests, such as those discussed in Chapter 3, usually require that respondents manipulate a set of test materials to solve a problem (for example, arrange blocks according to a prescribed design) within a time limit.

[5] For further information on essential attributes of psychological tests, readers should consult Anastasi (1976), Cronbach (1970), Kleinmuntz (1967), and Nunnally (1978).

tory. Nevertheless, personality testing during World War I was a success and subsequently, as a direct outgrowth of this development, hundreds of such personality questionnaires were constructed. The current *Eighth Mental Measurements Yearbook* (Buros, 1978) lists about 350 personality inventories.

The self-report inventory is essentially a standardized interview with such questions as these:

"Are your feelings easily hurt?"

"Do your interests change quickly?"

"Do you tend to get angry with people rather easily?"

or statements to which the respondent agrees or disagrees, such as "I daydream very little."

Instead of each person being interviewed individually, inventory statements are printed in a booklet and administered to many persons simultaneously.

The items presented to each respondent are identical, as are the administration and scoring procedures, and this equivalence for all subjects facilitates comparing scores.

Answers on inventories are limited to fixed alternative categories (Yes, No, or Cannot Say). The disadvantage of limiting alternatives is that it restricts freedom of response; the advantage, on the other hand, is that it eliminates the need for the tester's judgments in scoring and obviates the necessity for relying on memory to reconstruct responses.

The most carefully constructed and widely used self-report test is the *Minnesota Multiphasic Personality Inventory*, or MMPI (Hathaway and McKinley, 1943), which consists of 550 statements (for example, "Everything tastes the same") printed on separate cards, which the respondent sorts into three categories: True, False, or Cannot Say. A group form of the inventory, prepared after the first test, consists of 566 statements (550 separate items with 16 items repeated) printed in a test booklet. Subjects record their responses on answer sheets. MMPI statements cover a wide range of personal topics, including general

Table 4.4
Sample Items from the Woodworth Personal Data Sheet

Have you failed to get a square deal in life?
Is your speech free from stutter or stammer?
Does the sight of blood make you sick or dizzy?
Do you sometimes wish that you had never been born?
Do you find that people understand and sympathize with you?
Do people find fault with you much?
Do you suffer from headaches or dizziness?

Source: Woodworth, R. S. Personal data sheet. *Chicago: Stoelting, 1920.*

health, religious attitudes, gastrointestinal complaints, family and marital attitudes, moods, delusions, hallucinations, phobias, masculinity-femininity, and social interests.

Scoring the MMPI proceeds by tallying item responses according to ten *clinical scales* and four *validity scales*, and these responses are plotted on a profile sheet such as is shown in Figure 4.2. Raw scores on each of these scales are converted to and expressed as T-scores.[6]

The clinical scales, conventionally identified by their scale numbers, are arranged in a serial position from left to right on the profile sheet as follows: Scale 1, Hypochondriasis (Hs); Scale 2,

---

[6] Every distribution of scores can be expressed in terms of its arithmetic mean and standard deviation (the spread of variability of the scores). The status of an individual score can then be understood in terms of the mean and standard deviation of that distribution. Converting raw scores to a distribution with a mean and a standard deviation allows the use of standard scores. The T-score is a standard score that is derived by reducing measurements from raw scores to a common scale of units with the mean equal to 50 and the standard deviation equal to 10. Thus a raw score that is two standard deviations above the mean is equivalent to a T-score of 70. Similarly, raw scores at one standard deviation above the mean or at one and two standard deviations below the mean are equivalent to T-scores of 60, 40, and 30, respectively.

Starke R. Hathaway, cofounder of the Minnesota Multiphasic Personality Inventory and pioneer in self-report testing.

(Courtesy Starke R. Hathaway)

Depression (D); Scale 3, Hysteria (Hy); Scale 4, Psychopathic Deviate (Pd); Scale 5, Masculinity–Femininity (Mf); Scale 6, Paranoia (Pa); Scale 7, Psychasthenia (Pt); Scale 8, Schizophrenia (Sc); Scale 9, Hypomania (Ma); and Scale 0, Social Introversion (Si). Referring to the clinical keys by their numbers, according to their ordinal positions from left to right on the profile sheet, simplifies the coding of scores and eliminates unjustified psychiatric labeling (see p. 25ff.).

The four validity, or credibility, scales that appear to the left of the clinical scores on the profile sheet, are the following: Question Scale (?); Lie Scale (L); Fake Scale (F); and Correction Scale (K). The first of these reflects the number of items not answered by the respondent and is an index of evasiveness. The L scale is a measure of credibility in that it detects attempts at faking in the direction of "looking good." The F scale detects faking in the other direction, "looking bad," or it can be a sign that the examinee was confused about what he or she was to do on the test. The last validation scale, K, measures the defensiveness of the examinee who is generally guarded about personal affairs and discloses only as much as is absolutely unavoidable. Table 4.5 lists the validity and clinical scales, gives simulated sample items for each, and indicates typical interpretations associated with their elevations.

MMPI Interpretation

When the MMPI was being devised, its authors thought that specific scale elevations would correspond closely to diagnostic classification. For example, if a person's Scale 6, or Pa, was above a given criterion cutoff point, this would indicate paranoia. But with increasing experience in the use of the MMPI, it became clear that single scale elevations were not reliable indicators of diagnostic classes, and test users learned that the implications of scores had to be extended beyond their original psychiatric intent. That is, it became obvious that elevations on scales labeled "hysteria," or "schizophrenia" did not necessarily indicate that a person could be diagnosed as hysteric, depressed, or schizophrenic. Consequently MMPI scales began to be called by their ordinal numbers (Figure 4.2), and profiles were thereafter referred to by their codes rather than psychiatric labels. One example of such a code interpretation will be given here.

The most talked-about profile pattern among normal and hospitalized individuals is one called the "conversion V." It consists of elevations of Scales 1 and 3 (Hs and Hy), or 3 and 1, forming a

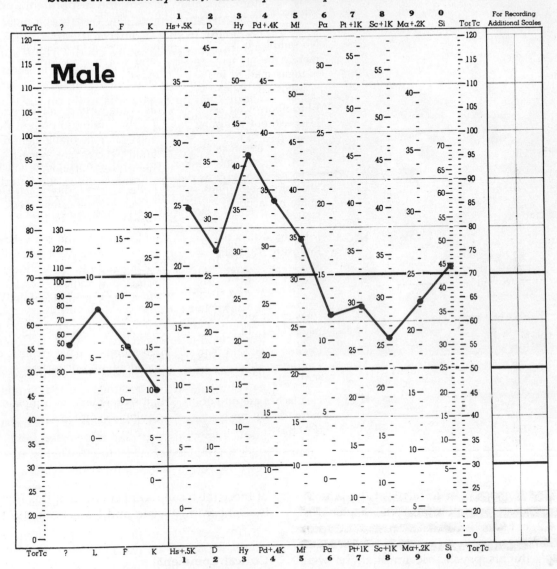

Figure 4.2

An MMPI profile form; the validity scales ?, L, F, and K are shown on the left-hand side; and clinical scales 1 to 0 are shown on the right-hand side. There are separate norms for males and females; this figure presents only the male norms. The interpretation of profile

patterns such as the one shown here is explained on p. 44ff.

Table 4.5

Items Similar to the Validity and Clinical Scales of the MMPI

Scale	Sample Item	Interpretation
?	No sample. It is merely the number of items marked in the "cannot say" category.	This is one of four validity scales, and a high score indicates evasiveness.
L	I have borrowed objects without returning them. (FALSE)	This is the second validity scale. Persons trying to present themselves in a favorable light (e.g., good, wholesome, honest) obtain high L scale elevations.
F	My voices sometimes guide my actions. (TRUE)	F is the third validity scale. High scores suggest carelessness, confusion, or "fake bad."
K	I do not always tell the truth. (FALSE)	An elevation on the last validity scale, K, suggests a defensive test-taking attitude. Exceedingly low scores may indicate a lack of ability to deny symptomatology.
Hs	I never get low back pains. (FALSE)	High scorers have been described as cynical, defeatist, and crabbed.
D	Friends have said that I am overactive. (FALSE)	High scorers usually are shy, dependent, and distressed.
Hy	Headaches are rare occurrences for me. (FALSE)	High scorers tend to complain of multiple symptoms.

valley or a V shape, with Scale 2 at the bottom. This configuration, or profile type, depicted in Figure 4.2, obtained its name because it was often found among people diagnosed "conversion hysteria." But its psychiatric implications were not always borne out in the many studies in which supposedly normal college men and women also obtained this profile pattern.

Many commonly recognized patterns exist in MMPI folklore, and Dahlstrom and Welsh's *MMPI Handbook* (1960) describes no less than 72

of these (also see recent revision of this *Handbook* by Dahlstrom, Welsh, and Dahlstrom, 1972).

Critical Comment

Item Format. One criticism leveled at self-report inventories is that test items are too restrictive. The MMPI item "I am an important person," to take just one instance, calls for a True, False, or Cannot Say response.[7] Many people would like

Table 4.5

Items Similar to the Validity and Clinical Scales of the MMPI (*continued*)

Scale	Sample Item	Interpretation
Pd	My parents and I get along fine. (FALSE)	Adjectives used to describe some high scorers are adventurous, courageous, and generous.
Mf	I am interested in automobiles. (FALSE)	Among males, high scorers have been described as aesthetic and sensitive. High-scoring women have been described as rebellious, unrealistic, and generous.
Pa	People tend to mind their own business. (FALSE)	High scorers on this scale were characterized as shrewd, guarded, and worrisome.
Pt	I have trouble starting projects. (TRUE)	Fearful, rigid, anxious and worrisome are some of the adjectives used to describe high Pt scorers.
Sc	Everyone hates me. (TRUE)	Adjectives such as withdrawn and unusual describe Sc high scorers.
Ma	Lots of things interest me. (TRUE)	High scorers are called sociable, energetic, and impulsive.
Si	I get along well with others. (FALSE)	High scorers: modest, shy, and self-effacing. Low scorers: sociable, colorful, and ambitious.

Note: The True or False responses, within parentheses indicate the scored direction of each of the items.

to qualify their answers by saying things like "sometimes" or "under certain conditions," but the test format simply does not permit these replies. The resultant difficulty is twofold. First, the constraint of fixed alternatives forces endorsement of, or disagreement with, items that are not applicable; or even worse, it endorses irrelevant items because disagreement may, at least on the surface, signify psychopathology. Second, if the test constructor did not adequately convey the intended meaning of the item, then the respondent's frame of reference is different from that of the constructor and either a Yes or a No reply is ambiguous.

Test Faking. Another disadvantage of self-report inventories is that they are highly susceptible to

[7] Our examples refer mainly to the MMPI because it is one of the most extensively researched psychiatric self-report inventories.

faking. The motivations for doing so are many (for example, to evade military recruitment, to obtain a medical discharge, to gain admission to a psychiatric hospital), but safeguards against faking are not easily constructed. Numerous studies have shown that personality test scores can be modified, sometimes radically, when subjects are instructed to do so.

In one of these studies (Bird, 1948) the MMPI was administered at the beginning of the semester to a college class in abnormal psychology, first under ordinary conditions, and then with instructions to simulate specific psychiatric disorders. Following the completion of their course, these students again were requested to sham abnormality. They were more successful in their second attempt. Their improvement was reflected in higher clinical and lower validity scale scores (lower ?, L, F, and K). In other words the course in abnormal psychology provided them with sufficient clinical information to fake psychopathology more expertly.

Response Styles. Not all test faking is intentional, however. Some people agree with items as self-descriptive regardless of content. This test-taking attitude has been called *acquiescence*. It is the tendency to agree rather than disagree with propositions in general (Block, 1965), and the result is that it casts doubt on the proper interpretations of test scores. One way to correct for the effect of this uncritical acceptance of all statements is to construct a test so that it has as many items tallied in the psychopathological direction when answered True as when answered False.

Another response style, called *social desirability* (Edwards, 1953), is reflected in some persons' endorsement of those items that place them in a socially favorable light. For example, on an item such as "In school I was sometimes sent to the principal for cutting up," a False response is socially desirable and the alternative response is not. Anyone who wants to favorably impress, say, a future employer would never endorse this item.

One other response style, *deviation*, is the tendency to answer personality test items in an unusual or uncommon direction. According to one researcher who has studied this tendency extensively and who has formulated the "deviation hypothesis" (Berg, 1955, 1959, 1961, 1967), respondents' answers are not related to item content; rather they are related to a tendency to behave atypically in other areas as well. From this standpoint response deviation on tests is a valuable index of personality deviation.

Test Instructions. Still another problem arises from the special test conditions of personality assessment. Typical instructions for achievement or intelligence testing read as follows: "You are to try your best, but you may not be able to answer all the items. If you do not know the answer to a question, you should guess" (or sometimes, ". . . you will be penalized for guessing a wrong answer"). These instructions are written to motivate the exertion of maximum effort.

But what is maximum effort in a personality test? It simply does not exist because personality testers try to measure *typical* rather than *maximum* performance (Cronbach, 1970). Consequently, psychologists disguise the purpose of personality tests by their instructions, "There are no right or wrong answers," and this deception, which incidentally is detected by most respondents, leads to resentment and faking.

Lack of Self-knowledge. But even if we assume that people want to tell the truth, it is naive to think that they understand their motivations or that they can report accurately their typical behavior. On theoretical grounds alone, as Freud made us well aware (see Chapters 6 and 22), self-knowledge is inversely related to severity of personality disturbance. Consequently, even when people are not motivated to disguise wishes, fantasies, and behavior, they simply may not have enough self-knowledge to render reliable reports about themselves.

Projective Techniques

Projective techniques consist of amorphous stimuli intentionally left ambiguous so that people can express themselves in any way they choose. Consider, for example, the inkblot shown in Figure 4.3. People often respond to this blot by describing it as "two clowns talking" or "two bears trying to pull apart. . . ." Since the inkblot in this figure does not really depict these scenes, such responses must originate from within. In other words, individuals project thoughts and feelings onto the stimuli. This suggests the derivation of the label for this type of test.

Projective techniques are administered in conjunction with interviews, case history data, and self-report inventories. Clinical practitioners prefer to use self-report inventories for more molecular personality descriptions (for example, response tendencies, habits, traits, or behavioral dispositions) and to administer projectives for information about deeper facets of personality (for example, needs, unconscious wishes, and fantasies).

Projection and Projective Techniques. The concept of *projection* was introduced by Freud. He defined it as a process of ascribing one's undesirable drives, feelings, and sentiments to other people or objects in an effort to defend against becoming aware of these threatening qualities in oneself.

The term *projective technique* gained its popularity because of L. K. Frank (1939), who called attention to the importance of a disguised personality measure.[8] Such a method, he believed, gives the tester a glimpse of a person's private world and the way he or she attributes meaning

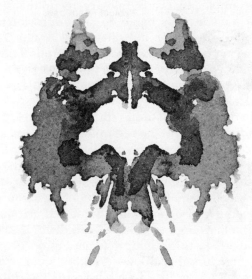

Figure 4.3
An inkblot similar to one used in the Rorschach Test.
(Courtesy Dorsey Press)

to, or projects content into, a relatively plastic field.

The Rorschach Inkblots. Projective methodology's greatest boost came in 1921 with a report by Hermann Rorschach (1884–1922), a Swiss psychiatrist, which described a technique for determining modes of behavior from verbal responses to inkblots. Rorschach believed clinicians needed a tool that afforded greater standardization than was possible by routine clinical observation and that could be used to study unconscious motives and personality. Accordingly, he devised a standard series of ten inkblot pictures.

The Rorschach Inkblot Test is the most widely used projective technique in clinical practice. It is administered by an examiner who presents each of ten cards to the subject with instructions to tell what the blot looks like and what it

---

[8] Until quite recently the origin of the term *projection*, when used to denote a form of test, was attributed to Frank (1939). However, the origin should be credited to H. A. Murray et al. (1938) who, in his volume *Explorations in Personality*, used the label "projection" tests (Lindzey, 1961).

Inkblot	Typical Responses

Two bears kissing
Two clowns clapping hands
A spinning top

A bear rug
A monster sitting on
a tree stump

Animals climbing
The insides of a
person

Two bugs biting
each other
Poached eggs

Figure 4.4
Four inkblots and some typical responses to each.

(Courtesy Dorsey Press)

might be. Responses, some of which are shown in Figure 4.4, are recorded verbatim.

Scoring is in terms of the particular blot areas used, adequacy of response form, use of color and shading, projection of movement and depth, qualitative content of responses, language used to describe what is seen, and many other interrelated characteristics. The Rorschach protocol can be scored and interpreted only by a trained clinician. Examples of interpretations of typical Ror-

schach responses are shown in Table 4.6.

These interpretations clearly do not yield the kind of information that can form the basis for psychiatric diagnostic classification. Rather Rorschach scores tend to provide interpreters with insight into other stylistic aspects of respondents. For example, responses that are formed by using the shape or outline of the blot are said to correspond to "intellectual control"; seeing movement in the blots presumably implies "inner emotional control"; and inclusion of a wide range of content (for example, humans, animals, inanimate objects, and original responses) is said to reflect wide interests.

Thematic Apperception Test (TAT). The other projective technique, almost as popular as the Rorschach, is the *Thematic Apperception Test*, or TAT (Murray et al., 1938; Murray, 1943), which consists of drawings and photographs. Compared with the Rorschach's amorphous blots, the identity of most objects in TAT pictures is obvious. Some ambiguity evidently does exist, however, since people interpret objects in some of the pictures differently; but almost everyone agrees that they depict people or familiar objects and scenes. For example, there is little question that the drawing shown in Figure 4.5, which resembles one TAT test stimulus card, represents a woman standing on the threshold of a half-open doorway and looking into a room. But enough ambiguity remains to allow the woman to be perceived as frowning or cheerful, coming into or leaving the room. Respondents are also free to imagine what the woman sees inside the room.

Test administration consists of presenting 20 cards, 19 having pictures on them and one blank. A total of 31 cards are available, but the tester selects a subset of these, depending on whether the respondent is a girl, boy, woman, or man. The pictures include such diverse content as a young boy contemplating a violin; a rural scene; a young woman staring off into space; spatially anomalous drawings like those of M. C. Escher; and apparent bedroom scenes.

Table 4.6
Examples of Interpretations of Rorschach Responses

Response	Inkblots	Nature of Interpretation
This is a butterfly. Here are the wings, feelers, and legs.		Using the whole blot in this way is considered to reflect the subject's ability to organize and relate materials.
This is part of a chicken's leg.		Referring to only a part of this inkblot is usually interpreted as indicative of an interest in the concrete.
This could be a face.		The use of an unusual or tiny portion of this blot may suggest pedantic trends.
Looks somewhat like a spinning top.		Persons who reverse figure and ground in this manner often are observed as oppositional, negative, and stubborn.

To show how a TAT is interpreted, we present below a response to one of the TAT pictures (Figure 4.6) and the interpreter's analysis of the response. The patient was a 12-year-old boy whose parents had brought him to a child guidance center because of his problems in school. The boy was repeating fifth grade for the second time, and his teachers agreed that the cause of his failure was not lack of intelligence. Here is his response, presented line by line for the purpose of the analysis that follows (Kleinmuntz, 1975, pp. 302–303):

LINE 1: "This boy was supposed to be practicing his violin but he really doesn't feel like it.

LINE 2: "If his mother catches him goofing off from practicing, he is going to get into a lot of trouble.

LINE 3: "She does a lot of yelling and screaming about these types of things and the boy has learned not to excite her.

LINE 4: "She really doesn't care whether he learns to play the thing or not, and as long as she doesn't catch him goofing off, she's satisfied.

Figure 4.5

A picture similar to one in the TAT. Although this picture is more structured than any of the Rorschach inkblots, the respondent still has the opportunity to "read into" various aspects of the stimulus task.

(Courtesy Dorsey Press)

LINE 5: "Right now the boy is trying to figure out how to fool his mother and he thinks maybe he'll tape-record his practice session and then in the future play back the tape recordings while he sneaks out the window and plays with his friends.

LINE 6: "Wait till he tells his friends about the tape recordings and the way he fooled his mother. They'll find out again how smart he *really* is."

In this boy's story there are numerous valuable clues to his personality, subsequently corroborated by his psychologist. Borrowing as little as possible from any particular personality theory, we can analyze each line of the narrative. In actual practice, of course, interpretation of the story proceeds in conjunction with consideration of other narratives and within the context of other assessment procedures:

LINE 1: The opening comment indicates that the subject perceives the violin accurately (most but not all subjects do), that he has been instructed to practice his lessons, and that he does not enjoy playing the violin.

LINE 2: Here the boy suggests that his behavior may make mother unhappy, and she may punish him.

LINE 3: There is some cynicism expressed in this remark, and the subject indicates that his mother is to be placated.

LINE 4: Mother is portrayed as being uninterested in his progress with the violin and will not reprove him so long as she is not confronted with his defiance. This remark probably reveals his opinion of her attitudes toward his violin lessons and seems to be a facet of their relationship worth exploring.

LINE 5: This boy's plan reflects ingenuity and suggests he is willing to take risks.

LINE 6: The final sentence indicates his exhibitionism, his concern about the opinions of others, and fear of being stigmatized as ignorant and mentally slow. It also suggests that he has planned similar deceptions prior to the one described.

In general, TAT interpreters' analyses are highly content-oriented and rely heavily on qualitative characteristics of the stories. They attend to the forces emanating from the "hero" (called *needs*) as well as from the environment (called *press*) and analyze these forces under several categories: the needs of the hero, the pressures of his surroundings, and outcomes of the stories, as well as the interests, sentiments, and relationships of the hero to people and objects in his environment.

The Thompson modification of the TAT, constructed specifically for administration to blacks (Thompson, 1949), portrays black figures rather than white. This test, sometimes called the T-TAT to reflect its author's name, has been found more productive than the TAT in eliciting fantasy material from black college students. (Figure 4.7 is a sample of a card similar to those appearing on this test.) Black students are more responsive to black figures in the stimulus cards because the black Americans' unique experience and history in this country make it all but impossible for them to identify easily with white heroes (see Cobbs, 1967; Coles, 1963; Fanon, 1963, 1967; Franklin, 1965; Grier and Cobbs, 1968, 1971; Guthrie, 1970).

Critical Comment

Detractors have also faulted projective testing for its demonstrated lack of two essential qualities of a good test: reliability (the ability to yield similar scores over time) and validity (assurance that it tests what it is designed to test). Most of these shortcomings may be due to the tests' complex nature and person-to-person administration.

The Rorschach Inkblot Test and TAT are not tests in the usual psychometric sense of the term. In contrast to self-report inventories such as the MMPI, which are group-administered in an impersonal way, these tests are presented one at a

Figure 4.7
A card similar to one that appears in the Thompson modification of the TAT.

(Courtesy Dorsey Press)

time in an interpersonal situation. This is time-consuming, sometimes requiring two or more hours of clinician and patient time. When this much time is spent on a procedure, one can reasonably ask whether the extra time is justified. The evidence is mixed.

In Defense of Projectives. Those who defend the Rorschach Inkblot Test and TAT have cited absence of structure as a feature that makes them resistant to faking. But even here there are problems. Although the ambiguity of the inkblots and to a lesser extent of the photographs and drawings presents a formidable challenge to those who

want to fake the projectives, the ambiguity and subtlety seem to be operating equally well against the tests' scorers and interpreters. Not only is there disagreement among interpreters about the scoring and interpretation of test protocols, but instructions about these procedures abound and no two schools seem to agree.

An Innovation. A promising attempt has been made to bring the Rorschach test closer to being a psychometric device. The *Holtzman Inkblot Technique* (Herron, 1963; Holtzman, 1958, 1959, 1965; Holtzman et al., 1961, 1963; Swartz and Holtzman, 1963), also known by its acronym, HIT, consists of 45 cards that are presented one at a time. The respondent makes one response to each card, and these responses are scored along 22 scales containing most of the information obtained from the Rorschach. By increasing the number of stimuli from ten to 45 and restricting the responses to each card, the HIT has increased the inkblot technique reliability and validity.

Behavioral Assessment

Before the 1960s psychodiagnostic assessment was most often associated with the observational interview and testing procedures just described. Since then a group of clinicians and experimentalists with empirical roots in the conditioning therapy of Joseph Wolpe (1958) and in B. F. Skinner's (1938, 1953, 1969) work with animals developed what is variously called "behavior modification," "behavior therapy," or "behavioral engineering." The conceptual frameworks guiding these new practitioners were classical and operant conditioning, orientations about which we shall have more to say in Chapter 6 and again in Chapter 23. Here it will suffice merely to say that two types of learning experiments have provided the scientific basis for behavioral treatment and assessment: *classical conditioning,* derived from Pavlov's famous studies demonstrating that dogs can be conditioned to salivate to a sound (the conditioned stimulus) that is repeatedly associated with a morsel of food (the unconditioned stimulus); and *operant conditioning*, which views behavior as an "operant" that is controlled and strengthened (or weakened) by its reinforcing (or nonreinforcing) consequences.

Problem Behaviors and Treatment

Behaviorally oriented assessors generally find psychodiagnostic labeling unnecessary. Instead they separate behavior problems into three general classes (see Ciminero, 1977; Goldfried, 1976;

Sundberg, 1977): *behavioral excesses*, which include such problems as overeating, hyperactivity, and nail-biting; *behavior deficits*, which include lack of social skills, poor eating habits (or none at all), and inability to communicate; and *inappropriateness*, which refers to behaviors that are socially unacceptable such as stealing, bowel or urinary evacuation in public, and talking to imaginary companions. Each of these behaviors calls for somewhat different approaches to treatment. Excesses suggest treatment through non-reinforcement; deficits suggest the learning of new skills; and inappropriate behaviors call for programs that teach discrimination between proper and

Behavioral Analysis

Behavioral analysis is a method of assessment quite distinct from psychological testing. It originated in the learning theory approaches of B. F. Skinner (see Chapter 6) and is used by behavior therapists (see Chapter 23) to help them decide which behaviors need changing. The method derives its name from Skinner's idea that behavior is a function of external cues or stimuli that must be discovered in order to predict and control that behavior. The procedure, sometimes also called functional analysis of behavior, and the questions it answers are described below (see Bijou, 1965; Ferster, 1965; Gottman and Leiblum, 1974; Peterson, 1968; Ullmann and Krasner, 1975).

Whereas interviewers and psychological testers are often interested in answering the question "why" something happened ("Why did you hate your brother?" "Why did you do that?"), behavioral assessors are more concerned about the "what" of behavior ("What would you like to change in your behavior?" or "What external stimulus led you to do that?"). The difference is one of orientation. The former technique is

grounded in Freudian and other psychodynamic views holding that behavior has antecedent, unconscious, or intrapsychic origins that must be discovered. Behavioral analysis, in contrast, makes no such assumptions and therefore focuses on the stimuli, situations, and reinforcing circumstances that trigger and sustain behavior.

Psychologists using behavioral analysis ask what the undesirable or abnormal behaviors are. Once they have identified them, they analyze the consequences or reinforcing stimuli that sustain the behavior and prevent other, perhaps more desirable, behaviors from emerging. The behavior identification itself often involves careful observation and control of environmental stimuli in order to determine the frequency of behavior under some specified set of conditions. This provides psychologists with a behavioral baseline from which they can measure subsequent progress. They can then decide how to alter the environment so that desirable rather than abnormal behavior is fostered, rewarded, and strengthened.

improper modes of action. But regardless of the treatment the behavioral assessor searches for the stimulus–response–reinforcement relationships in the environment that are the conditions under which these behaviors occur.

In addition, there are three major functions of behavioral assessment: (1) *description* of the problem, (2) *selection* of a treatment strategy, and (3) *evaluation* of the treatment outcome. The first of these requires the identification of the specific behaviors needing modification, as well as the variables (both antecedents and consequences) controlling these behaviors (see Goldfried and Sprafkin, 1974; Kanfer and Phillips, 1970; Kanfer and Saslow, 1969).

Selection of a treatment strategy, the second major function of behavioral assessment, is based on the finding that important relationships exist between assessment data and effective treatment programs. Some studies have shown that certain behavioral deficits may interfere with certain treatments. For example, one group of researchers (De Moor, 1970; Hain et al., 1966) found that the effectiveness of systematic desensitization (see Chapter 23) was limited if patients had difficulty with relaxation or visual imagery. And Borkovec (1973) reported that fear reduction techniques and direct modification by means of biofeedback may be most useful when the behavioral problems have their origins in the patient's physiological response system.

Evaluating the effectiveness of treatment, which is of great concern to many people doing behavior modification, has been called the *functional analysis of behavior.* Although the term was originally used by Skinner to refer to the analysis of behavior in terms of cause and effect, some behaviorally oriented psychologists (Bijou and Peterson, 1971; Peterson, 1968) describe, under this name, both such an analysis and an evaluation of treatment. Peterson (1968, p. 114) describes functional analysis of behavior below:

The central features of the method are (1) systematic observation of the problem behavior to obtain a

response frequency baseline, (2) systematic observation of the stimulus conditions following and/or preceding the behavior, with special concern for antecedent discriminative cues and consequent reinforcers, (3) experimental manipulation of a condition which seems functionally, hence causally, related to the problem behavior, and (4) further observation to record any changes in behavior which may occur.

Essentially, then, a functional analysis of behavior, by observing whether appropriate changes occur in the problem or target behavior, demonstrates whether a given treatment approach is effective.

One other important clinical theorist whose assessment methods have been considered behavioral was Julian Rotter (1954). He was an early proponent of the social learning approach to clinical problems. Rotter (1966) and his associates (Phares, 1972; Rotter et al., 1972) developed techniques for assessment and treatment that combine reinforcement concepts with cognitive elements. For example, Rotter and his associates conceptualize both an internal and an external *locus of control* of reinforcement, which refers to two types of personalities. Locus of control is a way of expressing the degree to which an individual sees himself in control of his life and the circumstances and events that influence it. People who see themselves as exerting a significant influence over their own lives are Internals (Is); people who believe that events in their lives are determined by forces outside themselves (fate, chance, the government) are Externals (Es). These people are assumed to differ in their generalized expectations or beliefs about causation and about the sources of their reinforcements.

Rotter's method for assessing whether a person attributes causes of his or her behavior to internal or external forces was to create measures from which I–E tendencies could be inferred. Then he observed behavior in real-life settings and contrived experimental situations to permit meaningful comparisons between the I- and

E-oriented individuals. His first measures resemble traditional psychometric self-report inventories: A person is instructed to choose one each from a series of item pairs, one of which reflects an expectation that one can control his or her life ("In my case, getting what I want has little or nothing to do with luck"), and the other an expectation that outside forces are in control ("Many times we might just as well decide what to do by flipping a coin").

Findings from observations in real-life situations and from experimental settings have suggested that perceptions of control influence a wide array of behaviors. For example, individuals scoring high on internality appear more active in their attempts to control and master the environment. They seek out more information relevant to their goals, are less subject to subtle social influence, are better adjusted, and can laugh at themselves in the face of failure, thus exhibiting frustration tolerance and the defenses necessary to cope with stress (Phares, 1972).

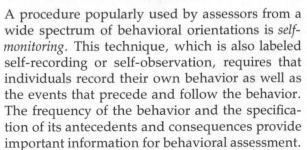

Self-monitoring

A procedure popularly used by assessors from a wide spectrum of behavioral orientations is *self-monitoring*. This technique, which is also labeled self-recording or self-observation, requires that individuals record their own behavior as well as the events that precede and follow the behavior. The frequency of the behavior and the specification of its antecedents and consequences provide important information for behavioral assessment.

This is not a new procedure; its origins have been traced to Benjamin Franklin (see Ciminero et al., 1977; Thoresen and Mahoney, 1974), but some of its current uses are unique. Three main current uses are common (Ciminero et al., 1977): (1) to obtain baseline frequencies of target behaviors; (2) to obtain a self-recorded report of progress (or lack of it) during therapy; and (3) to effect a behavior change, since the very act of self-recording has been shown to produce

changes in the frequency of behavior (Ernst, 1973; Maletzky, 1974; Rutner and Bugle, 1969; Sobell and Sobell, 1973).

A variety of self-recording techniques have been used, most quite crude compared to the sophisticated electronic equipment used by these same investigators in their laboratories. For example, the simplest of these methods involves the use of paper and pencil, with which the individual may be encouraged to keep a *behavioral diary* or to chart a *behavior graph*. The first of these, as the name suggests, merely requires the patient to record in a notebook or on cards when and where the behavior occurred and what happened before and after the response. The behavior graph (see Mahoney and Thoresen, 1974) requires charting of behavior on a standard sheet of graph paper. The graph is usually set up so that the horizontal axis is divided into units of time (for example, hours, days, weeks) and some measure of behavior strength (for example, frequency or duration) is placed on the vertical axis.

Somewhat less crude devices are the various mechanical counters that are manually operated by the subjects under study. These counters are generally used to collect frequency data and as such are of limited usefulness (see Lindsley, 1968; Mahoney, 1974a). In the same category of crudeness are the timing devices used to collect duration data. For example, Mahoney and Thoreson (1974) describe how an electric clock with a switch installed in the cord was used to help a student increase the amount of time he spent on his studies.

The most sophisticated self-recording devices currently in use are electronic video and audio tape recorders. Other, rather innovative devices are the cigarette case that automatically records the number of times it is opened (Azrin and Powell, 1968); a posture-detecting device to help straighten bad posture (Azrin et al., 1968); a gravity-sensitive watch to record hyperactivity (see Schwitzgebel and Kolb, 1974); and a stabilometric cushion that fits on the seat of the child's chair, also to measure hyperactivity (see

Table 4.7
Verbal Subtests and Representative Items of the WAIS

Subtests	Sample Items
Information	How many nickels make a dime?
	What is pepper?
Comprehension	What is the advantage of keeping money in a bank?
	Why is copper used in electrical wires?
Arithmetic	Sam had three pieces of candy and Joe gave him four more. How many pieces of candy did Sam have altogether?
	If two apples cost 15¢, what will be the cost of a dozen apples?
Similarities	In what way are a lion and a tiger alike?
	In what way are a circle and a triangle alike?
Vocabulary	This test consists simply of asking "What is a _____?" or "What does _____ mean?" The words cover a wide range of difficulty or familiarity.
Digit span	Repeat the following digits after me: 8–5–3–2–7
	Now say the following digits backwards: 3–6–2–1

Source: Reproduced with permission of the Psychological Corporation.

Miklich, 1975). The last of these devices was recently used in combination with radio-telemetry as an aide in the behavior modification of hyperactive children (Christensen and Sprague, 1973),

who were seated on the cushion and were told that they would receive rewards proportional to the number registered on a counter at their desk. Information from the cushion was transmitted to modular programming equipment located in another room. This equipment recorded the data and also determined when a child's activity was sufficiently reduced to deserve a reinforcement under the schedule in effect. When a reinforcement was due, a second transmitter was triggered and a signal was sent to a receiver–counter on the child's desk.

Several problems are associated with the use of the more crude types of self-monitoring devices. Among these are problems shared with many verbal self-reporting tests and inventories. Namely, aside from the possible distortions that result from conscious and unconscious motives of the self-reporter, inaccuracies result from the difficulties inherent in keeping recordings concurrent with the unfolding of behavior (Epstein et al., 1976). In an effort to improve the reliability of self-monitoring, several investigators have shown that accuracy increases if accurate self-monitoring is rewarded by some external means such as verbal feedback (Risley and Hart, 1968), tokens that purchase privileges and food (Fixsen et al., 1972), and good school grades (Flowers, 1972).

Intelligence Testing

The two main psychodiagnostic objectives of *intelligence testing* are to establish level of cognitive functioning, or IQ, and to estimate intellectual deterioration. The latter aim, probably more common in testing among adults, evaluates how far an individual's intelligence has fallen below an earlier level. Intellectual deterioration is most apparent in patients with central nervous system disorders (see Chapter 5) but may also be evident in other disturbed individuals, especially schizophrenics (see Chapter 12).

The Wechsler Tests

The intelligence tests in widest clinical use today are those of Wechsler and of Binet. The former series consists of the *Wechsler Preschool–Primary Scale of Intelligence,* or WPPSI (1967), intended for children from 4 to $6^{1}/_{2}$; the *Wechsler Intelligence Scale for Children,* or WISC (1949), and its 1974 revision, the WISC-R (Wechsler, 1974), appropriate for those whose ages fall between 7 and 16; and the *Wechsler Adult Intelligence Scale,* or WAIS, designed for adults over 16 (1955). All these yield verbal and performance IQs, together giving a full-scale IQ. Table 4.7 lists representative verbal subtests of the WAIS and several items similar to those that appear on these subtests.

The Binet Scales

One of the earliest tests of general intelligence was developed because in 1903 Alfred Binet (1857–1911) was asked by the Minister of Public Instruction in France to devise a method for identifying slow learners in the Paris schools. Together with Theodore Simon (1873–1962), Binet developed what was first called the Binet–Simon Scale and, after several revisions in the United States, has come to be called the *Stanford–Binet Scale.*

Binet conceptualized intelligence as a steadily growing power; he therefore proposed a scale, or ladder of tests, that allowed him to assess how far up a child could go before the tests become too difficult. For any level on this ladder Binet selected tasks that average children at that age are able to master. The tests for young children involve relatively simple discriminations and recall, whereas those for middle childhood require more complex reasoning. The Stanford–Binet is applicable for the ages $2^{1}/_{2}$ through average adult. Table 4.8 illustrates representative tasks similar to those that appear on this test (Terman and Merrill, 1960; Thorndike, 1973).

A child's score is the sum of the months for

Table 4.8
Representative Tasks Similar to Those of the Stanford–Binet

Year	Task
II-6	*Identifying Objects by Name:* Show the card with five small objects attached and say, "See these things? Show me the car." "Show me the window," etc.
	Obeying Simple Commands: Put objects on a table and say, "Bring me the doll." "Put the car in the box," etc.
IV	*Opposite Analogies:* (a) "Sam is a boy; Doris is a . . ." (b) "Children talk; dogs . . ."
	Memory for Sentences: Say, "Mary is getting the newspaper for her father."
VI	*Differences:* "What is the difference between glass and ice?" "Night and day?"
	Mutilated Pictures: Show a card with mutilated pictures and ask, "What is gone in this picture?"
VIII	*Similarities and Differences:* I want you to tell me how the things I will name are alike and how they are different. "In what way are a dog and a cat the same?" "How are they different?"
	Comprehension: Ask, "What should you do if someone you know tells you to skip school?"

Source: Adapted from Terman, L. M. and Merrill, M. A. Measuring intelligence. Boston: Houghton Mifflin, 1960.

which he or she received credit, and this total is called the *mental age* (MA). In some of the earlier revisions of the test, an *intelligence quotient* (IQ) was computed by dividing the MA by the CA (chronological age) and multiplying by 100. For example, a child with an MA of 12 and a CA of 10 would earn an IQ of 120. In later forms the mental age was transformed to an IQ by simply referring to a conversion table that takes the child's chronological age into consideration.

Interpretation of Test Scores

How is an IQ interpreted? We can obtain some idea of this by noting the adjectives commonly used to describe various IQ levels. Table 4.9 contains such descriptions and shows the percentage of the general population included within each group (see p. 64).

Intelligence tests, as mentioned at the outset of this section, are used in mental health settings mostly to assess level of thinking. This evaluation facilitates classification of children or adults according to what they can or should be expected to accomplish intellectually, an especially important consideration for people at the lower end of the intelligence distribution.

Jensenism

That there are measured IQ differences between black and white children of both sexes in America has, with some notable exceptions (Jones, 1972, p. 61), been repeatedly demonstrated by psychologists. But there is considerable controversy about whether these differences, which tend to be about ten to twenty points on the average in favor of white children, are due to environmental or hereditary determinants.

The central figure in this controversy is Arthur Jensen, a University of California (Berkeley) educational psychologist who, to support his heredity argument, invokes the concept of *heritability*. This is a technical term that he borrowed from quantitative genetics and that refers to the proportion of a trait that can be attributed to genetic factors. Using this concept, Jensen concludes that heredity accounts for up to 80 percent of the obtained IQ differences. His main thesis was contained in a lengthy article, "How Can We Boost IQ and Scholastic Achievement?" (Jensen, 1969), which appeared in the prestigious *Harvard Educational Review*. Its appearance, which stirred a considerable furor among psychologists and in the popular press, led one journalist (Edson, 1969, p. 10) to coin the term "jensenism," which he defined as a noun, describing "the theory that IQ is largely determined by genes."

Later, Jensen (1973) defended the herita-bility argument by placing the burden of the proof on the shoulders of the environmentalists. Thus he states, "Of course, they [environmental causes] may be *possible* explanations of the IQ difference, but that does not necessarily make them the *most probable*. . . . I am not saying that they have been proven 100 percent wrong, only that they do not account for all of the black IQ deficit" (Jensen, 1973, p. 81).

Jensen's arguments for the genetic hypothesis consist mainly of counterproposals to the cultural and environmental explanations. Thus, in answer to the argument that blacks do less well than whites on culture-biased tests because blacks do not know this culture, he contends that studies indicate that Arctic Eskimos, Orientals, and Mexican- and Native Americans do as well on IQ tests as white Anglos. He also discounts the effects of the tester's race as an influence lowering black children's scores, by pointing to a study of his own in which 9000 black and white children were administered a number of "standard mental tests" by both black and white examiners. No systematic differences could be attributed to the race of the examiner. All in all Jensen (1973, p. 80) believes that genetic factors have been ignored because of "fear and abhorrence of racism" and because research into the possible genetic influence has been considered "academically

A second purpose of intelligence tests, it will be recalled, is to estimate the extent of intellectual deterioration in brain-damaged or disturbed individuals. The most direct way to accomplish this, of course, would be to compare test scores obtained before and after the onset of the disorder; unfortunately, however, pre-illness tests are usually not available and, therefore, interpretations must be based on available test scores. This involves comparing current IQ with a reasonable estimate of past intellectual functioning. Thus if an individual has a college education and currently functions at an IQ level of 95, it is probably correct to infer that some loss has occurred.

There is also evidence to suggest that vocabulary declines less than speeded performance

and socially taboo."

Jensen's critics are far more sophisticated than he cares to admit. For example, the noted geneticist Theodosius Dobzhansky (1973, p. 98) contends that Jensen's use of the term heritability is faulty in that its application to the individual case is spurious. Moreover he notes that the "same gene constellation can result in a higher or lower score in different circumstances. Genes determine the intelligence (or stature or weight) of a person only in his particular environment. The trait that actually develops is conditioned by the interplay of the genes with the environment."

But perhaps even more convincing evidence of the fallacy of Jensen's heritability hypothesis can be found in a study by Sandra Scarr–Salapatek (1975), who demonstrated that different race and class IQ averages are less genetically determined than individual variations in IQ. Her study was conducted among 1521 pairs of twins attending public schools in Philadelphia. She compared test scores across races and socioeconomic levels and found that individual genetic differences show up more in persons who mature in favorable surroundings, but remain hidden or unused in individuals from adverse environments. Therefore, she concludes, both the percentage of genetic variance and the mean scores are very much influenced by the rearing condition of the population.

R. C. Lewontin (1976), a population geneticist, has criticized Jensen for equating "inherited" with "unchangeable," as well as incorrectly interpreting in several other respects the relationship among gene, environment, and organism. However, the most damaging objections to the biological determinist position grew out of an address to the American Psychological Association in 1973 in which psychologist Leon Kamin argued convincingly that Sir Cyril Burt, whose research supplied much of the "factual" basis for the genetic-determination-of-IQ hypothesis, had faked his data. In England Ann Clarke, a psychologist at Hull University, and her husband, Professor Alan Clarke, followed Kamin's lead and came up with additional evidence that Burt's data points had never existed outside his own mind. The crowning blow came when Oliver Gillie, the London *Sunday Times* medical correspondent, tried to locate two of Burt's collaborators, Margaret Howard and J. Conway, who should have been able to shed some light on the controversy. Gillie found that no one at University College (London) had any recollection of either of the two researchers, nor was there any official record that they had ever existed. Jensen himself first noted the difficulties with Burt's data, and has now conceded that Burt's data cannot be relied upon, but the controversy continues.

Some Sociopolitical Consequences of IQ Testing

Intelligence testing in America, according to two books, *The Politics of IQ Testing* (Kamin, 1975) and *Even the Rat Was White* (Guthrie, 1975), has been used more or less consciously to oppress the poor, the foreign born, and racial minorities. This misuse was not the doing of avowed racists or fascists; rather it was the work of America's leading pioneers of mental tests who probably believed that they were reporting sound scientific findings—Lewis Terman of Stanford; Robert Yerkes of Harvard; and Henry Goddard of Vineland, New Jersey.

In his 1916 book introducing the Stanford–Binet, for example, Terman described the poor performance of Indian and Mexican children (p. 92): Mental retardation "represents the level of intelligence which is very, very common among Spanish-Indians and Mexican families of the Southwest and also among negroes. Their dullness seems to be racial." What was his evidence? In addition to the use of a test that was constructed on a sample of 1000 children and 400 adults—none of them black, brown, or red—he cites his own random observations as follows (p. 92):

The fact that one meets this type with such extraordinary frequency among Indians, Mexicans, and negroes suggests quite forcibly the whole question of racial differences which cannot be wiped out by any scheme of mental culture.

These were the findings and conclusions of one of the foremost psychologists of this time, later to be elected president of the American Psychological Association. And what were this influential scientist's solutions? One was pedagogical (p. 92): "Children of this group should be segregated in special classes and be given instruction which is concrete and practical. They cannot master abstractions." The other solution was eugenic (p. 93): "There is no possibility at present of convincing society that they should not be allowed to reproduce, although from a

items, abstract reasoning, and concept attainment. Vocabulary is therefore taken as a measure of past intellectual level, and the discrepancy between the vocabulary score and levels achieved on other subtests suggests the amount of decline.

Intelligence testing has also been severely criticized. Among others, Kamin (1973) has pointed out that intelligence testing has repeatedly been turned into a political and social weapon for the suppression of minorities or other unfavored groups. The eugenics movement early in this century was one such instance; its simplistic thesis was that crime and delinquency could be prevented by mass sterilization of low-IQ individuals (who just happened to be mostly members of ethnic and racial groups other than white Anglo–Saxon Protestant). In particular, intelligence testing has had a long history of use in systematic discrimination against blacks (Guthrie, 1975). One group of black psychologists has argued that current practices in intelligence testing are harmful to the mental well-being of black children (see Barnes, 1972; Cleary et al., 1975; Jackson, 1975; Williams and Rivers, 1972). Some of these psychologists have called for a moratorium on the testing of these children.

eugenic point of view they constitute a grave problem because of their unusually prolific breeding."

At least Terman was a man of patience, a quality strikingly absent in Goddard and Yerkes, both of whom managed to exert a direct influence on America's immigration policies. Henry Goddard, who in 1912 was invited by the U.S. Public Health Service to apply the new mental tests to arriving European immigrants, reported that 83 percent of Jews, 80 percent of Hungarians, 79 percent of Italians, and 87 percent of Russians were "feebleminded." He was able to report triumphantly several years later, in 1917, that the use of mental tests "for the detection of feebleminded aliens" had vastly increased the number of aliens deported (Goddard, 1917, p. 243).

Similarly, as a result of the mass intelligence testing that was introduced by Colonel Robert Yerkes during the screening of American draftees in World War I, black–white dif-ferences were found as well as evidence that the "Latin and Slavic countries stand low." The Poles, it was reported, did not score significantly higher than the blacks. These results were published in 1921 in the prestigious *Annals* of the National Academy of Sciences, and became generally known in Congress. Consequently in 1924 Congress passed a law not only restricting the total number of immigrants, but also assigning national origin quotas as determined by the census of 1890. That is, immigration from European countries was restricted according to the proportion of persons represented in the American population in 1890. The intent of setting the quota on the basis of 1890 rather than 1920 was clearly to curtail "biologically inferior" immigration from southeastern Europe. That same law led ultimately to the deaths of tens of thousands of victims of the Nazi holocaust, denied entry to the United States because their quota had been filled.

Brain Damage Testing

Another type of testing that is of interest to clinical psychologists involves the detection of damage to the central nervous system, or brain damage. Although these measures are not without their critics (see articles by Billingslea, 1963; Mosher and Smith, 1965; Tolor and Schulberg, 1963; and Yates, 1954), many clinicians and researchers believe in their worth (see Russell et al., 1970).

The Bender Visual–Motor Gestalt Test

One of the most widely used brain damage tests is the *Bender Gestalt Test*, which is a measure of perceptual–motor skills. It was developed by Lauretta Bender (1938), a psychiatrist at Bellevue Hospital in New York City, and is administered as follows: patients are seated and given paper and pencils with erasers; they are instructed to copy nine designs shown to them; the card bearing the first design is presented, and after the patients have copied it, they are shown the second one; this continues until they have finished the entire series, after which some examiners ask the patient to reconstruct the entire series from memory.

Although an acceptable quantitative scoring system for the Bender Gestalt has not yet been successfully worked out for differentiating

Table 4.9
Distribution of IQs; Descriptive Adjectives and
Percentage in Each Category

IQ	Classification	Percent Included
130 and above	Very superior	2.2
120–129	Superior	6.7
110–119	Bright normal	16.1
90–109	Average	50.0
80–89	Dull normal	16.1
70–79	Borderline	6.7
69 and below	Mental defective	2.2

Source: Wechsler, D. WAIS Manual: Wechsler Adult Intelligence Scale. *New York: Psychological Corporation, 1955. Reproduced by permission. Copyright © 1955 by The Psychological Corporation, New York, N.Y. All rights reserved.*

brain-damaged from non-brain-damaged individuals, some helpful hints are obtained by attending to certain qualitative aspects of the drawings. Among the more important diagnostic signs on the Bender Gestalt are oversimplification, fragmentation, rotation, reversals, and, in some serious cases, complete inability to reproduce designs. Figure 4.8 illustrates these signs by showing some typical Bender Gestalt drawings found among persons with central nervous system disorders.

A Battery of Tests

A much more complex, and reportedly more valid, approach to brain damage testing was developed by three investigators (Russell et al., 1970). Using a series of tests developed by Ward Halstead (1951) and Ralph Reitan (1966), they developed objective decision rules, much like those described earlier for MMPI interpretation, for identifying the presence of neurological lesions. They apply their decision rules to inter-preting the configuration of scores that patients obtain on the battery of tests. In other words people are diagnosed as brain-damaged or not depending on the combination of scores they obtain on such tests as spatial relations, speed of finger tapping, several WAIS subtests, and such tests of abstract and concrete thinking as those of Goldstein and Scheerer (1941).

The validity of these decision rules for the purpose of identifying brain damage was established by comparing the descriptions made in terms of them with objective findings based on EEG (electroencephalogram) and other neurological tests. The advantage of using these interpretive rules rather than having clinicians use their intuitive judgments about score patterns is that, once they are devised, a clerk or computer can render decisions by using them, thus freeing the clinician for other jobs. Besides, if they are good rules, they can surpass the clinician's performance because they apply their logic more consistently.

Ethical Problems in Psychological Testing

Like observational and interview procedures, psychological testing is not without its difficulties. Aside from the many technical considerations and problems already mentioned throughout this chapter, there are numerous *ethical* ones associated with testing, especially personality assessment.

One of the most basic criticisms is that tests are an invasion of privacy.[9] Two reasons for this are given: first, personality inventory questions about sex and religion are personal and should only be asked in privileged communication relationships; second, these tests give government

[9] In addition to sources cited here, the interested reader is referred to the special issue of the *American Psychologist* (American Psychological Association, 1965).

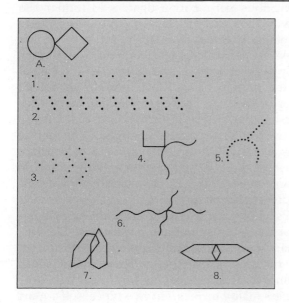

Figure 4.8
The figures for the Bender Visual-Motor Gestalt Test. They usually appear individually on nine separate cards, and the patient is instructed to copy each of them and then to recall the entire series.

(Bender, 1946. Copyright the American Orthopsychiatric Association, Inc. Reproduced by permission)

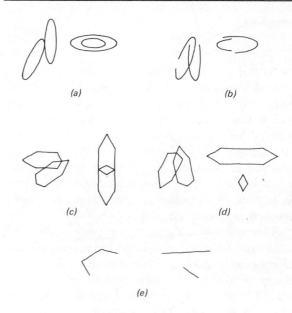

Figure 4.9
Representative Bender Gestalt drawings by persons with central nervous system damage. The five signs shown in these reproductions of two designs (7 and 8, Figure 4.8) include (a) oversimplification, (b) fragmentation, (c) rotation, (d) reversals, and (e) abortive reproduction.

administrators and law enforcement agents power over the individual. The following statement by a U.S. congressman makes these points (Gallagher, 1965, pp. 881–882):

Remember there is nothing voluntary about these tests . . . persons could not select their own private psychologists and doctors to conduct and evaluate the tests . . . I am sure that in some cases the tests are a useful tool in psychiatric evaluation when they are used in a clinical situation where there is a doctor-patient relationship. . . . What bothers me is that personnel people often are interpreting these tests, and the answers are reposing in some government file somewhere, all set to follow the person throughout his career or non-career.

The charge that personality inventory items probe into personal matters has an element of truth to it, but one must consider the rationale for doing so. Hathaway (1964), coauthor of the MMPI, draws the following analogy (pp. 206–207):

If the psychologist cannot use these personal items to aid in the assessment of people, he suffers as did the Victorian physician who had to examine his female patients by feeling the pulse in the delicate hand thrust from behind a screen . . . it is obvious that if we were making a new MMPI, we would again be faced either with being offensive to subgroupings of people by personal items they object to or, if we did not include personal items and were inoffensive, we would have lost the aim of the instrument.

And if personality tests do have an element of coerciveness about them, this must be weighed against the consideration that it may sometimes be essential to know whether or not a person is unsuited for an assignment because of a serious personality disorder. Tests such as the MMPI can be useful to help identify persons who may do serious harm to themselves and others (for example, in military or police settings) and who might benefit from psychological counseling.

The use of computers for personality and intelligence tests has also been the subject of ethical concern. Again the potential for invasion of privacy is amplified when computers are used because of their capacity for large-scale storage and rapid retrieval. It is apparent that a special subset of standards for ethical uses will have to be developed before widespread computer use becomes a reality.

To the charges made against the technical flaws of tests and their computer interpretations, the psychologist must reply with further research designed to improve measurement instruments and computer decision-making; to the accusations of misuse of tests and machines, the psychologist must be at the forefront in working to assure sound ethical practices.

Summary

In all the sciences, data are collected by observation. Observing human beings, is especially difficult, however, because they are more likely to react to being studied and because the observer is also a human.

Observations are of two types: naturalistic and controlled. Naturalistic observations are difficult to obtain without numerous hardware aids and rating scales to add precision to the way information is collected and recorded. Controlled observations permit investigators to induce the behavior they want to view. Both methods have advantages and disadvantages.

At least two types of interviews are commonly used in clinics and hospitals: the intake and the mental status. The first, which is the briefer of the two, collects initial data about patients and important information about the nature and course of possible treatment. The mental status interview delves into numerous sensitive areas having to do mainly with evaluating the person's speech, mood, orientation, and cognitive preoccupations.

Psychological tests systematically sample behavior that is presumably related to real-life situations. These tests add another dimension to psychodiagnosis by yielding information about personality, intelligence, and brain damage.

Personality tests are of two types: self-report and projective. Self-report tests confront subjects with objective items that require fixed alternative responses; projective techniques challenge subjects to create imaginative productions. Each type of test has its advantages and disadvantages: self-report inventories are too restrictive and they are susceptible to faking; projectives, although less vulnerable to faking, are difficult to score and interpret.

A recent addition to the clinician's tools for personality study is *behavioral assessment*. It's roots are in classical and operant conditioning.

Intelligence testing consists of the Wechsler series of tests and the Stanford–Binet scales. Their purpose is chiefly to evaluate level of intellectual functioning, although often they are also used to estimate cognitive deterioration. Separate procedures are also available for brain damage testing.

Aside from the many technical problems inherent in psychological testing, numerous ethical issues surround the use of tests and computers for psychodiagnosis. Mainly these moral considerations have to do with the problem of invasion of privacy. No doubt these issues are as important as the technical ones.

Terms and Concepts to Master

Acquiescence

Behavior sample

Behavioral assessment

Bender Gestalt Test

Brain damage

Clinical scales

Controlled observation

Deviation hypothesis

Intake interview

Intelligence quotient (IQ)

Intelligence test

Interviewee errors

Interviewer errors

Locus of control

Mental age (MA)

Mental status interview

MMPI

Naturalistic observation

Objectivity (of tests)

Projection

Projective technique

Psychological test

Response styles

Rorschach Inkblot Test

Self-report inventory

Situational tests

Standardization (of tests)

Stimulus ambiguity

Structure

Test faking

TAT

T-TAT

Validity scales

5 Biological Determinants of Behavior Disorders

Disordered behavior, like any other behavior, results from the complex interplay of motivational, sociocultural, and biological forces. No two individuals are alike with respect to these forces, nor is one individual subject to the same combination of forces at all times. The main biological determinants of abnormality are hereditary and brain factors, as well as endocrine imbalances, and physical deprivations and deficiencies. These may influence behavior singly or in combination, as we shall see.

Hereditary Factors

Heredity has an indirect role in the formation of behavior pathology: what is inherited is not pathology itself, but rather the underlying raw materials (temperament, constitution, biological makeup) that are partly responsible for its development.

How do we know whether a trait is hereditary? It is usually considered hereditary if its distribution in a family follows specific rules of genetic transmission. For example, a higher incidence of behavior pathology among a patient's closer relatives than among more distant ones is generally taken as a sign that a disorder is hereditary.

Unfortunately, this kind of evidence is easily and commonly misread. The fact often overlooked is that members of a family, especially close relatives, tend to share the same environment and to participate in the same patterns of communication (or non-communication). The complexity of behavior etiology makes it difficult for the clinician to separate the influence of genes from the influence of parent and sibling relationships, roles, and expectations.

Genes and Chromosomes

Each cell of the human organism carries 23 pairs of chromosomes. A chromosome[1] contains about twenty thousand genes; therefore, there are about one million genes in a human cell. Until recently the existence of a gene was hypothetical—that is, its existence was inferred rather than observed. The electron microscope made it possible to see genes, and subsequently the structure of the gene was discovered (Watson and Crick, 1953; Watson, 1968).

Germ Cells

Germ cells are produced in the male testis and female ovary in the form of sperm and eggs, respectively. During germ-cell formation, *meiosis*, or cell division, occurs, and the number of chro-

---

[1] Chromosomes are long, thin threads that can be seen under an electron microscope—they are called *chromo*somes because they color dark after staining.

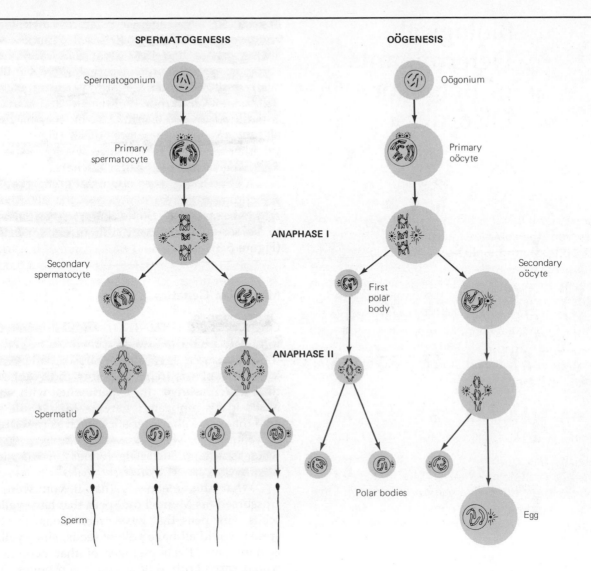

SPERMATOGENESIS

Spermatogonium

Primary spermatocyte

ANAPHASE I

Secondary spermatocyte

ANAPHASE II

Spermatid

Sperm

OÖGENESIS

Oögonium

Primary oöcyte

First polar body

Secondary oöcyte

Polar bodies

Egg

Figure 5.1

A diagram representing the meiotic sequence in the male and female animal; the process of spermatogenosis, resulting in the formation of four sperm; and oogenesis, resulting in the formation of one egg and three polar bodies.

(Gardner, 1960. Reproduced by permission)

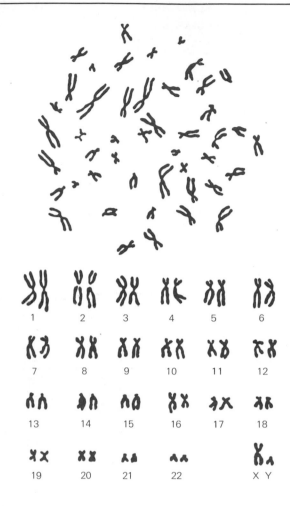

Figure 5.2
Chromosomes of the normal human male.

(From Recent Advances in Human Genetics, 1961. Ed.
L. S. Penrose, London: Churchill)

mosomes reduces from 23 pairs to 23 single chromosomes in each germ cell (Figure 5.1).

The fertilized ovum receives the full complement of genes and chromosomes, 23 from each parent. Of these 23 pairs, one pair (one chromosome from each parent) determines the sex of the child. Since a female has only XX chromosomes

in each cell, every egg she produces carries an X chromosome. Since a male's sex chromosomes are XY, about half his sperm cells carry an X chromosome, while the other half carry a Y. If an egg is fertilized by an X-bearing sperm, the child will be an XX and therefore female, and if an egg is fertilized by a Y-bearing sperm, the child will be an XY and therefore male (Figure 5.2). Whether an egg is fertilized by an X- or a Y-bearing sperm is a matter of chance.

A gene that causes abnormality may be in a sex chromosome, in which case the disorder is said to be *sex-linked*. Some characteristics are said to be *sex-influenced*, and others are *sex-limited* (Figure 5.3).

Mendelian Genetics

Gregor Mendel (1822–1884), an Austrian monk, formulated his now classic principles of genetic transmission in 1866 after years of patient and systematic observations of plants and vegetables that he crossbred. In experiments with peas raised in his monastery garden, Mendel discovered that some characteristics, such as roundness or yellowness, were carried by *dominant genes*, whereas others, such as greenness or wrinkledness, were carried by *recessive genes*.

What this means is that if you were to crossbreed (as Mendel did) peas that have yellow seeds with peas that have green seeds, the offspring would all have yellow seeds, since yellow is dominant. Each member of that generation would carry both yellow and green genes. The next generation would be a mixture of yellow and green, about three yellow to one green. If the yellow seeds were then planted, about one-third of them would produce only yellow seeds, and two-thirds would produce both yellow and green seeds. The green seeds would produce only green seeds.

Translating this into human genetics, we can observe that a person bearing only the genes for blue eyes will have blue eyes, and a person bearing only the genes for brown eyes will have brown eyes, but a person bearing both will also have brown eyes, since brown is dominant. Very few human traits are determined by a single gene pair, but most human traits are determined by several thousand pairs.[2] This is called *polygenic*, or multiple gene, *inheritance*; it occurs even in such characteristics as eye, skin, or hair color, as witnessed by the great variations in hues among offspring of the same parents. Therefore it is correct to say that there are gradations of characteristics, rather than discrete differences. The effects of polygenic inheritance are apparent in almost all human physical and some psychological traits, and the observed characteristics are the result of the complex interaction among the more than twenty thousand gene pairs in the chromosomes.

This does not mean, however, that the effects of dominance or recessiveness are not observable in human genetic research. Many such dominant and recessive characteristics have been isolated. Some of these are listed in Table 5.1, and it is apparent from inspection of this list that neither dominance nor recessiveness implies desirability. The gene producing six fingers on each hand, for instance, is dominant over the gene producing five fingers, yet the latter is considered the normal condition.[3]

Human Genetic Research

With these basic genetic concepts as background, we can now concentrate on the three main ways

---

[2] The entire genetic complement of a plant or an organism is its *genotype*, but strictly speaking, genotypes are not observable. Instead investigators can only view *phenotypes*, which are the surface, or observable, phenomena expressed by genotypes. From these observations, investigators infer specific genotypes.

[3] The reader will find more detailed discussions of basic genetics in Carter (1970), Dobzhansky (1962), Penrose (1961), and Rosenthal (1970, 1971).

Table 5.1

Some Traits Transmitted by Dominant and Recessive Genes

Dominant Traits	Recessive Traits
Brown, green, or hazel eye colors	Blue or gray eye colors
Dark hair	Blonde hair
Curly hair	Straight hair
Black skin	White skin
Normal pigmentation	Albinism
Migraine headache	Normal
Huntington's chorea	Normal
Hereditary tremor	Normal
Normal hearing	Congenital deafness
Six fingers each hand	Five fingers each hand
Webbed fingers or toes	Normal
Dwarfism	Normal

Source: After table "Some hereditary traits in man." In Health science, *2nd ed., by Kenneth L. Jones, Louis W. Shainberg, and Curtis O. Byer. New York: Harper & Row, 1971, p. 339.*

to investigate genetic transmission in human beings: *pedigree, family*, and *twin* studies. For many years the first two of these were the methods chosen; but recently they have come under increasing criticism because they rely so heavily on information gathered from hearsay and from less than completely credible sources.

Pedigree Studies. The most direct way to study genetic transmission of traits is to examine the pedigree, or history, of a family line that displays some characteristic or trait of interest. The assumption of such studies is that the genetic hypothesis (genetic determinism) is confirmed when a trait or disorder distributes itself according to Mendelian genetics.

Specifically in this method the investigators locate an *index case* that represents the disorder they are analyzing. They then search for relatives of the index case, distant and near, and after identifying all relatives, they examine and interview them in order to ascertain whether the incidence of the disorder in their pedigree is consistent with Mendelian dominant or recessive patterns.

Two families have become well known in the psychological literature because they were studied by this method: the Jukes, a family that was traced through several generations of feeblemindedness, crime, and disease; and the Kallikaks, a family whose feeblemindedness was derived from a female progenitor. Both families

The XYY Syndrome and Crime

There has been much interest in recent years in the so-called XYY syndrome, in which males possess an extra Y chromosome, giving them three sex chromosomes, or a total of 47 chromosomes (47,XYY). In the normal configuration there are two sex chromosomes, or a total of 46 chromosomes (46,XY). Little was known about the XYY male, a rather rare condition, until an unusual number of cases were discovered in a maximum-security prison in England.

Before the discovery of XYY males in prisons, only 11 cases had been identified, all had been found by chance, and criminality had not been associated with the condition. Although the condition was known to be rare, no one knew how rare. In order to determine the 47,XYY genotype, a complete karyotype had to be made, a difficult and time-consuming process that involves micrographic counting of chromosomes in a cell nucleus. In 1965 Patricia Jacobs and her colleagues (Jacobs et al., 1965) undertook such karyotyping among prisoners in a British institution for the criminally insane. The investigators had been searching for any type of chromosomal error among the criminals and found seven cases of XYY. Considering that only 11 cases had previously been observed, this discovery was quite unexpected. It attracted much attention, and other studies were made, first in Great Britain and then in the United States (Hope, 1967; Nielsen, 1968; Telfer et al., 1968; Marinello, 1969), and the picture that emerged was that of a taller than average man, usually with mild mental deficiency and a repeated history of aggressiveness. Nonetheless little was known for certain about the XYY syndrome's connection to criminality, except that chance alone could not account for the numbers of XYY prisoners.

Many other subsequent investigations were then conducted. The original phenotypic reports of tallness, aggressiveness, and borderline intelligence were substantiated, with some variations. A number of the individuals studied were observed to have severe acne well after puberty. No sexual defects were found, and no brain wave abnormalities were observed. Few cases had either siblings or parents with histories of criminality or mental illness, and no other environmental or inheritable factors were uniformly associated with XYY. A "typical" case history was described by Jarvik and associates (1973): the subject was uncontrollably antisocial from his early childhood. He attended school intermittently from age 6 thorough age 10, and was repeatedly found to be a hopeless disciplinary problem. Institutionalized at age 10, he escaped whenever possible, and compiled a long record of crimes against property. He was characterized as a loner, and was prone to unpredictable, impulsive violence.

What is the connection between the XYY syndrome and violence? One conclusion drawn by some researchers (Clark et al., 1970) on this matter was that the phenotype of an individual with an extra Y chromosome was produced feebleminded, antisocial descendants.

The Kallikak family was particularly interesting to proponents of the genetic hypothesis because Martin Kallikak, a soldier in the American Revolution, fathered children by both a feebleminded and an intellectually intact, or normal, woman. Only the descendants of the former were "feebleminded, alcoholic, insane, and morally defective"; the offspring of the normal woman showed no traces of such behavior.

subject to variable expressivity, meaning that in some individuals the chromosomal anomaly has its full effect, causing the deviant behavior and other characteristics, but that among others it has a lesser effect or none at all.

Another hypothesis is that the XYY person could be born in environments that are more conducive to crime. None of the investigations into the backgrounds of criminal and noncriminal XYY males, however, has offered any confirmation of this. A third hypothesis is that the physical traits of the XYY syndrome—tallness and severe acne—influence the way people react to the subject. This reaction, in turn, causes the XYY male to develop the characteristic aggressiveness. For this to be valid, though, it has to be generally believed that tall people or people with severe acne have a tendency toward aggressive behavior. It is not likely that such evidence can be found.

An intriguing hypothesis with some evidence in its favor is that the Y chromosome accounts for the aggressive behavior of the male. Thus two Ys in an XYY male would cause a "double dose" of aggressiveness. The hypothesis holds that the single dose of aggressiveness in a normal male can be controlled, but sometimes is not, leading to violent criminal behavior. In the XYY male, the double amount can also be controlled, but because of the extra inherited tendency to be aggressive, there is also a tendency to lose control more often, resulting in more occurrences of criminal behavior. The supporting evidence for this hypothesis (Clark, 1970) was that the XYY criminal was found to have a younger mean age for his first offense (12 years) than XY criminals (18 years). Clearly, however, much more information is needed about how the Y chromosome contributes to aggression before such meager evidence is accepted as fact.

But in another, much more comprehensive study (Whitkin et al., 1976), the *aggression hypothesis*, as it came to be called, received little support. Using data involving 28,884 Danish men born between 1944 and 1947 (out of a total potential sample of 31,436 men), these investigators found support for an *intellectual dysfunction* hypothesis. The evidence from this study showed that XYYs had appreciably lower intelligence test scores than control group subjects, a finding that readily lent itself to the conclusion that "people of lower intelligence may be less adept at escaping detection and so be likely to have a higher representation in a classificatory system based on registered crimes" (Whitkin et al., 1976, p. 553). In other words, all else being equal, the elevated crime rate found in many XYY groups may reflect a higher apprehension rate rather than simply a higher rate of commission of crimes.

Source: Kleinmuntz, D. N. Unpublished paper. University of Chicago, December 1978.

Figure 5.3
A father and son share a recessive genetic trait: baldness. Baldness is primarily found in men because it is a sex-influenced characteristic, which means that it behaves as a dominant in one sex and as a recessive in the other. Thus baldness would develop in a male if the gene for baldness were transmitted by either parent. In the female it will develop only if genes for baldness were received from both parents. Other factors, known as sex-limited, are present in both sexes, but their expression is inhibited in one sex by the presence of the sex hormones. An example of a sex-limited trait is beardedness in men.

Family Studies. According to one psychologist (Rosenthal, 1971), most investigators have given up hope finding pedigree patterns that follow the principles of Mendelian genetic transmission. Instead they have turned to *consanguinity*, or family studies in the search for abnormalities that occur more frequently in certain families than in the general population, the idea being that if the prevalence of a disorder is higher among close relatives (parents, siblings, children) than among distant ones (aunts, nephews, grandparents), one can infer a genetic etiology.

But once again, as we indicated earlier, evidence of an association between prevalence and consanguinity does not in itself warrant an inference of genetic causation. This association can result from a third variable, such as environmental stress, or from other factors totally unrelated to genetic transmission. For example, the finding that children speak their parents' language is not evidence that language or speech is inherited.

To summarize, then, we can say that with the exception of such clear-cut illnesses as Huntington's chorea, results from pedigree and consanguinity studies must be interpreted cautiously. The trouble with these studies, especially ones like those tracing the Kallikak family tree, is that the evidence is usually hearsay, and the studies and the information vague.[4]

Moreover, the criteria used for calling offspring "feebleminded," "alcoholic," "insane," and "morally defective" are ill-defined. Although feeblemindedness has subsequently been shown to be transmitted genetically, it is nevertheless unlikely that "alcoholism" and "moral defect," whatever that may be, are similarly inherited.

Because of these shortcomings, twin studies have been the preferred method of many investigators. At least in the study of twins, the investigators deal directly with their experimental subjects, although occasionally, even here, they must rely on secondhand information.

Twin Studies. Twins are of two kinds: those derived from a single fertilized zygote (egg), referred to as *monozygotic*, or MZ, twins; and those that develop from two fertilized zygotes, called *dizygotic*, or DZ twins. These types are also referred to, respectively, as *identical* and *fraternal* twins. Identicals are always same-sexed; the fraternal twins may be of the same or opposite sex; they are ordinary siblings who happen to be born at the same time.

Twin comparisons are usually expressed in terms of *concordance ratios*, which, as in family studies, signify the percentage of the persons related to the individual with the behavior disorder who also display it. It is assumed that MZ twins, as a result of their identical inheritance, will display the same phenotype. When they do, they are considered *concordant* with respect to it.

If twins (or others) differ with regard to a trait or disorder, they are *discordant* for that phenotype. Compared with MZ twins, DZs have varying concordance ratios, depending on the mode of inheritance of the traits in question (Rosenthal, 1971).

A basic assumption of twin methods is that any difference within MZ pairs is due to environmental, or at least nongenetic, causes; and differences within fraternal pairs result from both environmental and genetic influences.

In Chapter 1 we cited one set of studies, conducted by Franz Kallmann, that found higher concordance ratios of schizophrenia among relatives more genetically similar to one another than in the general population. These studies also demonstrated that MZ twins were much more likely to be both schizophrenic than DZ twins, full siblings, half siblings, and so on (Kallmann, 1946, 1953); we shall examine these studies more closely in our discussion of schizophrenia in Chapter 12.

More recently, one investigator (Smith, 1965), in attempting to pinpoint the effects of environment on MZ and DZ twins, deliberately selected traits expected to be highly modifiable by environmental influences. These included such items as "eating between meals," "time usually go to bed," "time usually get up," and the like. The results of this study, summarized in Table 5.2, suggest that even in these habits, MZs neverthe-

---

[4] Ideally, the investigator should interview each relative personally. Such interviews, however, in addition to being unfeasible, are themselves subject to many errors (see Chapter 4).

Table 5.2
Proportions of Twin Pairs Concordant for Selected Habits

Habit	Males		Females		Both Sexes	
	MZ	DZ	MZ	DZ	MZ	DZ
Eating between meals	72.5	66.7	77.1	57.5	75.0	61.6
Snack before bedtime	50.0	66.7	60.4	62.5	55.7	64.4
Time usually go to bed	50.0	72.7	72.9	57.5	66.7	64.4
Time usually get up	60.0	53.1	72.9	65.0	67.0	59.7
Dressing alike	59.0	57.1	68.7	33.3	64.4	40.3
Study together	23.1	9.1	54.2	20.5	40.2	15.3

Source: Smith, R. T. A comparison of socioenvironmental factors in monozygotic and dizygotic twins, testing an assumption. In Vandenberg, S. G. (ed.). Methods and goals in human behavior. New York: Academic Press, 1965.

less show greater intrapair similarity than DZs, possibly demonstrating the pervasiveness of genetic influences.

In still another twin study, a British psychologist, Sandra Canter (1971), reported some interesting findings. Using R. B. Cattell's Sixteen Personality Factor Text (16PF), which is a self-report inventory developed by the method of factor analysis (Cattell, 1965), she found higher correlations of test scores among MZ than among DZ twins on the following traits: intelligence, tough-mindedness, suspiciousness, and apprehensiveness.[5]

Twin studies, then, seem to be an improvement over those that focus on family trees and consanguinity because they provide more credible support for an inference of genetic causality. But the study of twins is not without its problems, and one investigator has called attention to four such problems (Mittler, 1971).

First, the reliability of determining zygosity—for example, by methods of blood grouping (serology), and finger and palm print analysis (dermatoglyphics)—although much higher than that achieved by merely asking people whether they have trouble telling twin pairs apart, still allows for a margin of error in twin classification.

Second, the fundamental assumptions of twin studies—that MZs are genetically identical and that any differences between them must be environmental, or at least nongenetic—are open to criticism. Differences between MZ pairs may originate early, because of gene mutations or chromosomal errors at mitosis, or they may occur during the later stages of gestation as a result of environmental anomalies, (*in utero* crowding or special conditions of implantation or delivery) within the mother's womb.

Third, because identical twins look so much alike, they may, as they become older, exaggerate any differences that exist between them. In other words each twin is more likely to be impelled to seek his or her own individuality by emphasizing traits that differ from the twin's. This may account for the general finding that twins are more alike in intellectual ability than in their personali-

[5] Factor analysis is a mathematical method used to simplify large arrays of variables. Further details may be obtained in texts by Cronbach (1970), Helmstadter (1964), and Nunnally (1978).

ties. Many clinical reports, for example, indicate that one twin is dominant over the other or tends to speak for the pair.

Fourth, twins are not a representative sample of the general population. According to Mittler (1971), they differ in the following ways (p. 55):

Not only are they subject to very different biological and developmental hazards from the moment of conception, but as a group, they show consistent, if slight, inferiority in respect of their intellectual, functional and educational skills throughout the whole of their childhood.

Brain Functioning ✱ know italicized words + what parts are controlled by them

Whereas heredity has an indirect role in the formation of behavior abnormalities, the functions of the brain are more directly involved in determining various emotional states. An understanding of how brain damage causes abnormal behavior (see Chapters 9 and 18) and of the relationships between various brain structures and the emotions requires some knowledge of the central and autonomic nervous systems. Because the anatomy of this system is complex, we shall discuss only the aspects of these systems that are specifically relevant to understanding the behavioral effects of brain damage (see Chapters 9 and 18) and certain biochemical theories of various disorders (see Chapters 12, 13, and 14). Our discussion will focus first on the gross features of the brain's structures.

The Nervous System's Gross Structures

The nervous system is the principal region involved in thinking, reasoning, comprehension, perception, orientation, movement, and emotion. It consists primarily of the brain and spinal

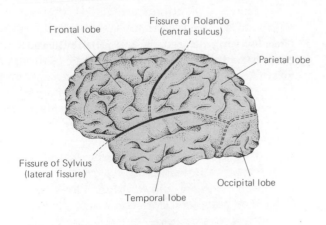

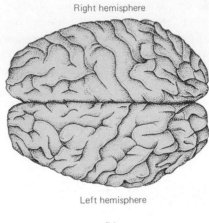

Figure 5.4
(a) The left hemisphere of the brain showing the four lobes: frontal, parietal, temporal, and occipital. (b) The right and left hemispheres, viewed from above.

(From Psychology, 2nd ed., by B. von Haller Gilmer. New York: Harper & Row, 1973, p. 139)

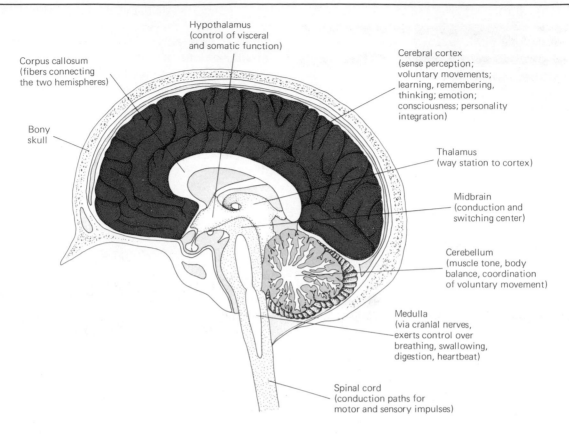

Figure 5.5
A cross-section of the brain showing some of the major parts.

(From Psychology, 2nd ed., by B. von Haller Gilmer. New York: Harper & Row, 1973 p. 135)

Figure 5.6
The shaded region of this diagram shows the names of the primary centers in the cerebrum that control motor functions.

(From Psychology, 2nd ed., by B. von Haller Gilmer, New York: Harper & Row, 1973, p. 138)

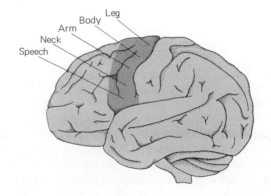

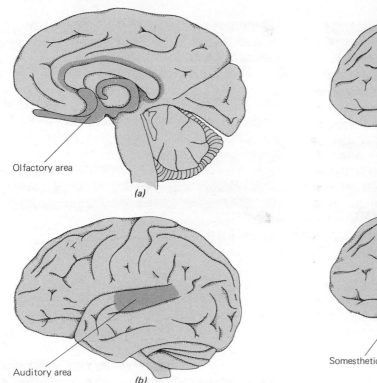

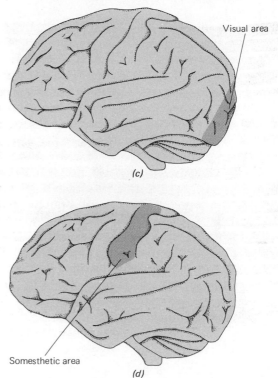

Figure 5.7
Sensory regions of the cerebral cortex. Diagram (a) shows a median section of the brain, with the olfactory section shaded; (b) is a side view of the auditory area in the temporal lobe. The shaded portions of diagrams (c) and (d) represent the visual center in the occipital lobe and the somesthetic area in the parietal lobe.

(From Psychology, 2nd ed., by B. von Haller Gilmer. New York: Harper & Row, 1973, p. 137)

cord. The brain is divided into left and right hemispheres of the *cerebrum*, which contain the frontal lobes and the motor and sensory areas. Just below the cerebrum and to the posterior is the *cerebellum*; it is involved in maintaining equilibrium, coordination, and balance. At the lower end of the brain, just above the spinal cord, is the *medulla*, which—with the *thalamus* and *hypo-* *thalamus*—controls autonomic functioning. Connected to the medulla at its lower end is the *spinal cord*, which is the coordinating center for some reflexes and a connecting cable to conduct impulses up to and down from the brain centers. All of these structures and some of their functions are shown in Figures 5.4, 5.5, 5.6, and 5.7.

The Peripheral Nervous System

The brain and spinal cord are usually called the central nervous system (CNS), and the portions of the nervous system lying outside the CNS are called the *peripheral nervous system*. The peripheral nervous system connects the CNS to other parts of the body through nerves, which transmit information away from the CNS (efferent) to the muscles, organs, and sensory receptors and also conduct information toward the CNS (afferent).

The peripheral nervous system has two divisions, the somatic and the autonomic. The somatic system conducts information from the brain to the skeletal muscles and from the skeletal muscles to the brain. The autonomic nervous system consists of nervous tissue that both innervates and receives messages from the internal organs, smooth muscles, and gonads. The autonomic nervous system is further subdivided into the *sympathetic* and *parasympathetic* systems, which we shall discuss in Chapter 8 in connection with its role in the psychophysiological disorders.

Blood Supply

The brain receives approximately 20 percent of the blood flow from the heart, and it receives this blood flow continuously (Carlson, 1977). Other parts of the body, like the skeletal muscles and internal organs, receive varying quantities of blood, depending on their needs relative to those of other regions. The brain, however, must always receive its share because it cannot store its fuel, nor can it temporarily extract energy without oxygen as the muscles can. Therefore a constant blood supply is essential. A one-second interruption in the blood flow to the brain uses up much of the dissolved oxygen; a six-second interruption produces unconsciousness. Irreversible damage occurs within a few minutes or as a result of long-term but gradual blood flow deprivation, as in alcoholism (see Chapter 9) or old age (see Chapter 19).

Neural Functioning

The brain and other nerve tissue of an adult human contain from ten to twenty billion neural cells, which vary widely in size and shape. The typical neuron is a cell with a membrane. The cellular parts are a cell body, one or more dendrites, and an axon (see Figure 5.8). The cell body regulates the metabolic functioning of the cell. The dendrites are specialized to receive extracellular influences (for example, from other cells or from the environment). The axon transmits impulses from the neuron to other cells. The region where nerve cells or neurons connect is called a *synapse*.

Synaptic Transmission

How neural activity is transmitted across the synapse is one of the most important questions in neurophysiology, and is currently a topic of active interest in the etiology of schizophrenia (see Chapter 12). The evidence indicates that in general such transmission is chemically mediated (Axelrod, 1974; M. Schwartz, 1973). Special transmitter substances are synthesized and stored in vesicles in the *presynaptic* nerve endings (at the end of the axon). The arrival of the neural impulse at these endings results in the release of transmitter substances into the synaptic space, where the transmitter reacts with a *postsynaptic* receptor (a specialized part of the dendrite or the cell body).

Most of what is known about chemical synaptic transmission is derived from the study of the peripheral nervous system, but at least the principles are believed also to apply to the CNS. Two transmitter substances have for some time been identified in the peripheral system: *acetylcholine* and *norepinephrine*. Synapses using acetylcholine are called *cholinergic*, and in general, acetylcholine is an excitatory transmitter substance. Synapses using norepinephrine are called *adrenergic*, and norepinephrine appears to have an inhibitory effect on neurons. A third transmitter substance, *dopamine*, once thought to be simply an intermediate in the synthesis of acetylcholine and norepinephrine, is also a neurotransmitter in its own right in the brain. There it functions in nerves that influence movement and behavior. Together, the norepinephrine and dopamine transmitters are called *catecholamines*.

In Chapter 12 we shall discuss speculations about another possible synaptic transmitter, *serotonin*, which is sometimes called 5-hydroxytryptamine and has been implicated in schizophrenia. Serotonin occurs in relatively fewer neurons than the other transmitters mentioned above. Serotonin neurons seem to regulate sleep and wakefulness. Thus, if serotonin neurons are selectively detroyed, animals become insomniac for prolonged periods of time.

Although the actions of many of the neurotransmitters at the synapses are still not well understood, specific drugs now used to treat schizophrenia, depression, and hypertension influence synaptic activity in various important ways. We shall have more to say about these drug actions in Chapter 21.

Endocrine Factors

The endocrine or ductless glands secrete hormones directly into the bloodstream. This has a regulatory effect on parts of the autonomic nervous system and, in turn, on the affected bodily organs. The principal endocrine glands of human beings and other mammals are the pituitary, thyroid, parathyroids, adrenals, pancreas, and ovaries or testes. Some of these glands and their hormones and principal functions are shown in Table 5.3 and discussed below. We shall return to a discussion of the importance of these and other endocrines later in this book, when we describe the so-called psychophysiological disorders (Chapter 8).

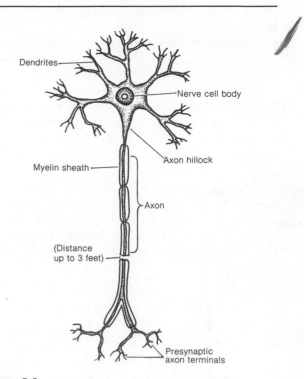

Figure 5.8
Human nerve cell. Impulses are received by the dendrites and transmitted by the axon. The nucleus (inside the cell body) controls metabolic processes within the cell.

(After Thompson, R. F. Foundations of physiological psychology. New York: Harper & Row, 1967)

The Pituitary

The pituitary, which is located at the base of the brain and is considered the master endocrine gland, controls several other endocrines, though it is itself controlled by feedback from other glands. Structurally, it consists of the posterior and anterior nuclei, both of which are intricately involved in behavior. The posterior nucleus secretes hormones that raise blood pressure, regulate the retention of body water, and induce uterine dilation and contraction during child delivery.

Table 5.3
A Portion of the Endocrine System and Its Functions

Gland	Hormones	Functions
Anterior pituitary	Somatotropic (STH)	Stimulates growth
	Adrenocorticotrophic (ACTH)	Stimulates adrenal cortex to produce its hormones
	Thyrotropic (TTH)	Stimulates production of thyroxin in thyroids
Posterior pituitary	Oxytocin	Excites nonstriated muscles (uterine contraction stimulates mammary glands in milk production)
	Vasopressin	Stimulates blood pressure and enhances body-water retention
Thyroid	Thyroxin	Stimulates metabolic rate
Parathyroid	Parathormone	Regulates calcium-phosphate metabolism
Adrenal medulla	Adrenalin	Stimulates "fight or flight" reactions
Adrenal cortex	Glucocorticoids	Helps maintain normal blood-sugar level; stimulates formation and storage of glycogen
Hypothalamus	Releasing hormones for the anterior pituitary	Regulates hormone secretion by the anterior pituitary

The anterior pituitary is involved in growth and stimulates the gonads, pancreas, and thyroids.

The anterior lobe of the pituitary is controlled by action from the hypothalamus, although no neural connections exist between these glands or between the brain and the pituitary. In the hypothalamus, the part of the brain to which the pituitary is connected, there are specialized neurons that secrete specific chemical substances into an elaborate network of blood vessels. These substances, called hypothalamic hormones, are the release or control factors for the hormones of the anterior pituitary.

The interactions between the hypothalamus and the anterior pituitary are important not only because of the target organs they affect, but also because these and other hormones are in the bloodstream and have a widespread influence on the brain and consequently on behavior. The importance of these and similar interactions has stimulated the formation of a new subdiscipline called behavioral endocrinology (Beach, 1975; Kimble, 1977).

The Thyroids

Thyroid functioning, which is indirectly influenced by pituitary secretions as a result of a complex feedback system, can be thrown off by hypothalamic or pituitary abnormalities. Its malfunctioning can also result from other physical causes and from psychological stress. *Hyperthyroidism* (overactivity of the thyroid) and *hypo-*

thyroidism (underactivity), the common thyroid disorders, are both responsible for numerous behavioral and personality anomalies. Overactivity of the thyroid tends to cause restlessness, irritability, sleeplessness, apprehension, and heightened reactivity to noises and other intense stimuli. Hypothyroidism, or underactivity of the thyroid, can lead to mental deficiency and to such behavioral symptoms as lethargy and depression.

The Adrenals

Of the remaining endocrine glands, we shall single out only the adrenals for consideration here. The adrenal gland consists of two parts, a cortex and a medulla. The adrenal cortex plays a vital role in metabolism and, in turn, in behavior. It is active in maintaining the sodium–potassium balance and in carbohydrate utilization.

The adrenal medulla secretes epinephrine and norepinephrine, hormones that act on the cardiovascular system to increase blood pressure. Epinephrine does this by increasing cardiac output, while norepinephrine does it by producing a general vasoconstriction. Both hormones also raise blood sugar levels. As we have noted, these hormones also influence neurotransmission. All of these actions, as we shall note throughout this book, exert a direct effect on several behavior disorders.

Homeostasis

The human biological organism has been genetically endowed with an intricate network of delicately balanced neurons, glands, muscles, organs, and other vital tissues. Disruptions among any of the complex interconnecting components cause imbalances in the system—imbalances the organism constantly strives to avoid. This attempt of the organism to maintain a continuous state of internal balance or equilibrium was first recognized in 1932 by Walter Cannon, who wrote *The Wisdom of the Body* and who called this self-regulating process *homeostasis*.

He described the automatic physiological processes by which the volume of blood and the concentrations in it of sugar, salt, oxygen, and carbon dioxide are kept constant; by which the temperature of the body is maintained within narrow limits; and by which foreign matter is removed from the bloodstream. These mechanisms are automatic in that they occur without the individual's awareness and without voluntary action.

Were Walter Cannon alive today, he would surely include in his list of self-regulatory functions the physiological mechanisms by which the central nervous system interacts with the peripheral nervous system, which in turn affects behavior directly and indirectly through hormone secretion and neural transmission.

Sometimes the automatic homeostatic mechanisms cannot maintain the necessary steady states in the body. One such emergency or crisis is stress, as we shall see in Chapter 8; other crises that disturb the equilibrium are the deprivations and deficiencies that are discussed below. The important thing to note for our purposes is that when homeostasis is disrupted, and when processes are set in motion to correct the disequilibrium and return the body to its normal balance, certain behavioral consequences may occur.

Physical Deprivations and Deficiencies

Of the many types of possible deprivations and deficiencies we shall discuss five basic ones: food, sensation, sleep, oxygen, and nutrition. Their specific influence on behavior cannot always be predicted by simply knowing the nature of the deprivation. Rather the influence depends on one's personality and prior experience with the environment, as well as present physical and psychological states. Nonetheless, dominant observable patterns do accompany many deprivations.

Food Deprivation

Personality changes experimentally produced by food deprivation were studied at the University of Minnesota, where conscientious objectors served as volunteer subjects during World War II.

This study, which demonstrated that a semi-starvation diet can lead to marked personality changes, used the following procedure: the subjects were first placed on adequate diets for three months, then given an extremely low-calorie diet for six months, followed by several months of nutritional rehabilitation. During the six-month semistarvation regimen, the subjects' average weight dropped from about 155 to 120 pounds, a considerable weight loss. Comparisons were then made between their personalities during the semistarvation and the other two periods (Guetzkow and Bowman, 1946; Keys, 1952).

Some startling findings were reported: although previously considered respected citizens of their communities, after a period of deprivation these men were caught stealing food from store counters and from one another, fighting among themselves, hoarding dishes and silverware, and lying to obtain additional food.

Other behavioral changes included a newly developed interest in reading recipes and cookbooks and pinning magazine pictures of lavish meals on walls. The men also reported a preoccupation with sumptuous feasts and suspicions of others' intentions toward their food rations. In addition their hunger drive became so compelling that other drives declined: sexual desires diminished, intellectual activities became major chores, and extreme apathy set in. Personality tests showed increased hypochondriacal preoccupation, depression, and other neurotic tendencies.

In short these men underwent severe personality changes as a result of their semistarvation. On measures of ability, aptitude, and intelligence, however, their scores were essentially the same after the food deprivation as before, suggesting that only personality is very much affected by such deprivation.

Sensory Deprivation

Research conducted at McGill University demonstrated that personality changes can be induced under conditions of "decreased variation in the sensory environment" (Heron et al., 1953; Heron, 1957; Wexler et al., 1958). In one of these studies volunteer subjects were placed in a tank-type respirator; their movements and tactile contacts were restricted by cylinders on their arms and legs, vision was confined to a view of only a small area of screening and ceiling, and auditory stimulation was limited to the droning of the respirator's motor.

Only six of the original 17 men could tolerate the deprivation long enough to complete the 36-hour observational period. Eight subjects reported auditory and visual hallucinations, and the temporal judgments of most men were so impaired that their estimates of time spent in the respirator were mistaken by as much as 50 percent.

In a second experiment, reported in *Scientific American* by Heron (1957), male college students were paid $20 a day to participate in a study in which they lay on a bed in a lighted cubicle 24 hours a day. The aim of the project was to obtain information on how human beings react when nothing at all is happening. They participated for as long as they wanted, with time out only for meals (while sitting at the edge of the bed) and elimination. They wore translucent plastic visors that transmitted light but prevented pattern vision. Their tactile senses were restricted by cotton gloves and cardboard cuffs, and auditory perception was likewise muted by a foam rubber pillow on which their heads lay and by the drone of the air conditioning equipment.

The results of this experiment were interpreted as indicating that exposure to monotonous environments definitely had deleterious effects: thinking was impaired, emotional responses became childish, visual perception became disturbed, and visual hallucinations occurred (Figure 5.9). One student repeatedly saw visions of a rock shaded by a tree; another saw pictures of babies, which he could not erase from his mind. Occasionally, also, subjects had auditory hallucinations, or a combination of auditory and visual ones. One man heard voices. Another saw the sun rising over a church and heard a choir singing "in full stereophonic sound." Other sensations reported were tactile and kinetic experiences such as being hit on the arm with pellets, electric shock, and a sense of movement. Brain wave patterns recorded on the electroencephalogram also indicated changes from the normal state.

These effects of sensory deprivation suggest that normal functioning depends on the continuing arousal reaction generated in portions of the brain, which in turn depends on constant sensory inputs. The principal investigator concluded from his findings that a changing sensory environment seems essential for human beings, and that without it abnormalities of behavior develop.

Nevertheless, the effects of sensory deprivation are not all negative. Some clinicians suggest, on the basis of later reports (McNeil and Rubin, 1977) and research (Suedfeld, 1975), that sensory deprivation may even facilitate intellectual functioning and that negative reactions reported during and shortly after sensory deprivation experiments may be due to the subjects' expectations. Suedfeld suggests that if sensory deprivation were experienced in calm surroundings, there would be few negative effects.

Suedfeld suggests also that the hallucinations experienced in sensory deprivation experiments are due to spontaneous firing of retinal nerves, are short-lived, and are not signs of emotional reactions to the experience. Subjects may

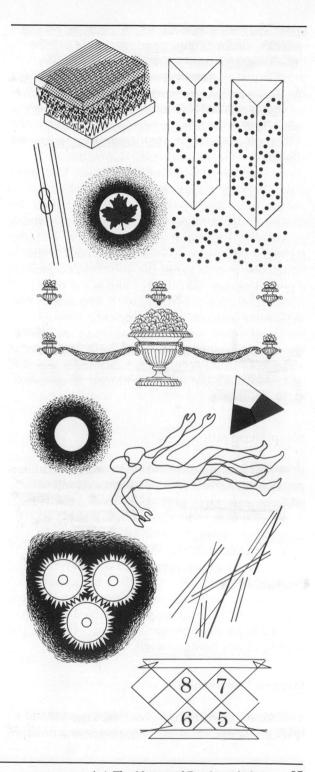

Figure 5.9

Drawings of the hallucinatory experiences reported by some subjects under conditions of sensory deprivation.

(From "The Pathology of Boredom," by Woodburn Heron. Copyright © 1967 by Scientific American, Inc. All rights reserved)

also experience sensations of hearing or smell resulting from stimuli within their own body, including yesterday's music or even dinner.

Finally, Suedfeld contends that sensory deprivation may be beneficial to some people. It may restore some of the individual's receptivity to new experiences, contributing to creativity and actually sharpening visual, auditory, and tactile sensitivity. This accords well with what we know about the physiology of sensation. The most acute hearing sensitivity has been observed in people who live in environments in which the silence is rich and pervasive. A popular sensory awakening technique used at Esalen and described by Gunther (1968) is the blind walk, in which one person keeps his or her eyes closed for a period of, say, 30 minutes and is led on a brief walking tour by a partner, with frequent opportunities to explore and experience through the senses of touch, smell, hearing, and taste. Participants commonly report not only heightened awareness in all of those sensory modes during the blind walk but also heightened visual sensitivity afterward.

Sleep Deprivation

Research has also shown that lack of sleep affects personality, either when experienced intensively or over extended periods of time. Individuals undergoing such deprivation are unable to concentrate on tasks, become restless and irritable, and experience hallucinatory episodes during which they cannot distinguish between real and imagined events. Occasionally a bandlike sensation around the head is reported, called the "hat illusion," which may be accompanied by subjective feelings of depersonalization—that is, the feeling of not being oneself.

Oxygen Deprivation

The most basic human need is oxygen, and of course a complete lack of it results in death within three to five minutes. But milder oxygen deprivation, or *anoxia*, is more common and may occur prenatally or after birth. Anoxia during the fetal stage or during the delivery of an infant may result in either a stillbirth, CNS damage (for example, cerebral palsy), or mental retardation.[6]

Less dramatic changes result from prolonged periods of anoxia, which may result from a reduction in the amount of oxygen circulated by the blood to the brain, as in anemia and cerebral vascular accidents, or from breathing air that has too little oxygen—a common phenomenon at increased altitudes or in smog-ridden cities. Some of these changes include memory deficit, fatigue, lassitude, and lack of emotional control; and depending on an individual's pre-anoxic personality, these changes may also include euphoria, irritability, and aggressiveness, or depression and apathy.

Malnutrition and Vitamin Deficiencies

Nutritional deficiencies can cause central nervous system damage and consequent behavioral and personality changes. Among the nutritive substances essential for adequate physical and psychological functioning are the energy-yielding carbohydrates, fats, and proteins. Without adequate amounts of them, as seen in the Minnesota semistarvation studies, the individual undergoes profound personality changes. The long-term effects of nutrient deficiencies, especially of the carbohydrates (which are converted to the glucose necessary for brain functioning), include confusion, intellectual deterioration, and poor judgment. Deficiency in vitamins results in restlessness, fatigue, release of latent behavior abnormalities, and elaboration of those already manifest.

---

[6]In Chapters 13 and 18 we discuss a childhood disorder, *infantile autism,* that is thought by some to be caused by exposing the neonate to an excess of oxygen.

Organic Brain Disorders

The term *organic brain disorder* is applied to acquired disorders of behavior and thinking that are believed to arise from altered structures of the nervous system, usually the brain. The damage to the brain may be general—as in aging, poisoning, alcoholism, drug abuse, and syphilis—or it may be more localized—as in brain abcesses, traumas, and tumors. Typically, the effects of localized damage are immediately reflected in behavior changes, whereas generalized damage is more insidious and manifests itself in slower and more subtle personality changes.

Injury to the Brain's Structure

Damage to the central nervous system usually, but not necessarily, occurs in the cerebrum and may be either *diffuse* or *specific*. Diffuse, or generalized, damage leads to widespread impairment of function. Typical symptoms include poor judgment; confusion; disorientation for person, time, and place; memory deficits; fluctuations of mood; and behavioral abnormalities. The latter need not necessarily occur with brain damage, but when they do, their manifestation is usually an exaggeration of lifelong maladaptive traits (for example, suspiciousness, querulousness, egocentricity, rigidity, depression), and may resemble the neuroses or, more commonly, the psychoses. Specific, or localized, brain damage results in behavioral symptoms that correspond closely to the function of the injured area.

Other factors that are important in determining the kinds and extent of behavioral change manifested are the amount of tissue destroyed, and the location of the destruction in the brain. There has been a long-standing argument among brain researchers about whether it is the location or the amount of damage that is more important.

On one side have been those who equated brain structure with specific behavioral functions and attempted to identify anatomical loci of particular functions in the brain. On the other side are those who agree with Lashley (1929) that all cortical regions of the brain are equally important for intelligence and other behavior and that the mass of brain tissue destroyed is therefore much more important than the location of the damage. The evidence seems to be that anatomical specialization does exist, but that it is not sufficient to provide functional divisions for many intellectual abilities.

Chapman and Wolf (1959) made the most extensive test of Lashley's hypothesis in human beings. Their study correlated measured brain tissue removal during surgery for tumors with postoperative intellectual deficiency. When damage was not extensive, adaptive capacities were found to be impaired, but memory and orientation remained intact.

The following presentation is further divided into disorders caused by generalized and localized brain injuries. It is important throughout this discussion to keep in mind that the symptoms displayed with either type of brain injury are not automatic consequences of the particular central nervous system damage incurred. Rather, these symptoms are almost always products of the complex interaction of life-long personality growth factors, environmental influences, and the nature of the injury.

Generalized Brain Damage

We shall describe three causes of diffuse brain damage: aging, poisoning, and syphilis.

Aging. The most common cause of brain damage is aging, a top in Chapter 19. As we behavioral changes as become more frequent modern medicine has p could be due either to of the cerebrum) or (hardening of cerebral ress insidiously and are accompanied by identifiable physical and, in some instances, personality changes.[7] The overall behavioral picture is one of restlessness, irritability, poor judgment, depression, and severe mood fluctuations. Subjective somatic complaints, which are often of hypochondriacal proportions, include headache, dizziness, and fatigue.

When the frontal lobes (see pages 77–79), particularly the area anterior to the motor region, are the region of destruction, large amounts can be destroyed with little or no disturbance of motor or sensory functions. But noteworthy behavioral changes occur. There may be a tendency toward inappropriate jocularity, alternate crying and laughing with minimal provocation, poor emotional self-control, and an inability to understand the consequences of actions. When the destruction is extensive, torpor and apathy are common, sometimes including speechlessness even in the face of painful stimuli.

Parietal lobe damage results in rather non-specific symptoms, such as speech difficulty if the lesion is in the dominant hemisphere and defective visual–spatial conceptualization if the damage is in the nondominant hemisphere.

Lesions in the temporal lobes, however, produce notable cognitive deficits and possibly hallucinations, depression, and sexual dysfunction. Parts of the temporal lobe, particularly the medial region and the rest of the limbic system, play an important role in memory. Consequently, damage to these regions causes disturbances, often permanent, to recent memory.

Although brain tissue degeneration usually begins well beyond the age of 60, there are three so-called *presenile psychoses* that have an earlier onset, typically in the 50s: *Alzheimer's, Pick's,* and *Jacob–Creutzfeld's* diseases, all named after the physicians whose observations at the turn of the century led to the original descriptions. These are characterized by premature brain atrophies of unknown origins, whose accompanying behavioral symptoms resemble those of the senile psychoses.

The prognosis for all of these progressively degenerative disorders is unfavorable, although temporary improvement occurs. It has been variously estimated that the time between the initial manifest symptoms and death is about five to ten years.

Poisoning. Three types of poisoning are commonly implicated in damage to the brain; these are lead, mercury, and carbon monoxide. *Lead poisoning* occurs as a result of swallowing lead paint from toys, furniture, or old dwellings; it is common among children in slum areas, who are left to chew on porch bannisters or other exposed areas where old paint has not been properly scraped. Adults are usually poisoned when they handle or inhale industrial leads. Filling station attendants who are daily exposed to leaded gasoline make up a sizable proportion of lead poisoning victims, as do ceramicists and paint factory workers who inhale either lead dusts or fumes (lead becomes volatile at very high temperatures —above 2400°—and gives off poisonous fumes).

Along with gastrointestinal symptoms (vomiting, stomach tenderness, constipation, or diarrhea), there are signs of fatigue, depression, and irritability; and in severe cases fits of delirium, progressive intellectual deficit, and coma may occur. The behavioral abnormality resembles psychosis-like symptoms that include delusions of persecution and visual hallucinations, as well as emotional outbursts that last anywhere from several minutes to hours.

Mercury poisoning was at one time confined to industrial workers who inhaled volatile mercury over extended periods of time. More recently, however, there have been increasing reports that it can come about as a result of eating fish, especially swordfish, that inhabit mercury-polluted

---

[7] For a complete clinical description of physical signs and [symp]toms, the reader may want to consult several other [sources] (Bannister, 1969; Batchelor, 1969; Wechsler, 1963).

Computerized Electrical Brain Stimulation and Strokes

Dr. Lawrence Pinneo and his associates (cited in Rubinstein, 1975) at the Stanford Research Institute are attempting to restore disrupted motor functions similar to those damaged during cerebrovascular strokes. Their intention is to help people whose limbs have been paralyzed through brain damage caused by stroke.

Bodily movement is directed by the motor areas of the cerebral cortex and is integrated in the brain stem. When a person suffers a stroke, the blood supply to the cortex is disrupted and cells in the motor areas are destroyed, causing paralysis in the limbs that these areas govern. Pinneo and his colleagues, in experiments on monkeys, discovered that there are some two hundred different sites in the brain stem that could be electrically stimulated to produce the movements controlled by the damaged cortex motor areas. In addition these researchers learned that the movements were even more precise than they would have been if the proper areas of the cerebral cortex itself had been stimulated. Next the researchers programmed a computer to fire electrodes in sequence to bring about purposeful motion in the paralyzed limbs of a monkey. For example, one program enabled the monkey to extend its arm, pick up food, and place the food in its mouth. Other programs, some under the control of the monkeys, allowed them to scratch themselves, climb, and select programs of their choice.

The implications of this work for humans are obvious, and Pinneo and his associates believe that with more research, this form of computerized stimulation can be applied to humans who have been partially paralyzed by strokes.

---

waters. The symptoms are similar to those of lead poisoning and frequently mimic the psychophysiological symptoms discussed in Chapter 8. A story that appeared in *Newsweek* (May 31, 1971) describes some of these symptoms:

Three weeks ago when the Food and Drug Administration urged that swordfish be crossed off the National menu because of mercury contamination . . . it became obvious that some Americans were going to have to review their past eating habits as carefully as they must now plan their future menus.

Mrs. N.Y. (from New York), was a 38-year-old short and unhappily fat, Long Island housewife when in 1964 she decided to go on a special weight-reduction diet. For nineteen months, she ate 10 ounces of swordfish daily as a principal staple and dropped from 165 lbs to 120 lbs. But with her slimmer figure came a host of ailments: dizziness, memory loss, hand tremors, tongue quivers, hypersensitivity to light, difficulty in focusing her vision, and physical uncoordination.

. . . "She was signed out in 1966 after a battery of tests at the Neurological Institute in New York City as suffering from psychosomatic complaints," Dr. Roger C. Herdman, a New York State Health Department Official, told the Senate's Environmental Subcommittee last week. "It was suggested that she seek psychiatric consultation." She did so for two and one-half years—"with no obvious benefit," in Herdman's words. Only when

Brain Damage and Behavior: A Classic Case

The behavioral effects of brain damage have provided much information about human brain functions. One of the earliest cases providing such information was that of Phineas Gage, a railroad work crew foreman, who was injured in a dynamite blast that rammed a three-foot iron spike through his face and head. The spike entered through his left cheek, passed through the brain, and emerged from the top of his skull. Gage survived the accident, but there was such a marked change in his personality that it inspired his physician, J. M. Harlow (1868, pp. 330–340) to describe the following series of events:

The patient was thrown upon his back by the explosion, and gave a few convulsive motions of the extremities, but spoke in a few minutes . . . an hour afterwards . . . [he] walked up a long flight of stairs . . . and seemed perfectly conscious. . . . He bore his suffering with

firmness, and directed my attention to the hole in his cheek, saying the iron entered there and passed through his head.

His physical health is good. . . . Has no pain in the head . . . [but] the equilibrium . . . between his intellectual faculties and animal propensities, seems to have been destroyed. He is fitful, irreverent, indulging at times in the grossest profanity (which was not previously his custom) . . . impatient of restraint or advice when it conflicts with his desires . . . yet devising many plans of future operations, which are no sooner arranged than they are abandoned in turn for others. . . . His mind is radically changed, so decidedly that his friends and acquaintances said he was "no longer Gage."

Gage's injury, we now know, was a manifestation of brain damage in the area of the frontal lobes that control emotional behavior and judgment.

---

the State Health Department expert tested a sample of Mrs. N.Y.'s hair did anyone realize that she was suffering from mercury poisoning.

Later it was established that mercury is also being found in halibut, bass, walleyed pike, and northern pike at levels in excess of the Federal Drug Administration's standard.

Carbon monoxide poisoning is the type that occurs most frequently, and may either be self-inflicted or a result of accidental coal-gas or car-exhaust inhalation. Carbon monoxide combines in the blood with hemoglobin, thus limiting the blood's capacity to take oxygen to the brain. This oxygen deficiency in the brain causes unconsciousness and coma, and if the person recovers,

he or she may become disoriented and delirious. Case Report 5.1 describes a poisoning that resulted from an unsuccessful suicide attempt (Maslow and Mittelmann, 1951, p. 549).

Case Report 5.1 *Carbon Monoxide Poisoning*

A 35-year-old woman who was depressed following a marital upset attempted suicide by turning on the gas. After being discovered, she remained unconscious for about 24 hours. During the next few days her temperature rose and she suffered abdominal pain. She later developed some stiffness and tremor in her extremities, accompanied by excessive salivation. She became apathetic and

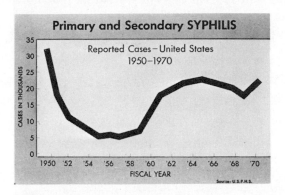

Figure 5.10

The reported cases of primary and secondary syphilis occurring in the United States, as indicated in this curve, show a steady decline during the 1950s, followed by a gradual increase during the 1960s.

(Courtesy Pfizer, Inc.)

neglectful of her appearance, and experienced time disorientation and memory defects. She would chat about having visited relatives or gone shopping the previous day or during the morning when in fact she had not left the house. She did not remember her suicide attempt and attributed her physical symptoms to having fallen or to being overworked.

SOURCE: *A. H. Maslow and B. Mittelmann.* Principles of abnormal psychology. *Rev. ed. Copyright © 1941, 1951 by Harper & Row, Publishers, Inc. By permission of the publishers.*

Although these acute occurrences almost always call for emergency treatments (artificial respiration, oxygen resuscitation), the real danger for most people is the inhalation of small amounts of gas over extended periods of time. In these cases, the manifest physical and neurological signs may not be so obvious, but numerous subtle psychological symptoms develop. Mental deficit, comprehension difficulty, and mutism are common; and in more severe instances, symp-

toms of parkinsonism ("pill-rolling" movement of thumb and forefinger, facial immobility, staring eyes, tremor, shuffling gait, explosive speech) may also develop. People suffering from gradual carbon monoxide poisoning also display depression, agitation, anxiety, headache, dizziness, and muscular pains as well as digestive disorders, difficult breathing, and heart palpitation (Kolb, 1968).

In all cases of poisoning the treatment involves removal of the responsible agent. This is sometimes difficult to accomplish because, as we saw in the *Newsweek* story cited earlier, correct diagnoses are not always made. Even when the person can be removed from exposure to the poisonous agent, brain damage is irreversible. The psychological symptoms, however, do begin to improve within a few weeks after the removal of the agent, and the person may recover completely from these within two years.

Syphilis. After World War II syphilis declined sharply for a time, and its long-term psychological effects were rarely seen. More recently, it has been on the increase, largely as a result of two byproducts of oral contraception: increased sexual freedom and decreased use of condoms, especially by teenagers.

Syphilis is caused by a microscopic organism, the *spirochete* (also called *treponema pallidum*), which is transmitted by an infected individual, usually during sexual relations (with or without intromission, since the infected site need not be in the genital area).[8] This microorganism enters the body through mucous membranes or abrasions in the skin. Immediately thereafter, the spirochetes multiply rapidly, and within two

---

[8] Congenital syphilis can also occur; in such cases the infected mother transmits the disease to the unborn child. Consequently, the child may be born mentally retarded, deaf, or blind, or may display symptoms similar to those described under *general paresis,* which is covered in the following paragraphs.

to three weeks a sore, or *chancre,* develops at the site of the infection.

This chancre disappears within about one month, even when untreated. From three to eight weeks after the chancre has appeared, a copper-colored rash resembling smallpox is evident, sometimes covering the whole body. All surface symptoms then clear up during a latency period, but it is during this stage that the microorganisms may attack any of the organs of the body such as the heart, spleen, liver, blood vessels, bones, spinal cord, or brain.

An attack by the spirochete on the spinal cord or brain is called neurosyphilis, a disease almost always accompanied by psychotic symptoms. Only about 10 percent of the individuals infected ever show evidence of neurosyphilis, but in those who do, it usually appears at least 10 to 20 years after the initial infection.

One common variety of neurosyphilis is called *general paresis* (GP) or *general paresis of the insane* (GPI); at its onset the patient has difficulty understanding what is said, or may not remember what has been said. Rapid intellectual and personality deterioration follow.

The intellectual deficit may involve total loss of all learned mental skills (arithmetic, spelling, counting); and the personality changes may be in the direction of gaiety, carelessness, and abandon; or, depending on the patient's previous personality makeup, may involve depression and suicide.

There is disorientation for time, and sometimes for place and person as well. Delusions of grandeur are common and are responsible for bizarre and silly behavior, especially since these delusions are not consistent from one time to the next. If left untreated, deterioration gradually occurs, and the patient dies within five years, or sooner, of the initial onset of symptoms.

Treatment of syphilis consists of vast numbers of penicillin injections, which halt the progress of the disease in almost any of its stages. The earlier the disease is recognized and treated, of course, the more favorable is the prognosis.

When neurosyphilis has already set in, it is more accurate to say that the disease has been arrested than that it has been cured.

Localized Brain Damage

The most common varieties of specific brain damage arise from abscess, tumor, and trauma. They are discussed separately below. Again we note that the resulting behavioral symptoms correspond closely to the function of the damaged area. It may be helpful to the reader to refer back to Figures 5.4, 5.5, 5.6, and 5.7 because they illustrate the relationships between specific structures and their functions.

Brain Abscess. With the advent of antibiotics, this once common threat to the central nervous system has been greatly reduced. A brain abscess consists of a proliferation of bacteria within the cerebral white matter, resulting in a disintegration and softening of the surrounding brain tissue. The most frequent causative agents of brain abscess are *Staphylococci, Pneumococci,* and *Streptococci* (Netter, 1962). Abscess may, however, develop following an untreated infection in the middle ear or the facial sinuses, as well as after any bacterial infections about the face or bony structure of the head, and it may spread to the brain. The location of the abscess in the central nervous system, as we said above, and the direction of its spread determine the type of mental symptoms seen.

The early mental and physical symptoms include malaise, nightly headaches, low-grade fever, stiffness of the neck, and vomiting. The specific neurological damage depends on the site of the infection, as do the behavior symptoms. Most often these symptoms consist of mental deterioration, poor judgment, thick or slurred speech, noncoordination, and changed personality, usually in the direction of lethargy and depression.

Brain Tumors. The salient symptoms of brain tumors or neoplasms are headache, vomiting, and slow pulse, and their severity depends on the size of the tumor and its location. There are various types of neoplasms (astrocytoma, oligodendroglioma, ependynoma glioblastoma).

The psychological symptoms accompanying neoplasms usually occur because brain tumors cause intracranial pressure. These symptoms include apathy, disinterest, confusion, perplexity, and disturbed consciousness, sometimes resulting in coma. The exact nature of the symptoms, of course, depends on the precise area of the neoplasm and they may include olfactory hallucinations, if the tumor is localized in the temporal lobe or olfactory bulb; visual hallucinations, if the tumor occurs in the temporal or occipital lobe, or in the thalamus; "Lilliputian" hallucinations, if it is in just the temporal lobes (the patient sees small figures that he usually knows are not real); and gustatory hallucinations, if the tumor is located in the basal ganglia and the thalamus. Occasionally euphoria or depression is seen, depending on the location of the tumor and the type of intracranial pressure it causes.

Mental symptoms frequently appear long before any convincing local signs. This is particularly true when the tumor is in the frontal lobe, because from there it may not extend back far enough to damage the motor area. Behavioral symptoms are also likely when the tumor is localized in the corpus callosum, the structure that connects the two hemispheres (see Figure 5.5).

Brain Trauma. Trauma to the head can precipitate or cause symptoms either immediately or shortly thereafter. The individual may be only temporarily dazed, or may remain completely unconscious for a few minutes or even several days. Shortly after sustaining injury, the victim may suffer nausea, headache, vomiting, or dizziness.

There are three common reasons for psychological symptoms following head injury: extradural hematoma (a blood clot between the skull and the cortex resulting from meningeal hemorrhage), intracerebral hematoma (bleeding inside the cerebral cortex), and traumatic pneumocephalus (air inside the central nervous system). *Extradural hematoma* is recognized by some typical behavior symptoms that include transient loss of consciousness, followed by a lucid interval during which the patient complains only of headache, nausea, and vomiting. The headache then increases, and the patient becomes drowsy and possibly stuporous, and eventually comatose. This hematoma is easily diagnosed by X-ray of the skull, and treatment consists of removal of the blood clot by suction (see Figure 5.11).

In *intracerebral hematoma*, the diagnosis may be more difficult, depending on the location and size of the affected area. Again the individual shows signs of increasing intracranial pressure, including headaches, dizziness, vomiting, and drowsiness. Thereafter, again depending on the site of the injury, the individual may be unable to speak or understand spoken language (aphasia), and hemiparesis may result. Such injury following a mild head trauma is rare; it is most often due to a severe blow to the head or wounds inflicted by knife or bullet.

Traumatic pneumocephalus is due to injury to one of the accessory nasal sinuses, which permits air and bacteria to enter the brain or the ventricular system. Although skull fracture is the most frequent cause of pneumocephalus, it may also occur after a severe sneezing spell. Such an injury is followed by complaints of severe headache, accompanied by discharge of clear fluid from the nostrils or middle ear. This condition, if caught early, is easily diagnosed and treated.

Any head trauma can produce chronic symptoms that resemble psychotic reactions. Usually the clinical picture is one of depression: the patient becomes apathetic and slow, shows no initiative, may be disoriented for time and place, and may not remember having been in an accident or having otherwise sustained a head trauma. Large memory gaps may also develop, which, if the condition improves, are gradually filled in (Case Report 5.2).

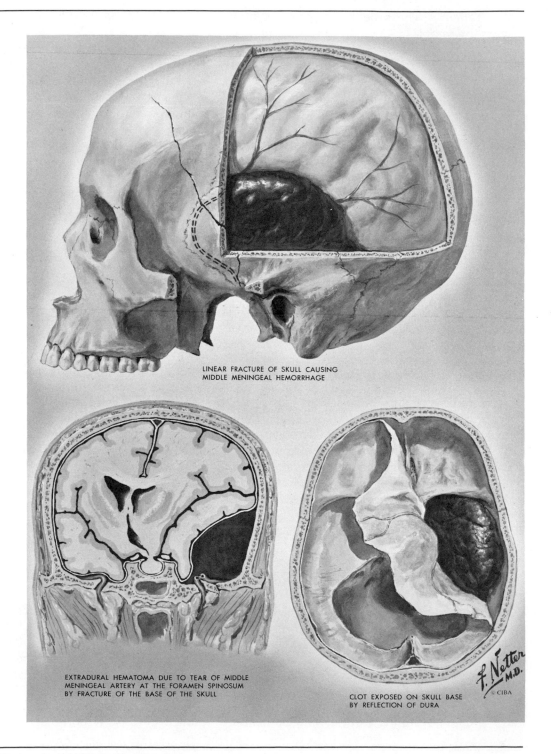

LINEAR FRACTURE OF SKULL CAUSING
MIDDLE MENINGEAL HEMORRHAGE

EXTRADURAL HEMATOMA DUE TO TEAR OF MIDDLE
MENINGEAL ARTERY AT THE FORAMEN SPINOSUM
BY FRACTURE OF THE BASE OF THE SKULL

CLOT EXPOSED ON SKULL BASE
BY REFLECTION OF DURA

Case Report 5.2 *Head Trauma*

A 28-year-old man suffered a severe head injury in an automobile accident. After being taken to the hospital, he remained unconscious for two hours, and an X-ray showed that his skull was fractured. In addition, the facial nerve on the right side was paralyzed, his spinal fluid was bloody, and he had a hearing difficulty in one ear.

After several days of drowsiness, the patient became talkative. Although he obeyed instructions to stay in bed, he had to be watched constantly because he repeatedly sat up in bed and offered advice to everyone. He calmed down after several days, but remained overtalkative. About a month later he grew even more talkative and showed flights of ideas and distractability. He talked about how well he felt and about a trip he planned. He would then describe his experiences on these supposed trips, as well as the political policies that prevailed at the places visited. A few weeks later he began to talk of being commissioned by the government to undertake various engineering projects to improve the conditions of the country, and described several visits to Washington that he had never actually made. He also believed he was in the best of health, even though his face was still paralyzed. He remained in this condition for about eight months, then gradually recovered under ordinary medical care and psychiatric counseling.

SOURCE: *A. H. Maslow and B. Mittelmann.* Principles of abnormal psychology. *Rev. ed. Copyright © 1941, 1951 by Harper & Row, Publishers, Inc. By permission of the publishers.*

Figure 5.11 (page 94)

An extradural hematoma such as appears here is due mainly to brain trauma and consists of a blood clot between the outer layer of the brain (dura) and the inner skull bone. The resulting behavior may include transient loss of consciousness, headache, nausea, and vomiting.

Specific Symptoms of Brain Damage

Another way to conceptualize the results of brain damage is to focus on specific symptoms that are observed clinically in patients. We shall discuss three such symptoms: aphasia, delirium, and epilepsy.

Aphasia

An impairment in language due to cortical damage is called aphasia. By studying the locus of the damage or lesion that accompanies aphasia, one can discern the regions controlling the language function. The first such observation associating a language disorder and brain damage was made in the middle of the nineteenth century by a French neurologist, Pierre Paul Broca. Broca described two patients who had difficulty speaking but who could understand language. He correlated this *expressive aphasia,* as it has come to be called, with lesions in the third frontal convolution (see Figure 5.4). This area is now called Broca's area.

Some years after Broca, another neurologist, Carl Wernicke, found that damage to another area, the primary auditory cortex, appeared to be correlated with another kind of aphasia. People in this group could speak relatively well but had a severe impairment in understanding language, both spoken and written. Wernicke called this *sensory aphasia,* and the region of the brain is now called Wernicke's area. This disorder is sometimes also called *receptive aphasia.*

For a language impairment to be classified as an aphasia, according to Gazzaniga (1973), the cause of the disturbance must be cortical and not peripheral impairment. For example, expressive aphasics are able to move the speech musculature. Their deficit arises from damage to the cortical area that initiates language production. Speech disturbances that result from damage to the speech apparatus (tongue, vocal cords, lips) or motor centers of the brain are called *dysarthria.*

Dysarthric speech is thick and slurred, with disturbances in timing and intonation. The speech of expressive aphasics, in contrast, sounds normal in quality.

Delirium

Organic brain disorders that are of acute onset, usually because of high fever or other sudden toxic or metabolic causes, are often characterized by delirium. Delirium is an acute state of disorientation and poor memory, interspersed by periods of lucidity and somnolence. Delirium can be mild, with a barely perceptible reduction in orientation and memory, or it can be severe and accompanied by tremulousness, visual hallucinations, incoherence, and impairment of motor functions. Delirium can culminate in stupor, unconsciousness, and coma.

Epilepsy

Sometimes also called convulsive or seizure disorder, epilepsy is defined as an organic disorder characterized by random neuronal discharges from a, hyperexcitable region of the brain. Approximately ten different types of clinical epilepsy have been classified. We shall describe only three: *grand mal, petit mal,* and *psychomotor* seizures. The many recognized varieties are usually classified in two ways, according to whether they are a result of brain damage (*symptomatic epilepsy*) or unknown etiology (*idiopathic epilepsy*) and on the basis of the type of seizure that occurs. Our listing follows the latter classification.

Grand Mal Epilepsy. This form of seizure disorder is characterized by a total loss of consciousness and stereotyped motor activity (Pincus and Tucker, 1978). Initially there is a *tonic* stage during which the body stiffens and breathing stops. This is followed by a clonic phase that includes rhythmic shaking of the extremities and trunk. This

sequence often lasts a minute or two and may repeat itself several times. After the convulsions, there is drowsiness, confusion, headache, and somnolence, all of which may last from a few minutes to a day or two.

Approximately one-half the grand mal patients experience warning symptoms, called an *aura,* prior to an oncoming attack. The aura is considered an integral part of the seizure, and is sometimes considered the seizure even if not followed by a grand mal attack. Typically, the aura is an ill-defined sensation of not feeling well accompanied by visual, olfactory, or auditory hallucinations. But the precise nature of the aura seems to be related to the locus of the damaged area of the brain.

Petit Mal Epilepsy. The seizures of the petit mal variety of convulsive disorder usually begin without warning and are characterized by a brief loss of awareness. There is usually no motor activity other than arching of the back and blinking or rolling up of the eyes. According to one source (Pincus and Tucker, 1978), these seizures occur in children and are rarely encountered in anyone over 15 years old.

Psychomotor Epilepsy. Attacks of psychomotor seizures are similar to the petit mal form in that there are brief interruptions of consciousness or awareness. But the psychomotor activity defining this order does differ from petit mal attacks in that it is manifested by repetitive lip-smacking, chewing, gagging, retching, or swallowing. Some individuals perform a repetitive series of more complicated motor acts such as repeating a phrase over and over again or buttoning and unbuttoning clothing. Others experience flights or fugue states in which they detachedly perform some acts, usually not antisocial, that they do not afterward remember having performed. These psychomotor activities may last several minutes or they may last hours or days.

Because much of the accompanying psychomotor behavior resembles everyday activities, it is often quite difficult to distinguish behavior caused by psychomotor seizures from episodic abnormal behavior caused by hysteria or even psychosis. Several distinguishing features are present, however, and these include momentary and subjective changes that are not typical of the person's usual way of behaving, confusion during the episodes, loss of memory for most actions except those that occurred at the beginning of the episode, and fatigue depression following the attacks.

Etiology of Epilepsy. The distinction referred to at the outset of this section on epilepsy between symptomatic and idiopathic seizures simply designates whether or not the brain damage has been identified. Pincus and Tucker (1978, p. 4) object to the indiscriminate use of the diagnosis of idiopathic epilepsy if it "becomes a subterfuge when a clinician lacks a clear-cut diagnosis." Used properly, the term should refer to inherited epilepsy, which is further defined by its childhood manifestation and a family history of epilepsy.

In the main, symptomatic epileptic seizures are caused by acquired brain damage in the form of toxic, tumor, or trauma agents. But the mechanism by which the identifiable damage results in seizures is not well understood. And not all persons with identifiable brain damage have seizures. But when the brain damage is accompanied by seizures, the discharge produces whatever activity is controlled by the particular area damaged.

Whether or not the brain damage is identifiable, the damage does not necessarily result in epilepsy. In fact, it has been a long-standing clinical observation that epilepsy is more common among close relatives of epileptics than in the general population. This, of course, suggests the possibility that the acquired brain damage itself, unless it is due to infection, trauma, or tumor, may be genetically transmitted.

The evidence for the genetic transmission of epilepsy, however, is far from clear. Although twin studies indicate a high concordance rate of

85 percent
twins comp
twins (Lenr
as low as 5
and DZ twi
theoretically
for MZ twi
the genetic
the incidenc
first-degree
percent) in a
the incidenc
than would
somal recess

Treatment. Although complete seizure control is sometimes not possible without some degree of drug toxicity, the treatment of choice is chemotherapy. Initially a moderate dosage of a simple drug is used, usually an anticonvulsant (for example, dilantin, phenobarbital, or valium), then the dosage is increased until either the seizures are controlled or toxic side effects of the drug appear. If it is not possible to control seizures at nontoxic doses, a second drug is added until control or toxicity is again achieved. In most cases complete seizure control can be achieved.

In any case the extent to which a convulsive disorder disrupts normal life varies considerably, depending on the nature and frequency of the seizure, as well as the person's emotional reaction to being epileptic (Kazniak and Reiss, 1977). In general, most epileptics lead normal lives.

Summary

The impact of heredity is indirect in that predispositions rather than psychopathology are inherited. These temperamental predispositions may in turn determine whether abnormalities develop.

Many behavior disorders are associated with changes in the functioning of various parts of the nervous system. The central nervous system con-

nal cord. Everything
ures is called the periph-
which is subdivided into the
ystem, which transmits neural
n the CNS and the skeletal mus-
autonomic nervous system, which
eural impulses between the CNS and
rnal organs, smooth muscles, and go-
. The autonomic nervous system is further
bdivided into the sympathetic and parasympathetic systems.

The brain requires a constant supply of
blood. A nerve cell consists of a cell body, one or
more dendrites, and an axon. Neural impulses
are received by dendrites and transmitted by
axons through synapses. Various transmitter
substances are involved in synaptic transmission.

Endocrine system dysfunctions, especially
those affecting the pituitary and thyroid glands,
also cause abnormalities. Some of the more
common endocrine-based disorders are hyperthyroidism, hypothyroidism, and extremes of
stature.

The foregoing are mostly predisposing
causes of abnormality, since their influences are
long-term. Precipitating causes are physical deprivations and brain damage. These disorders are
caused by deprivation of food, sensation, sleep,
and oxygen, as well as by central nervous system
damage caused by aging, poisoning, alcoholism,
syphilis, brain abscess, tumor, and head trauma.

Terms and Concepts to Master

Autonomic nervous
  system

Central nervous system

Chromosomes

Concordance ratio

Consanguinity

DNA

Dominant gene

Endocrine glands

Genotype

Heredity

Homeostasis

Index case

Mendelian genetics

Neural transmitter
  substances

Neuron

Pedigree method

Peripheral nervous
  system

Phenotype

Pituitary gland

Polygenic inheritance

Recessive gene

Somatic nervous system

6 Motivational and Sociocultural Determinants of Behavior Disorders

Human behavior is shaped not only by biological factors, but also by psychological and cultural forces, although sometimes the distinction between biological and psychological causes of behavior disorders cannot be easily or unambiguously drawn. For example, we might view maternal deprivation as a form of sensory deprivation and therefore a biological determinant, or we might view it as a psychological determinant, since it arises in the interpersonal relationship of mother and child. We could even see it as a sociocultural determinant if we were studying the Mundugumor, among whom some deprivation is the rule rather than the exception. In short our categories are not ironclad and not mutually exclusive. We shall call a determinant *motivational* if it is described in one of the existing psychological models, and *sociocultural* if it is mediated by subcultural or cross-cultural differences.

Motivational Determinants

The attempt to discover why people behave as they do has yielded an impressively large number of psychological hypotheses. Thus far, however, only those that grew out of the clinical observations of Freud and those that developed in the psychological laboratories of Pavlov, Watson, Thorndike, and Skinner have been fully accepted into the mainstream of American psychology. We shall give most of our attention here to those two models, with a brief summary of two other inter-

esting and rather loosely grouped alternatives, the interactive models and the humanistic-existential models. We shall discuss all of these models in greater detail in later chapters; our treatment here is intended primarily to introduce the models and to establish the context in which the behavior disorders will be presented.

Intrapsychic Models: Freudian and Neo-Freudian Approaches

Sigmund Freud (see *The standard edition* of the complete psychological works, 1953) formulated one of the most comprehensive theories of human motivation, which he based on his clinical observations of neurotics. If we examine the Freudian model of a human being, we see a driven creature, motivated by *unconscious* forces—forces that never appear, except in symbolic ways, in a human's waking consciousness. This person is a pleasure-seeking organism, whose actions are motivated (albeit unconsciously) by the desire to have pleasure and avoid pain, and whose pleasure-seeking is bounded by the recognition that reality places limits on the possibilities for immediate gratification. We shall present below several essential concepts of Freud's theory.

Primary and Secondary Process Thinking. To cope with the conflicting demands of unconscious desires and reality, thinking functions at

Freud (with cane and cigar) is shown in this well-known photograph taken at Clark University during his first visit to the United States. Seated next to Freud are the famed psychologist G. Stanley Hall and the psychiatrist Carl G. Jung. Standing are psychiatrists A. A. Brill, Ernest Jones, and Sandor Ferenczi.

(Courtesy Clark University)

the primary and secondary levels. *Primary process thinking* is the more primitive of the two and follows the pleasure principle. Traces of its existence are found in dreams, slips of the tongue, inadvertent gestures, and other clues of unconscious thinking. An example of cognition at this level is the reluctant after-dinner speaker who means to say, "I am most grateful for having been invited here," but instead says, "I am almost grateful for having been invited here." Since the speaker's apparent attitude toward the host and audience is completely friendly, the slip of the tongue provides important information about *unconscious hostility*.

Secondary process thinking, consisting as it does of inhibitions and constraining forces, develops later in one's childhood and represents preconscious and conscious thinking. It is full of doubt, uncertainty, contradiction, and other moderating influences, and its development may be seen in some children's tendency to chastise themselves with a "No, no, bad girl, don't do that."

Components of Personality. The idea that primary process thinking provides a key to unconscious motives was one of Freud's most important concepts. To develop his theory of unconscious motivation, however, Freud also needed separate components of personality. Therefore he posited three distinct hypothetical entities: id, ego, and superego (1927), all of which have made their way into common parlance. The *id* is the personality's pleasure-seeking source of psychic energy, totally unconscious and therefore inaccessible to a person's ordinary cognizance. It contains the "untamed passions" of the individual, including the *libido*, the instinctual sexual energy of humans. The id also contains such other *life instincts* as hunger and thirst, although Freud believed that the sex drive was the most significant of these motives.

In contrast to the id, which seeks immediate gratification, the *ego* serves as the mediator between inner impulses and external reality. It is

the executive portion of the personality and its functions include perception, conscious thought, memory, learning, choice, judgment, and action. The ego also detects and deals with threats in the environment, as well as dangerous unconscious impulses.

Unlike the id, which is totally unconscious, the ego functions also at preconscious and conscious levels. At the unconscious level, the ego deals with sexual and aggressive impulses originating in the id. At the preconscious and conscious levels it tests reality through secondary process thinking. Reality-testing helps the ego distinguish fact from fantasy and the rational from the wishful. After having made this distinction, it must decide upon a course of action that maximizes pleasure and minimizes pain (Blum, 1966).

The third personality component, the *superego*, embodies the sum of the parental and societal moral teachings internalized, or *introjected*, by the individual while growing up. In short it is the conscience. Accordingly it sets strict limits and strives for moral and ethical perfection. Because the superego was initially forged by parental authority, it behaves toward the ego and id as the parents once did toward the child. If properly internalized by the child, the superego becomes the part of the individual that is self-critical, prohibitive, and self-punishing, especially with regard to direct expression of sexual and—to a lesser degree—aggressive impulses. Its demands can be as irrational and insistent as the id's.

Psychosexual Stages. The core of Freud's theory was his attempt to explain unconscious mental processes from birth to maturity, and hence he formulated the *psychosexual stages* of personality development. This theory holds that the infant is born with a specific amount of sexual energy, or libido, which when discharged is pleasurable, but when blocked from discharge causes tension. The focus of libidinal discharge presumably shifts according to a person's physical and chronological age during three identifiable infantile stages, corresponding to their focal erogenous zones: oral, anal, and phallic.

The *oral stage* occurs during the first two years of the infant's life, when mouth and lips are the prime centers of gratification and when sucking is the predominant mode of pleasurable activity. The *anal stage* occurs during about the third and fourth years of life, and during this period fecal expulsion and retention become the focus of erotic pleasure. This is followed by the *phallic stage*, during which the genital region becomes the pleasure center. This is also the stage in which the *Oedipus complex* (from the Greek myth of Oedipus) occurs, and the child becomes enamored of its opposite-sex parent and hostile toward its same-sex parent. The boy, for example, wishes to marry his mother and therefore would like somehow to be rid of his father.[1] These are, of course, frightening desires, for they often involve death wishes toward the same-sex parent; and depending on how this complex is resolved, according to Freud, an individual's adult attachments are sexually normal or abnormal, and a person's adjustment is either neurotic or not.

The Oedipal period is followed by a *latency* stage, a relatively nonsexual phase of development achieved as a result of unconsciously motivated forgetting, or *repression*. During the final phase of psychosexual development, called the *genital* stage and occurring in adolescence, a person's self-love and self-attachments become channeled into love of others.

Personality Types. Everyone, according to Freud, has infantile sexual complexes. The difference between normals and abnormals is that the normals resolve them satisfactorily. If the complexes are not resolved, however, either because of excessive frustration or overgratification at particular developmental stages, *fixations* may occur, and the adult character structure displays symptoms that reflect *regression* to the unresolved conflicts that occurred at various developmental stages.

The *oral character's* conflicts, for example, were not satisfactorily resolved at the first stage of development and, as an adult, he is extremely dependent upon others for the maintenance of self-dignity. He tends to equate love with food and when depressed may eat to reassure himself of being loved. He may display several other oral preoccupations: excessive smoking, alcoholism, and nail-biting. This neurotic's chief characteristic is an insatiable desire to be reassured and an unrelenting demandingness.

The *anal character*, whose fixations, according to psychoanalytic theory, occurred during the second stage of psychosexual development, has been described as stingy, obstinate, and orderly. Presumably stinginess is a continuation of anal retentiveness; obstinacy dates back to refusal to give up a part of himself at his parents' request; and excessive orderliness and neatness derive from compliance and obedience to parental demands—all of these traits being related to toilet training.

The *phallic character*, who is basically narcissistic, self-loving, and vain, is the adult consequence of unresolved and infantile preoccupation with oneself as the object of love. Some adult manifestations include exhibitionism, bravado, and excessive personal sensitivity. These individuals are easily insulted, and criticism of them or their work can engender deep depressions.

The normal adult, or *genital character*, who has presumably passed successfully through each of the stages, is able to establish mature emotional ties with other individuals and with members of the opposite sex without being plagued by traces of earlier psychosexual conflicts. In a sense Freud's normal character resembles the ideal rather than the average person.

Several other concepts of Freudian theory are valuable in accounting for the origins of adult

---

[1] In the girl, this is sometimes called the *Electra complex*; however, the term Oedipal has generally been used to refer to both sexes.

psychopathological symptoms, and, indeed, as we mentioned earlier, psychoanalysis was formulated on the basis of observations and treatment of adult neurotics. Our discussion of these concepts is resumed in Chapter 11, which covers the origins and treatment of the neuroses, and again in Chapters 20 through 25, which deal with the psychotherapies.

Neo-Freudian Theories. Although Freud's theories, in their pure, unmodified form, do not play a large part in the diagnosis or treatment of behavior disorders today, his influence is so pervasive that variants of his ideas can be found in every model except the stimulus–response models. That influence is, of course, most obvious in the psychoanalytic school itself. Freud's former disciples broke with him over theoretical issues and went off to found other branches of that school. Most took issue with his insistence that childhood sexual conflicts were the crucible in which character is formed, and that libido was the primary motivating force. They also introduced interpersonal and cultural factors as motivating agents, and gave more attention to needs for power, security, individuation, self-esteem, and assertiveness.

Alfred Adler, for example, believed that social needs are primary, and that the strongest drive is the desire for power, which he felt arises from the need to overcome one's inferiority complex. Adler believed also in the uniqueness of every human and in the individual's capacity for self-determination; in this respect and in his emphasis on social intercourse, he foreshadowed the humanists.

For Otto Rank the birth trauma was the original catastrophe, and the central drive was the desire to return to the security of the womb. Pain is thus symbolic of separation, and pleasure is symbolic of intrauterine life, the Eden that existed before the Fall.

Karen Horney stressed cultural factors as the primary determiners of motivation, along with a need for security. She believed that childhood anxiety arose from feelings of helplessness, hostility, and isolation. She believed also that each person has a "real self" consisting of "particular human potentialities," and that within that self there was a "healthy striving toward self-realization." In this respect she was, like Adler, a forerunner of the humanists.

Erich Fromm also sees social factors as crucial to human motivation, in such forms as a taboo against self-love and a society in which "human relations are essentially those of alienated automatons."

Erik Erikson has drawn upon his own work with children as well as data from cultural anthropology in expanding Freud's psychosexual stages into eight "ages of man." According to Erikson the individual faces a characteristic conflict at each of these ages, and must resolve that conflict during that age in order to continue growing.

Most neo-Freudians turned outward to interpersonal and social clues to motivation, but Carl Jung turned to what has been described in another context as the "beyond within." Underlying the individual unconscious, he believed, was a *collective unconscious* shared by all humans, in which could be found the *archetypes* of dreams and myths. In his own time Jung's theories were often bypassed as being "mystical," an epithet that has recently lost some of its sting.

Whereas Jung had gone deeper into the unconscious than Freud, Wilhelm Reich (1970) went further into libido theory. A perpetual center of controversy, Reich saw sexual energy not in the abstract metaphorical sense in which Freud saw it but in a physical sense, as something that could be measured, like voltage or current. Reich believed that healthy functioning in a human organism consisted of the charging and discharging of this energy. Pathology, like energy, also had a physical reality for Reich. He believed that as children's emotional life (especially their natural sexuality) is crushed by a repressive society, their repeated tensing up to block feeling becomes a pattern of lasting muscular rigidities ("character armor") that continue to block the ebb and flow of energy and feeling.

Critical Comment. Freud's theories, and to a large extent, the theories of the neo-Freudians just discussed, are based exclusively on the case study method, a method fraught with inherent pitfalls (see Davison and Neale, 1978, pp. 39–40). One of these pitfalls is that clinical reporting is an unreliable way to obtain information about people. Patients do not often report what they really feel or think; rather they report what they believe the listener wants to hear. Another problem is that clinicians do not always have the opportunity to take careful notes during their sessions; therefore they have to rely on their recollections. This is less of a problem now that tape recorders are readily available, but it was certainly a factor when Freud and many of the neo-Freudians were originally formulating their theories about the person.

A second difficulty with Freudian theory is that research and social change over the past half-century have cast serious doubt on the validity and predictive value of many of the concepts of that theory (Mussen et al., 1979). Investigations have not shown, for example, that excessive pleasure or frustration during several of the psychosexual stages produces the particular symptoms that the theory predicted. Moreover, Freudian theory predicts that decreases in anxiety surrounding sexuality should inevitably lead to increased happiness and fewer neurotic defenses. Although there has apparently been a marked increase in anxiety-free sexual intercourse in contemporary America over the last half-century, there is still much anxiety and conflict surrounding commitment to goals and people, as well as an increased reliance on drugs and violence as ways of resolving conflict. Freud's theory has limited predictive value.

Finally, Freud's theory has limited generalizability because his sample of patients, and to a great extent the patient sample of most private practitioners of psychotherapy, was very special.

Most of Freud's patients were from the upper-middle classes of Vienna during the early 1900s. Nowhere is this exclusiveness more clearly stated than in Frantz Fanon's observation in *Black Skin, White Masks* (1967, pp. 150-151) that "Freud and Adler and even the cosmic Jung did not think of the Negro in all their investigations." Although Fanon, a black psychiatrist from Martinique, chose to focus on the plight of blacks, one could easily substitute for Negro the words poor, disenfranchised, uneducated, and inarticulate.

Stimulus–Response Models

Freudian theory is so firmly entrenched in the establishment now that it is hard to imagine the aura of radicalism that once surrounded it. It was, after all, of European origin and had its roots in clinical observation. Stimulus–response theory, on the other hand, grew up in the psychological laboratory and, Pavlov notwithstanding, has been a home-grown product, perhaps the very essence of American technological resourcefulness. We shall explore two stimulus–response models—classical conditioning and operant conditioning—and the social learning model, which emphasizes the role of imitation in learning.

Classical Conditioning. This approach, sometimes also called *respondent conditioning*, was introduced by Pavlov's well-known study (1927) demonstrating that dogs can be trained to salivate at the sound of a bell or metronome (see Figure 6.1). A review of this study will introduce several concepts that crop up throughout the text.

The procedure and terminology are as follows. For a hungry dog salivation at the sight of food is an *unconditioned response* (UR). When the dog learns to salivate at the sound of the bell that precedes the presentation of food, a *conditioned response* (CR) has been established. This means that the dog has acquired salivation as a response to a previously neutral stimulus.

Figure 6.1
*The Russian physiologist Ivan Pavlov photographed with
his students and an experimental dog used in his work
on respondent conditioning.*

In Pavlov's experimental conditioning procedure a bell is sounded immediately before presenting food to a harnessed, hungry dog. After several pairings of the bell with food, the dog salivates at the sound of the bell. The bell has become the *conditioned stimulus* (CS), which now has the power to elicit the conditioned response.

In classical or respondent conditioning, the unconditioned stimulus (US), or food, is also a *primary reinforcer*, in the sense that the organism's response would *extinguish*, or cease to exist, without its presentation. There are also *secondary reinforcers*, defined as any neutral stimuli that acquire reinforcing properties by virtue of their association with the primary ones. In the experiment with Pavlov's dog, for example, any of the cues in the laboratory (harness, color of the walls, laboratory coat) can, because of their contiguity to or association with food, acquire secondary reinforcing characteristics.

Two basic forms of respondent conditioning exist: *appetitive* and *aversive*. The first, already dealt with above, is illustrated by Pavlov's classical conditioning paradigm, in which dogs learn to salivate in response to a previously neutral stimulus.

Aversive conditioning is based on the less-well-known experiment of Bekhterev (1932), in

Ivan Pavlov, John B. Watson, and Edward L. Thorndike (from left to right), early contributors to a psychology of learning.

(Courtesy National Library of Medicine [l]; New York Academy of Medicine [r])

which a CS (any neutral cue) is paired with a noxious US (usually shock) and the organism attempts to *avoid* or *escape* its effects. Both appetitive and aversive conditioning have been demonstrated with many organisms, from flatworms to human beings, and a wide variety of involuntary responses have been conditioned—sweating, crying, decreased and increased heart rate, gastrointestinal secretions, nausea, vomiting, finger withdrawal, and muscular spasms.

The best-known illustration of respondent conditioning leading to phobia in human beings is Watson and Rayner's (1920) experiment with Little Albert. They taught Albert, an 11-month-old infant, to fear (CR) a rat (CS) by pairing a loud noise (US) with the rat whenever the boy

approached the animal. Albert had no prior fear (no UR) of rats. After several simultaneous presentations of the rat with a loud noise Albert developed a fear, or phobic response (crying, tremulousness), to the CS alone. The conditioned phobic response was so well established that it *generalized* or transferred to other furry animals and objects, so that Albert was also afraid of rabbits and dogs.

Operant Conditioning. *Operant conditioning,* which is most closely identified with the work of B. F. Skinner, differs from classical conditioning in that the organism must behave before it is reinforced. In this sense the reinforcement is said to be *contingent* upon the emission of a response.[2]

Skinner challenged the Pavlovian position that most responses are *elicited* by stimuli and that all learning occurs as a result of a chaining of associated reflexes. Proposing that most behavior was of the type in which emission of a voluntary response was *instrumental* in obtaining reinforcement, he called particular attention to such everyday behaviors as opening doors, shutting windows, dressing, and learning to talk. In each instance successful completion of the behavior causes consequences that are pleasant or satisfying. Such behaviors are more likely than others to occur again. Behavior that is not followed by positive consequences, or that leads to unsatisfying outcomes, is not likely to occur in the future and may eventually be *extinguished* from the organism's repertoire.

The prototype experiment to illustrate operant, or *instrumental*, conditioning usually takes place in an apparatus devised by B. F. Skinner and called a *Skinner box*. At one end of the apparatus there is a lever, or bar; when it is activated by a hungry organism (usually a rat or a pigeon), a pellet of food is automatically dispensed by a magazine in the tray below the lever. At first the organism depresses (responds to) the lever quite by accident and activates the food magazine, making food available immediately after the response. Once the subject has responded and received food, it soon depresses the lever again (and receives food and responds again, and so forth), and the probability of its responding, or its *operant rate*, is increased.

Because the rate of responding increases when behavior is followed by food, the latter is

B. F. Skinner, the famed Harvard behavioral psychologist.

(Courtesy B. F. Skinner)

said to reinforce the response (or reinforcement is said to be contingent upon the response), and food becomes a *primary*, or *unconditioned*, *reinforcer*. When the magazine has been operated many times, the organism responds immediately to the noise made by it and approaches and eats the pellet. Hence the noise (or a light, if the food magazine is illuminated) becomes a *conditioned*, or *secondary*, *reinforcer*, and subjects will respond to

---

[2] One of the first psychologists to call attention to the importance of the consequences of responses was E. L. Thorndike. His formulation, referred to as the *law of effect*, was based on the assumption that much of animal and human behavior occurs as a result of trial-and-error learning. The law of effect states that when an organism is first confronted with a new problem and has not previously learned the responses needed to solve that problem, it engages in trial-and-error behavior until it attains a solution.

it for long periods of time. If, however, responding ceases to produce food altogether, then the noise, through *extinction*, loses the power to reinforce and responding stops (see Holland and Skinner, 1961).

The concept of reinforcement is further elaborated by Skinnerians to include its positive, negative, and punishing consequences. A *positive reinforcer* is a stimulus whose presentation increases the operant rate; a *negative reinforcer* (or aversive stimulus), in contrast, is a stimulus whose withdrawal increases the probability of the response that preceded it. Punishment is defined as a positive reinforcer withdrawn or a negative reinforcer presented (see J. Cohen, 1969).

Skinnerians also pay attention to the stimulus conditions, or *discriminative stimuli*, that give rise to behavior; they pose most of their questions in the form of, "What stimuli and what consequences will maintain a given response?" The term *operant* itself, according to Skinner (1953, p. 65), "emphasizes the fact that the behavior *operates* upon the environment to generate consequences." And in their behavior therapy, as we shall see later in this book, Skinnerians find it important to bring behavior under the control of certain discriminative stimuli in the environment. Such behavior is said to be under *stimulus control*.

But what happens when the experimenter wants to reinforce a response that is not in a person's behavior repertoire? Then he must *shape* or create that response by reinforcing progressively closer approximations to it. Skinner wrote (1953, p. 91):

Operant conditioning shapes behavior as a sculptor shapes a lump of clay. Although at some point the sculptor seems to have produced an entirely novel object, we can always follow the process back to the original undifferentiated lump, and we can make the successive stages by which we return to this condition as small as we wish.

By this method, shaped conditioned operant responses have produced such unlikely behaviors as raccoons playing basketball and chickens walking a tightrope.

Throughout this book you will read of many applications of Skinnerian techniques in behavior modification and, indeed, it is in that domain that operant techniques have excelled. But this does not mean that the principles of instrumental conditioning have nothing to contribute to the analysis of the origins of behavior pathology. In fact some interesting illustrations of how these principles can be used to account for abnormal reactions are presented by Skinner (1953) in his *Science and Human Behavior*. One deals with anxiety (p. 178):

A stimulus that characteristically precedes a strong negative reinforcer has a far-reaching effect. It evokes behavior which has been conditioned by the reduction of similar threats and also elicits strong emotional responses. The bandit's victim not only turns over his pocketbook and displays a high probability of running away, he also undergoes a violent emotional reaction which is characteristic of all stimuli leading to avoidance behavior.

Our second illustration describes how alcoholism may develop (p. 230):

The individual often comes to control part of his own behavior when a response has conflicting consequences—when it leads to both positive and negative reinforcement. Drinking alcoholic beverages, for example, is often followed by a condition of unusual confidence in which one is more successful socially and in which one forgets responsibilities, anxiety, and other troubles. Since this is positively reinforcing, it increases the likelihood that drinking will take place on future occasions.

Social Learning. Classical and operant conditioning stress the importance of reinforcement and external rewards in learning. This follows from the fact that both had their origins in animal laboratories. In more recent applications of learning theory principles to complex human behavior

Separation Anxiety

A form of anxiety that appears in American infants at about 10 to 12 months of age and begins to disappear about one year later is described in Mussen et al. (1979, pp. 174–177) as *separation anxiety*. For example, a 12-month-old boy is playing in the living room with some toys; he sees his mother go to the front door and leave. As the door closes he begins to cry. A 5-month-old infant would typically not cry in this situation. Why, then, does the 1-year-old cry?

It should also be understood that infants are more likely to cry when their mothers leave them in an unfamiliar place than when they are left in a familiar one. Even in their own homes, they are more likely to cry if their mothers leave from a door they hardly use than from a typical exit. The explanation offered for this "separation from mother" is that, as children mature, they establish an idea or schema for their mothers or caretakers in particular places. It is a conceptualization of mother in particular contexts—in the kitchen, standing by the sink, leaving by certain doors. When this conceptualization is disrupted and children are unable to interpret the new events, they become afraid.

Crying as a response to separation seems to be influenced, therefore, by children's ability to recognize that they are in an unusual situation and, at the same time, their inability to grasp why or to do anything about it. Since this recognition ability requires a certain level of cognitive maturity, very young children do not display separation anxiety. Numerous verifications of this observation have been obtained by psychologists working among mothers and their infants in many parts of Africa (Ainsworth, 1969, 1973) and Latin America.

the possibility of internal events as mediating agents of self-reinforcement has been recognized. This formulation of *social learning theory*, as it has come to be called, emphasizes a cognitive orientation that includes the expectancies and values of the behaving person as determinants of actions. It also places less importance than the earlier learning theories on the role of direct rewards or reinforcement. People can learn, according to this view, by observing others and not only from the direct consequences of their own behaviors.

The major contemporary contributor to social learning theory has been Albert Bandura (Bandura, 1969, 1971, 1974; Bandura and Walters, 1963), whose approach emphasizes the importance of *modeling*, or imitation. According to his view, a person may form adaptive or maladaptive habits merely by observing others, without ever practicing the responses involved or being reinforced for eliciting them. If, however, the model is reinforced for behaving in certain ways, then the viewer is much more likely to imitate the observed behavior. We shall return to Bandura's theory in Chapter 23, where we discuss its application to behavior therapy; here we shall note only that one can learn (or unlearn) habits by observing a model who is acquiring (or eliminating) such behavior, a learning process that is believed to involve covert or cognitive mediation (Bandura, 1974; Meichenbaum, 1972; Meichenbaum and Cameron, 1974).

One other social learning theory is that of Julian Rotter (1954), whom we mentioned in Chapter 4 in connection with his work on internal and external locus of control measures. He was an early proponent of a social learning theory that holds that human behavior is complexly determined by several variables that include reinforcement value expectancies and the psychological situation (see Phares, 1976).

Rotter formulated "specific expectancies," which are a person's expectancies that specific behaviors will result in particular outcomes (reinforcements) in a specific situation. "Generalized expectancies," on the other hand, refer to somewhat broader expectations regarding the probable outcomes of the person's behavior on the basis of past experiences and total history in similar situations. Both kinds of expectancies, then, as defined by Rotter (1954, p. 107) are "the probability held by the individual that a particular reinforcement will occur," either as a function of specific behaviors in specific situations or as a function of past behaviors in related situations. The precise relationships between behavior, behavior feedback, and changes in the person's expectancies have been studied extensively (Davis and Phares, 1967; Weiner, 1972).

Interaction Models

The family is the matrix within which the individual passes through the developmental stages described by Freud and the learning experiences described by Pavlov, Skinner, and Bandura. It is the context in which an individual originally learns the rules of living, and in which the first interpersonal transactions are experienced. The infant's earliest encounter with the world is usually his contact with his mother, who normally satisfies his needs for nourishment, body contact, and emotional response. She is also usually the person who first exercises control over his behavior. Both the satisfactions and the controls play an important part in the child's development. The child's relationships with parents and siblings are considered by many to be among the most im-portant influences shaping his or her personality and ways of interacting with others.

We shall briefly mention here the family interaction model of behavior pathology that derives from the psychoanalytic theories of Harry Stack Sullivan and the researches of Gregory Bateson. We shall then discuss specific ways in which the family environment influences individual development.

Sullivan, to a greater extent than most personality theorists, understood the importance of language in personality development. As individuals pass from infancy to childhood, their efforts at learning to use their parents' language correctly almost always result in a measure of success. Such success, however, does not occur without at least some failures. For Sullivan these early failures were important because they caused anxiety. Furthermore, as psychologist Robert Carson has emphasized (1969, pp. 32-34), they teach the child to use a personal or autistic language. Parents are extremely likely to frown upon the "autistic performances of the infant, insofar as they become overt . . . (and) . . . the infant is going to experience anxiety promptly following any public display of his linguistic eccentricities."

Sullivan stressed the child's dependence on others to meet his needs, and his anxiety whenever any of those needs are not met. The child's self-concept is formed out of the reflected appraisals of these people. Thus love, acceptance, and support lead to a "good me" self-image, rejection to a "bad me" self-image, and disgust to a "not me" self-image. The parts of oneself identified as the "not me" tend to be repressed or attributed to others, and Sullivan saw this process as an element of behavior pathology.

Sullivan also considered the development of language a crucial tool for helping individuals fuse their infantile self-concepts with their later identities. Thus "good me" and "bad me" become just "me," and "good mother" and "bad mother" become just "mother," in each case, of course, with vestiges of the earlier infantile concepts remaining (1953).

Bateson (1972; et al., 1956) focused on the patterns of disturbed communication he found in studying the families of schizophrenics. On the basis of these studies Bateson formulated the highly controversial *double bind hypothesis*. A double bind is a damned-if-you-do, damned-if-you-don't situation, and it usually arises from a double message. (A common example of a double message is "Come love me/keep your hands off me.") Typically the person in a double bind is (a) strongly motivated to respond to the demands of a significant other person, who (b) makes conflicting, mutually exclusive demands, and (c) does not allow the person in the double bind to comment on the double message or withdraw from the situation. Bateson sees the steady repetition of this communication pathology as the major determinant in the development of schizophrenia.

Numerous studies have been made of the effects of various parental behaviors and attitudes on the development of children. We shall now examine some of those studies.

Parental Behavior. Particular parental behaviors have been shown to exert specific effects in causing behavior pathology. In investigating the relation of the family unit to the development of problem behavior, a group of psychologists at the University of Illinois (Becker et al., 1959) intensively studied two groups of families, one with children not in need of clinical services ($N = 25$), and the other with children who had behavior problems ($N = 32$). They asked, "Which aspects of parental behavior are most closely related to behavior disorders in children?" and their findings, presented diagrammatically in Figure 6.2, suggest that when one parent is punitive and frustrating toward the child (instigating aggression) and the other is lax about discipline, conditions are right for the development of an aggressive child. Moreover, when the parents are maladjusted and give vent to unbridled emotion, they provide for the child a *model* of uncontrolled behavior (see Figure 6.3).

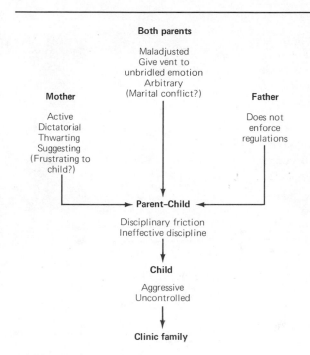

Figure 6.2

A diagram depicting the effects on children of the behaviors of mother, father, and both parents of clinic cases.

(Becker, et al., 1959)

Parental Attitudes. Studying parental behavior yields only half the family unit equation; it is equally important to attempt to comprehend the effects on behavior pathology of parents' *attitudes* toward their children. Several attitudinal dimensions have been identified, including the *warm–restrictive, warm–permissive, hostile–restrictive,* and *hostile–permissive* parent. Children raised in warm–restrictive homes, compared with those reared in warm–permissive homes, were likely to be more dependent, less friendly, less creative, and more hostile (Kagan and Moss, 1962).

The parent who is both hostile and restrictive, according to several investigators (Kessler,

Figure 6.3
In displaying aggression toward her brother, this girl is modeling her mother's behavior.

1966; Mussen et al., 1979), tends to encourage counterhostility within the child without allowing it to be expressed. This parental combination is often found among neurotic children with suicidal tendencies and accident proneness (Sears, 1961).

Whereas restrictiveness combined with hostility maximized self-aggression, the combination of permissiveness and hostility (hostile–permissive) encourages the child's "acting-out" of resentments. This interpretation makes psychological sense because one would expect hostile–restrictive parents to promote internalization of anger, since they do not permit children to express their hostility as their hostile–permissive counterparts do (Mussen et al., 1979). Studies with delinquent children tend to corroborate this

expectation, finding that aggressive, or "acting-out," boys most often come from homes in which severe punishment was common and permissiveness high (Sears et al., 1957).

Maternal Deprivation. The long-lasting effects of maternal deprivation in infancy were first called to our attention by René Spitz (1945, 1946, 1954) in a series of now highly controversial studies that investigated two groups: infants who were brought up in a foundling home since birth and were not carefully attended to; and a control group, who were also institutionalized but were visited and handled by their mothers. Both groups of infants received adequate diets and physical care.

Observations and tests over a two-year period showed that the two groups differed markedly in numerous important ways. The foundling group showed an intellectual decline, fell further behind in bodily, perceptual, and social functioning, and—most significantly—also had higher disease and mortality rates than the nursery children.

According to one of these studies (Spitz and Wolf, 1946) the critical period for emotional deprivation to take its toll seems to be the end of the infant's first year. If mothering is resumed shortly after the first year of deprivation, the depression and physical and psychological deficit in functioning can be reversed.

To illustrate the dramatic effects of such reversals, we present Case Report 6.1, a hospitalized 13-month-old infant who suffered maternal deprivation (Patton and Gardner, 1963), and Figure 6.4.

The infant received a program of 90 days of intensive mothering in the hospital, with one nurse providing most of the attention. The results, according to some authors (Kimble and Garmezy, 1968), were as follows (p. 419):

Within days after the mothering program was initiated, the infant's expression brightened; she began to say "mama" to her nurse-mother and started eating well and gaining weight. Several weeks later, she could sit upright without assistance and roll over with good motor control.

Black Ghetto Lifestyles

In his classic study, *The Nature of Prejudice*, Gordon Allport (1954) described some of the traits that can result from victimization. Following his lead, William McCord and John Howard (1969, pp. 76–77) have more recently examined some of the possible responses to aggression. Beneath the diversity of ghetto life, they say, people have consciously or unconsciously made one of three basic choices:

1. They can seemingly accept their roles as victims of the ghetto or they can, with switchblade or protest sign, rebel against their status.
2. They can channel their response through organized groups—gangs, churches, lodges—or they can go it alone on an individualistic path.
3. They can react to their situation in an overtly aggressive, violent manner or they can suppress whatever rage they feel and, perhaps, direct it against themselves.

Seven lifestyles, or perhaps, seven types of people, emerge as a result of these choices:

1. The *stoics*, who are outwardly apathetic and accepting and find some happiness in joining a traditional Negro church or simply resigning themselves to being invisible.
2. The *defeated*, who have been crushed by life and escape from a reality they can no longer tolerate into a world of drugs, alcohol, or psychotic hallucination.
3. The *exploiters*—the blockbusters, numbers runners, morticians—who have a stake in maintaining the status quo in the ghetto.
4. The *achievers* who seek to better their own lot in life but may have little concern for the collective condition of blacks.
5. The *rebels without a cause*, who reject existing society and express their rebellion through delinquency.
6. The *reformers*, who hope to change society by reform measures.
7. The *revolutionaries* who have rebelled militantly against American society and hope to effect a total change in the black way of life.

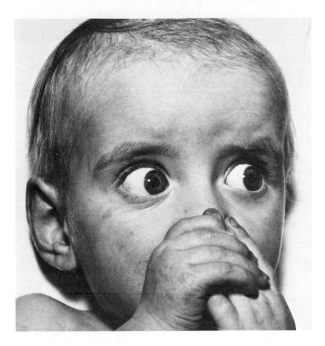 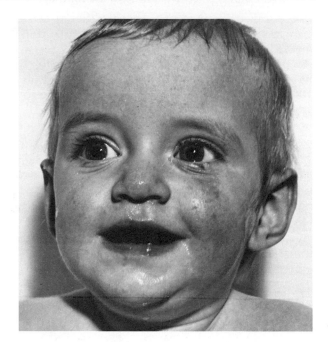

Figure 6.4

On the left is a maternally deprived 13-month-old infant. Note the frightened look and the hand biting. On the right is the same infant after about 60 days of intensive mothering in the hospital.

(Courtesy Lytt I. Gardner)

Some of these changes are clearly evident in Figure 6.4b (also see Kimble et al., 1974, p. 502).

Case Report 6.1 *Maternal Deprivation*

A 13½-month-old girl was brought to the hospital after an 11-month period of maternal deprivation. The mother, who was feebleminded, had been told during her infant's second month that too much attention might spoil her child. Subsequently she avoided physical contact with the infant in every way possible. The infant was visited only during feeding time, and otherwise was left to fend for herself, isolated from all human contact. The infant then became inert, grew listless, and could not hold down her food, and the mother brought her to the hospital complaining that "there's something wrong" with her child. Upon hospitalization, she weighed 10 pounds, lay on her back motionless, and bore an apprehensive expression on her face, cupping her hands over her mouth, and chewing her fingers constantly.

SOURCE: *Adapted from R. G. Patton and L. I. Gardner. Growth failure in maternal deprivation, 1963. Courtesy of Charles C. Thomas, Publisher, Springfield, Ill.*

While Spitz's work with human infants has come under considerable criticism over the years for its methodological shortcomings, and single case studies can be flawed because of the selective attention frequently paid by investigators to evidence confirming their hypotheses, work with animals has circumvented some of these problems and has shown clearly that the infant–mother relationship is crucial in the origins of behavior anomalies.[3]

In a fascinating series of well-known studies Harry Harlow and his associates at the University of Wisconsin Primate Laboratory reared infant monkeys with artificial, or surrogate, mothers. In one of the first of these studies a group of monkeys was separated from their mothers 6 to 12 hours after birth and supplied with wire "mothers"; a second group was given wooden "mothers" covered with foam rubber and terry cloth (Figure 6.5). Thus some monkeys had surrogate mothers who were hard, cold, and unresponding, and other monkeys had surrogate mothers who were merely unresponding. Each of the surrogate mothers was equipped with a nipple so that nursing was possible (Harlow, 1959, 1962; Harlow et al., 1971; Harlow and Zimmerman, 1959).

Harlow and his associates published a number of noteworthy findings in this and subsequent studies over the years. For example, terry cloth mothers were discovered to provide more warmth and security than wire mothers. Under conditions of threat infant monkeys normally seek out their primary source of sustenance (see Figure 6.6), but this does not happen with infants

Harry Harlow of the University of Wisconsin with one of his laboratory monkeys.

(University of Wisconsin Primate Laboratory)

raised on wire mothers. These monkeys, even when given the opportunity to cling to their original source of sustenance, prefer the cloth mothers, probably because of the greater warmth provided by them.

A follow-up study showed that both the monkeys raised on wire mothers and those raised on cloth mothers found it difficult later in life to develop normal social and sexual companionships with other monkeys. Only monkeys who were reared by their own mothers displayed normal patterns. The behavior of the others showed bizarre patterns: they were indifferent, sat listlessly with their heads covered by their hands, or rocked to and fro repetitively; they easily went into rages, often mutilating themselves in the process.

In other follow-up studies (Harlow and Harlow, 1971) these psychologists demonstrated that there was a critical period in the lives of infant

---

[3] Maher (1970) makes the point that many family studies must be interpreted cautiously because few tools are available to measure such elusive variables as "overprotection," "rejection," and so forth, and that investigators often make their observations with specific hypotheses in mind, which they seek to confirm. Frequently, also, investigators of families must settle for retrospective accounts by the patient, and these too are likely to be biased and therefore inaccurate.

Figure 6.5

A baby monkey clinging to its surrogate mother, which is made of wood and covered with foam rubber and terry cloth.

(University of Wisconsin Primate Laboratory)

monkeys during which they must engage in activities with other monkeys. They showed that when infant monkeys are allowed to play with other monkeys during the first half-year of life, regardless of the type of mothering received earlier, normal adult social and sexual behavior occurs later on. Of monkeys reared in complete isolation during the first 3, 6, or 12 months, however, those raised on the latter two schedules

were apprehensive and overaggressive and showed inadequate social interactions as adolescents and adults.

As might be expected, the combination of social isolation and surrogate mothering was found to be the most damaging. This was especially evident among female monkeys, who displayed inadequate social skills and sexual prowess. Compared with normal monkey mothers, these female monkeys as mothers ("motherless mothers") responded to their infants' needs indifferently and sometimes bit them severely, even killing them (4 out of 10 cases). Compare Figures 6.7 and 6.8.

Returning to human studies again, we can observe that Spitz's findings as well as those of Harlow have been corroborated by several well-controlled studies. Provence and Lipton (1962), for example, observed 75 babies living in an institutional environment in the United States where nutrition and bodily care were adequate and the infants were not physically ill, but where interactive play and opportunity to explore were inadequate.[4] The infants were also fed without the presence of adults and there was minimal adult contact and minimal variability in their experience. There were no vocalizations from other people and no close relationship between a child's crying and the reaction of someone else.

After four months of institutionalization, the institutionalized babies vocalized very little; they showed no cooing, no babbling, and little crying, as do family-raised infants. Moreover, they did not adapt their postures to the arms of an adult and, according to the researchers, reacted to adult warmth like sawdust dolls.

---

[4] Mussen et al. (1974) suggest that some of the ill effects of institutionalization among Spitz's children may have been due to their being physically ill, suffering from either serious malnutrition or chronic infectious diseases. Nonetheless, they concede (1974, p. 218) that Spitz's "observations alerted many psychologists and psychiatrists to the possible psychological consequences of institutional living."

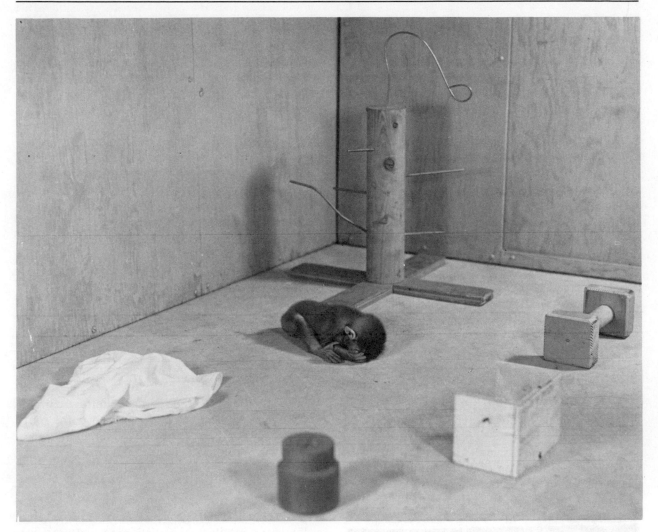

Figure 6.6
A terrified baby monkey in an unfamiliar playroom, in which there is no cloth surrogate mother.

(University of Wisconsin Primate Laboratory)

In another long-range follow-up study, ~~Skeels~~ (1966) ~~showed the differential effects of contrasting types of institutional experiences in childhood.~~ The study (reported in Davids, 1973) began in the early 1930s and covered 30 years. It involved 25 infants who were wards of the state and were placed in an orphanage in Iowa. Intelligence testing showed all to be mentally retarded. Because of crowded conditions at the orphanage, 13 of these children were transferred as "house

Figure 6.7
One of Harlow's motherless mothers, confused about what to do with her hungry infant.

(Courtesy National Institute of Mental Health)

guests" to an institution for the retarded. The children were all under 3 years of age at the time of this transfer. They were placed under the care of retarded women who showered them with attention and affection. The remaining 12 children stayed in the orphanage, where they received very little stimulation, attention, or love. Over a period of 2 years, the children in the group under the care of the retarded women showed an average IQ gain of 29 points, whereas the group that remained in the orphanage showed an average IQ loss of 26 points: quite a difference between two groups that only 2 years earlier had performed at a similar retarded level on intelligence tests.

An initial follow-up study conducted 3 years after termination of the original study found that 11 of the 13 children in the transferred group had maintained their earlier gains in intelligence. All children who had remained in the orphanage were still mentally retarded. In the few children in this group who showed some IQ point gains, there had been improved environmental experiences subsequent to the original study.

A long-range follow-up study, after a lapse of 21 years, located and obtained information on each of the original group of children. It was found that the two groups had maintained their divergent intellectual functioning patterns into adulthood. All 13 children of the transferred group were self-supporting and none was institutionalized. The findings among the orphanage children as adults were quite different. One died in adolescence following continued institutionalization, and four were still residents in state institutions. Those who were employed, with only one exception, were engaged in menial work with very limited incomes.

Although it is tempting to conclude from these human and animal studies on maternal

deprivation that the factors determining abnormality have been isolated, critics of these studies have pointed out that in most studies this variable is confounded with stimulus deprivation (Casler, 1968; Dohrenwend and Dohrenwend, 1969). Evidently the two influences are independent of one another, as one psychologist noted, and the im-

mediate effects of maternal deprivation become more severe as one moves up the evolutionary scale. But more importantly, in monkeys as well as in human beings, absence of the mother does not necessarily lead to behavior disorder so long as social relationships with peers are possible (Bronfenbrenner, 1968).

Humanistic–Existential Models

Third-force, or humanistic–existential models of motivation proceed from a set of beliefs and assumptions significantly different from those of either psychoanalysis or behaviorism. Third-force psychologists are less likely to see an individual's distress as resulting from failure to adjust to society, since they tend to see alienation as a major cause of distress and society as the major source of alienation. Furthermore, since they believe that the individual is free to make choices and is responsible for his actions, they are averse to regarding human behavior as *determined* by unconscious drives or external reinforcement.

Existential psychology originated in Europe and is best known in the United States through the writings of Rollo May and those of R. D. Laing. Laing concurs with Sullivan and Bateson in regarding disturbed communication within the family as the pivotal factor in neurosis and psychosis. In Laing's view, the child's authentic self-expressions are repeatedly invalidated because they do not match the values and expectations of the parents. Thus the child learns that his real feelings are not acceptable, that he cannot be himself and be loved, so he develops a divided self—a false, outer self hiding the real, inner self. If even this strategy fails (because of repeated double binds), the individual resorts to the desperate strategy of psychosis.

In the United States existential psychology has merged with humanistic philosophy, of which two important premises are that (a) human nature is intrinsically good and health-seeking, and (b) individuals have the power to shape their own lives. As we noted in Chapter 1, Abraham Maslow was one of the principal founders of third-force psychology. Maslow believed that most human problems resulted from blocking, rather than from expressing, natural human impulses. He also believed that people have a hierarchy of needs. Thus no energy is available to meet a particular need if a more basic need remains unmet.

Carl Rogers, about whom we shall also have much more to say in Chapter 24, was another founding father of third-force psychology. He associates pathology more with the internalization of negative self-images, which may block the release of inner strivings for self-realization.

Humanists believe that in his heart each person is already wise, wholesome, and loving, and that destructive behavior results from interfering with natural impulses, either by blocking them or by trying to force them. Thus pathology may result from learning repressive or manipulative modes of self-control. Unfortunately, an already socialized person cannot simply let go and expect nature to take over. What would take over is learned habit patterns, which are quite powerful. But humanists believe it is possible to cut through conditioning, to deprogram people, and to restore their authenticity. They believe that in the authentic person control flows outward from the organism itself as in the growth and blossoming of a plant, which is an example of spontaneous control. Control is then neither manipulative nor repressive, but *expressive*.

Sociocultural Determinants

A society's culture is its total way of life. It provides a blueprint for living, and its traditions help shape the people's beliefs, attitudes, and thinking, as well as governing their interpersonal affairs. Therefore, it comes as no surprise that a society's abnormalities closely parallel its culture.

Subcultural Influences

The family is only a single unit of culture, albeit an early and important one, in which behavior is learned. Other units, some subcultural and others more narrowly defined, include socioeconomic class, ethnic group membership, urban versus rural residency, employment status, and living conditions, as well as age, sex, and marital status.

Table 6.1

Distribution of Control and Psychiatric Populations by Social Level

Social Level	Normal Population		Psychiatric Population	
	Number	Percent	Number	Percent
I and II	1,284	11.3	150	7.9
III	2,500	22.0	260	13.3
IV	5,256	46.0	758	38.6
V	2,037	17.8	723	36.8
Unknown[a]	345	3.0	72	3.7

$\chi^2 = 281.0;$
$\quad p < 0.001$[b]

Source: Printed in original form in The American Journal of Psychiatry, *1953, 109, 729–734. Copyright 1953, the American Psychiatric Association.*

[a] The cases whose social level could not be determined because of paucity of data are not used in the calculation of χ^2.

[b] The χ^2, or chi square, is a statistic that indicates the probability that a result could have occurred by chance. In this case the probability is less than one in a thousand.

Socioeconomic Class. A question often asked is, "Do sick societies create sick people?" Several studies conducted in this century have found relationships between behavior pathology and aspects of the sociocultural environment, especially two aspects: *social isolation* and *social class.*

The first of these sociocultural variables was proposed as a cause for schizophrenia almost 40 years ago (Faris, 1934). The social isolation hypothesis holds that social disorganization in low socioeconomic areas leads to stress and social isolation, which in turn increases a person's likelihood of developing abnormal behavior. A related notion, prevalent among sociologists during the 1940s, was known as the "social drift" hypothesis. It explained the relatively greater incidence of behavior pathology in the lower socioeconomic groups on the basis of a drift downward of mentally ill persons from higher to lower socioeconomic areas (Myerson, 1941). We shall return to a lengthier discussion of social isolation as a determinant in schizophrenia in Chapter 12.

The classic studies linking low socioeconomic status with particular forms of mental illness are those conducted in New Haven by Hollingshead and Redlich (1958), the Midtown Manhattan study of Srole and his associates (1962), and the Stirling County (Canada) study of Leighton and his associates (1963), all of which reported a relatively higher incidence of behavior pathology in lower socioeconomic groups. We shall have more to say about these studies in later chapters, but here we shall merely cite some data that came out during the early stages of the New Haven study (Redlich et al., 1953).

For every patient in the New Haven area a research team of psychiatrists and sociologists obtained information on 44 items relating to social status and psychiatric condition. A total of 1963 cases were thus studied, and the data obtained about them included information on symptomatology and diagnosis, time of onset and duration of illness, reason for referral to the practitioner or

Table 6.2
Distribution of Neuroses and Psychoses by Social Level
(Psychiatric Census)

Social Level	Neuroses		Psychoses	
	Number	Percent	Number	Percent
I and II	98	65.3	52	34.7
III	115	44.2	145	55.8
IV	175	23.1	583	76.9
V	61	8.4	662	91.6
Total	449		1442	

$\chi^2 = 297.8$;
$\quad p < 0.001$

Source: Printed in original form in The American Journal of Psychiatry, *1953, 109,
729–734. Copyright, 1953, the American Psychiatric Association.*

hospital, nature and intensity of treatment, and such demographic data as their occupations, educational levels, nationalities, religious beliefs, parents, siblings, children, and spouses.

Of the 1963 cases, 50.7 percent were males and 49.3 percent were females. The distribution of the control and psychiatric populations, according to social levels, is presented in Table 6.1. It should be noted that level I families rank high in wealth, education, and social prestige. Level II includes families in which most adults hold college degrees and are in professional or high executive positions; level III consists of small-business people and white-collar and skilled workers; level IV consists largely of semiskilled workers and laborers; and level V includes unskilled laborers, who have an elementary education or less, and who live in the poorest areas of the community. The data of Table 6.1 show a significant correspondence between social level and incidence of psychiatric treatment, thus supporting the notion that prevalence of psychiatric disorders is related to social status of the patients.

Information presented in Table 6.2 reveals a marked inverse relationship between neuroses and psychoses by social level. Neuroses show a relatively high incidence in the upper social levels and a remarkably low incidence in social levels IV and V. The reverse is true for the psychoses. The researchers interpreted these findings as showing a relationship between a diagnosis of neurosis and socioeconomic status. This is somewhat confirmed by the data presented in Table 6.3, which establishes a relationship between the social stratification of the psychiatric population and the treatment agency in which they are found. These data indicate that some two-thirds of all upper-level patients are treated in private practice while patients of lower levels are concentrated in state hospitals.

We shall have further occasion, in Chapters 11, 12, 13, and 14, to interpret these differences and their implications for the diagnosis of neurosis and psychosis. It may suffice here to mention that there are three types of problems in these epidemiological studies, as Dohrenwend and Dohrenwend (1969) suggest:

(1) the validity of the measures used to determine psychological disorder is questionable and hence it is difficult to know what are the true

Table 6.3
Percentage Distribution of Patients by Social Level and Treatment Agency

Agency	Social Level			
	I and II	III	IV	V
State hospitals	14.0	41.9	68.5	84.5
Veterans hospitals	2.6	3.1	3.8	5.5
Private hospitals	14.7	3.1	0.9	0.0
Clinics	5.3	12.3	7.9	7.2
Private practitioners' cases	63.3	39.6	18.9	2.8

$\chi^2 = 871.1$; $p < 0.001$

Source: Printed in original form in The American Journal of Psychiatry, *1953, 109, 729–734. Copyright 1953, the American Psychiatric Association.*

rates of disorder in contrasting class and ethnic groups;

(2) the presence of symptoms is not necessarily an indication of the presence of disorder, because symptoms might be transient responses to life crises; and

(3) the secondary gain (sympathy, unemployment benefits) from symptomatology tends to be greater in lower- than in higher-class groups, and within classes among members of disadvantaged as opposed to advantaged ethnic groups, therefore serving to perpetuate abnormalities.

Another possible problem is that a greater reluctance of lower-class individuals to seek treatment for a neurosis could also be a variable.

Ethnic Group Differences. Just as there is a correspondence between prevalence of mental illness and social class, there is evidence of ethnic group patterning of behavior pathology. In the United States, for example, mental hospital admission rates are substantially higher for blacks than for whites in all psychodiagnostic categories. It is difficult to know, however, whether these differences are related to the stresses associated with membership in a disadvantaged group or with our society's tendency to hospitalize blacks more readily than equally disturbed whites; in general these studies are subject to the same criticisms as those showing class differences in the disorders.

There are notable subcultural differences in the rate of alcoholism, as we indicate in Chapter 9, and it has been repeatedly shown that chronic alcoholism occurs more frequently among Irish–Americans than among other groups. These differences hold for groups of comparable socioeconomic status.

Symptoms of a particular disorder can differ according to an individual's ethnic status. Opler (1956, 1959) compared Irish–American and Italian–American men who were hospitalized in New York with a diagnosis of schizophrenia. He found striking differences in their symptoms: more hostility, acting-out, elation, and bizarre mannerisms were seen among Italian schizophrenics than among their Irish counterparts. He attributed these clinical differences to the disparate family structures among these groups. For

Other- and Self-Control

Psychologists who spend their time trying to condition animals in the laboratory, according to Aubrey Yates (1975, p. 183), are usually chagrined when they visit the circus and discover the exquisite control exerted over the performing animals by trainers with no academic qualifications. Similarly, asserts Yates, psychologists who spend their time trying to improve self-control in clinical patients or teach various skills are embarrassed to see the quite extraordinary degree of body control exercised by circus performers as well as the equally extraordinary control over bodily functions that can apparently be sustained by yogis or by people who allow needles to be driven through their skin without bleeding.

One reasonable interpretation of these wonders is that psychologists have barely scratched the surface in their attempts to explain control of behavior. Another explanation is that most humans could, if they wished to do so and practiced hard enough, obtain much more control over their bodily functions than they normally achieve. Numerous ways of achieving that kind of control, from yoga to biofeedback, are currently being explored.

example, he found that the families of his Irish patients were run by mothers, who were strict and prohibitive, especially about matters pertaining to the display of emotions and to sex; and the families of his Italian patients, in contrast, were patriarchal, expressions of emotions were not suppressed, and talk about sex was more open than among Irish families.

The Effects of Urbanization. Admission rates to mental hospitals have always been about twice as high for urban as for rural Americans. In part this difference can be explained by the urbanites' easier access to mental health facilities and by the greater tendency of rural families to retain their mentally ill in the home. But that is not the whole story. Increased urbanization has accelerated the stresses and strains of city living, of which population density, or *crowding*, may be one of the chief offenders.

Most of the evidence concerning the effects of crowding comes, quite properly and understandably, from animal research. In a fascinating series of studies on the behavioral effects of population density among laboratory rats, Calhoun (1962) permitted six different populations of rats to increase to approximately twice the number that could comfortably occupy their living space. He found that the most apparent abnormalities developed among the females. Many were unable to carry pregnancy to full term, and if they did, an even greater number did not carry out their maternal functions (Figure 6.9). Among the males the behavior disorders included sexual deviation, cannibalism, and frenetic overactivity.

In another animal study two investigators (Bronson and Eleftheriou, 1963) showed that putting trained fighter mice together in an open cage for one minute, once, twice, four, and eight times a day for seven days increased their adrenal weight and hence their tendency to fight.

Evidence from human research has only recently attracted the attention of psychologists.[5] In

---

[5] There is also an extensive anthropological literature on people's use of space. See, for example, Edward T. Hall's *The Hidden Dimension* (1966).

Figure 6.9

The effect of population density on the behavior and social organization of rats was studied by confining groups of 80 animals in a 10-by-14-foot room divided into four pens by an electrified fence. Each pen (numbered 1, 2, 3, and 4 clockwise from door) was a complete dwelling unit. Conical objects are food hoppers; trays with three bottles are drinking troughs. As seen in pen 1, where the top of a burrow has been removed, elevated burrows reached by winding staircases each had five nest boxes. Ramps connected all pens but 1 and 4, and rats therefore tended to concentrate in pens 2 and 3. Development of a "behavioral sink," which further increased population in one pen, is reflected in pen 2, where three rats are eating simultaneously. The rat

approaching the ramp in pen 3 is an estrous female pursued by a pack of males. In pens 2 and 3, where population density was highest, males outnumbered females; in 1 and 4, a dominant male was usually able to expel all other males and possess a harem of females. Dominant males are sleeping at the base of the ramps in pens 1 and 4. They wake when other males approach, preventing incursions into their territories. The three rats peering down from a ramp are probers, one of the deviant behavioral types produced by the pressure of a high population density.

a personal account of his arrival in New York City Stanley Milgram (1970), professor of psychology at the City University of New York, had the following to say (p. 1461):

When I first came to New York it seemed like a nightmare. As soon as I got off the train at Grand Central I was caught up in pushing, shoving crowds on 42nd Street. Sometimes people bumped into me without apology; what really frightened me was to see two people literally engaged in combat for possession of a cab. Why were they so rushed? Even drunks on the street were bypassed without a glance. People didn't seem to care about each other at all.

The author of these observations then reports a number of studies relating the experience of city living to the effects of what he calls "urban overload." These include studies on deficiencies in social responsibility, which have shown that the larger the number of bystanders in an emergency situation, the less the likelihood that any of them will intervene (Latané and Darley, 1969); and, less dramatically, studies that have demonstrated that dwellers in large cities are unwilling to extend a helping hand to strangers (Altman et al., 1970); and those that indicate that the anonymity that large cities create may be responsible for the greater destructiveness and vandalism that occur there (Zimbardo, 1970).

How do urbanization and crowding relate to behavior pathology? In the first place the tempo and pace of large cities are more frenetic and hectic. This was shown in one investigator's find-

A typical noontime scene of crowding on a busy New York City street.

ings of relatively faster walking speeds of pedestrians on the streets of such large cities as New York, Philadelphia, and Boston compared with those of small and moderate-size towns (Berkowitz, 1970).

Second, as an article in *Science* (Galle et al., 1972) indicates, crowding in a dwelling increases the number of social obligations of each of its dwellers. Crowding also brings with it a marked increase in stimuli and noises, which are difficult to ignore. Therefore it would seem reasonable to propose that people would react to the escalation of social demands, increased stimulation, and lack of privacy resulting from overcrowding with irritability, weariness, and withdrawal.

The effect of density on psychiatric and social disorders, however, is not clear. Although it seems reasonable to anticipate a strong interrelation between persons per room and rate of admissions to mental hospitals, the opposite is actually the case. Rate of admissions to hospitals is highly correlated ($r = .72$) with the percentage of people living alone. This unanticipated relationship can be accounted for in terms of a self-selection factor, as the following explanation suggests (Galle et al., 1972, p. 29):

People who have a history of difficulty in getting along with others are likely to move to small apartments where they live by themselves, and these are the persons most likely to be admitted to mental hospitals.

But the relationship between population density and antisocial behavior (juvenile delinquency) is much clearer. The authors of the *Science* article attribute this to the breakdown of parental care that is attendant upon crowding. Children tend to receive less effective care under these circumstances, and, in general, these parents are likely to be irritable, weary, harassed, and inefficient. Children, in turn, are apt to seek relief from intolerable conditions by getting out of the home. All these factors contribute to the development in children of delinquent and aggressive behavior (see Chapter 19 for further discussions of the interrelationships of parents' attitudes and their children's behavior).

Demographic Differences. We conclude this section on the subcultural determinants of abnormality with a consideration of such demographic variables as *sex*, *age*, and *marital status*. The evidence for sex-linked differences among the behavior disorders indicates that there is a greater tendency for women to develop depression and other neurotic disorders, that men show a consistently higher incidence of antisocial disturbances, and that there are no sex-linked differences in the prevalence of total psychological abnormality (Dohrenwend and Dohrenwend, 1965, 1967). This suggests that cultural sex-role stereotypes may determine the type of disorder that occurs. For example, it is more acceptable in our society for women to display emotion, which could account for the greater prevalence of affective disturbances among them. Likewise, our culture encourages aggressiveness among males, and hence it is not surprising to find more men than women among those displaying socially undesirable acting out. Sex-role conditioning may in fact contribute to behavior pathology, as reported by Sandra Bem (1975a, p. 3):

High femininity in females has consistently been correlated with high anxiety, low self-esteem, and low social acceptance . . . and, although high masculinity in males has been correlated during adolescence with better psychological adjustment . . . , it has been correlated during adulthood with high anxiety, high neuroticism, and low self-acceptance.

The relationship between age and the incidence of mental disorders, as measured by age at first admission to a public or private hospital in the United States, shows that there is a steady rate increase per 100,000 of hospitalizations as age increases (Kramer, 1976). It is difficult to know, however, whether these age differences are due to the unreliability of diagnoses at earlier ages, or whether individuals are indeed more susceptible to disorders at particular ages. For example, some have speculated that the decline of first admissions between the ages of 35 and 64 is mainly due to the sharp decrease in prevalence of general paresis (Page, 1971). Similarly there may be critical ages during which individuals are more prone to develop psychological disturbances than at other times. In any event the incidence of disorders rises rapidly after the age of 65, no doubt because of the advances of medicine that have contributed to longevity; this, in turn, may be responsible for the increased prevalence of disorders associated with brain damage.

Mental disorder corresponds closely to marital status, in that it tends to occur more frequently among single persons and those who are divorced and separated than among marrieds living together. Although it is tempting to speculate that marriage contributes to the prevention of mental disorders, it is probably more correct to say that the mental disorders themselves may have led to the marital breakups that are reflected in these figures. It is also possible that people who were mentally disordered in the first place are less likely to marry.

Growing up Black. Frantz Fanon, in *Black Skin, White Masks* (1967, p. 43), states that "a normal Negro child, having grown up in a Negro family, will become abnormal on the slightest contact with the white world."

But if Fanon's use of the terms "slightest contact" seems to exaggerate somewhat the effects of exposure to the white world, the following passage from Grier and Cobbs (1968) leaves little question about its impact (pp. 58–59):

Thus the black boy in growing up encounters some strange impediments. Schools discourage his ambitions, training for valued skills is not available to him, and when he does triumph in some youthful competition he receives compromised praise, not the glory he might expect. In time he comes to see that

society has locked arms against *him, that rather than help he can expect opposition to his development, and that he lives not in a benign community but in a society that views his growth with hostility.*

Although the racist attitudes that prevailed when Grier and Cobbs wrote this passage have somewhat abated, blacks are still isolated from the larger community and hence have developed separate social institutions, which are economically and politically dependent on the white establishment's support. As a consequence of this dependence, many residents of the black community still provide a source of cheap labor, and—depending on the needs of the larger community—unemployment in black neighborhoods may be widespread. Furthermore conditions generally are far inferior to those of the community at large. Crowding, poor housing, lack of adequate city services, and schools that are inferior as well as white-controlled are only a few of the conditions that daily plague many citizens of the black community.

How do these conditions affect the individual black? Grier and Cobbs (1971) state it as follows in the opening paragraphs of *The Jesus Bag* (p. 1):

Black children from birth are exposed to heavily systematized hostility from the nation and for their own survival must reject the community's code of behavior, containing as it does the injunction that they themselves are to be the object of hatred. The formulation is simple. The community hates blacks and blacks return the favor.

In addition to this hatred the black ghetto is filled with the symptoms of social disorganization that have been called the *pathology of the ghetto* (Clark, 1965). These symptoms include high rates of juvenile delinquency, venereal disease, narcotics addiction, illegitimacy, homicide, and suicide—all of which contribute to the emotional ill health of ghetto life. In Kenneth Clark's words (1965, p. 82), the "harmful effects of American racism on personality development and psychological balance are unmistakable." Although this observation is less valid in the late 1970s than it was in 1965, and despite the burgeoning black middle class in our country, racism directly or indirectly still has an impact on black children.

Cross-Cultural Research

Cross-cultural studies of mental illness focus on primitive and non-Western societies in an effort to discover features in these societies that contribute to abnormality. The advantage of studying many cultures rather than a single one lies in the greater variation that is afforded for testing hypotheses about the interactions among societal and personality disorder variables.

A fundamental assumption underlying this research is that people as biological organisms have universal physiological characteristics (for example, the primary drives that lead people to eat, drink, eliminate waste products, and maintain homeostasis) and environmental characteristics that lead to cross-cultural similarities in behavior. In other words, as one psychologist (Sears, 1970, p. 167) phrased it, "when a given kind of organism has to interact with a given kind of environment, all organisms having the same general property will develop behavior repertoires that can be conceptualized in the same way."

Although investigators making cross-cultural studies of personality disorders have occasionally reported finding a society that at first glance seemed free of mental illness as we understand the term, the available evidence now suggests that all the traditional psychiatric abnormalities appear in non-Western groups. These abnormalities can be divided into two categories: those whose precise symptomatic expression is culture-bound and those that resemble Western psychiatric syndromes.

Culture-Bound Abnormality. The study of societies in which unique culture-bound pathologies occur is valuable, for it provides the investigator with a microcosm in which the unusual features of a society's customs and moral codes may be identified and implicated as causes of disorders. One example of a unique behavior disorder is *koro*, an abnormality occurring only in southeast Asia, especially among the inhabitants of the Malay Archipelago and among southern Chinese who migrated to this region. It is an anxiety state in which the individual is afraid that his penis will withdraw into his abdomen, resulting in his death. This syndrome usually has a sudden onset and is very intense. It may last for several days, or even weeks and months, and is attributed to sexual overindulgence, especially to excessive masturbation. It is believed to be avoidable by abstention from sex; if the affliction occurs, the accepted method of preventing withdrawal of the organ is to have the afflicted individual hold his penis in a viselike grip, possibly with the assistance of his wife, friends, and relatives. To release it even for an instant, according to this belief, would be disastrous (Wittkower and Dubreuil, 1968).

In many respects koro resembles what psychoanalysts call "castration anxiety," which is commonly seen in the West. But as one anthropologist indicates (Rin, 1963), the symptoms are also firmly rooted in fundamental Chinese concepts of sexuality. The Chinese believe that koro is due to an excess of what they call *yin*, the "female factor," and must be treated with *yang*, the "male factor."

Another unique disorder is so-called *susto*, or "magic fright," which has been reported among Central and South American Indian tribes and non-Indian inhabitants of the Andean Highlands of Peru, Bolivia, and Colombia. It most often afflicts infants and young children, although adolescents and, exceptionally, adults may also suffer an attack. *Susto* is closely tied to these Indian cultures and is attributed to contact with supernatural beings, breathing "bad air" in dangerous places such as cemeteries, or encountering strangers or animals that frighten the victim and cause him to fall to the ground.

The symptoms of this disorder are varied and can be divided into somatic symptoms (emaciation, loss of strength, rapid heartbeat, gastrointestinal disorders) and psychological symptoms (intense anxiety, hyperexcitability, generalized phobias, depression). Treatment consists of invoking the absent soul and cleansing the body by rubbing it with various plants or animals; especially palliative in this way is the guinea pig (Wittkower and Dubreuil, 1968).

Likewise, *amok*, which occurs among the Malayans and in some parts of Africa and has its counterparts in our society, has culture-specific features. It is characterized by a withdrawn, quiet, passive, and gentle behavior just prior to the onset of the disease proper. The disorder itself is manifested by greater withdrawal, during which afflicted people lose contact with the world around them, have ideas of persecution, and may assume a mood of anxiety and rage. This is followed by an excited stage, also called amok, during which the person suddenly jumps up, sometimes with a terrifying yell, grabs daggers or other weapons, and attacks anyone or anything he encounters. When such a person runs amok, he may commit homicide or mutilate himself. Often he is killed by frightened neighbors. This disorder has similarities to various disease categories known in our culture, especially to catatonic schizophrenia (see Chapter 12).

Amok's cultural components have been noted by some writers (Wittkower and Dubreuil, 1968; Yap, 1966), who attribute this rage reaction to the tolerance of some societies to such outbursts. For example, in Malaya and Java the incidence of this disorder fell after the authorities captured and jailed people stricken with the illness.

Similarities of Disorders Among Cultures.
There are many more similarities than differences in the symptoms of behavior pathology among diverse cultures. Research by several anthropologists (Leighton, 1969; LeVine, 1963), for example, compared abnormalities among Nigerian (Yoruba tribespeople) and rural North American cultures and found that the prevalence and the varieties of mental illness are similar in these widely disparate cultures.

Some of these similarities include, for example, talking to oneself; hearing voices and seeing imaginary people; refusing food because of the belief that it is poisoned; inappropriate affect; overconscientiousness in religious rituals; and sudden attacks on people, with loss of memory afterward. These abnormalities, as will be apparent later in this book, have their psychotic and neurotic counterparts in Western societies, although they are not always explained in the same ways in the two cultures. The Yoruba, for instance, believe that mental derangements are due to superhuman attacks from gods; the breaking of taboos and failures to observe ceremonial duties; and influences coming from human agents through witchcraft, curses, and the practice of magic (or *juju* as it is called throughout West Africa). They also believe that contagion plays a role and that disorders are transmitted from one sick person to the next, usually through direct contact with the fluids (foam at the mouth, mucus) of the ill person.

On the other hand, some societies exist in which Western symptomatology does not occur. Among the Yoruba, for example, the counterparts of phobia, obsessive–compulsive symptoms, and depression are virtually unknown. Certain characteristics of the ''Yoruba way of life'' may merit careful study if these disorders are to be prevented in our own society.

Summary

The principal motivational theories of abnormal behavior are those that originated with Freud and his followers and dissenters and the stimulus–response approaches to learning that arose in the psychological laboratories. The main contributions of Freud and his followers were the directing of attention to the importance of unconscious drives and behavior and the rich storehouse of clinical observation and inference it provided.

Stimulus–response theories found their proponents primarily among psychologists experimenting in laboratories and were solidly based on theories of learning established there. Two main types of learning were proposed—respondent and operant—and these make minimal assumptions about thinking or mind and, instead, focus on an individual's learning experiences. A third type, social learning, focuses on observation and imitation, and does recognize a cognitive element in learning.

The interactive model of psychopathology stresses the role of disturbed communication within the family, whereas the existential model emphasizes the alienation and fragmentation of the self arising from the conflict between the individual's strivings for self-realization and a desire to be accepted in the family and in society.

The search for psychogenic determinants of behavior also takes into account the context or culture within which the individual learns to function. The smallest unit and earliest of these cultures for each individual is the family. It is in this unit that the person originally learns the rules of living, and it is the experiences with parents and siblings that leave a lasting impression.

Other cultural influences are those of social class, ethnic group, type of residency (city or rural), and demographic status.

Cross-cultural research provides investigators with the opportunity to compare Western with non-Western societies in terms of the interrelationships among biological and environmental variables. In other words, the study of many cultures affords a large arena in which both unique and familiar behavior pathologies may be examined for the light they shed on etiology.

Terms and Concepts to Master

Authenticity	Primary process thinking
Classical conditioning	
Crowding	Psychosexual stages
Cue	Reinforcement
Culture	Stimulus–response theory
Double-bind	Secondary process thinking
Drives	
Ego	Social class
Id	Social isolation
Libido	Social learning
Modeling	Subculture
Operant conditioning	Superego

2   The Behavior Disorders

Subjective Distress and its Effects   The person whose behavior is abnormal is often *hurting*. And there is nothing exaggerated or figurative in our use of that term. Psychic pain is real pain, and everyone has felt it, especially in the form of anxiety, which we have chosen as the starting point for our discussion of the behavior disorders. Because anxiety is unpleasant—often in the extreme—people defend themselves against it; the mechanisms they use for that defense play a key role in the development of behavior disorders. We shall discuss anxiety and the defense mechanisms in Chapter 7. Another kind of subjective distress occurs when emotional stresses —or one's way of dealing with them—lead to physical illness, or psychophysiological disorders, which we shall discuss in Chapter 8.

Personally Maladaptive Behavior   Besides being painful, behavior disorders can interfere with a person's ability to live an effective and satisfying life. Consider, for example, the dependencies. That term itself contains a strong hint of the debilitating nature of alcoholism, which we discuss in Chapter 9, and drug abuse, which we discuss in Chapter 10. The neuroses and hysterias, which we discuss in Chapter 11, may or may not interfere with a person's ability to survive, to function, or to cope, but they can seriously hamper his or her enjoyment of life. And anyone suffering from schizophrenia or paranoia (see Chapter 12), from childhood schizophrenia or infantile autism (see Chapter 13), or from an affective disorder (see Chapter 14) is likely to have a difficult time living in the world as we know it.

Bear in mind that our system of organizing and arranging the behavior disorders is only an abstraction, albeit one that we feel is a useful learning device. It would be a mistake, for example, to fail to notice the very heavy burden of subjective distress in the alcoholic or to assume that psychotics are free of it. And the astute reader may already have noticed that anxiety and the psychophysiological disorders can handicap people. What we have done here is to try to focus on the most obvious qualities of each disorder and then locate it on a continuum that begins with the most familiar and subjective kinds of experience.

15. Sexual Dysfunctions and Divergent Sexual Patterns

16. The Antisocial Personality

17. Aggression and Violence

Social Variance and Deviance Disordered behavior may be painful or self-defeating, as we have seen. It may also bring the individual into conflict with society. However, as we suggested in Chapter 2, this is a criterion that ought to be applied with extreme caution. For example, all societies have codes of sexual behavior, but sex acts that are taboo in one society may be the norm in another. No form of sexual expression exists that has not been forbidden, or at least frowned upon, somewhere; no form of sexual expression

exists that has not been accepted somewhere. The very concept of sexual "deviance" therefore raises serious issues; we grapple with these issues in Chapter 15, following a discussion of sexual dysfunctions. In Chapter 16 we discuss the most obvious candidate for inclusion in this category, the antisocial personality. And in Chapter 17 we discuss what we consider the most maladaptive interpersonal behavior of all—aggression and violence. Physical violence has, in the last generation or so, taken hundreds of millions of lives and—we think—ought to be seriously examined by students of psychopathology.

18. Mental Retardation

19. Developmental Disorders

Organic and Developmental Disorders Mental retardation, which we shall discuss in Chapter 18, is an absence of certain intellectual and social capacities rather than a disturbance of an individual who is otherwise fully capable of functioning. Often these disorders require a different approach in treatment, care, and child-rearing practices. Moreover many of the emotional problems of retardates arise as a consequence of their repeated frustration and disappointment in trying to acquire ordinary living skills. In Chapter 19 we discuss behavior disorders that occur primarily during childhood and adolescence and that are, in some instances, unique to childhood. We conclude Chapter 19 with a discussion of the disorders of aging, a topic that has been receiving increasing attention in the last several years.

7 Anxiety and the Defense Mechanisms

That pain and distress play a significant role in the impairment of psychological health goes without saying, but what is that role? Almost everyone knows, or knows of, people who have suffered deep pain and severe distress without damage to their psychological health. Fear and guilt seem to be universal feelings, and some people seem none the worse for the experience. Yet anxiety and depression (see Chapter 14) are debilitating in themselves, as well as central to the formation of many behavioral disorders. Why?

In the first place, fear—when it is sustained—*can* cause noticeable damage to an organism. In a single episode fear mobilizes the body's flight and fight responses, supplying extra strength for survival. But repeated episodes of fear deplete the body's resources, with destructive effects, including some of the psychophysiological disorders we shall discuss in Chapter 8. Anxiety somewhat resembles sustained fear, although it can be felt in the absence of any identifiable danger. It too depletes the body's resources, and the way we defend against it determines the pattern of neurotic behavior that may follow, as we shall see in Chapter 11.

Humans usually cope with anxiety by means of one or more *defense mechanisms*. A defense mechanism, to the extent that it works, prevents the anxiety from incapacitating the person. Unfortunately the anxiety does not necessarily go away, and whether the defense mechanism does more good than harm is still an issue in psychology. Some psychologists see defense mechanisms as essential to survival; others see them as the core of neurosis. Either or both views may be correct; in any case an understanding of how people experience anxiety and how they defend against it is essential to understanding the behavior disorders.

Anxiety

Anxiety is a sense of threat or impending disaster; a gnawing feeling that despite your best efforts to protect yourself, some unforeseen danger will unpredictably strike out at you. It is a common experience, especially in fast-paced, competitive societies. Its most extreme form is panic.

The descriptions of anxiety that appear in the *Diagnostic and Statistical Manual of Mental Disorders*, and in the most recent draft of its revision, or DSM II and DSM III (APA, 1968, 1980), emphasize that it is a state of subjective distress from which the patient desires relief.

In general, experimentally produced anxiety, both for animals and for human beings, results from pairing a neutral stimulus (one that did not originally evoke anxiety) with an aversive one (a painful or noxious stimulus).[1]

---

[1] Fear and anxiety are often distinguished in the psychological literature. Fear is a reality-based response to a frightening stimulus or situation; anxiety is a *vague fear* in the sense that it is not a response to an identifiable object.

The main difference between experimentally induced anxiety and its everyday counterpart is that the latter is not as closely linked with physical objects or stimuli. For example, as we noted earlier, anxiety may occur when an individual is threatened with the loss of his job or when he thinks about an uncertain future. In either case the evidence of intense anxiety is unmistakable: the trembling legs, the dry mouth, the distant sound of one's tremulous voice, and the profuse sweating. In even more severe instances these experiences may be accompanied by urinary and bowel incontinence.

The outward appearance of the anxious person is that of someone who is trying to go in all directions at the same time, but who is too confused to settle on a particular course. Furthermore he may gasp for air and have difficulty in swallowing, and his face may reflect the panic of someone who needs immediate help. In short, the effects of anxiety are disruptive and disorganizing.

Most people, fortunately, undergo milder forms of these experiences; and when they do occur, they are transitory and disappear when the situation giving rise to them terminates. But for some neurotics these sensations are a constant part of daily existence, usually not occasioned by identifiable objects or situations, and they spend much of their time and energy combatting them.

Depending on the way they defend against anxiety, neurotics have more or less success in controlling it. If their control is minimal, they have to suffer the symptoms described above, but if their control is good, as we indicate shortly, they express their anxiety indirectly, typically in terms of rituals and somatic symptoms. Their success in controlling anxiety depends on the strength and choice of their *defense mechanisms*, which, in turn, are the end products of lifelong learning patterns. That success does not insure health or well-being, however. The person's status may be anywhere from excellent to highly symptomatic.

State and Trait Anxiety

An important distinction has been made between *state* and *trait* anxiety. State anxiety is a more transitory experience, as in the person who is anxious about an upcoming test, and trait anxiety is a more stable disposition of the person. This relation between the two concepts of anxiety has been described by one researcher (Spielberger, 1966, p. 16) as

analogous . . . to the relation between the physical concepts of kinetic and potential energy. State anxiety, like kinetic energy, refers to . . . a reaction which is taking place now *at a given level of intensity. Trait anxiety, like potential energy, indicates a latent disposition for a reaction of a certain type to occur if it is triggered by appropriate (sufficiently stressful) stimuli.*

Anxiety and Control

A crucial element in anxiety seems to be the anxious person's conviction that he or she cannot control the situation. Several experiments with animals (Liddell, 1956; Mowrer and Viek, 1948) and with humans (Haggard, 1943; Pervin, 1963; Neale and Katahn, 1968) showed that the more helpless subjects were, the more their anxiety incapacitated them. Geer et al. (1970) suggested that the individual's *perception* of helplessness, rather than actual helplessness, is the relevant variable. During the first part of their study they gave each subject a series of ten painful electric shocks, each 6 seconds long. Subjects were instructed to press a switch when the shock began so that reaction time could be measured. Sweat gland activity was measured to determine the amount of arousal. In the second part of the study half the subjects were told that they could cut the shock duration in half by reacting quickly, and the other half were told that the second series of shocks would be shorter. Actually all shocks were shortened to 3 seconds.

Measurements of sweat gland activity showed that the subjects who believed they could control the duration of the shocks were better able to tolerate the shocks.

In the social learning theory of Rotter (1954), anxiety is often seen as a series of responses indicative of a high expectancy for punishment or a low expectancy of success. For example, the student who expects to fail, the suitor who expects to be rejected, and the employee who expects to be fired all would be regarded as having a high expectancy for punishment. Anxiety might follow from such a high expectancy (for example, worrying, crying, withdrawing, inappropriate behavior). Social learning theorists (see Phares, 1976) predict that externally controlled individuals would exhibit relatively higher expectations for punishment and therefore display more anxiety than internally controlled individuals, a prediction that was supported in a study by Nelson and Phares (1971). These psychologists tested the idea that locus of control would be associated with both anxiety and needs. As anticipated by the investigators, individuals whose locus of control was perceived as externally imposed rated themselves as being more anxious than those who believed themselves in control (were internally controlled). A similar finding was supported by Strassberg (1973), who also argued for a complex relationship between anxiety, locus of control, and the perceived value of the expected goals.

Seligman (1975) has identified predictability as the key element differentiating anxiety from fear. Seligman defines fear in the animal laboratory as "the acute state that occurs when a signal predicts a threatening event, such as electric shock" and anxiety in the same context as "the chronic fear that occurs when a threatening event is in the offing but is unpredictable." Anxiety is the more emotionally disruptive experience because the organism receives no signal from its environment that it will be safe. Thus Seligman's *safety-signal hypothesis* holds that people and animals are afraid all the time, except in the presence of a stimulus that reliably predicts safety. They therefore seek out safety signals as predictors of avoidable danger because such knowledge also gives them information about safety.

Examples and implications of the role of unpredictability in anxiety come readily to mind. The terrorism by which totalitarian regimes have often subjugated people and paralyzed resistance has generally been unpredictable in the extreme. No one, no matter how scrupulously docile, could be certain not to be the next person dragged off to imprisonment, torture, or death. We might also speculate that some people who seem to court punishment do so to terminate the unpredictability and exercise some control.

Defense Mechanisms

Seeking or sustaining pleasure and recoiling from pain are basic human responses. Sudden and intense pain brings an instantaneous and automatic withdrawal—a reflex action that living organisms have evolved as a defense against injury. When an infant touches a hot stove, its hand pulls back without any intervening thought or exercise of will. The infant also learns something that will affect its future encounters with stoves. Without such defenses and such learning experiences, an individual's life and health would be in great jeopardy. But in the realm of thought and feeling defenses may sometimes be maladaptive. When an individual defends against psychic pain, the defensive patterns may, if they persist even after they cease to be needed, become obstacles to health—stereotyped and self-defeating patterns that block growth and aliveness.

Freud was among the first to recognize that unacceptable thoughts and impulses cause anxiety and, as we already noted, he introduced the concept of the defense mechanism, by means of which an individual blocks or distorts disturbing thoughts, feelings, or impulses. Since we all have thoughts and impulses whose existence we would rather not acknowledge, the use of defenses is not limited to neurotics, as we shall see.

Most of the defense mechanisms we will discuss were first described by Freud. Among the exceptions are compensation, which was described by Alfred Adler, and denial, which was described by Carl Rogers. We shall deal first with the most important Freudian defense mechanisms, and then briefly summarize several others. Our discussion is by no means exhaustive. There is no standard list of defense mechanisms to draw upon, and different theorists emphasize different combinations of defenses. Some, such as the behaviorally oriented clinicians and researchers discussed in Chapter 6, do not find it useful at all to think of behavior or personality in terms of defensive strategies. Our view is more positive, for we believe the work of Freud, Adler, and Rogers early provided the opportunity for studying the cognitive complexities of emotional and motivational forces.

Repression

Repression, according to Freud, is the underlying defense upon which most others are built. Its part in early personality development is attested to by the observation that most people cannot easily recall many of their early experiences and that traces of infantile recollections are still present in adult dreams and behavior. Later in life, according to psychoanalytic theory, repression permits individuals to thrust aside painful thoughts, desires, or impulses by rejecting them or by relegating them to the unconscious.

The mechanism of repression thus performs two functions: it *stops* ideas from attaining consciousness, and it *expels* those already there. This is accomplished without the individual's awareness and, as one writer notes (Cameron, 1963, p. 238), "Repression is silent. We only know that something that should be present has disappeared." When repression fails, anxiety crops up again; but the relationship is not a simple one. Although anxiety is the stimulus that brings re-

pression into play in the first place, the repressed material takes on an energy of its own, part of which, in turn, is transformed into anxiety. Excessive reliance on repression, according to this theory, may cause neurotic symptoms.

The symptoms most commonly associated with overreliance on repression include functional blindness (for example, loss of vision without organic basis), functional deafness, and function aphonia (or voice loss), as well as loss of memory. The disoriented person who is found wandering aimlessly in the streets, and whose memory loss was motivated by a desire to forget an unpleasant situation, is sometimes said to have repressed past experiences. The two syndromes, or disorders, most closely linked to the use of repression are the conversion and dissociative hysterias, to be discussed in Chapter 11.

Although repression is silent and elusive, its existence has been demonstrated in the laboratory. Among some 65 studies that have dealt with repression, 45 have found positive evidence for it and 20 have been negative or inconclusive. One of the main difficulties in studying repression in the laboratory is finding a way to create a sufficiently threatening situation to evoke it.

A study by Eriksen and Kuethe (1956) is typical of a majority of the more successful experiments. Its purpose was to see whether people would learn to avoid making those verbal responses that had previously been associated with a painful electric shock. They presented college students with a series of 15 words, one at a time, and told them to associate the first word that came to mind. Responses to five of these words were accompanied by a strong electric shock. The result was that in the future the experimental subjects avoided making the punished responses; see Eriksen (1966) and Martin (1971) for further details and a critique on these and similar studies.

Reaction Formation

Reaction formation serves to strengthen repression because people develop patterns of behavior

Repression

*"In a neurosis, however, the conflict found a
different outcome. The ego drew back, as it
were, after the first shock of its conflict with the
objectionable impulse; it debarred the impulse
from access to consciousness and to direct motor*
*discharge, but at the same time the impulse
retained its full charge of energy. I named this
process* repression."

SOURCE: *Freud, 1935, p. 54*

designed, albeit unconsciously, to reassure them
that they are not thinking unacceptable thoughts,
craving taboo gratifications, or giving in to unacceptable impulses. They accomplish this by
adopting ideas and behavior that are diametrically opposed to the natural and undefended
ones. For example, through the use of reaction
formation, hostile persons become softspoken
and kind, libertines become conservative, and the
sexually preoccupied launch antisex campaigns.

How does one distinguish between persons
who are truly inspired and those who are defending against unacceptable impulses? There are
several ways, the distinguishing feature being the
excessiveness with which the latter pursue their
campaigns. No one is more pious than a reformed
atheist; no one is more pristine than a former
profligate; and the staunchest teetotaler is the
cured alcoholic. It seems that their behavior,
which by any measure of normality is overdone,
serves to reassure them that they are indeed
pious, pure, and cured.

Undoing

The behavior carried out in conjunction with reaction formation is often repetitive and ritualistic
and is called *undoing*. Both reaction formation and
undoing, as we shall see later, have been cited as
causes of the obsessive–compulsive neuroses.

Undoing has its roots in infantile or childish
thinking. Many children believe that such behaviors as counting, tucking oneself completely in at
night, or not stepping on a crack in the sidewalk
will cause something else to happen (or not happen). Similarly some neurotic adults engage in
undoing—for example, blinking the eyes a certain number of times—to erase "impure" or
"sinful" thoughts or actions. It is not unusual to
find a person who uses a gesture or idiosyncratic
movement to cancel out an unacceptable thought:
for example, the teenage boy who would turn the
doorknob to the right, and then undo this by
turning it to the left, thus symbolically eradicating
the guilt associated with touching the doorknob
with his unwashed hands.

Undoing has its normal counterpart in magical or superstitious thinking. When, for example,
a baseball pitcher gets ready to deliver the ball
across the plate, he may go through elaborate
rituals, wiping his brow three times, doffing and
donning his hat twice, or chomping down hard
on his chewing gum or tobacco. Careful observation will confirm that given similar circumstances
(number of runners on base, type of pitch to be
thrown, number of outs), a pitcher goes through
his unique idiosyncratic rituals in exactly the
same way each time. His behavior is similar to
superstition in that it has become part of his repertoire as a result of having been associated with
success at one time. Furthermore, it may continue
even though it no longer has its former "magical
powers," because he believes in its magic and

feels uncomfortable and anxious when he does not carry it out.

Displacement

Displacement occurs when a person vents aggression, not at its real object—who seems too threatening—but at a harmless scapegoat. In colloquial language this is called "taking it out on someone else."

In a classic animal experiment on displaced aggression, Miller (1948b) taught one rat to strike another by reinforcing it for such aggression. The reinforcement consisted of turning off an electrically charged grill, thus permitting the attacking rat to escape shock. When the victim was replaced by a rubber doll, just an "innocent bystander" in the situation, it became the victim of the attacking rat's aggression (see Martin, 1973, 1977).

The clinical end products of unusual reliance on displacement are sometimes phobia and hypochondriasis, which, according to psychoanalytic theory, involve transferring energy from one object to another. These disorders are covered in greater detail in Chapter 11.

Projection

In projection, which always employs repression, an individual can rid himself of threatening desires, impulses, or traits by attributing them to others. Of course, as we shall show in our discussion of the paranoid states in Chapter 12, overreliance on projection assures the return of undesirable impulses in such disguised forms as others' hatred, malice, hostility, or ill-will, as well as in the form of unwanted sexual desires.

Everyday instances of projection may be seen in the hostile person who calls others hostile, the gossip who is reluctant to depart from a room full of people lest they talk about him, and the fearful child who calls others "chicken."

Projection is perhaps best exemplified in the depressed person's ascribing his self-critical conscience to others. He accuses people around him of seeing him as unworthy or contemptible, or finding it difficult, if not impossible, to go on loving, respecting, or emotionally supporting him. In this way, according to Cameron (1963), the depressive neurotic allows himself to protest openly that he is unloved.

In an early experiment designed to demonstrate the existence of projection among normals, one investigator had college fraternity men rate themselves and one another on such undesirable traits as disorderliness, obstinacy, bashfulness, and stinginess. Each man's actual possession of these characteristics was assumed to be the average of the ratings given him by his fraternity brothers. These average ratings were then compared with his self-ratings and the ratings he gave others. The findings indicated that those who did not recognize in themselves undesirable traits that others saw were especially likely to project these characteristics to others. For example, they would attribute disorderliness to others who were not so, when they were disorderly themselves but could not or would not admit it (Sears, 1936).

Fantasy

People often react to frustration of their needs and desires by slipping off into daydreams—wish-fulfillment fantasies in which they either conquer all obstacles or have their suffering recognized and appreciated and win the sympathy and consolation of the significant others in their lives.

Compensation

A person may defend against feelings of inferiority by struggling to overcome a physical or emotional handicap or by intense efforts to achieve success in some other area (and thereby distract people's attention from the handicap).

Denial

Denial, a refusal to acknowledge the truth, is closely related to repression, but denial is a more willful and less unconscious behavior. The function of denial is usually to avoid facing an unpleasant or unacceptable truth. An example might be the response of one woman in a therapy group when the group leader asked her how she felt about the statement her husband had just made to her [...]
with his mar[...]
of the proofs [...]
had a satisfa[...]
not be unha[...]
defend by de[...]
(men who h[...]
happy) to re[...]
just said he [...]
be the respo[...]
in her hom[...]
how she fe[...]
"My daugh[...]
eleven!" A [...]

ately broke in to say, "[...]
boys since I was ten[...]
Perhaps the [...]
is the reality of [...]
(1970) has no[...]
they are g[...]
against [...]
situa[...]
cra[...]

Psychological Defenses in Extreme Situations

Sudden personality changes are often the result of traumatic and extremely stressful experiences. In discussing the impact of the Nazi concentration camps on the prisoners, the initial shock of being torn away from one's family, friends, and occupation and then deprived of one's civil rights and subjected to extraordinary abuse, psychoanalyst Bruno Bettelheim (1960, pp. 175–231; also see Dimsdale, 1974) describes several psychological defenses of prisoners. Since Bettelheim was himself an inmate of one of these camps, he speaks from experience as well as from observations of others.

Some of these defenses were *early rationalizations* ("They tried to impress the guards with the important positions they had held or the contributions they had made to society. But every effort of this kind only provoked the guards to further abuse"), *atoning for others* (Feeling "newly important because their suffering protected others. After all, concentration camp prisoners had been singled out for punishment by the SS as representative of all the dissatisfied elements"), *emotional detachment* ("To avoid so much guilt, frustration, and pain, one withdrew emotionally from one's family and those aspects of the outer world one was still strongly attached to. But . . . the alternative of denying, repressing, and loosening [these attachments] robbed the prisoner of what might have been his greatest source of strength"), *selective amnesia* ("Many prisoners showed a tendency to forget names and places because of ambivalence toward important events of their previous lives, and the people in it"), *daydreaming* ("Prisoners daydreamed almost continuously in their efforts to escape a depressing reality"), *anonymity* ("To remain inconspicuous, and therefore unnoticed, was one of the best means of surviving in the camp"), and *projection* ("By projecting into the SS everything they considered evil, the SS became still more powerful and threatening. But the process of projection kept them from using to advantage any chance of viewing the SS man as a real person; it forced them to see him only as an *alter ego* of pure evil").

Mother! I've been kissing

most common subject of denial
death. As Elizabeth Kübler–Ross
ted, when people are informed that
oing to die, their immediate defense
the shock is to deny the reality of their
on. People discussing the news of an airline
sh often deny the horror suffered by the victims. For example, one person insisted that the
passengers of an airplane involved in a midair
collision were too busy fighting fires in the cabin
during the remaining few minutes of their flight
to experience any horror, despite the fact that the
newspaper accounts mentioned the screams of
the passengers. Another common response is to
cite actuarial statistics proving how safe flying is,
as if that made the fatalities less real.

Assuming that a person has acquired one or
more defense mechanisms and habitually uses
them in attempting to squelch anxiety (as most
people do), what does a therapist do about it? The
answer, as might be expected, depends on the
orientation of the therapist. Some therapists tend
not to deal with defenses, on the grounds that
specific problems can be solved without involving
the defenses at all. Psychoanalysts might be more
likely to seek the meaning and function of specific
defenses, attempting, for example, to bring repressed thoughts and feelings to the surface.
Reich believed that the defense mechanism *is the
neurosis*, and Reichian, as well as Gestalt, therapists try to break down the defenses and restore
the state of openness and vulnerability (and
aliveness) that existed before the defenses arose.
Rogerian therapists have a more noninterfering
approach, in keeping with their belief that change
must come from within the client at the client's
own initiative.

Summary

Anxiety is an intense experience in which one
may be overwhelmed by feelings of impending
disaster whether or not any disaster actually
threatens. It is the central concept in many models of neurosis, the nature of the neurotic symptoms presumably depending on the way in which
the individual defends against anxiety. State anxiety is a transitory experience that passes when
the situation changes, whereas trait anxiety is a
stable disposition. The more helpless a person
feels, the more intense the feelings of anxiety are
likely to be.

Defense mechanisms are patterns of behavior
people develop to ward off anxiety. A person
often continues to use a defense mechanism
whenever anxiety threatens, even though the
defense mechanism sometimes regenerates the
anxiety. Repression is a pushing out or walling
off from consciousness of threatening thoughts,
feelings, knowledge, or memories. Reaction formation is the replacement of an unacceptable
behavior by its exact opposite, usually exaggerated in intensity. Undoing is a ritualistic attempt
to control one's situation, either to ensure success
(as in many superstitious acts), to cancel out
unacceptable thoughts or wishes, or to remove
guilt (as in the case of Lady Macbeth's compulsive
handwashing). Displacement is the deflection of
aggressive impulses away from their real but
dangerous or powerful object toward someone
weaker. Projection is the attribution to others of
traits or feelings not accepted in oneself. Fantasy
is an escape into wish-fulfilling dreams. Denial is
a refusal to face unpleasant realities. Opinion
among therapists is divided on whether therapy
requires the removal or penetration of defenses.

Terms and Concepts to Master

Compensation	Fantasy	State anxiety
Defense mechanism	Projection	Trait anxiety
Denial	Reaction formation	Undoing
Displacement	Regression	

8 Psychological Factors in Physical Disorders

According to various estimates, 75 to 85 percent of the people seen by physicians have physical ailments with psychological causes. Typically, their complaints are backache, headache, breathing difficulties, chest pains, vomiting, constipation, or loss of appetite. Although some physicians are becoming more knowledgeable about possible links between these symptoms and the emotions, many of them are not, because most of these patients simply do not resemble psychotics or neurotics. They have no hallucinations or delusions and do not necessarily display neurotic symptoms.

Their conditions, formerly called psychophysiological disorders (and still earlier called psychosomatic disorders), are described in DSM II (APA, 1968, p. 46) as follows:

This group of disorders is characterized by physical symptoms that are caused by emotional factors and involve a single organ system, usually under autonomic nervous system innervation. The physiological changes involved are those that normally accompany certain emotional states, but in these disorders the changes are more intense and sustained. The individual may not be consciously aware of this emotional state.

In the most recent draft of DSM III (APA, 1978), this category is described as "Psychological Factors in Physical Conditions" and it is expanded to include many more physical ailments that are initiated, exacerbated, or perpetuated by psychological factors.

We can further clarify this definition by differentiating between psychophysiological symptoms and those of conversion hysteria. Whereas the symptoms of conversion hysteria involve peripheral areas (head, limbs, fingers, toes), psychophysiological symptoms affect, among other regions, the organs and tissues of the viscera (heart, stomach, intestines). The physical damage inflicted by the two ailments also differs. In the psychophysiological disorders, there is identifiable organ destruction that may threaten life; in the conversion hysterias organ involvement and structural changes are minimal and are rarely dangerous.

Essentially then, what happens in a psychophysiological disorder is that an emotional state (that in some cases the person is unaware of) acts through autonomic nervous system innervation to effect physiological changes in an organ system. These are the same changes normally caused by those emotional states but more intense and sustained.

Since the concept of emotion is generally taken for granted, and the nature of the autonomic nervous system is not widely understood, we shall briefly describe them.

The Nature of Emotion

Much has been written about emotion and many experimental studies have been conducted in an effort to formulate a generally acceptable defini-

Table 8.1

Sympathetic and Parasympathetic Functions of the
Autonomic Nervous System

Organ	Sympathetic Action	Parasympathetic Action
Eye pupils	Dilation	Constriction
Heart	Acceleration and dilation	Inhibition and constriction
Stomach and small intestine	Inhibition of secretion and of peristalsis	Secretion and peristalsis
Adrenal glands	Secretion	None
Colon	Inhibition	Increased tone
Rectum	Inhibition	Feces release
Bladder	Inhibition	Urine release
Genitals	Contraction of seminal vesicles (male) and vasoconstriction (female)	Erection (male) and vasodilation (female)
Liver	Sugar release	None
Sweat glands	Secretion	None
Hair	Erection	None
Blood vessels	Constriction (in skin and abdominal region)	Dilation
	Dilation (in heart and somewhat in striate muscles)	Constriction (in heart)

tion of it; most of this work is being pursued actively by contemporary physiologists and psychologists, but it is too extensive to review here.[1] We shall therefore adopt a definition that is currently gaining recognition and that suits our purposes.

The definition we have selected is one recently proposed by Izard (1971, Ch. 3), in his book *The Face of Emotion:* "emotion is a complex concept with neurophysiological, neuromuscular, and phenomenological aspects." The first of these aspects consists of the electrochemical activities that innervate the numerous organs and body tissues involved in reacting to evocative stimuli (Table 8.1). This is the aspect that interests us most in this chapter, for the relationship between the neurophysiology of the autonomic nervous system and emotion is responsible for psychophysiological symptoms. The second aspect, the neuromuscular aspect of emotion, involves facial, postural, gestural, and other expressions of emotion. And, finally, the phenomenological aspect consists of people's subjective experiences of emotion, although they

---

[1] The most recent extensive reviews of the emotions can be found in Bindra (1969, 1970), Goldstein (1968), and Izard (1971, 1972).

may not always be aware of what emotions they are feeling.

This definition is especially pertinent here because in a later work Izard (1972) formulates anxiety and depression in the same terms. For example, from among what Izard considers the nine major emotions—interest, enjoyment, surprise, distress, disgust, anger, shame, fear, and contempt—he holds that anxiety includes fear, distress, anger, shame, and interest. He defines depression in terms of fear, distress, inner- and outer-directed anger, disgust, and contempt.

These conceptualizations—somewhat simplified here—of anxiety and depression as complex emotional patterns allow us to view somatic symptoms as physical breakdowns resulting from long-term anxiety and depression that give rise to innervations by the autonomic nervous system.

The Autonomic Nervous System (ANS)

The autonomic nervous system includes all the nerve cells, or neurons, located outside the spinal cord and the brain (see Chapter 5 for a review of the central nervous system).[2] It has two main divisions: the sympathetic branch, which mobilizes a person's energy in the preparation for "fight or flight"; and the parasympathetic branch, which is involved more with the conservation of bodily resources.

---

[2] For still more information about the autonomic nervous system, the reader should consult the following basic physiological psychology textbooks: Deutsch and Deutsch (1973), Grossman (1967), Morgan (1965), and Thompson (1967). Izard (1972) discusses more fully the relationships between this system and emotions.

Voluntary Control of Some Regulatory Body Functions

Can body temperature and other basic regulatory body functions be brought under voluntary control? An early experiment that bears on this question was performed in 1938 by the Russian psychologist A. R. Luria (1969). He had been studying the mental feats of a man who had such excellent eidetic imagery (photographic memory) that he could evoke vivid images that changed his behavior. When he was instructed to modify the skin temperature in his hands, he could make one hand hotter by two degrees, while the other became colder by one and one-half degrees.

Similarly in a later study designed to gain hypnotic control of skin temperature Maslach et al. (1972) demonstrated that a person could simultaneously make one hand hotter and the other colder. Each subject was simply told to make an arbitrarily selected hand hotter, and the other colder, than normal. Experimenters also suggested several images that could be useful in producing this effect, and encouraged the subject to generate the personal imagery that might help achieve the desired result. All the subjects demonstrated the ability to significantly alter localized skin temperature. Large differences, in one instance as much as 4°C, were observed between identical skin sites on opposite hands within two minutes of the verbal suggestion. These differences were maintained for about ten minutes and then were rapidly eliminated upon the suggestion to normalize skin temperature. Temperature decreases in the "cold" hand were generally much larger than increases in the "hot" hand, the largest decrease being 7°C, while the largest increase was 2°C.

Can You Control Your Bodily Functions?

While reading this page you have engaged in a number of behaviors under your voluntary control. You have fixed your eyes on these words; you have used your arms to position the page; and you have adjusted your body into a comfortable reading position. Some of your other ongoing behaviors during this same period, however, have not been under your control. Try if you can to reduce your pulse, or set your blood pressure at 110/70; and while you are at it, tell your kidneys to decrease the rate at which they are forming urine. These functions, according to one psychologist's (Katkin, 1976, p. 203) description, are "controlled by a system of nerves that is virtually *autonomous*. For that reason this system is referred to as the *autonomic nervous system* (ANS)."

The autonomic nervous system was so named because its innervation was believed to be involuntary and therefore inaccessible to conscious control. In recent years many experiments have shown that ANS innervation *can* be consciously controlled. In other words the autonomic nervous system is not entirely automatic. The implications of this realization are far-reaching and have triggered a flurry of experiments in the control of ANS-mediated body functions by hypnosis (especially imaging), and by various conditioning techniques (especially biofeedback; see Chapter 23).

Among the organs affected by the distribution of the sympathetic and parasympathetic nerves are the heart, lungs, stomach, pancreas, liver, adrenals, rectum, bladder, and genitals, as we show in Figure 8.1.

The actions of the sympathetic and parasympathetic branches are generally antagonistic. The sympathetic branch, for example, accelerates heart rate, inhibits gastric secretion, and relaxes the smooth muscles of the bladder and rectum; generally, but not always, the parasympathetic branch has the opposite effect on these functions. Activation of the sympathetic system, which, as we will show shortly, occurs during emotion, produces effects similar to those obtained when adrenalin or epinephrine is injected into the bloodstream; activation of the parasympathetic system resembles the injection of an adrenalin-blocking or norepinephrine-blocking agent. Table 8.1 summarizes the functions of these separate branches of the autonomic nervous system for a select set of organs and body tissues.

The autonomic nervous system is controlled by nuclei in the hypothalamus, which send impulses to neurons that come from the spinal tract. The hypothalamus is involved in most visceral reactions, and it is the part of the central nervous system that helps keep the sympathetic and parasympathetic branches in balance. This balance becomes disrupted in the psychophysiological disorders, as we indicate shortly, and results in domination by either of its two branches, with consequent overstimulation of the circulatory, gastrointestinal, or other organs and tissues mentioned in Table 8.1.

Figure 8.1

The autonomic nervous system.

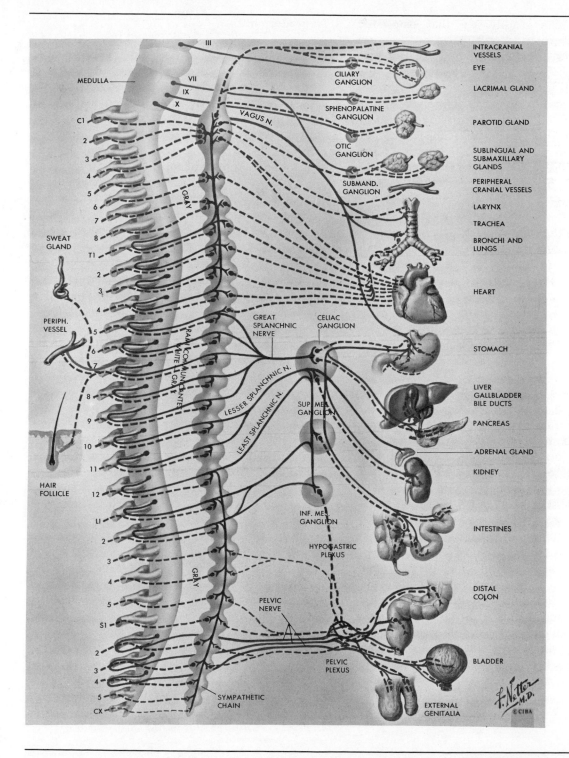

INTRACRANIAL VESSELS

EYE

CILIARY GANGLION

LACRIMAL GLAND

MEDULLA

III

VII

IX

X

SPHENOPALATINE GANGLION

PAROTID GLAND

VAGUS N.

OTIC GANGLION

SUBLINGUAL AND SUBMAXILLARY GLANDS

C1

2

3

4

5

6

7

8

T1

SUBMAND. GANGLION

PERIPHERAL CRANIAL VESSELS

LARYNX

TRACHEA

BRONCHI AND LUNGS

GRAY

SWEAT GLAND

2

3

4

HEART

GREAT SPLANCHNIC NERVE

CELIAC GANGLION

PERIPH. VESSEL

5

6

7

STOMACH

LESSER SPLANCHNIC N.

RAMI COMMUNICANTES

WHITE

GRAY

8

9

LIVER GALLBLADDER BILE DUCTS

LEAST SPLANCHNIC N.

SUP. MES. GANGLION

PANCREAS

10

11

ADRENAL GLAND

KIDNEY

HAIR FOLLICLE

12

LI

2

INF. MES. GANGLION

INTESTINES

HYPOGASTRIC PLEXUS

3

4

GRAY

5

DISTAL COLON

PELVIC NERVE

S1

2

3

PELVIC PLEXUS

BLADDER

4

5

CX

SYMPATHETIC CHAIN

EXTERNAL GENITALIA

F. Netter M.D.
©CIBA

Thus we can readily see that emotional states, when they are intense and persist over long periods of time, may seriously affect various organs and tissues of the body, sometimes causing irreparable damage that threatens life. Contrary to popular folklore, a psychophysiological disorder is not "all in your head." This misconception is as incorrect as the belief that the causes of physical ailments are always physical. The cause is emotional, but the result is quite tangible: an ulcer, hives, asthma, backache, tension, obesity, or worse.

As counter examples of these misconceptions, we note the following: difficulty in breathing may be predominantly emotional in one individual, a result of physical disease in another, and both in a third. Eczema may result from emotional stress, from an allergy, or from both allergy and stress, with the latter exacerbating the former. These interrelationships should become apparent from the following discussions.

Skin Disorders

Perhaps more than any other part of the human anatomy, the skin discloses emotional states. The most obvious instances of this are blushing or blotching when one is embarrassed, paling when frightened or weak, and perspiring when subjected to stress. The skin is such a good index of emotion because its surface is supplied by a multitude of small blood vessels that are under the control of the autonomic nervous system.

Common skin disorders include neurodermatitis, urticaria, angioneurotic edema, acne, and itching. These disorders, of which only the first two are discussed here, are psychophysiological in the sense that emotional states cause or aggravate them and that they desist, or improve, with psychotherapy, behavior modification, or hypnosis.

Neurodermatitis

This condition, sometimes also called *eczema*, is an inflammation of the skin characterized by itching and edema. Often it resembles poison ivy because scratching of the small blisters leads to an oozing sore spot. If the condition becomes chronic, the skin takes on a thick or horny appearance. Whether its causes are allergic or emotional is still a matter of considerable controversy. The evidence for its possible allergic origins stems from the observation that it appears in infants in the first several months of life, reaching its height around the ninth month and disappearing in about the second year. The evidence for a "neuro" or nervous origin (as its name seems to imply) is its frequent eruption and disappearance under emotional and relaxed conditions, respectively.

Case Report 8.1 *Neurodermatitis*

A 25-year-old married man with an apparent hostile and extroverted personality was referred for therapy because of recurring episodes of severe eczema. The rashes, which occurred mostly at the hairline in the back of the neck, consisted of raw, red blistering areas, which he would scratch incessantly. The redness, accompanied by frequent bleeding, especially after a scratching bout, was a source of constant embarrassment to him. After trips to the barber shop, the patient would report that the barber asked about the origins of his "infections." The patient, in fact, had the distinct impression that even when the barber was silent about his eczema, this in itself was an expression of his considerable curiosity.

His consultations with dermatologists occasionally relieved his symptoms, but they would return several months later. After his dermatologist suggested that the disorder had emotional components, the patient sought help. He had suspected an emotional basis all along because he also suffered from high blood pressure and had difficulty breathing. There were also periods when the patient's anxiety was unbearable. He observed a correspondence between these latter periods and the reappearance of his skin condition, high blood pressure, and respiratory difficulties.

He made an even stronger association between emotional factors and skin disorder when he observed that after he separated from his wife for several months the skin condition improved. When he visited her, the rash erupted again.

Psychotherapy was begun with the primary goal of helping the patient develop insight into the close correspondence between his physical symptoms and his emotional stresses and strains, especially in the interpersonal sphere.

SOURCE: *H. A. Abramson. Somatic and psychiatric treatment of asthma. Copyright © 1951. The Williams & Wilkins Co., Baltimore.*

Psychoanalytic theory emphasizes the importance of scratching in the skin disorders and interprets this as hostility directed toward oneself (Alexander, 1950). The self-aggression is punishment inflicted upon oneself to atone for the feelings of guilt experienced as a result of some real or imaginary wrongdoing. The self-mutilation occasionally borders on masochism (see Chapter 15) and has been known to do damage severe enough to be evident to the casual observer. Case Report 8.1 illustrates some of the factors operating in eczema, as well as the manifestation of several psychophysiological disorders in the same person under different circumstances.[3]

Experimental corroboration of the correspondence between neurodermatitis and life situations is reported in one set of studies in which 14 subjects were interviewed while their forearm skin temperatures were measured. There were increases in skin temperature of at least .3°C, and in some instances as much as 1.2°C (indicating dilatation of arterioles) when the subjects were discussing events in their lives known to have been associated with exacerbation of the dermatitis (Wolf and Goodell, 1968).

Urticaria

The symptoms of urticaria, or *hives*, include inflammatory wheals, spread over various portions of the body, which are accompanied by severe itching. The eruption of these wheals is sudden and general, each lesion lasting a few hours and being succeeded by new ones in other places. The association of hives with emotional factors has been noted for many years (Deutsch and Nadell, 1946; Saul and Bernstein, 1941), and some clinicians have observed a correspondence between them and suppressed weeping, so that when frustration was followed by weeping, hives did not occur; but when weeping was inhibited or was not possible for other reasons, urticaria would develop (Kepecs and Robin, 1950).

Respiratory Disorders

Emotional states affect breathing. Surprise, pleasure, and fear, to name just three emotions commonly experienced, are almost always correlated with variations in breathing. Thus rapid respiration accompanies surprises, shallow breathing is evident with pleasure, and sighing and breathlessness are associated with fear. Asthma, discussed below, in many respects represents an extension of common breathing irregularities.

Asthma occurs because of bronchial (tubes in the lungs) muscular spasms, resulting from imbalances of sympathetic and parasympathetic innervations. During an attack of asthma, the patient cannot get enough air, and therefore pants, wheezes, and has a feeling of asphyxiation. An adrenalin injection to stimulate sympathetic activity usually relieves the asthmatic attack.

---

[3] This may be a good place to reemphasize that, although our presentation may at times draw clear-cut distinctions between the various psychophysiological disorders, there is much overlap among the symptoms of these and other abnormalities.

Clinical and experimental studies of asthma are extensive, and several psychological factors have been isolated as aggravating and etiological agents.[4] At one time asthma was considered exclusively an emotional disorder, and in older medical textbooks it is still referred to as "asthma neurosa." But with the advent of modern immunology and the discovery of allergens, nonemotional factors were also implicated, although the past decade has witnessed a reemphasis on emotional influences. The emphasis on emotional factors is popular because of the close correspondence between asthmatic attacks and emotional states, as Case Report 8.2 illustrates.

Case Report 8.2 *Bronchial asthma*

Anita B., age 20, a college student, had suffered severe asthmatic attacks from age 3 to age 7. The attacks corresponded with recurrent quarrels between her parents, but grew less frequent after her parents divorced when she was 7. Thereafter she suffered occasional attacks when under pressure.

Her attacks became more frequent during the past year, and numerous consultations with her allergist culminated in a referral for psychotherapy.

Her attendance in college classes followed the pattern of irregularity she developed in elementary and high school, her absences coinciding closely with such stressful situations as examinations and project deadlines. Anita then met a boy whom she dated frequently, and upon their break-up, she suffered a severe attack that required emergency hospitalization and close care.

Although Case Report 8.2 implies that Anita's physical ailment was a direct consequence of emotional upset, it is important to note that in this instance, as in most psychophysiological and neurotic disorders, the symptoms fulfilled important needs. Thus her respiratory difficulties, which first occurred during quarrels between her parents, may well have served to call attention to herself in an effort to distract her parents from arguing, and perhaps from breaking up. Likewise, once she learned, perhaps unwittingly, that her symptoms exempted her from certain unpleasant chores and situations, she may have exploited them to excuse herself from facing such other unpleasant situations as school exams and project deadlines.

No doubt her illness earned her certain secondary rewards such as the sympathy and concern of her family, teachers, and friends. But lest we overplay the importance of asthma's emotional components, we hasten to add that her symptoms probably also had biological determinants that left her especially vulnerable to these attacks.

Among the many sources of emotional arousal implicated over the years in the causes of asthma, the following have been the most recurrent: sexual excitation, jealousy, rage, and anxiety. Psychoanalytically oriented clinicians tend to agree in their observations that asthmatics are ambivalent about their mothers in that they have an inordinate need for their mother's love and at the same time are afraid of "losing" or "destroying" them. Unfortunately such hypotheses, although interesting, are not easily testable.

Some promising clues about the etiology of asthma have come from conditioning studies.[5] In one such study (Dekker et al., 1957), experimenters conditioned an asthmatic attack in two volunteer subjects by pairing neutral stimuli (oxygen, neutral solvent) with inhalation of allergens to which the subjects were known to be highly susceptible. The allergens produced the expected

---

[4] See Abramson (1951) and Freeman et al. (1964) for a review of the clinical and experimental literature.

[5] For a more detailed review of the conditioning literature pertaining to asthma, see Yates (1970a, pp. 181 ff) and for a brief review of the biofeedback research, see Yates, 1975, pp. 206–207.

asthmatic attack, and evidence of conditioning was later obtained when the neutral stimuli were also able to trigger asthma.

Similarly, another study demonstrated that animals can also be conditioned to learn "asthma-like" responses. This was accomplished by gradually modifying the animal's normal breathing until it became a reasonable facsimile of asthma (Turnbull, 1962).

A third study (Luparello et al., 1974) measured the effect of suggestion on changes in airway resistance in the bronchial tubes among subjects with asthma, emphysema, and restrictive lung disease, as well as normal persons. The results demonstrated that suggestion is capable of influencing the airway diameter among almost half of the asthmatics investigated, with bronchoconstriction or dilation being accomplished, depending upon the suggestion used. This phenomenon was not observed among normals or subjects with bronchitis or restrictive lung disease.

But these are only leads that help corroborate the notion that learning is important in asthmatic episodes; they tell us little about how the disorder is caused. In other words we can produce a symptom in many ways, but we still do not know how it actually develops in those suffering from asthma (or other disorders; see especially the discussion beginning on p. 166).

Later studies have yielded evidence that infection in early life may render the respiratory system hypersensitive or vulnerable; conflict, frustration, and other emotional upsets can then interact with these damages to produce asthma (Lachman, 1972). A study by Rees (1964) supports the idea of such predisposing factors in the history of asthmatics. He found that 80 percent of a sample of asthmatics had previous respiratory infections compared with 30 percent of a nonasthmatic control group.

But still other studies have again implicated psychogenic factors as important triggering agents. Philipp (1970) presented subjects with saline, a neutral substance, and suggested that they would experience breathing difficulties. They did. He then presented subjects with another inhalant, mecholyl, a bronchospasm-inducing drug, and told them that it was a neutral substance that would not cause breathing difficulties. His subjects reacted less intensely to this substance than to the neutral one.

Subsequently, Philipp and his associates (1972) demonstrated that the expectancy of asthmatic attacks is an important factor in this respiratory disorder. He compared the reactions to bronchospasmatic and neutral substances of a group of allergic asthmatics (based on skin-test reactivity) to a group of nonallergic, or psychogenic asthmatics. The findings, based on measures of breathing capacity, were that the nonallergic group had more asthmatic attacks than the allergic group in response to both the bronchospasm-inducing and the neutral inhalants. The investigators interpreted these results as indicating that the psychogenic group's greater fear or expectancy of asthmatic attacks was responsible for these differences. They also learned that the nonallergic or psychogenic group also benefited more from relaxation training than the allergic group, suggesting again that fear of attack may be important in triggering the asthma attack itself.

Family interactions have also been implicated as significant factors in asthma (Purcell et al., 1969; Rees, 1963) and have been shown to be responsible for triggering asthma attacks. The first of these studies demonstrated that asthmatic children who have disturbed relationships with their parents and are separated from these parents show a dramatic drop on several measures of asthma (rapidity of air expulsion, wheezing, need for daily medication, frequency and intensity of daily asthma attacks). The study by Rees (1963) indicated that children of overprotective but rejecting parents had a greater incidence of asthmatic attacks than children whose relationships with parents were less disturbed. These and similar results led one observer (Martin, 1977, p. 331) to conclude that "when asthma develops without strong allergic predisposition, many features of antagonistic, mutually frustrating family interaction are present."

Other respiratory disorders in which emotion has been implicated include the *hyperventilation syndrome*, which is characterized by rapid breathing or panting; *hay fever*, which has a strong seasonal and allergic component, but nonetheless can be exacerbated by stress; and *pulmonary tuberculosis*, which cannot exist without the tubercle bacillus but is affected by many additional psychological and social forces that determine its time of onset and that, for better or worse, can influence its course.

Musculoskeletal Disorders

Increased emotion has frequently been associated with heightened tension in the skeletal muscles. Such tension is physiologically linked to the organism's state of alertness and is important for its performance in this state because it regulates efficiency of action.[6] A constant state of alertness may lead to difficulties, however, as the following description suggests.

The most common tension-produced musculoskeletal disorder is a pain in the small of the back—*backache*. Several "stress-interview" studies have demonstrated that sustained contraction of the skeletal muscles, such as occurs under emotional strain, plays an important role in the genesis of such backaches. In one of these studies (Holmes and Wolff, 1950) 65 patients with backaches were compared with nonbackache patients in situations that threatened their security and engendered apprehension, conflict, and anxiety (all of which were provoked by having an interviewer touch on sensitive and previously determined conflictive topics). Backache patients displayed a significantly greater muscular activity

than nonbackache patients, as measured by a muscle action potential recorder.

Presumably backaches are related to the "take action" posture that most individuals assume when threatened. This posture is similar to that of the competitive swimmer poised and waiting to uncoil at the sound of the gun, or of the automobile driver carefully groping through a blizzard or thick fog. Unfortunately, the backache patient does not relinquish this posture as most people do when it is no longer needed; instead, it persists as a chronic condition, almost as if the patient were in a constant state of vigilance. And because the musculature involved in this pattern is designed for short-term use, maintaining it over a longer period overloads a person's physical capacity to sustain it. The end result, as Holmes and Wolff (1950) explain, is as follows (p. 770):

Difficulties ensue in these patients when the usual behavior patterns of action upon which they depend so heavily for security prove ineffective. These difficulties are further enhanced when, because of the context of the setting in which their security is threatened, they are blocked in their efforts to take action to resolve their conflict; or they are unable to make a decision concerning what course of action to take.

Gastrointestinal Disorders

Although the complex cause-and-effect relationships between emotion and gastric disturbances are still not well understood, clinicians have for some time recognized their close ties. For example, Beaumont's direct viewing of digestive changes in men under stress (1833), Pavlov's classic demonstration (1927) of the influence of psychological factors on gastric secretion, and Cannon's classic report (1929) of the influence of emotion on gastric functions are instances of these early observations. More recently, Wolf's (1965), and Wolf and Goodell's studies (1968) on

---

[6] For a thorough review of several psychological processes from a physiological viewpoint, see Gellhorn and Loofbourrow (1963).

human gastric functions, Alexander's psychoanalytic studies (1950) of patients with ulcers, and Mahl's findings (1953) of increased gastric secretions among students during their final examination period have provided additional evidence of the complex interaction of emotion and changes in the digestive system.

The clinical and experimental literature in this area is enormous. We shall therefore limit our discussion to ulcers, especially the peptic ulcer, and to obesity, which has recently attracted much research interest and which some clinicians may classify in categories other than the psychophysiological.[7]

Peptic Ulcer

A peptic ulcer is a lesion in the lining of the stomach or the duodenum. Under some conditions it produces internal bleeding, dizziness, nausea, epigastric pain, and vomiting. Its mechanism is somewhat as follows.

In the normal individual hydrochloric acid is secreted when food enters the stomach and stops when digestion has been completed. But in the ulcer patient this acid is produced in larger quantities than is necessary for digestion, and its activity continues after the food has been digested.[8] The immediate result is hunger pangs, which for the healthy individual are a signal that the body needs food, but in ulcer patients leads to overeating. And the more they eat the worse they get because the excess acid has irritated and damaged the stomach linings. The stomach is then further irritated by vomiting, which invariably ensues, and by the food that is not expelled. After multiple recurrences, the sore becomes painful and infected and appears as an ulcer on X-ray examination.

Attempts to heal the symptoms of peptic ulcers still consist of prescribing bland, alkaline diets and sometimes call for surgical intervention. One common surgical procedure is to halt the production of gastric juices by severing the vagus nerve, which is known to transmit the impulse that triggers gastric oversecretion. Once the sore is healed, the method for treating ulcer patients is to determine the psychological causes responsible for the inflammation in the first place.

This disorder has often been called the "psychosomatic disease *par excellence*" because it is a chronic ailment characterized by remissions and flare-ups. Case Report 8.3, adapted from a write-up by Maslow and Mittelmann (1951, pp. 457–458), illustrates how an ulcer, once established, is maintained and reinforced by the stresses and strains of existence.

It seems evident, regardless of one's theoretical orientation, that this patient's flare-ups occurred when he experienced emotional upset and that his ulcers were occasioned by trips away from home. Whether they were the symptoms of his dependency or his guilt and resentment, as the psychoanalytic interpretations of Maslow and Mittelmann imply, are matters for theoretical conjecture.[9] Nor is it clear why this patient developed ulcer symptoms, while others who may have had similar life histories and constellations of problems suffer from different organic and nonorganic abnormalities. But interesting clues may be obtained from the animal and human experiments described below.

---

[7] Strictly speaking, obesity is not psychophysiological in the sense that it is accompanied by organ involvement or destruction. Its inclusion here, however, is justified by the fact that it is a condition in which physical changes are caused by emotional states.

[8] Ulcer patients are reported to secrete 4 to 20 times more acid at night than normals do, this secretion actually occurring when the stomach is relatively empty (Dragstedt, 1956).

[9] This is the same Maslow who, earlier in this book and again later, we mention in connection with nonpsychoanalytic theories. About four years after writing *Principles of Abnormal Psychology*, he formulated his own motivational theories (see Maslow, 1970).

Case Report 8.3 Ulcer

A 35-year-old electrician, who was conscientious, hard-working, and ambitious, had been suffering from an ulcer for five years. He was a devoted husband and the father of three children, who also enjoyed the company of his friends and was interested in labor problems. Outwardly he seemed always poised and calm.

Careful discussion of his life history and of the circumstances under which his complaint started revealed the following: frequently his work took him to another city for prolonged periods, during which he visited his family about once a month. He sent money home regularly. While away from his home, he sometimes had sexual relations with other women. When he was about 30 years old, and away from home, he had a serious accident in which a leg and an arm were broken. He was removed to the hospital and recovered fully. However, the next time he had to be away from home, he began to have pain a few hours after meals.

His life history further disclosed that he was the oldest child in his family and that his father, who was a good provider and a rather dutiful and strict man, died in an accident when the patient was 5 years old. From the age of 15, the boy supported his mother and his three younger siblings, yet his younger brother was the mother's favorite. Within a short period of time the patient's mother and one of his sisters also died in an accident, and he became the sole breadwinner.

In spite of the patient's apparent strength, he had a strong need to lean on and depend upon others, and this need clashed with his ideals and self-esteem. Further probing indicated that, beginning with his relationship with his parents, he had always expected rejection in close emotional relations, that he was in conflict about being away from his wife and family, and that his accident, together with guilt feelings about his relations with other women, threatened his emotional dependency upon his wife ("If she knew what I had done she would condemn me, repay me in kind, and abandon me"). This resulted in anxiety and resentment, which in turn caused the emotional upset and gastric disturbance. Each time he had to be away from home his stomach symptoms reappeared.

After psychotherapy was begun and dietary measures were taken, the patient's gastric complaints lessened considerably, and he became almost entirely free from symptoms. Then his wife suffered an attack of appendicitis and had to be operated on. She was reluctant to undergo the operation, but the patient reasoned with her, without anger or rancor, and persuaded her to submit; he handled the situation with his characteristic poise and in a very sensible manner. During this period, however, his ulcer symptoms returned in full force.

SOURCE: *Abridged and adapted from pp. 457–458 of* Principles of abnormal psychology. *Rev. ed. A. H. Maslow and Bela Mittelmann. Copyright 1941, 1951 by Harper & Row, Publishers, Inc. By permission of the publishers.*

Animal Experiments. Not all animals develop ulcers under emotionally straining conditions. In one study (Mahl, 1953) dogs were subjected to conditioned fear experiments in which a buzzer was followed at irregular intervals by a painful electric shock. Symptoms of chronic fear developed in these animals. These symptoms were associated with increased gastric secretion, but did *not* cause any ulcers. Mahl concluded that emotionally stable dogs evidently do not develop experimental neurosis under stress (see also Nikolaeva, 1959).

On the other hand, numerous experiments with rats indicate that situations arousing fear and conflict do lead to the formation of ulcers. Typically in these experiments the animals are kept in a box provided with a grid adjacent to the food and water supply. The grid is electrically charged for about 47 out of 48 hours, and the animals' attempts to get food are painful. These experimental animals almost always develop ulcers (Sawrey et al., 1956; Weisz, 1957).

Other experiments with relevance for the formation of ulcers in human beings are the now controversial studies of Brady and his associates on "executive monkeys" (Brady, 1958, 1964, 1970; Brady et al., 1958). In these studies monkeys were harnessed in restraining chairs so they could move only their hands and limbs but not their bodies. They were then given a series of shocks that might be avoided by pressing a lever every 20 seconds. If a period of 20 seconds elapsed without lever-pressing, shock was delivered to their feet. This procedure produced ulcers. But it was not clear that the electric shock was the major factor involved. The researchers hypothesized that electric shock was a necessary but not sufficient condition for producing the ulcers.

To test that hypothesis, the experimenters placed two monkeys in yoked chairs. Both animals received shocks but only one—the experimental, or "executive" monkey—could prevent them. The executives developed ulcers, but the controls did not.

The researchers later learned that 6-hours-on, 6-hours-off was the schedule that caused the greatest gastrointestinal destruction. They began to measure the gastric secretions of the animals living under this schedule by making a surgical opening (or fistula) in the abdominal and stomach walls through which the contents of the stomach could be sampled. They then studied gastric secretion during various periods of avoidance responding. The results indicated that a 1-hour session had no effect on secretion, but that there was a considerable rise in acidity after a 3-hour session and an even more apparent rise after a 6-hour session. The most crucial findings were that acid increases occurred at the end of avoidance sessions, reaching a peak several hours later when the animal was resting. These results led them to conclude that emotional stress, if it is to produce ulcers, must be intermittent and have the effect of turning the animal's system on and off.

Subsequent studies, however, have suggested that the way the monkeys were assigned to the executive and control groups may have caused an artifact in the experimental design. All eight monkeys were originally placed on the executive schedule. The first four to start pressing

the bar became the executives; the last four became the yoked subjects. It has been noted since then, with studies using rats, that the more emotional an animal is, the sooner it begins to press the bar when it is shocked (Sines et al., 1963). This suggests rather strongly that the four most emotional animals became the executives, and the four most phlegmatic became the yoked subjects (Seligman, 1975).

In a rather extensive series of studies J. M. Weiss (1971 a, b, c) randomly assigned three groups of rats to conditions in which they could or could not control the shocks. In these studies it was shown that the executive animals got fewer and less severe ulcers than the yoked animals. Furthermore the yoked animals lost more weight, defecated more, and drank less than the animals who could control their environments. In other words the more helpless animals were the more stressed ones. Weiss's studies (1970, 1971) also indicated that the ulceration differences apparently caused by controllability may actually reflect differences in predictability: when an animal engages in an activity to avoid shock, the feedback from bar-pressing predicts safety; the yoked animal cannot control shock, and also has no prediction of safety.

On the basis of these and similar studies conducted after Brady's, Seligman (1975, pp. 122–123) has concluded that "men and animals prefer predictable to unpredictable aversive events. I believe that this reflects the fact that no safety is available with unpredictable shock, while safety can be predicted by the absence of the signal for predictable shock. So acute fear is preferred to the anxiety or chronic fear that unpredictability produces."

Human Experiments. The best known of these studies are those with Tom, a patient who was observed from 1941 until his death in 1958. Tom's esophagus was badly burned when he swallowed hot clam chowder at the age of 9, which necessitated his being fed through a fistula, or surgical opening, into the stomach (Wolf, 1965; Wolf and

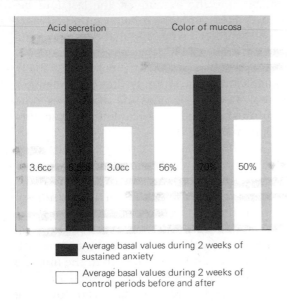

Acid secretion   Color of mucosa

3.6cc   6.6cc   3.0cc   56%   70%   50%

■ Average basal values during 2 weeks of
sustained anxiety

□ Average basal values during 2 weeks of
control periods before and after

Figure 8.2

*In this bar graph Tom's sustained hypersecretion of HCl
and his gastric hyperemia (abnormal supply of blood) are
depicted over a 2-week period of emotional upset (shaded
bars) and are compared with measures taken during the
preceding and following weeks (white bars).*

(From S. Wolf and H. Goodell. *Stress and disease*, 1968.
Courtesy Charles C Thomas, Publisher, Springfield, Ill.)

Wolff, 1942, 1947; Wolf and Glass, 1950; Wolf and
Goodell, 1968). When this patient became an
adult, he had to be hospitalized, which provided
an opportunity for keeping a thorough day-to-
day diary on him and for directly observing his
stomach under numerous conditions of emotional
stress and strain.

Comparisons made of the gastric mucosa of
Tom's stomach under these circumstances indicated that his stomach underwent apparent
physical changes that reflected his frustration and
moods. Thus when he was calm and relaxed, his
mucosa was seen to be of average appearance.
Observations and photos taken immediately after
Tom had had a transitory but intensely humiliat-

ing experience indicated greater activity of the
mucosa. Symptomatically this situation was accompanied by nausea and epigastric pain. And
observations and pictures taken when he was
tense, anxious, resentful, and guilty showed a
full pattern of overactivity, and the mucosa were
a deep red because of engorgement. (See the
graphic representations in Figures 8.2 and 8.3.)

In several other studies similar relationships
have been noted between stomach activity and
emotional states (Dragstedt et al., 1951; Mirsky,
1958). In one particularly interesting conditioning
experiment, for example, researchers demonstrated that gastric secretion could be conditioned
quite easily during a psychiatric interview (Sun et
et al., 1958) and that, for some patients, after
gastric flow had been evoked over a period of
several interviews, the *time of the interview* became
the conditioned stimulus for increased gastric
flow.

In light of the foregoing and similar observations and experiments, it has been suggested that
people with hypersecretion of gastric juice are the
most likely candidates for ulcers (Gellhorn and
Loofbourrow, 1963), but here a word of caution is
in order.

The observational and experimental procedures themselves may influence the kinds of gastric functioning noted. The study of fistulous
subjects, for example, although it permits the
direct observation and measurement of gastric
functioning, is affected by the very instruments
used and the conditions under which they are
measured. Moreover people who are studied
under these conditions are very special subjects,
if for no other reason than their surgical condition. Therefore one should not overextrapolate
from the correlations observed in these cases.

Caution should be exercised in assuming
psychogenic interpretation of many of these results because it has been shown that the level of
gastric juice secretion in any individual is determined quite early in life and hence may have
genetic origins. Therefore it is possible that those
who are susceptible to ulcers are those whose

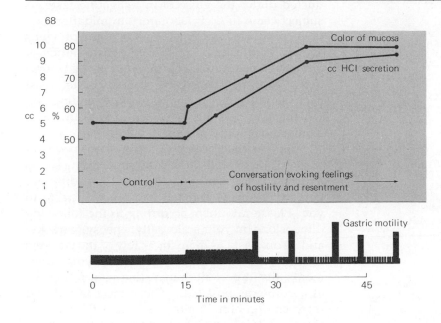

Figure 8.3

This graphic representation shows how short-term increases in color of mucosa, hydrochloric acid (HCl) secretion, and motor activity occurred when Tom was unjustly accused of irresponsibility and ineffectiveness.

(From S. Wolf and H. Goodell. *Stress and disease*, 1968. Courtesy Charles C Thomas, Publisher, Springfield, Ill.)

genetic predispositions cause high levels of gastric juice secretions. This may explain the finding of some researchers (Rosen et al., 1972) that the brothers of ulcer patients are almost twice as likely to develop ulcers as people selected randomly from the general population.

Obesity

A common psychophysiological disorder in children and adults is obesity, which is an excessive accumulation of fat in the body. Obese individuals gain weight without any apparent glandular or organic disturbances. The disorder is due mainly to lack of exercise and compulsive overeating.

That compulsive eating has emotional or psychological determinants in animals has long been known and has been shown in numerous experiments (Brooks and Lambert, 1946; Glad-

felter and Brobeck, 1962; Teitelbaum, 1955). But even more important, this has recently been demonstrated by Nisbett (1968) and by Schachter (1967, 1968, 1971a, 1971b) in a series of ingenious experiments. These experiments suggest that eating in the obese is unrelated to any internal visceral state but rather is determined by such external cues as the sight of food and social expectations; for normals, on the other hand, eating is related to *both* internal and external factors. That is to say, eating in the nonobese is also triggered by external cues, but they eat mainly when they are in a state of physiological hunger.

In one of these experiments Nisbett (1968) examined the effects of the sight of food. He reasoned that if food cues are important motivating stimuli for fat people, they should eat according to their physiological needs. To test this hypothesis, he provided college students who had not eaten lunch with either one or three roast beef sandwiches and casually told them that there

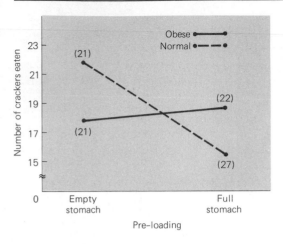

Figure 8.4

This experiment examined the effects of preliminary eating on amount eaten. It was shown that only normal subjects were influenced by preliminary eating—they ate more crackers when their stomachs were empty than when they were full. Obese subjects, in sharp contrast, ate as many crackers, if not more, when their stomachs were full. Numbers in parentheses are numbers of subjects.

(Schachter, 1971a)

were dozens of sandwiches in the refrigerator across the room: "Have as many as you want." As Nisbett had expected, the normals ate until they were no longer hungry and then stopped, even though this required some of them to leave uneaten sandwiches on their plates and others to go to the refrigerator for more. The obese subjects ate exactly what was on the plate, whether it was one sandwich or three. Nisbett concluded that the obese subjects were "plate cleaners" and that they were responding not to gastric secretions or neurological satiety signals (internal cues) but to a well-learned parental injunction to eat whatever was set before them (external cues).

Schachter (1968) and his associates carried this experiment one step further in a study con-

ducted under the guise of investigating taste. A subject came to their laboratory in midafternoon or evening. He had been telephoned the previous evening and asked not to eat the meal (lunch or dinner) preceding his appointment at the laboratory. When he arrived, he was fed either roast beef sandwiches or nothing, depending on whether he was being tested under the full-stomach or food-deprivation condition.

He was then seated in front of five bowls of crackers, presented with a long set of rating scales and told, "We want you to taste these different kinds of crackers and tell us how they taste to you. Please rate them according to the following dimensions on your scale: salty, cheesy, garlicky, and so on. Taste as many or as few of the crackers of each type as you want in making your judgments; the important thing is that your ratings be as accurate as possible." The subject tasted and rated crackers for 15 minutes, under the impression that this was a taste test, and the experimenters simply counted the number of crackers he ate.

In all there were 91 participants; they were divided into obese subjects (from 14 to 75 percent overweight) and normals (from 8 percent underweight to 9 percent overweight). The outcome of the experiment is summarized graphically in Figure 8.4, where it can be seen that the normal subjects ate considerably fewer crackers when their stomachs were full of roast beef sandwiches than when their stomachs were empty. This is in sharp contrast to the eating behavior of obese subjects, who ate as much (and in some cases more) when their stomachs were full as when they were empty. Evidently, for the obese, the actual state of the stomach had nothing to do with behavior.

In another set of experiments reported by Schachter (1971b), it was noted that obese subjects are more likely than normals to eat easily available food. The procedure here was to ask the subject, when he arrived at the laboratory, to sit at the experimenter's desk and fill out a variety of personality tests. Besides the usual office litter, there was a bag of almonds on the desk. The experimenter helped herself to a nut, invited the subject to do the same, and then left him alone with his tests and the nuts for 15 minutes. There were two sets of conditions. In one the nuts had shells; in the other the nuts had no shells. This procedure gave subjects the opportunity to eat almonds, with and without having to shell them.

The results, which are presented in Table 8.2, indicate that as many normals ate nuts with (50 percent) as without (55 percent) shells, but that many more of the obese ate shelled (19 out of 20 subjects) than unshelled (1 out of 20 subjects) nuts. In other words the finding was that when food is easy to get at, obese subjects eat more than normals.

Starting from the same observations Schachter used, Nisbett (1972, p. 433) concluded that "some individuals have no choice but to be fat . . . they are biologically programmed to be fat." His basic hypotheses are that obesity does not produce but rather results from an elevated baseline of fat stored in tissue cells, and that the central nervous system, via the ventromedial nucleus of the hypothalamus, adjusts food intake to maintain fat stores at the baseline. Schachter does not entirely reject the ventromedial arguments (1971b, p. 143), but he argues that there is a learned component to the hunger drive, although it "has . . . a physiological locus in the ventromedial hypothalamus," which makes organisms stimulus-bound. Thus the physiological drive may function through sensitizing the person directly to external cues related to food.

Nisbett's hypotheses led one psychologist (Yates, 1975, pp. 148–149) to speculate that "it may well be futile, if not positively dangerous, to attempt to induce weight reduction in some obese persons. On the other hand . . . it is not really surprising that behavior therapists have had little success with the problem of obesity as yet on a long-term basis and that there will have to be some radical rethinking of the approaches thus far adopted." It is unfortunately also true, however, that other therapies have not had any more

Table 8.2
Effects of Work on the Eating Behavior of Normal and Fat Subjects

	Number Who	
	Eat	Don't Eat
Nuts have	Normal Subjects	
Shells	10	10
No shells	11	9
	Fat Subjects	
Shells	1	19
No shells	19	1

Schachter, S. Some extraordinary facts about obese humans and rats. *American Psychologist, 1971(b), 26,* 129–144.

success than the behavioral ones.

To recapitulate, then, the foregoing experiments, as well as several others by the same group (for example, Johnson, 1970), suggest that the obese eat more than normals when food cues are prominent and eat less when the cues are remote; that the actual state of the stomach has nothing to do with fat people's eating behavior; and that they eat much more than normals when food is easily available. These conclusions do not tell us *why* obese individuals behave in these ways, but they suggest that treatment of the obese should include procedures that carefully regulate their daily contacts with food and its cues.

Genitourinary Disorders

Since the genitourinary functions are also under the control of the autonomic nervous system (Figure 8.1), emotional causes underlie such psychophysiological symptoms as bladder and urinary difficulties and sexual dysfunctions. We discuss some of these disorders below. Sexual dysfunctions are discussed in Chapter 15.

Urinary Disorders

The relation between bladder functions and emotion is evident in our day-to-day existence. For example, it is not uncommon for students to experience urinary urgency either just before or during an important school examination, and some people have difficulty urinating in strange and unusual settings. Evidence of the latter may be seen in individuals who, because of fear or shame, are unable to pass urine for specimen analysis in the doctor's office. Soldiers under battle stress, in contrast, may undergo urinary and bowel incontinence.

Menstrual Disturbances

Three types of conditions connected with menstruation have psychological and emotional origins: (1) amenorrhea, which is an abnormal suppression or absence of menstrual flow; (2) premenstrual or menstrual tension; and (3) dysmenorrhea, which is difficult or painful menstruation.

Amenorrhea. It is commonly known that emotional factors can cause a temporary delay in onset of the menstrual flow. A somewhat rarer instance of this phenomenon is "false pregnancy" (pseudocyesis), a condition in which menstrual flow is delayed for several months and which is accompanied by enlargement of the abdomen due to accumulation of gas; it is, of course, an extreme form of amenorrhea in that it involves a total psychopathology rather than just an isolated symptom. In this disorder the woman firmly believes that she is pregnant and develops the accompanying objective signs. Clinicians commonly classify this syndrome among the conversion hysterias, and psychoanalytic theory holds that the pseudocyetic woman is conflicted between the wish for, and the fear of, pregnancy.

Premenstrual or Menstrual Tension. The symptoms of premenstrual or menstrual tension are moodiness, irritability, and severe anxiety. Often these symptoms disappear with the onset of menstruation, although in more serious cases the moodiness continues throughout menstruation.

Dysmenorrhea. Dysmenorrhea is accompanied by cramp-like pains that, from a physiological standpoint, are due to increased contractions of the uterus. This occurs mainly on the first day of menstruation and is accompanied by such symptoms as fatigue, tension, insomnia, and headache. One clinician observed that reproduction and sexual function are also invariably disturbed in women who suffer from these symptoms and, because of the pain, sexual responsiveness is likewise impaired (Taylor, 1950).

That menstrual symptoms do not occur in isolation is amply evident from inspection of Figure 8.5, which is based on the summary of the symptoms of several hundred patients seen over several years at Columbia University's College of Physicians and Surgeons. These patients usually also complain of fatigue, sleeplessness, anxiety, and depression, among other bodily and emotional ailments.

General Causative Considerations

We have frequently mentioned psychoanalytic, behavioral, and miscellaneous other explanations for the development of psychophysiological disorders. We shall now review these hypotheses explicitly and present evidence in their support. Our coverage is again highly selective because the literature is extensive.

The Psychoanalytic Hypothesis

One emphasis of psychoanalysis has been on the importance of *regression* (see Chapter 6). The psychophysiologically ill person is said to have reverted to an earlier psychosexual stage of development and, according to this theory, the more severe the symptoms, presumably the more entrenched the regresssion. Psychoanalysis also stipulates that the emotions associated with the particular stage are crucial. For example, regression to the oral period might lead to dependency, which in turn causes gastrointestinal disturbances, and regression to the anal stage might manifest itself in rebelliousness and resentment leading to skin disorders.

Another common psychoanalytic theme has been that symptoms have symbolic significance. Thus peptic ulcers are assumed to symbolize internalized aggression against one's mother, persons with ulcerative colitis supposedly have deep disturbances in their key object relations, and asthmatics are presumably afraid of losing their mothers or destroying them. Many of these psychoanalytic hypotheses are derived from clinical experience and are couched in complicated, and often nontestable, terms. Maher (1966) aptly summarizes our view of the main shortcomings of this approach as follows (p. 263):

It is quite possible that all these observations are true, and useless. Loss of a significant relationship produces grief and general stress. The important ingredient of all these precipitating circumstances may well be simply that they are stressors, not that they specifically involve loss of relationships. The emphasis upon the local characteristics of the stressors may be quite misleading; it certainly has not led to any substantial addition to our knowledge of the mechanisms of psychosomatic illnesses.

A variation on the psychoanalytic theme is Franz Alexander's *specific emotion hypothesis* (1950), which asserts that for each disorder there is a typical conflict. As we saw earlier in the de-

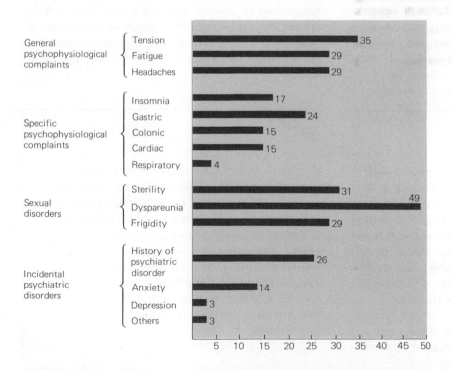

General psychophysiological complaints	Tension	35
	Fatigue	29
	Headaches	29
Specific psychophysiological complaints	Insomnia	17
	Gastric	24
	Colonic	15
	Cardiac	15
	Respiratory	4
Sexual disorders	Sterility	31
	Dyspareunia	49
	Frigidity	29
Incidental psychiatric disorders	History of psychiatric disorder	26
	Anxiety	14
	Depression	3
	Others	3

Figure 8.5
The incidence of other symptoms presented by women who were referred for gynecological problems is quite high. Not unexpectedly, there is a higher frequency of dyspareunia (painful coitus) than other disorders. Undoubtedly this is related to the pain that these women experience during menstruation.

(Taylor, 1950)

scription of the skin disorders, Alexander stressed the importance of scratching as a representation of hostile impulses turned inward. Unlike most psychoanalytic theorizing, many of Alexander's hypotheses have lent themselves to laboratory tests, and in some instances evidence has been brought to bear on their credibility.

Stress as a Causative Agent

One of the most important contributions to understanding human psychophysiological reactions was made by a University of Montreal endocrinologist, Hans Selye, who introduced the concept of *stress* into the life sciences. His books *The Physiology and Pathology of Exposure to Stress* (1950) and *The Stress of Life* (1956) were responsible for an unprecedented flurry of research in psychology (see also Selye, 1974).

Hans Selye was impressed by the fact that most human beings react to stress by developing nonspecific symptoms, and he based his concept of the *general adaptation syndrome* (GAS) on this observation. The GAS hypothesis holds that there are various forms of internal and external stress resulting from injury to tissue, infection from bacterial attacks, fatigue, hunger, and pain, as well as frustration and conflict, and that the organism responds to these stressors in three stages: (1) the alarm reaction; (2) resistance; and (3) exhaustion.

Although Selye's theory leaves many questions unanswered about why some individuals develop specific symptoms and others, under apparently similar circumstances, develop different ones, there is evidence in the research literature to suggest that stressors do result in the development of psychophysiological disorders. We shall summarize two studies that seem to support Selye's general hypothesis.

One of these studies (Liljefors and Rahe, 1970), conducted in Sweden, investigated psychosocial factors as influencing agents in the development of heart disease among identical twins. Thirty-two pairs of male identical twins, between the ages of 42 and 67, were studied to assess the effects of life-stress factors on coronary heart ailments. Only one twin in each of the pairs actually suffered from chronic heart disease. This type of study, especially since it used trustworthy criteria for monozygosity, offers an excellent opportunity to hold constant the contribution of genetic influences (see Chapter 5). The following

Noise as a Stressor

In a series of studies, two psychologists (Glass and Singer, 1972) have shown that noise can be a stressor with significant effects on task performance and physiology. Interestingly the cognitive context in which noise occurs and its unpredictability are more important than the intensity of the noise in disrupting subsequent functioning. On the basis of these findings, they assert (p. 162):

Yet it is these very factors which characterize the noisy environments to which most of us are exposed. Jets, air compressors, sirens, rock-and-roll music, automobile traffic are generally unpredictable and often uncontrollable sources of stimulation that contribute to making the sound of our environment almost unbearable and, indeed, dangerous for behavioral efficiency and mental well being. . . . Unpredictable and uncontrollable noise is a hazard of contemporary life that can and must be controlled—by personal measures, appropriate laws, and communication.

findings of this study have important implications for our daily existence: the members of the twin pairs with coronary heart disease showed significantly greater devotion to work and lesser tendencies to take leisure time, had more problems at home, and experienced greater dissatisfaction with life. Unexpectedly, however, there were no differences in the history of smoking, systolic or diastolic blood pressure, serum cholesterol, uric acid, height, weight, or obesity. These results strongly suggest not only that environmental factors may lead to coronary disorders, but also that some environmental determinants exert more potent influences than others.

The second set of studies showed that job dissatisfaction increases the probability of risk for coronary heart disease. In the first of these studies (Sales, 1969) individuals were asked to perform a laboratory task for one hour. Their enjoyment of the experiment was negatively and significantly correlated with increases in their levels of serum cholesterol. This means that the less they enjoyed the experimental task, the higher was their cholesterol level. In the second of these studies (Sales and House, 1971), in which coronary disease mortality rather than cholesterol level was the outcome measure, interviewers surveyed 12 different white-collar occupational groups by asking such questions as, "Does your job offer you the chance to use your skills and abilities?" Presumably what these questions measured was *intrinsic job satisfaction*. As an index of *extrinsic satisfaction*, the researchers asked questions about pay satisfaction, job security, work setting, and coworkers. Four-point scales, from "very good" (low score) to "very poor" (high score), were used to anchor the satisfaction items. The findings are presented in Table 8.3.

Inspection of Table 8.3 suggests that there is a substantial relationship between total job satisfaction and incidence of coronary heart disorder—namely, the greater the job satisfaction, the lower the likelihood of a coronary disease (the correlation coefficient, not shown in Table 8.3, was −.55 between these variables). Moreover, in other information collected in this study (also not presented in this table), there was a hint of a closer relationship between intrinsic job dissatisfaction and heart mortality than between extrinsic dissatisfaction and heart mortality.

In a more recent study a group of researchers at the University of Michigan (*Institute for Social Research Newsletter*, Spring 1975) found that high job satisfaction is associated with less anxiety, depression, or irritation and that, by implication, it reduces the likelihood of physical disorders due to psychological causes. For example, one psychology textbook (Smith et al., 1978) notes that physicians work long hours and carry large workloads, but report the greatest satisfaction with their jobs, as well as low levels of anxiety, depression, and irritation, and few somatic problems such as insomnia, loss of appetite, or fast heartbeat.

In contrast, assembly-line workers, whose workload is lighter and cognitively less demanding, typically report the most boredom and the greatest dissatisfaction with their workload, as well as the highest level of anxiety, depression, irritation, and physical disorders.

But perhaps the greatest single factor determining an individual's reaction to stress is personality makeup. Research evidence suggests that personality predispositions may be related to the incidence of heart disease and that self-imposed stress may be as important as environmental conditions surrounding the individual.

The most extensive program of research attempting to link behavioral variables to coronary heart disease has been undertaken by two heart specialists, Friedman and Rosenman (1974). These investigators have found that coronary-prone persons display a certain behavior pattern, which they call "Type A." Type A individuals operate under high pressure, are hard-driving, and are demanding of themselves and others. The list of characteristics believed to be associated with Type A people is as follows:

Table 8.3

Relationship between Job Satisfaction and Coronary Heart Disease

Occupational Group	Number in Group	Percent Satisfied	Intrinsic[a] Satisfaction Score	Extrinsic[b] Satisfaction Score	Number with Coronary Heart Disease (SMR)[c]
Professors, librarians	8	75	1.44	1.80	71
Advising professions	36	69	1.32	1.67	79
School teachers	54	74	1.32	1.98	75
Scientists, physicians	16	62	1.56	1.64	131
Accountants, auditors	13	46	1.66	1.84	133
Engineers	43	44	1.76	1.74	89
Technicians	33	39	1.94	2.15	119
Managerial	131	65	1.67	1.81	116
Bookkeepers	18	78	1.81	2.21	103
Other clerical	150	58	2.62	2.02	105
Sales	50	38	2.02	2.13	126
Other sales workers	7	58	2.22	2.38	136

Source: Robinson, J. Occupational norms and differences in job satisfaction: a summary of survey research evidence. In Robinson, J., Athanasiou, R. and Head, K., (eds.). Measures of occupational attrition and occupational characteristics. Ann Arbor, Mich.: Institute for Social Research, 1969. Used with permission of the publisher: Survey Research Center, Institute for Social Research, The University of Michigan.
[a] The data for intrinsic and extrinsic satisfaction are coded so that low scores imply high satisfaction.
[b] The instrument used to measure extrinsic satisfaction consisted of 4-point scales that respondents were asked to rate from "very good" (low score) to "very poor" (high score).
[c] The SMR, or standardized mortality ratio, is a measure of a tabulated deaths-per-occupation-cause group divided by expected deaths for this group and multiplied by 100. The SMR is standardized for age (Guralnik, 1963).

1. highly competitive
2. involved in many activities that have time pressure
3. extraordinarily alert
4. moving, walking, and eating rapidly
5. feeling guilty while relaxing
6. trying to do too many things at once

People who are characterized by Type B behavior are described as easygoing, not prone to hurry, and not inclined to become tense in response to time pressures. Essentially they are the exact opposites of Type A people.

Some authors (Weiner et al., 1977) have suggested that the ideal experimental procedure for determining the relationship between these two personality types and the incidence of heart disease would be to take a random selection of people, identify the Type As and the Type Bs, and then look for differences in rate of heart disease. Obviously this is not feasible. We are therefore left with correlational data.

Friedman and Rosenman developed a scale to assess a person's type of behavior pattern. Yes answers to such questions as, "Do you drive harder to accomplish things than most of your associates?" and "Do you have the impression that time is passing too fast for the things you'd like done?" indicate a Type A person. Obtaining replies to questions such as these from over 3,500 men (ages 35–59) who were free of heart disease, the Western Collaborative Group Study found that 50 percent were Type A persons.

Compared to Type Bs, Type As showed approximately a three times greater incidence of heart disease; larger increases in serum cholesterol, triglycerides, and Beta-lipoproteins (all associated with heart disease); smaller whole blood clotting times; and several other heart disease warning signals.

During the first five years of the study, up to six times more Type A than Type B men died because of heart disease. Furthermore the coronary arteries and veins of deceased Type As showed twice as much basic atherosclerosis as those of the deceased Type B men.

Rosenman and Friedman believe that the Type A pattern of behavior is related to environmental factors. They assert that the pattern emerges when the environment arouses particular facets of an individual's personality. In the most recent estimates reported in the newspaper, Friedman speculated that the incidence of Type A persons may be rising to 70 percent because of the increasing emphasis on competitiveness in our society. He was also quoted as saying that although women show a lower incidence of Type A behavior than men, women's increasing participation in business and the professions will add to their number of Type As.

Stress and Life Crises

The physical effects of stress can be profound. For example, when two researchers (Rahe and Holmes, 1965; Holmes and Rahe, 1967) interviewed 5,000 patients about life events that preceded physical illness, they uncovered a wide variety of prior stressors that were implicated. In order to study the extent of the stress and its impact, they constructed a scale of stress values measured in "life stress units." They predicted that too many changes, coming too close together and totaling more than 300 points within one year, could result in serious mental disorders.

To arrive at the scoring system, the researchers assigned an arbitrary baseline value of 50 to the act of marrying and then invited people from several countries to rate other actions and events in terms of it. The life events and their scale values are presented in Table 8.4. The reader may note that some of these changes are pleasant events.

This relation of illness to life crises was subsequently confirmed in a similar investigation involving 2,500 Navy officers and enlisted men aboard three cruisers. In this study (Holmes and Masuda, 1972) life change data were collected for six months and then health change records were collected after the men had spent six months at sea. In the first month of the cruise those who had been exposed to intense life changes before embarking had nearly 90 percent more illnesses than their less stressed counterparts. And the first group incurred significantly more new illnesses each month than the others.

Life stress has also been reported to influence psychological functioning. It has been shown to be significantly correlated with traffic accidents among male drivers, especially alcoholics (Selzer and Vinokur, 1974), and with feelings of depression, paranoia, aggression, anxiety, distress, and tension (Vinokur and Selzer, 1975). In related studies researchers found that women and poor people are exposed to significantly greater numbers of stressful life events than men and rich people (Dohrenwend, 1973); and that athletes with high life stress scores had twice the percentage of injuries of their low stress score counterparts (Bramwell et al., 1975).

Table 8.4
Life Events as Stressors

Life Event	Mean Value	Life Event	Mean Value
Death of Spouse	100	Son or Daughter Leaving Home	29
Divorce	73	Trouble with In-Laws	29
Marital Separation	65	Outstanding Personal Achievement	28
Jail Term	63	Wife Begins or Stops Work	26
Death of Close Family Member	63	Begin or End School	26
Personal Injury or Illness	53	Change in Living Conditions	25
Marriage	50	Revision of Personal Habits	24
Fired at work	47	Trouble with Boss	23
Marital reconciliation	45	Change in Work Hours or Conditions	20
Retirement	45	Change in Residence	20
Change in Health of Family Member	44	Change in Schools	20
Pregnancy	40	Change in Recreation	19
Sex Difficulties	39	Change in Church Activities	19
Gain of New Family Member	39	Change in Social Activities	18
Business Readjustment	39	Mortgage or Loan Less than $10,000	17
Change in Financial State	38	Change in Sleeping Habits	16
Death of Close Friend	37	Change in Number of Family Get-Togethers	15
Change to Different Line of Work	36	Change in Eating Habits	15
Change in Number of Arguments with Spouse	35	Vacation	13
Mortgage over $10,000	31	Christmas	12
Foreclosure of Mortgage or Loan	30	Minor Violations of the Law	11
Change in Responsibilities at Work	29		

Source: Reprinted with permission from the Journal of Psychosomatic Research, *Vol. 11 (Thomas H. Holmes and Richard H. Rahe,* "The social adjustment rating scale"), copyright 1967, Pergamon Press, Ltd.*

Evidence from Hypnosis Experiments

One particularly useful empirical approach for studying psychophysiological reactions is hypnosis, which, as we shall see in Chapter 11, is a convenient technique for producing a variety of emotional changes. These changes can be induced in a matter of minutes and can be easily terminated after a desired interval. "Before-and-after" studies can thus be conducted within a reasonable time span. This technique does have limitations, however, not least of which is that hypnosis may constitute a hazard to the emotional well-being of some subjects, especially when abnormal states are induced. Nonetheless, given trained and responsible hypnotists, this method is probably no more hazardous than some others involving experimental induction of emotion.[10]

In one set of hypnosis experiments, the Grahams and their associates (Grace and Graham,

---

[10] See Levitt et al. (1964) for a more complete discussion of the advantages and disadvantages of hypnosis as an experimental technique.

1952; Graham et al., 1958, 1962) postulated that people's characteristic attitudes in conflict situations determine the psychophysiological reactions they experience. Accordingly they conducted studies to demonstrate these relationships. Their technique consisted of manipulating attitudes by direct suggestion under hypnosis while making measurements of physiological responses.

Their hypothesis was that each psychophysiological disorder has associated with it specific attitudes toward life events and that these attitudes can precipitate and sometimes exacerbate psychophysiological symptoms. If their hypothesis is correct, they reasoned, then inducing a particular attitude should elicit its associated psychophysiological condition. A subject who is angered, for example, should show elevated blood pressure; and, conversely, when a specific physiological disorder is hypnotically suggested, individuals should show the hypothesized attitudes.

They tested the first of these notions (Graham et al., 1958) by hypnotizing normals and suggesting "pathogenic" attitudes of hives, Raynaud's syndrome (cold, moist hands), and hypertension (high blood pressure). Measurements of skin temperature reflected a rise in association with the suggested hives attitude and a fall with the suggested Raynaud's syndrome attitude. The hypertension attitude resulted in a significant rise in diastolic blood pressure. The subjects, of course, were never told what disorder their assumed attitude was related to, nor were they told the physiological manifestations of these disorders. Here are the instructions they gave their subjects (pp. 446–447):

For Hives Attitude. "Doctor X is now going to burn your hand with a match. When he does so, you will feel very much mistreated, but you will be unable to do anything about it. You can't even think of anything you want to do about it. You are thinking only what happened to you."
For Raynaud's Disease Attitude. Identical

instructions were given with this exception: "You feel mistreated and you want to hit Doctor X. You want to hit him as hard as you can, you want to hit him and choke him and strangle him. That's all you are thinking about, how much you want to hit him."

In another, though related, series of studies these investigators (Graham et al., 1962) used the interview to corroborate their findings from hypnosis experiments. First they obtained information from many people about 18 kinds of physiological symptoms and their corresponding attitudes. Then they used this information in interviews in which they elicited each individual's recall of his attitude at the time of the symptoms. They asked each subject to remember what it was that he most wanted to do at the time of the symptoms. They observed that different psychophysiological symptoms were indeed associated with different attitudes and that the relationships between these were so apparent that even nonmedically trained interviewers and naive judges could recognize them. Fifteen of the 18 disorders and their corresponding attitudes are listed in Table 8.5.

Finally, in another set of hypnosis studies, a group of investigators hypnotized 13 subjects in 40 experiments in an effort to demonstrate that they could produce skin disorders on a person's "vulnerable" arm. They proceeded by suggesting to the person under hypnosis that one arm was normal or anesthetic, numb, wooden, or otherwise devoid of sensation, and that the other arm was painful, burning, damaged, or otherwise sensitive and vulnerable. They systematically varied these numerous conditions in the 40 experiments, but in all of them they then exposed both arms to noxious allergens and subsequently assessed the extent of damage or inflammation to both arms.

Invariably the finding was that the arm rendered vulnerable under hypnosis displayed a significantly greater incidence of blisters, edema (accumulation of serous fluid), and necrosis (dead

Table 8.5
Psychophysiological Disorders and Their Associated Attitudes

Disorder	Attitude and Its Example
Hives	Feels he is taking a beating and is helpless to do anything about it. *Example:* "The boss cracked a whip on me. I couldn't do a thing about it."
Duodenal ulcer	Feels deprived, wants to get even. *Example:* "He didn't give me the raise I deserved. I'll get back at him one way or another."
Essential hypertension	Feels threatened with harm and has to be on guard. *Example:* "Come what may, I'm ready."
Asthma	Feels rejected and tries to shut out the person or situation. *Example:* "I wanted to bury my head in the sand."
Chronic ulcerative colitis	Believes he is being injured or degraded and wishes he could get rid of the responsible agent. *Example:* "He treats me like dirt; I'd like to get rid of him."
Eczema	Feels that he is being frustrated by an insuperable obstacle. *Example:* "I want to make her understand, but it's impossible."
Acne	Wants to cease being picked on. *Example:* "I wish she'd leave me alone."

tissue). They also noted a greater and more sustained temperature rise in the vulnerable arm and they explained their finding of skin disorders on the basis of this temperature elevation (Chapman et al., 1959).[11]

Some doubt has been cast on these studies (see Goldenberg, 1977, p. 401) by indications that the investigators in the hypnosis studies may not have screened their subjects sufficiently for hypnotic suggestibility and that it is the fact of hypnotic suggestion rather than the type of attitude induced that caused some of the psychophysio-

---

[11] In striking contrast to the findings reported in these studies, a later investigation (Beahrs et al., 1970) indicated that subjects who have had no history of skin reactions or allergies were not susceptible to hypnotically induced skin inflammations. Evidently studies such as those reported by the Chapmans and many others use subjects with histories of allergies and other psychophysiological ailments.

Table 8.5
Psychophysiological Disorders and Their Associated Attitudes (*continued*)

Disorder	Attitude and Its Example
Psoriasis	Feels picked on but thinks he has to put up with it. *Example:* "They are constantly nagging me, but I just have to put up with it."
Hyperthyroidism	Tries to prevent losing something or someone he loves. *Example:* "If I can only hold on to her for awhile longer we'll both have it made."
Nausea and vomiting	Is concerned about past mistakes for which he feels responsibility. *Example:* "I wish I didn't do that; I could've avoided it if I really tried."
Constipation	Perseveres in a hopeless situation. *Example:* "It's a bad job, but what can I do but stay with it?"
Migraine headache	Feels like relaxing after a particularly strenuous effort at meeting a deadline. *Example:* "Deadlines must be met."
Rheumatoid arthritis	Feels restricted and wants to get free. *Example:* "I've been tied down long enough."
Raynaud's disease	Wants to take aggressive action. *Example:* "I wanted to hit him."
Low backache	Feels like walking or running away from something. *Example:* "I just had to get out."

Source: Adapted from Grace and Graham (1952); Graham et al. (1958, 1962).

logical changes. Peters and Stern (1971) selected experimental subjects who had scored high on tests of hypnotic suggestibility and assigned them to one of four groups that were differentiated by the type of attitude that was induced in each (for example, hives as opposed to Raynaud's disease attitude) and by whether hypnosis was used. Each subject received a hives attitude suggestion in one session and a Raynaud's disease suggestion in the other, and each was hypnotized in one session but not in the other. Skin temperature readings showed decreases for the hypnotized groups throughout the experiment regardless of the type of suggestion they were given. Unhypnotized subjects, however, showed initial drops but then increases in skin temperatures that were well above their base levels.

Conditioning Experiments

Some evidence for the causes of the psychophysiological disorders has also come from laboratory conditioning studies. Some psychologists have argued that many of the physiological and psychological changes of hypnotized subjects can be obtained through nonhypnotic role playing (Barber, 1965; Orne, 1959, 1962; Sarbin, 1965), and indeed some of these changes have been observed in well-controlled conditioning experiments.[12]

Many of these experiments have demonstrated that subjects can control their autonomic activity when they are provided with feedback of their success and when their specific changes are rewarded. In one of these studies Neal Miller (1969) demonstrated that visceral and glandular responses can be learned in an experimental situation.[13] In several other experiments he and his associates (N. Miller et al., 1971) showed how subjects can produce autonomic changes within their cardiovascular system. In one of the latter studies subjects were conditioned to learn to increase or decrease their blood pressure without undergoing corresponding changes in the heart rate.

Likewise, in other conditioning studies, subjects' heart rates have been increased and decreased without corresponding changes in the systolic blood pressure (Shapiro et al., 1969,

1970). One experiment (Schwartz et al., 1971), which has considerable implications for both the etiology of the psychophysiological disorders and its therapy, demonstrated a method whereby conditioning of *both* blood pressure and heart rate can be accomplished so that subjects can exercise significant control over these functions. The entire conditioning procedure was accomplished in only one experimental session. In a clinical study designed to decrease blood pressure, four researchers (Benson et al., 1975) studied 14 hypertensive patients who had been taught in four consecutive daily lessons to relax by means of transcendential meditation (TM). The relaxation consists of constantly and silently repeating a word or sound called a mantra and assuming a passive posture in order to reduce the muscle tonus.

Repeated measures of the pretraining blood pressures of the 14 subjects had averaged higher than those obtained from persons with normal blood pressure. After the experimental period of TM, blood pressure was measured over a 30-day period. This time the averages indicated significantly reduced hypertension. We return to discussions of conditioning procedures, hypnosis, and TM in the Treatment section below and again in Chapter 23.

Concluding Comments

Our review of etiology so far has shown that although there is considerable appeal in the psychoanalytic idea that regression to infantile stages and their associated emotions may cause somatic symptoms, this conceptualization is not testable. It has also indicated that Hans Seyle's stress theory is much more amenable to empirical verification and finds considerable support in the research literature regarding the influence of stress on symptom development. Furthermore we showed how evidence from clinical interviewing and hypnosis implies interrelationships between attitudes and symptoms and how conditioning

---

[12] Anyone interested in exploring the issue of whether or not hypnosis is a necessary and sufficient condition for some of the dramatic phenomena induced under hypnosis should consult Rosenhan's excellent commentary (1967) on the social psychology of hypnosis research, and Barber's exhaustive review (1971) of the physiological effects of hypnosis and suggestion.

[13] The stimulus–response theory of Dollard and Miller, in this regard, simply holds that psychophysiological disorders are "innate physiological reactions to a state of high drive or to some consequence of a learned response" (Dollard and Miller, 1950, p. 193).

can produce autonomic changes.[14] The questions still left unanswered, however, are why symptoms develop in one organ or body system rather than in another, and why, under similar stressful circumstances, some people develop symptoms and others do not.

The simplest answer to these questions is that the kind of disorder that arises is determined by the special vulnerability of the organ or system involved, and that vulnerability may be transmitted genetically. This idea is called the *somatic weakness hypothesis*; according to the somatic weakness hypothesis, a person whose lungs are especially vulnerable may develop asthma in response to a given stressor, whereas a person whose gastrointestinal system is especially vulnerable may develop an ulcer in response to the same stressor.

Several studies by Wolf and Glass (1950) and by Wolf and Goodell (1968), whose studies with the fistulous patient were described earlier, suggest that each person has a characteristic mode of responding to stress, which remains dormant until a stressful situation occurs. Once the individual encounters the stressful stimuli, he reacts in a characteristic pattern that is determined as follows (Wolf and Goodell, 1968, p. 253):

The stimulus does not necessarily determine the pattern of response. The determinants include genetic equipment and other characteristics of the individual which may be acquired. Thus, the effect of the stimulus must depend heavily on the prevailing state of the organism.

And regarding the question why some persons are more vulnerable than others, it is often assumed that differences in genetic endowment make some people more vulnerable to somatic breakdown. In this respect Hans Selye postulated that each of us has a certain quantity of *adaptation energy*. This energy—which may be hereditary and therefore due to constitutional differences among people—can be used slowly, as in the case of people who lead uneventful lives, or rapidly, as among those whose lives are shorter, perhaps more colorful, and certainly more stressful. According to this theory, it should be possible to measure each person's adaptive defenses against stress and hence to lay the scientific foundation for treatment aimed at strengthening these adaptive–defensive mechanisms (Selye, 1956).

Treatment

At the beginning of this chapter we mentioned that many people who are referred to physicians probably have psychological rather than strictly physical ailments. We should like again to remind the reader that the psychogenic hypothesis should not be carried too far. High blood pressure can result from kidney or liver disorders; obesity may be due to glandular dysfunctions; and severe pain may occur as a consequence of organic damage in almost any bodily system. But along with this word of caution, we repeat that it is equally important not to overlook the possible psychological bases of some physical disorders, either as a direct cause of symptoms or as an important contributing element in their remission or exacerbation.

But even when psychogenic factors are apparent, treatment of the psychophysiological disorders often requires medical procedures. The ulcer patient, for example, needs a special diet and sometimes also requires delicate surgical intervention. Similarly, drugs, dietary changes, surgery, and other medical procedures are important in treating many of the psychophysiological disorders, In cases of minimal serious physical damage, however, or in nonemergency situations, psychological treatment methods are appropriate. Some of these therapies have already

---

[14] We reemphasize that the production of a symptom, although it may carry important implications for treatment, tells us little about how the symptom actually develops.

been mentioned or implied in passing; a brief review of them follows.

Hypnosis

The use of hypnosis as a therapeutic tool has been recognized for many years, either as a way to provide symptomatic relief through direct post-hypnotic suggestion or as an aid to other kinds of psychotherapy. Nevertheless, how hypnosis works is still a puzzle.

Some of the work being pursued at Hilgard's Laboratory of Hypnosis Research at Stanford University has direct therapeutic implications and includes personality development and changes under hypnosis (Hilgard, 1970): reducing snake phobias by having subjects relive snake-related events *with* and *without* experiencing emotion (Horowitz, 1970); the reduction of pain under hypnosis (Hilgard, E. R., 1967, 1969; Hilgard, J. R., 1970); hallucinated relief of pain (Hilgard, 1970); voluntary control of normally involuntary responses (Zimbardo and Maslach, 1970); and autohypnosis as a device to control sleep, pain, and tension. These therapeutic applications come about because of two practical features of hypnosis: (1) hypnosis can induce relaxation and thus reduce anxiety; and (2) physiological responsiveness can be altered under hypnotic suggestion.

For example, in one of the studies mentioned above (Zimbardo and Maslach, 1970), normally involuntary responses were controlled under hypnosis. It was shown that it is possible to selectively alter blood flow to the two hands simultaneously so that skin temperature is changed significantly between them. These studies have also demonstrated that under hypnosis it is possible to curtail the flow of blood to particular sites and organs of the body. The implications of this work are obvious for surgery (especially oral surgery, where it is extremely difficult to halt bleeding), bleeding ulcers, and other symptoms accompanying internal injuries.

Conditioning Procedures

The overall objective of conditioning studies, as implied earlier, is to bring the functions that are innervated by the autonomic nervous system under control of the individual or of external cues. Therefore conditioning techniques hold considerable promise in the treatment of psychophysiological disorders.

In this regard, the work of Miller (1969) and of Shapiro and his associates (1969, 1970) on controlling autonomic reactivity with reinforcement and feedback techniques has already been mentioned in the last section. Other conditioning studies have shown that vasodilation can be attained (Razran, 1961) and that increased and decreased heart rates can be achieved (Ascough and Sipprelle, 1968).

More recently, in a number of human conditioning experiments, people have learned feedback-induced muscle relaxation (Budzynski et al., 1971) and have been taught to control their own EEG patterns (Hardt, 1973; Nowlis and Kamiya, 1970). The latter studies, to which we return in Chapter 23, are of particular relevance to researchers who are interested in comparing conditioning and hypnosis studies.[15]

One early conditioning study (Jones, 1956) stands out in the psychological literature and will be detailed here because it illustrates one of the more manipulative procedures of behavior therapy. As we noted earlier in the section on the genitourinary disorders, some urinary dysfunctions are associated with emotional states (Chapman, 1959; Straub et al., 1950; Wolf, 1963). Excessive frequency of the urge to micturate is one such abnormality. The treatment procedures we are about to describe involved the case of a 23-

---

[15] The problem of how much control can be achieved over the behavior of hypnotic subjects (or their self-control under autohypnosis) has motivated Hilgard and his associates to conduct feedback studies, comparing control obtained by operant conditioning with that achieved by hypnosis.

year-old woman who had to give up her career as a dancer because her frequent urge to urinate interfered with her stage performance.

Using a manometer, the therapist asked the patient to view the pressure changes recorded on this device while warm water was introduced into her bladder. In this manner, she learned to associate the urge to urinate with specific pressure levels on the manometer. Then the experimenter falsified a lower reading on the measuring instrument while introducing the same amount of water into the bladder. Given such false feedback, which caused her to associate a higher instrument reading with lower bladder pressure, the patient was conditioned to tolerate increased amounts of fluid in the bladder without experiencing the urge to urinate. According to Yates (1970a), "a week after the cessation of the laboratory treatment, her urinary frequency had practically disappeared."[16]

Psychotherapy

Traditional psychotherapy also has its uses. In all of the psychophysiological disorders, at least at the onset of the disturbance, the individual seems to be enjoying the disability. That is to say, there is considerable clinical evidence to suggest not only that people's symptoms serve a primary gain function in the sense that the disorder removes them from a threatening or unpleasant situation, but also that these symptoms serve important secondary gain purposes. The mother who controls the household with her stomach symptoms and the father who has the family trembling lest he become totally incapacitated as a result of an impending coronary disorder often seem to be stubbornly holding on to their symptoms.

---

[16]This woman had numerous other neurotic and psychophysiological symptoms that interacted complexly. For further information on similar, but less manipulative forms of behavior therapy, see Jones (1956), Yates (1970a, pp. 184–185), and Chapter 23 of this book.

In this and similar cases, psychotherapy can be very helpful in pointing out how these people are using their symptoms to manipulate others and showing the trade-off between these gains and the physical harm they are inflicting on themselves. Moreover, psychotherapy may help improve the patient's life situation insofar as that situation may be responsible for symptoms. Finally, since the role of stress in the etiology of the psychophysiological disorders is important, psychotherapy often contributes to removing or attenuating the stresses and strains of a person's daily existence.

Summary

The psychophysiological disorders are characterized by somatic symptoms that have psychological or emotional bases. Emotion may be defined in terms of its neurophysiological, muscular, and subjective components. In this chapter we were concerned chiefly with the first of them, primarily the effects on the autonomic nervous system, which we depicted as the mediator between emotion and organic involvement. The autonomic nervous system has two main branches, the sympathetic and parasympathetic, which are thrown out of balance by the chronic "take action" dispositions of some organisms.

The main tissues and organs involved in the psychophysiological disorders are the skin, lungs, muscles, bones, intestines, stomach, bladder, rectum, and cardiovascular system. The chief evidence for the breakdown of these systems comes from clinical experience, mainly that of the psychoanalysts, and from stress theory (Selye), as well as from hypnosis and conditioning experiments. The latter carry especially important implications for treatment.

Terms and Concepts to Master

Autonomic nervous
  system   17 mins,

Emotion

Gastrointestinal
  disorders

General adaptation
  syndrome

Genitourinary disorders

Musculoskeletal
  disorders

Respiratory disorders

Skin disorders

Somatic weakness
  hypothesis

Stress

9 Alcoholism

Alcohol abuse and alcoholism constitute the largest single mental health problem in the United States today. They affect an estimated 9 million Americans, or 7 percent of the adult population (NIAAA, 1971). In one year alcohol abuse was implicated in 28,000 traffic deaths. The direct effects of alcohol on the liver, the heart, the brain, and other parts of the body also account for many deaths each year. And the estimated economic cost of alcohol misuse is $25 billion a year (NIAAA, 1974).

Patterns of Alcohol Use

Alcohol's social role, like the behavior of some people when they drink, has a Jekyll-and-Hyde quality: its usefulness as a social lubricant and ceremonial offering is sometimes exceeded by its power to disrupt and destroy social bonds. Fallding (1964), who sees alcohol as a dignifying or undignifying element in introducing individuals to civilized community, describes four types of drinking.

The first type, which he calls *ornamental*, *community-symbolic drinking*, is the most socially functional type. Ceremonial, symbolic, and integral to the culture, it builds solidarity based on trust. Drinking in religious ceremonies and by families during meals are examples of this type.

The second type, *facilitative drinking*, eases an individual's integration into society and is typified by peer drinking. Although trust is present,

the drinking can become dysfunctional, releasing hostile or other disturbing impulses.

The third type, *assuagement drinking*, substitutes for mutual trust and common purpose. People who feel deprived of membership in society become demoralized and give themselves up to insatiable drinking.

In the fourth type, *retaliative drinking*, "the person exploits the incapacitating power of alcohol in order to make himself a passenger on the system." These people drink to protest the community's failure to give them the security and rewards they believe they deserve. This is the type of drinking seen on skid row: it is vengeful and self-destructive. All these kinds of drinking can occur in a variety of contexts, as we shall see below.

Socially Approved Uses

Except where alcohol use is prohibited by religion, as it is among Moslems, the practice of social drinking and drinking with meals is woven into the fabric of civilization. Its association with cheerfulness, hospitality, sociability, and festivity has a long and almost universal history. Beer and wine have been made and consumed for more than eight thousand years, and their ability to induce changes in mood and behavior probably led very early to their use as libation and sacred drink, wherein the imbiber sought to incorporate the divine power of the alcohol (Goodenough, 1956). The aura of sanctity that beer and wine acquired through religious use may have contributed to their secularization in early civilizations, including the Greek, Roman, Hebrew, Egyptian, Sumerian–Akkadian, and Babylonian–Chaldean.

When distillation became popular in Europe in the fifteenth century, the spirits of fermented fluids quickly supplanted wine in magical and medicinal uses. Alcohol was for a long time the most effective anesthetic, but today it has little usefulness in medicine, at least when taken internally. However, wine still serves in a religious setting among Jews and, to a lesser extent, among Catholics.

Alcohol and Nutrition

The crude alcoholic beverages of primitive people supplied valuable nutrients, as does the present-day beer of the Bantu tribes. In these brews essential vitamins and minerals were conserved (McCarthy and Douglass, 1949). However, no such nutrients exist in the beverages produced by modern technology, with the exception of a small amount surviving from the original grain in beer. This small amount is currently being eliminated by brewers catering to calorie-conscious customers. Except for that vanishing cereal content of beer (about 4 calories per ounce), alcoholic beverages contain only empty calories. These calories are useful, nevertheless, for heat and energy, and they are present in abundance–about 100 calories per fluid ounce of 100-proof distilled spirits.

Alcohol also has a negative nutritional effect, for two reasons. Because it contains so many calories, it meets a drinker's caloric needs without providing other essential nutrients, such as vitamins, minerals, and proteins. By displacing nutritious foods from the diet, alcohol leads to malnutrition. But even if the drinker's diet is adequate, a large alcohol intake can cause malnutrition by interfering with the digestion and absorption of foods (Mezey et al., 1970). Further-

more, alcohol seems to have an adverse effect on the ability of the intestine to absorb certain nutrients, including vitamins B_1 and B_{12} and amino acids.

Alcohol as an Intoxicant

Ethyl alcohol, or ethanol (CH_3CH_2OH), the active ingredient in alcoholic beverages, is produced by the fermentation of sugar by yeasts. This process makes beer from barley, wine from grapes, and cider from apples, all relatively weak alcoholic beverages. Beer, for example, contains between 2.5 and 4.5 percent alcohol by volume; strong beers occasionally contain as much as 8 percent; and the ciders are of roughly comparable strength. Most wines contain between 10 and 12 percent alcohol.

The alcoholic strength of a beverage may be increased subsequently by distillation, a process that greatly concentrates alcohol to form the "hard" liquors. The alcohol content of distilled liquor is expressed as *proof*, which in the United States is the percentage of alcohol multiplied by two. Thus 100 proof liquor, not uncommon among the bourbons and Scotch whiskeys, means 50 percent alcohol content.

The behavioral signs of intoxication are due to alcohol's effect on the brain (see Table 9.1). Alcohol is a central nervous system depressant, and it produces slurring of speech, for example, by depressing the brain center that controls the motor functions involved in speech. Some people are surprised to find alcohol classed as a depressant because this seems to contradict their own experience of feeling more animated after a couple of drinks. Increased activity does often result from small doses of alcohol, but the reason is that alcohol's depressant action on the brain weakens inhibitions.

Degree of intoxication is a function of the relation between the rate at which alcohol is consumed and the rate at which it is metabolized, as well as the individual's drinking history. Alcohol

Table 9.1
Blood-Alcohol Levels (percentage)

Body Weight	Drinks[a]											
	1	2	3	4	5	6	7	8	9	10	11	12
100 lb	.038	.075	.113	.150	.188	.225	.263	.300	.338	.375	.413	.450
120 lb	.031	.063	.094	.125	.156	.188	.219	.250	.281	.313	.344	.375
140 lb	.027	.054	.080	.107	.134	.161	.188	.214	.241	.268	.295	.321
160 lb	.023	.047	.070	.094	.117	.141	.164	.188	.211	.234	.258	.281
180 lb	.021	.042	.063	.083	.104	.125	.146	.167	.188	.208	.229	.250
200 lb	.019	.038	.056	.075	.094	.113	.131	.150	.169	.188	.206	.225
220 lb	.017	.034	.051	.068	.085	.102	.119	.136	.153	.170	.188	.205
240 lb	.016	.031	.047	.063	.078	.094	.109	.125	.141	.156	.172	.188

Under .05[b]	.05 to .10	.10 to .15	Over .15
Driving is not seriously impaired.	Driving becomes increasingly dangerous. .08 legally drunk in Utah.	Driving is dangerous. Legally drunk in many states.	Driving is *very* dangerous. Legally drunk in any state.

Source: Reprinted through the courtesy of the New Jersey Department of Law and Public Safety. Division of Motor Vehicles. Trenton, New Jersey.
[a] One drink equals 1 ounce of 100 proof liquor or 12 ounces of beer.
[b] Recent information suggests that blood alcohol levels below .05 percent seriously impair drivers under age 25 and may be dangerous to older persons who drive under conditions other than "average" (Division of Motor Vehicles, State of New Jersey, 1972).

is absorbed through the stomach and the small intestine at a more or less constant rate. If it is being consumed more rapidly than it is being metabolized, the blood alcohol concentration (BAC) increases (see Table 9.1). More alcohol reaches the brain, and the degree of intoxication increases. Changes in mood and behavior sometimes appear with the first sips, but such changes are probably a conditioned response acquired during previous experiences. With small doses most people feel some relaxation, but some feel anxious and suspicious. These individual differences diminish as the dose increases and the pharmacological effects begin to predominate. As the BAC continues to increase, the drinker begins to feel tired, and may fall into a stupor. Even at high doses, however, responses vary, and the drinker may feel mellow or maudlin, irritable, or pugnacious.

BACs have become important for legal reasons. In most parts of the United States and in some European countries an individual with a blood alcohol level of 0.10 percent or more is considered legally intoxicated or "under the influence." A BAC of 0.05 percent or less is the legal measure for sobriety and fitness to operate a motor vehicle. Beyond the legal considerations, the resulting behaviors usually associated with 1, 2, 3, 4, and 5 "shots" of whiskey are, respectively, changes in feeling, sedation and tranquility, talkativeness (or moroseness), loss of coordination, and erratic behavior and considerable motor impairment. These estimates are based on relationships between BAC and behaviors in a

155-pound person with a history of moderate drinking who rapidly consumes 90-proof whiskey on an empty stomach. These effects may be slightly stronger if the drink is gin or vodka or if the drinker weighs much less than 155 pounds. In any event, after 25 shots of whiskey, unconsciousness and possibly death may occur, regardless of body weight and drinking history (*Alcohol and Alcoholism*, 1972).

Various bodily functions are affected to varying degrees by alcohol intoxication. The senses generally resist alcohol, but the effects that have been observed are depressant or detrimental. For example, resistance to glare is diminished, as is sensitivity to odors and flavors. Some studies indicate that time appears to pass more quickly and that speeds and distances tend to be underestimated.

Motor performance is more seriously affected than the senses, and swaying in the "standing steadiness" test increases considerably, especially with the eyes closed. Sensorimotor coordination is also impaired.

The chief emotional effect seems to be a decrease in feelings of self-criticism, which, coupled with the loss in inhibitions and a greater willingness to take risks, often makes people more outgoing and assertive after a drink or two. Alcohol has a mixed effect on sexual performance. To the extent that it releases inhibitions, it facilitates sexual behavior. But studies show that large doses impair sexual performance in both animals and humans. As Shakespeare observed, drink "provokes the desire, but it takes away the performance." Drinking before bedtime decreases the amount of rapid eye-movement (REM) sleep, and if a person drinks before bedtime several nights in a row and then stops, REM sleep will rebound, increasing to a level slightly above normal. REM sleep deprivation usually results in poor concentration and memory, as well as fatigue, irritability, and anxiety.

People differ in their ability to overcome the effects of alcohol and in their ability to recognize the extent to which their performance is impaired. One study (Drew et al., 1959) showed that bus drivers who had had several drinks were more likely to misjudge the space between movable posts and to try to drive their buses through spaces that were too narrow. Not only was their judgment impaired, but their certainty that they were right increased.

Not surprisingly, excessive alcohol intake is involved in a large proportion of auto and other accidents, as well as assaults, suicides, and homicides. Anything that impairs visual sensitivity, motor coordination, speed of response, or judgment deteriorates driving performance, and alcohol impairs all these. In one year excessive alcohol intake was reported in half the automobile fatalities recorded. According to a number of studies, drivers who drink heavily are much more likely to be involved in automobile accidents than are nondrinkers. Furthermore the blood alcohol levels of a large proportion of the drivers involved in fatal accidents are high enough to indicate a chronic drinking problem. Many of these accidents are single-car accidents, and many single-car accidents are believed to be consciously or unconsciously suicidal. According to one source (NIAAA, 1971), "Excessive alcohol intake, generally of a chronic, long-continued nature, is associated with one-third of all reported suicides."

Several studies show a link between alcohol intoxication and violent behavior. One study of home accidents (Wechsler et al., 1969) showed that 56 percent of the patients who had been injured in fights had positive blood alcohol levels and 39 percent had readings of 0.05 percent or higher. And a study of 588 criminal homicides reavealed that 55 percent of the offenders had been drinking (Wolfgang, 1958).

Alcohol Abuse and Alcoholism

Many drinkers who are not alcoholics have nevertheless experienced some of the effects of alcohol abuse—the memory lapses, the "dry heaves," and especially the hangovers. But only an alcoholic knows in its full magnitude the hell of being dependent on alcohol. Those who have had the experience have vividly described the panic, the resentment, the shame, and the sheer terror and pain they felt.

Research on alcoholism has failed thus far to yield a clear picture of the processes involved or the nature of the disorder. Individual patterns vary greatly, and neither a single determinant nor a single syndrome is likely to be seen. Jellinek (1960) describes four types of alcoholism, which he differentiates on the basis of various patterns of psychological dependence, physical dependence, medical problems, and history of use. He designates as *alpha* alcoholism a "purely psychological continual reliance on the effect of alcohol to relieve pain." *Beta* alcoholism involves physical complications such as liver disease or changes in nerve functions. In *gamma* alcoholism the individual is physically dependent on alcohol and has lost control over his or her drinking behavior. In *delta* alcoholism the individual is unable to stop drinking even for a day.

Jellinek's types of alcoholism are based almost exclusively on interpretations of questionnaire data and are therefore flawed by all the problems common to such data. Two types described above, *gamma* and *delta,* have already been called into question by later experimental work. Specifically, the idea that alcoholics lose control of their drinking has been seriously challenged by Marlatt et al. (1973), who permitted alcoholic subjects to drink as much of alcoholic or non-alcoholic beverages as they wished during several time periods. They discovered that initial drinks did not have a differential effect on the subsequent drinking behavior of alcoholics versus social drinkers. These researchers did find, interestingly, that the only important determinant of the amount of alcohol consumed was the subjects' expectations of what they were drinking, and that those subjects who expected alcohol on the basis of pre-drinking instructions did in fact drink more alcohol than those who had no such pre-drinking instructions.

The notion that alcoholics cannot be taught to drink in moderation has also been challenged by Sobell and Sobell (1973), who achieved significant success with a group of 40 chronic male alcoholics in a California state hospital. Sobell and Sobell taught half their subjects controlled drinking. The other half received conventional treatments such as group therapy. A year after treatment, the controlled drinkers had been functioning well (in the sense that they were either not drinking or drinking moderately) 70 percent of the time, while the other group functioned well only 35 percent of the time.

Because of the variety of patterns, alcoholism is not easily defined. Chafetz (1967) calls it a "chronic behavioral disorder manifested by an undue preoccupation with alcohol and its use to the detriment of physical and mental health, by loss of control when drinking has begun, and by self-destructive attitudes in dealing with personal relationships and life situations."

Prevalence

At the beginning of this chapter we mentioned that 9 million people have excessive drinking problems in the United States. This is only an estimate by a knowledgeable source (Chafetz and Demone, 1974). The precise number of Americans affected by drinking is not known, but a nationwide survey conducted in 1967 and again in 1972 by the Social Research Group of George Washington University is revealing (Cahalan, 1970; Cahalan and Room, 1974). On the basis of interviews with over two thousand subjects, this survey indicated that 68 percent of all American adults drink at least occasionally; that about 56 percent of these adults were infrequent to moderate drinkers; and that 12 percent were heavy drinkers (mostly problem drinkers or alcoholics). Regional differences were also found, with the highest proportion of drinking occurring in the Middle Atlantic and New England states, and the lowest in the southern and central states. A later study (Efron et al., 1974) indicated that the Pacific and New England regions have the highest rates of alcohol consumption and the east and south central region the lowest.

Cutting across the categories of regional and age differences, the survey disclosed that alcohol use was most widespread among residents of large communities and among those with higher education, income, and vocational status. Ethnic and religious background of Americans seems also to be correlated with drinking patterns. Generally, Italians, Chinese, and Jews rarely get drunk in public. Blacks, Chicanos, Native Americans, and Eskimos tend to have high rates of alcoholism. Heavy drinking is higher among Catholics than among liberal Protestants, whose rate is still higher than that among conservative and fundamentalist Protestants. Paradoxically Jews and Episcopalians have higher proportions of drinkers than other religious groups, but they have relatively few heavy drinkers (Keller and Rosenberg, 1971). In general, alcoholism (as distinguished from such other use patterns as heavy drinking and getting drunk in public) is more common among groups that are ambivalent toward alcohol and less common among groups with well-defined drinking customs and values (NIAAA, 1971).

In another study (Mulford, 1964), drinking was reported by 79 percent of those who were single, 72 percent of those married, 69 percent of those divorced, and 51 percent of those widowed.

These percentages are all in close agreement with earlier similar surveys of patterns of drinking in the United States; therefore they tend to confirm the widespread belief in the field that these patterns are stable over time. For example the earlier findings show that 65 percent of the adult population drinks; more than half these drinkers use distilled spirits; 17 percent are regular drinkers; and 48 percent are occasional drinkers. Additional findings of these earlier surveys also show that the percentage of people who drink is highest in big cities. Moreover, the percentage of drinkers increases from lower to higher economic levels.

A national survey conducted in 1973 (NIAAA, 1974) provided profiles of persons with high and low alcohol-related problems. People who had alcohol-related problems were more likely to be male; to be single, separated, or divorced; to have no religious affiliation; and to drink beer rather than wine or hard liquor. Those who did not have alcohol-related problems were more likely to be female; to be over 50; to be married or widowed; to be Jewish; to be residents of the South; to be at the postgraduate educational level; and to be wine drinkers.

The problem with survey statistics is that they tend to include reports of persons who use alcohol infrequently as well as those for whom drinking is a problem. In other words, they lump together the occasional social drinker with the homeless skid-row derelict who is repeatedly arrested for disorderly conduct; the laborer who stops at several saloons on the way home from work, spending his family's meager resources on alcohol; the heavy-drinking young executive who is a hazard on the highway; and the blue-collar worker who is constantly on the verge of being dismissed because of absenteeism or for lack of sobriety during working hours (Plaut, 1967). Therefore other approaches, preferably those using indirect methods of assessing alcoholism, are also important.

The number of alcoholics in America, on the basis of figures obtained from admission rates to several public and private community agencies, usually considered underestimates, has been placed at about 9 million, or 7 percent of the adult population. This is the figure given in the *First Special Report to the Congress on Alcohol and Health* (NIAAA, 1971). The risk of alcoholism—the number of alcoholics relative to the number of people who drink—is currently estimated at about 1 in 9, an estimate based on the assumption there are about 80 million drinkers and that 9 million of them are alcoholic. This is a risk rate of 11.2 percent (NIMH, 1969a).

Still other estimates, gathered from hospital

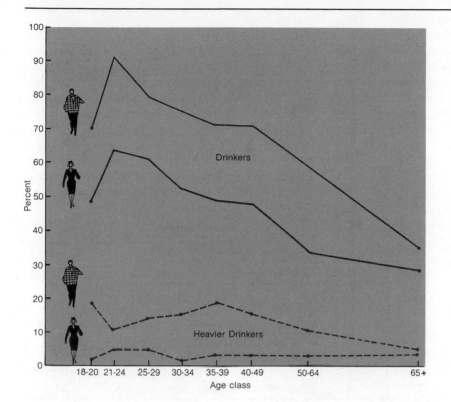

Figure 9.1

Percentage of drinkers and "heavier" drinkers among adults, by sex and age class, U.S.A., autumn 1972.

(NIAAA, 1974, p. 11)

admission rates, indicate that 22 percent of first admissions of male patients to three hundred state mental hospitals in the United States were given a diagnosis of alcoholism, and that the same percentage of men discharged from psychiatric wards of general hospitals were likewise diagnosed "alcoholic."

The percentage of people who drink, the percentage who drink heavily (Figure 9.1), and the prevalence of alcohol-related problems all vary considerably with age, most people reaching their peak between their late teens and middle twenties and tapering off rapidly thereafter. Although most drinkers do drink less as they grow older, part of the decline in prevalence figures

may actually reflect the higher mortality of heavy drinkers.

Two pronounced trends in drinking behavior have appeared during the last several years. The first of these is an increase in alcohol consumption by minors (Figure 9.2). A study by the San Mateo County (California) Department of Public Health and Welfare (1973) showed that during each year from 1968 to 1973 the number of students who reported they had begun drinking the previous year increased. For example, the percentage of seventh graders who reported they had started drinking the previous year rose from 52 percent of the boys and 38 percent of the girls in 1968 to 72 percent of the boys and 67 percent of

Figure 9.2

Percentage of teen-age drinkers who report getting drunk or very high, by frequency and school grade, U.S.A. 1974.

(NIAAA, 1974, p. 21)

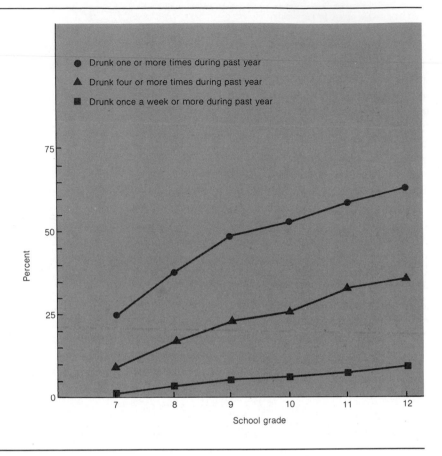

the girls in 1973. Similar increases have been reported elsewhere, and since school dropouts were not included, the data for students are likely to underestimate the extent of teenage drinking.

The second major trend, beginning after World War II, is the increase in alcohol consumption by women. Among adult women, some 47 percent now drink once a month or more.

Long-term Effects

Chronic alcoholism causes long-term physiological and behavioral symptoms, which arise because of the *withdrawal* of alcohol, vitamin defi-

ciency, or destruction of the brain cells. The first of these long-term symptoms is evident when the alcoholic abruptly stops drinking or his supply is suddenly and drastically reduced, resulting in a rapid drop in the blood alcohol concentration. Then, within a few hours to a few days thereafter, he experiences acute tremulousness, or "the shakes": a gross tremor of the hand, anxiety, physical restlessness, and weakness, which may be so pronounced that he is not able to sit still, dress himself, or pour liquids without spilling. During the day he experiences terrifying illusions and hallucinations, and at night he cannot sleep because of nightmares. This condition usually disappears rapidly as more drink is taken, but without alcohol it persists as long as two or three days.

At a more advanced stage of alcoholism, after vitamin deficiencies and brain damage have begun to take their toll, *delirium tremens* (the DTs) may occur. This is a much more serious condition. The early stages of the DTs are similar to the withdrawal illness described above, but as the condition progresses, its severity intensifies and the individual experiences distractibility, agitation, and overwhelming fear, as well as confusion, disorientation, and hallucinations.

This condition usually has its onset after the age of 30 and is characterized by coarse tremors, especially of the hands; frightening visual hallucinations; restlessness; sleeplessness; and fear. When the victim does sleep he has nightmares and wakes up in terror at the slightest noise. Auditory illusions are also common (for example, house noises heard as burglars or explosions), as are visual illusions (objects seen as insects or animals, sometimes crawling toward or on the individual). Occasionally the alcoholic is driven to such a panic by these threatening sights and sounds that he has to be restrained by two or more people.

This condition may follow a prolonged alcoholic binge or occur just after the withdrawal of alcohol. In either case the symptoms are due to a combination of alcoholic intoxication and vitamin deficiency, with the latter probably contributing more importantly. Fortunately alcoholics are highly suggestible during these attacks; they can be induced to eat and will readily permit physicians and family to administer vitamins and other nutrients and medicine to them. The usual duration of the DTs, if treated properly, is from three to six days, and improvement follows a prolonged period of sleep and rest. During the acute stage of the illness, pneumonia or heart failure is a high risk, and therefore nursing and special care are essential.

Another possible consequence of alcoholism is *Korsakov's psychosis,* named after the Russian physician Sergey Korsakov (1854–1900), who first described it. Korsakov's psychosis may follow the DTs and its cause is vitamin deficiency. It is characterized chiefly by memory impairment in which the individual attempts to "fill in the gaps" or *confabulate* in an effort to account for the missing periods of time in his or her life (Case Report 9.1). Disorientation, especially for time, is common; and visual and auditory hallucinations occur in approximately half the cases. Affective fluctuations with cycles of euphoria, irritability, and depression are frequently seen. In general Korsakov patients are much less suggestible or cooperative than those with the DTs, and hence are a greater management problem both at home and in hospitals.

Case Report 9.1 *Korsakov's Psychosis*

The patient, Henry, was born in a small farming community where he has always lived, except for frequent short periods of employment in other locations. Henry began to drink at age 16 and has been a heavy drinker all his life. He was 56 at the time of his admission to the hospital.

During his period of intoxication he frequently accused his wife of going out with other men, but during his sober periods he treated her well.

About three months before his admission to the hospital Henry complained of pains in his extremeties, although the pains were not severe enough to keep him in bed. At this time he became unsteady and did not walk very well. About a month before his admission he became confused. He claimed that he was not in his own home, failed to recognize his neighbors, and thought that his parents, who had been dead for some time, were visiting him. His physician advised that he be committed to a hospital.

After admission Henry was quiet and cooperative and ate fairly well. During the interview his conversation was relevant and coherent, but he showed marked defects in orientation. He knew that he was in a hospital but complained that it was not the one he said he helped to build. At one moment he claimed it was January 1935, and at other times

Alcohol use can serve as a social lubricant, fostering relaxation and conviviality, or it can be socially destructive, leading to dependence and despair.

he said it was March 1919. He insisted that the examining physician was his family doctor whom he had known for a long time and that another staff physician was the latter's son. He also claimed that he knew several of the attendants and that they owned property near his father's farm.

He showed a marked defect in memory for both past and recent events and filled in these defects with confabulations. At times he said that his father was still living and at other times that he was dead. At first he claimed that his mother died at the age of 65, but later he said he could hear her talk to him. He could not remember the ages of his children and did not remember when he came to the hospital.

He assured the examining physician that he had been "over at the club" and had a couple of drinks yesterday and that this morning he had a couple of glasses of beer. No delusions could be elicited. He claimed on one occasion he heard his mother and sister calling him from downstairs and that they were probably in the hospital. He denied hearing any other voices.

SOURCE: *Abridged and adapted from "Alcoholic Korsakov Psychosis" by Margaret Mercer and Saul Greizman. In* Case histories in clinical and abnormal psychology, *Arthur Burton and Robert E. Harris, eds. Copyright 1947 by Harper & Row, Publishers, Inc.*

Habitual drinkers, who over a period of 30 to 40 years have consumed alcohol heavily and almost daily, usually undergo gradual changes in intellect and personality, and sometimes manifest symptoms not unlike those experienced in DTs and Korsakov's psychosis, although less pronounced. In these cases, *chronic alcoholic deterioration* is the most probable diagnosis. Its symptoms include antisocial behavior, delusions of persecution and jealousy, and untruthfulness. Because of the untruthfulness, this type of alcoholic is frequently seen as cunning, twisting facts to suit personal ends and evading responsibilities at home and on the job. These people are much more difficult to live with or manage than alcoholics with DTs or with Korsakov's psychosis. Henderson and Gillespie (Batchelor, 1969) give the following description of the deteriorated chronic alcoholic (p. 409):

He is often able to carry on his ordinary work sufficiently well to make a fair appearance to the casual observer; but he never reaches a high pitch of energy or efficiency, and his history is one of gradual deterioration, moral and intellectual. To his companions he is usually pleasant, sociable and sympathetic, entering boisterously into his alcohol enjoyments and shedding a ready tear in commiseration of others' misfortunes. At home, on the other hand, he is irritable and careless of his family's welfare. Sometimes the chronic alcoholic goes so far as to sell his home and furniture, thrash his children and assault his wife. It is at this more advanced stage that sexual crimes and indecent assaults are especially frequent.

Some chronic alcoholics become depressed, and the risk of suicide is substantial. According to Robins and her associates (1959), 23 percent of suicides in St. Louis during one year were alcoholics; and Litman (1970), of the Los Angeles Suicide Prevention Center, mentions that overall among alcoholics, about 5 percent may be expected to commit suicide. The blood-alcohol level of many suicides has been found to be quite high,

between 0.20 and 0.36 percent (gross intoxication level is 0.15 percent); but some of these deaths result from a combination of barbiturates or other drugs and alcohol.

Causes of Alcoholism

Despite extensive research in several disciplines, the causes of alcoholism remain unknown. The failure of any model to fit all the relevant research results suggests that alcoholism is either a collection of disorders having different etiologies or a disorder that results from the interaction of several determinants. We shall briefly sketch the major models and discuss the available evidence.

Biological Models

Most biological research has focused either on attempts to find chemicals in specific beverages that might be responsible for alcohol addiction or on genetic, nutritional, or metabolic defects that would predispose organisms toward excessive drinking. So far it has not been possible to isolate chemical substances that produce clear-cut alcoholic addiction in experimental organisms (Mendelson and Ladou, 1964), but some aspects of the search are worth mentioning.

There is some evidence indicating that the incidence of alcoholism is higher among closer relatives, the most frequent observation being its occurrence in children of alcoholics. But this is hardly a convincing argument for its inheritance, since alcoholism also occurs in the children of abstainers (Bleuler, 1955) and abstinence also occurs among children who are raised separately from their alcoholic parents (Jellinek, 1960).

A strong suggestion that chronic alcoholism is influenced by genetic factors is a twin study conducted in Sweden by Kaij (1960). In summarizing this study in his book *Genetics of Psychopathology*, Rosenthal (1971, p. 149) observed that the difference between identical (MZ) and fraternal

(DZ) twin pairs with respect to concordance ratios (degree to which both members of a pair show the disorder) is highly significant. In other words Kaij's data suggest a greater intrapair similarity for MZ than for DZ twins. But the degree of similarity was also high for the DZ pairs, suggesting that environment is an additional important contributor. Even stronger evidence for the genetic hypothesis comes from a group of American and Danish investigators (Goodwin and Guze, 1974; Goodwin et al., 1973; Schukit et al., 1972) who studied adopted children in Denmark. The adopted children of natural parents who were alcoholic (high risk potential) differed from adopted children of nonalcoholic natural parents (low risk potential) in that they had significantly greater alcohol-related problems than the adoptees of natural nonalcoholic parents. Eighteen percent of the high-risk children became adult alcoholics; only 5 percent of the low-risk controls became alcoholic. This research is open to some criticism (see Chafetz et al., 1974) in that the controls had a greater proportion of "heavy drinkers" than the others. Furthermore, as Rosenthal (1970, p. 262) remarked in an earlier review of Kaij's work, "although his findings are strongly suggestive that genetic factors are implicated, the probable role of environmental influences in interaction with the inferred genetic factors cannot be estimated from this study."

There is some evidence that alcoholism runs in families. Cahalan and Room (1974) in their national survey reported that heavy drinking by parents is a good predictor of alcoholism among American men. Critics (cited in Goldenberg, 1977) have pointed out, however, that imitation or modeling rather than heredity can explain these results.

It has also been suggested that alcoholism is caused by vitamin deficiencies or hormone imbalances. Research by Roger Williams (1959) at the University of Texas suggests that some organisms have unusually strong congenital requirements for certain food elements (for example, vitamins, enzymes, or minerals), and that in-

creased alcohol intake may be induced by such deficiencies. Segovia–Riquelme and his associates (1970) at the University of Chile, demonstrated similar relationships between nutritional factors and appetite for alcohol; additionally they found that this appetite may be determined by two main genes, "one of them probably influencing the activity of an enzymatic system in the oxidative pathology of glucose" (p. 95).

Beerstecher and associates (1951), working in Williams' laboratory, reported increases in alcohol consumption by rats when deprived of thiamine, riboflavin, pyridoxine, and pantothenate. However, when Lester and Greenberg (1952) gave nutritionally deprived rats a choice of water, alcohol, and sugar solution, the rats chose the sugar solution. These findings are based on studies with experimental animals and their applicability to human beings is not yet established. So far, in studies with human beings, most nutritional and hormonal deficiencies observed in alcoholics appear to be the results rather than the causes of excessive drinking.

Alcohol addiction has also been said to be caused largely, and sometimes even entirely, by overexposure to alcohol. If this is the case, the highest rate of alcoholism should be expected among nationality groups with the greatest per capita intake of alcohol. Only a weak relationship of this sort exists. For example, in Italy, a country where alcohol intake is extensive, the rate of alcoholism is low. Table 9.2 lists the 20 countries with the largest apparent consumption of alcohol.

Psychological Models

Some clinicians believe that there is a prealcoholic personality and that alcoholics are psychologically different from others. Some of the personality traits attributed to alcoholics are low frustration tolerance, difficulty in controlling impulses, feelings of inferiority combined with attitudes of superiority, fearfulness, and dependency. However, what is not clear about these so-called traits

Table 9.2

Apparent Consumption, in 20 Countries, of Each Major Beverage Class, and of Absolute Alcohol from Each Class, in U.S. Gallons Per Person in the Drinking-age Population[a] (listed in descending order of total)

Country	Year[b]	Distilled Spirits	Absolute Alcohol	Wine	Absolute Alcohol	Beer	Absolute Alcohol	Total Absolute Alcohol
1. France	1966	2.35	1.18	43.03	4.52	20.10[d]	.83	6.53
2. Italy	1968	[1.11][c]	.55	41.29	3.30	3.54	.16	4.01
3. Switzerland	1966	1.53	.61	13.61	1.43	29.73[d]	1.35	3.39
4. West Germany	1968	[2.35]	.89	4.04	.40	44.65	1.97	3.26
5. Australia	1966	.54	.31	2.58	.44	42.86	2.14	2.89
6. Belgium	1967	.67	.33	3.14	.44	42.07[d]	2.10	2.87
7. U.S.A.	1970	2.56	1.15	1.84	.29	25.95	1.17	2.61
8. New Zealand	1964	.79	.45	.98	.17	39.28	1.96	2.58
9. Czechoslovakia	1968	[.83]	[.42]	[3.51]	[.49]	[30.91]	[1.54]	2.45
10. Canada	1967	[1.86]	.75	[1.12]	.18	[25.47]	1.27	2.20
11. Denmark	1968	.78	.34	1.53	.22	29.03	1.38	1.94
12. United Kingdom	1966	.51	.29	1.08	.18	31.77	1.43	1.90
13. Sweden	1968	2.13	.85	1.77	.24	15.57	.65	1.74
14. Japan	1968	[1.10]	.35	[5.10][e]	.81	8.22	.37	1.53
15. The Netherlands	1968	[1.38]	[.69]	[.86]	[.15]	[15.38]	[.69]	1.53
16. Ireland	1966	.70	.40	.56	.09	22.26	1.00	1.49
17. Norway	1968	1.20	.52	.70	.10	10.82	.51	1.13
18. Finland	1968	1.33	.52	1.06	.17	6.85	.34	1.03
19. Iceland	1966	2.11	.73	.62	.08	4.26	.15	.96
20. Israel	1968	.89	.44	1.66	.20	3.58	.18	.82

Source: NIAAA (1971).

[a] Age 15+
[b] Latest available year for each country
[c] [ ] Bracketed data converted from source terms
[d] Includes cider
[e] Includes saké

of the alcoholic is which came first—the alcoholism or the traits? The common experience of drinking and the consequent long-term effects of alcohol may in themselves lead to a similarity in behavior that has nothing to do with a person's prealcoholic personality. Alcoholics who come to the attention of professionals have been drinking steadily for many years. Moreover, in case studies in which clinical data are used as evidence, psychiatrists and psychologists often find whatever they are looking for. A clinician who happens to believe, for example, that alcoholics are neurotic, maladjusted, unable to relate effectively to others, or sexually and emotionally immature may *find* these characteristics in them.

Thus it is essential to study the prealcoholic personality. Unfortunately, however, such people do not often show up at clinics; or if they do, it is difficult to predict that they will become alcoholic. This problem was somewhat circumvented in a nationwide survey on problem drinking, in which specific attitudes and values associated with alcoholism were investigated by Cahalan (1970). This survey indicated not only that people's prealcoholic attitudes toward drinking and heavy drinking (can good things be said for drinking? do they enjoy drinking and getting drunk once in a while?) were important indices of later alcoholism, but also that attitudes favoring drinking were strongly correlated with problem drinking. To rule out the possibility that such favorable attitudes are attempts to justify one's drinking, a 3-year follow-up study was conducted, and this study indicated that, to a limited extent, prior attitudes can predict problem drinking. For example, if during his or her prealcoholic days an interviewee reported that persons who give up drinking probably miss it a lot, that drinking does more good than harm, and that it is important to have something to drink on social occasions, this person would be more likely than others to have drinking problems later. The other factors contributing to subsequent drinking problems, in decreasing order of importance (with attitudes toward drinking as the most important variable), were environmental support of heavy drinking, impulsiveness and nonconformity, alienation and maladjustment, unfavorable future expectations, and looseness of social controls (Cahalan, 1970, pp. 139–140).

Two reasons are commonly given by alcoholics themselves for their drinking: one is *dependency* on the bottle, and the other is the influence of *stress* as an initial factor. Regarding the latter, most of the research that supports the idea that stress plays a role in the etiology of this disorder is animal research; but even in animal studies there are contradictory findings. For example, one group of investigators (Casey, 1960; Dember and Kristofferson, 1955) correlated rats' alcohol intake with their level of emotionality, while another found no such relationships (Korman and Stephens, 1960; Rodgers and Thiessen, 1964). Myers and his associates at Purdue University have called attention to some of the difficulties inherent in such studies with rats and monkeys (Myers, 1966, 1970; Myers and Veale, 1972), sug-

gesting that the difficulties may be increased considerably as one moves from studying stress among infrahumans to studying it among human subjects.

Some animal experimental evidence has also been found to support the contention of alcoholics that they are physically dependent on the bottle (Isbell, 1970). The importance of such a finding is that the physically dependent alcoholic must then drink partly to prevent the symptoms of abstinence and this physical dependence in turn reinforces the psychological dependence already present.

McClelland and his associates (1972), in an effort to develop an improved method for measuring the need for power (*n* power), used a technique by which motives were experimentally aroused and then assessed in fantasy (see Atkinson, 1958). The researchers inadvertently stumbled upon the finding that under certain circumstances drinking is a behavior characteristic of young men high in *n* power.

What are the circumstances under which *n* power relates to drinking? For an answer to this question the researchers examined their college-student subjects' power-related fantasies. After distinguishing between two aspects of the power motives ("hope of impact" and "fear of impotence"), they obtained several important leads suggesting that drinking is directly related to power concerns when these concerns are negative, threatening, or fearful. In other words, according to this account (McClelland et al., 1972, p. 119), "Drinking may be directly related to fantasies of losing power, or fantasies of the power of another over the self."

Learning models stress the use of alcohol as a means of reducing a drive state such as fear or anxiety. When Conger (1951) injected rats with alcohol after training one group to avoid an electric shock and another group to approach a food goal, the avoidance response decreased but the approach to food did not. On the face of it learning theory seems to collide with the well-known fact that alcoholics suffer a great deal of pain, humiliation, and punishment, all of which ought to make drinking aversive. This objection is answered in the First Special Report to the U.S. Congress on Alcohol and Health (NIAAA, 1971, p. 65) as follows:

The role of punishment is becoming increasingly important in formulating a cause of alcoholism based on the principles of learning theory. While punishment may serve to suppress a response, experiments have shown that under some circumstances it can serve as a reward and reinforce the behavior (Solomon, 1964). Thus if the alcoholic person has learned to drink under conditions of both reward and punishment, either type of condition may precipitate renewed drinking.

But if the role of punishment is important in the cause of alcoholism, the significance of certain forms of anxiety in triggering drinking has also been shown. In one study (Higgins and Marlatt, 1973) researchers showed that whereas the physical threat of electric shock did not produce an increase in alcoholic drinking during an experimental "wine-tasting" session, the arousal of social anxieties did produce such an increase. Similarly, in another study (Higgins and Marlatt, 1975), heavy-drinking male subjects drank significantly more wine than a control group of matched males after only the former were told that they were to talk to a group of females about interpersonal attractiveness and were to be rated by them on a number of qualities. Several animal experiments have demonstrated that excessive alcohol consumption can be learned, but unfortunately the use of animals as models for human drinking may not be valid, since it has been demonstrated that alcohol is not necessarily a reinforcer for laboratory animals (Mello, 1973).

Experimental studies with humans, unlike some animal studies, suggest that alcohol may not be a tension reducer. Moreover, contrary to popular belief, a "craving" for alcohol may be more myth than reality. But if, as some authors (Nathan and Harris, 1975) suggest, alcohol is not

a tension reducer, how can we explain the persistence of the drinking response? Martin (1977) suggests the possibility that self-reports of such mood changes as tension, anxiety, or depression are an incomplete picture of the subjective changes of the alcoholic who takes a drink. In this regard Nathan and his colleagues (1972) suggest that most chronic alcoholics tend to forget many of the unpleasant events that occur while they are engaged in heavy drinking. Therefore they are relatively unaffected by such memories when they anticipate drinking again. Clearly, if there is to be an adequate behavioral explanation of alcoholism, the question of whether or not it is tension-reducing for human beings must be settled. After all, most behaviorists take the view that alcohol is a reinforcer because it is tension-reducing.

Sociocultural Models

While there are problem drinkers and alcoholics in all strata of American society, specific differences, as we noted earlier, exist among certain ethnic and cultural groups. In the United States, Canada, and other parts of the Western world, the most consistent and striking of these differences are those found between the drinking patterns of Americans of Irish or Anglo–Saxon backgrounds and those of Italian, Chinese, or Jewish backgrounds.

For example, in one cross-ethnic study conducted in New York City where available figures indicate that 10 percent of the total population is Irish, 15 percent Italian, and 25 percent Jewish, the proportions of alcoholics were as follows: 40 percent were Irish, 1 percent Italian, and none Jewish (Lolli et al., 1960). Similarly, another study, this time in California, again with large proportions of Irish, Italian, and Jewish inhabitants, indicated that 20 percent of the alcoholics were Irish, 2 percent Italian, and 6 percent Jewish (Terry et al., 1957). Likewise during World War II the military inductee rejection rates for alcoholism in the Boston area were 3 percent among the Irish, 1.2 percent among the Italians, and .2 percent among the Jews. The Irish rejection rate, in other words, was more than twice that of the Italians and 15 times greater than that of the Jews. Extremely low rates of alcoholism have also been found among Chinese–Americans (Barnett, 1955).

Contrary to popular belief, however, these low rates of alcoholism among some subcultures are not matched by low rates of psychological disorders generally. Thus alcoholism is not necessarily a consequence of the stresses experienced by minority groups.

Traditionally, hospital personnel have not been sympathetic to alcoholics and have treated them with hostility.[1] These feelings were evoked by the so-called typical alcoholic patient who, on admission to a hospital, often appeared dirty, disheveled, disruptive, and demanding. Unless alcoholics were wealthy or prominent and therefore admitted to a hospital under a camouflaged diagnosis, they would end up in the "drunk tank" of a local jail, on the psychiatric ward of a state institution, or on the emergency service of a local hospital. In all of these facilities the main concern was with sobering up the patients, treating obvious wounds or contusions, and discharging them as quickly as possible.

These attitudes, however, have changed somewhat over the past several years and general hospitals now play a crucial role in the treatment and management of alcoholics. Treatment consists mainly of alleviating the symptoms of alcohol withdrawal and of attending to the secondary medical complications of alcoholism. Traditional psychotherapy and behavioral approaches are now also tried more frequently.

---

[1]Morris Chafetz, head of the NIMH Division of Alcohol Abuse and Alcoholism, has been quoted as saying that his most disheartening failure in his 20 years in the field of alcoholism has been his attempts to change the expectations of physicians toward alcoholics: "They tend to feel it is something they should not dirty their hands with" (Chafetz, 1972, p. 8).

Treatment of Alcoholism

Any attempt to treat alcoholism faces several obstacles. In the first place so many factors and combinations of factors seem to be involved that no single treatment is likely to work for all alcoholics. In the second place the alcohol itself is already being used as a "self-treatment" and, in spite of its destructive effects on the individual, it has great power to solve problems momentarily. The First Special Report to the U.S. Congress on Alcohol and Health stresses this point (NIAAA, 1971):

The devastating effects of alcohol are so obvious that we are bewildered by patients apparently evading or frustrating the best treatment efforts. But when heavy drinking is seen as an adaptive phenomenon, we are not so perplexed that people can actually treat themselves this way.

Another obstacle is the failure to recognize the threat posed by the clinician's understandable angry response to the frustration of his or her efforts. The wish to punish the patient can arise easily, and if acted out consciously or unconsciously, it can distort the treatment program. And finally the alcoholic may find it even more difficult than most people to admit a need for help. The feeling of omnipotence many people have when drunk is not conducive to a search for help, and neither is the shame they feel while sobering up. Even after deciding to seek help, the alcoholic still must decide where to turn for that help and then often has no assurance of being greeted civilly.

Biological Treatment

Often patients must be treated for alcohol intoxication before they can be treated for alcoholism. This may include anticonvulsant drugs and sedative compounds to prevent seizures and delirium tremens during the withdrawal period, high-potency vitamins, and general supportive care. No effective remedy (other than the passage of time) exists for the aftereffects of intoxication, and complete recovery may require a week or longer.

Psychotherapy

Despite the doctrinal disputes among the various psychotherapeutic schools, most therapists agree on one point, according to the First Special Re-

People are less likely to become dependent on alcohol when they are introduced to it in a social setting that draws a clear distinction between acceptable and unacceptable drinking. That distinction is generally made in Italian-American, Chinese-American, and Jewish families, where moderate drinking is an accepted part of family life.

port to the U.S. Congress on Alcohol and Health (NIAAA, 1971):

A vital part of any treatment program is the opportunity offered the alcoholic person to develop trust in someone. The alcoholic individual generally appears to be lonely and guilt-ridden. Beneath a facade of conviviality, he yearns for a trusting and nonjudgmental person upon whom to become dependent. This dependency is often accompanied by such distrust from earlier disappointments in life that the alcoholic person must challenge any new-found helper to see if this caregiver will be found wanting—like all others who came before.

On other questions opinions are very sharply divided. Alcoholics Anonymous insists that alcoholism is a disease, that every alcoholic has a character defect, and that an alcoholic cannot take even one drink without losing control. But many psychotherapists disagree with one or more of these positions. Therapists trained in Transactional Analysis (TA) believe that alcoholism is a game. Other therapists take the position that it is neither a game nor a disease and that calling it a disease impedes the alcoholic's efforts to gain control of his drinking behavior.

The hottest controversy, however, is over the prospects of teaching an alcoholic to drink in moderation. A major objection to such attempts, shared by Alcoholics Anonymous and some professionals, is that alcoholic patients can easily convince themselves that they are among the select few capable of becoming controlled drinkers. Such rationalizations can easily pave the way for an uncontrolled binge. That view has been challenged, as we mentioned earlier, by Sobell and Sobell (1973), who found that a group of alcoholic patients who had been taught controlled drinking functioned well twice as much of the time as a control group that had been given conventional therapy.

The Sobells used a variety of behavioral techniques, including assertiveness training and monitoring the participants while the latter were drunk, then later having them view a playback of their drunken behavior while they were sober. What is especially encouraging in the Sobells' study is their report that alcoholic patients can maintain controlled social drinking over a period of time.

Also at issue is whether the treatment should be by someone who has "been through the mill" and already overcome alcoholism. Certainly the former alcoholic has a great advantage in establishing trust and in simply understanding what the patient is experiencing. Nevertheless individuals differ, and recovered alcoholics who lack professional training run the risk of imposing their own recollections and expectations on someone who is in a totally different place. Since there are not enough professionals to go around, the most likely resolution to this dispute is increasing cooperation between professionals and paraprofessionals, including recovered alcoholics.

Individual therapy may work best for some people. For others, couple or family therapy may be more productive, especially if the established pattern of family interrelationships supports the disorder or undermines the cure. On more than one occasion the long-suffering spouse has turned out to be an accomplice, even to the point of smuggling a bottle to a hospitalized patient. If the alcoholic's weakness is being exploited by a spouse, they may benefit most from being treated as a couple. Such a situation is the exception rather than the rule, however, and most husbands and wives of alcoholics warmly welcome their partner's recovery.

Group therapy has a sizable potential in the treatment of alcoholism. It is especially suited to the alcoholic's situation—loneliness, alienation, and self-punishment. If the other members are alcoholics or former alcoholics, they will also be especially adept at recognizing every rationalization for drinking. The patient might persuade himself that he could deceive the therapist, but he is much less likely to think he can fool another alcoholic. This fact clearly plays a large part in the apparent success of Alcoholics Anonymous.

Alcoholics Anonymous (AA)

The best-known approach to treating alcoholism is the group therapy method of *Alcoholics Anonymous* (AA). This approach involves having alcoholics help one another. It was started by a stockbroker, Bill W., and a medical practitioner, Dr. Bob, at Akron, Ohio, in 1935, and is a loosely knit voluntary fellowship of alcoholics who meet regularly to help themselves and each other get and stay sober.

AA, which also serves its members as a way back to life and prescribes a design for living, has been widely publicized since the early 1940s and has more than 28,000 active groups in more than ninety countries. Its world membership now exceeds one million. Its motto is "I am responsible. When anyone, anywhere, reaches out for help, I want the hand of AA always to be there. And for that, I am responsible."

To join AA a person need only get in touch with any member, or look AA up in the telephone directory. It is not necessary to have stopped drinking. Anyone who wants to stop drinking and is prepared to admit that he or she is "powerless over alcohol" can join. The AA approach is based on its famous Twelve Steps, whereby the alcoholic admits to having hit "rock bottom" and that he or she is in a desperate and totally intolerable situation. This program, almost a creed, is based on a pledge that the alcoholics make "to God, to ourselves, and to another human being" that they lack power over alcohol.

How does it work in practice? The "pigeon," a new AA member, receives encouragement from the "old timer" who, having taken him under his wing, permits and fosters an interpersonal dependency that replaces the former dependence on alcohol. With the new satisfactions of friendship and reliance on a "sponsor" for help and self-control, the pigeon can begin to reduce his or her drinking. Moreover, AA exerts group pressure on newcomers to dispel any idea they may have that someday they will control and enjoy their drinking and that, in this regard, they are like other people. Pigeons simply have to concede that they are alcoholics and therefore different. AA strongly believes, furthermore, that nothing can do so much to insure immunity from drinking as intensive work with other alcoholics.

During the early years of AA some members rigidly insisted that "only an alcoholic can understand another alcoholic," and there was minimal cooperation between AA workers on the one hand and physicians, clergy, and social workers on the other. With the accumulation of more experience and knowledge, however, most AA members no longer insist on this, and cooperation with psychotherapists and other professionals has been increasing. Thus, AA, which at one time prided itself on its program of effecting sobriety by itself, without the help of psychotherapy, now has become a valuable and widely accepted adjunct to most hospital and individual treatment programs.

Behavior Modification

Because the behavioral approach to alcoholism is a more manipulative procedure than traditional psychotherapy, it seems to have enjoyed more treatment successes. In Chapter 23 we detail two specific techniques used by behavior therapists to treat drinking problems; therefore, we shall deal here only with the generalities of these procedures and our discussion will depend heavily on analyses made by Bandura (1969, 1976), Franks (1970), Kanfer and Phillips (1970), Yates (1970a, 1975), Bootzin (1975), and O'Leary and Wilson (1975). These analyses take into account the important idea that alcoholism is more than just a symptom of a disorder and that it therefore requires a broad spectrum of behavioral approaches. We shall take note of five aspects of this spectrum.

First, this approach requires that a variety of deconditioning procedures be used to eliminate the undesired behavior of drinking. Second, if necessary, the alcoholic should be supplied with a variety of substitute need satisfiers. Third, behavior therapy aims at modifying or removing other deviant aspects of the alcoholic's behavior repertoire so that the alcoholic is not treated as a normal person who happens to have a drinking problem. This is especially important in view of our earlier discussion suggesting that there are aspects of prealcoholic personality that relate to drinking. Fourth, behavior therapists attempt to sustain the ex-drinker's newly acquired nondrinking patterns. Fifth, and perhaps most important of all, behavior modifiers attempt to intervene in the patient's private affairs, helping him or her search for more appropriate employment, in locating a new place of residence, in resolving interpersonal incompatibilities, in pursuing new leisure-time activities—in short, in effecting complete rehabilitation.

According to Franks (1970), the best example of a systematic application of this approach to the treatment of the alcoholic is the program developed by McBrearty and his associates (1968) in several state hospitals in Pennsylvania. This program involves as many of the following treatment steps as are considered essential. We have edited and condensed these procedures somewhat for convenience of presentation (Franks, 1970, pp. 468–469).

A. **Didactic Training for Behavioral Change**
   Regular group meetings to discuss and practice the principles of behavior modification.
B. **Aversive Conditioning Procedures**
   (see Chapters 6 and 23)
   1. *Visual-verbal sequence,* whereby the appearance of "alcohol" words causes the patient to receive an electric shock, whereas "relief" words (such as *relax*) bring with them orange juice and *no* shock.
   2. *Sip and Sniff Sequence.* Similar to the above except that actual beverages are used rather than "alcohol" words.
C. **Relaxation Procedures**
   Individual sessions in which the patient is taught how to acquire control over relaxation.
D. **Desensitization Procedures**
   During this time the various hierarchical proce-

dures of Wolpe are implemented (see Chapter 23).
E. **Training in Areas of Behavioral Deficit**
   1. This can involve any aspect of the patient's total behavioral repertoire and requires active collaboration with individuals such as an employer, other professionals, spouse, or parent (see Chapter 23).
   2. *In Vivo Training.* This involves the gradual real-life exposure of the patient to those situations that originally elicited the maladaptive behavior.
F. **Controlling Behavioral Excesses and Deficits by Systematic Application of Contingent Reinforcement Procedures**
   Essentially, this represents an attempt to apply behavioral engineering or token economy principles (see Chapter 23) in order to study the drinking process and to test whether moderate drinking is a possible alternative to uncontrolled alcoholism.

Other Treatment Resources

Many people recovering from alcoholism need help in staying sober while they begin therapy, as well as in making the transition back into society after recovery. One solution to the first problem is *disulfiram* (Antabuse), an otherwise inert substance that interferes with alcohol metabolism and increases the blood level of acetaldehyde, a highly toxic substance. Ingestion of alcohol produces severe and dangerous symptoms. Since disulfiram is removed slowly from the body, the patient cannot drink safely for several days after discontinuing the drug. The standing joke is that the patient on disulfiram therapy who takes a drink will get so sick that he or she will promptly and permanently give up disulfiram. Actually, disulfiram has been used with some success; its value lies in its ability to make drinking aversive long enough for psychotherapy to have a chance.

The halfway house (see Chapter 25) has helped ease the transition back into society for many alcoholics. It gives recovered alcoholics a breathing spell in an atmosphere in which they can continue therapy and enjoy the benefits of group support and confrontation.

Summary

Although our society condones some uses of alcohol, this beverage may lead to serious harm both to the individual who abuses it and to his or her family. Alcoholism is a widespread problem in this country (and others) involving several million people and affecting the lives of many more.

The physiological effects of ethyl alcohol are mainly on the central nervous system, where it reduces or depresses all functions. Its secondary effects, in terms of the damage it causes to the stomach and liver, lead to serious nutritional deficiencies that may produce further central nervous system damage.

The short-term behavioral influences of alcohol, well known to most of us, depend on the level of concentration of ethanol in the blood. In general, prelethal dosages result in impaired psychomotor functioning. The longer-term effects of years of alcohol consumption, usually the outcome of a combination of brain damage and malnutrition, are sometimes manifested in delirium tremens, Korsakov's psychosis, or a chronic deteriorated state involving symptoms of insidious brain damage.

The evidence for the biological origins of alcoholism consists mainly of studies that search for chemicals in alcohol that trigger predisposing genetic, nutritional, or metabolic defects. Some studies support a genetic–environmental interaction theory for the etiology of alcoholism. Psychological and motivational research have focused on the pre-illness personalities and attitudes of persons who later become alcoholic. The need for power among some individuals has been implicated as one possible motivating force leading to later alcoholism.

Treatment usually includes detoxification, followed by a period of abstinence during which patients are helped to find new ways to deal with their problems. Traditional psychotherapy and behavior therapy have had varying degrees of success in the treatment of alcoholism, but one of the most successful approaches seems to be that of Alcoholics Anonymous (AA), which stresses group interaction and development of trust in other people who are themselves former alcoholics.

Terms and Concepts to Master

Alcoholics Anonymous

Alpha alcoholism

Assuagement drinking

Beta alcoholism

Blood alcohol
concentration

Chronic alcoholic
deterioration

Delirium tremens

Delta alcoholism

Facilitative drinking

Gamma alcoholism

Korsakov's psychosis

Ornamental,
community-symbolic
drinking

Retaliative drinking

10 Drug Abuse

Anyone trying to gauge the dangers of drug use and abuse faces the task of sorting out fact from fiction in a jungle of conflicting claims and counterclaims, studies and counterstudies. A majority of people may agree that drug abuse is a serious problem, but then the value conflicts of the various subcultures in American society enter the picture. It is no longer even a simple conflict of a bourbon- and Valium-consuming establishment culture versus a dope- and acid-consuming counterculture, if indeed it ever was that simple.

Unfortunately the clouds of misinformation sometimes obscure the existence of very real dangers in the use or abuse of certain drugs, and the most dangerous drugs are not always the ones with the worst reputations. Inhaling hairspray can produce sudden death. "Speed kills," even though amphetamine therapy is sometimes still prescribed for hyperactive children because it calms them and makes them more manageable in school. Psychoactive drugs can be used for a multitude of purposes. Thus the willingness of different groups of people to accept a new drug (or their eagerness to condemn it) might be strongly influenced by whether the drug is described as "effective in reducing inhibitions" or as "effective in reducing antisocial behavior."

Drug abuse obviously has different meanings for different people. In a medical or legal context it tends to mean unauthorized drug use, whether or not such use is harmful. We shall define drug abuse here as any drug use that is physically or psychologically harmful.

Drug Effects

All chemical substances that alter mood, perception, or consciousness are *psychoactive drugs*. The alterations, or changes, are known as the drug's *psychoactive effects*. Alcohol is a psychoactive substance according to this definition.

Main and Side Effects of Drugs

There is no such thing as *the* psychoactive effect of a given drug. Every drug has a variety of effects that depend on internal and external states. Some of these effects are predictable; others are not. So-called *side effects* are merely those that the user (or his prescriber) is not interested in obtaining in a given instance; sometimes side effects become the *main* effects through a change of circumstances. For example, codeine may be prescribed by a physician as an analgesic (pain killer), but the patient may discover that he enjoys the mild euphoria or sedative effects of the drug and subsequently takes it to obtain this high. These variable effects are due to the complex interaction of the body's chemistry and the drugs' active ingredients, as well as to the effects of the social surroundings in which they are taken and the expectations of those who use them.

Nevertheless, we can make some generalizations about short- and long-term drug effects. Among the many variables that govern the drug experience are dosage level (all chemical substances are psychoactive when administered at very high dosages), method of administration (orally, subcutaneously, intravenously, inhalation), and the reasons for using the drug. Some of these factors, along with the short- and long-term effects of many drugs, are shown in Table 10.1. Also noted in this table, especially in the Usual Long-term Effects column, are the propensities of the drugs toward causing psychic and physiological dependencies; these terms are further clarified below. The "Long-term effects" should be interpreted cautiously, since they are often a function of the drug subculture, not of the drug itself. Figure 10.1 shows the spectrum and continuum of drug action.

The Nature of Drug Dependency

Traditionally the terms *addiction* and *habituation* referred to repeated abuse or misuse of a psychoactive chemical. These terms caused confusion, however, and did not accurately describe the problems of drug abuse. Consequently, the World Health Organization (WHO) Expert Committee on Addiction-Producing Drugs (1964) redefined and enlarged these concepts and recommended instead the term *drug dependence*, which it described as a state of physical or psychic dependence, or both, arising in a person following drug administration on a periodic or continuous basis.

Physical Dependence. *Physical dependence,* formerly known as *addiction,* is characterized by *tolerance* and *withdrawal.* Tolerance is a physiological survival mechanism of the body in which an organism adapts to a drug and thus becomes better able to withstand continual exposure to its toxic substances. This can have unfortunate and sometimes dangerous (or deadly) consequences because, as a user becomes accustomed to successive doses of a drug, similar amounts of it produce decreasing subjective effects. Therefore to maintain the same degree of psychological

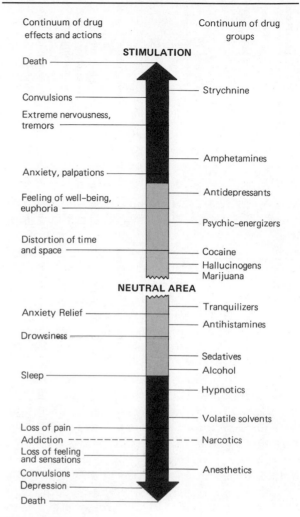

Figure 10.1

Spectrum and continuum of drug action.

(Courtesy Robert W. Earle, Ph.D., California College of Medicine, University of California at Irvine)

reaction (for example, euphoria, calmness, peacefulness), the user must increase dosage continually; and with certain drugs, ever-increasing amounts lead to overdose, sometimes

Table 10.1
Comparative List of Psychoactive Drugs and Their Effects

Drug Name	Slang Name	Number of Hours of Effect (and dosage)	Method of Taking	Reasons Drug Is Sought by Users	Usual Short-term Effects	Usual Long-term Effects
			Narcotics (opiates, analgesics)			
Opium	Op	4 (10–12 "pipes")	Smoking	To act "high" (euphoria)	Central nervous system depressed	Constipation; loss of appetite and weight; temporary impotence; sterility; psychic and physical dependence; withdrawal illness
Heroin	Horse, H, junk, scag, smack, stuff, shit, flea powder	4 (bag or paper with 5–10% heroin or 60 mg)	Injecting or sniffing	As an escape	Sedation Euphoria	
Morphine	White stuff, M, junk, fix, cap	4 (15 mg)	Swallowing or injecting	To avoid withdrawal symptoms	Relief of pain	
Codeine	Schoolboy	4 (30 mg)	Swallowing	Conformity to drug subculture	Disorientation	
Percodan[a] Demerol[a]		4 (1 tablet) 4 (50–100 mg)	Swallowing Swallowing	Rebellion Pain relief (medical uses)		
Cough syrup		4 (2–4 oz., for euphoria)	Swallowing			
Methadone	Dolly	4 (7.5–10 mg)	Swallowing	Pain relief; help withdraw from heroin		
			Stimulants			
Amphetamines	Speed, pep pills, uppers, whites		Swallowing pills or capsules, injecting in veins	Stimulation and relief of fatigue	Central nervous system stimulants	Restlessness, irritability, weight loss, toxicosis, paranoid episodes; psychic and possible physical dependece; extreme irritability
Benzedrine[a]	Bennies			Get high	Increased alertness	
Methedrine[a]	Crystal	4 (2.5–5 mg)		Drug subculture	Insomnia, loss of appetite	
Dexedrine[a]	Dexies, X-mas trees					
Cocaine	Coke, gold-dust, flake, snow, sniff, toot		Sniffing or injecting			

Sedatives, Depressants

Drug	Slang names	Dose	How taken	Reasons for use	Effects	Dangers / Dependence
Barbiturates Nembutal[a] Seconal[a] Phenobarbital Doriden[a] (glutethimide)	Barbs, downers Yellow jackets, nebbies Reds Phennies Goofers	(50–100 mg) 4 (500 mg)	Swallowing pills or capsules	To relax or sleep; euphoria; drug subculture	Central nervous system depressant; sleep; sometimes euphoria; drowsiness; decreased judgment, reaction time, coordination; muscle relaxation	Irritability, weight loss; physical dependence with severe withdrawal illness (like DTs); psychic dependence

Hallucinogens

Drug	Slang names	Dose	How taken	Reasons for use	Effects	Dangers
Cannabis (marijuana; hashish)	Dope, grass, pot, tea, weed, stuff, reefer, joint, hash	4 (1 cigarette)	Smoking, swallowing	To get high; escape; curiosity; to socialize; to conform to drug subculture; rebellion	Euphoria; alteration of time perception; production of visual imagery; impaired judgment and coordination	Usually none (for marijuana); can precipitate psychosis, panic reaction
LSD	Acid, sugar, trips	12 (150 micrograms)	Swallowing: liquid, capsule, pill, or sugar cube			
Psilocybin Mescaline	Mesc, lactus	6 (25 mg) 4 (350 mg)	Chewing plant			

Volatile Solvents

Drug	Slang names	Dose	How taken	Reasons for use	Effects	Dangers
Glue Gasoline		2 (1 tube or bottle) 2 (soaked rag)	Sniffing Sniffing	Curiosity; to get high; thrill-seeking; ready availability	Produces high with impaired judgment and coordination	Can damage liver, kidney, heart, brain

Legally Sanctioned Drugs

Drug	Slang names	Dose	How taken	Reasons for use	Effects	Dangers
Tranquilizers (meprobamates)		4 (200–400 mg)	Swallowing	To obtain calm; euphoria	Produces high, muscle relaxation; tremors	Can be physically and psychically addictive
Antihistamines		2 (25–50 mg)	Swallowing	Curiosity; sedation; to get high; ready availability; allergy relief	Produces high and euphoria	Can damage liver, kidneys

Table 10.1
Comparative List of Psychoactive Drugs and Their Effects (*continued*)

Drug Name	Slang Name	Number of Hours of Effect (and dosage)	Method of Taking	Reasons Drug Is Sought by Users	Usual Short-term Effects	Usual Long-term Effects
Aspirin		2 (variable)	Swallowing	To kill pain; ready availability	Headache, dizziness, ringing in ears, blurred vision, thirst, nausea, diarrhea, stupor, coma	Can damage fetus and produce malformation
Tobacco	Fag, coffin nail		Smoking, chewing, sniffing	Calmness, sociability	Nausea	Lung cancer, heart disease, emphysema and other lung diseases, loss of appetite, physical and psychic dependence

Source: *Adapted from* The pleasure seekers, *copyright © 1969, by Joel Fort, reprinted by permission of the publisher, The Bobbs-Merrill Company, Inc.*
[a] Trade name.

causing central nervous system and other organ damage.

For many but not all drugs, a physical need develops; that is, the user needs to have them constantly present in his or her system lest a *withdrawal illness* develop. The symptoms of withdrawal from barbiturates or from an opiate or its derivatives, for example, can be harrowing. They begin when the user misses a shot and senses that his/her "habit is coming on," and progress through states during which the user becomes increasingly restless, irritable, agitated, and anxious and suffers abdominal cramps, severe twitching of the muscles, loss of appetite, vomiting, and diarrhea; and they may end in convulsions, coma, or death.

The anticipation of the physical and subjective discomforts of withdrawal is a serious problem not only for the above reasons, but also because it often serves as a motive for using the drug. Even under rehabilitative supervision, during which the amount of the drug given is gradually reduced, withdrawal can be a frightening experience. It is often more feared by users than are the consequences attending the drug's illegal procurement or the personal losses (family, friends, job) they may incur to support the habit.

Psychological Dependence. The new term for drug *habituation* is *psychological dependence*, which is indicated by the person's repeated seeking out of a drug. This desire may range all the way from a fairly mild though persistent need for the effects of the drug to an uncontrollable craving. Psychological dependence is further characterized by its repetition, often at regular intervals, and a decreasing resistance to the temptation to repeat the act. The seriousness of psychological dependence is often underestimated, probably because it is overshadowed by the physical discomforts of withdrawal; but according to some accounts it is more difficult to overcome than the physical symptoms.

The degree of psychological dependence varies with the drug, and with the body chemis-

try and personality of the user. When the user discovers that pleasure or a sense of improved well-being may be derived from a drug, a desire to continue taking it may develop, and the user may frequently go to great lengths to obtain it, possibly disregarding all social and legal conventions. Such users become increasingly preoccupied with obtaining drugs and consequently may disregard the values they have held in the past. In a word the drug user may change his lifestyle to suit his particular psychological dependence (Houser, 1969; Jones et al., 1969; Lindesmith, 1968; Maurer and Vogel, 1967).

Types of Drugs

Several principal types of drugs are most often used for their psychoactive properties: *narcotics, stimulants, depressants, hallucinogens,* and *volatile solvents,* as well as numerous *legally sanctioned drugs,* including *tranquilizers.* Abuse of any substances falling under these categories may lead to unusual sensations, or may produce physiological or psychic dependence.

Narcotics

The term *narcotics* refers to the so-called hard drugs that characteristically relieve pain and produce a state of tranquility, elatedness, and sometimes sleep. This category consists largely of the opiates, the best known of which are opium, morphine, heroin, codeine, and methadone.

Prevalence. Narcotics addiction, although smaller in magnitude than it was in 1900, may be worse in terms of its total effect on society. Because the narcotics supply now comes almost exclusively from the underworld, today's users must spend most of their time scheming to get their drugs and the money to pay for them. As the cost of maintaining a habit mounts from a few dollars to as much as $75 or $100 a day, users typically resort to crimes of violence, or impoverish their families by exhausting their total resources.

It has been estimated that in New York City alone narcotics users must raise between $500,000 and $700,000 every day, most of it through shoplifting, burglary, forgery, prostitution, armed robbery, mugging, and other illegal activities. And in the United States, only three states—New York, California, and Illinois—account for approximately 77 percent of known narcotics addicts. Most of these come from the larger cities of those states, New York City itself accounting for more than half the addicts known to the Federal Bureau of Narcotics. But these estimates require careful interpretation, since crimes attributed to drug users are easily overestimated (Singer, 1971).

Once a problem only in the ghettos of our large cities, and perhaps for that reason easily ignored by the middle class, narcotics addiction has today spilled across racial, socioeconomic, and neighborhood boundaries. According to recent estimates, about 1.5 percent of elementary-school and high-school students have used narcotics, mostly heroin; and approximately equal percentages of college students have experimented with these drugs (see Blum et al., 1969a, 1969b; Goldstein et al., 1970; Goldstein, 1971b, 1973b). Again, though in numbers alone this is not a staggering abuse of narcotics, its high potential for inducing physical and psychic dependency and its attendant high rates of criminality create serious problems for the user and for society (Blachly, 1970; Brenner et al., 1970; Fort, 1969).

Types of Narcotics. The two main varieties of narcotics used in the United States today are *morphine* and *heroin*. *Morphine*, sometimes known as *M, white stuff, junk, fix, paper, poison,* or *cap,* was first thought to be a cure for *opium* addiction; it is about ten times stronger than opium and, like heroin, has a generally depressant action on the entire central nervous system, including the cen-

ter controlling the most vital physiological functions. Although smaller doses (5 to 29 mg taken orally, or less when injected subcutaneously or intravenously) result in the relief of pain, larger doses (120 mg taken orally, or more than 30 mg injected), depending on the tolerance of the individual, may result in a dangerous slowing of heart action and breathing.

Heroin, a morphine derivative, is the most popular narcotic in current use. It is technically known as diacetylmorphine hydrochloride, or more commonly, as *H*, or any word beginning with capital H (*Horse, Harry*). It goes by the additional names of *medicine, shot, stuff, junk, white stuff, shit, smack,* or *flea powder*. It is a white crystalline powder closely resembling morphine. When it was first produced in 1898 and sold as a substitute for morphine and codeine, it was promoted as a cure for morphine addiction. It was soon discovered, however, to be several times more powerful than morphine, and quite addictive. Narcotics peddlers, or *pushers*, prefer to deal in heroin because it is three times as powerful, and a given quantity is therefore worth three times as much on the illicit market; also it is more easily diluted than other narcotics, thus making the profits even higher.[1]

Heroin is taken in the same way as morphine, either orally or by injection, although in smaller doses because of its greater potency. Some addicts, especially beginners, inhale or "sniff" heroin; however, they are soon forced to inject it because of the inflammation of their nostrils and because of the greater "rush" obtained by injection. Just as with morphine, injection is

---

[1]The wholesale heroin pusher sells it by the kilogram, a kilo (2.2 pounds) of pure heroin being valued at somewhere between $10,000 and $15,000. Frequently wholesale heroin is sold in one-ounce or smaller plastic bags, which in turn are "cut" or diluted by retail pushers. When this kilo is diluted, usually with powdered milk, sugar, or other impurities, the mixture ends up containing 3 or 4 percent heroin. In this way the wholesaler's original kilo of heroin becomes worth $1 million on the illegal market.

the quickest way of getting it into the system (Figure 10.2), and many users force it directly into the body by opening a blood vessel with a pin or razor blade and administering the heroin into the opening with a medicine dropper.

According to Lingeman (1969), different routes of taking heroin play their part in the user's future relationship with the drug. The typical progression of street use is from sniffing to subcutaneous (*skin popping*) and intravenous injections (*mainlining*). Many users stay at the level of skin popping for several years or permanently, taking the drug occasionally on weekends for kicks (*joy pop*). But it is only a short step from skin popping to mainlining, which because of the telltale marks it leaves, alienates the heroin user from society. Mainlining is often the preferred method because it is a cheaper and faster way to get kicks.

Aside from the alienation, there are the dangers of contracting skin infections, abscesses, and hepatitis because of unsterilized needles, pins, or medicine droppers. Also, constant injection, or forcing the drug into the blood vessels, causes vascular breakdown and produces visible scars on the skin over the veins. The breakdown leads the user to seek new areas for injecting the drug until the entire lengths of the arms are marked by needle punctures; and because of the scar tissue, he selects new sites for injection, preferably those less exposed than arms and legs. Favorite spots are between the fingers or toes, in the neck above the hairline, and inside the mouth. Thus the narcotic-dependent individual is forever searching for sites that will hide the many clues of prolonged use.

A third type of narcotic is *methadone*, a synthetic opiate used in medicine as an analgesic, to suppress the cough reflex, and in the treatment of heroin or morphine withdrawal symptoms—so-called *methadone maintenance therapy*—which we discuss later in this chapter.

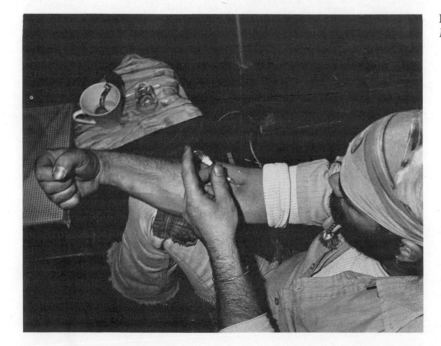

Figure 10.2
Heroin is typically injected intravenously.

This man's death resulted from a heroin overdose.

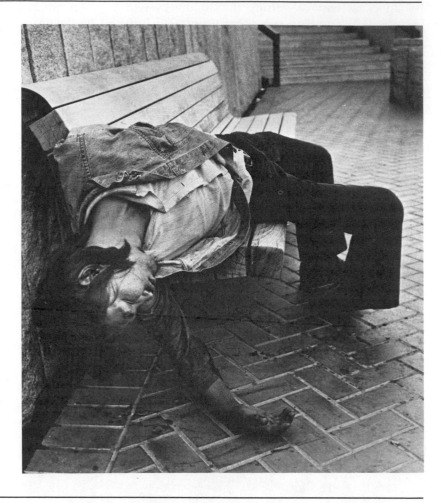

The Subjective and Physiological Experience of Narcotics. Narcotic drugs are central nervous system depressants whose immediate subjective effects, like those of alcohol, include a sense of well-being, serenity, and relief from fear and apprehension. These effects, however, wear off and the individual becomes apathetic. The transition is gradual and occurs as follows: a few seconds after the injection of a narcotic, the user's face flushes, pupils constrict, and a tingling sensation is felt, particularly in the abdomen. The tingling soon gives way to a feeling of elation (the "fix"),

which lasts about 30 minutes. The user later drifts into a somnolence ("going on the nod"), waking up, drifting again, all the while indulging in daydreams. During this phase, understandably, the user has no interest in anything and spends most of the time in bed. In this condition the user may be easily awakened and will answer questions accurately, but readily goes back on the nod. The drug effects wear off within about three to four hours, sometimes a little longer.

The regular narcotics user discovers early that unless the dose is increased, the drug no longer has the same effect. In other words, a *tolerance* for the drug has been developed and even large amounts of the substance no longer bring the same "fix." Many users who are suddenly cut off from narcotics, or try to "kick the habit" to escape its control, find shortly following the last dose that the "habit is coming on." They yawn, sweat, and experience a burning of the eyes and nose as in the onset of an acute head cold. These *withdrawal* symptoms increase in severity and are followed, after about 24 hours, by muscle spasms, waves of goose flesh, dilation of the pupils, vomiting, and diarrhea. In short, functions that had been depressed are now hyperactive.

Withdrawal symptoms may last for two or three days and then diminish gradually over a period of a week or more; or, in more chronic cases, the user may experience a general feeling of discomfort for several months thereafter. In the case of withdrawal from heroin, these symptoms reach a peak in 24 hours; with morphine, they peak in 36 to 48 hours; with methadone the symptoms are less severe but more prolonged. In any event, within a week or ten days after the last drug, the user has lived through the worst of the withdrawal sickness and may be well on the way to losing a physical dependence on narcotics. Complete recovery, however, requires from two to six months.

There appears to be little direct permanent physiological damage from chronic use of pure narcotics; adulterated street samples, however, do cause numerous complications, most of which are caused by the variable dosage levels, or as a consequence of contaminants in the diluter.[2]

Commonly reported complications include heart and lung abnormalities. Sudden collapse and death following intravenous injections are sometimes also reported.

Psychic Dependence. The psychological effects of narcotics vary considerably among different individuals and situations. Many people simply do not enjoy its effects and may avoid its repetition, while others describe feelings of serenity, warmth, and tranquility. Still others experience euphoria, nausea, drowsiness, confusion, apathy, and lethargy. Certain individuals, especially when fatigued, report feeling bursts of energy and strength; and some regular users even describe the "rush" of intravenous injection in ecstatic and often sexual terms.

Psychic dependence develops when the drug user increasingly turns to narcotics to shut out problems and quiet his or her anxieties. Unfortunately, however, the anguish or misery endured before taking the drug returns after its effects wear off. Furthermore, and here lies the danger, not only does the euphoria wear off, but the anticipation of the severe withdrawal illness drives narcotics users to seek out their next fix.

To illustrate the impact of heroin addiction on an individual, we present the following description of one day in the life of John—not his real name—who came to New York as a teenager. On his job as short-order cook, John quickly learned a new jargon: "shooting gallery," "white stuff," "skin popping," and so forth. He was frequently jailed for the thefts he committed to support his habit, and his life became a continuous round of peddling, stealing, and jail (Jeffee, 1966, pp. 49–51):[3]

7:30 A.M. An "eye opener"—not a shot of liquor but heroin.

8:30 A.M. Meets with friends—all addicts—in side-street

---

[2]Drug users on the street often say (and this is a view often shared by coroners, although they may not admit it publicly) that some heroin overdose deaths are actually murders. For example, a pusher may deliberately give someone a much stronger dose than usual in order to get rid of a troublesome junkie, perhaps because the latter threatened to inform the police (Goldstein, 1973b).

---

[3]Reprinted from *Narcotics—an American plan* by Saul Jeffee, © 1966, by permission of Paul S. Eriksson, Inc., New York, publishers.

taverns. Discusses possible "hits" to get merchandise to pawn.

9:30 A.M. *Gets burglar tools including small crowbar and screwdriver he hid the night before in tenement back hall garbage can.*

10:00 A.M. *Breaks into fourth floor apartment of downtown apartment house after knocking at door and getting no answer. . . . He makes off with some rings and a small TV set.*

11:00 A.M. *He pawns the TV and the rings at a downtown shop. Net proceeds: $50. Often he has to commit several additional robberies to net this amount.*

11:15 A.M. *Taxies to 125th Street, makes his connection with a pusher, buys nine bags of diluted heroin.*

11:34 A.M. *Goes to his apartment for a second shot. Goes out again.*

12:30 P.M. *Two burglaries. During one of these, an old man came into the room and John, suddenly terrified, struck. Later he was quoted as saying, "I hope that old man was okay. I didn't stop to look at him, man, I was scared. . . ."*

1:00 P.M. *After pawning more stolen goods, he goes for more heroin from the pusher.*

2:00 P.M. *John meets his wife and they go to a cheap downtown movie. Relax. John is high on heroin now and does not care about the movie. . . . He and his wife meet with other addict friends in "shooting gallery" uptown. . . .*

5:30 P.M. *Someone has lost his "hypo" needle. John lets the addict use his but will wash it carefully later. The danger of infection—and possibly death—from a contaminated needle is a high risk in the addict world.*

7:00 P.M. TO CLOSING. *This is dream time for John and his associates and friends. Now he loses himself and his pain in his world of dreams.*

A number of relatively permanent personality changes among narcotics users have been noted, including alterations of the individual's lifestyle until the need for drugs replaces all other motivations and modes of adjustive behavior; a loss of interest in productive labor, food, sex, companionship, family ties, and recreation; and unreliability, lethargy, and personal slovenliness. Moreover, so that addicts can procure their sup-

ply of drugs, they must maintain their contacts with the underworld characters who control the distribution of narcotics, which in turn, contributes further toward their socially unacceptable status (Ausubel, 1958; S. Cohen, 1969; Goldstein, 1971b; Laurie, 1967; Lingeman, 1969).

Stimulants and Depressants

The stimulants, such as Benzedrine, Dexedrine, and Methedrine (*amphetamines*), and the depressants, such as Nembutal, Seconal, and phenobarbital (*barbiturates*), are called "uppers" and "downers" to reflect their effects of speeding up and slowing down a person's activities. The use and abuse of these drugs are extensive; the best estimates indicate that over ten million people in the United States use them legally by prescription and that another half-million individuals, who spend no less than $25 million yearly on amphetamines and barbiturates, obtain them on the illicit markets. It has also been estimated that about 25 percent of the barbiturates and almost 50 percent of the amphetamines manufactured annually in the United States find their way into illicit outlets.

Stimulants. The most commonly abused stimulants—Benzedrine, Dexedrine, and Methedrine, also known as *bennies*, *pep pills*, *speed*, *crystal*, *meth*, *uppers*, or *eye-openers*—are used medicinally to combat depression and narcolepsy (attacks of involuntary sleep and weakness) and are therefore alternately known as psychic energizers or antidepressants. The *amphetamines*, as they are called generically, exert their central nervous system energizing action because they are closely related to adrenalin (epinephrine), and their effects, either taken orally or injected, are similar to those of sympathetic nervous system innervation (see Chapter 8). The resulting subjective experience usually includes feelings of elation, self-confidence, and heightened alertness and initiative. The latter two effects account for their frequent use among truck drivers trying to stay awake on long trips and among students cramming for examinations.

A side effect of the amphetamines is to reduce appetite; thus they are commonly recommended in the treatment of obesity. But many physicians do not like to prescribe these stimulants. While they have a tendency to suppress appetite, they also cause several undesirable side effects. For example, while losing weight, a person may also lose sleep, becoming agitated, irritable, and overtalkative; and as soon as the drug is withdrawn, appetite returns unless a new pattern of eating has been established. More frequently the amphetamine user resumes the old habit of overeating, which led to the original difficulties.

Amphetamines are usually taken orally; increasingly, however, among those who seek their side effects (kicks), they are being taken intravenously. (This is especially common in Methedrine abuse.) Injection results in more rapid absorption and hence causes a greater psychoactive effect, which is described as a sudden pleasurable "rush" or "flash" and accounts for some people's motivation to use the drug.

Those who "shoot up" amphetamines often take excessive and intoxicating doses in a very short period of time; this may lead to acute *amphetamine intoxication*, which is characterized by agitation, restlessness, sleeplessness, profuse perspiration, distractibility, and impaired judgment. Prolonged abuse may cause severe physical damage involving primarily the liver, which normally activates the amphetamines and is destroyed or impaired quite easily. Secondary damage to the heart and nervous system sometimes also occurs.

Although there is an absence of *physical dependence* in the sense of developing the withdrawal syndrome, *tolerance* for the drug does build up so that the user must take ever-increasing doses to obtain the desired subjective experiences. Hence some former amphetamine users are now wearing buttons that read "Speed Kills," a warning directed at "speed freaks" or "meth heads" who have become accustomed to taking massive doses for several days, which occasionally causes serious illness or death.

Psychic dependence on the amphetamines develops because of their capacity to produce feelings of energy, initiative, and self-confidence. Since these experiences are usually followed by a rebound effect leading to fatigue and depression, a return to the former high state is likely to be sought. This up-and-down cycle is heightened if the amphetamine causes insomnia, which in turn calls for a barbiturate to induce sleep. Many users are known to alternate these drugs with each other, hoping to find a psychological equilibrium somewhere between a pleasant high and a serene low. However, this can lead to abuse of both drugs because keeping them in balance is difficult, and it is not uncommon to find these people undergoing wide mood shifts, from excitement to depression.

The self-report of a 30-year-old divorced housewife, presented in Case Report 10.1, illustrates the way the user turns to ever-increasing doses of amphetamines as a result of the tolerance that builds up. She was able to overcome dependence on the drug, mainly because of the fears she had about what would become of her two daughters.

Both the physiological and the psychological responses to amphetamines vary considerably with dose; the effects of intravenous injection of large quantities, for example, may bear little resemblance to those of low amounts administered orally. At typical moderate doses (5–30 mg), they produce the adrenalin-like peripheral effects mentioned earlier; at chronic high-dose intravenous injections (several thousand mg), the reaction is entirely different. Initially most users feel energetic, talkative, enthusiastic, happy, confident, and powerful, and may begin and complete highly ambitious tasks. Many cannot sleep or eat; compulsively repeat meaningless acts; become irritable, suspicious, and self-conscious. Some experience hallucinations and/or paranoid delusions. Toward the end of the "run"—that is, at the time (about a week) the user "comes down" or "crashes" from intravenous amphetamine—fatigue sets in and prolonged sleep follows, sometimes lasting several days. Because of this post-run depression, the user may start the cycle again. Clinically these manifestations very much resemble the cyclic behavior of the manic-depressive.

Case Report 10.1 *Amphetamine Abuse*

At first I started taking Benzedrine tablets three or four times a day. That was about four years ago. It was the only way I could get through the day, what with my screaming, howling kids and all. These tablets made me feel fine and I was much better to get along with. I even began taking classes at night at the local college, determined to finally get my undergraduate degree in art history. Before taking the pills, I could barely get through the day—I was always drained of all my strength by midday.

Then, after about the first year on these tablets, I discovered that I needed more and more to get going. This was especially true mornings—I would feel completely exhausted, almost as though I hadn't slept at all, my mouth would be dry, my head spinning, and all I could think of was getting some sort of a lift again.

That's when I began scheming to get more and more Benzedrine. My doctor would not prescribe any more tablets, so I began to shop around for other doctors. Luckily, I was somewhat overweight, so I could always manage to obtain some amphetamine prescription. I then discovered that the usual tablet dosages were not strong enough to bring on the lift I needed so I increased the amount I took. This required still more scheming until I became so preoccupied with obtaining the drug that I could think of little else. I began to take such huge amounts that I became worried about my health and what would happen to the children if I were to become ill. While I was on the medication I just didn't care about anything, and I was very rough on the kids. That also worried me. It seems also that I never got anything done—housework,

schoolwork, shopping, and so forth. Oh, I expended a lot of energy, but as I look back, it was like random activity. What finally really got me worried were my constant battles with my neighbors who, I was convinced, were out to do me in. It all seems like a bad nightmare now.

Depressants. The chief central nervous system depressants used today, with the possible exception of the opiates and alcohol, are the *barbiturates*—Nembutal, Seconal, and phenobarbital. On the illicit market the argot for the barbiturates is *goof balls, yellow jackets, pink ladies, red birds, barbs, downers,* and similar names, often depending on the color of the tablets or capsules. These drugs are much less expensive than narcotics, yet similar in their depressant action. Many heroin users combine the barbiturates with alcohol for an added kick.

Taken in small doses and under the direction of a competent physician, they do no harm; taken in uncontrolled quantities, however, and at frequent intervals, they may create organic problems. The barbiturates are prescribed for, and widely used in, a large variety of diseases and disorders in which sleep or sedation is essential—that is, in cases in which agitation and anxiety are overwhelming, or on occasions when it is essential to protect the individual from disturbing emotional distress or other external stimuli that may precipitate tension and upset. They are also widely used in disorders marked by emotional tension combined with physical symptoms, such as in gastric ulcer, thyroid dysfunction, or convulsive seizures.

The organ most affected by the barbiturates is the brain, which is the primary site of their depressant action. The drug's action interferes with oxygen consumption and therefore with the mechanisms by which energy is derived, stored, and utilized within the brain cells. These cells develop a *tolerance* for barbiturates very rapidly, requiring ever-increasing dosages to accomplish their desired effects. This is why some people accidentally take lethal overdoses.

The depression of brain cell function results in a general slowing down of most, if not all, areas of the central nervous system. Such depression of cellular activity also helps to account for some of its anesthetic effects and for its ability to prevent epileptic seizures. At the extremely toxic dosages usually taken by the chronic barbiturate abuser, these drugs can produce a state of overactivity and excitement before the general suppression of the central nervous system occurs. As with alcohol this initial increased activity is due to the depression of the brain's inhibitory systems, which causes euphoria, excitement, and a feeling of liberation.

Barbiturate abuse is also accompanied by a *withdrawal* illness, which the World Health Organization Expert Committee (1964) describes as appearing within the first 24 hours of cessation of drug taking. The symptoms of the withdrawal illness, in approximate order of appearance, include anxiety, involuntary twitching of muscles, tremor of hands and fingers, progressive weakness, dizziness, distortion in visual perception, nausea and vomiting, insomnia, weight loss, and a precipitous drop in blood pressure. Convulsions of a *grand mal* type or hallucinations and illusions resembling those of alcoholic delirium tremens may also occur. Barbiturate withdrawal is more life-threatening than alcohol or heroin withdrawal.

The detrimental behavioral effects to individuals using barbiturates stem in part from their preoccupation with drug taking, but more particularly from the persistent physical and mental symptoms resulting from the drug: ataxia (muscular incoordination), dysarthria (speech difficulties), and impairment of the higher mental processes, causing confusion, loss of emotional control, and poor judgment. Occasionally, a toxic psychosis develops in which hallucinations and delusions of persecution are the most prominent features.

As with many other drugs, alcohol *potentiates* (makes the drug more potent or effective) the properties of barbiturates. Unfortunately in the case of barbiturates this is even more serious than with other drugs because alcohol is often taken in combination with them, usually to achieve greater sedative effects. This is an extremely hazardous practice, which, according to one psychologist (Lingeman, 1969, p. 18), may result in consequences "ranging from death by accident to death by respiratory failure."

One barbiturate that has been a repeated source of drug problems is phencyclidine. Dubbed PCP (for "PeaCe Pill") in the Haight-Ashbury during the 1960s, it reemerged in the 1970s with such street names as *angel dust, tic, tac, hog, busy bee,* and *goon.* It has, according to some popular news accounts, been so pervasive and deadly that the National Institute of Drug Abuse and other federal agencies have held priority meetings to decide how to cope with it.

PCP was developed as an anesthetic in 1956, but it produced side effects of agitation, delirium, and disorientation. Consequently its use was discontinued for humans, but it is approved as a tranquilizer for animals.

On the street PCP is sprinkled on marijuana, tobacco, mint, and parsley and is usually smoked. The drug can also be snorted or taken orally. Although originally used in conjunction with other drugs, it is also being used exclusively by some "PCP freaks."

Reactions to PCP vary. Most users report a pleasant sensation upon first using the drug. Thereafter the experience can be harrowing. Psychotic hallucinations are common and such self-destructive behavior as biting off parts of one's own fingers is also reported. Users may also suffer bowel and bladder incontinence as well as slurred speech, inability to walk, and immobility. Even after a month of nonuse, these symptoms can persist. Taken in large doses, PCP causes severe toxic reactions and can induce seizures, coma, and death.

The drug's effects seem to diminish with treatment by such minor tranquilizers as Valium and Librium, but there are some reports that these drugs only serve to potentiate PCP's undesirable effects. The most successful treatment of its ill effects seems to be through the use of large doses of vitamin C to acidify the urine and hasten its excretion from the body. Until more is learned about this drug's effects, the best course of action seems to be to follow "Baretta's" much-heard TV advice, "Don't go near it, it's a rattlesnake and it will kill you."

Hallucinogens: LSD

Few drugs have had so profound an effect on American culture in as short a time as the hallucinogenic (hallucination-producing) drugs, especially lysergic acid diethylamide-25, familiarly known as LSD, or "acid."

LSD is a tasteless, odorless, white powder prepared from ergot, a fungus growth on rye grain; or it may be prepared synthetically. It is variously called *acid, sugar,* or *sugar cube.* Sometimes it appears on the illicit market as sugar cubes treated with LSD solutions; as powder in capsules; and in vials of solution of 1 cc each for individual doses, selling for from five to ten dollars a dose. Since it is difficult to obtain from legitimate sources, LSD is now sold mostly on the illicit market. The result is uncontrolled or unsupervised use of the drug, which in its bootleg form may vary widely in dosage, purity, and strength.

LSD use began in the 1950s when its now well-known subjective consequences generated an initial optimism in the experimental laboratory about the potential research usefulness of its supposed *psychotomimetic* (psychosis-mimicking) and *psychotogenic* (psychosis-producing) characteristics. This led several researchers to believe that LSD produces a model psychosis, behavior that resembles disturbances seen in psychotic individuals. Hence, since this drug seemed to have the capacity to produce a model psychosis, it was reasoned, our understanding of severely psychotic individuals would be enhanced by experimentation with it. Subsequently interest was

centered on LSD as a psychotherapeutic agent in the treatment of alcoholism and other psychiatric disorders (see Chapter 21).

Matters took another turn, however, when in 1963 glowing reports by Timothy Leary and Richard Alpert, two Harvard psychologists, appeared in the *Harvard Crimson* and the *Harvard Review,* and an article in the *Reporter* in the same year lauded the "consciousness expanding" properties of LSD. Largely because of this publicity an increased popular interest in the drug developed; experimentation just for kicks followed shortly thereafter. At first this experimentation was carried on openly; but later its illegality forced LSD use underground.

Researchers soon discovered that the *model psychosis* produced in a normal individual (usually a self-experimenter) differs from schizophrenia in several important ways and shows closer resemblances to the experiences of sensory deprivation and the DTs. The main differences, as shown in Table 10.2, between the schizophrenic and LSD states lie in the spheres of perception and emotion. In other respects (body image, ideation, orientation, coordination) there are similarities; but the differences are crucial, and they, too, were partially responsible for abandoning the idea that LSD is a psychotomimetic (Laurie, 1967).

The pluses and minuses in Table 10.2 indicate the presence and absence of certain subjective experiences, and we may note that the LSD trip is marked by many more visual hallucinations and visual intensification experiences than schizophrenia. In addition the LSD state is predominantly characterized by acute hearing distortions and by gross distortions of touch, taste, and smell, all of which are rare among schizophrenics. The main similarities among the DTs, schizophrenia, sensory deprivation, and LSD are the anxiety, emotional instability, and inappropriate affect that they produce and the changes that occur in body image, ideation, orientation, and motor coordination.

The physiological and biochemical features of

Table 10.2
LSD State Compared with Other States

| Subjective Experience | Psychological States | | | |
	DTs	Schizophrenia	Sensory Deprivation	LSD
Perceptions				
Intensification of color and depth	—	rare	+	+
Visual illusions	+	rare	+	+
Visual pseudo-hallucinations	+	rare	+	+
Visual hallucinations	+	rare	+	+
More acute hearing	—	—	+	+
Auditory hallucinations	+	+	+	rare
Hallucinations of touch, taste, and smell	rare	rare	+	rare
Emotions				
Euphoria	rare	rare	rare	+
Anxiety	+	+	+	+
Emotional instability	+	+	+	+
Inappropriateness of feeling	+	+	+	+
Body Image				
Feeling that self is unreal	+	+	+	+
Feeling that world is unreal	+	+	+	+
Ideation				
Fantasies	+	+	+	+
Flight of ideas	+	+	+	+
Everything has personal meaningfulness	+	+	+	+
Delusions	+	+	+	+
Impaired concentration	+	+	+	+
Lower intelligence test scores	+	+	+	+
Orientation				
Poor for time	+	+	+	+
Poor for place	+	+	+	+
Motor Coordination				
Impaired	+	+	+	+

Source: Adapted from Tables 1 and 2 in Drugs of hallucination *by
Sidney Cohen. Published by Martin Secker & Warburg Ltd., 1965.
Reprinted by permission of Atheneum Publishers, New York.*

LSD are still not well understood. Some of its central nervous system concomitants have been studied, however, and it is known that LSD causes stimulation of electrical activity in the brain. This stimulation is reflected by activation of the electroencephalograph, particularly in the reticular formation. The net effects are *sympathomimetic,* or resembling stimulation of the sympathetic branch of the autonomic system, which causes increased pulse and heart rate; elevated blood pressure; pupillary dilation; elevated body temperature; hair standing on end; flushing, shivering, and chills; loss of appetite, nausea and vomiting; dizziness; headache; decreased muscular coordination; and fine tremor of the fingers and hands.

The *short-term psychological state* resulting from swallowing, inhaling, or injecting a minute quantity of LSD is known as the *trip.* Trips generally last from eight to ten hours and can be divided into four stages. The first stage extends from time of ingestion of the drug to the time when the full experience develops. If the dose is taken orally, symptoms appear in about 30 to 45 minutes; if it is injected into the bloodstream, the effects occur more rapidly, in a matter of several minutes.

The second phase, when the full subjective and physiological effects of the drug are felt, usually lasts about four to five hours, again depending on the size of the dose and the method of administration. In general the perceptual changes taking place during this phase are striking. Colors are brighter than ever, time hangs in limbo, objects move to and fro in an exaggerated and sometimes grotesque manner, all sense of self is lost, the limbs feel strangely unfamiliar, minor matters take on a tremendous importance.

During the third phase—that is, during the period of recovery when the effects of the drug begin to diminish—the person experiences alternating waves of LSD symptoms and waves of normal feeling. About seven to nine hours after the drug is taken, most people report that they still experience mild lingering symptoms.

The last phase, sometimes called the *aftermath,* produces a feeling of tension and fatigue. Usually this feeling lingers for several hours, but it is gone by the following day. But prolonged effects, such as recurring hallucinations and reactions of a psychotic type, do appear in some individuals. This recurrence, or *flashback,* can happen within several days or weeks and has been known to occur as long as two years after ingestion. Flashback symptoms, usually triggered by stress, fatigue, fever, or another drug, may cause people considerable anxiety about their sanity (see, for example, Brenner et al., 1970; Hoffer, 1970a).

The *long-term effects* of LSD are still not well documented, but some data are beginning to appear. Like many other drug users, chronic LSD users tend to drop out of society; but it is difficult to establish whether this is because many potential drop-outs gravitate toward these drugs, or because the drugs cause them to drop out.

Some data have also appeared linking LSD with genetic damage. Several investigators report having found that LSD causes an abnormal amount of breakage in the chromosomes of the white blood cells; if such abnormal chromosomal damage does occur, miscarriages and birth defects could result. There are several studies bearing on this point: one showing *in vitro* chromosomal abnormalities in lymphocytes exposed to LSD (Cohen et al., 1967), another reporting that LSD administered at critical stages during early pregnancy can produce serious birth defects in some mammals (Auerback and Rugowski, 1967), and a third extending these findings to humans by showing that a leg defect developed in an infant exposed early *in utero* to LSD (Zellweger et al., 1967).

While these reports are provocative, numerous other investigators have failed to observe similar genetic or congenital complications of LSD use (Bender and Sankar, 1968; Judd et al., 1968). And, after an extensive review of the genogenesis of LSD, Dishotsky and his associates (1971) concluded as follows (p. 439):

Of nine studies in vitro, *six have indicated some degree of induced chromosomal breakage after exposure to LSD; three failed to confirm these results. The damage when found was generally . . . the result of concentrations of drug and durations of exposure which could not be achieved in humans with reasonable dosages.*

In other words, according to this conclusion, chromosome damage is due to the abuse of LSD, and these investigators suggest that pure LSD ingested in moderate doses does not damage chromosomes *in vivo*, does not cause detectable genetic damage, and is not a teratogen (causing congenital malformations) or a carcinogen (causing cancer). Within these bounds, therefore, they further suggest that "other than during pregnancy, there is no present contraindication to the continued controlled experimental use of pure LSD" (Dishotsky et al., 1971, p. 439).

Marijuana and Hashish

No drug, not even LSD, has figured as prominently as marijuana in the clash of cultures that has shaken the foundations of our society in the last two decades. Marijuana is a politically explosive subject, and the passion (overt or covert) with which it is discussed seems to be surpassed only by the wealth of misinformation on all sides.

Marijuana is the dried leaves and buds of the hemp plant *cannabis sativa,* which grows in many parts of the world. It is usually smoked in cigarettes ("joints") or in pipes, but it is sometimes eaten in baked goods ("Alice B. Toklas brownies"). The active ingredient is tetrahydrocannabinol (THC), which is present in varying percentages, depending on the quality of the marijuana. Hashish is made from the resin of the hemp plant and has a much higher concentration of THC than marijuana.

In small doses, the short-term effects of marijuana vary considerably and seem to be influenced by the user's expectations, but the greater the dose the more the pharmacological properties predominate and the less diversity there is in its effects. The "high" resulting from low-quality (low THC) marijuana may sometimes be nothing more than an increase in heart rate and a general sensation of physical intoxication. Any mood already present tends to be intensified, whether it is depression or elation. A good high is reported variously as euphoria, release, heightened sense perceptions, intense sexual arousal, a slowing down of time, a feeling of no longer being intimidated by the fear of others' disapproval, an intense hunger ("the munchies"), or a tendency to see almost everything as hilariously funny ("the sillies"). Sometimes people hear complex passages of music in greater clarity and detail than ever before. Sometimes, also, people feel a leaden sense of alienation that borders on paranoia. Short-term memory lapses are common (for example, forgetting what one has just said), and the ability to perform reasoning processes that involve either a lengthy sequence of steps or a complex pattern of logical relationships is impaired.

The political significance of people's attitudes toward marijuana stems from its association with rejection of authority. It acquired that association in the fifties when it was called *pot* and was smoked by a handful of people identified as the "beat generation." In the sixties it was called *grass* and was closely identified with the hippie movement. By the seventies it was being called *dope* and seemed to have become popular, at least in urban areas, among many middle-class and middle-aged people as well as large numbers of high school students. By 1976 an estimated 50 million Americans had tried it, and according to the Shafer Commission surveys released in 1972, over 13 million Americans considered themselves regular users of marijuana. The conclusion the Commission drew from this was that "there are now three recreational drugs in this country: alcohol, tobacco, and marijuana."

One consequence of this popularity has been a weakening of legal prohibitions. Several states have reduced marijuana possession to the status of a misdemeanor, roughly equivalent to a parking violation. Alaska has removed all penalties for possession of small amounts in the home. And President Carter has suggested decriminalization at the federal level.

Still the debate continues. Is marijuana physically harmful or safe? Is it a threat to society or only to the values of some people? Opponents and proponents have produced an impressive array of studies with diametrically opposite results.

Those who are neither vehement opponents nor ardent proponents have often taken the position that too little is known about marijuana, and judgment should therefore be suspended until the results are in. Psychiatrist Norman E. Zinberg, in an excellent article called "The War over Marijuana" (1976), points out that in fact marijuana has been studied exhaustively. In our discussion of marijuana we shall draw heavily on the data cited by Zinberg.

Zinberg discusses the seven most publicized dangers attributed to marijuana, describing the studies in support of the danger claims and those in opposition, as well as events that drew considerable attention from the mass media—President Nixon's rejection of the Shafer Commission's report, a column by Ann Landers (later retracted) asserting that studies had proved that marijuana causes birth defects, and hearings held by Senator Eastland of Mississippi to give opponents of marijuana a chance to be heard.

The alleged dangers of marijuana fall into three categories: (1) physical or neurological consequences, such as birth defects, brain damage, interference with the immune response, sexual impairment, and psychosis; (2) the marijuana-is-a-steppingstone-to-heroin hypothesis; and (3) the claim that marijuana makes people less moral, productive, and socially useful (the "amotivational syndrome").

The amotivational syndrome argument is the one most clearly fraught with political overtones, for the simple reason that one's evaluation of

someone else's motivation depends entirely on one's set of values. A hedonistically motivated person may be seen as amotivational in the context of the Protestant ethic. Note that the disagreement here is not primarily over what happens while a person is stoned. Proponents as well as opponents agree that rational, analytical, linear thinking and perhaps other presumed left-brain processes are suppressed during marijuana intoxication. But the proponents of the amotivational syndrome hypothesis fear worse consequences. They assert that marijuana users lose their will and their ability to think straight even when they are not intoxicated.

The seesaw battle over the amotivational syndrome is typical of the more than ten years of marijuana research done thus far. The National Clearing House for Drug Information reported in 1970 that marijuana users and nonusers do about equally well academically. Less than a month later a report from the Federal Bureau of Narcotics and Dangerous Drugs asserted that marijuana users do not do as well academically as nonusers. This was followed by two reports in 1971 asserting that marijuana causes physical dependence, but the annual HEW Report on Marijuana and Health in 1972 reported that no difference between users and nonusers was found in several studies of high school and college students. Almost immediately an article appeared claiming that "primitive" countries in which marijuana users were not punished always accomplished less than countries that were less primitive and more punitive. Also in 1972 the Shafer Commission report found no evidence for an amotivational syndrome.

Next the Jamaica study, authorized by the Shafer Commission, found no differences in motivation between nonusers and users who smoked seven to 25 cigarettes a day of strong Jamaican marijuana for 10 to 25 years. The Jamaica study even hinted that the users might be better motivated. Hochman and Brill (1973; cited in Zinberg, 1976) found no differences between users and nonusers, but in the same year the

Army claimed that soldiers who used marijuana were less well motivated than those who did not. The Le Dain Commission in Canada, however, reported essentially the same results as the Shafer Commission. Then the amotivational syndrome was revived in the Eastland hearings. Next, the Drug Abuse Council reported in 1975 that after one year of decriminalization in Oregon neither marijuana use nor problems related to use had shown any increase. In July 1975 R. T. Jones, at Langley Porter Neuropsychiatric Institute, found tolerance and dependence in subjects who received 210 milligrams of THC a day for a month, an amount equivalent to 50 to 100 joints each day.

A similar pattern prevails in every other area of marijuana research. For example, the Federal Bureau of Narcotics and Dangerous Drugs found chromosome damage in marijuana users in 1970, but the Department of Health, Education and Welfare found none in 1971. Wesley Hall, at that time president-elect of the American Medical Association, stated at a news conference on March 6, 1971, that an AMA study showed that marijuana caused sterility and birth defects. After being severely criticized by the National Institute of Mental Health and the chairman of the AMA Committee on Drug Dependence, Hall admitted on March 25, 1971, that no evidence had been found that marijuana caused either birth defects or diminished sexual capacity. Hall's explanation: "I still care about morality and decency and I'm tired of phrases like 'credibility gap.'"

The chromosome break hypothesis was supported by two studies, but both have been criticized on methodological grounds. The first (Stenchever, 1973; cited in Zinberg, 1976) was done without obtaining any information on the subjects' condition before they used marijuana. The second, reported at the Eastland hearings by Akira Morishima, used only three subjects.

A. M. G. Campbell and his associates reported in 1971 that they had found evidence of brain damage in ten heavy smokers of marijuana. But in 1972 Lester Grinspoon pointed out that of Campbell's ten subjects, eight had used amphet-

amines; four had had head injuries; several had used heroin, morphine, sedatives, and barbiturates; and all ten had used LSD and alcohol (a drug that is known to cause eventual brain damage). In 1973 A. J. Stunkard and his associates found no neurological or neuropsychological differences between a group of 29 student marijuana users and a control group of nonusers.

The two claims against marijuana that are most difficult to evaluate are its alleged interference with the immune response and with sexual potency. S. Gupta and his associates reported in 1973 that T-lymphocytes of marijuana smokers had a weaker reaction to sheep red blood cells than those of nonusers. But in 1975 S. C. White and his associates examined microcultures of blood lymphocytes of 12 long-term users and a control group of nonusers and found no difference. Here, however, the picture is complicated by the fact that the studies are not quite parallel.

In 1974 R. Kolodny found the testosterone blood levels of 20 male users to be lower than those of 20 nonusers. E. M. Brecher pointed out that testosterone levels vary tremendously from month to month, day to day, and hour to hour. To check Kolodny's results, J. H. Mendelson tested 27 male subjects for 5 days, then gave them all the marijuana they wanted for 21 days, then tested them again for 5 days. (They were locked inside a hospital ward the entire time.) Mendelson reported that the testosterone levels of the heavy and occasional users were all in the normal range and not significantly different from each other. Kolodny then had 13 male subjects refrain from smoking for two weeks, after which they remained in a locked hospital ward for three months. For the first 11 days they were given no marijuana and then were given a fixed amount daily. From the fourth week on, their testosterone blood levels decreased.

Kolodny's latter study seems convincing, except for one fact: serum testosterone level is largely a function of sexual excitement. That is, the higher a male's sexual excitement, the higher his testosterone blood level. Assuming that

Kolodny's subjects were heterosexually oriented, locking them up together in a hospital ward for three months could easily have introduced a variable that had nothing to do with the effects of marijuana.

Finally, no convincing evidence has been produced that marijuana leads to psychosis or to heroin use. The steppingstone-to-heroin idea, which has been consistently discredited, rests on the assumption that sequence denotes causality. Furthermore, studies of heroin users show that the first intoxicant used by the overwhelming majority is alcohol. To argue that alcohol leads to heroin would, of course, be just as meaningless as arguing that marijuana leads to heroin.

The most that can be said at present about the physical dangers of marijuana is that inhaling any kind of smoke into the lungs can hardly be good for one's health. Moreover, any intoxicant impairs some mental and physical functions, and driving under the influence of an intoxicant is unquestionably dangerous. Nevertheless marijuana (in contrast to tobacco, alcohol, heroin, barbiturates, and amphetamines) has not produced one fatality attributable directly to use of the drug. No evidence of physical dependence has been found, nor does its already widespread use appear to have led to a significant amount of psychological dependence. Its popularity will probably continue to increase in the foreseeable future unless, of course, harmful effects begin to be uncovered as a result of long-term, carefully conducted research.

Other Psychoactive Agents

When most people talk about "drugs" they refer only to narcotics, LSD, and marijuana; but there are numerous other substances in everyday use, as well as a large variety of over-the-counter drugs, that are also psychoactive. These include the volatile solvents that are found in paint thinner, lighter fluid, gasoline, and airplane glue; and socially approved drugs, such as tranquilizers, aspirin, cough syrups, sleeping aids, laxatives, tobacco, and alcohol.

Volatile Substances. A particularly dangerous and not uncommon practice among today's youth is inhaling airplane glue, hairspray, or any of the other volatile chemicals. Typically the user empties a tube of glue into a rag, thereby saturating it, and sniffs the fumes; or he may inhale it from a plastic bag. In either case the effects produced are as potent and dangerous as those accompanying heroin or morphine use. In the case of hairspray, death may be almost instantaneous.

Volatile chemicals are central nervous system depressants, very much like alcohol, narcotics, and barbiturates; consequently their initial effects are exhilarating and create a feeling of release. Tolerance to these chemicals develops much more rapidly than to the other substances, however, usually within several weeks, and the habitual user must inhale increasingly larger amounts to obtain the initial high.

Because of their inexpensiveness and easy accessibility, the solvents tend to appeal to younger people and to those in the lower socioeconomic groups. According to one report, glue sniffers are usually boys, some as young as 8, with an average age of about 14, who are introduced to the habit by schoolmates and friends. Abuse of these solvents, which is almost always an inevitable consequence of use, is accompanied by truancy and other antisocial behavior, usually of a violent or erratic nature (Houser, 1969).

The *subjective* high obtained by sniffing lasts about thirty minutes to an hour and the effect resembles an acute alcoholic intoxication—the user talks nonsense, slurs his speech, is dizzy, and loses his balance. After about an hour, depending on the amount inhaled (or sometimes injected), he shows poor judgment, is nauseated, vomits, and sometimes loses consciousness or becomes stuporous. During this latter stage, lasting about an hour, he is unable to recall what he was doing. Habitual glue sniffers experience visual and auditory hallucinations that are as frightening as those of alcoholics.

The *physical damage* inflicted by solvents may take the form of organic lesions to body tissues. The mucous membranes and the respiratory tract become irritated, sometimes leading users to inject these substances directly into the bloodstream, hence accelerating some of their damaging effects to the liver, kidneys, heart, and brain. There have been reports of brain damage directly traceable to the use of these chemicals, and incidents of death due to plastic bag suffocation as well as cardiac and respiratory arrests are becoming common with their increasing abuse.

Tranquilizers. The use of tranquilizers in our society became fashionable almost immediately upon their introduction in 1955 as the pill that would bring new happiness to millions of people. Miltown and Equanil were the trade names by which these meprobamates,[4] as they are called generically, were marketed. Their main therapeutic use was and still is in the treatment of anxiety, muscular spasms, and minor convulsions. The most popular minor tranquilizers in recent years have been Valium and Librium. A Veterans Administration report, *Drug Treatment and Psychiatry* (VA, 1970, p. 15), for example, indicates that any of these antianxiety drugs "can modify crippling anxieties and diminish the mounting tension that often precedes and accompanies impulsive and "acting-out" behaviors."

Psychic dependence, or habituation, occurs with these drugs, especially among individuals who take them regularly to get through the day. When the daily dosage is abruptly halted, according to one source (Lingeman, 1969), these

---

[4]These are the *minor tranquilizers;* for information on the *major tranquilizers,* used mostly in the treatment of the psychoses, see Chapter 21 and other sources (Lingeman, 1969; Ray, 1972).

people may be afflicted with a *rebound* effect, which consists of a reemergence of their former symptoms, but this time in magnified form.

Prolonged and heavy use, which has become increasingly more common in recent years, may also result in physical dependence with withdrawal symptoms that include tremors, insomnia, gastrointestinal distress, hallucinations, convulsions, and sometimes death. Furthermore, as has been discovered on the street, alcohol may potentiate the drug's effects, thus increasing the danger of death from respiratory collapse.

Other Socially Approved Drugs. Of all the socially approved and legally sanctioned psychoactive drugs available today, *aspirin* (acetylsalicylic acid) is by far the cheapest, most accessible substance and, though it has been a very commonly used medicine since 1899, it is probably the least understood among chemical agents. Current American annual consumption of salicylate and other aspirin combinations amounts to an estimated 20 billion tablets. These compounds have three main medical actions: they reduce inflammation in tissue and joints, combat fever by influencing the balance between the production and loss of body heat, and relieve pain, possibly because of selective central nervous system depressant effects by mechanisms that are not yet understood (Hammond, 1971).

Although aspirin is considered a harmless household product by most people, some sources indicate that it is the most frequent cause of drug-induced disturbances resulting in hospital admissions (Nowlis, 1969). According to another report (Ogle, 1967), there were 5700 poison cases in Florida in 1966, of which 418 were reported by the four hospitals in Pinellas County. Of these 418, almost half were cases of poisoning from other medicines, and 92 were from aspirin.

For most people acute salicylate poisoning occurs at excessively high dosages. The symptoms of such poisoning may include headache, dizziness, ringing or buzzing in the ears, blurred vision, disorientation, lethargy, sweating, thirst, nausea, vomiting, and diarrhea. As poisoning progresses, the central nervous system effects set in, and they are marked by depression, stupor, and coma, possibly followed by respiratory collapse, convulsions, and sometimes death.

Fortunately, however, aspirin, unlike alcohol, narcotics, and other psychoactive agents, is not sought for the high it produces; and its abuse, when it occurs, is almost always a consequence of accidental therapeutic overdosage or intentional self-destruction.

Tobacco is another of our society's approved drugs and, although not generally regarded as a problem drug, causes more health problems and deaths than all drugs combined—with the possible exception of alcohol.

Unlike the use of many of the drugs covered so far, cigarette smoking yields no obvious pleasures or benefits to its user, except the anxiety that it allays *after* a user has become physically and psychologically dependent on nicotine. On the other hand its physiological effects, most of which are by now well known, are devastating. Cigarette smoking has been linked to an impressive increase in age-specific death rates, the risk being related to the amount smoked; it has been associated with a substantial increase in cardiovascular diseases and has been correlated with chronic bronchitis and coughing, as well as cancer of the lung, larynx, esophagus (Horn, 1968), lip, throat, and jaw. Freud's chain-smoking of cigars is a classic example of drug dependence. He continued his habit to the very end even though it led to excruciatingly painful jaw cancer, many operations, disfigurement, and eventually death.

Drug Users and Their Motivations

Thus far we have focused mainly on drugs as physiological and psychoactive substances; we turn now to the questions of who uses drugs and what motivates them to do so.

Surveys and Interviews

A number of surveys and door-to-door canvassing studies have been conducted on college campuses and among other drug users. Information gathered by either procedure is, of course, subject to a number of criticisms. For one, there is no way to know the extent of distortion that occurs as a result of over- or underreporting; for another, it is difficult to differentiate a "user" from an "abuser." As Baughman aptly observed (1972, p. 548), "Too often . . . surveys lump the chronic and deeply involved drug abuser with the 'spree' or very occasional user." On the other hand, however, Blum and his associates (1969b) reported data suggesting a high correspondence ($r = .78$) between people's stated willingness to take drugs and their response to social invitations to use them illicitly, thus validating somewhat the self-reports of admitted drug users.

College Campus Studies. Survey findings on drug use and abuse have been reported from several colleges and universities—Brooklyn College, Carnegie–Mellon University, Dartmouth, Yale, Wesleyan, and several other schools (Pearlman, 1968; Goldstein et al., 1970; King, 1969; Imperi et al., 1968; Robbins et al., 1970; Blum et al., 1969b). Predictably the data of these studies show a mix of information; but there are many similarities as well. We shall focus mainly on the reports of a survey conducted at Carnegie–Mellon University (Goldstein et al., 1970, 1975; Goldstein, 1971a, 1971b, 1972, 1973a, 1973b, 1975a, 1975b) and will emphasize the similarities of its findings to other studies rather than the differences.

Goldstein (1971b) found drug users to be more likely than nonusers to come from urban or suburban upper middle-class families; to have better educated parents; to have a higher family income; to have come from a Jewish background, or one with little or no emphasis on formal religion, rather than from a Catholic background; to be more liberal politically; to prefer humanities or fine arts to other academic fields; to believe that marijuana is not physiologically addictive and that it does not lead to use of LSD or heroin or criminal activity; and to estimate higher numbers of others who have used marijuana. No clear-cut relationships were uncovered between marijuana use and sex of the persons, grades earned in school, and frequency of participation in extracurricular activities either on or off the campus. The trends of the marijuana findings were even more pronounced for users of the more "exotic" drugs (LSD, amphetamines, barbiturates, heroin). Heavier users of stimulants and depressants had lower grades and were less likely than nonusers to participate in on-campus extracurricular activities.

But the most compelling motivation for all drug use was peer use. Goldstein (1975a) suggests that peers may serve as a source of reassurance to the novice and may provide knowledge of techniques. The presence of friends can be comforting because they are associated with previous pleasant experiences. Also, affiliation can reduce specific fears and provide help in reducing uncertainty about drug use.

Furthermore, Goldstein and his associates (Goldstein, 1975b; Goldstein et al., 1975) report in an extensive study, which included all students who entered Carnegie–Mellon in 1968 and again in 1972, that most marijuana users intended to continue with this drug but not with LSD or heroin. Typically they became marijuana users as a result of having been introduced to it by one or two same-sex peers who were present at the initiation, and this drug was the fourth of fifth psychoactive substance they tried (out of a possible 17 listed in the survey questionnaire). The most frequently mentioned reasons for using marijuana were "to get high, feel good"; "curiosity" (first use); and "to explore the inner self." Once the drug habit has begun, the students' evaluations of their drug experience depend in large part on their expectations, and users' expectations are largely determined by what they have heard from their friends or have previously experienced themselves. Beginning users, with less experience to draw on, reassure themselves that the experience will be positive by carefully preparing themselves. These preparations often include elaborate practices designed to give reassurance that use will be safe and beneficial. Such preparations lose importance once the weight of accumulated experience becomes largely positive.

Among those students who had previously decreased or ceased marijuana use, the reasons most commonly mentioned were that they no longer cared to experience its effects, that it was illegal, and that they had a negative experience with the drug. The starting times for various drugs were also revealing. In a 1968 survey, for example, among college students with more than one marijuana experience and no other illegal drug use, none had started their marijuana experiences in elementary school; 5 percent began to use it in high school or afterward, but before college; 28 percent during the freshman year of college; 26 percent during the sophomore year; 24 percent during the junior year; 6 percent in the senior year; and 11 percent after college or while in graduate school. In other words, at least during the period sampled, college was the place to initiate this practice.

The preceding figures as well as the following ones, also collected by Goldstein but relating to the use of other drugs, are remarkably consistent with the findings of other studies (see, for example, Eells, 1968). Users of amphetamines, barbiturates, tranquilizers, narcotics, and hallucinogens who had used one of these substances at least ten times began their drug experiences as follows: elementary school, 0 percent; high school or immediately thereafter, 19 percent; freshman year, 19 percent; sophomore year, 13 percent; junior year, 7 percent; senior year, 5 percent; and after college or while in graduate school, 5 percent (no reply, 31 percent). More recently Goldstein (1973b) found that first experiences with psychoactive drugs occurred earlier than in college. And even more recently Goldstein and his associates (Goldstein et al., 1975) report that cannabis use in college has increased, but that the percentage of these users wanting to progress beyond cannabis is actually decreasing (from 20 percent down to 10 percent between the classes of 1968 and 1972).

The Counterculture. A survey conducted by cultural anthropologist John Weakland (1969) among so-called hippies and flower children of the late 1960s, although more broadly focused on the meaning of this subcultural scene, is also of interest for the information it yields on the characteristics of and reasons given for drug usage. This information was collected by field workers at a campsite at Big Sur in northern California, in the Haight–Ashbury district of San Francisco, at several "be-ins" held in San Francisco and Palo Alto, and at Timothy Leary's public "Psychedelic Celebration." Some of the data are also based on interviews conducted in a variety of settings, including offices and among hippie hitchhikers, and from written materials such as may be found in the "underground press" (San Francisco *Oracle*, Berkeley *Barb*, Los Angeles *Free Press*, and Haight–Ashbury *Songbook*). We shall mention only a few of the more salient features from this vast array of information.

Drug use within the counterculture was mainly stated to be for the purpose of getting a "high," either for "kicks" or for "consciousness expansion." Many expressed the feeling that the straight world's attitudes toward their drug use were stupid, hypocritical, and motivated by false or nonrational concerns over the possible hazards of drug use. Again as with college student surveys, it appears that many of these users came from middle-class families and were themselves quite intelligent (but not always communicative). They tended to attribute their dropping out to such events as the Vietnam war, civil rights struggles (and frustrations), and widespread student dissatisfaction with the nature of the educational system.

More specifically, as when Weakland studied individual cases of drug users and their relationships with their authoritarian or permissive parents, the data seemed to indicate that drug use was simply another symptom of faulty family relationships and of intrafamilial frictions. For example, one high school girl described how her mother had encouraged her to read about the dangers of drug use and not to experiment with drug taking just because of peer group pressures. As a result the girl read rather extensively in the literature on drug use, and then reported to her mother that there was little evidence to support the popular notion of marijuana's harmful effects, although she had not yet tried it herself. Weakland's description of the mother's reaction is interesting (1969, p. 367):

Her mother's response was to hit the ceiling and to say she knew otherwise—on the basis of a couple of popular magazine and newspaper stories she had seen. In reporting this story, the girl made it clear that it was not simply her mother's position and authority she was complaining about, but the bind in which she had been put.

We might paraphrase this youngster's feelings somewhat as follows: "If my mother had made up her mind about the issue anyway, then why did she tell me to read up on the matter?" One might speculate also that the mother's hypocrisy in this instance was representative of the overall mother–daughter relationship, and that if drugs were not easily accessible to this youngster, she would express her defiance in some other antisocial way.

Personality Questionnaires

Many of the above survey studies included personality inventories as part of the procedure. On the basis of these tests Goldstein and his associates at Carnegie–Mellon (1970), for example, compared amphetamine and alcohol users with nonusers on the *California Psychological Inventory* (Gough, 1960), and on the Allport–Vernon *Study of Values* (see Allport, 1961). His results, which are congruent with those obtained by many others (Haagen, 1970; Hogan et al., 1970; Blum et al., 1969b) were as follows: users tend to score higher than nonusers in the direction of greater poise, but score lower on scales measuring well-being and self-satisfaction. Moreover users are inclined to be more nonconforming than nonusers, and more self-centered, less achievement-oriented by conforming means, less secure, less optimistic about vocational futures, and more disorganized under stress. Furthermore Goldstein reported that drug users were more likely than the others to be flexible in thinking, inclined toward aesthetic and social values, more apt to be rebellious toward rules and conventions, and less oriented than nonusers toward economic, political, and religious values.

Three salient facts emerge from these studies on drug users' motivations. First, it is apparent that in college and counterculture settings, drug users come from more privileged families than nonusers. Blum and his associates (1969b) theorize, in this regard, that people from higher socioeconomic groups use more drugs than others because drugs are more available to them in the home, because they have had more experience with the healing powers of drugs, and because they have somehow learned that drugs may fulfill certain of their intangible needs.

Second, the roles of the school and family in drug use may be important in that the school provides the setting for peer group pressures and the home lays the groundwork for subsequent participation in unapproved behaviors. It is easier, of course, to comprehend the force of the school than that of the home because the latter's influence is more subtle. But they both probably interact in a fairly complex way, with the home being the more important of the two. To assess the influence of the home, Smart and Fejer (1972) obtained data about the drug use patterns of nearly 10,000 Toronto students and their parents as reported by the students. They found a positive relationship between the parents' use of to-

bacco, alcohol, and tranquilizing drugs and the students' reported use of drugs of all kinds. These results can be interpreted to support a modeling theory of drug use in which young people may use their parents as models in deciding whether to use drugs.

Third, once drug use is begun, almost regardless of its original motivating source, the user learns of its anxiety-reducing and sometimes pleasure-inducing properties. Further drug use then becomes simply a product of the drug's self-reinforcing qualities.

In addition to these motivations Lipinski and Lipinski (1970) list the following factors as determining the drug use of some people: curiosity; the feeling of missing something or not being "with it"; a need to prove one's openness to new things and one's emotional maturity; a search for meaning; escape from feelings of inadequacy; and an end to interpersonal shyness and isolation.

Prevention and Treatment

Traditionally, two approaches have been used to prevent drug abuse. The first approach is to declare the drug illegal, hoping thereby to keep the addict or prospective user from getting the drug. The second approach is to preach mental health. Although neither solution is effective, it should be noted that both focus on the individual as the target for intervention.

A third approach, one that has not yet been tried, places the burden of drug prevention squarely on society. Its thesis, most ably proposed by Lennard and his associates at the University of California in San Francisco (1971, 1972), is that the individual is only one variable in this complex system and that any attack upon the problem of drug abuse must be launched at the complex interlocking system that involves, in addition, the drug industry, the medical profession, and the mass media (including the underground press). Such an approach should emphasize imaginative social engineering rather than attention to just one segment of these interrelationships; therefore it calls for a program that strikes at the very heart of the problem of contemporary drug abuse. In short it must shift the focus of attention from the user to the society that has created a need for drugs.

This view contrasts sharply with most current approaches to drug abuse, which pay little attention to the growing use and abuse of these agents by the society at large.

Before launching such a campaign, however, one must understand the background of drug use and abuse today; a good way to start is by taking a look at prevailing attitudes toward the use of approved drugs in our society. We are daily encouraged to solve our problems by taking drugs: pep pills to wake up in the morning or to stay awake late at night; tranquilizers and sedatives to relax us. The message is both persistent and clear—if you can't cope, drug yourself.

Children and adolescents are realists in the sense that they pay less attention to their parents' words of warning about the perils of drugs than to the martini in father's hand and the assortment of tranquilizers and sedatives in the drawer of mother's bed table. Middle-class parents often see drug abuse in terms of right and wrong, but their children sometimes see it more in terms of warfare between competing value systems. More than a few have expressed the view that the use of drugs to obtain pleasure (as opposed to a deadening of the senses) is what really seems threatening to their elders. That view may be simplistic, but it will undoubtedly persist until someone answers it effectively.

Treatment of drug abuse has usually meant helping individuals abstain from their former habits and controlling the symptoms of the drug's withdrawal. This may involve hospitalization, methadone treatment (for narcotics), tranquilizing drugs, recreational and occupational therapy, and, in some instances, psychotherapy upon release from the hospital. In the remainder of this chapter we shall focus first on the treatment of narcotics users in hospitals, then on one of the

self-help groups available to assist these and other drug-dependent types, and finally on methadone maintenance as an alternative program for narcotics users.

It is probably as difficult for a physician to recognize the narcotics abuser as it is to treat him or her. The abuser may be a patient in a doctor's office (perhaps even another physician), a member of a prominent family, or a stranger with a plausible story of needing drugs only until his or her own physician can be contacted. Occasionally the drug-dependent person has a good cover story, telling about angina pectoris, a kidney infection, migraine headache, or hemorrhoids, even detailing symptoms realistically, and then suggesting that his or her regular physician customarily prescribes narcotics to relieve the pain. The narcotics addict may even show a drug label based on another physician's prescription and claim that this drug had been very effective. The user will appear, in all likelihood, to be physically and mentally normal.

If drug abuse is suspected, the most important finding that the examiner may make will be the presence of needle marks on arms, legs, hands, abdomen, or any of the less obvious parts of the anatomy into which the narcotic has been injected; or if the user has been off drugs for a while, there may be signs associated with withdrawal.[5] The only sure way of demonstrating habitual narcotics use is to bring on the withdrawal sickness by injecting N-allylnormophine, a relatively new drug highly effective as an antidote for morphine, heroin, and similar narcotics. Injected into someone who has recently taken such drugs, it induces signs of withdrawal within 15 minutes.

Physicians do not usually treat narcotic users privately because they must control their intake of drugs completely; such control almost always

---

[5]Other signs of drug use include poor appetite, personal slovenliness, slow and halting speech, and blood spotting on clothes (Laurie, 1967).

requires hospitalization. Until quite recently the only institutions available for treatment, unless patients or their families could afford a private sanitarium, were the Public Health Service hospitals at Lexington, Kentucky, and Fort Worth, Texas. Now such treatment is available at an increasing number of municipal and state hospitals. Information about these installations can be obtained from local, county, and state health departments.

Treatment for narcotics dependency usually consists of several phases. First the individual is helped to overcome the symptoms of withdrawal illness. This is sometimes accomplished by substituting one drug for another. The substitute drug that is often used, *methadone*, has a drug-effect span of 24 to 36 hours compared to heroin's 8 hours. When given daily, methadone produces two effects: it relieves the persistent "drug hunger" that often plagues users withdrawing from narcotics; and it induces a *cross-tolerance* for heroin so that it prevents the addict from obtaining a heroin high during this period.[6] We shall discuss methadone maintenance shortly.

In the second stage of treatment there is a period of convalescence from withdrawal, during which the patient receives medical and surgical treatment for cuts and injuries that may have been self-inflicted during an attempt to force narcotics into the various openings in his or her body.

Following convalescence, a period that lasts about two weeks, the patient is put in an orientation ward. There normal appetite and strength are regained, although irritability and restlessness may still be experienced—symptoms that often last for several more months. In the orientation ward, the patient is interviewed by members of the vocational, correctional, social service, and psychiatric staffs, with a view toward preparing him or her for life outside. During this time the patient is assigned to jobs in the hospital and is counseled on how to find and hold a position when discharged. The primary purpose of this vocational program is to help patients establish steady work habits and, in general, to change their lifestyles. Unfortunately because of limited professional staffs in most hospitals, fewer than 25 percent of the patients receive psychotherapy or any direct psychological treatment. Moreover, some people resist such treatment and others are incapable of benefiting from it.

The last phase of hospital treatment, probably the most difficult to achieve, occurs after hospital discharge. No matter where the drug user is treated, whether in a private sanitarium, county or state hospital, or one of the federal centers, hospitalization is only the first step. Post-hospital supervision, or aftercare, is just as essential; if this is neglected, the ex-drug user simply reverts to his or her prior drug habit because the personality predisposition that originally led to drug use has not changed, and the same drug-taking companions and environmental conditions await the former drug user's return, usually with no job, and quite probably no home. Because our society still unfortunately considers drug dependency a crime rather than a disorder, the conditions that greet the patient on returning home may be worse after release from the hospital than before. It is precisely at this time that drug users need a group similar to Alcoholics Anonymous. There are several such self-help programs— Delancey Street, Daytop Village, Phoenix House, and Gateway House are just a few examples. Synanon, before its recent troubles, had helped many individuals outgrow their drug dependence through such techniques as the use of attack therapy in a group setting (the "square games") to destroy the addict's defenses.

Methadone Maintenance. Earlier we mentioned that methadone is often used during the first

[6]It should also be added that methadone does not produce cross-tolerance for the nonopiates (stimulants, barbiturates, alcohol), which are therefore sometimes used to gain the euphoria denied by the smaller oral doses of methadone (Lennard et al., 1972).

There are now a number of self-help clinics across the country. In this "open door" drug clinic, a young man's arm is being examined for track marks, the evidence of frequent intravenous injections.

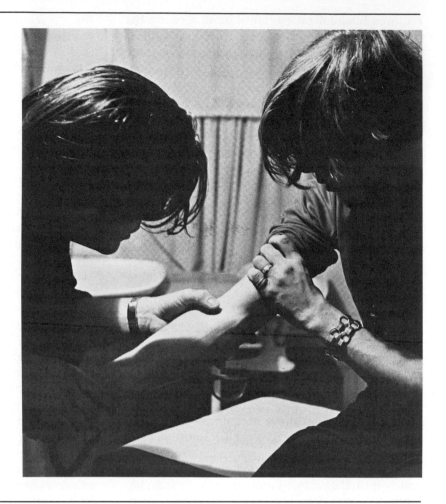

stage of hospital care; there are now more than five hundred community-based *methadone maintenance* centers in the United States. The idea of these federally supported centers is to make the narcotic readily available to the hundreds of thousands of heroin users who would never seek out a hospital program.

The methadone maintenance technique was developed in 1965 by two physicians, Vincent Dole and Marie Nyswander, a husband and wife research team who found that it was possible to persuade heroin addicts to substitute oral intake of methadone for intravenous heroin. They considered this substitution important because they believed that heroin addiction's permanent and irreversible changes cause the addict to experience a lifelong need for opiates.

But methadone maintenance as a program of treatment presents several problems not encountered in the self-help group approaches. First, as Lennard and his associates clarified in a *Science* article, "The Methadone Illusion" (1972), many of the beneficial effects of this synthetic substitute for heroin are due to the smaller oral doses given on the maintenance programs. When either drug is taken intravenously, the results are much more sudden and subjectively dramatic, and their physiological and subjective effects are roughly equivalent. Thus it is the oral administration and not the particular drug that produces the lesser effect during methadone maintenance.

Another problem that has recently emerged in many cities of the United States is that methadone has made its way, by one means or another, into the hands of illegal pushers. Consequently the federal government is now exercising tighter controls over the dispensation of this drug to the point at which physicians are no longer able to prescribe it and druggists may not sell it unless they are part of an approved program. But whether these controls will work is a moot question; in the meantime one of the major reasons for giving methadone—its legality—has been temporarily undermined. It is now available illicitly.

Still another problem of methadone maintenance is that ex-heroin users will have to keep taking the drug for the rest of their lives. This prospect raises an additional problem: if the government, for one reason or another, should abandon this program, this country will be confronted with many more persons who now have substituted one addiction for another. And considering the greater potency of methadone, present problems with heroin addiction will be minor compared with methadone dependence. Its price on the illicit market, of course, will also increase if the government discontinues its free distribution, and we will be where we are now with heroin.

And, finally, to quote Lennard and his colleagues (1972, p. 881), "If heroin use were 'the problem,' then methadone might well be the answer." But the methadone solution is just one more facet of the real problem, which is the "popular illusion that a drug can be a fast, cheap, and magical answer to complex human and social problems." Lennard and his coauthors then conclude as follows (p. 884):

What is required are profound changes in the professional and public understanding of the promotion and use of all psychoactive drugs. We need to concern ourselves with the entire spectrum of drug use, not just the use of heroin.

The new look in prevention will be educational and promotional, aimed at the society that produces drug users and not at the individual. Treatment, which for narcotics dependency consists mainly of hospitalization or methadone maintenance, is a difficult and lengthy process. Self-help groups such as Phoenix House, Delancey Street, and Daytop Village, with their emphasis on cold-turkey abstinence and changing the addict's lifestyle, are invaluable both as aftercare facilities for narcotics and other drug users and as viable alternatives for hospitalization or methadone maintenance. The general feeling of ex-addicts, in this regard, incidentally, is that drug maintenance programs are tempting (but dangerous) solutions to a difficult problem; invariably they advocate self-help group cures.

Summary

Virtually all drugs exert psychoactive effects; the precise effects of any given substance, however, are sometimes difficult to predict because, in large part, they depend on such additional factors as method of administration, dosage level, expectations, and setting.

Drug dependence may be of two types. The first is a physical dependence, which consists of tolerance and withdrawal. Tolerance is the organism's capacity to withstand ever-increasing dosages of some substances; withdrawal illness occurs after the drug has been abruptly withheld from the individual; it is characterized by restlessness, stomachache, and muscular twitching, as well as nausea and malaise. Sometimes the consequences are more serious. The second type of dependence is psychic, and it is manifested mainly by a need to repeatedly take some drugs in order to cope with reality.

The major chemical substances in use today include the narcotics, mainly morphine, heroin, and methadone; stimulants such as the amphetamines (Dexedrine, Methedrine, Benzedrine); depressants of the barbiturate type (Nembutal, Seconal, phenobarbital); hallucinogens (LSD); marijuana, which in high dosages is also a hallucinogen; such volatile solvents as glue and paint thinner; and the socially approved drugs (tranquilizers, aspirin, tobacco). Although each of these exerts its beneficial or deleterious effects, depending on the setting and the concentration of active ingredients, some are more dangerous than others.

Marijuana has been the topic of greatest recent controversy. The emotions surrounding marijuana research suggest that the drug is a symbol of a personal and intellectual freedom that our society is not yet prepared to condone. As in alcoholism, successful treatment for drug abuse often involves group interaction among drug addicts and former addicts.

Terms and Concepts to Master

Dependency	Stimulant
Depressant	Tolerance
Hallucinogen	THC
Methadone maintenance	Withdrawal

11 The Neuroses and Hysterias

Anxiety has traditionally been considered the chief characteristic of the neuroses.[1] How the individual defends against that anxiety determines the pattern of his or her disordered behavior, but whatever that pattern is, the defensive behavior is ultimately self-defeating.

Ironically the neurosis seems to perpetuate itself through its very ineffectiveness, like the drugs that reengender the stress they were supposed to relieve. The neurotic is thus caught in a vicious cycle, in which each failure of his defenses seems to reinforce the defensive behavior he has learned. Not surprisingly the neurotic feels increasingly powerless and inadequate. As the world repeatedly fails to respond to his frantic efforts to ward off the threats he senses, he is seized by feelings of futility and desperation. As long as the neurotic pattern persists, the individual's personal growth is blocked.

Major Disorders

Because of anxiety's central role in the formation and perpetuation of neurotic patterns of behavior, we shall describe those patterns in an order that proceeds from the least to the most success-

---

[1] The neuroses are no longer a classification category in DSM III (APA, 1980). Instead, some of the disorders covered in this chapter come under an "Anxiety Disorders" heading; others fall into "Somatoform," and "Dissociative" classifications.

ful defense against anxiety. First, however, a word of caution: although the clinical descriptions in this and other chapters tend to neatly categorize people into readily identifiable diagnostic classes, the actual clinical picture is rarely so clear-cut. Symptomatology in the behavior disorders overlaps considerably; our presentation simplifies for the sake of textbook exposition.

Anxiety Disorder

Anxiety disorder occurs when the defenses, especially repression, are functioning inadequately, or not at all. Although no two anxiety attacks are alike, they are generally marked by episodes of extreme apprehension and restlessness, accompanied by periodic attacks of heart palpitation and sweating, which may be so overwhelming that the individual panics. The panic reaction itself is an intensely frightening experience, as we mentioned earlier, that lasts several minutes or more and may recur several times during a day or night.

Anxious persons often talk of "climbing the walls" or believe that they are "going crazy"; and because of the accompanying subjective symptoms of rapid heartbeat, difficult breathing, and increased perspiration, they may also express concern about coronary or other somatic crises. Their other reported experiences include feelings of nausea, asphyxiation, gastrointestinal distress, and sudden severe headaches with stiffness of the neck and shoulders.

Decisions about minor matters may precipitate major crises for people with anxiety disorders because they are insecure. They simply do not trust their own ability or judgment. Paradoxically, however, though they may have difficulty making these routine decisions, they have little or no difficulty in deciding important matters. It is not uncommon, for example, for them to put off buying a particular suit of clothes or shoes because they cannot make up their minds about style or cost, but they can reach an instantaneous decision to change their jobs, even though this may involve uprooting and moving halfway across the continent.

The current DSM III (APA, 1980) description of anxiety disorder emphasizes its distinction from the phobias and from normal fear and apprehension; its essential features include motor tension, autonomic hyperactivity, apprehensive expectation, vigilance, and scanning.

An example of this disorder is presented as Case Report 11.1, and we call particular attention to the psychological functions of John L.'s symptoms. His anxiety attacks, which were almost always precipitated by such stressful circumstances as lecturing before a group or being teased by his fellow workers, served as an excuse for his incompetence. His reasoning, although possibly not at a conscious level, was that so long as he had these "attacks" he couldn't be held responsible for his poor performance. In other words his anxiety was a convenient alternative to facing up to the possibility that he might not pass muster. Ironically, however, in John's case this "insanity bit," as he called it, became the occasion for further anxiety.

Case Report 11.1 *Anxiety Disorder*

John L., a laborer at the United States Steel Plant, age 26, came to the Veterans Administration outpatient clinic because he feared he was losing his mind. Even before going into the military he had been having what he called "panic attacks" during which he would become dizzy and weak, and then completely immobile. During his two years of army duty he experienced these attacks most often while lecturing the troops on the dismantling and assembling of weapons. Afterward he showed great concern about their opinions of a "goofball" like him "trying to tell them how to do something."

Following his military service, he accepted a laborer's job at the steel mill, and while acknowledging that he was not intellectually challenged by the work, he explained that he would attend college and then seek other employment as soon as he overcame his "insanity bit." However, he feared being unable to compete with the others even in the present job, and he frequently complained that his coworkers teased and harassed him.

One day, during lunch break, while being ridiculed by some of his associates, he had his first real anxiety attack at work. He reported that something seemed to snap in his ears, after which everything sounded louder than usual, and he held his hands over his ears until he fell to the ground. Once down, he was seized by the fear that he might never get up again; but he jumped up suddenly and reassured everyone around him that he was all right. The first anxiety attack lasted about 60 seconds, but thereafter he had a constant fear of a recurrence, and he sought help because he was afraid that he was losing his mind.

Psychotherapy, conducted on a twice-a-week basis for about six months, disclosed that although his anxiety was of long duration, the immediate precipitants of his military and post-service attacks were related to his marriage just before entering the army. His wife was a vivacious young woman, who in sharp contrast to John, was self-confident and outgoing. During therapy, he began to understand the relationship between his anxiety and his lack of self-confidence as a lover, provider, and person. He had to learn also that his apprehension about future attacks was very much related to their actual occurrence.

Depressive Disorder

In this disorder one's defenses are also inadequate for coping with basic conflicts and the consequence, again, is anxiety. This time, however, the anxiety is turned inward or displaced onto the self and takes the form of sadness, dejection, and agitation; what is even more disheartening, the depressive by a process of projection finds support for his or her feelings of worthlessness in the statements of others. Therefore the depressed person is racked with feelings of guilt, discouragement, and worthlessness and is convinced that life is not worth the effort, a conviction that in day-to-day experience gains further support because of his or her repeated failures. In short, the depressive neurotic leads an inert and unhappy existence.

Except for the absence of hallucinations and delusions, this disorder resembles psychotic depression (see Chapter 14). People with either disorder cry frequently, are self-derogatory and uninterested in anything except their own preoccupations, and brood a good deal of the time, often looking as if the world had come to an end.

In contrast to psychotic depression, however, which seems to occur without any identifiable reason, this form of depression is frequently precipitated by a tangible event, such as loss of a job or the death of a close friend or relative. And in contrast to the normal's reaction, the neurotics have more than just ordinary grief. Their feelings of abandonment and hopelessness are out of proportion to the event. These features are illustrated in Case Report 11.2, the case of a divorced college student who had difficulty concentrating on her studies.

Case Report 11.2   *Depressive Disorder*

Mrs. Dorothy M., a 25-year-old divorced college student, outlined several problems she wanted help with. She said, "My relationship to boys is all fouled up." She was involved in a triangular affair

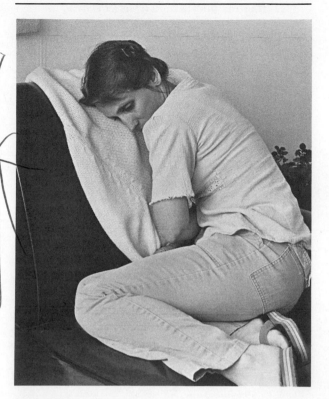

Figure 11.1
This patient's posture is typical of depressed people. The inertia that accompanies depression impedes efforts to motivate the depressed person to move from such a posture once it has been assumed.

(Courtesy of National Institute of Mental Health)

with two men, both of them under psychiatric care. She was concerned about the fact that she had "never been able to accept my responsibilities" (meaning her child and her financial responsibilities). Another problem was her difficulty in studying.

The patient felt that her problem began after going out with two young men for about ten months. Both of these men were quite disturbed emotionally, and she became upset about being a pawn between them. She expressed guilt about coming between these two friends.

*During the interview, she spoke evenly,
slightly dragging out the words, and with very little
expression in her face. She said nothing unless she
was asked and seemed to react automatically to what
she was told to do. The only evidence that she had
feelings about what she was doing was her quiet
comment, almost to herself, about the difficulty of a
task or the strain it was to do it. Her general
attitude seemed to be one of resigned compliance and
low mood.*

In terms of conspicuous symptoms a mixed-
neurosis *was an applicable diagnostic formulation.
Principally it was largely a reactive depression [the
older diagnostic label for depressive disorder (APA,
1952)] with secondary psychosomatic concomitants.
The patient had a strong feeling of guilt; she
intensely denied her aggressive impulses, but showed
hostile feelings that were especially strong toward
men and also (though she strongly denied them)
toward her child.*

*Concerning the future, she felt lost, deserted,
hopeless. In her depressed state she had considered
suicide but concluded that "it would have been an
ignominious death." However, she still had a strong
suicidal potential.*

*The treatment recommendations consisted of
psychotherapy of a supportive-counseling type with
a woman therapist.*

SOURCE: *Abridged and adapted from "Neurotic Depression and
Masochism" by Lester Luborsky, Richard Siegal, and George A.
Gross. In* Clinical studies of personality, Vol. 1, *edited by
Arthur Burton and Robert E. Harris. Copyright © 1955 by
Harper & Row, Publishers, Inc.*

Suicide is a real and present danger in all
people with depression, as we see in this case
report. We shall have more to say about suicide in
Chapter 14, in which we discuss psychotic depression.

Dorothy M.'s depression, at least to judge
from the limited information given in Case Report
11.2, may be explained in numerous ways. She
was depressed because her association with men
was unsatisfactory and because she was now
saddled with a child by her previous marriage.

These realities also contributed to her poor school
performance, which, in turn, might have engendered anger toward her child, and certainly had
to contribute to her feelings of worthlessness and
dejection.

But why guilt and worthlessness, one might
ask, rather than anxiety (as in Case Report 11.1)
or other symptoms? The answer requires close
analysis of the unique meaning depression has
for this person, and the purposes her symptoms
serve, information that can be obtained only from
a more careful study of the person than is possible here.

A feeling of worthlessness and loss of self-
esteem has been observed among black women
by Calvin Hernton in his *Sex and Racism in America*; he writes that the personality of the black
woman is a product of her response to the degra-
dation and belittling she has suffered in a white
society. This form of self-rejection involves, first,
an acceptance of another's criticism of her and,
second, an attempt to rid herself, by projection,
of her supposedly undesirable features. Thus,
according to Hernton (1965, p. 131), "Because
the Negro woman has been and is judged, by
whites and blacks alike, according to the Caucasian standard of beauty and femininity, the
American Negro woman hates herself."

That this tendency toward self-rejection has
been lessening since the 1960s (Figure 11.3)
is amply supported by two studies that have suggested that black school children no longer present a picture of self-devaluation and negative
self-esteem (see Baughman, 1972; McDonald and
Gynther, 1965; Wendland, 1967).

Obsessive–Compulsive Disorder

Obsessions are persistent and repetitive intrusions of unwanted thoughts; compulsions are
urges to do certain things or certain actions or
rituals. And in many respects these obsessive
symptoms resemble the unwanted thoughts that
most people experience: the irritating TV com-

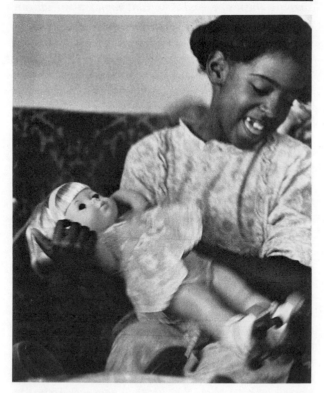

Figure 11.2
One by-product of being black in a white society is seen in this picture of a black girl playing mother to a white doll.

Figure 11.3
The self-rejection suffered by black people living in a predominantly white society has been lessened in recent years as social movements originating in the black community have inspired new pride and confidence.

mercial or jingle that persists in spite of efforts to banish it from memory; the gnawing uncertainty over whether the gas jet was shut off before leaving home; or the concerned preoccupation over minor details. Compulsive actions, likewise, plague most people: fussy tidiness; excessive attention to inconsequential matters; and fastidious dress of oneself and children. But for most people, these behaviors are transitory and temporary, whereas they are a constant part of existence for the neurotic, who is persistently burdened by unwanted thoughts and goads to action.

Paradoxically, if it were not for such actions, the obsessive–compulsive neurotic would be extremely anxious because of being forced to confront the real problems that are being avoided through the compulsive acts; but the intrusion of unacceptable thoughts and the urge to perform unacceptable actions make the individual anxious nonetheless. The neurotic abhors some of the thoughts that occur to him and is repulsed by some of his urges. More often he is simply annoyed by the silliness of his thoughts and rituals.

The obsessions and compulsions are frequently interrelated in their manifest and symbolic content, as, for example, in the case of a male college student whose obsessions consisted of intrusions of musical lyrics, which became especially strong during lectures and even stronger during important examinations. These tunes were so disruptive that he could not concentrate in class or on examination problems. His related compulsions included the urge to discard his textbooks, preferably in a place where he could not gain easy access to them (for example down the sewer or in the river). Clearly both symptoms jeopardized his success at school, and both seemed to be expressions of his concern over possible failure as a student at the university. It almost seemed as if his behavior symbolized his desire to fail by his own doing rather than by being flunked out by the school authorities.

Obsessions can also be terrifying experiences that one attempts to counteract by performing rituals. The young mother who, to take just one more example, is bothered by thoughts of killing her child may go through elaborate rituals designed to *undo* her horrible thoughts. She may also behave toward the child solicitously and display an overabundance of affection. The solicitous behavior is excessive because it is an expression of her *reaction formation,* which along with undoing is one of the principal defenses used by these neurotics, as is noted in Case Report 11.3 (Maslow and Mittelmann, 1951, pp. 429–430). Note here the extent to which husband and wife each participated in the other's maladaptive behavior.

Case Report 11.3 *Obsessive–Compulsive Neurosis*

A 30-year-old man sought treatment because he was afraid he would cut his child's, wife's, or mother's throat. He felt utterly contemptible and worthless for having such thoughts, was in constant dread of carrying them out, and even contemplated suicide. At times he did not dare touch a knife.

The patient had earlier been active in organizing his co-workers into a union. He had, however, refused an offer to be elected as their delegate to the union convention after his wife had become depressed at the thought of his being away from home for long periods of time. Shortly thereafter, in the fifth year of his marriage, his compulsive thoughts began. He had by that time stopped going out alone in the evenings, although he liked to attend political meetings, visit friends, and bowl. His wife never objected to his going out, but she became depressed whenever he did. He also gave up all his labor union activities.

When the patient came for treatment, he said his relationship with his wife was perfect and he had no criticisms of her. He claimed also to have an understanding attitude toward his mother. Only day-to-day observation enabled the therapist to determine that the patient resented both his wife and his mother and felt a great deal of conflict about them. The patient, with the aid of the therapist, was able to recognize that resentment and conflict, as well as his feeling that his wife dominated him, was unfair to him, and had interfered with his career and ambitions. He was able to see that his compulsive thoughts were especially intense whenever he stayed home to prevent his wife from becoming depressed. He also recognized the emotional trap he had put himself in: his high ideals and need for his wife's approval prevented him from allowing himself to feel his anger. If he felt angry, or if he failed to sacrifice himself for his wife, he felt worthless.

After one year of treatment the patient improved considerably. His condition then remained stationary until his wife agreed to be treated. At the end of three years the patient had recovered completely.

SOURCE: *Abridged from A. H. Maslow and B. Mittelmann. Principles of abnormal psychology. Rev. ed. Copyright 1941, 1951 by Harper & Row, Publishers, Inc.*

The Phobic Disorders

In the anxiety disorders apprehension seems to be freefloating in the sense that it is not attached to, nor apparently associated with, any event or object. This is less true among obsessive-compulsives; where anxiety does occur, it is usually tied to the individual's feelings about unacceptable thoughts, impulses, and actions. In the phobic disorders the anxiety is very much attached to events or objects, so much so that the individual becomes totally preoccupied with avoiding situations that bring him or her into contact with the feared objects.

Although the phobic's subjective experiences are similar to those of people afflicted with generalized anxiety, the phobic's tremulousness, perspiration, nausea, and even panic are associated with such objects or situations as open spaces (*agoraphobia*), closed spaces (*claustrophobia*), eating in public places, heights (*acrophobia*), airplanes, and germs, to name just a few of the many possibilities. The experiences are all alike: an intense and overwhelming fear, which the individual recognizes as *irrational* ("But why should I be afraid of a mouse?" or "I used to be able to swim; how can I possibly be so frightened of water?"), but over which he or she has little or no control.[2]

The phobic individuals have a distinct advantage over the anxious ones. Their energies are directed toward dealing with concrete, identifiable, and objective situations; and their tendency is to cope with the threat that is clearly present. Anxiety neurotics, it will be recalled, have no such clues about their discomforts and therefore have no target against which to mobilize their efforts.

In both cases, however, individuals are not able to see the connection between their reactions and the problems and stresses of daily existence. In this regard the phobic's ability to localize fear, or to focus it on a specific object, is merely a self-deception. Thus, when an unsuccessful musician says, "I am afraid of leaving the house; I fear nothing else," he or she is actually fearful of a very definite something else—an inability to compete in the world of music or a failure to build a solid career in the field. This is well illustrated in Case Report 11.4, in which Ronald H.'s expressed fear was leaving his college dormitory.

Case Report 11.4 *Phobic Neurosis*

For several months before coming to the student mental health center, Ronald H., an 18-year-old freshman at a midwestern university, panicked each time he left his dormitory room and headed toward his classes. He could not understand this since he was reasonably pleased and satisfied with his classes and professors. "It would get so bad at times," he told his freshman adviser, "that I thought I would collapse on the way to class. It was a frightening feeling and I began to be afraid to leave the dorm." Even after he returned to the dormitory, he would be unable to face anyone for hours or to concentrate on his homework. But if he remained in his own room, or not too far from it, he felt reasonably comfortable. His resident counselor suggested that he talk to someone at the student mental health center.

It became apparent during the interviews with Ronald that he had experienced similar fear reactions, although not as intensely, since about the age of 13. He also reported other fears, such as becoming contaminated by syphilis and growing prematurely bald. Both of the latter fears were sufficiently intense and persistent to cause him to compulsively scrub his hands, genitals, and head until these parts became red, and sometimes even bled. In addition, he touched doorknobs only reluctantly, never drank water from a public fountain, and only used the toilet in his home or on his dormitory floor.

Ronald understood that his fears were unfounded and exaggerated, but he also felt that

---

[2]Franz Fanon, the black psychiatrist cited earlier in this book, presents a masterful study of another variety of irrational fear, which he calls *Negrophobia* (1967, pp. 160 ff).

many of his precautions and constant worrying were necessary to avoid even greater "mental anguish" and discomfort. Sometimes, during the interviews, he could even laugh at his own behavior.

Ronald's past history indicated that since he was about 8 years old he had tended to avoid playing or competing with the other boys in the neighborhood. Because he could not run as fast or hit a ball as far as his peers, he chose to stay out of games. But more important, his mother strongly rewarded his tendency not to join the others because she was convinced that he would get hurt if he participated in their "rough-housing."

Several years later, at about the time that most boys have attained puberty, Ronald was packed off to summer camp against his better judgment. This experience was traumatic for him, because it was at camp that he began to entertain serious doubts about his completeness as a boy. At a time when most of the other boys in his cabin were completely at ease in the shower room and locker room, he discovered that he was still sexually underdeveloped. He worried a great deal about this seeming deficiency and wondered whether it signified that he was destined to become a girl. At one point he even became fearful that the other boys might attack him sexually.

Although his puberty made a belated appearance and he understood that such things could happen, he continued to worry about his masculine identity and, from time to time, even fantasized that he was a girl. At these times he became extremely anxious and seriously considered suicide as an alternative to a possible future as a homosexual. His greatest concern was that his mother would discover that she gave birth to, and raised, a monster.

The therapist's immediate goal was to remove Ronald's irrational fear of leaving the dormitory, which was accomplished with systematic desensitization (see Chapter 23). It was clear, however, that the phobias in this case were part of a deep-rooted problem of sexual identity which would require depth psychotherapy (see Chapter 22).

Phobic people's main defense mechanism is *displacement*, by means of which they are able to disconnect the actual problem in their lives from the new object that has become symbolic of it. For example, Ronald H., the young man discussed in Case Report 11.4, was fearful of leaving his dormitory, and that seemed to be his major preoccupation. This phobia, however, could have symbolized his unwillingness to place himself in any situation where he might meet someone, male or female, who might make sexual advances toward him. The precise symbolic meaning of any phobia, to repeat what we emphasized earlier, depends, of course, upon the individual's earlier experiences and family interaction patterns.

Many phobias, as in the experimental demonstration with "Albert" (see Chapter 6), can be traced to an earlier traumatic or frightening experience. For example, a child who is often punished by being locked into a dark closet may develop claustrophobia; likewise the youngster who is barked at or attacked by a dog may become frightened of animals, no matter how harmless they appear. But in many more instances the causes of the original fear-evoking stimulus are unknown.

Some phobias can also be learned by imitation, observational learning, or modeling. Bandura (1969) has argued that many of our fears are learned by observing the behavior of someone who is afraid of particular objects or persons.

Hypochondriasis

The main preoccupation of hypochondriacs is with diseases that they believe they are about to contract or from which they are actually suffering. Hypochondiacs' concern with somatic problems is so intense and so circumscribed that they suffer little anxiety about matters not related to their organs or health. They complain vaguely of multiple aches and pains, or report localized symptoms such as an aching back, bloated stomach, or, more seriously, pains in the chest radiating down the arms.[3]

One cannot easily engage the hypochondriac in conversation about anything except his or her somatic functioning. A casual "Hello, how are you" in the morning becomes the occasion for an interminable listing of the latest symptoms. After a physician has given the hypochondriac a "clean bill of health," this reassurance lasts only for a very short while. He or she soon doubts the validity of the physician's credentials and/or diagnostic acumen, and shops around for a sympathetic medical ear. Case Report 11.5 illustrates how reluctantly a hypochondriac surrenders the belief that his or her health is threatened (Maslow and Mittelmann, 1951, p. 444).

Case Report 11.5 *Hypochondriasis*

A college student complained of extensive gastric disturbances, indigestion, "weak stomach," belching, aches, and many other symptoms. Questioning showed that he had made a full-time job of studying his eating, his digestion, and his eliminative processes. For instance, he made up menus for a month in advance in which everything was weighed to the ounce. He always cooked his own meals, refusing to entrust this important task to his mother.

He spent several hours each day using muscle exercisers, breathing according to a special system, and reading medical books.

The problem that brought him to the psychologist was his relationship with his fiancee. Questioning revealed that she loved him intensely but had angered him by disparaging his symptoms.

He apparently did not love her at all but intended to marry her because "everybody gets married." He had broken off with her without any feeling of loss, even with relief, but he now wanted to know if marriage was necessary to health.

It took some time to convince him that he needed psychological treatment, and this was possible only after a very detailed examination by a medical specialist showed no medical problems. He never really made contact with the therapist and no results were being obtained by interviews; so he was sent to another therapist. This time he showed more progress, but after his therapist instructed him to give up his pills and laxatives, he did not return.

SOURCE: *Abridged from A. H. Maslow and B. Mittelmann. Principles of abnormal psychology. Rev. ed. Copyright 1941, 1951 by Harper & Row, Publishers, Inc. Reprinted by permission of the publishers.*

The dynamics of hypochondriasis are rather similar to those of the phobias in that the individual's concerns and anxieties are *displaced* to bodily functioning instead of to other objects and situations. To return to Case Report 11.5, we may note that the college student's loss of his fiancee did not ruffle him. This leads to the speculation that his hypochondriacal symptoms may have represented his anxieties about this relationship, or, still more significantly, may have been adopted to hasten the break-up. Again, like the phobias, hypochondriasis can be learned by observing others.

The Hysterias

In the hysterias, anxiety is more successfully avoided than in any of the disorders previously discussed. The behaviors of *hysteria*[4] include

---

[3]With the recent increased sophistication of the general public about medical matters, there has been a corresponding closer simulation of actual diseases. Whereas at one time physicians could easily distinguish between hypochrondriasis and bona fide physical disorders, the advent of medical articles in such popular magazines as *Reader's Digest* and *Newsweek* has made differential diagnosis more difficult.

[4] Although most clinicians agree that the prevalence of the classical or textbook varieties is diminishing, occurrences of the hysterical neuroses are still being actively reported in the psychological literature.

everything from severely incapacitating paralyses to sleepwalking. The term hysteria and many of its symptoms were described by Hippocrates, who believed it was a uniquely female disease. He ascribed the disorder to a wandering womb (*hysterikos* is Greek for uterus), and this notion was not abandoned for nearly two thousand years. Freud, in 1886, incurred the wrath of his colleagues when he lectured about a case of male hysteria.

Two types of hysteria are commonly recognized: conversion and dissociative. *Conversion hysteria* includes such somatic symptoms as blindness, deafness, aphonia, and the anesthesias and paralyses; *dissociative hysteria* includes alterations in the state of consciousness and identity, with such symptoms as amnesia, somnambulism (sleepwalking), and multiple personality (see also Chapter 7, p. 138).

As we indicated in Chapter 7, the principal defensive mechanism operating in both the conversion and the dissociative hysterias is *repression*. In the hysterias this defense is so successful in warding off anxiety that the conversion hysteric has often been described as displaying a *belle indifference*, or nonchalance, toward his disabilities. For example, rather than showing the alarm that some people may display upon discovering an infirmity, hysterics are apparently unconcerned about their aches, pains, paralyses, or sensory symptoms; moreover, they show an almost enviable optimism about their prognoses, an optimism usually not warranted by their debilitating condition.

This blandness is not entirely shared by the dissociative reactions, because in many instances, the somnambulism, amnesia, or multiple personality is itself cause for anxiety. Evidently there are strong psychological forces operating to retain one's identity; and the person becomes anxious when he realizes that the dissociations interfere with his desire to become himself again. The hysterias are extremely rare.

Conversion Hysteria. The term *conversion* was coined by Freud to convey the idea that there is a transformation of affective or psychic energy into somatic disabilities. In many cases these disabilities resemble real, organic disturbances, and it sometimes is difficult to make a differential diagnosis between the two. The key factor in these cases is that hysterical paralyses do not follow any known neuronal pathways. For example, in one type of anesthesia called "glove" paralysis, the individual feels neither pain nor touch in the area of the hand that would be covered by a glove. There is no single set of nerves that can easily be severed to cause this phenomenon.

Other sensory and perceptual phenomena include excessive sensitivity (hyperesthesia) or reduced sensitivity (hypoesthesia), the feeling of pins and needles (paresthesia), loss of feeling and sensation in one side of the body (hemianesthesia), inability to smell, deafness, tunnel vision, and blindness. These symptoms have been attributed by some to the autosuggestibility of hysterics. The exceptional suggestibility, according to one clinician (Batchelor, 1969), can be shown readily in those who are afflicted with hemianesthesia. Their anesthesias can be transferred from one side to the other side of the body by suggestion in the waking state. These sensory phenomena have also been observed to vary spontaneously from one neurological examination to the next.

Motor problems are also present in conversion hysteria, and these include tremors, especially of the hands; tics and twitching; cramps of the voluntary muscles, as in "writer's cramp"; aphonia, or the inability to talk above a whisper; and a feeling of having a lump in the throat. More serious conversion disabilities, at least in terms of their ability to incapacitate, are *astasia abasia*, in which the individual is able to sit but cannot stand or walk; *camptocormia*, or distortion of the spine, which forces the individual to assume a forward-bent posture; and *hemiplegia* and *paraplegia*, in which the individual is paralyzed on either side of the body in the first instance, or paralyzed from the waist down in the second. The latter two conversion disabilities are more difficult to distinguish from true neurological symptoms because there are nerve pathways in the brain and the spinal cord that when injured do produce hemiplegia and paraplegia, respectively; and to make the differential diagnosis even more difficult, many paralyses are accompanied by local physiological changes, the most common ones being bluishness and coldness in the affected limb and atrophy, or wastage, of the affected muscles. These changes come about because of the disuse of the affected limbs or muscles in both hysteria and actual nerve damage.

Other motor conversion disorders include choking sensations, coughing spells, difficult breathing, hiccoughing, belching, loss of appetite, nausea, headaches, and urinary and bowel retention. Some of these rather dramatic symptoms were discussed in Chapter 8, which covers symptoms of the psychophysiological disorders, a category into which they are often grouped.

Case Report 11.6 provides an unusually clear example of how conversion symptoms can supply clues to their function in a person's life situation.

Case Report 11.6 *Conversion Hysteria*

The client, a 20-year-old male college student, complained that he was unable to sit through any of his class examinations because of tremors in his writing hand, a twitching of both eyelids, and a rather severe case of "writers cramp," whenever he was able to control his tremor sufficiently to start writing. On the morning of an important test he often overslept and complained of headaches; he displayed similar incapacitating behaviors in other, nonschool situations as well.

Treatment sessions with his college counselor disclosed that he was extremely concerned about his ability to "hack it" at school, really would have preferred to be working and earning money, and was in school against his better judgment just to please

his parents. He also felt much resentment toward his parents but was somewhat ashamed of these feelings and also afraid to express them openly.

During psychotherapy, he learned that his incapacitating behaviors, maladaptive as they seemed on the surface, were actually face-saving devices that protected him against a seemingly irresolvable personal conflict. By using these symptoms, he learned, both in school and in many other situations, he was able to stay in the situation, thus avoiding displeasure to his parents, and yet to stay out of the situation, thus proving to himself that he was master of his own behavior.

Dissociative Hysteria. As the name indicates, this condition is characterized by a disunity of the individual's personality. Four major types of dissociation are recognized: somnambulism, fugue, amnesia, and multiple personality.

In *somnambulism*, or sleepwalking, a person spontaneously gets out of bed and performs various acts, almost as if searching for something specific. The sleepwalker may open a window or a door, usually on the ground floor, and leave the house and go for a short walk. On command from an authoritative voice, the person will stop what he or she is doing, or may return to bed spontaneously. If questioned closely without being awakened from this trance, the sleepwalker will mumble something that is probably related to a daytime event or conflict.

A *fugue* state, or flight, involves unexpected wandering off on lengthy journeys, during which the individual retains his or her own identity. Such a person resembles the sleepwalker who has carried over his somnambulism to the waking state in that his or her activities, like those of the somnambulist, serve wish-fulfilling ends. Thus, in addition to running from a stressful situation, the individual usually wanders purposively toward some significant object or situation.

Occasionally criminal acts are committed during one of these fugue states, and therefore it is often difficult to differentiate a fugue state from antisocial personality (see Chapter 16). The disunguishing feature is that the hysteric's destructive behavior is isolated and through repression he manages to forget it, while no such isolation or forgetting seems to occur to the antisocial personality. Moreover, for the hysteric the fugue state is a symptom that serves a particular purpose (escape from an intolerable family or job situation), although this distinction is not always easy to draw.

Amnesia, or loss of memory, the third of the

Figure 11.4
One psychoanalytic hypothesis about Adolf Hitler (Langer, 1972) holds that the German leader possessed a dual personality such that the same man who could cry over the death of his canary could also, at the slightest provocation, pronounce that "heads will roll."

dissociative hysterias mentioned above, is defined as the forgetting either of one's name, address, or family affiliation, or of all these. In some instances the complete past is forgotten, although memory for recent events remains intact. Amnesia may last for several minutes to a month or more. In contrast to fugue states, which are purposive flights toward or away from something, amnesic individuals have been known to wander the streets aimlessly because they have forgotten who they are or where they belong.

Massive amnesia, in which an individual blots out several unpleasant memories and experiences, is most dramatically manifested in *multiple personality*, the dissociative hysteria in which two or more separate and markedly different personalities coexist in the same individual. The most celebrated fictional case of multiple personality is Dr. Jekyll and Mr. Hyde. Hitler may have had a dual personality (see Figure 11.4). One of the earliest scientific write-ups of the disorder was that of Morton Prince, who described the case of Miss Beauchamp in *The Dissociation of a Personality* (1906). Later, *The Three Faces of Eve* caught the public's fancy first as a popular book and then as a movie (Thigpen and Cleckley, 1954, 1957; Lancaster, 1958).

Like somnambulism, fugue states, and amnesia, multiple personality is an escape reaction from stress or unhappiness. The separate personalities can be quite different from one another, each having its own memories and histories as well as its own identity. These personalities, although living in the same household, may not know of each other's existence, and maintaining these unique identities protects the individual from confronting an unhappy reality. This is illustrated in Case Report 11.7, which is a summary of the outstanding features of *The Three Faces of Eve*. (See Figure 11.5.)

Case Report 11.7 *Multiple Personality*

Description of Eve White (pp. 1–5): She did not at first appear to be an unusual or a particularly

Figure 11.5
Chris Sizemore, the subject of Thigpen and Cleckley's study, The Three Faces of Eve. *She discusses her famous case in her autobiography entitled* I'm Eve.

interesting patient. This neat, colorless young woman was . . . twenty-five years of age. . . . Demure and poised, she sat with her feet close together, speaking clearly but in soft, low tones. This superlatively calm, utterly self-controlled little figure of propriety showed no suggestion of anything that the layman might think of as nervousness. *Her hands lay still on the arms of her chair as she* spoke. . . . She was not undernourished but seemed somehow very delicate, the reticent, meticulous manner suggesting a physical fragility. . . . Her personal problems were complicated and serious, but by no means extraordinary.

Description of how Eve White suddenly changes to Eve Black (pp. 20–22): The brooding look in her eyes became almost a stare. Eve seemed momentarily dazed. Suddenly her posture began to change. Her body slowly stiffened until she sat rigidly erect. An alien, inexplicable expression then came over her face. This was suddenly erased into utter blankness. The lines of her countenance seemed to shift in a barely visible, slow, rippling transformation. . . . Closing her eyes, she winced as she put her hands to her temples, pressed hard, and twisted them as if to combat sudden pain. . . . Then the hands lightly dropped. . . . A pair of blue eyes popped open. . . . There was a quick reckless smile. In a bright unfamiliar voice that sparkled, the woman said, "Hi there, Doc!"

With a soft and surprisingly intimate syllable of laughter, she crossed her legs, carelessly swirling her skirts in the process. She unhurriedly smoothed the hem down over her knees in a manner that was playful and somehow just a little provocative. . . . The demure and constrained posture of Eve White had melted into buoyant repose.

The doctor handed her a cigaret, and then lighting it, said, "Who is 'she'?"

"Why, Eve White, of course. Your long-suffering, saintly, little patient."

"But aren't you Eve White?" he asked.

"That's for laughs," she claimed, a ripple of mirth in her tone. She tossed her head slightly again. "Why, you ought to know better than that, Doc!"

"Well who are you?" he asked incredulously.

"Why, I'm Eve Black," she said (giving Mrs. White's maiden name).

Description of Jane (pp. 139–141): Sometime after the returning of the headaches and blackouts, with Eve White's maladjustment still growing worse generally, a very early recollection was being discussed with her. The incident focused about a painful injury she had sustained when scalded by water from a washpot. As she spoke her eyes closed sleepily. . . . After remaining in this sleep, or trance, for perhaps two minutes, her eyes opened. . . . Slowly, with an unknown but curiously impressive voice and with immeasurable poise, she said, "Who are you?"

From the first moment it was vividly apparent that this was neither Eve White nor Eve Black. . . . This new woman showed herself ever more plainly and in all respects to be another entity. . . . She showed no evidence of Eve Black's obvious faults and inadequacies. . . . She also impressed us as being far more mature, more vivid, more boldly capable, and more interesting than Eve White. . . .

This third personality called herself Jane, for no particular reason she could give. . . . In her, early appeared the potential or the promise of something far more of woman and of life than might be expected from the two Eves with their faults and weaknesses eliminated and all assets combined.

SOURCE: Thigpen and Cleckley (1957).

While Eve White, Eve Black, and Jane were seeing her therapists (psychiatrists Thigpen and Cleckley), psychologists Osgood and Luria (1954) were given an opportunity to test the validity of a self-rating scale they had devised called the semantic differential.[5] Thigpen and Cleckley suggested that it would be interesting to collect semantic differential data from each of the personalities of their patient and have the psychologists interpret them on a blind basis—that is, without seeing her. Thigpen and Cleckley administered the semantic differential to their pa-

---

[5]The semantic differential consists of a set of seven-point scales, each defined by a pair of bipolar adjectives (for example, excitable–calm, strong–weak), in terms of which concepts or words can be rated. These ratings can be plotted in three-dimensional space by using a mathematical distance formula. The resultant semantic structures give an informative rendition of how individuals assign connotative meanings to concepts and terms. For further information on this technique see Osgood et al. (1957) and Kleinmuntz (1967).

tient while she was identified with each of her three personalities; subsequently, they discovered that the psychologists had approximated, in their blind analysis, the personality structures of these separate entities.

Although we have referred here to Eve's three personalities, in accordance with the original study, we note that she was eventually discovered to have seven sets of three personalities each—21 in all.

Causation

By far the most widely accepted explanations for the causes of these disorders hold that they are psychogenic—that is, that they originate in the individual's life experiences. Some evidence exists, however, for biological origins, and we shall begin our discussion with this evidence.

Biogenesis

Attempts to trace the origins of neuroticism to biological causes have been somewhat successful in showing that it has heritable components, and some confirming evidence for biochemical determinants has also been found. Most of these studies, however, have difficulties that detract from their scientific credibility (see Chapter 5). The genetic studies, for example, used procedures that have recently been discredited (family and pedigree), and the biochemical evidence is sparse.

Heredity. The genetics of neurosis has been studied by the *family* and the *pedigree* methods, although *twin* studies are currently the most favored form of research. The first of these is exemplified in an early study by Brown (1942), in which the incidence of neurosis was investigated among parents and siblings of three groups of neurotic target cases (also called *probands*): anxiety neurotics, hysterics, and obsessionals. The results obtained are presented in Table 11.1, where it can be seen that the incidence of neurosis among affected relatives is higher than the normal expectancy of 2 percent (Fremming, 1951).

At first glance these results would seem to favor a genetic explanation, but further reflection should reveal that these findings mean nothing more than that neurotic parents foster neurotic children. This observation permits both an environmental explanation and a genetic one, since the same parents who provide the genes also make up the environment. Moreover, these results are suspect because, as Rosenthal points out (1970, p. 243): "The author was the psychotherapist of most of the patients," and "he personally interviewed 500 of their 2,288 relatives." It comes as no surprise, therefore, that the author of this study "found" exactly what he was seeking since he served as both interviewer and data analyst. When this personal bias is added to the reliability

Table 11.1

Rates of Neuroses for Parents and Siblings of Target Cases

| | Percentage of Affected Relatives | | | | | |
| | Anxiety Neurotics | | Hysterics | | Obsessionals | |
Types of Target Cases	Parents	Sibs	Parents	Sibs	Parents	Sibs
Anxiety neurotics	21.4	12.3	1.6	2.2	0	0.9
Hysterics	9.5	4.6	19.0	6.2	0	0
Obsessionals	0	5.4	0	0	7.5	7.1

Source: F. W. Brown in Proceedings of the Royal Society of Medicine, *1942, 35, 785–790.*

problems inherent in interviewing (see Chapter 4), the conclusions about the contribution of either heredity or environment become even more tenuous.

The use of the pedigree method to prove genetic transmission of neuroticism has the same drawbacks as family studies, since these, too, as will be recalled from our discussion of the Kallikak family (see Chapter 5), rely on hearsay and depend on interview data for diagnostic evidence. Furthermore pedigree studies also lend themselves to both genetic and environmental interpretations.

Their dual interpretability is aptly illustrated by one investigator (Ehrenwald, 1960), who traced the *Obscomp* (which stands for obsessive–compulsive) pedigree over four successive generations and showed that obsessive–compulsive disorders can follow seemingly genetic transmission patterns (Figure 11.6). He derived the Obscomp pedigree by interviewing 14 family members. Although most of his evidence was gained from clinical interviews, he found that interpersonal attitudes and environmental influences were as important in causing the "minor psychiatric epidemic" as were genetics. He does admit,

however, "that even here gene-controlled variables may have contributed . . . to the existing patterns of psychological contagion and its perpetuation" (Ehrenwald, 1960, p. 235). A similar theme appears in a number of twin studies, to be discussed next.

The basic assumption of the twin method, it will be recalled, is that if differences between fraternal twins (dizygotic, or DZ) are greater than those existing between identical twins (monozygotic, or MZ), then heredity is a powerful causative factor; whereas if differences between DZs are small or nonexistent, the influence of genetics may be discounted.

Most twin studies tend to show that MZs are more alike than DZs in neuroticism, and presumably this favors heredity as an etiological agent; but precisely what is inherited is unclear. For example, in an early twin study, Eysenck and Prell (1951) postulated that the trait of neuroticism, as defined by a battery of personality inventories, is inherited. To test this hypothesis they selected 25 pairs of MZ twins and 25 pairs of DZ twins. Twenty-one neurotic children were also selected as a criterion group against which to compare the results of the MZ and DZ twin groups. Their findings, which showed that some 80 percent of individual differences in the neuroticism factor were due to heredity and only about 20 percent to environment, initially led them to conclude that neuroticism is inherited.

In a later publication (Eysenck and Rachman, 1965), however, Eysenck and another associate revised that conclusion and held that what is inherited in neuroticism is an autonomic system that predisposes some people more than others to react more vigorously, more lastingly, and more quickly to strong, noxious, painful, or sudden impinging stimuli (see Chapter 8 for a description of the autonomic nervous system).

The idea that there is a hereditary component in autonomic reactivity is corroborated in a study by two researchers (Lader and Wing, 1964), who compared 11 pairs of MZs with the same number of same-sex DZs (all between the ages of 17 and 26) and showed that the identical twins' galvanic skin response (GSR) and heart rates in response to high-frequency tones were significantly more alike than those of fraternal twins.[6] Similar supporting evidence, although not as convincing for reasons too numerous to list here, was also obtained in other studies (Block, 1967; Vandenberg et al., 1965).

It has been suggested, in criticism of findings that indicate higher similarity between MZ than DZ twins, that MZ likenesses result from their being treated more equally because of their greater resemblance to each other. This criticism, however, is hardly valid when autonomic correlates are the measures in question, since it is difficult to imagine how identical twins can influence these physiological variables. Moreover this objection has been convincingly countered in one study (Shields, 1962), in which personality tests were administered to 28 pairs of DZ twins and 44

[6]GSR changes can be detected by a galvanometer; they are commonly used as an indicator of emotion and are caused by alterations in the resistance of the skin (usually measured at the finger tips) to the passage of electric current.

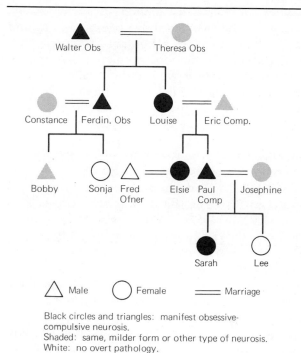

Figure 11.6

The Obscomp pedigree, illustrating transmission of familial contagion along genealogical pathways that may be explained by both hereditary and environmental causes.

(From J. Ehrenwald, ''Neurosis in the Family,'' *Archives of General Psychiatry*, 1960, 3, 232–242. Copyright 1960, American Medical Association)

pairs of MZ twins brought up apart and the same number reared together. The results indicated not only that the personalities of MZ twins were much more alike than those of the DZs, but that MZ twins raised apart were *more* alike than MZs raised together. A possible explanation for this unexpected finding might be that parents try especially hard to treat each member of an identical twin pair differently, and MZ twins are known to go out of their way to behave differently from each other.

In summary, our limited survey of family, pedigree, and twin studies suggests that, by and large, there may be a heritable component to neuroticism, but that environmental factors play an important role as well; and of the three methods used to study genetic transmission, the twin method holds the greatest promise for confirming or disconfirming the genetic hypothesis.

Biochemistry. The search for biochemical influences in neuroticism has linked excessive lactate (a salt of lactic acid) production during standard exercise with the presence of anxiety neurosis (Pitts and McClure, 1967). On the basis of the observation that the rise in blood lactate level of anxiety neurotics approximates that of atherosclerotic heart disease patients when both undergo standard exercises, two investigators developed the idea that lactate in itself could produce anxiety attacks in susceptible persons.

Accordingly, they conducted a double-blind study of the effects of sodium lactate infusion on patients suffering from anxiety neurosis and on normal control subjects.[7] The patients included people who showed at least ten of the following 16 symptoms:

headache	easy fatigability
dizziness	paresthesia
blurred vision	depression
chest pain	trembling
palpitations	shakiness
labored breathing	weakness
sighing	fears
tiredness, fatigue	insomnia

Among their experimental patients, the investigators included only those who had had anxiety attacks, which they defined as "an acute episode of extreme fearfulness, feeling of impending doom, fear of insanity, fear of 'having a heart attack,' or fear of other serious infection." A total of 14 patients and ten normal controls were thus selected, and each of these was interviewed by a psychiatrist, who was told (incorrectly) that the study was being conducted to investigate the effects of certain sugars in producing psychiatric symptoms.

After the conclusion of this study, patients with anxiety neurosis claimed that the symptoms produced by lactate infusion resembled those of their "worst attacks."[8] These symptoms were produced in 13 of the 14 neurotic patients, but in only two of the normals. Thus patients with anxiety neurosis responded characteristically and, more important, very differently from normal controls to infusion of lactate ion. Furthermore, 15 of the 16 symptoms listed above were produced by lactate in half the neurotic patients; glucose-in-saline solutions, used as a control procedure, produced no symptoms in either group. An important treatment implication of this study is that it is possible to prevent lactate-produced anxiety attacks by adding calcium ion to the infusion.

Regarding biogenesis of anxiety neurosis, Pitts and McClure propose the following theory: anxiety symptoms may occur in the normal person under stress because of increased lactate production that is triggered by epinephrine release.[9] The person with anxiety neurosis, according to this theory, might be someone especially vulner-

---

[7]Although more stringent criteria of the "double-blind" (when both the experimenter and subject are "blind" as to the purpose of the experiment), procedure are desirable, in this experiment it meant that "the psychiatrist [that is, interviewer] . . . knew nothing of the purpose of these investigations."

[8]The fact that the investigators demonstrated that they can produce anxiety symptoms exempts this study from the usual criticism launched at biochemical research: namely, that researchers investigate a disorder after its onset. The reader is invited to compare this procedure with those used in studying the biochemistry of schizophrenia, in which investigators attempt to extract chemical substances from the blood or urine of patients (see Chapter 12).

[9]Epinephrine is an adrenal hormone that stimulates autonomic action (see Chapter 8).

able to chronic overproduction of epinephrine who consequently produces unusual amounts of lactic acid, which, in turn, inhibits calcium metabolism. Since it is known that low blood calcium levels produce anxiety, this would explain the symptoms.

A possible alternative explanation that makes minimal assumptions about biogenic determinants holds that lactic acid or epinephrine produces only limited features of the physiological responses associated with anxiety and that *past conditioning* may be the crucial variable that distinguishes between those who have full-scale anxiety attacks and those who do not. It is possible also, according to this account, that once the person senses the initial phases of the attack coming on, anticipation and fear of the dreaded attack may facilitate a vicious circle (Martin, 1971).

In summary, the evidence for the biological origins of neurosis shows some connection between test-measured neuroticism and heredity, in that there may be predispositional differences in autonomic reactivity between neurotics and normals. At least one biochemical agent has been found that triggers anxiety and its inherited endogenous production may be responsible for the greater susceptibility of some persons to neuroticism. All in all, however, studies purporting to show the biogenesis of neuroticism are sparse, and most of these allow alternative explanations that implicate environmental and conditioning processes.

Psychogenesis

Our discussion of the psychogenesis of neurosis includes many of the motivational and sociocultural determinants covered in Chapter 6. Space limitations do not permit us to deal with the rather extensive area of animal research that has shed additional light on the psychological origins of neuroticism (see Amsel, 1971; Gantt, 1971; Masserman, 1971; Sandler and Davidson, 1971).

The Psychoanalytic Model. According to this theory, as we noted in Chapters 6 and 7, neurosis is rooted in childhood experiences. The anxiety that originates in later life is due to unresolved infantile sexual complexes, with too much libido being fixated or attached to early love objects. The ego denies expression of these anxiety-arousing impulses by repressing them, and neurotic symptoms signify the emergence of these repressed desires. Furthermore, symptoms serve as convenient symbolic fulfillments of infantile impulses and arouse less anxiety than their direct gratification would.

What determines which neurotic symptom will appear? In the Freudian view this is determined by individual differences in the degree of fixation upon early love objects, differences in childhood experiences, and the extent of subsequent regression to earlier psychosexual stages. Since everyone is subject to infantile complexes, all adults display some neurosis-like symptoms, but only a subset of people are so markedly disturbed as to qualify for the classification of neurosis.

The purpose of the defense mechanisms, as we saw in Chapter 7, is to cope with threats to the self or ego. Their defensive success may be minimal, as in freefloating anxiety; may result in displacing anxiety onto external objects or internal organs, as in phobia and hypochondriasis; or may produce repetitive and unwanted thoughts and urges, as in the obsessive–compulsive neuroses. On the other hand the success of the mechanisms may be maximal in the sense that they help convert anxiety into hysterical symptoms. In any event it is these mechanisms, in Freudian theory, that are used to compromise between the impulses of the id and the strictures of reality. Illustrations of how these mechanisms operate in the neuroses were given earlier in this chapter.

Essentially, then, Freudian theory is a developmental one holding that the individual, while growing up, passes through various stages of interaction with the environment. Whether one develops a disorder depends in large measure on what happens at each stage; and the type of symptom one displays depends on the adequacy of one's defenses.

The Operant Conditioning Model. The learning approach that totally rejects Freudian theory and makes no assumptions about thinking or unconscious processes is that of B. F. Skinner (see Chapter 6).[10] According to Skinner (1953, pp. 375–379) concepts such as ego, superego, and id are unnecessary. Instead of talking about repression, he would rather ask why the response was emitted in the first place, why it was punished, and what current environmental conditions are active in supporting it. Whereas in the Freudian model behavior is only the symptom of the real problem—the neurosis—the Skinnerian model sees behavior as the only reality and regards underlying psychological processes as unnecessary fictions.

Skinner's (1953) account of the acquisition of hysteria is instructive because it demonstrates how one can trace the environmental origins of a neurosis without resorting to inner mechanisms (p. 381): "Thus when a solicitous parent supplies an unusual measure of affection and attention to a sick child, any behavior on the part of the child which emphasizes his illness is strongly reinforced." And regarding its treatment, he goes on to say: "One obvious remedial technique for behavior which is the product of excessive reinforcement is to arrange new contingencies in which the behavior will be extinguished."

Mowrer's Two-Factor Model. Some learning theorists explain neurotic symptoms as an avoid-

ance or escape from high levels of anxiety. According to this view, which has been most clearly articulated by O. H. Mowrer (1939, 1950, 1960b, 1965), the learning of neuroticism involves two factors: instrumental or operant and respondent processes. In his early conceptualization Mowrer (1939, 1950) held that instrumental processes govern voluntary events and represent the means by which the individual learns which responses produce pleasure and avoid anxiety or pain. Thus the person responds to a threatening situation in a certain way, avoids or escapes the anxiety of the situation, and hence attains his or her goal. The probability of similar responding in the future is also thereby increased. Respondent or classical processes govern involuntary, reflex events that result in sign learning; sign learning is the process by which previously neutral stimuli acquire conditioned stimulus properties.

Most reflex events, according to one interpretation of Mowrer's two-factor theory (see Sandler and Davidson, 1973), are related to potentially dangerous situations, and sign learning is critical in the acquisition of nonneurotic or normal and efficient responding. Inappropriate sign learning interferes with adequate solution learning, thus restricting the person's behavior repertoire, and eventually contributing to maladaptive behavior. Consider the person who has failed in a number of college courses. This produces conditioned fear or anxiety in the presence of those stimuli (classroom, content, or teacher of those courses) that accompany or signal certain courses. By not attending school or class, the person can avoid the anxiety conditioned to these situations. In the process, however, many other stimuli may acquire the signs for danger, and the avoidance behavior may begin to appear as a response to many situations other than school.

For Mowrer, then, the central factor in neuroticism is anxiety, a conditioned emotional reaction that is aroused in the presence of specific danger signs or stimuli. Behavior that avoids or escapes the danger is reinforced because of its immediate relief-giving properties. But such be-

---

[10]There are a number of other learning theory approaches to the neuroses. Some of these partially accept psychoanalytic theory (Mowrer, 1950), and others reject it totally (Bandura, 1969; Eysenck, 1957, 1960b; Wolpe, 1958). The interested reader is again invited to consult these primary sources, or several excellent secondary works that summarize these various positions (Bischof, 1970; Buss, 1966; Hall and Lindzey, 1978; Kanfer and Phillips, 1970; Maher, 1966; Yates, 1970a).

havior provides no long-term solution. Neurotics, in other words, are people who have learned how not to learn. Instrumental responses enable them to avoid the anxiety associated with the danger signs in the environment, but in the process the source of the anxiety remains untouched.

Subsequently Mowrer (1960, 1965) revised his two-factor learning model by dropping the operant or instrumental stage and invoking the concepts of shame, guilt, and moral fear. We shall not discuss these modifications here.

Existential Models.   Humanistic and existential, or third-force, psychologists have postulated still another model of neurosis, in which the roots of neurosis are found in an early childhood conflict: the child's own actions and feelings are not ac-

ceptable to his parents, and he repeatedly faces punishment or disapproval for his spontaneous and expressive behavior. Because he needs his parents' love and approval, he learns to block expressions of feeling (and therefore to block awareness of feeling). He learns, for example, not to seek bodily (especially genital) pleasure, not to strike out or scream out when he is angry, and not to cry when he is hurt, frustrated, or grief-stricken. The essential lesson he is learning is that he cannot be himself and be loved. Usually his need for love is so great that he betrays himself to be acceptable, and sacrifices his own authenticity.

As we noted in Chapter 6, R. D. Laing (1970) believes that the result is a "divided self." The personality splits into an outer, false self that behaves in ways likely to gain love and approval,

---

Another View: The Behavioral Theory of Neurosis

Most psychodynamic theorists agree that the neuroses are manifested by defensive behavior designed to allay anxiety caused by unconscious conflicts. This view implies that neurotic behavior is merely a symptom of an underlying difficulty that must be resolved before the neurotic behavior is banished.

The behaviorists, in contrast, postulate no unconscious causes of neurotic behavior. Behavioral theory holds that the neuroses consist of bad habits, developed and maintained in much the same way as other learned responses. The difference is that the neurotic either has learned the wrong responses or has failed to learn the appropriate ones.

How do the neurotic responses come about? Through learning, which is either deliberate or accidental, the individual discovers that a certain situation produces anxiety. Rather than dealing directly with the situation, the person may try to avoid or es-

cape it by responding in some way that either prevents the situation from occurring or that takes him out of the situation. The consequent relief of anxiety caused by this avoidance or escape behavior is reinforcing, and the newly learned behavior becomes strengthened and may be used again the next time the situation presents itself. These indirect modes of dealing with the threatening situation are extremely difficult to extinguish because the individuals may never learn that the threat he is avoiding or escaping no longer exists and because the newly learned behavior continues to be highly charged with emotion. The reinforcing properties of the avoidance behavior, plus the fact that the individual believes the threat is still present, therefore make neurotic behavior exceedingly persistent, no matter how maladaptive it may be (adapted from McNeil, 1974, p. 446).

and an inner, real self harboring the renounced and repressed impulses. This split is maintained at considerable cost in body tension and psychic energy.

A parallel can be seen between these models and the Reichian model, which also sees the origin of neurosis in the child's blocking of unacceptable feelings, but emphasizes the physiological nature of neurosis: one blocks feelings by tensing muscles. For example, to stifle an impulse to cry, one must tense the diaphragm, chest, and neck. Both the feeling and the tension that blocks it are physiological processes; Reich (1970) believed that the two opposing energies become "frozen" into the musculature as rigidity ("character armor") and that this rigidity continues to block energy and feeling. Similar models exist in Chinese medicine and in some of the meditative practices of India. Practitioners of the form of physical therapy called structural integration ("Rolfing" in popular parlance) sometimes report the release of emotional material in patients when muscle fascia are loosened by this form of deep massage, but as of this writing no experimental work has been reported that either substantiates or refutes Reich's hypothesis. Some third-force psychologists have adopted the Reichian model, especially the concept of armor. Reichian therapy is sometimes done in combination with third-force approaches, such as Gestalt therapy.

The Gestalt model of neurosis (Perls et al., 1951) begins with the assumption that the organism has a drive toward wholeness, toward experiencing the events of life whole (as Gestalten) with no split between thought, feeling, and activity. The repressed material of early childhood, in this view, is not fantasies but organismic needs. In contrast with Freudian psychoanalysis, which aims at recovering repressed material, Gestalt therapy seeks to expand consciousness into a total awareness of whatever is happening here and now. Frederick Perls, the founder of Gestalt therapy, saw the neurotic personality as being fragmented in many ways—a tyrannical "topdog" split from an obsequious "underdog,"

thought split from feeling, and so on.

Stress. The stresses of war combat and civilian catastrophies have long been recognized as catalysts for neurosis—so much so that many mental health writers refer to these as separate psychopathological disorders (*combat* or *traumatic neuroses*). Here, however, we discuss stress as simply another etiological force, and because of space considerations we limit our comments to combat as a cause.

Military combat as a source of neurosis usually takes two forms: *acute* combat exhaustion and a more *chronic* type of reaction (see Figure 11.7). The first of these is characterized by the victim's inability to relax, disorientation, sensitivity to noise, and insomnia. In some people these reactions often crystalize into chronic neurosis, and some writers hold that this occurs particularly among people who are psychologically vulnerable because of their prior life experiences.

The chronic reaction, then, can best be defined as neurosis precipitated by combat stress in predisposed persons. A good description of this neurosis is given by one writer who did mental status interviews (see Chapter 4) with evacuees on a hospital ship returning from Vietnam. Case Report 11.8 is an abbreviated version of this write-up. This case describes the interaction of specific combat stress and the not-uncommon mixture of neurotic and psychophysiological symptoms in a neurotic patient whose symptoms had not previously been conspicuous (Strange, 1969, pp. 85–86).

Case Report 11.8 *Stress as a Causative Factor*

This 30-year old U.S. Marine Corps staff sergeant was initially placed on the sick list because of "nervousness," headache, and gastrointestinal complaints following several mortar attacks on his unit. When his acute symptoms did not improve under treatment, he was transferred to the hospital ship for further psychiatric care.

At the time of admission his psychomotor activity was retarded and there was little spontaneity in his movement or speech. He had a tremor and his mood was obviously depressed and apprehensive. Thought content was dominated by preoccupation with the mortar attacks along with his own sense of worthlessness, hopelessness, and futility. He also complained of vague headache and abdominal discomfort.

His background indicated a relatively unremarkable childhood and adolescence marked only by compulsive traits and somewhat excessive dependency needs. He had an excellent military record, but there was evidence of excessive perfectionism, rigidity, and tenuous self-esteem, especially in his personal life. His first marriage failed, largely because of his neurotic needs and demands, and shortly before he departed for Vietnam and his initial combat experience his second wife had threatened separation.

During his three months in the combat area he had been appalled by the uncertainties and seeming disorganization of actual war, and he began to be preoccupied with a sense of inadequacy in managing the responsibilities of his job. He was plagued with headaches and abdominal discomfort, and all of his symptoms became suddenly worse following the succession of mortar attacks.

In psychotherapy his concern about the mortar attacks and combat soon proved superficial, and his more significant problems of dependency, guilt, self-esteem, and perfectionism were explored.

SOURCE: *R. E. Strange (1969), pp. 85–86.*

Sociocultural Variables. The smallest subcultural unit of our society, it will be recalled, is the family (see Chapter 6). This unit is an early and important context for the learning of maladaptive behaviors, and its importance for the development of neurosis is corroborated by most theorists and by a considerable store of empirically derived knowledge.

Not surprisingly most of the evidence reinforces the observation that neurotic parents foster neurotic individuals (Dohrenwend and Dohren-

Figure 11.7
Military combat stress frequently leads to neurosis. Upon return from a mission in Vietnam, this marine was in a state of acute exhaustion.

wend, 1969; Ehrenwald, 1960; Jenkins, 1966). This evidence is predominantly based on statistical surveys or on case-history data and, as such, tells us little about the relative contribution of hereditary and environmental factors. As in the case of the Obscomp family, the number of possible psychopathogenic familial patterns are infinite; we shall mention only five of them:

1. A parent may displace his own hypochondriasis onto a child as, for example, in the case of a mother who is overly concerned about her child's health. A typical mother–child interaction in this instance

Neurotic parents often displace their neuroses onto their children. For example, the hypochondriacal woman may assume the overprotective mother role, and the child soon learns to go through each day haunted by the feeling of being continually on the brink of illness, injury, or death. Similarly, the man who cannot accept his failure to meet his own unattainable goals may subject his children to unrelenting pressure to achieve.

may be for the mother to go through a checklist of possible symptoms each morning before the child leaves for school. Before long, the child may begin to share his mother's concern over him. Other neurotic behaviors may be similarly acquired.

2. Parents may promote sibling rivalry inadvertently by favoring one child in the family and ignoring, perhaps even belittling, others.

3. A parent may attempt to have the child live the life that he or she could not, possibly setting unattainable goals for the child. For example, the father who flunked out of law school and became a real estate agent may insist that his son take up where he left off. If the child has other plans or, even worse, if he does not have the aptitude for that work, his sense of competence may be seriously undermined by his failures.

4. Parents may use the child as a weapon in their conflicts with each other, and their threats to "walk out" can be traumatic to the child and cause feelings of insecurity.

5. A child may learn from his parents' frequent marital conflicts that close heterosexual relationships are not gratifying and are to be avoided whenever possible.

The search beyond the family for sociocultural influences indicates that neurosis occurs in all cultures (Eaton and Weil, 1955; Opler, 1959; Plog and Edgerton, 1969; Norbeck et al., 1968), although its symptomatic expression has strong

---

[11]The Hutterites live in the northern United States and in Canada and are social isolates in the sense that they do not marry outside their sect; they also maintain distinctive social traditions.

culture-bound features. In one of these studies (Eaton and Weil, 1955), for example, it was found that among the Hutterite sect[11] the overall incidence of neurosis was lower than for many other cultures, and neurotic patients have mild and benign symptoms. Moreover patients in this sect had chiefly those symptoms that are socially acceptable in their culture. They expressed their tensions by internalizing them as depressive or psychophysiological responses. Phobic and obsessive–compulsive reactions, which would violate strong cultural taboos, were rare.[12]

Cross-cultural research further discloses that gross forms of hysteria, such as hysterical blindness, deafness, convulsions, and paralysis, which are on the decline in Europe and America, are common in such developing countries as India, Lebanon, Egypt, and Tunisia; and that within these countries, there is a greater incidence of obsessive–compulsive neurosis in urban than in rual areas (Wittkower and Dubreuil, 1968).

In our own culture reviews of most epidemiological studies (Dohrenwend and Dohrenwend, 1969) show that the maximum prevalence rates of neurosis occur as often in the lowest as in the other social classes. But there are differences, nonetheless, in the types of neuroses found among the various classes and in the number of neurotic patients in treatment. Regarding the first of these differences, Hollingshead and Redlich's social stratification studies (1958) indicate that hysterical and somatic reactions were present in the lowest two classes but were essentially absent in the upper three classes. Obsessions and compulsions, by contrast, were not often found in the lower classes but were present in the upper strata. These differences can be explained in terms of the emphasis on success and competitiveness in the higher socioeconomic groups, an emphasis that probably fosters the obsessive–compulsive neuroses, and in terms of the remunerative compensation that lower-class persons receive for being and staying somatically ill. These explanations, although some support is found in the rural–urban differences of the above cross-cultural studies, are highly speculative and need to be pursued further before much credence is placed in them.

Less speculative, however, are notions regarding treatment differences between patients in upper and lower classes. Even though the prevalence rates and the number of cases admitted each year are about the same at all social levels (Hollingshead and Redlich, 1958; NIMH, 1972), there is a lower rate of treatment among persons in the lower strata. One explanation for this may be the greater distrustfulness toward psychiatric treatment among lower socioeconomic groups and their tendency to view neurotic symptoms as physical ailments; but in large part the economics of obtaining treatment determines these differences. The costs for psychotherapy are prohibitive to all but the most affluent, and, as Hollingshead and Redlich (1958) suggested, physicians readily accommodate the lower-class patient's somatic complaints by prescribing medication, whereas the upper-class patient is pampered with more lengthy treatment procedures.

In summing up the evidence for the psychogenesis of neurosis, we see that Freudian as well as some stimulus–response and existential models emphasize early experiences and motivational factors. The evidence from hypnosis suggests that hysterical symptoms can be produced, eliminated, or transferred by means of hypnotic induction, but such demonstrations are not to be misconstrued as evidence for their hypnotic origins. As we emphasized in Chapter 8, symptoms can be produced in many ways, but this does not establish that individuals acquire them in these ways. Finally stress and sociocultural variables have important influences on the development of neurosis, but the dynamics of these variables are still not well understood.

---

[12]It is difficult to know the extent to which genetics contributes to these differences, since inbreeding within this sect is high. More than 60 percent of its members carry the surnames of Hofer, Waldner, Wipf, Stahl, and Kleinsasser.

Treatment and Outcome

It is not possible to provide a detailed presentation of treatment procedures within the limits of this chapter; our comments here are brief and we defer detailed discussion of the therapies until Part Three.

Psychotherapy

The treatment applied most often to the neuroses is individual psychotherapy—that is, the form of therapy in which a patient talks to a therapist about his problems. The names usually associated with the founding and popularization of psychotherapy are Freud, Horney, Fromm, Erikson, Adler, Jung, Rogers, Maslow, and Sullivan— all of whom formulated their treatment theories in clinical settings.

Although these various approaches differ in objectives and techniques, they do share the common goals of probing beneath the surface of the patient's manifest expressions of neurosis (hence the name "depth" therapy) and attempting to restructure his personality so that he gains increasing awareness of the functions of his symptoms (hence "insight" therapy). For example, in Freudian treatment of neurosis, the therapist pays minimal attention to the apparent content of the patient's verbalizations and attempts to remove his symptoms by restoring to consciousness the repressed memories that gave rise to the symptoms in the first place.

Behavior Therapy

By contrast, the behavior therapies, relatively recent arrivals, have their origins in the psychological laboratory and apply principles of learning to the modification of unwanted behavior. Ayllon, Azrin, Bandura, Eysenck, Ferster, Krasner, Lovaas, Skinner, Ullmann, and Wolpe are just a few of the names frequently associated with be-

havior therapy, and, although there are important differences among some of their approaches, all of them pay particular attention to understanding the conditions in the environment that maintain and perpetuate maladaptive responses. Their aim, almost without exception, is to extinguish these responses.[13]

Physical Treatments

The physical, or somatic, methods sometimes used in treating the neuroses include *tranquilizing drugs* and *electroshock therapy* (EST). These are administered to anxious and depressed patients and are usually given in combination with some form of psychotherapy. The anxious person is helped by sedatives or minor tranquilizers to relax sufficiently to function adequately at home and at work without experiencing intense panic reactions.

EST, which consists of applying electrical current through two electrodes attached to the patient's temples, is used mostly for treating depressives. Its precise effect on the central nervous system and the reason for its reported success are still not well understood, although it has been in use for about forty years.

Outcome

A number of clinical and social history variables have repeatedly been found to correspond to particular outcomes of neurosis. Most of these arise in the context of claims for the success rates of various psychological and somatic therapies. We shall examine these claims in Part Three; here, however, we shall describe one of the few thor-

---

[13]There are at least two distinct types of behavior therapy: *classical* and *operant conditioning*. This distinction will be developed more fully in Chapter 23.

ough studies to appear in the literature on the prognosis of neuroticism (Gunderson and Arthur, 1968).

This study, which also has implications for the recovery of psychotics, followed up 88 diagnosed neurotics for a period of five years after they had been admitted to naval hospitals. Unfortunately complete follow-ups were available for only 57 of these 88 patients, but partial information was obtained for the remainder. *Outcome*—degree of improvement or recovery—was measured by the amount of change in disability ratings noted by a group of psychologists, psychiatrists, and physicians over the five-year period.

The results indicated that the most important predictor of improvement was the age of the person at the time of hospitalization (*onset*). Older patients were less likely to recover than younger ones. Other significant indicators of outcome were adequacy of social life and history of medical treatment—the more withdrawn people were prior to hospitalization and the more extensive the pre-hospital medical care, the more unfavorable were their chances for recovery.

Most of these results tend to corroborate findings previously obtained in psychosis and neurosis outcome studies (see Huston and Pepernick, 1958; Marks et al., 1963; Nameche et al., 1967; Schofield et al., 1954; Stephens et al., 1966; Vaillant, 1964), but there were some surprises. For example, it was learned that the amount of anxiety manifested during hospitalization was not related to recovery, and first-borns are less likely to recover than those having other birth orders. Most surprising of all was the finding that improvement was more predictable for psychotics than for neurotics. In general, however, recovery or improvement was more rapid and complete for neurotic patients.

Summary

Prolonged use of each of the defenses against anxiety may culminate in characteristic neurotic symptoms, and the neuroses are often ranked according to the success a person has in dealing with anxiety. The order of neuroses, beginning with the disorder in which the greatest anxiety is manifested (for example, in which a person has no success in dealing with anxiety), is as follows: anxiety, depressive, obsessive–compulsive, phobic, hypochondriacal, and hysterical.

Numerous etiological agents have been ascribed to the development of neuroticism. The most common among these are psychogenic agents; these disorders are learned within the context of a person's family, subculture, and total life experiences. Some evidence has also pointed in the direction of possible biogenic origins (heredity and biochemistry) of the neuroses, but this evidence is unconvincing.

Treatment of these disorders has traditionally been of the psychotherapy or "talking cure" variety, although behavior therapy has lately made important inroads into this area. In general the outlook for neuroticism is more favorable than for, say, the so-called psychotic and other disorders, and outcomes can be predicted from numerous demographic variables. The highest recovery rate is usually achieved by younger persons whose social lives were active prior to hospitalization and among those who have a short history of prior medical care.

Terms and Concepts to Master

Anxiety neurosis	Phobic neurosis
Depressive neurosis	Semantic differential
Hysteria	
Obsessive–compulsive neurosis	

12 Schizophrenic and Paranoid Behavior

Being crazy is like one of those nightmares where you try to call for help and no sound comes out. Or if you can call, no one hears or understands. You can't wake up from the nightmare unless someone does hear you and helps you to wake up.

These are the words of a 26-year-old woman who—after 34 electric shock treatments and 60 insulin shock treatments—had been declared hopelessly psychotic.[1] Her description of psychosis (Hayward and Taylor, 1956, p. 221) carries the authority of personal experience:

When I was catatonic, I tried to be dead and grey and motionless. I thought mother would like that. She could carry me around like a doll.

I felt as though I were in a bottle. I could feel that everything was outside and couldn't touch me.

I had to die to keep from dying. I know that sounds crazy but one time a boy hurt my feelings very much and I wanted to jump in front of a subway. Instead I went a little catatonic so I wouldn't feel anything. [I guess you had to die emotionally or your feeling would have killed you.] That's right. I guess I'd rather kill myself than harm somebody else.

Of all the people who are hurting psychologically, psychotics have been driven furthest from

---

[1]She was diagnosed as a catatonic schizophrenic.

being able to satisfy their own wants and needs. Much of their behavior seems to make no sense in any context visible to others. They may speak in "word salads" (seemingly meaningless sequences of words and phrases). They may address beings visible only to them. They may be rigid and suspicious, or absurdly grandiose or silly. They may, like the woman quoted above, withdraw completely. Today more and more clinicians, whatever model of behavior pathology they subscribe to, seem to be agreeing that there is usually some context in which some of the psychotic's behavior makes sense.

That the psychotic is more disturbed than the neurotic or the psychophysiologically ill is evident in the comparisons made in Table 12.1. In particular, psychotics are less willing to acknowledge their disorders, more withdrawn and disoriented, and less likely to benefit from available methods of treatment.

Two Types of Psychosis

There are two general categories of psychosis: the first includes the psychoses associated with central nervous system damage (sometimes called organic brain damage). Examples are the behavior changes that accompany senility, alcoholism, drug addiction, and many other disturbances mentioned in Chapter 5, where we listed several forms of injury to the brain's structure. The second group consists of psychoses not attributable to brain damage; these include the affective disorders, the paranoid disorders, and the schizophrenias.

The distinguishing feature between what DSM II calls the "psychoses associated with organic brain syndromes (APA, 1968, p. 24) and those "not attributed to physical conditions" (APA, 1968, p. 32) is that people in the latter category have no identifiable brain tissue damage.[2] Another noteworthy difference is that some people with tangible organic destruction show good recovery after the precipitating agents are removed. For example, someone whose psychosis is associated with an intracranial infection (abscess or syphilis) may show good behavioral improvement after the infection is cleared up,

even though the brain damage is irreversible.[3] Such recovery is less common among individuals whose psychotic behavior is not organically based.

---

[2]In DSM I (APA, 1952), the nonorganic psychoses were referred to as "functional disorders" and were believed to be due to psychogenic factors, or at least not proved to be caused by structural or physical changes. Increasing recognition of the possibility that all psychotic behavior may be caused by nonpsychogenic agents is responsible for the new categorization. DSM III (APA, 1980) simply separates the schizophrenic from the paranoid disorders and implies that these are psychoses.

[3]This recovery of function occurs because of the brain's facility to compensate for destruction of some of its cells by having neighboring tissue take over. Of course this becomes less true as the initial, or ongoing, damage becomes more extensive.

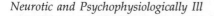

Table 12.1

Comparison of Characteristics of Neurotics and Psychophysiologically Ill with Those of Psychotics

Neurotic and Psychophysiologically Ill	Psychotic
Frequently talks about his symptoms and does not accept his condition. Talks about how healthy he used to be and anticipates the day when he will return to his normal self.	Often denies that there is anything wrong with him and tends to accept his illness as inevitable. If someone calls attention to his unusual behavior, he defends it. He lives his psychosis.
Does not lose contact with reality. If reality testing is at all impaired, it is in the direction of overactivity—he or she can't seem to ignore reality.	In sharp contrast, he or she has lost contact with or has a tenuous reality and substitutes fantasy for it.
Orientation for person, place, and time is intact.	Orientation is poor or entirely gone.
Although she complains that she is "falling apart," she rarely does.	Her total personality may be disorganized by her illness and her lifestyle is chaotic.
Continues to function socially and on the job.	He may harm himself or others. Consequently he often requires close care or hospitalization. His close relatives are among the first to insist that he seek help because they are often the victims of his behavior.
The prospects for recovery of acceptable functioning are favorable.	Although many psychotics benefit from treatment (sometimes recovery is spontaneous), most benefits consist of temporary cures of particular symptoms or improvement of behavior.

Psychotic Behavior Patterns

Although specific behavior does vary with particular psychotic disorders, the following description, taken from DSM II (APA, 1968), and closely paralleled in DSM III (APA, 1980), applies to all the psychoses (p. 23):

> *Patients are described as psychotic when their mental functioning is sufficiently impaired to interfere grossly with their capacity to meet the ordinary demands of life. The impairment may result from a serious distortion in their capacity to recognize reality. Hallucinations and delusions, for example, may disturb their perceptions. Alterations of mood may be so profound that the patient's capacity to respond appropriately is grossly impaired. Deficits in perception, language and memory may be so severe that the patient's capacity for mental grasp of his situation is effectively lost.*

Many of the behaviors mentioned in this definition will be clearly recognizable in the following survey of psychotic behaviors especially relevant to the psychoses.

The psychoses involve disturbances of perception, thinking, affect, communication, motor activity, and motivation. As in other disorders these are not all-or-none phenomena; they may be present in some psychoses but not in others, or they may occur in the same person in varying degrees from time to time. The following discussion will cover some of the distinguishing behaviors. The paranoid behaviors will be discussed separately later in the chapter. Other psychotic behaviors will be discussed in Chapters 13 and 14.

Perceptual Distortions. *Hallucinations*—experiencing imaginary objects or phenomena—are the main perceptual behaviors in psychoses. Typically psychotics may hear voices, have visions, or smell peculiar odors; less commonly, their sense of taste is distorted or they report that things are crawling on or touching them.

Even though it is commonly believed that hallucinations are experienced mainly by psychotics, it has been shown that they can be produced in almost anyone either in the classroom (Slosson, 1899) or under hypnosis (Barber, 1971). The first of these demonstrations is more interesting for our purposes because the reader can easily replicate it. This classroom performance was first conducted by a psychologist who, during one of his lectures, showed how an odor (olfactory hallucinations) can be easily suggested to a large group of persons (Slosson, 1899, p. 407):[4]

> *After some experiments, I stated that I wished to see how rapidly an odor would be diffused through the air, and requested that as soon as anyone perceived the odor he should raise his hands. I then unpacked the bottle in the front of the hall, poured the water over the cotton, holding my head away during the operation and started a stop watch. . . . In 15 seconds most of those in the front row had raised their hands, and in forty seconds the "odor" had spread to the back of the hall.*

Similarly, hallucinations of temperature and pain are easily induced by such suggestion or by hypnosis (Hilgard, 1969), as are visual and auditory hallucinations (Barber, 1971; Spanos and Barber, 1968).

Thought Disturbances. *Delusional thinking* comes under this category, and it is probably the one feature of psychotic behavior that makes psychotics so very difficult to live with. Not only is the psychotic convinced of his or her false beliefs but, at best, works hard to persuade others to share them. At worst, a psychotic may injure him

---

[4]In light of what we know today about subjects' compliance with experimenters' expectations, we might suggest an alternative explanation—that the students did not hallucinate but merely raised their hands because they believed it was expected.

Thought Experiment

A basic fact about human communication is that listening is selective. Your assumptions, mental set, expectations, and previous experience all influence the way you listen. The result is that you may hear only part of what is being said, or you may hear something totally different. Part of the clinician's skill is the ability to shift ground while listening, instead of remaining locked into old habits of perception. For example, it is easy to see the characteristic disorientation and negativity in the words of the patient (diagnosis: schizophrenia, hebephrenic type) in the following exchange:

Dr.: *Can you state your name?*
Pa.: *I can and I cannot.*
Dr.: *What is your name?*
Pa.: *The same as yours, only different.*
Dr.: *Do you know who I am?*
Pa.: *Of course, you are you and I am I.*
Dr.: *That is very good, but it is important for our records to obtain correct information.*
Pa.: *Then write in your records that I am the King of Kings and you are my servant.*
Dr.: *You are not answering my questions.*
Pa.: *I am, but you are not listening.*
Dr.: *I'll try again. What is today's date?*
Pa.: *Oh, that's easy—it is the 33rd of June, 1933.*
Dr.: *What time of day is it?*
Pa.: *Tulip day, late evening.*
Dr.: *And why are you here?*
Pa.: *To talk to you.*
Dr.: *But I can't get any information from you.*
Pa.: *That's because you are doing all the talking. Besides you are blowing my brain.*

Is what the patient is saying totally meaningless? Given certain assumptions, we could perceive it as such. But what if we changed our assumptions? To explore this possibility, reread the passage, making the following assumption:

(1) The patient is aware of the doctor's expectations and is putting the doctor on.

Does a different picture emerge? Try it again, making this assumption:

(2) The patient is feeling angry, frustrated, and impatient in his attempt to communicate an agonizing and difficult truth about his anguish and despair.

Now try this assumption:

(3) The patient perceives the doctor as incredibly naive, petty, rigid, tradition-bound, and unimaginative.

And this one:

(4) The patient is locked into a desperate struggle between the desire to reveal his suffering and the fear of being judged and punished.

All of these assumptions are pure fantasy; they are not presented as "accurate" or "clinically sound" descriptions of the patient's state. Adopting them does not change the patient's behavior, nor does it in any way contradict the diagnosis. The patient is still disoriented, but we have changed some of the meanings we assign to his behavior by changing our assumptions.

There is much that resembles psychotic art in this section of a picture of Hell, painted by the sixteenth-century Dutch painter Hieronymus Bosch. Especially noteworthy are the mutilated portions of human and animal anatomy, the tightly packed canvas, and the artist's apparent association of eroticism with filth, decay, and mutilation.

(Museo del Prado)

or herself or others through following the dictates of these unfounded convictions. For example, the person who believes others are out to get him may, in self-defense, strike out at them.

Another thought disturbance is called *autistic thinking*, or *autism*. Autism follows its own idiosyncratic logic and disregards almost entirely the constraints of reality. Signs of autism are usually found in language and speech and consist of mixing up words and using nonstandard patterns of phonation, rhythm, articulation, and gestural communication.

Most of us approach autistic thinking when we become so engrossed in our nightmares or daytime fantasies that we talk aloud or make strange gestures that only we understand. The difference, of course, between this behavior and that of psychotics is the psychotics' more frequent use of it and their greater tendency to become totally absorbed in the autistic experience.

Disorientation is another distinguishing disturbance of thought in the psychoses, and it is marked by confusion about time, place, and person. If one were to ask the disoriented psychotic why he is where he is, his reply might conform more to his current thinking than to the actual situation.

Language and Speech Disturbances. We shall have more to say about communication disturbances at appropriate points throughout our later descriptions of specific psychoses. A listing of the several qualitative and quantitative speech and language disorders should suffice here; they include circumstantiality, neologisms, word salad, clang associations, echolalia, mutism, and retarded and accelerated speech. For some psychotics, particularly schizophrenics, we can even evaluate the extent of disturbance simply by judging their verbal productions.

Motor Anomalies. This aspect of psychotic behavior is displayed by rocking to and fro, exaggerated gait, frequent stopping and turning, or prolonged staring into space. Other unusual motor activities include maintaining a posture for extended periods of time, facial grimacing, leering, stereotyped gesturing, or unusual movements.

Motivational Anomalies and Decompensation. Finally, McNeil (1970) mentions these two features as prominent processes in psychotic behavior. Disorders of *motivation* may take a number of forms. A person's desire to act may be totally lacking, as it is among some psychotic depressives and schizophrenics; or it may be overly stimulated, as it is among some manics.

Decompensation is a person's inability to mobilize enough energy to meet the ordinary demands of daily existence. Most people, for example, when confronted with a situation requiring immediate action, respond rationally and quickly do what has to be done under the circumstances; their thinking, feeling, and behavior are integrated, calculated, and purposive. Psychotics, in contrast, react in an anxious, agitated, noncontrolled, and disconnected way, almost as if they had no physical or psychological resources available to meet their daily challenges.

Incidence of Psychoses

In both state and county mental hospitals, as well as in those run privately or by the city (psychiatric wards), psychotics account for the greatest number of first admissions. This is shown in Table 12.2, which presents comparable data for these patients and for outpatient clinics. Note also that psychotic patients show up relatively infrequently in outpatient centers (NIMH, 1972).

The average readmission rates to state, county, and private hospitals for psychotic patients are also comparatively higher than those of patients with other disorders. This is shown in Table 12.3 (NIMH, 1972).

As impressive as these figures may be in terms of their implications regarding comparative severities of psychotic and other disturbances,

This painting, The Triumph of Death, *by the Flemish artist Pieter Brueghel, also has elements that resemble the schizophrenic's use of art—for example, the extreme attention to minute detail and the desire on the painter's part to make his comment as comprehensive as possible. The themes of death and horror are also quite evident in the artwork of schizophrenics. (Partial work shown.)*

(Museo del Prado)

they should be interpreted cautiously. No doubt many of the observed differences result from the interaction of several of the following extraneous factors that determine what types of patients are admitted to a specific facility and what will be their length of stay:

The referral practices of various health, educational, welfare, and correctional agencies

Different frames of reference for diagnoses among psychologists, psychiatrists, and physicians in private practice

The varying administrative, legal, fiscal, and clinical policies of different types of facilities

Table 12.2

Incidence of Psychoses and Other Diagnostic Types in Hospitals and Clinics

Type of Mental Health Facility	Disorder	Percent
State and county hospital	Brain syndromes	11
	Schizophrenia	30
	Alcoholic disorders[a]	18
	Personality disorders[b]	10
	Depressive disorders[c]	10
	All others	21
Private mental hospitals	Depressive disorders[c]	37
	Schizophrenia	19
	Psychoneurotic disorders[d]	7
	Alcoholic disorders[a]	11
	Personality disorders[b]	6
	All others	20
Psychiatric services in general hospitals	Depressive disorders[a]	34
	Psychoneurotic disorders[d]	12
	Schizophrenia	17
	Alcoholic disorders[a]	8
	Brain syndromes	7
	All others	12
Outpatient clinics	Personality disorders[b]	18
	Transient situational personality disorders	6
	Schizophrenia	22
	Depressive disorders[c]	7
	Psychoneurotic disorders[d]	22
	All others	25

[a] Includes brain syndromes associated with alcohol and the category alcoholism from the personality disorders.
[b] Includes all personality disorders except alcoholism.
[c] Includes affective reactions and neurotic depressive reactions.
[d] Includes all neurotic disorders except neurotic depressions.

The availability and effectiveness of different types of programs to meet the needs of different kinds of patients

The extent to which alternative forms of care are available in a given area

The attitudes of patients and their families toward treatment and toward particular types of facilities

Health insurance coverage

In general, however, institutionalization for psychotic individuals has followed the dramatic shift in patterns of use of mental health facilities noted for all psychiatric patients, a shift from inpatient to outpatient care (see Keith et al., 1977). Whereas in 1955, 77 percent of all patient-care episodes were in inpatient settings, the proportion dropped to 32 percent by 1973. Moreover, the average length of inpatient stay shortened from 41 days in state and county hospitals to 20 days. These shifts have been attributed to the greater use of community-based treatment facilities and the usefulness of major tranquilizers in controlling the symptoms of the psychoses.

Patterns of care for schizophrenic patients do differ from the care provided for all psychiatric patients. Schizophrenic patients usually have longer stays than other psychiatric patients except those with depressive disorders. For example, in 1970–1971, the average length of stay for a schizophrenic was 12.9 days compared with 11.4 days for all patients in state and county facilities (Taube, 1973, 1976). Moreover the majority of schizophrenics (62 percent) still receive inpatient treatment.

In the remaining pages of this chapter we shall discuss schizophrenia, one of the most prevalent and also most interesting types of psy-

Table 12.3
Readmission Rates for Varying Groups of Patients
in Long-term Mental Hospitals

Type of Hospital	Disorder	Percent
State and county	Schizophrenia	48
	Brain syndromes	23
	Mental deficiency	8
	Depressive disorders[c]	5
	Alcoholic disorders[a]	5
	All others	11
Private	Schizophrenia	26
	Depressive disorders[c]	20
	Brain syndromes	17
	Personality disorders[b]	9
	Psychoneurotic disorders[d]	5
	All others	23

[a] Includes brain syndromes associated with alcohol and the category alcoholism from the personality disorders.
[b] Includes all personality disorders except alcoholism.
[c] Includes affective reactions and neurotic depressive reactions.
[d] Includes all neurotic disorders except neurotic depressions.

chosis, and paranoia. In Chapter 13 we discuss childhood and adolescent schizophrenia, and in Chapter 14 we shall conclude our discussion of psychoses with the affective disorders.

Categories of Schizophrenia

The earlier classification of the American Psychiatric Association lists 11 categories of schizophrenia (simple, hebephrenic, catatonic, paranoid, acute schizophrenic episode, latent, residual, schizo-affective, childhood, chronic undifferentiated, and other) and describes their common characteristics as follows (APA, 1968, p. 33):[5]

This large category includes a group of disorders manifested by characteristic disturbances of thinking, mood and behavior. Disturbances of thinking are marked by alterations of concept formation which may lead to misinterpretation of reality and sometimes to delusions and hallucinations, which frequently appear psychologically self-protective. Corollary mood changes include ambivalent, constricted and inappropriate emotional responsiveness and loss of empathy with others. Behavior may be withdrawn, regressive and bizarre.

And regarding the distinctions between these disorders and the affective and paranoid ones, the APA classification continues (p. 33):

The schizophrenias, in which the mental status is attributable primarily to a thought disorder, are to be distinguished from the Major affective illnesses which are dominated by a mood disorder. The Paranoid states are distinguished from schizophrenia by the narrowness of their distortions of reality and by the absence of other psychotic symptoms.

From among the 11 categories of schizophrenia described above, we shall consider four: *simple, hebephrenic, catatonic,* and *paranoid.* Although the symptoms vary from one form to another, and one patient may display a variety of symptoms during the course of the illness, most varieties of schizophrenia are marked by looseness of thinking, bizarre behavior, chaotic lifestyle, and withdrawal. In severe cases regressive behavior is common, as are gross personality disorganization, unsystematized delusions of persecution, and bizarre auditory hallucinations. All these symptoms may appear at any time in life, but commonly first occur between 15 and 25 years of age. The condition usually persists, although with fluctuations, throughout the individual's life (also see APA, 1980).

Simple Schizophrenia

Simple schizophrenia develops slowly and insidiously, usually beginning during adolescence. It often involves reduction of external attachments and interests, apathy and indifference, impoverishment of interpersonal relations, mental deficit, and lower levels of adjustment and functioning than the individual experienced prior to its onset. This condition is the least dramatically psychotic among the four types of schizophrenia to be discussed; but in contrast to the *schizoid personality,* who is a secluded and withdrawn type of social isolate familiar to most of us, the simple schizophrenic's total lifestyle is more profoundly disrupted.

The simple schizophrenic wants to be alone and, in his quest for seclusion, may wander off to strange places or spend nights sleeping in parks or abandoned houses. When questioned about his lack of ambition or aimless wandering, he is likely to be vague, evasive, monosyllabic, and even perplexed about his condition. He seems to

---

[5] The most recent draft of DSM III (1980) retains seven categories: disorganized (hebephrenic); catatonic; paranoid; schizo-affective, depressed; manic; undifferentiated; and residual.

have difficulty focusing or sustaining his attention and may sit in one place, grimacing for hours at a time. Such behavior becomes especially noticeable if his prepsychotic personality contained no traces of it.

His relatives, especially members of the immediate family, realize that something is wrong when he does not live up to expectations based on earlier accomplishments. Hallucinations, although rare, are auditory and manifest themselves as a "buzzing" or "ringing" in the ears. Delusions are absent. Consequently these patients are sometimes misclassified as mental retardates; and frequently it is only after brain damage has been ruled out by psychological tests and other examinations that the diagnosis of simple schizophrenia is made.

Uncomplicated environments frequently enable the simple schizophrenic to make the minimal adjustments necessary for survival, and thereby many of them avoid identification and hospitalization. For example, the population of street people, the flower children of the late 1960s, and more recent commune dwellers have included in their ranks many simple schizophrenics. Case Report 12.1 describes a typical form of this disorder in an adult who, in his earlier years, might easily have wandered off to live in the once seemingly protective environments of the Haight–Ashbury, Berkeley, and the East Village.

Case Report 12.1 *Simple Schizophrenia*

Albert S., the 35-year-old, unmarried son of a wealthy midwestern shoe manufacturer, had been in and out of a VA hospital several times since his discharge from the army ten years earlier. His service record indicated nothing unusual, and his pre-service schooling earned him a bachelor's degree in business administration. Since his military discharge, Albert had been handling the bookkeeping in his father's factory, except during his stays in the hospital.

Albert's father reported that he began to notice irregularities in his accounts about five years before Albert's first hospital admission and that at about the same time Albert began to show a pattern of absenteeism. Close questioning was unproductive except that Albert created the distinct impression, at least in his father's mind, that he resented working for him. When Albert was encouraged to try to go out on his own, he became evasive and replied cryptically, "I'll haul the load." The family became increasingly concerned when Albert's previous tidiness deteriorated first to slovenliness and then to a complete neglect of even the rudiments of personal hygiene.

His absence from work and the family home increased, and it was discovered that he spent these times wandering through the city streets. He spent many nights sleeping in the back of parked trucks or almost anywhere that provided free space. At about this time Albert would show up for work, collect his wages, and promptly go to the city's downtown section to distribute his money dollar by dollar to passers-by. With each dollar gift he would say, "What's mine is yours—God bless," Albert's most recent hospitalization occurred at about this time.

His behavior in the ward during each of his hospitalizations was similar, without any deterioration over the 10-year period. He had a look of perplexity about him; didn't mix easily with other patients; spoke reluctantly, slowly, and cryptically; and showed no signs of being hallucinatory or delusional. A model patient in every way except that he would not participate in any activities, Albert was content to sit and stare blankly in the direction of a television set that might be tuned in to a program or not, or might even be disconnected. Toward the end of each of his hospital stays, usually after about 60 days of hospitalization, he expressed some interest in going back to his family and job, only to return three months later without any apparent goals in life.

Arthur H. Bremer, 21, the would-be assassin of Alabama Governor George Wallace during his 1972 presidential campaign tour, is shown in this picture with his characteristic enigmatic grin. This grin, which in many psychotics may change to a grotesque grimace within moments, is similar to one that hebephrenic schizophrenics often display.

In the hospital the hebephrenic can be a serious problem because of regressive behavior, which in the more advanced stages of the disorder, includes wetting and soiling, licking and biting of his or her hands, and constant rocking to and fro accompanied by head banging against a wall. The following excerpts, taken from the administration of the Wechsler Adult Intelligence Scale to a 40-year-old woman, illustrate a predominantly hebephrenic mood:

Ex.: *What are the colors in the American flag?*
Pa.: *Well, I think they are red. Let's see now, oh yes, they're quite red, red, red, red.*
Ex.: *How many months are there in a year?*
Pa.: *Some years have many [crying] and some have more. There aren't many more, are there?*
Ex.: *Why do we wash clothes?*
Pa.: *That's a communist conspiracy [laughs, and then sings some verse she composed]. The communist powers have perverted our minds with mindless sexism that subverts the sexless mindlessness that sucks the soul [patient doubles up with laughter].*
Ex.: *Okay, but can you tell me why we wash clothes?*
Pa.: *We don't wash clothes no more.*
Ex.: *Now, let us try these. How much is four dollars and five dollars?*
Pa.: *Now I remember. . . . Let's see now, well, I had this friend who borrowed, florrowed, and sorrowed till she could pay no more, and then she up and died, penniless as a pauper, get it?*

Hebephrenic Schizophrenia

Hebephrenic schizophrenia also has an early onset, frequently in the teens. The hebephrenic is characterized by impulsive conduct, sudden spontaneous laughing and crying, grotesque grimacing, and silly grinning. Hebephrenics' hallucinations are often pornographic ("two cats screwing on your writing pad, Doc"), and their delusional thinking is fragmented and inconsistent from one moment to the next.

Catatonic Schizophrenia

Catatonic patients will display, in addition to some of the other behaviors of schizophrenia, a fluctuation of affect that includes depression, stupor, and excitement. The excitement may occur after long periods of apathy during which these patients may have sat idly in one position or remained in bed. During this seemingly depressed or stuporous stage, they may be mute, refuse to eat, be totally unresponsive to their surroundings, and be incontinent or totally retentive; they may maintain one posture for hours or days. During this period others may have to feed them, sometimes intravaneously, and attend to all their physical needs.

Except for his odd posturing, the catatonic resembles a deeply depressed patient. A distinguishing diagnostic feature, however, is his *waxy flexibility*, which allows him to maintain any posture, no matter how uncomfortable, that he is placed in, either by himself or by someone else. His experiences are vivid during these periods: after emerging from them, he frequently tells of having heard and experienced things but of being unable to respond because he was convinced that talking would cause "something catastrophic" to occur.

During the *catatonic excitement* episode, which, as we stated earlier, often follows stupor, the patient is agitated and hyperactive, flails out wildly at anyone within range, talks excitedly and incoherently, and may assault someone or mutilate himself severely. Later he may report having been completely under the command of his voices or having been divinely inspired.

In spite of the dramatic aspects of catatonic schizophrenia—certainly in many respects more dramatic than the other varieties of schizophrenia dealt with so far and the paranoid forms to be discussed next—catatonic patients do have a greater likelihood of recovery. This is more true if the patient's illness is of sudden onset, if it is in later life, and if he has had no history of previous withdrawal and apathy.

Case Report 12.2, written up by Maher (1966, pp. 305–306) and based on a description by Meehl (1947), illustrates most features of catatonic schizophrenia. This case is unusual in two respects, however, because the woman's psychosis began with an excited episode and because her mood swings were so rapid. More commonly catatonia commences with an episode of inert posturing, usually accompanied by mutism, and

the cycles of waxy flexibility and excitement are not of such short duration.

Case Report 12.2 *Catatonic Schizophrenia*

A 45-year-old unmarried schoolteacher was hospitalized following complaints by her family that she was overactive and assaultive, talked irrationally, acted peculiarly, and was generally "out of her head." Her psychotic behavior had developed only four days before admission to the hospital, after she had come to her parents' home from the town in which she was employed. At first she seemed to them to be unwell; her complaints were largely somatic and seemed to involve a headache. A local physician prescribed medicine for her condition, but the next day grossly psychotic symptoms appeared.

She first began to mumble somewhat unclearly about having stolen or lost one hundred dollars from the school milk fund. The family went to the trouble of checking this with the school superintendent, who reported that there was no money missing. She would stand motionless for long periods of time staring vacantly into space; then she would suddenly become active and talk vaguely about someone coming to take her away. At times she would creep around the floor, on her knees with her hands outstretched, exclaiming repeatedly, "A child is born! A child is born!" (possibly a connection with a Christmas play she was directing). With considerable difficulty her parents managed to get her back into bed.

Later she continued to behave peculiarly. She wandered aimlessly around the house, whined and cried a good deal, and said puzzling things. On one occasion she knelt before her mother and cried, "Mother, mother—come!" She still seemed to be under the impression that someone was coming to take her away. Various members of the immediate family would remain at her bedside all night, when on the whole she was reasonably peaceful. She was able to carry on a more or less lucid conversation with her sister, although she was not very voluble and still stared into space for extended intervals.

When she awoke Sunday morning, she had a difficult time putting on her stockings. She ate a hearty breakfast and then at her parents' suggestion lay down for a nap. Upon awakening from this nap, she called her parents into the library, saying that she had something important to talk to them about. However, when they came in to listen, her words were blocked by what seemed to be a speech difficulty. She grasped her father's hand without saying anything and squeezed it so hard that he cried out in pain. When her mother asked her what was the matter with her, she said that her stomach hurt and that she wanted a hot-water bottle for it. Upon being given a hot-water bottle she began to "tear it apart." Then she suddenly became "stiff and rigid." This phenomenon alarmed the mother, who ran to the telephone, saying that she was going to call the physician, whereupon the patient again became active and fought to keep her mother from the telephone. When the physician arrived he decided to administer an intravenous sedative; this required the combined efforts of four people to hold the patient down. During the half hour or so before this injection took effect, she ran and rolled "all over the floor," bumping into furniture and grabbing at people, so that it was necessary to keep objects clear of her to prevent her from injuring herself. Late that afternoon she was brought to the university hospital and admitted to the psychiatric ward.

Once in the hospital this patient's behavior was marked by negativism. Whatever the nurse requested, she would do the opposite. When her temperature was to be taken, she would close her mouth tightly. She would sometimes spit out the food that she had allowed to be put into her mouth, and it was necessary to catheterize [insert a tube in] her because of urinary retention. At times she would be fairly quiet and able to speak easily but within a short time would become tense and hold her arms rigid; then two hours later she would have to be put into restraints because of violent activity and assaultiveness.

SOURCE: *Adapted from* Principles of psychopathology *by B. A. Maher. Copyright © 1966 by McGraw-Hill, Inc. Used with permission of McGraw-Hill Book Company.*

Paranoid Schizophrenia

Of all of the schizophrenias, the paranoid type is the most common. It is characterized chiefly by delusions of persecution and auditory hallucinations. Often delusions of grandeur and an excessive religiosity are also evident. The patient's attitude is usually hostile and aggressive, and behavior tends to be consistent with this animosity. In this regard, DSM II (APA, 1968) differentiates three subtypes of this disorder, depending upon the predominant symptoms—hostile, grandiose, or hallucinatory.

In general paranoid schizophrenia does not involve the gross personality disorganization seen in the hebephrenic and catatonic schizophrenias; this has been attributed to the patient's use of *projection*, by means of which he ascribes to others the characteristics he cannot accept in himself, and as a result of which he may focus on some group of persons he believes are persecuting him.

Its typical onset and course are as follows: first, the individual displays the moodiness, preoccupation, and suspiciousness that resemble simple schizophrenia. Then, gradually, his lifestyle becomes increasingly chaotic, and he withdraws from social contacts, gives up or loses his job, gets into constant battles with others whom he accuses of plotting against him, refuses to eat outside the home, questions the contents of food given him at home, becomes abusive, and assaults those around him.

In the more advanced stages of active paranoid schizophrenia, the person may attack members of his family because he is convinced that they are conspiring with others to do him in, or he may do so because his voices advise him to. His speech may be voluble and hoarse because of excited shouting; he may ramble incoherently, make strange gestures with his hands that have special significance for him, and occasionally utter magical phrases that make sense only to him. At this active stage of the disorder it is impossible to be around him without becoming a target of his delusional thinking; if he is grandiose, he expects others to treat him in a manner appropriate to the role he has adopted; if he feels persecuted, he accuses everyone of plotting against him.

Some of the following ideas often expressed by paranoid schizophrenics may serve to illustrate the type of thinking prevalent in this disorder:

My voices keep calling me "dirty dog." . . . He stole my childhood innocence and then some. . . . Even the reporters on TV steal my ideas. . . . I have X-ray vision. . . . The medirulers inject urine in my blood to influence my thinking. . . . I am no longer real. . . . My stomach is stone. . . . The system punishing me will be punished in return.

The following dialogue between a 60-year-old paranoid schizophrenic man in a state hospital and a clinical psychologist also captures the tenor of this form of thinking and behaving:

Dr.: *Can I get you to join the group therapy session this afternoon? You know, Herbert, you're the only holdout from among the guys on your ward.*

Pa.: *So be it doc, so be it. You're not gonna get me in on one of those crazy groups. I got enough troubles keeping away from those guys as is.*

Dr.: *Why do you want to do that?*

Pa.: *They're fixing to get rid of me.*

Dr.: *How do you know that?*

Pa.: *Why, didn't you see David looking at me funnylike when he passed here before? And you know, they're all spying on me again — through the mirrors that they put around my room at night. Do you like my shave?*

Dr.: *Your shave?*

Pa.: *Yeah, my shave. That crazy guy came around last night and pasted hair all over my body again. I'll get it off. He's got one of them hair-pasting dingoes.*

Dr.: *Do you think if you joined the group, maybe that would stop?*

Pa.: *What are you talking about? He'd never tell*

me it was him. He wouldn't even look at me — they're all in on it.

Dr.: *What about Jack? You seem to get along O.K. with him. He's in the group.*

Pa.: *Jack! He's the worst of the lot.*

Dr.: *I'd really like to help you get out of here. You've been here more than 15 years. We've got this resocialization program. . . .*

Pa.: *Oh, I'll get out. Don't you worry. I'll escape out of this crazy place.*

Dr.: *But you don't have to escape. I can help you get out.*

Pa.: *What? And get on the outside where they can really foul me up. No sir, not me. Besides, you need a cure so badly by your method that you want to use me. I'm not gonna be your first cure. No sir, I'll do it my own way.*

The noteworthy points about this conversation are that Herbert, the patient, has delusions of persecution that include the psychologist and several imaginary and real people who spy on him and who cover his body with hair. Because he believes that others are out to get rid of him, he does not participate in group activities and he finds significance in other people's gestures and looks. And although he does talk about leaving the hospital, he is ambivalent about the prospects because of his fear of what may happen to him on the outside.

It is important also to note that his delusional thinking is an integrating part of his personality because it allows him to focus on one or two aspects of his environment rather than to show concern about a host of problems. It could be argued, for example, that Herbert really doesn't want to leave the hospital for fear of all the adjustments he would have to make after 15 years of institutionalization. Instead he blames his reluctance to face the outside world on the fact that it is a place "where they can really foul me up." In one sense, of course, Herbert may be making a realistic assessment of the outside world's likely impact on him, on the basis of his early experiences.

Process and Reactive Schizophrenia

In addition to the categories of schizophrenia discussed above, there is another widely accepted distinction—between *process* and *reactive schizophrenia* (Kantor et al., 1953), first noted by Bleuler in 1911 but not followed up by him. The process schizophrenic has a life history of psychological difficulties, withdrawal from people, ineffectuality, and an unfavorable prognosis. The reactive schizophrenic, in contrast, has a history of better social adjustment and competence, experiences a more sudden onset of symptoms, shows a lesser degree of thought disturbance, and has a more favorable prognosis (Phillips, 1966).

Earlier formulations held that the process disorders were of genetic and constitutional origin, the reactive disorders of psychogenic origin. More recent theorists tend to discount this view and propose, instead, that they are two endpoints on a continuum of greater (process) to lesser (reactive) psychopathology. Some theorists place the process and reactive types on a malignant–benign, or a chronic–acute, scale. These demarcations point to differences that may have etiological and prognostic significance.

Some of the differentiating characteristics between these endpoints on a continuum are shown in Table 12.4, where it can be seen that the two groups, at least from the evidence of clinical studies, are quite different. Caution should be exercised, however, in interpreting a number of the case history items presented in this table. For example, some of the items used to describe process schizophrenia have not been supported by recent evidence. Thus, as we show in our discussion of etiology, it is not a foregone conclusion that "early psychological trauma," "physical illness," "family troubles," an "overprotective or rejecting mother," or a "rejecting father" are necessarily a part of the background of schizophrenics. Some of the items presented in Table 12.4 emerged from one study (Kantor et al., 1953), and should be interpreted with caution.

Several studies on the prognosis of the two types of schizophrenia have been conducted and, as we said earlier, they have indicated that reactive types have more favorable outcomes. We shall have more to say about these studies in a later discussion.

Unfortunately most patients do not display symptoms as clear-cut as the categories and illustrative cases described above seem to imply. The result is that experts sometimes disagree on the diagnosis of schizophrenia (see Salzinger, 1973). In one review of studies on the reliability of diagnoses of schizophrenia (Zubin, 1967), agreement between any two psychiatrists varied from no agreement at all to 80 percent agreement. This unreliability of diagnosis is due in part to the variability of specific symptoms from one schizophrenic patient to another, but there is also evidence that the diagnostic system and errors of observation and interpretation contribute to the unreliability.

That the nosological system is faulty has been argued most convincingly by Zubin (1967), who mentions that the system was decided on by majority vote rather than by an empirical approach to diagnosis. But errors of observation and interpretation made by individuals have perhaps played an even greater part in disagreements among diagnosticians. In one interesting study (Langer and Abelson, 1974) on the effects of contextual factors in diagnosis, two psychologists asked two groups of clinicians to evaluate the psychopathology of a man being interviewed. Half of each group of clinicians was told that the man was a patient, the other half that he was a job applicant. They were asked to rate the man on a 10-point scale in which 1 indicated he was very disturbed and 10 very well adjusted. The clinicians to whom the man had been identified as a patient gave him an overall rating of 3.47; when he was presented as a job applicant, they gave him a rating of 6.2. Thus the context or suggestion of psychopathology led to the discovery of it for some clinicians.

Table 12.4
Items Defining Frame of Reference for Case History Judgments

Process Schizophrenia	Reactive Schizophrenia

Birth to the Fifth Year

Process Schizophrenia	Reactive Schizophrenia
a. Early psychological trauma	a. Good psychological history
b. Physical illness–severe or long	b. Good physical health
c. Odd member of family	c. Normal member of family

Fifth Year to Adolescence

a. Difficulties at school	a. Well adjusted at school
b. Family troubles paralleled by sudden changes in patient's behavior	b. Domestic troubles unaccompanied by behavior disruptions; patient "had what it took"
c. Introverted behavior trends and interests	c. Extroverted behavior trends and interests
d. History of breakdown of social, physical, mental functioning	d. History of adequate social, physical, mental functioning
e. Pathological siblings	e. Normal siblings
f. Overprotective or rejecting mother, "momism"	f. Normally protective, accepting mother
g. Rejecting father	g. Accepting father

Adolescence to Adulthood

a. Lack of heterosexuality	a. Heterosexual behavior
b. Insidious, gradual onset of psychosis without pertinent stress	b. Sudden onset of psychosis; stress present and pertinent; later onset
c. Physical aggression	c. Verbal aggression
d. Poor response to treatment	d. Good response to treatment
e. Lengthy stay in hospital	e. Short course in hospital

Adulthood

a. Massive paranoia	a. Minor paranoid trends
b. Little capacity for alcohol	b. Much capacity for alcohol
c. No manic-depressive component	c. Presence of manic-depressive component
d. Failure under adversity	d. Success despite adversity
e. Discrepancy between ability and achievement	e. Harmony between ability and achievement
f. Awareness of change in self	f. No sensation of change
g. Somatic delusions	g. Absence of somatic delusions
h. Clash between culture and environment	h. Harmony between culture and environment
i. Loss of decency (nudity, public masturbation, etc.)	i. Retention of decency

Source: Kantor, R. E., Wallner, J. M., and Winder, C. L. Process and reactive schizophrenia. Journal of Consulting Psychology, 1953, 17, 157–162.

Causes of the Schizophrenias

As we indicated earlier, despite the long history of schizophrenia, its causes remain undiscovered. Indeed it is not yet clear whether its origins are biological or whether a combination of biological and other factors interact in complex ways.

Genetic Factors

In his presidential address to the American Psychological Association, Paul E. Meehl (1962, p. 827) posed the following question:

Suppose that you were required to write down a procedure for selecting an individual from the population who could be diagnosed as schizophrenic by a psychiatric staff; you have to wager one thousand dollars on being right; you may not include in your selection procedure any behavioral fact, such as a symptom or a trait manifested by the individual. What would you write down?

His answer: "There is only one thing you could write down that would give you a better than even chance of winning such a bet—namely, 'find an individual X who has a schizophrenic identical twin.'" More specifically, Meehl's conclusion is that "schizophrenia, while its content is learned, is fundamentally a neurological disease of genetic origin."

Thus Meehl considers the inherited brain defect a necessary condition for schizophrenia; without it schizophrenia is not possible. This leads him to suggest that the neurological defect, while it may always be present in schizophrenia, is most likely to lead to clinical schizophrenia when an individual with this defect is reared in a stressful environment. In ordinary, nonstressful life situations, according to Meehl, a person with this biochemical defect displays *schizotypic* behavior, which, although it resembles schizophrenia, is much milder and manifests itself in a tendency toward withdrawal and inappropriate emotional expression.

The distinction that Meehl draws is between *necessary* and *sufficient* causation; we want to emphasize its importance, for it is relevant to the remainder of our discussion of causation. Very simply paraphrased, the point is that heredity (or any other agent) may play an important part in causing a disorder, in that it may be a necessary condition for it to occur, but heredity alone may not be adequate or sufficient to trigger schizophrenia. This suggests that the necessary causal agent interacts with a number of other conditions to produce the observed disorder, an especially interesting hypothesis in view of the finding that situational stresses can trigger schizophrenic episodes (Birley and Brown, 1970).

The Evidence from Adoption Studies. For more than a decade investigators interested in the genetic causation of schizophrenia have taken advantage of the excellent record-keeping system of Denmark to study the effects of heredity and environment, specifically where records were carefully kept on adopted children. In a cross-fostering study, for example, Wender and his associates (1974) compared three groups of "adopted-away" offspring: (1) children ("adoptive-index") who had one biological parent with a schizophrenia diagnosis and were raised by parents who had never received a psychiatric label; (2) children ("adoptive-control") with psychiatrically well biological parents and normal adopting parents; and (3) children ("cross-fostered") with normal biological parents raised by parents one of whom received a diagnosis of schizophrenia.

The adoptees underwent three to five hours of a semistructured psychiatric interview and one and a half days of psychological tests. The interviewing psychiatrist summarized his data on a card, and the cards of all subjects were then sorted on a 20-point scale from "least ill" to "most ill" without knowledge of the group from which the subject came.

The results indicated that 18.8 percent (total $N = 69$) of index adoptees fell into the "most ill" upper quartile of the rank, whereas 10.1 percent (total $N = 79$) of adopted controls and 10.7 percent (total $N = 28$) of cross-fostered subjects fell into the same quartile. When the adopted control and cross-fostered groups are combined (both have psychiatrically well biological parents), the difference is even more striking, with 19.7 of the adopted index group as compared to 9.4 of the adopted control and cross-fostered groups falling into the "most ill" quartile. These results imply that offspring of schizophrenic parents reared by normal adoptive parents had a greater probability of receiving a schizophrenia diagnosis than the cross-fostered or control adoptees.

Critical Comment. These findings were admittedly fraught with problems. The authors pointed out that it was difficult to get adequate samples for all the groups. But even among the participating subjects, the mean age was such that an appreciable risk remains that some children from any of the groups could still develop the disorder. Another criticism was that the age of transfer to the adopting parents varied from 5 days to 7 years and, in some instances, more than one set of possible adopting parents refused to adopt the child. And finally, as Wender and his associates (1974) and Rosenthal (1973) note, since an adopted-away child receives half his genes from each parent, a genetic study that does not include an assessment of the nonschizophrenic parent is subject to the unknown effects of that parent's genes. They conclude, therefore, that it is essential to examine both parents, an investigation Rosenthal (1973) undertook.

Rosenthal studied the co-parents of the adopted-away offspring of a schizophrenic parent. In all there were 79 co-parents. The major findings as summarized by Keith and his colleagues (1977) are as follows: when the index parent is female, the co-parent is diagnosed as having either a schizophrenic or other psycho-pathic disorder in 56 percent of the matings (divided about equally between the two diagnoses). When the index parent is male, almost half the female co-parents have schizophrenia diagnoses. When both parents have schizophrenia diagnoses, 9 of 17, or 53 percent of the offspring, had schizophrenia diagnoses. Among those who had only one parent with a diagnosis of schizophrenia, about 10.5 percent had such a diagnosis.

The Evidence from Twin Studies. The idea that schizophrenia is transmitted genetically has traditionally been supported by twin studies, especially those in which the incidence of the disorder among identical twins (monozygotic, or MZ) is greater than among fraternal twins (dizygotic, or DZ), ordinary siblings, and other close and distant relatives. Identical twins, it will be recalled from our earlier discussion (Chapter 5), have the same genetic endowments, since they result from the splitting of a single fertilized ovum (hence *monozygotic*); fraternal twins are as similar genetically as any two siblings born of the same parents, and they result from the simultaneous fertilization of two separate ova (hence *dizygotic*); and, because sex is genetically determined, MZs are always same-sexed, while DZs may be of different sexes. Therefore, since MZ twins are of identical heredity, a disorder with a purely genetic origin should show up in both members of the pair. Likewise the incidence of a genetic disorder should be much lower among DZ twins. These twin comparisons, which presuppose that inherited disorders appear with greater frequency among genetically similar persons, are usually expressed in *concordance ratios* — the percentage of relatives of schizophrenic persons who also have the disorder.

Some of the findings from genetic studies are summarized in Table 12.5, where we see that the average concordance ratio for MZ twins is about 50 percent (with a range from 6 to 69 percent); for DZ twins the average ratio is considerably lower, at about 12 percent (with a range from 0 to 19);

and for opposite-sex DZ twins, examined in another study by the same researchers (Gottesman and Shields, 1966), it is still lower, at about 5 percent (range: 0 to 11 percent).

The lower concordance ratios among opposite-sex than among same-sex DZs suggest that strong environmental factors are also operating, since opposite-sex siblings are usually treated more differentially than same-sex DZ twins.[6] But the findings in general tend to support the inheritability of schizophrenia, by showing a sig-

nificantly greater probability among MZs than among DZs that when one twin has the disorder, the other will also have it.

In a later comprehensive review of many twin studies Rosenthal (1970, 1971), who is much in agreement with Meehl, leans toward a heredity–environment interactive theory of the origins of schizophrenia. On the basis of his review he proposes that a psychopathological constitutional predisposition is inherited and that manifestations of the disorder depend on whether or not predisposed persons encounter stressors. Likewise, according to this formulation, the nature and severity of the symptoms depend on an individual's predisposition and the form of stress encountered.

---

[6] An excellent review of the state of concordance ratio studies appears in Heston's article on the genetics of schizophrenia (1970).

Table 12.5
Studies of Schizophrenia in Twins

		Concordance	
		MZ Twins	*DZ Twins (same sex)*
Investigator	*Country*	*Percent/N* [a]	*Percent/N* [a]
Kallmann (1946)	USA	69/174	11/296
Allen et al. (1972)	USA	27/95	5/125
Slater (1953)	UK	65/37	14/58
Essen–Möller (1941)	Sweden	64/11	15/27
Rosanoff et al. (1934)	USA	61/41	13/53
Inouye (1961)	Japan	60/55	18/11
Luxenburger (1928)	Germany	58/19	0/13
Gottesman and Shields (1972)	UK	40–50/22	9–10/33
Kinglen (1967)[b]	Norway	25/38	4–10/90
Tienari (1971)[b]	Finland	6–36/16	5–14/20
Fischer et al. (1969)	Denmark	24–48/21	10–19/41

Source: Adapted from Gottesman, I. I. and Shields, J. Schizophrenia and genetics: a twin study vantage point. New York: Academic Press, 1972. References to the studies mentioned can be found in this source.
[a] N = number of sets of twins studied.
[b] Male subjects only and without age correction.

The theory further suggests that the precipitating factors may be head trauma, disease, alcohol, drugs, childbirth, exhaustion, or other stressors; and that remission, or recovery, from schizophrenia may occur when the physiological aspects of the disease or the stressors are reduced.

In view of Rosenthal's conclusions the next question is, "How does one study predisposition toward schizophrenia?" This is an especially difficult problem because clinicians and researchers do not usually see prepsychotic people, but only individuals who have developed their disorders. Two investigators bypassed this difficulty, as we indicate below, by locating children whose parents are schizophrenic. Such research, of course, presupposes the inheritance of the characteristic under investigation.

Evidence about Genetic Predisposition. One method of studying prepsychotic characteristics (Mednick and Schulsinger, 1965; Mednick, 1970), involves follow-ups of a population having a *high risk* for the disorder. After defining the high risk population as normally functioning children who have chronic and severely schizophrenic mothers, these psychologists located 207 high-risk subjects and compared them with 104 normal controls in terms of autonomic responsivity. The researchers found highly significant differences between these two groups in galvanic skin response latency (time that elapses from the onset of a stimulus to the organism's reaction), with high-risk children showing shorter latency periods than controls to stress stimuli. This has led Mednick and his associates to conclude tentatively that high-risk individuals have more volatile autonomic nervous systems than normals.[7]

In a long-term study underway at the University of Pittsburgh, Schachter and his associates (1972) are also studying high-risk subjects. The latter are infants of schizophrenic parents, and degree of risk is defined by whether the child has two schizophrenic parents (very high risk) or only a single such parent. The investigators' main intent is to learn whether high-risk subjects are neurophysiologically more responsive than low-risk subjects.

Their preliminary results, as indicated by higher tonic heart rates measured among high-risk infants and electroencephalograph (EEG), or brain wave, differences between the high-risk offspring and low-risk subjects, suggest that the high-risk subjects may be neurophysiologically more responsive. Similar differences between normal and high-risk schizophrenic offspring have been reported by others who have studied infants (Yarden and Suranyi, 1968), children (Fish, 1971), and adolescents and adults (Ax and Bamford, 1970; Mednick, 1970).

Thus we see that the findings of studies with high-risk-for-schizophrenia subjects suggest a relatively greater autonomic and central nervous system reactivity in prepsychotic individuals. This area of research is only now receiving the attention it deserves, and it is still too early to know whether it will solve the mysteries of schizophrenia. But even if further studies corroborate the findings of greater autonomic and central nervous system volatility among preschizophrenics, another part of the mystery still remains: namely, what environmental stressors interact with psychotic predisposition to trigger the disorder. The way to answer this question is to examine the backgrounds of high-risk and normal subjects many years before they either develop or do not develop the disorder. This is a quite different approach from retrospectively focusing on the family backgrounds of schizophrenics (see the discussion of Schofield and Balian's study, 1959, p. 277).

---

[7]The investigators intend follow-up studies of 20 to 25 years and estimate that from among their 311 subjects, 100 will succumb to some form of mental illness and that 25 to 30 will become schizophrenic. Mednick (1970) also reported that a significant number of their high-risk subjects had undergone complications at the time of their birth delivery, a finding that may be important.

Critical Comment. While the genetic risk strategy seems to be valuable, Keith et al. (1977) suggest that since 90 percent of persons diagnosed as schizophrenic do not have parents so labeled, the findings of the high-risk studies may be generalizable to a minimum of 10 percent of schizophrenics. This potential limitation of applicability must be kept in mind as the original sample of high-risk subjects begins to move into the period of risk.

Of perhaps greater importance than the limited generalizability of these studies are the ethical issues they raise. These issues are of growing concern to high-risk researchers and fall into two separate but related areas: (1) the unintended effects of research itself on the subjects; and (2) the question of intervention with persons who did not originally come for treatment but who may (or may not) need help. Guidelines are now being developed to deal with the issues (see Keith et al., 1977, p. 543).

Biochemical Factors

Discovering biochemical substances in abnormal persons has always appealed to behavioral scientists because it carries the implication that therapy could be aimed at removing or destroying these substances. A major impetus to this research occurred with the discovery of the psychological effects of the hallucinogens (hallucination-producing drugs), among which the best known were mescaline and lysergic acid diethylamide (LSD-25).

At first these drugs were called *psychotomimetic* drugs because of their seeming ability to induce model psychoses in normals. Researchers seized upon the possibility that psychosis could be induced in the laboratory where it could be studied exhaustively, and that eventually these studies could isolate some process whereby the psychotic's body manufactured its own hallucinogen. Unfortunately, however, the basic assumption of much of this work—that the mental states produced by hallucinogens are truly comparable to naturally occurring psychoses (see Chapter 10)—has been seriously challenged. There are many superficial resemblances but, as one researcher suggested, "the total clinical syndrome is considerably different" (Hollister, 1968, p. 122).

The search for the biochemical origins of schizophrenia was also inspired by the reports of Heath and his coworkers that schizophrenic patients have abnormal EEG spiking in the septal region of the brain, a locus important in the production of emotions, particularly pleasure (Heath et al., 1954; Heath and Leach, 1962). The same researchers also reported that schizophrenic patients produce an abnormal blood substance, *taraxein* (derived from the Greek word meaning "to be disoriented or disorganized"), which is a protein that combines with other bodily substances to become toxic to the central nervous system (Heath, 1963, 1966; Heath et al., 1970).

When this substance was injected into monkeys, their EEG brain wave recordings resembled those of psychotic patients; and after it was introduced into the blood of 32 human volunteers, it produced a clinical picture of schizophrenia with symptoms of catatonia-like behavior, suspiciousness, autism, grandiosity, and many other psychotic mannerisms and patterns.

Attempts to replicate the preceding findings in other laboratories, however, have not been successful (Robins, 1957; Siegel et al., 1959; also see Mosher and Feinsilver, 1970). This raises the question of what role suggestion may have played in the original experiments. As Robert Rosenthal (1966) has made us well aware, an experimenter's biases not only can influence his or her perception of results in many subtle ways, but can also be transmitted to the experimenter's subjects. Even without such subtle communication of expected outcomes, the individual's knowledge that he or she has been injected with taraxein, or with any serum of schizophrenics, may in and of itself produce symptoms in suggestible subjects.[8] Therefore, it is essential that these and similar studies be replicated under rigorous experimental conditions.

Later experiments provided some evidence for the theory that chemical damage to the noradrenergic (sympathetic) reward system by a substance called 6-hydroxydopamine (6-HD) causes schizophrenia (Stein and Wise, 1971). Much of the evidence in support of this theory has come from work in which catatonia-like behavior (waxy flexibility) was induced in rats by injecting 6-HD intraventricularly (into the ventricles of the brain).

According to the theory, the damage is inflicted in the organism's reward system of the brain. Electron microscope evidence revealed that specific nerve terminals in the brain degenerate and eventually disappear after repeated doses of 6-HD. The most promising aspect of this work is that the investigators found that Chlorpromazine, the drug used in the treatment of schizophrenia, prevents the damage. Evidently this drug protects the reward system because it blocks the uptake of internally produced 6-HD into the nerve endings. Therefore, even if schizophrenics can be assumed to continue to produce 6-HD endogenously, perhaps because of a genetic predisposition to do so, the toxic substance can no longer gain entry to the vulnerable site.

The predominant biochemical hypothesis of schizophrenia is currently the "dopamine (DA) hypothesis" (see Meltzer and Stahl, 1976). In its simplest form this hypothesis states that schizophrenia may be related to a relative excess of DA-dependent neuronal activity. It is derived from pharmacologic evidence that drugs that decrease DA activity (for example, phenothiazines) may be antipsychotic and drugs that promote DA activity (for example, amphetamines) may be psychotomimetic. The means by which too much

dopamine is produced are not yet known.

To summarize, we can say that although the preceding biochemical studies are extremely important in the search for the origins of schizophrenia, several methodological problems still have to be overcome, especially in work with human beings.

First, as we already indicated, the symptoms of schizophrenia and those produced by the hallucinogenic drugs are easily differentiated and therefore bear a questionable equivalence (Hollister, 1968).

Second, schizophrenia is a lifelong disorder, and therefore it seems unlikely that the implicated chemical substances could be produced within the body in adequate quantities continuously without the person developing a tolerance.

Third, the presence of certain substances such as taraxein and copper in human blood and urine has not always been replicated; and in some instances it has even been traced to the effects of hospital diets and routine.

And, finally, even after it has been demonstrated that specific biochemical changes are unique to schizophrenia, it is still not known how the substances are produced, how they do their damage, and why toxic quantities of these substances are found only in schizophrenics.

Intrapsychic Models

Besides contributing to the classification of schizophrenia, Eugene Bleuler is also closely linked with early attempts to understand the disorder. He coined the term *autism* (Bleuler, 1913), which he conceptualized as a form of schizophrenic thinking marked by the individual's creating a world of fantasy.

Although he rejected the notion that schizophrenia could have psychological origins, Bleuler believed that the manifest content of schizophrenic thinking could be understood in terms of Freudian theory. Psychiatrist Silvano Arieti carried this notion one step further and applied

---

[8]Orne (1962) and Webb et al. (1966) also have much to say about subjects' awareness of the "demand characteristics" of experiments and their desire to behave in prescribed ways.

Freud's concept of the unconscious to schizophrenia; he proposed that the schizophrenic's "inability to make things unconscious" is one of the important characteristics of this psychosis (Arieti, 1959c, p. 457). Freud himself said that projection played an important part in this disorder (1896) and postulated that the schizophrenic withdraws his libido from external objects and redirects his energy into the ego or self (1955b).

Interpersonal Models

The depth theorist who formulated his own non-Freudian concepts of this disorder, and who had more to say about schizophrenia than most others, was Harry Stack Sullivan (see also p. 110). Sullivan introduced the idea of interpersonal psychiatry and, within this framework, held that schizophrenia was an indirect result of faulty interpersonal relations between the child and its parents (Sullivan, 1946, 1953, 1956).

Especially crucial in the child's growing up, according to this view, is the anxiety it picks up from its mother, through the process of *empathy*. This anxiety may cause the schizophrenic to avoid persons and situations that evoke it. In turn such avoidance prohibits the establishment of patterns of interpersonal responses that for most people serve to eliminate anxiety. Consequently people avoid anxiety by means of what Sullivan called *parataxic distortions*: they perceive everyone in terms of significant figures in their past.

The Double-Bind Hypothesis. According to anthropologist Gregory Bateson and his associates (Bateson, 1972), an important determinant of schizophrenia is a repetitive pattern of disturbed intrafamilial communication that produces *double binds*. Bateson defines the double bind as "a situation in which no matter what a person does, he can't win" (p. 201). The double bind has the following elements:

1. The victim is in an intense relationship in which it is vital that he or she discriminate message types (see below) accurately and respond appropriately.
2. The other person in the relationship is giving two kinds of message, one denying the other (double messages).
3. The victim cannot comment on the messages to correct his or her interpretation of them.

Typically, the victim receives such messages from his mother, and they contain three kinds of negative injunction:

a. "Do not do so and so, or I will punish you." Or "If you do not do so and so, I will punish you."
b. (Also enforced by the threat of punishment) "Do not see this as punishment" or "Do not see me as the punishing agent" or "Do not submit to my prohibition" or "Do not think of what you must not do" or "Do not question my love of which the primary prohibition is (or is not) an example."
c. "You may not escape from the field." (This is not stated but is understood.)

How do double binds produce the disordered thinking of schizophrenia? Bateson draws on linguistics and communication theory to analyze the disturbances in the schizophrenic's communication. Noting that schizophrenics are said to have ego weakness, he defines ego weakness as "trouble in identifying those signals which tell the individual what sort of a message a message is" (p. 194). Those signals are at a level of abstraction that Bateson calls *metacommunication*. They are the usually nonverbal messages that say "This is play" (for example, when kittens play at fighting) or "I'm kidding" or "I mean for you to take what I'm saying figuratively."

The ability to correctly interpret such signals is necessary not only in play, kidding, teasing, and the use of metaphor, but also in bluff, threat, histrionics, humor, and paradox.

To discriminate between play and nonplay, according to Bateson, one must use "secondary process" thinking (waking consciousness). But the primary process (the unconscious) is operating all the time, in play certainly, and most especially in dreams: "Within dream or fantasy the dreamer does not operate with the concept 'untrue'" (p. 185). All of us sometimes have difficulty deciding whether a dream was a dream or not. Bateson relates this kind of discrimination to semanticist Alfred Korzybski's concept of language having the same relation to events that a map has to a territory. Thus, in primary-process thinking, the map and the territory are not discriminated. In secondary-process thinking they are discriminated; and in play, which Bateson sees as a possible step in the evolution of communication, they are at the same time equated and discriminated. The kind of thinking needed in play is the kind of thinking needed for handling frames and paradoxes.

But this is precisely where the schizophrenic is on thin ice. Bateson asks, rhetorically, whether certain forms of psychopathology are specifically characterized by abnormalities in the patient's handling of frames and paradoxes, and answers Yes (p. 190). The schizophrenic cannot or will not recognize the frame that defines the nature of the message, the "as if" element without which metaphor ceases to be metaphor and becomes a direct statement about reality. Most people understand the "as if" in such metaphors as "My love is like a red red rose." But that playful, poetic marking of similarity is taken literally by the schizophrenic, and becomes an identity—a statement that his or her love object is in fact a flower. To use Korzybski's metaphor, the schizophrenic treats the map as if it were the terrain.

Psychotics are not the only people who confuse metaphor and reality. We all lose our "as if" grip on fantasy and imagination in the dreaming state, and some of us do so even in the waking state. For example, when Great Britain and the American colonies adopted the Gregorian calendar in 1752, an 11-day discrepancy between the old and new calendars was accommodated by simply skipping 11 numbers in the calendar for September of that year. This brought a storm of protest from people who complained bitterly that

their lives were being shortened by 11 days. During World War II an attempt to conserve energy by extending daylight saving time ("war time") was protested by people who insisted that standard time was God's time and that the government had no right to tamper with nature. And more than 250,000 people wrote to "Marcus Welby, M.D." during the first five years of that television series, most of them asking for medical advice. Even today many people consider "dirty words" a threat to family stability. We all use metaphors, but in the speech of schizophrenics (and sometimes other people) the metaphors are *unlabeled:* "The pathology enters when the victim himself either does not know that his responses are metaphorical or cannot say so" (p. 210). When one begins thinking of schizophrenia in this way, Bateson asserts, "a great deal of what the schizophrenic says falls into place as a description of his life experience. . . . In a schizophrenic salad, he is describing a traumatic situation that involves a metacommunicative tangle" (p. 115).

Noting that normal people also sometimes take refuge in metaphorical language when they feel threatened, Bateson argues that the schizophrenic's behavior is defensive, and infers that *"he must live in a universe where the sequences of events are such that his unconventional habits will in some sense be appropriate"* (p. 206): a universe containing repeated double binds.

One of Bateson's examples of a double-bind situation involves a mother who feels threatened either by her hostility toward her son or by her affection for him, and therefore feels compelled to withdraw from him. She might say, "Go to bed, you're very tired and I want you to get your sleep." She is using a false loving message to deny a true hostile message. If the boy discriminates the messages accurately, he has to face both the rejection and the deception, which are traumatic for him. Instead, he accepts the idea that he is tired, deceiving himself about his own internal state. "To survive with her, he must falsely discriminate his own internal messages as well as falsely discriminate the messages of others."

Thus, Bateson continues (p. 214),

The problem is compounded for the child because the mother is 'benevolently' defining for him how he feels. . . . To put it another way, the mother is controlling the child's definitions of his own messages, as well as the definition of his response to her (e.g., by saying, 'You don't really mean to say that,' if he should criticize her). . . . The result is that the mother is withdrawing from him and defining this withdrawal as the way a loving relationship should be.

But if he accepts her false loving behavior as real and approaches her, her feelings of fear and helplessness will be aroused and she will withdraw. If he then responds by withdrawing, she will either punish him for withdrawing, since she interprets his withdrawal as a statement that she is not a loving mother, or she will approach him, trying to draw him closer. If he moves closer, she will put him at a distance. He is punished for reading her messages accurately, and he is punished for reading them inaccurately. He is caught in a double bind.

The end result of a continued pattern of this kind of interaction is that the boy "behaves in such a way that he shall be responsible for no metacommunicative aspect of his messages" (p. 261). That is, he behaves schizophrenically.

For the breakdown of the child's ability to read message-identifying signals, Bateson uses the term "overt schizophrenia." For the mother's constant switching of message-identifying signals in her own and other people's messages, he uses the term "covert schizophrenia."

Bateson believes that genetic factors may be involved in the etiology of schizophrenia but that they have not yet been identified. He also believes that the schizophrenic has been cast in a role by his or her parents, and that this explains the fact that many siblings of schizophrenics are normal. The double-bind hypothesis is based solely on clinical observation, although Bateson does cite (p. 223) an experiment by Milton H. Erickson, in which a hypnotically induced double bind ("Your hand cannot move, but it will when I give the signal") resulted in a hallucination.

One of Bateson's associates, Jay Haley (1960), has suggested that the parents of schizophrenics repeatedly contradict and countermand, qualify and disqualify, their own and others' messages, making the transmission of an unequivocal message virtually impossible. In particular, their actions totally contradict their words.

A study on the effects of double-bind communications on normal college students suggests that those effects are potentially disruptive, although its implications for the etiology of schizophrenia must be interpreted cautiously. Smith (1976) administered punishment (noise) to four groups of college sophomores, two of which received contradictory communications. The results quite clearly indicated that repeated double-bind messages are disruptive and that college normals seem unable to adapt to this situation. These results led Smith (p. 362) to conclude that "normals are greatly affected by double binds [which] . . . suggests that double binds are not a common part of their life experience."

Thus far the double-bind hypothesis has not had much impact on the treatment of schizophrenia, but it has had a considerable impact in other areas, such as the practice of conjoint family therapy (Satir, 1967) and the teaching of communication skills, especially to parents. Family patterns and parent–child relations may not be as crucial as the interaction hypothesis claims, however. Rogler and Hollingshead (1965) found that childhood and adolescent experiences of schizophrenics do not differ noticeably from those of normals. A study by Schofield and Balian (1959) of 150 normals and 178 hospitalized schizophrenics also failed to reveal any differences between families of normals and those of schizophrenics. Whether these findings actually contradict the interaction hypothesis is not certain, however, since the factors studied were poverty, divorce, and invalidism rather than disturbed communication, double messages, and double binds.

Other Cognitive and Communication Factors.
Several researchers have theorized that schizophrenia is primarily a thought disorder. Thus Chapman and his associates (1964, 1973) maintain that schizophrenic thinking differs from that of normals in that associations between words and things have a personal rather than the usual agreed-upon meaning. According to this theory a normal person responds to a word with a graded series of meaning responses, depending on the context in which the word is being used. The schizophrenic, however, displays an excessive tendency to respond to the strongest meaning (sometimes to the most personal meaning) of a word, with relative neglect of weaker meanings.

On the basis of Chapman's idea, one researcher (Mourer, 1973) predicted that schizophrenics would demonstrate a greater tendency than normals to respond to a word's strongest meaning. In addition this research predicted that schizophrenics would display more generalization errors for words sharing stronger meaning responses than normals, where generalization errors were defined as the incorrect inclusion of words that had not previously appeared. Both predictions were confirmed: unlike normal subjects, schizophrenics made significantly more errors on words sharing strong meaning responses than on words sharing weak meaning responses and they also made more generalization errors than normals. Similar findings have been reported by other researchers (Cohen and Camhi, 1967; Cohen et al., 1974).

Several investigators studying the cognitive factors in schizophrenia (Koh et al., 1973; Koh and Kayton, 1974; Nachmani and Cohen, 1969) have theorized that schizophrenics are impaired in their ability to organize information in memory. A distinction is made between "recall" performance, which requires an organized retrieval system and should therefore be susceptible to dysfunction in schizophrenics, and "recognition" performance, which is unimpaired in these patients. In an attempt to study this process Koh, Kayton, and Berry used a test of "free recall" of 20 words that could conceptually be organized into five categories, and 20 unrelated words. They tested 12 nonpsychotic schizophrenics, 12 nonschizophrenic psychiatric patients, and 12 normals and found that the recall performance of the schizophrenic group was significantly worse than that of the normals and nonsignificantly worse than that of the nonschizophrenic patients. As the trials were repeated, the normals and, to a lesser degree, the nonschizophrenic psychiatric patients were able to form meaningful clusters of words to aid in their recall; the schizophrenic patients were not.

Although clear differences were found between normals and schizophrenics on these tasks, the nonschizophrenic patients as a group showed results midway between (but not significantly different from) those of the other two groups. These findings would be compatible with the conclusion that schizophrenics are quantitatively but not qualitatively different from patients with other psychiatric disorders and that these tests of recall may indicate only relative levels of psychopathology.

In a second series of experiments using single-trial recall with multiple-word lists, Koh and Kayton (1974) concluded that the recall performance of schizophrenics is impaired for the following reasons: they take less information into their memories; they do not use strategies (for example, associating adjacent words on the list) that help organize information in memory; they are easily distracted; and they respond very slowly. Koh and his associates are currently testing the hypothesis that it is the schizophrenics' overall approach to the task rather than their memory capacity that significantly influences the ability to recall.

Experimental Investigations

Psychophysiological research has focused on the schizophrenics' apparent inability to respond appropriately to incoming stimuli. Whereas normals, for example, have many associations to stimuli but somehow manage to select the single most appropriate response, schizophrenics seem unable to make this choice.[9] Instead, their selection process resembles randomness. Some support for this idea may be gleaned from self-descriptions of schizophrenics, such as the following one taken from an article by McGhie and Chapman (1961, pp. 105–109):

I can't concentrate on television because I can't watch the screen and listen to what is being said at the same time. I can't seem to take in two things like this at the same time especially when one of them means watching and the other means listening. . . . When people are talking, I just get scraps of it. If it is just one person who is speaking that's not so bad, but if others join in then I can't pick it up at all. I just can't get in tune with the conversation. . . . Half the time I am talking about one thing and thinking about half-a-dozen other things at the same time. It must look queer to people when I laugh about something that has got nothing to do with what I am talking about, but they don't know what's going on inside and how much of it is running around in my head.

This self-description and the observation of random schizophrenic response suggest that a schizophrenic's deficit should be greater in complex environments than in simple ones because of the more intense competition among responses to be selected. Support for this prediction was found in a study (Chapman and McGhie, 1962) in which subjects were asked to repeat sets of six numbers or letters with different series presented to the subject visually and auditorily. The finding was that when visual and auditory presentations were concurrent and subjects were asked to respond selectively to one or the other, schizophrenics did less well than normals and non-

---

[9]An excellent review of many stimulus–response approaches to understanding schizophrenia appears in Broen (1968).

schizophrenic psychiatric patients. These subjects were also instructed, in another experiment, to turn a wheel at a constant rate that was comfortable for them. They were then asked to repeat the task while listening to a variable auditory rhythm. The experimenters then compared the variability in turning rates between the two conditions and found the schizophrenics significantly more distractible than either normals or other nonschizophrenic hospital patients.

But even when the attentional task is relatively uncomplicated, as in simple eye-tracking tasks, schizophrenic patients seem to have difficulty. Holzman and his associates (1973, 1974), for example, reported that schizophrenics showed unusual deviations in eye-tracking records obtained during pendulum pursuit. Instead of the smooth curve seen in normals, schizophrenics displayed a ragged pattern suggesting an uneven tracking procedure with many erratic stops and starts. Furthermore a high proportion (44 percent) of first-degree relatives of schizophrenics showed a similar uneven pattern. Similar findings were also reported by other investigators (Shagass et al., 1974, 1976), suggesting that the study of attentional factors in schizophrenia may be worth pursuing.

Abnormalities of heart rate and respiration have also been widely observed, leading many investigators to suspect that the arousal activity of the sympathetic nervous system may be impaired. In one study (Zahn, 1975) a researcher noted that schizophrenics and normals did not differ in their physiological reactions to unimportant tones but did differ significantly when the tone was important in that it was a signal to respond to a reaction time task. Schizophrenic subjects failed to show greater arousal when the tone was important.

Another kind of experimental study, described by Garmezy (1966), focuses on the discrepant effects produced by rewards and punishments on the behavior of schizophrenics. After showing in a series of experiments that schizophrenics are inflexible, exhibit a persistent with-

---

Aversive Maternal Control: A Psychogenic Theory of Schizophrenic Development

Alfred B. Heilbrun, professor of psychology at Emory University, has proposed an aversive maternal control theory of schizophrenia for which he has collected a modest amount of support (Heilbrun, 1973, p. 251). According to this theory, as the child develops from the completely dependent stage of infancy to the relatively independent adult stage, the mother comes to represent the critical socialization agent. The child's characteristic mode of responding, this theory holds, is influenced in important ways by dealings with the female parent. If the mother permits the child to assume increasing autonomy while continuing to nurture it affectionately and with trust and respect, the child will learn to transact effectively with its expanding social environment. In contrast, if the mother does not communicate love and esteem during this critical period and if the child's sense of worth is further reduced by perception of maternal rejection, the child may conclude it is unlovable and unworthy of esteem. Thus the combined experience of sustained maternal control and maternal rejection act together to shape a self-concept that mirrors the mother's disparagement and distrust.

This aversive maternal control, as Heilbrun calls it, introduces a form of circularity into the child's development so that initiation of new relationships is deterred by its poor self-image, which increases its expectancy of rejection, which in turn entrenches it more firmly in the very relationship that instigated the problem. The mother, for her part, then comes to regard the child with even greater disapproval as it reaches the stage at which more autonomous functioning is expected (adolescence). The child's fear in forming new and better interpersonal relationships is magnified by the mother's more obvious control and rejection, which derive from her growing realization that her developing child is psychologically deviant.

drawal from psychologically noxious events, and display a lessened responsiveness to social rewards, Garmezy offered two learning formulations about the origins of their avoidance behavior. First, he proposed that the schizophrenic is brought up in "an environment in which the ratio of rewards to punishments was so heavily weighted in favor of the latter that there would be little likelihood that approval or praise would develop strong secondary reinforcing properties" (Garmezy, 1966, pp. 170–171). Second, he speculated that schizophrenics' behavior is strongly resistant to extinction because their prepsychotic responses have often been both rewarded and punished. Garmezy cites as an example of this the kind of situation Bateson describes as a double bind.

Larger Sociocultural Influences

Do sick societies produce sick people? The answer to this question is probably Yes; it is difficult, however, to specify precisely which aspects of the sick society are responsible.[10] Several factors have

---

[10]In assessing the effects of urbanization on mental health, Srole (1972, p. 582) suggests that the prime research question should be, "What kinds of people differentially stay in or are drawn to various kinds of community milieus?"

been mentioned (Buss, 1966), as we indicated in Chapter 6, and they include *social disorganization, social isolation,* and *social class.*

Social Disorganization. The basic assumptions here are that social disruption leads to personality disorder because of the chaos created by social change and that the accompanying chaos causes psychopathology. If these suppositions are valid, we should be able to predict that unstable communities foster more schizophrenic children than stable ones. There is some support for this prediction.

Using poverty level, cultural confusion, absence of religious values, and high crime rate as indices of social disintegration, one group of investigators (Leighton, 1959; Leighton et al., 1963) found a considerably higher percentage of abnormal individuals in socially more disorganized regions. Other researchers (Clausen, 1966; Clausen and Kohn, 1959; Jaco, 1954, 1960) have also reported a higher incidence of schizophrenia in disorganized communities.

But in these studies it is difficult to separate cause and effect. For example, does social disintegration lead to psychopathology, or is it the other way around? Many authorities speculate that the causal ties may be indirect in the sense that social disorganization could affect a family's outlook on its place in society, which in turn could influence personality development within that family (Roman and Rice, 1967).

Social Isolation. Social isolation was first suggested as a cause of schizophrenia in 1934 by a sociologist, Faris (1969), who proposed that being rejected or otherwise restricted from contacts with people outside the individual's family leads to the "shut-in" personality of the schizophrenic. Faris offers the following in support of this hypothesis (1969, pp. 161–162):

Long-term prisoners show little joy when their sentences expire. . . . Frequently they desire to return to their cells . . . they were nearly all described as "thoughtful, subdued and languid."

Class, Family, and Schizophrenia

Which is most important for the development of schizophrenia: social class, family factors, or genetic inheritance? The latest sociological thinking on this topic tends to implicate all three factors, plus a fourth—stress. Thus, in a review of the relevant literature in the field, Melvin Kohn (1972a) asserts that to try to explain the relationship of class to schizophrenia without considering genetics and stress would be extremely difficult. There seems to be a contradiction in the literature, which Kohn attempts to resolve. The contradiction is that, although poorer conditions of life seem conducive to schizophrenia, the absolute incidence of the disorder in even the lowest class is small. The resolution of this contradiction occurs when one considers the roles of genetics and stress.

Kohn's formulation is that the more constricted living conditions experienced by lower-class people more rapidly impair their ability to deal resourcefully with problematic and stressful events. Such impairment, in conjunction with genetic vulnerability to schizophrenia and the experience of great stress, combine to disable lower-class members to the disorders. Since both genetic vulnerability and stress seem to occur disproportionately at lower social class levels, according to Kohn, people in these segments of society may be at triple jeopardy (also see Mechanic, 1972; Kohn 1972b).

Sheepherders and other isolated persons are said to develop similar traits after long periods of enforced solitude. . . . The schizophrenics, however, are for the most part neither prisoners nor sheepherders. . . . Cultural isolation—that is, lack of intimate social contacts—may also cause the same type of seclusiveness.

Proponents of this hypothesis have collected corroborating data that are mostly clinical and observational, but others (Clausen, 1966; Kohn and Clausen, 1955) believe that the schizophrenic behavior was apparent in the childhood of many patients before social isolation took place. Thus social isolation, rather than being a cause of schizophrenia, could also be a symptom indicating that one's interpersonal difficulties have become so great that one can no longer relate to others.

Social Class That social class is correlated with incidence of schizophrenia has been well documented in the epidemiological studies of Hollingshead and Redlich (1958). These investigators located all residents of New Haven, Connecticut, who were in psychiatric therapy during the period between May 31 and December 1, 1950. They reported a substantially greater number of psychotics in the lower than in the upper socioeconomic classes (Figure 12.1).

Similar findings were obtained in the Midtown Manhattan study (Srole et al., 1962), indicating that the incidence of psychoses was 13 percent in the lowest socioeconomic group and only 3.6 percent in the upper class and showing that 33 percent of lower-class individuals were judged to be "impaired" compared with 18 percent in the highest level (Table 12.6).

In many of these and similar epidemiological studies (Dohrenwend and Dohrenwend, 1969) the findings are the same: the incidence of neurosis increases from lower to higher socioeconomic groups, with notable class differences in the way neurotic symptoms are expressed (see Chapter 11); the trend is reversed for schizophrenia.

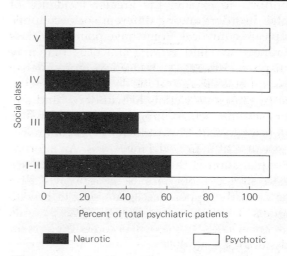

Figure 12.1
The percentage of neurotics and psychotics among total psychiatric patients. Class I–II includes patients from well-established families, with college educations and holding managerial and professional jobs. Class III includes small-shop owners, white collar and sales personnel, and skilled manual laborers with high school educations. Class IV includes semiskilled workers with elementary and high school backgrounds. And Class V includes mainly semiskilled and unskilled laborers.

(Adapted from Hollingshead and Redlich, 1958)

Table 12.6
Mental Health and Socioeconomic Class

Mental Health Status	Socioeconomic Class		
	Highest	Middle	Lowest
	%	%	%
Well	24	20	10
Mild symptoms	36	37	33
Moderate symptoms	22	23	25
Impaired mental health	18	21	33

Source: Srole, L., Langner, T. S., Michael, S. T., Opler, M. K., and Rennie, T. A. C. Mental health in the metropolis: the Midtown Manhattan study. New York: McGraw-Hill, 1962.

Efforts to explain the greater incidence of mental disorders among different socioeconomic groups are equivocal. Some have pointed to class differences in child rearing practices that may predispose lower-class children to more intense stress; others believe that the devastating effect of poverty causes its victims to withdraw; and still others say that schizophrenic types have greater tendencies to *drift* toward lower-class communities because of their social ineptness. An alternative explanation is that the class differences are due to simple economics: schizophrenics who come from the upper classes are sent to private hospitals. There they are less likely than patients from lower-class homes to become subjects in epidemiological studies.

The *social drift hypothesis*, first proposed by Myerson (1941b), was popular for a time and received some support in a study in which investigators examined the lifestyles and residential stability of 305 male schizophrenics admitted to a Massachusetts state hospital between 1931 and 1950. Corroborating the drift hypothesis were the findings that the highest rates of schizophrenia occurred in the areas of the city with the poorest living conditions and that those people who came from the poorest district had only lived there a short time (Gerard and Houston, 1953).

In an almost identical study, however, another group of investigators found no evidence of drift (Lapouse et al., 1956). And in a more direct test of it, two researchers, who compared the occupations of schizophrenics to those of their fathers, and contrasted this finding with the intergenerational mobility of normals (Clausen, 1966; and Clausen and Kohn, 1959), found no significant differences between schizophrenics and normals. Their studies cast serious doubt on the idea that schizophrenics drift down toward lower social strata.

Cross-cultural Evidence Researchers have long been fascinated by psychoses in different societies and, as we noted in Chapters 1 and 6, nu-merous *culture-bound* and unique syndromes have been described. But it has also been reported that the delusional content of schizophrenics in varying cultures is significantly different. According to Kiev (1972) careful examination of these delusional systems has revealed their close adherence to the belief system prevalent in the culture. Thus schizophrenic symptoms among some African societies contain mythological content as well as delusions of becoming a chief or a witch doctor or being poisoned or bewitched. Delusions of people in Western societies, by contrast, include influences operating from a distance, through electricity, X-rays, hypnotism, and outer-space vehicles.

And within African societies of varying degrees of westernization, the delusional content also differs accordingly. For example, one anthropologist (Tooth, 1950) found that among the "bush" people in the north of Ghana the delusions dealt with the ramifications of the fetish system, whereas in the south of Ghana, where Western influences are more apparent, the delusions are about control of electricity and radio.

Closer to home, as we already indicated in Chapter 6, symptom differences have been noted among schizophrenics of different ethnic backgrounds (see Opler, 1956, 1959). Thus Irish-American schizophrenics were reported to be less hostile, more subdued, and less bizarre than their Italian-American counterparts. These symptom differences seemed to be related to varying family patterns among these groups. Similar ethnic diversity in symptoms was found between Japanese schizophrenics raised in Japan and those of Japanese descent in Hawaii. Those in Japan were described as physically assaultive, while those in Hawaii were suspicious and brooding.

The importance of finding symptom differences between these groups, as well as between Irish-Americans and Italian-Americans, is that it dispels the idea that these differences are due to genetic factors and tends to support the hypothesis that "persons of the same racial stock, carrying the same diagnosis, develop different kinds of symptoms depending upon the society in which they live" (Phillips, 1966, p. 478).

Treatment of the Schizophrenias

know 5 pts.

In general, regardless of the kind of treatment applied, the prospects for recovery from schizophrenia depend on several conditions, among which the following are the most important:

1. The likelihood of recovery is better if the diagnosis is reactive rather than process schizophrenia.
2. The more withdrawn the person is from social contact, the poorer the prospects are (Sherman et al., 1964).
3. If there is a clear precipitating event, the outlook is more favorable (Vaillant, 1966).
4. Schizophrenics with good pre-illness adjustment patterns are more likely than others to recover (Nameche et al., 1967; Vaillant, 1966).
5. If the patient is not a paranoid schizophrenic, is Caucasian, and has had a history of much prior medical treatment and of anxiety, his or her chances for recovery are good (Gunderson and Arthur, 1968).

Treatment of schizophrenia is divisible into two categories: somatic and psychological. Somatic treatment involves the use of *major tranquilizing drugs*, mainly phenothiozines, and the application of *electroshock treatment*. We have already mentioned these treatments in earlier chapters and will elaborate on them later (see Chapter 21). The psychological treatment methods include variations of the *psychodynamic psychotherapies* (Chapter 22), *behavior modification* (Chapter 23), and *humanistic-existential* psychotherapies (Chapter 24).

Paranoid Disorders

The distinctions between paranoid schizophrenic behavior (see p. 266–267) and the paranoid disorders are rather unclear. Clinical lore has it that the personalities of the paranoiacs are less disorganized and more intact, and that their delusions of persecution are more focused on a single theme or series of connected themes. The persecutory delusions associated with the paranoid disorders in most other respects, however, resemble those of the schizophrenias in that the person believes he or she is being conspired against, cheated, spied upon, followed, poisoned or drugged, harassed, or obstructed. Small slights may be exaggerated and form the nucleus of a delusional system. But these distinctions between paranoid schizophrenia and the paranoid disorders are difficult to draw in practice. We shall make them for purposes of textbook exposition.

Three main types of paranoid disorders are recognized by DSM III (1980): paranoia, shared paranoid disorder (*folie à deux*), and paranoid state. In addition there is the paranoid personality disorder. We shall take up the first and second of these after a few words about some clinical and literary differentiations.

People with a *paranoid personality disorder* are presumably not as psychotic, in the sense of having an airtight delusional belief system, as the true paranoiacs to be discussed shortly; rather they closely resemble the everyday hypersensitive, suspicious, jealous, or envious individual. The psychotic paranoiacs' delusional systems are more unshakable than those of the paranoid personalities, even when massive counter evidence indicates clearly and objectively that the basic paranoid premise is invalid; and the delusions are more intricate and highly systematized. They "know" who is responsible for their harassment and persecution, and they relentlessly devise complex measures to counterattack their enemies.

Two other distinctions help separate psychotic paranoia from paranoid personality and from ordinary suspiciousness. The first of these is the psychotic's all-consuming preoccupation with defending against betrayal or conspiracy. No matter what the occasion or the conversation, the paranoid always manages to return to the subject of how he or she was wronged. Once the paranoid's first premise is granted, the remaining behavior follows quite logically and unequivocally. The paranoid psychotic jealous husband, for example, reacts the same way upon returning from work (perhaps an hour or a day early) whether he finds his wife in a happy or sad mood. If she is happy, he reasons, it is because her lover just made it out the back door; if she is sad, it is because her husband has returned and she is trapped with him for the remainder of the day or weekend.

Of course, such delusional thinking may become self-fulfilling in that the paranoid sooner or later finds in it a basis in reality. In other words the husband (or wife) who continually reasons from these and similar paranoid premises may become so objectionable that his or her spouse will indeed pursue other companionships—which is just another way of saying that the person who expects the worst may influence the reactions of others to him so that his expectations become self-fulfilling prophecies.

Paranoia. This is a category of disorder rarely found in hospitals, probably because paranoiacs somehow evade and effectively fight "giving in" to their persecutors. But in those cases of paranoia that have been carefully studied, it is clear that the condition is characterized by the gradual development of a complex, intricate, and elaborate *delusional system* that is based on, and often follows logically from, misinterpretations of actual events.

The prepsychotic personalities of paranoiacs are usually described by relatives and close acquaintances as having been predominantly rigid, uncompromising, and humorless. They are often reported to have been aggressive individuals who were not easily disciplined by their superiors and who were exceedingly sensitive to insults.

Once their psychotic personalities take shape, usually after the age of 40, these people spend much time brooding over wrongs and become preoccupied with their delusions of persecution. They talk about plots and conspiracies, complain of trespassers and prowlers, and are concerned about being watched. In more extreme cases, sometimes bordering on the schizophrenic, these individuals talk about remote mind control and being influenced by fluids or rays. A substantial number of these individuals are grandiose in that they see themselves as endowed with special ability and as being thwarted by those around them.

Occasionally these persons, if they are sufficiently frightened and think they know who is responsible for their troubles, may litigate in a court of law, defend themselves by bombing or otherwise destroying the property of their persecutor, or even assault their imagined enemy with intent to kill. Case Report 12.3, taken from our experience in a Veteran's Administration Hospital, illustrates many of the symptoms of paranoia.[11]

Case Report 12.3 *Paranoia*

A married man, 48 years old, whose wife described his prehospitalization personality as naturally suspicious, jealous, hostile, and distrusting ("likely to pick a fight with a neighbor over minimal provocation") reportedly tried many times to telephone the President of the United States during a six- to eight-month period. The incident that precipitated his hospitalization was an attempt by his wife to prevent one of these calls. She pleaded with her husband that such a call would once again bring the FBI to the house and would subject the family to precisely the type of surveillance he constantly feared. The wife's behavior infuriated him and he threatened to slit her throat if she tried to stop him this time. She called the police, who had

---

[11]Henderson and Gillespie also emphasize that the illness is more common among women than men and that it affects more single than married patients (Batchelor, 1969, p. 294).

to subdue him forcefully and take him to the hospital.

Three years before his admission, he had begun to talk about the large sums of money and prestige his "new invention" would bring the family. At first these glowing accounts, although tedious because he dwelt on the subject for hours at length, were interesting because of his obvious enthusiasm and cheerfulness. After several months, however, when it became apparent to the wife that his invention was a gadget to "repair the vision of the blind"—an area of expertise far removed from his profession, real estate brokerage—she attempted to discourage him. Then, after about a year of these painful discussions, in which the husband would insist that his wife and two children listen to his talk of the "invention," he began trying to telephone the patent office in Washington. Although he was repeatedly invited by someone there to file for a patent, he refused and insisted that this was a ruse to "steal his ideas for their own profits."

He then became convinced that he must talk to the "top man in the country" because this discovery was too important to be put in the trust of "a bunch of bungling bureaucrats." It was apparent to the wife from the beginning that her husband's invention, the sketch of which he showed her in strict confidence, was merely the scribblings and annotations of a troubled man. However, she was afraid of him and feared that if she did not go along with his delusions, he might become violent with her and the children. Then, when his telephone calls began to bring the family under surveillance—a state of affairs that contributed even more to his feelings of persecution—she objected vehemently to his conversations in the family and his telephone calls. Finally he became increasingly more abusive until she was forced to call the police.

At the time of his admission to the hospital (his third in ten years) he was in fine physical health. He stated that he had decided to let his wife hospitalize him because he had been very nervous and because here he could work on his invention in peace and quiet. He would not show the drawings to anyone in the hospital, not even his therapist.

Although his personality was well maintained during his six-month hospital stay, it was apparent that his grandiose ideas about his invention continued undiminished. When he began to talk about it, he became hoarse and somewhat incoherent. His antagonism toward being "cooped up like a common criminal," became increasingly more vocal until he reported he could not stay any longer and wanted to leave. Since he was in no condition to be discharged from the hospital, consultations with his wife and other members of his immediate family were held. These resulted in a decision to commit him to long-term hospitalization so that he could be treated intensively with a combination of psychotherapy and drugs. Surprisingly he was not as upset over this turn of events, as his family and others had anticipated.

Folie à Deux. When the same delusional system is shared by two persons, usually with the dominant individual influencing the submissive one's thinking, the condition is called *folie à deux (à trois, à quatre,* and *en famille,* for three, four, and the family). The most common "shared insanity" is sister-to-sister, in which both sisters are spinsters living together. Other but less frequent combinations, usually also within the family, are husband-to-wife, and mother-to-child.

These *folies* involve genuinely shared delusional systems in which the participating parties cooperate to ward off their persecutors. Most of the delusions are persecutory, and clinical lore has it that women show a greater susceptibility than men to adopting a partner's delusional ideas. According to Cameron (1959, 1963) this greater vulnerability may be the result of our culture's expectation of relatively more dependency and submissiveness in women.

An interesting facet of this form of paranoia is that when the dominant person is removed from the situation, because of work transfer, hospitalization, or death, the submissive one recovers rather quickly and ceases to be concerned about the intentions of other people. This is described in Case Report 12.4, where it may be seen how the delusions of an older sister were adopted by her younger siblings and dropped rather quickly after her death.

Case Report 12.4   *Folie à Trois*

Three elderly spinster sisters, aged 72, 68, and 65, were admitted to a psychiatric hospital after a neighbor called the police to report that one of them threatened to "slit the throat" of a 10-year-old neighbor boy. These sisters had worked, eaten, and lived together for more than 40 years.

When interviewed in the hospital, each of the sisters told an almost identical story about how this 10-year-old boy had been "sent by them" to remove the No Trespassing sign from their front lawn. Close questioning revealed that many years earlier these women had posted such a sign on their lawn because both their neighbors "were spying" on them by coming on their lawn and looking through the front window. It was also learned that the sisters had sued one of their neighbors over a boundary dispute. They lost the suit and attempted to find another lawyer to take their case, but no lawyer would do so. The boy they had threatened was the grandson of their neighbor, and they described him as "rotten to the core from the day he was born."

The two younger sisters also said that they and their sister had a good deal of trouble at vacation spots, usually rooming houses near resort areas, because other people were after their money and belongings. The oldest sister vehemently denied having had such difficulties and explained that her younger sisters occasionally "told such lies," but that she would "set them right" as soon as she saw them on the ward.

When the younger sisters were again interviewed several days later, they both volunteered the information that their story about their rooming house troubles was untrue and that their neighbor had a way of influencing them to tell such stories. They then disclosed that they thought the doctor was conspiring with their neighbor against them and that he had better not ask them any more

questions because he was being paid to keep the three in the hospital.

About three weeks after admission, the oldest sister had a massive stroke and died within hours of the attack. The two younger sisters at first became severely depressed, but then, as often happens with separation from the dominant person in such folies, several weeks after the death, they began talking about going back to their home and "letting bygones be bygones."

Causes of the Paranoias

Most theorists and clinicians do tend to agree that, with the possible exception of organically induced paranoid states (see Chapters 9 and 10), these disorders have psychological origins. Let us examine some of the evidence for both biological and psychological causes.

Biological Origins. Attempts to link paranoid behavior to genetic, or other biological, causes have been sparse and hardly noteworthy. Craike and Slater (1945) report a case of *folie à deux* in monozygotic female twins reared apart. The twins, separated at the age of nine months, were brought up in different families and met for the first time at age 24. Each in due course had developed a paranoid psychosis, with each sister involving the other in her own delusional systems.

Most other accounts of the genetics of the paranoid disorders tend to deal with this category in conjunction with the paranoid schizophrenias, which we covered earlier in this chapter (see Rosenthal, 1970, 1971).

We mentioned several biological contributors to paranoid symptoms earlier when we briefly discussed the effects of aging, endocrine disorders, alcohol, and drugs. To this we should add a note about Pavlov's attempt (1934) at a physiological account of paranoia. His theory, based on laboratory observations of animals, was that a *pathological inertness* developed in organisms that paid undue attention to certain stimuli. He believed that the inertness was a cortical phenomenon, in which brain cells were affected, and that this could lead to a paranoid delirium.

A theory based on this notion was further developed by Maller (1956), who proposed that the cause of this delirium was a disturbance in the transmission of impulses; this, in turn, was responsible for the paranoid's disturbed interpretation of incoming stimuli. But it should be noted that even if these formulations are correct, they provide evidence only for the possible cortical changes that occur as a consequence of exogenous (externally induced) events. And as we noted in several prior sections on the etiology of other disorders, producing symptoms by a particular procedure does not demonstrate that actual cases originate in the same way.

Intrapsychic Models. The most frequent explanation of the paranoid states is in terms of their psychological origins. Freud proposed *projection* as an important defense leading to this disorder (see Chapter 7). The formula for projection, as conceptualized by Freud (1959b), is, for instance, a latent homosexual male who thinks, ''I don't love him; I hate him.'' Because this is threatening to the individual's self-concept, he turns it into the more acceptable ''I don't hate him; he hates me.'' According to Freud these projections begin as a consequence of the repressed homosexuality of the male and his attempt to escape the self-condemnation attendant upon being homosexual. Evidently it is more acceptable for the male to hate another male than to love him; and it is even more acceptable to be hated than to hate.

Although this causal relationship between homosexuality and paranoia has been all but abandoned, even by the staunchest psychoanalysts, for lack of supporting evidence, Freud's formulation of the role of projection in paranoia is still accepted by many clinicians.

A more recent theory of paranoia, also conceptualized within a psychoanalytic framework, attempts to account for the patient's hostile behavior in terms of the *paranoid pseudocommunity*. This is psychiatrist Norman Cameron's concept

(1963, pp. 486–488), which he defines as follows: ''The paranoid pseudocommunity is a reconstruction of reality. It organizes the observed and the inferred behavior of real and imagined persons into a conspiracy, with the patient as its focus.''

According to this idea, the community does not correspond to reality, although it does include real people and their actual behavior, along with imagined people and their inferred behaviors. The patient ascribes motives to both the real and the imagined persons, and the pseudocommunity serves the purpose of binding together his projected fears and wishes to justify his own hostile aggression and to give it a tangible target.

Stimulus–Response Models. Curiously, the stimulus–response advocates have little to say about the origins of paranoia. Dollard and Miller (1950) are the exceptions, but they give it short shrift and essentially follow the Freudian thinking that posits its beginnings in a male homosexual conflict (pp. 183–184):

The thought of hate tended to eliminate any thoughts of love because of the logical incompatibility of the two and the emotional responses of hate may also have had some tendency to inhibit the appearance of incipient homosexual feelings. Inhibiting these responses reduced the anxiety they elicited and thus produced additional reinforcement for the thoughts and emotions of hate.

Shame–Humiliation Theory. In an appraisal of four theories of paranoid phenomena, K. M. Colby (1977) has proposed what he calls a shame–humiliation theory of paranoid phenomena. This theory assumes that the person has a model of himself that he uses to simulate experience, to try anticipatory alternatives, and to react to a future in his simulation before it arises in actuality. Then when a belief in the self's inadequacy is activated by relevant input, the paranoid uses defensive procedures to forestall a threatened unpleasant experience of humiliation, which is detected as shame in the anticipatory simulation. To prevent humiliation, the paranoid uses a strategy of blaming others for wronging him.

Colby argues that his model has greater explanatory power than Freudian homosexual theory (see above), hostility theory (paranoids have a high degree of hostility or unconscious hate, which, to avoid conflict, is disavowed and attributed to others), and homeostatic theory (an organism pursues equilibrium; a threat to equilibrium is explained as "others threaten me"; this threat must be eradicated to restore equilibrium, to achieve security, and to protect the self). The shame–humiliation theory incorporates the other theories, according to Colby (1977, pp. 58–59),

as special cases that are derivable from its hypotheses and assumptions. For example, it would assert that only when homosexual concerns are a source of shame and humiliation to the individual does he become hypersensitive to homosexual topics. . . . Shame-humiliation theory considers hostility not a primary but a second-order reaction to believed threats and harms. Attempts to manage threats and restore imbalances, as postulated by homeostatic theory, are simply taken for granted by the shame-humiliation theory.

Sociocultural Variables. Several sociocultural factors have been implicated in the causation of paranoid states. These include family, socioeconomic status, and birth order. One study (Kay and Roth, 1961) that compared 99 paranoid patients admitted to Swedish and British hospitals showed that a significantly higher percentage of paranoids than other patients lived alone and had no friends at the time they became ill.

A second study (Lucas et al., 1962) linked types of delusions with the variables of age, birth order, and marital and socioeconomic status. In this study the researchers observed that delusions with religious or supernatural content, as well as grandiose ones, were more frequent in persons of high social status and in the unmarried than among lower-status and married individu-als; that grandiose delusions occurred in eldest rather than youngest siblings; and that delusions of inferiority were more common among lower than higher social levels and were prominent among youngest siblings. As might be expected also, persecutory delusions were found more frequently in youngest siblings, probably because they are typically exposed to such indignities as hand-me-downs and having more privileged, older, and sometimes stronger brothers or sisters. Some of the other findings also make psychological sense in that one would expect grandiosity to be associated with high status and wealth and would expect feelings of persecution to accompany low-status memberships.

But family, socioeconomic status, and birth order are only part of the explanation of paranoia. Pettigrew (1964), when writing about psychoses among blacks in America, points out how the behavior of some patients was directly related to their racially restricted experiences, and thus for blacks to see hostility in their environment is a normal perception. Moreover it is often incorrect to call Afro–Americans paranoid, since they live in a culture that in fact persecutes them.

Grier and Cobbs (1968, p. 178) make this point somewhat more forcefully in *Black Rage* when they suggest that it is essential for American blacks to distrust their white fellow citizens. They then describe the *cultural paranoia* we mentioned in Chapter 2:

If he does not so protect himself, he will live a life of such pain and shock as to find life itself unbearable. For his own survival, then, he must develop a cultural paranoia *in which every white man is a potential enemy unless proved otherwise and every social system is set against him unless he personally finds out differently.*

Cross-cultural Research. Identifying paranoia in cultures other than our own is difficult. In many societies hostility, suspicion, and delusions of persecution are a way of life, without which individuals might not survive the onslaughts of rival groups. The question then arises, as one group of researchers phrased it (Savage et al., 1965, p. 46): "If it is a cultural pattern, how can one ever identify the truly paranoid in such a context?"

The same problem has been addressed by Kiev (1972, p. 17), who pointed out, "While basic personality patterns have been usefully related to cultural experiences in particular societies, there has been a tendency to use psychological labels to describe what are characteristically normal behavior patterns for certain societies." For example, the well-accepted patterns of feeling persecuted by spirits or witches noted among the Kwakiutl Indians of Canada has often been mistakenly described as paranoid by Western observers.

The only way to determine who is paranoid, evidently, is to judge whether a person's beliefs are out of tune with his culture, because the "sociocultural environment and the patient interact continually and predictably within cultural contexts" (Kiev, 1972, p. 20). Unfortunately crosscultural studies of paranoia that adopt these standards are still to be conducted. The only available cross-cultural data on paranoid ideation are reports that the content of psychotic delusions and hallucinations is influenced by the societies in which these occur (Parsons, 1961; Wittkower and Dubreuil, 1968), and that delusions within our own culture have changed over the past 50 years from persecution by devils or God to persecution by nonsupernatural forces (Lenz, 1964).

You may recognize here an echo of a question we posed in Chapter 2: how, in the face of a virtually infinite spectrum of possible cultural patterns, can we judge an individual's behavior abnormal? We seem to be caught between ethnocentrically judging other cultures by what are ultimately the values of our culture, and saying that whatever is the norm in each culture is correct—two equally unenlightened positions. Common sense tells us that behavior of deviants can be either adaptive or maladaptive, and the cultural pattern they deviate from can be either adaptive or maladaptive. In discussing paranoia,

we face the further complication that most societies persecute deviants, thus giving credence to the paranoid delusion. Unfortunately we do not have a measure of cultural adaptiveness that is free of any taint of ethnocentrism, and perhaps we never will. In the meantime, it would be unwise to assume that an individual behavior and a cultural manifestation result from the same process. The paranoid person in our culture may be responding to intrapsychic factors that are not involved in the behavior of the Kwakiutl.

Thus the answer to the question of how a person becomes paranoid is that it is learned within the person's family and within the larger cultural context. Several demographic variables seem to make a difference. These include marital status, birth order, and socioeconomic group membership, and paranoia seems to occur more frequently among the married, the youngest siblings, and people in the lower strata of our society.

From a depth psychology standpoint the paranoid disorders occur as a result of a person's lifelong pattern of projecting unacceptable traits onto others. One particularly elaborate psychodynamic formulation suggests that paranoids build up an imaginary community of persons who are the recipients of their hostility and animosity.

Evidence regarding the biological origins of these disorders is sparse.

Treatment of the Paranoias

Because of the quite unshakable suspiciousness of paranoid patients, psychotherapy is all but impossible. It is difficult, especially in the advanced states of the disorder, to get the paranoid individual to enter into a psychotherapeutic relationship, and it is even more difficult for the therapist not to get drawn into the patient's delusional system. When the paranoid begins to understand that the therapist is not there to help him in his fight for "justice," he loses interest or becomes suspicious of the therapist's motives. In short, although the traditional psychotherapies are often tried, the prognosis is poor.

Somatic therapies such as electro-shock therapy (EST) and drugs have been equally unsuccessful in changing the delusional systems of intact paranoids, and, generally, recovery rates are poorer for paranoid states than for paranoid schizophrenia. But again, as we shall see in the treatment of schizophrenia (Chapter 21), the period just following EST is marked by temporary subsidence of symptoms.

Drug therapy has its own drawbacks, most of which are peculiar to the nature of the paranoid condition. Paranoid patients can be coerced into going along with a drug regimen while in the hospital, and drugs do calm their agitation somewhat, but once out of the hospital, these patients refuse to "swallow the medical poisons" that their relatives might instruct them to ingest.

There is some evidence to suggest that symptoms of paranoia can be attenuated by behavioral techniques. For example, Ullmann and Krasner (1975, p. 413) call attention to a case treated by Davison (1966), in which paranoid symptoms were moderated somewhat by a combination of relaxation and desensitization (see Chapter 23).

In general, the treatment of paranoia is beset with special problems that arise from the nature of these disorders, and it has not been successful.

Summary

Psychotic behavior is more disordered than any that we have discussed thus far. Two types of psychoses exist: those caused by identifiable tissue damage and those that are not obviously determined by organic factors. In both varieties the behaviors include perceptual, cognitive, affective, communicative, motor, and motivational anomalies. In this chapter we discussed schizophrenia and the paranoid disorders, two of the categories of nonorganic, or functional, psychoses.

Schizophrenia has long been recognized as a disorder, but its origins and cure have so far eluded discovery. There are currently four major forms of schizophrenia—simple, hebephrenic, catatonic, and paranoid—each of which has its predominant and distinctive features. Process and reactive schizophrenia are its chronic and acute manifestations, respectively.

Numerous causes have been postulated for schizophrenia; these include genetic and biochemical models, as well as intrapsychic, stimulus–response, interaction, and sociocultural models. The weight of evidence seems to favor a biological–environmental interactive explanation, requiring that both a genetic predisposition and an environmental stressor be present for the disorder to occur.

Treatment of schizophrenia is mainly by the application of drug or electroshock therapy, although several specific psychological methods have been designed especially for this disorder.

We also discussed three main psychotic paranoid states: paranoia, shared paranoia (*folie à deux*), and paranoid state. All three are marked by delusional ideation (persecutory and grandiose) that tends to render the paranoid individual frightened and overly reactive to real or imagined indignities.

The origins of the paranoid disorders, it is generally agreed, are traceable to psychological causes. Projection is one of the chief defenses used by paranoids and its end result is that the cast-off and unacceptable impulses return to plague the individual. Family constellations and other demographic variables (marital and social status, birth order) also seem to make a difference.

Treatment of the paranoid disorders is exceedingly difficult because the paranoid person's suspiciousness precludes trust and his or her airtight delusional system blocks change.

Terms and Concepts to Master

Autism

Catatonic schizophrenia

Decompensation

Delusional system

Double bind

Folie à deux

Functional psychosis

Hebephrenic
  schizophrenia

Organic psychosis

Paranoia

Paranoid schizophrenia

Paranoid state

Process schizophrenia

Pseudocommunity

Reactive schizophrenia

Simple schizophrenia

Social drift hypothesis

Waxy flexibility

13 Childhood and Adolescent Schizophrenia and Infantile Autism

Unlike its adult counterpart, childhood and adolescent schizophrenia is not marked by hallucinations and delusions. Instead its main features are withdrawal, inability to distinguish between fantasy and reality, disturbance in emotional attachments to people, bizarre behavior, and preoccupation with morbid thoughts or interests. Other features associated with this disorder include unexplained panics, illogical rage reactions, extreme instability of mood, ritualistic and repetitive behavior, peculiar posturing, and a questionlike melody in the speech. Occasionally in the more severe cases, biting and hitting occur, as well as head-banging and other forms of self-mutilation.

This extremely rare disorder is twice as prevalent among boys (about five cases out of every 10,000) as among girls, according to DSM III (APA, 1980) and Werry (1972). Because of its frequent outgrowth from, and continuity with, infantile autism, we shall discuss that disorder first.

Infantile Autism

Infantile autism is also a rare disturbance, but it has attracted a great deal of interest and is the subject of many papers and books (Kanner, 1943, 1944, 1946, 1949, 1957; Des Lauriers and Carlson, 1969; Rimland, 1964; Wolman, 1970). This interest is probably due to its rather dramatic nature. Unlike other childhood behavior disorders, it has an early onset, usually during the first year of life, and a distinctive pattern of behaviors.

Before the onset of the disorder, the infant is usually healthy and attractive; in the words of its parents, it is a "good baby." Being good may mean, however, only that it makes few demands on its parents. When the infant is about 4 months old, its mother begins to notice that something is amiss. The infant does not cuddle; in fact, it struggles vigorously to remove itself from human contact. Furthermore its social smile does not develop, and it makes no anticipatory movements when it is about to be picked up. Typically it does not develop speech, at least not as communication. It may make bizarre sounds or develop a parrotlike habit of imitating speech, and this is likely to be its only imitation of adult activity. It seldom if ever engages in thumbsucking or other autoerotic activities. Although it manipulates its body, it does so in a way that seems to have no relation to bodily pleasure. In short it seems to have no positive sensory, affective, or social responses.

As the infant grows into a toddler, its movements develop into a bizarre pattern of repetitive, stereotyped, stimulus-seeking behaviors, such as head-banging, rocking, whirling, pacing. It may relate to inanimate objects, especially mechanical ones like vacuum cleaners, the way a normal child would relate to human beings. It seems to have an intense need for sameness in its environment, and may panic or rage if a piece of furniture is moved even an inch from its usual position.

It is not long before parents begin to show concern about this behavior, especially if there is another child in the household for comparison. They note that the normally developing child is not content, as is the autistic one, to sit motionless for hours staring into space, as if deep in thought; and they may observe that the normal child, even if considerably younger than the autistic one, shows a responsiveness and interest in other people that the latter never displays (see Des Lauriers and Carlson, 1969, pp. 19–24).

Causes

The origins of infantile autism are unknown. Genetic, psychological, and organic determinants have been suggested. The evidence for its genetic origins is found in studies showing that concordance for autism is high in both twins of monozygotic pairs but is rare among dizygotic twins (Ornitz and Ritvo, 1968). Moreover proponents of a genetic hypothesis argue that the symptomatology in all cases is so highly unique and specific that only a hereditary explanation is plausible.

The arguments against a psychological formulation are strong (Kanner and Eisenberg, 1957; Ornitz and Ritvo, 1968; Rimland, 1964) and are based on findings showing that some clearly autistic children are born of parents who do not fit the alleged autistic parent personality pattern, that most siblings of autistic children are normal, and that autistic children are behaviorally unusual from the moment of birth.

The organic hypothesis rests mostly on the evidence that autism is closely simulated in children with known brain damage and that autistic children display a "cognitive dysfunction" that resembles such injury. Rimland, in his book *Infantile Autism* (1964), sets the locus of this damage in the reticular formation of the brain and cites as evidence for his hypothesis experimental lesions produced in the brain stems of cats whose subsequent behavior resembled symptoms of children with early infantile autism. These animals became

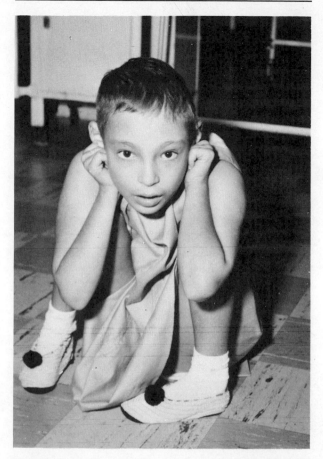

An autistic child in a characteristic posture. Other children often describe such youngsters as "spooky."

(Courtesy Dr. Charles H. Carter, Sunland Hospital, Orlando, Florida)

highly inaccessible and undistractable; engaged in ceaseless stereotyped behavior; assumed blank-staring and masklike facial expressions; became mute, unaffectionate, and unresponsive to pain; mouthed many kinds of objects; and became either anorexic or voracious. Rimland (1964, p. 119) concludes that such damage is due to an "excess of oxygen given in early infancy."

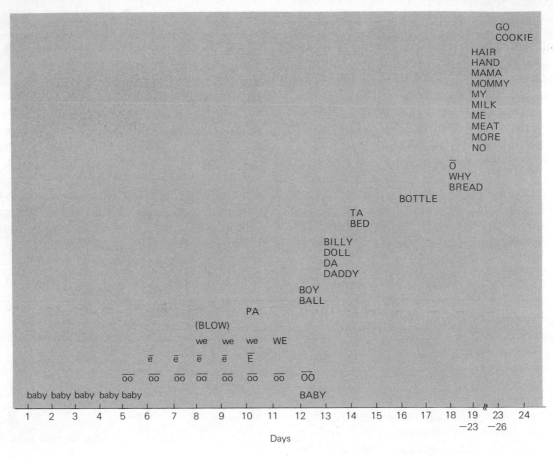

Figure 13.1

The rate of verbal acquisition by a previously mute autistic child during the first 26 days of training. The abscissa denotes training days. Words and sounds are printed in lower case letters on the days they were introduced and in capital letters on the days they were mastered.

(Lovaas et al., 1966. Copyright 1966 by the American Association for the Advancement of Science)

Treatment

The prognosis for autism has not been favorable because of these children's extreme inaccessibility to human contact, failure to use speech to communicate, and lack of spontaneity. These characteristics conspire to make them extraordinarily difficult patients in conventional therapy (Wolman, 1970).

Numerous psychotherapy follow-up reports indicate that although some limited improvement in social conformity and adaptability was attained by autistic children, most of them (about two-thirds) later developed adult schizophrenia and only a negligible number achieved "good" adjustment (Bender, 1953; Eisenberg, 1956; Brown and Reiser, 1963).

Some encouragement has been expressed in

the favorable reports of behavior therapists who have worked with autistic children. One of the earliest such reports by a Skinnerian psychologist, Charles Ferster (1961), laid the groundwork for subsequent therapy with these difficult children. He isolated numerous basic variables in the environment responsible for sustaining the child's autistic behavior and identified specific factors in the autistic child's home life that reinforce the symptoms of the disorder.

Subsequently Ivar Lovaas and his associates (Lovaas et al., 1966; Lovaas, 1967), also Skinnerians (see Chapters 6 and 23), demonstrated in a series of studies that they could shape social behavior in autistic children by Skinnerian operant conditioning techniques. In one of these demonstrations, they treated two autistic children who learned imitative speech after being rewarded for increasingly finer verbal discriminations and closer reproduction of their adult model's speech. Their procedure consisted of giving two autistic children 26 days of imitation training, until these patients had learned to imitate "with such ease and rapidity that merely adding verbal responses to their imitative repertoire seemed pointless" (Lovaas et al., 1966, p. 707). The rate of progress for one youngster is shown in Figure 13.1, in which lower-case letters signify introduction and training and capital letters signify mastery. In this figure it can be seen that as training progressed during the 26 days, the rate of mastery increased. Whereas at first this previously mute child took

A child at a computer teletype similar to the one used to treat nonspeaking autistic children.

(Courtesy Pennsylvania Department of Public Welfare)

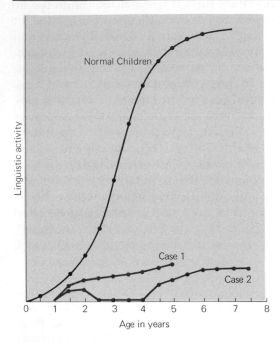

Figure 13.2

The linguistic activity of two nonspeaking autistic children compared with that of normal children of the same chronological ages.

(Colby and Smith, 1971. In J. H. Masserman, ed., *Current psychiatric therapies*, vol. 2, New York: Grune & Stratton, 1971. By permission)

several days to learn a single word, during the last two weeks he required only a single day to master several words.

More recently, Kenneth Colby devised a computer-aided treatment method for nonspeaking autistic children (Colby and Smith, 1971). This procedure consists of a series of eight computer-controlled "games," which the child plays twice a week in half-hour sessions. The computer displays on a paper printout or a TV-like screen a series of letters, words, numbers, pictures, phrases, sentences, and so forth, and simultaneously plays sounds of human voices, animals, and machinery through its speakers. The child's task is to imitate the sounds he hears and label the objects he sees. A sitter helps the child play these games, if such aid is necessary.

The underlying assumption of this computer-display system is that children like to make things go. This seems to be a justified assumption, as we can see in Figure 13.2, because the learning curves of two treated autistic children show that although their learning does not compare well with the learning of normal children (also shown), they can be taught to talk. Furthermore, Colby and Smith report that over a period of 3 years, 13 out of 17 treated cases (76 percent) have been successes, with success being defined as developing language in previously nontalking children.

Childhood and Adolescent Schizophrenia

Because, as we indicated earlier, childhood and adolescent schizophrenia often appears to grow out of infantile autism, many psychologists do not differentiate between the two disorders, classifying infantile autism as "schizophrenia in early childhood" (Bender, 1953, 1959; Wolman, 1970). Nevertheless we find it useful to distinguish between them on theoretical and clinical grounds (see also Weiner, 1966, 1968, 1970) and therefore deal separately with adolescent schizophrenia.

Onset and Course

The usual time of onset for most categories of schizophrenia is adolescence (Weiner, 1958), although in its initial stages adolescent schizophrenia does not show a clear clinical picture of the adult variety.[1] These youngsters tend to resemble

---

[1] Paranoid schizophrenia, perhaps because it represents a more developed psychotic syndrome, appears, according to most authorities, at about the age of 30.

antisocial personalities or brain-damaged or other emotionally disturbed individuals, and it is perhaps because of this confused clinical picture that relatively few children under the age of 15 are diagnosed as schizophrenics. Beyond this age, however, especially between the ages of 15 and 29, schizophrenia has been well established as a disorder of adolescence and early adulthood (Neubauer and Steinert, 1952; Verville, 1967).

The behaviors usually considered precursors of schizophrenia include interpersonal difficulties, daydreaming, withdrawal from work, personal neglect, and a tendency toward antisocial acting-out. According to one survey, conducted by Spivack et al. (1967), in which ratings of 640 13- to 18-year-old boys and girls were collected, the following characteristics were also noted in the 93 schizophrenic adolescents who were studied (Weiner, 1970, p. 97):[2]

1. **Bizarre Cognition** The adolescent in this group substitutes, confuses, or misuses pronouns in conversation; uses his name rather than "I" when referring to himself in conversation; his speech is disconnected, incoherent, or not sensible; he reports hearing voices or other hallucinations.

2. **Bizarre Action** This group displays odd facial grimaces, postures, or movements; puts inedible, unhealthy, or even dangerous things into the mouth; shuts out sounds by lifting shoulders or putting fingers in ears; rocks while sitting or standing.

3. **Schizoid Withdrawal** The patient has a blank stare or faraway look in eyes, day dreams, walks around oblivious, as if wrapped up in his own thoughts; looks puzzled or confused by things happening around him, talks to himself.

4. **Emotional Detachment** The patient keeps his distance or reserve with adults; has a fixed facial expression that lacks feeling; is unemotional, rarely shows feelings; is unaware of how adults feel toward him.

5. **Poor Emotional Control** The youngster in this group gets very upset or overemotional if things do not go his way; often expresses anger; is easily upset by peers; expresses anger in poorly controlled fashion; reacts with anger if having difficulty in mastering or learning something.

Several researchers have attempted to identify preschizophrenic signs in adolescents who later became schizophrenics. The most detailed study of this kind, conducted by Bower et al. (1960), reviewed the high school records and interviewed the teachers of 44 19- to 26-year-old hospitalized schizophrenics. They compared these records with those of 45 nonpatient controls (Table 13.1) and found that the pre-morbid personalities of schizophrenics were more peculiar, shy, dreamy, and withdrawn than the controls; and were less well integrated and less popular than the others. All these differences are reported in Table 13.1 and are statistically significant.

The potential schizophrenic has also been described as unemotional and aloof, having severely limited social contact and activities and an ineptitude for self-management. Preschizophrenics dread being forced into demanding situations, and are highly vulnerable and easily hurt. Life for them seems to be a series of crises. Other adolescents around them are quick to detect that something is wrong, and are usually not reluctant to poke fun at them. As one 17-year-old schizophrenic male high school student put it when he was told by his teacher that his erratic behavior only caused others to laugh at him: "Oh, I'm used to that, kids are always laughing and making fun of me." Here is an excerpt of a dialogue between this student (Pa.) and a therapist (Th.):

Th.: *How many friends do you have?*
Pa.: *Not too many.*
Th.: *Can you name a few?*
Pa.: *No, not really.*
Th.: *Do you have one close friend?*

---

[2] Adapted from *Psychological disturbance in adolescence* by I. B. Weiner. Copyright © 1970 by John Wiley & Sons, Inc. By permission.

Table 13.1
Personality Descriptions of 44 Preschizophrenic High School Students and Their Controls

| | Incidence | |
Personality Description	Preschizophrenic Group (N = 44)	Control Group (N = 45)
Unusually striking personality, noted by others to be odd, peculiar, queer, or at times crazy	9	2
Slight personality problems, different but not markedly so; shy, dreamy, lacked concentration, temperamental, and stubborn	19	3
Apparently well-adjusted and well-integrated; moderately popular, sociable; no apparent school difficulty	9	31
Qualities of leadership in athletics or scholarship, "pride of school," eager or overeager for success	3	9
No problem, seldom noticed, seclusive, and quiet; often hazily remembered by teachers; sensitive, shy, passive, and colorless	4	0

Source:·*E. M. Bower, T. A. Shellhamer, and J. M. Daily. School characteristics of male adolescents who later became schizophrenic.* American Journal of Orthopsychiatry, *1960, 30. Copyright © the American Orthopsychiatric Association, Inc. Reproduced by permission.*

Pa.: *The last friend I had was in third grade. Ever since that time kids have been teasing me and pushing me around and laughing at me.*
Th.: *Why do you think they do a thing like that?*
Pa.: *I guess they think I'm a "mental."*
Th.: *What is it about your behavior that makes them think that?*
Pa.: *I guess I sort of walk funny, and sometimes talk different. Anyway, that's what they tell me. I walk sort of a little bent over to the left, and I talk poetry. Besides, I don't like them copying answers from my papers anyhow.*
Th.: *Do you think they might like you more if you let them?*
Pa.: *I once tried that. It didn't work either.*

Causes

In general, the information about the causes of childhood and adolescent schizophrenia is about the same as that for its adult counterpart. For example, the family backgrounds of these youngsters sometimes show marital disharmony and an enduring atmosphere of unhappiness and stress, as well as an overcontrolling mother, but, as we noted in Chapter 12, these features are also present in the families of nonschizophrenics. Likewise biological explanations are subject to the same criticisms cited in Chapters 5 and 12, and the reader may want to review these accounts and critiques at this time.

Treatment

The outlook for recovery from schizophrenia, according to some evidence (Pollack et al., 1968), is less favorable among adolescent and young adult schizophrenics than among patients with later onset. This information was obtained from a 3-year follow-up study, which indicated that schizophrenic patients whose first hospitalization occurred between the ages of 16 and 29 fared less well than those whose first admission was between the ages of 30 and 57. Similar findings were also reported in other research (Colbert and Koegler, 1961; Eisenberg, 1956; Symonds and Herman, 1957), and were corroborated in studies conducted by others (Gunderson and Arthur, 1968).

In general, favorable outcome indications for adolescent schizophrenics are the same as those for adults (see Chapter 12). They include the following (Gunderson and Arthur, 1968; Vaillant, 1964): acute onset, less than six months elapsing between the onset of difficulty and full-blown schizophrenia, absence of prodromal adjustment problems, disorientation and confusion, clear precipitating factors, a family history of psychotic depressions, and preoccupation with death—all of which are good signs probably because they are symptoms of disorders other than schizophrenia and hence suggest the possibility of misdiagnoses.

Summary

Instead of the delusions and hallucinations of adult schizophrenia, childhood and adolescent schizophrenia usually involves withdrawal, inability to distinguish between fantasy and reality, disturbance in emotional attachments to people, bizarre behavior, and morbid preoccupations. It often appears to be an outgrowth of infantile autism, and some psychologists do not differentiate between the two disorders. Infantile autism commonly has its onset in the first months of life. The baby does not respond, physically or emotionally, to other people and does not develop speech. As a toddler it has repetitive, stereotyped, stimulus-seeking movements, and may relate to inanimate objects the way a normal child would relate to human beings.

The causation of infantile autism is unknown. Genetic, psychological, and organic determinants have been suggested. Treatment is difficult because of the autistic child's extreme inaccessibility to human contact, failure to use speech to communicate, and lack of spontaneity. About two-thirds of the autistic children treated eventually develop adult schizophrenia. Behavior therapy has had some success in attempts to teach autistic children to use language.

Most types of schizophrenia have their onset in adolescence, although the clinical picture seldom resembles the adult form at that age. Early symptoms usually include interpersonal difficulties, daydreaming, withdrawal from work, personal neglect, and a tendency toward antisocial acting-out.

The etiology of childhood and adolescent schizophrenia is generally the same as that of the adult form. The prognosis for recovery from schizophrenia is poorer among child and adolescent schizophrenics than among those in whom the onset is later.

Terms and Concepts to Master

Autism	Poor emotional control
Bizarre action	Schizoid withdrawal
Bizarre cognition	Stereotyped behavior
Emotional detachment	Stimulus-seeking behavior
Imitative speech	

14 The Affective Disorders

In contrast to schizophrenia and paranoia, which are thought disorders, the *affective disorders* are—as the name implies—primarily disturbances of mood or feeling. Although depression and mania (overactivity, euphoria), the two main disorders to be discussed in this chapter, can occur as normal states, they are sometimes labeled neurotic or even psychotic, depending on their severity. Having already discussed so-called neurotic depression in Chapter 11, we shall emphasize here mainly its more psychotic forms.[1]

We shall discuss three main varieties of psychotic affective disorders: *psychotic depression, involutional melancholia,* and *manic-depressive psychosis.* Their common bond is that each is a disturbance of mood and motivation. Since the risk of suicide is considerable among depressives, we shall also discuss that topic.

Depression

According to DSM II (APA, 1968), the following definition of *psychotic depression*[2] is currently used (p. 38):

This psychosis is distinguished by a depressive mood attributable to some experience. Ordinarily the individual has no history of repeated depressions or cyclothymic mood swings. The differentiation between this condition and Depressive neurosis depends on whether the reaction impairs reality testing or functional adequacy enough to be considered a psychosis.

Both as an experience and as a concept, depression seems to be a hazier entity than anxiety. Like anxiety it is more of a mood than a feeling and like anxiety it can be free-floating, although "floating" would be a strange word to describe anything as leaden as depression. It is a sense of hopelessness, in which the world seems totally unresponsive to one's efforts to meet one's needs. It seems to have elements of sadness or grief, but often also involves guilt, self-punishment, and self-dislike. According to Mendels (1970), "The central symptoms of depression are sadness, pessimism, and self-dislike, along with a loss of energy, motivation, and concentration." Mendels also lists the following behaviors (p. 7):

Mood Sad; unhappy; blue; crying

---

[1] The latest draft of DSM III (1980) distinguishes between episodic and chronic affective disorders, with the episodic label replacing the former "neurotic" label, and the chronic label replacing the former "psychotic" label.

[2] Strictly speaking, DSM II now refers to this as *Psychotic depressive reaction* and lists it under the larger category of *Other psychoses*; but this distinction, which takes it out of its DSM I classification with the affective psychoses, is not important for our purposes of description.

327

Thought Pessimism; ideas of guilt; self-denigration; loss of interest and motivation; decrease in efficiency and concentration

Behavior and appearance Neglect of personal appearance; psychomotor retardation; agitation

Somatic Loss of appetite; loss of weight; constipation; poor sleep; aches and pains; menstrual changes; loss of libido

Anxiety features

Suicidal behavior Thoughts; threats; attempts

Not all these symptoms are likely to be observed in one person. Thus one person may show psychomotor retardation (a general slowing down of movement, speech, and thought) and another person may show agitation.

Classification of Depression

Agreement between clinicians in diagnosing a depressive patient is poor, barely exceeding 50 percent in controlled studies (Mendels, 1970). This low rate of agreement is probably due, at least in part, to the lack of general agreement on definitions and classification schemes. We shall briefly describe some of the ways in which depression has been classified.

Reactive and Endogenous Depression. *Reactive* depressions, the more common type, are reactions to external events, such as the loss of a loved one or a disaster. According to Seligman (1975), they do not cycle regularly in time, are not usually responsive to physical therapies (drugs or electroconvulsive shock), seem not to be genetically determined, and are usually milder in their symptoms than endogenous depressions. *Endogenous,* or autonomous, depressions are a response to some as yet unknown internal process. They are not associated with any external event, but simply sweep over the sufferer. They usually cycle in time, with regular alternation between

despair and neutrality. Fortunately endogenous depressions often respond to drugs and shock treatments, suggesting that they may be hormonal or perhaps genetically predisposed. Symptoms are often more severe than those of reactive depressions.

Bipolar and Unipolar Depression. Perris (1969) found significant differences between two groups of patients whose depressions he classified as bipolar and unipolar. A person suffering a *bipolar* depression alternates between depressive and *manic* episodes. (Mania looks like extreme elation and excitement, a mirror image of depression, although some clinicians see it as a desperate attempt to deceive oneself by denying the depression.) A person whose depression is *unipolar* may have several depressive episodes but no manic episodes.

Grinker's A, B, C, and D Syndromes. Grinker and his associates (1961) applied factor-analytic techniques to the study of the feelings, concerns, and behavior of a group of depressed patients. They found four distinct patterns, which they called Type A ("empty"), Type B ("anxious"), Type C ("hypochondriacal"), and Type D ("angry"). The four patterns are summarized in Table 14.1.

Continuity Versus Discontinuity of Depression

Some theorists consider depression a unitary disorder that occurs in various degrees of severity, from the mildest neurotic disturbances to severe psychotic depressions. Other theorists consider neurotic depression a distinct entity different from psychotic depression. As Reiss and his associates (1977) point out, the crucial issue in this controversy is whether the distinction between neurotic and psychotic depression is quantitative or qualitative.

The usual distinction, to which we shall adhere in this book, is that in neurotic depression

Table 14.1
Four Factor Patterns of Depressive Syndromes

	Type A ("empty")	Type B ("anxious")	Type C ("hypochondriacal")	Type D ("angry")
Feelings	Dismal, hopeless, low self-esteem, guilt	Dismal, hopeless, low self-esteem, anxiety	Deprivation of love	Gloomy, hopeless, guilt, anxiety
Behavior	Withdrawn, apathetic, retarded	Agitation, clinging, demands for attention	Agitation, demanding, hypochondriacal, psychosomatic symptoms	Demanding, provocative
Treatment response	Poor to psychotherapy, better to somatic therapy	Often good to psychotherapy and tranquilizers	Poor to ECT, better to pharmacological therapy and supportive psychotherapy	Poor to psychotherapy because of danger of "rage suicide"; somatic therapy often required

Source: Grinker, R. R., et al. The phenomenon of depression. *New York: Harper & Row, 1961; as adapted by Lehmann, H. E., Pharmacotherapy of depression, Cole, J. O. and Wittenborn, J. R. (eds.). Springfield, Ill.: Charles C Thomas, 1966.*

there are no hallucinations or delusions. But the evidence for such a discontinuity theory (Eysenck, 1970; Grinker et al., 1961; Mendels, 1970) is as unconvincing as that for the continuity theory (Beck, 1967). The critical factors for a resolution of the debate would seem to be, as some experts have argued (Reiss et al., 1977, p. 399), that "the continuity position would be confirmed if neurotic and psychotic depression have common etiologies; the discontinuity position would be confirmed if they have different etiologies."

Depression and Self-esteem

Clinical descriptions of depression frequently — though not always — mention low self-esteem as a symptom. Freud (1917) considered the "fall in self-esteem" that occurs in depression one of the chief differences between depression and grief. Related terms used by clinicians to describe depression include guilt, self-judgment, self-blame, self-reproach, bad self-concept, and self-punishment. Arieti (1959) suggested that manic-depressive illness develops in childhood when parents are dissatisfied and resentful either because of their overall life situation or because of their increased family responsibilities. Instead of expressing their resentment and aggression directly, the parents increase their expectations of the child. The child then feels the need to earn their love or be rejected, and feels responsible for losing their love. As a result, he or she feels that parental punishment for being unworthy of love is good, since it gives the child a way to recover that love, or at least not slip further from parental good graces. He or she feels guilty (having taken on the responsibility for being loved), and developes a need to be punished, hoping that punishment will absolve him or her of this guilt and earn back the lost love.

Hidden Depression

Especially among the elderly and among people in their teens and early twenties, depression is often masked by persistent complaints of physical symptoms such as headache, backache, tiredness, or abdominal pains. No organic cause for these symptoms can be found, and the symptoms of depression are not obvious to the physician making the examination. Sometimes a person with a hidden depression relies increasingly on alcohol and drugs to relieve distress, and may easily be incorrectly diagnosed as an alcoholic or drug addict instead of a depressive. Since the two diagnoses call for different treatment, the error can be significant.

Depression as "Giving Up"

Depression appears to be an important factor in triggering many physical illnesses as well as in determining their outcome (NIMH, 1975, p. 180). "Giving up" may lead to death. Evidence sug-

gests that patients who suffer from depression after a heart attack, for instance, develop a large number of physical complications during the ensuing recovery period that not only prolong convalescence but increase the likelihood of a fatal outcome.

Episodic and Chronic Depression

The latest revision of the DSM III (APA, 1980) distinguishes between episodic and chronic depression. It describes both varieties as being characterized by a loss of interest or pleasure and suggests that the episodic type, as the name implies, is recurrent and involves periods of recovery to normal functioning. Chronic depression is characterized by a disturbance that persists for perhaps two or more years, depression being the predominant mood for 50 percent or more of the time. Other characteristic behaviors include sleep disturbance, appetite loss, change in weight, agitation or slowing down, thought disturbance, decreased energy, feelings of worthlessness or guilt, and thoughts of suicide or death.

Age-specific Factors of Depression

Although the basic features of depression are the same in children, adolescents, or adults, there are some differences in the associated circumstances and features. For example, the precipitating con-

Depression and Aggression

Anger and bitterness are frequently observed in depressed patients. Many clinicians have suggested that one of the factors in depression may be an inability to handle feelings of aggression and a denial of those feelings, although others see the anger as a result rather than a cause. Bonine (1966) points out that depression has a punitive and revengeful effect on people with whom the depressive lives, and argues that depression is "one of the forms of expressing hostility."

dition for a child might be a fear that the parents or the child may die, or that the parents may leave or may break up the marriage. The behaviors associated with such fears may be clinging, or refusal to eat or go to school, depending on the age of the child and other circumstances. Teenage boys have been known to display antisocial behavior when depressed, but more commonly, for both adolescent boys and girls, the salient picture is sulkiness, reluctance to cooperate in family outings, and withdrawal from social activities. School difficulties are likely, and there may be a neglect of personal appearance, and possibly even alcohol or drug abuse.

People in middle age, between about 45 and 60, also may experience depression, formerly called *involutional melancholia*, which is often associated with specific endocrine changes accompanying the menopause in women and retirement in men.

Aside from the hormonal changes, middle age may also bring the inclination to take inventory of one's accomplishments and failures and to redefine familial and employment roles. During this period some people face the ending of their child-bearing years; others face the end of their children's dependence on them. For those who have not had children, this can be an intensely lonesome period of life, especially if one's spouse has died.

On the job there may be the realization that the prime of productivity has long since passed, or regrets over having entered the wrong occupation. In either event there is the harsh reality for some persons in middle age that job opportunities elsewhere are severely limited.

Common Clinical Features of Depression

Regardless of age and no matter what the classification, depressions are more alike than different. Their clinical features include changes of mood, thought, behavior, and appearance; in addition depressives are characterized by somatic symptoms as well as anxiety.

In one study (Beck, 1967) the frequencies of some of the preceding and other clinical symptoms were tallied among 486 nondepressed patients, as well as mildly, moderately, and severely depressed patients. These tallies are summarized in Table 14.2, where it is apparent that even though nondepressed psychiatric patients suffer from some of the same symptoms, these features become more readily apparent as the depression becomes deeper. The really significant differences are that the deeper the depression, the sadder will be the facial expression, the more stooped the posture, the greater the likelihood of suicide, the greater the loss of interest, and the greater the disturbance in the appetitive and other physiological functions.

Manic-Depressive Psychosis

The word *mania* is derived from the Greek and is synonymous with madness, but the term is used today to describe a behavior disorder in which three main symptoms predominate: euphoria, heightened psychomotor activity, and flight of ideas. Not every manic patient displays euphoria, but restlessness and overtalking are almost always present among the clinical features. Other essential features noted in DSM III (APA, 1980) are irritability, inflated self-esteem, decreased need for sleep, and expansiveness.

Manic speech is typically loud, rapid, and difficult to understand. Often it is full of jokes, puns, plays on words, and amusing irrelevancies, and it can become theatrical, with singing and rhetorical mannerisms. If the mood is more irritable than expansive, the person may complain, make hostile comments, and go on tirades. Often there are abrupt changes from topic to topic that are based on understandable associations and distracting stimuli. This distractibility and flight of ideas from topic to topic are responsible for much of the incoherent speech observed in manics and are due to attending to various irrele-

Table 14.2
Frequency of Clinical Features Among Variously Depressed Patients

| Clinical Feature | Depth of Depression | | | |
	None (%)	Mild (%)	Moderate (%)	Severe (%)
Sad face	18	72	94	98
Stooped posture	6	32	70	87
Crying in interview	3	11	29	28
Slow speech	25	53	72	75
Dejected mood	16	72	94	94
Diurnal mood variation	6	13	37	37
Suicidal wishes	13	47	73	94
Indecisiveness	18	42	68	83
Hopelessness	14	58	85	86
Inadequacy	25	56	75	90
Conscious guilt	27	46	64	60
Loss of interest	14	56	83	92
Loss of motivation	23	54	88	88
Fatigability	39	62	89	84
Disturbed sleep	31	55	73	88
Appetite loss	17	32	61	88
Constipation	19	26	38	52

Source: After Beck, A. T. Depression: clinical, experimental, and theoretical aspects. *New York: Harper & Row, 1967.*

vant external stimuli such as background noise or people passing by. The following is an excerpt of a manic patient's reply to the question, "How do you feel today?"

I feel like a million bucks without a cent in my pocket or yours. Nice clothes you got on, on, on, and on until I called this guy downtown about the deal with. . . . Hey, John. Where the hell are you going? It's not feeding time yet. So I have these four telephones in my room and only two ears to listen with. Need more ears, more time, more money, more deals, more whores coming in here to cheer up the place.

Typically also there is inflated self-esteem, which is marked by uncritical self-confidence and grandiosity. It is not unusual for these people to offer advice and consultation on matters about which they have no special knowledge, such as how to fix an automobile or run the government. In the absence of any particular artistic talent, they may write a novel, compose music, or paint a picture. Common grandiose delusions involve their being put on earth to accomplish a special mission, usually by order of God or some potentate.

Frequently the manic person's need for sleep decreases, and he or she awakens after two hours of sleep, full of energy, and ready to pursue some mission or transact some deal. Paradoxically the more severe the sleep disturbance, the more well-rested the manic may feel, even after days without any sleep at all.

Contemporary Description

According to Winokur et al. (1969) the description of the manic-depressive disorders has undergone little improvement since Kraepelin's work. They are divided into three types in DSM II (APA, 1968, pp. 36–37):

Manic-depressive illness, manic type This disorder consists exclusively of manic episodes. These episodes are characterized by excessive elation, irritability, talkativeness, flight of ideas, and accelerated speech and motor activity. Brief periods of depression sometimes occur, but they are never true depressive episodes.

Manic-depressive illness, depressed type This disorder consists exclusively of depressive episodes. These episodes are characterized by severely depressed mood and by mental and motor retardation progressing occasionally to stupor. Uneasiness, apprehension, perplexity, and agitation may also be present. When illusions, hallucinations, and delusions (usually of guilt or of hypochondriacal or paranoid ideas) occur, they are attributable to the dominant mood disorder. Because it is a primary mood disorder, this psychosis differs from *Psychotic depressive reaction,* which is more easily attributable to precipitating stress.

Manic-depressive illness, circular type This disorder is distinguished by at least one depressive episode *and* one manic episode. This phenomenon makes clear why manic and depressed types are combined into a single category.

This classification scheme was refined somewhat in the 1980 version of DSM III (APA, 1980), where a distinction was made between single and recurrent episodes of the disorder and between patients whose current or most recent episode was manic (bipolar affective disorder, manic) and those whose current or most recent episode was depressive (bipolar affective disorder, depressed). A category was also established for patients whose most recent episodes involve both manic and depressive symptoms, thus recognizing that mixed cases often appear. Other distinctions included various forms of episodic, intermittent, and psychotic manic disorders.

The differentiations of DSM II and the latest draft of DSM III are quite subtle and in practice often difficult to draw. As with depression, the diagnosis of manic-depressive psychoses is made on the basis of observation, history, and interview—in short, from clinical observation, interviews, and tests.

Redlich and Freedman (1966), authorities in this area, base their diagnosis on four considerations: (1) the presence of a distinct and marked phasic disturbance of mood without accompanying cerebral pathology and without intellectual deterioration; (2) well-defined attacks of mood change; (3) the presence of other manic-depressive and cyclothymic persons in the family; and (4) no conspicuous precipitating psychogenic factors.

Other Clinical Features

An articulate description of a manic episode was written by John Custance (1952, p. 55), who, in the midst of his psychosis, gave the following account:[3]

I am at the moment in a typical state of hypomania, and am a patient in a Mental Hospital. One result of my condition is that I am writing with far greater ease than in normal circumstances. Usually I am a very slow-brained writer, whereas now my pen can scarcely keep up with the rapid flow of ideas.

He then goes on to describe the main features of the manic state:

(1) Intense feeling of well-being, (2) heightened sense of reality, (3) breach in the barriers of individuality, (4) inhibition in the sense of reality, (5) release of sexual and moral tension,

---

[3] Additional firsthand accounts are presented by Kaplan (1964), in *The Inner World of Mental Illness,* and by Landis and Mettler (1964), in *Varieties of Psychopathological Experience.*

(6) *delusions of grandeur and power,* (7) *sense of ineffable revelation.*

Many of the clinical features of this disorder are further illustrated in Case Report 14.1, the description of the dentist who was suddenly inspired to enlarge his practice. In this case the dentist's prior hospitalizations also resulted from his manic episodes, and evidently his depressions were not considered sufficient to warrant hospitalization.

The depressive phase of this disorder resembles the previously described clinical picture of depression; therefore when a depressed person turns up at a hospital, it is difficult to know whether he or she belongs in the manic-depressive or other depressive categories. In this regard Clayton et al. (1965) report finding a previous history of depression in 22 of 31 manic patients they examined. Such a finding, of course, serves to clinch the differential diagnosis. That it is important to distinguish between the two for more than just academic reasons should become apparent in our discussion of the treatment of affective disorders.

Case Report 14.1 *Manic-Depressive Psychosis*

Robert B., 56 years old, was a dentist, who for most of his 25 years of dental practice provided well for his wife and three daughters. Mrs. B. reported that Robert had at other times behaved as he did immediately before his hospitalization, but that this was the worst she had ever seen.

About two weeks prior to hospitalization, the patient awoke one morning with the idea that he was the most gifted dental surgeon in his tri-state area; his mission then was to provide services for as many persons as possible so that they could benefit from his talents. Consequently he decided to remodel his two-chair dental offices into 20 booths so that he could simultaneously attend to 20 patients. That same day he drew up the plans for this arrangement, telephoned a number of remodelers,

and invited them to submit bids for the work. He also ordered the additional necessary dental equipment.

Toward the end of that day he became irritated with the "interminable delays" and, after he attended to his last patient, rolled up his sleeves and began to knock down the walls of his dental offices. When he discovered that he couldn't manage this chore with the sledge hammer he had purchased for this purpose earlier, he became frustrated and proceeded to smash his more destructible tools, washbasins, and X-ray equipment. He justified this behavior in his own mind by saying, "This junk is not suitable for the likes of me; it'll have to be replaced anyway."

He did not tell any of his family about these goings-on for about a week, and his wife began to get frantic telephone calls from patients whom he had turned away from his office. During this time she realized something was "upsetting him" because he looked "haggard, wild-eyed, and run-down." He was in perpetual motion, and his speech was "overexcited." One evening Robert's wife mentioned the phone calls and his condition and he launched into a 15-minute tirade of "ranting and raving." She said later that he stopped shouting only because he became hoarse and barely audible.

After several more days of "mad goings-on," according to Mrs. B., she telephoned two of her married daughters for help and told them that their father was completely unreasonable and that he was beyond her ability to reach him. Her daughters, who lived within a few minutes' drive, visited their parents, bringing along their husbands. During their visit Robert—after bragging about his sexual prowess—made aggressive advances toward his daughters. When his sons-in-law tried to stop him, Robert assaulted them with a chair and had to be forcefully subdued. The police were called and he was admitted to the hospital several hours later.

During the interview with Robert it was apparent that he was hyperactive and overwrought. He could not sit in his chair; instead he paced the office floor like a caged animal. Throughout his pacing he talked constantly about his frustrated plans and how his wife and two favorite daughters double-crossed him. It was also learned, both from him and subsequently from Mrs. B., that this was not the first episode of this sort and that he had had three previous hospitalizations.

He responded well to lithium treatment (see pp. 318–320 and 476–477) and was discharged within several weeks of admission to the hospital.

Course and Outcome of the Affective Disorders

Although most studies have not separated the varieties of affective disorders—no doubt because of the difficulty involved in making accurate differential diagnoses—some distinguishing information can be gleaned from the early and recent literature on the topic.

The average age of onset for the depressive disorders is later than for the manic-depressive ones. This average is probably influenced by the late onset of the involutional psychoses; but, in general, the depressions also occur later. For example, in one study it was found that the average age of manic patients was 28 years, and of depressive patients 35 years (Clayton et al., 1965). In a more recent and more extensive study in which 59 manics and 353 depressives participated, it was found that the age of onset was 34.6 years for manic-depressives and 39 years for depressives (Winokur et al., 1969). Similar findings were also reported in other studies (Perris, 1966; Wertham, 1929).

Regarding the course of these disorders, one early study found that among 2000 cases of manic patients the duration of the first attack frequently was from 60 to 180 days, with over 50 percent of their illnesses lasting less than 6 months, and with only 15 percent lasting more than 18 months. Some had durations of more than 5 years (Wertham, 1929).

Information on the outcome of depressive illnesses is sparse; more data are available on the manic-depressive psychoses. After reviewing this literature, Winokur et al. (1969) drew the following conclusions (pp. 20–31):

In general, it would appear that manic depressive disease is more likely to be associated with relapses than depressive disease. However, a considerable number of patients will experience only one attack. . . . It is possible to characterize manic depressive disease as an episodic illness with good social functioning between episodes. . . . In a significant number of patients, only one episode of illness occurs . . . an episode may go on to chronicity in the unusual case.

Causes of the Affective Disorders

Some of the psychological and biological variables relevant to the origins of the affective psychoses have already been covered, especially those pertaining to middle age. As indicated, this is the stage of life when people take inventory of their past accomplishments and failures, and it is the time when endocrine and other biochemical changes may influence behavior. We shall now consider several other possible explanations.

Intrapsychic Model

Among the first and most extensive efforts to find the causes of the manic-depressive disorders were those of Karl Abraham. In 1911, after intensively treating six of these patients, he was impressed by their similarities to obsessional neurotics (Abraham, 1927). Specifically he was struck by the manic-depressives' ambivalent attitudes of hate and love. This simultaneous hate and love, he proposed, makes it difficult for them to feel one way or another about others and, what is worse, the hatred is turned inward against themselves so that they exhibit depression. Another psychoanalyst, Sandor Rado (1928, 1954), later elaborated on this theory by noting that depression is a person's desperate cry for love and that the plea is an angry as well as a pleading one.

Freud, in his paper *Mourning and Melancholia* (1917), also amplified Abraham's position and held that depressed people suffer an object loss and displace the consequent grief onto themselves. The main difference between normal grief and depression, according to this theory, is that the loss is conscious in the first instance but unconscious in the second. Freud therefore suggested that in order to head off depression one ought to experience grief consciously. This would involve attempts to recall and to express repressed memories and fantasies associated with the lost object.

Depression and External Reinforcers

The apathy and unresponsiveness often associated with depression have been explained by some social-learning-oriented theorists as being due to a lack of positive reinforcers in the depressed person's environment. For example, Lewinsohn and Libet (1972), in a study involving three groups of college students, found that a depressive group engaged less in pleasant activities than a neurotic nondepressed group and a normal group. This finding was obtained by having each person rate his or her moods for a month while at the same time recording on a checklist the number of pleasant activities in which they participated each day. "Pleasant" was defined as being relaxed, having spare time, having people show interest in what one said, being with happy people, and many similar items.

Ferster (1973) has expanded the positive-reinforcement etiology of depression somewhat, contending that there are a number of additional components at play. In his view depression can also result from a high level of exposure to unpleasant or aversive situations; a drastic change in the environment, such as the death of a loved one, a change of job, or retirement; and the need to work very hard for limited reinforcements. Both Lewinsohn (1974) and Ferster (1973), then, can be said to favor a social learning theory of depression by arguing that depression results from a decreased schedule of positive reinforcements, an argument that has been tentatively challenged by a study (Price et al., 1978) that supports the learned helplessness model of depression described below.

The Cognitive View

Beck (1967, 1974) is the main exponent of a cognitive model of depression. Depressed people, according to this view, are those who have a negative opinion of themselves, the world, and the future. The depressed affective state is secondary to these negative cognitions. Depressive episodes may be externally precipitated, but it is the person's negative perception and appraisal of the event that render it depression-inducing. According to Beck, depression-prone persons suffer from three major cognitive patterns that compel them to view themselves, the world, and the future through a constellation of enduring negative attitudes. These attitudes, which Beck calls the primary triad in depression, are assumed to exist latently and may not be discerned by the person until the proper set of antecedents triggers their appearance in consciousness. The three components of the triad are (1) construing experiences in a negative way; (2) regarding oneself in a negative way; and (3) having primarily negative expectations of the future. We shall have more to say about the last of these components in our section on suicide.

In the meantime we shall note that, although Beck provides clinical and correlational evidence that depressives are more responsive to selective environmental inputs than nondepressives (see Becker, 1977, pp. 68–69), Blaney (1977) has suggested that such clinical and research evidence fails to prove that the negative cognitive sets are results rather than causes of depression.

Depression and Learned Helplessness

A belief in the futility of one's actions pervades depression, just as it does anxiety. Anxious people feel that regardless of the choices they make—the efforts to placate nature or society, the defensive maneuvers and fortifications—they will be booby-trapped by a whimsical, implacable, and unpredictable fate. In depression the seemingly futile actions are those aimed at gratifying one's needs. Depressed people believe they are helpless to control the elements of their lives that soothe, gratify, or nurture—the world does not respond. Seligman (1975) believes that this belief is the cause of depression, and that the same behaviors—the hopelessness and despair—are produced in the laboratory as learned helplessness (pp. 105–106).

Seligman originally demonstrated the laboratory phenomenon of learned helplessness with dogs. The dogs were placed in a harness and given a shock from which they could not escape. Later the same dogs were placed in a shuttlebox and shocked again, but this time they could terminate the shock by jumping over a barrier in the box. Untrained dogs had no trouble learning to escape. But the dogs that had earlier been given the inescapable shocks howled at first and then sat passively, enduring the shock. These dogs had learned that they were helpless, and so they remained passive and suffered even though they could have taken some action to relieve their pain.

Similar results have been obtained with humans, Seligman reports, in a study by two psychologists (Roth and Bootzin, 1974) in a Northwestern University laboratory. College students received solvable or unsolvable problems, then were taken to a second room in which a new set of problems, all solvable, appeared on a TV screen. On every tenth trial, the screen blurred. The students who first had unsolvable problems were the first to go get the experimenter to fix the screen; it seemed that this group was made anxious and frustrated, rather than helpless, by the unsolvability, at least as measured by readiness to seek help. But these students were poorer at solving the problems on the screen, and the authors speculated that uncontrollability first produces frustration, which gives way to helplessness as more uncontrollability occurs. Confirming this, according to Seligman, two investigators (Roth and Kubal, 1975) observed helplessness, not facilitation, when they increased uncontrollability, or when the subject perceived the failure as more significant.

Several laboratory studies (McNitt and Thorton, 1978; O'Leary et al., 1978; Smolen, 1978; Willis and Blaney, 1978) as well as some critical evaluations of the learned helplessness model of depression (Buchwald et al., 1978; Costello, 1978; Rizley, 1978; Teasdale, 1978; Wortman and Dintzer, 1978) have cast serious doubt on the relationship of depression to learned helplessness and controllability. In the main these studies replicated several of the experiments conducted in Seligman's laboratory (Klein and Seligman, 1976; Miller and Seligman, 1976; Miller et al., 1975) and either failed to find any evidence of depression among individuals who displayed laboratory-learned helplessness or failed to find full support for earlier research showing relationships between depressions and subjects' perceptions of controllability. In one study (Willis and Blaney, 1978), however, there was a successful replication of Seligman's (Hiroto and Seligman, 1975; Klein et al., 1976; Miller and Seligman, 1975) earlier findings that learned helplessness and depression interfere with solving anagram problems. But this replication did not support the claim that the inferior performance was accompanied by the subjects' reports of noncontrol over the outcomes of their laboratory behavior.

Partly because of the nonconfirming laboratory findings reported above, and partly as a result of his own realization that his original formulation was based on experiments with animals rather than humans, Seligman and his colleagues (Abramson et al., 1978; Seligman, 1978) reformulated their theory of learned helplessness. The reformulation, which itself has been criticized (Wortman and Dintzer, 1978), is made in terms of attribution theory. (Attribution theory was first introduced by Fritz Heider (1958) and is currently very influential among social psychologists. This theory holds that people behave as they do because of their perceptions of causality.)

According to Seligman's reformulation individuals in the laboratory first learn that certain outcomes and responses are related to one another, and then make an attribution about the cause. This attribution affects their expectations about future relationships between their actions and the probable outcome of these actions. In turn these attributions determine the chronicity, generality, and to some extent the intensity of the behavioral deficits people experience. Seligman cites an example similar to the following one in illustrating his reformulation in terms of this theory: a college student submits a midterm paper to a teacher and it is scathingly criticized. The student might make two possible attributions: "I am stupid," or "the teacher is stupid." The first of these has much more disastrous implications for the endterm paper (and future ones) than the second. If "I am stupid" is true, the endterm paper is likely to be just as severely criticized. If "the teacher is stupid," is true, future papers stand a better chance of receiving favorable comments as long as the student doesn't submit them to the same teacher. Seligman then demonstrates the complexity of the different kinds of attributions that can be made and their various implications for learned helplessness in specific and general situations (also see Weiner et al., 1978).

Seligman's studies raise other interesting questions. Is the learned helplessness induced in the laboratory identical to clinically observed depression, or merely similar? Even if it is identical, we cannot be certain that depression experienced "in real life" is induced in the same way, since a given result can often have more than one possible cause. Some studies suggest that genetic, biochemical, and psychophysiological determinants are involved, at least as predisposing factors, in the etiology of depression.

Nevertheless the learned helplessness hypothesis suggests some promising avenues of inquiry. What, for example, are the conditions in a person's home, school, or job environment that teach helplessness? And is the greater prevalence of depression among women related to the way in which sex-role conditioning discourages girls from exercising their own ability to explore and test reality? Given the importance of these questions for understanding depression and its possible causes, and given the controversy reviewed above about the validity of the theory for human subjects, we can safely predict that the last word on learned helplessness has not yet been written. In the meantime it is probably also true, as one psychologist (Huesmann, 1978) noted, that learned helplessness investigators will have to attend to two related lines of cognitive research: (1) how people make subjective probability judgments (see Hogarth, 1975; Tversky and Kahneman, 1974) and (2) how people infer functional relations from observations (see Egan and Greeno, 1974; Huesmann and Cheng, 1973; Simon and Lea, 1974).

Family Factors Model

Maternal-social deprivation is another favorite psychological explanation for the origins of various affective disorders. For example, in one study, already encountered in Chapter 6, René Spitz (1946) reported a syndrome of severe depression in hospitalized infants. He called this the *anaclitic depression* and explained that it developed in infants after an abrupt separation from their mothers. This syndrome occurred because their mothers were replaced by strange and unfamiliar figures; it was marked by a period of distress during which the infants silently cried, protested, and became generally colicky, apathetic, unresponsive, and sad. Upon reunion with their mothers, they usually showed significant improvement in their mood and behavior, although there were occasional periods of unresponsiveness even to their mothers (see Chapter 6 for additional comments on these studies). Several writers (Becker, 1977; Granville–Grosman, 1968; Heinicke, 1973) have noted a positive relation between death of a parent before the patient is 15 years old and the development of later psychiatric disturbances, including depression. Early death of a parent may also be related to severity of depression and to suicidal tendencies. This correlation is especially evident where the parent was the mother. Loss of either parent from ages 0 to 5, and of fathers from ages 10 to 14, especially seem to predispose to depression.

Other family factors leading to affective disorders are feelings of inferiority and parental demandingness. In one study (Cohen et al., 1954), for example, the family backgrounds and interpersonal relationships of 12 hospitalized manic-depressives were analyzed. The findings indicated that all the patients came from families whose members considered themselves socially undesirable and all of them belonged to racial minorities. But even more significantly, the authors of this study discovered that these families harbored a desire for upward mobility and placed the responsibility for this striving on one child. They concluded that this child, selected because he or she was the oldest, youngest, most promising, or perhaps the only child in the family, was subjected to considerable pressure to surpass his or her peers.

In another series of studies of interest here, a group of psychologists (Becker, 1960; Becker et al., 1963) paid particular attention to the role of parental demandingness in the etiology of the manic-depressive disorders. In one of these studies they were able to demonstrate the predicted differences between manic-depressives and non-psychiatric controls; but they later discovered that these differences were related more to being psychiatrically ill than to the specific diagnosis of manic-depressive disorder. This suggests, as Mendels (1970, p. 54) points out, that the background and personality characteristics ascribed by Cohen and her associates "may, in fact, simply have been a background basis for the experience of psychiatric illness in general."

Social and Cultural Influences

Although it has often been reported that psychosis in our culture is more frequent among lower

Hi Paula—

than higher socioeconomic groups, a review of many of these studies suggests that there is no consistent relationship between overall rates of psychosis and social class (Dohrenwend and Dohrenwend, 1969). This review also reports that the relationship between class and rate of manic-depressive psychosis is not consistent. However, the symptoms of depression do vary as a function of social class (Schwabb et al., 1967). Upper-class depressives feel loss of interest in life, middle-class depressives feel loneliness, guilt, and grief; and lower-class depressives feel futility and self-hatred.

In some societies interesting trends of the affective disorders are discernible. For example, among the Hutterites, a group we described earlier (see Chapter 11), depression was the most common reaction to stress (Eaton and Weil, 1955). Moreover, in sharp contrast to the finding that schizophrenia is the most common psychosis in our own culture, among the Hutterites manic-depressive illness is four times as frequent. Evidently there is something about the experiences of the Hutterites that predisposes its members to a comparatively higher incidence of affective disorders. Mendels (1970) suggests that this may be due to their tendency to be inner-directed, but he wisely counsels caution about overinterpreting the psychological significance of these results (p. 66):

consideration must be given to the possibility that the significant inbreeding that occurs . . . may have been responsible for the high incidence of manic-depressive illness. It is well known that this inbreeding within a small group of people increases the likelihood of any genetic (hereditary) factors emerging.

Biological Origins

The evidence supporting biological etiology has been of various kinds. One study suggests that depressives undergo metabolic changes. It is not

Table 14.3
Symptoms of Depression with Physiological Basis

Diurnal mood swing	Impotence
Early morning waking	Menstrual changes
Loss of weight	Diminished pulse rate
Constipation	Lowered blood pressure
Loss of appetite	Lowered body temperature
Inability to weep	Loss of facial flush
Dry mouth	Cold extremities
Decreased sexual desire	

Source: Pollitt, J. D. Suggestions for a physiological classification of depression. British Journal of Psychiatry, 1965, III, p. 489.

clear, however, whether these changes precipitate the depression or result from it. For example, Pollitt (1960, 1965) suggests that certain depressive illnesses appear independently of psychological stress and result from alterations in biological rhythms and from changes in metabolic and autonomic balance. He labels these endogenous depressions and attributes them to a "depressive functional shift" to distinguish them from other, more psychologically caused symptoms of depression. He believes these symptoms, listed in Table 14.3, have a physiological basis.

According to Pollitt, the functional shift results from damage in the hypothalamus, which is responsible for homeostasis. To support his theory, he draws on evidence from animal studies in which resemblances appeared between a functional shift and physiological disturbances. Thus he draws an analogy between periodicity of manic-depressive illness and the physiological changes accompanying hibernation (for example, lower metabolism, weight loss, hypothermia), these changes presumably being similar to those observed in dysfunctions of the hypothalamus. In human beings, according to this investigator, similar functional shifts are seen in depressives after midlife and develop because of altered hypothalamic functioning. Table 14.4 summarizes the determinants that, according to Pollitt, are

Table 14.4
Development of the Depressive Functional Shift

Predisposing Factors

1. Heredity
2. Influences serving to establish habitual inhibition of emotional expression
    (a) Civilization
    (b) Mode of upbringing
    (c) Obsessive personality
    (d) Social position
    (e) Advanced age

Precipitating Factors

Natural Life Situations	*Physiological Changes*
Circumstances calling out emotion in settings requiring inhibition of its expression:	Premenstrual phase
Grief	Pregnancy
Heightened sexual feelings	Puerperium [woman's state immediately after childbirth]
Anger	Menopause
	Oophorectomy [removal of the ovaries]
	Virus infections
	Reserpine and phenothiazines
	Debilitation
	Lesions of the hypothalamus

Functional Shift and Depression Characterized By:
    Loss of biological defense mechanisms
    Lack of emotional expression
    Disturbance of metabolic regulators
    Secondary hypochondriasis
    Depressive stupor
    Death

Source: Pollitt, J. D. Suggestions for a physiological classification of depression. British Journal of Psychiatry, 1965, III, p. 492.

involved in causing depressive functional shifts. Since sleep disturbances are a common clinical observation among depressed persons, with sleep being shallow and sporadic, the relationship between rapid eye movement (REM) sleep and depression has been studied. The results (Mendels et al., 1969) are ambiguous. Most so-called psychotic depressives in this research have exhibited reduced REM; less chronic kinds of depressives have increased REM.

Studies of visual evoked potential (a regular series of alterations in the slow electrical activity recorded from the brain, produced by a visual stimulus) in unipolar and bipolar patients have yielded some differences (Buchsbaum et al., 1971). Bipolars tend to augment the evoked potential—their cortical brain activities increase in direct relation to the magnitude of the visual stimulus. The brighter or more salient the visual stimulus, the larger the evoked potential activity.

An inverse relationship occurs among unipolar patients; their electrical brain activity reduces as the stimulus becomes larger. These findings have not yet been replicated, and no adequate theoretical explanation has been offered (see Becker, 1977, pp. 180–181).

Several other studies have attempted to demonstrate how biochemical anomalies might account for the affective disorders. One likely possibility is that depression involves a depletion of norepinephrine, a chemical conveying impulses from one neuron to another in the brain and nervous system (see Chapter 5). This may cause an inhibition or slowing down of neural transmission, which in turn gives rise to periods of depression. Evidence in support of this is that low levels of norepinephrine have been found in animals that have received inescapable shocks in learned helplessness experiments (Weiss et al., 1977); this evidence has been offered as a more adequate explanation of learned helplessness than attribution or cognitive theory.

Evidence that norepinephrine may be the critical substance in depression also comes from research into reserpine-induced depression in monkeys (Redmond et al., 1971). Reserpine, a drug that is used in treatment of hypertension and that has often been observed to cause depression in humans, has been shown to deplete norepinephrine stores, and this has a sedating and slowing-down effect.

It is difficult to specify at this time whether these reported biochemical changes result from the depression or trigger the depression. Clearly more work in this area is needed.

Evidence for hereditary determinants of the affective disorders is much more suggestive than that for biochemical origins. It has been repeatedly shown in family and twin studies of affective psychotics that the expectancy percentages for affective disorders are higher among relatives of those diagnosed manic-depressive or affective psychotic. Table 14.5 summarizes these findings (see also Gottesman and Shields, 1966, 1972; Kallmann, 1953; Rosenthal, 1970, 1971). Family studies also seem to indicate that while both unipolar and bipolar depressions are familial, there is no genetic overlap between the two (Pincus and

Table 14.5
Expectancy Rates for Affective Disorders Among
Relatives of Index Cases Diagnosed as
Manic-Depressives or Affective Psychotics

Kinship	Number of Studies	Median Expectancy Rate (%)	Percentage Range
MZ twins	6	70	50–93
DZ twins	6	20	0–38
Parents	10	8	3–23
Siblings	9	9	3–23
Children	6	11	6–24
Uncles and aunts	2	3	1–4
Grandchildren	2	3	2–3

Source: Reprinted from J. D. Page. Psychopathology, *Chicago: Aldine, 1975.*

Tucker, 1978); that is, bipolar disorders do not occur in families of unipolar probands and vice versa. The parents and siblings of bipolar patients have a 20 percent risk of bipolar illness, and the parents and siblings of unipolar patients (three or more episodes of depression) have a 12 to 14 percent risk of unipolar depressive disease (Slater and Cowie, 1971).

These percentages, according to Page (1975), indicate rather clearly that the manic-depressive and affective disorders occur more often among closer than among distant relatives. Thus if an identical twin has an affective psychosis, the likelihood that his or her brother or sister will develop a similar disorder (the concordance ratio) is 70 percent. The concordance ratios drop to 20 percent for fraternal twins; to about 10 percent for other immediate family members; and to 3 percent for extended family relatives.

A review by Becker (1977, p. 166) of the evidence for genetic transmission of the affective disorders led him to conclude that indirect evidence strongly suggests a hereditary etiology. But he cautions that thus far "there is neither an identified genetic anomaly that mediates these disorders, nor an established pattern of transmission (e.g., dominant or recessive, sex-linked or autosomal)." Current evidence, according to Becker, rests primarily on concordance-consanguinity studies, though more adequate adoptee studies are currently being done in Denmark by Seymour Kety and his associates. In the absence of identified anomalous genes or biological mechanisms in people with affective disorders, many investigators have focused on attempting to forge finer distinctions among several subtypes of the disorder and linking these with various biological findings.

At this point, only very tentative subtype-differences evidence is available, and it seems to suggest that the genetic component is greater for bipolar (with alternative manic episodes) than for unipolar depression (no manic episodes). Further evidence for the usefulness of the bipolar–unipolar dichotomy comes from the psycho-pharmacological work, which shows that bipolars respond better to lithium carbonate whereas unipolars respond better to tricyclic and MAO inhibitor antidepressants (see below and Chapter 21).

Some new but indirect evidence suggests that bipolar patients suffer a deficit of REM and of deep sleep, and following treatment, these patients display more REM and deep sleep than normals (Gillin and Wyatt, 1975; Huri et al., 1974; Lewinsohn, 1977; Wyatt et al., 1971). The precise meaning of these findings is not yet known.

Treatment of the Affective Disorders

The prognosis for those with affective disorders is highly favorable, and many are good candidates for spontaneous recovery without therapy. This is especially true for manic-depressives, who are believed to have episodes of spontaneous remissions every six months to one year.

It has been estimated that the symptoms of about 80 percent of affective psychotics terminate within nine months. Compared with schizophrenics, then, this is a relatively good remission rate. Nevertheless affective psychosis is a serious illness and, as we shall see shortly, one in which suicide is a constant possibility. Consequently even such short durations may be intolerable for both patients and their families, and therapeutic intervention is therefore essential.

Psychological Treatment

Traditional psychotherapy has been virtually useless for the affective disorders, but behavior therapy shows much more promise. Three possible behavioral treatments have been outlined by Lazarus (1968). The first consists of having patients imagine future activities that produce positive reinforcement ("time projection with positive reinforcement"; see Yates, 1970a, p. 417); the second consists of having patients verbally express moods that are opposite to—and hence designed to inhibit—depression; and the third consists of depriving patients of sensory inputs on the premise that following a period of such deprivation almost any stimulus will be reinforcing.

More recently (see Wilcoxon et al., 1976), behavioral treatment strategies for the affective disorders, particularly depression, have emphasized techniques that either divert the patient's verbalizations and attention away from depressive topics or focus on the patient's environment as a means of modifying behavior. For example, Lewinsohn (1974) has reported a technique for identifying activities that seem especially important to the way a particular person feels. In a study with ten depressed college students Lewinsohn and Graf (1972) tested the effectiveness of increasing the student's participation in pleasant activities as a means of relieving a depressed mood. For each subject the ten activities that correlated most highly with nondepressed mood over a 30-day period were selected as target behaviors. Subjects were then reinforced with therapy time for increasing the frequency of these activities. The result was that the target or pleasant behaviors increased substantially more than ten "control" behaviors, and positive changes in mood paralleled these increases.

Focusing on the depressed person's environment as a means of modifying behavior, three psychologists (Hersen et al., 1973) set up a token economy program (see Chapter 23) that reinforced nondepressive behaviors in several areas: work assignments, occupational therapy, responsibility, and personal hygiene. A behavior rating scale used by the nursing staff on a time-sampling basis assessed depression in three major categories: talking, smiling, and motor activity. The psychologists made token reinforcements and privileges contingent upon performance of the target or desired behaviors (for example, talking, smiling, and activity). When these behaviors ceased (when original baseline behaviors were resumed), the psychologists withheld the token reinforcements and hence the privileges they bought. The authors reported increased activity and increased range of social contacts, as well as more smiling and nondepressed behaviors. Thus it seems that behavior therapy is an improvement over conventional psychotherapy. But this will remain a matter for conjecture until some evidence is collected. In the meantime the somatic treatments are preferred.

Physical Treatment

The method of choice for treating depression has been electroshock therapy (EST), with drug therapy running a close second. Approximately 90 percent of psychotically depressed and older chronic patients who receive about six to eight EST treatments at the rate of about three a week tend to improve dramatically in less than one month (Zung, 1968).

Drug therapy is recommended for manic-depressives, who do not respond as well to EST. For them, as for schizophrenics, Chlorpromazine, a major tranquilizer, has been reported to be the most effective drug. On the other hand, tranquilizers have been relatively ineffectual for depressives and may even slow them down more. Consequently a number of antidepressant drugs (Tofranil, Parnate) are commonly used instead of tranquilizers. The therapeutic efficacy of the so-called tricyclic antidepressants (imipramine and amitriptyline) has also been reported (Pincus and Tucker, 1978). Whether they are older patients with psychotic depressions or young patients with less severe depressions, 60 to 70 percent of depressed patients benefit from the use of these drugs.

The really promising development in drug therapy with patients in the manic state has been lithium carbonate. Since its introduction in 1949, numerous encouraging results have been reported from around the world. Original use of lithium chloride as a salt substitute, according to Winokur and his associates (1969), led to lithium's disrepute as a safe drug in the treatment of anything. But with increasing experience with its combination with carbonate, and with constant monitoring of serum blood lithium levels, it can now be used safely. It is not indicated for patients who have cardiovascular, renal, or central nervous system pathology. There is now general agreement that episodes of mania can be shortened to within ten days by the administration of lithium carbonate and that continuous lithium therapy prevents the recurrence of manic episodes in most individuals with bipolar affective disorders (Davis et al., 1973).

The Veterans Administration and National Institute of Mental Health are currently conducting joint studies of lithium treatment for mania and depression, and the results should be of considerable interest to all mental health professionals. Research interest in the biology and pharmacology of lithium is currently very high (Schou, 1976) as is the interest in its therapeutic effectiveness (Braceland, 1977; Gershon and Shopsin,

1973; Johnson, 1975). The evidence to date strongly suggests that it is highly effective in the treatment and prevention of both manic and depressive episodes. We shall have more to say about lithium in Chapter 21.

In evaluating the treatment of the affective disorders, there are two main difficulties: the absence of a definitive classification system, and the fact that even chronic, recurrent affective disorders usually have time-limited episodes.

The Problem of Suicide in the Affective Disorders

Suicide is always a possibility with the affectively disturbed. It is an especially attractive alternative to the person who has given up hope, whose sleepless and agitated nights have become unbearable, and who believes in his or her own worthlessness.

The depressed person's sense of futility in life often evolves into the contemplation of suicide.

Incidence

There are about twenty thousand suicides in the United States each year; this does not include people who are unsuccessful in their attempts. The number of potential suicides is considerably higher, the best estimates indicating that there are about five to eight times as many as actual suicides (Shneidman et al., 1970).

Several generalizations about suicide have been supported by research (Lester and Lester, 1971). Men tend to complete suicide, whereas women tend to attempt suicide. For whites, middle and old age are the most common times for suicide; blacks tend to commit suicide in their 20s. It has also been found that people who threaten or attempt suicide are more likely than others to successfully commit suicide. Moreover suicide is more common among persons who have a history of psychological disturbances than among those who do not. And behavioral indicators such as sleep disturbances and loss of appetite are better predictors of suicide than psychological tests.

It is difficult to assign direct causal relationships between depression and suicide, but the findings of several studies are illuminating. In one of these studies (Robins et al., 1959), which investigated the backgrounds of 134 successful suicides, 94 percent were found to be psychiatrically ill and 45 percent of those had been depressed. In another study (Pokorny, 1965), in which the suicides among veterans were traced over a 15-year-period, the incidence per 100,000 each year was 566 for depressive patients, which was more than four times higher than that for normal controls. Similar findings were reported from the Los Angeles Suicide Prevention Center (Wold, 1970).

In another study of suicides and attempted suicides, a group of investigators followed up 138 depressives with histories of manic episodes (bipolar patients) and 139 depressives without such histories (unipolar patients). They found that after 20 years only 2 percent of the former and 10

An 11-year-old girl is pulled to safety after threatening to jump from a fifth-floor window.

percent of the latter committed suicide. Likewise the incidence of suicide attempts was considerably higher for patients whose only disorder was depression (26 percent) than for those who also had a history of manic episodes (D'Elia and Perris, 1969; Perris, 1969).

In this context it may be illuminating to consider Beck's idea of negative expectations, mentioned earlier, which holds that suicide is the most logical alternative for a person whose forecast for the immediate and distant future is bleak and negative.

Beck (1967) states that the depressed person's major complaint is often a sense of futility about life expressed as, "I don't have any goals anymore," or "I don't see any point in living." He notes that 78 percent of depressed hospitalized patients report a negative outlook; this compares with 22 percent of a nondepressed patient group. He also notes that clinical ratings of depression correlate highly with patients' self-reports of negative expectations. It is also Beck's contention, on the basis of clinical observations, that negative expectations, as a component of the depressive disorders, are a stronger predictor of suicidal intent than depression itself.

Several empirical studies (Bjerg, 1967; Ganzler, 1967; Beck and Beck, 1973) support the statistical relationship between negative expectations and suicide. In a factor analysis of test items on Beck's Depression Inventory (Beck, 1961), two investigators (Pichot and Lemperiere, 1964) found a factor that contained two main components: negative expectations and suicide. Other investigators also reported the importance of negative expectations for suicidal wishes (Cropley and Weckowicz, 1967).

While depression is the main cause associated with suicide among adults, this disorder may not be as important a factor in younger groups. According to a review of the literature on adolescent suicide by Seiden (1974a), self-inflicted death may occur among children because they identify with, imitate, or follow the suggestions of people close to them who have died, attempted suicide, or are preoccupied by suicidal thoughts. Usually the child does not intend to die, but because of an unrealistic assessment of immortality due to an incompletely developed concept of death, the child does not fully anticipate that he may indeed kill himself. The method chosen, however, which is commonly jumping from a window, hanging, or running in front of a car or train, may not leave any chance for rescue.

Among young people, accidental overdoses of such psychoactive drugs as LSD and PCP (see Chapter 10) have also been frequently linked with suicide. Several varieties of drug-related suicides have been isolated (Seiden, 1974a, b). One is the accidental suicide of the person who, under the influence of a delusion, believes he or she can fly and jumps from a roof or out a window. The idea that a "bad trip" will never end can also lead to suicide. This is an agitated depression type of suicide, not unlike that of many clinically depressed persons.

Then there is the flashback suicide, so called because it follows a recurrence of the effects of LSD or PCP. The person may panic because of a confusion over what brought on the delusional or hallucinatory episode and concern about whether it can be ended. Attempts at suicide in this state may be marked by the same motivation to escape psychic pain that occurs in the drugged state.

Many socially determined suicides also occur among children as well as adults. Loss of a parent or a loved one can lead to suicide. Homesickness among younger people is not an uncommon reason for suicide. Among all ages social isolation is an important influencing factor leading to suicide, and its attendant problems in communicating with others have also been associated with suicide.

Cultural determinants may also influence the suicide rate in two basic ways: (1) by the acute psychological stresses produced in people; and (2) by the degree of acceptance of suicide. Instances of the first type were found in a comparison of suicide rate differences among the Scandinavian countries of Denmark, Sweden, and Norway (Hendin, 1964). These rates were related to national differences in child-rearing orientations. In Sweden, where the suicide rate is relatively high, suicide was characterized by high achievement expectations, self-hatred for failure, and problems with depression resulting presumably from early maternal separation. Denmark, where the suicide rate is also high, had a similar configuration of influences. But in Norway, where the suicide rate is relatively low, mothers were found to be more accepting, less concerned with their children's achievement, and more tolerant of aggression and strivings for independence than Swedish or Danish mothers.

Cultural acceptability of suicide is best exemplified in countries such as Austria, Germany, and Japan, where suicide is regarded as an honorable way to die. Unlike such countries as England and the United States, where self-destruction is considered abnormal or even cowardly, these cultures have favorable attitudes toward suicide and, not surprisingly, they produce a higher incidence of suicide.

Suicide among Afro-Americans, although not relatively higher than among whites (see Clark, 1965; Pettigrew, 1964), is twice as frequent among black men between the ages of 20 and 35 as it is among whites of the same age. Again it is difficult to say whether this is due to the *cultural depression* mentioned earlier in this book or to other causes, but Herbert Hendin (1969) in his study *Black Suicide*, suggests several possibilities. After intensively interviewing and analyzing the backgrounds of 25 black patients who made suicide attempts, Hendin reports that among older black men, whose lifelong obedience and submissiveness served to mask their rage and guilt, there are strong feelings of deserving punishment. Consequently they anticipated their punishment by attempting to destroy themselves. Among the younger men—those who fall within the 20–35 age group—the suicide attempts represented a turned-inward expression of their murderous rage and self-hatred, an integral part of the burden of being black in America. Of this Hendin writes as follows (p. 138):

If the Negro has grown up hating his mother and father for rejecting him and later feels bitter at society's rejection, he seldom sees beyond his own anger to become conscious of the ways in which society has shaped and directed his mother's and father's treatment of him and each other. In fact the culture's overt rejection of the Negro all too often reinforces feelings of rage and worthlessness that are already present—feelings that the culture, operating through the family, has insidiously helped to produce.

The Prediction of Suicide

Depressed patients seldom commit suicide when seriously ill. Evidently their psychomotor activities are so severely slowed that they are incapable of mobilizing enough energy to attempt the act. According to Mendels (1970), the danger period comes after treatment or partial recovery, when the patient is able to mobilize enough energy to make the attempt. Some support for this notion comes from a study showing that among a group of psychiatric patients who committed suicide, 30 percent did so while hospitalized and 63 percent succeeded within one month of being discharged from the hospital (Wheat, 1960).

The most intensive effort to understand suicide has grown out of the work at the Los Angeles Suicide Prevention Center. The authors of *The Psychology of Suicide* (Shneidman et al., 1970), which summarizes much of this work, emphasize what they term *suicidal logic* and the content analysis of suicide notes (Figure 14.1). Their system of analyzing these notes and the reasoning upon which it is based, evolved from the study of several hundred suicide notes, are too elaborate to explain here. But a summary of the varieties of logic uncovered is illuminating; it appears in Table 14.6, along with the personal characteristics of suicidal types and suggested modes of treatment (Shneidman and Farberow, 1961).

Table 14.6 describes *catalogic*, the thinking of the helpless and forlorn; *normal logic*, the reasoning of those who arrive at their self-destructive conclusions rationally; *contaminated logic*, the reasoning of those who think that suicide will speed their entrance to a new and better life in the hereafter; and *paleologic*, the disorganized thinking that characterizes many psychotics.

Suicide Prevention

There are now more than 100 suicide prevention centers throughout the United States, and in 1966 the National Institute of Mental Health estab-

lished a Center for Studies of Suicide Prevention, which supports research into suicide's clues, causes, and prevention. One of its tasks is to educate the public about the facts of suicide. Table 14.7, based on information distributed by the Los Angeles Suicide Prevention Center (Shneidman and Mandelkorn, 1970), is a summary of facts and fables about suicide.

Summary

The main affective disorders are psychotic depression and manic-depressive psychosis.

Depression, like anxiety, need not have an external referent. When it does, it is called reactive depression, which is analogous to state anxiety. It is endogenous when it is triggered by some unknown internal mechanism. Bipolar depression is depression alternating with mania (manic-depressive illness), and unipolar depression is a series of depressive episodes with no manic episodes. Depressions have also been classified as empty, anxious, hypochondriacal, and angry. Depression has also been characterized as "learned helplessness" because of its similarity to symptoms produced in laboratory animals in experiments that induced feelings of helplessness. Manic-depressive psychosis differs from the psychotic depression in that it is marked by severe mood swings from deep depression to elated euphoria. In general the manic-depressive disorders have a more favorable course, outcome, and prognosis than the depressions, although drug and shock treatments have contributed considerably to earlier remission of depression.

Intrapsychic, stimulus–response, and interactive models to account for the affective disorders abound. These tend to focus on the depressed person's inner-directed hostility and to emphasize his or her deprivations. Biological formulations are sparse, but there seems to be some solid evidence suggesting a genetic basis for the manic-depressive psychoses. Unfortunately in both types of studies—that is, in those that pro-

Dear Folks:

I know this won't seem the right thing to do but from where I stand, it seems like the best solution, considering what is inevitably in store for the future.

You know I am in debt. Probably not deeply compared to a lot of people but at least they have certain abilities, a skill or trade, or talents with which to make financial recovery. Yes, I am still working but only "by the grace of the gods". You know how I feel about working where there are a lot of girls I never could stand their cattiness and I couldn't hope to be lucky enough again to find work where I had my own office and still have someone to rely on like Betty...

Some girls can talk about their work to their girl friends and make it sound humorous. But I guess it sounds like complaining the way I talk...

But just what is there to talk about when you get tired of the same old questions and comments on the weather "how are you," "Working hard or hardly working?" and you know better than to say very much about things they are interested in or concerned about... Due to these, and many, many more frustrations... and other causes I have become much more nervous than I was...

How I wish I could make "small talk" or "party chatter" like some girls do. But I can't compete with most of them for many reasons and after trying to enter social activities with kids in my age range, especially the past year, I find I can't compete with most of them. Even if I had all the clothes to look the part I still wouldn't be able to act the part. Sorry I am such a disappointment to you folks.

I am saying these things so you'd understand why it's so futile for me to even hope for a better job. As long as I go on living there will be "working conditions" when there are so many other better places for the money.

One reason for doing this now is that Bill will be back and may want his .22. But the primary reason is one I think you already know — Mike. I love him more than anyone knows and it may sound silly to you but I can't go on without him. What is there that's worth living for without him?

Table 14.6
Types of Suicide and Suggested Treatments

Logical Type	Personal Characteristics	Psychologic Label	Suggested Mode of Treatment
Catalogic: the logic is destructive; it confuses the self as experienced by the self with the self as experienced by others	Individuals who are lonely, feel helpless and fearful, and feel pessimistic about making meaningful personal relationships	*Referred suicides:* the confusion in logic and in the identification is "referred" (like referred pain) from other root problems	Dynamic psychotherapy wherein the goal would be to supply the patient with a meaningful, rewarding relationship, so that his search for identification would be stabilized
Normal logic: the reasoning is acceptable according to Aristotelian standards	Individuals who are older, or widowed, or who are in physical pain	*Surcease suicides:* persons desire surcease from pain and reason that death will give them this	Treatment is in terms of giving freedom from pain through analgesics and sedatives and providing companionship by means of active milieu therapy
Contaminated logic: the logical or semantic error is in the emphasis on the self as experienced by others	Individuals whose beliefs permit them to view suicide as a transition to another life or as a means of saving reputation	*Cultural suicides:* their concept of death plays a primary role in the suicide	Treatment has to do with deeply entrenched religious and cultural beliefs and would have to deal with and clarify the semantic implications of the concept of death
Paleologic: makes logical identifications in terms of attributes of the predicates rather than of the subjects	Individuals who are delusional and/or hallucinatory	*Psychotic suicides:* not all suicides are psychotic, but psychotics can be unpredictably suicidal	Treatment has to do primarily with the psychosis and only subsequently with suicidal tendencies; treatment would include protecting the individual from his or her own impulses

Source: Shneidman, E. S., and Farberow, N. L. The logic of suicide. In Shneidman, E. S., Farberow, N. L., and Litman, R. E. (eds.). The psychology of suicide. New York: Science House, 1970, p. 68.

Table 14.7
Facts and Fables About Suicide

Fable	Fact
People who talk about suicide do not commit suicide.	Of any ten persons who kill themselves, eight have given definite warnings of their suicidal intentions.
Suicide happens without warning.	Studies reveal that the suicidal person gives many clues to and warnings of suicidal intentions.
Suicidal people are fully intent on dying.	Most suicidal people are undecided about living or dying, and they "gamble with death," leaving it to others to save them. Almost no one commits suicide without letting others know how he or she is feeling.
Once a person is suicidal, he or she is suicidal forever.	Individuals who wish to kill themselves are suicidal for only a limited period of time.
Improvement following a suicidal crisis means that the suicidal risk is over.	Most suicides occur within about three months following the beginning of "improvement," when the individual has the energy to put morbid thoughts and feelings into effect.
Suicide strikes much more often among the rich—or, conversely, it occurs almost exclusively among the poor.	Suicide is neither the disease of the rich nor the curse of the poor. Suicide is very "democratic" and is represented proportionately among all levels of society.
Suicide is inherited or "runs in the family."	Suicide does not run in families. It follows an individual pattern.
All suicidal individuals are mentally ill, and suicide always is the act of a psychotic person.	Studies of hundreds of genuine suicide notes indicate that although potential suicides are extremely unhappy, they are not necessarily mentally ill.

Source: Adapted from Shneidman, E. S., and Farberow, N. L. Some facts about suicide. Washington, D.C.: Government Printing Office, 1961.

pose psychogenic causation and those that support biogenic causation—the sampling procedures tend to combine the psychotically depressed and the involutional (unipolar) patients with those who are manic-depressive (bipolar).

Although the threat of suicide is constantly present among the affectively disordered, there has been some encouraging work both in suicide prevention and in the treatment of these disorders.

Terms and Concepts to Master

Bipolar depression

Endogenous depression

Functional shift

Involutional melancholia

Learned helplessness

Lithium treatment

Manic-depressive psychosis

Reactive depression

Safety-signal hypothesis

Suicidal logic

Unipolar depression

15

Sexual Dysfunctions and Divergent Sexual Patterns

In this chapter we shall examine two aspects of human sexuality. The sexual dysfunctions, which we discuss first, are, almost without exception, psychophysiological disorders (see Chapter 8). The rest of the chapter is an examination of forms of sexual behavior that conflict with the values of this culture. What the two topics have in common is the word *sex*. They are, however, traditionally taught as a single topic, and we bow to tradition by combining them.

Sexual Dysfunctions

All human beings are sexual beings. Frequently a newborn boy's first response to the world is an erection, and orgasms are known to occur as early as age four months in both boys and girls. Not only do we enter the world sexually alive, but as children we "explore in indiscriminate and anarchistic fashion all the erotic potentialities of the human body" (Brown, 1959). Freud (1953f) described this as "polymorphous perverse sexuality"; he called it "perverse" because it has many forms, whereas he believed adult sexuality was not perverse because it was (he thought) concentrated in the genital organ to serve primarily what he called the "genital function"—procreation.

Much of our new understanding of human sexual responses and sexual difficulties is the direct result of the pioneering work of sex researchers, especially William H. Masters and Virginia E. Johnson.[1] Partly as a result of their ef-

forts, we are beginning to see, for example, the extent to which we may have mistaken the effects of nurture for those of nature.

Human sexual response, according to Masters and Johnson, has four stages: *excitement, plateau, orgasm,* and *resolution,* the first and last stages accounting for the largest segment of time. If an adequate intensity of stimulation is maintained, excitement increases rapidly, and the plateau stage may be reached quickly. If the stimulation is physically or psychologically objectionable, or if it is interrupted, the excitement stage may be prolonged or terminated.

The effectiveness of stimuli and the individual's drive for release determine the duration of the plateau stage.[2] If the stimulation stops, or if the stimulation or the drive is inadequate, there is no orgasmic release, and sexual tension drops slowly through an extended resolution stage.

If both stimulus and drive are sufficient, there is a brief period of supersensitivity during

---

[1] Their early studies, reported in two of their books, *Human Sexual Response* (1966) and *Human Sexual Inadequacy* (1970), were so comprehensive, unprecedented, and well done that they still serve as the foundation for the work of many other sex researchers and sex therapists. There is a scarcity of attempts to replicate these studies; thus authors of textbooks tend to rely rather heavily on Masters and Johnson. Sex research is still in its infancy and its results should be approached cautiously.

[2] Within limits, it can also be lengthened to prolong pleasure.

which arousal and pleasure are extremely intense, followed by the moment in which release can no longer be resisted, and then by orgasm. Both major components of sexual arousal—the muscular tension (myotonia) and the engorgement of genital tissues with blood (vasocongestion)—are unlocked in a succession of rhythmic contractions. The sensations of orgasm are concentrated in the pelvic area—in the clitoris, vagina, and uterus of the female and the penis, prostate, and seminal vesicles of the male.

Tension continues to ebb away during the resolution phase. Some females respond to stimulation during the resolution stage and have repeated orgasms. Most males enter a refractory period, during which penile stimulation is not pleasant and does not induce arousal. If the orgasmic release is unusually intense, there will be less residual tension to be drained off during the resolution. The speed at which an individual moves through the response cycle is extremely variable.

Psychosocial interference with this natural process can take various forms. If vasocongestion is blocked, erection does not occur in the male and vaginal lubrication does not occur in the female. The causes of interference are numerous, but the results are invariably, physically and emotionally, stressful to the individual and injurious to a relationship.

Negative action in the psychosocial system is not always due to early learning. For example, unexpressed anger can block sexual feeling, and the release of anger through fighting may be one explanation for the intense lovemaking that often follows a fight. Thus, even though learned social and sexual values contribute heavily to any blockage of arousal, that blockage must be treated as a disorder of the couple's interaction.

Many individuals experience temporary loss of the capacity to be sexually aroused—for example, after heavy drinking—but for a few the loss is a continuing, often worsening, condition, diagnosable as *impotence* in the male or as *vaginismus* (a painful contraction of the vagina) or dys-

Parental Sex Education

A parent cannot choose whether to give or not to give sex education; he is giving it involuntarily from moment to moment. Communication may be nonverbal—but the child reads the message loud and clear.

—*Mary S. Calderone,* Sex education for young people —and for their parents and teachers, *in Brecher and Brecher (1966).*

pareunia (painful intercourse) in the female. We shall now examine those conditions.

The physiology of arousal is almost the same in both male and female: the two major components of arousal are *vasocongestion* and *myotonia*. Vasocongestion is the engorgement of tissues with blood. In the male it produces penile erection. In the female it produces erection of the clitoris and a kind of "sweating" through the vaginal tissues that dampens and lubricates the vagina. Myotonia is the muscular tension that makes genital and surrounding tissues taut in both sexes. Both myotonia and vasocongestion bring more nerve endings into play and thereby heighten sensitivity to pleasurable touching. Both also contribute to the development of the "orgasmic platform," contraction of the outer third of the vagina, and a stiffening and swelling of the pelvic floor. The orgasmic platform plays an important part in the female orgasm.

Inhibition of Arousal

A continued unblocked input of sexual stimulation to any healthy human organism should induce a steadily increasing state of arousal culminating in orgasm. At first, stimulation increases the tension—the energy charge—until the level of tension reaches a critical point, and then any additional input, no matter how small, produces a discharge of energy and tension. At that moment of supersensitivity the slightest movement, or even a look or a word, can be so powerfully erotic as to tip the scales.

Some people have never reached that point. Others reach it too quickly to enjoy it. The reason, in the absence of physical pathology, is interference by a negatively conditioned psychosocial system.

Primary Impotence. Masters and Johnson *"arbitrarily"* define the primarily impotent male as "a male never able to achieve and/or maintain an erection quality sufficient to accomplish successful coital connection." They add, "No man is considered primarily impotent if he has been successful in any attempt at intromission in either heterosexual or homosexual opportunity." Like most sexual difficulties, primary impotence is a problem, not merely of one partner, but of the couple, and successful therapy requires a change in the behavior of both partners. If both partners' sexual value system and sexual experience have been severely limited by what Masters and Johnson call "adherence to demanding forms of religious orthodoxy," their plight is especially pathetic (1970, pp. 139–140):

When premarital sexual expression has been restricted to handholding, the first fumbling, bumbling, theologically and legally acceptable attempts at sexual connection are often unsuccessful. This psychosocial diversion of the natural biophysical process may evolve into the disastrous combination of a severely shredded male ego further traumatized by the unreasonable, but so understandable female partner's virginally blind insistence that he 'do something.'

Other factors in the etiology of primary impotence include a conflicting sexual orientation (as when the male's previous experience has been passively homosexual) or any traumatic experience in a male's first attempt at coitus.

A vicious spiral operates in primary impotence, as it does in most sexual difficulties: any unsuccessful attempt at coition is likely to instill performance fears, and performance fears are in turn likely to demoralize and incapacitate the individual.

Secondary Impotence. Secondary impotence is distinguished from primary impotence by the presence in a man's history of at least one successful penetration of his partner. A single erective failure does not constitute a case of secondary impotence, since many men are occasionally unable to achieve erection, usually as a result of fatigue, distraction, or heavy drinking. Only when such an episode triggers performance fears is there much likelihood of secondary impotence. Masters and Johnson accept a diagnosis of secondary impotence only when such episodes approach 25 percent of the person's opportunities.

A crucial element in the stress felt by the impotent male seems to be the fact that to conceive the male must perform, whereas the female need only be there. In other words culture places the full responsibility for "successful" coital connection on the male partner.

If all males are subject to performance fears, why do only a few become impotent? Apparently as in many other psychological difficulties a precipitating or potentiating factor interacts with predisposing factors to trigger the disturbance. In the case of secondary impotence the most common potentiators are premature ejaculation and excessive alcohol intake. (Alcohol depresses the brain centers involved in sexual arousal.)

Often the premature ejaculator becomes impotent, ironically, by trying to overcome an ejaculatory difficulty (see pp. 332–334). His repeated attempts to delay his orgasm by dulling his awareness of his own and his partner's sexual excitement inhibit and ultimately wreck his capacity for arousal.

Negative psychosocial input is the chief predisposing factor in secondary impotence, and these environmental factors are especially destructive in the formative years. Such factors may include parental imbalance (for example, maternal dominance), "religious orthodoxy," and homosexual orientation. Masters and Johnson also found several cases of secondary impotence due to inadequate counseling. Case Report 15.1 is adapted from one of these.

Case Report 15.1 *Secondary Impotence Resulting from Inadequate Counseling*

A couple who had been having intercourse about once a day during their three-year marriage were advised by their friends that this was an unusually high frequency. Despite their lack of problems and their great delight in their intimacies, they decided to consult a professional. The professional they consulted told them that at such a high frequency the male would wear out rapidly; he also expressed his surprise that the husband was not already having difficulty keeping an erection, and advised reducing their coital frequency to a maximum of twice a week. He concluded with the hope that it was not already too late.

For 48 hours after this consultation the husband worried about what he now believed was his impending sexual demise. His erective response was considerably slowed when the couple had intercourse two nights after the consultation. One night later he had serious difficulty attaining an erection, and three days after that he was totally impotent. Except for managing intercourse with a partial erection six to eight times a year, he remained impotent for seven years before seeking treatment for that condition.

SOURCE: *Adopted from Masters, W. H., and Johnson, V. E., Human sexual inadequacy, p. 191. Boston: Little, Brown, 1970. Reproduced by permission.*

Vaginismus. Instead of contracting rhythmically, as it does in orgasm, the musculature of the perineum and the outer third of the vagina may contract spastically. This contraction is an involuntary reflex due to a negative emotional response to real, imagined, or anticipated penetration. When this syndrome is fully developed, penile penetration is impossible.

A pelvic examination is required to establish a diagnosis of vaginismus, which is usually a surprise to both partners. In a high percentage of cases, vaginismus in the female partner is associated with secondary impotence in the male partner, and the number of cases in which the vaginismus occurred first is about equal to the number in which the impotence occurred first.

The two major causes of vaginismus are male sexual difficulties, as indicated above, and severely controlled social conduct resulting, according to Masters and Johnson, from the strictures of religious orthodoxy. Less common causes are prior sexual traumas and prior homosexual orientation. It is not always possible to determine, when both vaginismus and secondary impotence are present, whether the secondary impotence is caused by the male's frustration or the vaginismus by his inept attempts at penetration.

When prior sexual trauma is the cause, the trauma may be, variously, rape, dyspareunia (painful intercourse), or laceration during childbirth of the broad ligaments supporting the uterus. One woman who came to Masters and Johnson for treatment had suffered such lacerations when, during childbirth, two nurses held her legs together to halt delivery until her obstetrician arrived. Other researchers have noted that the pubococcygeus muscle, which plays a vital role in female sexual response, as well as in bladder control and childbirth, can be damaged by an improperly performed episiotomy (a surgical incision in the perineum usually made just before delivery), and such damage may disable a woman's sexual response (Kegel, 1952; Sherfey, 1972).

Dyspareunia. Dyspareunia can occur in either male or female and has been classed as a psychophysiological disorder. Before a diagnosis of dyspareunia can be made, a pelvic and rectal examination is necessary to rule out physical causes. The most common physical cause in women is chronic vaginal irritation, which may be due to a decrease in the acidity of the vaginal environment. The body naturally maintains an acid environment (pH 3.5 to 4.0) as a protection against infection, but this protection can break down during menstrual flow, especially when a tampon is present.

Usually this irritation is due to vaginitis—a bacterial, trichomonal, or fungal infection. Fungal infections are becoming more common because of changes in the vaginal environment resulting from the use of antibiotics and oral contraceptives, and also from the wearing of nylon pantyhose or undergarments that, because of their inability to "breathe," create an airless, ultrahumid environment in which yeast fungi thrive.

Painful intercourse in the male can also have many physical causes, including bowing of the penis due to illness or injury, irritation caused by the effect of douches or spermicides on the vaginal environment, urethritis, prostatitis, or venereal disease. Whether due to physical or emotional causes, painful intercourse is not a natural occurrence.

Pain can also result from the absence of sexual release. For example, maintaining erection for long periods of time can cause testicular pain, and because there is no mechanism for reabsorbing prostate fluid into the body, extended intervals of time between ejaculations can cause prostate congestion, a painful buildup of pressure in the prostate.

When painful intercourse in the female is not due to physical causes, its immediate cause is insufficient vaginal lubrication. This is a classic example of what Masters and Johnson characterize as the biophysical system responding to psychosocial influences. The result is burning, itching, or aching during coitus, but the most common cause is the woman's lack of interest in her partner or in the particular opportunity. Fear is another cause; it reduces receptivity to sensory stimulation, and thus interferes with arousal.

Inhibition of Release

The French describe orgasm as *le petit mort*—the little death. It is one of the most involuntary human activities—total loss of control, the original act of "letting go." It has also been described as a dissolving of ego boundaries, the nearest most people come to what mystics call "cosmic consciousness."

In both sexes orgasmic contractions occur at intervals of about four-fifth of a second. Multiple orgasms have been widely reported by females, and recently some males have also been found to be multiply orgasmic. The male orgasm has two stages—the moment of ejaculatory inevitability, and the ejaculation itself, which follows after a brief interval. Orgasm may occur without ejaculation, and commonly does so in prepubescent boys and in men who have had prostatectomies.

In most males erection is usually lost immediately afterward, and there is a refractory period during which penile contact is painful rather than pleasurable. For this reason males are seldom capable of a succession of *genital* coital episodes. A male can only dream of satisfying a procession of female partners in this way, whereas a procession of male partners in genital coitus would be well within the biophysical capacity of the average female. Masters and Johnson see this inequality as the motive for much male fear of women and for adhering to a double standard. (There are, of course, other ways of satisfying a partner, but the alleged male fear of female sexual capacity may be associated with a penis orientation that overlooks the possibilities of other than penile/vaginal coitus.)

As in the case of arousal, difficulties of release are often due to interference from a negatively conditioned psychosocial system.

Premature Ejaculation. No satisfactory definition for premature ejaculation has been found. Some clinicians have defined it as the inability of a male to maintain ejaculatory control for some arbitrarily selected period of time—30 seconds or

60 seconds—after intromission. The hapless male is thus pitted against the stopwatch even by his counselor. Masters and Johnson substitute the also arbitrary qualification that the male be unable to satisfy his partner in at least 50 percent of their coital episodes (assuming that the female partner is not nonorgasmic for other reasons).

Whether either partner should be so completely charged with the responsibility for satisfying the other is a moot question. Most women are orgasmic, or at least "preorgasmic," but many are not *coitally* orgasmic—they can be brought to orgasm manually or orally but not coitally. To call the male partner a premature ejaculator in such an instance would be a mistake.

Nevertheless the problem does exist. Some males are not able to retain ejaculatory control beyond the first few thrusts after intromission, and the results are distressful to both partners. The woman's inevitable frustrations can lead to the complaint that she is "just being used." Next she may try to resolve those frustrations, perhaps in an extramarital affair or through psychotherapy. What follows that is usually the "don't touch" approach: all the foreplay is aimed at maximum arousal for her and minimal arousal for him, followed by a frantic mounting in which both partners desperately try to trigger her release in advance of his, but always without success. Then they reduce the frequency of their coital attempts—exactly the tactic most likely to intensify, not diminish, his sexual volatility. Gradually she loses confidence in his consideration and appreciation of her. Finally the pressure of performance demands may lead to erective failures, and in a few cases, to secondary impotence.

Sex is anything but pleasurable and free for the premature ejaculator trying desperately, repeatedly, and unsuccessfully to delay his orgasms by distraction. The moment he penetrates his partner's vagina, he drives himself into distracting fantasies—his work, unpaid bills, the major league standings, counting backward, and so on. He becomes a spectator in his own sex life, and a distracted one at that.

The causation of premature ejaculation seems simple. It is, according to Masters and Johnson, learned behavior, usually acquired in the male's earliest coital experiences. If the first coital experience was with a prostitute, as is sometimes the case, especially among the older generations, rapid ejaculation may have been a response to the prostitute's demand to hurry. If the first coital experience was in a parked car, the fear of discovery may also have put a premium on speed. Rapid ejaculation is also a likely result of using withdrawal as a means of contraception.

Other explanations have also been given. Psychologist James McCrary (1971), for example, suggests that many men expect too much of themselves as lovers, and therefore feel ashamed and sexually inadequate if their "staying power" after penile penetration is minimal. Whatever the cause, premature ejaculation is not a rare disorder. Kinsey and his associates (1948) found that about three-fourths of all men ejaculate within two minutes after penile insertion.

Ejaculatory Incompetence. The victim of ejaculatory incompetence is unable to ejaculate intravaginally. Like the premature ejaculator, he has no difficulty with arousal, but unlike him, he does not ejaculate, even in prolonged intercourse. The cause is usually either a sexually repressed childhood, especially one in which ejaculation was seen as sinful or semen regarded as repugnant, or a traumatic experience such as the one described in Case Report 15.2.

Of the 17 men treated for ejaculatory incompetence by Masters and Johnson, three had never been able to masturbate to ejaculation. For the others masturbation had been the usual method of sexual tension release, but

the men had infrequently included their wives as contributors to their release mechanisms (4 out of 17). By denying their wives the privilege of participating in the ejaculatory experience, even if occasioned manually, they further froze the possibility of a successful sexual relationship.

Graham Crackers and Corn Flakes

It is popularly—and incorrectly—believed that traditional sexual morality has existed since the dawn of recorded time. Thus both aspects of the sexual revolution—the rejection of traditional sex roles and the greater freedom of sexual expression—are seen as an attack on "eternal verities."

While it is true that sexual repression has a long history, the eternal verities in question actually date from about 1830, the beginning of what we call "Victorian morality." Earlier Americans, even the Puritans, lived a lusty life, and the Founding Fathers were no exception. Much has been written, for example, about Benjamin Franklin's sexual adventures, and Franklin was also outspoken in his views, as when he suggested that the way to find out whether a man is a liar is to ask him if he masturbates and consider him a liar if he says no.

All of that changed in the 1830s, and the change is described by Stephen Nissenbaum in a paper called "The new chastity in America, 1830–1840" (quoted in Leonard, 1972). At that time temperance lecturers looking for wider horizons began attacking the alleged evils of sexuality and all other forms of sensory pleasure. Foremost in popularity and power among these lecturers was Dr. Sylvester Graham, the inventor of the Graham cracker.

Graham's basic premise was that the natural environment is hostile and will destroy people unless they mobilize all their faculties to oppose it. Therefore all attention must be focused on external reality and all inner life censored or ignored. Dreams, fantasies, religious exaltation, mental images arising from memory or imagination, and most of all, bodily sensations were seen as a threat to survival. Graham wrote, "When . . . we are *conscious* that we have a stomach, or a liver from any *feeling* in those organs, we may be certain that something is wrong." Needless to say, any consciousness of sensation in the genitals was a sign of peril. The nerves of those organs "are, in their natural state, entirely destitute of animal sensibility." In contrast to our present view of sex as a healthy activity, Graham considered

---

The female partner's attitude is crucial, since treatment depends on the success with which the male partner surrenders his ejaculatory control to her.

Case Report 15.2 *Ejaculatory Incompetence*

The patient, age 31, had been suffering from ejaculatory incompetence since a traumatic incident that occurred when he was 18: he was surprised by the police in a "lovers' lane" while a young woman was manually stroking him to ejaculation. He was, *in fact, on the verge of ejaculation at the moment they were interrupted. His own embarrassment and fear, coupled with young woman's terror, "left an indelible residual." Through two subsequent engagements and many other coital opportunities, the patient was not able to ejaculate intravaginally.*

SOURCE: *Adapted from Masters, W. H. and Johnson, V. E., Human sexual inadequacy, p. 124. Boston: Little, Brown, 1970. Reproduced by permission.*

Primary Orgasmic Dysfunction. A diagnosis of primary orgasmic dysfunction is made only if a woman has never had an orgasm by any method

---

even marital sex catastrophically destructive to body and mind. Since he believed not only that any sensory stimulation was dangerous, but also that any food that stimulated the sense of taste would stimulate genital sensations, he invented Graham flour in an attempt to create a nourishing meatless diet that would be as bland as possible.

Graham's appeal has to be seen in the context of the two major social movements of his time, Manifest Destiny and the Industrial Revolution. The first demanded that Americans conquer and tame every inch of the wilderness that stretched to the Pacific. Nature itself, as well as the Indians and their way of life, had to be seen as the enemy.

The second movement, perhaps anticipating Freud, demanded sublimation. Since energy released in sex was not available as work, sex was a threat to industrial expansion. Desensitized men who could function like machines were the best source of labor.

The excesses of the New Chastity are almost unbelievable today. George Leonard (1972) notes that in the nineteenth century:

respected physicians in the United States and Europe regularly recommended clitoridectomy, circumcision, infibulation (putting a silver wire through the foreskin), wearing of locked chastity belts or spiked penile rings, blistering the penis with red mercury ointment, cauterization of the spine and genitals, surgical denervation of the penis and, in extreme cases, removal of both penis and testes.

Many of these operations were performed on children with the full approval of well-meaning parents genuinely concerned for the moral and physical health of their offspring.

Some of the measures were less extreme. William Acton recommended that adults sleep with their hands tied behind their backs. And Grahamite sanitariums were established to provide an atmosphere free of sexual stimulation. Dr. John Harvey Kellogg, in his Grahamite Battle Creek Sanitarium, tried to cure neurasthenia by feeding his patients cold breakfast cereal. Thus the corn flake, like the Graham cracker, was originally an attempt to overcome sensory pleasure.

of stimulation. In their strongest language, Masters and Johnson cite the culture as the source of the trouble (1970, p. 215):

It is obvious that man has society's blessing to build his sexual value system . . . in an appropriate, naturally occurring context and woman has not. . . . During her formative years the female dissembles [hides] much of her developing functional sexuality in response to societal requirements for a "good girl" facade. Instead of being taught or allowed to value her sexual feelings . . . she must

attempt to repress or remove them from their natural context of environmental stimulation.

A girl is allowed the aura of romanticism that surrounds sexual feelings but not the sensory development that is normally at the heart of those feelings, since society cannot accept the fact that sexual feelings are a natural part of the healthy development of *any* girl, not just "disturbed," "precocious," or "culturally deprived" girls. This point has also been made by John H. Gagnon (1965):

Distraction in the Classroom

Most parents and teachers nowadays would be horrified by the efforts of nineteenth-century Americans and Europeans to curb a child's masturbation by such extreme measures as removal of a girl's clitoris or a boy's penis. Nevertheless, many adults are uncomfortable in the presence of a child's genital play and respond covertly—they attempt to stop the child's behavior by distraction, mystification, or other forms of manipulation. A. S. Neill, founder of the world-famous Summerhill School in England, has this to say about such attempts (1960, p. 226):

When baby includes his genitals in the play scheme, parents meet the great test. Genital play must be accepted as good and normal and healthy; and any attempt to suppress it will be dangerous. And I include the underhand, dishonest attempt at drawing the child's attention to something else.

I recall the case of a self-regulated little girl who was sent to a nice day school. She seemed unhappy. She had christened her genital play snuggling in. When her mother asked her why she didn't like school, she said, 'When I try to snuggle in, they don't tell me not to—but they say Look at this *or* Come and do this, *so I can't ever snuggle in at the kindergarten.'*

The shock for adults of Freud's discoveries was not that children might be involved in sexual activity, but that this activity was not confined to a few evil children and was, in fact, an essential precursor and component of the character structure of the adult.

One result of adult refusal to validate the sexuality of girls, according to Masters and Johnson, is that every generation makes the same sexual mistakes. And they believe the needed freedom of communication between parents and children will not be achieved "until the basic component of sexuality itself is given a socially comfortable role by all active generations simultaneously." Our sexual taboos have also distorted the female's sex role into that of a breeding machine. Since her sexual responsiveness and expressiveness are not necessary for fulfillment of her breeding function, they have either been assigned no value at all or have been considered shameful.

The attempt to belittle, from infancy on, the sexuality of the female may, according to Masters and Johnson (1970, p. 218), result from fear of the real potential of female sexuality, which they believe exceeds the male:

Sociocultural influence . . . places woman in a position in which she must adapt, sublimate, inhibit, or even distort her natural capacity to function sexually in order to fulfill her genetically assigned role. Herein lies a major source of woman's sexual dysfunction. . . . The human female's facility of physiological response to sexual tensions and her capacity for orgasmic release have never been fully appreciated.

What direct effect does the cultural invalidation of the girl's sexuality have? She pretends, usually from the time she reaches school age if not earlier, not to feel anything sexual. Thus, among nonorgasmic women, the denial of sexual feelings is a requirement imposed by early learning. Patients did, however, reveal much variation in the origins of the negative conditioning. At one pole parents deliberately omitted any verbal reference to sexual function as a component of living and the girl had no model to emulate—no woman who was secure in the expression of her sexuality. At the other pole acknowledging or overtly expressing sexual feeling was rigidly and consistently forbidden by parental or religious authority or both.

Thus the woman in the sex therapist's office voicing "the time-worn cry of 'I don't feel anything'" (Masters and Johnson, 1970, p. 223) is the ultimate result of a lifetime of dissimulation of sexual feelings. In short the pretense of not feeling anything sexual has materialized into a very real sexual anesthesia (see Case Report 15.3).

The basic difficulty for most women who have not had orgasms is that (Masters and Johnson, 1970, p. 225)

the requirements of their sexual value system have never been met. Consequently the resulting limitations of the psychosocial system have never been overcome.

There are many women who specifically resist the experience of orgasmic release, as they reject their sexual identity and the facility for its active expression.

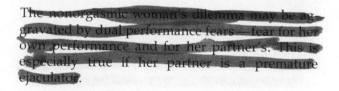

The nonorgasmic woman's dilemma may be aggravated by dual performance fears—fear for her own performance and for her partner's. This is especially true if her partner is a premature ejaculator.

Case Report 15.3 *Primary Orgasmic Dysfunction*

Mrs. B, an only child, had played the role of a "doll" in her parents' lives. Both teachers in a small, religiously oriented college, they were restrained more by habit and lifestyle than by religious commitment. Throughout her childhood she was impeccably dressed, seldom handled, and disregarded emotionally. She had no positive female role model, no woman comfortable with her own sexuality, with whom she could identify. There was

no nurturing ground in which her sexual value system could develop.

Whenever a decision was to be made in her behalf, two alternatives were presented to her in a theoretically objective manner, but her parents' preferences—primarily her mother's—were always emphasized. Mrs. B could not recall making a single decision on her own before her sophomore year in college, when she decided to marry an older man who was a graduate student at the time. "With this one decision she again relinquished all opportunity for self-determination."

More by default than by preference, Mr. B assumed total authority in the marriage, which at the time they began treatment had lasted eleven years and produced two children. The motivation to seek treatment was Mrs. B's keenly felt desire, during the last six years of the marriage, for full sexual expression for herself, as well as for increased sexual pleasure for her husband. He, in spite of a warm and protective attitude, was highly restrained in both his sexual and his nonsexual behavior toward her. He had no primarily negative attitudes, but neither did he have any feeling for personal interaction.

Despite her enthusiasm for attaining a more effective sexual relationship, Mrs. B was not able to "overcome anesthesia to any sensory perception that she can relate to erotic arousal. She has been unable to establish sensory reference within which to relate her well-defined affection and regard for her husband." Her biophysical and psychosocial systems were still displaced relative to each other.

SOURCE: *Adapted from Masters, W. H., and Johnson, V. E.* Human sexual inadequacy, *pp. 233–234. Boston: Little, Brown, 1970. Reproduced by permission.*

Situational Orgasmic Dysfunction. Masters and Johnson consider a woman's orgasmic dysfunction situational rather than primary if she has "experienced at least one instance of orgasmic expression, regardless of whether it was induced by self or by partner manipulation, developed during vaginal or rectal coital connection, or stimulated by oral–genital exchange." They further categorize the difficulty as *masturbatory* if she has not had orgasm through manual stroking by herself or a partner, *coital* if she has not had orgasm during coitus but has had orgasm triggered by manual or oral stimulation, and *random* if she has had orgasm at least once each in the coital and the manual or oral mode.

The masturbatory form results from either of two childhood patterns: (1) the girl's early attempts at masturbation failed to produce orgasm and were followed by guilt and termination of the practice; or (2) the "don't touch" syndrome. Parental attitudes taught her, either explicitly or implicitly, that masturbation was evil, and she avoided it.

Very often a woman has orgasmic difficulties simply because her partner has a low value in her eyes. If his ability as a provider falls short of her expectations, if he has physical or behavioral characteristics that antagonize her, if he is in the unfortunate position of substituting for the man she really wanted but couldn't have, or if she does not accept and value him as a sexual being, then his masculine image will not meet the requirements of her sexual value system, and his touch will not stimulate her to orgasm.

Sexual Dysfunctions and Other Behavior Disorders

In some cases the sexual dysfunction may be a symptom of some other behavior disorder. For example, two Yale University researchers (Weissman and Paykel, 1974, 1975) found that depressed married women showed widespread impairment involving almost every aspect of their marital and sexual relationships, including, of course, the inability to achieve orgasm and the occurrence of dyspareunia.

The main difference between these women and a control group was in their *feelings* about sex rather than actual behavior. The depressed women reported marked disinterest in sex and greater incidence of situational orgasmic dys-

function, whereas the difference in frequency of sexual intercourse between the two groups was less marked.

Sex Therapy

Sex therapy is a relatively recent development, for the simple reason that its emergence depended on social changes. As long as sex was supposed to be only for procreation, the only sexual dysfunction was impotence, and that was generally treated as a medical problem. But the sexual revolution has created—and the culture seems to be moving toward—a value system in which a central belief is that every person is entitled to sexual pleasure and every couple is entitled to mutually fulfilling sexual communication.

Masters and Johnson

The work of Masters and Johnson has contributed much to improving the possibilities of successful sex therapy. First, they took the unprecedented step of subjecting human sexual responses to empirical observation (1966). Then they studied human sexual dysfunctions and established a rather successful program of sex therapy (1970).

Traditional psychotherapy often proceeds on the assumption that sexual dysfunctions are symptoms of underlying personality disorders. Presumably the sexual dysfunction will clear up after two or three years of psychotherapy has restructured the personality, or after a couple has overcome the maladaptive ways of relating to each other that are being reflected in their sex life.

Masters and Johnson insist on treating the relationship, not either individual, and they limit the treatment at their clinic to two weeks, using primarily behavior-directive methods. They regard sexual dysfunctions as learned behavior and point out that sexual problems are often the *cause* of other problems in a relationship rather than the result (1970, pp. 14–15):

The ultimate level in marital-unit communication is sexual intercourse. When there is marital-unit complaint of sexual dysfunction, the primary source of absolute communication is interfered with or even destroyed and most other sources or means of interpersonal communication rapidly tend to diminish in effectiveness. . . . Usually the failure of communication in the bedroom extends rapidly to every other phase of the marriage. When there is no security or mutual representation in sexual exchange, there rarely is freedom of other forms of marital communication.

The sex therapy of Masters and Johnson aims at inducing a good deal of unlearning and a certain amount of relearning. It attempts to take the threat of the unknown (and unspoken) out of sex, largely through simple educational and desensitization processes. It attempts to decondition people whose socialization has left them with a devaluation of their sexual feelings and desires. It also attempts to remove learned mental sets that stand in the way of spontaneous sexual behavior.

To accomplish these aims, the therapists rely heavily on the power of authority in influencing people, placing their authority against that of parental, peer, and other social influences that conditioned the original maladaptive pattern. Both partners are given strong support for taking pleasure in their sexual interaction and for listening to their bodies and allowing them to respond instead of commanding them to perform. This permission-giving helps to restructure the social value system, which forms the individual's image of what is acceptable sexual behavior and what is taboo. Changes in the social value system may then be reflected in the sexual value system, which determines what sexual stimuli the individual will allow himself or herself to be excited by. Most important of all, perhaps, the therapists' authority is placed squarely behind an effort to open up the greatest possible degree of physical and verbal communication between the partners.

Performance fears are a major focus in therapy, since such fears become self-fulfilling prophesies. For example, the man who is afraid of impotence becomes a divided person—the mind alienated from the body, making demands and watching for results. The surest result is a loss of receptivity to sensory input, and that loss of receptivity leads to impotence. One of the first tasks of therapy in such a case is to familiarize the other partner with the details of the fear component. Another is to remove all suggestion of goal-oriented behavior, since goal-seeking is a large part of the problem. The partner of an impotent male or nonorgasmic female is also likely to have performance fears, usually of the "what's wrong with me that I can't satisfy my partner?" variety.

The basic method by which the therapists try to restore their patients' openness to sensory input is the application of the "give-to-get" principle. Basically the principle seems to be that a person's sensory receptivity can be effectively freed if he or she becomes absorbed in giving sensory pleasure to another person, while being guided by that person's expressed wants. The basic technique for applying the method is the *sensate focus*, which we shall discuss later.

The first two days of therapy are devoted entirely to history-taking, which is done by the same-sex therapist on Day 1 and by the opposite-sex therapist on Day 2. Day 3 begins with a medical history, followed by a physical examination, and concludes with a roundtable discussion. At this discussion the entire history is summarized and the couple encouraged (as they have been throughout the history-taking) to make corrections and express disagreements. Next the cotherapists explain the role of sensory appreciation in human sexual response "as a medium of social exchange vested primarily in touch."

Then sensate focus is explained: the couple is asked to take two segments of time before the next day's session, while in their private quarters, and to remove their clothes at the beginning of each such segment (and before every "homework" session). The "giving" partner (chosen arbitrarily by the cotherapists) is then to "trace, massage, or fondle the 'getting' partner with the intention of giving sensate pleasure and discovering the receiving partner's individual levels of sensate focus." During the second segment they reverse roles. Until they are directed otherwise, the touching is not to include either partner's genitals or the woman's breasts. The only other rule is that each partner is to protect the other from any error that "discomforts, distracts, or irritates." For many people this is the first opportunity to have a sensuous experience at leisure with no pressure for "end-point release." All other exercises are preceded by sensate focus, in a cumulative pattern likened to that of the song "The Twelve Days of Christmas."

During sensate focus the giving partner applies a moisturizing lotion to the skin of the receiving partner. This helps people work through any negative feelings they may have about pelvic organs and reproductive fluids. Furthermore the instruction to apply the lotion is another way of giving permission to touch and to give and receive tactile pleasure. It also provides in some cases an early indication of treatment failure. Out of 23 people who reported a disinterest in or an objection to using the lotion, failure to reverse symptoms occurred in 19. This is 400 percent above the 20 percent failure rate expected.

During the next day's sensate focus the touching is to include both partners' genitals and the woman's breasts. The receiving partner is also instructed to place his or her hand lightly on the partner's hand, guiding direction, pressure, timing, and the like. Verbal communication, if spontaneous, is encouraged as a supplement to the physical communication. The object of these exercises is "sexual responsivity spontaneously developing."

Beyond the second day of sensate focus specific directions depend on the nature of the presenting complaint. We shall next summarize those specific treatments.

Treatment of Impotence. The three primary goals in treating impotence are (1) to remove the male's sexual performance fears; (2) to reorient his behavioral patterning so that he becomes an active participant instead of a spectator; and (3) to relieve the female partner's fears for the male's sexual performance.

Masters and Johnson maintain (1970, p. 199) that "the secret of successful therapy is not to treat the symptoms of impotence at all." The impotent male's erective failure is the direct result of his effort to achieve erection by an act of conscious will. Sensate focus makes a major contribution to the strategy of avoiding such goal-seeking because it shifts the couple's attention from performance to pleasing each other. It gives *"opportunity to think and to feel sexually without orientation to performance"* (1970, pp. 201–202). Performance is in fact specifically forbidden, thus increasing the male's freedom to receive sensory input in both modes. The couple next moves, in a succession of gradual steps, to nondemanding coital play.

Treatment of Premature Ejaculation. The first step in treating premature ejaculation is to assure both partners that the dysfunction can be reversed successfully. During sensate focus the woman is encouraged to use "any acceptable form of pelvic stimulation." This is a direct reversal of the couple's usual "don't touch" pattern. She sits with her back against pillows propped up on the headboard of the bed, feet apart. He lies on his back, head toward the foot of the bed and legs drawn up over hers, giving her free access to his genital organs. She approaches him directly to stimulate his erection, then uses the squeeze technique to forestall ejaculation. In the squeeze technique, developed by James Semans, the woman places her thumb on the frenulum (just under the tip of the glans) and her first two fingers on either side of the coronal ridge, applying rather strong pressure for three or four seconds. When this is successful, the man loses his urge to ejaculate, as well as perhaps some of his erection. The woman waits 15 to 30 seconds after releasing pressure and then continues stimulation until full erection returns. Repeating this process through four or five applications of the squeeze technique permits 15 to 20 minutes of sex play without ejaculation. This technique improves both control and communication.

After two or three days of practice with the squeeze technique, the next step is nondemanding penetration. During this phase of treatment the woman quite commonly becomes stimulated to unusually high levels of sexual tension, for several reasons, including the encouragement of seeing her partner's progress and the permission she has been given (for the first time in many instances) to think and feel sexually. Extremely high levels of sexual arousal for the giving partner are a common occurrence in treating many sexual dysfunctions, and Masters and Johnson urge the receiving partner to provide orgasmic release by whatever method is acceptable to the couple.

As the man's control increases, the woman is encouraged to begin pelvic thrusting, first in a slow, nondemanding way, then "with full freedom of expression." Finally they are urged to convert to the lateral coital position, in which both partners have full freedom of pelvic motion.

Of 186 prematurely ejaculating men who were seen by Masters and Johnson, only four failed to learn ejaculatory control. Two of these four had accompanied their nonorgasmic wives and refused to be treated for premature ejaculation.

Treatment of Ejaculatory Incompetence. The "give-to-get" principle is especially important for both partners in the treatment of ejaculatory incompetence. The woman stimulates her partner by whatever means is acceptable to her, asking for verbal and physical direction from him. Once she has succeeded in obtaining his ejaculation manually or orally, the next step is to bring him to the point of ejaculatory inevitability and then quickly mount him in the female-superior position with immediate pelvic thrusting. If ejaculation does not occur, the process is repeated. Even a few drops of semen released inside the vagina

constitute a major step in overcoming the man's mental block against intravaginal ejaculation. After three of four such episodes, the major obstacle to communication between the partners has been removed.

Treatment of Female Orgasmic Dysfunction. In treating female orgasmic dysfunction, the cotherapists try to discover what expectations and experiences have positive or negative significance for the woman in her sexual exchanges. Both the history-taking and the daily reports and discussions reveal how well the basic requirements of her sexual value system are being met and how well she is able to adapt those requirements.

When there is little or no cultural interference with natural processes, the basis for orgasmic response is "infantile imprinting of sexually undifferentiated sensory receptivity to the warmth and sensation of close body contact" (1970, p. 295). Just as a man cannot will an erection, a woman cannot will an orgasm. Sexual responses are not voluntary and they are not learned (1970, p. 297):

It seems more accurate to consider female orgasmic response as an acceptance of naturally occurring stimuli that have been given erotic significance by an individual sexual value system than to depict it as a learned response.

And when a woman's receptivity to sexual stimuli is blocked, it is because she has been deprived "of the capacity to value the sexual component of her personality" and prevented from "placing its value within the context of her life" (1970, p. 315).

The cotherapists' initial directions to the couple include "developing a nondemanding, erotically stimulating climate in the privacy of their quarters." They are urged to set aside tension-provoking forms of interaction and to create an atmosphere in which the woman has permission to express her sexual feelings spontaneously without focusing on her partner's sexual function except for enjoying the direct contribution that awareness of his sexual excitement makes to her own level of excitement.

During the second phase of sensate focus (genital manipulation) the instructions to the partners give the woman "permission" to enjoy genital play, as well as providing specific details of position, approach, and the like, and ways of avoiding the usual pitfalls of the man's failure to provide the stimulation she prefers.

Sensate focus is extended on the second day to include genital stimulation and on the third day to include mounting in the female-superior position. The woman is instructed to remain still and "absorb the awareness of penile containment." She may then experiment with pelvic thrusting. Her partner remains still, contributing only his erect penis, which cotherapists have encouraged the woman to think of as hers "to play with, to feel, and to enjoy." Once sensate focus is developed vaginally, the male begins slow, nondemanding pelvic thrusting at a pace communicated by the female.

Group Treatment Methods

Many individuals are not able to take advantage of the therapy offered by Masters and Johnson, either because the cost is beyond their means or because they do not have a partner. To meet the needs of these people, the Human Sexuality Program at the University of California Medical Center in San Francisco has initiated group treatment programs. We shall summarize two of these programs, one developed by L. G. Barbach (1974) for "preorgasmic" women and one developed by B. Zilbergeld (1975) for sexually dysfunctional men.

Treatment of Preorgasmic Women. To avoid the negativity of such words as *nonorgasmic* or *anorgasmic,* and to express the great optimism of the staff, Barbach uses the term *preorgasmic* to describe the women treated by her program. Six women meet with two female cotherapists twice a week for six weeks. The authoritative influence of the cotherapists is thus buttressed by peer-group support in the all-important function of permission-giving. "Homeplay" is based on a nine-step masturbation desensitization program developed by Lobitz and LoPiccolo (1972).

During meetings the women explore the impact of subtle messages they have received all their lives from family and society and are encouraged to recognize "that they have a right to sexual pleasure and that their bodies and sexuality is a positive thing." They also discuss their experiences in their homeplay assignments, which are identical for the first few sessions and are then tailored to the specific needs of individuals. The first assignment is for each woman to examine her nude body in a full-length mirror to become more comfortable and more accepting of her body. The assignment also includes the Kegel exercises (1952) and readings in *Our Bodies Ourselves* (Boston Women's Health Book Collective, 1971). (The Kegel exercises are designed to strengthen the pubococcygeus muscle, which plays a vital role in female sexual response.)

The second meeting includes an explanation of the anatomy of the female genitalia and the sexual response cycle. For her homeplay assignment each woman examines her genitals carefully with a hand mirror.

In the third session a female masturbation movie from the National Sex Forum is shown to help demystify the orgasmic process. The homeplay assignment is to masturbate, but not to the point of orgasm. Subsequent homeplay assignments are tailored to the individual's specific problems and pace.

No restrictions are placed on sexual intercourse. Once a woman has acquired skill in masturbating to orgasm, homeplay assignments include the partner, if there is one. The woman is first instructed to masturbate to orgasm while her partner is watching. This is followed by nongenital and genital exploration with the woman guiding her partner's hands over her body. If the woman wants to become orgasmic during coitus, she masturbates while her partner's penis is in her vagina.

By the end of the 10 sessions, 91.6 percent of the first 83 women had become orgasmic. A follow-up study of 17 of those 83 women (Wallace and Barbach, 1974) showed that over 87 percent of the women were capable of orgasm with their partners eight months after treatment. They also showed increased enjoyment of coitus and improvement "of life in general, sex, communication with their partner, and overall level of happiness and relaxation." Changes were also reported in their attitudes toward traditional roles, interest in politics, and a number of body acceptance scales.

Treatment of Sexual Dysfunction in Men. Group treatment has also been used in reversing premature ejaculation and impotence. These groups met for 12 two-hour sessions, at a rate of one session per week decreasing to one session every two or three weeks at the end. Six or seven members met with two coleaders. In three groups both coleaders were male, and in one group one of the coleaders was female. Most of the group sessions were devoted to discussing homework assignments. Masturbation is the main form of homework, employing Semans's start–stop technique instead of the squeeze technique. Stimulation stops each time ejaculatory inevitability is approached, until the man can masturbate for 15 minutes while sustaining high levels of sexual excitement and without ejaculating. The next step is to masturbate using lotion or oil. For those with partners the next step is dry stimulation by the partner. For those without partners, an entire sexual episode is fantasized. If a man's presenting complaint is impotence, he is instructed to stop from time to time and lose, then regain, his erection.

Once he is confident that he can get and maintain erections, he is asked to fantasize, while masturbating, a series of anxiety-provoking sexual situations, starting with the one that is least anxiety-provoking. Whenever he begins to feel anxious, he stops masturbating and "focuses on a relaxing image." He continues this until he can masturbate without any anxiety while fantasizing the most anxiety-provoking situation in the series. "Thus, sexual arousal is paired with images of situations that formerly inhibited sexual response in the natural environment" (Zilbergeld, 1975).

Other methods used in these groups are self-disclosure (encouragement to discuss fears with partners and with group members); assertiveness training; relaxation training to increase awareness of tensions and permit more relaxation and comfort; and debunking of male sexual mythology. The last subject is broached by asking the group members to list "all the things that a real man has to accomplish in a sexual situation." The absurdity of the myths soon becomes obvious.

Results, based on leaders' evaluation of members' self-reports, were as follows: about two-thirds of the members felt that they had achieved their goals completely by the end of therapy. Most of the remaining one-third had learned some ejaculatory control or were getting erections in appropriate situations. Until controlled studies are done, conclusions can only be tentative, but most of the group members, like those in women's groups, reported improvements in other areas of their lives as well.

Divergent Sexual Patterns

Psychologists have more difficulty defining abnormality in sexual expression than in any other aspect of human behavior, and the reason should be obvious. It is here that we have the least assurance that our perceptions are not being shaped by culture-biased presuppositions. Sexual taboos are so thoroughly learned and the learning so thoroughly forgotten that many people cannot even comprehend that their culture's sexual taboos are not universal laws of nature.

One way to try to minimize the effects of this

bias is to study the taboos themselves. Unfortunately their origins are lost in antiquity, but we can easily guess their overriding objective: sexual taboos attempt to block sexual alternatives to procreation.

Certainly changing attitudes toward sexual pleasure have coincided with changing attitudes toward population growth and, more importantly, with the increasing power of women to choose not to conceive without also having to choose not to be sexually active. As sexual expression is increasingly released from its traditional role of serving procreation exclusively, the "crimes" and "perversions" of yesterday are becoming the joyful and imaginative play of today. Consequently the discussion of "sexual deviations" must be placed in a context of changing values and becomes largely an excursion into anthropology.

Only a few years ago most sexual variations were considered not merely abnormal but "unnatural," as if cultural norms were biological facts. And in the dawn of the new sexual freedom people often sought reassurance that what they were doing was normal. The first official word that statistical norms did not match the previously accepted cultural norms was provided by Kinsey and his associates (1948, 1953), who showed that actual behavior was far more varied than most people had supposed.

On what basis do we draw the line between variation and deviation? We are not likely to discover such a line in nature, which knows only biological possibilities, not cultural limitations. Even if there were a single cultural norm, it would rest only on the force of consensus, but what confronts us instead is a seemingly infinite assortment of norms, all changing from time to time and from place to place. Sociologists have shown how these sexual norms vary among different ethnic, socioeconomic, and age groups (Reiss, 1970). The reports by Kinsey and associates (1948, 1953) showed an extreme discrepancy between the sexual norms of people in the upper and those in the lower socioeconomic strata of American society. For example, couples in the lower strata often went through elaborate rituals to avoid nudity in each other's presence, while upper-strata couples tended to accept nudity as the natural condition for lovemaking. And among upper-strata people a man who mounted his partner without first stimulating her manually and perhaps orally was behaving grossly, while lower-strata people considered such foreplay perverted. These differences between value systems have apparently diminished to some extent since the Kinsey Reports.

Furthermore cross-cultural studies by anthropologists show an almost infinite range of norms and and practices in courtship; premarital, extramarital, and nonmarital coitus; homosexuality; masturbation; and incest (Lindzey, 1969; Mann, 1967; Seal, 1971; Malinowski, 1927). In America sexual intercourse between children occurs, but adults react to it with horror and disgust; in the Trobriand Islands (Malinowski, 1955) childhood sex is universal, and adults neither disapprove nor interfere.

Legal definitions are even less useful than cultural ones. In the first place legal definitions are most often merely a codification of cultural definitions. They are slower to reflect change, and they too vary widely from place to place. Thus in some states even private sexual communication between husband and wife is narrowly circumscribed by laws (for example, prohibiting orogenital and anogenital coitus), whereas in other states no sex act is illegal if it is performed in private between consenting adults. Similarly a man may be found guilty of statutory rape if his partner has not reached the age of consent, but the age of consent varies greatly from state to state.

In the second place transgression cannot be equated with deviance. A given act may be immoral, or illegal, or deviant, or any two or all three of these, but the three concepts are not identical and should not be confused. Legal concepts of "sex crimes," like legal definitions of insanity, have no scientific basis.

In the third place legal definitions, perhaps even more than cultural ones, draw arbitrary and categorical distinctions. But human behavior reflects a continuum of responses and occurs in unique situations. Either/or thinking is not appropriate to the study of human behavior.

Is a culture-free definition possible? If sexual deviance is nothing but an unwillingness or inability to conform to the sexual values of one's culture, a discussion of sexual deviance can do nothing but describe the prevailing sexual taboos of a society. Therefore a definition ought to be applicable independently of the culture's sexual values. It should also be nonjudgmental, focusing not on wrongdoing but on maladapative behavior. Such a definition would thus meet these two tests:

1. Even if the act classed as deviant did not violate a sex taboo, it would still be clearly maladaptive.
2. The person's supposedly deviant sexual behavior is clearly damaging to himself or to his partner.

Various definitions that might meet these tests have been proposed by people involved in feminist, sexual freedom, and gay liberation movements. Those definitions could be summarized as follows:

Sexual behavior is deviant if it is (a) harmful, physically or emotionally, to oneself or one's partner; or (b) forced on one's partner; or (c) self-defeating.

Like most definitions, this one is subject to a great deal of interpretation. It represents the thinking of the sexual avant-garde and has not been accepted by the majority of professionals or by the general public. A more traditional definition is given in DSM II (APA, 1968):

This category is for individuals whose sexual interests are directed primarily towards objects other than people of the opposite sex, toward sexual acts not usually associated with coitus, or toward coitus performed under bizarre circumstances as in necrophilia, pedophilia, sexual sadism and fetishism. Even though many find their practices distasteful, they remain unable to substitute normal sexual behavior for them. This diagnosis is not appropriate for individuals who perform deviant sexual acts because normal sexual objects are not available to them.

Reduced to its simplest terms, this definition identifies sexual deviation as an interest primarily in (a) an inappropriate object, or (b) an inappropriate act, where the individual is not able to substitute an appropriate object or act, and where appropriate objects willing to cooperate in appropriate acts are available. It limits the class of appropriate objects to adults of the opposite sex and the class of appropriate acts to those usually associated with coitus, presumably meaning genital coitus and foreplay that leads to genital coitus. It excludes coitus from the class of normal acts when the partner is a child or a corpse or when the act is performed in a sadistic or fetishistic way.

The DSM II definition presents several problems, and we shall try to examine the most apparent of these.

1. **Exclusion of Same-Sex Partners.** When DSM III appears, the limitation of appropriate partners to the opposite sex will possibly be gone. Homophile groups campaigned vigorously against the classification of homosexuality as a mental disorder, and they were increasingly supported by clinicians. On December 15, 1973, the APA voted, after a stormy debate, to remove homosexuality from the list of mental disorders.

2. **Exclusion of Acts Other Than Coitus.** The language of the definition is vague. *Webster's New Collegiate Dictionary* (1974) defines coitus as "the natural conveying of semen to the female reproductive tract," but then defines it broadly as "sexual intercourse." If the broader meaning is assumed, this part of the definition becomes circular to the point of absurdity. But if the narrow meaning was intended, what about the couple who have a profound desire to make love but who can-

not risk pregnancy and, for whatever reason, are not able to use reliable means of contraception? Many people would quarrel with the notion that it would be maladaptive for such a couple to substitute (at least temporarily) orogenital, anogenital, or manual/genital intercourse.

3. **The Question of Availability.** Exactly what constitutes an *available* normal sexual object is not entirely clear. It seems safe to assume that under this qualification a prisoner in a penitentiary or a sailor at sea would not be considered deviant for turning to a same-sex object, and that masturbation would not be seen as deviant for an individual living in isolation and cut off from any possibility of coitus. But what about the woman who is not attracted to any of the available men? Would she be considered deviant for choosing masturbation when there are men willing to have coitus with her? Perhaps the framers of the definition had only men in mind, but if so, the reason for the double standard is not clear, nor is it clear whether the substitution of celibacy is considered nondeviant.

Because of these and other failings, the DSM II definition leaves something to be desired. Defining sexual deviance will probably continue to be a murky area for some time to come, not only because of the effects of cultural conditioning, but also because of a widespread tendency to assume that any sex act that is immoral or illegal must ipso facto be deviant as well. Yet as sociologist Leslie White (1949) pointed out in reference to the incest taboo, societies do not have strong taboos against behavior that has no natural appeal; the presence of a strong taboo indicates the presence in most people of a strong desire. Most people do at some time in their lives have "deviant" fantasies or desires, but to call everyone deviant clouds the meaning of deviance.

The alternative is to stop seeing sexual phenomena as peculiar and remote from the rest of human experience. Psychology then has ample resources to draw upon. There is nothing inherent in sexuality that exempts it from the concepts that define healthy or maladaptive behavior in any other aspect of human life. All that is necessary is to apply to sexual behavior the same principles we apply to other behavior. This would, for example, make it easier to see the difference between the person who sometimes feels forbidden desires (as most of us do) and the person who is obsessed with one sexual object or act to the exclusion of all else.

Along those lines, it might help to recall Freud's distinction between behavior that appears "beside the normal" and behavior that "has under all circumstances repressed and supplanted the normal." He identified *exclusiveness* and *fixation* as the distinguishing features of sexually deviant behavior (1938, p. 572).

Variations No longer Classed as Deviant

Two generations ago many Americans considered even genital coitus normal in only one of the numerous possible positions. Since then a major shift in attitudes has taken place, and varied, imaginative, and playful forms of sexual contact are now seen as an essential and basic ingredient of sexual fulfillment. There has also been an increasing recognition that exploration of one's own body may be a healthy part of human growth.

Orogenital and Anogenital Coitus. As the taboo against nonprocreative sex began to weaken in America, the idea that the only appropriate object for a penis was a vagina, and vice versa, also began to weaken. A significant factor in this change, at least in recent years, may have been the growing acceptance of the woman's right to sexual satisfaction, including orgasms, and the discovery by sex researchers that a significant number of women can reach orgasm only through oral or manual stimulation of the clitoris. Furthermore fewer people nowadays consider genitals dirty or semen repugnant, and the mouth is increasingly accepted as a sexual organ, as is the rectum.

It is hard to believe now that only a few decades ago in many states orogenital and anogenital coitus were "sex crimes" subject to draconian punishments. The laws, many of which are still on the books, did not even name or describe the offense, referring to it usually as "the infamous crime against nature."

Masturbation. For most people in sexually restrictive societies the conflict between nature and culture begins very early in life, when they begin to notice that touching their own genitals is a pleasurable experience. Self-discovery is likely to be cut short by a slap on the hand, an angry word, or an attempt at distraction. The incident is usually forgotten, but the message is not. Perhaps because autoeroticism is the most accessible form of sexual experience, it is the most common target of the taboo against nonprocreative sex. In the nineteenth century it was referred to, not as self-pleasure, but as "self-abuse." Even in our own time children have been subjected to all sorts of horror stories. They have been told that their hair would fall out, that they would get acne, that they would go insane, or simply "you'll wear it out." All these are myths, of course, but old beliefs die hard, and the taboo against masturbation has been part of Judeao–Christian civilization for more than 2000 years. Even the word masturbation, derived from the Latin *mastubari*, meaning to defile or taint oneself, is judgmental.

Masturbation is more socially acceptable in some other cultures than it is in ours. For example, in the Trobriand Islands children commonly masturbate in public, and adults take no notice. But the taboos of most Western cultures force people to masturbate only in solitude, and then ironically the practice may be criticized as being antisocial. The DSM II definition of sexual deviance makes masturbation a deviant act if it is practiced when other outlets are available. Unless that part of the definition is abandoned in DSM III, still in press at this time, the APA will have to reconcile it with the dramatic successes of some sex therapies that employ masturbation as part of the therapeutic method.

Masturbation can still be a problem for the person who feels guilt about doing it. After all guilt is one of the most basic and debilitating kinds of subjective distress. In the past most clinicians might have tried to "cure" the person's autoeroticism, but now they would probably try to help the patient deal with his or her negative feelings toward it.

Variations Proscribed by Recently Weakened Taboos

Two kinds of diversity can be seen in recent patterns of sexual behavior. One is a tendency of the whole society to be heterogeneous—to contain many individual patterns. The other is the presence within that society of many different groups, each relatively homogeneous in itself. For example, many people whose sexual orientation is homosexual move within a homosexual subculture, but not all the time. Others with the same orientation live apart from the homosexual subculture. Troilism (multiple-partner or nonprivate sex) and communal sex are associated with the counterculture, but are certainly not limited to it, nor are they universal or even necessarily widespread practices within that subculture. Transvestism, transsexualism, and prostitution all exist on the fringes of the mass culture but are not always associated with identifiable subcultures.

Homosexuality. With the increasing recognition that normal human beings are a mixture of "male" and "female," many people have become more accepting of homosexual acts and homosexually oriented people. Among young people, fewer "straight" males still feel called upon to shun the company of "gay" males. In fact to do so may be taken as a sign of doubt about one's own gender identity. Also on the decline are the stereotyped images of the male homosexual as a flamboyantly effeminate "flying queen," and the female homosexual as an aggressively masculine "bull dyke." Most homosexuals, male or female, look and act like most other people. They are also no more likely than anyone else to behave in maladaptive ways (Hooker, 1957; Thompson et al., 1971; Weinberg and Williams, 1974; Freedman, 1975). This fact is largely responsible for the controversial 1974 APA decision to drop homosexuality from its list of mental disorders.

Homosexuality is practiced, according to one admittedly biased source (Abbott and Love, 1972), by no less than 20 million Americans. The term *homo* (Greek for "same as") is intended to describe erotic love between two same-sex persons, male or female. In the discussion that follows, we shall distinguish between male and female homosexuality, mostly because their lifestyles differ.

Male Homosexuality. At one time homosexuality was thought to be the result of excessive debauchery, a depraved predisposition brought on by autoerotic practices, or the placement of a female soul in a male body. The homosexual was an object to be despised, rather than understood, and no doubt this condemnation has its roots in theological teachings: "You shall not lie with a man as with a woman: that is an abomination" (Leviticus 18:22). Thus early misinformation, when coupled with Biblical condemnation, made the homosexual easy to despise, for not only was he freakish, but his acts were sinful and degenerate (Cantor, 1971).

The earliest impetus for the emergence of the homosexual from this moral disenfranchisement was supplied by the Kinsey Reports and by several homophile organizations, including the Mattachine Society of New York and Washington, the Homosexual Law Reform Society of America in Philadelphia, and the gay liberation organizations on many campuses and in many communities. Their efforts in behalf of members have made homosexuality more acceptable and have led to legal changes that will have widespread consequences. For example, in 1969 Connecticut amended its criminal statutes and now does not treat adult, private, and consensual homosexual acts as crimes. Similar changes have been made in the laws of Illinois and California.

The progress made by homosexuals toward equality has been assisted by several sympathetic plays ("A Taste of Honey," "Staircase," "The Boys in the Band"), movies ("Victim," "Therese and Isabelle," "Sunday Bloody Sunday"), television drama ("Quentin Crisp's Naked Civil Servant"), nonfiction (Tobin and Wicker, 1972; Murphy, 1971; Abbott and Love, 1973), and fiction by such well-known writers as Gore Vidal, James Baldwin, and Jean Genet.

Homosexuality is common among male adults whose access to the opposite sex is limited for any reason. It is also not an unusual form of sexual expression among children and young adolescents, whose sex play is exploratory or experimental and hence indiscriminate.

No clear-cut line of demarcation exists between the male homosexual and his heterosexual counterpart. Some male homosexuals are married to women, but prefer men; others are exclusively homosexual and are repulsed by women; still others are frankly bisexual and enjoy sexual contacts with men and women, either sequentially or simultaneously.

Some writers have distinguished between latent and overt homosexuality: overt homosexuals are aware of their sexual orientation, but latent homosexuals are not. The assumption was that latent male homosexuals "unconsciously" adopt feminine mannerisms and styles of dress, and that they have "feminine" interests, such as cooking, sewing, keeping house, and the like. A much more sophisticated concept of latent homosexuality focuses on reaction formation: the loud, aggressive, *macho* male and the Hemingway-hero type who wants nothing more than to be off in the woods hunting and fishing with "the boys" are perceived as trying to conceal or deny their own homosexual leanings. The classic example of this kind of reaction formation is the "Let's go beat up some fags" syndrome.

Four types of male homosexuals were described by sociologist Laud Humphreys in a study described in his book, *Tearoom Trade: Impersonal Sex in Public Places* (1970).[3] These categories, which use the argot of the male homosexual subculture, are the *trades, ambisexuals, gays,* and *closet queens.* The trades are mostly unhappily married men, blue-collar or clerical workers, who, according to Humphreys, may be further described as follows (pp. 116–117):

They are almost uniformly lonely and isolated; lacking success in either marriage bed or work, unable to discuss their three best friends (because they don't have three), enroute from the din of factories to the clamor of children, they slip off the freeways for a few moments of impersonal sex in a toilet stall.

The ambisexuals are less confined than the trades to tearooms, are less likely to be fleeing from an unhappy and loveless home life, and are more candid in their recognition of homosexuality as a lifestyle. They tend also to read extensively about homosexuality and discuss it with their friends.

The third type, the so-called "gay" homosexuals, are usually single and are open participants in a male homosexual subculture. They are also often supported by older male lovers, have a median age of 24 (the range is from 19 to 50), are well-educated, have effeminate mannerisms, are careful of their appearance, and keep immaculate and well-furnished apartments or houses. They speak of marrying the men they love and, Humphreys reports (p. 124), "in a surprising number of cases they take their lovers 'home to meet mother.'"

The closet queens, so-named because they keep their orientation hidden, parallel the trades

in that they usually have blue-collar and clerical jobs, and are lonely and less educated than ambisexuals or gays. Their distinguishing feature is that they prefer teenage boys as sex objects and frequently cruise the streets in search for boys thumbing rides home from school. Among the bar set of the homosexual subculture, "closet queen" is a pejorative term because their activities frequently result in the sort of scandal feared by the gay community.

Female Homosexuality (Lesbianism). The term *lesbian* derives from the Greek island of Lesbos, home of the poetess Sappho, who was herself a homosexual. The lesbian sometimes engages in homosexual relationships because of the inaccessibility of men. For example, Ward and Kassebaum (1970, p. 126), two sociologists who closely studied the behavior of inmates at the California Institution for Women (interviews, questionnaires, personal observation, and analysis of official records), learned that "there is a greater amount of homosexuality among female prisoners than among male prisoners—much of it reflected in manner and dress." But there is less coerciveness in the relationship than among male prisoners,"[4] and estimates of the total amount of such activity varied from 50 percent (inmates' estimates) to 60–75 percent (staff estimates).

Much less has been written about the lesbian than about the male homosexual. This is possibly due to society's greater concern with suppressing male homosexuality than its female counterpart. Male homosexuality causes more anxiety than lesbianism in a society that is clearly male-oriented, and in which the lesbian can still be seen as an erotic object by heterosexual males. Nonetheless its incidence is higher than was

---

[3] *Tearooms,* in the language of male homosexuals, refers to public restrooms; and *trade,* in one meaning of the term, refers to transactions and agreements between consenting partners.

[4] For an account of sexual assaults among male prisoners, see Davis (1970).

Table 15.1

Incidence of Homosexual and Heterosexual Experience Among Males and Females

Scale Value	Scale Description	Cumulative Percent	
		Males	Females
0	Entirely heterosexual experience		
	Single	53–78	61–72
	Married	90–92	89–90
	Previously married	–	75–80
1–6	At least some homosexual experience	18–42	11–20
2–6	More than incidental homosexual experience	13–38	6–14
3–6	Homosexual as much or more than heterosexual	9–32	4–11
4–6	Mostly homosexual experience	7–26	3–8
5–6	Almost exclusive homosexual experience	5–22	2–6
6	Exclusively homosexual experience	3–16	1–3

Source: Kinsey, A. C. et al. Sexual behavior in the human female. Philadelphia: Saunders, 1953.
Note: Female data apply only between ages 20 and 35, and percentages apply only to single individuals unless otherwise indicated.

once commonly believed. For example, the Kinsey Report *Sexual Behavior in the Human Female* (1953) indicates that 11 to 20 percent of the females in their sample claimed "at least some homosexual experience" and that as many as 11 percent reported "homosexual as much or more than heterosexual" experiences. Some of these figures are shown in Table 15.1, which compares the incidence of male and female homosexuality (Kinsey et al., 1953).

Contrary to an assumption commonly held by straight people, a polarized relationship in which one person is always "butch" and the other always "fem" is not usual in lesbian (or male homosexual) relationships. Such a polarity of sexual roles sometimes occurs, but it is rarer among lesbians than among male homosexuals. Furthermore, according to one writer (Storr, 1964), some female homosexual relationships involve no physical contact more intimate than the warm embraces society generally accepts as a natural accompaniment of friendship between women.

Another popular belief that may turn out to be a myth is the notion that a trade-off exists between heterosexual and homosexual impulses, and that the stronger a person's heterosexual drives are, the less likely he or she is to enjoy homosexual contacts. According to several reports (for example, Bartell, 1971) on group sex activities, it is often the woman most sexually responsive to men who is also most able to enjoy sexual contact with another woman. Many men report being intensely turned on by the sight of two women making love, so such an event is likely to elevate the sexual excitement of everyone present. Whether this phenomenon can be accounted for in terms of the supposed greater sexual potential of women, no one knows.

Transvestism and Transsexualism. Transvestites (from the Latin word meaning "across-dressing") are people who dress in clothing that is ordinarily associated exclusively with the opposite sex. This concept does not apply to the "unisex," or androgynous patterns of casual dress—the tendency for young people of both sexes to wear identical jeans, shirts, and shoes. A male transvestite would be more likely to wear a dress, nylons, nylon panties, a garter belt, and other garments that are part of the more conventional attire of women in our culture. Similarly a female transvestite is likely to wear coarser clothes and a shorter haircut than most males.

Transvestites are not always homosexuals. Many male homosexuals are attracted to maleness, and they do not perceive their relationships as anything other than two men loving each other. In contrast a male transvestite is apparently drawn to the feminine, or at least to the trappings of the female. Thus some transvestites are heterosexual males whose cross-dressing serves as a "turn-on" prior to heterosexual coitus. Others are homosexual males "in drag." Storr (1964, p. 64) reports the case of a happily married heterosexual male transvestite who dressed in his wife's clothes about once a week and claimed that it not only excited him intensely but also increased his potency.

Transsexuals are people who believe they were born with a body of the wrong sex. For example, a transsexual born male believes he is really a female. Through sex reassignment surgery, some transsexuals have been able to acquire the sex of their choice. For a male seeking reassignment as a female, the operation involves removal of the penis and testicles and in some cases fabrication of an artificial vagina. Hormone therapy fosters breast development and other female secondary sex characteristics, but the patient's genetic identity is not changed, nor is she able to bear children. The reverse operation—reassignment from female to male—has been somewhat less successful. The male turned female can experience genital coitus as a female, with orgasm, but medical science has not yet succeeded in enabling the female turned male to function to the same extent in genital coitus.

The traditional view of homosexuality and transvestism as totally abnormal and unnatural phenomena is changing. Nature seems not to have shared the traditional view, since humans are biologically well-equipped to enjoy both heterosexual and homosexual intercourse, and since transvestism obviously depends on culturally defined sex-appropriateness of dress. As the prevailing models change, scientists are (not surprisingly) beginning to see homosexual behavior in other species, sometimes even when heterosexual partners are available. Some people believe that humans are bisexual, and Kinsey (et al., 1948, 1953) seems to have suggested that this is what his data were saying. Bisexuality is, in fact, more widespread than exclusive homosexuality, and one researcher (Churchill, 1967) has suggested that some bisexuals may be driven into exclusive homosexuality by society's rejecting attitude toward homosexuality and the resulting barriers between straight and gay people. It may be too early to tell whether the extent of exclusive homosexuality is being reduced by the increasing tendency of young people to think less in terms of heterosexual or homosexual people and more in terms of heterosexual or homosexual acts as simply parts of people's sexual repertory.

Satyriasis and Nymphomania. Satyriasis and nymphomania are commonly defined as excessive sexual drive or desire in males and females, respectively. That concept stands on rather shaky ground, since we cannot easily answer the obvious question, "excessive in comparison with what?" No one can say how much is too much; hence the intensity of a person's sexual drive or desire is a meaningless criterion. However if we focus on the insatiability rather than the intensity of the drive, we can get a better clue to the way in which the behavior may be maladaptive. The satyr and the nymphomaniac never achieve resolution emotionally (or in many cases physically), perhaps because they are using sex to try to satisfy a nonsexual need. Such behavior is inherently self-defeating.

Satyriasis. The classic satyr is the Don Juan whose compulsion to succeed sexually with every

Dr. Richard Raskin before sex reassignment surgery.

Renée Richards after sex reassignment surgery.

woman in sight preoccupies him to the exclusion of almost everything else. Often this pursuit is a desperate attempt to prove his virility and blot out underlying feelings of inadequacy.

The satyr is often brilliantly adept at making a woman feel wanted, but she has value to him only as an object to be conquered. Once conquered she loses her value in his eyes. Many satyrs are misogynists (woman-haters) whose sexual behavior is really a form of aggression aimed at denigrating women. In such cases the satyr is really the standard old-fashioned moral prude to whom any woman who surrenders sexually is worthless. He usually has no difficulty finding willing women.

Nymphomania. The double standard is nowhere more obvious than in society's attitudes toward sexual promiscuity. The man who sets out to emulate Don Juan is, at worst, seen as a dashing, virile, romantic scoundrel. If anything, the scoundrel part intensifies the attraction women feel for him and the envious admiration with which other men regard him. But the woman who would emulate Cleopatra fares badly, at least in conventional society. Women regard her with malice and contempt, and her availability arouses fear and repugnance in many of the men.

The nymphomaniac's behavior may be a desperate bid for attention and love. She may also, like the satyr, be trying to overcome feelings of sexual inadequacy. The literature repeatedly mentions that a sizable majority of nymphomaniacs come from families that lack emotional warmth and that many of these women are sexually unresponsive (Rosen et al., 1972; Thorpe et al., 1964).

Prostitution

Although there are no precise figures available regarding the prevalence of prostitution, Kinsey's statistics (1948), which indicate that about 69 percent of his white male population reported having had some sexual experience with prostitutes, suggest that it is widely practiced in the United States. Its prevalence and acceptance in primitive societies (Davenport, 1965) and throughout history (Durant, 1954) are well corroborated. Here is an excerpt from a description of early Sumerian history (Durant, 1954, p. 129):

Women were attached to every temple, some as domestics, some as concubines for the gods or their duly constituted representatives on earth. To serve the temples in this way did not seem any disgrace to a Sumerian girl; her father was proud to devote her charms to the alleviation of divine monotony.

It was also a lucrative enterprise in early times, as the following excerpt from an account of early Egyptian history aptly shows (Durant, 1954, p. 166): "Blood ran warm along the Nile . . . premarital morals were free and easy; one courte-

san, in Ptolemaic days, was reputed to have built a pyramid with her savings."

In prostitution the choice of a sexual object is made on the basis of a business transaction; and therefore both sides of this unusual partnership must be examined closely to determine who is the deviant party.

The buyer, who is almost always a male, typically has contracted for the sexual services of another human being. If we assume that he has other outlets for sexual gratification, we may speculate that he has chosen a prostitute either because he must degrade, humiliate, or otherwise dehumanize the object of his choice, or because his current mates do not adequately gratify him. In either event his relationship with the prostitute is part of a business contract, and he considers all his requests legitimate.[5] Consequently prostitutes have become the targets for a wide range of unusual sexual practices that the conventional members of the buyer's larger community would not tolerate. Perhaps this last point is best made in a self-report by an anonymous prostitute, who describes one of her experiences in this passage taken from *Streetwalker*:[6]

I follow the little man on tiptoe into his room. . . . He is a nice, considerate person after all. I must have been crazy to have thought otherwise. . . . Still, I shall be on my guard. . . . He's all right, this little man. I might even stretch a point and stay here till morning. . . . After the low, expected noises . . . [of undressing], his voice sounds harsh and loud. . . . My eyes meet his. . . . This is no nice little man. This is trouble. . . . It is his wit

---

[5] This is an opinion evidently shared by the prostitute. Kinsey et al. (1953) noted that quite commonly a prostitute would indignantly reject as perverted a boyfriend's request for her to participate with him in a sex act (for example, fellatio) that she routinely performed for her customers.

[6] From *Streetwalker*. Anonymous. Copyright © 1959 by The Bodley Head. Reprinted by permission of The Viking Press, Inc.

against mine, and I must win. . . . He isn't even aware of me as an individual. . . . He looks at me as if I were a beetle, to be squashed at will. I'm scared. . . .

"Get on that bed."

Get on, get on it. . . . Don't shut your eyes. . . . Don't let your concentration waver. . . . Relax for a second. Not your mind! But your body. There may be more to come.

"Over."

"No. Oh, no."

This is too much. . . . No. . . . He's hurting. . . . I can't stand it. . . . That's it, keep your eyes on his face. Smile. Talk! . . . Now lie down beside him. . . . Wait for his breathing to get even. Not yet, it may be too soon. All right, take a chance. . . . He's stirring. . . . Danger. . . . He's awake. . . . He hit you. Move. . . . Don't give him a chance of grabbing. . . . Take the chair with you. . . . Careful, he's grabbed the legs! . . . He's out cold. . . . He's moaning. . . . Dress, quick. Out.

The prostitute, who in our society is almost always a female, is also engaged in a form of sexual deviation. Although it is commonly assumed that the prostitute is motivated primarily by money, Hollender (1961) has presented evidence that at least some prostitutes enter these transactions because they have no other way of relating to people and obtaining love. It is probably also true that some prostitutes, perhaps as a consequence of having been subjected to sex-is-dirty training, are incapable of entering sexual relations without the prospect of being degraded by their partners. Of course among their ranks are also those women whose prostitution is a symptom of such other disorders as mental retardation, schizophrenia, and antisocial personality.

But whatever the motivation or psychopathology, it is evident that prostitutes have entered an apprenticeship (see Bryan, 1967, for a description of this apprenticeship) in which they have either wittingly or inadvertently excluded themselves almost entirely from society. Unlike the homosexual, who is only excluded *as* a homosex-

ual but is accepted in most other roles, the prostitute is totally unaccepted.

Troilism and Communal Sex. A female who has sexual contact with multiple partners, either simultaneously or in rapid succession, or who experiences any sex act in the sight of someone other than her partner in that act, is violating a strong taboo of our culture. A male is less likely to suffer disapproval for the same behavior. The term *troilism* is rather loosely applied to all such acts, but whether troilism is deviance per se is not clear. In the first place the obvious double standard is grounds for suspicion that no clear-cut psychopathology is involved. In the second place the majority of the world's cultures do not share this taboo with us. Neither exclusivity nor privacy is universally seen as a necessary condition for sexual intimacy.

During the 1960s some people eager to explore their new-found sexual freedom experimented with nonexclusive and nonseclusive patterns of sexual behavior. Troilistic fantasies are common among people of both sexes, and in the permissive atmosphere of communes and, sometimes, large outdoor rock concerts the sex-before-an-audience fantasy became for some a reality.

Multiple-partner sex generally takes one of three forms. The *triad* is an extension of the couple by the addition of one more person. FMF (two females and one male) triads are more common, although MFM triads are more in keeping with the greater sexual capacity of the female. The *tetrad* consists of two couples who trade partners. Wife-swapping, the troilism of the middle class, is tetradic. In the third form of multiple-partner sex, one female has sex, simultaneously or consecutively, with several male partners. Cleopatra's accomplishments in this last form have been well noted by historians. All three forms have homosexual equivalents, the equivalent of the third form being especially common among males cut off from female company. People who are uneasy about close contact with members of the same sex may have some difficulty enjoying troilistic sex, especially in triads.

The classical "everybody-love-everybody" orgy is not a common occurrence, and "swinging" parties tend to consist mainly of many couples coupling in adjacent spaces. Such events may serve a function similar to that of the pagan rites of an earlier time, which allowed everyone complete sexual license on certain annual holidays. The permission given by the mistletoe, which is a relic of those rites, once extended far beyond kissing.

Long-term inclusive sexual relationships include group marriage, mostly tetradic but sometimes triadic (Constantine and Constantine, 1973), and communal sex. Communal sex is not a new concept, having had a long history, including some of the nineteenth-century utopian communes. Different communes have evolved different patterns. In some the strains resulting from jealousy have led to reimposition of strict monogamy. In others (Kincade, 1973) people at first paired off into monogamous couples, which then began to split up as new liaisons were formed, until finally the sexual relationships of members ceased to be exclusive.

Although multiple-partner sex is generally associated with the counterculture, it is probably far less common than monogamy, even there. For many people the increase in the range of possible partners and experiences is offset by the fact that rivalries, jealousies, and insecurities are also multiplied.

Patterns Still Classed as Deviant by Most Clinicians

There is no common denominator apparent in the patterns of sexual behavior most commonly considered deviant. Some fit the "nonprocreative sexual outlet" criterion, but four exceptions to that rule are also included. As in the two previously discussed categories, the list shows a mixture of acts considered inappropriate and objects considered inappropriate. Some of these patterns, such as voyeurism and exhibitionism, seem to be unique to modern technological societies, but other patterns are age-old and worldwide.

Voyeurism and Exhibitionism. Some confusion surrounds the use of the terms *voyeur* and *exhibitionist*, since very many people of both sexes and all ages find it erotically pleasurable to see nude people of the opposite sex and to be seen nude by people of the opposite sex (or of the same sex if one's orientation is homosexual). Even by a narrow definition of sexual normalcy, it would be hard to see such pleasure as maladaptive.

What makes the voyeur and the exhibitionist different is that they are furtive intruders, and that they avoid, rather than seek, intimacy. Most men will not look away if an attractive woman next door forgets to draw the drapes before undressing, but the voyeur will climb a tree to look into a second-story window. Furthermore this is likely to be his only source of sexual gratification. Similarly many people enjoy watching sexual activities but do not violate the privacy of others to do so.

There is also a clear distinction between the person who simply enjoys being seen nude and the exhibitionist. The true exhibitionist is the "flasher," who suddenly opens his raincoat to display his genitals to a strange woman. Like the voyeur the exhibitionist is often psychosexually immature and unable to seek and obtain sexual pleasure in other ways.

Incest. The taboo against sexual union of close relatives is one of the strongest in our culture. According to many writers (Ferracuti, 1972; Weiner, 1962; Weinberg, 1955) it is virtually universal. The word is from the Latin *in* + *castus,* meaning "unchaste," but the exact definition of the excluded relationships depends on the culture. In many cultures kinship is defined in ways that have little to do with our concept of genetic relation, and an individual may find that dozens of people are taboo as possible sex partners. In Western societies the breadth of the taboo has also varied, extending as far as sixth cousins in the tenth and eleventh centuries. Marriage between first cousins is forbidden in some states on the basis of the incest taboo, but in other states first cousins may marry. The taboo is most vigorously applied to brother–sister, father–daughter, and mother–son relationships.

Sociologist William Graham Sumner, in his classic *Folkways* (1906), was one of the first to point out that there is no natural abhorrence toward incest (p. 480) and that although very widespread, the taboo was not quite universal. Sumner cited reports of permissive attitudes in some cultures toward brother–sister marriages, father–daughter marriages, mother–son marriages, and in a few cultures toward two or all three of these forms. Sumner lists eight cultures that seem to have had no incest taboo at all. In one case, incest was forbidden among coastal tribes but not inland, suggesting that cultural diffusion may be a factor (that is, the taboo may have been acquired through contact with the outside world). Incestuous marriages among royal families were common in ancient Egypt, as well as in Peru, Burma, Siam, and Hawaii.

Anyone seeking explanations for the incest taboo can find them in abundance. Incestuous marriages are forbidden because such marriages are sterile (Pope Gregory I), because they would be without love (Martin Luther), because they would lead to excessive love within the family (Aristotle, St. Chrysostom), because if sexual love were added to familial love, there would be so much human love that God would be forgotton (St. Thomas Aquinas). The explanation Margaret Mead got from an Arapesh elder was that if a man married his sister, he would have no brothers-in-law to visit, whereas if he and she both married outside the family, he would have at least two (quoted by Weinberg, 1955). Other explanations are that close family habituation creates an aversion to intrafamilial sex (Westermarck, 1934),[7] that in primitive societies intertribal marriages are economically desirable (Fortune, 1932), that intrafamilial sexual rivalries would destroy family bonds (Malinowski, 1961), and that erotic impulses within the family need to be controlled to promote fuller socialization outside the family (Parsons, 1954).

In present-day America the most frequently given explanations of the incest taboo are genetic: incest leads either to an accumulation of genetic defects or to a diminished genetic pool. According to the accumulated-defect model, many of us carry recessive genes for undesirable traits (for example, predispositions to certain diseases). Outbreeding increases the chances of those genes remaining recessive and therefore "hidden" from natural selection. The more closely people inbreed, the greater the chance of a child receiving the same defective gene from both parents. Inbreeding also intensifies genetic traits at the expense of vigor. The chances of inbreeding producing genetically defective children have been variously assessed as very great (Lindzey, 1967) and very small (Alström, 1976).

The diminished pool model holds that a continued pattern of inbreeding would produce so much sameness in the population that there would be little chance of producing the rare genius whose innovative thinking is needed if society is to survive serious crises.

Statistics on incest in America should be approached cautiously, since cases occurring in lower-class families are much more likely to come to the attention of medical, social, or law-enforcement agencies. Incest in middle- or upper-class families is less likely to be reported, except to the family physician or a therapist in private practice.

Common denominators in reported incest cases include alcohol and crowded housing conditions. According to a Swedish study of 100 cases of father–daughter incest (reported in Ferracuti, 1972), the significant precipitating factors included inferior socioeconomic conditions,

---

[7] It is not clear whether the especially close family habituation of husband and wife creates an aversion to intrafamilial sex between them. If it does, its possible role in marital sex problems might be worth exploring.

unstable work records, and obstacles to normal conjugal intercourse. In these cases the father took the initiative, the daughter stepped into her mother's sexual role, and the mother did not interfere. The average age of the daughters in this study was 15 years, and many of them were pre-pubertal.

Weiner (1962) reported that girls in father–daughter incest cases are characteristically precocious in their sexual sophistication and eager to assume an adult role. They enjoy the father's attention and express hostility toward the mother through the relationship with the father. Private physicians report a different picture, in which the girl is not sexually precocious and is forcibly raped by her father. The subsequent sexual behavior of these girls seems to cluster at the ends of the spectrum—either promiscuity or a fearful withdrawal from sexuality. In some cases of father–daughter incest, the father's behavior is a symptom of psychopathology. He may be schizophrenic or brain-damaged, and his sexual behavior may be part of a pattern of impaired judgment.

Brother–sister incest is less often reported than father–daughter incest. Most often it consists of prepubertal and pubertal sex play and experimentation between a girl and her (usually older) brother. In adult sexual relationships between brother and sister, the brother usually takes the initiative and again is usually older. The range of the brother's aggressiveness in these cases is from seduction to rape.

Pedophilia. *Pedophilia* (literally "child love") is a sexual preference for children, expressed sometimes by kissing or caressing a child, or by various forms of sex play, including coitus. The offender is usually a man and the victim usually a girl, and they usually know each other.

Physical coercion is seldom employed by pedophiliacs, and the relationship often continues for a period of time. But even if the child provokes or initiates, welcomes, and enjoys the intimacies (as sometimes happens), the adult is held responsible for a crime and is considered deviant. (Sometimes, in fact, he is considered guilty until proven innocent.) In our culture no child is considered competent to give her consent for sexual contact.[8]

Pedophiliacs, whose preferences may be heterosexual, homosexual, or bisexual, are considered by some to be chronologically adult but psychosexually infantile (Reinhardt, 1957). It is assumed that the pedophiliac chooses children because he is incapable of having satisfactory sexual relations with adults.

Sadism. *Sadism* is named after the Marquis de Sade (1740–1814), who attained sexual gratification from fantasizing or inflicting punishment and cruelty. He recorded his sadistic fantasies in his novel *Justine and Juliette, or The Curse of Virtue and the Blessing of Vice.*

The punishment and pain inflicted by the sadist may be of a physical or a verbal nature, the latter including abusive language, teasing, denigrating, and threatening. The physical punishment commonly includes kicking, biting, whipping, and slapping, and occasionally results in the murder of the victim.

The type and frequency of sadism practiced differs widely from one person to another and, even within the same individual, from one situation to the next. In its least deviant form mild sadism is expressed when sexual intercourse is accompanied by pinching, biting, or scratching the sex partner. Some sadists derive pleasure simply from imagining the infliction of pain on the sex object; this is usually a masturbatory fantasy.

The following is an excerpt from an Associated Press report of how one sadist made his fantasies come true. Not all victims get off as easily as the ones reported here:

---

[8] As previously noted, the age of consent varies widely from state to state.

Heinrich Himmler, shown here with Hitler and other top-ranking Nazis, was the Gestapo chief who, according to Erich Fromm, derived sexual pleasure from observing nude women being exterminated in gas chambers.

EVANSTON, ILL., MARCH 5, 1971. SPANK RESEARCH BRINGS 13 UNHAPPY END RESULTS. . . . *Would you agree to accept a spanking for $15, in the interest of scientific research . . . ? Thirteen coeds . . . did.*

Some said later they became suspicious, after a couple of half-hour research sessions, of the young spanker's unprofessional conduct and enthusiasm for his work, and even more so when their $15 checks bounced. . . .

It began with an advertisement in the . . . student newspaper. It offered girls 18 to 26 a chance to earn $15 for a half hour participation in "research discussion groups."

Of 100 girls who responded, the group leader selected 13 for his scholarly work on their sexual response to spankings while lying across his knee. He said the research was in behalf of G & S Love Industries. Each girl was to tell him of some recent misbehavior and was to receive the number of spanks he thought the offense deserved.

He warned them they must not discuss the project with outsiders. That, he said, was a 20-spank offense. . . .

Some coeds protested that the spankings hurt, but their main complaint was that their first $15 checks were no good.

They consulted the security office, which in turn consulted the state's attorney and the researcher. The settlement was $30 in the form of cashable checks for each subject.

According to some psychological interpretations, sadism is based on people's feelings of insecurity, which compel them to overpower their sexual partners, and psychoanalytic theory holds that sadism can be traced to a fixation on an early misinterpretation by the child of the male role in coitus. This view assumes that the child has witnessed sexual intercourse between parents and has interpreted the male role as a brutal attack on the female.

But not all theorists believe that sadism is just a sexual deviation. For example, Erich Fromm suggests that it is all-pervasive in that it is the passion to have absolute control over another living being. And according to this view, sadism is a compensation for the inability to have the power to create or to love, the compensation being in the form of forcing, hurting, and controlling another person. The personality of Heinrich Himmler, the Nazi Gestapo chief who amused himself by viewing nude women being gassed to death, was a textbook case of sadism (Fromm, 1973).

Masochism. Masochism, the enjoyment of pain, punishment, and humiliation, is named after Count Leopold von Sacher-Masoch (1836–1895), an Austrian writer who sought out women to inflict pain on him. He obtained sexual satisfaction from the mistreatment he received from them and from having his wives engage in sexual liaisons with other men.

Like voyeurism and exhibitionism, masochism sometimes resembles behavior that is part of the sexual repertory of healthy individuals. It is not necessarily abnormal for a person to feel erotic arousal when being spanked, and this apparently happens to children quite regularly. The human body contains a vast network of nerve endings that may respond erotically to various kinds of touch. Alex Comfort, in *The Joy of Sex* (1972), claims that either partner's orgasm can be intensified if the person is bound while being genitally stimulated by the other partner. Another suggestion is that being in an inverted position (feet higher than head) intensifies orgasm. Both methods are well known to masochists, but the masochist relies almost exclusively on such devices, often as part of a full-scale ritual of "S & M" (sadism and masochism) or "B & D" (bondage and discipline) practices.

The part of masochism that clearly is not part of the normal range of erotic sensations is the enjoyment of being humiliated, mistreated, or punished. Sometimes sadism and masochism appear as caricatures of the conventional male and female sex roles in our society. The totally compliant female thus seems to be the perfect partner for the totally domineering male. She may complain that he is mistreating her, but she keeps coming back for more. A culture that encourages male aggressiveness and female submissiveness is also one that fosters amplifications of these behaviors in deviant sex practices.

But matters are not always so straightforward; sadistic and masochistic behaviors are often present in the same person. Cameron (1963) explains this form of *sadomasochism* as follows (p. 671):

> Sadistic and reciprocal masochistic attitudes of abnormal intensity are usually present in the same person—that is, if a person fantasizes sadistic acts, he also fantasizes the masochistic experiences which they would arouse, and vice versa. . . . Even when sadism appears alone, the sadistic person seems to identify strongly with his victim; and where it is masochism that prevails, the masochist seems to experience pleasure in fantasizing about what sadists do.

The roots of masochism, according to many psychodynamic accounts, are to be found in early childhood when attitudes of shame and guilt develop toward sexual matters. Again the sex-is-dirty theme is so common in our culture that few individuals escape its influence. This is often evident even in so-called normal sexual functioning, the sentiment being that if sex is indeed dirty, one ought to suffer the penalty of pain for participating in it. Occasionally, when the masochist is guilt-ridden but cannot find someone to inflict pain on him, he may inflict the punishment on himself in the form of self-mutilation, which often causes serious injury, especially around the genitals, and sometimes even culminates in accidental or intended suicide.

Rape. Violence is the element in rape that makes it both criminal and deviant. The rapist forcibly deprives his victim of her freedom of choice and also physically assaults her, turning his penis from an instrument of love into an instrument of aggression. Indeed, for many rapists sex is only the means to the end of defiling, degrading, humiliating, and dominating the victim. Such rapists often use more force than is needed. In some cases, however, the rapist seems to employ force to satisfy a basically sexual need. He may even try to establish a relationship with his victim (Astor, 1974).

For the victim the trauma often does not end with the act itself. Her husband or boyfriend may subsequently regard her as defiled, may reproach her for not having offered more resistance, or may suspect her of having provoked the rape. If she reports the rape to the police, her humiliation may be compounded, for in many places the police, who are predominantly male, are insensitive to the victim's feelings and question her in a way that reflects either a prurient interest in the details or a suspicion that the victim provoked the rape. Rape trials in the past have been notorious for the brutal callousness with which defense attorneys have tried to destroy the victim's reputation. Any evidence that the victim has ever been sexually active has been offered as proof that she must have provoked the rape.

Fortunately treatment of rape victims is improving. Any woman who is raped is well advised to seek counseling, which is offered in many places by feminist groups and social service agencies. Many police agencies have reformed their treatment of rape victims, both through better training of police and through the use of female interrogators. Finally evidence of prior sexual activity by a rape victim is, in most cases, no longer admissible in court.

Fetishism. The term fetish denotes, according to most dictionaries, an object of irrational attention or reverence. Originally the word described primitive religious articles of worship. From this, the meaning has been extended to include objects on which some people exclusively fasten their erotic attention.

The fetishist gains sexual gratification from the sight of, or contact with, certain objects such as shoes, gloves, or underwear. Some fetishists also attain sexual excitement from viewing or touching a particular part of the human body, such as hair, hands, feet, ears, legs, or in some instances from focusing on a deformity or bodily damage (Storr, 1964).

Fetishists are almost always males, and the symbolic sex object usually belongs to a female. It is impossible to estimate the extent or prevalence of this deviation because to some degree it is present in most males. Like voyeurism it does serve a normal excitatory function during the foreplay period of heterosexual coitus. Moreover some degree of fetishism is actively promoted and reinforced by the fashion industry, whose purpose it is to focus attention on one part of the body at a time (the "shifting erogenous zone").

The fetishist presents an annoying problem to the police because he sometimes steals to obtain the sexually arousing object. It is not difficult to identify a burglary or theft committed by a fetishist. The kinds of items stolen and the manner in which the crime is committed characterize the person involved. Reinhardt (1957, pp. 240–241) describes the case of a milkman who claimed that he stole shoes because his "wife likes high-heel shoes and he couldn't resist stealing them." A police search of his home turned up 79 pairs of women's shoes, many of which were not his wife's size.

How do fetishes arise? The fetishist, afraid of being rejected by the person to whom he is attracted, fixates on an article of clothing or on a portion of the body because this fixation does not involve sexually approaching the real person and therefore remains under his complete control.

An experiment reported by Rachman (1966) suggests that conditioning plays an important role in acquiring fetishes. Using three unmarried male psychologists as subjects, Rachman presented to them colored slides of a pair of black, knee-length woman's boots as the conditioned stimulus (CS). The unconditioned stimulus (US) consisted of colored slides of nude women, which for these men were sexually arousing. The conditioned response (CR) was penis-volume changes. A CR was defined as five successive reactions above a given magnitude to the CS. Rachman found that all these subjects were successfully conditioned to react sexually (for example, penis-volume changes were measured) to the pair of black, knee-length woman's boots, which prior to the experiment were neutral stimuli. This experiment has been successfully replicated by Rachman and Hodgson (1968).

Necrophilia. *Necrophilia*, a sexual interest in corpses, is believed to be quite rare, and its very nature expresses the individual's profound sense of personal inadequacy. Almost all necrophiles are males.

Zoophilia. This practice, sometimes also called *bestiality*, involves obtaining sexual gratification through contact with an animal. In the United States this form of contact is not unusual among adolescent males in rural areas. The most common animals used for sexual gratification are cows, sheep, goats, dogs, and cats.

Summary of Etiological Considerations

Because we find the evidence for the biological etiology of the sexual "deviations" unconvincing, we concur with the following statement of Ullmann and Krasner (1975, p. 423):

As one moves up the phylogenetic scale, the role of instinctual patterns and hormonal control diminishes to such an extent that even in cases of extreme physiological anomalies, social training takes precedence over the physiological limitations. . . . Hormonal, genetic, and physiological deviation theories are contraindicated by current research.

That psychological factors are the predominant determinants of deviant (and normal) sex functioning is further corroborated by evidence that suggests that a person's background exerts an important influence on modes of sexual gratification. Socialization and environmental forces shared by all categories of deviates include poor same-sex models, association of fear with sex, traumatic and unpleasant sexual experiences, pleasant sexual experiences under unusual circumstances, remuneration for perverted sex experiences, a sense of personal inadequacy, and many other, perhaps less apparent, frightening and reinforcing circumstances that foster deviant sexual expression.

Treatment

Often in our culture the attitude of the public toward the "sexual deviates" is one of outrage and contempt; it is commonly believed that they should be severely punished. The futility of this attitude and approach is aptly described by Karpman (1954, p. 614):

Since his reactions are expressions of unconscious urges, it is no more possible to cure the sexual psychopath of his impulses by repeated punishment than to cure a schizophrenic of his delusions by like means. Punishing a man's exhibitionism cannot change the basic force driving him to exhibitionism; punishing a man for homosexual acts cannot turn him into a heterosexual. Punishment is useless and irrational.

It is undoubtedly true that the public should seek protection from certain types of violent and dangerous acting-out sexual deviates; but distinctions should be made between these people and those who present more of a nuisance than a danger. For example, with some exceptions, homosexuals, fetishists, and voyeurs present no danger to anyone. On the other hand, those who practice pedophilia, necrophilia, and sadism are often dangerous.

General Considerations. One of the chief obstacles to treating sexual abnormalities, however, lies in the fact that the deviate, unlike those with other psychopathologies, derives conscious gratification from his or her symptoms. This may help explain why deviates rarely seek therapy.

Typically, they complain of other ailments and indicate that they are not interested in changing their deviant lifestyles. Many stay away from psychoanalysis because it usually imposes upon them a period of absolute abstinence, which is difficult to sustain after 10, 20, or 30 years of pursuing deviant modes of sexual gratification. And successful psychoanalytic therapy has almost always occurred among younger deviates who were strongly motivated to change their ways of sexual functioning. Such motivation is often due to the severe humiliation to which some individuals have been subjected by their families and associates, and only secondarily to the personal dissatisfactions and anxieties that their sexual patterns engender.

Behavior Therapy. Alternatives to traditional psychotherapy include surgical sex reassignment and behavior therapy. The first of these alternatives, as we saw earlier, is a rather radical form of treatment that most people do not care to undergo. For them, assuming that they are not resigned to their existing sexual lifestyles, behavior therapy is a viable alternative.

Behavior therapy is particularly suited to treating sexual deviates because of the specific and identifiable symptoms involved that can be dealt with individually; we shall discuss a behavioral technique used to cure the symptoms of fetishism. Our presentation, which is a preview of a more extensive discussion in Chapter 23, draws heavily upon sources cited in Bandura (1969), Kanfer and Phillips (1970), Ullmann and Krasner (1975), and Yates (1970a).

Earlier we noted that fetishes can be learned by conditioning; here we present a method found useful in the treatment of fetishism—*aversive counterconditioning*. By means of this technique the patient is taught to attach negative value (aversion) to previously attractive stimuli (the fetish object); concurrently he is presented with alternatives for securing sexual gratification. For example, Oswald (1962) reported the case of a fetishist who, because of his attraction for rubberized garments, required that his wife wear to bed a rubberized mackintosh without which he could not become sexually aroused. This was bothersome to his wife, and she thus persuaded him to seek treatment. The aversive counterconditioning therapy consisted of having the fetishist wear the rubber mackintosh in the laboratory while experiencing apomorphine-induced nausea. The erotic arousal properties of rubber

were eliminated, and a 21-month follow-up indicated that "he feels . . . indifferent to rubberized clothes . . . and his wife confirms that they are normal and happy in their general and sexual life" (Oswald, 1962, p. 201).

As an addendum, however, it should be noted that treatment of fetishism by conditioning procedures is more successful when the patient does not rely entirely on his fetish for sexual gratification. This is easily understood in terms of the reinforcing properties of the orgasm. In other words, when alternative means of sexual gratification can be reinforced by orgasm, it is easier to extinguish the undesirable practice.

Summary

Human sexual response normally progresses through four stages: excitement, plateau, orgasm, and resolution. Multiple orgasms are possible for many females and some males. Physiologically arousal in either male or female consists largely of vasocongestion (blood engorgement) and myotonia (muscular tension). Both the congestion and the tension are released during orgasm and resolution.

Primary impotence is the inability to attain or keep an erection sufficient to accomplish coitus. It may be caused, according to Masters and Johnson, by the demands of religious orthodoxy, a conflicting sexual orientation, a traumatic experience with a prostitute, or any traumatic experience in the male's first attempt at coitus. Performance fears are aroused, and they in turn aggravate the problem.

Secondary impotence is the inability to attain or keep an erection adequate for coition in 25 percent of the male's coital opportunities. Major possible causes, according to Masters and Johnson, are negative psychosocial input during the formative years, parental imbalance, a conflicting sexual orientation, and the demands of religious orthodoxy.

Vaginismus is a spastic contraction of the

muscles of the perineum and the outer third of the vagina that prevents penetration. It may be a response to male erective difficulty or the result of severely controlled social conduct, prior sexual trauma, or a conflicting sexual orientation.

Dyspareunia is painful intercourse, and it can occur in either sex. The major cause in females is insufficient vaginal lubrication, most commonly due to lack of interest in the partner or the occasion.

Premature ejaculation is the male's inability to delay ejaculation long enough to satisfy his female partner in more than 50 percent of their coital opportunities. It is invariably the result of earlier coital experiences in which hurrying was an adaptive behavior.

Ejaculatory incompetence is the inability to ejaculate intravaginally. It may result from a sexually repressive childhood or from a traumatic experience.

Primary orgasmic dysfunction is a history of never having had an orgasm by any method of stimulation. One of its main causes is the habit, acquired in childhood, of pretending not to have sexual feelings.

Orgasmic dysfunction is situational if there has been at least one orgasm. A common cause is a low sexual value placed on the partner.

Since they regard sexually dysfunctional behavior as learned behavior, Masters and Johnson attempt to remove old learned patterns and to teach new ones. They use authoritative direction to encourage greater communication, especially physical communication, between partners. Clients are seen only as couples, on the grounds that "there is no such thing as an uninvolved partner in any marriage in which there is some form of sexual inadequacy." Patients are seen daily for two weeks by a dual-sex therapy team. The approach is based on the "give-to-get" principle — that sensate input becomes unblocked when one becomes absorbed in giving sensual pleasure.

Group treatment methods are designed for people who are partnerless and are unable to afford the therapy offered by Masters and John-son. One of the basic techniques for both pre-orgasmic women and sexually dysfunctional men is masturbation. The supportive influence of the group is placed firmly on the side of the individual member's attempts to recover his or her capacity for bodily pleasure without paying for it in guilt or shame and without feeling pressured to perform.

Abnormality in sexual behavior is especially difficult to define because everyone tends to assume that the sexual values of his or her culture are universal truths about the human species. That assumption is contradicted by anthropological evidence indicating that virtually every form of sexual expression that is physically possible has been part of the accepted norm of some culture at some time, and conversely, virtually every form of sexual expression has been forbidden by a sexual taboo in some culture at some time. With very few exceptions, the sexual taboos of our society are aimed at preventing sex acts that have no likelihood of resulting in pregnancy.

Sexual radicals have tried to limit the definition of abnormal sex behavior to acts that are harmful, coercive, or self-defeating. Traditional definitions stress inappropriate objects or acts and tend to relect the cultural bias against non-procreative sexual outlets.

Sexual values and sex taboos in our culture are changing rapidly. Only two generations ago orogenital coitus, anogenital coitus, and masturbation were considered deviant behavior by many professionals as well as laypeople, whereas today they are accepted and even recommended by most sex educators. Taboos still exist but in considerably weakened form against homosexuality, transvestism, transsexualism, satyriasis and nymphomania, prostitution, and troilism.

The strongest taboos are those against voyeurism and exhibitionism, incest, pedophilia, sadism and masochism, rape, necrophilia, and zoophilia.

Biological theories of the "deviations" are not well founded. Contemporary opinion tends to favor the importance of psychological influences, such as modeling, association of fear with appropriate and pleasure with inappropriate sexual behavior, and family socialization patterns.

The traditional therapies are successful when the motivation to change is present; but behavior therapy is ideally suited when such motivation is not present. Furthermore behavior therapy succeeds because the identifiable symptoms-to-be-changed are easily isolated.

Terms and Concepts to Master

Aversive counterconditioning

Dissimulation of sexual feelings

Dyspareunia

Ejaculatory incompetence

Excitement stage

Exhibitionism

Gay Liberation movement

Give-to-get principle

Kegel exercises

Myotonia

Orgasm stage

Performance fears

Plateau stage

Premature ejaculation

Primary impotence

Primary orgasmic dysfunction

Pubococcygeus muscle

Refractory period

Resolution stage

Secondary impotence

Sensate focus

Sex reassignment

Sexual value system

Situational orgasmic dysfunction

Social value system

Squeeze technique

Vaginismus

Vasocongestion

16 The Antisocial Personality

Of all the clinical types confronting the psychologist, the *antisocial personality* is the most baffling. Here we have individuals who exhibit none of the usual neurotic symptoms, are completely rational, show no psychotic signs, but nonetheless behave in a clearly maladaptive and disabling way. Paradoxically, also, they seem to have insight into others' behavior but not into their own; they are capable of describing their conduct as "awful" and "shameful," yet this insight is superficial and these expressions of remorse lack feeling. For example, they may talk of "guilt," "mistakes," "repenting," and about "starting life all over again," and occasionally may even be convinced of their own sincerity, but their subsequent actions disclose that it was all sham.

People who have dealt closely with antisocial personalities tend to emphasize either their intelligence, charm, and personableness or the intense disappointment they have experienced in them. Antisocial individuals' good reputations are earned because such people function well interpersonally, are often quite entertaining, and typically are articulate and considerate. They occasionally work steadily toward socially acceptable goals, some of which are attained, but they almost always display an uncanny facility for bungling things and getting sidetracked. People who know them casually are usually led to expect more of them, begin to believe in them, and almost always find it difficult to understand why such human potential should be wasted. On the other hand, the people who know antisocial individuals well have learned to expect little of them and are well aware of their emotional and intellectual shallowness.

Description

Generally, the behavior patterns of an antisocial personality become evident by the time the person reaches adolescence and usually follow a predictable course of increasing and unremitting acts against society, as described below (APA, 1968, p. 43):

This term is reserved for individuals who are basically unsocialized and whose behavior pattern brings them repeatedly into conflict with society. They are incapable of significant loyalty to individuals, groups, or social values. They are grossly selfish, callous, irresponsible, impulsive, and unable to feel guilt or to learn from experience and punishment. Frustration tolerance is low. They tend to blame others or offer plausible rationalizations for their behavior. A mere history of repeated legal or social offenses is not sufficient to justify this diagnosis. Group delinquent reaction of childhood (or adolescence) and Social maladjustment without psychiatric disorder should be ruled out before making this diagnosis.

The distinction made in the last sentences of this description refers, in part, to the earlier DSM I (APA, 1952) classification of *sociopathic personality disturbance*, which was divided into *antisocial* and *dyssocial reactions*. The latter label was reserved for those individuals whose disregard for social codes and mores was traceable to environmental influences. This would include, for instance, the racketeer or burglar whose socialization fostered such behavior. Moreover, according to the earlier description, dyssocial types are capable of forming group loyalties, which antisocial personalities presumably cannot manage. For the remainder of this chapter, unless otherwise indicated, we deal only with the antisocial personality;[1] and, for convenience we shall use this term interchangeably with *sociopath* and *psychopath*.

Historical Background

The concept of antisocial personality originated with Phillipe Pinel's description and diagnosis of a case of *psychopathic state* (Kavka, 1949). Pinel (1745–1842) wrote a lengthy article describing a disorder he called *manie sans délire* (insanity without delirium), which shed new light on a type of personality to which none of the usual psychiatric classifications applied, but which nonetheless displayed maladaptive behavior.

Pinel's observations and conceptualizations were subsequently picked up by an English psychiatrist, J. C. Prichard; in 1835 he depicted a "form of mental derangement" in which intellect seemed unimpaired but the "power of self-government" was lost or lacking, so that the individ-

ual was incapable of "conducting himself with decency and propriety in the business of life" (Prichard, 1835). He coined the phrase *moral insanity* to describe these individuals in whom

the moral and active principles of the mind are strongly perverted or depraved; the power of self-government is lost or greatly impaired and the individual is found to be incapable, not of talking or reasoning upon a subject proposed to him, but of conducting himself with decency and propriety in the business of life.

Prichard's 1835 paper was followed by M. Gouster's 1878 presentation of the first clinical picture of the symptoms found in moral insanity and the new name subsequently given to the disorder was *psychopathic inferiority*, a label invented by J. A. Koch in 1888 (Koch, 1891; McCord and McCord, 1964).

Since 1888, according to one authority (Cleckley, 1959, p. 571), there have been numerous attempts to classify and reclassify "essentially dissimilar entities under a single and vaguely defined label." For example, Kraepelin (1915) listed no less than seven types of sociopaths, and Schneider (1934) expanded the list to ten. Among the more important contributions toward developing the current conceptualization of the disorder were those of Adolf Meyer (1904–1905), who separated these personality types from the neuroses; G. E. Partridge (1930), who further clarified the characteristics of this entity and suggested the term *sociopathic personality*; Benjamin Karpman (1941, 1961), who described the sociopath's unique inability to develop major and permanent emotional ties to others; and Hervey Cleckley (1959, 1964), who offered the most comprehensive current descriptions of the antisocial personality as a separate mental disorder.

Current Conceptualization

In the following discussion and in Table 16.1, we draw heavily on the descriptions of sociopathy

---

[1] According to the DSM II's classification (APA, 1968, pp. 41–46), *antisocial personality* is an abnormality that belongs to a group of "certain other nonpsychotic mental disorders" characterized by "ingrained maladaptive patterns of behavior." Other personality disorders included under this heading are the *paranoid, cyclothymic* (recurring periods of depression and elation), *schizoid* (seclusive, shy, oversensitive), *explosive, obsessive–compulsive, hysterical, asthenic* (low energy), *passive–aggressive* and *inadequate* (emotional, social, intellectual, and physical ineptness) types. The current DSM III classification (APA, 1980) places these types under a conduct disorder heading which includes undersocialized aggressive and unaggressive categories as well as a socialized variety.

Table 16.1
Characteristics and Typical Behavior of the Antisocial Personality

Characteristic	Typical Behavior
Inability to form loyal relationships	Treats persons as if they are objects; might marry but often deserts family
Inability to feel guilt	Feels no pangs of remorse, although he or she can express sorrow and other emotions.
Inability to learn from experience, special attention, or punishment	Commits repeated crimes, and neither rewards nor severe deprivations seem to be deterrents
Tendency to seek thrills and excitement	Behaves bizarrely and sometimes grotesquely as a rule rather than as an exception
Impulsiveness	Like a child, cannot defer immediate pleasures, cannot tolerate long-term commitments
Aggressiveness	Reacts to frustration with destructive fury
Superficial charm and intelligence	Often qualified for the confidence rackets because of winning personalities and astuteness
Unreliability and irresponsibility	Unpredictably responsible during some periods, but completely irresponsible during others
Pathological lying	Plays many roles—doctor, lawyer, soldier—according to his whims; often confused himself about what he or she has accomplished or who he or she really is
Inadequately motivated antisocial behavior	Impulsively steals and destroys "just for the hell of it"
Egocentricity	Behaves parasitically because of an insatiable need to be believed, served, and supported
Poverty of affect	Incapable of true anger or genuine grief
Lack of insight	Can analyze the motivations underlying the behavior of others—and often does—but has no appreciation of the impact he or she has on others
Casual but excessive sexual behavior	Has a casual attitude toward sex; and sexual contacts, like most behavior, are outlandish and erratic
The need to fail	Has no apparent life plan, except perhaps the need to be a failure

provided by Cleckley (1959, 1964), Hare (1970), Karpman (1961), and McCord and McCord (1964). These descriptions, which are somewhat laden with moral overtones, are, of course, not without their critics; but they constitute an impressive body of information on the phenomenology of this disorder.

Inability To Form Loyal Relationships. The antisocial personality has been described as a "loner." A man with such a personality would seem incapable of sustaining warm relationships with others, treat them as if they were things, and seem unable to share their feelings, except in the most superficial way. If he marries or forms business partnerships, he soon deserts his wife or exploits his associates. In short he cannot maintain loyalties or other close bonds. Some of these characteristics are illustrated in Case Report 16.1.

Inability To Feel Guilt. After a review of the clinical literature, McCord and McCord (1964) concluded that the two salient features of the antisocial character are *lovelessness* (see Case Report 16.1) and *guiltlessness.* Such a person can commit the most unkind acts without the uneasiness most people experience. Some writers (Rosen et al., 1972) compare this behavior with that of the infant who has no standards of right or wrong. The difference, of course, is that the normal infant grows out of this stage; the sociopath does not.

Inability to feel remorse, however, does not mean an inability to express it. As we mentioned at the outset of this chapter, this person speaks of sorrow and morality but the talk is hollow. Cleckley (1964) has referred to the discrepancy between what the sociopath feels and says as "semantic dementia," which he describes as a dissociation between rational faculties and emotional inner control.

There is evidence, however, to suggest that some sociopaths rationalize their antisocial actions. Consider the following passage from a book describing the professional thief (Sutherland, 1937, p. 176):

The con-man [confidence man] has little difficulty in easing his conscience, for in the con the sucker [the victim] is always beaten while he was trying to beat someone else. The sucker is generally gloating over his prospective gain and has no sympathy for the person he expects to victimize, so that the thief gets a feeling of sweet vengeance in beating him.

Inability To Learn from Experience or Punishment. Antisocial personalities do not learn from their past failures nor do they profit from punishment or special attention. These features of their behavior have led to the hypothesis that they have a low level of anxiety. David Lykken (1957) compared groups of prison inmates, whom he divided into "primary psychopaths" and "dyssocial" types, with one another and with normal subjects. He found that compared with the nonpsychopathic control groups *primary psychopaths* displayed lesser levels of GSR reactivity to a conditioned stimulus associated with electroshock and were relatively less able to learn to avoid previously punished responses. We shall return to a discussion of Lykken's experiment later in this chapter. In the meantime, Case Report 16.2 will serve as a clinical example of the sociopath's unresponsiveness to either punishment or social rewards.

Tendency To Seek Thrills and Excitement. It is difficult for society to disregard psychopaths, for their behavior is dangerously disruptive. They may burglarize a home or mug someone on the street, and unlike the professional thief, may murder a victim "just for the hell of it." They have been described as asocial characters for whom no rule, no matter how important, is a deterrent (McCord and McCord, 1964).

Psychopaths seem almost incapable of finding pleasure in stability and therefore are willing to sacrifice everything for excitement, change, and repeated thrills. A paragraph from Cleckley's description of a psychopathic physician illustrates this quest for excitement (1964, p. 218):

This man's history shows a great succession of purposeless follies dating from early manhood. He lost several valuable hospital appointments by lying out sodden or by bursting in on serious occasions with nonsensical uproar. He was once forced to relinquish a promising private practice because of the scandal and indignation which followed an escapade

*in a brothel where he had often lain out
disconsolately for days at a time.*

Case Report 16.1   *Disloyalty in a Sociopath*

*A 42-year-old sociopath had a criminal record which
dated back some 30 years. He had worked with
partners, but only for short periods and for particular crimes. He had a long succession of "affairs"
with women from one end of the United States to
the other, and at the time of hospitalization was discovered to have legally married five women. When
confronted with the fact that his marital and extramarital behavior was unusual he said, "I'm an unusual person with a tremendous capacity to love.
Hell, think of all the women I made happy."*

Case Report 16.2   *Inability To Learn from Punish-
ment*

*A 17-year-old male psychopath, who had an IQ of
132 as measured on the Wechsler Adult Intelligence
Scale, broke into several gasoline stations along a
major highway skirting Pittsburgh. After a night's
work of breaking-and-entering into these stations, he
parked his car alongside the highway, leaving his
booty of tires, batteries, and automobile parts in
clear view of passing cars. When he was later asked
to explain his behavior, he shrugged the whole incident off by saying, "You can't win 'em all. Besides, a
short rest period in the cooler never hurt anyone. I
know because I've been in the cooler several times."*

Impulsiveness.   The antisocial personality's
craving for change may indicate a total lack of
internal or external controls. An example of this
form of impulsiveness is the case of a 32-year-old
man who became bored with the everyday routine
of playing husband and father and one day went
out for a "cup of coffee" and never returned.
After five years he was apprehended and questioned by the police; he explained his disappear-

ance by saying, "I just wanted to leave the rat
race behind me. I got bored with the whole bit."

There are many similar instances: bus drivers
who detour several hundred miles from their
usual route; entertainers who suddenly decide
not to show up on opening night; and professors
who impulsively decide to leave town for several
weeks, leaving their students stranded.

Aggressiveness.   McCord and McCord describe
this feature of sociopathy as follows (1964, pp.
10–11):

*He is not the passive neurotic who hurts no one but
himself, nor the anxious psychotic who withdraws
from human contact. . . . The normal man has
learned to control aggression. He reacts to
frustration with sublimation, with constructive
action, with withdrawal—less often with
aggression. The psychopath, on the other hand,
characteristically reacts to frustration with fury.*

Much of this aggression may be due to the
psychopath's history of being rejected, abused,
and sometimes physically beaten by parents and
others whom he/she now imitates. This hostility
may generalize or transfer to others in the environment, especially authority figures. But it is
difficult to know which came first—the sociopath's behavior or others' reaction to it.

Some writers on psychopathy consider impulsive aggressiveness the most striking feature
of the disorder. Anthony Storr (1972), for instance, draws a distinction between deliberate
cruelty and the casual, unpremeditated violence
of psychopaths, which seems to be provoked by
some obviously frustrating cause in the immediate environment. Moreover it is indifference to
the effect of violence upon others that chiefly
characterizes psychopaths, not pleasure in its
use. Storr attributes this form of impulsive violence to a "childlike" emotional makeup in which
conscience has not developed adequately.

Superficial Charm and Intelligence. Charm and intelligence are the most striking features of the sociopath's clinical picture and, in many respects, they add to the characteristics that make him or her so dangerous to society. Combined with guiltlessness, warped capacity for love, and antisocial aggressiveness, the sociopath's apparent allure to others and cleverness at manipulating them truly make him or her a threat to the unsuspecting. The following description of a successful confidence man illustrates these points (Sutherland, 1937, p. 56):

Not all persons can be good con men. They generally must have a winning personality, shrewdness, agility, like the good things in life, and be too lazy to work for them, and have great egotism. They must, first of all, be good actors. The whole con game is a matter of acting. If they cannot put on this veneer of culture, they cannot make it go. A confidence man must live by his wits.

These characteristics—winning personality, shrewdness, and agility—are undoubtedly all called into play in a successful confidence game. Below is a story of an incident that appeared in the *Pittsburgh Post-Gazette* that illustrates how these skills are utilized:

Con Men Bilk Two Women of $10,000 Here
Bunco Duet Uses "Bank Examiner" Scheme in Swindle

PITTSBURGH, *Feb. 11, 1971.* Two skillful con men, using the well-worn "bank examiner" dodge, have been loose again in Pittsburgh—this time bilking an elderly East Liberty woman and her daughter of $10,000. . . .

The latest case was disclosed after a telephone inquiry was made to a bank by the victims, Mrs. Pearl Oliver, 88, and her daughter, Mrs. Roberta Johnston, 66, both of the 1000 block of N. Negley Avenue. Detectives described the operation yesterday this way:

Mrs. Oliver received a phone call Feb. 1 from a man who said he was a state bank examiner investigating "some trouble" at the bank involving reported thefts from savings accounts by tellers.

"Examiner asks help"

The caller inquired about her bank balance, saying her assistance was needed in investigation of a suspected teller. He asked her to withdraw $2,500 and to be photographed with the suspect.

Mrs. Oliver said she was told the money would be redeposited and she would be issued a new account book.

She went to the bank, she said, and withdrew $100, but when she returned home she received another call from the "bank examiner." At the same time, another man, who said he represented the bank, arrived at her apartment.

"Very good job"

The visitor said the investigation could not proceed unless she withdrew $2,500.

She agreed, and the next morning he took Mrs. Oliver and Mrs. Johnston downtown. However, he said there "might be the same trouble" with Mrs. Johnston's account at another bank. The daughter withdrew $2,500 there.

The women were told they did a "very good job." The next day, however, the women were asked to repeat the $2,500 withdrawals. They complied, turned the money over to the "examiners" and were sent home in a taxi.

When their promised new bank books did not arrive, they waited until this week to call the banks and notify police.

In conversation and dress, they said, the swindlers were "very businesslike."

Unreliability and Irresponsibility. In a society that emphasizes integrity and reliability, sociopaths pose a special problem, for they do not feel bound by the rules that govern most people. Agreements in situations of mutual trust are violated as easily as they are entered; promises are broken; money is borrowed and never returned; and chores and responsibilities, no matter how important, are shunned more often than they are fulfilled. Cleckley (1964) points out that if such conduct occurred always, others would quickly learn not to trust sociopaths; but that is not what happens, and in this sense their cleverness pays off. They may have periods during which they show up regularly for work, meet financial obligations, and do not pass bad checks; but just as soon as one's confidence in them is built or restored, they commit some bizarre and grotesquely irresponsible act.

The sociopath's unreliability and irresponsibility render him or her as unfit for the underworld as they do for ordinary interpersonal relations (Sutherland, 1937, p. 38):

A mob must be a unit and work as a unit. . . . In spite of the rules and understandings, there are some persons who are hard to get along with and who tend by their actions to disrupt any mob. In such a case the procedure is to have nothing to do with them, especially if the difficulty concerns business rather than social relations.

Pathological Lying. Closely related to the psychopaths' irresponsibility is their total disregard for the truth. They feel no compunction about lying, and sometimes even they find it difficult to disentangle truths from fabrications. This characteristic too disqualifies them for the work of professional thieves (Sutherland, 1937, p. 36):

Members of the mob are to deal honestly with one another. One of the most heinous crimes in the mob is for a member to burn the others, that is, report that a score showed less than it actually did and hold out the difference. When this occurs, the first
offense is the last. Lying is perhaps considered by thieves to be more unethical than it is by the law abiding.

It is from the ranks of these pathological liars that imposters are drawn. These people assume others' identities and disguises so that they may play out the social roles that happen to catch their fancy: professors, lawyers, surgeons, tycoons, statesmen, and warriors. The most celebrated imposter of recent years was Ferdinand Demara, the subject of a book and a film. During his career he has posed as a Trappist monk, teacher, Ph.D. in psychology, and combat surgeon (Crichton, 1959).

Inadequately Motivated Antisocial Behavior. The sociopath's crimes are the same as those committed by others and range from embezzling to more violent crimes. What distinguishes those offenses is that they are committed without any apparent goal. For example, the ordinary citizen may cheat on his income tax or may misappropriate public funds; but these behaviors are almost always inspired either by a tangible need for funds or simply by greed. Not so with the sociopaths. Somehow they do not share these motivations. They may steal, lie, cheat, or murder just for the fun of it. This characteristic is well illustrated in Case Report 16.3, which describes the inadequately motivated thefts of a 16-year-old youngster.

Case Report 16.3 *A Theft Without a Clear Motive*

The mother of a 16-year-old boy telephoned to report that her son often stole objects from five-and-dime stores, but the situation was brought to a crisis when he heisted several expensive jewelry pieces from the mother's weekend house guests.

The mother explained that not only are they well-to-do, but her husband is president of a large and reputable local corporation and her son has access to anything he wants "just for the asking."

It was evident from the interview with the son

that this rather personable youngster had no particular need for the objects he stole, nor was he addicted to expensive drugs that might explain the thefts. Rather he vaguely explained his behavior by saying that "some people deserve what they get — besides it is not fair that so few have so much."

Questions about the likelihood that he was altruistically or politically motivated yielded even vaguer explanations than those offered at the outset; the possibility of schizophrenia was also ruled out, since he displayed no psychosis-like symptoms. Further probing disclosed that he often also engaged in "hell-raising" and thefts "just to stir up a little excitement."

Egocentricity. The unabashed self-interest of the sociopath is legendary. He expects his family or friends to help him out; should they demur in any way he becomes indignant and flies into a rage. To justify his demands, he complains about a multitude of physical ailments, which usually have no adequate physical basis; but should he become physically ill, he malingers. His headache is a brain tumor, his low back pain is a slipped disc, and he expects to be treated accordingly. Sometimes his physical complaints are an excuse for not working; but more often he would rather let others carry the major burden of work. In short, he demands much but gives little in return.

Several psychologists (Buss, 1966; Craft, 1965; Foulds, 1965) consider egocentricity and lack of empathy largely responsible for the psychopath's disturbed interpersonal relations. Being unable to place himself in another's position, he is able to manipulate people as he would inanimate objects. In this way, he can achieve short-term satisfactions without concern for the consequences of his actions; and, being unable to identify with the feelings of others, he lacks the capacity to grasp their reactions to his unusual behavior.

Poverty of Affect. Although, as we noted earlier, some sociopaths can show remorse, rage, excitement, and, at times, even enthusiasm, this display is empty. They are incapable of real anger, true indignation, sincere joy, or genuine grief; but they do talk about these emotions as if they experienced them. McCord and McCord (1964) recorded the following remarks by a sociopath who was able to steal and kill with conscienceless abandon (p. 13):

Life can at times be a problem — and a laugh. For me, there have been a great many laughs and tears only make the laughter sweeter. . . . But all men, whatever their fate, could take a good lesson from the Bible — the fundamental truths of religion must guide us all.

Lack of Insight. Because of his singular inability to feel deeply or to empathize with others, the sociopath has no capacity to see himself as others see him. Cleckley (1964, p. 384), who finds this lack of insight more puzzling than any of the symptoms of schizophrenia, says, "here is the spectacle of a person who uses all the words that would be used by someone who understands, and who could define all the words but who still is blind to the meaning."

The following letter from a 27-year-old former graduate student to his adviser illustrates clearly this lack of insight. The student had dropped out of graduate school several times, on each occasion neglecting several prior commitments. After having been given numerous opportunities to return, each of which he accepted with promises of "this is really it — this time I am going to make a go of it," he had the following to say two years after his final mysterious disappearance:

Dear Prof:
I'll bet you are surprised to hear from me after all these years. No, I am not asking for readmission to the program — God knows I don't deserve it but I am writing to inform you that I appreciate all you did for me. I thought also that you might be interested to learn that because of your efforts in my behalf I am now another person. In fact, you will be

pleased to know that I am counseling my kid brother who has gotten a little sidetracked in pursuing his own career goals.

But should you care to reconsider my case, I would be most appreciative. Really, it's been a difficult haul uphill . . . but I think I finally know where I am at. I don't want to bore you with the details. I know it sounds corny, but please . . . please give me one more chance.

Predatory Sexual Behavior. The shallowness of affect that is a part of the sociopath's interpersonal contacts also characterize his sexual life. He has a casual attitude toward sex, a take-it-or-leave-it approach, and is not motivated by the sexual desires apparent in most persons. This is not surprising in view of his incapacity for love and his tendency to treat persons as objects. Cleckley (1964) has the following to say about the sociopath's sexual behavior (p. 398):

To casually "make" or "lay" the best friend's wife and to involve a husband's uncle and/or one of his business associates in particularly messy triangular or quadrilateral situations are typical acts. Such opportunities, when available, seem not to repel but specifically to attract the psychopath.

The Need To Fail. Most of the sociopath's behavior seems to suggest that he is driven by a need to fail, almost as though it were his master life plan. Cleckley (1964) cites numerous instances of how the psychopath as businessman, statesman, scientist, physician, and psychiatrist, by his fantastic and often nonsensical buffoonery, somehow manages to abort what seems to be the beginning of a brilliant career. And he concludes (p. 400) that it is hard to avoid the observation that "here is true madness—madness in the sense quite as vivid as that conveyed to the imaginative layman by the terrible word *lunatic*."

In summary then, after considering all the foregoing traits, we cannot help being impressed by the dangerously disruptive menace to society that the antisocial personality poses. He is an impulsive, guiltless, and loveless loner whose constant search for thrills and excitement throws him headlong into conflicts with society. Consequently his behavior attracts the attention of law-enforcement agencies and occasionally of mental health professionals. His aggressiveness is almost incorrigible because he does not have the ability to learn, like most people, from rewards and punishments. Because of his apparent charm and intelligence, he frequently wins the confidence of those around him, but his irresponsible and often fantastic behavior sooner or later betrays his true shallowness and inability to carry on normal interpersonal relationships.

Causes

The question of how a person can become a sociopath is closely linked to another question: what is antisocial behavior a symptom of?[2] We have dealt with this disorder thus far as if it were a symptom syndrome in the same sense as the neuroses and psychoses. We shall now introduce a number of distinctions that have been drawn in the psychological literature.

Other Antisocial Types

Earlier we referred to the differences that were attributed in DSM I (1952) to the *antisocial* and *dyssocial* types and noted that the latter includes sociopaths whose delinquency resulted from having been reared in subcultures where antisocial behavior is, if not encouraged, certainly not

---

[2] The incidence and prevalence of this personality disorder are difficult to estimate because antisocial behavior, defined as the violation of legally established codes of conduct, often results in detention of these individuals in juvenile courts and in prisons. Moreover, the estimates available tend to cluster together under the heading of personality disorders those who are diagnosed within any of the various subtypes.

penalized. These distinctions have been made by Weiner (1970, pp. 289–347), who also differentiates between the so-called primary psychopath's delinquent behaviors and his sociologically and psychologically determined behaviors. These are useful distinctions, and in what follows we shall briefly outline the major contributing factors to the noncharacterological types of sociopathy.

Sociological and Psychological Contributors. Three main distinctions are drawn within this category: *adaptive* versus *maladaptive, social* versus *solitary,* and *lower-class* versus *middle-class* delinquency. *Adaptive delinquency* refers to antisocial behavior motivated by goal-oriented needs (money, food, recognition) or by frustrating circumstances with which the individual cannot cope (see Jenkins, 1957, 1960; Jenkins and Boyer, 1968). Adaptive delinquency is sometimes also called *socialized delinquent behavior* and is comparable to dyssocial sociopathy. *Maladaptive delinquency* is frustration-induced behavior or, as it is sometimes called, *unsocialized aggression,* which is the closer of the two to the DSM II classification of antisocial personality.

Social delinquency is distinguished from solitary delinquency by whether this antisocial behavior is pursued within or without a subgroup context. In this regard sociologist Howard Becker (1963) observed that noncriminal behavior within a delinquent group may be just as deviant as antisocial behavior in our society. As Becker states it (pp. 7–8):

[*The*] *sociological view is . . . relativistic. It identifies deviance as the failure to obey group rules. Once we have described the rules a group enforces on its members, we can say with some precision whether or not a person has violated them and is thus, on this view, deviant.*

In classifying lower- and middle-class delinquency, antisocial behavior is usually described as a lower-class phenomenon. For example, Wei-

ner (1970) observed that most studies of delinquency are conducted in disadvantaged neighborhoods and therefore disregard the antisocial behavior of middle-class youths; but when the variables of educational, social, and economic disadvantages are controlled (accounted for), "It is apparent that lower class and middle class youths commit essentially the same kinds of delinquent acts" (p. 299).[3]

In a book on the psychopathic personality, Alan Harrington (1972) refers to another form of the antisocial personality, which he calls "functional psychopathy." This form may arise from some sort of oppression that breaks or warps family life so that the child grows up neglected, abused, or without a stablizing adult model to imitate. Perhaps this type of psychopathy is best described by Malcolm X in his autobiography (1964, p. 311):

Actually the most dangerous black man in America was the ghetto hustler . . . [who] is internally restrained by nothing. He has no religion, no concept of morality, no civic responsibility, no fear—nothing. To survive, he is out there constantly preying upon others, probing for any human weakness like a ferret. The ghetto hustler is forever frustrated, restless, and anxious for some "action."

Delinquency as a Neurotic or Psychotic Symptom. Neurotic delinquency, according to Weiner (1970, pp. 300–314), may have one of two origins. The first is the youngster's communication of a need to be punished (out of a sense of guilt), recognized (through personal or group status), or helped (in a plea for added attention); and the second type of neurotic delinquency may be due

---

[3]Herskovitz and his associates (1959) found no differences between the number of delinquent behaviors of middle-class and lower-class youths, with the exceptions of auto thefts (slightly more common among middle-class offenders) and burglary (committed more often by lower-class delinquents).

to a parent's subtle or inadvertent reinforcement of antisocial behavior.

The latter type of delinquency, according to a psychoanalytic hypothesis formulated by Adelaide Johnson (1949), is due to a *superego lacunae* (a gap in one's conscience) caused by a parent's covert or unintentional rewarding of his or her offspring's delinquency. For example, the father who often boasts of his uproarious drinking bouts in his youth, even though he is now an upstanding citizen, may be responsible for similar antisocial behavior in his son or daughter. The same antisocial behavior may also be fostered by a parent who, because of oversight or a lapse of attention, sanctions antisocial behavior. In either case this parent tacitly communicates approval of sociopathic behavior.

Another variety of neurotically motivated delinquency occurs among obsessive–compulsives who feel compelled to steal, aggress, or otherwise commit acts that our society judges unacceptable. For example, some obsessive–compulsives cannot control their need to shoplift, even though they consider their behavior abhorrent and do not need the items they steal.

Symptomatic delinquency is also seen among psychotics, usually among schizophrenics; and it may be caused by the tenuous hold they have on reality, which may distort their perceptions and judgments about what is antisocial behavior. For example, a deluded paranoid schizophrenic may strike out against imagined persecutors to defend him- or herself.

Finally, noncharacterological delinquency may also occur as part of an organic disturbance that affects the central nervous system (see Chapter 5). Almost any form of brain damage may be responsible for impulsive or poorly controlled aggressive behavior, and there is a sizable psychological literature that also implicates the endocrine system in this type of aggression (see especially Moyer, 1971).

Origins of Primary Psychopathy

Having digressed briefly to consider the non-characterological causes of psychopathy, we can now return to the question, "How does one become a psychopath?" Although there are still no definitive answers to this question, evidence is beginning to mount on the nature of its cause. As with all disorders we have discussed so far, evidence points to both biological and environmental origins.

The Biogenesis of Antisocial Personality

The search for biological determinants of sociopathy has included investigations of brain defect, autonomic reactivity, and genetic contributors. Although some interesting etiological leads have been found among these studies, the overall results are equivocal.

Evidence of Brain Abnormality. Early studies of the biological causation of sociopathy attempted to correlate it with brain defects. One of the main inspirations for such research was the observation that the electroencephalograms (EEGs) of sociopaths displayed deviant brain wave activity. In a pioneering study of EEG waves and antisocial disorders, for example, Hill and Watterson (1942) discovered that the records of many sociopathic adults were indistinguishable from those of normal young children. Therefore they suggested the possibility that the psychopath's brain may be immature. Unfortunately, however, the criteria for sociopathy is this early study were not sufficiently clear to rule out the inclusion of other diagnostic types, and therefore it is difficult to know how many of these subjects were true or "primary" psychopaths and how many were noncharacterological.

Later studies (Arthurs and Cahoon, 1964; Ehrlich and Keogh, 1956; Gottlieb et al., 1946; Hill and Pond, 1952; Knott and Gottlieb, 1943; Knott et al., 1953; Silverman, 1943) used more reliable criteria for sociopathy. These tended to support the earlier findings with some consistency, for they indicated that between 30 and 60 percent of adult and adolescent psychopaths had EEG abnormalities consisting of *theta*, or slow, rhythms. One study, however, which was also designed adequately, reported no such differences between sociopaths and normals (Simon et al., 1946).

What are the implications of these findings? The most tempting formulation, of course, especially in view of the clinical observation that the antisocial personality is egocentric, lacking in inhibitions, impulsive, and self-indulgent, is that he or she is very like a child. This formulation, however, must be made cautiously for several reasons. First, despite the high incidence of abnormal EEGs among psychopaths, not all of them have abnormal EEGs, nor do all law-abiding citizens have normal EEGs. To state this matter differently, there is no proof that either brain damage or an abnormal EEG is a necessary condition for the development of antisocial personality (Robins, 1966).

Second, as mentioned above, not all EEG studies indicate distinguishable differences between sociopaths and normals. This would be reason enough for caution; but an even more important consideration is that EEG abnormalities also correlate with other behavior pathologies (Zax and Cowen, 1972).

A third reason to be cautious about these findings relates to the nature of the EEG recording itself. There is still much debate among electroencephalographers about the EEG's accuracy in locating central nervous system damage. Thus EEG abnormality does not necessarily mean that a brain abnormality has been identified; nor does normal brain wave activity necessarily indicate the absence of a central nervous system disorder (Hare, 1970; Kiloh and Osselton, 1966).

Abnormal Autonomic Reactivity. Our earlier clinical description of sociopaths depicted them as displaying, among other traits, tendencies toward pathological lying and emotional unresponsiveness. This clinical observation has raised the possibility of an autonomic nervous system disorder. We shall sample only a few salient selections of the extensive literature that now exists on this topic.

An undisputed classic piece of research in this sphere is the study of David Lykken (1957) of the University of Minnesota, which showed that psychopaths were less likely than other prisoners and normals to display anxiety on a lie-detector test. An important feature of this study was Lykken's attempt to separate his antisocial study samples into *primary sociopaths* and the clinically similar appearing subtypes such as the *dyssocial* and *neurotic* sociopaths.

Specifically, he provided his psychologist judges with a 14-item criterion checklist to be used for identifying primary sociopaths who fitted Cleckley's prototype descriptions of "pure psychopathy." In this way two experimental prisoner groups and one control group were selected. Group I (12 males and 7 females) consisted of primary sociopaths; group II (13 males and 7 females) was made up of inmates who did not meet these criteria; and group III (10 males and 5 females) was selected from among normal high school and general college (junior college) students, matched with the other subjects for age, intelligence, and socioeconomic background.

The experimental hypothesis was that group I subjects would not easily develop anxiety in the laboratory, that they would show abnormally little manifest anxiety in real-life situations, and that they would be relatively incapable of *avoidance learning* in the laboratory (see pp. 129–130). To test the last part of this hypothesis, Lykken took a GSR measure of the blindfolded subjects, who were seated in the lab, while administering

to them buzzer (CS)–shock (US) combinations. He found that group I showed significantly less GSR reactivity to the CS than the other two groups. Of all the tests used, according to Lykken (1957, p. 10), this was the most important one because it showed that if a person "does *not* produce a GSR to a stimulus, one can be sure that he has not 'reacted emotionally' to that stimulus."

In the avoidance conditioning situation primary psychopaths (group I subjects) showed the least avoidance, and hence the least anxiety; neurotic and other types (group II) were next in amount of avoidance exhibited; and the normals (group III) showed the most avoidance behavior. These results suggest that primary sociopaths are autonomically less reactive than normals or secondary antisocial types.

To test the second part of this hypothesis—namely, that primary sociopaths have less real-life anxiety than others—subjects were administered such self-report questionnaires as the *Anxiety Index*, or AI, of the MMPI (Dahlstrom et al., 1972), the *Taylor Manifest Anxiety Scale* (Heineman, 1953; Taylor, 1953), and an "anxiety scale" especially constructed by Lykken for this study. The results on all tests except the last were that group II, as would be expected because of their neurotic anxiety, achieved the highest anxiety scores, with group I, unexpectedly, showing slightly higher scores than group III. But on Lykken's special anxiety scale, the primary psychopaths showed the least anxiety, the scores being significantly lower than those of normals, with the neurotic and other sociopaths falling somewhere between the primaries and normals.

In another ambitious study, Hare (1968a) tested the hypothesis that primary psychopaths are both sympathetically and parasympathetically underreactive (see Chapter 8). Accordingly he measured skin resistance, heart rate, digital vaso-constriction, and respiration rate of three groups of prisoners. This was, again, a well-designed study because *primary* and *secondary* psychopaths were differentiated and a third group of nonpsychopaths was used. Physiological measures were taken under several conditions: during the resting state; while blowing up a small balloon (presumably requiring maximal autonomic reactivity); while listening to a series of fifteen 900-cycles-per-second tones followed by a sixteenth novel tone; and while solving a series of simple arithmetic problems. His findings strongly suggested that levels of autonomic reactivity in the psychopathic groups were comparatively lower than in any of the other groups, at least during states of relative inactivity. In a second study, also well designed, Hare (1968b) measured the electroshock detection thresholds of the three groups of subjects, and he found, as Lykken had, that conditioning the fear response is more difficult in primary than in other types of sociopaths or in normals.

The findings of these two studies by Hare, when considered together with those of Lykken, support the hypothesis that primary psychopaths are both sympathetically and parasympathetically underreactive. This, in turn, supports the clinical observations of Cleckley (1964), Karpman (1961), and others who have described psychopaths as physiologically unresponsive in situations ordinarily considered emotional.

A word of caution, however: when one deals with a primary psychopath in the laboratory, one is not experimenting with just another laboratory subject. In this regard, Lykken (1968) and Hare (1970) have speculated that psychopaths are likely to view experimental situations as more of a game than a threat. This means that in their experiments, primary psychopaths might have accepted the challenge of the "lie detector and [were] motivated to 'beat' the device as a matter of pride, therefore showing a mild degree of (nonanxious) excitement throughout this part of the experiment" (Lykken, 1968, p. 173).

Hereditary Determinants. What part does heredity play in determining both the clinically and experimentally observed differences between sociopaths and others? This question has repeatedly cropped up in discussions of the etiology of the other disorders, and, again, we must admit that no definitive answers have as yet been uncovered. Nevertheless, some interesting leads for a genetic hypothesis are available. Most of them were obtained from twin studies and, since 1965, from findings showing that there is an extra Y chromosome present in some male criminals. As we noted in Chapter 5, however, the evidence linking the extra Y chromosome to crime is extremely weak.

Rosenthal, in an evaluation (1971) of the findings from twin studies, suggests that both heredity and environment are implicated in the development of criminal types, but concerning the role of genetics in primary psychopathic or antisocial personality, his conclusion is (p. 137): "We know all too little about the heritability of this personality type. Its study has been limited by the constant confounding of hereditary and environmental variables." Rosenthal then indicates that good adoption studies are needed to clarify this confusion.

The Psychogenesis of the Antisocial Personality

Psychogenic hypotheses have included parental, stimulus-response, and other environmental models of behavior. None of these, as we shall see, offers a definitive answer to the question of causation.

Evidence of Parental Influences. Among the most popular theories that attempt to account for the origins of sociopathy are those that relate the phenomenon to some form of familial influence. Early writers on the subject emphasized parental rejection (Greenacre, 1945; Haller, 1942; Partridge, 1930) and emotional deprivation (Bender, 1947; Bowlby et al., 1956; Davis, 1940; Freud and Burlingham, 1944; McCord and Zola, 1959); more recently, researchers have focused on the specific type of parental rejection and deprivation that may be responsible for the formation of sociopathy. For example, a survey by Oltman and Friedman (1967)

Table 16.2

A Comparison of Psychopaths with Other Psychiatric and Nonpsychiatric Groups on Incidence and Type of Parental Loss

		Incidence and Type of Parental Loss			
Psychiatric Group	Total N	Mental Illness %	Separation %	Death %	Total %
Psychopaths	301	0.7	27.9	20.6	49.2
Drug addicts	69	0.0	20.3	23.2	43.5
Psychoneuroses	363	0.3	14.9	25.3	40.5
Alcoholic states	1103	0.6	7.9	29.3	37.9
Organic conditions	341	2.3	11.4	22.9	36.7
Neurotic depressions	377	1.3	13.5	20.4	35.3
Schizophrenia	2921	2.8	8.9	23.4	35.0
Affective psychoses	829	2.4	7.1	23.9	33.4
Normals	350	0.0	7.4	26.9	34.3

Source: Adapted from Oltman and Friedman (1967).

indicates that sociopaths are much more likely than drug addicts, psychotics, and neurotics to have suffered from parental loss by separation than for other reasons (Table 16.2) and that the separations have predominantly involved fathers rather than mothers leaving the household. The importance of these separations lies in the emotional and physical disturbance that they cause.

Specific parent–child relationships have also been cited as important in the development of aggressive behavior (Becker et al., 1959; Sears et al., 1957). Most of these studies have indicated that mothers who are permissive toward aggressive acts by their children but also behave punitively toward those children tend to have the most aggressive children; and that when one parent is punitive and frustrating toward the child (possibly instigating aggression), and the other is lax about discipline, conditions are optimal for the development of an aggressive child.

That parental influences play an important role in antisocial behavior was further corroborated in an extensive study reported by sociologist Lee N. Robins in *Deviant Children Grown Up* (1966). Robins and her associates followed up 524 children who had been seen 32 to 37 years earlier in a child guidance clinic. This study also included 100 control subjects selected from public school records. The follow-up diagnosis of sociopathic personality was determined by demonstrating the presence of at least five of the symptoms listed below; it is apparent that not all of these subjects were of the "pure" antisocial variety (O'Neal et al., 1962):

poor work history
poor marital history
excessive drugs
excessive alcohol
repeated arrests
aggression or
  belligerency
sexual promiscuity
  or perversion
suicide attempts
marked impulsiveness
poor school history
  (with truancy)

financial burden
  on society
poor army records
vagrancy
numerous somatic
  symptoms
pathological lying
lack of friends
use of aliases
lack of guilt about
  sexual exploits
  and crimes
reckless youth

The findings of Robins's study suggest that the single most reliable predictor of antisocial behavior is growing up in a home in which the parents, particularly an alcoholic father, display sociopathic symptoms. These results are summarized in Table 16.3, where it can also be seen that when neither the father nor the mother was known to have behavior or psychiatric problems, about one in every seven children developed sociopathic symptoms as adults, and that the incidence increases to one in every three children when both parents exhibit antisocial behavior.

Modeling and Stimulus–Response Studies. More recent formulations have stressed the role of modeling and socialization in the development of psychopathy (Aronfreed, 1968; Bandura and Walters, 1963; Bandura, 1969; Buss, 1966; Ullman and Krasner, 1975; Wiggins, 1968; Yates, 1970a). For example, according to Buss (1966), two types of parental behavior may be important in the development of antisocial personalities. One is the parent who is cold and distant toward the child, permitting no warm, close relationship to develop. In this case the child who imitates the parent will also be-

Table 16.3
Parental Behavior and Offsprings' Diagnosis of Sociopathic Personality

Parents' Problems	Number[a]	Percentage Diagnosed Sociopathic Personality When	
		Father Exhibits	Mother Exhibits
Antisocial behavior			
Arrests	51; 22	35[b]	32
Chronic unemployment for reasons other than incompetence	92; –	34[b]	
Desertion	94; 25	33[b]	36
Excessive drinking	143; 19	31[b]	26
Failure to support	116; –	30[b]	
Extravagance	39; –	28	
Neglect of housekeeping	–; 99		27
Cruelty	93; 17	24	29
Illicit sex	80; 84	22	25
Other problems			
Incompetent worker	29; –	24	
Nervousness or mental disease	104; 221	18	19
Cold and unaffectionate	31; –	6[c]	
No known problems	141; 154	16	18

Source: L. N. Robins, Deviant children grown up. *Copyright* © 1966, *The Williams & Wilkins Co., Baltimore.*
[a] The first figure is the number of fathers showing this behavior; the second the number of mothers showing this behavior. Figures omitted when the number is less than 15.
[b] Significantly high.
[c] Significantly low.

come cold and distant. The second is the parent whose behavior is inconsistent in the way he or she provides affection, warmth, rewards, and punishment. In this instance the child lacks a consistent model to imitate, and consequently his or her concept of "self" remains diffuse and inconsistent.

An interesting variation of the inconsistency pattern is the bidirectional formulation suggested by Wiggins (1968). This hypothesis asserts that the child's maladaptive behavior, no matter what its source, may augment the very inconsistency on the part of the parents that in turn triggers the child's further maladaptive acts. For example in dealing with a difficult child the parents may try various disciplinary techniques, shifting to and fro between punishment and overindulgence until the "parents' inconsistent socialization practices . . . represent both a cause and effect of the child's maladaptive behavior, the parental and child behaviors reciprocally augmenting one another to culminate in a vicious spiral" (p. 325).

Still another variation on the modeling hypothesis is that of Bandura (1969, pp. 37–38). After citing research evidence indicating that people usually adopt for self-reinforcement those standards exhibited by exemplary models, he writes that

social behavior is usually regulated to some extent by covert self-reinforcing operations which rely upon symbolically generated consequences in the form of self-commendation, esteem-enhancing reactions, or self-depreciation. Persons who have failed to develop self-monitoring reinforcement systems or those who make self-reward contingent upon skillful performance of anti-social behavior require considerable social surveillance.

Aubrey Yates (1970a), whose book *Behavior Therapy* we have already cited, makes the following broader generalization (p. 210):

Socialization essentially . . . involves training and conformity to certain rules of behavior laid down by society as essential to its own preservation, rules which often conflict with the child's natural urges, and this

training requires that the child's fear be aroused so that avoidance training can occur. Thus, when the child is about to perform an undesirable act, the . . . fear can then produce inhibition of the act at its inception.

And, by implication, the converse is also true. That is to say, if socially approved behavior is to occur and "conscience" to be developed, the individual must internalize those stimuli that promote conditioned fear during the socialization process (see Solomon, 1960; Solomon et al., 1968).

Socioeconomic Differences. Earlier, in our discussion of the sociological and psychological contributors to delinquency, we indicated that antisocial behavior is usually conceptualized as a lower-class phenomenon, and we suggested that this observation may be related to the fact that delinquent behavior is studied only among people of that social class.

Conclusions

What conclusions can we draw about the causes of sociopathy? EEG studies indicate that there may be similarities between brain wave patterns among sociopaths and children, suggesting that psychopathy may be due to cortical underdevelopment. But these studies are fraught with design problems that seriously impair their credibility.

Somewhat more solid research evidence exists that so-called primary psychopaths are autonomically less responsive than either secondary psychopaths or normals. Of course this raises the question of whether such unresponsiveness is inherited or acquired, and the evidence on either side is sparse. Neither the twin nor the chromosomal studies in support of the heritability of sociopathy were adequately designed, since the two types of studies tended to lump together in one group both the primary and the dyssocial sociopaths.

A similar confounding of diagnostic categories, unfortunately, has also occurred in studies that have attempted to link the disorder to environmental influences; but some good evidence exists that antisocial behavior (for example, delinquency) occurs more frequently among children of antisocial parents. The important role of modeling in such instances is unquestionable, and there are numerous types of parental behavior that foster various forms of antisocial acting-out. Whether such acting-out constitutes primary sociopathy, however, is questionable. Obviously more and better research is needed here.

Treatment

Traditional psychotherapy in the form of the "talking cure" has largely failed with antisocial personalities, because, in part at least, of their superficial emotionality, disparaging attitudes toward treatment, lack of insight, impulsive acting-out, and general lack of motivation for treatment. Cameron's opinion (1963), although more representative of the psychoanalytic than of other schools, reflects many clinicians' doubts about psychotherapy with sociopaths (pp. 652–653):

It should be said at the outset that current psychotherapy and psychoanalysis have little success in dealing with adults in this group . . . it is difficult for a therapist to tolerate situations in which therapeutic failure is so consistent and the disorder seems so completely irrational.

There are exceptions to this viewpoint, however, and there are carefully documented empirical studies on the success of some clinicians with psychotherapy of sociopaths (see Patterson, 1972; Persons, 1965, 1966; Persons and Pepinsky, 1966; Truax et al., 1966).

Not surprisingly, since the history of psychiatric opinion is closely linked with constitutional and biogenic explanations of sociopathy, *somatic* treatments of it abound. In one report electroshock therapy was used with 24 psychopaths (Green

et al., 1943). Each of these patients was given a series of at least five treatments. The reported result was that in some patients both behavior and EEG records improved; for other patients, however, no such improvement was evident, and in some cases the EEG actually changed for the worse. In addition to these ambiguous findings this report reflects the poor sampling procedures we noted earlier, which confused the diagnoses of primary and other forms of psychopathy. Its results, therefore, are of questionable value.

Pharmacological approaches have also been tried. Since abnormal EEGs had been observed, it was reasoned, perhaps anticonvulsant drugs could be successfully used in the treatment of sociopathy. Dilantin, the most frequently used anticonvulsant agent, was therefore tried and several enthusiastic testimonials about its efficacy were reported some 35 years ago (Silverman, 1943, 1944a). But inadequate diagnostic criteria for determining psychopathy, as well as slovenly research procedures, again raised serious questions about the significance of these findings.

Psychosurgery has been used (Darling and Sandall, 1953), prefrontal lobotomies having been performed on 18 "severe psychopaths." It was reported that 17 of these patients improved sufficiently to be able to return to their families. Again numerous objections can be raised to the diagnostic criteria that were applied in the sampling procedure and to the criteria of improvement that were used. Therefore available evidence does not warrant the use of such radical surgical procedures.

Behavior modification, although it holds considerable promise, has been applied only to the treatment of *delinquent* behavior and not to the cure of the antisocial personality. The distinction is an important one, as we have suggested, because not all delinquents are sociopaths. Delinquency is merely a wastebasket category that includes, along with primary sociopaths, persons whose behavior is antisocial but who may be drawn from a variety of diagnostic classifications. With these disclaimers in mind, we shall now discuss the application of behavior modification.

In one study, the subjects were 12 delinquent boys assigned to a special intensive training unit. The therapist (Burchard, 1967) rewarded their *prosocial*, or socially acceptable, behavior with tokens and punished their antisocial behavior with seclusion and loss of tokens. He defined antisocial behavior as responses "acquired, maintained, and modified by the same principles as other behavior," and therefore he rewarded or punished it systematically on a response-contingent basis (versus haphazard, indiscriminate, and noncontingent reinforcement or punishment). The therapist selected specific and identifiable behaviors to be reinforced or punished in the delinquents' daily environment. For example, in a workshop setting he administered tokens if the youngsters remained seated at a job and finished particular tasks; and isolated them or withheld tokens for not working. He then compared positive reinforcement procedures with aversive (punishing) ones and found that positive reinforcement was the more beneficial in controlling antisocial behavior. Similar findings of the greater worth of rewarding behavior were reported by others who treated delinquency in less programmed settings (Wetzel, 1966), as well as in similarly programmed laboratories (Cohen et al., 1968; Fixsen et al., 1973; Tyler and Brown, 1967).

A quite different and somewhat unusual approach to developing prosocial behavior was used in studies by the Schwitzgebel brothers and their associates (Schwitzgebel, 1960, 1961, 1963, 1964, 1967; Schwitzgebel and Kolb, 1964; Schwitzgebel et al., 1964). In one of these studies (Schwitzgebel and Kolb, 1964) chronic delinquents were cajoled into coming to the laboratory to tape-record interviews. During these interviews socially acceptable verbalizations were reinforced. The results, over a period of one year of treatment, showed significant declines in the number of arrests and prison terms for this group compared with an untreated group of delinquents.

In a second set of studies (Schwitzgebel, 1967, 1969) similar procedures were used to compare three groups of delinquents. In the first study one group was given positive reinforcement for statements of concern about other people and for dependable and prompt arrival at the laboratory; the second group was given negative contingencies for hostile statements about people and positive reinforcement for socially acceptable nonverbal behavior; and the third group served as controls,

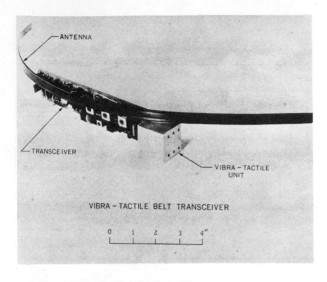

VIBRA – TACTILE BELT TRANSCEIVER

Figure 16.1
*Therapist-controlled positive reinforcement was provided by
Robert L. Schwitzgebel for juvenile delinquents. This
picture shows the miniature two-way radio unit housed in
a wide leather belt; it also shows a subject wearing the
belt. The therapist usually sends messages to the
delinquent by activating a small coil on the receiver's unit
that is transmitted as a tap on the abdomen, accompanied
by a small light.*

(Courtesy Robert L. Schwitzgebel)

being seen only twice, once at the beginning and
once at the end of therapy for experimental
groups. The results indicated that there was a significant increase in prosocial behaviors if it was followed by reinforcement and that there was no decrease in antisocial behavior if it was followed by
punishment. In the second study prosocial behaviors were shaped by positively reinforcing the delinquents via a two-way system of radio communication, housed in the recipient's wide leather belt.
By virtue of this system, the delinquent can be
"tuned in" by the receiving unit, which transmits
messages from the therapist in the form of taps in
the delinquent's abdominal region (see Figure
16.1). For a more complete description of behavior
therapy, see Chapter 23.

In summary the treatment of antisocial behavior has mainly been attempted with five procedures: psychotherapy, behavior modification,
psychosurgery, drugs, and electroshock therapy.
Behavior therapy is the most recent and perhaps
most promising of these approaches, although it
has not been applied to purely characterological
disorders.

Summary

The antisocial personality is a puzzle for psychologists because, even though his or her behavior is
unmistakably maladaptive and irrational, the antisocial personalities share none of the symptoms of
people with other behavior pathologies. Their
characteristic traits include getting into constant
trouble with the law, inability to form loyal relationships, selfishness, egocentricity, guiltlessness, low frustration tolerance, unreliability, and
impulsive and destructively aggressive behavior.

There seem to be two kinds of antisocial personalities: one is characterized by unsocialized aggression and is often called a primary, or endogenous (originating from within), sociopath; the
other is marked by socialized delinquency and is
referred to as a dyssocial, or exogenous (from
without), sociopath.

These distinctions, however, are often blurred in the research literature. At the present time research indicates that the origins of sociopathy lie in the complex interaction of biological and environmental forces.

Psychotherapy with sociopaths has presented a special set of problems because of their emotional shallowness, egocentricity, and inability to relate to others on any but the most superficial plane. Some success has been reported by behavior therapists in promoting prosocial behavior and in extinguishing antisocial acts. Unfortunately these therapists tended to combine cases of primary and dyssocial forms of this disorder, thus obscuring the real significance of their results.

Terms and Concepts to Master

- Adaptive delinquency
- Antisocial personality
- Dyssocial personality
- Maladaptive delinquency
- Moral insanity
- Primary sociopath
- Prosocial behavior
- Superego lacunae

17 Aggression and Violence

They were supposed to go after what they called a Viet Cong whore. They went into the village and instead of capturing her, they raped her—every man raped her. As a matter of fact, one man said to me later that it was the first time he had ever made love to a woman with his boots on. The man who led the platoon, or the squad, was actually a private. The squad leader was a sergeant but he was a useless person and he let the private take over his squad. Later he said he took no part in the raid. It was against his morals. So instead of telling his squad not to do it, because they wouldn't listen to him anyway, the sergeant went into another side of the village and just sat and stared bleakly at the ground, feeling sorry for himself. But at any rate, they raped the girl, and then, the last man to make love to her, shot her in the head.

The Winter Soldier Investigation: An Inquiry into American War Crimes (Beacon Press, Boston, 1972)

A more maladaptive form of behavior than violence would be hard to find, whether we view it from the standpoint of the individual, or of the species, or of society. It harms the offender as well as the victim, and the emotional suffering it produces often extends far beyond the offender and the victim. Everyone complains about the problem, and many are ready with solutions— usually violent ones.

Violence is also one of those issues on which people divide along predictable philosophical lines. Those who subscribe to an "evil human nature" model see violence as an innate disposition programmed into every person's genes and reducible only by keeping human impulses under the strictest rein and diverting energy through harmless safety valves. Those who subscribe to a "good human nature" model see violence as a result of thwarting natural impulses, and see the solution in terms of freeing those impulses. Those who subscribe to a "no human nature" model see violence as a result of ineffective socialization and believe it can be prevented by applying the right techniques.

Unfortunately most of the literature on the subject suffers from a confusion of terms and an absence of clear and consistent definitions. *Aggression* can mean violence, assertiveness, hostility, or anger, and a common fallacy is to cite a fact about one of these to make a point about another while calling them both aggression. Not only is the distinction among anger, hostility, and violent impulse often lost, but even the difference between feelings and behavior is slighted.

Erich Fromm, in a book called *The Anatomy of Human Destructiveness* (1973), tries to overcome this confusion by sorting out the many referents of the term aggression and examining each as a distinct phenomenon with its own etiology. Fromm also distinguishes between *benign* (helpful) and *malignant* (hurtful) aggression, and discusses the derivation of the word *aggress,* which originally meant "to step forward," just as *regress* means "to move backward." Assertiveness is thus the original meaning of aggression. Fromm suggests that the connotation of violence grew out of the fact that an army must move forward to attack.

Since assertiveness is adaptive behavior, we shall not discuss it here. Nor will we examine the subject of violence to the spirit, important as it is, though we touch on it in several other chapters. We shall focus our attention here on behavior intended to do physical harm.

Instinct Models

During the late nineteenth and early twentieth centuries human behavior seemed easily explainable in terms of instinct and heredity. If people behaved in a certain way, their behavior was presumed to be driven by an instinct—an inherited inner tension that could only be relieved by a specific outward action. In the heyday of instinct theory, many psychologists assumed that different actions must express different instincts, and the catalogues of instincts swelled to the hundreds. If people were thieves, they were inborn thieves. If they herded sheep, it was because they were innate sheepherders. We can easily see the absurdity of such thinking, but the models that shape our perceptions now were not current then.

The instinct boom collapsed in the 1920s,

Is Aggression Psychopathology?

One way of looking at the relation between aggression and psychopathology is to administer a personality test to persons judged by their peers as high or low in aggressiveness and to find out whether these two groups differ in measures of psychopathology. This was done in a study (Lefkowitz et al., 1977) in which boys and girls were administered the Minnesota Multiphasic Personality Inventory (MMPI). In terms of IQ and social class, the findings for boys were as follows:

(1) low-aggressive boys have higher IQs;
(2) high-aggressive boys have a larger number of physical complaints;
(3) high-aggressive boys have a greater tendency toward antisocial behavior;
(4) high-aggressive boys display more obsessive-compulsive behavior;
(5) high-aggressive males admit to more bizarre behaviors.

The results for girls showed some similar tendencies, but also displayed some distinctive features:

(1) high-aggressive females are more masculine in interests, attitudes, and behaviors;
(2) low-aggressive girls tend to withdraw from social interaction more than high-aggressive girls;
(3) high-aggressive females tend to say more unusual things about themselves.

The authors of this study emphasize that the obtained relationships between psychopathology and aggression are not necessarily relevant to the incidence of violent acts among mentally ill persons. According to the reports of the National Task Force on Individual Acts of Violence (Mulvihill and Tumin, 1969, p. 444), "All studies to date indicate that the mentally ill are no more likely than the general population to be involved in such crimes as assault, rape, or homicide." Moreover, none of the boys or girls in the above study was diagnosed as mentally ill.

Source: Lefkowitz et al. (1977).

aided no doubt by some persuasive criticisms by the behaviorists of that time. Freud was then just beginning to think in terms of a death instinct as the polar opposite of a life instinct, but he was a good deal more cautious in his approach to instinct than many of his contemporaries.

Except for its limited application in Freudian theory, instinct became unfashionable until it came into vogue again in the 1960s, spurred by a series of popular books (Lorenz, 1966, 1974; Ardrey, 1961, 1966; Storr, 1968; Morris, 1968).

The Freudian Model

In contrast to most earlier instinctivists, Freud tried to limit the notion of instinct to a simple dualistic system. At first he recognized only the sexual instinct and the instinct for self-preservation. Then with the publication of *Beyond the Pleasure Principle* (1953a) and *The Ego and the Id* (1927), he began to postulate a death instinct in opposition to the life-serving instincts of sex and self-preservation. He later (1953b) described the change as follows:

Starting from speculations on the beginning of life and from biological parallels, I drew the conclusion that, besides the instinct to preserve living substance and to join it into ever larger units, there must exist another, contrary instinct seeking to dissolve those units and to bring them back to their primaeval, inorganic state. That is to say, as well as Eros there was an instinct of death.

Against the drive to live there was a drive to die; against Eros there was Thanatos; against libido there was aggression. The events that changed Freud's perceptions are not hard to guess. He grew up during *la belle epoque*, a time of what seemed to be enduring peace. (There had not been a major European war since 1871.) Against this background the fury of World War I came as a stunning shock.

Freud saw the death instinct as a drive either to destroy oneself or to destroy others. Because it was an instinct, it would arise with or without an external stimulus. Its power could be reduced, but it could not be escaped. Powered by the libido, this drive is the cause of war and a cause for pessimism about humanity's future. In a letter to Albert Einstein in 1932 concerning war, Freud (1959c) argued against the feasibility of ridding human beings of their aggressive instincts. The diversion of aggressive impulses so that they would be expressed in other forms than war would be enough of an accomplishment (see Lefkowitz et al., 1977).

Like the earlier instinctivists Freud retained a hydraulic model of motivation: instinct likened to a fluid accumulating in a reservoir. By building up pressure—for example, in the form of bodily tension—it would sooner or later force its own release through specific forms of action. Freud's dualism avoided the proliferation of instincts that eventually proved an embarrassment to the early instinctivists, but it lost precision by ignoring the distinctions between different kinds of aggressive behavior. Moreover little experimental support can be found for the psychoanalytic theory of aggression as an innate force seeking vicarious expression. What evidence there is for such theorizing comes primarily from the analysts' clinical hunches.

The Lorenzian Model

In the Freudian model the dynamics of human motivation arise from the conflict between a life-serving and a death-serving instinct. The picture presented by Lorenz, Ardrey, Storr, and Morris is simpler: the human animal is innately destructive—a killer by instinct. Their view has frequently been likened to Thomas Hobbes's view of humans as innately depraved creatures whose natural state is war. For example, the Lorenzians assert that the aggressive drive is "still a hereditary evil of mankind" and that "an evil intraspecific selection must have set in" (Lorenz, 1966); that "it is no use supposing that we can change human nature into something pacific and gentle" and that "we know in our hearts that each of us harbors within himself those same savage impulses which lead to murder, to torture and to war" (Storr, 1968); that "man is a predator whose natural instinct is to kill with a weapon" (Ardrey, 1961); and that man's intelligence will never be capable of ruling his "raw animal nature" (Morris, 1968). It is not hard to see why Ashley Montagu (1973) calls this viewpoint "original sin revisited."

The reason for the popularity of such harsh protrayals of human nature is itself the subject of some speculation. The most commonly given explanation is that many people welcome the chance to deny responsibility for their own actions by simply saying, "my genes made me do it." And indeed, according to ethologist Konrad Lorenz, aggression is genetically programmed into every human. Arguing by analogy from the behavior of greylag geese and other birds and fishes (mostly in captivity), Lorenz postulates a hydraulic model of *action-specific energy* that builds up and eventually explodes, even in the absence of an external stimulus.

In lower forms of animal life, according to this hypothesis, innate aggression is a life-serving mechanism. It allows an animal to defend itself from attack and to achieve various other supposedly desirable ends, which we shall discuss shortly. This instinct to kill others usually does not cause an animal to kill members of its own species because, supposedly, other instinctual patterns provide escape mechanisms—ritualized fighting and appeasement gestures. But at some point in the evolution of the human species these protective devices were lost, weapons came into use, and the once life-serving instinct became cruel, evil, and destructive. Indeed, according to Ardrey, the human species emerged *because* weapons had been invented.

A more moderate ethological approach to aggression is that of Niko Tinbergen (1968). Tinbergen attempts to reinterpret Lorenz's idea of an internal urge to attack as the cause of aggressive behavior in animals and people (see Lefkowitz et al., 1977). He considers Lorenz's use of the term "spontaneity of aggression" unfortunate. In his view both instinct and external stimuli produce fighting. Thus fighting originates as much from the situation as it does from an aggressive drive. Moreover, there is a great deal of variability in aggressive drive and in the situational stimuli that combine to produce aggressive behavior. Therefore, according to this modified view, aggression is by no means reflexive; rather it is the result of a complex interaction between aggressive drive and environmental stimuli. In this respect Tinbergen agrees with Desmond Morris (1968) who, in *The Naked Ape*, proposes that aggressive acts are genetically governed responses to stimuli originating in others.

To see why the controversy over the innate aggression hypothesis has generated so much heat, we need only examine some of its implications. As we mentioned earlier, the Lorenzians see the aggression of lower animals as serving desirable ends other than defense. What are these desirable ends? By a remarkable coincidence they turn out to be values highly prized by political and social conservatives: social distance, dominance, competition, hierarchy, monogamy, nationalism, and private property. Humans too are inherently territorial animals in this model. By keeping each other at a distance and defending their "turf," Lorenz says, they survived on the available natural resources until about forty thousand or fifty thousand years ago, when they purportedly began to form tribes and to fight wars to defend their territory and resources. Now, the theory goes, we are all instinctive killers without any internal inhibitory mechanisms to save us from ourselves.

In case anyone might miss the most obvious implication, Lorenz spells it out repeatedly:

It is the spontaneity of the instinct that makes it dangerous. (1966)

Man must know that the horse he is riding may be wild and should be bridled. (1974)

Among the many phylogenetically adopted norms of human behavior, there is hardly one that does not need to be controlled and kept on a leash by responsible morality. (1966)

A formidable number of psychologists, cultural anthropologists, neurophysiologists, paleoanthropologists, zoologists and other behavioral scientists have taken Lorenz and his fellow instinctivists to task for their premises, their logic, their conclusions, and their supporting evidence (or lack of it). Many of these criticisms have been collected by Montagu (1973). Other critical works include Fromm (1973), Berkowitz (1970), Montagu (1976), Bandura (1973), Feshbach (1970), and Kaufmann (1970).

A complete list of the criticisms would fill several pages, so we shall mention only a few:

1. Lorenz's argument from analogy requires a huge leap of faith. The fact that he sees a similarity between the behavior of a fish in an aquarium tank and the behavior of humans does not establish a genetic connection, or even an instinctive etiology, for either behavior.
2. Aggression has been loosely defined, and the term is used to cover a multitude of actions that do not all have the same cause. Fromm (1973) points out that the term aggression can refer to accidental aggression, playful aggression, self-assertive aggression, defensive aggression, conformist aggression, instrumental aggression, vengeful destructiveness, ecstatic destructiveness, destruction

Aggression and Obedience to Authority

Under what conditions will ordinary human beings knowingly inflict pain on other human beings? One of those conditions appears to be (for many people) a command from authority to do so. This conclusion is pointed to by a series of now-famous studies conducted by social psychologist Stanley Milgram (1963, 1964, 1965) and later published in a book called *Obedience to Authority* (1974).

Milgram's subjects were hired to participate in what each was told would be an experiment to study the effects of punishment on learning. The subject was to be the teacher, and another subject (actually an accomplice of the experimenter) was to be the student. The student was directed to answer a series of test questions, and the teacher was directed to punish each wrong answer by pressing a button that (each teacher was told) would deliver an electric shock to the student. With each wrong answer the voltage was to be increased, from a level labeled "Slight Shock—15 volts" to one labeled

"Danger: Severe Shock—450 volts." The experimenter made it clear that the teacher was under orders and was expected to comply.

And 65 percent of the subjects did comply. As the supposed shock (no shock was actually delivered) reached higher and higher voltages, the "student" would cry out, plead for the shocks to be stopped, refuse to go on answering, and finally fall silent. The naive subjects (the teachers) often broke into a cold sweat, trembled, begged to be excused from the experiment—and continued to obey the experimenter. Even after being informed of the deception, some subjects were so severely troubled that they required therapy.

Another experimenter (Kaufmann, 1968) found, in a series of follow-up studies, that most college students, when they become bystanders in a similar situation, do not attempt even minimal steps to interrupt or terminate the proceedings. As in Milgram's studies, these subjects based their compliance idolatry, sexual sadism, nonsexual sadism, and necrophilia.

3. The term "instinct" is loosely and inaccurately used. Lorenz has conceded this point, excusing it as a kind of "shorthand."

4. It is anthropomorphic to attribute human feelings and motivation to birds and fish simply because the observer sees a similarity in outward behavior.

5. No neurophysiological mechanism has been demonstrated or even identified as the locus of the alleged instinct.

6. Many events, such as paleolithic or neolithic wars, are assumed in the absence of evidence or in the face of contradicting evidence. Stone Age people did not live in an overcrowded world short of natural resources. They were few in number, and their natural resources were virtually limitless.

7. The Lorenzians ignore a wealth of anthropological data describing numerous thriving cultures that have a cooperative, nonviolent way of life.

8. Defensive aggression is only part of a system of "flight or fight" responses, in which flight is at least as likely as fight and often more adaptive, yet the Lorenzians do not posit a flight instinct.

Learning Models

External stimuli, which the Lorenzians discount, assume a significant role in learning theory. These stimulus–response approaches are somewhat less monolithic than the Lorenzian position, and few of them proceed from the radical behaviorist position that excludes any mention of inter-

on the ostensible demand characteristics of the alleged "learning experiment." Kaufmann later (1970) wrote that these findings strongly supported the thesis that aggression often occurs as a function of situational demands (rather than as a response to frustration or an expression of anger).

Milgram's and Kaufmann's results can, of course, be interpreted in more than one way. They also raise some interesting questions. Why, for example, does it not occur to most people that they have the option of openly disobeying authority when ordered by that authority to commit an act perceived as immoral? Does the influence of authority block out even the recognition that that alternative exists? In a way this is analogous to the Zen master's double-bind described by Bateson (1972, p. 208): "If you say this stick is real, I will strike you with it. If you say this stick is not real, I will strike you with it. If you don't say anything, I will strike you with it." In this case the aim of the double-bind is therapeu-

tic, and—as Bateson points out—the master might accept the response of simply taking the stick out of his hand. In the Milgram experiment the subject always has the option of simply refusing to push the button.

Milgram's study is relevant to, and was motivated by, the central issue of the Nuremburg War Crimes Trials: does the individual have the moral responsibility to disobey an order to commit an immoral act even when that order is issued by a legally constituted authority? The precedent-setting answer at Nuremburg was yes, and it was affirmed later in the trial of Adolph Eichmann and in the trial of William Calley.

One more question is raised by the Milgram and Kaufmann experiments: do most people cease to see violence as violence when it is done at the command of a legitimate authority and labeled as punishment? Certainly a study of the effects of legitimizing violence would be well worth pursuing.

nal states, although A. H. Buss argues (1961) that "*intent* is both awkward and unnecessary in the analysis of aggressive behavior."

The Frustration–Aggression Model

In 1939 Dollard and his associates wrote that "the occurrence of aggressive behavior always presupposes the existence of frustration and contrariwise, the existence of frustration always leads to some form of aggression." One of those associates, Neal Miller, later conceded (1941) that frustration could lead to a number of other responses besides aggression. Miller's revised position on the relation of frustration to aggression was that frustration results in an instigation to aggression but that the instigation may be too weak to cause aggressive behavior. Berkowitz (1969b) subsequently revised the model further, saying that a person's emotional state resulting from frustration may or may not be sufficiently strong to lead to aggression but environmental cues such as a threatening or angry gesture can increase the probability of an aggressive response.

Some doubt has been cast on the frustration–aggression model by studies with both humans and animals showing that aggression is only one of many responses elicited by frustration; by the fact that the terms "frustration" and "aggression" have become so loosely defined that any antecedent situation can be interpreted as frustrating and any response can be called aggressive; by the observation that aggression may occur without any visible or detectable antecedent frustration; by the fact that many aggressive acts, such as wars, result from calculated decisions rather than frustrations; and by the fact that the most frustrated people are not always the most aggressive.

The Social Learning Model

Aggression is effective behavior—it gets results. It is therefore likely to be reinforced at an early age. Whether acquired through imitation or shaping or a combination of the two, it can be seen as a learned response like any other learned response, and its sources can be found in the matrix of child-rearing and socialization.

Several experiments have been cited in support of this model, including a study of imitative aggression in nursery school children done by Bandura and his associates (1970). The 96 subjects, whose mean age was 52 months, were divided into the following four groups:

Experimental group 1, which observed live aggressive acts

Experimental group 2, which observed filmed aggressive acts

Experimental group 3, which observed aggressive acts in an animated cartoon

Control group, which observed no aggressive acts

There was a further subdivision into male and female groups. Half of each male and half of each female experimental group saw same-sex models; the other half saw opposite-sex models.

Experimental group 1 watched live models punching a "Bobo doll," pounding its head with a mallet, and kicking it around the room. Experimental group 2 watched the same people performing the same actions on film. Experimental group 3 watched an animated cartoon of a cat attacking a Bobo doll. Each group was then taken into a room in which there were toys—both aggressive and nonaggressive—and tested for the amount of both imitative and nonimitative aggressive behavior they showed in the absence of models. The control group was similarly tested. All groups, including the control, were frustrated before testing. The mean total aggressive scores were as follows:

Experimental group 1: 83

Experimental group 2: 92

Experimental group 3: 99

Control group: 54

Boys showed more total aggression, imitative aggression, and nonaggressive gunplay than girls, and subjects who had seen male models showed a larger amount of aggressive gunplay than those who had seen female models.

In the face of these and other experimental results it is hard to resist the conclusion that at least some violence is stimulated by observing violence. And if violence teaches violence, some serious questions are raised about the consequences of punishment, especially in view of a study by Berkowitz (1969), in which violence was more strongly stimulated by watching "justified" violence. But the effects of punishment on aggression are less than clear. The animal literature, according to one source (Reiss et al., 1977), suggests that the effects of punishment depend on many variables, including the nature of the punishment, its intensity, the type of aggression punished, the organism's prior learning history, and the availability of an alternative, non-punished response. Thus, under these varied circumstances, the effects of punishment have been both to increase and to decrease the punished response, depending on the preceding variables. The effects of punishment on aggression in young children have generally indicated that parental punishment for aggressive behavior increases aggression. But again the interaction between punishment and aggression is complex, as the following conclusion by Lefkowitz and his associates in the longitudinal study of the development of aggression (1977, p. 192) attests:

From our earlier work (Eron et al., 1971) . . . we found that punishment reduced aggressive behavior only for certain boys who were strongly identified with their fathers. When high identification was not present, punishment (especially physical punishment) was positively and strongly associated with aggression. . . . The [present] longitudinal data indicate that moderate punishment by parents in the long run produces less aggressive children than either no punishment or harsh punishment.

The Ventilation Hypothesis Versus the Circular Effect Hypothesis

Proponents of a hydraulic model of aggression believe that the accumulated aggressive energy is dissipated, or ventilated, in the violent act. They also believe that aggression can be ventilated by participating in, or even watching, contact sports such as football or soccer (Lorenz, 1966; Ardrey, 1966; Storr, 1968). Learning theorists, on the other hand, argue that the violent act, instead of ventilating the violent impulse, reinforces it,

Anonymity and Aggression

Sometimes people choose to enter a situation of anonymity (and unaccountability) through being part of a group. Examples of chosen anonymity are seen in the exuberance (and often destructiveness) at large conventions, as well as in fraternity hell-nights, costume parties, the Mardi Gras, and Ku Klux Klan activities. . . . Anonymity is but one of many conditions that can foster the subjective state of deindividuation, with its weakening of the usual controls that restrain impulsive and antisocial behaviors. . . . If anonymity is conducive to deindividuation and, in turn, to greater susceptibility to aggressive and other antisocial actions, it is in society's interest to discover what conditions prevent deindividuation and foster individuation instead (Zimbardo and Ruch, 1975, pp. 634–635).

Diffusion of Responsibility

In 1964, early one morning in the streets of Kew Gardens, New York, an assailant repeatedly attacked and then stabbed Kitty Genovese as she screamed for help that never came. A subsequent investigation disclosed that about one-fourth of her neighbors had witnessed the attack. None of these neighbors came out of their apartments to help, nor did any call the police—even after the attacker had fled and had left Ms. Genovese to die. This apparent indifference of neighbors toward someone in distress was blamed by some people on the reputed indifference of New Yorkers toward their fellow citizens.

Two social psychologists, John Darley and Bibb Latané (Darley and Latané, 1968; Latané and Darley, 1968, 1970), suggest that one reason for the failure of each person to act was his or her awareness that a large number of other people were also watching, a condition that permits each onlooker to reason that someone else will probably take action and that therefore one does not need to act. Darley and Latané call this *diffusion of responsibility*. They believe it occurs when onlookers are physically separate from one an-other, unable to communicate directly, but aware of the presence of other onlookers.

In an experiment designed to test this hypothesis, Darley and Latané recruited male college students to participate in a discussion group. The experiment was conducted in such a way that at times subjects could communicate with other participants, and other times they could not. During a conversation the subject suddenly heard another participant, in still another room, who was apparently in distress and perhaps experiencing (it was suggested) an epileptic seizure.

The results were revealing and confirmed the investigators' expectations. Of the subjects who believed that they were the only people to overhear the emergency, 85 percent reported it to the experimenter. Of those who believed there was one other bystander, only 62 percent reported it. Among those who believed there were four other witnesses, only 31 percent reported it. Hence there seemed to be a diffusion of responsibility directly proportional to the number of witnesses to an emergency.

stimulating more violence—hence creating a circular effect.

Numerous experiments, including the one by Bandura and his associates that we cited earlier, appear to support the circular effect hypothesis. Berkowitz (1970) reviews a number of these studies, including several done in his own laboratory. These studies showed, for example, that watching "justified" violence increases aggressive behavior, that identifying with the winning side in a fight increases aggressive behavior, that the presence of guns heightens aggressive behavior, and that seeing someone injured reinforces aggressive behavior.

As for watching athletic contests as a safety valve for aggression, that too has been studied, and once again the evidence supports the circular effect hypothesis. Not only do sports events not prevent wars and riots, they may even instigate them. A referee's decision in a soccer match in Lima, Peru, in May 1964 precipitated a riot in which several spectators were killed. And a soccer match between El Savador and Honduras erupted into a war between those two countries

(Lever, 1969). Numerous other examples are cited in a study by Goldstein and Arms (1971).

Also supporting, and refining somewhat, the circular effect hypothesis is an experiment in which Feshbach (1972) tested the differential effects on aggressive behavior of real versus fantasy film depiction of violence. In this experiment 40 grade school children were shown a six-minute film of a campus riot in which police march in formation to attack and arrest the campus demonstrators. Half the children were assigned to a "reality" group: these children were told that they would be shown a newsreel of a campus riot. The 20 subjects in the "fantasy" group were told that the film they would view was part of a movie about a campus riot made by a Hollywood studio. Thus the same film was used for both groups, but the instructions were different. The measures of aggression consisted of several psychometric devices and a behavioral index of aggressive actions.

The results of this experiment reflected large differences between the reality and fantasy depictions of violence. Children who thought the film was a newsreel became significantly more aggressive than the control group; children who thought this same film was fictional were significantly less aggressive than the controls. Moreover there was an increase in anger arousal *without* an increase in aggressive behavior even when the children believed that the film was fictional. These findings led Feshbach (1972, p. 340) to conclude that "when an event is fictional, subjects can 'leave their feelings in the theater' . . . the 'message' of a newsreel, however, goes beyond the context in which the film is observed. By definition, the newsreel has meaning for events beyond the theater or living room. . . . We suggest that the observation of socially approved . . . 'real violence' . . . generalizes to 'real' aggressive behavior."

A Neurological Model

As persuasive as it is, the social learning model does not explain all aggressive acts. For example, among isolation-reared female rhesus monkeys the few who are able to procreate become punitive mothers, and their offspring later become aggressive. Social learning theory can account for the behavior of the offspring but not for that of the mother, who was cut off from the social situations in which aggression could have been learned by imitation or shaping. Furthermore, even though normal human behavior does not seem to fit the Lorenzian notion of spontaneously exploding innate aggression, some violent acts *are* spontaneous outbursts that apparently cannot be accounted for by learning processes.

A case in point is the incident in which Charles Whitman shot 14 people to death and wounded 31 others at the University of Texas. Whitman had a fast-growing tumor near a part of the brain called the *amygdala*. The significance of this is that electrical stimulation of the *amygdala* has been shown to elicit instantaneous hostile feelings and violent behavior, which experimenters are able to turn on or off with the flick of a switch (King, 1969). In other experiments aggression has been elicited in a cat by stimulation of the reticular formation of the brain (Sheard and Flynn, 1967; cited in Prescott, 1975) and inhibited in psychotic patients by stimulating the septal region (Heath, 1963).

Other studies of brain functioning and aggression also suggest that the temporal lobes and the limbic system of the brain are integrally involved in both eliciting and suppressing aggressive behavior (Boelkins and Heiser, 1970; Mark and Ervin, 1970; Moyer, 1971). As indicated by the implantation of electrodes in these areas, the focus for eliciting or suppressing is extremely narrow, often within fractions of a millimeter. Stimulation of certain regions of the hypothalamus or the amygdala will provoke rage attacks in cats and other organisms, whereas the removal of these organs will reduce aggression.

How are these brain centers activated or de-activated in real life? No one knows, but some researchers are studying developmental processes, especially in the first months of life, for clues to factors that may predispose a person to violence. One of the starting points for this research is the work of the Harlows with maternal deprivation in monkeys, which we discussed in Chapter 6. These studies demonstrated that the infant–mother bond was based on warmth and softness rather than nourishment. The emotional value of nursing, in other words, is not in the milk the infant receives but in the intimate contact with the mother (Harlow and Harlow, 1962).

Monkeys reared without such contact show a variety of abnormal behavior, and those who become mothers batter their offspring. A similar situation among humans was revealed in a study by Steele and Pollack (1968), who found that the parents of battered children had a history of maternal and somatosensory deprivation. Without exception the parents studied had been deprived of physical affection in their own childhood, and almost without exception the battering mothers had never experienced orgasm. Sexual adjustment of the battering fathers was also poor.

Citing these studies and his own cross-cultural study of 49 cultures showing a high correlation between the absence of violence and the presence of either physical affection in infancy or sexual permissiveness in adolescence, Prescott (1975) has proposed a pleasure–violence reciprocity hypothesis:

Laboratory experiments with animals show that pleasure and violence have a reciprocal relationship, that is, the presence of one inhibits the other. A raging, violent animal will abruptly calm down when electrodes stimulate the pleasure centers of its brain. Likewise, stimulating the violence centers in the brain can terminate the animal's sensual pleasure and peaceful behavior. When the brain's pleasure circuits are "on," the violence circuits are "off," and vice-versa. Among human beings, a pleasure-prone personality rarely displays violence or aggressive behaviors, and a violent personality has little ability to tolerate, experience, or enjoy sensuously pleasing activities. As either violence or pleasure goes up, the other goes down.

Prescott, a developmental neuropsychologist for the National Institute of Child Health and Human Development, believes that "sensory stimulation is a nutrient that the brain must have to develop and function normally." He points out that the brain is immature at birth, with new brain cells developing up to 2 years of age, and that "the complexity of brain cell development continues up to about 16 years of age." At about 3, 7, 11, and 15 years, growth spurts occur in the brain. The final growth spurt, according to some data, may be prevented by early sensory deprivation.

That sensory stimulation is a factor in brain growth has also been demonstrated in experiments showing that rats reared in a sensory-enriched environment have a larger number of branches of dendrites in the visual cortex than rats reared in an ordinary or a sensory-deprived environment (Volkmar and Greenough, 1972). Prescott contends that isolation rearing of an animal interferes with normal development of the cerebellum and that the cerebellum is involved in violent and aggressive behavior. Cerebellar surgery can change the behavior of isolation-reared rhesus monkeys from aggressive to peaceful, and stimulation of a part of the cerebellum called the cerebellar fastigial nucleus can induce predatory killing behavior in an ordinary house cat.

The sense that is deprived in isolation rearing is the sense of touch. Whether Prescott is correct in equating sensory stimulation with body pleasure may be arguable, at least until the effects of painful and neutral stimuli on brain development have been compared with those of pleasurable ones. No one should be astounded, however, at the suggestion that body pleasure may be biologically adaptive.

Aggression and Hormones

Males have long been observed to be more aggressive than females, and that difference has not been accounted for by sex-role learning (see Maccoby and Jacklin, 1971). Consequently some researchers have investigated the possibility of a connection between male hormones and male aggressiveness.

In animal experiments, treating pregnant rhesus monkeys with testosterone during the second quarter of fetal development resulted in more masculinized and aggressive social behavior in female offspring (Young et al., 1964). Castration has been shown to reduce fighting in animals (Sigg, 1968), and the introduction of estrogens has been shown to reduce aggressive behavior in males.

Research with human subjects has shown that the behavior of a majority of girls ($N = 10$) between the ages of 4 and 14 whose mothers received treatments with androgen-like hormones during pregnancy was classified as quite masculine and tomboyish (Ehrhardt and Money, 1967). These characterizations were based on sex-role preference tests showing that these girls selected boys' toys, showed outdoor interests, and had minimal interest in typical girls' activities and pursuits.

Finally, there is evidence from research among inmates in a women's prison showing that 62 percent of the crimes of violence were committed during the premenstrual week compared to 2 percent committed at the end of the period (Hamburg, 1966). In another study 49 percent of all crimes were committed by women during the menstrual period or premenstrum (Dalton, 1964), times during which there is a drop in the progesterone hormone level in the blood. In this connection it has also been noted that women who take oral contraceptives containing progestagenic agents are significantly less irritable (and perhaps less aggressive) than women using other forms of contraceptives or no contraceptives (Hamburg et al., 1968). But the physiological relationships between premenstrual tension and irritability and between estrogens in the bloodstream and irritability are far from clear, although they are suggestive. A great deal more research in this area seems needed.

Control of Aggression

Whether one favors the ventilation or the circular effect hypothesis, one thing is certain: aggression and violence must be controlled. The most common control of persistently violent behavior seems to be penal or mental hospital institutionalization. Available research (Lefkowitz et al., 1977) suggests, however, that aggression and violence do not decrease and perhaps even increase in these institutions. Moreover there is no evidence (Lefkowitz, 1975) that the unfocused treatment programs (work, education, religious activities, recreation, individual and group psychotherapy) usually provided in institutions actually mitigate violent behavior, nor that the programs that do reduce violence generalize to the community after an individual's discharge. More likely institutional experience that is not designed to modify a specific target behavior, such as aggression, will have no effect on this behavior in the community.

Behavior modification that focuses on specific violent target behaviors among juvenile delinquents has had some success (Davidson and Seidman, 1974), but the outcomes are ambiguous, since many of the studies conducted in this area have lacked adequate control group information. The available evidence suggests, however, that behavior modification is effective in reducing aggression in the institutional setting. Whether this reduction will generalize to the community is still an open question.

Treatment of violent behavior has also been attempted by psychosurgery and pharmacotherapy. In the 1950s, prefrontal lobotomy and temporal lobectomy were widely used techniques, but these have been largely replaced by stereotaxic surgery, a procedure in which tiny electrodes are implanted in the brain and guided to deep target structures by a stereotactic machine. The electrodes, which are inserted through a small opening in the skull, are used to destroy a very small number of cells in a precisely specified area. Mark and Ervin (1970), two users of the stereotaxic technique, claim that they can initiate and terminate violent behaviors in patients suffering from temporal lobe disease by stimulating different loci in the amygdala and hippocampus. These researchers summarize the state of the art in stereotaxis as follows (Mark and Ervin, 1970, p. 87): "There is a significant and growing body of clinical and especially surgical evidence to indicate that the production of small focal areas of destruction in parts of the limbic brain will often eliminate dangerous behavior in assaultive or violent patients."

The control of violence and aggression in state institutions has also been effected by the use of major tranquilizers classified under the phenothiazines (see Chapter 21). The minor tranquilizers classified under the benzodiazepines have also been shown to be fairly effective in reducing aggressive excitability, hostility, and irritability (Moyer, 1971).

Among children suffering from "hyperkinesis," temper tantrums, rage, and other outbursts of violent behavior have been reduced by certain psychomotor stimulants such as amphetamines and methylphenidate (Conners, 1972), but the meaning of the results is highly controversial (see Chapter 19).

But psychosurgery, pharmacotherapy, and —to a lesser extent—behavior modification have come under considerable criticism on technical as well as ethical grounds. From a technical standpoint the main criticisms are that behavior modification results are equivocal and, so far at least, not applied systematically and with scientific rigor to appropriately selected samples of subjects. Regarding psychosurgery, even with the new stereotaxic methods, not enough is known about the precise areas that need to be assaulted and stimulated in order to achieve optimal results with a minimum of damage to surrounding brain cell structures. And pharmacotherapy suffers similarly in that not enough is currently known about the physiochemical mechanisms that mediate aggression and violence, although theories about these matters abound (see Avis, 1974; Crane, 1973).

The ethical objections to these direct treatments of aggression and violence are that these are a form of mind control and that such techniques are used mainly against the poor, the black, the female, the helpless, and the institutionalized (see Holden, 1973). It is also often argued that these techniques, once developed for use with the institutionalized, can easily and indiscriminately be used for political or personal purposes. Certainly the disclosures of CIA research with mind control methods attest to the credibility of some of these objections.

Thus we see that the treatment and reduction of violence has thus far met with limited success. Lefkowitz and his associates (1977, pp. 207–210) endorse another approach—prevention. We agree with the conclusion to their extensive longitudinal study:

To produce a diminution in the level of violence, a broad change in values must be effected, hopefully through socioeducational means. In contemporary American society, aggression and violence are glorified and celebrated in major areas of endeavor: industry and commerce, labor, military, politics, and most forms of entertainment. When violence is successful in winning a cause, the perpetrators are reinforced and a model for emulation is created. . . . Celebrating violence by publicizing and glorifying . . . [it] must be regulated. [Since] aggression is a socially learned phenomenon . . . manipulation in certain ways of a set of social conditions will produce an aggressive individual, whereas manipulation of these conditions in another way will produce a nonaggressive individual.

Summary

Instinct models of aggression employ a hydraulic analogy: aggressive energy accumulates until body tension forces its release through aggressive behavior. Freud postulated a perpetual struggle between life-serving instincts (sex and self-preservation) and a death-serving instinct (aggression). The Lorenzians believe that aggression is programmed into the genes of every human and that it builds up until it explodes with or without an external stimulus. Learning theories include two models of aggression: the frustration–aggression model, in which aggression is a response to frustration, and the social-learning model, in which aggression is learned by imitation or shaping. A neurological model has been proposed in which aggression results from the failure of certain brain centers to develop properly because of inadequate sensory stimulation during the formative years. According to the ventilation hypothesis, performing or watching aggressive acts releases aggression, but most experimental evidence supports the circular effect hypothesis, which states that aggressive behavior incites further aggressive behavior.

Terms and Concepts to Master

Action-specific energy	Lorenzians
Circular effect	Sensory deprivation
Death instinct	Social learning
Frustration–aggression	Territorial animals
Hydraulic model	Ventilation

18 Mental Retardation

Mental retardation strikes children without regard for class, creed, or economic level. Each year sees an estimated 126,000 new cases. But it hits more often—and harder—at the underprivileged and the poor; and most of all—and most severely—in city tenements and rural slums where there are heavy concentrations of families with poor education and low income.

There are very significant variations in the impact of the incidence of mental retardation. Draft rejections for mental deficiency during World War II were 4 times as heavy in States with low incomes as in others. In some slum areas 10 to 30 percent of the school-age children are mentally retarded, while in the very same cities more prosperous neighborhoods have only 1 or 2 percent retarded.

There is every reason to believe that we stand on the threshold of major advances in this field. Medical knowledge can now identify precise causes of retardation in 15 to 25 percent of the cases. This itself is a major advance. Those identified are usually cases in which there are severe organic injuries or gross brain damage from disease. Severe cases of mental retardation of this type are naturally more evenly spread throughout the population than mild retardation; but even here poor families suffer disproportionately. In most of the mild cases, although specific physical and neurological defects are usually not diagnosable with present biomedical techniques, research is rapidly adding to our knowledge of specific causes: German measles during the first 3 months of pregnancy, Rh blood factor incompatibility in newborn infants, lead poisoning in infants, faulty body chemistry in such diseases as phenylketonuria and galactosemia, and many others.

John F. Kennedy, 1963

Underprivileged people and poor people are still the hardest hit by mental retardation. Sociocultural factors account for the majority of cases of mild retardation, and mild retardation represents an estimated 90 percent of the total number of cases of all kinds of mental retardation. Many of the organically caused cases are also linked to such socioculturally influenced factors as malnutrition and a lack of prenatal care.

Mental retardation is defined by the American Association on Mental Deficiency (AAMD) as "significantly subaverage general intellectual functioning existing concurrently with deficits in adaptive behavior, and manifested during the developmental period" (AAMD, 1973). Thus a diagnosis of mental retardation means not only low intelligence (that is, an IQ of less than 69), but also poor social adaptiveness and the presence of these impairments early in life.

Social adaptiveness, or SQ (social quotient), is often measured in terms of Doll's Vineland Social Maturity Scale, and more recently by the Adaptive Behavior Scale, prepared by the AAMD (1974). This scale provides ratings of the child's ability to perform a variety of nonacademic tasks. The rating is usually done by a person familiar with the child's behavior, such as a parent or teacher. Designed primarily for mental retardates, this scale can also be used with other kinds of problem children and with normals. Some typical Adaptive Behavior Scale domains are the following: independent functioning (eating, toilet use, cleanliness), physical development (sensory, motor), language, responsibility, socialization, violent and destructive behavior, withdrawal and hyperactive tendencies.

Levels of Retardation

The AAMD classification system recognizes four levels of mental retardation—mild, moderate, severe, and profound. The cutoff points are, of course, arbitrary, and the descriptions are necessarily generalizations in that not all mentally retarded are equally deficient in all areas. Not only is there general variability from individual to individual, but there is also considerable variability in each individual's levels of achievement on different measures (Hutt and Gibby, 1965). A study by Klausmeier and Check (1959) illustrates this point. Klausmeier and Check studied the rela-

tionships among 16 measures of physical, mental, achievement, and personality traits of children, about $9\frac{1}{2}$ years old, in low, average, and high intelligence categories. These investigators learned that children with low intelligence (IQ 55–80) did not differ significantly from either the average children (IQ 90–110) or the high-intelligence children (IQ 120 and higher) in most of these measures. But the low IQ group was lower than both the average and high IQ groups in reading achievement, arithmetic achievement, and language achievement. Also Klausmeier and Check found that variability within each child in three functions (reading, arithmetic, and language) was less for the average than for the low and high IQ groups.

Mild Mental Retardation (IQ 52–68)

People in this group occasionally also show signs of physical deformity or brain pathology. They are considered "educable" and are often placed in

---

An Alternative View of Retardation

The conceptualization of retardation by Dorothea and Benjamin Braginsky in their studies of children in institutions for the mentally retarded (1971) contradicts some widely held assumptions about mental retardation and leads them to the conclusion that "there is nothing particularly different about 'retardates' but that they are very much like everyone else" (p. 178). The Braginskys do not deny the importance of institutions for these children, because "it would be criminal to insist that they stay in a home where they are humiliated, abused, and degraded." But they do believe that it is even more criminal that the "channels society now provides . . . offer no respite for the child [who] . . . is viewed

by the staff as homogeneous, defective, maladaptive . . . [and is] degraded, and, at times, abused."

Moreover, the Braginskys believe that the mentally retarded as well as brain-damaged children are often "rejected because parents cannot [rather than do not want to] maintain or care for their children. But here again, there is no place for such children except the institutions for the retarded— thus, they are labeled, incarcerated, and treated for their retardation. There is no reason, however, to assume that mental retardation is a relevant concept even for brain-damaged children" (p. 179).

special learning disability classes. They often need extra help and supervision but are able to function in unskilled trades and to support themselves.

Moderate Mental Retardation (IQ 36–51)

Individuals in this category are considered "trainable," and most can perform useful work in a sheltered work situation. Many are awkward, poorly coordinated, and physically deformed. A substantial number are institutionalized.

Severe Mental Retardation (IQ 20–35)

Most of these people are institutionalized and need constant supervision. Sensory, motor, and speech handicaps are common, but with training many of these individuals can accomplish minimal amounts of self-care and personal hygiene.

Profound Mental Retardation (IQ less than 20)

Adaptive behavior is extremely limited in this group, although some individuals can be trained to use the toilet and to eat without help. Many have severe physical and neurological abnormalities. The average life expectancy of this group is low.

Abilities of Retardates

Abstract reasoning, creative thinking of any sort, and any kind of behavior that requires initiative are especially difficult, and in many cases impossible, for the mentally retarded. Consequently rote learning, which is the most primitive and often least effective kind of learning in the normal classroom, is frequently the only kind of learning possible with retardates. But again we cannot generalize about all retardates without also emphasizing that there are important differences within and between the various groups described above.

Thus mildly and moderately retarded individuals do much better on tasks requiring motor coordination and control than on those demanding verbal skills. The more concrete the task, the more effectively they function. Compared to severely and profoundly retarded people, the mildly and moderately retarded do not require continued custodial care. Such people usually can be taken care of at home, attend school or a job, and usually come into contact with a wide range of people and social agencies. Nevertheless, mildly and moderately retarded people can present continuing problems to their parents and families, to the community in which they live, and to themselves. The following five specific problem areas have been identified, particularly among mildly and moderately retarded children (Hutt and Gibby, 1965, pp. 59–67).

Speech and Communication. Even the most retarded of the group can communicate some of their needs to other people. Their vocabulary and range of interests are at a considerably lower level than those of average children, but they do respond to others and can express themselves in a limited way. The least retarded of the group do rather well on the whole, and are capable of initiating and sustaining adequate conversation.

Social Interaction. The most limited individuals of the moderately retarded group relate to other people only at the most elementary level. They tend to be totally lost in more complex social situations, being ill at ease and not perceptive of the nuances of interpersonal relationships. They do, however, learn the most important social customs and behaviors. They find it very difficult to participate in group activities, and are unable to comprehend fully the responsibilities of group membership. Those at the upper end of the mildly retarded group, however, can develop a considerable degree of social interaction skill. The kind of achievement they tend to attain at this upper level of ability seems to be dependent upon the treatment accorded them as children.

Self-Care. Individuals at the lower end of the moderately retarded group can learn, with difficulty, to take care of their bodily needs. They can learn to feed and dress themselves adequately, but only after much repetition. At this level they cannot "hold things in mind," and have little ability to undertake several tasks simultaneously. It is best, when teaching them as children to care for themselves, to focus on a particular aspect of self-care, then move on to the next when the first has been established.

People at the upper end of the group do not have such great problems in this area, but even they learn more slowly than normals, and need a thorough program of habit training for adequate self-care.

Motor Skills. This term refers to one's ability to use muscular control in handling or manipulating objects. People at the lower end of the intellectual scale have considerable difficulty in establishing such muscular and movement controls, particularly in the use of finer muscles. Gross muscular control is also difficult for them to establish, but eventually they gain adequate competence in this sphere. At the upper levels of mild retardation, these people can develop such skills to a relatively high degree. For example, in one study of such children (Hutt and Gibby, 1965, p. 65), a group of boys trained to play volleyball were able to do more than hold their own with a group of "average" high school boys of their chronological age and above.

Vocational Adjustment. Mildly and moderately retarded individuals are capable of holding a great many types of jobs. This is becoming increasingly apparent where such vocational education programs as sheltered workshops and other vocational services provide them with suitable preparation. Many former special-class pupils are successfully holding jobs as general and skilled factory workers, messengers, foundry workers, clerks, restaurant workers, butchers, farm helpers, and many others that do not require a high level of intellect.

Identification of Retardation

The clinical psychologist uses several methods for identifying and diagnosing mental retardation (see Clarizio and McCoy, 1976). These methods include (1) taking a familial and developmental history; (2) administering measures of intelligence; (3) assessing social competence; (4) identifying particular personality factors; and (5) evaluating performance and learning abilities. The first of these requires an account of the individual's development and family background. A majority of the mentally subnormal have close relatives who are also of below average intelligence. The search should include examining possible sources of trauma from illness and injuries incurred from birth on. Rounding out the history-taking is a detailed review of the developmental attainments of the individual. The mental retardate consistently lags in age of sitting up, feeding self, talking, and toilet training, and in fact tends to be slower in all anatomical, physiological, motor, and social functions.

Scores from scales of intelligence, as we noted earlier, are the single most commonly used criterion for rendering a diagnosis of mental retardation. In fact it was in the diagnosis of subnormality that psychological measurement first achieved general acceptability. Some psychologists and educators, however, rely too heavily on these tests, and as Guilford (1967) has noted, "intelligence" measurement deals with too narrow a range of mental processes. It is also essential to sample the person's perception of a given situation, attitudes about self, and effects on other people.

Another way of identifying mental retardation is to assess an individual's social competence. There is some justification for expecting a greater percentage of the mentally retarded to fail in meeting social demands and expectations. Identification of social incompetence is often difficult, however. What, for example, constitutes a good parent, a steady worker, or a solid citizen? As with the other indices below and those covered so far, social competence must be evaluated in the context of other information.

The search for the typical personality associated with mental retardation has not met with much success, but those traits most frequently cited include perseveration, a preference for dealing with the concrete and tangible, and dependency. But it has been pointed out that some of these characteristics may be a consequence of the experience of being retarded. For example, a study conducted by two psychologists suggests that dependency among some retardates is a consequence of the docile adjustment demanded by institutionalization (Zigler and Butterfield, 1968).

Finally, a difference in the ability to learn a task is the most consistently observed quality of the mentally retarded. As a result they take longer to learn, reach peak performance at a lower attainment level, and seem to retain less. The distinction becomes more obvious as the task becomes more complex and abstract.

Statistical Estimates

It has been variously reported over the years (President's Panel, 1962; Schlanger, 1973) that approximately 3 percent of the population of the United States is considered mentally retarded. This has usually been broken down to include 2.6 percent of the total population, or 85 percent of the mentally retarded, who are labeled "mildly retarded," 11.5 percent "moderately–severely retarded," and 0.1 percent "profoundly retarded."

Most of these estimates are based on the institutionalized retarded. Of the almost 6 million mentally retarded, about 200 thousand are in institutions. These are principally from the "severely" and "profoundly" retarded groups (Baumeister, 1970). Extrapolations beyond the institutionalized retarded may be biased, since there are usually selective debilitating factors that send the person to the institution initially and also keep him or her there.

The presence of emotional disturbance among the retarded has also interested some workers in this area. The best estimates suggest that about 10 percent of educable mentally retarded high school students have emotional problems (Gorelick, 1966), that 11 percent of children seen in an outpatient clinic have emotional disturbances or major personality disorders associated with mental retardation (Koch et al., 1969), and that 16 percent of institutionalized retarded residents revealed some type of neurotic or psychotic behavior (Penrose, 1963). Moreover many institutionalized retardates have been found to present a mixed diagnostic pattern as well as a diagnostically confusing pattern of retardation plus antisocial and rebellious behavior at early adolescence (Conrad, 1970).

In a recent summary of the relationship between mental retardation and emotional disturbance Balthazar and Stevens (1975) suggest that emotional disorders of one sort or another have been observed among 10 to 44 percent of the retarded, but that these estimates are somewhat flawed in that they were made among groups under stress (military discipline, prison environment, psychiatric hospital regimen). In addition it is often difficult to discriminate between organically induced psychoses and some forms of retardation associated with organic causes. These authors then conclude that "the knowledge is certain that there is a relatively high predisposition for emotional disturbance among the mentally retarded. The character and frequency of stress situations, however, as well as the problems incurred by definition, make it difficult to determine the degree of involvement with exactitude" (p. 9).

Organic Causes

In cases of profound, severe, or moderate retardation, the cause is usually organic. The problem may be a genetic or chromosomal abnormality, in which case it is determined at the moment of conception. Or it may result from disease or trauma either *in utero* or at the time of birth.

Chromosomal Anomalies

Down's syndrome, also called mongolism, is the most common single cause of mental retardation. It was first described by J. Langdon H. Down (1866), who saw such cases as furnishing "some arguments in favor of the unity of the human species." The typical physical features are almond-shaped eyes; thick eyelids; a broad, flat nose and face; short, broad neck and hands; stubby fingers; creases in the palms; L-shaped loops in the fingerprints; and a thick tongue that is sometimes creased. Retardation is usually moderate, and many mongoloid children are aided in their social adaptation by a tendency to be extremely playful and affectionate.

About 95 percent of the people having Down's syndrome have 47 chromosomes instead of the usual 46. The cause is a failure of chromosome pair 21 to separate in the egg. Union of the sperm and the egg thus results in a *trisomy*—three chromosome 21s instead of two.

Other anomalies involve the sex chromosomes. Instead of the normal XY (male) or XX (female) pair, a person may lack one member of the pair or have an extra sex chromosome, or even two extra ones. For example, a male with *Klinefelter's syndrome* may have XXY or XXXY. Klinefelter's syndrome is usually not noticed until puberty, when the testes remain small, and in some cases feminine secondary sex characteristics appear. In *Turner's syndrome* a female has only a single X chromosome instead of the XX pair. A few cases of *Triple X* have also been reported; these are XXX females. Intelligence is reduced in many chromosomal anomalies, but not in all. For example, only about 25 percent of males having Klinefelter's syndrome are retarded, and their retardation is usually mild or moderate.

Genetic Defects

Metabolic disorders sometimes result from the failure of genes to direct the body's production of certain enzymes. The absence of an enzyme may influence the formation of the embryo, or it may not begin to have an effect until after the baby is born. An example of the second type is *phenylketonuria* (PKU), a rare disorder occurring in about 1 in 20,000 births. The infant with PKU appears normal at birth, but lacks a liver enzyme needed to convert phenylalanine, an amino acid found in protein foods, to tyrosine. The phenylalanine and a derivative, phenylpyruvic acid, accumulate in body fluids and cause brain damage. The first signs may be vomiting, seizures, or a strange odor in the urine, or they may be symptoms of mental retardation—unresponsiveness or a defi-

ciency in motor development. Brain damage can be minimized by early detection and treatment. A test given four or five days after birth detects excessive phenylalanine in the blood. A diet low in phenylalanine maintained for the first six years shows great promise of alleviating some of the intellectual deficit (since brain differentiation is largely complete by the sixth year). If the disorder goes untreated, the child will be severely to profoundly retarded.

Maple Syrup Urine disease is a disorder of amino acid metabolism. Cerebral and muscular deterioration usually lead to death within the first year. *Gargoylism* is characterized by physical deformities, including an oversize head, bushy eyebrows, and a protruding forehead. Life expectancy sometimes extends into the teens.

Trauma

Disease or injury can cause brain damage at almost any stage of development. The embryo or fetus may be traumatized through the mother—for example if she ingests a toxic substance or is exposed to excessive radiation—or the infant may be injured during birth, as when anoxia results from tangling of the umbilical cord. Injury or illness may occur during the early years of life, when the brain is still differentiating. The following sources of trauma can lead to mental retardation.

Deficiency. If the mother suffers from malnutrition during pregnancy, the infant may be born with a smaller than normal number of brain cells, and extreme malnutrition in the developing child can have a similar effect. Protein deficiencies are especially harmful, particularly if they occur during the perinatal period. An iodine deficiency in the diet of a pregnant woman can cause the baby's thyroid glands to be underdeveloped or atrophied. The resulting thyroid deficiency causes *cretinism*, a deficit in both intellect and physical stature. The cretin is typically dwarflike, with coarse features and short, stubby limbs. Retardation is usually moderate to severe. The use of iodized salt has reduced the incidence of cretinism considerably. Early detection and treatment with thyroid gland extract can arrest the disorder.

Infection. Brain damage to the fetus can occur if the mother has German measles in the first trimester of pregnancy. The danger is greatest during the first month and diminishes during the second and third months. In cases of Rh incompatibility the mother's immune system forms antibodies that attack the red blood cells of the fetus, resulting in oxygen deprivation and brain damage. Rh incompatibility can be prevented by a vaccine given to the mother within 72 hours after her first childbirth, miscarriage, or abortion. When that measure is no longer possible, a complete blood transfusion for the baby can minimize brain damage. Meningitis contracted early in life can also cause mental retardation.

Injury and Prematurity. A small number of cases of mental retardation result from injuries during birth or early in infancy. Premature babies are more likely to be retarded than full-term babies, but the reasons are not yet understood.

Toxic Agents and Radiation. Mental retardation can also result from lead poisoning, carbon monoxide poisoning, or other toxic agents. Any toxic substance (including alcohol and drugs) entering the pregnant woman's bloodstream reaches the fetus effectively multiplied in dosage because of the fetus's much smaller body weight. Radiation from X-rays or any other source during pregnancy can cause mutation and retardation.

Cranial Abnormalities

Gross distortions in the shape and size of the head are another cause of mental retardation. *Microcephaly* is a condition in which failure of the brain to develop leads to a failure of the cranium to grow normally. Except for their small heads and receding chins and foreheads, microcephalics are normal in stature and proportions. The range of their retardation is from moderate to profound. *Macrocephaly* is an enlargement in brain size and weight and consequently in the size of the head. Symptoms include convulsions and visual impairment. *Hydrocephalus* is a condition in which brain damage and enlargement of the cranium result from an excess of cerebrospinal fluid accumulating inside the cranium. Early detection and surgical treatment can prevent severe brain damage.

Sociocultural Causes: Cultural–Familial Retardation

The more we learn about mental retardation, the more the data refute the myth that "feeble-mindedness comes from faulty breeding." Such a generalization would be unwarranted even for the organic causes we have already discussed, and those causes are involved in only a small percentage of the total. Most mental retardates, especially in the mild-to-moderate range, show no signs of cerebral or other physiological pathology. What these retardates do have in common, to a considerable extent, is low socioeconomic status. A disproportionate number of them (about three-fourths) come from homes that are characterized by economic, social, emotional, and intellectual deprivation. They are classified as cultural–familial retardates.

Cultural–familial retardation is due to an assortment of related factors. The child growing up in poverty is more likely to suffer the effects of malnutrition in both prenatal and postnatal life, to be left unattended, to ingest harmful substances, and probably most important of all, to be deprived of stimulation. Especially in the formative years, the brain needs stimulation that can only come from the child's physical, verbal, social, and intellectual contact with other human beings. When the father is absent physically or emotionally and the mother inaccessible physically or emotionally, the child's development suffers. Deprivation is repeatedly mentioned in studies of cultural–familial retardates. According to one such study (Tarjan and Eisenberg, 1972), these children are not exposed during infancy "to the same quality and quantity of tactile and kinesthetic stimulations as other children . . . the number of words they hear is limited, with sentences brief and most commands carrying a negative connotation."

Studies of cultural–familial retardates have also provided convincing evidence that IQ is not fixed and immutable. For example, as the cultural–familial retardate grows up, his/her IQ may decline. This frequently observed fact is consistent with a sociocultural etiology but not with a biological one. Furthermore, enriching the environment produces dramatic increases in IQ. In one study (Skeels and Dye, 1939) 25 individuals in an orphanage who had been classified as mentally retarded were divided into an experimental group of 13 and a control group of 12. Those in the experimental group were moved to an institution for the mentally retarded where they shared a ward with older (and less retarded) girls who gave them a great deal of love and attention. Those in the control group remained in the orphanage. Two years later, the average IQ of the experimental group had risen 27 points and the average IQ of the control group had fallen 26 points. A follow-up after another 20 years (Skeels, 1966) showed that the experimental group had achieved a much higher level of adaptation than the control group. Although open to some criticism on methodological grounds, these studies argue strongly for the importance of early stimulation in determining the individual's cognitive and social development.

Some Similar Diagnostic Categories

The retarded child may display all the signs and symptoms associated with other handicapping conditions, just as the child designated as emotionally disturbed, learning impaired, or deaf may also be functionally retarded. It is often not possible to separate one condition from another without lengthy and detailed diagnostic workups. Some of the literature on the most confusing overlapping categories is summarized elsewhere (Schlanger, 1973, pp. 10–12).

Infantile Autism

The autistic child may be differentiated from the retarded on the basis of early skilled performance, memory, and spatial and musical ability. The autistic child early displays an extreme self-isolation and an insistence on the preservation of sameness. Avoidance of contact with people is frequently observed among autistic but not among primarily retarded children. There is also a marked failure among the autistic to develop speech and language for communication purposes, and little interest in learning. This pattern is complicated somewhat, however, by the finding of one investigator (Eisenberg, 1958), who followed up 63 autistic children to an average age of 15, that 73 percent were mentally retarded (see Chapter 13 for a more detailed discussion).

Aphasia

Aphasic children are children who, because of brain injury (usually during the prenatal period), fail to develop the ability to use and understand language. Asphasics are often able to function at normal levels on tasks that do not require language expression and are therefore differentiated from retardates, whose performance is subnormal in most if not all spheres of functioning.

Childhood Schizophrenia

Many characteristics present in the schizophrenic are not so readily detected among retardates. These are hallucinations and delusions, return to earlier behavior, increased activity, immobility, and bizarre or stereotyped behavior. In addition the communication of the schizophrenic child is more disturbed and less related to the context of the environment than that of the retarded child (see Chapter 13 for a more detailed discussion).

Prevention and Management

Down's syndrome and other chromosomal anomalies can now be detected as early as the thirteenth week of pregnancy by a process called *amniocentesis*. A small quantity of amniotic fluid is obtained with a hollow needle. Fetal cells present in the amniotic fluid are then cultured and a chromosomal analysis is done. If Down's syndrome is present (trisomic chromosome 21), the mother may then decide whether to carry the baby to term or obtain a therapeutic abortion. PKU can be detected by a blood test usually given four or five days after birth, and brain damage can be minimized by a diet low in phenylalanine. Improved nutrition and prenatal care can reduce the incidence of cretinism and other conditions caused by deficiencies. When cretinism does occur, it can be arrested if it is detected immediately and treated with thyroid gland extract.

The effects of prematurity are just beginning to be understood. For example, a premature baby placed in an incubator that does not move is deprived of balancing, or vestibular stimulation normally provided during the last weeks before birth by the mother's movements. To provide that vestibular stimulation some hospitals now have incubators that rock. Cultural–familial retardation may be reduced to some extent by educating parents about the needs of children and a greater extent by eliminating poverty, but the most effective answer may be to increase the availability of competent day care for children who live in a deprived environment.

Whether to institutionalize a retarded child is always an agonizing decision for the parents. Generally the less retarded the child, the more it will benefit from the love and stimulation that a caring person can provide and that is extremely scarce in a crowded institution. But in extreme cases of retardation the strain on the family of providing full-time custodial care in the home may be too much for anyone to bear.

Whether a mildly retarded child should be placed in a special class for the educable mentally handicapped (EMH) remains an open question. Some studies (cited in Meyerowitz, 1962; Thurstone, 1959) suggest that retarded children in EMH classes are better adjusted socially than those who remain in regular classes. Jordan and deCharms (1959) attributed this better social adjustment to freedom from the fear of failure that pressure for academic achievement generates in the regular classroom. If this is true, according to Meyerowitz (1962), it should follow that EMH children will be more derogatory in their self-evaluations than normal children and that EMH children in regular classrooms, where feelings of inadequacy are fueled by competition with normal children, will be more self-derogatory than EMH children in special classes. Since self-esteem is a crucial factor in learning and in social adjustment, this kind of information is useful as well as interesting.

Meyerowitz tested the two hypotheses as follows: all the entering first-grade children in three geographic areas were tested to determine their IQs. The 120 children whose IQs were 60 to 85 were randomly and evenly divided into an experimental group assigned to special EMH classes and a control group remaining in the regular classroom. A third, "criterion" group of 60 normal children matched to the EMH group was also selected. At the end of the first school year all three groups completed the Illinois Index of Self-Derogation.

The results (Table 18.1) confirmed the first hypothesis and denied the second. Both groups of retarded children attributed more self-derogatory statements to themselves than normal children did, but the children in the EMH class chose nine self-derogatory statements in larger numbers than the retarded children in the regular classrooms, while those in the regular classrooms outnumbered those in the EMH classes on only two self-derogatory items. The implication of Meyerowitz's study is that placement of a mentally retarded child in a special learning disability class is detrimental to the child's self-image.

Treatment

Unfortunately institutionalization and management are often the treatment of choice for the retarded. Some authorities in the field (Thompson, 1972) attribute this state of affairs to the many misconceptions about retardation that have prevailed throughout history. Others (Balthazar and Stevens, 1975) believe that an attitude of defeatism among institutional administrators, psychiatrists, and clinical psychologists is responsible. Nevertheless the goals for treatment of the retarded should generally be similar to those for treatment of others in our society, and the institution, as we indicate in Chapter 25, may not be the treatment *place* of choice.

Present thinking on the education of the retarded emphasizes the maximization of each person's potential—or *self-actualization*. This objective is not different from that of therapy with normals except that in the case of retardates its attainment is far more complicated. As Hutt and Gibby (1965) repeatedly note throughout their book on the *Mentally Retarded Child*, retarded individuals are more likely to have been blocked in their development by their special handicaps (physical as well as intellectual), conditions in the home, and emotional withdrawal as a result of repeated failures. Such people need intensive and continuing assessment in order to discover possible assets that adverse experience may have covered or inhibited.

The retarded also need to learn *social competence*—for both interpersonal and intrapersonal adjustment, for effective relationships with others, and for internal harmony and peace of mind. These related objectives are intertwined in the sense that personal adjustment depends on interpersonal skills. Retarded people usually have a unique history of problems in their personal

Table 18.1
Proportion of Each Population Ascribing Each Derogatory Choice
To Themselves

	Population		
	Normal "Criterion"	Experimental	Control
1. The mother of this child does not miss him when he is in school	20	54[a]	52[a]
2. There are many things that this child does not know	9[b]	8[b]	28
3. The mother and father of this child wish he would do better	16[b]	35[b]	58
4. This child is going to have a hard time in school	2	27[a,b]	6
5. This child still won't be reading next year	2	21[a,b]	6
6. The mother of this child does not love him	5	27[a,b]	8
7. Kids like to make this child cry	9	33[a,b]	18
8. People do not say nice things about this child	9	3[a]	22
9. Some kids say nasty things about this child	11	35[a,b]	10
10. This child cannot run as fast as other children	27	41[b]	18
11. This child is not the same as other children	25	43[b]	20
12. The mother and father of this child are proud of his brother or sister	50	86[a,b]	66

Source: Reproduced by permission from Meyerowitz, J. H. Self-derogations in young retardates and special class placement, Child Development, *June 1962, 33.*
[a] Difference from normal group significant beyond .05 level.
[b] Difference from control group significant beyond .05 level.

adjustment—some of them unnecessary consequences of society's unfortunate attitudes toward them—and therefore special emphasis needs to be placed by the school or therapist on the simultaneous and complementary processes leading to overall general social competence. This form of training should prepare the educable retarded for community living. But since the trainable retardate will not be able to live independently as an adult, special emphasis must be placed upon minimal skills for living and working in sheltered environments.

Another reason for education and treatment is to teach vocational and economic competence. Hutt and Gibby (1965, pp. 339–340) state that "whether the expected outcome will be complete or relatively complete economic independence, or whether it will be living under sheltered and protected conditions, a major objective of all retarded individuals, educable and trainable, will be the attainment of some degree of vocational competence and economic productivity."

Psychotherapy

Much pessimism has been expressed over the years about the probable benefits of psychotherapy for retarded individuals. The attitude generally seems to have been that little could be done beyond institutional commitment and special education, although several therapists have reported successful outcomes of psychotherapy with emotionally disturbed mental retardates. But if individual psychotherapy has had only a qualified success, the behavioral approach to retardation (Bigelow, 1972) has enjoyed considerable success.

Unlike the conventional psychotherapies, with their emphases on insight, behavior modification is a teaching procedure (see Chapter 23). The aim is improvement, not insight. The behavioral approach attempts to teach individuals the specific skills that will help them function more effectively, enjoy a wider range of experiences, and continue learning other valuable skills. Particularly noteworthy have been behavior modification programs that have replaced disruptive with constructive group participation behavior, and taught mastery of numbers and letters as well as reading skills to the mentally retarded (Thompson and Grabowski, 1972). In special schools behavioral approaches have taught neatness in grooming, dependability, and punctuality to the mentally retarded—skills that may be val-

uable to them in postschool settings (Clarizio and McCoy, 1976). As a result of behavior modification the severely retarded, formerly confined to custodial institutions, now actively participate in programs in which their destructive or aggressive responses have been supplanted by self-care and language skills (Thompson, 1977).

The important ingredient of behavior therapy for retardates is that it always focuses on enhancing the individual's behavioral repertoire. No limit is set on what a person can learn, other than the limits of individual rate of progress. According to Bigelow (1972, p. 18), the behavioral approach focuses on teaching specific skills "that minimize the frustration and pessimism of the therapists who can readily see the learning occurring." And regardless of the "particular behavior . . . selected to be taught . . . it must be specified clearly and precisely." Thus having a precise behavioral goal is an essential first step for any successful treatment program.

Certain general principles of behavior modification must be applied in the home or in institutionalized settings if therapy is to be effective. These principles, formulated by several therapists (Baumeister, 1967; Bucher and Lovaas, 1968; Gardner, 1970), are as follows:

1. *The desired response must be potentially available.*
2. *Desirable behaviors should be rewarded and undesirable ones ignored.*
3. *Reinforcement should be immediate and should be given whenever the desired response occurs.*
4. *Behavior should be shaped by reinforcing "successive improvements" in the components of the behavior.*

Since most treatment occurs in an institutional setting, the negative effects on children of living in these institutions are important information. The available studies suggest the following effects (Hobbes, 1975, pp. 142–148).

Unless the child comes from an extremely deprived home environment, institutionalization has a negative effect on intelligence. Verbal ability is most seriously affected, and—not surprisingly—the longer the child is institutionalized and the younger he is when placed, the greater the negative effect is likely to be.

Institutionalized children are more likely than noninstitutionalized children to have personality disorders (Heber, 1964, p. 144). Moreover institutionalization stigmatizes. Former retarded residents of institutions trying to make it in the community spend much time and energy trying to conceal their past (Edgerton, 1967).

A great percentage of persons discharged from institutions fail to remain in the community because they lack the skills required for coping with everyday life. Having adapted to institutional life, they have become maladapted to the world outside. The mildly retarded are more likely to remain in the community than the more seriously handicapped, but even these individuals tend to settle at the lower end of the social and economic continuum.

Finally, there is some evidence to suggest that individuals who as adults are identified as mentally retarded on the basis of an IQ test but were not so identified as children tend to make better social adjustments than those who were identified earlier in life (Haywood, 1971, pp. 12–13). This finding has been interpreted by one expert (Hobbes, 1975, p. 143) as suggesting the destructive power of labels and stereotypes.

Summary

Four levels of mental retardation are recognized: mild (IQ 52–68), moderate (IQ 36–51), severe (IQ 20–35), and profound (IQ less than 20). Organic causes include chromosomal anomalies such as Down's syndrome (mongolism), in which chromosome 21 is trisomic; Klinefelter's syndrome, in which a male has one or two additional X chromosomes and does not mature sexually; and Turner's syndrome, in which a female has only one X chromosome. Genetic defects include phenylketonuria (PKU), in which a missing liver enzyme results in an accumulation of phenylalanine in the body, causing brain damage. Retardation may also result from nutritional deficiency, as in cretinism, in which an iodine deficiency in the mother results in a thyroid deficiency in the child, who remains dwarflike and retarded. Brain damage to the fetus can result when the mother has German measles during the first trimester of pregnancy. Rh incompatibility can also cause brain damage. Retardation is more common among premature babies, and may also be caused by injury at birth or during early childhood, by radiation, or by ingesting toxic substances. Cranial abnormalities include microcephaly (failure of the fetal brain and cranium to grow normally), macrocephaly (enlarged brain and head), and hydrocephalus (brain damage and cranium enlargement due to accumulating cerebrospinal fluid). Most retardation is mild and results from sociocultural factors usually linked to poverty and especially to deprivation. The cultural–familial retardate typically has not been sufficiently held, fondled, smiled at, talked to, and otherwise stimulated with human contact and interaction.

In the past it has generally been assumed that nothing can be done for retardates beyond institutionalization and special education. Nevertheless, some success has been reported with conventional psychotherapy and considerable success has been reported with behavior modification, which is used to teach the retardate the needed skills. Personality disorders are more common among retardates who have been institutionalized than among those who have not.

Terms and Concepts to Master

Amniocentesis	Macrocephaly
Cretinism	Microcephaly
Cultural–familial retardation	Mild/Moderate/ Profound/Severe retardation
Down's syndrome	
Hydrocephalus	PKU

19 Developmental Disorders

One of the side effects of the socialization process is its tendency to put adults out of touch with what it felt like to be a child. The result is that the adult image of childhood is often unrealistic. Eighteenth-century adults saw the child as a scaled-down adult. In the nineteenth century this distortion gave way to the opposite one: the child was seen as a fairylike, helpless, incompletely human creature—an image that could be expected to make life difficult for any real, flesh-and-blood human child. The nineteenth-century image has not entirely departed, with the result that parents and teachers (and sometimes clinicians) may be locked into a set of presuppositions that obscure their perception of the actual child.

One reason parents often do not recognize psychopathology in their offspring is that, being agents in the child's socialization, they cannot see what they have helped to create. Furthermore what they are transmitting is essentially the conditioning they themselves have been given, and few people ever understand that part of what they see as "facts" consists of projections into the real world of beliefs, attitudes, and habits of perception invented by the culture and then learned by the individual.

The diagnosis and treatment of early childhood disorders are also complicated by the possible involvement of maturational processes that are not yet fully understood. For example, some evidence suggests that sensorimotor stimulation may be a necessary condition for normal proliferation of brain cells, at least in the cerebellum, reticular formation, and cerebral cortex of the embryo and infant. Thus a premature baby in an incubator may fail to develop normally unless special attention is given to its tactile and kinesthetic needs.

Another factor differentiating the child patient from the adult is the presence of the parents in its daily life. As we indicated in Chapter 13, family interaction patterns may play a big part in the child's difficulties. For this reason clinicians may insist on seeing the entire family, and they may be careful to refer to the child as the *identified* patient.

Our perception of older people, like our perception of children, is often distorted. We tend to see people in both categories as incompetent, asexual, and a little too prone to foolishness to be taken seriously. The cultural dynamics that result in those perceptions are a matter for sociologists and anthropologists. We shall not explore them here beyond pointing out that the culture itself is part of the problem.

The Politics of Child Rearing and Education

Many of the conflicts between different psychological viewpoints are political in the sense that they reflect different value systems. For example an analysis of the writings of A. H. Maslow and B. F. Skinner strongly suggests that the two men are proceeding from completely different sets of tacit basic assumptions and that their basic assumptions are inseparable from their values, especially regarding the proper relation between the individual and society.

The hottest political issues, in and out of psychology, are often those involving the birthing, rearing, and educating of children. This is not surprising, since most parents are deeply concerned about their children's well-being. Their expectations and fears tend to focus on their children's performance in school, and professionals—medical or psychological—are often drawn into that arena of conflict.

Whatever the surface issues, the underlying issues are frequently achievement, responsibility, and control. These are age-old issues, but they

have only recently been addressed by the massive application of medical, pharmacological, and behavioral technology. The use, or possible misuse, of that technology has become an issue in itself, for example, in the treatment of hyperactivity with amphetamines. As we shall see, critics have charged that these children are simply being drugged to make them more manageable in school. At least some of the controversy is probably attributable to the difficulty of classifying this and other disorders in the young.

Classification Problems

Childhood and adolescent disorders, unlike those already discussed, are not easily classified be-

---

Child–Adult Differences That Have Child Psychotherapeutic Implications

Factor	Adult	Child	Treatment Implication for Child
motivation for treatment	often self-referred and therefore better motivated	referred by others, usually parents; lacks motivation to work on own problems	need to motivate child
insight into treatment objectives	tends to share goals of therapist and to be aware of his own role in therapy	more apt to lack common goals with therapist and resist own role	must make therapy intrinsically rewarding. Can be achieved by using needs for play, exploring, and manipulation
linguistic development	usually satisfactory verbal skills	limited verbal facility	emphasis can be placed on nonverbal communication (action, play, experiencing)
dependence on others	usually minimal	very dependent on significant others	treatment must attend to outside pressures and dependencies, physical and psychological
plasticity of personality	better established defenses; more rigid	more pliable; still developing	less need for depth-therapy approaches

Source: Clarizio and McCoy (1976, p. 388).

Table 19.1

Frequency of Undesirable Childhood Behaviors at Various Ages as Reported in a Survey of 275 Parents (in percentages)

Behavior	Age Groups (years)				
	3–5	5–7	7–10	11–14	14–18
Disobedience	46.6	52.6	39.8	33.3	28.0
Temper tantrums	24.4	10.5	9.7	5.6	4.0
Shy, uncommunicative	0.0	7.9	7.1	20.4	20.0
Thumbsucking	20.0	10.5	13.3	5.6	2.0
Bedwetting	17.8	9.2	2.6	1.8	0.0
Many fears	11.1	14.5	23.0	7.4	10.0
Overconscientiousness	4.4	15.8	18.6	37.8	14.0

Source: From A. Long. Parent's reports of undesirable behavior in children. Child Development, 1941, 12, 43–62.

cause children's symptoms do not cluster cohesively, their significance for the overall developed personality is not yet clear, and the criteria of abnormality vary according to the child's stage of development. Bedwetting, for example, is always abnormal for adults but is not considered abnormal for children until they reach a certain age; and other behaviors such as tantrums and thumb sucking, as we indicate in Table 19.1 (see also Long, 1941), can be normal or abnormal, depending on age.

Nevertheless various traditional classification schemes have been used, with some modifications, for diagnosing children. Lippman (1956), for example, recommends the following four categories: the neurotic child, the child with personality problems, the child who acts out, and the child who has a tenuous hold on reality. And in 1966 the Committee on Child Psychiatry of the Group for the Advancement of Psychiatry proposed a classification system based on traditional diagnostic categories:

healthy responses
reactive disorders
developmental deviations
psychotic disorders
psychophysiological disorders
psychoneurotic disorders
personality disorders
brain syndromes
mental retardation
other disorders

The *Diagnostic and Statistical Manual of Mental Disorders* (APA, 1968, pp. 49–51) refers to these disturbances as *hyperkinetic* (overactive, restless, distractible), *withdrawing, overanxious, runaway, unsocialized,* and *group reactions* of childhood and adolescence. But all groupings of this nature are necessarily superficial, for, as Ross indicated (1974, p. 18), ". . . [what] we wish to classify is . . . not an entity . . . it is the behavior . . . [of] children whose social environment [is] . . . deviant."

Then how are we to communicate systematically about childhood disorders? The method we have adopted in this chapter consists of grouping disturbances according to the types of cases encountered in child guidance practice.[1] Again, ad-

---

[1] Other schemes might include objectionable behaviors reported by mothers (Lapouse and Monk, 1958), teachers (Valentine, 1956), and mental health professionals (Roach et al., 1958), although there are considerable differences of opinion among these groups about what constitutes a behavioral disorder (Schrupp and Gjerde, 1953).

mittedly, these categories are arbitrary and hence subject to the same criticisms as the others; but they do provide us with a convenient way to arrange the material without resorting to conventional classification systems. Table 19.2 summarizes our classification scheme; we call attention to its limited coverage, which is essential if we are to keep the size of this chapter within reasonable bounds.[2]

Disorders of Childhood

From the moment of birth the infant displays certain innate emotional reactions (crying, thrashing about, rage) when it experiences any of its several basic drives (hunger, thirst, pain, cold); the expression of these emotions brings it into direct contact with others in its environment. Much of its subsequent normal and abnormal development depend on how these and later needs are met and on early interpersonal relationships. Let us see how this works in several crucial developmental experiences.

Feeding and Eating

The infant's first reflex response is getting food at its mother's breast or from a bottle. This is also its earliest complex social experience, the first opportunity to interact with another person. During this feeding period the infant learns to associate people (usually the mother) with the relief of the discomforts associated with hunger and thirst. From this experience, according to Mussen et al.

(1979), the infant learns two things: first, it learns to associate pleasant and comfortable sensations with the tactile, kinesthetic, visual, vocal, and auditory stimuli of the mother; and second, it learns to babble, smile, cling, and make body adjustments in response to the person holding it. These are important lessons.

If there are no major difficulties directly associated with feeding, the infant's first trauma will occur when it is separated from close contact during feeding with its mother or caretaker. This separation, usually called *weaning*, is the time when sucking is relinquished and a new mode of getting food is adopted. This, according to Sears et al. (1957, p. 69), "denotes the end of a way of life. The old habits must be replaced by the new; loving nurturance is no longer the inevitable accompaniment of eating; the suckling becomes a child."

Weaning usually occurs between the ages of 8 to 14 months, and it is at this time that problems associated with eating become apparent. The infant may be reluctant to relinquish the breast or bottle, may retain its infantile clinging to the mother, and may refuse to learn to feed himself or herself. These problems, which become more pronounced as the individual reaches childhood, may have any of several later manifestations, two of which are discussed below.

Refusal of Food. There are at least two ways to refuse food. The first way, by far the more frequent, is by dawdling: the child takes two or three bites, holding each one in his mouth for long periods of time without attempting to chew or swallow. This child may simply not be hungry, may be too busy to eat, may be trying to hold the attention of his assembled parents and siblings, or may be trying to avoid what invariably follows the meal—naptime, bedtime, cleaning up his room, or having to sit on the toilet.

The other form of food refusal, somewhat more serious, is vomiting. If we assume that the child is not physically ill, the chances are good that he has learned that this behavior is effective in

---

[2] In accordance with our intent to limit this book's coverage to disorders not clearly associated with organic involvement, we have elected to omit several areas traditionally discussed in chapters on childhood and adolescent psychopathology. The omitted topics are the brain dysfunctions, reading disabilities, and language disturbances. Interested readers are referred to the following sources for more information on these matters: Kessler (1966), Knopf (1979), Wender (1971), and Werry (1972).

making his parents anxious. At first the child may vomit accidentally as a consequence of crying or gagging after being forced to eat against his will; but after he notices the parental concern and anxiety that his behavior causes, he learns to produce it almost at will, to make his parents anxious or to attract attention.

Refusal to eat can become the basis of a

Table 19.2
Disorders of Childhood and Adolescence

	Disorder	Characteristic Manifestations	Typical Parental Presenting Complaints
Problems of Childhood	Feeding	Food refusal	My child fusses for hours over a meal; he gets rid of food by dumping it in the garbage; he vomits up more than he eats
		Obesity	Johnny constantly eats; he'd rather eat than socialize; it's almost as though food means more than just nutrition; if we deny him a snack, he becomes unmanageable
	Elimination	Enuresis	My boy never stopped wetting the bed; or after his sister was born, he resumed wetting
		Encopresis	It's in the family—his father was also a soiler; I think he's too busy to go to the toilet properly, therefore he has trouble holding it between trips
		Constipation	My daughter has always been reluctant to go to the toilet, especially in strange places
Problems of Adolescence	Aggression	Assault of parents and siblings	Even as an infant, the slightest frustration sent him into a rage and tantrum
		Destruction of property	Al hits the other neighborhood children and doesn't know how to play with them; if an adult tells him to play elsewhere, he picks up a brick and hurls it through a window
	Overactivity	Hyperkinesis	(Teacher's complaint) She has a short attention span and poor concentration. Her actions are often purposeless and frantic. She disrupts the class in sometimes provocative ways

power struggle between parent and child. Rudolf Dreikurs, the Adlerian psychiatrist (see Chapter 22 for a description of Adler's personality theory), describes one such case, "Little John," a 7-year-old boy who was brought to his summer camp after having just recovered from whooping cough (1958, pp. 224–228). John coughed and vomited not only when he started to eat but also

Table 19.2
Disorders of Childhood and Adolescence *(continued)*

	Disorder	Characteristic Manifestations	Typical Parental Presenting Complaints
Problems of Adolescence (continued)	School phobia	Refusal to attend school	My son has not attended school more than three times this month; he seems to get halfway through dressing, then returns to bed and sleep
	Depression	Dejection, indecisiveness, suicidal preoccupations	Ever since she lost her boyfriend, she has been brooding and you can't reach her; she should be concentrating on her school work; she was once such a good student
	Schizophrenia	Daydreaming, withdrawal from daily activities	He was such an alert child, and now he can't get going and acts so strange; almost as though he's lost interest in people and things
	Neuroses — Hypochondriasis		He is a fussy eater and bundles himself up in clothes even in the summertime; when he catches cold you'd think it was double pneumonia
	Hysteria		It all started when she tried to keep her hair out of her eyes; now she has the oddest jerking movement of the head I've ever seen; and she flutters her eyelids constantly
	Obsessions and compulsions		She's a real busybody and worries about everyone's affairs; and lately she's become super-moralistic, you can't even enjoy a TV show without her referring to it as "smut"

when he became excited or exerted himself physically.

Dreikurs, in keeping with the Adlerian tradition, traced the source of the boy's eating trouble to the power struggle between parent and child, from which the child gained the impression that eating was not for his own interest, but for his parents' sake: "Thus eating becomes a ready weapon to be used against them, especially if the child feels neglected or slighted" (1958, p. 224).

The treatment of "Little John" consisted of starving him until he understood that he had lost the power struggle. This contrasts sharply with the behavior modification approach to therapy in a case of *anorexia nervosa* (inability to take in food) that will be discussed in Chapter 23. Whereas behavioral methods focus on rewarding appropriate responses and eliminating undesirable ones, Adlerian therapy emphasizes eliminating objectionable behavior. Both approaches, however, rely heavily on programming the environment (for example, gaining the cooperation of relatives, working within a special setting) to accomplish their ends.

Obesity. Obesity, which is a consequence of overeating, may also have its origins during weaning; or it may be a symptom of a number of other psychopathologies. For boys obesity often interferes with getting around easily and hence keeping up with peers in athletics; for girls obesity may lead to social isolation. In either event these children become increasingly alone; they acquire a habit of eating for consolation, thus gaining more weight, and hence further diminishing opportunities to associate with peers.

Three factors have been implicated as possible causes of obesity. First, overeating may develop in a child of 5 to 8 years old, as he attempts to replace the immediate members of his family with friends. If he fails, he is lonely; then he seeks food as a consolation for his isolation.

Second, according to the psychoanalytically oriented, maternal overprotection is at the root of obesity, so that overfeeding the child is the mother's symbolic attempt to make up for her own loveless childhood, or to defend against her rejecting feelings toward the child. According to this theory mother equates food with love and lavishes it on her child as she would love. A related psychoanalytic theory, described by Hilde Bruch (1970), is that eating may be the obese child's expression of an insatiable desire for unobtainable love and may thus be a symbolic form of self-indulgence.

And third, in the opinion of many authorities (Burchinal and Eppright, 1959; Juel-Neilson, 1953; Quaade, 1953; Tolstrup, 1953), family patterns of abnormal food intake are responsible for childhood obesity. Since such children always have large quantities of food available, they reason, and because everyone around them is constantly eating, they acquire the habit of overeating by imitation, encouragement, and sometimes even pressure from parents. This explanation is made more plausible by the observation that in some families obesity is considered a sign of good health and nourishment.

The experiments of R. E. Nisbett and those of Stanley Schachter, already encountered in Chapter 8, are relevant here. These studies, it will be recalled, indicated that eating for normal (nonobese) college subjects was closely tied to hunger; whereas eating for the obese was less related to visceral states and more to the presence of such external cues as the ready availability of food (Nisbett, 1968; Schachter, 1971a, 1971b).

Internal cues include the presence or absence of hunger pangs, as well as signals from a hunger center and a satiety center in the brain. Whether childhood overfeeding disturbs a person's ability to detect or attend to these signals is not known. Overfeeding in infancy can, however, cause multicell obesity—an excess in the *number* of fat cells rather than in the size of fat cells. An obese person can lose weight by reducing the size of fat cells but can never reduce the number of fat cells; hence multicell obesity is extremely difficult to overcome.

Obesity does not present the medical emergency of anorexia nervosa, but, as we indicated before, it may cause the child serious emotional and social concerns. Unfortunately the obese child is a difficult patient in psychotherapy. He or she is often demanding and seems to crave the therapist's love in the same way food is craved. Hence the child is bound to be disappointed with traditional individual psychotherapy. The methods of choice, therefore, for treating overweight adults and children are either behavior therapy (see Chapter 23) or self-help groups such as Weight Watchers, which operates on principles similar to those used by Alcoholics Anonymous or Synanon (see Chapters 9 and 10).

Problems Associated with Elimination

A child's eliminative functions are like those of feeding in the sense that he (or she) is born with reflexes to rid himself of waste matter but must be trained in later childhood to perform this act in appropriate places at particular times. This *toilet training* is again a situation of significant social interaction between parent and child, one that is loaded with potential for pathology. Like weaning, toilet training demands that the child change his infantile ways of meeting natural needs to ones that are approved by adults.

Few teaching chores produce as much animosity between parent and child as toilet training. Often, because the child is not yet physiologically and intellectually ready to control his sphincters or prepared to signal his mother, he is punished for his failure to evacuate properly. Consequently both child and mother become increasingly angry and disappointed with each other and with themselves, which produces a pattern of self-propagating behavior: punishment leads to more failures, which, in turn, lead to a total breakdown of the toilet-training process. How unnecessary this is was demonstrated by two behavioral psychologists (Foxx and Azrin, 1973). Using a modeling strategy that involved

having children toilet-train dolls, they showed that it is possible to toilet train children who are at least 20 months of age in one day.

The two most clear-cut failures of learning proper forms of elimination are enuresis (bedwetting) and encopresis (soiling). Other problems are associated with the struggles emanating from toilet training, as we shall see.

Enuresis. *Enuresis* is a disorder of elimination, usually psychogenic, in which the child fails to learn control of daytime and nighttime urination.[3] In many respects nighttime control is the more difficult to learn because sleep interferes with and blurs the none-too-distinct internal signals that the child must notice if he is to exercise sphincter control (Sears et al., 1957). Enuresis can also result from physical malfunctioning; therefore enuretic children are usually examined by physicians to rule out this possibility.

Nocturnal enuresis, the most common form, may vary from slight bedwetting to complete bladder emptying. It is more frequent among boys than girls and in most cases stops after puberty, but occasionally it continues throughout life.

Many psychological factors have been implicated in its occurrence. For example, some cases of enuresis result from overtolerant parents who were indifferent to bedwetting, never really emphasizing to the child the appropriateness of retaining urine at night; and other cases have been traced to the parents' reassuring the child that his or her condition is a result of an inherited weak bladder and that his or her forebears had similar problems. Under these circumstances, the child either as a result of neglect in the first instance or because he wants to uphold the family tradition in the second, may be enuretic for years. There are even some cases reported of males who were

---

[3] Clinicians disagree about the exact age after which enuresis becomes pathological, but no one seems to set the age at younger than 3 or older than 8 (Kessler, 1966; Knopf, 1979).

inducted into the army and discovered only then that bedwetting was not an acceptable practice.

Enuresis is particularly common among children who are suddenly confronted with the arrival of a new sibling, are separated from family or loved ones, are placed in a new home, or have moved with the family to new surroundings. In these cases the enuresis is almost always accompanied by other signs of emotional upset such as shyness and anxiety; it is short-lived and tends to disappear when the emotional upset subsides.

The most difficult form of nocturnal enuresis to treat is the type that occurs in adults during periods of ordinary stress. Typically these adults have had a continuous history of occasional wetting since childhood, and it is associated with daytime anxieties and pressures. Case Report 19.1 illustrates this category of wetting.

Case Report 19.1 *The Enuretic Football Star*

Tom, a 230-pound defensive tackle for a large midwestern university, sought help at the campus counseling center for what he called "an embarrassing problem." Ever since he could recall, he had been an occasional bedwetter. Tom listed the types of situations that would precipitate his enuresis: they included overnights away from home, exams in elementary and high schools, approaching birthdays, and other minor and major occasions that might cause him apprehension. In high school, Tom explained, he was especially likely to wet his bed the night before a big football game.

During his freshman year in college his bedwetting followed a predictable pattern: he would thoroughly wet the bed the night before a game. This caused him much concern, for he was afraid that if the others in the dorm discovered his enuresis, "they'd haze the daylights out of this 230-pound baby." During that first year Tom tried almost everything to prevent this confrontation with his peers. He would stay up most of the night before a game. When this worked, he said, he was so tired the next day that anyone could get past him during

the game. If, however, he did get more than just a catnap, he would wet the bed.

Just before he sought help, his enuresis had intensified until the slightest daytime upset was sufficient to trigger it. He was especially concerned at this time because his sophomore year of football was about to get under way, and he felt he could not endure another season of "hiding my wet linens and night things." Tom was now seriously considering dropping out of school because of his problem.

At the insistence of the coach, who was one of the few people to whom Tom spoke about his problem, he had consulted a psychiatrist in the community and was given tranquilizers and short-term psychotherapy, to no avail. With the cooperation of the coaching staff and the school authorities, a special bed was then arranged for Tom in which conditioning procedures could be carried out without causing undue commotion, attention, and fussing about his enuresis. Tom's bedwetting was deconditioned by this technique within a period of two weeks.

Freudians, not surprisingly, tend to attribute enuresis to sexual motives; that is, wetting becomes a substitute for such repressed genital activity as masturbation. According to this interpretation urinary incontinence is the less-prohibited sexual outlet because it offers the child the opportunity to disclaim responsibility for his guilt-laden and anxiety-arousing genital activity. Presumably this form of enuresis tends to disappear at about the time of puberty when genitality takes over more completely.

One of the most common interpretations of bedwetting is that it symbolizes aggression. This interpretation has undoubtedly gained support over the years from the incident related by Swift in *Gulliver's Travels*, in which Gulliver, a prisoner of the Lilliputians, inundates the Empress's palace apartment with urine, presumably to extinguish a fire.[4] One expert (Pearson, 1949) even coined the term *revenge enuresis* to describe this type of aggressive wetting, which represents the child's unconscious expression of anger.

When enuresis is not symptomatic of a more serious personality disorder, the child usually gains control spontaneously during development and is praised for any successes (Salfield, 1954; Verville, 1967). And in the case of children who have not been encouraged to stop, either because of the parents' tacit permission to wet (for example, allowing them to sleep with diapers) or because of their neglect to train them, additional training sessions have usually helped. In some instances training plus conditioning procedures have worked satisfactorily.

Conditioning methods, first introduced to the United States by two psychologists in the 1930s (Mowrer and Mowrer, 1938), usually adhere to Pavlovian learning principles and generally involve waking a sleeper when he wets his bed. This is accomplished by sounding an alarm or buzzer or by administering a slight shock when his urine comes in contact with the electrically wired mattress on which he sleeps. Thus a full bladder becomes the conditioned stimulus (CS); the shock or alarm the unconditioned stimulus (US); and waking, which at first is an unconditioned response (UR) to the alarm, buzzer, or shock, becomes the conditioned response (CR) associated with the full bladder.

Follow-up information on conditioning therapy with enuretics suggests that these procedures are satisfactory in a majority of cases (Martin and Kubly, 1955; Baller and Schallock, 1956; Tapia et al., 1960) and that even when the enuresis is a symptom of another personality problem, conditioning is successful. In this regard one psychologist responded to the common criticism of depth theorists that behavior therapy cures only symptoms by calling attention to the possibility that if

enuresis is allowed to persist "over a long period the child *may* develop personality disturbance" (Yates, 1970a, p. 97).

Encopresis. *Encopresis,* persistent soiling by a child over two years of age, is a rarer and much more serious condition than enuresis. Occasional relapses occur in many children to about the age of 3 and sometimes, as during a period of diarrhea, up to the ages of 12 or later. Encopresis in the nonretarded and physiologically normal child, which usually involves daytime soiling, is often an expression of the child's defiance, especially toward the person who trained him and is an infantile mode of expressing hostility and aggression for someone who senses that no other weapon will be as effective. According to some clinicians, this form of hostility resembles magical thinking in that the child is saying, "I am angry at so and so, and if I do this-and-this, it will harm him." An extreme instance of such soiling is presented as Case Report 19.2, which shows that encopresis may signify a mixture of aggression and fear.

Case Report 19.2 *Encopresis*

Charles was a 12-year-old boy whose school work was not progressing satisfactorily. Whereas his neighborhood acquaintances had all made it to the sixth and seventh grades, he was still in the fifth grade, and not doing well. One day Charles's home room teacher asked to see his mother about a disciplinary matter at school. Charles was instructed to accompany his mother on the designated evening.

When Charles and his mother showed up at the teacher's room, they discovered that there were two or three other parents and children ahead of them and they waited behind them. After a 15-minute wait, and just moments before their turn came, Charles's mother hastily took her son by the hand and accompanied him to the nearest toilet. She returned shortly thereafter, by herself, and somewhat embarrassedly explained to the teacher

---

[4] Gulliver's afterthought, in this regard, is also interesting: "It was now daylight, and I returned to my house without waiting to congratulate with the Emperor; because, although I had done a very eminent piece of service, yet I could not tell how his Majesty might resent the manner by which I had performed it. . . ."

that her son had had a full bowel movement while waiting. She also related that this was a problem of long-standing between them, that he was always defiant and "never did let me toilet-train him," and that his soiling was his way of "shaming me in front of strangers."

Charles's version of this story was that his bowel movement was a result of his fear about what the teacher would tell his mother.

Various conventional psychotherapeutic approaches, such as are discussed in Chapters 22 and 24, are often attempted with the encopretic. Unfortunately, however, there is no information available about its success, nor are there data about spontaneous remission. There is some indication in the research literature, however, to suggest that behavior therapy (see Chapter 23) has enjoyed some treatment success (Gelber and Meyer, 1965; Keehn, 1965; Neale, 1963; Peterson and London, 1964; Yates, 1970a), the method of choice usually consisting of social learning techniques (see O'Leary and Wilson, 1975, pp. 111–130; Yates, 1970a, pp. 102–103).

Constipation. Defiance, rejection, and hostility toward the toilet trainer sometimes also lead the child to express animosity by withholding his or her feces instead of soiling, although the two are frequently seen together. *Constipation* can also develop in a small child who is too busy playing to go to the toilet or, again, when toilet facilities are not readily accessible to him. In either event, if signals from the sphincter are continually ignored, the sensation of contracting bowel muscles ceases, and fecal material is retained for long periods of time. Subsequently, because of the retention, the bowel movement is large and painful and the child in turn postpones this unpleasant task as long as possible, thus setting up a condition that perpetuates constipation (Verville, 1967).

This disorder may also occur in another way, according to one psychologist (Kessler, 1966). If parents express extreme disgust, or if they punish

their child severely for soiling accidents, the youngster may erroneously learn that defecation is bad. Although this is more likely to occur in the retarded, almost any child at about the age of 2 can easily get the idea that feces are disgusting and dirty and consequently may try to hide them or hold them back. In this case the child's reaction is docile rather than hostile.

Of the two failures in training—soiling and withholding—withholding can lead to more serious physical consequences because it may cause fecal impaction in the colon, which often requires surgical intervention. Therefore it should be treated as early as possible. Its treatment, as in the case of soiling, usually requires investigation of the method of toilet training as well as of the availability and condition of toilet facilities. Classical conditioning principles have also been used here, with some reported success (Quarti and Renaud, 1962).

Aggressive Behavior

Aggression (see also Chapter 17) is an almost universal characteristic among children. At first it is expressed as rage and anger and consists mainly of the infant's crying and using random overall body movements, such as kicking, flailing its arms and legs, arching its back, and twisting its body. Then, at about age 1, these random movements become more directed expressions of aggression and, among other purposive acts, include deliberate attacks on the offending person, usually a parent or sibling, and kicking, biting, striking, and screaming.

As the child acquires language, he turns to refusing food, name-calling, and arguing. Still later, usually at about 18 months, the child deliberately does whatever is forbidden and whatever he knows will annoy the parents. By about the third year, the child learns that he can physically hurt others and he may injure others with intent. When he reaches middle childhood, his attacks become less physical and more verbal and psychological; and during adolescence, these verbal and psychological expressions include name-calling, swearing, sarcasm, and ridiculing and humiliating others.

The first targets of a child's aggression are in the home and are generally parents (usually the mother) and siblings. We have already seen that the mother is the natural object of aggression because of her role in raising the child; this aggression is easily transferred toward siblings and, in this form, is somewhat more difficult to control than attacks on parents. The aggression that the child learns to express in the home is later easily displaced to other situations.

The Aggressive Child. This category includes the child whose aggression, either in the home or outside, becomes so disruptive that parents and society feel treatment is necessary. This behavior may consist of physical assaultiveness, verbal abusiveness, and generally hostile or destructive acts; it may include overtly antisocial actions such as stealing, lying, or fire-setting; or it may manifest itself in temper outbursts, sulking, or pouting. The younger aggressive child is often a disruptive influence in the classroom, and therefore school authorities are the first to detect the need for treatment. The older antisocially aggressive child or adolescent may come to the attention of law enforcement agencies that deal with his "predelinquent" or delinquent actions.

Training the child not to be aggressive is probably as essential as teaching it proper eating and elimination habits, although this is a part of upbringing often overlooked. The obvious place to start, as with other training, is in the home. That this is not a simple matter is suggested by Sears et al. (1957, p. 266), whose research findings indicate that parents may produce nonaggressive children by frowning upon aggression, stopping it when it occurs, and avoiding punishing the child for it. Other aspects of its causes and dynamics are discussed in Chapter 17 and elsewhere throughout this book.

Treatment of Aggression. In a fascinating series of studies too detailed for discussion here, two psychologists, Gerald Patterson and Joseph Cobb (1971), demonstrated that some environments are inadvertently programmed to promote aggression and that behavioral analyses and deconditioning techniques can be used to diminish the likelihood of such aggression. They also hypothesized that mothers teach children to become aggressive by punishing them and, perhaps more important, that mothers learn from interactions with their children to carry out assaults that subsequently cause bodily injury or more serious harm to their young children.[5]

Withdrawal

When confronted with threatening situations or strange people, young children frequently avoid, flee from, or withdraw from the scene. Such withdrawal comes naturally to them and is considered normal reactions of inexperienced, small, and generally helpless organisms. They may also express withdrawal by hiding their faces in their hands when strangers approach, leaving the room, disappearing behind a sofa or drapes when adults enter the house, or, depending on their age, by shouting, pulling at or clinging to their parents, slamming doors, or doing somersaults, or by being passive, shy, quiet, or unassertive.

---

[5] The battered-child syndrome, first reported in the early 1960s by Helfer and Kempe (1968), was based on observations of pediatricians that a large number of children admitted to pediatric services suffer from nonaccidental injury at the hands of their parents and caretakers. The incidence of such child abuse runs into the tens of thousands of children being severely battered or killed in the United States each year. The role of parental psychopathology in inflicting such abuse is receiving increasingly more attention in research and professional literature. See Bakan's *Slaughter of the Innocents* (1971) and Steele and Pollack's "A Psychiatric Study of Parents Who Abuse Infants and Small Children" in Helfer and Kempe's *The Battered Child* (1968).

Withdrawal is often a reaction of a young child in the presence of strange people or threatening circumstances.

Many children also display fears, or phobias, as a withdrawal reaction and may develop such other symptoms as tics, speech disorders, asthma, excessive masturbation, eating difficulties, and insomnia. When accompanied by these disturbances, the withdrawal is viewed as a somewhat more serious sign of personality disorder.

Hyperkinesis and "Hyperactivity"

Some confusion surrounds the exact nature and definition of the disorder commonly called "hyperactivity." One reason for this may be that present definitions are often an amalgam of psychological, medical, pharmacological, and pedagogical concepts: psychological because hyperactivity is a behavior disorder, medical because the problem is often diagnosed as minimal brain dysfunction and treated with drugs, pharmacological because the diagnosis is often believed to be validated if the ingestion of CNS stimulants reduces symptoms, and pedagogical because the starting point for the diagnosis is often a teacher's report of "learning disabilities."

Another problem is that the term *hyperkinesis* seems to have both a narrow definition and a broad one. It may refer to a rare neurological disease that affects about one out of every 2000 people (Rutter et al., 1970; Bax, 1972) and that causes people to be overactive all the time rather than just in school. Or it may refer to a disorder that is supposed to afflict a large percentage of school-age children (3 to 40 percent, according to various estimates). In this broader sense the term is sometimes used interchangeably with *hyperactivity* and with *minimal brain dysfunction*. Children suffering from this disorder are also sometimes called *learning disabled*.

Some clinicians report qualitative rather than quantitative differences between the activity of the hyperactive child and that of the normal child. Typically the behavior of the hyperactive child is characterized as impulsive, frenetic, and disruptive. Often control seems to be an issue, as when the child plays dumb when a demand is made on him or engages in provocative behavior, or when his poor impulse control provokes the imposition of control by others. Often there is significant body tension, which the child seems unable to reduce. He or she is also likely to be unaffectionate and to resist the holding and comforting that reduce tension in normal children.

The body tension and inconsolability mentioned above are especially noticeable in infancy. The infant is often colicky and extremely resistant to eye contact and body contact, pushing others away. Premature babies are a high risk for hyperactivity.

The Minimal Brain Dysfunction Model. At one time brain damage was believed to be the cause of hyperactivity. When it became clear that no brain damage could be demonstrated in most hyperactive individuals, the hypothesis was modified; a functional rather than organic disturbance was postulated, and since no measurable brain pathology could be found, the disorder was called *minimal* brain dysfunction (MBD).

The most widely used definition of minimal brain dysfunction seems to be that given in a 1966 monograph based on a study led by S. D. Clements of Arkansas Medical Center. According to this definition (pp. 6–7) minimal brain dysfunction affects children

of near average, average, or above average general intelligence with certain learning or behavioral disabilities ranging from mild to severe, which are associated with deviations of function of the central nervous system. These deviations may manifest themselves by various combinations of impairment in perception, conceptualization, language, memory, and control of attention, impulse, or motor function. . . . These aberrations may arise from genetic variations, biochemical irregularities, perinatal brain insults or other illnesses or injuries sustained during the years which are critical for the development and maturation of the central nervous system, or from unknown causes. . . . During the school years, a variety of learning disabilities is the most prominent manifestation of the condition which can be designated by this term.

Most children receiving the MBD diagnosis show no evidence of brain damage. A small number have some irregularities in their EEG traces, but no connection has been found between such traces and any known brain pathology. When a learning disability is present, it is believed to be caused not by any deficit in intelligence or general ability but by the child's behavior problem. However, learning disabilities are not always present, and some of these children do well academically. And the behavior problem may be overactivity; underactivity; slowness in finishing work; sleep abnormally light or deep; socially bold and aggressive; physically immature, or physical development normal or advanced for age; possibly negative and aggressive to authority; sweet and even-tempered, cooperative and friendly; or any of 91 others listed in Clements' monograph. Prevalence estimates for MBD vary from 3 to 40 percent of the school-age population. Screening programs are used to permit "early intervention," and the director of one such project in Muncie, Indiana, claims to have found a learning disability in every child in the district (Schrag and Divoky, 1975, p. 22).

Proponents of amphetamine therapy claim that the drugs have a "paradoxical effect." Instead of producing hyped-up behavior, as they do in normal adults, the drugs apparently calm children who are hyperactive. Therefore, it is argued, any child who is calmed by an amphetamine must be hyperactive. Although Ritalin was placed on the federal government's "hard narcotics" schedule in 1972, its use to treat hyperactivity continued to increase.

The Allergenic Model. Immunologist Ben F. Feingold believes that hyperactivity is caused by the immune system's response to food additives, particularly artificial colorings and synthetic flavorings. These chemicals are *haptens*—low-molecular-weight chemicals. According to Feingold (1974, p. 6),

The chemicals man uses as drugs and chemicals used as food additives are both low-molecular compounds. . . .

An artificial color, such as the chemical tartrazine—Food, Drug, and Cosmetic (FD&C) 'Yellow #5'—can behave within the human body in the same manner as a 'drug' used for medication—a fact some physicians have overlooked.

The implication is that food dyes and synthetic flavorings may function as psychoactive drugs.

Feingold's hypothesis rests partly on clinical observation and partly on circumstance, the circumstance being the similarity between graphs showing the increase of hyperactivity in the 1960s and graphs showing the increase in the amounts of food additives used during the same years. The clinical support consists of a small number of cases in which Feingold (he is also a pediatrician) placed a hyperactive child on a diet free of synthetic food additives. Feingold claims that the symptoms disappeared and that they returned whenever foods containing additives were reintroduced into the diet. The smallness of the sample makes the findings inconclusive; a large-scale study with controls is now underway.

The Sensory Input Reduction Model. A hypothesis arising from a study of pain tolerance has some interesting possible implications for the study of hyperactivity. According to Petrie (1960), some people seem to consistently reduce the intensity of their perceptions, while others consistently augment the intensity of their perceptions. People who reduce sensory inputs tolerate pain well and are more extraverted, less tolerant of sensory deprivation, and more mesomorphic than those who augment sensory inputs. Reducers also tend to judge time as passing more slowly and are more likely to be delinquents. (Some clinicians claim an association between hyperactivity and delinquency.) Ryan (1969, p. 95), commenting on Petrie's studies, noted that

At the elementary or junior high school level the reducer would tend to be male, extraverted, loud (whether he sees himself this way or not), unable to sit in one place too long, always going to get a drink or going to the toilet, often poking the person in front or back of him, and unable to concentrate or pay attention for extended periods of time . . . in the typical classroom the young reducer would appear to be at a decided disadvantage. Here is a person who reduces all stimulation. He is placed in a setting where stimulation is typically at a

minimum. . . . Thus we would predict that the reducer would need to seek additional stimulation of one kind or another . . . we would expect the reducer to be more of a behavior problem, at least in the younger years, and we would expect his academic achievement to be less than it should be in relation to his ability.

Petrie and her associates (1962, p. 421) also express concern about the classroom environment:

We suggest that the education of such delinquents and predelinquents needs to make allowances for their vulnerabilities and strengths. They need change, movement, and speed, actual rather than 'symbolic' instruction, bright colors, music, and company.

Neither Petrie nor Ryan refers to hyperactivity as such, yet much of what they say about sensory input reducers matches, almost word for word, some of the descriptions of the hyperactive child. We introduce it here partly to point up the difficulty of diagnosing some childhood disorders, especially when any part of the diagnosis rests on the child's response to a school situation, which is an uncontrolled variable. Before accepting at face value a child's inability to attend or to concentrate, the clinician might consider what it is that adults are demanding the child attend to or concentrate on. We are confronted here by one of the political issues we mentioned at the beginning of the chapter. Does the child have a right to ignore material that bores him? Certainly even the most interesting prepared learning materials are not likely to engage the attention of every child in a normally distributed population. Apropos of this, one of the behaviors often mentioned in the literature on hyperactivity is "selective inattention": the child tunes out except when something catches his or her interest. And Rie (1979) reports that medicated children perform better than unmedicated ones in repetitious and mechanical tasks but unmedicated hyperactive children perform as well as normals in tasks that are pleasurable and stimulating. It might therefore be worthwhile to ask, "What is a healthy child's response to material that does not interest him or her?"

The Somatosensory Deprivation Model. Developmental neuropsychologist James Prescott (1969) notes similarities between the behavior of isolation-reared animals such as Harlow's monkey's and a variety of human behavior patterns variously labeled hyperactive, autistic, schizophrenic, or violent–aggressive. He argues that the maternal-social deprivation described by Harlow is actually a special case of somatosensory deprivation—a deficit of both sensory stimulation and kinesthetic stimulation during the perinatal period.

In other words the person, as embryo and infant, does not get enough input from touch and movement to permit normal development of brain cells. The mechanism Prescott proposes is Cannon's Law of Denervation Supersensitivity. The poverty of inputs at a critical time results in hyperexcitability in the cerebellum, and the resulting self-stimulating behaviors reflect "the general principle that sensory deprivation experiences produce stimulus-seeking behaviors that are related to the sensory system that is deprived."

In this model the sensory deficit that resulted from insufficient movement (as in premature babies kept in incubators) or from insufficient handling may be responsible for the rocking and head-banging of the autistic child, as well as the fidgeting, kicking, and poking of the hyperactive child.

The Invented Disease Model. Although the MBD hypothesis has been warmly accepted by an impressive number of parents, teachers, and school administrators, as well as by some professionals in medicine and psychology, a substantial minority of people in all those groups have strenuously objected to the medical model as a way of per-ceiving, and attacking, the problems of classroom learning and behavior. Their objections have appeared in medical and psychological journals and in an angry book called *The Myth of the Hyperactive Child* (1975) by Peter Schrag and Diane Divoky.

Schrag and Divoky allege that MBD's status as a disease rests on flimsy and doubtful evidence. "It has no single name, no universally accepted symptoms, and no discernible anatomical or biochemical characteristics which can be diagnosed in a clinic or a laboratory." (The physician's diagnosis is based largely on reports of classroom performance.) Furthermore, the studies cited in support of the MBD hypothesis are flawed by (p. 20)

inadequate statistical methods, skewed population samples (mostly ghetto blacks), miniscule control groups, and an almost total absence of long-range follow-up . . . also by an almost totally arbitrary set of definitions which in many cases represented nothing more than the bias of teachers or cops translated into scientific jargon.

Schrag and Divoky see the epidemic of hyperactivity that is supposedly sweeping the country as an artifact of labeling, arguing that any healthy child is overactive by adult standards and pointing to a 1958 study (Lapouse and Monk, 1958) showing that half of a representative group of mothers considered their own children overactive. Schrag and Divoky assert that "What is new, however, is the increasingly fashionable attribution of common problems to neurological abnormalities." Thus an observation of behavior ("The kid can't sit still") translates into disease ("hyperkinesis"), and "every annoying habit has now been honored with a pseudo-scientific designation." These syndromes "simply reflect behavior that some adult doesn't like."

Conceding that a small percentage of these children do in fact suffer from a diagnosable medical ailment serious enough to justify the use of drugs, Schrag and Divoky claim that most "are being drugged, often at the insistence of schools or individual teachers, to make them more manageable." What began as a well-meaning attempt to make adequate schooling available for genuinely handicapped children has grown into a "comprehensive screening and sorting game in which new categories of problems and new labels are continually being created, and in which children are being found to fit them."

Besides assuming that neurological pathology underlies underachievement and annoying classroom behavior, the proponents of the MBD hypothesis are also, according to this view, assuming

(1) that every child should progress academically at the same rate as every other child of the same age; in other words only the mean score is normal, and the rest of the bell-shaped curve represents a pattern of deviance
(2) that every child should do equally well in all academic subjects at all times
(3) that IQ tests have an absolute power to gauge innate intellectual capacity

Typically, a child whose reading ability is below the level predicted by his IQ score is classed as "dyslexic." But just as many children read *better* than their IQs indicate and are therefore "hyperlexic." Studies are cited that indicate that "hyperactivity is a normal variant of temperament," that the symptoms listed by Clements could not be related to "any single syndrome," and that reading ability is a normal physiological variant (Thomas et al., 1968; Silberg and Silberberg, 1967, 1968–1969, 1971; Routh and Robert, 1972). According to one clinical psychologist (Stone, 1974), hyperkinesis "is often a social term which calls for a definition based on the acceptability of certain behavior in [a] specific situation." Child psychiatrist R. D. Freeman states flatly that there is no such thing as MBD (Hobbs et al., 1973).

The "paradoxical effect" premise has been attacked by L. A. Sroufe and M. A. Stewart (1973), who noted that the reasoning is circular—hyperactivity is assumed to be a sign of brain damage, and brain damage is then assumed to be the cause whenever hyperactivity is observed. Sroufe and Stewart add that normal children have the same response to stimulant drugs as brain-damaged children, yet that response is still taken as evidence that the subject must have the ailment for which the drug was prescribed. They point out also that neurological "soft signs" and irregular EEGs are not good indicators of brain damage, although they are used in MBD diagnosis, that no current neurological test or combination of tests can differentiate hyperactive children from controls, and that no unitary MBD syndrome has been found. W. M. Cruickshank (1972, pp. 6–7) writes that

teachers have questioned me about disrespectful children, children who will not listen to the adult, children who cry, children who hate, children who are sexually precocious, children who are aggressive—all in the belief that they are learning disability children. One parent asked me if the fact that his college student son wore long hair and, he suspected, lived with a girl outside his dormitory was the result of a learning disability.

As for Ritalin's effect on performance, H. E. Rie, after two years of a long-term study, told Schrag and Divoky (1975, p. 89) that the drug had no positive effects on the academic achievement of children diagnosed as hyperactive.

At first, teacher ratings indicate an improvement, Rie told us, because 'the kids slow down dramatically and are out of people's hair, but when objective testing is done, they're not performing one bit better. In fact, what we're observing on this round of measurement is that the youngsters on drugs are far less responsible and enthusiastic, and are far more apathetic, humorless and zombie-like.'

One other aspect of the criticism is worth noting. A report of a federal study on labeling of children (Hobbs et al., 1973) concludes with the observation that, according to critics, "learning disabilities spring from a discrepancy between parental expectation, which is sometimes unrealistically high, and the performance of the child, which may be at his level of capacity." We could perhaps sum up the critics' view of hyperactivity by saying that in their eyes a hyperactive child is a child with normal childhood levels of energy and excitement who is (a) required to sit still for long periods of time in school and (b) under strong pressure to achieve academically.

Critical Comment

Until hyperactivity is more precisely defined, the controversy is likely to continue. Past approaches have given little assurance that the behavior being labeled hyperactive was not, in many cases, a function of classroom environment, adult expectations, or a combination of the two.

Even if we identify a population of children who are hyperactive independently of external pressures, we still face the central question raised by the critics: how appropriate is the medical model for dealing with a disorder manifested as unruly classroom behavior? If hyperactivity is a behavior disorder, some doubts may be raised about the desirability of a teacher and a physician, neither of whom necessarily has any background in the behavioral sciences, assuming responsibility for diagnosis and treatment. Currently the MBD model seems to be losing favor among clinicians, but as yet no other model has superseded it. Deprivation models such as Prescott's have an intuitive appeal but are not yet supported by the weight of clinical observation or laboratory experiment. Certainly the possible role of contact comfort and other forms of sensory stimulation in the infant's development is well worth studying.

Disorders of Adolescence

With the approach of adolescence, childhood disorders begin to take on more adult forms. Several of them are discussed here; we begin with school phobia, which straddles these two developmental periods.

School Phobia

School phobia, which commonly occurs in the lower elementary grades and is usually accompanied by crying, trembling, somatic complaints, and pleas to stay home, takes on a somewhat different form among adolescents. At the younger ages it is traceable to fears of separation from mother, and anxiety about eating in the lunchroom or going to strange toilets. For the adolescents, school phobia is usually a symptom of a larger neurosis-like personality behavioral pattern and as such is more resistant than the childhood variety to environmental manipulation. In general this type of adolescent tends to avoid unpleasant situations because he has no skill in coping with them; and school just happens to be one among many of these situations. In addition he tends to be demanding, especially at home, and to pout when he cannot have his way; he accuses others of selfishness when they disappoint him, is negativistic, and seeks attention by annoying and intruding on others.

The adolescent usually attributes this fear of school to any one of a series of precipitating incidents, which are exaggerated out of all proportion to their actual importance. But the incident is used to justify the irrational behavior. A typical example is the case of Harry (Case Report 19.3), a 14-year-old boy whose school phobia was only one symptom in a general pattern of withdrawal.

Case Report 19.3 *School Phobia*

Harry, a 14-year-old, huskily built white male, was a freshman in high school when he decided one day that he'd "had it" and would not "go back to that crazy place." He said his teacher had wronged him in front of his friends by sending him out of the room as a disciplinary measure for "doing nothing." Closer questioning disclosed that Harry's past record of attendance and comportment at school had indeed been exemplary, but that on this occasion, although the teacher was reputedly a disciplinarian, Harry deserved what he got.

At the time he was referred to the child guidance center, Harry had been out of school for more than three months. During that time he had made several abortive attempts to return to school, both alone and with the help of a social worker and a school psychologist. But to no avail. One time he came so close that he was able to peek into his homeroom, whereupon he began to cry, turned pale, and trembled all over. He left the building in a panic.

Harry was seen at the child guidance center for about six months. During that time interviews with him disclosed that he felt inadequate in many ways and that school was the place where many of his inadequacies were brought to the fore. He couldn't climb the ropes in gym or run the 60-yard dash within the required time limit, and he did not know what to do in a football huddle or when given the ball in basketball. Moreover he was extremely self-conscious about his looks and clothes and resentful because his parents could not afford to furnish him with a wardrobe comparable to those of his peers.

At home he was a demanding youngster who had been until the last three years the object of their smothering affection and dominance. His parents reported that over the last several years Harry had become an isolate and spent most of his time locked in his room listening to records.

The treatment of cases such as Harry's depends largely on whether the therapist prefers to have the patient return to school immediately or elects to defer his return until the youngster has achieved some insight into his difficulties. A major disadvantage of the latter strategy is that the longer the return to school is delayed, the more difficult it becomes for him to give up his pleasant existence at home for the seemingly un-

pleasant one awaiting him at school.

Some therapists consider it so important not to delay the adolescent's return that they sometimes accompany him to the school and use every stratagem at their disposal to get him into the building. If he is incapable of entering the classroom they may allow him to stay in the principal's or counselor's office and encourage him to return to class gradually, perhaps to only one period at a time, letting the adolescent decide the order of return himself.

In some urban centers because of the recent availability of funds for community mental health action programs (see Chapter 25), transitional facilities, sometimes called *workshops*, have been made available to school-phobic children and adolescents, who can regularly be in a classroom-like situation without actually being in school. The advantages of these workshops over psychotherapy alone are that they provide a regular schedule for the adolescent and offer a constructive alternative to staying at home or becoming an inmate in a detention facility. Occasionally also, because it is illegal to quit school before the age of 15 or 16, these workshops enroll many borderline mental defectives and tough juvenile delinquents, who make it so unpleasant for disturbed adolescents that a return to the regular school situation may seem the lesser of two unpleasant situations.

Depression and Suicide

From a clinical standpoint adolescent depression is similar to adult neurotic and psychotic depression in that it is characterized by dejection, low self-esteem, indecisiveness, loss of motivation, disturbed sleep, and sometimes suicidal preoccupation. Presumably because they are more unstable in mood and temperament than adults, adolescents are more vulnerable to depression when faced with disappointment, crisis, or failure.

Depression. Adolescent depression is often precipitated by such specific events as rejection by a girlfriend or boyfriend, failure to make the football team, or an eruption of acne. Sometimes it is a consequence of nothing more than such unconscious or unrealistic fantasies as "My parents don't love me anymore," "I'll never be able to succeed at anything," or "My body is weak and unattractive" (Weiner, 1970, p. 167).

Depression in early adolescence is characterized by boredom and restlessness, consisting of alteration between total disinterest and intense preoccupation with activities and events; fatigue and bodily preoccupation, which can be a consequence of these extreme swings in mood; difficulty in concentrating, which often shows up in declining school performance; acting-out, including temper tantrums, running away, defiance, rebelliousness, and delinquency; and a turning away from people. In later adolescence, the clinical manifestations of depressive disorders closely resemble those of adults.

Suicide. Suicide among adolescents accounted for approximately 3.5 percent of the 22,970 self-destructive deaths reported for the entire population during 1971. It is usually precipitated by a specific distressing problem or event. Most commonly it is a consequence of conflicts within the family, particularly revolving around disciplinary action taken, in which the adolescent feels wrongly chastised. But here, as in the case of the precipitating incident between the school-phobic adolescent and his teacher, the actual situation is amplified by the victim and is just one symptom of a larger underlying personality disorder.

The suicidal adolescent, whose success at taking his or her life is often unintentional, usually has a previous history of either talking about or attempting self-destruction. The actual attempt seems to occur at the point at which he or she feels completely helpless to alter a situation that has become intolerable and represents his or her last desperate appeal for love, help, pity, and attention. Occasionally suicides are merely attempts to influence others' actions and attitudes toward the adolescent (Jacobs, 1971; Stengel, 1964).

Except in instances where the adolescent verbalizes his or her intention (see the suicide letter in Chapter 14), it is seldom possible to predict an adolescent suicide attempt or its consequences. Some guidelines for anticipating suicidal behavior are available, however. These are summarized below (Weiner, 1970, pp. 189–195).

1. The possibility of suicide should *always* be considered when a youngster begins to exhibit a depressed mood, eating and sleeping disturbances, withdrawn or rebellious interpersonal behavior, and declining school performance.
2. The risk of suicide is particularly serious when there has been a recent and marked breakdown in previously existing communication channels.
3. The potential for suicide in a troubled adolescent is heightened by a previous history of suicide at-

tempts or accident-proneness.
4. It is important to know the lethality of the means used for previous suicide attempts in order to assess the possibility for future success (attempts to hang or shoot oneself have greater lethality than aspirin overdosage or superficial scratches of the wrist).
5. Most serious of all is the adolescent whose suicide attempt occurred in total isolation from others and was accompanied by conscious wishes to die.[6]

Treatment for the potentially suicidal adolescent, especially one who is playing for attention, help, or understanding, is usually best accomplished by any of the traditional psychotherapeutic methods discussed in Chapters 22 and 24. When suicide seems imminent, the crisis intervention center is the place where treatment should first be initiated (see Case Report 25.1 in Chapter 25). In this regard one sociologist recommends that formerly suicidal persons answer the telephones instead of psychiatric social workers or other "trained" volunteers, who may be less apt to understand or sympathize with the problems of the suicidal adolescent (Jacobs, 1971).

Drugs, electroshock therapy, and hospitalization in general are not recommended for the treatment of suicidal adolescents because they provide little more than temporary alleviation of problems that often require immediate resolution. For these reasons conventional psychotherapy may be the method of choice, for it aims at changing the person and his behavioral patterns so that he can cope with formerly intolerable situations (Litman, 1970).

General Causative Considerations

Essentially the origins of childhood and adolescent disorders resemble those of adults; therefore

---

[6] From *Psychological disturbance in adolescence* by I. B. Weiner. Copyright © 1970 by John Wiley & Sons, Inc. By permission.

we shall focus on causes that are particularly germane to children.

With the possible exceptions of infantile autism and schizophrenia—for which the most likely determinants are biogenic—the causes of most childhood and adolescent abnormalities, as we already indicated at appropriate points throughout this chapter, may be traced to family influences: the kind of family a youngster is born into determines the sort of person he or she will be, an observation already noted in Chapter 6. Similarly, in this chapter we also indicated that the attitudes and behaviors of parents determine their offspring's aggressiveness and assertiveness. In what follows, we shall first call attention to the complexity of these interrelationships, and then cite several other studies that bear on childhood and adolescent disorders.

Parental Patterns and Home Atmosphere

Concerning the complexity of the cause-and-effect linkages between parental (especially maternal) practices and subsequent pathology, we want to reemphasize the idea that overall parental attitudes are more important than specific child-rearing techniques in determining the personality development of offspring. This is in sharp contrast to earlier, predominantly psychoanalytic views, which tended to oversimplify these relationships. The contemporary approach is to view specific parental behaviors simply as indices of larger attitude patterns. On this point, R. I. Watson has the following to say (1965, p. 208; also see Mussen et al. 1979, pp. 368–370):[7]

Another approach to maternal influences of infant socialization is through studying patterns of *maternal behavior. For example, a mother's feeding behavior, cleaning, caressing, and moving the infant*

about *may be studied to see if they form a pattern, instead of being examined one at a time as is done in specific practice studies.*

Intrapsychic and Environmental Variables

It would be a mistake, however, to suggest that an individual's personality is entirely the product of family interaction patterns. Several additional *endogenous* (originating from within) and *exogenous* (originating from without) forces also influence the formation of personality. Thus the child's unique biological and physical endowments play an important role in his growing up, as do the extrafamilial demands of teachers and peers.

As an instance of the former consider the relation between physical makeup and personality, on which Alfred Adler (see Chapter 22) had much to say in his early writings. His theory about *organ inferiority*, which originally was narrowly conceptualized to account for psychosomatic symptom selection (see the discussion of the *somatic weakness hypothesis* in Chapter 8), was that the individual strives to *compensate* for this real or perceived inferiority. He later extended this view to include any feelings of inferiority, whether they arise from physical or from psychological and social disabilities (Adler, 1917, 1927).

But regardless of one's theoretical orientation on this matter, it is difficult to deny the overwhelming importance of a disability for a person's personality development or the way he subordinates all other matters to the one relating to compensating for his defect. One of the more famous examples of such compensation was Demosthenes, a stutterer as a child, who became noted for his oratory. More recent examples are the many Olympic athletes, especially weightlifters and track stars, whose daily physical exercises were efforts to overcome disabilities caused by childhood illnesses.

In addition to the effects on personality of these endogenous factors, there are many external forces with which the youngster must cope in

---

[7] For an excellent review of family interaction and psychopathology of children see Hetherington and Martin (1972).

order to meet and master his environment. These forces, most of which are extrafamilial, begin to take on a special significance as the child's social world expands beyond the bounds of his home into the neighborhood, nursery school, elementary school, and beyond (Mussen et al., 1979).

Diagnosis and Treatment of Childhood and Adolescent Disorders

The diagnosis and treatment of behaviorally disturbed children and adolescents may take place in a child guidance clinic or in a hospital. We shall focus primarily on the first of these facilities, where the youngster and his family are seen by a psychiatrist, psychiatric social worker, and clinical psychologist. The typical diagnostic and therapeutic procedures are somewhat as follows.[8]

Diagnosis

After the family is either referred to, or makes contact with, a child guidance center, perhaps having learned of the clinic from newspaper articles, friends, or relatives, the parents are usually seen first by the psychiatric social worker, who arranges an intake interview between the parents (either separately or together) and any of the other mental health professionals assigned to the case. During this interview the worker tries to understand the problem as it is viewed by the parents, attempts to clarify for them what they might expect from the clinic, and interprets its function to them. If the family has indeed come to the right place, arrangements are made to bring the youngster in for his first visit; but if the family could receive more appropriate attention else-where, the parents are referred to another agency (for example, a clinic for the deaf or mentally retarded or a residential treatment center).

Following the intake and after the staff's decision to accept the case for further evaluation or for therapy, the mother supplies the clinic with a complete life history of the child-patient. A separate interview is also conducted with the father in order to involve him in the family's problems and to allow him to express his views and feelings about the child's difficulty. (Many fathers still regard raising children as "woman's work.") The child is then interviewed; depending on the child's age, this takes the form of either a play session (see p. 439) or a purely verbal interchange between the child and the professional.

At some point, either simultaneously with the parents' interviews or shortly thereafter, but following the initial contact between the child guidance worker and the youngster, the clinical psychologist tests the child. This assessment usually consists of administering intelligence and personality measures (for a review of appropriate tests for children and adolescents, see Anastasi, 1976; Buros, 1978; Cronbach, 1970; Kleinmuntz, 1975). Occasionally also, and especially when the presenting problem involves learning difficulties, a battery of tests designed to diagnose learning disabilities may be administered. All these tests, when considered together, help assess the child's scholastic potential, the content of his or her conflict, and the organization of his or her personality.

In this team effort to diagnose the family's problem, the psychologist obtains one type of data, the psychiatrist another, and the psychiatric social worker a third.[9] Although these data often differ, possibly because of the different techniques used to obtain them, they often supplement rather than conflict with one another.

---

[8] For excellent accounts of the prevention of childhood and adolescent disorders, see Chapter 17 in Kessler (1966) and Chapter 14 of Knopf (1979).

[9] For further descriptions of these and other members of the mental health team, see Chapters 1 and 25.

In conjoint family therapy, as practiced here by Virginia Satir, the therapist works with the entire family.

Beyond the initial goal of diagnosing the child's (and the family's) problem, an objective that is by no means shared by all child guidance workers, most clinics attempt to evaluate the nature of family interrelationships. The basic assumption of this assessment, of course, is that the child-patient's conflicts originated in, and are being sustained by, his family (see Santostefano, 1971, *Miniature Situations-Parent-Child Interaction* method, or MS-PCI).

Case Report 19.4 *Presentation of a "Problem Child"*

Mrs. Z, a 30-year-old housewife, brought Susan, her 7½-year-old daughter, to a clinic with the following main complaints. Susan was doing very poorly in school, she refused attention from mother, and she was generally immature and a loner. When Mrs. Z discussed Susan's problems with the social worker, Mrs. Z emphasized how difficult it was for her to reach Susan, and said that in spite of her motherly overtures, Susan seemed to reject her for some unknown reasons. Mrs. Z also stressed that Susan's 6-year-old sister, Helen, was functioning quite adequately, was doing well in school, and responded well to mother's affection and disciplining. The social worker found Mrs. Z a warm, outgoing, articulate person in the interview situation and had the impression that Mrs. Z's observations could be accepted as reasonably valid. In a play interview the diagnostician found Susan quiet, guarded, and inhibited. She spoke only a few words spontaneously and seemed to avoid interacting with the interviewer. She engaged the toys with what seemed to be little interest, and she failed to develop themes in her play.

The diagnostic team decided to introduce the MS-PCI into the diagnostic study, in part because the information gathered did not suggest a confident disposition to the diagnostic team and in part because the procedure was available at the clinic in an ongoing project. They also decided that the MS-PCI would be administered in one situation to Mrs. Z and Susan, and in another situation to Mrs. Z and Susan's sister, Helen. This decision was made because Mrs. Z emphasized in her interview with the social worker that she experienced her two daughters differently and observed her daughters responding to her mothering in very different ways. Accordingly the diagnosticians felt that observations of mother negotiating with the identified patient, when compared with observations of mother negotiating with the well-adjusted sibling, should contribute diagnostic information that would aid in understanding the problem and in selecting a disposition.

SOURCE: *Santostefano, S.* Beyond nosology: Diagnosis from the viewpoint of development. *Adapted from Herbert E. Rie, ed.,* Perspectives in child psychopathology. *Chicago: Aldine-Atherton, Inc., 1971. Copyright © 1971 by Aldine-Atherton, Inc. Reprinted by permission of the author and Aldine Publishing Company.*

Case Report 19.4 describes a housewife who was referred to the clinic with a typical problem—a child who was doing poorly in school. We shall use this case to illustrate one assessment situation involving the MS-PCI, the *mutual transactions* portion (Type I). This situation offered options to the child of guiding mother through a pencil-and-paper maze (while mother, with eyes closed, held a pencil) or of being guided by mother through a maze. Both Susan, the identified patient described in Case Report 19.4, and her younger sister, Helen, chose to be guided by mother. While guiding Susan, mother held the top of the pencil, making no contact with Susan's hand; she performed the act stiffly and did not comment spontaneously. Susan was solemn throughout. With Helen, the mother held her hand while guiding her through the maze, smiling and commenting freely. Helen reciprocated

with bursts of laughter. After completing the task, mother spontaneously and enthusiastically noted that Helen does "A" work in school and that she happened to have brought along one of Helen's school papers.

The critical observation here, obviously, is that mother behaved one way toward the identified patient and another way toward her sister—or as Santostefano expressed it (1971, p. 170): "The diagnostic team concluded that much of Susan's problem lay in the give and take which had been established between mother and Susan."

That diagnosis and treatment are a routinuum is evident from Santostefano's concluding remark about this case (p. 170):

It was decided that given the limited clinic time available for individual psychotherapy, it would be most effective if a therapist worked intensively with mother with the specific goals of familiarizing her with the restrictions she is placing on Susan's efforts to gain nurture, and of uncovering, if possible, some of the dynamics and unconscious factors in mother's personality which were contributing to the particular caretaking role she manifested in her negotiations with Susan.

Several alternatives to traditional psychotherapy, especially as far as the child-patient is concerned, are described next.

Treatment

After the decision is made to continue a particular family in treatment, the youngster becomes the focal point of therapy. Because the other members of the family, especially the parents, are considered an integral part of the youngster's behavior problems, they, too, as we indicated above, are often seen for treatment in the clinic.

Psychoanalytic Child Therapy. The first systematic treatment of a child, according to one source (Rosenblatt, 1971), was carried out by a parent. Under the direction of Sigmund Freud, a father (Freud, 1909) treated his 4-year-old son—the now celebrated case of "Little Hans" —for a phobia in which the child was afraid to go out in the street for fear that a horse would bite him. The father acted as the child's analyst, reporting to Freud regularly and receiving written instructions by return mail on ways of dealing with and interpreting Hans's behavior.

But the person most responsible for the development of child analysis as a discipline was Sigmund Freud's daughter, Anna, who in 1926 gave her famous series of lectures introducing the technique of child psychoanalysis. These lectures were later published (Freud, 1946), and they were responsible for a great "outpouring of activity" in the techniques of child analysis (Rosenblatt, 1971), a flurry of literary activity that to this day is still unmatched.

But because children do not easily verbalize their problems or conflicts, child psychoanalysis is not considered applicable to most cases. Children often require special therapeutic techniques, usually the action-oriented or play therapies described below. Through his actions or free play, the child reveals much about his fears, anxieties, aspirations, feelings, and frustrations; and because a child does not control his or her life situation, they usually involve his relationships with his parents and siblings.[10] The older the child, of course, the more closely therapy resembles the "talking cure" of adults (see Chapter 22), even though in many instances action orientation still remains a useful catalyst for verbalization.

Play Therapy. Children's primary mode of expression and activity is play, and therefore *play therapy* is the natural technique to apply when approaching them. Various media of play are used;

In play therapy the child's feelings and conflicts are expressed through play, which can serve as a diagnostic or a therapeutic device. Here clinicians watching through a one-way mirror record their observations on a child who is attacking an inflated doll.

for the younger child they include the standard toys, clay, and water and finger paints, as well as miniature household furniture, dolls, and punching bags; older children and adolescents are usually engaged in board games, billiards, or Ping-Pong and the like.

Play and action serve a number of functions in therapy. At the outset they can be valuable "icebreakers" because few children can just sit down and talk their problems over with a total stranger; throughout therapy they permit the

---

[10] This action-oriented play does not rule out psychoanalytic interpretations and handling of treatment. In fact, theorists of many depth-psychological approaches use play therapy as a means of communicating with younger children.

Table 19.3
Data Obtained from 24 Studies on Success of
Treatment in Childhood Disorders

Disorder	Number of Studies	Number of Cases	Percent Total Improvement
Psychosis	5	252	65
Neurosis	3	230	61
Acting-out	5	349	55
Special symptoms	5	213	77
Mixed cases	6	697	68
Total	24	1741	65

Source: Levitt (1963).

child and adolescent to express their most secret wishes and feelings. The aggressive or hostile child, for example, can express his or her animosities by punching or dismembering dolls or dummies; and the frustrated and anxious one can release his pent-up emotions by reenacting with the surrogates numerous scenes that involve members of his or her family. Some patients even attain therapeutic "release" merely by throwing darts, smashing objects, or smearing paint all over a canvas or themselves.[11]

The therapist may or may not elect to interpret these expressions to the patient, depending on his or her theoretical biases, the stage of therapy, and the child's readiness to accept such interpretations; but regardless of the immediate use the therapist makes of the material, he or she has gained important information about the child that might not have been obtained otherwise. With older children, however, especially those over the age of 10, the therapist may elect not to withhold interpretations and often tries to help the child to be aware of his or her own feelings on a conscious level.

Behavior Therapy. Increasingly play therapy is being replaced by behavior therapy. As we will show in the theoretical discussion in Chapter 23, it deals more directly with the control of conditions that reward both the adaptive and maladaptive behaviors of children.

Behavior techniques are particularly valuable in the treatment of conditions that have identifiable symptoms requiring modification: for example, phobias, compulsions, tics, stuttering, thumb-sucking, enuresis, and autism. This finding was clearly supported by one reviewer, who noted an overall comparative improvement rate of 65 percent for the psychotherapies, which is about the same rate found among untreated children with similar disorders (Table 19.3). But the highest rate of improvement, 77 percent, occurred in children with special symptoms (tics, enuresis, school phobia); according to the reviewer this improvement was probably due to the greater use of behavior modification techniques to treat these cases (Levitt, 1963).[12]

The current interest in the applications of behavior therapy to children's disorders, according to one group of psychologists (Miller et al., 1971), is due to a general disillusionment with the efficacy of psychodynamic theory to account for known facts of human behavior and to its failure to deal with a wider variety of behavior disorders, especially the more profoundly disturbed types (autism and schizophrenia). In Chapter 13 we indicated how this technique had been successfully used in shaping language in autistic children. One more illustration of its use to treat a more

---

[11] This form of *release therapy*, as it is sometimes called, was first developed by Levy in 1938 and operates on the assumption that the release itself is therapeutically valuable and cathartic.

[12] A thorough theoretical and methodological review of behavioral treatment techniques may be found in Ross's chapter on behavior therapy (1972).

common phenomenon, the *brat syndrome,* follows (Bernal et al., 1968).

According to Bernal and her associates (1968) and others (Anderson and Dean, 1956; Miller et al., 1971), brats are the garden-variety patients of child guidance clinics. The typical brat dominates the family with tantrums; aggresses against parents, siblings, and peers; and is a disruptive influence on the family, neighborhood, and school. Case Report 19.5 briefly illustrates the use of behavior modification in the treatment of a brat. Our write-up is based on a condensation provided by Miller et al. (1971) in their review of behavior therapy with children.

Case Report 19.5 *Behavior Therapy of a Brat*

Jeff, an 8¹/₂-year-old boy, was destructive and disruptive. The therapist's first move was to insist that Jeff's parents clarify their deteriorated marital situation by having the father live apart from the mother. This reduced much of the strain in the family interactions. Then on the basis of a careful analysis of mother's dealings with Jeff, it was learned that mother's clues about her displeasure with Jeff's misbehavior were unclear and that she was not always consistent in differentiating her expressions of displeasure, affection, and warmth. The therapists decided that she would be taught to provide clear cues about her anger when her son misbehaved, that she was to spank him if it continued, and that she should be certain that Jeff understood which behavior earned spanking. Finally, and perhaps equally important, Jeff's mother was taught to identify acceptable behaviors and to reinforce them with warmth and affection.

SOURCE: *M. Bernal, J. Duryee, H. Pruett, and B. Burns. Behavior modification and the "brat syndrome."* Journal of Consulting Psychology, *1968, 32, 447–455. Copyright 1968 by the American Psychological Association. Reproduced by permission.*

The principles of learning applied in this treatment case are simple: identify the contingen-

cies associated with one kind of response, differentiate stimuli associated with different responses, reward the desired response, and punish the undesired ones. To accomplish this, videotapes were made of the sessions, in which the identified patient's mother carried out the therapist's instruction. These provided the necessary feedback to the behavior modifiers, and enabled them, within 25 weeks, to help mother gain control of her brat. "Beyond this," according to Miller and his associates (1971, p. 364), "Jeff's mother replaced her terror of him with genuine affection."

Hospitals and Residential Treatment Centers. Some children are sufficiently disturbed to require hospitalization or the services of a residential treatment center. These cases usually include children with autistic disorders or extreme feeding problems, and others whose disorders require round-the-clock observation and care. The decision to institutionalize children or adolescents is usually made on the basis of the severity of the youngster's symptoms and the degree of psychopathology of his or her parents. For example, a severely disturbed child being reared by a schizophrenic mother would invariably require hospitalization. Less obvious instances are children whose parents simply cannot manage them.

Follow-up studies of children placed in treatment centers, according to one psychologist's review of the literature (Kessler, 1966), are poorly designed but tend to corroborate the personal conviction by the therapy staff that the hospital treatment improved the child's condition more than could be expected from maturation alone. We shall have more to say about these hospitals and several contemporary alternatives to them in Chapter 25.[13]

---

[13] A recent historical review of traditional child guidance facilities and other community alternatives for treating the behaviorally deviant child may be found in Knopf (1979) and Rhodes and Gibbins (1972).

Disorders of Aging

At the other end of the developmental continuum —beyond what Gail Sheehy (1974) in her popular book, *Passages*, calls the "deadline" or "midlife" decades—is old age. Precisely what old age is varies from person to person, depending on overall physical health and psychological outlook on life; but in general people in the United States are considered elderly if they are over 65.

This elderly population is becoming larger mainly as a result of new lifesaving drugs and techniques. For example, in 1940 only 6.8 percent of the population was 65 or older; by 1970 this percentage climbed to 9.9. A recent projection indicates that this percentage will be about 10.5 by 1984 but should remain relatively constant thereafter.

Gerontology (the study of the elderly) is a relatively recent development; it is society's acknowledgment that we now have a large segment of the population that needs social and psychological attention, a segment that is particularly susceptible to a whole new set of stresses and strains.

Attitudes Toward Aging

The way younger people perceive the elderly is related to the way young and middle-aged people view their own prospects of aging, as well as the way the elderly perceive themselves.

Research evidence indicates that elementary school children view older people as feeble, unable to get around, and mean (Hickey et al., 1968), and that high school and college students viewed them even more negatively (Hickey and Kalish, 1968). The trend, however, is in the direction of more favorable attitudes toward the elderly (Kalish, 1975), attitudes perhaps fostered by sympathetic media presentations of this group. In another study (Ahammer and Baltes, 1972) adolescents and young and middle-aged adults placed greater value on their own autonomy and independence than the elderly did, which led one expert (Meyer, 1977) to conclude that young people attempt to mold the elderly into a stereotype that elderly people resist.

How do the elderly perceive themselves? An extensive lifespan study involving 4000 people, ages 9 to 89, provides some answers to this question (Monge, 1976). In this study participants were asked to rate the concept *my characteristic self* on 21 polar adjective pairs. Interestingly, the age trend for one factor, "congeniality–sociability," is in the unpredicted direction in that older people viewed themselves as more congenial and more sociable than adolescents and adults did. The investigator suspected that this age effect was due to sampling procedures rather than to real age differences between these groups. (The elderly were selected from Senior Citizen centers and social clubs, settings that attract congenial and sociable people rather than the alienated and incapacitated.) A question that can be answered in future research, however, is whether the social settings attract sociable and congenial people or produce them.

Findings in the expected direction in this study were the self-concept ratings of adjustment. Adjustment was rated least positively during the years 20 to 34, with a steady decline beginning at adolescence, but with consistently increasing positive self-concept until the mid-sixties. Thereafter, at about retirement age and beyond, there is a decline in self-perception of adjustment, a decline that is understandable in view of the many new adjustments that need to be made during this stage. We shall elaborate on some of these in the following sections.

Family Relationships

Older people are reluctant to live with their children and prefer to maintain their own households (Troll, 1971). In part this is based on their desire to permit younger people to live their own lives, but mainly it seems to reflect a need of the elderly to retain their former independence, demonstrate their competency, and assert their self-determination. And indeed available studies indicate that the elderly in the United States do generally live in their own homes (Shanas et al., 1968; Streib, 1958; Sussman, 1965).

Unfortunately, however, this independence is often undermined by circumstances not under the control of older people. Financial stringencies, chronic ill health, and the death of a spouse may force an older person to seek new living arrangements. For the elderly, who may have become set in their ways, these altered arrangements present a host of new problems and are often seen as signs of being abandoned and betrayed by their children and spouses.

Usually they are moved into a home for the aged, where they must depend on someone else to attend to their physical needs. This loss of independence—even when they move in with relatives—is a major stressor for the aged. Furthermore they are isolated from the rest of the community. Because they spend most of their time with contemporaries, they lose touch with the outside world and are deprived of contacts with younger, more active people. Consequently such homes can become way-stations to death. Children often suffer guilt because they have had to "put a parent away." This guilt may make visits unpleasant—and hence infrequent—leaving the old person to face new despair at what is interpreted as rejection.

Loss of a Spouse

Perhaps the greatest crisis confronting the older person is the loss of a spouse. Since men tend to die younger than women (a trend that seems to be changing as women increasingly enter the "man's" workaday world) and because women usually marry men older than themselves, it is far more likely that women will lose their husbands than that husbands will lose their wives.

Loss of a spouse usually causes deep bereavement, often accompanied by guilt and by loss of companionship and sexual satisfaction, as well as changes in friendship and social patterns. Again these readjustments, never easy even at earlier stages of life, are extremely difficult for the elderly.

Retirement

For people with adequate incomes retirement may bring opportunities for a variety of new activities, especially if they have planned in advance to occupy themselves with such activities. For most older people, however, perhaps because of their feelings of uselessness as a result of being "set out to pasture," the new leisure is accompanied by boredom and depression. Whether the adjustment to retirement will be satisfying or not is influenced by the older person's health, alternative sources of satisfaction, and financial security (Streib, 1956).

Like their male counterparts, career or working women undergo an abrupt change of status upon retirement. But for women who are homemakers, a form of retirement usually occurs earlier, at about the time their children leave home. This may be accompanied by boredom and unhappiness; but again, if properly planned for, it can also be a time to embark on a new career.

For both men and women the level of active engagement in life's affairs seems to be a good index of positive adaptation to aging (Maddox, 1963). A study of 250 older people showed that morale levels were directly related to activity levels: increasing activity levels were indicative of increasing morale, and decreasing activity levels were associated with decreasing morale. This study reversed the findings of an earlier one (Cumming and Henry, 1961), which suggested that disengagement, or withdrawing from activities, by the elderly was a positive adaptive approach. The relationships between these variables are complex and still need sorting out (see Havighurst et al., 1968; Neugarten et al., 1968).

Menopause

The menopause, or "change of life," occurs at about the time children may be leaving home. This physiological period during a woman's life, usually beginning between the ages of 46 and 50, when menstruation gradually ceases and the child bearing capacity comes to an end, can be accompanied by physical changes and discomforts as well as psychological readjustments. The degree to which these reactions are disruptive varies considerably among women, depending again upon prior planning, but has been estimated to be as low as 10 percent of women undergoing the menopause. The simultaneous departure of children from the home at this time has obscured the psychological consequences of menopause, but generally women who earlier had perceived their lives as happy and meaningful are less likely to experience serious adverse effects during menopause.

Questionnaire evidence about women's attitudes toward menopause (Neugarten et al., 1968) indicates strong age differences in the perception of menopause. More younger (21 to 44) than older (45 to 65) women viewed menopause as a significant event. The investigators speculated that these differences were due to a lack of concern among older women about the loss of reproductive capacity, and that a generally positive attitude toward life helps to minimize adverse effects of menopause.

Anxiety about Death and Dying

Contrary to the popular belief that one of the greatest anxieties of the aged is death and dying, some recent evidence (Kastenbaum and Aisenberg, 1972) suggests that most old people are not afraid of death. Death seems to be feared most by young people, who seem also to express more hostility toward dying than do the elderly. But since death and dying are still relatively unstudied topics, more questions than answers are available, and not all of them are relevant for the aged. Some of the more pertinent questions for our purposes are (Kastenbaum and Aisenberg, 1972, pp. 107–108): "How does aversion . . . to death develop? What stages does it pass through? What are the critical factors which influence its scope, particularity, and intensity? . . . From what standpoint can we say that one orientation toward death—fearing, sorrowing, overcoming, participating—is 'better' than another?" Answers to some of these questions can be useful in helping the elderly cope with one of their greatest crises mentioned earlier, the loss of a spouse.

Psychopathology

It is difficult to determine whether certain forms of psychopathology are consequences or correlates of some of the aforementioned social crises of aging, or whether psychopathology is due to a deficiency in biological functioning (Gurland, 1973). Clearly anxiety and apprehension in the elderly that may seriously affect their adjustment can result from the loss of job, close friends, spouse, relatives, association with young people, independence, social status, or health. A common expression of anxiety among the elderly is *hypochondriasis* (Busse, 1970). This is more common among women, but for either sex at these advanced ages it is difficult to separate the part of hypochondriasis that is attributable to failing health from what is a channeled outlet for anxiety.

In view of the many losses incurred by the aged, it is also not surprising to find that *depression* is common. This variety of psychopathology, formerly considered a psychosis and called "involutional melancholia" (APA, 1968), is now simply differentiated on the basis of whether or not it is episodic or chronic and age-related (APA, 1980). Depression that is associated with old age is considered by some to be a normal reaction to aging (Meyer, 1977) and by others to be related to psychological changes (Gurland, 1973). But regardless of its etiology, depression is common in this age group (Busse and Reckless, 1961; Zinberg and Kaufman, 1963), a fact that makes suicide a real possibility for some elderly people (see Chapter 14).

Among the aged there is also a high incidence of psychopathology directly related to a deficiency in biological functioning, especially to accidents of a cerebrovascular nature. The terms dementia and organic mental disorders are often applied to behavioral and cognitive disturbances associated with the brain damage that results from these accidents, although the organic disorders can result from nonaging causes.

The two main organic mental disorders that are of interest to us here are what DSM III (APA, 1980) labels the *senile* and *presenile* dementias (also called Alzheimer's, Pick's, or Jacob–Creutzfeldt disease). The essential feature of senile dementia is the appearance after age 65 of a gradual onset of decreased intellectual functioning sufficiently severe to interfere with social or occupational functioning. The deficits usually involve memory and problem-solving judgment, as well as personality changes that include poor impulse control and a withdrawal from social interactions.

Although the course of the deficits accompanying senile brain damage is steadily progressive and presumably irreversible, each case is different, often depending on how much brain tissue is affected. In most cases, however, memory failure is the most prominent feature, and this involves anterograde and retrograde amnesia. That is to say, the older person so afflicted has both an inability to reason new things (anterograde amnesia) and difficulty in recalling past events (retrograde amnesia). Past events may be remembered well, but the person may forget names, telephone numbers, directions, and recent events and conversations.

Previous personality traits of the senile elderly may become accentuated. Hence a previously compulsive individual may become more so, and one who was slovenly may become more unkempt, careless, and sloppy. In the most severe cases there is increasing apathy, slovenliness, and helplessness, and only the simplest vegetative functions are preserved.

Affect and mood may be labile in the organically damaged elderly; their moods may vary quickly from euphoria to calm to tears. However, the predominant feature is depression, marked by notable slowing down of most psychomotor functions (for example, speech, gait, or gestures).

The personality and cognitive functioning of people with presenile dementia are similar to those just described. The main difference between the two is one of age, the age of onset being before 65 for presenile disorders. Although the prevalence of the presenile disorders is unknown, they are usually considered rare conditions, and their cause, in contrast to senile dementia, is almost always rapid deterioration, or atrophy, of the entire brain.

While people with these conditions often show schizophrenic-like and psychotic behavior—hallucinations, delusions of persecution, and other cognitive disturbances—they rarely mimic the symptoms of schizophrenia exactly (Pincus and Tucker, 1978). Disorientation, confusion, and fluctuating states of alertness and apathy are rarely present in schizophrenia, but are often present in behavior disorders associated with brain damage.

Environments and Treatment for the Aged

Obviously there is no cure for aging; nor has any one therapy orientation been found most suitable for this group. Nonetheless there are optimal environments for the aged in terms of both the seemingly impossible physical demands that they must meet in old age and the psychological adjustments that must be made.

One such model environment, based on the work of the Environmental Psychology Program of the City University of New York (Kiritz and Moos, 1974; Proshansky et al., 1970; Schwartz, 1975), provides essential cues and aids to help the aged get around (easily read signs), avoid hazards (texture markers), and locate service areas (color-schemes). In addition this environment is designed to encourage the use of all senses (bright colors, music, nonbland foods, textured surfaces), to maintain variety (opportunities to adjust and regulate sensory inputs), and to challenge the elderly with activities that are interesting (TV, radio, books, and magazines as well as crafts, hobbies, pets, and exposure to babies, children, and young adults). And most essentially, perhaps, the design of this model environment includes physical support features that assure the aged of safety (oversize knobs, controls that are regulated by arm or leg pressure), easy

access to communication (in-house phones), and privacy (locks on doors, entering a room only when invited).

But this is an ideal environment only now beginning to be promulgated for the aged. In the meantime several housing possibilities are available for ambulatory older people, though they are less than ideal. For example, a relatively recent development is the so-called senior citizen's community. Typically such a planned community provides elderly people the opportunity to gather together socially and to help one another cope with some of the physical and psychological threats of the outside world. Most such communities restrict residency exclusively to the aged. Many of the elderly find these communities objectionable, for ironically such an environment throws together people whose only common bond is old age. Others feel cut off from the mainstream of society. For these people there are other planned arrangements where care is taken to include, within the bounds of the community, younger families with children and other residents of various ages and occupations. This microcosm of the "real world," however, has been deemed too expensive for older people whose sole source of income is pensions.

Federal and state housing projects have been largely unsuccessful in relieving the living and housing problems of the elderly. Most low-rent, high-rise apartments have been designed for the entire low-rent group, rather than specifically for the elderly. One consequence is that the elderly cannot cope in an environment designed for younger people; another consequence, particularly in large cities such as New York, Chicago, Detroit, and Philadelphia, is that the elderly are victimized and often brutally beaten and killed by younger people who are determined to take advantage of these easy and vulnerable targets. Therefore, aside from the intense loneliness and isolation experienced by these people thrown into unplanned housing projects, most of the elderly are terrified at the prospects of leaving, or even unlocking the doors of, their apartments.

Dignity, humanity, and love can be realized at any age.

There are other state and federal programs, the latter being administered mainly by the Administration on Aging, that provide elderly people with information relevant to their lives. Some of these programs include Meals-on-Wheels, providing food for the nonambulatory aged; centers for health and education services; day-care facilities for outpatient medical services and physical therapy; a foster grandparent program that pays nominal fees to the elderly in return for services they render to institutionalized children; and the Retired Senior Volunteer Program, which places the elderly in unpaid community service capacities in libraries, hospitals, etc.

For the totally nonambulatory elderly there are mainly hospitals and nursing homes. At best these can be pleasant way-stations for people who are helpless and are awaiting death; but very often, particularly in the many poorly administered nursing homes now being exposed for their corruption and obscene neglect of the aged, they are unpleasant, foul-smelling quarters that rob the aged of their dignity and humanity.

Summary

The problem in classifying psychopathological disorders of childhood is that symptoms are not yet well formed and do not present cohesive clusters or syndromes. Here we grouped together the two childhood disturbances associated with feeding and elimination and the two aggressive and withdrawal behaviors that youngsters often display against their trainers. We also described four adolescent disturbances—school phobia, depression, schizophrenia, and neurosis; these adolescent disorders resemble their adult counterparts more closely than childhood abnormalities do.

With the possible exception of infantile autism and schizophrenia, the origins of childhood and adolescent disorders were traced to family and other environmental influences. We noted that the contemporary trend is toward attending to patterns of influences rather than to specific parent-to-child interactions.

The definition and etiology of hyperactivity

are still controversial. The most commonly used hypothesis is minimal brain dysfunction, but others include drug effects of food additives and incomplete brain cell proliferation due to somatosensory deprivation during the perinatal period. Some clinicians doubt the existence of such a disease.

The diagnosis and treatment of childhood and adolescent disorders occur in child guidance clinics, residential treatment centers, and, more recently, in other community-based action programs.

Aging may bring with it a new set of problems, some arising from people's attitudes toward aging and the aging person's self-perception. Elderly people are often segregated from the rest of society and face rejection and despair. Other factors in disorders of aging include be-reavement following the loss of a spouse, anxiety about dying, depression, and disorders resulting from physiological deficits.

Terms and Concepts to Master

Aggression	MS-PCI
Anorexia nervosa	Play therapy
Anterograde amnesia	Presenile dementia
Brat syndrome	Release therapy
Encopresis	Retrograde amnesia
Enuresis	School phobia
Gerontology	Senile dementia
Menopause	

3

Behavior Change

The tendency of problematical or unsatisfying behavior to perpetuate itself is often outweighed by the impetus for change that it generates. Sometimes that impetus is strong enough to produce a spontaneous remission—the organism heals itself, as it does when it recovers from an infection or a laceration. In many instances, however, outside help is desirable or necessary, and the individual makes a commitment to use some form of counseling, psychotherapy, or self-help technique. In Chapter 20 we look at the essential elements of psychotherapy, and in the following four chapters we explore a selected sample of the great variety of therapeutic approaches derived from four major models of human nature. We discuss physical treatments in Chapter 21, psychodynamic therapies in Chapter 22, behavior therapy in Chapter 23, and humanistic–existential therapies in Chapter 24. In Chapter 25 we explore the history and present status of community mental health care.

20 Elements of Psychotherapy

Once a person has made the decision to seek help, either out of distress or because of a desire for a more rewarding life, what options are available? In subsequent chapters we shall discuss the approaches offered by different schools of psychology, reflecting the various models of human nature and human pathology. Here we shall examine the forms in which those differing contexts of therapy may be presented.

Ultimately, of course, the personality and experience of the therapist are likely to count more than ideology or format. Nevertheless some forms and methods seem to be more useful than others for particular problems or goals. For example, the degree of intervention attempted by therapists runs the gamut from a completely noninterfering, Taoist stance (Taoism is essentially trust in the way of nature) among Rogerians to very forceful direct manipulation in some medical and behavior-directive therapies. It is doubtful that any one point on that spectrum marks the best approach to *all* problems. The presence of such a bewildering array may be confusing, but it has the advantage of increasing the likelihood of finding the most appropriate path for an individual. Besides, if psychotherapy were less diverse, it might not be nearly as interesting.

What Is Psychotherapy?

All psychotherapies begin with an inquiry into the nature of the problem and then attempt to change behavior or personality. Nearly all psychoanalytic therapies rely on verbal give-and-take, as do Rogerian and similar humanistic–existential therapies. At the other extreme the medically based therapies attempt to change the person physically through drugs, shock, or surgery. An increasing number of therapies fall somewhere near the middle of that spectrum. For example, behavior therapies restructure the person's environment, thus compelling him to alter his responses. Some therapies, such as Gestalt and psychodrama, involve the person in an enactment of his conflicts. Therapies with a Reichian orientation attempt, using a variety of physical and verbal techniques, to free the person of the body tension with which he holds back feeling. Some combine the Reichian and Gestalt approaches in such a way that the work is physical and verbal at the same time. And an increasing number of therapists are able to move freely back and forth between directive and nondirective, verbal and nonverbal approaches as the needs of the patient or client dictate.

Commonalities

Psychotherapies have the following qualities in common:

First the therapist always *accepts* the person for what he or she is. Regardless of the therapist's biases and standards, and no matter what the patient says or claims to have done, the therapist does not make moral judgments. Occasionally this raises difficult ethical issues, as, for example, when a patient discloses plans to injure someone. Should the therapist be neutral under these circumstances? Or should the therapist attempt to dissuade or even report the patient?

Fortunately these cases are rare, and in most instances the therapist can be totally accepting of the patient—an acceptance that is essential if the patient is to develop trust and respect for the therapist and a willingness to disclose his or her most personal feelings.

A second common feature of individual psychotherapy, which arises because all therapeutic systems are outgrowths of the interview, is its emphasis on *verbal communication* as a means for establishing connections between the patient's inner and outer worlds. The therapist needs considerable listening skills and the ability to facilitate free expression. Therapy demands more than just listening and responding; it requires the ability to grasp meanings from minimal cues—it calls for what Theodor Reik (1948, p. 145), a Freudian psychoanalyst, refers to as "receiving, recording, and decoding these 'asides,' which are whispered between sentences and without sentences." Reik calls this "listening with the third ear." Such sensitivity facilitates understanding, and the feeling of being understood is a powerful motivator for a troubled client, often encouraging him or her to communicate freely and without constraint.

The third common feature of individual psychotherapy is its two-way commitment, in which each participant performs according to an unwritten agreement. The therapist agrees to assume responsibility for the patient's psychological well-being; in return, the patient is expected to be completely honest, insofar as possible, about his feelings and actions and to be committed to devoting a great deal of energy to changing. This unique relationship, which has been called a *contract* by some (Menninger, 1958) and a *partnership* by others (Sundberg et al., 1973), often requires the therapist to remain aloof from the patient and his problems, lest he (or she) become emotionally involved and hence render himself unable to help.

Not all therapists, however, agree on this point, and some interpret the rules of this contract to suit their own unique styles. Sidney Jourard (1971) believed that the best way to help others is to be honest with them (pp. 139–140):

Effective *therapists . . . follow this simple hypothesis: If they are* themselves *in the presence of the patient, if they let their patient and themselves be, avoiding* compulsions *to silence, to reflection, to interpretation, to impersonal technique . . . but instead striving to know their patient, involving themselves in his situation, and then responding to his utterances with their spontaneous selves, this fosters growth. . . .*

But this . . . relationship is a far cry from the impersonal administration of reflections, interpretations. . . . [He] is quite free and spontaneous in his relationship; his responses are bound only by his ethics and his judgment. He may laugh, scold, become angry, give advice—in short, break most of the rules laid down in psychotherapy training manuals.

A fourth common factor is the *unique interaction* that develops between patient and therapist. It is unlike any other two-person relationship; and whether it is called transference, rapport, spontaneity, or whatever, the intense interpersonal communication that is established is considered essential by most psychotherapists.

Fifth, individual psychotherapy usually aims to provide patients with *insight*. This is implemented differently by each school of therapy and carries various meanings for all of them, but usually refers to the person's achieving a greater understanding of himself or herself in relation to others. Whether the individual is able to apply to everyday affairs the insight gained in therapy is another matter and depends largely on the skills of the therapist.

Goals

Therapeutic goals can be as narrow as the elimination of a tic or as broad as the restructuring of one's personality. Narrow goals are usually pursued most successfully through behavior-directive therapies, such as systematic desensitization, hypnosis, or biofeedback. Transactional Analysis, an analytic therapy that focuses on ego states, self-esteem, "life scripts," and group support, is also often directed toward narrow goals, usually specified in a contract between patient and therapist. Psychoanalysis usually is directed toward broader goals, with an emphasis on the relief of pathology. The humanistic–existential therapies overlap to some extent with both the behavioral and the psychoanalytic approaches, but their emphasis is on growth, on becoming more alive rather than less sick.

Common general or underlying goals are greater ability to cope with everyday affairs, greater awareness of what one is doing and of its significance and consequences, and a greater willingness to accept responsibility for one's own feelings and actions. A more specific goal might be to overcome a phobia or a sexual dysfunction, to relieve anxiety, or to change any habit such as a dependency. Sometimes the goal is educative in the usual sense, as in learning better communication skills to improve one's interactions with others. Sometimes it is educative in a more oriental sense, similar to the sudden freshness of perception associated with the *satori* (enlightenment) experience of Zen.

The Setting

In recent years there has been a proliferation of therapeutic approaches and of the settings in which therapy occurs. Treatment of behavioral disorders is no longer limited to the ward of a mental hospital and the psychoanalyst's office. As we shall see in Chapter 25, a variety of innovative settings are being used, including community mental health centers, halfway houses, and crisis intervention centers.

Perhaps the most novel of the new settings is the growth center, which resembles a health resort more than a hospital. The prototypical growth center is, of course, Esalen Institute at Big Sur, California. People who want to get more out of life and have the money to pay for it can spend a weekend or a week or longer at Esalen in any of a staggering variety of activities—encounter, Gestalt, massage, movement, sensory awareness, yoga, Rolfing, aikido, jogging, Feldenkrais exercises, T'ai Chi Chuan, psychosynthesis, fight training for couples, psychodrama, polarity therapy, Reichian therapy, biofeedback training, or any of several dozen other ways of expanding one's experience. Esalen also conducts shorter and less expensive seminars and workshops in San Francisco and elsewhere. Smaller growth centers and holistic health centers have appeared throughout the country, with the greatest concentration in California.

The Psychotherapist

The mental health team in institutional settings has traditionally consisted of the psychiatrist, the clinical psychologist, and the psychiatric social worker.

Psychiatrist

The psychiatrist is a medically trained specialist who holds an M.D. degree. His (or her) education was in medicine (anatomy, neuroanatomy, biochemistry, pathology, physiology), and his experiences include internships within the various medical specialties of surgery, gastroenterology, obstetrics, and so on. After medical school the aspiring psychiatrist undergoes specialized training, or a "residency," in neuropsychiatry, during which time he spends about three years taking courses and acquiring practical experience in psychodiagnosis, psychotherapy, and various special physical or somatic treatment methods.

His unique contribution to the mental health team consists of the medical care of the patient and, as Schofield (1964, p. 119) indicates, this domain "has historically extended to a quasi-legal responsibility (final authority) for such psychological procedures as prescribing changes in activity programs, giving or withholding passes, allowing or disallowing visitors." But increasingly, partly as a result of manpower shortages and partly as a function of the team approach, such decisions are becoming a group responsibility, including the patient (see Chapter 25), or are transferred to the other two members of the team.

Clinical Psychologist

The clinical psychologist holds a Ph.D. degree in psychology, which means that in addition to his (or her) undergraduate and graduate education in personality theory and measurement, abnormal psychology, psychodiagnosis, and psychotherapy, he has also received clinical training in testing, interviewing, and therapy. But instead of medicine the clinical psychologist's main focus is on experimental design, statistics, psychological testing, and research methodology. Because of these latter skills he is better equipped than either the psychiatrist or the social worker for both psychodiagnostic testing and conducting research; often these are his singular contributions to the team effort.

Psychiatric Social Worker

The third member of the team holds an M.S. degree, having completed a two-year graduate course of study that included a formal and practical training similar to that of the psychiatrist and the clinical psychologist. Unique to his or her training is intensive field experience obtaining *in situ* (in the original place) family background data and his knowledge of the functions and policies of various community resource agencies.

Each of these professionals, although equipped somewhat differently to specialize in particular aspects of mental health care delivery, is also trained to conduct psychotherapy. The extent to which each is successful in effecting therapeutic change is more a function of individual skills and experience than of training and educational background.

Although the division of labor we have described is still the pattern in many hospitals, academic credentials often tell very little about the approaches, skills, and methods of therapists in private practice. Only the psychiatrist is authorized to prescribe drugs, but otherwise the three kinds of credentials are often interchangeable in terms of impact on the client.

The Patient

Considerable evidence supports most psychotherapists' belief that therapeutic progress depends on patients' motivation for therapy, and their readiness to confront and communicate their feelings openly (see Korchin, 1976, pp. 446–450). Some of the more specific factors identified include experiencing guilt and anxiety, acknowledging dependency feelings, wanting help, liking the therapist and his or her work, accepting personal responsibility for problems, and seeing them in psychological rather than medical terms. Evidence also suggests that patients regarded by their therapists as attractive have better outcomes and patients rated more likable do better in therapy. Likability or attractiveness, which are to a large extent in the eye of the beholder, probably reflect other qualities valued by therapists, such as motivation, alertness, and psychological mindedness.

But other patient factors also play an important role in the success of psychotherapy. The patient's hopes and expectations, according to J. D. Frank (1973) and his associates at Johns

Psychotherapy was originally created for the relief of the emotional problems of rich clients, mused psychologist George Albee (1976) in a recent paper. He also reminded his audience that Freud's first clients were largely middle- and upper-middle-class women suffering from pseudoneurological ills that Freud, as a neurologist, discovered were due to the conversion of unconscious sexual conflicts into mystifying paralyses and anesthesias. In short the first subjects for psychoanalysis were overcontrolled and neurotic women who were undoubtedly suffering from the sexist, repressive forces characteristic of industrializing societies.

In a later part of the same paper, the main theme of which was Albee's argument that including psychotherapy in national health insurance represents a subsidy to the rich from the poor, he points out that psychotherapists prefer people with the Yavis syndrome (young, attractive, verbal, intelligent, and successful [see Schofield, 1964]). He argues that the training of psychotherapists makes them unsuited for any kind of intervention except one-to-one psychotherapy with middle-class clients.

Hopkins University, influence the course and success of therapy. Intelligence and education seem to influence patients' expectations and motivations and, in turn, affect their acceptance of therapy, their continuing in it, and their gaining from it (Luborsky et al., 1971).

Such demographic variables as age, sex, intelligence, social class, and race are often believed to make a difference in a patient's success in therapy, but the evidence suggests that only the last three factors matter. It is probably true that the brighter, better-educated person can communicate more easily with and better understand the therapist, although the evidence is not entirely clear in this regard. It is evident, however, that lower-class patients are less likely to be referred for psychotherapy than their upper-class counterparts (Hollingshead and Redlich, 1954), and when referred, they are sent for medical or drug therapy. Moreover therapists regard lower-class patients as less interesting, more pathological, and—if offered psychotherapy—more likely to refuse such treatment or break off prematurely. These considerations led one community psychiatrist to comment wryly (Dumont, 1968, p. 25) that "psychotherapy, as generally practiced, requires a patient who is verbal, insightful, and motivated, one who can delay gratification, and who, more or less, shares the values of the therapist, thereby virtually excluding the lower-class person from treatment."

Format

One-to-one interaction for 50 minutes once a week is the traditional format for psychotherapy, and still a popular one, but it is only one of a wide range of possibilities. One may be seen individually or in couple, family, or group therapy, by one or two therapists, once a week, twice a week, for two or two and a half consecutive days in a weekend workshop, for 24 or more continuous hours in a marathon, or every day for a week in some growth center workshops. We shall discuss examples of many of these formats in the chapters that follow.

Individual Therapy

Psychoanalysis is, of course, the classic example of individual therapy. One sees a therapist, usually a psychiatrist with analytic training, for one or more 50-minute sessions a week for several years. Many Rogerian therapists expect therapy to be complete in one year or less. Behavior-directive therapies are often limited to a few sessions.

Couple and Family Therapy

Often the causes of human distress lie not so much in the character or personality of the individual as in the interactive patterns of a couple or a family. In such cases the most effective therapy format is to see the entire unit—the couple or family—in therapy. Marriage counseling is the most familiar form of couple therapy. Rather than depend entirely on the inevitably biased reports of one individual or the other, the therapist is able to see the actual interactions between the two people, and to call their attention to their ways of relating and communicating. Many approaches to sex therapy, including that of Masters and Johnson, employ couple therapy. Still another form of couple therapy is the couples group. This is the format used by George Bach in his popular fight training for couples (Bach and Wyden, 1968; Bach and Deutsch, 1970). Bach teaches couples nondestructive ways to express their angry feelings toward each other as an alternative to conflict avoidance and destructive fighting.

Family therapy proceeds somewhat as follows: first, the therapist meets with the member who seeks help at the clinic. Nathan Ackerman, one of the earlier contributors to family therapy, refers to that person as the "primary patient" and considers him or her the ticket of admission to the clinic of "an emotionally warped family group" (Ackerman, 1958, p. 104).

The therapist subsequently meets with the family as a unit and becomes a participant observer of their interactions. Occasionally, especially at the outset, the therapist may invite himself to the home where he can observe, firsthand, conflicts and exchanges as they develop *in vitro*. Once in the home, he also has the opportunity to view the living conditions of the family and may meet with and involve in the interview other significant persons such as grandparents, aunts, or servants. Regardless of setting, however, the main purpose is to interview "all the people living under one roof: there may be three generations with a grandmother; there may be an aunt or uncle" (Ackerman, 1961a, p. 241).

As he succeeds in establishing a working relationship with the family, the therapist may alternate its various units; he may elect to see one parent at a time, both parents, or any combination of parent or sibling, as he sees fit, all the while attempting to gain an understanding of what makes the family tick.

The therapeutic goals consist mainly of fostering greater family equilibrium, promoting improved communication among its members, and remedying the circumstances that brought in the primary patient in the first place. These aims may involve manipulation of undesirable environmental conditions or simply strengthening each family member's ability to cope with situations in and outside the home.

There is one notable exception to the usual format of family therapy. Whereas traditional approaches assume that deviant behavior results from long-term family conflicts, and that change can only be brought about by altering these conflicts, most therapists working within the behavioral, or more specifically within the operant conditioning, framework (see Fontana, 1966; Patterson and Cobb, 1971) make no such assumptions. Instead they attempt to modify the reinforcing conditions within the family that serve to sustain maladaptive behavior. The goals in these instances are to train family members to alter the reinforcement schedules that foster deviant behavior; such goals are often achieved by teaching parents to observe and then to alter their own and their children's behaviors and reinforcement contingencies.

An illustration of how family behavior therapy operates is presented in Case Report 20.1, which indicates how a mother was trained to extinguish the temper tantrums, aggressiveness, and bizarre verbal behavior of her 8-year-old-son. This case was discussed in Chapter 19 as an example of the ''brat'' syndrome.

Case Report 20.1 *Family Behavior Therapy*

The first step in training was to teach the mother to reduce her verbal output and to selectively ignore all of Jeff's abusive behaviors, from sulking to direct physical assault. This plan was intended to help her to make decisions about her own behavior as she and Jeff interacted, and to extinguish his abuse.

Step two was to establish certain maternal behaviors as conditioned negative reinforcers by associating them with physical punishment. The behaviors, or cues, consisted of ignoring abuse and if ignoring did not stop it, the mother was to express anger and order him to stop. Finally, if he did not stop, she was to spank him. Hopefully, these cues—ignoring, frowning, angry tone of voice, the word ''don't'' etc.—if clearly presented and consistently paired with punishment when the boy did not obey, would take on properties of conditioned negative reinforcers.

SOURCE: *M. Bernal, J. Duryee, H. Pruett, and B. Burns. Behavior modification and the ''brat syndrome.'' Journal of Consulting Psychology, 1968, 32, 447–455. Copyright 1968 by the American Psychological Association. Reproduced by permission.*

Group Psychotherapy

Group psychotherapy, which has been with us for over fifty years,[1] gained increasing recognition

immediately after World War II because of the growing demands of large numbers of people for whom individual care was impossible. This recognition contributed to a rapid rise in the development and acceptance of group methods in state and private institutions and especially in the armed forces. Subsequently the use of group therapy in the mental health services of the Veterans Administration hospitals had an important impact on its growth.

Classroom Beginnings. Many forms of early *group therapy* resembled classrooms in which the therapist was the lecturer. He introduced an agreed-upon topic and tried to stimulate student-like participation among patients. The main object of these groups was to help participants achieve better motivation for living and to impart information about good mental health practices.

These groups were often referred to as *inspirational* or *fellowship* groups, and they were formed because people had a common problem that needed solution (like Alcoholics Anonymous or Synanon; see Chapters 9 and 10). Invariably these sessions stirred intensive emotional interactions among participants, and gradually the classroom procedure gave way to a less rigid group structure in which feelings were expressed more readily.

Contemporary Group Therapy. Today group psychotherapy involves as many variations as there are different points of view, and its main objective is to help the individual, within the group context, gain insight into his or her own personality and behavior. How this is accomplished varies greatly with the orientation of the leader. Some follow classic Freudian or Adlerian models, while others prefer less interpretive approaches. Freudians, for example, see themselves as authority or father figures, perceive group members as siblings acting out with one another, and engage freely in the interpretation of feelings. Everything a patient does and says is treated as *transference* and is subject to analysis in

---

[1] Rudolf Dreikurs (1969), an Adlerian therapist, mentions that Adler and his coworkers had used group approaches in their child guidance centers in Vienna since 1921.

terms of the patient's internal dynamics (Coffey, 1966; Slavson, 1969).

Adlerians, on the other hand, with their emphasis on social interest, eschew internal states and use the group session to promote reorientation, altruism, and healthy interpersonal relationships. The differences between Adlerian individual psychotherapy and its group counterpart in this regard, according to Dreikurs, is that in the group "the patient's goals and movements become much more obvious in the interaction with his fellow group members than in the limited interaction between him and the therapist" (1969, pp. 44–45).

But considerations of orientation aside, all group leaders attempt to foster fundamental behavior and personality changes and to investigate reasons for emotional difficulties; and all groups provide for members social stimulation and support that encourage them to experiment with and test relationships with one another. In most groups the therapist's main responsibility is to stimulate discussion and to see to it that the interactions are therapeutic and minimally damaging.

Relationships among group members understandably become intense because of the nature of their mutual self-disclosures and because of the multiple opportunities to react to one another in previously learned maladaptive ways.[2] But the group affords each member the opportunity to modify and clarify feelings, provides an incentive for this by open discussion, serves as a catalyst for self-disclosure, encourages each member to discuss personal problems with others and to try out new behavior with others in the group. The presence of others can be a protection against (or a problem because of) being the only object of the therapist's attention, and peer identification and acceptance is often a gratifying experience for participants.

Types of Groups. The varieties include *insight* groups and *supportive, activity, educational, and social-action*-oriented groups (Scheidlinger, 1969). Insight therapy usually allows the members of the group to interact freely with each other, with minimum interference from the leader. Each participant quickly learns that he is his own and others' therapist, and that the leader's main function is to interpret or reflect feelings and interactions. This type of group functions best when its members are highly verbal. When used with the less educated or the inarticulate, it usually requires a more empathic and sensitive therapist. Instead of the typical stance of nondirectiveness the therapist does well to adopt a more active role during the early sessions and to clearly structure the situation so that channels of communication are opened.

Supportive groups are ideally suited to reach a maximum number of people. Their major goal, with some exceptions, is symptom relief; and their mainstay is guidance and reassurance (support) from the leader and peers. Sometimes medication is dispensed under medical supervision. According to one report the short-term management and supportive technique sometimes give way to traditional intensive group therapy (Bloch, 1968).

Activity groups emphasize the use of arts and crafts, of materials and other action-oriented tasks. Their main value lies in combining work with verbalization of problems, an especially welcome combination for people who are unaccustomed to talking freely about their problems. Often these groups include work and socializa-

---

[2] Because of the intensity of these interrelationships and the problem-centeredness of these sessions, patients in some groups are discouraged from seeing one another socially. Of course this is more difficult to accomplish when they are in the same hospital than when they are outpatients meeting in a mental hygiene clinic, but the idea is to discourage such sociability because it may be countertherapeutic to the orientation of the working sessions. The motivation to socialize may be powerful. When the group process works well, it shatters social barriers and nurtures emotional intimacy and self-disclosure. As a result group members sometimes feel a closeness to each other that they have not experienced "outside."

tion programs as well as the prescription of drugs and therapeutic discussions (Christmas, 1967).

Social action groups are (Peck et al., 1967) staffed by nonprofessional community mental health workers selected from their neighborhoods. These groups may serve as go-betweens for the professionals and the community. We will encounter these social action programs again in Chapter 25.

Human Relations Training

Group interactive situations are not necessarily confined to people with emotional problems. There are many groups whose aims are to change interpersonal skills rather than personalities. The earliest of these, the T-groups (T for training), started just after World War II and began as a response to the wishes of educators, managers, and others to learn new skills or to improve their skills in interpersonal communication. During the 1960s and into the 1970s many people became increasingly interested in these groups as vehicles for *human relations training*. With this increased popularization there has been a proliferation of growth centers. A classification of the wide range of activities called alternately by any of numerous names—sensitivity group, T-group, marathon, microlab—is presented in Table 20.1.

As is apparent from Table 20.1, the goals of human relations training differ from those of group psychotherapy. The human relations training group emphasizes the here and now rather than historical data or family life; it focuses more on corrective treatment; it pays more attention to available interpersonal data than to unconscious or motivational material; and it lays greater emphasis on group processes and member interactions than on leader–member relationships.

The therapeutic goals of human relations training are expressed in the following passage by a group leader; the similarities to the third-force therapies are apparent (Bach, 1969, pp. 305–306):

Marathons are not tension-relieving, cathartic acting-out groups. They generate rather high levels of emotional tensions which stimulate cognitive reorientation for their relief! Generally two new modes of acting, feeling, and being emerge during a marathon: (1) transparency of the real self, which (being accepted and reinforced by the peer-group) leads to (2) psychological intimacy within the peer-group. This sequence from transparency to intimacy is a natural development because what alienates people from one another are the masks they put on, the roles they take, the images they try to create, and many of the games they play.

In the course of the long work hours of marathon therapy, a transition from this self-defensive alienation and exploitive game-playing to psychological intimacy is revealed for everyone present to see.

Thus, *encounter groups*, as they are sometimes called, are closely related to the humanistic psychotherapies we shall discuss in Chapter 25, especially to the Gestalt-oriented approaches (see Ruitenbeek, 1970). Much like them, they emphasize, according to one knowledgeable source (Mintz, 1971, p. 24), "the values of love, creativity, and self-fulfillment which is viewed as including an active concern for the welfare of society as well as for the self and which also implies an awareness of values transcending the search for immediate material satisfaction."

Techniques. As in Gestalt therapy, which is also usually applied as a form of group experience, marathon participants engage in a series of *games* designed, for example, to enhance awareness of feelings, to make people conscious of effects on others, to encourage the expression of emotion, and to foster self-understanding and self-acceptance. The games, according to Mintz (pp. 48ff), may be separated into five categories and include preliminary games (*self-description*: "Give each participant an identical slip of paper. Ask them to write down three self-descriptive adjectives. Scramble the slips of paper . . . and let each par-

Table 20.1
Categorization of Human Relations Groups

Treatment Designation	Central Aims	Definitive Activities or Characteristics	Description[a]
1. Creativity–growth	Creativity Awareness Releasing human potential	Induced experiences designed to expand human awareness	Otto and Mann (1968)
2. Marathon	Personal growth Greater capacity for being intimate	Uninterrupted interpersonal intimacy	Stoller (1968)
3. Emergent	Personal growth Group growth	Absence of leader Nonprogrammed, unpredictable, emergent activities	Gibb and Gibb (1968b)
4. Authenticity	Openness Authentic encounter	Interventions and experiences focused on openness and consonance	Bugental (1965)
5. Sensitivity	Personal competence Group effectiveness Organizational effectiveness	Focus on here-and-now experiences, and on group processes	Bradford, Gibb, and Benne (1964)
6. Programmed	Personal growth and/or competence Group effectiveness Organizational effectiveness	Experiences initiated and/or directed by absent leaders	Berzon and Solomon (1966)
7. Microexperience	Interpersonal skills Group effectiveness Organizational effectiveness	Limited time (2 to 20 hours; 1 to $2^1/_2$ days) Restricted depth	Bradford, Gibb, and Lippitt (1956)
8. Inquiry	Skills of inquiry Group effectiveness System effectiveness	Data-gathering, quasi-structured experiences Focus on explicit and predictable individual and group learnings	Miles (1965)
9. Embedded	Team effectiveness Organizational effectiveness Problem-solving skills	Training experience embedded in sequential and continuous organization-based program of inputs, data-gathering, and experiences	Argyris (1962) Friedlander (1968)

Source: J. R. Gibb. The effects of human relations training. In A. E. Bergin and S. L. Garfield, eds., Handbook of psychotherapy and behavior change: an empirical analysis. © *1971, John Wiley & Sons, Inc. Reprinted by permission of John Wiley & Sons, Inc.*
[a]*For complete citation, refer to the original source.*

ticipant speculate about what kind of person is described"); and games of interpersonal contact (*eye contact*: "This exercise rarely fails to elicit surprise and delight at the richness of an interpersonal experience which comes about through eye contact alone"); conflict (*arm squeezing, hand slapping,* and *hand pressing*); dialogue (*foot dialogue, role playing*); and resistance (*three-wishes* and other parlor games to draw out those "who find it more difficult than others to reveal themselves and to participate").

A personal account of the worth of these games is given in Case Report 20.2, in which a male group member relates how someone was encouraged to expose his deformed leg. The apprehensions that these games may evoke are also reflected in this account.

Case Report 20.2 *A Marathon Group Experience*

The game that affected me most was when Nicholas was asked to affirm his deformed leg as a part of him even if unsightly because of the paralysis. He was asked to sit in the center of the room without his shoe and sock and let us all see it. His deep resentment of this as a shame was about to preclude him from continuing when, almost as one, the group went to him to give their love and encouragement. At this point I sat behind him and when somebody first touched his foot, he fell back almost in agony into my arms. He was encouraged to speak words of acceptance to his leg as they finally bared it and laid their hands on it and caressed it. After a while I laid his head in the lap of one of the women and continued to stroke his shoulder as others in the group used physical touch to affirm their support of him and their loving acceptance. I had never expressed love in a physical way to a man before this day, I myself, in a certain sense also "crippled" by my phobia against physical contact, was freed to experience its rightness and genuine human warmth. My "homo hang-up" disappeared as a result of this experience. It was the involvement of the entire group that made it possible

for me to act and feel as I did.

SOURCE: *Mintz (1971), p. 125.*

Problems. With the increasing interest of the general public in these groups, and because their goals are sometimes similar to those of group therapy, there has been an attendant concern that they are potentially dangerous, for they do attract people who need psychotherapy. The concern is that these people are not sufficiently girded emotionally for the trauma that such encounters may engender.

Unfortunately there is a dearth of published research on this matter, but even if such research were to validate this concern, it is still easier to identify casualties than those who are improved by the group experience (Yalom, 1971). Besides, most attempts to uncover harmful effects of group training have been more hortatory than substantive. It is probably safe to say that since there are no stringent admission screening requirements, some people will be hurt, but group experience enthusiasts answer, "So what? If the psychosis was there, it might have surfaced at a worse time. This way, the person may receive treatment earlier."

There is some evidence, on the other hand, to suggest that people undergoing training in these groups develop increased openness, greater tolerance for new information, and greater acceptance of human differences (Bunker, 1965). And there is substantial support for the belief that, compared with controls, group participants develop greater personal growth (Argyris, 1965); "take charge of their own lives" to a greater degree (Byrd, 1967); become less authoritarian, more democratic, and participative (Bake and Mouton, 1966); and in general, "that changes do occur in sensitivity, feeling management, directionality of motivation, attitudes toward self, attitudes toward others, and interdependence" (Gibb, 1971, p. 855).

Some of the potential negative outcomes of encounter groups[3] have also received attention

(Hartley et al., 1976). By far the most numerous so-called casualties were those in which a "more than mild exaggeration of typical psychopathological traits of the participants" occurred. This form of casualty was noted in a study conducted among 32 business and professional people who attended a human relations laboratory conducted by trained National Training Lab (NTL) leaders (Gottschalk, 1966) and reportedly experienced psychopathological reactions that were directly traceable to their encounter group experience. Some other reported casualties were defined as follows: stressed enough to leave a workshop, negative feelings about the experience, lasting psychotic reaction, felt worse after the experience, increased anxiety or depression, and emotional disturbance related to T-group experience.

Two findings from some of these outcome studies are particularly noteworthy. Specifically Lieberman and his associates (1973) reported that some leaders were unaware of casualties in their own groups. Even after being informed about the casualties, they could identify only two of 16 members harmed by participation. The second finding was that two leader orientations, "energizer" and "laissez faire," were associated with higher casualty rates. In the first instance the problem was traced to the leader's verbal aggressiveness and style of intensive emotional stimulation, and in the second instance the casualties resulted from the absence of protective vigilance and adequate feedback.

Additional research is obviously needed. Questions worth investigating include the following (Brammer and Shostrom, 1977, p. 323). What personality changes are effected by the group process? How do these changes modify behavior and how enduring are they? What are the adverse "side effects" of the group experience? Are group experiences not indicated for some persons? What kinds of persons profit most from group experiences? Which groups are best for which persons? What is the effect of leadership style on group outcomes?

Brief Psychotherapy

The conventional psychotherapies are time-consuming, expensive, and sometimes superfluous for solving the problem at hand. Each session runs about 50 minutes, and the average number of sessions, over a two- or three-year period, may be between 750 sessions for Freudian psychoanalysis and 200 sessions for most other forms. Such treatment, with its emphasis on insight and self-knowledge, is usually accessible only to the wealthy and to those who have much leisure time to devote to themselves. Clearly it is not geared to handling emergency situations or to the indigent. For these reasons and because of recent federal legislation that has encouraged the opening of community mental health centers in urban areas (see Chapter 25), brief psychotherapy, the so-called 15- or 20-minute hour, has received the attention it deserves among workers in mental health (Aguilera et al., 1970; Barten, 1969).

Brief psychotherapy as a treatment form is not exactly new—its ideas date from the 1920s (Ferenczi, 1926)—but as a result of the increased demand for mental health services and the lack of personnel to meet this demand, it has enjoyed a recent surge of interest. In contrast to long-term psychotherapy with its unhurried pace and detailed exploration, brief therapy quickly focuses on specific, usually crucial, problems to be solved and allows the patient little meandering from this focal point. Its limited, and sometimes only, goals are to abate the patient's symptoms and to restore his or her ability to function adequately.

In brief psychotherapy the therapist assumes a more active role than in traditional methods

---

[3] An encounter group is a group in which the members are given permission to verbally express their feelings, positive or negative, toward each other as they become aware of those feelings, and are usually encouraged to take responsibility for those feelings—for example, by saying, "I feel left out," instead of, "You two are excluding everyone else."

because he systematically probes all facets of the patient's situation relating to the problem that led him to seek help. The first interview is the most important one, for it is here that the therapist develops his theory about the patient's problem. Throughout this session the therapist avoids digressions and focuses only on issues, or on the patient's comments that bear directly on the present problem. Subsequent sessions, of which there should be no more than seven or eight, might help the patient acquire some insight about his inability to cope with difficulties and concentrate on having the patient translate these insights into action.

Because of the brief nature of this method, some writers emphasize the importance of having the patient feel relief as rapidly as possible (Aguilera et al., 1970). But not all patients are capable of benefiting from this treatment, and those who are can be identified on the basis of several characteristics. For example, brief therapy is likely to succeed if the patients' disruption is of recent onset (Bellak and Small, 1965; Gottschalk et al., 1967; Straker, 1968; Wolberg, 1965), if his or her previous adjustment was satisfactory (Gillman, 1965; Sifneos, 1967), if the environment in which he or she functions is stable (Pumpian–Mindlin, 1953), and if the degree of precipitating stress was not overwhelming (Alexander, 1944; Sarvis et al., 1958). On the other hand brief therapy is not likely to succeed among paranoid schizophrenics or other patients with long-standing illnesses (Wolberg, 1965).

We shall again discuss brief psychotherapy in Chapter 25, where we deal with crisis intervention.

The Problem of Evaluation

How can a person seeking help decide which kind of therapy is best suited to his or her needs? Unfortunately there is no clear-cut answer to this question; the evidence of the comparative worth of the psychotherapies is conflicting, and re-search on the topic is beset by three main difficulties: the criterion problem, the placebo effect, and the complexity of the interaction of the therapeutic process. In group therapy, of course, the interactive complexity is even more profound.

Criteria of Cure or Growth

How do we know a person is cured or has grown? Two main sources of information are available—the patient and the psychotherapist—neither of which is reliable. In contrast to physical illness, where one can usually rely on the patient's statements (if the patient says he feels better and the pain is gone, treatment was successful), the client's report in psychotherapy cannot be trusted, for many reasons. There is the phenomenon, for example, that Starke Hathaway (1948) called the "hello–goodbye" effect, which refers to the patient who upon the initial contact (hello) tries, albeit unconsciously, to demonstrate to the therapist that he is ill enough to need help. He has learned somewhere that psychotherapists apply rather stringent criteria for admission to their service, and therefore he tries to impress upon the therapist that he is ill. When the decision is later reached to end treatment, either because the therapist feels he has exhausted every means at his disposal or because the patient claims he no longer needs help, the patient reports that he is feeling much better, appreciates the help he has received, and thanks the therapist for a job well done (goodbye). Does this mean he is better? Or is this self-report motivated by the same social expectations that had led him originally to believe that he had to be genuinely sick to gain admission to treatment (Sundberg et al., 1973)?

The second criterion of cure—the psychotherapist—cannot be relied upon for information about the patient's improvement because he has a vested interest in believing that the patient is better, that the therapist is the agent responsible for this improvement, and that the patient's condition probably would not have changed had he not been consulted. Unfortunately, as we indicate later, these testimonials and claims are not bolstered by credible research.

Placebo Effect

Another difficulty in assessing the worth of psychotherapy is the *placebo effect*. We have already encountered this phenomenon with respect to the influence of set and setting on the way people experience psychoactive drugs (Chapter 10). That it is equally important in medical and psychological treatment was noted by Frank (1961), who reported on studies by Gliedman and his associates (1958), in which more than half of 56 psychiatric patients showed significant improvement after receiving pharmacologically inert substances. Frank attributes this placebo phenomenon to patients' anticipation of relief. Similarly the mere introduction of a research project in the ward of a psychiatric hospital is sometimes followed by considerable behavioral improvement in patients, an improvement that Frank attributes to the "therapeutic zeal" of the staff (Frank, 1961, p. 68). That zeal is likely to be communicated as more attention paid to the patients, and the extra attention is a key factor in their improvement.

The ability of placebos to heal was also illustrated dramatically in a study by Volgyesi (1954), who found that 70 percent of hospitalized patients with bleeding peptic ulcers were cured by placebos. In this study the doctor injected the patients with distilled water, telling them that it was a beneficial new medicine. A control group, which received the same injection from a nurse with the information that it was an experimental medication of unknown potency, showed a remission rate of only 25 percent.

More recently Arthur Shapiro (1971), in a careful analysis of the reasons for placebo effects, set down the following elements that contribute to the success of Freudian psychoanalysis (pp. 459–463): selection of patients (the careful selection maximizes response to therapy); reassurance about guilt ("he was listening, what I said was worthwhile, I am worthwhile"); and discharge from treatment ("the most powerful reassurance and final *coup de grace* . . . occur when treatment has been completed and the therapist certifies that the patient is cured").

Interactive Complexity

And then there is the problem of the complex interplay between patient and psychotherapist. The interaction of the two participants and their relation to the outcome of psychotherapy present the researcher with a constant stream of activity that makes it almost impossible to assess progress at any point in time. This area of research has only recently attracted the attention of investigators and, as a result of numerous content-analysis studies of psychotherapy, is currently beginning to yield information showing which characteristics and functioning of therapists and patients influence the outcome of treatment (Luborsky and Spence, 1971; Marsden, 1971).

Empirical Evidence

Despite the foregoing difficulties, however, a number of psychotherapy outcome studies have been conducted over the years. In a well-known early summing up of these studies, Hans J. Eysenck in 1952 issued a formidable challenge to psychotherapists, proclaiming that only two-thirds of the patients undergoing treatment show improvement. A careful comparison of these studies led him to conclude that the more intensive and prolonged therapies were producing poorer results than the briefer ones and that the highest proportion of improved cases was found among groups that had received minimal treatment from physicians, nurses, or aides in mental hospitals.

Later, in reviewing updated outcome studies, Eysenck again called attention to the disap-

Table 20.2

Outcomes of 48 Studies (52 Groups) as a Function of Quality of Design and Nature of Therapy

	Positive Outcome	In Doubt	Negative Outcome	Totals
Experienced therapists	20	8	10	38
Inexperienced therapists	2	5	4	11
Control group	11	4	8	23
No control group	11	11	7	29
Design adequacy 1	5	2	3	10
Design adequacy 2	12	4	9	25
Design adequacy 3	5	9	3	17
Brief duration (5–20 hours)	3	5	2	10
Moderate duration (12–49 hours)	7	5	3	15
Long duration (50–600 hours)	9	1	6	16
Analytic therapy	11	3	8	22
Eclectic therapy	9	8	6	23
Client-centered therapy	1	4	1	6
Group of therapists	16	13	12	41
One therapist's report	6	2	3	11

Source: A. E. Bergin. In A. E. Bergin and S. L. Garfield, eds., Handbook of psychotherapy and behavior change. © *1971, John Wiley & Sons, Inc.*
Note: Totals sometimes do not add up to 52 because of missing information.

pointing overall improvement rate of 67 percent, asserting that this did not exceed the spontaneous remission rate—the rate that may be expected with *no* treatment. This led him to the following observation (1966, p. 40):

The writer must admit to being somewhat surprised at the uniformly negative results issuing from all this work. In advancing his rather challenging conclusion in the 1952 report, the main motive was one of stimulating better and more worthwhile research in this important but somewhat neglected field. . . . Such a belief does not seem to be tenable any longer in this easy optimistic form, and it rather seems that psychologists and psychiatrists will have to acknowledge the fact that current psychotherapeutic procedures have not lived up to the hopes which greeted their emergence fifty years ago.

In a later survey, however, Bergin (1971) reassessed many of the outcome studies criticized by Eysenck and also reviewed numerous new ones, including those of the brief psychotherapies. He reported evidence indicating that psychotherapy does, after all, "work," but that treatment outcomes depend to a large extent on the experience level of the therapist; hence the more experienced the psychotherapist, the more favorable the outcome. This evidence is presented in Table 20.2, where it can be seen that in 20 of the 22 studies reported, positive outcomes were obtained by experienced therapists. Though this 90 percent figure is impressive, a careful reanalysis of the data indicated that 71 percent of the negative outcomes also occurred with experienced therapists.

But the most important challenges to Eysenck's critique and conclusion about the ineffectiveness of psychotherapy are contained in reviews by Kiesler (1966) and by Meltzoff and Kornreich (1970).[4] The former argued that the question, "How effective is psychotherapy?" is meaningless and only makes sense if one refers specifically to a particular form of psychotherapy. Moreover, since the term psychotherapy is often used to describe a great diversity of types of counseling administered by persons of all degrees of experience and training, it is misleading to criticize it without specifying these factors. Also the characteristics of patients may differ greatly,

---

[4]Excellent reviews of these and similar critiques may be found in Bergin and Garfield (1971), Brody (1972), Garfield and Bergin (1978), Strupp (1971), and Strupp and Bergin (1969).

Does Psychotherapy Work?

The question of whether psychotherapy works, according to one viewpoint (Strupp and Hadley, 1977), is inherently difficult to answer because the problems in living that bring patients to psychotherapists are no longer necessarily viewed as an "illness" for which psychotherapy is prescribed as a "treatment." In increasing numbers patients enter psychotherapy not for the cure of traditional "symptoms" but for the purpose of finding meaning in their lives, for actualizing themselves, or for maximizing their potential.

Moreover, according to this view, there is no single criterion that can be applied consistently to patients because mental health judgments can be made from three major perspectives: society, which bases its judgments largely on the adaptive qualities of *behavior*; the individual, who bases his judgments on a sense of *well-being*; and the mental health professional, whose judgments are grounded in the assessment of the soundness of psychological *structure*.

The implication of this for psychotherapy researchers is clear: assessments of therapy outcome must be comprehensive; that is, they must consider all three areas of functioning. And they must be based wherever possible on standardized, generally accepted criteria of "good functioning" in each of the three areas.

Some studies that have met these two requirements have yielded encouraging results. For example, in a brief review of nearly 400 controlled evaluations of psychotherapy and counseling, two University of Colorado psychologists (Smith and Glass, 1977) concluded that the findings provide convincing evidence of the efficacy of psychotherapy. On the average, they found, the typical therapy client is better off than 75 percent of untreated individuals. Few important differences in effectiveness could be established among many quite different types of psychotherapy. More generally, almost no difference in effectiveness was found between the behavioral therapies (systematic desensitization, behavior modification) and the nonbehavioral therapies (Rogerian, psychoanalytic, rational–emotive).

as may those of therapists and their methods of proceeding. Consequently the question should be, "What kinds of therapy administered by whom are effective for which patients?"[5]

Meltzoff's and Kornreich's claim (1970) about the effectiveness of psychotherapy is even stronger than Kiesler's and, from their extensive review of 101 outcome studies, they found that most have yielded positive results. A careful breakdown of this research, however, indicated that 44 of the 101 studies had design flaws; of the remaining 57 studies, 48 indicated the positive effects of psychotherapy and reported no significant differences or any negative effects of psychotherapy. Thus even if we consider their report too biased in the direction of favoring the efficacy of psychotherapy (see Bergin, 1971; Brody, 1972) there still remains some modest evidence that psychotherapy, after all, does benefit some people.

In a somewhat similar vein one earlier researcher found evidence suggesting that the experience of therapists is more important than their theoretical orientation. For example, the fact that one is a Freudian, Adlerian, or Rogerian does not influence the outcome of psychotherapy as much as the amount of experience one has gained as a psychotherapist. Furthermore actual samples of psychotherapeutic interviews conducted by neophyte and expert representatives of the orthodox Freudian, Adlerian, and Rogerian schools indicated that in crises the verbalization and behavior of experienced psychotherapists of different schools resemble each other more than they do those of nonexperts of the same theoretical orientation (Fiedler, 1950).

The situation is somewhat the same in evaluating group therapy. Its effectiveness, too, depends on the skills of the therapist more than on his or her theoretical orientation. Research com-

paring the usefulness of group and individual psychotherapy indicates that there are a number of prerequisites for healthy involvement in group psychotherapy—the most basic one being a nonpsychotic disorder. Group psychotherapy is less successful with severely psychotic patients, probably because of their difficulty in establishing interpersonal relationships (Bednar and Lawlis, 1971).

Among some of the group therapy successes reported in the research literature were the following: treated juvenile and adult delinquents tend to show less personality test pathology and anxiety than those who are not treated (Persons, 1966; Truax et al., 1968), and they show more awareness of social approval and disapproval after therapy than before (McDavid, 1964); sex offenders who participate in groups have a lower rate of return to hospitals after treatment than before (Cabeen, 1961); treated schizophrenics show better hospital adjustment than nontreated controls (Boe et al., 1966; Sacks and Berger, 1954; Simon and Goldstein, 1957); treated psychiatric patients in general made better inpatient and post-hospital adjustment than controls (Fairweather and Simon, 1963); among university students of high ability, those who receive group therapy improve their academic grades more than a control group drawn from the same population (Teahan, 1966). In one of these studies, however—perhaps the only one in which researchers collected good follow-up data—improvement tended to disappear after 18 months following treatment (Fairweather and Simon, 1963). This suggests that those investigators who report success on the basis of short-term information may be judging this outcome prematurely.

Summary

Regardless of training or ideological differences, therapists always try to accept patients for what they are—that is, nonjudgmentally. They all rely heavily on verbal communication with their pa-

---

[5] Kiesler (1966) also argues that the evidence for spontaneous remission was based on Eysenck's naive interpretation of two poorly designed and ambiguous studies.

tients or clients. They all operate within the framework of some sort of contract with the client. They all have a unique kind of interaction with their clients, and they all try to help the patient or client gain insight or change behavior.

Therapeutic goals may be narrow or broad. Common overriding goals are increased ability to cope, greater awareness of what one is doing, and a greater sense of responsibility for one's own feelings and actions. The setting may be a mental hospital ward, a therapist's counseling room, a community mental health center, a halfway house, or a growth center. The therapist may be a psychiatrist, whose training includes medical school; a clinical psychologist, who has specialized training in testing, interviewing, and experimental psychology; or a psychiatric social worker, who has special training in studying the way a family functions and in working with various community agencies. All may practice psychotherapy in its various forms, although only the psychiatrist may provide medical service.

Therapy may be individual, couple, family, or group therapy, for an hour a week, for only one weekend, or over a variety of different time schedules. Couple and family therapy attempt to improve interactions between people in family units. Group therapy, in its many forms, involves the individual in ongoing interaction with others as well as with a therapist, thereby introducing a social dimension into therapy and helping the individual see how he or she appears to others. Brief psychotherapy is designed to deal with an immediate situation in a few short sessions. Studies disagree on the effectiveness of therapy, but there are indications that it is helpful for many people.

Terms and Concepts to Master

Activity groups

Brief psychotherapy

Couple therapy

Educational groups

Encounter groups

Family therapy

Individual therapy

Insight groups

Marathons

Placebo effect

Social action groups

T-groups

21 The Medical Therapies

Unlike the psychological forms of treatment that we shall discuss later, the medical or physical methods of intervention discussed in this chapter involve direct assaults on the organism. There are basically three such approaches: shock therapy, pharmacotherapy (or chemotherapy), and psychosurgery. By federal and state statutes these methods are defined as medical and therefore can be administered legally only by a physician or a psychiatrist.

Psychologists are nonetheless interested in these approaches because some of them, particularly pharmacotherapy, have provided important scientific data about the possible interactions between biochemical and behavioral effects of psychopathology. Psychologists are also often in contact with patients receiving these therapies, and not infrequently are asked to predict and evaluate patients' readiness for particular physical therapies. As an outsider to the medical field the psychologist can also serve as a constructive critic of these procedures, a criticism that has already contributed to the conduct of many rigorous studies on the "cost–benefit" aspects of many of these physical treatment procedures.

Shock Therapy

The idea of inducing shock in severely psychotic patients was introduced by a Hungarian psychiatrist, Von Meduna, in 1933. He based his theory on two observations: that schizophrenic patients lose their psychotic symptoms when they have convulsions, no matter what causes the seizures; and that epilepsy and schizophrenia rarely coexist in the same person. Although these observations are basically correct, the second phenomenon can be easily explained (see Reiss et al., 1977). Because the probability is low that a randomly chosen person will have *either* schizophrenia or epilepsy, the probability is lower still that a randomly chosen individual will have *both* schizophrenia and epilepsy.

Thus Von Meduna's observations may be correct, but his inference that one disorder precludes the other is wrong. Nevertheless, he observed, correctly again, that chemically inducing convulsions (Meduna, 1937) in schizophrenic patients does improve their condition. At first he used camphor and oil to induce seizures, but the side effects in the form of subsequent convulsions were intolerable. Then he tried Metrazol, another seizure-inducing drug, but that too had to be abandoned because of its high rate of fatalities.

At about the same time, Sakel, a Polish psychiatrist, observed that it was possible to modify and improve the condition of many victims of schizophrenia by insulin shock therapy (IST), sometimes also called insulin coma therapy. His observation led him to speculate that psychotic behavior was caused by an excess of adrenalin in central nervous system tissue that, in turn, caused hyperactivity. Although this notion was later easily disproved, the treatment was continued because it did seem to produce a favorable reduction of symptoms in many psychotic patients. Why it did work is still a matter of puzzled conjecture. One of the drawbacks of IST and the reason it is now seldom used is that the mortality risk during treatment is considerable, as high as one in one hundred treatments being fatal, according to one source (Nathan and Harris, 1975). The shock therapy of choice today is electroshock.

Electroshock Therapy (EST)

Sometimes also called electroconvulsive therapy, this form of treatment (like IST) produces convulsions and unconsciousness. EST, first introduced by two Italian physicians, Cerletti and Bini (1938), has virtually replaced IST and other shock therapies in the treatment of schizophrenia.

Before EST is administered the patient is injected with curare to immobilize his muscles so that he does not harm himself during the convulsive state. Then electrical current is applied through two electrodes placed against his temples. The resulting seizure, depending on the voltage used (65–140 volts for about 0.5 second), resembles a *petit mal* or *grand mal* epileptic convulsion.

EST is usually administered in a series of 10 to 12 shock sessions, given over a two-week period; when a state of greater amnesia or regression is desired, however—and this use is now becoming rare—EST may proceed on a daily (or more frequent) basis until the patient is reduced to a totally vegetative state. The state most often following EST is similar to that of insulin therapy; and the patient shows similar aftereffects and temporary improvement. Its main success has been in the treatment of depression, as we indicated in Chapter 14, and its effectiveness in treating other psychoses is also of short duration. Nevertheless, a survey conducted in Michigan and reported in the 1977 *Year Book of Psychiatry and Applied Mental Health* (Braceland et al., 1977, p. 244) indicates that electroshock therapy is

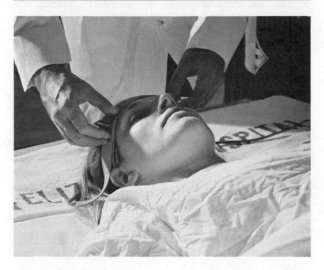

Electroshock therapy (EST) being administered to patient at St. Elizabeth's Hospital in Washington, D.C.

(Courtesy National Institute of Health)

"widely used in the treatment of psychoneurotic depressions and depressive personality disorders, besides affective psychoses and schizophrenias." And despite the scanty evidence of EST's effectiveness, the *Year Book* concludes, "It is time for psychiatrists to acknowledge openly that electrotherapy is used in the treatment of depressions of psychosis, neurosis or personality disorders in the modern practice of eclectic psychiatry."

Pharmacotherapy

Until the arrival of the drug therapies in the mid-1950s, IST and EST were the standard treatments. Soon the shock therapies were considered outdated, a notion strongly supported by the pharmaceutical industry. Although the initial enthusiasm that heralded the so-called miracle drug has waned as a result of more careful experimentation, the tranquilizers, or ataractics (from the Greek *ataraxy*, meaning freedom from confusion), and antidepressants have contributed considerably to the management of most distressed persons, and of schizophrenics. Formerly intractable and uncontrollable patients have become manageable and sometimes rational, and as a result of the introduction of these drugs there has been a steadily decreasing number of hospitalizations since about 1955.

Table 21.1
Some Drugs Used in Pharmacotherapy and Their Effects

Chemical Name (manufacturer's trade name)	Clinical Name	Drug Group	Primary Clinical Uses	Primary Target Population
Meprobamate (Equanil; Milltown)	Antianxiety or minor tranquilizer	Dial-carbanate	To relieve tension, anxiety; produces relaxation	Conditions characterized by tension, anxiety
Chlordiazepoxide hydrochloride (Librium)	Antianxiety or minor tranquilizer	Benzodiazepine	To relieve tension, anxiety; produces relaxation	Conditions characterized by tension, anxiety
Diazepam (Valium)	Antianxiety or minor tranquilizer	Benzodiazepine	To relieve tension, anxiety; produces relaxation	Conditions characterized by tension, anxiety
Chlorpromazine (Thorazine, Lagactil)	Antipsychotic or major tranquilizer	Phenothiazenes	Counteracts anxiety, hallucinations, agitation	Schizophrenia
Trifluoperazine (Stelazine)	Antipsychotic or major tranquilizer	Phenothiazenes	Counteracts anxiety, hallucinations, agitation	Schizophrenia
Thioridazine (Mellaril) Haloperidol (Haldol)	Antipsychotics or major tranquilizers	Phenothiazenes Butyrophenomes	Counteracts anxiety, hallucinations, agitation	Schizophrenia
Reserpine (Serpasil)	Antipsychotic or major tranquilizer	Rauwolfia alkaloids	Counteracts anxiety, hallucinations, agitation	Schizophrenia
Phenelzine (Nardil)	Antidepressant	MAO inhibitor	Elevates mood, improves appetite	Depression
Imipramine (Torfranil)	Antidepressant	Tricyclic	Elevates mood, improves appetite	Depression
Amitroptyline (Elavil)	Antidepressant	Tricyclic	Elevates mood, improves appetite	Depression
Lithium carbonate (Eskalith, Litonate)	Antimania	Lithium salts	Reduces euphoria, counteracts agitation	Manic–depressive, depression

These drugs, some of which are described in Table 21.1, are used in combination with psychotherapy or with electroshock therapy. We now present a brief discussion of the effects of different kinds of drugs on people in particular diagnostic categories (also see Cole and Davis, 1972; Dally, 1967; Kalinowsky and Hippins, 1969; Klein and Davis, 1969; Ray, 1972; Solomon, 1966; Freedman, 1977; Cain and Cain, 1975a, 1975b; Prien and Caffey, 1976).

Minor Tranquilizers

In Chapter 10 we mentioned that the use of tranquilizers in our society became commonplace in about 1955 when the meprobamates (marketed as Equanil and Miltown) were introduced as the new "happy pills." The main therapeutic application of these pills, however, is in the treatment of anxiety, muscular spasms, tension, and minor convulsions, any of which may accompany the neuroses.

These tranquilizers, sometimes also called *antianxiety drugs*, share the sedative, depressant, and habituating characteristics of the barbiturates and, as we noted in Chapter 10, after long administration their sudden withdrawal may cause convulsions. Under supervised and prescribed conditions, however, they are effective in controlling acute anxiety (see Chapter 7) and delirium tremens (Chapter 9). For example, in several well-controlled studies, Rickels (1966) showed the efficacy of several minor tranquilizers for the alleviation of neurotic symptoms. But these improvements are often unpredictable, may be due to placebo effects, and depend largely on a combination of the patient's personality and demographic and symptom characteristics. Whatever beneficial effects are derived from the minor tranquilizers, however, seem to be caused by their facility in inducing musculoskeletal relaxation. The precise mechanism of action is still not well understood (see Ray, 1972, pp. 154–155).

The more commonly prescribed tranquilizers include Librium (chlordiazepoxide), Serax (oxazepam), Valium (diazepam), Tranxene (chlorazepate), Miltown and Equanil (meprobamate), and Tyvatran (tybamate). The first four of these belong to the family of drugs called the benzodiazepines, and the last two to the family of mephenesin-like drugs. Prescription of tybamate and, especially, the meprobamates has been largely discontinued because they have been found to cause psychological and physical dependence, as well as convulsions and delirium when discontinued after prolonged use in high doses.

Although the risk of lethal effects with use of the minor tranquilizers is low, these drugs do have numerous adverse effects. These effects include central nervous system side effects (drowsiness, confusion, slurred speech, headache, lethargy, tremor, muscular uncoordination), au-

---

Valium: No. 1 on the Best-Seller List

Although alcohol is probably America's favorite "tranquilizer," the anti-anxiety drugs (minor tranquilizers) are the only ones prescribed for this purpose by physicians. Among *all* prescription drugs in the United States in 1974, Valium was number one. Librium followed close behind, and was number five on the best-seller list. One estimate (Belknap, 1978) is that about one adult in twelve has had a prescription for an anti-anxiety drug within the past year (or now has one), and the use of these drugs has doubled within the past five years (a problem that is currently under Congressional investigation).

tonomic nervous system symptoms (dizziness, incontinence, urinary retention, impaired visual accommodation), cardiovascular disturbances (hypertension, hypotension, fainting), behavioral disorders (euphoria, fatigue, weakness, depression), and numerous other systemic irregularities (anemia, nausea, vomiting, rashes, menstrual irregularities, and chills and fever). For most side effects, reduced doses are the usual treatment. Occasionally drug therapy must be stopped altogether if reducing the dose does not eliminate the side effects.

Major Tranquilizers

These compounds, sometimes also known as the phenothiazines[1] (marketed under their generic names as chlorpromazine, thioridazine, promazine), produce sedation without sleep or confusion and reduce chronic anxiety. Clinically they are often used to reduce excitement, overactivity, and hallucinations in acute schizophrenia and mania; to treat the paranoid delusions of paranoiac and schizophrenic patients; and to attenuate the apathy and withdrawal accompanying other psychotic disorders. Their mechanism of action is too complex to detail here (see Ray, 1972, pp. 148–149), except to say that their beneficial effects are due to their depressant action on the hypothalamus and the reticular activating system of the brain (see Chapter 5). Both of these parts of the central nervous system, it will be recalled, are intimately involved in autonomic reactivity and cortical arousal.

In several well-controlled and large-scale hospital studies that compared the effects of major tranquilizers and of placebos in changing the behavior of schizophrenics, Cole and Davis (1972) found that the phenothiazines resulted in clinical improvement. Drug-induced improve-

ments were greater for female patients than for hospitalized males, although men "improved" more than women on placebos. In addition both male and female patients did better on the following behaviors when they were administered drugs than when on placebos: social participation (increased), self-care (better), agitation and tension (reduced), indifference to environment (less), and nurses' ratings of improvement.

Some of the more common side effects of these major tranquilizers include central nervous system effects (Parkinson's syndrome [drooling, muscular rigidity, tremor] seizures, respiratory depression), autonomic nervous system symptoms (blurred vision, dry mouth, constipation, diarrhea, inhibition of ejaculation), allergic reactions (dermatitis, photosensitivity), and behavioral disturbances (fatigue, lethargy, insomnia, depression). There are also some serious adverse effects such as agranulocytosis (pronounced reduction of leukocytes in the blood), jaundice, and "extrapyramidal crises" (profuse perspiration, drooling, fever, tachycardia), but these are rare and can almost always be reduced by stopping medication.

In a review of 24 controlled studies on the use of maintenance antipsychosis drugs (Freedman, 1977), John Davis of the University of Chicago notes that although many schizophrenic patients still return to the hospital with relapses, drug therapy has replaced long-term custodial treatment programs. Specifically his review disclosed that 698 (65 percent) of 1068 patients who received placebo relapsed, compared with 639 (30 percent) of 2127 who received maintenance antipsychosis drugs. Thus these drugs prevented relapse in a substantial number of patients. However Freedman also suggested that most patients are at risk of relapse for some time after discontinuance of medication and that a relapse is a relatively more serious event for outpatients because a wide variety of social variables become involved (family, job, social situation). By contrast the relapse of a chronically ill inpatient, where an increase in symptoms can be easily

---

[1] Other major tranquilizers are the butyrophenones, thiozanthenes, and reserpines.

Side Effects of Antipsychotic Drugs

Some common side effects of antipsychotic drugs include autonomic, cardiovascular, and allergic, as well as extrapyramidal and other central nervous system (CNS) effects (Davis and Casper, 1977). The autonomic side effects include dry mouth and throat, blurred vision, flushing of the skin, constipation, urinary retention, and confusion.

Among the cardiovascular changes observed are low blood pressure, electrocardiogram disturbances of unknown origin, and (rarely) sudden death due to ventricular fibrillation (heartmuscular fiber twitching).

Jaundice and other skin and eye reactions are the allergic side effects of the phenothiazines and, again rarely, agranulocytosis can develop. Agranulocytosis is serious and it usually occurs within four to eight weeks of treatment. Its onset is abrupt and consists of a sudden sore throat with ulcerations of the throat, intestines, and other mucous membranes. These infections must be treated immediately by discontinuance of the antipsychotic drugs and by antibiotic medication.

The extrapyramidal side effects occur mainly in the form of Parkinson's disorder, which consists of motor retardation, masklike facial expressions, tremor, rigidity, and shuffling gait. Some of the other CNS complications are seizures, insomnia, bizarre dreams, confusion, and impaired psychomotor coordination.

tolerated and therapy can be reinstated, may entail less risk for the patient.

Furthermore two researchers (Hogarty and Goldberg, 1973) have shown that of 374 chronic schizophrenics briefly treated on maintenance phenothiazene on an outpatient basis and then separated into maintenance chlorpromazine and placebo patients, and further subdivided into psychotherapy versus nonpsychotherapy groups, most did not get well on placebo drugs. Specifically, at the end of one year after hospital discharge, 73 percent of the placebo patients without psychotherapy had relapsed. Of their drug maintenance counterparts only 33 percent and 26 percent had relapsed. These are highly significant differences between patients on pharmacotherapy and those not so treated. Psychotherapy also seemed to make some difference.

Antidepressants

As we mentioned in Chapter 14, the depressions are debilitating in that patients are often so wracked with guilt and worthlessness that they cannot mobilize enough energy to attend to even their slightest needs; and suicide is frequently a real possibility. What is needed, then, is a drug that will exert uplifting effects.

Such a compound was accidentally discovered in 1952 when preliminary reports suggested that a new chemical, *isoniazid*, was effective in treating tuberculosis (Ray, 1972); and when used with another drug, *iproniazid*, which is a *monoamine oxidase* (MAO) inhibitor,[2] the combination

---

[2] Monoamine oxidase is an enzyme involved in reducing or deactivating serotonin in brain neurons, and therefore inhibition of this deactivator results in high levels of serotonin in the cerebrum. Such high levels are thought to disrupt normal brain functioning, thereby causing psychotic symptoms.

was observed to be mood-elevating in tubercular patients. But its clinical efficacy with psychiatric patients, unfortunately, has been marked by toxic side effects as often as by success. For example, shortly after its initial introduction, the fatality rate (from liver toxicity) was as high as 25 percent. Currently, according to Cole and Davis (1972), the death rate varies from 1 in 3,000 to 1 in 10,000 patients. Less serious effects are also common, and they include dry mouth, dizziness, gastric distress, constipation, urinary retention, and impotence.

The other antidepressants in use, the *imipramines*, of the family called the tricyclics, are structurally similar to the phenothiazines and were accidentally discovered in 1957 when Kuhn (1958) was searching for an antipsychotic drug. It was found ineffective in schizophrenia, except that it seemed to alleviate the depression of schizophrenics. The imipramines were subsequently found effective with depressed patients and in more than one hundred studies were shown to have substantial benefits beyond those obtainable by placebos (see Klein and Davis, 1969, pp. 192ff).

The side effects of these compounds, although not as great as those of MAO inhibitors, are similar to those listed earlier for the phenothiazines. In addition patients must be cautioned that alcohol potentiates the effects of tricyclics and that the interactions of these compounds with MAO, minor tranquilizers, or other hypnotics and phenothiazines are contraindicated and may be dangerous. Several well-controlled double-blind studies conducted in Finland (Friend, 1976), for example, strongly indicated that the tricyclics alone did not affect psychomotor skills in driving and occupational performance. But tricyclics with alcohol increased reaction times and inaccurate responding, especially in driving, although this is less true of some tricyclics (chlorimipramine, nortriptyline) than of others (amitriptyline, doxepin).

According to one report (Davis, 1973), the tricyclic antidepressants benefited about 70 percent of depressed hospitalized patients, and these benefits seem to occur within about seven to 14 days after therapy is started. Some of the evidence (Paykel, 1972), with 86 female depressives, showed that psychotic depressives responded best to amitriptyline and anxious depressives responded least well. Other evidence by the same researcher indicated that the classification of a person as a psychotic or neurotic depressive had no value in predicting improvement.

As with the phenothiazines for schizophrenic patients, the tricyclic drugs are indicated for maintenance treatment after hospital discharge. In one study (Mindham et al., 1972) data were collected from among 34 psychiatrists in Great Britain, who compared improvement maintenance in treatment of depressives with tricyclics versus placebo for a period of six months. By that time 22 percent of the tricyclic maintenance group had relapsed in comparison with 50 percent of the group treated with placebo, although many of the latter did not relapse on placebo. It is not clear from these findings what long-term effects either the tricyclic or the placebo therapy would have.

Antimanic Compounds

As we mentioned in Chapter 14, the primary treatment for manic patients is *lithium ion*, which, unlike any of the drugs discussed so far, is a salt. Since it has been approved for use with mania only since 1970, there are not many adequate clinical or controlled studies available on its efficacy.

There have been some favorable experimental studies among both depressed and manic patients, however, that support the early enthusiasm for the compound. In a study conducted at the New York State Psychiatric Institute (Freedman, 1977, p. 293), the effectiveness of lithium was compared with that of a placebo in a double-blind study of 28 depressed patients who were followed up from 3 months to 4 years. The number of depressive episodes per patient-year was 2.7 times greater among the placebo group than among lithium carbonate patients.

In two carefully controlled double-blind studies, the effectiveness of lithium treatment of manic patients was compared with that of two major tranquilizers (chlorpromazine and haloperidol). One of these studies (reported in Freedman, 1976, p. 277), conducted in a hospital in New York, compared the relative efficacy of these treatments among 30 severely manic persons. Three groups of patients each received lithium carbonate, chlorpromazine, and haloperidol in maximum doses. Seven of the ten patients given lithium could be discharged after three weeks of treatment, compared with only two of those taking haloperidol and one of those taking chlorpromazine.

In the second double-blind study, conducted in Japan (Freedman, 1977, p. 295), this time using a larger sample of 80 manic patients, it was again shown that lithium carbonate was significantly superior to chlorpromazine in efficacy. Moreover evidence was also obtained in this study that adverse effects during therapy with lithium were rarer and milder than those found among chlorpromazine-treated patients.

Some undesirable side effects have been reported in the literature, however, and these consist mainly of motor disturbances characterized by fine, rapid tremors and some muscular rigidity. Equally disturbing has been one report from a Los Angeles hospital (Freedman, 1976, p. 287) that about 20 to 30 percent of patients with manic–depressive illness discontinue lithium treatment against medical advice. It has been postulated that they may refuse to take lithium carbonate because they do not want to be deprived of periodic manic episodes, which, it is argued, may be pleasant. A more plausible explanation for this phenomenon might be that lithium actually causes depression, which is unpleasant. There have been some favorable reports, but they have been mostly anecdotal. Oakley Ray (1972, p. 151), of Vanderbilt University, however, does report one double-blind study, conducted in Denmark, in which good antimania effects were obtained in 80 percent of the cases.

Psychedelics as Therapeutic Agents

According to one source (Dally, 1967) exaggerated claims have been made about the therapeutic usefulness of LSD. It has been given to patients in individual and group therapy, with the claim that it shortens the time required for these treatments since it quickly brings repressed materials into consciousness; also, since it reportedly heightens suggestibility, it has been used in aversion conditioning of alcoholism.

One writer (Caldwell, 1968) believes that its greatest virtue in therapy is its hallucinogenic quality, because it shifts thoughts from the "verbal rational" to the "eidetic." And others (Masters and Houston, 1970) see the psychedelics as adjuncts and facilitating agents to a variety of existing psychotherapeutic procedures.

Several prominent authorities in alcoholism therapy (Abramson, 1967; Hoffer, 1970; Hoffer and Osmond, 1968; Hollister, 1968), who are also known for their early contributions to the biochemistry of schizophrenia (see Chapter 12), have been in the forefront of scientists suggesting that psychedelics be used for inducing sobriety. These researchers have focused mainly on the similarities among alcoholic DTs (a toxic psychosis), schizophrenia, and the LSD trip. They recommend a combination of psychotherapy and psychedelic therapy (using such drugs as mescaline, LSD, or psilocybin) and claim, after having treated about one thousand patients, that "whether the experiments were considered controlled or not, about 50 percent were able to remain sober or to drink much less" (Hoffer, 1970, p. 361).

But properly controlled studies remain to be conducted. To dismiss the psychedelics as therapeutically ineffectual would be as mistaken as to uncritically endorse their efficacy. Clearly what is needed is several double-blind studies that differentiate the effects of psychedelic therapy from those obtained with placebos, other drugs, and no drugs.

Psychosurgery

Various forms of brain surgery have been used, the most common involving either cutting into or removing portions of the frontal lobes (prefrontal lobotomy, lobectomy, or topectomy), or severing the corticothalamic neurons that connect portions of the frontal lobes to the thalamus. Such surgery has the effect of changing the patient's emotional reactivity, usually inhibiting anxiety by disconnecting certain crucial nerve bundles.

Although psychosurgery has been reported to calm some patients, its side effects, which sometimes include amnesia and a regression to vegetativeness, are so consequential and severe that it must be ruled out except in the most grave situations. It is only used after everything else has failed and in cases in which it is apparent that

---

Psychosurgery: Harmful or Helpful?

Psychosurgery presents one of the most dramatic and difficult dilemmas of medical ethics. Its aim is to change the behavior of severely disturbed individuals by removing portions of the brain. According to one source (Trotter, 1976) there are some 400 such operations performed each year in this country. Opinions differ widely on the scientific justification for psychosurgery. Given its frequently unpredictable outcome, the most serious disputes over psychosurgery center around the degree and direction of emotional and intellectual changes produced, and the extent of adverse side effects.

In a series of studies performed under the support of the National Commission for Protection of Human Subjects of Biomedical and Behavioral research, scientists evaluated the outcome of four different psychosurgical procedures in 61 patients who had undergone operations between 1965 and 1975. The patients studied had had various long-standing illnesses that had been unresponsive to other psychiatric treatments including EST and chemotherapy. All were white and middle class. Most were female.

One of the studies was carried out under the supervision of neuropsychologist Hans–Lukas Teuber and two of his associates at MIT. They examined and tested 34 patients, all of whom had undergone cingulotomy, an operation in which small lesions are made to interrupt the cingulum, the bundle of nerve fibers connecting the frontal lobes with various structures of the limbic system, which is thought to control emotions.

The patients seen by Teuber had all suffered from a variety of disabling conditions including intractable pain, which was usually mixed with depression; depression alone; obsessive–compulsive symptoms; severe anxiety; and schizophrenia. The results were mixed. Of the 11 cases of severe pain nine patients and their relatives claim either complete or near complete relief from pains that had lasted many years. Five of seven patients with depression also claimed either full or partial relief. The rest of the patients did less well.

But even when the patient's original condition did not improve, Hans–Lukas Teuber reported, no additional deficits were detected that could be attributed to the psychosurgery per se. This finding surprised Teuber, who for 30 years had been studying the aftereffects of brain injuries incurred in accidents or military combat. On the basis of this study Teuber now concedes that psychosurgery may have some therapeutic value, a major reversal of his position of many years.

the patient will seriously harm himself or others without such surgery (Greenblatt, 1972). Case Report 21.1 describes a successful treatment by psychosurgery.

Case Report 21.1 *Successful Psychosurgery*

T. M. is a married woman of 37, with a history of schizophrenia and depressive hallucinations. The first psychotic episode occurred when she was in her early twenties.

She was married shortly afterward, at the age of 22. Soon after that, during her first and only pregnancy, she grew increasingly suspicious and agitated. She was given three to four ESTs and hospitalized for two years. She had her first psychosurgery at age 30—because of suicidal tendencies—and reportedly felt tremendous relief. She was still suspicious, but no longer felt "as if encased in a plastic cube." There were no side effects, except perhaps for a weight gain (80 pounds in the first postoperative six months).

T. M. says that she functioned fairly well for five years as a schoolteacher, but then got worse again and began drinking heavily. She then received a "multiple target stereotaxic procedure" (extensive lesions were made in the limbic system [see Chapter 5]). Immediately afterward she reported that she was no longer suspicious but still felt fearful. She then received a third psychosurgical operation, about eight months later, after which, except for a six-week regression, she reports being entirely well.

Previously this patient had received 27 ESTs and 60 insulin coma treatments. Asked for her views of psychosurgery and whether she would recommend it to others, she says emphatically, "I would tell them to snap it up as quickly as they could. . . . I don't know why they work or how they work, but they are truly a godsend. They gave me back my life."

SOURCE: *Trotter, S. APA Psychology Monitor, 1976, 7 (11), 4–5. Reproduced by permission.*

Critical Comment

Do the medical therapies work? As we have suggested, many of the medical therapies are effective, sometimes in combination with psychotherapy and often better than a placebo alone. Surprisingly, also, some recent evidence indicates that psychosurgery is more effective than was once believed, and that the "costs" in terms of irreparable intellectual and motor damage to the individual may not be intolerable.

But what are the long-term effects of the medical therapies? Most of the research on the efficacy of the medical therapies tends to confine follow-ups to one year or at most 18 months after hospitalization. Consequently there is little evidence that these treatments have any but the most ephemeral values. In fact there is ample evidence to suggest that patients on drugs, for example, generally make unsatisfactory post-hospitalization adjustments. Often they have to be rehospitalized (Durel, 1970; cited in Calhoun, 1977). The same problem exists, as we have just seen, with other therapies. Thus the medical therapies have substituted a "revolving door" policy for long-term hospitalization.

On the more positive side, however, is the fact that these therapies have provided symptomatic relief to people who previously suffered psychological as well as intractable physical pain. Thus, even though the early hopes of complete cures have not been realized, it does seem clear that partial cures have been produced.

Aside from the questions of the extent and duration of cures, however, there has been opposition to the physical therapies on ethical grounds. These objections (Reiss et al., 1977) have been based mainly on (1) the absence of a sound theoretical rationale for the effects of some treatment procedures; (2) beliefs that certain medical therapies (particularly psychosurgery) produce harmful effects in too many patients; and (3) concerns that there will be abuses in the practice of particular treatments. In regard to the first objection it should be emphasized that the effects of treatment procedures can be realized in the absence of adequate theoretical rationales. That realization, which can be empirically established, should be sufficient to justify treatment. In regard to the second objection (possible harmful effects) we previously noted that careful research planning can provide some pleasant surprises. Even though clinical lore has always had it that EST and psychosurgery are formidable treatments that invariably have harmful side effects, this lore seems to have been an exaggeration of the facts, particularly pertaining to psychosurgery. Clearly more evaluative research needs to be conducted with all the medical therapies to determine whether they can withstand the rigors of a "cost–benefit" analysis.

Finally, the fear is well founded that there will be abuses in applying some of the medical therapies, particularly those that are potentially the most physically damaging. Consider the scenario in a large mental hospital where a male patient may behave aggressively against a psychiatrist or one of the psychiatric aides—perhaps even justifiably or possibly because he resents being institutionalized. Angered by the patient's aggressiveness, the psychiatrist or an aide may seek to punish the patient. They can easily rationalize their obviously punitive "treatment" by noting that the patient's aggression is a sign of worsening "illness." Then they can drug, shock, or lobotomize the patient at will.[3] Unlikely? Possibly. But safeguards must nonetheless be provided against these unlikely but still possible eventualities.

Summary

Four somatic treatments were discussed in this chapter, most of which have at least temporary beneficial effects. These treatments include insulin, which induces comas and is used mainly in schizophrenia; electroshock, which induces convulsions and is used in schizophrenia and depression; the drug therapies, which are applied to all varieties of disorders; and brain surgery, which is used for severely disturbed and self-destructive patients. All these therapies are administered by physicians, and in most instances their precise mechanisms of action are not known.

Terms and Concepts to Master

- Antianxiety drugs (minor tranquilizers)
- Antidepressants
- Antimania compounds
- Antipsychotic drugs (major tranquilizers)
- Chemotherapy (pharmacotherapy)
- Electroconvulsive therapy (ECT)
- Electroshock therapy (EST)
- Insulin shock therapy (IST)
- Lithium carbonate
- Placebo
- Psychosurgery

---

[3] Many readers will recognize this scenario in fictional form as a key plot element in Ken Kesey's novel, *One Flew Over the Cuckoo's Nest.*

22 The Psychodynamic Therapies

Modern science is said to have grown out of the repeated interplay of theory and experiment, idea and verification. Belief in the fruitfulness of that interplay is often associated with scientific development since the Copernican revolution, but it predates Copernicus. Roger Bacon, who learned it from his Sufi teachers, stated the idea as follows in 1268:

There are two modes of knowledge, through argument and experience. Argument brings conclusions and compels us to concede them, but it does not cause certainty nor remove doubts in order that the mind may remain at rest in truth, unless this is provided by experience.

For the psychodynamic models of human nature, the experience consists of the practice of psychotherapy. The clinical observations of Freud, Jung, and Adler were shaped by their theoretical constructs, and what they saw and heard in the counseling room in turn prompted them repeatedly to modify and amend their theories. One of the basic links between psychodynamic argument and psychotherapeutic experience is the assumption that if repression, faulty lifestyles, self-deception, and unconscious motivations cause abnormal behavior, then insight into one's own interior processes is a logical goal of psychotherapy. This is such a central theme in the psychodynamic therapies that they are sometimes called "insight therapies."

Sigmund Freud and Psychoanalysis

We have already mentioned that Sigmund Freud's most basic discovery was that people *repress*, or relegate to unconsciousness, their unacceptable and threatening thoughts and im-

Reality Principle: The Education of the Pleasure Principle

Human activity, Freud (1953b, p. 76) wrote, develops in two directions, according to whether it seeks to realize the experience of pleasure or the absence of pain. For an organism that is without a preformed, adapted identity and subject to prolonged dependence, the capacity to feel pleasure, anxiety, and pain is a critical safeguard of adaptation. The structuring and education of the pleasure potential are at the heart of what Freud went on to call the "reality principle."

pulses. Once in the unconscious, these imponderables become forces that distort perceptions of reality and cause many psychopathological symptoms. Now we shall see how Freud utilized these and other concepts in the practice of psychotherapy. Recall also that it was in the clinic, while listening to the verbalizations of neurotic men and women, that Freud formulated his theory of personality.

The major aim of *psychoanalysis*, according to Freud, is to help the individual gain conscious access to his or her repressed self so that his or her miseries, conflicts, and anxieties can be banished. And, since the roots of symptoms are found in early childhood, the place to begin searching for them is there (see Chapter 6). Accordingly Freudian psychoanalysis focuses on childhood relationships and tries to help the individual achieve an emotional understanding of significant early experiences. The analyst's main tools for accomplishing these ends are *free association, dream analysis, transference,* and *interpretation.*

Regarding the first of these tools, Freud laid down a *fundamental* or *basic rule* for patients in psychoanalytic therapy: they are to say whatever comes to mind without censoring it, no matter how painful, trivial, or inane it seems at the moment. To facilitate free association the patient relaxes on a couch, with the analyst sitting behind him, out of his line of vision, taking notes. When the patient complains that there is nothing left about which to free-associate, this too takes on a special significance because it is interpreted as a symptom of unconscious *resistance* toward the therapist or toward disclosing important material. This in itself and the contexts within which it occurs also become topics for analysis.

The end result of free associations is a stream of thoughts that provides valuable clues about important wishes and impulses that were repressed while the individual was growing up. According to Freud nothing that is said or done occurs accidentally; therefore, even a person's most undisciplined cognitive meanderings have psychological significance. In other words because statements are related in meaningful ways to preceding ones that, in turn, are influenced by prior thinking and actions, this continuous stream of associations "adds up," in the sense that it follows logically from and provides valuable clues about the individual's total personality.

Freudians also use dream analysis because they consider the dream the key to the unconscious. The patient's dreams, and his or her associated feelings about them, are considered especially revealing because he or she can exercise little control over their unfolding. In *The Interpretation of Dreams* (Freud, 1900), Sigmund Freud calls attention to their significance by indicating that dream content stems from the events of the day and represents, often in disguised form, wish-fulfilling expressions of unconscious and unacceptable thoughts.

Transference occurs during psychoanalysis when the patient attributes to the therapist feelings, reactions, animosities, and affections that he now holds or has held toward important people in his life. Freud considered this an irrational, but highly significant, part of psychotherapy. In fact the therapist structures the situation in a way that almost assures the occurrence of such a relationship: the professional and social distance that he maintains; his positioning behind the patient during therapy; his interpretation of the patient's seemingly most inconsequential remarks and actions—all contribute to the transference. In a sense the therapist becomes an inkblot toward which the patient reacts, albeit unconsciously, as he did vis-à-vis important figures in his life. For example, the therapist may be perceived as the patient's mother, spouse, or sibling, sometimes even becoming the recipient of the same love or hate that the patient held for them.

The development and resolution of the transference is a major part of psychoanalysis because the patient-to-therapist relationship is primarily a product of the patient's imagination and therefore provides the therapist with invaluable information about the patient's basic conflicts and infantile responses. It also affords opportunities to help the patient gain awareness of these reactions so he or she will learn to discriminate between old conflicts and the new ones directed toward the therapist. The best way to facilitate such discrimination is to react neutrally, and hence differently, from early figures in the patient's life.

But transference can also create difficulties during psychoanalysis. The therapist must guard against reciprocating the patient's feelings by "acting-out" with his or her own *countertransference*, or emotional reactions. This requires that the psychoanalyst have a thorough understanding of his or her own motivations and personality.[1]

Finally *interpretation* is the psychoanalytic process whereby the therapist helps the patient understand the transference relationship. This is accomplished by explaining that his feelings and conflicts are rooted in his own past and are not rational reactions to the therapist.

To illustrate how psychoanalytic therapy proceeds, we have selected an excerpt from a case analyzed by Theodor Reik, an orthodox Freudian psychoanalyst (Case Report 22.1). This excerpt, though not a transcription of the dialogue be-

---

[1] Psychoanalysts undergo lengthy periods of *didactic* and *control* analysis. The first of these involves actual psychotherapy, in which the aspiring analyst is the patient. Control analysis consists of a period of supervision, during which the neophyte's tape-recorded cases are closely monitored by a senior psychoanalyst who understands the candidate's personality.

Insights and Feelings

The primary emphasis in psychoanalytic therapy is to help patients attain a series of *insights*. For example, a male patient may discover that his relationship with women parallels his feelings about his mother, that his conflicts with authority are similar to previous conflicts with his father, and so on. Freud's early emphasis on catharsis has been almost entirely superseded by his later emphasis on insight.

Insights are attained, among other ways, through the clarification of feelings. These *feelings* include (among others) anxiety, hostility, love, resentment, joy, revenge, shame, and guilt. As the feelings are brought to light, the defenses that have kept them under cover are also brought to light (Fine, 1973).

tween patient and psychotherapist, furnishes a glimpse of the entire process. The patient is a man in his early thirties, who had told Reik that he had become increasingly nervous and depressed during the previous year and had to interrupt work for a few months. During the early sessions of psychoanalysis, the man gave an autobiographical sketch that reached from his childhood to the time when the present crisis came into his life. From the beginning the patient emphasized that he had been lucky because he had an excellent position, that his marriage had been fairly good, and that he loved his children. He also mentioned that his parents had made considerable sacrifices for his education and that he had been successful in high school and especially in college, where he had made social connections that became useful in his later life. The remainder of this patient's analysis is described in Case Report 22.1.

Especially noteworthy in this case is the analyst's emphasis on the importance of the man's unconscious conflicts and guilt in producing behavioral symptoms. This case also demonstrates several other typical features of psychoanalysis that can be summed up as follows: early in the analysis the therapist claims to know what is wrong with the patient and he will then seek clinical "proof" during subsequent sessions; but he will defer disclosing his knowledge until he senses that the patient is emotionally ready to accept his interpretations.

Case Report 22.1 *Psychoanalytic Therapy*

The father of a friend had given him a small job in the big manufacturing company in which he had a leading position. A department chief in the company asked him after a short time in the office whether he would like to work for him. The young man accepted the offer gratefully, and his work was so good that he was promoted. His patron died and was replaced by an older man, who also liked the young, efficient, and well-mannered clerk. He soon became not only the assistant of his new boss but

also his confidential adviser. The old man made many complaints about the management of the company and about some of his superiors, including the man who had first helped the patient to get his job. Also his original benefactor had remained friendly with the ambitious young man and had confided in him, among other things, his growing dissatisfaction with the department chief, the patient's boss. Thus the patient was in an ambiguous situation; he had to listen for hours to complaints and accusations from both sides. Finally his boss, who was a grumbling and dissatisfied man, was removed from his office to another branch of the company and the young man was asked to take his place.

Now a strange thing happened; slowly, and at first imperceptibly, a change in his attitude took place. He began to doubt his ability to handle the position and became afraid of the great responsibility connected with it. He felt an increasing apprehension and nervousness. . . . He felt increasingly reluctant to go to the office where he had to take over his new position. He was afraid to face the task that awaited him. He stayed away. At the end he refused to leave the house.

While I listened to the patient's report, I felt some hidden emotional connections. . . . It was obvious that the man became ill when a wish that he had nursed for a long time became a reality. He had been very ambitious and had certainly wished to take the place of the old man and thus obtain a prominent position in the company. . . . No doubt, I said to myself, here are powers of conscience operating in the dark.

The patient had wished for a long time that the old man who had been so kind to him would be removed from the position that he wanted for himself. He must have listened to the complaints of the old man and to the expressions of dissatisfaction of his chief with great suspense, and always with the wish that the outcome of the conflict would be that he himself would succeed his boss. And when the old man was finally removed, an unconscious moral reaction set in.

My impression that my patient broke down

under the assault of unconscious-guilt-feeling on account of his wishes will have to wait for proof. When I shall tell him much later what I discovered about his own hidden character, he will, I am sure, deny his unconscious conscience got the better of him. Yet he will at the end admit that he must have thought he did not deserve the position. Doesn't his behavior already amount to an unconscious confession of his guilt in thoughts?

STOP

Erik Erikson and Developmental Theory

Of all the neo-Freudians Erikson (1963, 1964, 1968) is closer to Freud's position than any of the other traditional therapists covered in this chapter; he is also the theorist best known on college campuses.

Erikson's similarity to Freud stems mostly from his *eight stages of ego development*, which are similar to Freud's psychosexual stages. His developmental theory is outlined in Table 22.1, where it may be seen that failures and successes at each stage result in corresponding psychological states. Thus early infancy lays the foundation for either trust or mistrust, later infancy may cause subsequent autonomy or self-doubt, and so on, through the eighth stage, late adulthood, which may be marked by integrity or despair (also see Bischof, 1970; Maddi, 1972).

What made Erikson so popular on college campuses was his recognition that many young people have difficulty in developing a sense of *identity* (see fifth stage, Table 22.1). According to Erikson, the chore of finding one's identity is full of pitfalls because it involves a complex process of integrating all the identifications a person has made during the first 12 to 20 years of development. This stage corresponds in part to many college student's ages, and Erikson himself, according to one source, knew firsthand what it

meant to have an identity crisis (Freedman and Kaplan, 1972, p. 102) because of

his being a Dane living in Germany, a country that resented Denmark for its designs on Schleswig-Holstein; his being the son of an absent Danish father, and a Danish mother with both a rabbi and a minister in her ancestry; and his being a stepson of a German Jew, a pediatrician who wanted Erikson to become one too.

For Erikson the mentally healthy individual is one whose ego is well equipped to meet new challenges throughout life; the unhealthy person is one whose childhood anxieties persist into adulthood. Such anxieties undermine adult security and identity and are attended by mistrust, shame, doubt, guilt, inferiority, role confusion, isolation, stagnation, and despair. And the treatment of these anxious individuals, to quote Erikson's *Insight and Responsibility* (1964, p. 97), consists of the following:

Whether, as clinicians or administrators, we are charged with the cure, the transit, or the rehabilitation of others, we become the guardians of lost life stages: ideally speaking, our work of rehabilitation should at least provide a meaningful moratorium, a period of delay in further commitment.

And in discussing the treatment of many of society's hospitalized patients, Erikson continues as follows, striking a sensitive chord that we shall echo in our consideration of alternatives to hospitalization in Chapter 25 (p. 97):

Hospitalized patients, having been committed, are often ready to commit themselves. They expect "to go to work," both on themselves and on whatever task they may be asked to do. But too often they are met by a laborious process of diagnosis and initiation which emphasizes the absolute distance of patienthood from active life. Thus . . . the uprooted one, already considered expendable or abnormal by

Table 22.1
Erikson's Eight Stages of Ego Development

Success Brings		Failure Brings
First Stage *Early Infancy (birth to about 1 year)* *(corollary to Freudian oral sensory stage)*		
Basic Trust Result of affection and gratification of needs, mutual recognition	vs.	**Mistrust** Result of consistent abuse, neglect, deprivation of love, too early or harsh weaning; autistic isolation
Second Stage *Later Infancy (about ages 1 to 3 years)* *(corollary to Freudian muscular anal stage)*		
Autonomy Child views self as person in his own right apart from parents but still dependent	vs.	**Shame and Doubt** Feels inadequate, doubts self, curtails learning basic skills like walking, talking, wants to "hide" inadequacies
Third Stage *Early Childhood (about ages 4 to 5 years)* *(corollary to Freudian genital locomotor stage)*		
Initiative Lively imagination, vigorous reality testing, imitates adults, anticipates roles	vs.	**Guilt** Lacks spontaneity; infantile jealousy; "castration complex"; suspicious, evasive; role inhibition
Fourth Stage *Middle Childhood (about ages 6 to 11 years)* *(corollary to Freudian latency stage)*		
Industry Has sense of duty and accomplishment, develops scholastic and social competencies, undertakes real tasks, puts fantasy and play in better perspective, learns world of tools, task identification	vs.	**Inferiority** Poor work habits, avoids strong competition, feels doomed to mediocrity; lull before the storms of puberty; may conform as slavish behavior; sense of futility

Source: Reprinted from Childhood and society, *2nd ed. revised, Erik H. Erikson, by permission of W. W. Norton & Company, Inc. Copyright 1950, © 1963 by W. W. Norton & Company, Inc. After table "Erikson's Eight Ages of Man's Ego Development," in* Interpreting personality theories, *2nd ed., by Ledford J. Bischof, Harper & Row, 1970.*

Table 22.1
Erikson's Eight Stages of Ego Development, *Continued*

Success Brings		*Failure Brings*
	Fifth Stage *Puberty and Adolescence (about ages 12 to 20 years)*	
Ego Identity Temporal perspective; self-certain; role experimenter; apprenticeship; sexual polarization; leader-followership; ideological commitment	vs.	**Role Confusion** Time confusion; self-conscious; role fixation; work paralysis; bisexual confusion; authority confusion; value confusion
	Sixth Stage *Early Adulthood*	
Integrity Capacity to commit self to others, "true genitality" now possible, *Lieben und Arbeiten*—"to love and to work"; "mutuality of genital orgasm"	vs.	**Isolation** Avoids intimacy, "character problems," promiscuous behavior; repudiates, isolates, destroys seemingly dangerous forces
	Seventh Stage *Middle Adulthood*	
Generativity Productive and creative for self and others, parental pride and pleasure, mature, enriches life, establishes and guides next generation	vs.	**Stagnation** Egocentric, nonproductive, early invalidism, excessive self-love, personal impoverishment, self-indulgence
	Eighth Stage *Late Adulthood*	
Integrity Appreciates continuity of past, present, and future, acceptance of life cycle and lifestyle, has learned to cooperate with inevitabilities of life, "state or quality of being complete, undivided, or unbroken; entirety" (Webster's Dictionary); "death loses its sting"	vs.	**Despair** Time is too short; finds no meaning in human existence, has lost faith in self and others, wants second chance at life cycle with more advantages; no feeling of world order or spiritual sense, "fear of death"

his previous group of affiliation, finds himself categorized and judged by those who were expected to show him the way through a meaningful moratorium.

Carl Jung and Analytical Psychology

Jung was a contemporary of Freud who at first was quite favorable to the older man's ideas but who later parted company with him and formulated his own theory of personality. Jung's *analytical psychology,* as he called it, de-emphasizes sexuality as a central theme. For many years it was dismissed as being too mystical by clinicians who were put off by Jung's excursions into religion, art, oriental philosophy, and mythology. Our brief presentation of this position touches on only a few of its concepts and principles.

For Jung the *libido* is a life energy that originates from the body's processes and that may force the person into one of two directions. The first direction is *introversive* (inner-oriented) and is evident in the person whose world centers on subjective experiences that are personal; the second direction is *extroversive* (outgoing) and is manifested by the individual who is more concerned with objects and people.

Another important concept for Jung was the *objective psyche,* which in his early writings was called the *collective unconscious.* It has an autonomous existence independent of a person's subjective being and is the sum total of inherited memory traces. These memories, according to Hall and Lindzey (1978, p. 119), "are not inherited as such; rather we inherit the *possibility* of reviving experiences of past generations."

Among the various components of the objective psyche are the *archetypes,* which are like templates stored within each person to produce *images* of things that correspond to his or her conscious situation. For example, the archetype of the father creates the image that is then identified with the real father. These archetypes are a storehouse of latent emotions and may be further

subdivided into the *persona, self,* and *complexes.*

The persona, which is the Latin word for mask, refers to the masks worn by the actors of ancient Greece and represents the outer appearance that each individual shows the world. In a sense it is the individual's response both to society's prescriptions and mores and to his or her own archetypal demands.

Jung defined the self as a striving toward an ideal personality; in this sense it is not the real person but rather a motivating force that constantly undergoes modification by the person's conscious and unconscious experiences. And complexes, according to one of his posthumous works, are each individual's "agglomeration of associations," which are directly involved in his or her becoming neurotic or psychotic (Jung, 1968, p. 188):

A neurosis is a dissociation of personality due to the existence of complexes. To have complexes is in itself normal; but if the complexes are incompatible, that part of the personality which is too contrary to the conscious part becomes split off.

In large part, Jung's theory consisted of uncovering his patient's complexes, for he believed that each complex has tensions and energies of its own. A complex has a little personality of its own and can "upset the stomach . . . breathing . . . and heart" (1968, p. 80). Like Freud he uncovered complexes by interpreting dreams, fantasies, and artistic productions. But unlike Freud Jung did not see these productions as expressions of unconscious or repressed impulses; rather they are like Latin, Greek, or Sanskrit texts that must be studied carefully to be understood. An excerpt from Jung's analysis of a dream may serve to clarify his approach to patients. We include only pieces of Jung's account in Case Report 22.2, which describes this patient's malady, his dream, and portions of Jung's analysis; but they will illustrate his method.

It is apparent from this excerpt that Jung placed much value on what the patient claims to be the importance of a particular dream. This is no doubt related to Jung's conviction that each person holds the key to deciphering or decoding his or her own text. But he also interpreted the symbolism of dreams. Unlike Freud, however, he delved into the "psychic facts" of "archetypal dreams." This is not illustrated in Case Report 22.2; it relates to his theory that all people emerge from a deeply unconscious world of which we still contain traces that show up in dreams.

Case Report 22.2 *Jungian Interpretation of a Dream*

This is a case of a man 40 years old, a married man who has not been ill before. He looks well, but recently he had been badly troubled by neurotic symptoms, suffering from a form of vertigo (dizziness), heart palpitation, nausea, and exhaustion. His dream was as follows:

> *I am in the country, in a simple peasant's house, with an elderly, motherly peasant woman. I talk to her about a great journey I am planning; I am going to walk from Switzerland to Leipzig. She is enormously impressed, at which I am very pleased. At this moment I look through the window at a meadow where there are peasants gathering hay.*

The analysis of this dream proceeded by having the patient associate to the "simple peasant's house" to which he replied, "It is the lazar-house of St. Jacob near Basel," which was once a leprosarium. Thus, in the context of this dream, he has leprosy, which is a contagious and dangerous disease and renders him an outcast from human society.

The trip to Leipzig, according to his free association, is his desire to get a distinguished professorial chair at the University of Leipzig. Jung relates this ambition to the man's symptoms which resemble a mountain sickness and interprets this portion as representing the patient's wanting to climb too high; and he relates the peasant woman's being impressed by the patient to his boasting to an

inferior, uneducated person, which in turn is related to his own distorted value system: "he is inferior in his feeling life."

SOURCE: *C. G. Jung.* Analytical psychology: its theory and practice, © 1968 *Pantheon Books, a division of Random House, Inc.*

As a general rule, analytical psychotherapy does not have a theory. Jung the therapist, according to Whitmont and Kaufman (1973), was a pragmatist whose motto was "anything goes as long as it works," all within the framework of his larger theory as sketched above. For example, when faced with a woman whose main symptom was that she had not slept for several weeks, Jung sang a lullaby and thus put her to sleep. In another case, confronted by a woman unable to get in touch with her own inner religious experience, Jung literally taught her the scriptures, each session handing her an assignment and then testing her at the next session. In Jung's office people danced, sang, acted, painted, and modeled with clay, the media of expression being limited only by Jung's inventiveness and ingenuity.

Nevertheless, there are some guidelines. Typically therapy starts with a thorough exploration of the patient's conscious state. Since the unconscious is viewed as compensatory to the conscious state, the latter must first be established. The same dream, for example, can have quite different meanings with various conscious attitudes. The investigation must include past history, various important influences, attitudes, values, and ideas. Without this investigation, as we saw in Case Report 22.2, the analyst would not be able to attach the proper contextual meanings to subsequent dreams and free associations. In addition the past history of the patient permits the analyst to point out inconsistencies and contradictions, and peculiar reactions and behavior patterns. Most important, analytical therapy teaches the patient the slow and difficult path to his or her inner world. The patient may then find many assumptions challenged and questioned. The patient also learns to introspect, which often leads to considerable confusion.

Dreamwork is then introduced, thus launching the patient on the road to an awesome encounter with his or her unconscious. The patient who rises to this challenge is soon confronted with the disagreeable realization of not being in charge of his or her own house, and of having to contend with forces not under his or her control. With this encounter with the workings of the unconscious, the patient becomes acquainted with the compensatory nature of the unconscious: no sooner has a firm attitude been established in consciousness than the unconscious seems to bring out its opposite, and the patient is soon caught up between pairs of opposites. This creates tension and anxiety, but it also presents the opportunity for resolution of the opposites by the emergence of a new entity that transcends them.

On the other hand, while the initial period of therapy for most people is devoted to helping them get in touch with their inner world, for people who are overly absorbed in their introversion the effort will be to put them in touch with external reality.

The cardinal rule in Jungian analysis is that the basis of that analysis is experiencing; mere intellectual understanding is insufficient. For example, a depressed patient may be discouraged from attempting to do away with the depression (or having it drugged away); instead the patient will be asked to stay with the depression, to let it be, accepting it as an unconscious message.

One of the main techniques of analytical therapy, as we noted in Case Report 22.2, is dream interpretation. The main difference between the Freudian and Jungian approaches to a dream is their divergent views of repression. To Freudians, it will be recalled, a dream results from the emergence of repressed contents from the unconscious. As a result it is viewed as a distortion that must be unravelled. Thus the apparent theme of the dream is its *manifest* content, behind which lurks the dream's *latent* content. Jungians, in contrast, view the dream phenom-

enologically. The theme of the dream *is* the unconscious message expressed in symbolic form, a message that is trying to reveal meaning.

Alfred Adler and Individual Psychology

Alfred Adler was also a contemporary of Freud. At first he was a member of Freud's psychoanalytic circle and worked closely with him, even becoming the older man's successor as president of the Vienna Psychoanalytic Society and coeditor of its journal; but then, like Carl Jung, he broke away from Freud's tutelage and founded what he called the school of *individual psychology*. Even though Adler's theory of personality and methods of treatment are less well known than those of Freud, many of its terms and constructs have made their way into the vernacular—organ inferiority, compensation, lifestyle, feelings of inferiority and superiority.

Adler's social psychological theory contrasts strikingly with Freud's, Erikson's, and Jung's instinctual models, in that it rests on the assumption that human beings are motivated primarily by social urges, that they are social beings who relate to other people, that they engage in cooperative social activities, and that they place social welfare above selfish interests. His major theoretical concepts were *fictional finalism*, *striving for superiority*, *style of life*, *inferiority feelings*, and *compensation*.

Fictional finalism refers to the idea that people live by many purely fictional notions that have no counterpart in reality, an idea that Adler borrowed from Hans Vaihinger's philosophy of the "as if" (1925). According to Vaihinger, fictions are ideas, including unconscious notions without counterpart in reality, that serve the useful function of enabling us to deal with reality more effectively than we could otherwise. Similarly Adler believed people are motivated more by their ideals and expectations of the future than by experiences of the past. If a person believes, for instance, that he is destined to become great, this belief will influence his conduct, perhaps by spurring him on to attempt to live up to this fiction. These fictional goals, for Adler, were the true determiners of personality, which, when they have outlived their usefulness, may be discarded. In fact the distinction Adler makes between a normal person and a neurotic one is that only the former can be free from the influence of these fictions and face reality when confronted by it.

Striving for superiority, the second of Adler's constructs, does not mean, as the terms may imply, aspiring toward social distinction, leadership, or preeminent position in society. By superiority Adler meant the aspiration of each individual to overcome the weakness of the child, his or her ever-present inferiority feeling—a striving for perfection that the person carries from one state of development to the next higher state and may manifest itself in a thousand different ways (Adler, 1927).

Adler's conceptualization of the style of life can best be understood by considering his own analogy (1929, pp. 98–99):

If we look at a pine tree growing in a valley we will notice that it grows differently from on top of a mountain. It is the same kind of a tree, a pine, but there are two distinct styles of life. . . . The style of life of the tree is the individuality of a tree expressing itself and molding itself in an environment.

It is much the same way with human beings. We see the style of life under certain conditions of environment. . . . A trained psychologist could perhaps understand the style of life in a human being even in a favorable situation, but it becomes apparent to everybody when the human subject is put into unfavorable or difficult situations.

This distinctive lifestyle, according to Adler, begins to appear very early in childhood, by about the age of 4 or 5, and from then on the individual expresses himself and assimilates experiences according to his unique style.

Feelings of inferiority come about because of a sense of incompletion or imperfection inherent in most people, which motivates them to overcome their shortcomings so that they can master their environments and cope with problems. These feelings serve as goads to action, and Adler viewed them not only as inevitable and necessary to human survival, but as motivating forces for some of the greatest human achievements in medicine and science.

Disordered behavior, according to Adler, has its roots in the early stages of development when people acquire a set of faulty responses in trying to compensate for their increased states of discomfort. The faulty responses consist of exaggerated strivings for superiority, underdeveloped social interest, and listlessness, all of which are signs of neurosis. Moreover neurotic individuals are people who have acquired mistaken opinions about themselves and the world and who expend much time and energy in maladaptive behaviors aimed at safeguarding these opinions. When confronted with situations they feel they cannot meet successfully—perhaps because of their mistaken views and the faulty lifestyle they have adopted—the neurotic safeguards rather than abandons these views. Consequently such people strive for goals that are unattainable, perhaps because of their false sense of superiority, and lead a socially useless life.

Adlerian therapy includes three major objectives: (1) understanding the lifestyle of the patient, his (or her) specific problem situation, and the significance and meaning of the symptoms; (2) explaining the patient to himself by communicating with him in such a way that he accepts this interpretation, despite the initial negativism and lack of cooperation that are a part of the neurotic personality; and (3) strengthening the patient's social interest by giving him the experience of a "fellow human" and a feeling of cooperation in the joint task of treatment. In what follows, we draw heavily from Ansbacher and Ansbacher (1956), whose excellent book *The Individual Psychology of Alfred Adler* is essential reading for students of this approach.

The first of these three objectives is understanding the occurrence that precipitated the patient's current *dilemma*. Adlerians try to identify this dilemma, along with the patient's inappropriate responses, by attending carefully to the way in which he or she reports them. Following this *general diagnosis* the therapist formulates a *special diagnosis* by eliciting from the patient behaviors and reports about early childhood recollections, critical childhood disorders, aggravating life conditions (organ inferiorities, pressures in the family, pampering, sibling rivalry, or a neurotic family tradition), and content of daytime fantasies and nighttime dreams, and by carefully examining all expressive movements observable by him during the therapy sessions.

Explaining the patient to himself, in Adlerian therapy, is a verbal *tour de force,* in which the therapist hopes to convince the patient by sheer logic that his coping mechanisms are not up to the task of facing life's hardships. But because neurotics are presumed to cling to their faulty lifestyles, Adlerians often resort to overwhelming their patients by correctly predicting behavior that they, the therapists, have not had occasion to witness. In this way they hope to convince patients that there is a self-consistency and goal-directedness about behavior that makes it transparent or predictable and that they, the therapists, are truly expert at understanding such behavior.

The third objective of Adlerian therapy—the strengthening of social interest—is analogous to the function of the parent, who interprets society to the child. In fact Adler relegates this task to the mother, and his attitude toward the mothers of neurotics is reflected in his statement that if she "fails in this, the task is likely to fall much later to the physician, who is heavily handicapped for it. The mother has the enormous advantage . . . [because] she represents the greatest experience of love and fellowship that the child will ever have" (Ansbacher and Ansbacher, 1956, p. 341).

Perhaps the best way to illustrate how Adlerian therapy works is to let Alfred Adler speak for himself, as he does in Case Report 22.3, when he describes a woman who had been very pretty and had been spoiled by her mother and ill-used by a drunken father. She became an actress and had many love affairs, one of which culminated in her becoming the mistress of an elderly married man. Her mother reproached her for her bad judgment, and even though the man loved her, he could not get a divorce from his wife. She then began to suffer from headaches and heart palpitation and became irritable toward the man. Case Report 22.3 contains the rest of the description and Adler's interpretations.

Some striking differences between Freudian, neo-Freudian, Jungian, and Adlerian therapy are evident in this case. Not only do the terms differ, but the explanations given for the etiology and functions of symptoms are entirely at variance. Whereas the others talk of conscience, unconscious conflict, and guilt, Adlerians explain symptoms as products of competitiveness, self-absorption, and useful modes of manipulating others. The pace and tenor of therapy are different also. Adlerians display none of the hesitancy and deliberation of the Freudians and others (see especially Reik's remarks on p. 485: "When I shall tell him much later what I discovered about his own hidden character . . ."); instead they immediately explain to the patient the connection between symptoms and early and current behaviors ("I explained to her the connection between her headaches and the competitive attitude. . . . She felt incapable of obtaining her goal of superiority by normal means . . ."). Nor are Adlerians as reluctant as the others to give advice and to prescribe whatever changes they deem necessary to achieve a resolution of immediate and long-term problems. Whereas the others plod through the analysis of dreams and transference relationships, Adlerians lay down a set of rules for living that they strongly advise the patient to follow.

Case Report 22.3 *Adlerian Psychotherapy*

The girl's condition was the result of a neurotic method of striving to hasten her marriage, and was not at all ineffective. The married man, who was greatly worried by her continuous headaches, came to see me about my patient, and said that he would hurry the divorce and marry her. Treatment of the immediate illness was easy—in fact it would have cleared up without me, for the girl was powerful enough to succeed with the help of her headaches.

I explained to her the connection between her headaches and the competitive attitude with her sister; it was the goal of her childhood not to be surpassed by her younger sister. She felt incapable of obtaining her goal of superiority by normal means, for she was one of those children whose interest has become absorbed in themselves, and who tremble for fear that they may not succeed. She admitted that she cared only for herself and did not like the man she was about to marry.

Her palpitation was due to the fact that she had twice been pregnant and both times had resorted to abortion, when she justified herself to the doctor by saying that her heart was too weak to bear children. It was true that her heart was irritated by tense situations and suppressed anger, but she used this symptom increasingly and exaggerated it to justify her intention never to have children. Self-absorbed women generally show their lack of human and social interest by unwillingness to have children; but sometimes, of course, they desire children for reasons of ambition or for fear of being considered inferior.

SOURCE: *Used by permission of Dr. Kurt A. Adler. From* The science of living *by Alfred Adler. Copyright 1929, 1957 by Dr. Kurt A. Adler.*

Erich Fromm

Like Adler and Jung, Fromm was dissatisfied with Freud's personality theory, particularly with his concept of the libido; and much like Adler, he believed that a person's relatedness to the world

is more important than his or her sexuality. Of major importance to Fromm, as the list of his books readily discloses, is that "a person feels lonely and isolated because he or she has become separated from nature and from other people" (Hall and Lindzey, 1978, p. 170).[2]

Becoming abnormal in the Frommian sense means not having learned to cope adequately with the demands of society. But society often plays an important role in psychopathology, for it makes demands contrary to a person's nature. The individual would like to escape from such a society, and toward this end he uses such neurotic mechanisms as *masochism*, which is characterized by feelings of helplessness and insignificance; *sadism* and *destructiveness*, marked by a need for domination; and *automaton conformity*, in which a pseudo-self is created that has a slavish dependency on society's fashions and cultural patterns (Nagler, 1972).

In spite of his voluminous writing, Fromm has not developed a method of psychotherapy essentially different from that of Freud, although he labels his school of thought *humanistic psychoanalysis*. In a sense, therefore, he straddles the often fuzzy line that divides the psychoanalytic theorists from the humanistic–existential theorists to be discussed in Chapter 24.

Critical Comment

The main objection to the dynamic psychotherapies by the scientific community has been that its founders were practicing clinicians and, consequently, its theories were developed primarily on the basis of clinical observations and philosophical beliefs. Their theories, like those of the humanistic–existential therapists to be dis-

---

[2] Fromm's most important works, in chronological order, are *Escape from Freedom* (1941), *Man for Himself* (1947), *The Sane Society* (1955), *Beyond the Chains of Illusion* (1962), *The Heart of Man* (1964), and *The Revolution of Hope* (1968).

cussed in Chapter 24, suffer scientifically from vaguely defined constructs that are neither confirmable nor disconfirmable by evidence other than clinical observation.

In an attempt to further the growth of psychoanalysis as a science, some of its proponents (Holt and Peterfreund, 1972) have argued that it needs, first, an atmosphere that encourages innovation. Accordingly these proponents publish an annual series of volumes on *Psychoanalysis and Contemporary Science*, which has become a vehicle for theoretical and empirical contributions to psychoanalysis. Second, psychoanalysis needs rigorous standards of scholarship, since new advances, they argue, presuppose a thorough knowledge of the development and present status of psychoanalytic method and theory. Third, and perhaps most important, psychoanalysis needs clarity about the nature and meaning of scientific theory. And, finally, psychoanalysis needs stimulating ideas from other sciences, such as psychology, zoology, genetics, psychopharmacology, history, sociology, and the information and systems sciences.

In reflecting on his own uneasiness about the current status of the dynamic therapies and their future prospects, one psychoanalyst (Dahl, 1972, p. 237) had this to say: "We cannot live off the genius of Freud forever, nor off the second generation of truly gifted and creative clinicians whose insights we still feel but whom we have begun to lose. All current signs point to a steady decline in creative innovation and fresh clinical insights." Nevertheless, these psychotherapies continue in their clinical tradition and their chief research method is to test psychodynamic hypotheses by means of the case history study.

The use of case histories as the primary source of support for psychodynamic theory has been objected to on three main grounds (Reiss et al., 1977):

1. The therapist is a biased observer who is aware of the hypotheses being investigated and can elicit certain kinds of information from the patient. Moreover the data that are collected in the clinic, even when they are not subject to biased interpretations, are full of recording errors, as well as errors resulting from fallible memories. There is a need to make these data public, so that therapists other than the one taking the notes can have access to what was said by patient and therapist. The other therapists, in turn, must critically examine these audiotape recordings and invent methods for reducing the enormous amount of data thus collected. Some progress has been made in this area (see Dahl, 1972; Spence and Lugo, 1972), but progress in content analysis and clinical listening is only just beginning.

2. Case histories cannot be replicated because each case represents a unique set of circumstances and psychological dynamics. This need not be an insurmountable deterrent, however, for (as we noted above) the audiotapes can be subjected to careful and quantitative scrutiny.

3. Case history data permit inferences of correlations between two events; such correlations do not necessarily imply causation. For example, when a patient recalls an argument with his or her mother and recalls developing at the same time a fear of high places, these recollections are only correlated. It is possible that the argument with the mother caused a fear of high places, it is also possible that the fear of high places caused an argument with the mother, but it is more probable that some third factor caused both the argument and the fear.

Summary

The traditional approaches stem from Freud, Erikson, Jung, Adler, and Fromm. Freud formulated the familiar concepts of repression, dream analysis, and transference. Erikson's approach has become well known among the younger generation because it deals with the problems of seeking identity. Jung's mysticism and analytical psychology, also not without appeal on college campuses, delve deeply into the inner reaches of the unconscious. And Adler's and Fromm's social psychological theories come closest to recognizing and dealing with people as a product of their society.

Terms and Concepts to Master

Analytical psychology

Archetypes

Catharsis

Compensation

Countertransference

Dream analysis

Extroversion

Fictional finalism

Free association

Individual psychology

Inferiority feelings

Insight

Introversion

Objective psyche

Persona

Psychoanalysis

Repression

Stages of ego development

Striving for superiority

Style of life

Transference

23 Behavior Therapy

Behavior therapy—the application of conditioning or learning principles to the modification of behavior—is a development of the 1960s. Its difference from other therapies is not its conceptualization of psychopathology or therapy in learning theory terms because this was already accomplished in the 1950s by Dollard and Miller (also see Mowrer, 1950, 1960a).

What is different is that its practitioners modify human behavior, especially abnormal behavior, according to these principles. This approach has particularly appealed to experiment-minded psychologists and psychiatrists, for they see it as a natural outgrowth of years of work in the laboratory.

At the present time at least four general types of behavior therapies trace their origins to the psychological laboratory and to the learning principles developed there. One approach, currently represented by Eysenck, Franks, Lang, A. Lazarus, Lazovik, Rachman, Thorpe, Wolpe, and Yates, borrows much from Dollard and Miller and has its roots in the learning theories of Pavlov (1927), Hull (1952), and Spence (1956). Throughout this chapter we shall refer to it as *respondent behavior therapy*.

This mode of therapy has its roots in *classical*, or *respondent*, conditioning, which, as we noted in Chapter 6, was introduced by Pavlov's demonstration that dogs could be taught to salivate to the sound of a bell. In general terms this procedure consists of pairing a *conditioned stimulus* (CS) with an *unconditioned stimulus* (US) in order to elicit an *unconditioned response* (UR) that, after frequent associations, becomes the *conditioned response* (CR). By means of classical conditioning principles it is possible to explain why some people salivate at exactly noon and why others are attracted to or repelled by certain circumstances or objects. Earlier in this book, for example, we showed how Watson's Albert acquired his animal phobia (Chapter 6).

The other form of therapy has its beginnings in the behaviorism of John Watson (1924) and the work of E. L. Thorndike (1932) and B. F. Skinner (1938, 1953, 1971). The names commonly associated with it are Skinner, Ayllon, Azrin, Baer, Bernal, Bijou, Ferster, Goldiamond, Kanfer, Keller, Krasner, Lindsley, Lovaas, G. Patterson, and Ullmann (see Goodall, 1972). This form of therapy traces its principles mainly to *operant*, or *instrumental*, conditioning procedures, which are based on the observation that organisms must respond before being reinforced (see Chapter 6). In other words, whereas in classical conditioning responses are elicited by and associated with reinforcing stimuli, Skinner emphasizes the importance of the events that follow and are the consequences of a response.

Both forms of behavior therapy, respondent and operant, share as their main objectives the modification of maladaptive responses and the elimination of distressing emotional states by means of active manipulation of environmental conditions that contribute to the persistence of undesirable behavior.

The main difference between the two therapy approaches, however, is that respondent therapy focuses on involuntary, or autonomic, responses, and the Skinnerians focus on voluntary behavior: respondent therapy emphasizes manipulations of eliciting stimuli and autonomic responses leading to fear and anxiety and tends mainly to treat neurotic behaviors, while Skinnerians have traditionally concerned themselves with stimuli that set the occasion for and control responding, and with creating behavior formerly absent in the organism. Moreover operant behaviorists apply their methods principally to psychotic, autistic, and self-destructive behaviors. But neither method is restricted to any one type of disorder; nor is the autonomic–voluntary dichotomy entirely accurate, as we shall see in the discussion of biofeedback in a later section of this chapter.

A third type of behavior therapy, with solid roots in both the respondent and operant forms, is the *observational* or *vicarious learning*, or *modeling*, approach that we also discussed as one form of social learning theory. In observational learning an individual observes a model's behavior but need not practice the overt responses nor receive any apparent reinforcement for behaving. By observing a model the observer may vicariously learn a response without actually performing it. Bandura (1969, 1970, 1971) and Richards (Bandura and Richards, 1963) are associated with this therapy.

The fourth form of behavior modification uses concepts from the learning laboratory as well as from cognitive psychology. Several investigators and clinicians have emphasized the role of cognitions (perceptions, thoughts, beliefs) on behavior. Again the contributions of Bandura are important here, but so are those of Ellis (1962), Kanfer and Phillips (1970), Meichenbaum (1974, 1977) and Mahoney (1974, 1977).

With this background we can now consider in detail some applications of these four behavioral techniques. It must be said at the outset that the types of cases selected by behavior therapists are very much influenced by their adoption of the S–R, or stimulus–response, learning theory approach; and it is therefore not surprising to find that most of their treatment reports deal with such clear-cut behavior anomalies as phobias, obsessions, compulsions, tics, stuttering, and similar other symptoms that lend themselves to the application of learning principles for their modification (see, for example, cases reported in Chapters 8, 11, 15, and 19).

Respondent Behavior Therapy

According to Wolpe, a maladaptive response such as anxiety can be extinguished as follows (1958, p. 71):

If a response antagonistic to anxiety can be made to occur in the presence of anxiety-evoking stimuli, so that it is accompanied by a complete or partial suppression of the anxiety responses, the bond between those stimuli and the anxiety responses will be weakened.

This technique, variously called *deconditioning, reciprocal inhibition,* or *desensitization*[1] was known more than fifty years ago when Watson and Rayner (1920) recommended ways for removing Little Albert's conditioned fear response. In fact Jones (1924a, 1924b), who several years later treated a phobia for rabbits in a 3-year-old boy, Peter, quite probably used techniques based on those suggested by Watson and Rayner. Her study served as a springboard for new and recent

---

[1] For finer discriminations of these terms, the reader is referred to Evans's, and Wilson's article (1968) and to Bandura (1969), Franks (1969), Eysenck and Rachman (1965), Kanfer and Phillips (1970), Lazarus (1971), Meyer and Chesser (1970), and Yates (1970a). For our purposes, it is sufficient to say that all the techniques of respondent behavior therapy are intended to achieve *counterconditioning;* that is, their goal is to eliminate disturbing emotional components of behavior by conditioning eliciting stimuli to positive emotions.

interest in behavior modification, and therefore is worth recounting here.

Peter, like Albert, was experimentally conditioned to fear rats and other furry things such as a rabbit and a fur coat (Jones, 1924a). His fear was then extinguished by giving him food he liked while the experimenter introduced a rabbit (the feared object) at a sufficient distance so that it would not interfere with his eating response. The animal was then brought even closer, and occasionally other children were introduced into the experimental setting to show him that they were also not afraid of the animal.[2] Eventually the phobia was eliminated in favor of a more positive response toward the animal, which generalized, without additional training, to other feared objects resembling it.

Of the various other modification methods tried, Jones (1924b) found disuse (not exposing the child to the feared object), ridicule, starving, and verbal appeal ineffectual in removing the conditioned response. She also discovered that negative adaptation (constantly exposing the child to the feared object)[3] was somewhat successful in eliminating the response but that the most desired effects were accomplished by a combination of deconditioning and distraction, in which the phobic stimulus was placed in the context of a desired goal while being associated with another stimulus capable of arousing pleasant reactions.

Returning now to Wolpe's work, we shall list a number of techniques that he and his associates described in several books (Lazarus, 1971; Wolpe,

1958, 1961, 1969; Wolpe and Lazarus, 1966).

Assertiveness Training

As the name implies, this form of therapy is intended for individuals whose interpersonal and other behaviors are inhibited by anxiety. The therapist's goal in these cases is to augment "every impulse towards the elicitation of these inhibited responses, with the expectation that each time they do, there will, reciprocally, be an inhibiting of the anxiety, resulting in some degree of weakening of the anxiety response habit" (Wolpe, 1969, p. 62).

The therapist implements these goals first by asking questions designed to establish how the patient behaves passively in a number of situations ("Suppose that arriving home after buying an article you find it slightly damaged. What will you do?") and then by informing the patient that the outward expression of his or her resentment will reciprocally inhibit anxiety. The therapist also points out how the patient's (or others') behavior is maladaptive and may even argue with the patient until able to convince him or her of the logic of becoming more assertive. Wolpe and Lazarus (1966, p. 44) indicate that "such discourse . . . usually results in enough augmentation of resentment to quell the restraint of fear and permit the emergence of some assertive responses."

The patient is then encouraged, in various real-life situations, to try some of the following types of *assertive statements* (Wolpe, 1969, pp. 66–67):

Please don't stand in front of me.

I hate your duplicity.

I would rather not say.

Why are you late?

Pardon me—I was here first.

I like you.

---

[2] Social *imitation* was also recommended by Watson as a technique for removing fears, and it plays an important role in the behavior modification theory of Albert Bandura (see pp. 509–513), who states that Peter was cured as effectively by observing "the positive response of other children as they played with the feared animal" (1969, p. 451).

[3] In its modern form, this method is similar to the *implosive* therapy of Stampfl and Levis (1967, 1968), which we will discuss later.

I love you.

I admire your tenacity.

Although the idea of trying out these assertive responses in progressively more demanding or stressful real-life situations may be easy for some, not everyone can manage to be assertive without practice. Therefore this training may also involve *behavioral rehearsal,* which is a form of role-play. In these instances the therapist may play the part of the person who usually evokes anxiety in the patient's life, and the patient's role is to be assertive. Wolpe mentions that "a good deal of deconditioning of anxiety frequently takes place during the behavior rehearsal itself" (1969, p. 68). The trick, of course, is to get the inhibition of anxiety to generalize to real-life situations (see Friedman, 1971).

In this regard Ullmann and Krasner (1975, p. 234) observe that what has been learned in the role-expressive behavior can and should be applied in real-life situations. The favorable experiences resulting from each application should then generalize to other situations and the "individual can enter into and make adaptive responses in progressively more difficult situations. As in all behavior-change procedures, the person acts differently, and people, in turn, respond differently to him. This may well lead to further favorable changes in self-concept."

Systematic Desensitization

In another behavioral technique Wolpe and his associates attempt to reinstate a situation similar to the one in which the patient presumably acquired his or her neurosis. In this way, during the unlearning of maladaptive behavior, new responses can be associated with old cues. This aspect of behavior therapy, called *systematic desensitization* by Wolpe (1958, 1969), has its roots in animal experiments in which he noted that the fear response of extremely hungry cats who refuse to eat can be extinguished by feeding them in situations similar to the original fear-evoking ones.

In applying this technique to human beings, the behavior therapist first obtains a detailed history from the patient so that he or she can subsequently reinstate as many fear-evoking situations as possible. The therapist then constructs a hierarchical list in which items are ranked from minimal to maximal fear-evoking status. The items are written on separate pieces of paper and the patient is asked to rank them in order. The construction of this hierarchy usually takes from one to three interviews, depending on the nature of the phobia, the patient's verbal facility, and the therapist's skills.

The initial interviews are further used to train the patient in *progressive muscular relaxation,* usually an abbreviated form of Jacobson's method (1938), in which the patient first learns to contract and then to relax particular muscles while being attuned to discriminate the different sensations accompanying tension and relaxation. The patient is instructed to practice relaxation at home between treatment sessions. Then, during later sessions, when the therapist decides that the patient can successfully attain states of complete relaxation, the desensitization procedures are begun.

During desensitization, the patient is instructed to relax in the way he or she has learned and is asked to signal the therapist by raising a finger when feeling anxious or distressed. He or she is encouraged to imagine a neutral scene, one that does not elicit discomfort; the therapist then suggests one or two of the frightening situations that appear lowest on the hierarchical list of items. In the first of these sessions, the therapist ascertains how vividly the patient is able to imagine the fear-evoking stimuli and notes the associated feelings toward them. Later sessions consist of presenting patients with ever-increasing anxiety-arousing items until they no longer have any effect. Therapy continues until the most disturbing stimuli or the highest items on the list can be imagined without fear. In treating a snake phobia, for example, behavior therapy would continue until imagining snakes no longer frightened the individual—that is, until the individual has been desensitized to the previously fear-evoking stimulus of snakes.

Systematic desensitization has also been used to treat cases of impotence, premature ejaculation, and orgasmic dysfunction. The goal here is to reduce the anxiety associated in the patient's mind with the approach of sexual intercourse (Cooper, 1963, 1968; Kraft and Al-Issa, 1968; Lazarus, 1965, 1971; Wolpe, 1958, 1969). For example, in treating a man who had been impotent a number of years, Wolpe (1958, 1969) reports how he trained the patient in progressive relaxation so that he could learn to control his anxiety in the sexual setting. Once this was learned, the patient was instructed on how to relax while in bed with his partner and was told to confine his sexual advances to preliminary foreplay in order to preclude any possibility of reinforcing anxiety associated with sex. Wolpe also discouraged his patient's attempts at intromission until he thought that the anxiety associated with sex had been entirely removed. Subsequently, after the male reported increased sexual responsiveness, he was gradually encouraged to attempt intromission and coitus. Similar systematic desensitization procedures have been used in much the same way to treat orgasmic dysfunction and other sexual disorders.[4]

How effective is systematic desensitization? In a major review of the treatment results of this technique University of Illinois psychologist Gordon Paul (1969, p. 159) concluded: "The findings were overwhelmingly positive, and for the first time in the history of psychological treatments, a specific treatment package reliably produced measurable benefits for clients across a broad range of distressing problems." Several other controlled outcome studies demonstrating the efficacy of systematic desensitization are also described in Marks et al. (1971), Meichenbaum et al. (1971), and O'Leary and Wilson, (1975).

Despite the evident success of systematic desensitization, its theoretical mechanisms have been less than clear. Psychologist Aubrey Yates of the University of Western Australia, for example, in a chapter called "The Birth, Life, and Death of Systematic Desensitization" (Yates, 1975, pp. 152ff), suggests that although the technique apparently "works," its critical factors remain unclear and the theoretical explanations conflicting and indecisive. In his analysis Yates (1975, pp. 162–163) concluded: "Systematic desensitization seems to work, but there seem to be no component parts that cannot be removed, and the technique will then fail or be significantly reduced in its efficacy."

Implosive Therapy

Implosive therapy is a variation of Wolpe's desensitization technique. Instead of proceeding systematically through a graded hierarchy of least to most fear-producing stimuli, Stampfl and his colleagues (Levis and Stampfl, 1969; Stampfl and Levis, 1967, 1968) have suggested exposing the patient constantly, either in imagination or reality, to the most anxiety-evoking stimuli. This technique, which is also called *flooding*, consists of having the patient vividly imagine the feared situation and maintaining his or her anxiety at as high a level as possible with the idea of demonstrating to him that the resulting experience is not unbearable.

Implosive therapy starts with diagnostic interviews aimed at discovering which of the patient's internal and external cues evoke avoidance responses. Then, as with Wolpe's desensitization

---

[4] Essentially, as we saw in Chapter 15, with the addition of some suggestions for "training positions" and the "penile squeeze technique," these are the techniques now being used by Masters and Johnson (1970; see also Robbins and Robbins, 1970) at their Reproductive Biology Research Foundation in St. Louis.

procedure, a list is constructed in which the subtle avoidance cues are placed at the top and overt cues (those the patient is aware of as sources of his or her anxiety) are put at the bottom. The therapist next maintains the patient's anxiety at a high level, which, according to Meyer and Chesser (1970), is accomplished by describing progressively more fearful scenes to be imagined.

The evidence of the advantages of implosive therapy over other behavioral methods is still contradictory. In one study Barrett (1969) compared this technique with desensitization and found that implosive therapy was completed in almost half the time but that its effects also deteriorated more quickly (also see DeMoor, 1970). A few studies show more beneficial results with implosion (Hogan, 1968; Hogan and Kirchner, 1967; Smith and Shappe, 1970), but several others do not (Fazio, 1970; Hodgson and Rachman, 1970).

The main drawback of implosive therapy, according to a critical review (Mikulas, 1972), is that presenting fearful stimuli to the subject may actually result in conditioning more anxiety rather than extinguishing it. For example, one investigator (Fazio, 1970) tried to cure a patient of an insect phobia and discovered that the procedure led to more and not less anxiety associated with insects. On the other hand more recent reports (Romano, 1977, pp. 240–241) suggest that although anxiety was usually pronounced during treatment and sometimes even shifted to intense anger, patients who remained in therapy for the prescribed time experienced dramatic relief from the phobia with which they entered treatment. It is possible to reconcile some of these discrepant findings when one considers that the inconsistencies may be due to procedural differences. In contrast to the well-established procedural rules for systematic desensitization, according to O'Leary and Wilson (1975), the therapeutic guidelines for administering implosive therapy are unclear.

Aversive Conditioning

This form of respondent behavior therapy has been known for some time. This method has been applied, for example, to the treatment of homosexuality and fetishism in a study by Feldman and MacCulloch (1964, 1965) in which patients received electric shocks when they continued to view same-sex or fetish sex objects (see Chapter 15). This procedure, sometimes also called *instrumental avoidance therapy*, which is somewhat harsher than those already discussed, has often also been used successfully to treat alcoholics. The idea of aversive methods is to present, in the context of the response that is to be extinguished, the stimulus to a strong avoidance response, the most typical stimulus being strong electric shock.

In treating alcoholics the therapist first gives the patient a verbal description of what is about to occur. The patient then receives two 10-ounce glasses of warm saline solution (sometimes with whisky in it) containing drugs designed to cause vomiting (emesis). Immediately before vomiting occurs, the patient is also served a 4-ounce glass of whisky (to cause gastric irritation), which he or she is required to smell, taste, swill around in the mouth, and then swallow. If vomiting has not occurred, another straight whisky is given. Then, in order to prolong nausea, he or she is given a glass of beer containing tartar emetic. Subsequent treatments involve larger dosages of injected emetine, increases in the length of treatment time, and a widening range of hard liquors.

In conditioning terminology, the unconditioned stimulus (US) is the drug that produces vomiting; the conditioned stimulus (CS) is the sight, taste, and smell of alcohol; and the unconditioned response (UR) is the vomiting and nausea that occur as a result of the drug. After repeated pairings of the US and CS, the UR becomes a conditioned response (CR), and the alcoholic vomits each time he or she sees, tastes, or smells alcohol. It is *aversive conditioning* (see

Figure 23.1

A histogram showing drug abstinence rates. Rates are calculated as percentages at six-month intervals over a ten-year follow-up period.

(Voegtlin and Broz, 1949)

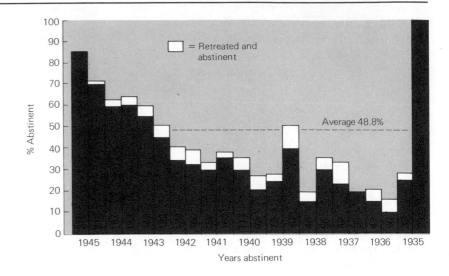

Chapter 6), because the CS, or the eliciting stimulus, has been associated with a US that has noxious or aversive properties.

The results obtained by classical aversive conditioning with drugs, ranging over a period of more than ten years, have yielded some encouraging results. For example, in one early study (Voegtlin and Broz, 1949) of over two thousand cases the overall abstinence rate attained was 44.8 percent in the early years, with the rate falling to 25 to 30 percent at the end of ten years (Figure 23.1). In this study abstinence was defined by strict criteria and excluded all those cases who subsequently relapsed to even the mildest form of drinking. But even the relapsed patients were reported to have enjoyed some period of abstinence before they resumed drinking (of 868 relapsed subjects, 640 were abstinent for at least 3 to 6 months, and 276 for over 12 months). Unfortunately, though, because aversive conditioning is a harsh form of treatment, therapists usually avoid prescribing it and patients are sometimes reluctant to submit to it.

Another technique, *covert sensitization*, which is a variation of aversive counterconditioning, has also been described (Cautela, 1967; Gottman and Leiblum, 1974). This is a combination of the aversive technique and systematic desensitization. In many ways it is the reverse of systematic desensitization, since covert sensitization is designed to foster an avoidance response rather than encourage approach behavior. It is therefore particularly suited to treating undesirable high-approach behaviors (overeating, alcoholism, drug abuse).

The term "covert" refers to the fact that both the behavior to be decreased and the aversive stimuli to be associated with it are to be imagined by the patient. Thus, after being taught to relax, the patient is instructed to visualize the events leading up to the initiation of the undesirable act. Just as the patient begins to imagine engaging in the undesirable behavior, he or she is asked to imagine nausea or other aversive sensations. The "sensitization" is then accomplished by associating the undesirable act with an exceedingly disagreeable consequence.

Variations on this technique have been reported. For example, Foreyt and Kennedy (1971) had a client imagine eating favorite foods while being subjected to extremely noxious odors. Tyler and Stranghan (1970) used an aversion-relief technique in which the subject imagined being tempted by food, then held his breath until he felt uncomfortable. Finally, Gottman and Leiblum (1974, p. 72) cite the following fictional example to illustrate the potential of this technique:

Ray Ugghill was an alcoholic of seven years. He wanted to stop drinking since he was in danger of losing his third job. Covert sensitization was employed. Mr. Ugghill was told to close his eyes and concentrate on the scene the therapist described. He was told to picture himself reaching for and pouring a fresh, frosty glass of beer. As he swallows the drink, it tastes bitter and putrid. He feels nauseous and dizzy. His body trembles, his face sweats and suddenly he begins vomiting. . . . People start moving away from him. . . . He . . . runs out of the bar, hoping to cool off his perspiration-drenched body. As soon as he reaches the street, he experiences . . . relief. He feels calm and relaxed.

Operant Behavior Therapy

According to Ullmann and Krasner (1965, p. 29), who are among the pioneers of operant behavior therapy, "all behavior modification boils down to procedures utilizing *systematic environmental contingencies to alter the subject's response to stimuli.*" This can be accomplished first by making a "thorough analysis of the interaction between the behavior organism and the environment in which the behavior occurs" (Kanfer and Phillips, 1970, p. 242), then by having the therapist understand and bring the consequences of given forms of behavior under control, and finally by transferring this control to the patient. In order to show the application of these behavior modification principles, we have selected for detailed discussion two illustrative cases.

Environmental Engineering To Extinguish Responses

The first example involves the treatment of alcoholism in a way that contrasts strikingly with the respondent aversive therapy and the covert sensitization just described. This is the case of a chronic alcoholic (Sulzer, 1965), who often got into trouble while drunk. Just as often he vowed to stop drinking but was not able to break the habit. He tried traditional psychotherapy, without success. Moreover aversive conditioning with an emetic was proposed to him but he rejected it because his job required that he enter taverns and cafes where alcohol is served.

The therapist treating this case enlisted the cooperation of two friends whom the patient was concerned about losing because of his frequent drunkenness and objectionable behavior. Evidently this cooperation was crucial to the treatment, since these friends created a situation in which social reinforcement for nonalcoholic drinking might be developed. The course of his therapy is described further as Case Report 23.1, which the reader should read before continuing.

Case Report 23.1 *Behavior Modification in an Alcoholic*

The primary goal of therapy was to reduce or stop the patient's drinking behavior. Solitary drinking did not appear to be a serious problem, because he did not often drink alone. Interviews with him suggested that he was concerned about losing the friendship of two men he had known throughout life who now found his frequent drunken states so objectionable that they avoided him. Neither friend was a teetotaler, nor drank heavily.

The patient contacted his friends, who agreed to the following plan. After working hours they would meet at a conveniently located tavern, where the three could drink for a time before going home. The patient was to order only soft drinks. If he ordered or drank hard liquor, the friends would leave immediately. They could drink anything they wished. This plan was to continue, on a once-a-week basis, for an undetermined period of time. Also the patient agreed to invite his friends to his home on all occasions that might call for serving alcoholic beverages. They agreed to come and remain only so long as he took no alcohol. They would also invite him to their homes on similar occasions but would not serve him alcohol.

The first planned accompanied "drinking" occurred without incident and the patient reported that his initial discomfort quickly disappeared. The bartender, somewhat unexpectedly, served as an additional source of social reinforcement by acting more friendly than he had during the patient's previous visits.

The following day the patient, at the therapist's instructions, planned no business visits to taverns and restricted himself to other eating places not serving hard liquor. Several days thereafter, however, for business reasons, the patient had to visit taverns; and on these occasions, he drank liquor again, but less than his previous amounts. On the last day of that week, he contacted his friends to meet him for a "drink," which they did. The patient was found to have already drunk several glasses of liquor when they arrived. The friends were uncertain as to whether they should stay but decided to remain with the patient while he sobered up. As he did so, the patient reported to his friends that he felt quite comfortable and felt little desire to drink with them present. After almost two hours the group broke up. That was the last day the patient had been known to drink any alcoholic beverage.

During this period the therapist met with the patient twice weekly, always expressing approval of reported nondrinking behavior. Also during this time the patient and his wife considered moving to a somewhat larger apartment in a different neighborhood. The therapist supported the proposed move because most of the patient's neighbors responded to him and his family in a way that strained interpersonal relationships and made sobriety more difficult.

The move was made a little over a month after the beginning of therapy and appeared to have very favorable consequences. The patient remained sober and his contacts with new neighbors did not include the kinds of responses he had encountered in his old neighborhood, where most people acted with mild disgust and open disapproval of him.

SOURCE: Adapted from Behavior modification in adult psychiatric patients, by Edward S. Sulzer. In Case studies in behavior modification, edited by Leonard P. Ullmann and Leonard Krasner. Copyright © 1965 by Holt, Rinehart & Winston, Inc. Reprinted by permission of Holt, Rinehart & Winston, Inc.

Careful reading of this case reveals several essential elements of operant behavior therapy: the engineering approach to the study of behavior so that stimulus control is gained, the use of friends as social reinforcers, overt attempts at extinction of undesirable responses, and selective reinforcement of acceptable behaviors. In a word, this case illustrates how the behavior therapist applies operant conditioning techniques to shape and reinforce more adjustive behavior in and out of the therapeutic environment (Ullmann and Krasner, 1965).

The Use of Shaping to Restore Behavior

Our second example of operant therapy is the well-known case of anorexia nervosa treated by Bachrach, et al. (1965). The reader may recall from our discussion in Chapters 8 and 19 that anorexia nervosa is a disorder marked by prolonged cessation of appetite and eating, which causes severe weight loss. In the case presented here, the weight loss was 73 pounds in a woman who had formerly weighed 120 pounds. The question the therapists had to answer immediately was, "How do we get her to eat?" And the more theoretical problem was, "Under what conditions will eating occur?" Solutions to both these problems required information about what manipulations will lead to restoring eating behavior and what events are most likely to increase and maintain her rate of eating.

The patient, a divorced, childless, 37-year-old 5'4'' female, was admitted to the University of Virginia Hospital Medical Service on December 14, 1960. Her weight loss began in about September 1943, and by January 1944, she weighed 110 pounds. Five years later, by 1949, her weight had gradually dropped to about 65 pounds. By the time she was admitted to the hospital in 1960 she had lost an additional 18 pounds. At that time she could stand only with assistance and weighed only 47 pounds. All the physical test results were within normal limits, and the only abnormalities detected on laboratory examination were traceable to her decreased food intake.

No specific attempt was made to take a psychiatric history from the patient, nor was any psychotherapy attempted, because the therapists considered the major objective to be that of restoring eating behavior, a critical goal in view of her very poor prognosis and the great risk of death. Furthermore they believed that a more effective technique for treatment than conventional psychotherapy would be to obtain a current evaluation of those conditions under which eating could be brought under stimulus control. Thus she was not given any drugs except for an occasional hypnotic for sleep and vitamins for her poor health.

For this special form of therapy the woman was transferred to the psychiatric service and assigned to a resident physician (Erwin), who consulted a staff psychologist (Bachrach); both of them arranged for a medical student (Mohr) to collaborate with them on the behavioral program of therapy. The treatment that followed is presented as Case Report 23.2, which describes how the woman's eating was restored and how this behavior was transferred to the home setting (see also Table 23.1).

This case highlights several salient features of the operant approach: programmatic arrangement of the stimulus environment (including the instructions to the parents to avoid reinforcing maladaptive responses); emphasis on the response to stimuli, not the specific response per

Table 23.1

Monthly Progress Report of Weight in an Anorexic Woman

	Date	Weight (lbs.)
1	12/16/1960	47
2	1/ 3/1961	50
3	2/ 1/1961	53
4	2/10/1961	59
5	2/20/1961	61
6	3/ 1/1961	60
7	3/10/1961	63
8	3/20/1961	64
9	3/30/1961	$64^{1}/_{4}$
10	4/14/1961	63
11	4/18/1961	64
12	4/22/1961	$65^{1}/_{2}$
13	5/ 6/1961	66
14	5/10/1961	$68^{1}/_{2}$
15	5/13/1961	67
16	5/17/1961	70
17	7/ 8/1961	70
18	7/15/1961	71
19	7/29/1961	72
20	8/12/1961	71
21	9/30/1961	72
22	10/14/1961	$75^{1}/_{2}$
23	11/11/1961	$75^{1}/_{4}$
24	11/25/1961	$76^{1}/_{2}$
25	12/ 2/1961	76
26	12/ 9/1961	$77^{1}/_{4}$
27	1/18/1962	$74^{1}/_{2}$
28	1/27/1962	77
29	2/ 3/1962	$77^{1}/_{2}$
30	2/10/1962	$77^{1}/_{2}$
31	3/31/1962	88
32	4/21/1962	84
33	5/14/1962	85
34	5/21/1962	$86^{1}/_{2}$
35	6/16/1962	85

Source: From Case studies in behavior modification, *edited by Leonard P. Ullmann and Leonard Krasner, Copyright © 1965 by Holt, Rinehart & Winston, Inc. Adapted and reprinted by permission of Holt, Rinehart and Winston, Inc. [See Bachrach, Erwin, and Mohr (1965).]*

se; behavior shaping; hospital and home environmental engineering to maintain learned adaptive behaviors; and transfer of stimulus control from therapist to patient.

Some therapists believe that for a disorder as complex as anorexia, behavior modification should be integrated with psychotherapy. A treatment program of this type with a case similar to the one just described has been reported (cited in Freedman, 1977, pp. 315–316). Behavior therapy was used to modify the life-threatening non-eating behavior and psychotherapy was useful in exploring the thoughts and feelings that precipitated the disturbance.

Case Report 23.2 *Behavior Modification of Anorexia Nervosa*

At first the patient was placed in an attractive hospital room with pictures on the wall, flowers on the table, and a lovely view of the university grounds from the window. She was given free access to visitors, books, records and record player, television and magazines. She had considerable difficulty reading because of her generalized debility; therefore the people who visited would read to her. These visitors also helped adjust her television and work her record player. In discussions with her the therapist discovered that she looked forward to these activities and seemed to welcome visitors as well. These activities apparently provided enjoyment for her and thus could subsequently be considered as response-contingent reinforcers—that is, as reinforcers contingent upon her eating behavior and nothing else.

She was then removed from her pleasant hospital room and transferred to a ward, which was barren and furnished only with a bed, nightstand, and chair, with only a sink available at one end of the room. Her window view was of the hospital courtyard. Fortunately her family and the hospital administration cooperated in this treatment. The nurses and other staff were told and readily understood that behavior modification was being

used and not some form of "inhumane treatment." Of course the patient was not told anything of the plan, which would consist of returning her to her former surroundings as reinforcement for eating.

Subsequently all meals were brought to her by a nurse and were to be taken in her room. The experimenters set up a reinforcement schedule which consisted of verbal rewards for any movements associated with eating. For example, when she lifted her fork to move toward spearing a piece of food, the experimenter would talk to her about something in which the patient was interested. The required response was then shaped by reinforcing successive movements associated with raising or lifting food toward her mouth, chewing, and so on.

The same reinforcement procedures were followed to increase the amount of food consumed. At first any portion of the meal that was eaten would be rewarded by having the nurse come into her room with a radio, TV set, or phonograph; if she did not touch any of the food before her, she received no reinforcement, and she would be left alone until the next meal. As time went on, more and more of her meal had to be eaten, until eventually she had to finish everything on the plate in order to be reinforced. Her meals were slowly increased in caloric value, with the cooperation of the dieticians, and her weight gradually rose to a level of 85 pounds.

After discharge from the hospital, the question became "How does one generalize the eating response acquired under controlled conditions to a situation in which such controls are lacking?" This problem was solved by enlisting the help of the patient's family. They were instructed specifically: (1) to avoid reinforcing any irrelevant behavior or complaints; (2) not to make any issue of eating; (3) to reinforce maintenance of her weight gain by compliments about her beginning to fill out her clothes; (4) not to prepare any special diet for her; (5) to refrain from weighing her at home because this was to be recorded only when she made periodic visits to see the medical student; (6) to discuss only pleasant topics at meal times; (7) never to allow her to eat alone; (8) to follow a rigid schedule for meals, with an alarm clock to be present for each meal; (9) to use a purple table cloth initially as a discriminative stimulus for mealtime table behavior associated with eating; and (10) to encourage her to dine out with other people under enjoyable conditions.

SOURCE: *From* Case studies in behavior modification, *edited by Leonard P. Ullmann and Leonard Krasner. Copyright © 1965 by Holt, Rinehart & Winston, Inc. Adapted and reprinted by permission of Holt, Rinehart & Winston, Inc. [See Bachrach, Erwin, and Mohr (1965).]*

Token Economy Procedures

The *token economy* procedure is a somewhat different conditioning treatment procedure from that given in the two illustrations above. The first step in this method is to explain to patients what is expected of them in a particular setting and to indicate that their receipt of reinforcements is contingent on their compliance with these rules.

The best-known contingency contracting program is one that provides tokens (poker chips, point tallies, money) as reinforcers for desirable behaviors. These tokens can later be exchanged for other reinforcers. For example, in Chapter 12 we noted the use of this system by Ayllon and Azrin (1965, 1968a, 1968b), in which they rewarded schizophrenics' socially acceptable behavior with tokens; and in Chapter 16 we encountered another use of tokens when one therapist (Burchard, 1967) reinforced the prosocial behaviors of delinquents. The details of the first of these uses are worth describing (see also Mikulas, 1972).

Ayllon and Azrin, pioneers in the use of token economies to reinforce the behavior of psychotics, reported in a 1965 paper that when tokens were distributed, there was a relatively higher output of work, but when reinforcements were withheld, work declined radically (Ayllon and Azrin, 1965). These investigators later de-

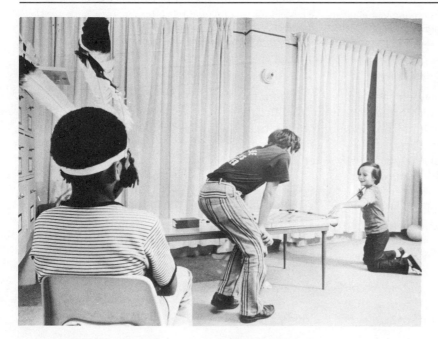

In a unique use of the token economy procedure, Paul Clement of the Child Development Center in Pasadena, California, usually places a parent and child in a play setting, observing them from behind a screen or viewing mirror and instructing the parent, via a signal audible only to the parent, when to reinforce the child with a token. In this photograph Clement is using another child as the therapist to provide reinforcement for the patient. The therapist is dressed as an Indian chief to set him apart from his peers; he receives instructions about reinforcing the patient from Clement, who is attempting to shape outgoing behavior in the shy youngster (kneeling at the right).

Table 23.2

Types of Jobs and Tokens Paid per Duration of Work

Types of Jobs	Duration	Tokens Paid
Waitress		
During Meals	10 minutes	2
Empties trays left on tables and washes tables between each of 4 meals		
In Commissary	10 minutes	5
Cleans tables, washes cups and glasses used at commissary; places cups and glasses in rack ready for automatic dishwasher		
Secretarial Assistant		
During Exercises	30 minutes	3
Assists recreational assistant with exercises; writes names of patients participating in exercises		
In Commissary	30 minutes	5
Assists sales clerk assistant; writes names of patients at commissary; records number of tokens spent; totals all tokens spent		

Source: T. Ayllon and N. H. Azrin. The token economy: a motivational system for therapy and rehabilitation. *New York: Appleton-Century-Crofts, 1968, pp. 244–250. Adapted by permission of Prentice-Hall, Inc.*
Note: Additional information and related research can be found in The token economy *as cited above.*

scribed a token economy system in which chronic psychiatric hospital patients were reinforced for performing specific jobs such as waiting, busing tables, and secretarial work. A sampling of the types of jobs and the number of tokens paid per duration of time is given in Table 23.2 (Ayllon and Azrin, 1968b).

The types of privileges that patients could purchase with their tokens included walks on the hospital grounds (2 tokens for a 20-minute walk), escorted trips to town (100 tokens), movies in the ward (1 token), and exclusive use of a radio (1 token). In this way some patients gradually acquired socially desirable behaviors. Of course the problem thereafter is to transfer the control of

behaviors from tokens to social reinforcers within and ultimately outside the hospital. The latter transfer may be implemented in halfway houses and community live-in arrangements (see Chapter 25).

Although the success of token economy programs was taken for granted since their inception in 1965, questions about their efficacy have been raised more recently. Two main concerns have been expressed. One of these concerns has been the high rehospitalization rate (O'Leary and Wilson, 1975) and, related to this observation, these patients' inability to function outside the hospital once released. The main reason for the high recidivism rate is probably that the prime focus in the hospital is on removing or modifying undesirable behaviors without preparing the patient with the necessary social and behavioral skills to function independently outside the hospital environment.

The other concern has been the exclusive focus of token economy therapists on changing target behaviors rather than on increasing the number of patients who leave the hospital or are transferred to better wards (Freedman, 1976). There is a need for more carefully controlled studies on the efficacy of token economy programs that investigate more than just the modification of specific behaviors.

Modeling

Techniques of behavioral therapy somewhat distinct from the respondent and operant paradigms, although with solid roots in both, are those that rely on *modeling* to modify behavior. The chief proponent of modeling has been Albert Bandura (Bandura and Walters, 1963; Bandura, 1965, 1969, 1976), who has argued that imitation or modeling may be as fundamental a form of learning as reinforcement (see also Aronfreed, 1968, 1969; Tharp and Wetzel, 1969). Modeling, which has its roots in animal experiments on imitation (Miller and Dollard, 1941), is also variously known as *social learning, observation learning,*

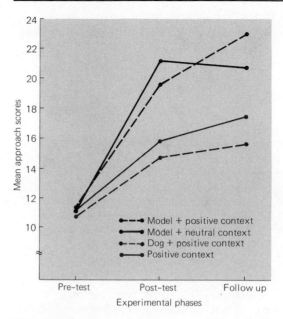

Figure 23.2
The average approach scores of dog-phobic children are shown in this graph. It may be seen that the most beneficial treatment for dog phobia is the one in which children are exposed to a nonfrightened model who handles dogs within a pleasant context, although the context is not as important as the presence of the model.

(Bandura et al., 1967)

Psychotherapy as a Learning Process

In what has now become a landmark paper in the history of behavior therapy, Albert Bandura (1961, p. 143) wrote:

While it is customary to conceptualize psychotherapy as a learning process, few therapists accept the full implications of this position. Indeed, this is best illustrated by the *learning theorists themselves. Most of our current methods of psychotherapy represent an accumulation of more or less uncontrolled clinical experiences and, in many instances, those who have written about psychotherapy in terms of learning theory have merely substituted a new language.*

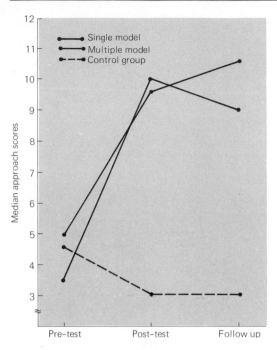

Figure 23.3

In this graph the median dog-approach scores of children are shown. This time the models were presented to the children in a film depicting dog handling by one and by several models. It may be seen from this graph that the films with models and dogs were more effective in augmenting an approach to dogs than films without dogs (controls). This symbolic, or film, procedure is not as effective as live modeling.

(Bandura and Menlove, 1968)

and *vicarious no-trial learning.*

Modeling is a more efficient means than shaping for getting behavior to occur. It may be used in a number of situations, usually in conjunction with some other techniques, such as vicarious desensitization of fears. Bandura (1969) cites as an example of modeling the treatment of autism by Lovaas and his colleagues (see Chapter 13), in which autistic mute children were taught to talk through stepwise reinforcement.

Perhaps a better example than the one given above may be found in Bandura's own work (Bandura et al., 1967; Bandura and Menlove, 1968), in which he extinguished children's fears of dogs. In the first of these studies 48 children with dog phobias were separated into four groups, each of which was treated differently: the first group members participated in eight sessions, during which they observed a fearless peer model exhibit progressively more fear-evoking interactions with a dog within a pleasant or party context; the second group witnessed the same performance, but in a neutral context; the third group witnessed the dog in a pleasurable setting, but with no peer model; and the fourth group engaged in pleasurable activities without exposure to the dog or peer model. All groups benefited from these procedures in that they showed a reduction in avoidance behavior in the presence of the test dog and an unfamiliar dog a month later, but both modeling conditions led to significantly greater and more stable improvement (Figure 23.2). This illustrates the principle of *vicarious extinction.*

In a second controlled study Bandura and Menlove (1968) compared the effects on dog-avoidance behavior of watching films of one model with one dog versus watching films of several models with a variety of dogs. The subjects in this study were 48 3- to 5-year olds; the purpose was to study the efficacy of a variety of symbolic modeling techniques that might lend themselves conveniently to psychotherapeutic applications. One group of children watched films of a fearless male model displaying the same progressively fear-provoking interactions with a dog as in the preceding experiment. The second group watched films of several different girls and boys of varying ages interacting positively with many dogs. A third group of children, serving as controls, was shown films without dogs. Although there was a significant reduction in fear among treated children compared with untreated children immediately after therapy (Figures 23.3 and 23.4), there was no difference upon follow-up of

Figure 23.4

In this series of photographs a girl who was previously apprehensive about dogs engages in fearless interactions with them after exposure to a series of films in which she viewed the fearless behavior of a peer model. Photographs

a–d show the model's behavior; and photographs e–l show the girl's interactions with dogs after she completed treatment.

(Bandura and Menlove, 1968)

the multiple- versus single-model condition. Bandura's conclusion on the basis of these and other data in which he compared live modeling with film (symbolic) procedures, was that "symbolic modeling is less powerful than live demonstrations" (1969, p. 131).

Subsequent experiments have shown that vicarious extinction is enhanced when multiple models are shown interacting with the feared object (cited in Bootzin, 1975). The model's similarity to the subject might also be expected to enhance effectiveness, but this has not been the case, at least not for physical attributes such as age. Modeling, according to some studies (Bandura and Barab, 1973; Weissbrod and Bryan, 1973), is just as therapeutic when the model and the patient are of different ages as it is when model and patient are peers. But a different dimension of similarity—the extent of fearfulness displayed by the model—does produce differences in effectiveness.

Modeling is also used to modify behavior in the so-called *instigation therapies*, in which patients learn to become their own therapists as a result of modeling after some of their therapists' appropriate behaviors (Kanfer and Phillips, 1966); for example, curing snake phobias among college females who witnessed male models handling snakes fearlessly (Geer and Turteltaub, 1967), and a modeling program for institutionalized juvenile offenders, who are provided with opportunities to identify with the socially acceptable behaviors of older persons who accept them and whom they respect (Sarason, 1968; Sarason and Ganzer, 1969).

Cognitive—Behavioral Approaches

According to recent surveys (Garfield and Jurtz, 1976; Mahoney, 1977), contemporary clinical psychology is moving in three general directions in its approach to therapy: (1) toward increased use of the theory and techniques of behavior therapy, as just described; (2) toward increased reliance on the theory and techniques of humanistic–existential perspectives, the therapies we shall present in Chapter 24; and (3) toward an increased emphasis on a flexibility that combines the other two trends and integrates these with cognitive psychology. We shall focus here on the third form of therapy, which has variously come to be called *cognitive–behavioral* or *cognitive–learning* to reflect the integration.

Rational Emotive Therapy. Albert Ellis, the founder of *rational emotive therapy* (1962, 1973), was probably among the first therapists to emphasize the importance of the role of irrational thoughts in the behavior disorders. This irrational thinking, according to Ellis, leads to a self-defeating internal dialogue, which consists of negative self-statements. This position is very close to that of Alfred Adler (see Chapter 22), who also held that a person's behavior springs from his ideas but who, unlike Ellis, did not formalize the notion that these ideas and the accompanying self-statements must be changed in therapy. But whereas Adler and Ellis listened for the pattern of the patient's thinking in order to discern and then restructure the maladaptive thinking that underlay his or her self-statements, the cognitive–behavioral therapist views the client's covert behaviors, such as ideas, self-statements, and images, as behaviors that are subject to the same laws of learning. Thus the behavior modification techniques that have been used to change overt behaviors, such as respondent and operant conditioning and observational learning, may be applied to covert processes.

For illustrative purposes imagine a classroom exam situation in which some students hand in their exams early. The differential thinking styles, and the self-statements that reflect this thinking, for the high and low test-anxiety individuals, are instructive. For the high test-anxiety individual this event provokes worry, and he or she is likely to say, "I must be doing something wrong. What's taking me so long. I must be dumb. How can those guys be done?" These statements elicit even more anxiety and further task-irrelevant behaviors and self-defeating thoughts. Compare this to the low test-anxiety student, who may readily dismiss the others' early exam performance by saying to him- or herself: "Those people only think they're done. If they understood the implications of the problem, it would take them twice as long. They're dumb."

In short, as Meichenbaum (1974) has asserted, high test-anxiety individuals tend to be self-oriented and to personalize the situations with which they are confronted. There is evidence to this effect (Sarason, 1972). There is also evidence that high test-anxious students are strongly self-deprecating and ruminative and that low test-anxious students plunge into the task at hand and are problem-oriented. How do we change these behaviors?

Cognitive–Behavior Therapy. The crux of the cognitive–behavior therapies is *self-instructional*

training, a method that has been most thoroughly explored by psychologist Donald Meichenbaum and his associates (Meichenbaum, 1973; Meichenbaum and Goodman, 1971). For example, in the 1971 study, impulsive and hyperactive children were trained to administer self-instructions for tasks on which they had previously made frequent errors. It had been discerned that these errors were due to rapid and careless performance. During self-instructional training the therapist modeled ways to perform various tasks such as coloring figures and copying lines. While performing each task, the therapist described its performance. By talking while working, the therapist verbally reinforced working carefully, as follows (Meichenbaum and Goodman, 1971, p. 117): "Okay, draw the line down, down, good; then to the right, that's it; now down some more and to the left. Good, I'm doing fine so far. Remember go slow. . . . Finished. I did it."

The children were then trained to instruct

The Things People Say to Themselves

The current resurgence of interest in using cognitive processes and verbalizations in modifying behavior (Craighead et al., 1976; Mahoney, 1974) raises an old question in psychology: to what extent do conscious cognitive processes influence human learning? According to one view, it is quite unnecessary to consider these private experiences in accounting for performance in learning situations. This is not to deny that such private experiences exist, but it does deny that they explain the ensuing behavior. The argument holds that both conscious experience and its report are themselves determined by the same variables that occasion the behavior they purportedly explain (see Skinner, 1953).

Adopting a second view, one observer (Farber, 1964) noted that reportable mediat-

ing events are important in accounting for the behavior of human subjects (1964, p. 196):

Subjects may not know exactly what is going on in an experiment or, for that matter, in a therapeutic session, but very few have no ideas at all. They may be mistaken, or they may be concerned with irrelevant matters, such as whether participation in the experiment is worth the time and trouble, or whether the counselor is as blasé as he seems, or what's for lunch. The one thing psychologists can count on is that their subjects or clients will talk, if only to themselves. And, not infrequently, whether relevant or irrelevant, the things people say to themselves determine the rest of the things they do.

themselves out loud while performing the task. Eventually they were trained to instruct themselves covertly without talking but only by moving their lips, and finally without lip movements.

There are many other self-training methods in cognitive–behavior therapy. Some involve the pairing of covert behaviors with external consequences, in the sense of associating positive thinking with treating oneself to food, cigarettes, or money. Others entail pairing covert behaviors with other covert behaviors. Joseph Cautela (1973) demonstrated the latter, also called *covert sensitization*, in a case in which a client was asked to imagine a maladaptive form of behavior needing change (for example, overeating or smoking) and then to imagine in detail a noxious or aversive scene such as vomiting. This conditioning process of contiguously pairing the two images results in a reduction of the maladaptive behavior. Still other self-training techniques have included pairing covert behaviors with an overt behavior, such as pairing the self-instruction "relax" with the actual response of relaxing. Not all these are, strictly speaking, self-management techniques, but in principle they are all amenable to the self-instructional mode.

Zen Meditation and Behavioral Self-Control. Still another extension of cognitive-behavior therapy was an attempt to link it with Zen meditation (Shapiro and Giber, 1978; Shapiro and Zifferblatt, 1976). The techniques developed within the Eastern Zen Buddhism tradition have their roots in methods that have been in use for thousands of years. For example, formal Zen breath meditation is a technique developed for breaking out of the symbolic, abstract world into the world of direct, immediate experience. By viewing this type of meditation as just another set of behaviors, psychologists believe they have removed it from the realm of "mystical practice" and redefined it as a technique that can be useful in cognitive behavior change.

Viewed as behavior in its own right, Zen breath meditation may be conceptualized as a five-step process that begins with some breathing techniques aimed at clearing the mind of competing stimuli all the way to increasing the receptivity of individuals to internal covert behaviors typically ignored.

Although this form of Zen requires practices that are quite different from self-management training, it is possible to combine the two to modify maladaptive behaviors. For example, other techniques, such as self-hypnosis (Paul, 1969) and relaxation with covert self-statements (Meichenbaum, 1973), employ certain covert images and self-statements (for example, "I'm feeling warm; my eyelids are getting heavy; I am feeling relaxed). In Zen meditation, although the individual does not silently say anything, it is the absence of the preprogrammed covert thoughts and images that seems to allow the meditator to observe and to become desensitized to "what's on his or her mind" and also to empty the mind of irrelevant verbal behaviors and images. This "empty mind" may be important for hearing certain newly programmed internal cues ("I'm okay; nothing upsets my stomach; slow down"), a particularly important state of mind for acquiring new self-management strategies.

Evaluation of the Behavior Therapies

Since its inception and popularization, behavior modification has had both defenders and detractors. Some of its advantages and disadvantages are worth considering.

Advantages

The behavior therapies have several distinct advantages over verbal therapies. First, because they rely less heavily on talking as a means of achieving a cure, the behavior therapies are more widely applicable. For example, as we note repeatedly throughout this book, conventional psychotherapy is not easily available to individuals of the lower socioeconomic groups nor is purely verbal therapy feasible for persons who are unable or unwilling to verbalize their feelings and emotions. Behavior modification, on the other hand, because of its emphasis on stimulus control and environmental manipulation, can reach such persons.

Second, it is less time-consuming and certainly less difficult to train professionals in the techniques of behavior therapy than it is to teach them the theoretical and, sometimes, arcane abstractions of psychotherapy. This is important because manpower shortages have so long been critical deterrents to proper treatment for those who need it. Behavior therapy is easier to teach because it uses specific and tangible manipulations, which means that it can be taught more easily than other conventional treatments to nonprofessional personnel (psychiatric aides, nurses, family, and friends). In this regard programmed instruction, which traces its origins to the same psychological laboratories responsible for the recent upsurge of behavior therapy (Skinner, 1968), can be used for mass training.

Finally, the advantage of behavior therapy over other therapies is that it takes less time. This efficiency results from its focus on particular problems of the patient and contrasts markedly with the time-consuming investment that many kinds of psychotherapy demand. From this standpoint, as noted by several proponents (see Ullmann and Krasner, 1975, pp. 231–232), behavior therapy is much like brief psychotherapy in that it places a premium on "purposeful selection" of specific problems to be solved.

Disadvantages

Some of the critics of behavioral treatments have argued that behavior modification is all right in animal experiments, where most of its learning principles were discovered, but irrelevant to human beings and, moreover, that it is dehumanizing to subject people to such manipulations. This type of argument has been most often

advanced by therapists who have aligned themselves with the humanistic–existential, or third force, movement in psychology (see Chapter 24). But the counterargument is that nothing in behavior modification requires the practitioner to denigrate patients and that, in the balance, the degree of dehumanization that occurs in treatment is more dependent on the personality of the therapist than on the technique.

It has also been argued by critics of behavior therapy that it utilizes a mechanistic language, conceptualizing behavior in terms such as *stimulus, response, reinforcement,* and *shaping*. But the counterargument has been that these words are best viewed as scientific metaphors useful in understanding behavior in order to increase the therapist's ability to help people. The principles arising from a behavioral analysis of actions are used to identify environmental events that control human behavior, focusing on efforts to change these events so that actions can be more personally satisfying and socially constructive (Davison and Stuart, 1975).

At a somewhat different level of consideration, the ethics of *behavior control technology,* as Perry London (1969, 1971) refers to it, have been questioned; the argument is that this form of control presents a threat to traditional ideas of personal responsibility. This issue was particularly stirred up by the appearance of B. F. Skinner's *Beyond Freedom and Dignity* (1971), a book that proposed the design of a culture to be based almost entirely on a programmed behavioral engineering approach. Proponents of such a system, Skinner included, have argued that they have in mind a benevolent social scheme (see Skinner, 1948, 1971) and besides, they maintain, since people have always been controlled by education and propaganda, why not also settle for a well-planned social system? But Skinner also argues that "such a technology is ethically neutral. It can be used by villain or saint. There is nothing in a methodology which determines the value governing its use" (1971, p. 150).

Inevitably, however, a behavioral technology

does raise several imponderables. Will people become automatons? Who is to design this culture (or any environment)? Can we trust the designer's good intentions, or will his or her environmental programming be self-serving? The ethics of using behavior modification in clinical practice raise similar questions in that patients come under the control of therapists who use scientific means to condition and extinguish responses. These patients are then at the mercy of therapists who could force upon them their interpretations of society's acceptable behaviors. These arguments, however, are based on several shaky assumptions.

First, they presuppose a therapeutic efficacy not yet supported by evidence (see below). Second, as Kanfer and Phillips have observed (1970, p. 534), the same degree of therapist control is present in all psychotherapies and the objections seem to be directed at "the novelty of emphasis on positive reinforcement." Third, there is nothing really novel in, or terribly potent about, the behaviorist's manipulations since they are frequently used to teach vocational or driving skills; thus it seems that when objections to the application of the same techniques are raised when they are used to control interpersonal behaviors that it is the domain rather than the method that is criticized. Finally, all psychotherapists—not just those who use behavioral principles—are interpreter-agents of society because they are products of the environments in which they operate.

But quite aside from these issues of the ethics of behavior modification is the question of the effectiveness of its techniques, an area which we now briefly consider.

Effectiveness

How effective are the behavior therapies? As with the traditional psychotherapies the answer depends largely on whom you ask. Not surprisingly most behavior therapists claim a high rate of success and compare their techniques favorably with the traditional approaches. Thus, out of approximately 75 cases presented in Ullmann and Krasner's two volumes on behavior modification (Krasner and Ullmann, 1965; Ullmann and Krasner, 1965), success is reported in most cases.

In a somewhat more empirical approach to the problem of success rates, Wolpe (1958, 1961, 1969) reports a 90 percent recovery rate of patients treated by his methods. These claims, however, are not supported by solid evidence, and the research designs used by him and his associates did not include adequate control groups (Yates, 1970a). Wherever carefully controlled studies of the efficacy of behavior modification are available, and unfortunately they are not as frequent as one might expect in an area dominated by research-oriented psychologists, favorable outcomes have been reported only in cases in which specific and easily identifiable problems—phobias, obsessive rituals, tics, stuttering, and other isolated symptoms—were the main source of difficulty. Ultimately, perhaps, it may turn out that for these seemingly monosymptomatic cases, behavior therapy is the method of choice and that for other and more complex problems behavior therapy is inappropriate. In the meantime, however, it is essential that many more controlled studies be conducted to compare the relative superiority of one method over the other (see Urban and Ford, 1972).

What then may we say about the worth of the behavior therapies? Although the advantages (require less patient verbalization, easy to learn and teach, time and cost economical) and disadvantages (dehumanizing, unethical, too controlling) of behavior modification are quite apparent to its users and detractors, the matter of its effectiveness is somewhat less obvious. For the most part its practitioners are enthusiastic about its worth, but so far have not come up with any well-designed comparative studies. Such studies are essential for this important technology, and public discussion of behavior modification techniques is needed to serve both society and the individual (Stolz et al., 1975).

Hypnosis

The therapeutic use of hypnosis was first reported in the eighteenth century by Franz Mesmer (1734–1815), who referred to it as "animal magnetism" and who, in his medical practice in Vienna, cured a young woman of hysterical symptoms (convulsions, earaches, toothaches, fainting spells, urine retention, paralysis). In his cure Mesmer used magnets and explained the phenomenon in terms of atmospheric and celestial forces (Mesmer, 1775).

Uses of Hypnosis in Psychotherapy

Most depth-oriented, or insight, therapists recommend using hypnosis only as an adjunctive treatment tool, "for the purpose of facilitating psychotherapy" (Schneck, 1963, p. 169), the consensus being that hypnosis enables the therapist to remove bothersome symptoms, thus more quickly focusing the patient's attention on relevant areas.

But in another sense *hypnotherapy*, as it is sometimes called, may also be viewed in its own right. In large part the difference between its adjunctive and its treatment uses depends on one's opinion about what success and failure can be attributed to, which is certainly not agreed upon by all clinicians. Marcuse has delineated this problem as follows (1959, p. 121):

Supposing a patient who visits his therapist a few times a week has the habit of . . . discussing his problems in a chit-chat fashion before traditional therapy is started. Supposing also that some type of cure has been effected—what has caused this? Is it the traditional procedure, or is it the chit-chat or both? In the therapeutic situation there are many factors at work. There is the . . . sympathetic non-critical listener . . . reassurance . . . airing of problems . . . and many other subtleties of interpersonal relationships that cannot be ignored.

Furthermore the notion of success or failure of psychotherapy, unless stipulated by specific criteria, is meaningless. Achieving insight and personality restructuring may not always be necessary. Many therapists treat people whose lives are made unbearable by habits they have acquired that are quite amenable to removal by either hypnosis or behavior therapy. On this topic Lewis Wolberg (1972, p. 229), who believes that depth interviewing is essential for many cases, makes this observation: "If the symptom is relieved, and the person is able to function again, then often his self-respect is restored, and he can go about improving his interpersonal relationships in the interests of a better total adjustment."

Symptom Removal by Hypnosis. Those who favor using hypnosis as an adjunct to depth therapy have reported the following benefits: it may be used to uncover memories the patient has repressed; to facilitate *abreaction*, or the release of repressed material that the patient has bottled up; to suggest topics about which the patient should dream; to remove an amnesia for particular names and places; to hasten the transference in psychoanalytic therapy; and to reassure the patient of the reversibility of his or her condition.

Symptoms that have been removed by direct hypnotic or posthypnotic suggestion include headache; neck, shoulder, and back strain; nail-biting; facial tic; some skin disorders or the itching attending them; peptic ulcer (by teaching the patient self-relaxation techniques); and fatty food preferences.

A recent description (Lourie, 1976, p. 23) of symptom removal by self-hypnosis reports on the removal of nocturnal enuresis among 40 children. This study was conducted at George Washington University with 20 children who had primary nocturnal bedwetting and 20 whose enuresis occurred after they already were toilet-trained. The age range was 4½ to 16 years, and some of these children also had daytime dribbling. Organic causes of enuresis were ruled out before self-hypnosis was taught. Two teenagers were taught a standard hand levitation technique of self-hypnosis. The 38 younger patients were instructed to focus on a quarter placed in the hand and told that the quarter would become heavy and fall and they would feel relaxed. Relaxation and heaviness of the coin were suggested, and the children were told to do the trick each night at bedtime. They were also told to tell themselves that when the quarter fell down, they would awaken for urinating and go to the bathroom by themselves. The children were followed up for 6 to 28 months. Thirty-one children were cured of bedwetting, six were improved, and three did not improve. All but three of those who were cured ceased bedwetting in the first month of treatment and all but two of the 38 children who learned the coin technique became proficient at achieving self-relaxation after one or two visits. The children seemed also to have acquired self-confidence from having achieved the cure themselves.

Biofeedback

The *reward learning*, or so-called *biofeedback* methods, are designed to provide *knowledge of results* to subjects who are controlling internal biological processes with the aid of monitoring equipment. This knowledge, which is the feed-

back to the organism, is usually presented in the form of an auditory or visual signal.

Earlier in this book (Chapter 8), we cited an unsophisticated example of a feedback technique as it was used in a behavior therapy context to cure a woman's enuresis. It will be recalled that Jones (1956) instructed a patient to watch a manometer for the pressure changes it recorded while he introduced warm water into her bladder. Gradually she was conditioned to associate urinary urges with specific pressure levels. Then Jones falsified lower pressure readings on the manometer while introducing ever-increasing amounts of water into the bladder. Given such false feedback the patient was conditioned to tolerate greater bladder pressures without experiencing urinary urgency. Considerably more sophisticated feedback procedures began to appear in the late 1960s, and the antecedents of biofeedback are generally traced to some startling experiments by Neal Miller and his colleagues on the instrumental conditioning of autonomic functions in rats (Miller and DiCara, 1967, 1968).

Psychotherapeutic Implications

One of the major promises of biofeedback research is the hope it offers for people to help

A Word of Caution About Biofeedback

When I began work on visceral learning, the general climate was so skeptical that it was difficult to get students to try any experiments. Now the climate has completely changed; there is a great deal of interest in this kind of work. But I deplore the exaggerated publicity in the popular press about this and other kinds of work

commonly called biofeedback. I fear that such exaggerated articles are raising impossible hopes which will inevitably result in a premature disillusionment that may interfere with the hard work that is necessary and desirable to explore this new area of research (Miller and Dworkin, 1975, p. 96).

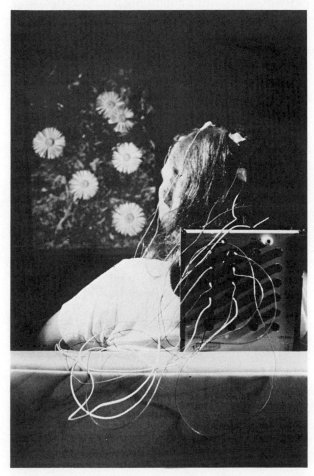

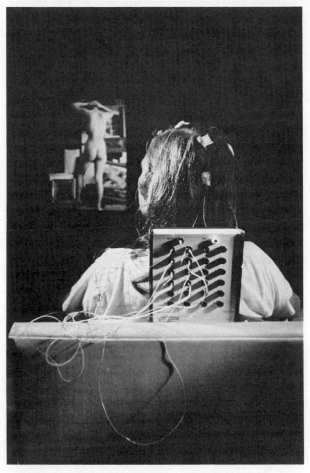

Whether the young man in this picture is paying attention can be determined by brain wave feedback (as registered on an electroencephalograph or EEG). When his brain shows alpha rhythm—a state associated with inattention and

meditation—a slide of a nude or a flower is projected before him. The slide automatically disappears if he leaves the alpha state, which in almost all young men occurs when they notice the nude, not when they see the flower.

themselves, rather than depending entirely on psychotherapists and others. We offer the following list of possible therapeutic applications, most of which require equipment, sometimes expensive, for successful self-help augmentation:

1. *Anxiety.* Paul Grim (1971) has lowered anxiety in subjects by self-induced muscle tension and by relaxation with respiration feedback. Of course relaxation techniques, as we saw earlier in this chapter, have been reported since the

1930s (Jacobson, 1938); but the addition in Grim's study of a respiration feedback device is new. In this study each of 95 nursing students was administered a test to measure level of anxiety and was then hooked up to the electronic equipment he designed to amplify breathing. The idea was to train each person to breathe more and more smoothly until a state of complete relaxation was achieved. Grim then retested the students with self-report anxiety measures and noted their reduced scores.

2. *Epileptic Seizures.* Working with an 18-year-old female convulsive patient, two clinicians (Johnson and Meyer, 1975) used a combination of relaxation, electromyograph (EMG) training, and electroencephalograph (EEG) training to control her epileptic seizures. The last of these procedures involved providing the patient with alpha feedback (33 sessions), followed by alpha–theta feedback (15 sessions), and lastly theta feedback (9 sessions). She was instructed to practice the relaxation exercises daily and told that when she sensed the aura, which usually preceded her *grand mal* convulsions, she was to try to relax and stay calm as if she were in the feedback situation.

Prior to these training sessions the patient had kept records that showed that over a 2-year period she had had 67 seizures, a mean of 2.79 per month. During the 12 months of treatment this was reduced to 18 seizures, or a mean of 1.50 seizures per month. This constituted a 46 percent decrease in seizures. A 3-month follow-up report indicated no significant seizure increase.

It is difficult, of course, to know from this clinical study whether to credit the relaxation, EMG, EEG, or a combination of all three methods. Careful experimental analysis of this and similar cases reported in the literature (Sterman et al., 1975) may disclose that the overwhelming portion of the improvement can be attributed to a placebo effect.

3. *Hypertension.* This disorder, or high blood pressure, could cause dizziness and nausea and is a serious problem for many people in that it may culminate in cerebrovascular accidents (strokes) and death. Following the leads of others who have applied operant techniques to modify autonomic functions (see Miller et al., 1970, above), David Shapiro of the Harvard Medical School demonstrated that human beings can be taught, through operant biofeedback procedures, to raise or lower their blood pressures.

In one such study (Shapiro et al., 1970), Shapiro worked with 21 male college students, each of whom was placed in a light- and sound-proofed room. A conventional blood-pressure cuff was wrapped around the upper arm of the student and a crystal microphone was mounted inside the cuff to amplify sounds from the brachial artery. A red flashing light also signaled lowered blood pressure. The sounds gave information about relative upward and downward changes in systolic blood pressure. Under one of the reinforcement conditions studied, subjects were rewarded for lowering their blood pressure. The reinforcer was a slide projected on a screen, and subjects were told that successes (lowered pressure) would be rewarded by viewing slides of nude females and by receiving bonus sums of money in addition to the $3.00 per hour they received for participating. Almost all subjects learned to lower their blood pressure by themselves. The work to be pursued now, according to Miller and his associates, "might best be carried out in hypertensive patients or in older persons in whom blood pressure levels are much higher and the possibility of sizable reductions might be greater than in . . . normal college students" (Shapiro et al., 1971, p. 398).

4. *Tension Headache.* As another illustration of therapeutic application we have chosen the work of Budzynski and his associates (1970, 1973), who use a feedback-induced muscle relaxation technique to reduce tension headache.

They described the application of their method to five patients with such headaches. Their procedure was somewhat as follows: patients were given EMG feedback information from activity in a relevant muscle group area. In the case of headache Budzynski decided to use the

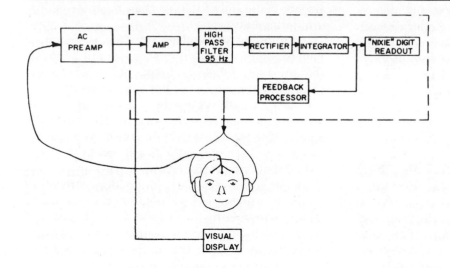

Figure 23.5

A diagram of the EMG information feedback system designed to reduce tension headaches.

(Budzynski et al., 1970)

frontalis (forehead) muscle group, and the feedback was a tone that rose in pitch as EMG activity increased and dropped as EMG activity decreased. This apparatus is shown in Figure 23.5.

During the training session each patient reclined on a couch in a dimly lighted room. The first two sessions consisted of practicing relaxing without feedback; and from the third session on (training consisted of two or three 30-minute sessions and the total training time varied from four weeks to two months) the patient was instructed to try to keep the tone low in pitch and was told that the tone followed his tension level. Case Report 23.3 describes on instance in which this feedback training was used, with partial success, to relieve the tension headaches of a hard-driving businessman. Budzynski omitted from this report the fact that he made it increasingly difficult for the patient to reduce his EMG activity after he had achieved a criterion level of relaxation: he adjusted the volume gain on the feedback amplifier so that the patient was forced to achieve even greater amounts of relaxation. Budzynski likens this procedure to *shaping* and notes that the re-

laxation response is not different from other responses.

Case Report 23.3   *Biofeedback Training for Tension Headache*

Patient G. A. was a dynamic, middle-aged businessman who, ever since early adolescence, had suffered from frequent, severe tension headaches. He had previously received some training in deep relaxation while undergoing behavior therapy. Consequently he learned to relax his frontalis muscle very quickly and was able to maintain low EMG levels at all times during feedback training. Although his baseline headache activity was very high, it decreased rapidly during the second week of training and remained low for the duration of the training.

After his fourth week of feedback training, the patient went on a five-week vacation. Upon his return to work his headaches also returned. Significantly the patient had neglected his daily relaxation session. He reported he had to "get things back in order" after his vacation, and was in a state of high tension. He was then given two more feedback sessions and was strongly advised to schedule a period of relaxation practice every day. His headache activity then returned to low levels and has remained there for the rest of the three-month post-training period.

SOURCE: *Budzynski et al. (1970).*

5. *Heart Rate.* Heart rate has also been brought under voluntary control in a recent study by Blanchard et al. (1975). In this study the effects on heart rate changes of varying types of correct information, incorrect information, and lack of information were tested with 64 subjects aged 16 to 45. These subjects were given different instructions consisting of informed–feedback ("the response we want you to control is your heart rate. . . . As your heart rate increases, the pen will move to the right. . . . Your job is to increase your heart rate when the right hand light is on"); informed–no feedback ("The response we want you to control is your heart rate. We want to see how well you can control it without any external feedback. Previous research has shown that most people are fairly good at this. Your job is to increase your heart rate"); uninformed ("So that you can control your bodily process solely through mental means, we are not telling you what the response is. . . . As your internal response increases, the pen will move to the right. . . . Your job is to increase the response"); misinformed ("The response we want you to control is skin resistance. . . . As your skin resistance increases, the pen will move to the right. . . . Your job is to increase your skin resistance"). The results indicated that subjects informed of the response and receiving feedback of it can alter their heart rates significantly and can lower it better than those who were misinformed, uninformed, or informed but without feedback. When raising heart rate, however, informed persons who receive feedback do better than those who are informed but receive no feedback, but

are not better able to do so than misinformed or uninformed subjects.

Although biofeedback has been generally hailed as a new and promising form of behavior therapy (see Yates, 1975, pp. 183–225), some cautionary notes have been sounded. In an *American Psychologist* article of several years ago, Yale psychologist Gary Schwartz (1973) outlines some of the problems that must be solved, particularly when the technique is applied to the individual patient. Biofeedback, according to this view, should be used in conjunction with other medical and psychological methods and never alone, particularly in treating chronic physical disease. Schwartz sees biofeedback as serving the same role as a "scale that helps direct the therapist and his obese patient in learning to . . . control weight. . . . By means of immediate augmented feedback . . . the patient may be able to learn new ways of coping *behaviorally* with his environment, or he may be able to alter his *lifestyle* in such a way as to keep his physiological processes within safer limits. In this respect biofeedback is really similar to current psychotherapies, for they all provide corrective feedback" (Schwartz, 1973, pp. 672–673).

A somewhat more recent and optimistic statement has been made by psychologist Katkin (1976, p. 225), who claims that much of the theoretical work has been done and that the "groundwork has been laid for an exciting future in which our innermost functions may be subject to modification by appropriate applications of external reward." And in an uncharacteristic moment of enthusiasm Katkin proclaims that "between now and 1984, you may well discover that you can voluntarily reduce your blood pressure, set your heart to beat at any rate you desire, and tell your kidneys just how fast to produce urine for your maximum convenience."

Summary

The main types of direct treatment covered in this chapter are behavior therapy, hypnosis, and bio-feedback. Behavior therapy, the application of conditioning principles to the alteration of behavior, uses respondent, operant, modeling, and cognitive procedures to accomplish its objective.

Hypnosis, which has been a controversial change agent from the time it was first reported, has lately become a domain of lively research interest. Its main usefulness seems to lie in the state of heightened suggestibility in which symptoms may be either produced or removed.

Biofeedback is a relatively new concept and involves training persons to track and modify their internal responses. Thus far it has been applied in the treatment of a variety of autonomic reactions that were hitherto believed inaccessible to conditioning methods.

Terms and Concepts to Master

Alpha wave
  conditioning

Assertiveness training

Aversive conditioning

Biofeedback

Cognitive–behavior
  therapy

Implosive therapy

Modeling

Operant behavior
  therapy

Respondent behavior
  therapy

Systematic
  desensitization

24 Humanistic–Existential Therapies

People enter therapy because they want changes in their lives, and all therapists try in some way to induce or facilitate change. They differ profoundly, however, in the way they perceive the desired goal, direction, and source of change. If a therapist's model of human nature embodies the traditional Western religious doctrine of original sin, he may strive to help the patient recognize and cope with chaotic or destructive inner impulses. If the model of human nature is based on the *tabula rasa* concept—that nothing exists but what has been learned—he may try to help the patient extinguish old habits and acquire new ones. In either case the source of change is outside the person.

But in the humanistic and existential approaches to therapy human nature is perceived as being, at its deepest levels, essentially loving, cooperative, wise, and health-seeking. Therefore, instead of trying to impose order from without, the therapist tries to make it easier for the person to discover what is already present inside, to get in touch with himself, to accept and fully experience his own feelings, and to be open instead of controlled.

Several other aspects of these therapies are logical consequences of adopting the model of a positive human nature. Therapy tends to be nonanalytical: instead of an interpretive cure, a direct and immediate experience of self-awareness. It also strives to be nonmanipulative: the therapist obviously exerts some influence, but very carefully avoids doing anything that would seem to take the responsibility for change out of the client's hands. Since the change has to come from inside the person, the initiative for change must remain in his or her own hands.

Personal growth, rather than the abatement of illness or the reduction of symptoms, is usually the immediate objective. If this has done nothing else, it has removed some of the stigma from seeking or obtaining help. If neurosis consists of being divided from oneself, most of us can be seen as neurotic (the "normally neurotic"). The real madness is then in the system that divides each of us, and entering therapy is a revolutionary act—a bold assertion of the will to be free.

Not surprisingly almost every form of humanistic therapy has been accused of being more religious than scientific. That objection is of course not new, having been raised earlier against Jung, who had no reluctance to call therapy a spiritual journey. Likewise humanists, perhaps the most unabashed eclectics of all, are willing to draw insights from religion when it seems appropriate, and point out that the word *wholeness,* which describes one of their ultimate goals, is derived from the same root as *holy, holistic,* and *hale,* as well as *healthy.*

Perhaps most important, the humanistic and existential therapies are designed to foster a positive self-image. They are not the only therapies ever to accomplish that result, but more than the others, they have elevated it to the status of a cardinal principle.

Origins and Assumptions

Existential therapy is not so much a different *system* of therapy as it is a different way of experiencing the therapeutic process. At the very great risk of being simplistic, we shall try to sketch the outlines of that approach.

Existentialism and Phenomenology

Alienation, anguish, and despair are seen, in existential therapy, not as a deviation from normality but as part of "being-in-the-world." What follows immediately from this is a recognition that therapist and patient stand on the same ground. Thus the existential therapist enters into an active dialogue with the patient, not to help him recover long-repressed thoughts, but to achieve a sense of shared immediacy in which the patient confronts his own anxiety head-on. All attempts to analyze, to explain, or to talk *about* the patient's feelings are pushed aside as distractions.

We shall not dwell on the philosophical roots of this approach, except to say that it derives from certain common elements in the widely diverse strains of existentialist philosophy, in particular the emphasis on direct experience as opposed to abstraction. In this context neuroticism is the avoidance of feeling, and an assumption is made that the patient can gain something by facing his alienation and working through it.

Another important element is the existentialist approach to science, which is based mainly on philosopher Edmund Husserl's *phenomenology* (Kockelmans, 1967), an attempt to reach the ultimate ground of science by stripping away all presuppositions until there is nothing left but the "thing-in-itself." Phenomenologists contend that much of what they call "naive" or "mechanistic" science is built on a foundation of such presuppositions, which are so taken for granted that they are not mentioned or even noticed, but which are open to challenge. Rather than assuming that their observations are objective, phenomenologists regard their subjectivity as conscious and intentional. Rather than excluding consciousness from the subject matter of psychology because it is not empirically verifiable, as Watson and Skinner did, Husserl insisted that nothing comes to us *except* through our consciousness and therefore the only way to get to the thing-in-itself (as distinct from our presumed objective but in fact subjective perception of it) is to study consciousness. This is consistent with Husserl's definition of psychology as a science of experience.

Thus the phenomenologist's attempt to cut through what he or she sees as an alienated science is paralleled by the existential therapist's attempt to cut through an alienated existence. He or she resists any attempt to impose an abstract order on the spontaneous moment (for example, by trying to explain it); he or she can only point and share. One element here has a correlate in psychoanalysis: opening yourself up has a liberating effect. To the existential therapist, that effect is due not simply to removing something unhealthy, but to the experience of coming into contact with one's own estranged self. The "rush" that the patient feels at such moments is often described as a joyful experience; it is also a key element in the human potential movement.

The existential therapist does not try to be distant, authoritarian, or unfeeling. Existential psychotherapy is, according to Laing (1967), *"an obstinate attempt of two people to recover the wholeness of being human through the relationship between them"* (italics Laing's).

Laing sees both the alienation and the therapy as political events. In childhood the individual's experience is mystified. That is, well-meaning parents and others manipulate the child, through disapproval or the withholding of affection or other pressures, into rejecting the evidence of his or her own senses and denying the reality of many of his or her feelings, since the authentic self is not socially acceptable. What the child disavows (there is a great deal of both Sullivan and Reich in this) may be any sexual feelings or fears, his or her grief or rage. It is one of Laing's premises—and an easy one to substantiate—that the socialization process often carries with it a cargo of lies that must be believed. The end result is a deadened person—one who is playing the role in which he has been cast but who is no longer in contact with his own feelings and senses. He is also quite probably divorced from any sense of responsibility for his own actions, since he is, after all, only playing the role demanded of him. The crucial fact is that he is unaware of all this. Such an individual is an easy mark for manipulation and exploitation.

To Laing it is the system itself that is mad, and "going crazy" may be, for some people, a way to end the self-betrayal and opt out of the system. The significant point for students of abnormal psychology is that this completely overturns the value system on which many traditional notions of normality and abnormality are based.

Not all existentially oriented therapists would state their position quite that strongly, but many would probably agree that once an individual has recognized that he has control over his own life he is likely to be freer and less easily exploited.

According to the late Sidney Jourard, who studied with Laing, the patient's newfound contact with himself can be observed as self-disclosure, "the act of making yourself manifest, showing yourself so that others can perceive you" (Jourard, 1971, p. 19). Jourard sees neurosis and psychosis as "smoke screens interposed between the patient's real self and the gaze of the onlooker. We might call symptoms 'devices to avoid becoming known'" (p. 32).[1]

Jourard suggests that the patient's self-disclosure is more likely if the therapist is able to show his or her *transparent self*. This is not likely to happen if the therapist shows any of these four signs of resistance (p. 149): "(1) Having fantasies during the session, and not disclosing them; (2) chronically giving technical responses rather than spontaneous responses; (3) lying to the patient about one's opinions, attitudes or feelings; and (4) withholding expressions of like, dislike, boredom, irritation."

Concerning the techniques of psychotherapy, he believes that people resent being manipulated, and that therapists who habitually withhold their real selves from others violate the dignity and integrity of their patients. His philosophy of dealing with patients is summarized in this passage (pp. 146–147):

My actual disclosures to the patient are still checked by common sense or by my judgment·(I sometimes suspect that this is automatic and unconscious checking, though I realize this sounds mystical), but increasingly I find myself being more unpremeditated and spontaneous in my responses to the patient.

When I become strictly technical and hence impersonal with my patients, I have learned it is usually because I have become anxious. When I am lucky enough to recognize my anxiety, I will sometimes say, "You are making me anxious." If I am angry, I let this be known. If I am concerned or worried, I let this be known.

If a patient asks me a question that I genuinely would rather not answer, I tell him, "I'd rather not answer." I give him true reasons, too. The most succinct way I have of describing what I do is that I strive to give the patient an openness of myself in that moment. I believe that he is entitled to an honest expression of myself as a professional man, and this is what I give him. This is the transparency, the "congruence," which Rogers has so lucidly described.

Humanism and Optimism

Despite the efforts of a few American therapists such as Rollo May (May et al., 1958) to introduce

---

[1] Quotations on this and following pages from *The transparent self*, 2nd ed., by Sidney M. Jourard. © 1971 by Litton Educational Publishing, Inc. Reprinted by permission of D. Van Nostrand Company.

existential therapy to their colleagues, it has never achieved any popularity here, at least in its original form. Its failure to do so has sometimes been attributed (Kovel, 1976) to its peculiarly European aura of despair, which seems alien to the American temperament.

Nevertheless it has had a considerable influence, resulting from a cross-fertilization with the indigenous American philosophy of humanism. Like behaviorism humanism is infused with the vitality of an optimistic belief that all things are possible. When existentialism and humanism converged, the emphasis shifted from the despair that the patient must grapple with to the joy that might follow. The result was humanistic psychology, an odd hybrid that, like its European counterpart, resisted codification and sought to begin with a new set of basic premises about human nature.

Abraham Maslow was one of the chief architects of humanistic psychology, and his own experience reflected the existential journey from despair to joy. He had been both an experimental psychologist (a behaviorist) and a clinician working with "mentally ill" patients. Seriously disillusioned as a result of the horrors of World War II, Maslow gave up his previous studies, "finding them insufficiently related to the struggle for human survival that was going on" (Maddi and Costa, 1972, p. 145). It was common at that time to cite the brutality of the war and the concentration camps as proof that humans are born evil, and an example of what happens when human impulses are allowed to break loose. Maslow argued that the brutality was instead the result of *preventing* the expression of human impulses, and called for a psychology that would foster the expression of the inherent goodness of humans. He also listed a hierarchy of needs that he believed had to be satisfied if humans were to actualize their potential. First, they must satisfy their *physiological needs* (homeostasis, food, water) and *safety needs* (security, stability, dependency), for without gratification of these "all other needs may become simply nonexistent or be pushed into the background" (Maslow, 1970, p. 37). Second, each of the following needs must also be met if the next higher ones are to be satisfied: *belongingness* and *love needs* (affectionate relations with people, a place in a group or family); and *esteem needs* (desire for strength, achievement, feelings of adequacy, prestige, fame, dignity). Then come the penultimate and final needs for *self-actualization* ("what a man *can* be, he *must* be" p. 46), and *knowledge, understanding,* and *aesthetic* enjoyment ("What for instance, does it mean when a person feels a strong impulse to straighten the crookedly hung picture on the wall?" p. 51). Maslow called humanistic psychology the *third force* in psychology (the other two being psychoanalysis and behaviorism).

The Therapies

We shall discuss three therapies associated with humanistic psychology. Carl Rogers's client-centered therapy and Frederick ("Fritz") Perls's Gestalt therapy are by now well established in the mainstream of humanistic psychology. Arthur Janov's primal therapy is newer and seems to have less in common with the first two as methods, though they have many of the same premises and assumptions. We shall also briefly discuss the expressive therapies, which, because of their emphasis on immediate action and on the client rather than the therapist, are closely associated with the humanistic–existential therapies.

Client-Centered Therapy

All the elements that went into the fusion of existentialism and humanism can be seen in the life and work of Carl Rogers. Always willing to follow his interests—and the truth—wherever they might lead him, he majored in agriculture and then history at the University of Wisconsin, then went to Union Theological Seminary to study for the ministry, next studied child guid-

Carl Rogers, the famed psychologist who founded the client-centered approach to psychotherapy.

(Courtesy Carl Rogers. Photo by John T. Wood)

ance at Teachers College, Columbia University, and then obtained a fellowship to the Institute for Child Guidance, from which he emerged as a clinical psychologist and began working with delinquent children.

In his work with delinquents and their families, Rogers found repeatedly that he had to rethink his views, which were based partly on his Freudian training at the Institute for Child Guidance and partly on the rigorous scientific approach he had learned at Teachers College. More and more he felt that he had been pushing too hard in clinical relationships and that as a result he was not being effective. The turning point came when, after a lengthy series of interviews with the mother of a delinquent boy, Rogers gave up. He had not been able to help her to the insight he believed she needed to reach, so he suggested they terminate the process, and she agreed. They shook hands and walked to the

door, whereupon she turned and asked, "Do you ever take adults for counseling here?" Rogers said yes, and she replied, "Well then, I would like some help." Rogers continues (1961, pp. 11–12):

She came back to the chair she had left, and began to pour out her despair about her marriage, her troubled relationship with her husband, her sense of failure and confusion, all very different from the sterile "case history" she had given before. Real therapy began then, and ultimately it was very successful.

This incident was one of a number which helped me to experience the fact—only fully realized later—that it is the client *who knows what hurts, what directions to go, what problems are crucial, what experiences have been deeply buried. It began to occur to me that unless I had a need to demonstrate my own cleverness and learning, I would do better to rely upon the client for the direction of movement in the process.*

The result was client-centered therapy, or—as it is sometimes called—Rogerian therapy. The primary objective of Rogerian therapy is to create conditions that allow the client to perceive and accept his or her unique self without the anxiety that comes from self-evaluation. This nonevaluative atmosphere in therapy is important because behavior pathology is presumed to result from a conflict between a person's two fundamental evaluative processes—those based on self-evaluative tendencies and those based on the values of other persons. It is furthermore the purpose of client-centered therapy to create a situation in which the client feels understood (*empathic understanding*) and accepted as a whole person (*unconditional positive regard*). Under these circumstances, he will be able to examine those experiences that are inconsistent with his self-concept and those that were previously perceived in a distorted way or not at all.

The Rogerian's main therapeutic technique is to *reflect* the client's feelings, which first consists of sensing the client's meaning and then involves putting it into words as clearly as possible; perhaps the therapist even asks questions to show that he or she is trying to understand and to follow the client rather than to lead. How this is actually accomplished during the interview is difficult to describe and probably is best exemplified by a transcription from one of Rogers's sessions. For this purpose we have selected an excerpt taken from the concluding portion of the thirteenth interview between Rogers and a married woman (Case Report 24.1). This turned out to be her third-from-last session.

Case Report 24.1 *Client-Centered Therapy*

Client: *I'll tell you how I feel about my coming here. I don't think I have to come twice a week. I would like to come once a week for the time being and see and just talk over my problems once a week. And then, if everything goes smoothly on the once a week deal, why then I think I'm through. The only reason I'm not stopping now, although I feel right now I don't need any more, is that I just want to feel a lasting final few licks, shall we say.*

Therapist: *You want to feel quite sure that you are really through before you quit.*

Cl.: *Or if this is one of these quiet weeks, if it is, why then I'll have to start coming back twice, maybe three times, I hope not.*

Th.: *By and large you feel that you are getting close to the end.*

Cl.: *I think so. How does one determine?*

Th.: *Just the way you are determining.*

Cl.: *Oh, is that so, just by feeling that you don't have to come as often?*

Th.: *When you are ready to call it quits, why we'll call it quits.*

Cl.: *Uh huh, and then no return, uh?*

Th.: *Oh yes, if you feel you want to.*

Cl.: *And then I'd have priority on you, is that it?*

Th.: *Oh, yes, yes. We don't close the door and lock it, we just say good-bye and if you want to get in touch with me again, why feel free to do so.*

Cl.: *I mean, I feel as if I have just about covered almost every phase of my difficulty and, uh, I think one could keep going talking and talking and talking about it, if it weren't doing any good. What I mean to say, if the cure hadn't been started, and I think it has—I sort of have leveled off, quite suddenly it seems to me, because last week, why is it, last Tuesday when I was here I was in a terrible state, this terrible state. I thought of suicide, which I hadn't even thought of for almost a year or so, and yet Tuesday night, maybe it's darkest before dawn or something like that, you know, platitudes.*

Th.: *Sometimes it is; (Cl.: It is?) sometimes not, I mean, it's interesting.*

Cl.: *Yes, but I had really reached a low, and it seems maybe superficial to say that in three or four days I come back and I feel like a different person, but I think maybe I was reaching a certain emotional—setting myself for an emotional revelation, subconscious revelation which I didn't know but that it was just coming to the top like a boil.*

Th.: *Getting to the point where you had to do something about the whole business.*

Cl.: *Yes, I realized the position, that I had to get it out, and I did, Tuesday night, and it wasn't that I sat down and I said, "Well, Arnold, let's talk it out. . . ." I didn't do that. My feeling of hatred towards him was so intense that I was weak already, really I was so weak—I said something and he misunderstood me. And then I misunderstood him and I said, "Arnold, we just don't meet at all, do we, Arnold?" Then he said, "Well, let's talk" so we sat down and talked. So he took the initiative, and I started to talk to him for a whole hour and a half. Before it opened up I hated him, I couldn't talk, "Oh, he won't understand." "We don't meet on the same level." To myself, "Let's get away from each other. I can't stand to be with you, you irritate me. . . ." Then all of a sudden, I said, "Arnold, do you know that I feel sexually* *inferior to you," and that did it. The very fact that I could tell him that. Which was, I think that was the very thing, the whole thought to admit, not to admit to myself, because I knew that all the time, but to bring it up so that I could have admitted it to him, which I think was the whole turning point.*

Th.: *To be able to admit what you regarded as your deepest weakness.*

Cl.: *Yes.*

Th.: *Just started the ball rolling.*

Cl.: *This feeling of sexual inadequacy, but now that he knows it—it isn't important any more. It is like I carried a secret with me, and I wanted somebody to share it and Arnold of all people, and finally he knows about it so I feel better. So I don't feel inadequate.*

Th.: *The worst is known and accepted.*

SOURCE: Client-centered therapy *by Carl R. Rogers. Houghton Mifflin Company, 1951, pp. 85–87. Copyright © 1951 by Carl R. Rogers. Reprinted by permission of the publisher.*

The most noteworthy features of this dialogue are the way the therapist leads the client to assume the major responsibility for her progress by encouraging her to reach her own decisions; and the way the client, rather than her therapist, makes all the important interpretations. These differences set the Rogerian approach apart from some of the therapies discussed in earlier chapters.

Gestalt Therapy

Although the Gestalt therapy of Frederick Perls (1970; Perls et al., 1951) shares many of the beliefs, assumptions, and goals of Rogerian therapy, the differences are striking. Rogerian therapy is ordinarily done within a traditional one-hour-a-week format; Gestalt is often confined to a workshop format—typically a single weekend. Rogerian therapy is done either individually, or as couple, family, or group therapy; Gestalt therapy is almost always done in a group.

When Rogerian therapy is done in a group, the essential ingredient is the interaction between group members (what Rogers calls the *group process*), and the leader, or *facilitator*, to use Rogers's term, does little "leading." Instead he reveals his own feelings and helps to clarify and focus what others are saying. The Gestalt leader, in contrast, takes a highly aggressive role, working with one person at a time (usually) and at times disabling one after another of that person's defenses until there is no place to go but the here and now. The goals are *awareness* and here-and-now *authenticity*.

One of the Gestalt therapist's chief functions is to give active *permission* for the person to express his or her feelings, including personal needs and resentments, in the group context. Thus both authority and social pressure are brought to bear in support of honesty and against the person's defenses, especially against *projection*, which Perls considered a major source of disturbed communication.

Perls, who had once been a Freudian training analyst, differed sharply with the Freudian viewpoint on several issues. He believed, for example, that the Freudian practice of keeping the patient immobilized on a couch and requiring him or her to verbalize only perpetuated the split between thought and feeling. Although Gestalt therapy is not as body-oriented as Reichian therapy, the Gestalt therapist pays a great deal of attention to everything that the person communicates with his or her body, and repeatedly calls his attention to these signals. According to Perls (1969, p. 57), "Verbal communication is usually a lie. The real communication is beyond words."

Perls also believed that Freud had overlooked the structure of awareness, and that awareness leads to *Gestalten*—patterns of experience in which there is a unity of thought, feeling, and activity. Anxiety arises, in this view, when the person senses the struggle toward this unity.

Gestalt therapists use a sizable repertory of tactics to bring a person to a state of here-and-now awareness and authenticity. Instead of describing a troublesome situation or event in his or her life, the person is asked to enact it. Thus if a person's objective is to feel more autonomous and free of his mother's influence, he may be seated facing an empty chair, asked to imagine that his mother is sitting in that chair and urged to address himself directly to her. From time to time, the therapist (who stays slightly out of the person's line of sight, occasionally prompting) may suggest that the person switch chairs, assume the mother's role, and answer. If the person senses that the conflict is within himself (as it is ultimately, in any case), he is asked to play the different parts of himself. For example, he may play his overbearing conscience, or "topdog," shouting demands and criticisms at the empty chair, and then switch chairs and play the obsequious and devious "underdog."

Like other ex-Freudians, Perls retained some Freudian concepts, but with significant differences. For example, he saw the forbidden material that the neurosis guards against not as repressed fantasies but as organismic needs. There is also, as we suggested, some of Reich in Gestalt therapy, especially the attempt to repair the mind–body split. The Gestalt approach to dream work is based on Jung's concept that all the elements of the dream represent parts of the self. And Gestalt psychology is seen as part of the theoretical and experimental framework of Gestalt therapy, but in Gestalt therapy the search for *wholeness* is applied more to feelings and sensations than to perceptions.

The crucial point in Gestalt therapy is the "impasse" (Perls, 1970, pp. 18–19):

especially in therapy, we come to the "sick point," to the point where we are stuck, to the impasse. The impasse occurs where we cannot produce our own support and where environmental support is not forthcoming. Gestalt therapy . . . [helps us] get through the impasse and through the frustrations of the impasse . . . [by] . . . uncovering our own ability, our own eyes, in order to find our potential, to see what is going on, to discover how we can

enlarge our lives, to find means at our disposal that will let us cope with a difficult situation.

Gestaltists formulated their therapy around *rules* and *games*. The rules are the *principle of the now* ("What is your present awareness?"); *I and thou* ("To whom are you saying this?"); *"it" language* versus *"I" language* (change the comment "There is some hostility in his statement" to "I don't like what you said to me"); *use of the awareness continuum* (the "how" of experience); *no gossiping* ("direct confrontation of feelings"); and *asking questions* ("change that question into a statement"). The games are numerous and an innovative therapist may well devise new ones from time to time. Of the dozen or so games listed, the following two are typical (Levitsky and Perls, 1970, pp. 146–149):

Unfinished business . . . *is the Gestalt therapy analogue of the perceptual or cognitive incomplete task of Gestalt psychology. Whenever unfinished business (unresolved feelings) is identified, the patient is asked to complete it. Obviously all of us have endless lists of unfinished business in the realm of interpersonal relations, with, for instance, parents, siblings, friends. . . . Resentments are the most common and important kinds of unfinished business.*

Marriage counseling games. *The partners face each other and take turns saying sentences beginning with, "I resent you for . . . ," "What I appreciate in you is . . . ," "I spite you by . . . ," "I am compliant by. . . ."*

As an illustration of Gestalt therapy, we have selected yet another game, called *exaggeration*, as it was played with a schizophrenic patient who is described in Case Report 24.2. This game involves asking the patient to amplify a particular abortive or partial movement repeatedly until the inner meaning is more apparent, or, as in Case Report 24.2, it can be used in a verbal interchange.

The rationale for the type of verbal interaction that transpired between patient and therapist in this case, according to Gestaltists, is to allow the therapist to make explicit the patient's internalized conversation. Or, couched in terms of the *double bind theory* of Bateson and his associates (see Chapter 12), the therapist places the patient in another double bind, whose significant instructions are (Close, 1970, p. 196): (1) display no aggression; make no noise (with coat hangers); (2) display much aggression; make much noise (setting fire to lobby); (3) do not take any of this literally; do not obey me; and (4) recognize that all of this is sarcasm. In short the exaggeration of the therapist makes it impossible for the patient to avoid recognizing this as an impossible message, which he or she can respond to with pleasure and humor rather than anxiety.

Case Report 24.2 *Gestalt Therapy (exaggeration) with a Schizophrenic Patient*

The patient discussed here is a 24-year-old male who had dropped out of several colleges, finally suffering a severe breakdown shortly after being drafted into the army. He had recently been driving his parents to distraction by his incessant rambling and incoherent communications, which were full of bizarre sexual symbolism. Two incidents will serve to introduce him: His first appointment with me was with his parents for the evaluation interview. I asked them, "What brings you here?" The patient volunteered, "We got this letter that said to be here at 8:30." On another occasion, he and his parents walked into the office for a family interview; and he opened the conversation by saying, "Mamma told me not to say anything to open the conversation today."

After two months of outpatient therapy, the patient was hospitalized. I had seen him daily for two months preceding the following interchange, which occurred during a session in his room.

The patient reported feeling that he was a nothing and had to bend over backward to avoid offending people. He said that he was keeping his shirts in his drawer instead of hanging them up in the closet because the rattling of the coat hangers might disturb the patients in the other rooms.

Th.: (With exaggerated affect and gestures)
I certainly agree with you. I can't imagine anything worse than your disturbing the tranquility of the ward by rattling your coat hangers. After all, what right do you have to make all the racket?

Pa.: *I can hear M——— when he rattles his coat hangers in his room.*

Th.: *That is different! M——— is somebody. He has a right to make noise. You do not! You certainly don't think that you are as good as he is, do you? It would be terrible for you to make that kind of noise. You will just have to keep your shirts in the drawer.*

Pa.: *But even the drawer makes some noise when you open it and close it.*

Th.: *By golly, you're right. I'd forgotten about that. I guess the only thing for you to do is pile your shirts over there on the floor—but don't unwrap them—the crumpling of the paper would make way too much noise!*

Pa.: *That's right! I remember once I unwrapped a big package, and instead of crumpling up that big piece of paper, I laid it under the bed. I did right, didn't I?*

Th.: *You sure did. That was absolutely right. The only thing you should have done differently is to have covered it with a blanket, lest a mosquito land on it.*

Pa.: (Warm, spontaneous laughter.)

Th.: *Look, I'll tell you one way you might be able to get your shirts hung up. If you will go out to the TV room and turn the TV up full blast, then you could dash madly back to your room before anybody turned it down, and the TV would drown out the rattling of the hangers. Or, even better than that, turn up the stereo and the TV, and make this coincide with R———'s singing (a constant nuisance on the ward), then dash madly back to your room.*

I'll bet you could get your shirts hung up before all the chaos outside subsided. No one at all would hear the coat hangers.

Pa.: (Smiling warmly, starts to make some comment.)

Th.: *Wait a minute. I've got another idea. If you really wanted to do this right, you could set off the* fire alarm—*that would get the staff all upset, as well as the patients, and you would have plenty of time to hang up your shirts.*

Pa.: (Laughs warmly.)

Th.: *An even better way than that would be to turn up the stereo and the TV, get R———— to start singing, and then* start *a fire in the sitting room. That would* really *cause a racket, and while everybody was running around widly, screaming and hollering, you could be in here hanging up your shirts in complete serenity.*

The patient appeared to enjoy this interaction very much. Following the interview, staff members commented that he seemed to be a bit more assertive with other people, and a few days later it was noticed that his shirts were hanging in the closet.

SOURCE: *Close (1970), pp. 194–196.*

Primal Therapy

Primal Therapy is the invention of psychologist Arthur Janov, who introduced it in two books, *The Primal Scream—Primal Therapy: The Cure for Neurosis* (1970) and *The Anatomy of Mental Illness: The Scientific Basis of Primal Therapy* (1971).

Janov practiced traditional psychotherapy for about seventeen years until, according to his account, he heard "an eerie scream welling up from the depths of a young man lying on the floor during a therapy session. I can liken it only to what one might hear from a person about to be murdered" (1970, p. 9). Janov regards this scream as the product of central and universal pains that he calls *Primal Pains* (1970, p. 11). He believes these are the original, early hurts that form the

core of all later neurosis. The main objective of Primal Therapy is to help the patient feel his pain.

Primal Therapy, as Janov calls it, assumes that we are all born with certain basic Primal Needs (hunger, warmth, privacy, to be held and stimulated, to develop according to our natural abilities). When these needs are not met in early childhood, the result is pain. But, Janov contends, if the child is prevented from feeling the pain (for example, by parental threats to punish him if he cries) he blocks the feeling by tensing up. The tension remains, as an enduring block against feeling. Unmet primal needs reach a point at which the pain of "chronic unfulfillment" shuts down even the need for feeling (1971, p. 23). Eventually an event (not necessarily traumatic in itself) in the child's life causes him to turn a good part of himself off. Janov calls this event the *Primal Scene.*

Since Primal Therapy involves overthrowing the neurotic system by a forceful upheaval, new patients are prepared in advance for this extraordinary treatment procedure. They are told about the technique and required to undergo a thorough physical exam; they are then isolated in a hotel room for 24 hours prior to the first session and may not read, watch television, or make telephone calls during this period. They may even be asked to stay up all night. The rationale for this is as follows (Janov, 1970, p. 80):

The isolation and sleeplessness are important techniques which often bring patients close to a Primal. The aim of the isolation is to deprive the patient of all his usual outlets for tension, while the sleeplessness tends to weaken his remaining defenses; he has fewer resources to fight off his feelings.

The patient then enters the "intensive," three weeks of full-time therapy.

Considerably less verbalization occurs in Primal Therapy than in any of the other psychotherapies covered so far. This is illustrated in Janov's write-up of the case of Laura, a 30-year-old woman whose self-description is reproduced, with considerable editing, as Case Report 24.3. It should be evident also from this report that Primal Therapy resembles the methods used in the traditional schools in that it stresses the importance of past experiences in the formation of neuroses.

The Primal Scream is not a response to the present, nor is it necessarily used to release tension; it is only one expression of the pain. The pain is the curative agent because its expression means that the person is *feeling* at last. The patient must be brought gradually to this point because most people avoid or resist this feeling state. In Janov's words (1970, p. 82), "when I see that he is into the feeling and is holding on tight, I will ask him to breathe deeply and hard from the belly. I will say, 'Open your mouth as wide as possible and keep it that way! Now pull, pull that feeling from your belly!'"

Case Report 24.3 *Primal Therapy*

I am a typical example of the failure of "insight" therapies, since after seven years (on and off) of basic techniques and three different therapists, I came to Primal Therapy not even feeling. In other words, seven years of therapy had not even broken down the first barrier toward "making me well" (that is, real and feeling).

I have learned in Primal Therapy, only by way of feeling (and not by any figuring out), that at the bottom of everything is my unsatisfied need for my mother and then for my father to have loved me. . . . It became clear that I could not get what I needed—just being me—so I stopped feeling and started acting. . . . Everything I did from that time on was more and more removed from who I really was and what I really needed.

Once I felt my first Primal experience in Primal Therapy, I knew that it was the truth, and that I was alone, that there was nothing I could get from anyone else that would satisfy that basic need. Once I felt the real need, no substitute would do.

The Primal experience is a deep feeling and expressing of the deepest needs we have. I have *never felt anything like it before, except perhaps an orgasm. . . . It is as if all the pain were running out of me. My eyes weep, my nose runs heavily, my mouth is open and saliva runs out, my pores sweat, and my vagina secretes . . . it is the greatest relief I've ever felt; the words and sobs and noises come rushing out of me. . . . There is no thinking, only feeling.*

After the Primal I lay there for awhile. It is quite a draining experience, and I couldn't do or say anything for a while. My hands were warm for the first time I can remember and they have been warm most of the time since.

SOURCE: *Adaptation by permission of G. P. Putnam's Sons from* The primal scream *by Arthur Janov. Copyright © 1970 by Arthur Janov.*

The Expressive Therapies

Verbal therapy has obvious limitations. As we have indicated, some therapists believe that it diverts the person's attention from his or her feelings and present awareness. Another limitation is that it is useless with preverbal children. Consequently various methods have been devised for allowing the person to express his conflict through action. Such therapies are often used as diagnostic tools, but they may also provide direct therapeutic benefit simply by virtue of the self-expression they stimulate.

Play Therapy. Play is the child's primary mode of expression, as well as his or her main instrument for learning. Through play children explore, form perceptions of, and are initiated into the world. A sensitive observer can see in a child's play his or her fears, resentments, wishes, and dreams. Even in working with older children, who are more capable of communicating their feelings verbally, the therapist may learn much from the way a child arranges or moves toys, and action may still serve as a catalyst for verbalization.

Play materials and formats are selected to

suit the child's age. A small child may be provided blocks, dolls, punching bags, boxing gloves, clay, finger paint, and miniature cars and furniture. An older child or adolescent may be encouraged to play a board game, billiards, or table tennis.

Play often serves as an icebreaker between the child and the therapist, as well as revealing much of what is troubling the child. Children may express rage or resentment by punching or dismembering dolls, or may express anxiety by reconstructing the anxiety-provoking situation, or simply find release from the pressures of adult expectations by smearing themselves with paint.

Psychodrama. In 1925 J. L. Moreno hit upon the idea of asking people to act out, or "role play" their conflicts. The basic idea of role playing has since become a staple in Gestalt therapy and in alternative approaches to education. Moreno saw from the start that he was dealing with a social situation and that a group setting would therefore be needed. He was the first, in fact, to use the term "group therapy."

Psychodrama and Gestalt overlap to some extent, but psychodrama makes considerable use of the group members, who play the other people in the protagonist's conflict situation (or even the protagonist, when the director calls on them to "switch"). Another group member may also take up a position close to the protagonist, mirroring his or her posture and actions, and attempting to verbalize the protagonist's unspoken feelings. The protagonist and others may also play parts of the protagonist's self, and this aspect of psychodrama is perhaps closest to the role playing of Gestalt therapy.

Unlike other role playing techniques, psychodrama often draws extensively on the full resources of the theater. In a matter of moments costumes and props are handed to the actors, appropriate music is played on the sound system, houselights go down and stagelights up, and a drama materializes on stage. Quite often these dramas, and the Gestalt role plays as well, have every bit as much impact as anything one might see on a commerical stage. Part of the benefit in both kinds of therapy is the "chain reaction," in which watching the action on stage may release feelings in people and put them in touch with their own similar conflicts.

Summary

Existential therapy draws from existential philosophy the emphasis on direct experience as opposed to abstraction, and from phenomenology the attempt to use rather than repress subjectivity on the way to undercutting all presuppositions. It also borrows and enlarges upon the psychoanalytic idea that opening oneself up can have a liberating effect. The existential therapist enters into an active dialogue with the patient, with the objective of helping the patient directly experience his or her anxiety and alienation. When the attempt is successful, the patient is in touch with himself and no longer hides himself. He freely allows himself to be "visible" to others.

Existentialism in its European form has never been popular in the United States, but its fusion with humanism, a basically optimistic American philosophy, resulted in humanistic therapy, which has been quite popular.

Rogerian, or client-centered, therapy is the result of Carl Rogers's realization that ultimately the client knows more than anyone else "what hurts, what direction to go, what problems are crucial, what experiences have been deeply buried." The Rogerian therapist reflects the client's feelings as accurately as possible in a way that helps the client feel accepted as a whole person.

Gestalt therapy, whose chief founder was Frederick Perls, uses a variety of tactics to support honest expression of feelings in order to achieve a sense of here-and-now authenticity. The emphasis is on action rather than verbalization, and the tactics include role playing and games such as "exaggeration."

Primal Therapy, the invention of Arthur

Janov, is based on the idea that when a small child's needs are repeatedly not met, he or she feels pain. At some point he defends against the accumulated pain by blocking feeling through tensing his muscles, and the tension remains, continuing to block feeling. Janov strips away the patient's defenses and requires him to breathe in a way that makes it difficult to maintain the tension. If the person experiences the pain, there is a scream or some other outward expression of the pain; this event is called a *Primal*.

Many of the humanistic therapies downplay verbalization because it can easily be used to maintain defenses. The expressive therapies try to use action rather than words as much as possible, not only for the above reason, but also to work with preverbal children. In play therapy the therapist allows the child to play freely with toys that have been placed in the counseling room. Because a child's play expresses much of the child's feeling or imagining, it serves as a useful diagnostic (and sometimes therapeutic) tool. Psychodrama, invented by J. L. Moreno, is a way of facing conflicts by dramatizing them. Members of the group play the parts of people in the protagonist's life, or parts of the protagonist's self.

Terms and Concepts to Master

Authenticity	Primal therapy
Client-centered therapy	Psychodrama
Exaggeration	Topdog
Existentialism	Transparent self
Humanism	Unconditional positive regard
"I" language	
Phenomenology	Underdog
Play therapy	Unfinished business

25 Community Mental Health

Many individuals who want or need help are not likely to see a therapist in private practice. People who can barely make ends meet often cannot afford the fees, and most medical insurance plans are not designed by people favorably inclined toward paying for the treatment of emotional problems—at least not until those problems have had catastrophic results. Plans that do provide coverage for psychotherapy generally stipulate that the therapist must be an M.D., which limits one's choice of therapist.

Cultural factors are also involved. Private therapy tends to be geared to highly verbal, highly educated people, and on the other side of the coin, many people in the lower economic strata are suspicious or disdainful of anyone who regularly visits a therapist.

Fortunately there are some alternatives to private therapy, and we shall examine those alternatives in this chapter. Treatment is provided by various county, state, and federal agencies (the Veterans Administration), as well as by such private agencies as the Family Service Association and by numerous volunteer organizations. We shall discuss first the care provided on a full-time inpatient basis for patients in mental hospitals and then the various kinds of outpatient care available throughout the community.

Inpatient Treatment

Behavior pathology is traditionally treated in the mental hospital. To place that institution in a meaningful context, we shall describe its evolution and early history. Our account draws on information that may be found in Brown and Greenblatt (1955), Deutsch (1949), Hobbs (1969), Mora (1971), Whitwell (1936), and Zilboorg and Henry (1941).

Biblical and Ancient Times

Isolating the mentally disturbed from society is as old as history itself. The Bible tells us, for example, that King Nebuchadnezzar of Babylon, whose "mind was so troubled that he could not sleep" (Daniel 2:1) was "banished from the society of men and ate grass like oxen; his body was drenched by the dew of heaven, until his hair grew long like goats' hair and his nails like eagles' talons" (Daniel 4:33). and "at the end of the appointed time . . . Nebuchadnezzar . . . returned . . . [to his] . . . right mind" (Daniel 4:34).

And among the ancient Egyptians, the care and treatment of mental illness, in keeping with the then prevailing idea of demoniacal possession by evil spirits, consisted of "banishing," "driving out," "terrifying," "shattering," and "destroying" the disease. The art of *exorcism*, or of expelling evil spirits, was practiced exclusively by priests, who plied their sacred craft in the temples. Those suffering from mental ailments came to hear invocations intended to strike terror into the spirits possessing the ill. Another common practice among the ancients was *trephining* (Figure 25.1), an operation in which holes were

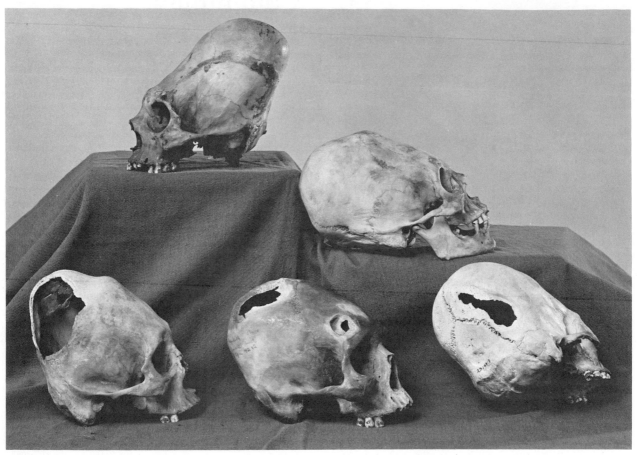

Figure 25.1

Archeological evidence of trephining, *a primitive form of treatment for mental disorders in which holes were burred in the skull of the patient. Evidently it was believed that* *these holes permitted the evil spirits and demons to leave.* (University Museum, Philadelphia)

chipped or burred in the skull to permit the escape of the brain's demons.

Among the early Greeks, as among the Hebrews and Egyptians, behavior deviations were perceived as demoniacal visitations that resulted from the anger of the gods (in this case the goddesses Mania and Lyssa). A well-known instance of such possession in classic mythology is that of Hercules, whom the goddess Hera afflicted with madness because she was jealous of his marriage to the Theban princess Megara.

The introduction of pharmaceutic remedies occurred somewhat later in Greek civilization, at about the time of Hippocrates (ca. 460–370 B.C.), who is known as the father of medicine. It was then that medicine freed itself from the domination of religion and began to recognize that natural phenomena cause mental disease. Subsequently an attempt was made to formulate specific remedies for their treatment, and there was also a movement at that time, as may be recalled from our discussion in Chapter 3, to classify the various abnormalities. Hippocrates explained mental illness in terms of disproportions among the four humors—black bile, yellow bile, mucus, and blood. And for the particular diseases he prescribed specific treatments. Thus, in addition to the administration of purgatives (bloodletting, diarrhetics) and drugs in the treatment of the insane, Hippocrates and the Roman physician Asclepiades (124–40 B.C.) after him berated their contemporaries for placing mental patients in dark chambers (presumably to quiet their minds) and recommended instead that they be housed in sunlit rooms and given proper diets, massage, and exercise.

At a somewhat earlier time in Greek history Plato (ca. 429–327 B.C.) attempted to explain irrational behavior as an inevitable consequence of human life and advocated treating the disordered by removing them from the streets of the city and letting their relatives watch over them. And Plato's student, Aristotle (384–322 B.C.), emphasized the importance of providing a *catharsis*, or natural outlet, for disturbing passions. He also recommended that such cathartic experiences occur in specially designated places, away from the inquisitive scrutinies of other citizens.

Galen (A.D. 130–200), like Asclepiades before him, advocated the humane handling and sequestering of patients and believed that "errors in judgment were made unconsciously . . . [and] . . . might be corrected by proper education" (Mora, 1971, p. 18). During late Roman civilization, the so-called *methodical school* continued application of humanitarian principles in the treatment and management of the mentally ill (Mora, 1971, p. 19):

Rooms were to be kept free from disturbing stimuli; visiting by relatives was restricted; the personnel

responsible for the care of patients were instructed to be sympathetic; during lucid intervals mental patients were encouraged to read and then discuss what they had read, to participate in dramatic performances (tragedy was prescribed to counteract mania, comedy to counteract depression), and to speak at group meetings. These procedures are basic to the therapeutic regimen in the modern mental hospital.

The Middle Ages

But with the fall of the Greek and Roman cultures the humanitarian ideas of Hippocrates, Plato, Aristotle, Asclepiades, and Galen gave way to a return to the occult and the practice of witchcraft and exorcism. During the early years of the medieval era the mentally ill were considered misdirected souls and were treated by the clergy. But later, because the great majority of the population was ignorant and still under pagan influence, witchcraft became the accepted explanation.

During this era humanitarian treatment was replaced once again by a mixture of superstition, astrology, alchemy, and magical rituals. For example, one nineteenth-century historian (Gundry, 1885, pp. 124ff) noted that a tenth-century prescription for insanity was as follows: "In case a man be a lunatic, take a skin of mereswine [whale] or porpoise, work it into a whip, swing the man therewith, soon he will be well. Amen." In addition, descriptions of signs useful for detecting those who were possessed by demons were widely circulated; in 1487, after much of Europe had been ravished by disease, famine, and pestilence, two northern German Dominican monks, Sprenger and Kramer, issued the *Malleus Maleficarum* (witches' hammer), a manual commissioned by Pope Innocent VIII. This was the first time the Christian church officially linked mental disorder with demonology.

The *Malleus Maleficarum* prescribed precise methods for dealing with or, more accurately, for finding, indicting, trying, judging, and torturing the alleged witches. The various means for exorcising them included the standard torture devices of the day and—if confessions were not forthcoming—burning at the stake, asphyxiation, strangulation, beheading, or for the lucky ones, brain surgery followed (Figure 25.2). Undetected mentally ill people were imprisoned by their relatives in cellars and attics; but many others were abandoned to wander aimlessly.

The Renaissance and Changing Attitudes

But if the *Malleus Maleficarum* was the low watermark in the history of the treatment of mental

Figure 25.2
In this sixteenth-century painting by the Dutch artist Hieronymous Bosch, a quack surgeon is depicted plucking the "stone of folly" from a patient's head. Bosch was lampooning a prevalent theory of his day, which held that madness was caused by such stones.

(Museo del Prado)

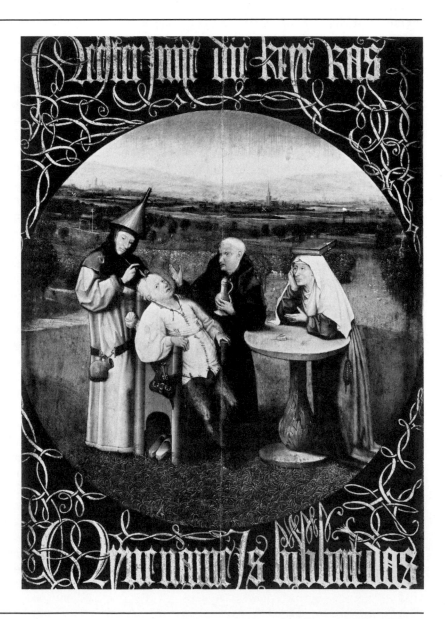

illness, it must also be remembered that it was written at the end of a period of general social and physical upheaval, at about the same time the writings of other philosophers and theologians were beginning to reflect changed attitudes toward these unfortunates. In fact, prior to the issuing of that dread document, numerous institutions for the custody of mental patients were being established (Mora, 1971): at Metz, Germany (1100); Uppsala, Sweden (1305); and Bergamo (1325) and Florence (1385), Italy.

Other treatises that reflected the changing times were written shortly after the appearance of the *Malleus*. The Spanish philosopher Juan Luis Vives (1492–1540), generally recognized as the first among several champions of the new humanitarian era to come, wrote a tract in 1538 that linked mental conditions to the instincts and emotions. In it he recommended that the mentally disordered be treated humanely.

The next notable figure on the scene was Johann Weyer (1518–1588), a Dutchman, who in 1563 published a treatise *De Praestigiis Daemonum*, which vigorously challenged the validity of demonology for many mental diseases. Being a product of his period, he did not entirely reject supernatural phenomena, but he argued that the demons rather than the possessed should be punished, since the latter are blameless. Further he held that there were a variety of mental disorders that called for a careful psychological examination of the patients. On the basis of his own clinical experience he described "a wide range of diagnostic entities and their associated symptomatology, and these included toxic psychoses, epilepsy, senile psychoses, nightmares, hysteria and delusions, as well as paranoia, *folie à deux*, and depression" (Mora, 1972, p. 31).

Weyer's ideas and work were so far ahead of their time that they were vehemently rejected by most of his contemporaries. Only Reginald Scot (1538–1599), an Englishman who in 1584 published his *Discovery of Witchcraft*, supported Weyer's position and strongly championed the humane treatment of "the poor creatures accused

of witchcraft" (Figure 25.3). They required treatment, he wrote, rather than exorcism for alleged sins, and they deserved physicians to help them rather than torturers and executioners to burn and hang them. King James I personally condemned the book and ordered it burned.

But interest in the psychological phenomena outlined by Weyer increased, and gradually others began to favor more humane treatment, including such noted physicians, philosophers, and mathematicians as Paracelsus, Cardan, Leonardo da Vinci, Galileo, and Bacon.

The layman's view of mental illness, however, remained essentially unchanged. As a result, according to Mora (1972, p. 35), there was no evidence of improvement in the facilities provided for the care of the mentally ill:

When they were kept at home, their families frequently resorted to the use of chains. And, with few exceptions, the conditions to which the hospitalized mental patient was exposed were equally deplorable.

This sad state of affairs, as we shall show shortly, continued well into the present century.

The Asylums of the Thirteenth Through Eighteenth Centuries

During these centuries such famed philosophers as Hobbes, Locke, Spinoza, Descartes, and Leibnitz did much to advance interest in psychological and naturalistic phenomena. But most important in the history of treatment facilities during these centuries was the establishment of mental institutions throughout Europe and the American colonies.

Historians say that the first institutions exclusively intended for the reception of lunatics, as they were called, were the monasteries of the late fourteenth and early fifteenth centuries. And in 1302 "there were at least six male lunatics in confinement" at Bethlehem Hospital, London

Figure 25.3

The title page of Reginald Scot's The Discovery of Witchcraft, *published in 1584, which referred to the "unchristian practices and inhumane dealings" of those who believed that demons cause mental illness.*

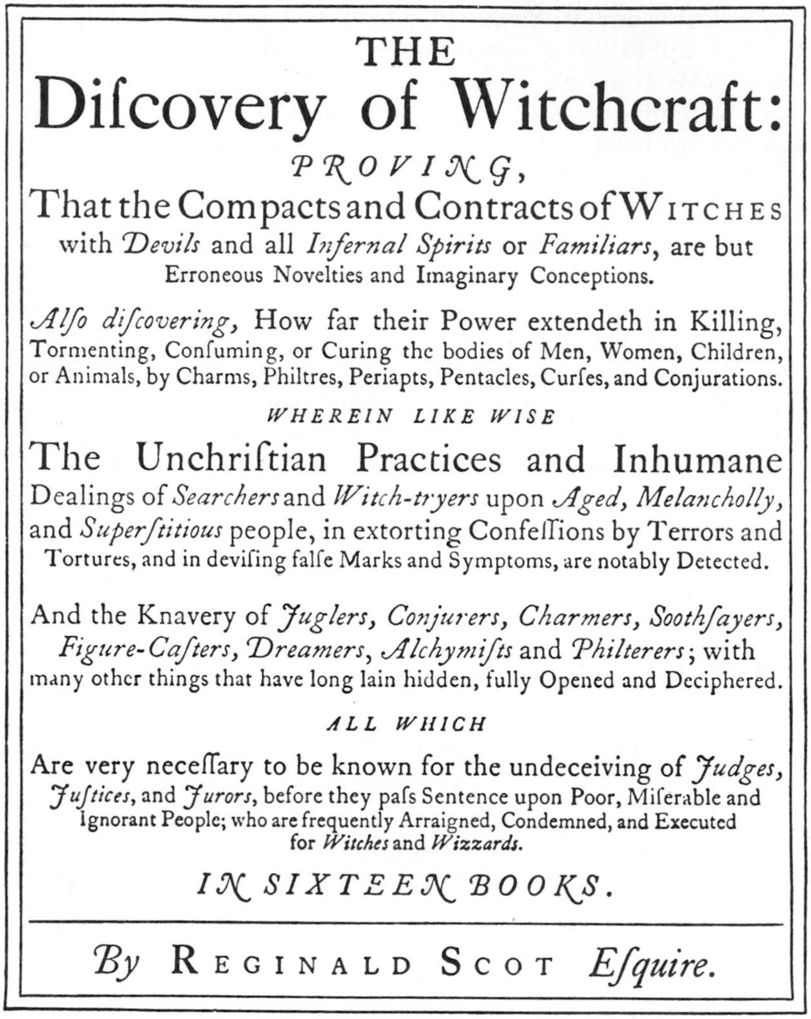

THE
Diſcovery of Witchcraft:

P R O V I N G,

That the Compacts and Contracts of WITCHES
with *Devils* and all *Infernal Spirits* or *Familiars*, are but
Erroneous Novelties and Imaginary Conceptions.

Alſo diſcovering, How far their Power extendeth in Killing,
Tormenting, Conſuming, or Curing the bodies of Men, Women, Children,
or Animals, by Charms, Philtres, Periapts, Pentacles, Curſes, and Conjurations.

W H E R E I N   L I K E   W I S E

The Unchriſtian Practices and Inhumane
Dealings of *Searchers* and *Witch-tryers* upon *Aged, Melancholly,*
and *Superſtitious* people, in extorting Confeſſions by Terrors and
Tortures, and in deviſing falſe Marks and Symptoms, are notably Detected.

And the Knavery of *Juglers, Conjurers, Charmers, Soothſayers,*
Figure-Caſters, Dreamers, Alchymiſts and *Philterers*; with
many other things that have long lain hidden, fully Opened and Deciphered.

A L L   W H I C H

Are very neceſſary to be known for the undeceiving of *Judges,*
Juſtices, and *Jurors,* before they paſs Sentence upon Poor, Miſerable and
Ignorant People; who are frequently Arraigned, Condemned, and Executed
for *Witches* and *Wizzards.*

I N   S I X T E E N   B O O K S.

By R E G I N A L D   S C O T *Eſquire.*

(Deutsch, 1949, p. 15). Bethlehem, originally founded as a general hospital in 1247, came to be called Bedlam in later centuries, a word synonymous with maltreatment of the mentally ill.

The first European asylum was founded in Valencia, Spain, in 1409, by a priest who had reportedly witnessed a street scene of mockery and sadism directed at the mentally ill. In the years immediately following, five similar hospitals were built in various other cities of Spain, and, in 1567, under Spanish influence, the first such hospital was established in Mexico City. According to Mora (1972, p. 30), the attitude of the Spaniards toward mental patients had been profoundly influenced by the Arabs, whose Moslem faith taught that the deranged person is loved by God and particularly chosen by Him to tell the truth.

The first hospital to accept mental patients in

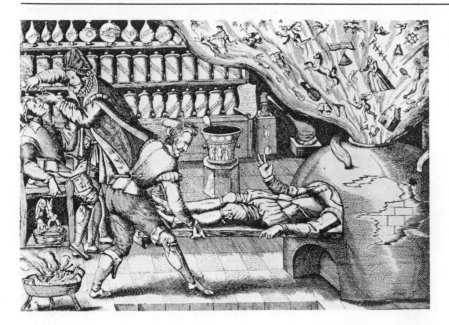

This seventeenth-century German lampoon of the medical practice of the time depicts treatment of mental illness by the administration of purgatives (left) and the driving out of demons by putting the patient into an oven.

An eighteenth-century characterization by Hogarth of a scene in Bedlam.

A statue of Philippe Pinel, shown freeing a patient from her chains. He broke the tradition of his day when in 1793 he freed many patients at La Bicêtre hospital in Paris.

(Deutsch, 1949, p. 58). It was called the Pennsylvania Hospital, and its founding was followed by the constuction, in 1773, of the Eastern Lunatic Hospital in Williamsburg, Virginia, for the exclusive treatment of the mentally ill.

The Nineteenth Century and Moral Treatment

But it was not until the end of the eighteenth century, when Philippe Pinel (1745–1826) broke through the inhumane atmosphere existing both in this country and abroad, that treatment methods began to improve. In 1793 Pinel obtained permission from the French government to free the patients from their chains at La Bicêtre hospital in Paris. Much to everyone's surprise at that time the freed patients were not violent or assaultive—in fact they were a docile and frightened lot.

Pinel's reforms ushered in an era of so-called *moral treatment*, a form of therapy that was based on Aristotle's theory of mental illness as an imbalance of the passions. In order to restore a proper balance, Pinel believed, the therapist had to treat patients firmly and subdue them until they were entirely under the control of the healer. Then they could be treated with kindness, firmness, and reason. One of the main benefits of this approach was "that the patient's participation in various activities within a structured environment greatly contributed to the success of Pinel's moral treatment" (Mora, 1972, p. 47).

The achievements and reforms of Pinel were paralleled at about the same time in England, mostly under the leadership of William Tuke (1732–1819), the prominent Quaker who opened a retreat at York in 1796 for the treatment of mental patients. He called it the Retreat to differentiate it from the Lunatic Asylum of York and to remove the stigma associated with the common terms of that day—insane asylums, lunatic asylums, madhouses. The Retreat admitted about thirty patients in its first few months, and they were treated as guests in a friendly and warm

colonial America was established in 1756, under the influence of Benjamin Franklin, and it differed from other such institutions in America in that "it was the first institution where cure, rather than custody and repression, was the underlying principle in the treatment of the insane" atmosphere free from medical influences, an idea that is only now beginning to take shape in this country.

Immediately following the reforms of Pinel and Tuke, the influence of the latter reached this country with the establishment of the Friend's Asylum, opened at Frankford, Pennsylvania, in 1817. This institution, which was about five miles north of Philadelphia, was situated on 52 acres of land and offered a sheltered location, "where the mentally ill could be protected from the gaze of the idly curious" (Deutsch, 1949, p. 96).

Among the most important figures in the American moral treatment movement was the versatile and energetic physician Benjamin Rush (1745–1813), who was educated in Edinburgh, Scotland, and who introduced the new methods of treatment at the Pennsylvania Hospital. He is widely acclaimed as the father of American psychiatry and, although his treatment methods were for the most part humanitarian, he was a product of his times with regard to certain specific therapies. For example, he invented the "tranquilizer chair," to which a patient was strapped hand and foot and in which his head was restrained in one position. The purpose of this chair, based on the notions of humane coercion, was to reduce muscular and motor activity, which, in turn, was supposed to slow the patient's heartbeat and pulse.

But he is best known for his insistence on treating patients with the same regard and dignity as that accorded to others. He recommended that patients be encouraged to be gainfully employed while hospitalized and that they be shown little acts of kindness from time to time. In this regard, "recognizing the evils arising from the universal practice of hiring ill-paid, coarse and often brutal attendants, he recommended, in 1803, the employment of a well-qualified person . . . as a friend and companion to the lunatics, whose business it shall be to attend them" (Deutsch, 1949, p. 85).

Somewhat later, in about 1840, Dorothea Dix (1802–1887) observed that the emotionally dis-

Until well into the nineteenth century, the mentally ill were often kept in chains in order to restrain them.

turbed were abused and mistreated in the jails and almshouses of Massachusetts, and she began actively to campaign for more humane treatment, a campaign that lasted almost forty years. Her efforts were directly responsible for the establishment of more than thirty state hospitals and probably laid the groundwork for mental hospitals as we now know them.[1]

---

[1] Not everyone agrees that Dorothea Dix's efforts were entirely in the best interests of the mentally ill. For example, Bockoven (1963) suggests that she was largely responsible for the stagnation of hospital life and the authoritarianism of hospital personnel, which still exists in many so-called modern facilities. Ullmann and Krasner (1975), who hold a similar opinion, describe her as a woman of "imperious manner, rigid opinions, and attitudes of censorship" and "credit" her with introducing to mental hospitals "petty fault-finding and punishing authority" (1975, p. 137).

The Twentieth Century

The next important impetus to the mental health movement, both in this country and abroad, was the 1908 publication of Clifford Beers's autobiographic account, *A Mind That Found Itself.* In it he wrote of his experience as a patient in three mental hospitals in Connecticut, all of which (two private and one state hospital), according to him, dealt with him in the harsh and crude way that was still prevalent at the time. He was beaten mercilessly, choked, spat upon, and reviled by attendants; and he was imprisoned for long periods in dark, dank, padded cells and at one point spent as many as 21 consecutive nights in a straitjacket (Deutsch, 1949).

Beers's book, which appeared with an introduction by the famous philosopher and psychologist William James, won immediate acclaim in America and Europe. Reviews, editorials, and articles on the book and its author were powerful instruments for progressive social change. Beers's book was a masterful indictment of the asylum system of the time, and it was a highly literary and articulate presentation that could not fail to impress readers with its ring of sincerity and truth. Adolf Meyer, who was considered the "dean of American psychiatry," was impressed by Beers's account of hospital conditions and exerted his considerable influence in behalf of hospital reforms.

But Beers's book did not stop merely with an indictment: it proposed a concrete program for the alleviation and reform of the shabby and inhuman conditions that existed. In addition the circumstances of his own illness convinced him that mental disease was not only curable in many cases, but also preventable. Therefore Beers outlined a plan for the establishment of a national society whose purposes would be to initiate and further reforms in the care and treatment of the mentally ill; to disseminate to the public information designed to create a more humane and intelligent attitude toward them; to encourage and carry on research into the causes and nature of mental disorder; and finally to create more services directed toward the treatment and prevention of mental illness.

In many respects Beers was half a century ahead of his time. The hospital reforms proposed by him are only beginning to take shape; resources for large-scale dissemination of information to the public were made available as recently as 1963; and public concern for hospital care for the mentally ill has lagged even further behind these developments. Nevertheless the mental hospital of today is a far more humane and efficient treatment center than it was during his day, and Clifford Beers was largely responsible for this development.

The Modern Mental Hospital

Most modern mental hospitals offer their patients pleasant surroundings and an interested and devoted staff, although even today there is a wide range of inpatient services, from the low-budget drab installations of some counties and states to the plush private hospitals of large urban centers. Our account will dwell mainly on the well-run hospital.

General Considerations

There are about one and a half million people in the United States in mental hospitals. These are people so burdened by their problems that they cannot cope with the routine demands of everyday living. Of course there are many more people (about three million) who do not need hospitalization and who can be treated in the many outpatient centers springing up around the country; but for those persons who are not functioning in society or are a threat to themselves and others, hospitalization can have many advantages.

The modern, humanely administered mental

hospital provides patients with round-the-clock care and an environment totally designed to help them reestablish routines of living that were disrupted by their problems. The advantage of such a hospital for the psychotically depressed or the schizophrenic patient, to take just two examples, is that it does not surround them with the anxieties that make them desperate. While their families may appeal to them to "snap out of it," professional and other trained personnel know that such exhortations only increase already existing anxieties and that they would snap out of it if they could. Moreover, for patients too distraught to look after themselves, the hospital is one of the few places that offer assistance in meeting such essential everyday needs as eating, drinking, evacuating, sleeping, and exercising.

The Hospital as a Therapeutic Community

This type of modern hospital, in addition to serving as a place where troubled people can spend time removed from their cares, is also a *therapeutic community,* a concept popularized by the psychiatrist Maxwell Jones (1953) to describe its treatment and environment (also see Main, 1946; Rossi and Filstead, 1972; Taulbee and Wright, 1971). The term *therapeutic community,* according to one source (Stainbrook, 1972), refers to those aspects of psychiatric hospital practice that aid in reducing patients' behavioral disturbances; it is historically related to the moral treatment of the early and middle nineteenth century, when respect for human rights, humane and dignified handling of patients, and a structured regimen all contributed to behavior improvement (Kraft, 1966).

The main elements of the modern therapeutic community are the staff, patients, and environment. Regarding the first it is recommended that in relation to each patient "everyone in contact with him should . . . be able . . . to answer the question, 'What sort of human experience does this patient need with me now?'" (Stainbrook, 1972, p. 387). And in this milieu great value is placed on having patients share in the responsibility of administrative hospital decisions, the rationale being that it offers them the opportunity for involvement in their own destinies and sets the stage for their subsequent decision-making outside the hospital.

The total environment of the therapeutic community, in addition to its focus on easy communication betwen staff and patients, should reflect the needs and aspirations of its constituents. According to Kraft (1966, p. 549) this means that the physical plant has a homelike quality and that it resembles, as much as possible, an open setting. Moreover the general hospital decor, inasmuch as it reflects the hospital's attitudes toward the patient, should be as pleasant as possible. The interiors of a hospital can easily clue the patient to the kind of behavior expected. For example, crude furnishings, doorless rooms, seatless toilets, open toilet stalls, and bare walls tell the inmate that the hospital administrators believe they must protect themselves against him.

The overall objectives of this community, then, are to promote a total environment in which patients are encouraged to communicate easily with one another and with the staff; are surrounded by interested and devoted people; and, most important, are prepared for life outside the hospital by being allowed to participate in decisions about their welfare.

But these are only ideals toward which some hospital administrations strive; the realities of modern hospitals are often far different. For example, many patients still feel that they sit out their lives in drab surroundings, sometimes exposed to uninterested (even sadistic) personnel. They complain of the tedium of hospital routine, and say that they feel abandoned by unsympathetic relatives. This point is forcefully driven home in the following excerpts from a dialogue between a psychologist and a schizophrenic woman in a ward of one of the better-run hospi-

The Right to Treatment

Kenneth Donaldson, a former carpenter, was involuntarily committed by his father to the Florida State Hospital at Chattahootchee in 1957. At that time a Florida county court judge assured Donaldson that he was being sent to the hospital for a few weeks for medication and psychiatric observation and that he would be out in a "few weeks." Instead Donaldson was diagnosed as "paranoid schizophrenic" and spent the next 15 years at Chattahootchee. Finally, in 1971, after numerous unsuccessful attempts to obtain his release, Donaldson was reclassified as mentally healthy and released. He immediately filed suit in a Florida Appeals Court charging violations of his federal civil rights and claiming damages for having been kept in the hospital without receiving adequate treatment. Some of the Chattahootchee Hospital doctors defended their actions with the claim that Donaldson received "milieu therapy," but they were unable to prove that the hospital milieu was in any way therapeutic. In fact, according to Donaldson and his attorneys, the hospital was countertherapeutic in that he was confined to a 60-bed locked hospital ward, denied ground privileges, and not permitted to attend occupational therapy groups. Evidently, Donaldson claimed, the hospital doctors feared that he would try to escape if given ground privileges or that he might learn to use the typewriter in occupational therapy and then prepare legal petitions for his release. Perhaps the most convincing evidence in Donaldson's behalf was the hint of evidence that came out at his trials that his several prior unsuccessful attempts at obtaining a release from the hospital qualified him as a troublemaker and as "mentally ill." The doctors' reasoning seemed to be that anyone who is confined to a mental hospital must be "crazy" if he tries to get out—a sort of "Catch-22" in reverse. A jury awarded Donaldson $38,500 and in July 1975 that award was upheld by the United States Supreme Court, which ruled that a state may not confine anyone involuntarily merely to provide custodial care.

Donaldson's case, which has far-reaching implications for mental health care,

---

tals in this country, which the authors called "A Day in the Life of a Schizophrenic" (Braginsky et al., 1969, pp. 16–23):

Qu.: *What do most of the patients do in these places? For example, the canteen, the coffee shop.*

An.: *Waste time! That's the biggest thing on our hands. It's just a matter of wasting time.*

Qu.: *What do most patients do on the ward?*

An.: *Watch television or just sit there. Some of them just sit there, and you wonder how they can sit there for five, six, seven hours just looking into space and not doing anything. They're just living vegetables!*

Qu.: *What do you generally do on the ward?*

An.: *Watch television. I do a lot of reading. I have the* Reader's Digest *sent up here every month, and I have taken books from the library. And later on watch television. I do a lot of letter writing, and as I say, my husband comes three times a week, and neighbors and relatives come once a week, and my family comes once a week.*

Qu.: *When they come, do they usually come in the evening?*

is now called the "right to treatment" case because he claimed, and the Supreme Court agreed, that if an individual is deprived of freedom for the express purpose of "treating" him, he must be treated. And if treatment is not given, the ruling indicates, the patient must be released unless the state can prove that he is dangerous and cannot function in society.

If the Supreme Court ruling and the awarding of damages to Donaldson do not immediately open the doors for the release of other mental patients, they will at least serve as incentives to hospitals to provide treatment. But this case also raises some questions that will not easily be resolved by court rulings. How can a clear distinction be made between custodial care and treatment? Must patients accept any treatment? Can they refuse treatment, even if this may mean longer hospitalization? And, finally, who is to decide what is good treatment? The patient? The doctors? Society? The courts?

The decision in the Donaldson case prompted the following memo, which might serve as a model for the staffs of mental hospitals.

NOTICE TO PATIENTS

The United States Supreme Court recently ruled that a mental patient who has been involuntarily hospitalized, who is not dangerous to himself or to others, who is receiving only custodial care, and who is capable of living safely in the community has a constitutional right to liberty—that is, has a right to be released from the hospital. The Supreme Court's opinion is available for patients to read.
If you think that the Supreme Court ruling may have a bearing on your present status, please feel free to discuss the matter with the hospital staff. In addition, if you wish to talk with an attorney about the meaning of the Supreme Court decision and how it may apply to you, the Superintendent has a list of legal organizations that may be of assistance. The staff will be glad to aid anyone who wishes to contact a lawyer.

Source: Brown (1976).

An.: *My husband comes in the evening, and so do the neighbors. The relatives and my mother and father, you can never tell. They come whenever they can. I very seldom go to any of the activities here. I used to when I first came here, but it gets to be old hat with you after awhile.*

Qu.: *What are you supposed to do while you're in the hospital?*

An.: *Rest. That is the main thing that I had to do. I was completely run-down, both physically and mentally, and I had to rest. And, of course, that's just about all I did was sit on my butt and rest, and it got pretty . . . tiresome after awhile.*

This patient's boredom and sense of uselessness are also articulated by sociologist Erving Goffman in his essays on asylums (1961, pp. 151–152):

In the mental hospital, the setting and the house rules press home to the patient that he is, after all, a mental case who has suffered some kind of social collapse on the outside, having failed in some overall way, and that here he is of little social weight, being hardly capable of acting like a full-fledged person at all. These humiliations are likely to be most keenly felt by middle-class patients, since their previous condition of life little immunizes them against such affronts, but all patients feel some downgrading.

And Thomas Szasz, whose objections to the "myth of mental illness" we already mentioned in Chapter 3, launches an even stronger indictment at the modern mental hospital. In his book, *The Manufacture of Madness*, he compares institutionalization with the Inquisition (1970, pp. xxiv–xxv):

To maintain that a social institution suffers from certain "abuses" is to imply that it has certain other desirable or good uses. This, in my opinion, has been the fatal weakness of the countless exposés, old and recent, literary and professional — of private and public mental hospitals. My thesis is quite different: Simply put it is that there are and can be, no abuses of Institutional Psychiatry, because Institutional Psychiatry is itself, an abuse; similarly there were, and could be no abuses of the Inquisition, because the Inquisition was, itself, an abuse.

A series of studies that at first seemed to be a devastating attack on the labeling and classification procedures in mental hospitals appeared in *Science* (Rosenhan, 1973). In these studies eight normal people, or so-called "sane pseudopatients," gained admission to 12 different hospitals. Among the eight pseudopatients were one psychology graduate student, three psychologists, a pediatrician, a psychiatrist, a painter, and a housewife; three were women, five were men. Their assignment was to call an assigned hospital for an appointment and then to present themselves to their respective hospital complaining of having heard voices. Once admitted to the hospital, each patient ceased simulating any symptoms of abnormality.

Despite their normal behavior, according to Rosenhan (p. 252) "the pseudopatients were never detected." Most were admitted with a diagnosis of schizophrenia, and each was discharged with a diagnosis of schizophrenia "in remission." In other words none of the pseudopatients was detected as normal nor, in the institution's opinion, had he or she ever been normal.

Rosenhan's article, which he called, "On being sane in insane places," and the conclusion he drew ("It is clear that we cannot distinguish the sane from the insane in psychiatric hospitals.") caused a considerable stir. Since then several clinicians have raised serious questions about the relevance of these studies. For example, R. L. Spitzer (1976) argued that nothing in Rosenhan's study supports his statement that "psychiatric diagnoses, in this view, are in the minds of the observers and are not valid summaries of characteristics displayed by the observed." The diagnostic category "schizophrenia, in remission," Spitzer points out, is not a common one, as one might assume, but is extremely rare. Therefore, he contends,

the diagnoses given to the pseudopatients were a function of the patients' behaviors and not of the setting (psychiatric hospital) in which the diagnoses were made. In fact, a moment's reflection may cause many a reader familiar with usual diagnostic practice to marvel that so many psychiatrists acted so rationally as to use at discharge precisely the same diagnostic category, in remission, that is so rarely used with real patients.

Spitzer notes also that the psychiatrist who believes a pseudopatient who is feigning a symptom "is responding to the patient's *behavior*," and that, since the patient is seeking admission to a hospital, "it is reasonable to conclude that the symptom is a source of significant distress." Perhaps the most interesting of Spitzer's comments is the one point he concedes to Rosenhan (also see Farber, 1975; Rosenhan, 1975):

Rosenhan presents one way in which the diagnosis did affect the psychiatrist's perception of the patient's circumstances—historical facts of the case were often distorted by the staff to achieve consistency with psychodynamic theories. Here, for the first time, I believe Rosenhan has hit the mark. What he described happens all the time and often makes attendance at clinical case conferences extremely painful, especially for those with logical minds and research orientations. Although his observation is correct, it would seem to be more a consequence of individuals attempting to rearrange facts to comply with an unproven etiological theory than a consequence of diagnostic labeling. One could easily imagine a similar process occurring when a weak-minded, behaviorally oriented clinician attempts to rewrite the patient's history to account for "hallucinations reinforced by attention paid to patient by family members when patient complains of hearing voices." Such is the human condition.

No doubt the range from the worst to the best of our mental hospitals is extremely wide. Periodically scandals surface, during which we discover that many mental patients are subjected to unbelievable brutality or neglect.[2] In fact the history of mental hospitals is studded from its beginnings with scandals and reforms, and with the introduction of nonpejorative terminology that becomes pejorative overnight. Where the idea of a therapeutic community has been applied by a sensitive and enthusiastic staff, a sense of community has indeed been achieved, as well as a

pattern of honesty in interpersonal relations that has given some patients second thoughts about the desirability of returning to the "real world." Nevertheless, as the data of Fairweather and his associates (Fairweather, 1964; Fairweather et al., 1969) suggest, the treatment programs of most hospitals, even when they consider themselves therapeutic communities, are ineffectual. Chronic patients tend to return to the hospital at the rate of about 70 percent within 18 months, and there are sizable numbers of persons who never leave the hospital at all. Fortunately some alternatives are available, and we shall consider them later in this chapter.

Outpatient Treatment

Outpatient services include public and private mental health clinics as well as the offices of clinical psychologists and psychiatrists. They are equipped mainly to serve the less seriously distressed, who hold jobs and function in society—the so-called ambulatory cases—and offer a wide range of services including psychotherapy, behavior modification, marital and family counseling, child guidance, and vocational and educational rehabilitation. Often they will provide treatment just short of hospitalization or assist the former patient in adjusting to the community after his release from the hospital.

Home treatment and halfway houses, are two alternatives to conventional hospitalization. As we indicate below, each holds considerable promise as a substitute for the often drab environment of the mental hospital.

Home Treatment

The ideal substitute for institutionalization, of course, would be to care for the emotionally troubled in the *home*. Such a system has been functioning in Amsterdam for more than thirty

---

[2] In an article on the contractual model for the protection of the rights of institutionalized mental patients, one psychologist (Schwitzgebel, 1975) argues that the use of contracts between hospital and patient in treatment could extend free choice and greatly clarify mutual expectations of patients and therapists. Even a simple contract stating that the institutional therapist will provide treatment that is "customary and usual in the profession" could vastly improve the situation of patients who are often neglected or given treatment of obviously inferior quality.

years (see Weiner et al., 1967), where professional personnel are available 24 hours a day to evaluate and treat psychiatric emergencies in the home. Originally set up to alleviate a psychiatric hospital bed shortage, it has been retained and expanded and is now an integral part of the mental health delivery system of that city. The goal of the service is to treat people in the home as soon as a call for help is received. The home visits are usually short, drug therapy is the treatment of choice, and no psychotherapy is given (Egan and Robinson, 1969).

The first comprehensive home treatment service established in the United States was set up in 1957 at Boston State Hospital in Massachusetts. Its intent from the outset, in contrast to that of the Amsterdam services, was to offer treatment in the home as a feasible alternative to hospitalization. The *Psychiatric Home Treatment Service*, as it was called, opened in Boston State Hospital and functioned in a research and demonstration capacity for its first five years. In 1962, through state legislative support, it was made a permanent facility of the hospital.

The main aims of this service are to provide psychiatric evaluation (and treatment when needed) to patients suffering from serious mental illness who, because they are either unable or unmotivated, do not seek help. In addition it supplies home service teams whose members offer consultation and seminars to community workers and other care-taking agencies (for example, clergy, police, volunteers), and it provides training in community mental health to other mental health professionals. To date the Psychiatric Home Treatment Service of Boston has had over two thousand patients referred to it during its several years of existence and has served in a consultative capacity to many professional and lay groups. Preliminary research on its treatment effectiveness indicates that for many patients, it is a feasible alternative to hospitalization (see Weiner et al., 1967, pp. 25–62).

Halfway Houses

A second alternative to hospitalization is the *halfway house,* a transitional living facility that serves as an intermediate stopping point between mental hospital and community. We discussed a similar type of residential arrangement earlier in this book when we described Synanon and other self-help residential treatment arrangements (see Chapter 10); but halfway houses differ from these in that they do not confine their activities to alcoholism or drug addiction; rather, they deal with all people who have recognized psychiatric problems and take them in as residents during their transitional period, usually immediately after discharge from a hospital.

The halfway house, usually located in an urban community, provides room and board and a measure of comfort, support, and supervision to its residents. It has a democratic, informal, and relaxed atmosphere that, in virtually every aspect of living, permits the resident to assume a far greater degree of autonomy than is afforded by a hospital. Although the halfway house does not force the patient into the fixed routines of hospitals, it is in many respects like a hospital because it retains similar rehabilitative goals and emphasizes the same therapeutic functions; but in some other ways it is closer to a boarding house because it offers a greater semblance of family life and demands more participation by its members than hospitals do (see Doniger, 1970).

The purpose of the halfway house, according to Raush and Raush (1968), who obtained their information by examining the survey responses of halfway house personnel, is to provide a place for the ex-hospitalized and for upset people to live in order to avoid the necessity for future hospitalization. It is also a residence where patients may live uncontaminated by the stigma of a hospital, and where they have more opportunity to influence their environment than in the larger, more highly structured organization of a typical institution. But most importantly it is a place free from association with past difficulties and old intense relationships, which at the same time provides opportunities to readjust to societal norms.

Among the first to propound the idea of a community transitional lodging were psychologist G. W. Fairweather and his associates (Fairweather, 1964; Fairweather et al., 1969), whose study of the ineffectiveness of traditional hospital treatment procedures we cited earlier. Their idea was based on an extensive Veterans Administration hospital study, which tested the feasibility of forming an autonomous group within the hospital. The purpose of organizing this group was to explore the possibility of moving it to the community as a unit to serve as a "bridge" to the outside world. Their research showed not only that such a group could be formed, but also that patients within such groups, when compared with those who receive traditional treatment, were more socially active in hospital affairs, had higher morale, gave more help to their fellow patients, and were more optimistic about future employment and marriage. Most important of all, however, was their discovery that later community adjustments of former task group members were superior to those of their traditional-treatment counterparts.

In a later project Fairweather and his associates (1969) extended their earlier work somewhat. They moved a cohesive group of chronic patients from a hospital into a community lodge and then demonstrated that these patients could administer their own halfway house. Originally this experimental group received the help of a research staff psychologist, but later it ran its own affairs. After they were given full responsibility for the functioning of the lodge, the patients formed a handyman service that in three years produced an income of fifty thousand dollars, which was allocated to group members according to their productivity.

More than three years later this group was compared with a matched group that had been discharged from the hospital after having participated in the type of small-group program described earlier (see Chapter 20). The results were clear-cut. On six-month and 40-month post-discharge follow-ups, members who had the self-governed halfway house experience were better able to hold income-producing jobs, were more capable of managing their daily lives, and could more easily adjust to the outside world than their control counterparts.

Today there are about fifty halfway houses in this country, operating primarily under private auspices. In addition to evidence found by Fairweather and his coworkers, other research evidence (Goertzel et al., 1960) indicates that halfway houses are effective in attaining their intended goals. One follow-up evaluation, conducted at Conrad House in San Francisco, reports that two years after departure, 80 percent of 52 former residents were living independently, 15 percent with parents and one person in a family-care home; moreover 31 percent of these people had been rehospitalized at least once, their length of stay varying from four days to 13 months. Somewhat more encouraging was the finding about former residents' work status, which, like the Fairweather study, indicated that 50 percent of former residents were employed full time, having stayed more than six months at the same job, while 23 percent were attending college or were in vocational training (Ross, 1970).

The Community Mental Health Movement

Nicholas Hobbs, a pioneer in community psychology, called the community mental health movement "mental health's third revolution" (Hobbs, 1964, 1969). He saw as the first revolution the work of Pinel, Tuke, Rush, and Dix, which was based on the notion that the mentally ill should be treated kindly and humanely. This belief, incidentally, has not yet gained wide acceptance with the general public, and in this sense the first revolution remains unconsummated.

The second revolution was marked by the writings of Freud and his followers and their interest in intrapsychic events and personality restructuring (see Chapters 6 and 22). The third revolution includes the *community mental health center* concept that we are about to outline, as well as the developments we have already mentioned (therapeutic community, home treatment, halfway houses, and so on). It also encompasses other services to be discussed shortly (open hospitals, crisis intervention centers, nonprofessional psychotherapists).

The chief emphasis of the community mental health concept is on the idea that abnormal behavior can be prevented. Three forms of prevention have been delineated (Cowen, 1973; Denner and Price, 1973; Reiss et al., 1977) as *primary*, *secondary*, and *tertiary* prevention. Primary prevention consists of steps that may be taken to prevent disturbed behavior before it begins. Considering the present limited state of knowledge about the etiology of the disorders, as we have noted throughout this book, our efforts would be mostly confined to reducing environmental stress factors, to genetic counseling, to providing early counseling programs and educational programs designed to promote psychological health in young children, and to assure proper diets for all people (also see Albee, 1979).

Secondary prevention is intended to provide early detection procedures so that potential or incipient disturbances do not magnify into severe disorders. This concept would encourage the early use of screening and identifying devices to help predict who will develop behavioral problems. A particularly useful research strategy falling under this heading would be the "high risk" for schizophrenia work that we discussed in Chapter 12. But again, given the state of knowledge in abnormal psychology at present, only limited steps in the direction of secondary prevention can be taken.

The third type of prevention, tertiary prevention, is essentially treatment designed to minimize the effects and consequences of already developed psychopathologies. Toward these ends the various therapies and rehabilitation discussed in previous chapters are more or less effective, as are the community mental health centers we shall now discuss.

We shall discuss first the community mental health center, which is the prototypic development of this third revolution (see Adelson and Kalis, 1970; Carter, 1968; Cook, 1970; National Clearinghouse, 1969).

Mental Health Centers

Community mental health centers are a direct outgrowth of the "bold new approach" outlined by President John F. Kennedy in his message to Congress in February 1963, which led to the passage of the Community Mental Health Centers Act in 1963 and its amendments in 1965 and 1967. This legislation focused the nation's attention on the inadequate care available to the mentally ill. In doing so, it further emphasized the need to develop a new vehicle for the organization and delivery of mental health services. The real significance of this legislation, however, was that it provided the guidelines and funds for such a vehicle.

Functions and Organization. Under this legislation flexible new programs for community mental health centers were planned and are still being built. These plans provide for treating the mentally ill close to their homes, and sometimes even in their homes; for working with troubled people, directly or through other agencies; for preventing, relieving, or removing conditions leading to illness or to unproductive lives; for bringing the principles of mental health to those people—such as teachers, judges, ministers, and employers—most likely to affect the lives of other people; for training professionals and nonprofessionals; and for doing research.

These programs are being funded by the federal government through the National Institute of Mental Health. At present they are organized through partnership arrangements between the private and public sectors and among federal, state, and local agencies. These sources are cooperating to provide facilities and services as well as to finance them. The whole idea of this new organization is to reach those for whom services have not been readily available in the past because of inaccessibility or prohibitive costs. Now these people can obtain help, without making appointments, simply by walking into any one of several hundred thousand neighborhood centers currently operating.

The network of community mental health services includes *outpatient* and *inpatient* care, *emergency services*, *consultation*, and *education*.

These five essential services are required for federal assistance under the Community Mental Health Centers Act. They may be expanded into a comprehensive program that includes, in addition, partial hospitalization, diagnostic and rehabilitation services, precare and aftercare services, training of personnel, and research and evaluation. We shall discuss only outpatient and inpatient care here.

The Outpatient Clinic. The outpatient service of the mental health center is the primary and most used facility of the community system. It is the place where most people first turn for help, and it is now uniquely equipped to offer such help in the following five ways.

First, like the entire center program, outpatient services are easily available to *all* who live within the center's service area, regardless of ability to pay or educational level.

Second, the outpatient clinic offers continuity of care for someone recovering from a stage of illness that required hospitalization.

Third, it provides immediate help to those who may be undergoing a short-term crisis.

Fourth, by establishing storefront outposts and traveling teams who may go into homes, it extends mental health services to those who would not ordinarily walk into a clinic.

And fifth, to carry out the goals of prevention and treatment, the outpatient service helps to operate the center's consultation and education program for community professionals—educators, police, lawyers, physicians, clergy (National Clearinghouse, 1969).

Predictably, because outpatient clinics have become the largest service and the key service in the community system, they are also the most extensively used. More than one million individuals are now obtaining help in such clinics, including children, adolescents, and adults for whom such service would not have been available otherwise.

Inpatient Services. Community mental health centers have not done away with the need for hospitals. Psychiatric inpatient care, as we indicated earlier, is one of its five essential services; patients are still being referred to public (mainly state) hospitals, especially those who are seriously disordered and cannot cope with everyday existence on the outside.

And because mental hospitals will continue to serve large numbers of these patients for a long time to come, the federal government, through NIMH, has tried to raise the quality of care. For example, it has launched new programs, the Hospital Improvement Project (HIP) and the Hospital Staff Development Program (HSD), with grants of large sums of money to approximately 85 percent of the state and county mental hospitals in the United States. These programs are part of a new concerted campaign to improve hospital facilities and to provide patients with personnel who are motivated, interested, and devoted to understanding them and helping them return to their families and society. It has also freed extra resources for novel alternatives to long-term institutionalization.

Innovative Inpatient Services: The Open Hospital

Because of increased federal funding several partial or open hospitalization schemes have been made increasingly available. Although they are not the alternative solutions to institutionalization that home treatment or cooperative retreats offer, they are steps in that direction.

Mental health authorities are now coming around to the views expressed by such critics as Goffman, Szasz, and others that hiding the patient behind the walls of an institution isolated from the rest of the world is not necessarily therapeutic. They have come to realize that many people can be more readily treated, even when hospitalization is indicated, if they are not severed from their accustomed surroundings. Three variations of the *open hospital* idea are discussed below.

The Day Hospital. The *day hospital* offers hospitalization from 9 A.M. to 5 P.M., with the patient spending the day in group activities, treatment, and occupational therapy. At night the patient goes home to spend time with his or her family (see Kramer, 1972; Zwerling, 1966).

The day hospital movement was initiated in Russia in 1933, and its first major use in the Western world occurred in Montreal in 1946 at the Allan Memorial Institute of Psychiatry. In the United States it was initiated somewhat later, in 1948 and 1949, at such private institutions as the

Yale Psychiatric Center and the Menninger Clinic. Since then many varieties of day hospitals have been developed in a host of different settings, including state hospitals, state departments of mental health, the Veterans Administration, and the psychiatric wards of general hospitals.

In the United States the original rationale for the development of the day hospital was the acute shortage of inpatient beds, which frequently led to the discharge of patients before the full benefit of hospitalization had been obtained; unfortunately this often also led to the necessity for readmission to the hospital. It was then felt that the day hospital could become a place where patients make a more gradual transition from the ward to the community (Kramer, 1972).

Currently the day hospital is being tried increasingly as an alternative to total institutionalization. One of its main advantages is that patients can maintain their family ties, no longer returning as strangers from long stays in the hospital. Moreover, under the day hospital method, the family itself can become involved in the day-to-day job of bringing the patient back to good health.

The Night Hospital. The *night hospital* is an equally interesting variation on the open hospital theme, and its permits the mentally ill to spend the day pursuing their jobs or other interests and then to go directly to the night center. Like the day center, the night hospital provides part-time hospitalization to those who need occasional respite from a stressful home environment. It also offers them therapeutic surroundings with the full range of psychiatric treatments available in other hospitals. Working patients can thus be involved in an active treatment program without disruption of gainful employment. Like its day hospital counterpart, this arrangement is economical to both patient and institution and still provides safeguards against some of the drawbacks of full-time hospitalization.

An outstanding example of night hospital care is the unit that has been functioning at the Montreal General Hospital since 1954 (Kinder and Daniels, 1962; Moll, 1963). With 15 beds, it offers an active program five nights a week from 6:30 P.M. until 11 P.M., including psychotherapy, drug therapy, electroshock, modified insulin therapy, and psychodrama. Under this arrangement patients may have their treatment after the evening meal, go to bed at about 11 P.M., rise about 7 A.M., and have breakfast and go to work.

In the past, one of the major drawbacks to partial hospitalization was the presumed risk involved in keeping disturbed persons outside a custodial setting; however, the introduction of the tranquilizers has decreased considerably the dangers involved (also see Chapters 10, 11 and 21). Moreover recent studies have shown that the risks to patient, family, and community are well within the range of tolerance and acceptance (Pasamanick, 1968).

Unfortunately no definitive evidence has been found to support the effectiveness of such partial hospitalization compared with its full-time counterpart. According to several studies cited by one reviewer (Kramer, 1972, p. 399), the most valid conclusion would seem to be that day or night care is no less effective than traditional methods of patient care. Clearly the effectiveness of the open hospital should be determined by well-designed studies similar to those conducted by Fairweather and his associates.

General Hospital Care. An arrangement related to the day or night hospital involves sending mental patients to a general hospital where they can be treated intensively for a week or two and then returned home to convalesce as they might well do if they had any other type of disorder. The attraction of such care is that it eliminates much of the stigma associated with the concept of mental illness. Moreover, compared with total institutionalization, it is reasonably inexpensive, and part or all of the costs could be defrayed by hospital insurance plans.

Innovative Outpatient Services: Crisis Intervention Centers

In addition to searching for expedient alternatives to traditional inpatient arrangements, psychiatric professionals and others have also sought novel approaches to meeting the ever-increasing need for outpatient services.

Crisis intervention, according to one authority (Parad, 1965), means entering into the life situation of an individual, family, or group for the express purpose of ameliorating the effects of traumatic stress. The dual purpose of the intervener is to reduce the impact of the stressful event (for example, earthquake, fire, financial straits) and to utilize the crisis situation to help the victims solve their present and future problems. In most instances the stationary clinic or center is still the place where such intervention occurs, although its setting is not its most important feature.

It is a logical extension of brief psychotherapy, which in turn evolved from the therapies discussed in Chapter 22. While these therapies realize their goals (alleviation of symptoms, personality change, enhanced self-image) through an extended, unhurried, and detailed exploration, brief therapy attempts to delineate quickly a specific problem dimension without allowing the patient leeway for digressing in other directions. The same holds true for crisis intervention, which has as its principal goal the resolution of an individual's immediate crisis and restoration of functioning to at least the level that existed before the onset of the crisis. Optimally, of course, given the time and opportunity, the next goal is to elevate functioning above the precrisis level.

The duration of such intervention, according to some experts (Caplan, 1964; Jacobson, 1965), is characteristically self-limiting and lasts from four to six weeks; it can, however, be a one- or two-shot affair, sometimes requiring no more than a telephone session and an immediate follow-up the next day. In either event the intervener exerts every effort to obtain as much information as

possible about the patient and his problem in a short period of time. In crisis situations, time is the crucial variable, often making the difference between life and death.[3]

Some of the most influential concepts in crisis intervention were formulated by psychiatrist Gerald Caplan in *An Approach to Community Mental Health* (1961). His work was influenced by Lindemann's classic study (1944) of normal and pathological grief reactions in relatives of victims of the Cocoanut Grove nightclub fire near Boston. Shortly after the fire, Lindemann described both the immediate and the abnormally prolonged reactions that occurred in different individuals as a result of losing a significant person in their lives. He observed that when a person's problem-solving capacities are overtaxed by life stress, there is a rise in tension, which in turn impedes the search for a solution. This may result in personality disorganization, which further leads to paralysis of action, symptom formation, and maladaptive behavior (Rappaport, 1965).

As a result of his collaboration with Lindemann in 1946 in establishing a community-wide program of mental health, and his subsequent work in Israel in community child psychiatry, Caplan became interested in the theory and practice of crisis intervention. A crisis, according to Caplan, occurs when a person faces seemingly insurmountable obstacles to important life goals, followed by a period of disorganization and upset during which he makes abortive attempts at solution (1951, 1964).

His theory is that during this crisis a person undergoes a period of emotional disequilibrium and becomes quite susceptible to influence (becomes more suggestible). This is therefore an optimal time for intervention to restore the equi-

---

[3] Bellak and Small (1965), in discussing brief psychotherapy, emphasize how much can be learned from a single initial probing interview, and describe how causal relationships can be quickly ascertained because of the therapist's knowledge of behavioral psychodynamics and "profiles of disturbance."

librium to an adaptive level higher than existed previously. We shall describe three facilities in which such intervention may occur.

The All-Purpose Crisis Intervention Center.
One of the earliest brief therapy clinics was the Benjamin Rush Center for Problems of Living, a division of the Los Angeles Psychiatric Service, which opened in January 1962. At the center a person applying for treatment could obtain it usually on the same day, but almost always within one week, and there was a maximum treatment period of six visits. Eligibility was open to persons over the age of 13½ in some branches and 17½ at others. The Benjamin Rush Center charges a nominal flat fee per visit if a person can afford it but renders services free of charge if not. The clinic's major treatment emphasis is on specific problems of living, including life crises and psychiatric emergencies. Admission to the center occurs without psychodiagnostic screening, hence it treats persons regardless of their psychiatric classification (Aguilera et al., 1970; Morley, 1965).

To illustrate the kind of situational crisis handled by such a center, we have selected the case of Tom, a young college student, who called a crisis intervention center, saying he knew he was "going to die; I can't control it. . . . I must!" Attempts on the part of the receptionist to elicit more information from the young man merely resulted in his repeating, "I need help, or I'll die!" This was followed by sobbing and repetitions of "I don't know. . . . I don't know." After the second telephone call he was connected directly to a nurse–therapist, who saw that Tom was confused and disoriented and suspected that he was under the influence of drugs. Tom acknowledged that he had taken LSD the week before but said he had not taken any drugs since. He added that he had had a bad trip: "I feel the same way now. . . . I'm so depressed . . . life isn't worth living. I've tried three times to jump out of the window of the dorm, but I can't do it . . . but I know I will." The therapist then gave him de-

tailed directions to the center and emphasized that she would be waiting for him. Additional excerpts are presented as Case Report 25.1.

Case Report 25.1 *Crisis Intervention*

Tom arrived ten minutes after he telephoned the Crisis Intervention Center. Because of the urgency of the situation, he was able to bypass the usual admission procedure and was seen immediately by the therapist. He was very anxious and was almost incoherent. The therapist managed to find out his age, address, and names of friends and family. After Tom explained about his trip on LSD the week before and that he was feeling "the same way" now, he was reassured that it was possible he was "reliving" the previous experience. A medical consultation was arranged and he received medication.

His roommate, Jake, was contacted and came immediately. The therapist used Jake to gain more knowledge about Tom's previous experience with drugs and his habitual patterns of coping with stress. Jake cooperated and stated that both he and Tom had tried "pot" a few times but did not use it regularly because it "didn't turn us on." When questioned about the LSD experience, he stated that about a week ago Tom had come to their room at the dorm with two other students who had LSD with them. Jake refused and advised Tom not to try it. But Tom thought "it might be fun." When he began to feel the effects of the drug, he apparently became frightened and panicked. He kept repeating, "I want to die . . . I want to die . . . I'm not fit to live!" He began crying and asking Jake to help him. After the effects wore off, Jake urged Tom to talk about what had happened, but he refused. He acted depressed and began withdrawing from social contacts and school activities, cutting classes and staying in the dorm, where he usually lay in bed staring at the ceiling.

When asked about Tom's previous patterns of interaction and reacting to stress, the therapist discovered that Tom and Jake had roomed together for two years, and Jake thought that basically Tom was a very lonely person, all of his relationships seeming superficial. Jake believed he was the only real friend that Tom had at school and that Tom usually accepted his decisions and opinions when he was undecided what to do.

When Tom returned to the therapist the following week, he was calm and his perception and thinking were clear. He seemed emotionally flat and he spoke in a low monotone. He slumped in the chair and said he wanted help because "I'm so depressed." When asked to be more specific he said he could not: "I just feel so dead, I can't really put my finger on any one thing."

In the ensuing sessions his feelings of depression remained, although they had lessened somewhat in intensity. He was able to discuss them freely with the therapist and at the dorm with Jake. During the third and final session Tom and the therapist discussed the advisability of his continuing in longer-term therapy. Tom stated that he felt that he was "just beginning to recognize and understand his feelings of depression, and wanted more help." He was referred outside the center for longer-term therapy.

SOURCE: *From D. C. Aguilera, J. M. Messick.* Crisis intervention, Second edition. *St. Louis: C. V. Mosby, 1974.*

It is evident from the description of this case that Tom's already precarious emotional stability deteriorated after his bad LSD trip and that his ability to cope with this crisis was inadequate and he panicked. The goals of intervention, which in this case stemmed the tide of the immediate crisis, were to reduce his intense anxiety, arrange a medical consultation, render situational support, obtain more information about him and his usual pattern of coping with stress, and refer him to a facility where more time could be spent exploring personality traits that were only touched on lightly at the center.

The Suicide Prevention Center. Another kind of crisis intervention service is one that deals with *suicide* as its only type of emergency. In Chapter 14, we referred to the service rendered by the Los Angeles Suicide Prevention Center; we shall expand on this coverage here.

This center was opened on September 1, 1958, and now offers around-the-clock, no-waiting, unrestricted-intake, walk-in service to people whose primary problem is a suicidal urge. Its opening was preceded by about ten years of interest, study, focus, and concern with suicide as well as suicide prevention by its three founders—Edwin Shneidman, Norman L. Farberow, and Robert E. Litman. Much of their work was supported by funds awarded by the National Institute of Mental Health, and in large measure the center grew out of their experience under that research grant.

The center's switchboard is staffed by nonprofessional mental health volunteers who are carefully selected, trained, and supervised. It has two main aims: to educate the public about suicide and to intervene directly to try to prevent acts of suicide. How such crisis intervention works in practice is described in the following excerpts, which tell in detail how active suicide prevention begins from the moment the telephone rings (Shneidman and Mandelkorn, 1970, pp. 134–136):[4]

When a worried man or woman calls . . . just to talk to someone to share his problems, the staff person on duty begins immediately to assess the caller's degree of "lethality." Cold statistics help at the outset. The staffman knows that elderly, single men are more apt to commit suicide than young married women callers. He tries to evaluate the stress the person making the call is under . . . and asks questions gauged to uncover whether the caller is stable or not, if he has a history of suicide attempts, what his life style is, and if there are any symptoms that would indicate that suicide is imminent. Finally, and most important, the staff

---

[4] © Science House, 1970, *The Psychology of suicide.*

member must discover just how specific is the caller's plan to kill himself. Has he planned the day and hour of the suicide? And just how will he accomplish it? Here, it is important to know which method the caller has chosen; shooting one's self with a gun that lies loaded in the next room at the moment of the call is a much more lethal scheme than a vague plan to purchase some sleep medicine at a drug store.

. . . The first telephone interview often spells the difference between life and death. The staff person who answers the phone must immediately establish some continuing communication with the caller, maintaining even the most tenuous of relationships: ("How did you get into trouble?" he'll ask the caller. "What are some of the solutions that you've thought about?") . . .

If the situation is highly critical the staffer must come up with an answer right there on the telephone. Frequently, with suicidal persons, life has lost its shadings. Every issue is either black or white, yes or no, life or death. Sometimes a caller can be persuaded to see his problem in a broader perspective. In other cases the staff therapist would be able to "arrange" things for the suicidal caller. Simply setting up an interview with a staff psychiatrist, psychologist, social worker, or volunteer may provide the tension relief needed to ease a critical suicidal situation.

Suicide crises are similar to those that occur at other intervention centers. They almost always concern two people, the suicidal person and the significant other, and the telephone worker attempts to ascertain who this is—father, wife, mother, lover, or whoever. An interview is arranged, if possible, to see both protagonists at the center. The significant second person in the prospective suicide must be made aware of the situation and, if possible, become involved in the life-saving efforts. In most cases, according to Shneidman and Mandelkorn (1970, p. 137), "these others" show surprise, concern, and a willingness to help—at least to some extent; in other cases they must be disregarded or cir-

cumvented—they may do more harm than good.

Once the troubled person is at the suicide prevention center, a worker attempts to persuade him (or her) to see the problem in perspective, or to find a novel solution to problems with which he has struggled. Sometimes the staff therapist or nonprofessional is even able to "arrange" things for the suicidal person that help him overcome seemingly insurmountable obstacles. On other occasions just setting up an interview with a staff psychiatrist, psychologist, social worker, or volunteer may provide the tension relief needed to ease the critical situation.

The Peer Help Center. Peer help centers are staffed exclusively by students trained and advised by interested mental health professionals on and around campuses. They became especially popular in the late 1960s and early 1970s because of radical changes of lifestyle among college students. As a result of these changes, which in many instances have polarized into conflicts between school personnnel and the so-called counterculture, some students felt that establishment clinics simply did not understand, or deal effectively with, their problems. This was especially true among those students who were using drugs and those whose living arrangements clashed with middle-class morality.

At Carnegie-Mellon University this problem was resolved by setting up a peer help center located in a readily accessible and well-publicized office. It is staffed 24 hours a day by student volunteers. When the crisis requires that a staff member appear at the scene (for example, dormitory or downtown), a two-person team proceeds to the individual in need and evaluates the situation to ascertain whether a supportive "talk-down" is sufficient or whether immediate professional help is needed. In either case appropriate help or transporation is furnished to the caller (Prestia et al., 1971).

In addition to rendering such on-the-spot assistance, workers at the center stand ready to follow up these team efforts at its office location.

The usual modes of contacting this center, like those of the previous ones discussed, are telephone calls, office drop-ins, prior contacts, and referrals from the campus counseling center or other sources. The student who contacts the center and is wary of the "worth" of the volunteer assistance offered may be assured by the staff that the peer helper does meet with a member of the counseling center to aid in the proper management of the relationship. He or she is also reassured that, if desired, his or her anonymity will be preserved.

Consultation. Four functions of mental health consultation have been distinguished (Altrocchi, 1972; Korchin, 1976), all of which have in common a process in which one person or agency (the consultee) seeking a solution to a problem, turns to either another person or an agency (consultant) with the ability to aid in that solution. First, the consultant may *teach* or *train* consultees, perhaps bringing to their attention special skills in handling particular cases, or the results of appropriate research, literature in the field, comparable solutions found in other agencies, or other material of relevance.

Second, the consultant can serve as a *communication facilitator*, either among consultees within an agency, or between agencies, or between the agency and the larger community. For example, in one study with group consultation in a small community, a number of workers from different agencies were seen simultaneously in group sessions (Altrocchi et al., 1965, reported in Korchin, 1976). The workers found that this procedure had facilitated communication among the various agencies by reducing communication barriers, reducing competition and mutual fear, and encouraging collaboration.

The third function of consultation takes advantage of the consultant's role as outsider, and uses him or her as a *human relations* mediator. As an outsider the consultant is in a position to detect interpersonal conflicts and problems that impede the work of the consultee agency. Thus a psychologist may be consulted by a principal of a school to discuss the relationship among teachers and between teachers and the administration. Similar consultations may be offered to hospital staff as well as police departments, court systems, civil service organizations, and so on. As a partial by-product of the consultant-as-human relations mediator, *T-group* arrangements (see Chapter 20) have been developed that, among other functions, have facilitated sensitivity training, interpersonal competence, and consciousness raising.

The fourth function of consultation is to aid the consultee in planning research of all kinds, but particularly in planning short- and long-term follow-up studies designed to evaluate the effectiveness of the agency's program in accomplishing its missions. This function is especially relevant to community mental health centers where evaluation research studying their effectiveness as agents of change is needed periodically. Unfortunately, as one authority (Bloom, 1972) has amply documented, evaluation research is often a secondary and neglected activity in community programs.

The Use of Nonprofessional Psychotherapists

Several of the foregoing community-oriented approaches to inpatient and outpatient care used nonprofessionals as psychotherapists. This was most apparent, for example, in the peer help center concept just discussed and perhaps least apparent in the halfway house movement mentioned earlier. This use of nonprofessionals as agents of behavior change is very much in keeping with the new spirit of mental health action, and in the next few pages we shall outline several additional roles nonprofessionals have played as psychotherapists.[5] They include the use of parents, volunteers, and teachers as agents of change. Of course the best-known nonprofessionals are found among such self-help groups as Alcoholics Anonymous and Delancey Street, discussed in Chapters 9 and 10.

Parents. The use of parents as therapists of their own emotionally troubled children—sometimes called *filial therapy* (see Andronico and Guerney, 1969; Fidler et al., 1969)—is an approach reminiscent of Freud's remote-control psychoanalysis of "Little Hans" (see Chapter 19). The children themselves are not seen in therapy; instead therapists train the parents to effect the necessary changes themselves. Much of the training involves teaching the parents to conduct play sessions with their children so that they can set the stage for letting the children communicate their wishes and needs through action-oriented play.

The main advantages of this approach over the traditional approaches are that parents become more ego-involved in the changes that occur in their children; they cooperate more readily with the therapist; and the therapist's sympathy and understanding for the children need not be transferred to the parents because the parents acquire these attributes directly by working with their children. In addition, filial therapy is economical in that it allows for the training of six to eight parents and their children while using only one office and many fewer hours of professional time. Filial therapy has another likely advantage: it may be a subtle way of educating parents to become better parents and thus remove a probable cause of the child's difficulty.

The evidence for its effectiveness, however, is sparse and consists mainly of testimonials by its users based on "experience to date with nine such groups, two of which have ended, while the other seven are in various stages," which indicates "that the same characteristics that seem to raise or lower probability of success in more tra-

---

[5] One of the earliest published programs to use nonprofessionals was that of Yale's Psychoeducational Clinic (see Sarason et al., 1966).

ditional therapies . . . also tend to do so in this form of therapy" (Andronico and Guerney, 1969, p. 134). In other words the technique is too new to yield definitive answers about its strengths and weaknesses (see also the work by Patterson discussed in Chapter 19).

An unanticipated problem of deinstitutionalization has been the reaction of families to their returning relatives (Kolb, 1977, p. 399). "Significant others" of 125 mental patients released from state hospitals were interviewed, and it was learned that although families often displayed a high tolerance of deviant behavior with little shame, continuance of severe symptoms troubled them. The least sympathetic reactions were in families whose relatives displayed the most symptoms. At best, it was reported, the former mental patient faces an ambivalent emotional atmosphere.

Volunteers. One type of volunteer program will be discussed briefly—the so-called *Big Brother* approach—which draws its members from an organized welfare-oriented group. There are many other volunteer help approaches, and the reader may want to consult other sources for information about them (see Guerney, 1969; Rappaport et al., 1971; Zax and Cowen, 1972).

The Big Brother program, in existence since the late 1950s (Lichtenberg, 1969), was designed to provide friends for boys who are emotionally deprived. Its purpose is to have the Big Brother provide a substitute for the relationship that a boy normally has with his father, a brother, an uncle, or a friendly neighbor. The volunteers, in this case drawn from a service arm of the Jewish Board of Guardians, are usually interviewed by a social worker in an effort to determine their suitability for this kind of program. The main emphasis of this screening is to ascertain the volunteers' motives for seeking their assignments and to suggest to them that their understanding of themselves is important in helping the boys.

Once a volunteer is selected, he is prepared for his assignment by a professional worker, who

The main elements of the therapeutic community are the humane and dignified handling of the psychiatrically disturbed and an all-staff effort to rehabilitate the patient. This photograph shows patients and staff engaged in a geography lesson.

usually explains some of the difficulties of this type of caretaking assignment. Regarding this matter Lichtenberg writes (1969, p. 118) that it is often wise to prepare the volunteer for the worst. He should be told that the boy will not necessarily seem to like him just because he is well intentioned and may well interpret as a rejection the Big Brother's busy schedule, which does not permit unlimited attention. Above all the volunteer is cautioned that he is not to assume the attitude that he is doing the boy a big favor, because this attitude will be detected and resented.

Meetings between the Big Brother and the boy usually occur once a week; and the volunteer is seen immediately after the first two contacts, and then once a month. Written reports are submitted after each session. It is also important for the Big Brother to meet from time to time with other men who are doing the same kind of work— to give the volunteer the opportunity to exchange his views and feelings about his disappointments and successes.

Although this program has been in effect among social workers since the late 1950s, no data are available on its successes or failures. Obviously the technique has possibilities for many phases of mental health service delivery, but its value has not yet been assessed.

Teachers. Teachers also deliver mental health services but are not trained primarily to do so. In one particularly well-known study conducted in a nursery school, Harris et al. (1969), working within the operant conditioning context, systematically examined the effects of using teachers as reinforcers of desired behaviors in a child. Specif-

In a token economy, patients are rewarded for approved behavior.

ically this case involved a boy who, according to teachers' reports, was passive and refused to participate in any play activities regardless of their coercions, friendly or otherwise. The behaviorist therapists therefore selected a particular form of active play, which they, along with the teachers, attempted to strengthen.

The vehicle they chose was a wooden frame with ladders and platforms, called a climbing frame. The method used to *shape* the child's responses was to reinforce successive approximations to climbing behavior. Thus at first teachers reinforced (by showing approval) the child's mere proximity to the frame; then, as he came closer, they reinforced his touching it; and finally they rewarded his climbing. In all instances the reinforcement consisted of the pleased attention of adults. Figure 25.4 reports this study's results.

Five different phases of the conditioning of this child are reflected in Figure 25.4. First, there was an eight-day *baseline* observation period, during which he climbed the frame (open bars) or any other equipment in the play yard (shaded bars) less than 10 percent of the time. This was followed by a nine-day period of reinforcement, which was marked by days in which more than 60 percent of the child's time was spent in climbing the frame (climbing on other objects was not scored during this period). Next there were five days during which the teachers ignored frame climbing, which resulted in almost total extinction of all climbing activities. The second reinforcement period of five days brought immediate recovery of frame climbing, to a high and stable level. After this the teachers began an intermittent program of reinforcement for climbing on

Figure 25.4

This bar diagram reflects five phases of several teachers' attempts to reinforce climbing behavior in a preschool child. The open bars refer to all climbing responses; the shaded ones only to frame climbing. It may be seen that during the baseline period, when no social reinforcements were delivered to the child, he climbed less than 10 percent of the time. Subsequently, when he was given extensive reinforcements, he climbed more than 50 percent of the time, and this response extinguished (eighteenth through twenty-second days) after his climbing was ignored. During the second reinforcement phase, climbing resumed to a high and stable level, and this generalized to other playground apparatus when such responses were intermittently rewarded.

(Reprinted with permission from *Young Children*, Vol. 20, No. 1, October 1964. Copyright © 1964, National Association for the Education of Young Children)

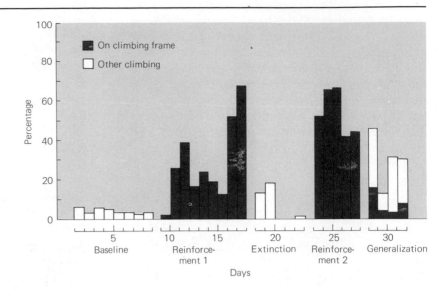

any other suitable object, as well as for vigorous and active play of all sorts. And, as may be seen from the final four-day period recorded in Figure 25.4, frame climbing weakened considerably, being largely replaced by other climbing activities. Generalizations of the reinforced activity to other play objects were not recorded by the investigators, but they reported "that climbing activities were thoroughly generalized" (Harris et al., 1969, p. 351).

Other studies that employed teachers or parents as reinforcing agents in behavior-oriented treatment programs have met with equally dramatic successes (see, for example, O'Leary et al., 1969; Patterson and Brodsky, 1969; Urban and Ford, 1972; Wolf et al., 1969).

Future Trends and Needs

Bert Brown, former head of the National Institute of Mental Health, once prophetically said that the new action programs for mental health will no longer be centered in the traditional clinics and hospitals, but rather in the cities and communities of our nation. Accordingly his advice to the mental health worker of the future was "go out into the community" (Brown, 1961, pp. 5–9).

This advice, as we indicated earlier, has not gone unheeded; various community-oriented innovative programs have been developed during the last decade. The main thrust of these programs has been to deliver mental health services to all the people, and as early as possible. But most of these approaches have been aimed at treatment, even, as was often the case, when they paid lip service to prevention as their primary goal. The goals for the future, in contrast, should be in the direction of prevention; or, to extend Brown's terse advice, we would suggest that the mental health worker of the future do as follows: "Go out into the community to solve the problems that predispose people to mental illness; and, while you're out there, get as much help as you can from available resources in the community."

Accomplishing these goals will require extensive *social planning, interagency cooperation, training of nonprofessionals,* and well-designed *planning and evaluative research* (NIMH, 1969, 1975). Let us look at these factors in turn to see how each could contribute to preventive mental health.

Social Planning

The history of many urban development projects and highway construction programs, to take just two examples, suggests that past social designing has not taken into consideration the consequences of such changes for people. If the cities are going to be fit for healthy human habitation, future planning must look beyond the bricks, mortar, concrete, and costs of such building programs.

Toward these ends the National Institute of Mental Health has made major commitments to support social policy training programs designed to equip city and community planners with a broad civic outlook. Furthermore NIMH has funded research aimed at teaching urban and regional planners how to build cities to meet people's interpersonal and psychological needs. These training and teaching programs are inter-disciplinary and involve architects, transportation experts, and administrators, as well as operations researchers, city planners, and psychologists.

A partial outgrowth of this concern about the effects on people of poor social design has been a relatively new subdiscipline of psychology variously called *environmental* or *ecological* psychology. Ecology is of course not a new discipline. In biology it is a well-established branch concerned with the mutual relatedness of species and their physical and biological environments. The community of plants and animals together with the corresponding inorganic environment is called the *ecosystem.* The fundamental basis of an ecosystem is a voluntary and involuntary cooperation that keeps flora, fauna, and other members of the system in perfect balance. The introduction into the ecosystem of a new or foreign agent, such as a pest or virus, can throw it out of balance.

The concern of ecological psychologists has been with the alterations and design of the human specie's environment that have damaged its survival capacities and have caused identifiable behavior abnormalities. Of particular concern have been the effects of increasing organization on people's behavior (Craik, 1970), and the central emphases have been on their capacities to *adapt* within these environments and the *interdependence* of living and nonliving elements within the ecosystem.

The environments within which the ecological perspective can be taken have been as large as the city (Craik, 1970) and as limited as public housing projects (Cooper, 1964), university dormitories (Hsia, 1967), elementary schools (Krasner and Krasner, 1973, 1978; Reiss, 1974), high schools (Kelly, 1966, 1968, 1969), and psychiatric wards (Ittelson, 1967). An example of one such approach, with the limited perspective of the classroom as environment, is presented below.

Inspired by the work of psychologist J. G. Kelly (1966, 1968, 1969), Steven Reiss and his associates (O'Neill, 1974; Reiss, 1974; Reiss and Dyhdalo, 1975) at the Chicago Circle campus of the University of Illinois conducted a number of studies in the classrooms of the Oak Park elementary school system. Their studies tested the effects of *open space* classroom environments and *open education* on children's adjustment in school. The term "open space" refers to an architectural concept in which several teachers and classes meet in a large area without walls; "open education" refers to a variety of practices that include self-directed learning and a humanistic attitude toward students (Walberg and Thomas, 1972). According to a series of studies, many of which are still in progress, some types of children fare better in open classes and others fare better in traditional classes. For example, creative children have healthier self-images in open classes than in traditional ones, whereas "nonpersistent" children have lower achievement in open classes than in traditional ones. Thus the ideal educational format would seem to be one that provides different types of environments for different types of children.

Interagency Cooperation

Among the major difficulties that joint social planning projects will encounter is gaining the cooperation of the various agencies and governmental groups that must inevitably become involved. For example, mental health agencies, public health services, schools, courts, churches, police, urban renewal planners, public housing authorities, and economic opportunity programs must cooperate with one another if progress is to be made. Such cooperation will not be easily achieved because the mix of workers is public, private, and voluntary, and the agencies are local, state, and federal.

Since most of these agencies are run by civil servants and others who are arranged in careful hierarchical relation to each other and are well trained to know and apply specific rules governing the allocation of money, land use, privilege, and influence, the directors of community mental health programs will need to know how to oper-

ate within these bureaucracies (Costello, 1970). This has been referred to as the "politics of mental health" (Connery, 1968), and understanding its intricacies will be essential for successful future programming.

Enlisting and Training Nonprofessionals

As we mentioned earlier in this chapter, there are a variety of ways in which personnel not primarily trained in mental health can be profitably used. We referred to parents, volunteers, and teachers as three possible kinds of resource personnel; but many more such nonprofessionals will be needed. Preferably they might be drawn from among the ranks of other "front line" social change agents and should include physicians, nurses, clergy, and police.

A most important resource, and one that has only recently begun to be tapped, is the worker who is indigenous to the locale. So far these people have been trained on the job mainly for work with delinquents, alcoholics, and drug users; in the future, they should also be employed for the care of the aged, infirm, physically handicapped, and unemployed—all of whom are prime candidates for emotional disruption.

The Training of New Professionals

Understandably many minority-group people will not or cannot go to therapists who are not familiar with their cultures. Many black patients, for example, will not willingly go to white therapists, although many black patients must go if black therapists are not available (cited in Kolb, 1977, pp. 371–372), and black clinicians are in short supply. One consequence has been that many mental health professionals have referred treatable black patients to state hospitals for custodial care.

A just solution to this problem would entail upgrading educational efforts available to blacks from prekindergarten through professional and graduate schools, but these efforts are floundering because of inadequate funding. In view of this situation it appears reasonable to use capable paraprofessionals as therapists, but, unfortunately, those working without adequate training, or without professional supervision, constitute an incomplete, second-class mental health delivery system.

Research

Clearly, the effectiveness of the preceding plans and programs must be stringently assessed beforehand by well-designed research. All too often, unfortunately, the plans have not been evaluated or have been evaluated long after the programs were launched. The Joint Commission on Mental Health of Children (1970, p. 22), recognizing the poor planning that has gone into many existing programs for children, made the following observation (also see Rhodes and Gibbins, 1972, p. 348):

They have been poorly coordinated with one another, meager in kind, and sometimes short lived. Often they have failed to reach those most in need. Too frequently they have been directed to special and separate problems rather than to the whole child and his family.

And looking beyond the child and the family, future research should be aimed at the *whole* community and its environs. One area of the community, for example, in which research is sorely needed is the human condition of those who are socially disenfranchised because of other people's attitudes toward members of their age, sex, social class, or race. In this regard Charles W. Thomas, a black psychologist at the Los Angeles Center of Racial and Social Issues, made the following observation (1971, p. 166): "No amount of humanistic disguise, in the way of social penalty for being too old, non-white, female, or having low test scores, will lessen the trauma for receiving treatment at an infrahuman level."

Thomas is particularly concerned with the black ghetto vis-à-vis the future of community

Community Mental Health Services to Minority Groups

It has become increasingly clear that minority group clients who seek psychotherapy receive discriminatory treatment from white therapists (see Padilla et al., 1975; Sue, 1977). Analyses of the services received by minority clients in numerous communities with mental health facilities suggested that ethnics received differential treatment and poorer outcomes than whites. But even in instances where black, Asian–American, Chicano, and native American clients receive treatment equal to that of white clients, poorer outcomes were reported, as measured by premature or abrupt termination rates. The factors believed to be responsible for these differential treatments and poorer outcomes are unresponsiveness of service modalities (even when equal) to ethnic clients' special needs, wide discrepancies in the socioeconomic and educational backgrounds of professionals and clients, and racism. (These explanations are highly speculative.) Solutions offered have been to extend the number of facilities available for minority groups, perhaps even building "separate but equal" agencies in order to cater to the special needs of some minorities, and to give special training to professional and paraprofessional staffs of existing community mental health centers.

psychology, and he suggested that community services include a variety of research activities in numerous locations: schools, social agencies, churches, health centers, housing projects, storefronts, or mobile units. Specifically he recommended that one of the main objectives of psychologists must be to gather, translate, and transmit research information.

Thus the community agency should be a place for "disseminating social science information through continuing education or cultural programs for children, youth, and adults"; it should serve "as a resource center for planning and developing programs based upon social science knowledge for community organizations and institutions"; it should be "an agency to evaluate new knowledge and to act upon it in developing pilot or demonstration programs"; and it should increase "social science utilization for achieving desired goals at the community level" (Thomas, 1971, p. 175). And in this regard Bert Brown (1975, p. IV) wrote that "it is through the close interplay between professionals interested in the community and the community's reciprocal interest and involvement . . . that programs can be translated into operational reality. It is only through this close interweaving between the community and the practitioner, the community and the researcher, and the community and the policymaker, that a relevant, significant, and meaningful mental health program can evolve."

In general, then, the task ahead for research is a formidable one. New avenues of investigation must be opened and older ones more fully explored; new preventive methods must be found and existing treatments must be further refined. Specifically we must also learn more about the effects of standard TV fare on violence in the streets, about human responses to social and physical density, and about the effects of increased urbanization on emotional stability. We must uncover the relationship between predisposition to psychiatric disorder and the present intrafamilial social structure, and we must be prepared to experiment with new modes of coping and living. And finally we must accept the tenet, as NIMH emphasized (1969, p. 120), that "the mental health of each citizen is affected by the maturity and health of our society—from the smallest unit to the largest."

Summary

Contemporary mental health services are the culmination of a long past of maltreatment for the emotionally disturbed. Almost from the beginning of recorded history, the mentally troubled person was banished from society and often cruelly treated because mental illness was thought to be caused by evil spirits. It was not until the third century B.C., at about the time of Hippocrates, that behavior abnormalities were thought of as consequences of natural phenomena and that the mentally ill began to be treated humanely.

But not long after the fall of the Greek and Roman cultures—during the Middle Ages—the longest period of recorded maltreatment of the mentally ill began and lasted well into the nineteenth and twentieth centuries. Of course there were gradual improvements in the official attitude, especially during the Renaissance, but it was not until the nineteenth century that the era of humane treatment began. This development was spurred by Pinel and Tuke in Europe and by Rush and Dix in the United States. But conditions were still deplorable in the twentieth century, according to Clifford Beers's autobiographical account, and did not improve until about 40 years ago.

The modern mental hospital, which has often been called a therapeutic community, still continues to provide a drab and tedious existence for many patients. Contemporary alternatives to complete institutionalization, mostly products of the 1960s, include home treatment, halfway houses, and open hospitals.

Another development of the 1960s and the 1970s is the community mental health concept:

that is, delivery of mental health care and consultative and educational services to all who seek it. Among the innovative outpatient facilities that have become possible as a result of large federal funding programs have been the all-purpose crisis intervention services, suicide prevention centers, and the use of nonprofessionals as psychotherapists.

Several future trends are discernible from developments that have occurred during the past several years: using local people to deal with the problems of their own communities and paying greater attention to considering the consequences of urban projects (buildings, highways) for the people. At the base of all future planning, however, is a continuing need to carry forward imaginative and thorough research that not only assesses the impact of mental health care and preventive programs, but also reaches out and includes the needs of all citizens.

Terms and Concepts to Master

Community mental
  health

Crisis intervention

Halfway house

Home treatment

Inpatient psychiatric
  services

Open hospital

Outpatient psychiatric
  center

Peer help center

Suicide prevention
  center

Therapeutic community

Glossary

abreaction. The release of previously repressed feelings and emotions (see *catharsis*).

acetylcholine. A chemical believed to transmit nerve impulses across neuronal gaps and used to lower blood pressure and increase digestive functions.

acrophobia. An irrational fear of height.

acute. Sudden in onset and of short duration. (see *chronic*).

adrenalin. Sometimes also called epinephrine, it is the hormone secreted by the adrenal glands.

affect. Emotion, feeling, or mood.

affective psychosis. A severe disturbance of mood accompanied by other psychotic symptoms (hallucinations, delusions).

agoraphobia. An irrational fear of being in open or public places.

alienation. A loss of involvement in or commitment to the world one lives in.

alpha wave conditioning. The process of learning to control one's EEG alpha waves (8 to 13 cycles per second) when provided with knowledge of results (see *alpha waves* and *biofeedback*).

alpha waves. The brain wave rhythm recorded on an *EEG* (see) when a person is in a state of wakeful relaxation.

Alzheimer's disease. A *presenile psychosis* (see) caused by early *atrophy* (see) of the brain.

amnesia. A loss of memory.

amotivational syndrome. A loss of interest and drive for doing things, supposedly as a result of recreational drug use.

amphetamines. Energizing drugs that cause euphoria, excessive self-confidence, and bursts of activity.

anaclitic depression. Dejection after separation from the mother in children between the ages of 4 and 10 months.

anal character. In psychoanalytic theory, the stingy, obstinate, and orderly adult whose fixations occurred during the second stage of psychosexual development.

anal stage. In psychoanalytic theory, the second psychosexual stage of development during which the anus is the child's focal area of erogenous interest.

analytical psychology. The name given by Jung to his theory of personality.

androgens. The hormones that develop and maintain masculine secondary sex characteristics.

androgyny. Behavior in which both the male (*andro-*) and the female (*-gyn*) sides of the personality are allowed expression, as opposed to behavior that is bent into conformity to a culturally prescribed sex role.

anogenital coitus. *Coitus* (See) in which a male achieves orgasm by penile thrusting in his partner's rectum.

anomaly. Something that doesn't fit, or doesn't

seem to make sense. Science historian T. S. Kuhn uses the term to describe an event that cannot be explained by existing scientific models, such as the apparent retrograde motion of planets, which did not fit the original Ptolemaic model of the solar system.

anorexia nervosa. An inability to take or to hold food in one's system.

anterograde amnesia. A memory loss for things that occurred *after* trauma or stress (see *retrograde amnesia*).

✳ **antisocial personality.** A disordered individual who manifests unreliable, irresponsible, and impulsive behavior (see *dyssocial personality*.)

✳ **anxiety disorder.** A disorder marked by chronic apprehension and panic.

aphasia. A language impairment due to cortical damage.

aphonia. A loss of voice.

archetypes. In Jung's theory of personality, the storehouses of unconscious images or thoughts that correspond to conscious happenings, and are presumably inherited from the cumulative experience of a person's ancestors and race and are believed to guide his modes of perceiving the world around him.

assertiveness training. A form of therapy for persons inhibited in their interpersonal aggressiveness, the goal being to elicit the inhibited responses under nonanxiety-evoking circumstances.

ataractics. See *major tranquilizers* and *minor tranquilizers*.

atherosclerosis. The hardening of the arterial walls—a lifelong process whose effects begin to show up in old age.

atrophy. Any diminution, wasting, or shrinking of muscle or organ tissue (see *Alzheimer's disease* and *presenile psychosis*).

authenticity. Genuineness; freedom from falseness, pretense, and self-reflexive censoring of speech and actions. Authenticity is the usual state of small children and can sometimes be seen in adults.

✳ **autism.** A form of fantasy thinking, sometimes denoting a particular infantile disorder marked by unusual and seemingly unmotivated strange behavior (see *infantile autism*).

autonomic nervous system. The part of the nervous system that includes all the neurons outside the spinal cord and brain, and which is divided into the *sympathetic* and *parasympathetic* branches (see).

aversive conditioning. The administration of a strong stimulus (usually electric shock) at the occurrence of undesired behavior for the purpose of extinguishing it.

BAC. Blood alcohol content. (See *blood alcohol level*.)

barbiturates. Depressant drugs that cause sedation and sleep.

behavior. Any response made by an organism, the responses of most interest to abnormal psychology being feelings, drives, impulses, emotions, and conscious and unconscious thinking.

behavior modification. See *behavior therapy*.

behavior therapy. A form of treatment in which principles of learning are applied to the removal of symptoms; alternatively called behavior modification.

behavioral assessment. A behaviorally oriented approach to psychodiagnosis, in which problem behaviors are classed as behavioral excesses, behavioral deficits, or inappropriateness.

behaviorism. A school of psychology that maintains that the most important units of behavior are observable responses.

biofeedback. A method of providing knowledge of results of internal responses by electronic means (sometimes also called reward learning).

✳ **bipolar depression.** An alternation of depressive and manic episodes.

blood-alcohol level. Alcohol concentration in the bloodstream.

brief psychotherapy. A shorter and more focused version of traditional psychotherapy.

castration anxiety. A psychoanalytic concept to describe a male's fear of emasculation.

catatonic schizophrenia. A category of schizophrenia in which the patient shows *waxy flexibility* (see) and, sometimes, a deep stupor followed by a stage of excitement.

catharsis. The release of pent-up feelings and emotions through either talking or acting-out.

central nervous system (CNS). The portion of the nervous system that includes the brain, spinal cord, and cerebrospinal fluid.

cerebellum. The brain structure that regulates voluntary movements and psychomotor balance.

cerebral cortex. The cerebrum's outer layer.

cerebrum. The main organic structure of the brain.

chemotherapy. See *pharmacotherapy*.

chorea. Irregular and spasmodic movements of the extremities or body.

chromosomes. Long, thin strands in each cell of an organism that contain *genes* (see).

chronic. Long standing and usually permanent. (see *acute*).

chronic alcoholic deterioration. Long-term effects of alcoholism; often marked by antisocial behavior, delusions of persecution, and lying.

clang association. Disordered speech marked and controlled by rhyming.

classical conditioning. A form of learning that takes place after a previously neutral stimulus is repeatedly paired with a response-evoking one (sometimes also called respondent conditioning).

claustrophobia. Irrational fear of being in closed places.

client-centered counseling. A form of *nondirective therapy* (see), most often associated with Carl Rogers, in which the client is given every opportunity to find his own solutions to his life problems.

closet queen. A homosexual who hides his sexual orientation.

coitus. Sexual intercourse, defined either narrowly as penile/vaginal coupling or broadly as any contact between the penis or clitoris of one person and any organ of another person, resulting directly in orgasm for at least one partner. (If it does not trigger an orgasm, it is usually classed as petting or foreplay.)

collective unconscious. See *objective psyche*.

coma. A state of profound loss of consciousness.

compensation. A defense mechanism designed, according to Alfred Adler, to help the individual overcome real or imaginary defects (see *overcompensation*).

compulsion. An urge to carry out some act or ritual.

concordance ratio. The percentage of persons related to a target individual who display traits similar to him.

conditioned response (CR). The response elicited as a result of repeated pairings of a *conditioned stimulus* with an *unconditioned stimulus* (see).

conditioned stimulus (CS). A previously neutral stimulus that, as a result of pairing with an *unconditioned stimulus* (see), acquires the property of eliciting a response.

confabulation. A main symptom of *Korsakov's psychosis* (see), in which a person fills in the gaps of his or her memory loss with false information.

congenital. Present at birth and possibly incurred during labor or while in the mother's body.

conversion hysteria. A disorder characterized by paralysis or loss of vision, hearing, or other sensory processes.

counterconditioning. Any of a number of procedures in which an antagonistic response is conditioned in order to compete with and eliminate an undesired response (see *reciprocal inhibition*).

countertransference. In psychoanalytic theory, the tendency of the therapist to allow his own feelings and personality traits to determine some of his reactions to his patient.

cue. According to Dollard and Miller's personality theory, any stimulus (internal or external), that directs the person's behavior.

culture. A society's shared beliefs, attitudes, and behaviors.

cyclothymic personality. A personality type whose behavior alternates between elated and dejected moods.

decompensation. An inability to mobilize sufficient energy to function properly.

deconditioning. See *extinction*.

defense mechanism. In psychoanalytic theory, the ego's ways of defending itself against threatening or anxiety-evoking thoughts and impulses.

delirium. The confusion and disorientation often associated with high fever or drug states.

delirium tremens (DTs). An advanced stage of alcoholism characterized by frightening hallucinations and coarse tremors (the shakes).

delusion. A false but persistent belief.

delusion of grandeur. The false belief that one is a great or wealthy person.

delusion of persecution. The false belief that others intend to harm one.

denial. An ego-defense mechanism that involves a refusal to acknowledge the reality of certain threatening circumstances (see *repression*).

deoxyribonucleic acid (DNA). The determinant of heredity within the genes.

dependency. When physical, characterized by *tolerance* to and *withdrawal* from a substance; when psychological, by a repeated seeking out of alcohol or other drugs in order to cope with everyday existence.

depersonalization. A belief that one has undergone a profound change, referring sometimes to an organ, or organ system, and at other times to the loss of one's identity.

depressants. See *barbiturates*.

depression. Feelings of dejection, sadness, and worthlessness.

depressive disorder. A disorder in which sadness, dejection, and agitation predominate.

depth psychology. A school of psychological thought that probes into the motivational bases for behavior (see *intrapsychic model*.)

desensitization. See *systematic desensitization*.

deviance. Departure from the *norm* (see).

displacement. A defense, according to psychoanalytic theory, by means of which one may express anger or any other emotion toward a substitute (and safer) figure.

dissociative hysteria. A form of neurosis marked by sleepwalking, loss of memory, or multiple personality (see *amnesia, conversion hysteria, fugue, hysteria, multiple personality, somnambulism*).

dizygotic (DZ) twins. Fraternal twins.

DNA. See *deoxyribonucleic acid*.

dominant gene. The gene that determines the *phenotype* (see) regardless of the nature of the gene with which it is paired (see *recessive gene*).

dopamine (DA). The precursor of the neurotransmitter norepinephrine. Low levels of dopamine are associated with Parkinson's disease, and high levels may be associated with schizophrenia.

double bind. A term coined by Gregory Bateson to describe a situation in which a person is "damned if he does and damned if he doesn't."

double-blind. A research design in which both the subjects and the experimenters do not know (that is, are blind to) which treatment is being given to which subject.

drives. May be separated into *primary drives* (hunger, thirst, warmth) and *secondary drives* (money, prestige, power), but usually referring to any condition that impels the organism in certain directions.

drug therapy. See *pharmacotherapy*.

dysfunction. The disordered functioning of a bodily organ or system.

dyspareunia. Painful intercourse.

dyssocial personality. A disordered individual whose destructive acts are a product of his or her environment. (see *antisocial personality*).

echolalia. The repetition of another's word or phrase.

echopraxia. The repetition of another's action or gesture.

EEG. The abbreviation for *electroencephalogram*, which is the graphic record of brain wave activity taken by the *electroencephalograph*.

ego. The mediator between inner impulses (*id*) and external reality (*superego*), according to Freudian psychoanalytic personality theory.

ejaculatory incompetence. Inability of a male to ejaculate intravaginally.

Electra complex. Female counterpart of the *Oedipus complex* (see).

electroencephalogram (EEG). See *EEG*.

electroencephalograph. The instrument to record the *EEG* (see *EEG*).

electroshock therapy (EST). A somatic treatment in which convulsions are produced by electroshocking the individual's temporal areas.

emetic. Having the ability to cause vomiting.

emetine. A bitter alkaloid that can cause vomiting and is used as an *emetic*.

empirical. Based on experience rather than theory.

encopresis. Persistent soiling by a child over 2 years of age.

encounter group. A group experience designed to foster greater interpersonal competence (an outgrowth of group therapy and social psychological theory).

endocrine glands. Ductless glands that regulate bodily organs involved in emotion by secreting hormones directly into the blood stream or lymphatic system.

endogenous. Originating within the person (see *exogenous*).

endogenous depression. Depression in response to an as yet unknown internal process, as opposed to *reactive depression* (see).

enuresis. Failure to control daytime and nighttime urination in a child older than about 5 years.

epidemiology. The study of the spread, incidence, prevalence, and distribution of illness among people.

epilepsy. An organic disorder characterized by random neuronal discharges from a hyperexcitable region of the brain.

epinephrine. See *adrenalin*.

erogenous zones. Any areas of the anatomy particularly susceptible to sexual arousal.

estrogens. The hormones that are responsible for and control feminine secondary sex characteristics (see *androgens*).

ethnocentrism. The habit of assuming that the patterns of one's own culture are the only way humans can behave and that if a different pattern exists anywhere, it is due to deficiency or aberration.

ethology. The branch of zoology that studies animal behavior, usually in its natural setting.

etiology. The science of the study of causation; also refers to the identification of causal agents.

euphoria. Elatedness.

exhibitionism. Deriving erotic pleasure by publicly displaying one's body or genitals.

existential therapy. A form of treatment that places great emphasis on the here and now and on fully participating in being.

exogenous. Originating from without the organism (see *endogenous*).

exorcism. The expulsion of evil spirits either by

ritual or, as in medieval Europe, by torture and burning at the stake.

experience. Whatever enters into an individual's awareness, including sensations, feelings, perceptions, thoughts, and memories. Experience (as opposed to unverified theory) is also the basis of all empirical approaches to knowledge.

extinction. The elimination of a conditioned response by the withholding of reinforcement.

extraversion. Outer-orientedness (see *introversion*).

family therapy. A form of treatment in which the whole family is seen either together or separately for the purpose of helping one or more of its problem members.

fantasy. The gratification of one's desires by creating an imaginary world.

fetishism. Sexual gratification through erotic attachments to inanimate objects or to portions of the body.

flight of ideas. Disordered thinking characterized by speech that digresses from one topic to the next.

flooding. See *implosive therapy*.

folie à deux. Two persons (usually related) who live together sharing the same paranoid delusional ideas.

free association. A psychoanalytic technique in which the patient is encouraged to tell everything that comes into his or her mind.

fugue. A form of "flight" that involves unexpected wandering off.

functional psychosis. A severe behavior disorder in which organic factors are not implicated (see *organic psychosis*).

functional shift. A physiological change of the organism to which depressive disorders have been attributed.

general adaptation syndrome. Hans Selye's concept that describes the organism's reaction to excessive or traumatic stress.

general paresis. The third stage of syphilis, which is manifested by intellectual and personality deterioration.

genes. Molecular structures located in the chromosomes that transmit physical and psychological characteristics from one generation to the next.

genotype. One's entire genetic complement, including observable and hidden physical and psychological characteristics (see *phenotype*).

Gestalt therapy. A type of treatment that emphasizes the here and now and restoring a person's wholeness by getting him in touch with all the fragmented parts of his personality (see *existential therapy*).

grand mal. An epileptic seizure marked by violent spasmodic convulsions (see *petit mal*).

group therapy. A form of treatment that deals with two or more patients at a time and is intended to complement individual psychotherapy.

halfway house. A transitional residential facility that serves as a bridge between the hospital and the community.

hallucination. The perception of nonexistent stimuli: auditory, visual, olfactory, gustatory, or tactile.

hallucinogens. Hallucination-producing drugs (see *psychotomimetic drugs*).

hebephrenic schizophrenia. A disorder in which inappropriate affect, impulsiveness, and silliness are the chief symptoms.

homeostasis. A drive of the organism to maintain a state of equilibrium.

hormone. Substance secreted into the blood stream by the endocrine, or ductless, glands (see *endocrine glands*).

human relations training. See *encounter group*.

humanistic-existential therapies. The name sometimes given to the newer psychotherapies that emphasize the importance of positive mental health, *authenticity*, and *self-actualization* (see).

Huntington's chorea. A hereditary condition carried by a single dominant gene, which does not usually show up until about the fifth decade of life and is marked by involuntary spastic movements and mental and personality deterioration.

hyperactivity. A supposed neurological impairment proposed as an explanation for high levels of activity in some children in the classroom.

hyperglycemia. A high concentration of sugar in the blood serum, which may cause behavioral symptoms.

hyperkinesis. A rare neurological disease characterized by high levels of activity independent of the setting or situation.

hypertension. Elevated blood pressure.

hyperthyroidism. An endocrine disorder in which there is an overactivity of thyroid secretion; characterized by restlessness, irritability, insomnia, and heightened reactivity (see *hypothyroidism*).

hypochondriasis. An irrational fear that one is afflicted with a disorder.

hypoglycemia. Low concentration of sugar in the blood serum, which may cause shock and coma (see *hyperglycemia* and *insulin shock therapy*).

hypomania. A mild degree of overactivity.

hypothalamus. The nuclei of the brain, just below the thalamus, that control most autonomic functions.

hypothyroidism. An endocrine disorder in which there is underactivity of the thyroid; marked by emotional dulling and a decline in intelligence (see *hyperthyroidism*).

✳ **hysteria.** A form of neurosis in which the person suffers a loss of function without any organic basis or in which he or she loses memory or develops a multiple personality (see *conversion hysteria* and *dissociative hysteria*).

id. A component of personality, which, according to psychoanalysis, is the pleasure-seeking source of psychic energy and houses the *libido* (see) and other instinctual forces of humans.

identification. In psychoanalysis, the adoption of another's qualities and behaviors (see *introjection*).

illusion. A misperception of stimuli.

impasse. In Gestalt therapy, the point at which a person is stuck.

implosive therapy. A method for extinguishing anxiety by a saturation exposure to the feared stimulus situation or its substitute (also called flooding).

impotence. Inability of a male to acquire an erection and retain it long enough to complete an act of *coitus* (see).

incidence. The number of new cases of a disorder during a specified time period, such as a year. (see *prevalence*.)

individual psychology. The name given by Alfred Adler to his personality theory.

infantile autism. Extreme fantasy and bizarre behavior in a young child.

inferiority feelings. An Alderian concept that traces man's inherent feelings of helplessness to his relative smallness.

instrumental conditioning. See *operant conditioning*.

✳ **insulin shock therapy (IST).** Now used infrequently, and mostly with schizophrenics, a procedure that involves inducing hypoglycemic comas to shock the system.

intelligence quotient (IQ). A concept that takes into account one's mental age (MA) and one's chronological age (CA), the ratio between them yielding an approximate assessment of the level of intellectual functioning.

interaction model. An explanation of human behavior in terms of the impact on a child of his or her family's patterns of interaction, especially their patterns of communication and their role expectations.

intrapsychic model. An explanation of human behavior in terms of largely unconscious drives or motivations.

introjection. The process of incorporating, according to Freudian theory, another person's behaviors, ethos, and characteristics (see *identification*).

introversion. Inner-orientedness (see *extraversion*).

involutional melancholia. Depression during the mid-life years.

ischemic pain. A type of pain induced by cutting off the supply of blood to a region of the anatomy.

kleptomania. An overwhelming urge or compulsion to steal.

Korsakov's psychosis. An advanced stage of chronic alcoholism marked primarily by memory defects and hallucinations (see *confabulation*).

labile. Emotionally instable and experiencing rapid and apparently unmotivated mood swings.

latency stage. A relatively nonsexual phase of development, according to psychoanalysis, that is a result of repressing prior impulses and experiences.

leucotomy. See *lobotomy*.

libido. A psychoanalytic concept to represent the portion of the *id* (see) that is the sexual energy of the human personality.

lithium carbonate treatment. Treatment of manic episodes by using a salt substance.

lobectomy. Now a rarely performed operation, it involves the removal of a portion of the cerebral (usually frontal) lobe in order to alter undesired behavior (see *psychosurgery*).

lobotomy. A surgical procedure, (see *psychosurgery*) now rare, that usually involves severing the corticothalamic nerve fibers in order to alter undesired behavior.

LSD. A hallucinogenic substance that produces psychosis-like reactions in some persons.

lysergic acid diethylamide-25. See *LSD*.

manic-depressive psychosis. Although often diagnosed while a person is in the elated (manic) phase of this disorder, it is also characterized by a deep mood swing into the depressed phase.

masochism. Obtaining sexual gratification by being bound, whipped, humiliated, or otherwise subjected to pain.

maternal deprivation. Absence in an infant's life of the kind of loving, nurturing care normally provided by a mother.

medical model. A view in abnormal psychology that uses the disease concept of mental illness.

mental age (MA). The level of one's intellectual functioning without regard to one's chronological age (see *intelligence quotient*).

meprobamates. The generic term for antianxiety muscle-relaxing drugs; sometimes called *minor tranquilizers*.

methadone maintenance. A program of drug treatment that uses methadone, a narcotic, to cure the heroin habit; its effects are supposedly weaker than those of heroin.

milieu therapy. A treatment similar to that occuring in a *therapeutic community* (see) in that several people make a concerted effort to help the patient recover.

model, behavioral. A person whose behavior is observed and imitated in social learning.

model, scientific. A pattern, schema, or formula that is believed to represent the way some part of the natural world works.

modeling. A behavior modification technique that provides patients with examples of persons performing the desired responses. Sometimes also called vicarious learning.

monoamine oxidase (MAO) inhibitors. Psychoactive substances used to treat depression.

monozygotic (MZ) twins. Identical twins.

multiple personality. A form of massive amnesia in which a person's memory for his identity is partially or totally lost and he adopts new identities.

mutism. An inability to talk, but usually referring to the seemingly negativistic tendency of some catatonic schizophrenics to refuse to speak despite the presence of normal speech mechanisms.

myotonia. Muscular tension, usually in the genitals and elsewhere in the pelvic region, as a component of sexual arousal. (See *vasocongestion.*)

necrophilia. Sexual interest in corpses.

negative reinforcement. The application of a noxious or aversive stimulus in association with an undesired response in order to extinguish it.

neo-Freudians. A term reserved for many of the personality theorists whose orientation, with minor or major modifications, is still psychoanalytic.

neologism. A new word, especially if coined by a psychotic person.

neurosis. An abnormality marked by maladaptive coping mechanisms designed to defend against anxiety. (Plural is neuroses.)

neurotransmitter. A substance synthesized and stored in the presynaptic nerve ending at the end of the axon and released into the synaptic space upon arrival of the nerve impulse, whereupon it reacts with a postsynaptic receptor in the dendrite of the next neuron, thereby transmitting the impulse to that neuron.

nondirective therapy. Sometimes alternatively called *client-centered counseling* (see), an approach in which the therapist encourages the client to determine the direction of therapy.

noradrenalin. See *norepinephrine.*

norepinephrine. A hormone found at the nerve endings of the *sympathetic autonomic nervous system* (see).

norm. A comparison group in terms of which the test scores of new respondents may be compared.

normal distribution. (or *normal curve*). The bell-shaped arrangement of scores or traits along a continuum.

nosology. The study of the classification of things, objects, or diseases.

nurture. The influence of environment on development ("nature versus nurture" is the controversy over the relative importance of heredity and environment in causing abnormalities or any other traits).

nymphomania. An "excessive" sexual drive in a female.

objective psyche. Jung's term for the sum total of a person's inherited memories; earlier called the collective unconscious.

objectivity (of tests). A test is objective when its administration, scoring, and interpretation are independent of the tester's subjectivity.

obsession. A recurring thought, idea, or tune that intrudes itself against one's will.

obsessive-compulsive disorder. A form of disorder in which a person must cope with persistent and repetitive intrusions of unwanted ideas and urges.

Oedipus complex. The psychoanalytic notion that sons fall in love with their mothers (and daughters with their fathers) during the phallic stage of psychosexual development.

operant behavior therapy. A form of *behavior therapy* (see) that has its origins in the principles of learning developed by B. F. Skinner and his followers.

operant conditioning. A form of learning that occurs as a result of obtaining reinforcement after a response is emitted; the response is said to be instrumental in obtaining reinforcement (sometimes also called instrumental conditioning).

opiates. Drugs resembling or derived from opium (see *narcotics*).

oral character. In psychoanalytic theory, one whose sexual conflicts were not satisfactorily resolved during the first stage of psychosexual development.

oral stage. In psychoanalytic theory, the first phase of psychosexual development, marked by the organism's main erotic interest in sucking.

organic psychosis. A severe behavior disorder triggered by identifiable organ (usually brain) damage or by toxicity (see *functional psychosis*).

orgasmic dysfunction. Inability of a female to experience orgasm through specified forms of sexual stimulation.

orogenital coitus. *Coitus* (see) in which one partner uses his or her lips and tongue to bring the other partner to orgasm, specifically by sucking a male partner's penis (fellatio) or by licking a female partner's clitoris (cunnilingus).

overcompensation. The defense mechanism, according to Alfred Adler, used by some persons to more than counterbalance a perceived or real defect (see *compensation*).

paradigm. (See *model, scientific*.)

paranoia. A form of psychosis in which the individual entertains a complex and intricate persecutory delusional system.

paranoid personality. The type of person whose suspiciousness, jealousies, and feelings of persecution are somewhat more intense than those of most people (see *paranoia, paranoid states*).

paranoid schizophrenia. The most common form of schizophrenia, characterized primarily by suspiciousness that is not necessarily focused on one person.

paranoid states. Psychotic disorders in which delusions, usually persecutory, predominate.

parasympathetic autonomic nervous system. The division that conserves body energy and operates antagonistically to the sympathetic branch.

pathology. An undesirable deviation from the norm (see *deviance* and *norm*), or the presence of an unhealthy laboratory or clinical finding.

PCP. Phencyclidine, also called "angel dust." A barbiturate with dangerous side effects.

pedophilia. A preference for children as sex objects.

peer counseling. Counseling of students by student volunteers who are trained and supervised by professionals.

peptic ulcer. A psychophysiological symptom marked by inflammation of the stomach walls.

petit mal. An epileptic seizure that is less violent than the convulsions of a *grand mal* (see).

phallic stage. In Freudian theory, the third infantile psychosexual stage when the genitals are the center of libidinal discharge and when the Oedipus (male) and Electra (female) complexes occur.

chemo

pharmacotherapy. The use of psychoactive drugs to treat behavior disorders.

phenomenology. An attempt, formulated largely by Edmund Husserl, to cut through the numerous presuppositions on which existing sciences are built to an absolutely valid knowledge of things that would be grounded in experience itself and expressed in philosophy, which would also be a rigorous science.

phenotype. The surface, or observable components, of one's genetic endowment (see *genotype*).

phobia. Irrational fear of objects, events, or situations (see also *anxiety* and *fear*).

phobic disorder. A type of abnormality in which one is preoccupied with disease, germs, and diet.

pituitary gland. The master endocrine gland that controls other endocrines and influences metabolism, growth, and other autonomic functions.

placebo effect. In experiments, the therapeutic effect gained through the use of harmless substances given as drugs to patients.

play therapy. An action-oriented treatment approach often used with children.

pleasure principle. According to Freudian theory, the guiding force that influences some persons to pursue gratifying experiences and avoid pain.

polymorphous perverse sexuality. Freud's term for the normal sexuality of an infant. It is polymorphous (having many forms) in the sense that an infant responds erotically to many different kinds of contact. It is also therefore—in Freud's eyes—perverse, since it is operative with many objects and in many acts as opposed to adult sexuality, which Freud saw as limiting itself to genital activity aimed at procreation.

posthypnotic suggestion. The mechanism that produces behaviors that have been suggested to subjects during their trance states.

precipitating cause. The conditions immediately preceding a behavioral abnormality (see *predisposing cause*).

preconscious. Areas of the mind not immediately accessible to the organism, but containing desires, wishes, and thoughts that may be made easily available.

predisposing cause. Any combination of long-term factors, either physical or psychological, that makes someone vulnerable to a behavioral abnormality.

premature ejaculation. A persistent pattern in a male of ejaculating either before penetrating his partner or so soon thereafter that the partner is denied the opportunity to enjoy the act.

presenile psychosis. A severe behavior abnormality caused by premature *atrophy* (see) of brain tissue, usually occurring at about the fifth or sixth decade of life (see *Alzheimer's disease*).

prevalence. The number of cases of a disorder (including both new and old cases) during a specified time period. (see *incidence.*)

primal scene. In Freudian theory, the first time that the child views his or her parents making love, but according to Janov's *Primal Theory*, any significant traumatic event early in the child's life.

Primal Therapy. Janov's treatment form in which early significant and traumatic experiences are the focus of therapeutic attention.

primary process thinking. According to Freud, a form of thinking guided by the pleasure principle.

primary reinforcer. Any stimulus that directly satisfies any of the organism's basic needs—for example, food, water, heat.

proband. A target, or index, case in genetic research.

process schizophrenia. An endpoint on a continuum of schizophrenia, characterizing the more chronic form of the disorder, the other endpoint being *reactive schizophrenia,* which is marked by an acute onset of the psychosis.

prognosis. The forecast of the probable course and outcome of an abnormality.

progressive muscular relaxation. A technique that involves tensing and then relaxing a series of muscles.

projection. A psychoanalytic term to describe the attribution to others of one's own undesirable wishes, thoughts, and traits.

projective technique. Any of a number of techniques that use ambiguous, or unstructured stimuli such as inkblots, pictures, or incomplete sentences to reveal personality.

psychedelic drug. Any of the *hallucinogens* (see) or so-called mind-expanding psychoactive substances (see *LSD*).

psychoactive drugs. The chemical substances that alter mood, perception, or consciousness.

psychoanalysis. Freud's term for the therapy that he devised, which is also a research method and a theory of personality.

psychodiagnosis. The process of identifying and labeling psychological disorders.

psychodrama. A form of role-playing therapy: each person is given scenes in which he or she may act out parts that are personally meaningful.

psychogenic. Having psychological or environmental origins.

psychomotor epilepsy. An epileptic seizure

similar to a petit mal seizure except that it involves repetitive lip-smacking, chewing, gagging, retching, or swallowing.

psychopath (or **sociopath**). See *antisocial personality.*

psychopathology. The study of abnormal behavior.

psychopharmacology. Study of the effects of drugs on behavior.

psychophysiological disorders. Somatic symptoms, usually in the viscera, that have psychological causes.

psychosexual stages. The chronological periods through which, according to Freud, each person passes, with corresponding shifts in the focus of erogenous interest—the mouth, anus, and genitals—as the center of erotic pleasure.

psychosis. A disorder marked by severe disturbances of perception, thinking, and communication.

psychosurgery. A form of brain operation, now rare, in which fibers are severed in order to change undesired behavior (see *lobectomy* and *lobotomy*).

psychotherapy. A psychological treatment method that evolved from the two-person interview.

psychotic depression. A deep dejection accompanied by defective reality testing.

psychotomimetic drugs. Psychoactive substances that produce symptoms similar to those of the psychoses.

rationalization. The giving of good rather than correct reasons for one's behavior.

Raynaud's disease. A psychophysiologial disorder marked by cold hands and feet caused by poor blood circulation to the extremities.

reaction formation. In psychoanalytic theory, a defense mechanism in which one behaves in a manner that conceals one's real, but unconscious, intention.

reactive depression. Depression in reaction to external events such as a personal loss. (See *endogenous depression.*)

reactive schizophrenia. The acute form of schizophrenia, at the opposite end of the continuum from *process schizophrenia* (see).

recessive gene. The gene that does not produce the phenotype when paired with a *dominant gene* (see).

reciprocal inhibition. The name given by Wolpe to a form of behavior therapy that involves pairing nonanxiety-evoking responses with anxiety-eliciting stimuli (see also *counterconditioning* and *systematic desensitization*).

regression. A retreat to an earlier stage of psychosexual development.

reinforcement. A reward that serves to strengthen the conditioned response.

reliability. Psychometric terminology for a test's ability to yield consistent results with repeated trials.

remission. The improvement or reduction of symptoms (see *spontaneous remission*).

repression. The most basic of defense mechanisms, by means of which, according to Freudian theory, one unconsciously denies, ignores, or forgets threatening memories.

resistance. In psychoanalytic therapy, the tendency of some patients to hold back from disclosing important information.

respondent behavior therapy. A form of *behavior therapy* (see) that has its origins in Pavlov's classical conditioning experiments.

respondent conditioning. See *classical conditioning.*

reticular formation. Nuclei in the brain that control the organism's arousal mechanisms.

retrograde amnesia. A forgetfulness for events or things that were known before sustaining physical or psychological trauma.

reward learning. See *biofeedback.*

sadism. Obtaining sexual gratification through cruelty to one's partner.

satyriasis. An "excessive" sexual drive in a male.

schizoid personality. A withdrawn and shy disposition.

schizophrenia. A large category of psychoses that includes a group of disorders marked by severe disturbances of thinking, mood, and behavior.

school phobia. An irrational fear of attending school.

secondary process thinking. In Freudian theory, thinking that is inhibited by constraining forces.

secondary reinforcer. A stimulus that takes on its reinforcing properties because of association with a *primary reinforcer* (see).

self-actualization. The realization of one's full potential as a human being.

self-monitoring. A technique in which an individual under treatment records his or her own behavior and events that precede and follow the specified behavior.

sensate focus. A homework assignment given by Masters and Johnson to couples in sex therapy and aimed at developing moment-by-moment awareness of sensory pleasure partly by the permission given to enjoy it and partly by removing the distraction of goal-seeking behavior, such as pressure to maintain erection or achieve orgasm.

sensory deprivation. The restriction of sensory stimulation so that one's experiences are limited.

serotonin. An organic substance present in the limbic system of the brain and other tissue that is believed to be important in the regulation of emotional states.

sex reassignment. A surgical procedure designed to transform people into anatomic approximations of the opposite sex.

shaping. A procedure of Skinnerian, or operant, conditioning in which a response is created by reinforcing successive approximations of the behavior desired.

shared paranoid disorder. See *Folie à deux*.

simple schizophrenia. A disorder involving a reduction of interests in things and people.

social learning. Learning by observing and imitating others.

socialization. The process by which a child learns to be a member of his or her society.

sociopath (or **psychopath**). See *antisocial personality*.

somatic treatment. Any of a number of therapies that use physical means to produce behavior change.

somnambulism. Sleepwalking, which is commonly seen among those suffering from *dissociative hysteria* (see).

spontaneous recovery. A learning term that refers to the tendency of responses to recur after they have been extinguished (see *extinction*).

spontaneous remission. The improvement of a condition or the reduction of symptoms without therapy.

standard deviation. A computed departure of many scores from a given arithmetic mean.

standard scores. The arrangement of a set of raw scores according to a common average and *standard deviation* (see).

standardization (of tests). The creation of uniform conditions for test administration, scoring, and interpretation.

stimulus generalization. The tendency of stimuli similar to the conditioned one (see *conditioned stimulus*) to elicit a *conditioned response* (see).

stress. A traumatic physical or psychological circumstance that strains one's adaptive mechanisms.

stupor. A state of reduced consciousness just short of *coma* (see).

sublimation. A psychoanalytic term to describe the channeling of forbidden impulses into socially approved activities.

superego. In psychoanalytic theory, the sum total of the parental and societal teachings incorporated during growing up.

suppression. A conscious pushing out of memory (see *repression*).

sympathetic autonomic nervous system. The division that readies the organism for "fight or flight" and is antagonistic to the parasympathetic branch.

symptom. A clinically observable clue of a larger disturbance.

symptomatic alcoholism. The form of alcoholism that occurs when drinking is a symptom of neuroticism, psychoticism, or some other type of psychiatric disorder.

synapse. The gap between one neuron (nerve cell) and another, across which neural impulses must be transmitted.

syndrome. A cluster of symptoms that form a behavior disorder.

systematic desensitization. The gradual exposure of a patient to a feared stimulus or its substitution in an effort to extinguish his or her anxiety response.

taraxein. A toxic substance found in the blood of some schizophrenics.

taxonomy. The science of classification.

T-group. See *encounter group*.

Thanatos. The death instinct, as postulated by Freud.

THC. Tetrahydrocannabinol, the psychoactive ingredient in marijuana and hashish.

therapeutic community. A psychiatric hospital environment that aids in reducing behavior pathology.

tic. An involuntary spasmodic movement.

token economy. A behavior modification technique in which redeemable tokens are given as reinforcements for desired responses.

tolerance. A physiological adaptation to a substance.

topectomy. See *lobectomy*.

transactional analysis (TA). A form of therapy developed by psychiatrist Eric Berne and usually done in a group setting, with an emphasis on "parent," "child," and "adult" as components of the personality, as well as learned roles. One of the techniques is "scripting," an analysis of the life script that a person is acting out.

transference. In psychoanalytic theory, the patient's tendency to attribute characteristics of significant others in his or her life (e.g., parents or spouses) to the therapist.

transsexual. One who has undergone surgery to change his or her sex.

transvestism. The desire or need to dress in the clothing of the opposite sex.

troilism. Sexual intercourse among at least three persons or in the presence of at least one spectator.

unconditioned response (UR). An innate, or reflex, reaction.

unconditioned stimulus (US). A stimulus that has the property of eliciting a reflex or unlearned reaction.

unconscious. In Freudian theory, the inaccessible portions of personality, which can be brought into consciousness.

undoing. The performing of a ritual in order to wipe out a previous thought or action.

unipolar depression. A succession of depressive episodes with no manic episodes.

vaginismus. A spasmodic contraction of the vaginal orifice that makes sexual intercourse difficult and painful.

validity. A psychometric term that refers to a test's ability to measure what it sets out to measure.

vasocongestion. Engorgement of the genitals and other pelvic tissues with blood, as a component of sexual arousal. (See *myotonia*.)

vicarious learning. See *modeling*.

voyeurism. The obtaining of erotic pleasure by viewing the body or genitals of another.

waxy flexibility. A malleability displayed by catatonic schizophrenics that allows them to be placed and to remain in any position, no matter how uncomfortable.

withdrawal illness. A physical manifestation following cessation of drug use and characterized by anxiety, restlessness, nausea, and sometimes death.

word salad. Words thrown together by a disordered person in a way that seems meaningless to others.

XYY syndrome. A chromosomal anomaly among some males presumably related to delinquent behavior.

zoophilia. Sexual interest in animal species other than the human.

References

AAMD (American Association on Mental Deficiency). *Manual on terminology and classification in mental retardation*. Rev. ed., Grossman, H. J. (ed.). Special Publication Series No. 2, 11+. Washington, D.C., 1974.

AA World Services. *Alcoholics Anonymous: the story of how thousands of men and women have recovered from alcoholism.* 3rd ed. New York: AA World Services, 1976.

Abbott, S., and Love, B. Lecture on lesbianism at the University of Pittsburgh Student Union, February 1972.

———. *Sappho was a right-on woman: a liberated view of lesbianism.* New York: Stein & Day, 1973.

Abraham, K. *Selected papers on psychoanalysis.* London: Hogarth, 1927.

———. The influence of oral eroticism on character formation (1924). In Jones, E. (ed.), *Selected papers of Karl Abraham, M.D.* The International Psychoanalytic Library, Vol. 13. London: Hogarth, 1949.

Abramson, H. A. *Somatic and psychiatric treatment of asthma.* Baltimore: Williams & Wilkins, 1951.

———. *The use of LSD in psychotherapy and alcoholism.* Indianapolis: Bobbs-Merrill, 1967.

Abramson, L. Y., Seligman, M. E. P., and Teasdale, J. D. Learned helplessness in humans: Critique and reformulation. *Journal of Abnormal Psychology*, 1978, 87, 49–74.

Achilles, N. The development of the homosexual bar as an institution. In Gagnon J. H., and Simon, W. (eds.), *Sexual deviance.* New York: Harper & Row, 1967, pp. 228–244.

Ackerman, N. W. *The psychodynamics of family life.* New York: Basic Books, 1958.

———. Emergence of family psychotherapy on the present scene. In Stein, M. I. (ed.), *Contemporary psychotherapies.* New York: Free Press, 1961(a), pp. 228–244.

———. Further comments on family psychotherapy. In Stein, M. I. (ed.), *Contemporary psychotherapies.* New York: Free Press, 1961(b), pp. 245–255.

Adams, R. D. The anatomy of memory mechanisms in the human brain. In Talland, G. A., and Wangh, N. C. (eds.), *The pathology of memory.* New York: Academic Press, 1969.

Adelson, D., and Kalis, B. L. (eds.). *Community psychology and mental health: perspectives and challenges.* New York: Intext, 1970.

Adler, A. *Study of organ inferiority and its physical compensation.* New York: Nervous and Mental Diseases Publishing, 1917.

———. *Practice and theory of individual psychology.* New York: Harcourt Brace Jovanovich, 1927.

———. *The science of living.* New York: Greenberg, 1929.

———. *Social interest.* New York: Putnam, 1939.

Aguilera, D. C., Messick, J. M., and Farrell, M. S. *Crisis intervention: theory and methodology.* St. Louis: Mosby, 1970.

Ahammer, I. M., and Baltes, P. B. Objective versus perceived age differences in personality: How do adolescents, adults, and older people view themselves and each other? *Journal of Gerontology*, 1972, 27, 46–51.

Ainsworth, M. D. S. The development of infant–mother attachment. In Caldwell, B. M., and Riccuiti, H. N. (eds.), *Review of Child Development Research*, Vol. 3. Chicago: University of Chicago Press, 1973.

Albee, G. W. Emerging concepts of mental illness and models of treatment: the psychological point of view. *American Journal of Psychiatry*, 1969, 125, 870–876.

———. Does including psychotherapy in health insurance represent a subsidy to the rich from the poor? *American Psychologist*, 1977, 32, 719–721.

———. The next revolution: primary prevention of psychopathology. *The Clinical Psychologist*, Spring 1979, 32, No. 3, 16 and 23.

Alcohol and Alcoholism. Washington, D.C.: Government Printing Office, 1972.

Alcohol and Health. Washington, D.C.: Government Printing Office, 1974.

Alexander, F. The indications for psychoanalytic therapy. *Bulletin of the New York Academy of Medicine*, 1944, 20, 319–332.

———. *Psychosomatic medicine: its principles and applications.* New York: Norton, 1950.

Allgeyer, J. Using groups in out-patient settings. *International Journal of Group Psychotherapy*, 1973, 23, 217–222.

Allman, L. R. Apple consciousness: a contextual analysis of alcohol. In Allman, L. R. S., and Jaffe, D. T. (eds.), *Readings in abnormal psychology: contemporary perspectives.* New York: Harper & Row, 1976, pp. 280–283.

Allport, G. *The nature of prejudice.* Boston: Beacon Press, 1954.

————. *Pattern and growth in personality.* New York: Holt, Rinehart and Winston, 1961.

————, **and Vernon, P. E.** *Studies in expressive movement.* New York: Macmillan, 1933.

Alström, C.–H. Testimony before the Sexual Offenses Commission, cited in Engström, L.–G. New penal provisions on sexual offenses proposed in Sweden. *Current Sweden* (Stockholm), 1976, 118, 6.

Altman, D., Levine, M., Nadien, M., and Villena, J. Unpublished research, Graduate Center, City University of New York (cited in Milgram, 1970).

Altrocchi, J. Mental health consultation. In Golann, S. E., and Eisdorfer, C. (eds.), *Handbook of community mental health.* Englewood Cliffs, N.J.: Prentice-Hall, 1972.

————, **Spielberger, C. D., and Eisdorfer, C.** Mental health consultation with groups. *Community Mental Health Journal*, 1965, 1, 127–134.

American Association on Mental Deficiency. *Adaptive behavior scale: manual.* Washington, D.C.: American Association on Mental Deficiency, 1974.

American Psychiatric Association. *Diagnostic and statistical manual of mental disorders* (DSM I). Washington, D.C.: American Psychiatric Association, 1952.

————. *Diagnostic and statistical manual of mental disorders* (DSM II). Washington, D.C.: American Psychiatric Association, 1968.

————. *Diagnostic and statistical manual of mental disorders* (DSM III). Washington, D.C.: American Psychiatric Association, 1980. (Drafts of the work in progress (1/15/78 draft) were made available by Dr. Robert L. Spitzer, Chairman, Task Force on Nomenclature and Statistics, American Psychiatric Association.)

American Psychological Association. Special issue: testing and public policy. *American Psychologist*, 1965, 20, 857–993.

Amir, M. The role of the victim in sex offenses. In Resnick, H. L. P., and Wolfgang, M. E. (eds.), *Sexual behaviors: social, clinical and legal aspects.* Boston: Little, Brown, 1972, pp. 131–167.

Amsel, A. Frustration, persistence and regression. In Kimmel, H. D. (ed.), *Experimental psychopathology: recent research and theory.* New York: Academic Press, 1971, pp. 51–69.

Anastasi, A. *Psychological testing.* 4th ed. New York: Macmillan, 1976.

Anderson, F. N., and Dean, H. C. Some aspects of child guidance clinic intake policy and practices. *Public Health Monograph*, 1956, 42, 1–16.

Andronico, M. P., and Guerney, B. G. The potential application of filial therapy to the school situation. In Guerney, B. G. (ed.), *Psychotherapeutic agents: new roles for nonprofessionals, parents, and teachers.* New York: Holt, Rinehart and Winston, 1969, pp. 371–377.

Ansbacher, H. L., and Ansbacher, R. R. (eds.). *The individual psychology of Alfred Adler.* New York: Harper & Row, 1956.

Anthony, W. A. Psychological rehabilitation: A concept in need of a method. *American Psychologist*, 1977, 32, 658–662.

————, **Buell, G. J., Sharratt, S., and Althoff, M. E.** Efficacy of psychiatric rehabilitation. *Psychological Bulletin*, 1972, 78, 447–456.

Appley, M. H., and Trumbull, R. On the concept of psychological stress. In Appley, M. H., and Trumbull, R. (eds.), *Psychological stress: issues in research.* Englewood Cliffs, N.J.: Prentice Hall, 1967.

Ardrey, R. *African genesis.* New York: Atheneum, 1961.

————. *The territorial imperative: a personal inquiry into the animal origins of property and nations.* New York: Atheneum, 1966.

Argyris, C. Explorations in interpersonal competence I. *Journal of Applied Behavioral Science*, 1965, 1, 58–83.

Arieti, S. (ed.). *American handbook of psychiatry*, Vol. I. New York: Basic Books, 1959(a).

————. Manic–depressive psychosis. In Arieti, S. (ed.), *American handbook of psychiatry*, Vol. I. New York: Basic Books, 1959(b).

————. Schizophrenia: the manifest symptomatology, the psychodynamic and formal mechanisms. In Arieti, S. (ed.), *American handbook of psychiatry*, Vol. 1. New York: Basic Books, 1959(c), pp. 455–484.

Arnhoff, F. N., and Speisman, J. C. Summary and conclusions. In Arnhoff, F. N., Rubinstein, E. A., and Speisman, J. C. (eds.), *Manpower for mental health.* Chicago: Aldine, 1969.

Aronfreed, J. *Conduct and conscience: the socialization of internalized control over behavior.* New York: Academic Press, 1968.

————. The concept of internalization. In Goslin, D. (ed.), *Handbook of socialization theory and research.* Chicago: Rand McNally, 1969.

Arthurs, R. G. S., and Cahoon, E. B. A clinical and electroencephalographic survey of psychopathic personality. *American Journal of Psychiatry*, 1964, 120, 875–882.

Ascough, J. C., and Sipprelle, C. M. Operant verbal conditioning of autonomic responses. *Behavior Research and Therapy*, 1968, 6, 363–370.

Aserinsky, E., and Kleitman, N. Regularly occurring periods of eye motility and concomitant phenomena during sleep. *Science*, 1953, 118, 273–274.

————. Two types of ocular motility occurring in sleep. *Journal of Applied Physiology*, 1955, 8, 1–10.

Astor, G. *The charge is rape.* New York: Playboy Press, 1974.

Atkinson, J. W. (ed.). *Motives in fantasy, action and society.* New

York: Van Nostrand Reinhold, 1958.

Atthowe, J. M., Jr. Behavior innovation and persistence. *American Psychologist,* 1973, 28, 34–41.

———. Treating the hospitalized person. In Craighead, W. E., Kazkin, A. E., and Mahoney, M. J. (eds.), *Behavior modification: principles, issues, and applications.* Boston: Houghton Mifflin, 1976, pp. 243–259.

———, **and Krasner, L.** Preliminary report on the application of contingent reinforcement procedures (token economy) on a "chronic" psychiatric ward. *Journal of Abnormal Psychology,* 1968, 73, 37–43.

Auerback, R., and Rugowski, J. A. Lysergic acid diethylamide, effects on embryos. *Science,* 1967, 157, 1325–1326.

Ausubel, D. P. *Drug addiction, psychological and sociological aspects.* New York: Random House, 1958.

———. Personality disorder *is* disease. *American Psychologist,* 1961, 16, 69–74.

Avis, H. H. The neuropharmacology of aggression: a critical review. *Psychological Bulletin,* 1974, 81, 47–63.

Ax, A. F., and Bamford, J. L. The GSR recovery limit in chronic schizophrenia. *Psychophysiology,* 1970, 7, 145–147.

Axelrod, J. Neurotransmitters. *Scientific American,* June 1974.

Ayllon, T., and Azrin, N. H. The measurement and reinforcement of the behavior of psychotics. *Journal of Experimental Analysis of Behavior,* 1965, 8, 357–383.

———. Reinforcer sampling: a technique for increasing the behavior of mental patients. *Journal of Applied Behavioral Research,* 1968(a), 1, 13–20.

———. *The token economy.* Englewood Cliffs, N.J.: Prentice-Hall, 1968(b).

Azrin, N. H., and Powell, J. Behavioral engineering: the reduction of smoking behavior by a conditioning apparatus and procedure. *Journal of Applied Behavior Analysis,* 1968, 1, 193–200.

———, **Rubin, H., O'Brien, F., Ayllon, T., and Roll, D.** Behavioral engineering: postural control by a portable operant apparatus, *Journal of Applied Behavior Analysis,* 1968, 1, 99–108.

Azumi, K. A polygraphic study of sleep in schizophrenics. *Seishin Shinkeigaku Zasshi,* 1966, 68, 1222–1241.

Bach, G. The marathon group: intensive practice of intimate interaction. In Ruitenbeek, H. M. (ed.), *Group therapy today: styles, methods and techniques.* New York: Atherton, 1969, pp. 301–309.

———, **and Deutsch, R. M.** *Pairing.* New York: Wyden, 1970.

———, **and Wyden, Peter.** *The intimate enemy: how to fight fair in love and marriage.* New York: Morrow, 1968.

Bachrach, A. J., Erwin, W. J., and Mohr, J. P. The control of eating behavior in an anorexic by operant conditioning techniques. In Ullmann, L. P., and Krasner, L. (eds.), *Case studies in behavior modification.* New York: Holt,

Rinehart and Winston, 1965, pp. 153–163.

Back, K. Intervention techniques: small groups. In Rosenzweig, M., and Porter, L. (eds.), *Annual review of psychology.* Palo Alto, Calif.: Annual Reviews, 1944.

Bakan, D. *Slaughter of the innocents.* San Francisco: Jossey–Bass, 1971.

Baldwin, A. L., Kalhorn, J., and Breese, F. H. Patterns of parent behavior. *Psychological Monographs,* 1945, 58, No. 268.

———. The appraisal of parent behavior. *Psychological Monographs,* 1949, 63, No. 299.

Ball, J. C., and Chambers, C. D. *The epidemiology of opiate addiction in the United States.* Springfield, Ill.: Thomas, 1970.

Baller, W., and Schallock, H. Conditioned response treatment of enuresis. *Exceptional Child,* 1956, 22, 233–236, 247–248.

Baltes, P. B., Schaie, K. W., and Nardi, A. H. Age and experimental mortality in a seven-year longitudinal study of cognitive behavior. *Developmental Psychology,* 1971, 5, 18–26.

Balthazar, E. E., and Stevens, H. A. *The emotionally disturbed, mentally retarded: a historical and contemporary perspective.* Englewood Cliffs, N.J.: Prentice-Hall, 1975.

Bandura, A. Psychotherapy as a learning process. *Psychological Bulletin,* 1961, 58, 143–159.

———. Influence of model's reinforcement contingencies on the acquisition of imitative responses. *Journal of Personality and Social Psychology,* 1965, 1, 589–595.

———. *Principles of behavior modification.* New York: Holt, Rinehart and Winston, 1969.

———. Psychotherapy based upon modeling principles. In Bergin, A. E., and Garfield, S. L. (eds.), *Handbook of psychotherapy and behavior change: an empirical analysis.* New York: Wiley, 1971(a), pp. 653–708.

———. *Social learning theory.* Morristown, N.J.: General Learning Press, 1971(b).

———. *Aggression—a social learning analysis.* Englewood Cliffs, N.J.: Prentice-Hall, 1973.

———. Behavior theory and the models man. *American Psychologist,* 1974, 29, 859–869.

———. Social learning theory. In Spence, J. T., Carson, R. C., and Thibaut, J. W. (eds.), *Behavioral approaches to therapy.* Morristown, N.J.: General Learning Press, 1976, pp. 1–46.

———, **and Barab, P.** Processes governing disinhibitory effects through symbolic modeling. *Journal of Abnormal Psychology,* 1973, 82, 1–10.

———, **and Menlove, F. L.** Factors determining vicarious extinction of avoidance behavior through symbolic modeling. *Journal of Personality and Social Psychology,* 1968, 8, 99–108.

———, **and Walters, R. H.** *Social learning and personality devel-*

opment. New York: Holt, Rinehart and Winston, 1963.

————, **Grusec, J. E., and Menlove, F. L.** Vicarious extinction of avoidance behavior. *Journal of Personality and Social Psychology*, 1967, 5, 16–23.

————, **Ross, D., and Ross, S.** Imitation of film-mediated aggressive models. In Wertheimer, M. (ed.), *Confrontation: psychology and the problems of today*. Glenview, Ill.: Scott, Foresman, 1970.

Banks, W. M. The black client and the helping professions. In Jones, R. L. (ed.), *Black psychology*. New York: Harper & Row, 1972, pp. 205–212.

Bannister, R. *Brain's clinical neurology*. 3rd ed. New York: Oxford University Press, 1969.

Barbach, L. G. Group treatment of preorgasmic women. *Journal of Sex and Marital Therapy*, 1974, 1, 139–145.

Barber, T. X. Experimental analysis of "hypnotic" behavior: review of recent empirical findings. *Journal of Abnormal Psychology*, 1965, 70, 132–154.

————. Physiological effects of hypnosis and suggestions. In Barber, T. X., DiCara, L. V., Kamiya, J., Miller, N. E., Shapiro, D., and Stoyva, J. (eds.), *Biofeedback and self-control, 1970*. Chicago: Aldine, 1971, pp. 188–256.

Barnes, E. J. Cultural retardation or shortcomings of assessment techniques? In Jones, R. L. (ed.), *Black psychology*. New York: Harper & Row, 1972, pp. 66–76.

Barnett, N. Alcoholism among the Cantonese of New York City. In Diethelm, O. (ed.), *Etiology of chronic alcoholism*. Springfield, Ill.: Thomas, 1955.

Barrett, B. H. Reduction in rate of multiple tics by free operant conditioning methods. *Journal of Nervous and Mental Disease*, 1962, 135, 187–195.

Barrett, C. L. Systematic desensitization versus implosive therapy. *Journal of Abnormal Psychology*, 1969, 74, 587–592.

Barry, H., Buchwald, C., Child, I. L., and Bacon, M. K. A cross-cultural study of drinking. IV. Comparisons with Horton ratings. *Quarterly Journal of Studies on Alcohol*, 1965, Supplement No. 3, 62–77.

Bartell, G. D. *Group sex: a scientist's eyewitness report on the American way of swinging*. New York: Wyden, 1971.

Barten, H. H. The coming age of the brief psychotherapies. In Bellak, L., and Barten, H. H. (eds.), *Progress in community mental health*, Vol. 1. New York: Grune & Stratton, 1969, pp. 93–122.

Bassuk, E. L., and Gerson, S. Deinstitutionalization and mental health services. *Scientific American*, 1978, 238, 46–53.

Batchelor, I. R. C. *Henderson and Gillespie's textbook of psychiatry*. 10th ed. London: Oxford University Press, 1969.

Bateson, G. *Steps to an ecology of mind*. New York: Ballantine Books, 1972.

————. The cybernetics of "self": a theory of alcoholism. In Allman, L. R., and Jaffe, D. T. (eds.), *Readings in abnormal*

psychology. New York: Harper & Row, 1976, pp. 284–291.

———— (ed.). *Perceval's narrative*. Stanford, Calif.: Stanford University Press, 1961.

————, **Jackson, D. D., Haley, J., and Weakland, J.** Toward a theory of schizophrenia. *Behavioral Science*, 1956, 1, 251–264. Reprinted in Buss, A. H., and Buss, E. (eds.), *Theories of schizophrenia*. New York: Atherton, 1969, pp. 128–155.

Baughman, E. E. *Personality: The psychological study of the individual*. Englewood Cliffs, N.J.: Prentice-Hall, 1972.

Baumeister, A. A. Learning abilities of the mentally retarded. In Baumeister, A. A. (ed.), *Mental retardation: appraisal, education and rehabilitation*. Chicago: Aldine, 1967, pp. 181–211.

————. The American residential institution: its history and character. In Baumeister, A. A., and Butterfield, E. (eds.), *Residential facilities for the mentally retarded*. Chicago: Aldine, 1970, pp. 20–26.

Bax, M. The active and the over-active school child. *Developmental Medicine and Child Neurology*, 1972, 14, 83–86.

Beach, F. A. Behavioral endocrinology: an emerging discipline. *American Scientist*, 1975, 63, 178–186.

Beahrs, J. O., Harris, D. R., and Hilgard, E. R. Failure to alter skin inflammation by hypnotic suggestion in five subjects with normal skin reactivity. *Psychosomatic Medicine*, 1970, 32, 627–631.

Beaumont, W. *Experiments and observations on the gastric juice on the physiology of digestion*. Plattsburg, N.Y.: Allen, 1833.

Beck, A. T. An inventory for measuring depression. *Archives of General Psychiatry*, 1961, 4, 561–571.

————. Reliability of psychiatric diagnosis: a critique of systematic studies. *American Journal of Psychiatry*, 1962, 119, 210–216.

————. *Depression: clinical, experimental, and theoretical aspects*. New York: Harper & Row, 1967.

————. *Depression: causes and treatment*. Philadelphia: University of Pennsylvania, 1972.

————. The development of depression: a cognitive model. In Friedman, R. J., and Katz, M. M. (eds.), *The psychology of depression: contemporary theory and research*. New York: Halsted Press, 1974.

Becker, H. S. *Outsiders: studies in the sociology of deviance*. New York: Free Press, 1963.

Becker, J. Achievement-related characteristics of manic-depressives. *Journal of Abnormal and Social Psychology*, 1960, 60, 334–339.

————. *Affective disorders*. Morristown, N.J.: General Learning Press, 1977.

————, **Spielberger, C. D., and Parker, J. B.** Value achievement and authoritarian attitudes in psychiatric patients. *Journal of Clinical Psychology*, 1963, 19, 57–61.

Becker, W. C., Peterson, D. R., Hellmer, L. A., Shoemaker, D. J., and Quay, H. C. Factors in parental behavior and personality as related to problem behavior in children. *Journal of Consulting Psychology,* 1959, 23, 107–118.

Bednar, R. L., and Lawlis, G. F. Empirical research in group psychotherapy. In Bergin, A. E., and Garfield, S. L. (eds.), *Handbook of psychotheraphy and behavior change: an empirical analysis.* New York: Wiley, 1971, pp. 812–838.

Beers, C. W. *A mind that found itself: an autobiography,* New York: McKay, 1908.

Beerstecher, E., Jr., Reed, J. G., Brown W. D., and Berry, L. J. The effect of single vitamin deficiencies on the consumption of alcohol by white rats. In *Individual metabolic patterns and human disease,* Publication No. 5109. Austin: University of Texas, 1951, pp. 115–138.

Bekhterev, V. M. *General principles of human reflexology.* New York: International Universities Press, 1932.

Belknap, J. K. Drugs and human behavior. In Holtzman, W. H. (ed.), *Introductory psychology in depth: developmental topics.* New York: Harper & Row, 1978, pp. 253–293.

Bellak, L., and Small, L. *Emergency psychotherapy and brief psychotherapy.* New York: Grune & Stratton, 1965.

Bem, S. L. Training the woman to know her place: the social antecedents of women in the world of work. Department of Psychology, Stanford University, 1971.

———. Beyond androgyny: some presumptuous prescriptions for a liberated sexual identity. Keynote Address for APA–NIMH Conference on the Research Needs of Women, Madison, Wisconsin, May 31, 1975(a).

———. Sex-role adaptability: one consequence of psychological androgyny. *Journal of Personality and Social Psychology,* 1975(b), 31, 634–643.

Bender, L. A visual-motor gestalt test and its clinical use. *Research Monographs of the American Orthopsychiatric Association,* No. 3, 1938.

———. *Visual-motor Gestalt test.* Beverly Hills, Calif.: Western Psychological Services, 1938–1964.

———. Psychopathic behavior disorders in children. In Lindner, R., and Seliger, R. (eds.), *Handbook of correctional psychology.* New York: Philosophical Library, 1947, pp. 360–377.

———. Childhood schizophrenia. *Psychiatric Quarterly,* 1953, 27, 663–681.

———. Concept of pseudopsychopathic schizophrenia in adolescents. *American Journal of Orthopsychiatry,* 1959, 29, 491–512.

———, **and Sankar, D. V. S.** Chromosome damage not found in leukocytes of children treated with LSD-25. *Science,* 1968, 159, 749–750.

———, **and Schilder, P.** Suicidal preoccupations and attempts in children. *American Journal of Orthopsychiatry,* 1937, 7, 225–234.

Bennett, I. *Delinquent and neurotic children.* New York: Basic Books, 1960.

Benson, H. Rosner, B. A., Marzetta, B. R., and Klemchuk, H. M. Decreased blood-pressure in pharmacologically treated hypertensive patients who regularly elicited the relaxation response. In DiCara, L. V., Barber, T. X., Kamiya, J., Miller, N. E., Shapiro, D., and Stovya, J. (eds.), *Biofeedback and self-control, 1974.* Chicago: Aldine, 1975, pp. 501–507.

Berg, I. A. Response bias and personality: the deviation hypothesis. *Journal of Psychology,* 1955, 40, 61–72.

———. Deviant responses and deviant people: the formulation of the deviation hypothesis. *Journal of Counseling Psychology,* 1957, 4, 154–161.

———. The unimportance of test item content. In Bass, B. M., and Berg, I. A. (eds.), *Objective approaches to personality assessment.* Princeton: Van Nostrand Reinhold, 1959, pp. 83–99.

———. Measuring deviant behavior by means of deviant response sets. In Berg, I. A., and Bass, B. M. (eds.), *Conformity and deviation.* New York: Harper & Row, 1961, pp. 328–379.

———. The deviation hypothesis: a broad statement of its assumptions and postulates. In Berg, I. A. (ed.), *Response set in personality assessment.* Chicago: Aldine, 1967, pp. 146–190.

Bergin, A. E. The evaluation of therapeutic outcomes. In Bergin, A. E., and Garfield, S. L. (eds.), *Handbook of psychotherapy and behavior change: an empirical analysis.* New York: Wiley, 1971, pp. 217–270.

———, **and Garfield, S. L.** (eds.), *Handbook of psychotherapy and behavior change: an empirical analysis.* New York: Wiley, 1971.

Bergstrand, C. G., and Otto, U. Suicidal attempts in adolescence and childhood. *Acta Paediatrica,* 1962, 51, 17–26.

Berkowitz, L. Simple views of aggression: an essay review. *American Scientist,* 1969, 57, 372–383.

———. Experimental investigations of hostility catharsis. *Journal of Consulting and Clinical Psychology,* 1970, 35, 1–7.

——— (ed.). *Roots of aggression.* New York: Atherton, 1969.

Berkowitz, W. Personal communication (cited in Milgram, 1970).

Bernal, M. E., Duryee, J. S., Pruett, H. L., and Burns, B. J. Behavior modification and the brat syndrome. *Journal of Consulting and Clinical Psychology,* 1968, 32, 447–455.

Berne, E. *Games people play: the psychology of human relationships.* New York: Grove, 1964.

Bernheim, H. *Hypnotisme, suggestion, psychothérapie.* Paris: Etudes Nouvelles, 1891.

Bernheim, K. F., and Lewine, R. R. J. *Schizophrenia: symptoms, causes, treatments.* New York: Norton, 1979.

Bettelheim, B. *The informed heart: on retaining the self in a dehumanizing society.* New York: Avon Books, 1960(a).

———. *The informed heart.* New York: Free Press, 1960(b).

Biblow, E. Imaginative play and the control of aggressive behavior. In Singer, J. L., *The child's world of make-believe.* New York: Academic Press, 1973.

Bigelow, G. The behavioral approach to retardation. In Thompson, T., and Grabowski, J. (eds.), *Behavior modification of the mentally retarded.* New York: Oxford University Press, 1972, pp. 17–45.

Bijou, S. W. Experimental studies of child behavior, normal and deviant. In Krasner, L., and Ullmann, L. P. (eds.), *Research in behavior modification.* New York: Holt, Rinehart and Winston, 1965, pp. 56–81.

———, **and Peterson, R. F.** Functional analysis in the assessment of children. In McReynolds, P. (ed.), *Advances in psychological assessment,* Vol. 2. Palo Alto, Calif.: Science & Behavior Books, 1971, pp. 63–78.

Billingslea, F. Y. The Bender-Gestalt: a review and a perspective. *Psychological Bulletin,* 1963, 60, 233–251.

Bindra, D. A unified interpretation of emotion and motivation. *Annuals of the New York Academy of Sciences,* 1969, 159, 1071–1083.

———. Emotion and behavior theory. In Black, P. (ed.), *Physiological correlates of emotion.* New York: Academic Press, 1970, pp. 3–20.

Bird, C. MMPI patterns under instructions to deliberately fake various psychiatric syndromes. Unpublished materials, University of Minnesota, 1948.

Birley, J. L. T., and Brown, G. W. Crises and life changes preceding the onset or relapse of acute schizophrenia: clinical aspects. *British Journal of Psychiatry,* 1970, 116, 327–333.

Bischof, L. J. *Interpreting personality theories.* 2nd ed. New York: Harper & Row, 1970.

Bjerg, K. The suicidal life space. In Shneidman, E. S. (ed.), *Essays in self-destruction.* New York: Science House, 1967.

Blachly, P. H. *Drug abuse: data and debate.* Springfield, Ill.: Thomas, 1970.

Black, S., and Wigan, E. R. An investigation of selective deafness produced by direct suggestion under hypnoses. *British Medical Journal,* 1961, 2, 736–741.

Blackwell, B., and Shepherd, N. Prophylactic lithium: another therapeutic method? *Lancet,* 1968, 1, 9–68.

Blake, R. R., and Mouton, J. S. Some effects of managerial grid seminar training on union and management attitudes toward supervision. *Journal of Applied Behavioral Science,* 1966, 2, 387–400.

Blanchard, E. B., Scott, R. W., Young, L. D., and Edmundson, E. D. Effect of knowledge of response on the self-control of heart rate. In DiCara, L. V., Barber, T. X., Kamiya, J., Miller, N. E., Shapiro, D., and Stovya, J. (eds.), *Biofeedback and self-control, 1974.* Chicago: Aldine, 1975, pp. 188–202.

Blaney, P. H. Contemporary theories of depression: critique and comparison. *Journal of Abnormal Psychology,* 1977, 86, 203–223.

Bleuler, E. *Dementia praecox oder die Gruppe der Schizophrenien.* Leipzig: Deuticke, 1911.

———. Autistic thinking. *American Journal of Insanity,* 1913, 69, 873.

Bleuler, M. Familial and personal background of chronic alcoholics. In Diethelm, O. (ed.), *Etiology of chronic alcoholism.* Springfield, Ill.: Thomas, 1955, pp. 110–166.

Bloch, H. S. An open-ended crisis-oriented group for the poor who are sick. *Archives of General Psychiatry,* 1968, 18, 178–185.

Block, J. *The challenge of response sets: unconfounding meaning, acquiesence and social desirability in the MMPI.* Englewood Cliffs, N.J.: Prentice-Hall, 1965.

Block, J. D. Monozygotic twin similarity in multiple psychophysiologic parameters and measures. In Wortis, J. (ed.), *Recent advances in biological psychiatry,* Vol. 9. New York: Plenum, 1967.

Bloom, B. L. Mental health program evaluation. In Golann, S. E., and Eisdorfer, C. (eds.), *Handbook of community mental health.* Englewood Cliffs, N.J.: Prentice-Hall, 1972.

Bloomquist, E. R. *Marijuana: the second trip.* New York: Free Press, 1971.

Blum, G. S. *Psychodynamics: the science of unconscious forces.* Belmont, Calif.: Wadsworth, 1966.

Blum, R. H., and Associates. *Society and drugs.* San Francisco: Jossey-Bass, 1969(a).

———. *Students and drugs.* San Francisco: Jossey–Bass, 1969(b).

———. *Horatio Alger's children: the role of the family in the origin and prevention of drug risk.* San Francisco: Jossey–Bass, 1972(a).

———. *The dream sellers: perspectives on drug dealing.* San Francisco: Jossey–Bass, 1972(b).

Bockoven, J. S. *Moral treatment in American psychiatry.* New York: Springer-Verlag, 1963.

Boe, E. E., Gocka, E. F., and Kogan, W. S. The effect of group psychotherapy on interpersonal perceptions of psychiatric patients. *Multivariate Behavioral Research,* 1966, 1, 177–187.

Boelkins, R. C., and Heiser, J. F. Biological bases of aggression. In Daniels, D. N., Gilula, M. F., and Ochberg, F. M. (eds.), *Violence and the struggle for existence.* Boston: Little, Brown, 1970.

Bogen, E. The human toxicology of alcohol. In Emerson, H. (ed.), *Alcohol and man.* New York: Macmillan, 1932, pp. 126–152.

Bonine, W. The psychodynamics of neurotic depression. In Arieti, S. (ed.), *American handbook of psychiatry,* Vol. III. New York: Basic Books, 1966.

Bonner, H. *Psychology of personality.* New York: Ronald Press, 1961.

Bootzin, R. R. *Behavior modification and therapy: an introduction.* Cambridge, Mass.: Winthrop, 1975.

Borgatta, E. F. Some notes on the history of tobacco use. In Borgatta, E. F., and Evans, R. R. (eds.), *Smoking, health and behavior.* Chicago: Aldine, 1968.

Borkovec, T. D. The effects of instructional suggestion and physiological cues on analogue fear. *Behavior Therapy*, 1973, 4, 185–192.

Boston Women's Health Book Collective. *Our bodies, ourselves: a book by and for women.* 2nd ed. New York: Simon & Schuster, 1976.

Bower, E. M., Shellhamer, T. A., and Daily, J. M. School characteristics of male adolescents who later became schizophrenic. *American Journal of Orthopsychiatry*, 1960, 30, 712–729.

Bowlby, J. Separation anxiety. *International Journal of Psychoanalysis*, 1960, 41, 89–113.

——, Ainsworth, M., Boston, M., and Rosenbluth, D. The effects of mother-child separation: a follow-up study. *British Journal of Medical Psychology*, 1956, 29, 211–247.

Bowman, K. M. Sakel and biological treatment of schizophrenia. In Rinkel, M. (ed.), *Biological treatment of mental illness.* New York: Farrar, Straus & Giroux, 1966, pp. 54–61.

Braceland, F. J. Clinical psychiatry. In Braceland, F. J., Freedman, D. X., Friedhoff, A. J., Kolb, L. C., Lourie, R. S., and Romano, J. (eds.), *Year book of psychiatry and applied mental health, 1977.* Chicago: Year Book Medical Publishers, 1977, pp. 271–313.

——, Freedman, D. X., Friedhoff, A. J., Kolb, L. C., Lourie, R. S., and Romano, J. (eds.). *Year book of psychiatry and applied mental health, 1976.* Chicago: Year Book Medical Publishers, 1976.

——, Freedman, D. X., Friedhoff, A. J., Kolb, L. C., Lourie, R. S., and Romano, J. (eds.). *Year book of psychiatry and applied mental health, 1977.* Chicago: Year Book Medical Publishers, 1977.

Brady, J. P. Brevital-relaxation treatment of frigidity. *Behavior Research Therapy*, 1966, 4, 71–77.

Brady, J. V. Ulcers in "executive" monkeys. *Scientific American*, 1958, 199, 95–100.

——. Behavioral stress and physiological change: a comparative approach to the experimental analysis of some psychosomatic problems. *Transactions of the New York Academy of Sciences*, 1964, 26, 483–496. Also appears in Palmer, J. O., and Goldstein, M. J. (eds.), *Perspectives in psychopathology: readings in abnormal psychology.* New York: Oxford University Press, 1966, pp. 196–208.

——. Endocrine and autonomic correlates of emotional behavior. In Black, P. (ed.), *Physiological correlates of emotion.* New York: Academic Press, 1970, pp. 95–125.

——, Porter, R. W., Conrad, D. G., and Mason, J. W. Avoidance behavior and the development of gastroduodenal ulcers. *Journal of Experimental Analysis of Behavior*, 1958, 1, 69–72.

Braginsky, B., Braginsky, D., and Ring, K. *Methods of madness: the hospital as a last resort.* New York: Holt, Rinehart and Winston, 1969.

Braginsky, D., and Braginsky, B. *Hansels and Gretels: studies of children in institutions for the mentally retarded.* New York: Holt, Rinehart and Winston, 1971.

Brammer, L. M., and Shostrom, E. L. *Therapeutic psychology: fundamentals of counseling and psychotheraphy.* 3rd ed. Englewood Cliffs, N.J.: Prentice-Hall, 1977.

Bramwell, S. T., Masuda, M., Wagner, N. N., and Holmes, T. H. Psychosocial factors in athletic injuries. *Journal of Human Stress*, 1975, 1, 6–20.

Brannon, E. P., and Graham, W. L. Intensive insulin shock therapy: a five year survey. *American Journal of Psychiatry*, 1955, 11, 659–663.

Brecher, R., and Brecher, E. *An analysis of human sexual response.* Boston: Little, Brown, 1966.

Brehm, M. L., and Back, K. W. Self-image and attitudes towards drugs. *Journal of Personality*, 1968, 36, 299–314.

Brenner, J. H., Coles, R., and Meagher, D. *Drugs and youth.* New York: Liveright, 1970.

Breuer, J., and Freud, S. Studies on hysteria (1895). In *Standard edition,* Vol. 2. London: Hogarth, 1955.

Brill, H. Contributions of biological treatment to biology. In Rinkel, M. (ed.), *Biological treatment of mental illness.* New York: Farrar, Straus & Giroux, 1966, pp. 62–70.

Brion, S. Korsakoff's syndrome: clinico–anatomical and physiopathological considerations. In Talland, G. A., and Wangh, N. C. (eds.), *Pathology of memory.* New York: Academic Press, 1969.

Brody, N. *Personality: research and theory.* New York: Academic Press, 1972.

Broen, W. E. J. *Schizophrenia: research and theory.* New York: Academic Press, 1968.

Bronfenbrenner, U. Early deprivation in animals and man. In Newton, G. (ed.), *Early experience and behavior.* Springfield, Ill.: Thomas, 1968, pp. 627–764.

Bronson, F. H., and Eleftheriou, B. E. Adrenal responses to crowding to *Peromyscus* and C. 57 BL/10 J mice. *Physiological Zoology*, 1963, 36, 161–166.

Brooks, C. M., and Lambert, E. F. A study of the effect of limitation of food intake and the method of feeding on the rate of weight gain during hypothalamic obesity in the albino rat. *American Journal of Physiology*, 1946, 147, 695–707.

Brooks, R., and Kleinmuntz, B. Design of an intelligent computer psychodiagnostician. *Behavioral Science*, 1974, 19, 16–20.

Broverman, I. K., Broverman, D. M., Clarkson, F. E., Rosenkrantz, P. S., and Vogel, S. R. Sex-role stereotypes and clinical judgments of mental health. *Journal of Consulting and Clinical Psychology*, 1970, 34, 1–7.

Brown, B. Recognition aspects of consciousness through association with EEG alpha actuity represented by a light signal. *Psychophysiology*, 1970, 6, 442–452.

——. Awareness of EEG—subjective activity relationships

directed within a closed feedback system. *Psychophysiology,* 1971, 7, 451–464.

Brown, B. S. Philosophy and scope of extended clinical activities. In Mitchell, C. F. (ed.), *Extending clinic services into the community.* Austin: Texas State Department of Health, 1961, pp. 5–9.

———. Memo from the director to the staff of the National Institute of Mental Health, Washington, D.C.: Government Printing Office, 1976.

Brown, E. L., and Greenblatt, M. Social treatment. In Greenblatt, M., York, R. H., and Brown, E. L. *From custodial to therapeutic care in mental hospitals: explorations in social treatment.* New York: Russell Sage Foundation, 1955, pp. 407–427.

Brown F. Depression and childhood bereavement. *Journal of Mental Science,* 1961, 107, 754–777.

Brown, F. W. Heredity in the psychoneuroses. *Proceedings of the Royal Society of Medicine,* 1942, 35, 785–790.

Brown, J. L., and Reiser, D. E. Patterns of later development in children with infantile psychosis. Paper presented at Fortieth Annual Meeting of American Orthopsychiatric Association, Washington, D.C., March 1963.

Brown, N. O. *Life against death: the psychoanalytic meaning of history.* Middletown, Conn.: Wesleyan University Press, 1959.

Brown, R., and Herrnstein, R. J. *Psychology.* Boston: Little, Brown, 1975.

Bruch, H. Eating disorders in adolescence. In Zubin, J., and Freedman, A. M. (eds.), *The psychopathology of adolescence.* New York: Grune & Stratton, 1970, pp. 181–197.

Bruner, J. S., and Postman, L. On the perception of incongruity: a paradigm. *Journal of Personality,* 1949, 18, 206–223.

Bryan, J. H. Apprenticeships in prostitution. In Gagnon, J. H., and Simon, W. (eds.), *Sexual deviance.* New York: Harper & Row, 1967, pp. 146–164.

Bucher, B., and Lovaas, O. I. Use of aversive stimulation in behavior modification. In Jones, M. R. (ed.), *Miami symposium on the prediction of behavior, 1967: aversive stimulation.* Coral Gables, Fl.: University of Miami, 1968, pp. 77–145.

Buchsbaum, M. S. Psychophysiology and schizophrenia. *Schizophrenia Bulletin,* 1977, 3, 7–14.

Buchsbaum, M., Goodwin, F., Murphy, D., and Borge, G. AER in affective disorders. *American Journal of Psychiatry,* 1971, 128, 19–24.

Buchwald, A. M., Coyne, K. C., and Cole, C. S. A critical evaluation of the learned helplessness model of depression. *Journal of Abnormal Psychology,* 1978, 87, 180–193.

Buck, R. W., Savin, V. J., Miller, R. E., and Caul, W. F. Communication of affect through facial expression in humans. *Journal of Personality and Social Psychology,* 1972, 23, 362–371.

Budzynski, T., Stoyva, J., and Adler, C. Feedback-induced muscle relaxation: application to tension headache. *Journal of Behavior Therapy and Experimental Psychiatry,* 1970, 1, 205–211.

———. Feedback-induced muscle relaxation. In Barber, T. X., DiCara, L. V., Kamiya, J., Miller, N. E., Shapiro, D., and Stoyva, J. (eds.), *Biofeedback and self-control, 1970.* Chicago: Aldine, 1971, pp. 447–460.

———, and Mullaney, D. M. EMG biofeedback and tension headache: a controlled outcome study. *Psychosomatic Medicine,* 1973, 35, 484–496.

Buehler, R. E., Patterson, G. L., and Furniss, J. M. The reinforcement of behavior in institutional settings. *Behavior Research and Therapy,* 1966, 4, 157–167.

Bunker, D. R. Individual applications of laboratory training. *Journal of Applied Behavioral Science,* 1965, 1, 131–148.

Burchard, J. D. Systematic socialization: a programmed environment for the rehabilitation of antisocial retardates. *Psychological Record,* 1967, 17, 461–476.

Burchinal, L. H., and Eppright, E. S. Test of the psychogenic theory of obesity for a sample of rural girls. *American Journal of Clinical Nutrition,* 1959, 7, 288–294.

Burma, J. H. Self-tattooing among delinquents: a research note. *Sociology and Social Research,* 1959, 43, 341–345.

Buros, O. K. (ed.). *The sixth mental measurements yearbook.* Highland Park, N.J.: Gryphon, 1965.

———. *The seventh mental measurements yearbook.* Highland Park, N.J.: Gryphon, 1972.

———. *The eighth mental measurements yearbook.* Highland Park, N.J.: Gryphon, 1978.

Burton, A. (ed.). *Modern psychotherapeutic practice: innovations in technique.* Palo Alto, Calif.: Science and Behavior Books, 1965.

———, and Harris, R. E. (eds.). *Clinical studies of personality,* Vol. 1. New York: Harper & Row, 1966.

Buss, A. H. *The psychology of aggression.* New York: Wiley, 1961.

———. *Psychopathology.* New York: Wiley, 1966.

———. *Psychology—man in perspective.* New York: Wiley, 1973.

———. *Psychology—behavior in perspective.* New York: Wiley, 1978.

———, and Plomin, R. A. *A temperamental theory of personality development.* New York: Wiley, 1975.

Busse, E. W. Psychoneurotic reactions and defense mechanisms in the aged. In Palmore, E. (ed.), *Normal aging.* Durham, N.C.: Duke University Press, 1970.

———, and Reckless, J. B. Psychiatric management of the aged. *Journal of the American Medical Association,* 1961, 175, 645–648.

Butcher, J. N. *Abnormal psychology.* Belmont, Calif.: Wadsworth, 1971.

———, and Maudal, G. R. Crisis intervention. In Weiner,

I. B. (ed.), *Clinical methods in psychology*. New York: Wiley, 1976.

Byrd, R. E. Training in a non-group. *Journal of Humanistic Psychology*, 1967, 7, 18–27.

Cabeen, C. W. Group therapy with sex offenders: description and evaluation of group therapy programs in an institutional setting. *Journal of Clinical Psychology*, 1961, 17, 122–129.

Cadogan, D. Marital group therapy in the treatment of alcoholism. *Quarterly Journal of Studies on Alcohol*, 1973, 34, 1187–1194.

Cahalan, D. *Problem drinkers*. San Francisco: Jossey–Bass, 1970.

———, and **Room, R.** *Problem drinking among American men*. New Haven: College & University Press, 1974.

———, **Cisin, I. H.,** and **Crossley, H. M.** *American drinking practices: a national study of drinking behavior and attitudes*. Monograph No. 6. New Brunswick, N.J.: Rutgers Center of Alcohol Studies, 1969.

Cain, N. N., and **Cain, R. M.** A compendium of psychiatric drugs, part II. *Drug Therapy*, 1975, 6, 77–83.

Cain, R. M., and **Cain, N. N.** A compendium of psychiatric drugs, part I. *Drug Therapy*, 1975, 5, 105–124.

Calderone, M. S. Sex education for young people—and for their parents and teachers. In Brecher, R., and Brecher, E. (eds.), *An anlysis of human sexual response*. Boston: Little, Brown, 1966, pp. 267–273.

Caldwell, W. F. *LSD psychotherapy: an exploration of psychedelic and psycholytre therapy*. New York: Grove, 1968.

Calhoun, J. B. Population density and social pathology. *Scientific American*, 1962, 206, 139–146.

Calhoun, J. F., Acocella, J. R., and **Goodstein, L. D.** *Abnormal psychology: current perspectives*. 2nd ed. New York: Random House, 1977.

Cameron, N. Paranoid conditions and paranoia. In Arieti, S. (ed.), *American handbook of psychiatry*, Vol. 1. New York: Basic Books, 1959, pp. 508–539.

———. *Personality development and psychopathology: a dynamic approach*. Boston: Houghton Mifflin, 1963.

Campbell, M., and **Small, A. M.** Chemotherapy. In Wolman, B. B., Egan, J., and Ross, A. O. (eds.), *Handbook of treatment of mental disorders in childhood and adolescence*. Englewood Cliffs, N.J.: Prentice-Hall, 1978.

Cannon, W. B. *Bodily changes in pain, hunger, fear, and rage*. 2nd ed. Englewood Cliffs, N.J.: Prentice-Hall, 1929.

Canter, S. Personality traits in twins. Unpublished paper reported in Mittler (1971).

Cantor, D. J. The homosexual revolution: a status report. In Kirkendall, L. A., and Whitehurst, R. N. (eds.), *The new sexual revolution*. New York: Scribner, 1971, pp. 85–95.

Caplan, G. A public health approach to child psychiatry. *Mental Health*, 1951, 35, 235–249.

———. *An approach to community mental health*. New York: Grune & Stratton, 1961.

———. *Principles of preventive psychiatry*. New York: Basic Books, 1964.

Capgras, J., and **Carrette, P.** Illusion des sosies et complexe d'oedipe. *Annals Medical-Psychologie*, 1923, 82, 48.

Capra, F. *The tao of physics*. Boulder, Colo.: Shambhala, 1975.

Carlson, N. R. *Physiology of behavior*. Boston: Allyn & Bacon, 1977.

Carpenter, W. T., Jr., Strauss, J. S., and **Bartko, J. J.** Use of signs and symptoms for the identification of schizophrenic patients. *Schizophrenia Bulletin*, 1974, 11, 37–49.

Carroll, J. B. *Language, thought, and reality: selected writings of Benjamin Lee Whorf*. Cambridge, Mass.: M.I.T. Press, 1956.

Carson, R. C. *Interaction concepts of personality*. Chicago: Aldine, 1969.

Carter, J. W., Jr. (ed.). *Research contributions from psychology to community mental health*. New York: Behavioral Publications, 1968.

Carter, C. O. *Human heredity*. Middlesex, England: Penguin Books, 1970.

Casy, A. The effect of stress on the consumption of alcohol and reserpine. *Quarterly Journal of Studies on Alcohol*, 1960, 21, 208 ff.

Casey, J. F., Bennett, I. F., Lindley, C. J., Hollister, L. E., Gordon, M. H., and **Springer, N. N.** Drug therapy in schizophrenia. *Archives of General Psychiatry*, 1960, 2, 210–220.

Casler, L. Perceptual deprivation in institutional settings. In Newton, B. (ed.), *Early experience and behavior*. Springfield, Ill.: Thomas, 1968, pp. 573–626.

Cassie, A. B., and **Allan, W. R.** Alcohol and road traffic accidents. *British Medical Journal*, 1961, 2, 1668.

Castaneda, C. *A separate reality*. New York: Simon & Schuster, 1972.

———. *Journey to Ixtlan*. New York: Simon & Schuster, 1973(a).

———. *The teachings of Don Juan: a Yaqui way of knowledge*. New York: Simon Schuster, 1973(b).

———. *Tales of power*. New York: Simon & Schuster, 1974.

———. *The second ring of power*. New York: Simon & Schuster, 1978.

Cattell, R. B. *The scientific study of personality*. Middlesex, England: Penguin Books, 1965.

———. Anxiety and motivation: theory and crucial experiments. In Spielberger, C. D. (ed.), *Anxiety and behavior*. New York: Academic Press, 1966, pp. 23–62.

———, and **Scheier, I. H.** *The meaning and measurement of neuroticism and anxiety*. New York: Ronald Press, 1961.

Cautela, J. Covert sensitization. *Psychological Reports*, 1967, 20, 459–468.

———. Covert processes and behavior modification. *Journal of Nervous and Mental Disease*, 1973, 157, 27–35.

Caveny, E. L., Wittson, C. L., Hunt, W. A., and **Herman,**

R. S. Psychiatric diagnosis, its nature and function. *Journal of Nervous and Mental Disease*, 1955, 121.

Cerletti, U., and Bini, L. L'Elettroshock. *Archives de Psicologia et Neurologia Psichiatria*, 1938, 19, 266.

Chafetz, M. E. Addictions. III: alcoholism. In Freedman, A. M., and Kaplan, H. I. (eds.), *Comprehensive textbook of psychiatry*. Baltimore: Williams & Wilkins, 1967.

———. Misconceptions about alcoholism mar therapeutic effectiveness. *Roche Report: Frontiers of Psychiatry*, 1972, 2, 2–8.

———, **and Demone, J. W., Jr.** Programs to control alcoholism. In Arieti, S. (ed.), *American handbook of psychiatry*, Vol. 2. 2nd ed. New York: Basic Books, 1974.

———, **Hertzman, M., and Berenson, D.** Alcoholism: a positive view. In Arieti, S., and Brady, E. B. (eds.), *American handbook of psychiatry*, Vol. 3. 2nd ed. New York: Basic Books, 1974.

Chance, E. Implications of interdisciplinary differences in case description. *American Journal of Orthopsychiatry*, 1963, 33, 672–677.

Chapman, A. H. Psychogenic urinary retention in women. *Psychosomatic Medicine*, 1959, 21, 119–122.

Chapman, J., and McGhie, A. A comparative study of disordered attention in schizophrenia. *Journal of Mental Science*, 1962, 108, 487–500.

Chapman, L. F., and Wolff, H. G. The cerebral hemispheres and the highest integrative functions of man. *Archives of Neurology*, 1959, 1, 357.

———, **Goodell, H., and Wolff, H. G.** Augmentation of the inflammatory reaction by activity of the central nervous system. *Archives of Neurology*, 1959, 1, 557–582.

Chapman, L. J. Disordered thought in schizophrenia. Englewood Cliffs, N.J.: Prentice-Hall, 1974.

———, **Chapman, J. P., and Miller, G. A.** A theory of verbal behavior in schizophrenia. In Maher, B. A. (ed.), *Progress in experimental personality*, Vol. 1. New York: Academic Press, 1964, pp. 49–77.

Chapple, E. D. "Personality" differences as prescribed by invariant properties of individuals in interaction. *Proceedings of the National Academy of Sciences*, 1940, 26, 10–16.

———, **Chamberlain, A. S., Egger, A. H., and Kline, N. S.** Measurement of the activity patterns of schizophrenic patients. *Journal of Nervous and Mental Disease*, 1963, 137, 258–267.

Chomsky, N. A review of B. F. Skinner's *Verbal Behavior*. *Language*, 1959, 35, 26–58.

Chopra, I. C., and Chopra, R. N. The use of the cannabis drugs in India. *U.N. Bulletin on Narcotics*, 1957, 9, 4–29.

Chopra, R. N., Chopra, G. S., and Chopra, I. C. Cannabis sativa in relation to mental diseases and crime in India. *Indian Journal of Medical Research*, 1942, 30, 155–171.

Chorover, S. The participation of the brain. *Psychology Today*, May 1974.

Christensen, D. E., and Sprague, R. L. Reduction of hyperactive behavior by conditioning procedures alone and combined with methyl phenidate (Ritalin). *Behavior Research and Therapy*, 1973, 11, 331–334.

Christmas, J. J. Sociopsychiatric treatment of disadvantaged psychotic adults. *American Journal of Orthopsychiatry*, 1967, 37, 93–100.

Christozov, C. L'Aspect marocain de l'intoxication cannabique d'après des études sur des malades mentaux chroniques: première partie et deuxième partie. *Maroc Médical*, 1965, 44, 630–642, 866–900.

Churchill, W. *Homosexual behavior among males: a cross-cultural and cross-species investigation*. Englewood Cliffs, N.J.: Prentice-Hall, 1967.

Ciminero, A. R. Behavioral assessment: an overview. In Ciminero, A. R., Calhoun, K. S., and Adams, H. E. (eds.), *Handbook of behavioral assessment*. New York: Wiley, 1977, pp. 3–13.

———, **Nelson, O. R., and Lipinski, D. P.** Self-monitoring procedures. In Ciminero, A. R., Calhoun, K. S., and Adams, H. E. (eds.), *Handbook of behavioral assessment*. New York: Wiley, 1977, pp. 195–232.

Clarizio, H. F., and McCoy, G. F. *Behavior disorders in children*. 2nd ed. New York: Crowell, 1976.

Clark, G. R., Teller, M. A., and Baker, D. Sex chromosomes, crime, and psychosis. *American Journal of Psychiatry*, 1970, 126, 1659–1663.

Clark, J. and Mallett, B. A follow-up study of schizophrenia and depression in young adults. *British Journal of Psychiatry*, 1963, 109, 491.

Clark, K. B. *Dark ghetto: dilemmas of social power*. New York: Harper & Row, 1965.

Clark, L. D., Hughes, R., and Nakashima, E. N. Behavioral effects of marihuana: experimental studies, *Archives of General Psychiatry*, 1970, 23, 193–198.

Clausen, J. A. Family structure, socialization, and personality. In Hoffman, L. and Hoffman, M. (eds.), *Review of child development research*, Vol. II. New York: Russell Sage, 1966.

———, **and Kohn, M. L.** Relation of schizophrenia to the social structure of a small city. In Pasamanick, B. (ed.), *Epidemiology of mental disorders*. Washington, D.C.: AAAS, 1959.

Clayton, P. J., Pitts, F. N., and Winokur, G. Affective disorder. IV. Mania. *Comprehensive Psychiatry*, 1965, 6, 313–322.

Cleary, T. A., Humphreys, L. G., Kendrick, S. A., and Wesman, A. Educational uses of tests with disadvantaged students. *American Psychologist*, 1975, 30, 15–41.

Cleaver, E. *Soul on ice*. New York: Dell, 1968.

Cleckley, H. Psychopathic states. In Arieti, S. (ed.), *American handbook of psychiatry*. New York: Basic Books, 1959, pp. 567–588.

———. *The mask of sanity*. 4th ed. St. Louis: Mosby, 1964.

Clements, S. D. Task force 1: minimal brain dysfunction in children: terminology and identification. National Institute of Neurological Diseases and Blindness, Monograph No. 3. Washington, D.C.: U.S. Department of Health, Education and Welfare, 1966.

Close, H. T. Gross exaggeration with a schizophrenic patient. In Fagan, J., and Shepherd, I. L. (eds.), *Gestalt therapy now: theory, techniques, applications.* New York: Harper & Row, 1970, pp. 194–196.

Cobbs, P. M. Journeys to black identity: Selma and Watts. *Negro Digest,* July 1967.

Cofer, C. N., and Appley, M. H. *Motivation: theory and research.* New York: Wiley, 1964.

Coffey, C. W. A 100 million dollar hangover for Texas. *Texas Business Review,* 1969, 43, 1–8.

Coffey, H. S. Group psychotherapy. In Berg, I. A., and Pennington, L. A. (eds.), *An introduction to clinical psychology.* 3rd ed. New York: Ronald Press, 1966.

Cohen, B. D., and Camhi, J. Schizophrenic performance in a word-communication task. *Journal of Abnormal Psychology,* 1967, 72, 240–246.

——, **Nahmani, G., and Rosenberg, S.** Referent communication disturbances in acute schizophrenia. *Journal of Abnormal Psychology,* 1974, 83, 1–3.

Cohen, H. L., Filipczak, J., Bis, J., Cohen, J., Goldiamond, I., and Larkin, P. *Case II—model: a contingency oriented 24-hour learning environment in a juvenile correctional institution.* Silver Spring, Md.: Facility Press, 1968.

Cohen, J. *Operant behavior and operant conditioning.* Chicago: Rand McNally, 1969.

Cohen, M. B., Baker, G., Cohen, R., Fromm-Reichmann, F., and Weigert, E. An intensive study of twelve cases of manic-depressive pyshosis. *Psychiatry,* 1954, 17, 103–137.

Cohen, M. M., Marinello, M. J., and Bock, N. Chromosomal damage in leukocytes induced by lysergic acid. *Science,* 1967, 155, 1417–1419.

Cohen, S. *Drugs of hallucination.* London: Martin Secker & Warburg, 1965. (The American title is *The beyond within.* New York: Atheneum, 1964.)

——. *The drug dilemma.* New York: McGraw-Hill, 1969.

Colbert, E. G., and Koegler, R. R. The child schizophrenic in adolescence. *Psychiatric Quarterly,* 1961, 35, 693–701.

Colby, E. (ed.), *The life of Thomas Holcroft, continued by William Hazlitt,* Vol. II. London: Constable, 1925.

Colby, K. M. Computer simulation of neurotic processes. In Stacy, R. W., and Waxman, B. (eds.), *Computers in biomedical research,* Vol. 1. New York: Academic Press, 1965, pp, 491–503.

——. Simulations of belief systems. In Schank, R. C., and Colby, K. M. (eds.), *Computer models of thought and language.* San Francisco: W. H. Freeman, 1973, pp. 251–286.

——. Appraisal of four psychological theories of paranoid phenomena. *Journal of Abnormal Psychology,* 1977, 86, 54–59.

——, **and Smith, D. C.** Computers in the treatment of nonspeaking autistic children. In Masserman, J. H. (ed.), *Current psychiatric therapies,* Vol. 2. New York: Grune & Stratton, 1971, pp. 1–17.

——, **Weber, S. and Hilf, F. D.** Artificial paranoia. *Artificial Intelligence,* 1971, 2, 1–25.

——, **Hilf, F. D., Weber, S., and Kraemer, H. C.** A resemblance test for the validation of a computer simulation of paranoid processes. *Stanford Artificial Intelligence Project. Report No. CS-246,* November 1971.

Cole, J. O., and Davis, J. M. Antidepressant drugs. In Freedman, A. M., and Kaplan, H. I. (eds.), *Treating mental illness: aspects of modern therapy.* New York: Atheneum, 1972, pp. 310–335.

Coleman, J. *Abnormal psychology and modern life.* 4th ed. Glenview, Ill.: Scott, Foresman, 1972.

Coles, R. Racial identity in school children. *Saturday Review,* October 19, 1963, 46, 56–57.

Comfort, A. (ed.). *The joy of sex: a Cordon Bleu guide to lovemaking.* New York: Simon & Schuster, 1972.

Conger, J. J. The effects of alcohol on conflict behavior in the albino rat. *Quarterly Journal of Studies on Alcohol,* 1951, 12, 1–29.

Conners, C. K. Pharmacotherapy of psychopathology in children. In Quay, H. C., and Werry, J. S. (eds.), *Psychopathological disorders of children.* New York: Wiley, 1972.

Connery, R. (ed.). *The politics of mental health: organizing community mental health in metropolitan areas.* New York: Columbia University Press, 1968.

Conrad, R. W. Needed: programs for the disturbed retarded. In Gardner, J. M. (ed.), *Mental retardation 1970:* selected papers from the 94th Annual Meeting of the American Association on Mental Deficiency, Vol. 2. Orient, Ohio: Orient State Institute, Department of Research and Development, 1970, pp. 72–83.

Constantine, L. L., and Constantine, J. M. *Group marriage: a study of contemporary multilateral marriage.* New York: Macmillan, 1973.

Cook, P. E. (ed.). *Community psychology and community mental health: introductory readings.* San Francisco: Holden-Day, 1970.

Cooper, A. J. A case of fetishism and impotence treated by behavior therapy. *British Journal of Psychiatry,* 1963, 109, 649–652.

——. A factual study of male potency disorders. *British Journal of Psychiatry,* 1968, 114, 719–731.

Cooper, C. C. *Some social implications of house and site plan design at Easter Hill Village: a case study.* Berkeley: Institute of Urban and Regional Development, University of California, 1965.

Cormier, B. M. The dilemma of psychiatric diagnosis. In

Resnick, H. L. P., and Wolfgang, M. E. (eds.), *Sexual behaviors: social, clinical and legal aspects.* Boston: Little, Brown, 1972, pp. 41–61.

Costello, C. G. A critical view of Seligman's laboratory experiments on learned helplessness and depression in humans. *Journal of Abnormal Psychology,* 1978, 87, 21–31.

Costello, T. W., and Zalkind, S. S. Cities, behavioral research and community mental health. In Adelson, D., and Kalis, B. L. (eds.), *Community psychology and mental health perspectives and challenges.* New York: Intext, 1970.

Cowen, E. L. Social and community interventions. In Mussen, P. H., and Rosenzweig, M. R. (eds.), *Annual review of psychology,* 1973, 24, 423–472.

Craft, M. J. *Ten studies into psychopathic personality.* Bristol, England: Wright, 1965.

Craighead, W. E., Kazdin, A. E., and Mahoney, M. J. *Behavior modification: principles, issues, and applications.* Boston: Houghton Mifflin, 1976.

Craik, K. H. Environmental psychology. In Craik, K. H., Kleinmuntz, B., Rosnow, R. L., Rosenthal, R., Cheyne, J. A., and Walters, R. H. *New directions in psychology,* Vol. 4. New York: Holt, Rinehart and Winston, 1970, pp. 1–121.

Craike, W. H., and Slater, E. Folie à deux in uniovular twins reared apart. *Brain,* 1945, 68, 213–221.

Crane, G. E. Clinical psychopharmacology in its 20th year. *Science,* 1973, 181, 124–128.

Crichton, R. *The great imposter.* New York: Random House, 1959.

Crider, A., Schwartz, G., and Schnidman, S. On the criteria for instrumental autonomic conditioning: a reply to Katkin and Murray. *Psychological Bulletin,* 1969, 71, 455–461.

Crocetti, G. M., Spiro, H. R., and Siassi, I. *Contemporary attitudes toward mental illness.* Pittsburgh: University of Pittsburgh Press, 1974.

Crompton, E. The marijuana problem. UCLA Interdepartmental Conference. *Annals of Internal Medicine,* 1970, 78, 449–465.

Cronbach, L. J. *Essentials of psychological testing.* 3rd ed. New York: Harper & Row, 1970.

Cropley, A. J., and Weckowicz, T. E. The dimensionality of clinical depression. *Australian Journal of Psychology,* 1966, 18, 18–25.

Cruickshank, W. M. Field of learning disability. *Journal of Learning Disabilities,* 1972, 5, 6–7.

Cumming, E., and Henry, W. H. *Growing old.* New York: Basic Books, 1961.

Cummings, N. A. The anatomy of psychotherapy under National Health Insurance. *American Psychologist,* 1977, 32, 711–718.

Custance, J. *Wisdom, madness and folly.* New York: Pelligrini and Cudahy, 1952.

d'Abro, A. *The rise of the new physics: its mathematical and physical theories.* New York: Dover, 1951. (Formerly titled *Decline of mechanisms.*)

Dahl, H. A quantitative study of a psychoanalysis. In Holt, R. R., and Peterfreund, E. (eds.), *Psychoanalysis and contemporary science.* New York: Macmillan, 1972, pp. 237–257.

Dahlstrom, W. G., and Welsh, G. *An MMPI handbook: a guide to use in clinical practice and research.* Minneapolis: University of Minnesota Press, 1960.

———, **and Dahlstrom, L. E.** *An MMPI handbook. Vol. 1: Clinical interpretation. Rev. ed.* Minneapolis: University of Minnesota Press, 1972.

Daily, C. A. The life history as a criterion of assessment. *Journal of Counseling Psychology,* 1960, 7, 20–23.

Dally, P. *Chemotherapy of psychiatric disorders.* New York: Plenum, 1967.

Dalton, K. *The premenstrual syndrome.* Springfield, Ill.: Thomas, 1964.

Darley, J. M., and Latané, B. Bystander intervention in emergencies: diffusion of responsibility. *Journal of Personality and Social Psychology,* 1968, 8, 377–383.

Darling, H. F., and Sandall, J. W. Treatment of the psychopath. *Journal of Clinical and Experimental Psychopathology,* 1953, Vol. 13.

Davenport, W. Sexual patterns and their regulations in a society of the southwest Pacific. In Beach, F. (ed.), *Sex and behavior.* New York: Wiley, 1965.

Davids, A. Digest of crisis in child mental health: the challenge for 1970s. In Davids, A. (ed.), *Issues in abnormal child psychology.* Monterey, Calif.: Brooks/Cole, 1973.

———, **and Engen, T.** *Introductory psychology.* New York: Random House, 1975.

Davidson, W. S. II, and Seidman, E. Studies of behavior modification and juvenile delinquency: a review, methodological critique, and social perspective. *Psychological Bulletin,* 1974, 81, 998–1011.

Davis, A. J. Sexual assaults in the Philadelphia prison system. In Gagnon, J. H., and Simon, W. (eds.), *The sexual scene.* Chicago: Aldine, 1970, pp. 107–124.

Davis, J. M. Drug therapy. In Spiegel, E. A. (ed.), *Progress in neurology and psychiatry.* New York: Grune & Stratton, 1973, pp. 423–448.

———, **and Casper, R.** Antipsychotic drugs: clinical pharmacology and therapeutic use. *Drugs,* 1977, 14, 260–282.

———, **Bartlett, E., and Termini, B. A.** Overdosage of psychotropic drugs: a review. *Disease of the Nervous System,* 1968, 29, 246–286.

———, **Janowsky, D. S., and El-Yousef, M. K.** The use of lithium in clinical psychiatry. *Psychiatry Annals,* 1973, 3, 78–99.

Davis, K. Extreme social isolation of a child. *American Journal of Sociology,* 1940, 45, 554–565.

Davis, W. L., and Phares, E. J. Internal-external control as a determinant of information-seeking in a social influence situation. *Journal of Personality*, 1967, 35, 547–561.

Davison, G. C. Differential relaxation and cognitive restructuring in therapy with a "paranoid schizophrenic" or "paranoid state." *Proceedings of the 74th Annual Convention of the American Psychological Association*, 1966, 177.

———, and Neale, J. M. *Abnormal psychology: an experimental clinical approach*. 2nd ed. New York: Wiley, 1978.

———, and Stuart, R. B. Behavior therapy and civil liberties. *American Psychologist*, 1975, 30, 755–763.

de Beauvoir, Simone. *The second sex*. New York: Bantam Books, 1952.

———. *The coming of age*. New York: Warner, 1973.

Dekker, E., Pelser, H. E., and Groen, J. Conditioning as a cause of asthmatic attacks. *Journal of Psychosomatic Research*, 1957, 2, 97–102.

Delgado, J. M. R. Permanent implantation of multilead electrodes in the brain. *Yale Journal of Biological Medicine*, 1952, 24, 351–358.

———. Chronic implantation of intracerebral electrodes in animals. In Sheer, D. E. (ed.), *Electrical stimulation of the brain*. Austin: University of Texas Press, 1961, pp. 25–36.

———. *Physical control of the mind: toward a psychocivilized society*. New York: Harper & Row, 1969.

———, Mark, V., Sweet, W., Ervin, F., Weiss, G., Bach-Rita, G., and Hagiwara, R. Intracerebral radio stimulation and recording in completely free patients. *Journal of Nervous and Mental Disease*, 1968, 147.

D'Elia, G., and Perris, C. Suicidal attempts in bipolar and unipolar depressed psychotics (cited in Winokur et al., 1969).

Dember, W., and Kristofferson, A. The relation between free-choice alcohol consumption and susceptibility to audiogenic seizures. *Quarterly Journal of Studies on Alcohol*, 1955, 16, 86 ff.

Dement, W. C. Psychophysiology of sleep and dreams. In Arieti, S. (ed.), *Handbook of psychiatry*, Vol. 3. New York: Basic Books, 1966, pp. 290–332.

———, and Fisher, C. Experimental interference with the sleep cycle. *Canadian Psychiatric Association Journal*, 1963, 8, 400–405.

———, and Kleitman, N. Cyclic variations in EEG during sleep and their relation to eye movement, body motility, and dreaming. *Electroencephalography and Clinical Neurophysiology*, 1957, 9, 673–690.

DeMoor, W. Systematic desensitization versus prolonged high intensity stimulation (flooding). *Journal of Behavior Therapy and Experimental Psychiatry*, 1970, 1, 45–52.

Dengrove, E. Behavior therapy of the sexual disorders. *Journal of Sex Research*, 1967, 3, 49–61.

Denner, B, and Price, R. H. *Community mental health*. New York: Holt, Rinehart and Winston, 1973.

De River, J. P. *The sexual criminal: a psychoanalytical study*. Springfield, Ill.: Thomas, 1950.

DesLauriers, A. M., and Carlson, C. F. *Your child is asleep: early infantile autism*. Homewood, Ill: Dorsey, 1969.

Detre, T., Himmelhoch, J., Swartzburg, M., Anderson, C. M., Byck, R., and Kupfer, D. J. Hypersomnia and manic depressive disease. *American Journal of Psychiatry*, 1972, 128, 1303.

Deutsch, A. *The mentally ill in America*. 2nd ed. New York: Columbia University Press, 1949.

Deutsch, F., and Nadell, R. Psychosomatic aspects of dermatology with special consideration of allergic phenomena. *Nervous Child*, 1946, 5, 339–364.

Deutsch, J. A., and Deutsch, D. *Physiological psychology*. Rev. ed. Homewood, Ill.: Dorsey, 1973.

DiCara, L. V., Barber, T. X., Kamiya, J., Miller, N. E., Shapiro, D., and Stovya, J. (eds.). *Biofeedback and self-control, 1974*. Chicago: Aldine, 1975.

Dimsdale, J. E. The coping behavior of Nazi concentration camp survivors. *American Journal of Psychiatry*, 1974, 131, 792–797.

Dishotsky, N. I., Loughman, W. D., Mogar, R. E., and Lipscomb, W. R. LSD and genetic damage. *Science*, 1971, 172, 431–440.

Division of Motor Vehicles. Alcohol countermeasures project of the state of New Jersey. Personal communication, 1972.

Dobzhansky, T. *Mankind evolving*. New Haven, Conn.: Yale University Press, 1962.

Dohrenwend, B. P. and Dohrenwend, B. S. The problem in validity in field studies of psychological disorder. *Journal of Abnormal Psychology*, 1965, 70, 52–69.

———. Field studies of social factors in relation to three types of psychological disorder. *Journal of Abnormal Psychology*, 1967, 72, 369–378.

———. *Social status and psychological disorder: a causal inquiry*. New York: Wiley, 1969.

Dohrenwend, B. S. Social status and stressful life events. *Journal of Personality and Social Psychology*, 1973, 28, 225–235.

Dole, V. P., and Nyswander, M. E. A medical treatment for diacetylmorphine [heroin] addiction. *Journal of the American Medical Association*, 1965, 193, 646–650.

Doll, E. A. Programs for the adult retarded. *Mental Retardation*, 1968, 6, 19–21.

Dollard, J., and Miller, N. E. *Social learning and imitation*. New Haven, Conn.: Yale University Press, 1941.

———, and Miller, N. E. *Personality and psychotherapy: an analysis in terms of learning, thinking, and culture*. New York: McGraw-Hill, 1950.

———, Miller, N. E., Mowrer, O. H., Sears, G. H., and Sears, R. R. *Frustration and aggression*. New Haven, Conn.: Yale University Press, 1939.

Doniger, J. Is a halfway house therapeutic?—the Woodley House. In Sinett, E. R., and Sachson, A. D. (eds.),

Transitional facilities in the rehabilitation of the emotionally disturbed. Lawrence: University of Kansas Press, 1970, pp. 63–71.

Dougherty, F. E., Bartlett, E. S., and Izard, C. E. A cross-cultural study of the responses of schizophrenics to facial expressions of the emotions. Unpublished manuscript, Vanderbilt University, Nashville, Tenn., 1969.

Down, J. L. H. Observations on an ethnic classification of idiots. *Reports of Obstetrics London Hospital,* 1866, 3, 259–262.

Doyle, W. Recognition of sloppy, hand-printed characters. *Proceedings of the Western Joint Computer Conference,* 1960, 17, 133–142.

Dragstedt, L. R. A concept of the etiology of gastric and duodenal ulcer. *American Journal of Roentgenology,* 1956, 75, 219–229.

————, **Oberhelman, H. A., and Smith, C. A.** Experimental hyperfunction of the gastric antrum with ulcer formation. *Annals of Surgery,* 1951, 134, 332–345.

Dreikurs, R. *The challenge of parenthood.* New York: Duell, Sloan & Pearce, 1958.

————. Early experiments with group psychotherapy: a historical review. In Ruitenbeek, H. M. (ed.), *Group therapy today: styles, methods and techniques.* New York: Atherton, 1969, pp. 18–27.

Drew, G. C., Colquhoun, W. P., and Long, H. A. Effects of small doses of alcohol on a skill resembling driving. Great Britain Medical Research Council Memorandum No. 38. London: H. M. S. O., 1959.

DuBois, P. *The psychic treatment of mental disorders.* New York: Funk & Wagnalls, 1909.

DuBois–Reymond, E. *Untersuchungen über thierische Elektricität,* Vols. 1 and 2. Berlin: Reimer, 1848–49.

Dumont, M. P. *The absurd healer: perspectives of a community psychiatrist.* New York: Science House, 1968.

————. The junkie as political enemy. In Allman, L. R., and Jaffe, D. T. (eds.), *Readings in abnormal psychology.* New York: Harper & Row, 1976, pp. 292–295.

————, **and Aldrich, C. K.** Family care after a thousand years—a crisis in the tradition of St. Dymphna. *American Journal of Psychiatry,* 1962, 119, 116–121.

Durant, W. *The story of civilization: our oriental heritage,* Pt. 1. New York: Simon & Schuster, 1954.

Eaton, J. W., and Weil, R. J. *Culture and mental disorders: a comparative study of the Hutterites and other populations.* New York: Free Press, 1955.

Edgerton, R. B. *The cloak of competence.* Berkekey: University of California Press, 1967.

Edson, L. "Jensenism," n. The theory that I.Q. is largely determined by the genes. *The New York Times Magazine,* August 31, 1969, p. 10.

Edwards, A. L. The relationship between the judged desirability of a trait and the probability that the trait will be endorsed. *Journal of Applied Psychology,* 1953, 37, 90–93.

Eells, K. Marijuana and LSD. A survey of one college campus. *Journal of Counseling Psychology,* 1968, 15, 459–467.

Efron, V., Keller, M., and Gurioli, C. *Statistics on consumption of alcohol and on alcoholism.* New Brunswick, N.J.: Rutgers Center of Alcohol Studies, 1974.

Egan, D. E., and Greeno, J. G. Theory of rule induction: knowledge acquired in concept learning, serial pattern learning, and problem solving. In Gregg, L. N. (ed.), *Knowledge and cognition.* New York: Wiley, 1974.

Egan, M. H., and Robinson, O. L. Home treatment of severely disturbed children and families. In Bindman, A. J., and Spiegel, A. D. (eds.), *Perspectives in community mental health.* Chicago, Aldine, 1969, pp. 538–544.

Ehrhardt, A. A., and Money, J. Progestin induced hermaphroditism: IQ and psychosexual identity in a study of ten girls. *Journal of Sex Research,* 1967, 3, 83–100.

Ehrenwald, J. Neurosis in the family. *Archives of General Psychiatry,* 1960, 3, 232–242.

Ehrlich, S. K., and Keogh, R. P. The psychopath in a mental institution. *Archives of Neurology and Psychiatry,* 1956, 76, 286–295.

Einhorn, H. J., Kleinmuntz, D. N., and Kleinmuntz, B. Linear regression *and* process tracing models of judgment. *Psychological Review,* 1979, 86, 465–485.

Eisenberg, L. The autistic child in adolescence. *American Journal of Psychiatry,* 1956, 112, 607–612.

————. School phobia: a study in the communication of anxiety. *American Journal of Psychiatry,* 1958, 114, 712–718.

Eisenson, J., Auer, J. J., and Irwin, J. V. *The psychology of communication.* Englewood Cliffs, N.J.: Prentice-Hall, 1963.

Ekman, P. Body position, facial expression and verbal behavior during interviews. *Journal of Abnormal and Social Psychology,* 1964, 68, 295–301.

————. Differential communication of affect by head and body cues. *Journal of Personality and Social Psychology,* 1965, 2, 726–735.

Ellis, A. *Reason and emotion in psychotherapy* New York: Lyle Stuart, 1962.

————. Rational emotive therapy. In Corsinic, R. (ed.), *Current psychotherapies.* Itasca, Ill.: Peacock, 1973, pp. 167–206.

Engstrom, D., London, P., and Hart, J. Hypnotic susceptibility increased by EEG alpha training. *Nature,* 1970, 227, 1261–1262.

Epstein, A. W. The relationship of altered brain states to sexual psychopathology. In Zubin, J., and Money J. (eds.), *Contemporary sexual behavior: critical issues in the 1970's.* Baltimore: Johns Hopkins University Press, 1973, pp. 297–310.

Epstein, L. H., Miller, P. M., and Webster, J. S. The effects of reinforcing concurrent behavior on self-monitoring. *Behavior Therapy,* 1976, 7, 89–95.

Eriksen, C. W. Perception and personality. In Wepman, J. M., and Heine, R. W. (eds.), *Concepts of personality.* Chicago: Aldine, 1963.

———. Cognitive responses to internally cued anxiety. In Spielberger, C. D. (ed.), *Anxiety and behavior.* New York: Academic Press, 1966, pp. 327–360.

———, **and Kuethe, J. L.** Avoidance conditioning of verbal behavior without awareness: a paradigm of repression. *Journal of Abnormal and Social Psychology,* 1956, 53, 203–209.

Erikson, E. H. *Childhood and society.* 2nd ed. New York: Norton, 1963.

———. *Insight and responsibility.* New York: Norton, 1964.

———. *Identity, youth and crisis.* New York: Norton, 1968.

Ernst, F. Self-recording and counterconditioning of a self-multilative compulsion. *Behavior Therapy,* 1973, 4, 144–146.

Eron, L. D. (ed.). *The classification of behavior disorders.* Chicago: Aldine, 1966.

———, **Huesmann, L. R., Walder, L. O., and Lefkowitz, M. M.** Does television violence cause aggression? *American Psychologist,* 1972, 27, 253–263.

———, **Laulicht, J. H., Walder, L. O., Farber, I. E., and Speigel, J. P.** Application of role and learning theories to the study of the development of aggression in children. *Psychological Reports,* 1961, 9, 261–334.

———, **Walder, L. O., and Lefkowitz, M. M.** *Learning of aggression in children.* Boston: Little, Brown, 1971.

Evans, D. R. Masturbatory fantasy and sexual deviation. *Behavior Research and Therapy,* 1968, 6, 17–19.

Evans, I., and Wilson, T. Note on the terminological confusion surrounding systematic desensitization. *Psychological Reports,* 1968, 22, 187–191.

Eysenck, H. J. The effects of psychotherapy: an evaluation. *Journal of Consulting Psychology,* 1952, 16, 319–324.

———. *The dynamics of anxiety and hysteria.* London: Routledge, Kegan Paul, 1957.

———. Classification and the problem of diagnosis. In Eysenck, H. J. (ed.), *Handbook of abnormal psychology,* London: Pitman, 1960(a), pp. 1–31.

———. *The structure of human personality.* London: Methuen, 1960(b).

———. *The effects of psychotherapy.* New York: International Science Press, 1966.

———. The classification of depressive illness. *British Journal of Psychiatry,* 1970, 117, 241–250.

———, **and Prell, D.** The inheritance of neuroticism: an experimental study. *Journal of Mental Science,* 1951, 97, 441–465.

———, **and Rachman, S.** *The causes and cures of neurosis.* San Diego: Knapp, 1965.

Fagan, J., and Shepherd, I. L. (eds.). *Gestalt therapy now: theory, techniques, applications.* New York: Harper & Row, 1970.

Fairweather, G. W. (ed.). *Social psychology in treating mental illness: an experimental approach.* New York: Wiley, 1964.

———, **and Simon, R.** A further follow-up comparison of psychotherapeutic programs. *Journal of Consulting Psychology,* 1963, 27, 186.

———, **Sanders, D. H., Maynard, H., and Cressler, D. L.** *Community life for the mentally ill: an alternative to institutional care.* Chicago: Aldine, 1969.

Falek, A., Craddick, R., and Collum, J. An attempt to identify prisoners with an XYY chromosome complement by psychiatric and psychological means, *Journal of Nervous and Mental Disease,* 1970, 150, pp. 165–170.

Fallding, H. The source and burden of civilization illustrated in the use of alcohol. *Quarterly Journal of Studies on Alcohol,* 1964, 25, 714–723.

Fanon, F. *The wretched of the earth.* New York: Grove, 1963.

———. *Black skin, white masks.* New York: Grove, 1967.

Farber, I. E. The things people say to themselves. *American Psychologist,* 1964, 19, 18–197.

———. Sane and insane: constructions and misconstructions. *Journal of Abnormal Psychology,* 1975, 84, 589–620.

Faris, R. E. L. Cultural isolation and the schizophrenic personality. *American Journal of Sociology,* 1934, 40, 155–164. Reprinted in Buss, A. H., and Buss, E. (eds.), *Theories of schizophrenia.* New York: Atherton, 1969, pp. 156–167.

Fazio, A. F. Treatment components in implosive therapy. *Journal of Abnormal Psychology,* 1970, 76, 211–219.

Feinberg, I., and Evarts, E. V. Some implications of sleep research for psychiatry. In Zubin, J., and Shagass, C. (eds.), *Neurobiological aspects of psychopathology.* New York: Grune & Stratton, 1969, pp. 334–393.

———, **Koresko, R. L., Gottlieb, F., and Wender, P. H.** Sleep EEG and eye-movement patterns in schizophrenic patients. *Comprehensive Psychiatry,* 1964, 5, 44–53.

Feingold, B. *Why your child is hyperactive.* New York: Random House, 1974.

Feinsilver, D. B., and Gunderson, J. G. Psychotherapy for schizophrenics—is it indicated? A review of the relevant literature. *Schizophrenia Bulletin,* Issue No. 6, 1972, 11–23.

Feldman, M. P. Aversion therapies for sexual deviations: a critical review. *Psychological Bulletin,* 1966, 65, 65–79.

———, **and MacCulloch, M. J.** A systematic approach to the treatment of homosexuality by conditioned aversion: preliminary report. *American Journal of Psychiatry,* 1964, 121, 167–171.

———. The application of anticipatory avoidance learning to the treatment of homosexuality. *Behavior Research and Therapy,* 1965, 2, 165–183.

Ferenczi, S. *Further contributions to the theory and technique of psychoanalysis.* London: Hogarth, 1926.

Ferracuti, F. Incest between father and daughter. In Resnick,

H. L. P., and Wolfgang, M. E. (eds.), *Sexual behaviors: social, clinical and legal aspects.* Boston: Little, Brown, 1972, pp. 169–183.

Ferster, C. B. Positive reinforcement and behavioral deficits of autistic children. *Child Development,* 1961, 32, 437–456.

———. Classification of behavioral pathology. In Krasner, L., and Ullmann, L. P. (eds.), *Research in behavioral modification: new developments and implications.* New York: Holt, Rinehart and Winston, 1965, pp. 6–26.

———. A functional analysis of depression. *American Psychologist,* 1973, 28, 857–870.

Feshbach, S. Aggression. In Mussen, P. H. (ed.), *Carmichael's manual of child psychology,* Vol. 2. 3rd ed. New York: Wiley, 1970.

———. Reality and fantasy in filmed violence. In Murray, J. P., Rubinstein, E. A., and Comstock, G. A. (eds.), *Television and social behavior. Reports and papers, Vol. 2: Television and social learning.* A technical report to the Surgeon General's Scientific Advisory Committee on Television and Social Behavior. Washington, D.C.: Government Printing Office, 1972.

Fidler, J. W., Guerney, B. G., Andronico, M. P., and Guerney, L. Filial therapy as a logical extension of current trends in psychotherapy. In Guerney, B. G. (ed.), *Psychotherapeutic agents: new roles for nonprofessionals, parents, and teachers.* New York: Holt, Rinehart and Winston, 1969, pp. 47–55.

Fiedler, F. E. A comparison of therapeutic relations in psychoanalytic non-directive and Adlerian therapy. *Journal of Consulting Psychology,* 1950, 14, 436–455.

Field, F. B. A new cross-cultural study of drunkenness. In Pittman, D. J., and Snyder, C. R. (eds.), *Society, culture, and drinking patterns.* New York: Wiley, 1962, pp. 48–74.

Fine, R. Psychoanalysis. In Corsini, R. (ed.), *Current psychotherapies.* Itasca, Ill.: Peacock, 1973, pp. 1–133.

Fish, B. Contributions of developmental research to a theory of schizophrenia. In Hellmuth, J. (ed.), *Studies in abnormalities. Exceptional infant,* Vol. 2. New York: Brunner/Mazel, 1971, pp. 473–482.

Fixsen, D. L., Phillips, E. L., and Wolf, M. M. Achievement place: the reliability of self-reporting and peer-reporting and their effects on behavior. *Journal of Applied Behavior Analysis,* 1972, 5, 19–30.

———, **Phillips, E. L., and Wolf, M. M.** Achievement place: experiments in self government with pre-delinquents. *Journal of Applied Behavior Analysis,* 1973, 6, 31–47.

———, **Phillips, E. L., Phillips, E. A., and Wolf, M. M.** The teaching family model of group home treatment. In Craighead, W. E., Kazdin, A. E., and Mohoney, M. J. (eds.), *Behavior modification.* Boston: Houghton Mifflin, 1976, pp. 310–320.

Flowers, J. V. Behavior modification of cheating in an ele-

mentary school student: a brief note. *Behavior Therapy,* 1972, 3, 311–312.

Fontana, A. F. Familial etiology of schizophrenia: is a scientific methodology possible? *Psychological Bulletin,* 1966, 66, 214–277.

Footlick, J. K., Howard, L., Camper, D., Sciolinos, E., and Smith, S. Rape alert. *Newsweek,* November 10, 1975, 70–78.

Ford, C. S., and Beach, F. A. *Patterns of sexual behavior.* New York: Harper & Row, 1951.

Ford, D. H., and Urban, H. B. *Systems of psychotherapy: a comparative study.* New York; Wiley, 1963.

Foreyt, J. P., and Kennedy, W. A. Treatment of overweight by aversion therapy. *Behavior Research and Therapy,* 1971, 9, 29–34.

Fort, J. *The pleasure seekers.* Indianapolis: Bobbs-Merrill, 1969.

Fortune, R. Incest. In *Encyclopedia of the social sciences,* Vol. 7. New York: Macmillan and Free Press, 1932, 620 ff.

Foulds, G. A. *Personality and personal illness.* London: Tavistock, 1965.

Fowler, R. D., Jr. Automated interpretation of test data. In Butcher, J. N. (ed.), *MMPI research developments and clinical applications.* New York: McGraw-Hill, 1969, pp. 105–126.

Foxx, R. M., and Azrin, N. H. Dry pants: a rapid method for toilet training children. *Behavior Research and Therapy,* 1973, 11, 435–442.

Frank, J. D. *Persuasion and healing: a comparative study of psychotherapy.* Rev. ed. Baltimore: The Johns Hopkins University Press, 1973.

Frank, L. K. Projective methods for the study of personality. *Journal of Psychology,* 1939, 8, 349–413.

Frankl, V. E. *Man's search for meaning.* Boston: Beacon, 1962.

———. *The doctor and the soul.* 2nd ed. New York: Knopf, 1965.

Franklin, J. H. The two worlds of race: a historical view. *Daedalus,* 1965, 94, 899–920.

Franks, C. Alcoholism. In Costello, C. G. (ed.), *Symptoms of psychopathology.* New York: Wiley, 1970, pp. 448–480.

——— (ed.). *Behavior therapy: appraisal and status.* New York: McGraw-Hill, 1969.

Freedman, A. M., and Kaplan, H. I. (eds.). *Interpreting personality: a survey of twentieth-century views.* New York: Atheneum, 1972.

Freedman, D. G. *Synopsis of comprehensive textbook of psychiatry.* 2nd ed. Baltimore: Williams and Wilkins, 1976.

Freedman, D. X. Pharmacotherapy. In Braceland, F. J., Freedman, D. X., Friedhoff, A. J., Kolb, L. C., Lourie, R. S., and Romano, J. (eds.), *Year book of psychiatry and applied mental health, 1977.* Chicago: Year Book Medical Publishers, 1977, pp. 271–313.

Freedman, M. *Personal definition and psychological function.* New York: Harper & Row, 1975.

Freeman, E. H., Feingold, B. F., Schlesinger, K., and Gor-

man, E. J. Psychological variables in allergic disorders: a review. *Psychosomatic Medicine,* 1964, 26, 543–575.

Fremming, K. H. The expectation of mental infirmity in a sample of the Danish population. *English Society of Occasional Papers on Eugenics,* 1951, 7.

Freud, A. *The psycho-analytical treatment of children* (1946). New York: International Universities Press, 1965.

———, **and Burlingham, D.** *Infants without families.* New York: International Universities Press, 1944.

Freud, S. *Mourning and melancholia.* In *Collected papers,* Vol. 4. London: Hogarth, 1917.

———. *The ego and the id.* London: Hogarth, 1927.

———. *An autobiographical study.* New York: Norton, 1935.

———. Mourning and melancholia (1917). In *Collected papers,* Vol. 4. London: Hogarth and the Institute of Psychoanalysis, 1950, pp. 152–172.

———. *Beyond the pleasure principle* (1920). In *Standard edition,* Vol. 18. London: Hogarth, 1953(a).

———. *Civilization and its discontents* (1930). In *Standard edition,* Vol. 21. London: Hogarth, 1953(b).

———. *A general introduction to psycho-analysis.* New York: Perma Giants, 1953(c).

———. *The interpretation of dreams* (1900). In *Standard edition,* Vols. 4 and 5. London: Hogarth, 1953(d).

———. *The standard edition of the complete psychological works.* Strachey, J. (ed.). London: Hogarth, 1953(e).

———. *Three essays on sexuality* (1905). In *Standard edition,* Vol. 7. London: Hogarth, 1953(f).

———. *Analysis of a phobia in a five-year-old boy* (1909). London: Hogarth, 1955(a).

———. On narcissism: an introduction (1914). In *Standard edition,* Vol. 14. London: Hogarth, 1955(b), pp. 67–107.

———. Further remarks on the defense neuro-psychoses (1896). Reprinted in *Collected papers,* Vol. 1, New York: Basic Books, 1959(a), pp. 155–188.

———. Psycho-analytic notes upon an autobiographical account of a case of paranoia (Dementia Paranoides) (1911). In *Collected papers,* Vol. 3. New York: Basic Books, 1959(b), pp. 385–470.

———. Why war? In *Collected papers,* Vol. 5. New York: Basic Books, 1959(c).

———. *Civilization and its discontents* (1930). Standard edition, Vol. 21, London: Hogarth, 1961, pp. 64–145.

———. *Three essays on the theory of sexuality* (1905). New York: Basic Books, 1976.

Friedman, M., and Rosenman, R. H. *Type A behavior and your heart.* New York: Knopf, 1974.

Friedman, P. Sexual deviations. In Arieti, S. (ed.), *American handbook of psychiatry,* Vol. I. New York: Basic Books, 1959, pp. 589–613.

Friedman, P. H. The effects of modeling and role-playing on assertive behavior. In Rubin, R. D., Fernsterheim, H., Lazarus, A. A., and Franks, C. M. (eds.), *Advances in behavior therapy.* New York: Academic Press, 1971, pp. 149–169.

Friend, D. G. (ed.). Neuropsychiatric disease. In *The year book of drug therapy, 1976.* Chicago: Year Book Medical Publishers, 1976, pp. 297–316.

Fromm, E. *Escape from freedom.* New York: Holt, Rinehart and Winston, 1941.

———. *Man for himself.* New York: Holt, Rinehart and Winston, 1947.

———. *The sane society.* New York: Holt, Rinehart and Winston, 1955.

———. *Beyond the chains of illusion.* New York: Simon and Schuster, 1962.

———. *The heart of man.* New York: Harper & Row, 1964.

———. *The revolution of hope.* New York: Harper & Row, 1968.

———. *The anatomy of human destructiveness.* New York: Holt, Rinehart and Winston, 1973.

Fromm–Reichmann, F. *Principles of intensive psychotherapy.* Chicago: University of Chicago Press, 1950.

Fry, L., Mason, A. A., and Bruce–Pearson, R. S. Effect of hypnosis on allergic skin responses in asthma and hay fever. *British Medical Journal,* 1964, 1, 1145–1148.

Gagnon, J. H. Sexuality and sexual learning in the child. *Psychiatry,* August 1965.

Gallagher, C. E. Special issue: testing and public policy. *American Psychologist,* 1965, 20, 881–882.

Galle, O. R., Grove, W. R. and McPherson, J. M. Population density and pathology: what are the relations for man? *Science,* 1972, 176, 23–30.

Galvani, L. De viribus electricitatis in motu musculari: commentarius. *Proceedings Academie de Bologna,* 1791, 7, 363–418.

Gantt, W. H. *Experimental basis for neurotic behavior.* New York: Harper & Row, 1944.

———. Experimental basis for neurotic behavior. In Kimmel, H. D. (ed.), *Experimental psychopathology: recent research and theory.* New York: Academic Press, 1971, pp. 33–48.

Ganzler, S. Some interpersonal and social dimensions of suicidal behavior. *Dissertation Abstracts,* 1967, 288, 1192–1193.

Gardner, J. M. Differential effectiveness of the methods for teaching behavior modification techniques to institutional attendants. Paper presented at American Association for the Mentally Deficient. Washington, D.C., 1970.

Gardner, R. A, and Gardner, B. T. Teaching sign language to a chimpanzee. *Science,* 1969, 165, 664–672.

———. Early signs of language in child and chimpanzee. *Science,* 1975, 187, 752–753.

Gardner, W. I. Use of behavior therapy with the mentally retarded. In Menolascino, F. J. (ed.), *Psychiatric approaches to mental retardation.* New York: Basic Books, 1970, pp. 250–275.

Garfield, S. L., and Bergin, A. E. *Handbook of psychotherapy and behavior change.* 2nd ed. New York: Wiley, 1978.

———, and Kurtz, R. Clinical psychologists in the 1970's. *American Psychologist*, 1976, 31, 1–9.

Garmezy, N. Children at risk: the search for the antecedents of schizophrenia. I. Conceptual models and research methods. *Schizophrenia Bulletin*. Rockville, MD: Center for Studies of Schizophrenia, MIMH, Spring 1974, pp. 14–90.

———. The prediction of performance in schizophrenia. In Hoch, P. H., and Zubin, J. (eds.), *Psychopathology of schizophrenia*. New York: Grune & Stratton, 1966, pp. 129–181.

Gauron, E., and Dickinson, J. K. Diagnostic decision making in psychiatry. *Archives of General Psychiatry*, 1966, 14, 233–237.

Gaver, K. D. Today's drug problem; what's happening. In Blachly, P. H. (ed.), *Drug abuse: data and debate*. Springfield, Ill.: Thomas, 1970.

Gaylin, W. In matters mental or emotional, what's normal? In Milgram, S. (ed.), *Psychology in today's world*. Boston: Little, Brown, 1975, pp. 212–217.

Gazzaniga, M. S. The split brain in man. *Scientific American*, August 1967.

———. *Fundamentals of psychology: an introduction*. New York: Academic Press, 1973.

Gearing, F. The response to a cultural precept among migrants from Bronzeville to Hyde Park. Unpublished master's thesis, University of Chicago, 1952 (cited in Webb et al., 1966).

Geer, J. H., and Turteltaub, A. Fear reduction following observation of a model. *Journal of Personality and Social Psychology*, 1967, 6, 327–331.

———, Davison, G. C., and Gatchel, R. I. Reduction of stress in humans through nonveridical perceived control of aversive stimulation. *Journal of Personality and Social Psychology*, 1970, 16, 731–738.

Gelber, H., and Meyer, V. Behavior therapy in treatment. *Behavioral Research and Therapy*, 1965, 2, 227–231.

Gellhorn, E., and Loofbourrow, G. N. *Emotions and emotional disorders: a neurophysiological study*. New York: Harper & Row, 1963.

Gerard, D. L., and Houston, L. G. Family setting and the social ecology of schizophrenia. *Psychiatric Quarterly*, 1953, 27, 90–101.

Gericke, O. L. Practical use of operant conditioning procedures in a mental hospital. *Psychiatric Studies and Projects*, American Psychiatric Association, 1965, 3, 2–10.

Gershon, S., and Shopsin, B. (eds.). *Lithium: its role in psychiatric research and treatment*. New York: Plenum, 1973.

Geschwind, N. Language and the brain. *Scientific American*, June 1972.

Gibb, J. R. The effects of human relations training. In Bergin, A. E., and Garfield, S. L. (eds.), *Handbook of psychotherapy and behavior change: an empirical analysis*. New York: Wiley, 1971, pp. 839–862.

Gillin, J. C., and Wyatt, R. J. Schizophrenia: perchance a dream. *International Review of Neurobiology*, 1975, 17, 297–342.

Gillman, R. D. Brief psychotherapy: a psychoanalytic view. *American Journal of Psychiatry*, 1965, 122, 601–611.

Gilmer, B.v.H. *Psychology*. 2nd ed. New York: Harper & Row, 1973.

Gladfelter, W. E., and Brobeck, J. R. Decreased spontaneous locomotor activity in the rat induced by hypothalamic lesions. *American Journal of Physiology*, 1962, 203, 811–817.

Glass, D. C. and Singer, J. E. *Urban stress: experiments on noise and social stressers*. New York: Academic Press, 1972.

Glasser, W. *Reality therapy*. New York: Harper & Row, 1965.

Glatt, M. M. Group therapy in alcoholism. *British Journal of Addiction*, 1958, 54, 133.

Gliedman, L. H., Nash, E. H., Imber, S. D., Stone, A. R., and Frank, J. D. Reduction of symptoms by pharmacologically inert substances and by short-term psychotherapy. *Archives of Neurology and Psychiatry*, 1958, 79, 345–351.

Glynn, J. D., and Harper, P. Behavior therapy in a case of transvestism. *Lancet*, 1961, 1, 619.

Goddard, H. H. Mental tests and the immigrant. *Journal of Delinquency*, 1917, 2, 243–277.

Goertzel, V., Beard, J. H., and Pilnick, S. Fountain House Foundation: case study of an ex-patients' club. *Journal of Social Issues*, 1960, 16, 54–61.

Goffman, E. The moral career of the mental patient. *Psychiatry*, 1959, 22, 123–142.

———. *Asylums: essays on the social situation of mental patients and other immates*. New York: Doubleday (Anchor Books), 1961.

Goldenberg, H. *Abnormal psychology: a social community approach*. Monterey, Calif.: Brooks/Cole, 1977.

Goldfried, M. R. *Behavioral assessment*. In Weiner, I. B. (ed.), *Clinical methods in psychology*. New York: Wiley, 1976, pp. 281–330.

———, and Sprafkin, J. N. *Behavioral personality assessment*. Morristown, N.J.: General Learning Press, 1974.

Goldman, A. R., Bohr, R. H., and Steinberg, T. H. On posing as mental patients: reminiscences and recommendations. *Professional Psychology*, 1970, 1, 427–434.

Goldstein, J. H., and Arms, R. L. Effects of observing athletic contests on hostility. *Sociometry*, 1971, 34, 83–90.

Goldstein, J. W. Motivations for psychoactive drug use among students. Paper delivered at the annual meeting of the Eastern Psychological Association, April 15, 1971(a).

———. *Narcotics and alcoholism, I: testimony and summary of research on youthful drug use before the United States Senate Subcommittee on Alcoholism and Narcotics*. Washington, D.C.: Government Printing Office, 1971(b).

———. Drug education worthy of the name. *Impact: The*

Magazine for Innovation and Change in Counseling. 1972, 1(4), 18–24.

——. On the explanation of student drug use. In Goode, E. (ed.), *Marijuana revisited*. Chicago: Lieber-Atherton, 1973(a).

——. Personal communication, 1973(b).

——. Assessing the interpersonal determinants of adolescent drug use. In Lettieri, D. J. (ed.), *Predicting adolescent drug abuse: a review of issues, methods and correlates*. Washington, D.C.: Government Printing Office, 1975(a), pp. 47–52.

——. Students' evaluations of their psychoactive drug use. *Journal of Counseling Psychology*, 1975(b), 22, 333–339.

——, Gleason, T. C. and Korn, J. H. Whither the epidemic? Psychoactive drug use career patterns of college students. *Journal of Applied Social Psychology*, 1975, 1, 16–33.

——, Korn, J. H., Abel, W. H., and Morgan, R. M. *The social psychology and epidemiology of student drug usage: report on phase one*. Carnegie-Mellon Psychology Department Preprint Series, Report 70–18, June 1970. (Also abstracted in *Research in education*, 1972, 7, 24).

——, and Sappington, J. T. Personality characteristics of students who became heavy drug users: an MMPI study of an avant-garde. *American Journal of Drug and Alcohol Abuse*, 1974, 4, 401–412.

Goldstein, K. The effect of brain damage on personality. Paper delivered to the American Psychoanalytic Association, Atlantic City, May 1952.

——, and Scheerer, M. Abstract and concrete behavior: an experimental study with special tests. *Psychological Monographs*, 1941, 53.

Goldstein, M. L. Physiological theories of emotion: a critical historical review from the standpoint of behavioral theory. *Psychological Bulletin*, 1968, 69, 23–40.

Gomes–Schwartz, B. Personal communication, 1978.

Goodall, K. Who's who and where in behavior shaping? *Psychology Today*, 1972, 6, 58–63.

Goode, E. *The marijuana smokers*. New York: Basic Books, 1970.

——. *Drugs in American society*. New York: Knopf, 1972.

Goodenough, E. R. *Jewish symbols in the Greco-Roman period. Vol. 5: Fish, bread, and wine*. New York: Pantheon, 1956.

Goodwin, D. W., and Guze, S. B. Genetic factors in alcoholism. In Kissin, B., and Begleiter, H. (eds.), *Clinical pathology*, Vol. 3. New York: Plenum, 1974.

——, Schulsinger, F., Hermansen, L., Guze, S. B., and Winokur, G. Alcohol problems in adoptees raised apart from alcoholic biological parents. *Archives of General Psychiatry*, 1973, 28, 238–243.

Gordon, D. C. *Self-love*. New York: Macmillan, 1968.

Gorelick, M. C. *An assessment of vocational realism of high school and post high school educable mentally retarded adolescents*. Los Angeles: Exceptional Children's Foundation, 1966.

Gorman, M. Community mental health: the search for identity. *Community Mental Health Journal*, 1970, 6, 347–355.

Gorton, B. E. The physiology of hypnosis. *Psychiatric Quarterly*, 1949, 23, 317–343.

Gottesman, I. I. Schizophrenia and genetics: toward understanding uncertainty. *Psychiatric Annals*, 1979, 9, 26–37.

——, and Shields, J. Contribution of twin studies to perspectives in schizophrenia. In Maher, B. A. (ed.), *Progress in experimental personality research*, Vol. 3. New York: Academic Press, 1966, pp.1–84.

——. Schizophrenia in twins: sixteen years' consecutive admissions to a psychiatric clinic. *British Journal of Psychiatry*, 1966, 112, 809–818.

——. *Schizophrenia and genetics: a twin study vantage point*. New York: Academic Press, 1972.

Gottlieb, J. S., Ashley, M. C., and Knott, J. R. Primary behavior disorders and the psychopathic personality. *Archives of Neurology and Psychiatry*, 1946, 56, 381–400.

Gottman, J. M., and Leiblum, S. R. *How to do psychotherapy and how to evaluate it: a manual for beginners*. New York: Holt, Rinehart and Winston, 1974.

Gottschalk, L. A. Psychoanalytic notes on T-groups at the Human Relations Laboratory, Bethel, Maine. *Comprehensive Psychiatry*, 1966, 7, 472–487.

——, Mayerson, P., and Gottlieb, A. A. Prediction and evaluation of outcome in an emergency brief psychotherapy clinic. *Journal of Nervous and Mental Disease*, 1967, 144, 77–96.

Gough, H. G. *California Psychological Inventory*. Palo Alto; Calif.: Consulting Psychologists, 1960.

Gouster, M. Moral insanity. *Revues des Sciences Médicales*, 1878, 5, 181–182.

Grace, W., and Graham, D. T. Relationship of specific attitudes and emotions to certain bodily diseases. *Psychosomatic Medicine*, 1952, 14, 243–251.

Graham, D. T., Stern, J. A., and Winokur, G. Experimental investigation of the specificity of attitude hypothesis in psychosomatic diseases. *Psychosomatic Medicine*, 1958, 20, 446–447.

——, Kabler, J. D., and Graham, F. K. Physiological response to the suggestion of attitudes specific for hives and hypertension. *Psychosomatic Medicine*, 1962, 24, 159–169.

Gralnick, A. Folie à deux: the psychosis of association. *Psychiatric Quarterly*, 1942, 16, 230–263.

Granville–Grossman, K. L. The early environment in affective disorder. In Coppen, A., and Walk, A. (eds.), Recent developments in affective disorders. *British Journal of Psychiatry*, special publication No. 2, 1968.

Graziano, A. M. Behavior therapy. In Wolman, B. B., Egan, J., and Ross, A. O. (eds.), *Handbook of treatment of mental disorders in childhood and adolescence*. Englewood Cliffs, N.J.: Prentice-Hall, 1978.

Green, B. F. *Digital computers in research: an introduction for behavioral and social scientists*. New York: McGraw-Hill, 1963.

Green, E., Silverman, D., and Geil, G. Petit mal electroshock therapy of criminal psychopaths. *Journal of Criminal Psychopathology,* 1943, 5, 667–695.

Greenacre, P. Conscience in the psychopath. *American Journal of Orthopsychiatry,* 1945, 15, 495–509.

Greenberg, L. Alcohol in the body. *Scientific American,* 1953, 189, 86 ff.

Greenblatt, M. Psychosurgery. In Freedman, A. M., and Kaplan, H. I. (eds.), *Treating mental illness: aspects of modern therapy.* New York: Atheneum, 1972, pp. 372–381.

Grier, W. H., and Cobbs, P. M. *Black rage.* New York: Basic Books, 1968.

——. *The Jesus bag.* New York: Bantam, 1971.

Grim, P. Anxiety change produced by self-induced muscle tension and by relaxation with respiration feedback. *Behavior Therapy,* 1971, 2, 11–17.

Grinker, R. R., Sr. A transactional model for psychotherapy. In Stein, M. I. (ed.), *Contemporary psychotherapies.* New York: Free Press, 1961, pp. 197–227.

——, Miller, J., Sabshin, M., Nann, R., and Nunnally, J. C. *The phenomena depression.* New York: Paul B. Hoeber, 1961.

Grinspoon, L. *Marihuana reconsidered.* New York: Bantam, 1971.

——, and Bakalar, J. B. *Cocaine: a drug and its social evolution.* New York: Basic Books, 1976.

Grossman, S. *A textbook of physiological psychology.* New York: Wiley, 1967.

Grosvenor, D. K., and Grosvenor, G. M. Ceylon, the resplendent land. *National Geographic,* 1966, 129, 447–497.

Guerney, B. G. (ed.). *Psychotherapeutic agents: new roles for nonprofessionals, parents, and teachers.* New York: Holt, Rinehart and Winston, 1969.

Guetzkow, H. S., and Bowman, P. H. *Men and hunger: a psychological manual for relief workers.* Elgin, Ill.: Brethren, 1946.

Guilford, J. P. *The nature of human intelligence.* New York: McGraw-Hill, 1967.

Gulevich, G. D., Dement, W. C., and Zarcone, V. P. All-night sleep recordings of chronic schizophrenics in remission. *Comprehensive Psychiatry,* 1967, 8, 141–149.

Gunderson, E. K. E., and Arthur, R. J. Prognostic indicators in psychosis and neurosis. *Journal of Abnormal Psychology,* 1968, 73, 468–473.

Gunderson, J. G., and Mosher, L. R. The cost of schizophrenia. *American Journal of Psychiatry,* 1975, 132, 901–905.

Gundry, R. L. Nonrestraint in the care of the insane. *Proceedings of the National Conference of Charities and Correction,* 1885, 124 ff.

Gunther, B. *Sense relaxation: Below your mind.* New York: Macmillan, 1968.

Guralnik, L. Mortality by occupation and cause of death among men 20 to 64 years of age: United States, 1950. *Vital Statistics Special Reports,* 1963, 53.

Gurel, L. A ten-year perspective on outcome in functional psychosis. Highlights of the 15th Annual Conference, VA Cooperative Studies in Psychiatry, Houston, Texas, 1970.

Gurland, B. J. A broad clinical assessment of psychopathology in the aged. In Eisdorfed, C., and Lawton, M. P. (eds.), *The psychology of adult development and aging.* Washington, D.C.: American Psychological Association, 1973.

Guthrie, R. V. *Being black: Psychological-sociological dilemmas.* San Francisco: Harper & Row (Canfield Press), 1970.

——. *Even the rat was white: a historical view of psychology.* New York: Harper & Row, 1975.

Haagen, C. H. *Social and psychological characteristics associated with the use of marijuana by college men.* Middletown, Conn.: Office of Psychological Services, Wesleyan University, 1970.

Haggard, E. Some conditions determining adjustment during and readjustment following experimentally induced stress. In Tomkins, S. (ed.), *Contemporary psychopathology.* Cambridge, Mass.: Harvard University Press, 1943.

Hain, J. D., Butcher, H. G., and Stevenson, I. Systematic desensitization therapy: an analysis of results in 27 patients. *British Journal of Psychiatry,* 1966, 112, 295–307.

Haley, J. Direct study of child-parent interactions. *American Journal of Orthopsychiatry,* 1960, 30, 460–467.

Hall, C. S., and Lindzey, G. *Theories of personality.* 2nd ed. New York: Wiley, 1970.

Hall, E. T. *The hidden dimension.* New York: Doubleday, 1966.

Hall, R., and Joffe, J. Aberrant response to diazepam: a new syndrome. *American Journal of Psychiatry,* 1972, 129, 738–742.

Haller, B. L. Some factors related to the adjustment of psychopaths on parole from a state hospital. *Smith College Studies of Social Work,* 1942, 13.

Halstead, W. C. Biological intelligence. *Journal of Personality,* 1951, 20, 118–130.

Hamburg, D. A. Effects of progesterone on behavior. In Levine, R. (ed.), *Endocrines and the central nervous system.* Baltimore: Williams & Wilkins, 1966.

——, Moos, R. H., and Yalom, I. D. Studies of distress in the menstrual cycle and postpartum period. In Michael, R. P. (ed.), *Endocrinology and human behavior.* London: Oxford University Press, 1968.

Hammond, A. L. Aspirin: new perspective on everyman's medicine. *Science,* 1971, 174, No. 10, 48.

Hansell, N. Casualty management method. *Archives of General Psychiatry,* 1968, 19, 231–239.

Hanson, D. R., Gottesman, I. I., and Heston, L. L. Some possible childhood indicators of adult schizophrenia inferred from children of schizophrenics. *British Journal of Psychiatry,* 1976, 129, 142–154.

——, and Meehl, P. E. Genetic theories and the validation

of psychiatric diagnoses: implications for the study of children of schizophrenics. *Journal of Abnormal Psychology,* 1977, 86, 575–588.

Hardin, H. *Suicide in Scandinavia.* New York: Grune & Stratton, 1964.

Hardt, J. Personal communication, 1973.

Hare, R. D. Psychopathy, autonomic functioning, and the orienting response. *Journal of Abnormal Psychology.* Monograph Supplement, 1968(a), 73, No. 3, Pt. 2, 1–24.

———. Detection threshold for electric shock in psychopaths. *Journal of Abnormal Psychology,* 1968(b), 73, 268–272.

———. *Psychopathy: theory and research.* New York: Wiley, 1970.

Harlow, H. F. Love in infant monkeys. *Scientific American,* 1959, 200, 68–74.

———. The heterosexual affectional system in monkeys. *American Psychologist,* 1962, 17, 1–9.

———, and **Harlow, M. K.** The effect of rearing conditions on behavior. *Bulletin of the Menninger Clinic,* 1962, 26, 213–224.

———, and **Harlow, M. K.** Psychopathology in monkeys. In Kimmel, H. D. (ed.), *Experimental Psychopathology: recent research and theory.* New York: Academic Press, 1971.

———, **Harlow, M. K.,** and **Suomi, S. J.** From thought to therapy: lessons from a primate laboratory. *American Scientist,* 1971, 59, 538–549.

———, and **Zimmerman, R. R.** Affectional responses in the infant monkey. *Science,* 1959, 130, 431–432.

Harlow, J. M. Recovery from the passage of an iron bar through the head. *Publication of the Massachusetts Medical Society,* 1868, 2, 327.

Hardt, J. Personal communication, 1973.

Harrington, A. *Psychopaths.* New York: Simon & Schuster, 1972.

Harris, F. R., Wolf, M. M., and **Baer, D. M.** Effects of adult social reinforcement on child behavior. In Guerney, B. G. (ed.), *Psychotherapeutic agents: new roles for nonprofessionals, parents, and teachers.* New York: Holt, Rinehart and Winston, 1969, pp. 342–354.

Hartley, D., Roback, H., and **Abramowitz, S.** Deterioration effects in encounter groups. *American Psychologist,* 1976, 31, 247–255.

Harway, N. I., and **Iker, H. P.** Objective content analysis of psychotherapy by computer. In Enslein K., and Kinslow, J. F. (eds.), *Data acquisition and processing in biology and medicine. Proceedings of the 1964 Rochester Conference.* New York: Pergamon, 1965.

Hathaway, S. R. Hypochondriasis. In Burton, A., and Harris, R. R. (eds.), *Case histories in clinical and abnormal psychology.* New York: Harper & Row, 1947, pp. 246–256.

———. Some considerations relative to nondirective counseling as therapy. *Journal of Clinical Psychology,* 1948, 4, 226–231.

———. MMPI: professional use by professional people.

American Psychologist, 1964, 19, 204–210.

———, and **McKinley, J. C.** *Manual for the Minnesota Multiphasic Personality Inventory.* New York: Psychological Corporation, 1943.

Hauri, P., Chernik, D., Hawkins, D., and **Mendels, J.** Sleep of depressed patients in remission. *Archives of General Psychiatry,* 1974, 31, 386–391.

Havighurst, R. J., Neugarten, B. L., and **Tobin, S. S.** Disengagement and patterns of aging. In Neugarten, B. (ed.), *Middle age and aging.* Chicago: University of Chicago Press, 1968.

Hayward, M. L., and **Taylor, T. E.** A schizophrenic patient describes the action of intensive psychotherapy. *Psychiatric Quarterly,* 1956, 30, 211–248.

Haywood, H. C. Labeling: efficacy, evils, and caveats. Paper presented at the Joseph P. Kennedy, Jr. Foundation International Symposium on Human Retardation and Research, Washington, D.C., 1971.

Heath, R. G. (ed.). *Serological fractions in schizophrenia.* New York: Harper & Row, 1963.

———. Schizophrenia: biochemical and physiological aberrations. *International Journal of Neuropsychiatry,* 1966, 2, 597–610.

———, and the Department of Psychiatry and Neurology, Tulane University. *Studies in schizophrenia.* Cambridge, Mass.: Harvard University Press, 1954.

———, and **Leach, B. E.** Brain recordings with schizophrenic behavior. Some metabolic factors responsible for physiological alterations. *Annals of the New York Academy of Sciences,* 1962, 96, 425–437.

———, **Guschwan, A. F.,** and **Coffey, J. W.** Relation of taraxein to schizophrenia. *Diseases of the Nervous System,* 1970, 31, 391–395.

Heber, R. F. Personality. In Stevens, H. A., and Heber, R. F. (eds.), *Mental retardation: a review of research.* Chicago: University of Chicago Press, 1964.

Heidel, F. *The psychology of interpersonal relations.* New York: Wiley, 1958.

Heilbrun, A. B., Jr. *Aversive maternal control: a theory of schizophrenic development.* New York: Wiley, 1973.

Heineman, C. E. A forced choice form of the Taylor Anxiety Scale. *Journal of Consulting Psychology,* 1953, 17, 447–454.

Heinicke, C. M. Parental deprivation in early childhood: a predisposition to later depression. In Scott, J. P. and Senay, E. C. (eds.), *Separation and depression.* Washington, D.C.: AAAS, 1973.

Helfer, R. E., and **Kempe, C. H.** (eds.). *The battered child.* Chicago: University of Chicago Press, 1968.

Helmstadter, G. C. *Principles of psychological measurement.* Englewood Cliffs, N.J.: Prentice-Hall, 1964.

Helper, M. M., Wilcott, R. C., and **Garfield, S. L.** Effects of chlorpromazine on learning and related processes in emotionally disturbed children. *Journal of Consulting Psychology,* 1963, 27, 1–9.

Hendin, H. *Suicide and Scandinavia.* New York: Grune and Stratton, 1964.

———. *Black suicide.* New York: Basic Books, 1969.

Henry, J. *Culture against man.* New York: Random House, 1963.

Hernton, C. C. *Sex and racism in America.* New York: Grove, 1965.

Heron, W. The pathology of boredom. *Scientific American,* 1957, 196, 52–56.

———, **Bexton, W. H., and Hebb, D. O.** Cognitive effects of a decreased variation in the sensory environment. *American Psychologist,* 1953, 8, 366 (abstract).

Herron, E. W. Psychometric characteristics of a thirty-item version of the group method of the Holtzman Inkblot Technique. *Journal of Clinical Psychology,* 1963, 19, 450–453.

Hersen, M., and Eisler, R. M. Social skills training. In Craighead, W. E., Kazdin, A. E., and Mahoney, M. J. (eds.), *Behavior modification.* Boston: Houghton Mifflin, 1976, pp. 361–375.

———, **Alford, G. S., and Agnas, W. S.** Effects of token economy on neurotic depression: an experimental analysis. *Behavior Therapy,* 1973, 4, 342–397.

Herskovitz, H. H., Levine, M., and Spivack, G. Antisocial behavior of adolescents from higher socio-economic groups. *Journal of Nervous and Mental Disease,* 1959, 125, 1–9.

Hess, E. H. Attitude and pupil size. *Scientific American,* 1965, 212, 46–54.

———. The role of pupil size in communication. *Scientific American,* 1975, 233, 110–119.

Hess, W. R. *Bertrage zur Physiologie d. Hirnstammes.* Leipzig: George Thieme, 1932.

Heston, L. The genetics of schizophrenia and schizoid disease. *Science,* 1970, 167, 249–256.

Hetherington, E. M., and Martin, B. Family interaction and psychopathology in children. In Quay, H. O., and Werry, J. S. (eds.), *Psychopathological disorders of childhood.* New York: Wiley, 1972, pp. 30–82.

Hewes, G. W. World distribution of certain postural habits. *American Anthropologist,* 1955, 57, 231–244.

Hickey, T., and Kalish, R. Young people's perceptions of adults. *Journal of Gerontology,* 1968, 23, 216–219.

———, **Hickey, L., and Kalish, R.** Children's perceptions of the elderly. *Journal of Genetic Psychology,* 1968, 112, 227–235.

Higgins, R. L., and Marlatt, G. A. The effects of anxiety arousal on the consumption of alcohol by alcoholics and social drinkers. *Journal of Clinical and Consulting Psychology,* 1973, 41, 426–433.

———. Fear of interpersonal evaluation as a determinant of alcohol consumption in male social drinkers. *Journal of Abnormal Psychology,* 1975, 84, 644–651.

Hilgard, E. R. A quantitative study of pain and its reduction through hypnotic suggestion. *Proceedings of the National Academy of Sciences,* 1967, 57, 1581–1586.

———. *The experience of hypnosis.* New York: Harcourt Brace Jovanovich, 1968.

———. Pain as a puzzle for psychology and physiology. *American Psychologist,* 1969, 24, 103–113.

———. Personal communication, 1971.

———, **Atkinson, R. C., and Atkinson, R. L.** *Introduction to psychology,* 6th ed. New York: Harcourt Brace Jovanovich, 1975.

Hilgard, J. R. *Personality and hypnosis: a study of imaginative involvement.* Chicago: University of Chicago Press, 1970.

Hill, D., and Pond, D. A. Reflections on one hundred capital cases submitted to EEG. *Journal of Mental Science,* 1952, 98, 23–43.

———, **and Watterson, D.** Electroencephalographic studies of the psychopathic personality. *Journal of Neurology and Psychiatry,* 1942, 5, 47–64.

Hiroto, D. S., and Seligman, M. E. P. Generality of learned helplessness in man. *Journal of Personality and Social Psychology,* 1975, 31, 311–327.

Hobbs, N. Mental health's third revolution. *American Journal of Orthopsychiatry,* 1964, 34, 822–833.

———. Mental health's third revolution. In Bindman, A. J., and Spiegel, A. D. *Perspectives in community mental health.* Chicago: Aldine, 1969, pp. 29–40.

———. *The futures of children.* San Francisco: Jossey-Bass, 1975.

Hoch, P. H., and Zubin, J. (eds.). *Psychopathology of schizophrenia.* New York: Grune & Stratton, 1966.

Hodgson, R. J., and Rachman, S. An experimental investigation of the implosion technique. *Behavior Research and Therapy,* 1970, 8, 21–27.

Hoff, H. The invention of insulin shock treatment of schizophrenia, a milestone in the development of psychiatry. In Rinkel, M. (ed.), *Biological treatment of mental illness.* New York: Page, 1966, pp. 45–53.

Hoffer, A. Treatment of psychosis with LSD. In Gamage, J. R., and Zerkin, E. L. *Hallucinogenic drug research: impact on science and society.* Beloit, Wisc.: Stash, 1970(a), pp. 69–82.

———. Treatment of alcoholism with psychedelic therapy. In Aarons, B., and Osmond, H. (eds.), *Psychedelics: the uses and implications of hallucinogenic drugs.* Cambridge, Mass: Schenkman, 1970(b), pp. 357–365.

———, **and Osmond, H.** *New hope for alcoholics.* New York: University Books, 1968.

Hoffman-LaRoche, Inc. *Roche Report: Frontiers of Psychiatry,* 1971, 1, No. 8, 1–2.

Hogan, R. A. The implosive technique. *Behavior Research and Therapy,* 1968, 6, 423–431.

———, **and Kirchner, J. H.** A preliminary report of the extinction of learned fears via a short-term implosive therapy. *Journal of Abnormal Psychology,* 1967, 72, 106–109.

Hogan, R. T., Mankin, D., Conway, J., and Fox, S. Personality correlates of undergraduate marijuana use. *Journal of Consulting and Clinical Psychology,* 1970, 35, 58–63.

Hogarth, R. M. Cognitive processes and the assessment of subjective probability distributions. *Journal of American Statistical Association,* 1975, 70, 271–289.

Hogarty, G. E., and Goldberg, S. C. Drugs and sociotherapy in the aftercase of schizophrenic patients. *Archives of General Psychiatry,* 1973, 54–64.

Holcomb, R. L. Alcohol in relation to traffic accidents. *Journal of the American Medical Association,* 1938, 3, 1076.

Holden, C. TV violence: government study produces more evidence, no verdict. *Science,* 1972, 175, 608–610. (See also *Television and growing up: the impact of televised violence.* Washington, D.C.: Government Printing Office, 1972.)

———. Psychosurgery: legitimate therapy a laundered lobotomy? *Science,* 1973, 179, 1109–1112.

Holland, J. G., and Skinner, B. F. *The analysis of behavior.* New York: McGraw-Hill, 1961.

Hollender, M. H. Prostitution, the body, and human relatedness. *International Journal of Psychoanalysis,* 1961, 42, 404–413.

Hollingshead, A. B., and Redlich, F. C. Schizophrenia and social structure. *American Journal of Psychiatry,* 1954, 110, 695–701.

———. *Social class and mental illness: a community study.* New York: Wiley, 1958.

Hollister, L. E. *Chemical psychoses: LSD and related drugs.* Springfield, Ill.: Thomas, 1968.

Holmes, T. H., and Wolff, H. G. Life situations and backache. In *Life stress and bodily disease: proceedings of the Association for Research in Nervous and Mental Diseases,* Vol. 29. Baltimore: Williams & Wilkins, 1950, pp. 750–772.

———, and Rahe, R. H. The social adjustment rating scale. *Journal of Psychosomatic Research,* 1967, 11, 213–218.

———, and Masuda, M. Psychosomatic syndrome: when mothers-in-law or other disasters visit, a person can develop a bad, bad cold. Or worse. *Psychology Today,* 1972.

Holmes, T. S., and Holmes, T. H. Short term intrusions into the life style routine. *Journal of Psychosomatic Research,* 1970, 14, 121–132.

Holt, R. R. *Assessing personality.* New York: Harcourt Brace Jovanovich, 1971.

———, and Peterfreund, E. (eds.). *Psychoanalysis and contemporary science.* New York: Macmillan, 1972.

Holtzman, W. H. *The Inkblot Test: a provisional manual for research purposes only.* Austin: University of Texas, 1958.

———. Objective scoring of projective techniques. In Bass, B. M., and Berg, I. A. (eds.), *Objective approaches to personality assessment.* New York: Van Nostrand Reinhold, 1959, pp. 119–145.

———. Personality structure. In Farnsworth, P. R., Mc-

Nemar, O., and McNemar, Q. (eds.), *Annual review of psychology,* Vol. 16. Palo Alto, Calif.: Annual Reviews, 1965, pp. 119–156.

———. The changing world of mental measurement and its social significance. *American Psychologist,* 1971, 26, pp. 546–553.

———. Personal communication, 1973.

———, Moseley, E. C., Reinehr, R. C., and Abbot, E. Comparison of the group method and the standard individual version of the Holtzman Inkblot Technique. *Journal of Clinical Psychology,* 1963, 19, 441–449.

———, Thorpe, J. S., Swartz, J. D., and Herron, E. W. *Inkblot perception and personality: Holtzman Inkblot Technique.* Austin: University of Texas Press, 1961.

Holzman, P. S. *Psychoanalysis and psychopathology.* New York: McGraw-Hill, 1970.

———, and Levy, D. L. Smooth pursuit eye movements and functional psychoses: a review. *Schizophrenia Bulletin,* 1977, 3, 15–27.

———, Proctor, L. R., and Hughes, D. W. Eyetracking patterns in schizophrenia. *Science,* 1973, 181, 179–181.

Hood, A. A study of the relationship between physique and personality variables measured by the MMPI. *Journal of Personality,* 1963, 31, 97–107.

Hook, E. B. Behavioral implications of the human XYY genotype. *Science,* 1973, 179, pp. 139–150.

———, and Kim, D. S. Height and anti-social behavior in XY and XYY boys. *Science,* 1971, 172, pp. 284–286.

Hooker, E. The adjustment of the male overt homosexual. *Journal of Projective Techniques,* 1957, 21, 18–31.

———. The homosexual community. In *Personality research. Proceedings of the XIV International Congress of Applied Psychology,* Vol. 2. Copenhagen: Munksgaard, 1962.

Hope, K., Philip, A. E., and Loughran, J. M. Psychological characteristics associated with the XYY sex-chromosome complement in a state mental hospital. *British Journal of Psychiatry,* 1967, 113, pp. 495–498.

Horn, D. Some factors in smoking and its cessation. In Borgatta, E. F., and Evans, R. R. (eds.), *Smoking, health and behavior.* Chicago: Aldine, 1968, pp. 12–21.

Horney, K. Culture and neurosis. *American Sociological Review,* 1936, 1, 221–230.

———. *Our inner conflicts.* New York: Norton, 1945.

———. *Neurosis and human growth.* New York: Norton, 1950.

Horowitz, S. L. Strategies within hypnosis for reducing phobic behavior. *Journal of Abnormal Psychology,* 1970, 75, pp. 104–112.

Horton, D. The functions of alcohol in primitive societies: a cross-cultural study. *Quarterly Journal of Studies on Alcohol,* 1943, 4, 199–320.

Hosarth, R. M. Cognitive processes and the assessment of subjective probability distributions. *Journal of the American Statistical Association,* 1975, 70, 271–289.

Houser, H. W. *Drugs: facts on their use and abuse.* Glenview, Ill.: Scott, Foresman, 1969.

Howes, D., and Solomon, R. L. A note on McGinnies' emotionality and perceptual defense. *Psychological Reivew,* 1950, 57, 229–234.

Hsia, V. *Residence hall environment: a comprehensive study in architectural psychology.* Salt Lake City: University of Utah, 1967.

Huesmann, L. R. Cognitive processes and models of depression. *Journal of Abnormal Psychology,* 1978, 87.

———, **and Cheng, C. M.** A theory for the induction of mathematical functions. *Psychological Review,* 1973, 80, 126–128.

Hull, C. L. *A behavior system.* New Haven: Yale University Press, 1952.

Hum Lee, R. *The Chinese in the United States.* New York: Oxford University Press, 1960.

Humphreys, L. *Tearoom trade: impersonal sex in public places.* Chicago: Aldine, 1970.

Hunter, R., and Macalpine, I. *Three hundred years of psychiatry, 1535–1860.* London: Oxford University Press, 1963.

Husserl, E. *The idea of phenomenology* (1913). Atlantic Highlands, N.J.: Humanities Press, 1964.

Huston, P. E., and Pepernick, M. C. Prognosis in schizophrenia. In Bellak, (ed.), *Schizophrenia.* New York: Logos, 1958.

Hutchins, R. M. Farewell address to the students, February 2, 1951. In Levi, E. H., The legacy of Robert M. Hutchins. *University of Chicago Magazine,* 1977, LXIX, p. 27.

Hutt, M. L. and Gibby, R. W. *The mentally retarded child: development, education and treatment.* Boston: Allyn & Bacon, 1965.

Ikemi, Y., Akagi, M., Maeda, J., Fokumoto, K., Kawate, K., Hirakawa, K., Gondo, S., Nakagawa, T., Honda, T., Sakamoto, A., and Kumagai, M. Hypnotic experiments on the psychosomatic aspects of gastrointestinal disorders. *International Journal of Clinical and Experimental Hypnosis,* 1959, 7, 139–150.

Imperi, L. L., Kleber, H. D., and Davie, J. S. Use of hallucinogenic drugs on campus. *Journal of the American Medical Association,* 1968, 204, 1021–1024.

Indian Hemp Drugs Commission Report, 1893–1894. *Marihuana* (introduction by J. Kaplan). Silver Spring, Md.: Thomas Jefferson Publishing, 1969.

Inoye, E. Observations on forty twin index cases with chronic epilepsy and their co-twins. *Journal of Nervous and Mental Diseases,* 1960, 130, 401.

Institute for Social Research Newsletter. Boring jobs are hardest on health, a study of 23 occupations reveals. Ann Arbor, Michigan, Spring 1975.

Interim Report of the Canadian Government. *The non-medical use of drugs.* Middlesex, England: Penguin, 1970.

Isbell, H. Experimental physical dependence on alcohol in humans. In Popham, R. E. (ed.), *Alcohol and alcoholism.* Toronto: University of Toronto Press, 1970, pp. 106–110.

Ittlelson, W. H. Environmental psychology of the psychiatric ward. In Taylor, C. W., et al. (eds.), *Second National Conference on Architectural Psychology.* Salt Lake City: University of Utah, 1967, pp. 2–21.

Izard, C. E. *The face of emotion.* Englewood Cliffs, N.J.: Prentice-Hall, 1971.

———. *Patterns of emotions.* New York: Academic Press, 1972.

———, **and Tomkins, S. S.** Affect and behavior: anxiety as a negative affect. In Spielberger, C. D. (ed.), *Anxiety and behavior.* New York: Academic Press, 1966, pp. 81–125.

Jackson, G. D. Rejoinder to Cleary, T. A., Humphreys, L. G., Kendrick, S. A., and Wesman, A. Educational uses of tests with disadvantaged students. *American Psychologist,* 1975, 30, 88–96.

Jackson, J. The adjustment of the family to the crisis of alcoholism. *Quarterly Journal of Studies on Alcohol,* 1954, 15, 562–586. Also reprinted in Rabkin, L. Y., and Carr, J. E. (eds.), *Sourcebook in abnormal psychology.* Boston: Houghton Mifflin, 1967, pp. 313–325.

Jaco, E. G. The social isolation hypothesis in schizophrenia. *American Sociological Review,* 1954, 19, 567–577.

———. *The social epidemiology of mental disorders.* New York: Russell Sage Foundation, 1960.

Jacobs, A., Brunton, M., and Mellville, M. M. Aggressive behavior, mental subnormality, and the XYY male. *Nature,* 1965, 208, 1351–1352.

Jacobs, J. *Adolescent suicide.* New York: Wiley, 1971.

Jacobson, E. *Progressive relaxation.* Chicago: University of Chicago, 1938.

Jacobson, G. Crisis theory and treatment strategy: some sociocultural and psychodynamic considerations. *Journal of Nervous and Mental Disease,* 1965, 141, 209–218.

Jaffe, J. H. Development of a successful treatment program for narcotic addicts in Illinois. In Blachly, P. H. (ed.), *Drug abuse: data and debate.* Springfield, Ill.: Thomas, 1970, pp. 48–63.

Jahoda, M. *Current concepts of positive mental health.* New York: Basic Books, 1958.

James, J. F., and Wilson, I. C. Lithium therapy in manic states: prediction of therapeutic effect. *Activitas Nervosa Superior* (Praha), 1972, 14, 52–57.

Janis, I. L. *Psychological stress.* New York: Wiley, 1958.

———, **Mahl, D. F., Kagan, J., and Holt, R. R.** *Personality: dynamics development and assessment.* New York: Harcourt Brace Jovanovich, 1969.

Janov, A. *The primal scream—Primal Therapy: the cure for neurosis.* New York: Dell, 1970.

———. *The anatomy of mental illness: the scientific basis of Primal Therapy.* New York: Putnam, 1971.

Jarvik, Lissy F., Klodin, V., Matsuyama, S. S. Human aggression and the extra Y chromosome, fact or fantasy?

American Psychologist, 1973, 28, 674–682.

Jeffee, S. *Narcotics—an American plan.* New York: Erickson, 1966.

Jellinek, E. M. Phases of alcohol addiction. *Quarterly Journal of Studies on Alcohol,* 1952, 13, 673–684.

——. *The disease concept of alcoholism.* Highland Park, N.J.: Hillhouse Press, 1960.

Jenkins, R. L. Motivation and frustration in delinquency. *American Journal of Orthopsychiatry,* 1957, 27, 528–537.

——. The psychopathic or antisocial personality. *Journal of Nervous and Mental Disease,* 1960, 131, 318–334.

——. Psychiatric syndromes in children and their relation to family background. *American Journal of Orthopsychiatry,* 1966, 36, 405–457.

——, **and Boyer, A.** Types of delinquent behavior and background factors, *International Journal of Social Psychiatry,* 1968, 14, 65–76.

Jensen, A. R. How much can we boost IQ and scholastic achievement? *Harvard Educational Review,* 1969, 39, 1–123.

——. The differences are real. *Psychology Today,* December 1973, 79–86.

Jessor, R., Young, H. B., Young, E., and Tessi, G. Perceived opportunity, alienation and drinking behavior among Italian and American youth. *Journal of Personality and Social Psychology,* 1970, 13, 215–222.

Johnson, A. M. Sanctions for superego lacunae of adolescents. In Eissler, K. R. (ed.), *Searchlights on delinquency.* New York: International Universities Press, 1949.

Johnson, F. N. (ed.). *Lithium research and therapy.* New York: Academic Press, 1975.

Johnson, J. H., and Williams, T. A. The use of on-line computer technology in a mental health admitting system. *American Psychologist,* 1975, 30, 380–390.

Johnson, R. K., and Meyer, R. G. Phased biofeedback approach for epileptic seizure control. In DiCara, L. V., Barber, T. X., Kamiya, J., Miller, N. E., Shapiro, D., and Stovya, J. (eds.), *Biofeedback and self-control, 1974.* Chicago: Aldine, 1975.

Johnson, W. G. The effect of prior-taste and food visibility on the food-directed instrumental performance of obese individuals. Unpublished Ph.D. dissertation, Catholic University of America, 1970.

Johnson, W. R. Hypnosis and muscular performance. *Journal of Sports Medicine and Physical Fitness,* 1961, I, 78.

Joint Commission on Mental Health of Children, Inc. *Crisis in child mental health: challenge for the 1970's.* New York: Harper & Row, 1970.

Jones, H. G. The application of conditioning and learning techniques to the treatment of a psychiatric patient. *Journal of Abnormal and Social Psychology,* 1956, 52, 414–420.

Jones, K. L., Shainberg, L. W., and Byer, C. O. *Drugs and alcohol.* New York: Harper & Row, 1969.

——. *Health science.* 2nd ed. New York: Harper & Row, 1971.

Jones, M. *The therapeutic community: a new treatment method in psychiatry.* New York: Basic Books, 1953.

Jones, M. C. The elimination of children's fears. *Journal of Experimental Psychology,* 1924(a), 7, 383–390.

——. A laboratory study of fear: the case of Peter. *Journal of Genetic Psychology,* 1924(b), 31, 308–315.

Jones, N. F., Kahn, N. W., and Langsley, D. G. Prediction of admission to a psychiatric hospital. *Archives of General Psychiatry,* 1965, 12, 607–610.

Jones, R., and Stone, G. Psychological studies of marijuana and alcohol in man. *Psychopharmacologia,* 1970, 18, 108–117.

Jordan, T. E. (ed.). *Perspectives in mental retardation.* Carbondale, Ill.: Southern Illinois University Press, 1966.

——, **and deCharms, R.** The achievement motive in normal and mentally retarded children. *American Journal of Mental Deficiency,* 1959, 55, 60–89.

Jourard, S. M. *The transparent self.* 2nd ed. New York: Van Nostrand Reinhold, 1971.

Judd, L. L., Brandkamp, W., and McGlothlin, W. H. Comparison of the chromosome patterns obtained from groups of continued users, former users, and non-users of LSD-25. Presented at the 124th annual meeting of the American Psychiatric Association. Boston, Mass., 1968.

Juel-Nielson, N. On psychogenic obesity in children. II. *Acta Paediatrica,* 1953, 42, 130–146.

Jung, C. G. *Analytical psychology: its theory and practice.* New York: Vintage Books, 1968.

Kagan, J., and Moss, H. A. *Birth to maturity: a study in psychological development.* New York: Wiley, 1962.

Kaij, L. *Alcoholism in twins: studies on the etiology and sequels of abuse of alcohol.* Stockholm: Almquist & Wiksell, 1960.

Kalin, R. Self-descriptions of college problem drinkers. In McClelland, D. C., Davis, W. N., Kalin, R., and Wanner, E. *The drinking man: alcohol and human motivation.* New York: Free Press, 1972, pp. 217–231.

Kalinowsky, L. Insulin coma therapy. In Freedman, A. M., and Kaplan, H. I. (eds.), *Psychiatry.* Baltimore: Williams & Wilkins, 1967, pp. 1285–1291.

——. The convulsive therapies. In Freedman, A. M., and Kaplan, H. I. (eds.), *Treating mental illness: aspects of modern therapy.* New York: Atheneum, 1972(a), pp. 345–359.

——. Insulin coma treatment. In Freedman, A. M., and Kaplan, H. I. (eds.), *Treating mental illness: aspects of modern therapy.* New York: Atheneum, 1972(b), pp. 360–367.

——, **and Hippins, H.** *Pharmacological, convulsive and other somatic treatments in psychiatry.* New York: Grune & Stratton, 1969.

Kalish, R. *Late adulthood: perspectives on human development.* Monterery, Calif.: Brooks/Cole, 1975.

Kallmann, F. J. The genetic theory of personality. *American*

Journal of Psychiatry, 1946, 103, 309–322.

———. *Heredity in health and mental disorder.* New York: Norton, 1953.

———. The genetics of human behavior. *American Journal of Psychiatry,* 1956, 113, 496–501.

———. The genetics of mental illness. In Arieti, S. (ed.), *American handbook of psychiatry,* Vol. 1. New York: Basic Books, 1959, pp. 175–196.

Kamin, L. Heredity, intelligence, politics, and psychology. Mimeographed. Princeton, N.J.: Princeton University Press, 1973.

———. *The politics of IQ testing.* Hillside, N.J.: Lawrence Erlbaum Associates, 1975.

Kamiya, J. Conditional discrimination of the EEG alpha rhythm in humans. Paper presented at the meeting of the Western Psychological Association, April, 1962.

———. Conscious control of brain waves. *Psychology Today,* 1968, 1, 57–60.

Kane, F. Clothing worn by outpatients to interviews. *Psychiatric Communications,* 1958, 1 (cited in Webb et al., 1966).

———. Clothing worn by an outpatient: a case study. *Psychiatric Communications,* 1959, 2 (cited in Webb et al., 1966).

———. The meaning of the form of clothing. *Psychiatric Communications,* 1962, 5 (cited in Webb et al., 1966).

Kanfer, F. H. The maintenance of behaviors by self-generated stimuli and reinforcement. In Jacobs, A., and Sachs, L. B. (eds.), *The psychology of private events: perspectives and covert response systems.* New York: Academic Press, 1971, pp. 39–59.

———. Self-management techniques. In Kanfer, F. H., and Goldstein, A. P. (eds.), *Helping people change: a textbook of methods.* New York: Pergamon, 1975.

———, **and Phillips, J.** Behavior therapy. *Archives of General Psychiatry,* 1966, 15, 114–128.

———, **and Phillips, J.** *Learning foundations of behavior therapy.* New York: Wiley, 1970.

———, **and Saslow, G.** Behavioral diagnosis. In Franks, C. M. (ed.), *Behavior therapy: appraisal and status.* New York: McGraw-Hill, 1969, pp. 417–444.

Kanner, L. Autistic disturbances of affective contact. *Nervous Child,* 1943, 2, 217–250.

———. Early infantile autism. *Journal of Pediatrics,* 1944, 25, 211–217.

———. Irrelevant and metaphorical language in early infantile autism. *American Journal of Psychiatry,* 1946, 103, 242–246.

———. Problems of nosology and psychodynamics of early infantile autism. *American Journal of Orthopsychiatry,* 1949, 19, 416–426.

———. *Child psychiatry.* 3rd ed. Springfield, Ill.: Thomas, 1957.

———. Parent counseling. In Rothstein, J. H. *Mental retardation: readings and resources.* 2nd ed. New York: Holt, Rinehart and Winston, 1971, pp. 503–509.

———, **and Eisenberg, L.** Early infantile autism, 1943–1955.

Psychiatric Research Reports, 1957, 7, 55–66.

Kantor, R. E., Wallner, J. M., and Winder, C. L. Process and reactive schizophrenia. *Journal of Consulting Psychology,* 1953, 17, 157–162.

Kaplan, A. *The conduct of inquiry: methodology for behavioral science.* New York: Intext, 1964.

Kaplan, B. (ed.). *The inner world of mental illness.* New York: Harper & Row, 1964.

Kaplan, J. *Marijuana—the new prohibition.* New York: Harcourt Brace Jovanovich, 1970.

Karpman, B. On the need for separating psychopathy into two distinct clinical types: symptomatic and idiopathic. *Journal of Criminology and Psychopathology,* 1941, 3, 112–137.

———. *The sexual offender and his offenses.* New York: Julian Press, 1954.

———. The structure of neurosis: with special differentials between neurosis, psychosis, homosexuality, alcoholism, psychopathy, and criminality. *Archives of Criminal Psychodynamics,* 1961, 4, 599–646.

Kastenbaum, R., and Aisenberg, R. *The psychology of death.* New York: Springer, 1972.

Katkin, E. S. Instrumental autonomic conditioning. In Spence, J. T., Carson, R. C., and Thibaut, J. W. (eds.), *Behavioral approaches to therapy.* Morristown, N.J.: General Learning Press, 1976, pp. 203–226.

———, **and Lachman, R.** Concerning instrumental autonomic conditioning: a rejoinder. *Psychological Bulletin,* 1969, 71, 462–466.

———, **and Murray, N. E.** Instrumental conditioning of autonomically mediated behavior: theoretical and methodological issues. *Psychological Bulletin,* 1968, 70, 52–68.

Katz, I., Robinson, J. M., Epps, E. G., and Waly, P. The influence of race of experimenter and instructions upon the expression of hostility by Negro boys. *Journal of Social Issues,* 1964, 20, 54–59.

Kaufmann, H. The unconcerned bystander. In *Proceedings of the Annual Convention of the American Psychological Association,* 1968.

———. *Aggression and altruism.* New York: Holt, Rinehart and Winston, 1970.

Kavka, J. Pinel's conception of the psychopathic state: an historical critique. *Bulletin of the History of Medicine,* 1949, 23, 461–468.

Kay, D. W., and Roth, M. Environmental and heredity factors in schizophrenias of old age ("late paraphrenia") and their bearing on the general problems of causation in schizophrenia. *Journal of Mental Science,* 1961, 107, 649–686.

Kazniak, A. W., and Reiss, S. Organic brain syndromes. In Reiss, S., Peterson, R. A., Eron, L. D., and Reiss, M. M. *Abnormality: experimental and clinical approaches.* New York: Macmillan, 1977.

Keehn, J. D. Briefcase report: reinforcement therapy of incontinence. *Behavioral Research and Therapy*, 1965, 2, 239.

Kegel, A. H. Sexual functions of the pubococcygeus muscle. *Western Journal of Surgery*, 1952, 60, 521–524.

Keith, S. J., Gunderson, J. G., Reifman, A., Buchsbaum, S., and Mosher, L. R. Special report: schizophrenia 1976. *Schizophrenia Bulletin*. Washington, D.C.: NIMH, 1977.

Keller, M. The definition of alcoholism and the estimation of its prevalence. In Pittman, D. J., and Snyder, C. R. (eds.), *Society, culture and drinking patterns*. New York: Wiley, 1962, pp. 310–323.

———, **and Rosenberg, S. S.** (eds.). First special report to the U.S. Congress on alcohol and health from the Secretary of H.E.W. Washington, D.C.: Government Printing Office, 1971.

Kelly, E. L., and Fiske, D. W. *The prediction of performance in clinical psychology*. Ann Arbor: University of Michigan Press, 1951.

Kelly, G. A. *The psychology of personal constructs*. New York: Norton, 1955.

Kelly, J. G. Naturalistic observations in contrasting social environments. In Willemg, E. P., and Raush, H. L. (eds.), *Naturalistic viewpoints in psychological research*. New York: Holt, Rinehart and Winston, 1969.

Kennedy, J. F. A national program to combat mental retardation. *Mental illness and mental retardation*, House Document No. 58. Washington, D.C.: U.S. Congress, 1963.

Kennedy, M. and Cormier, B. M. Father-daughter incest: treatment of family. Presented at the Annual Meeting of the American Society of Criminology, Montreal, Canada, 1964.

Kepecs, J. G., and Robin, M. Life situations, emotions, and atopic dermatitis. In *Life stress and bodily diseases: proceedings of the Association for Research in Nervous and Mental Diseases*, Vol. 29. Baltimore: Williams & Wilkins, 1950, pp. 1010–1015.

Kessel, N., and Walton, H. *Alcoholism*. Baltimore: Penguin Books, 1969.

Kessler, J. W. *Psychopathology of childhood*. Englewood Cliffs, N.J.: Prentice-Hall, 1966.

Kety, S. S. Biochemical hypotheses and studies. In Morris, R. J. (ed.), *Perspective in abnormal behavior*. New York: Pergamon, 1974, pp. 237–251.

Keys, A. Experimental induction of psychoneuroses by starvation. In *The biology of mental health and disease*. New York: Harper & Row, 1952.

Kiesler, D. J. Some myths of psychotherapy research and the search for a paradigm. *Psychological Bulletin*, 1966, 64, 114–120.

Kiev, A. *Transcultural psychiatry*. New York: Free Press, 1972.

Kiloh, L., and Osselton, J. W. *Clinical electroencephalography*. Washington, D.C.: Butterworth, 1966.

Kimble, D. *Psychology as a biological science*. 2nd ed. Pacific Palisades, Calif.: Goodyear, 1977.

Kimble, G. A., and Garmezy, N. *Principles of general psychology*. New York: Ronald Press, 1968.

———, **and Zigler, E.** *Principles of general psychology*. 4th ed. New York: Ronald Press, 1974.

Kimura, D. The asymmetry of the human brain. *Scientific American*, 1973.

Kincade, K. *A Walden Two experiment: the first five years of Twin Oaks Community*. New York: Morrow, 1973.

Kinder, E., and Daniels, R. S. Day and night psychiatric treatment centers. I. Description, organization and function. *American Journal of Psychiatry*, 1962, 119, 415–420.

King, F. W. Marijuana and LSD usage among college students: prevalence, rate, frequency, and self-estimates of future use. *Psychiatry*, 1969, 32, 265–276.

Kinsey, A. C., Pomeroy, W. B., and Martin, C. E. *Sexual behavior in the human male*. Philadelphia: Saunders, 1948.

———, **and Gebhard, P. H.** *Sexual behavior in the human female*. Philadelphia: Saunders, 1953.

Kiritz, S., and Moos, R. Physiological effects of social environments. *Psychosomatic Medicine*, 1974, 36, 96–114.

Klausmeier, H. and Check, J. Relationships among physical, mental, achievement, and personality measures in children of low, average and high intelligence at 113 months of age. *American Journal of Mental Deficiency*, 1959, 63, 1059–1068.

Klebanoff, L. B. Parental attitudes of mothers of schizophrenic, brain-injured and retarded and normal children. *American Journal of Orthopsychiatry*, 1959, 29, 445–454.

Klein, D. C., and Seligman, M. E. P. Reversal of performance deficits and perceptual deficits in learned helplessness and depression. *Journal of Abnormal Psychology*, 1976, 85, 11–26.

Klein, D. F., and Davis, J. M. *Diagnosis and drug treatment of psychiatric disorders*. Baltimore: Williams & Wilkins, 1969.

Kleinmuntz, B. An investigation of the verbal behavior of paranoid psychotic patients and normals. Unpublished doctoral dissertation, University of Minnesota, 1958.

———. Two types of paranoid schizophrenia. *Journal of Clinical Psychology*, 1960, 16, 310–312.

———. MMPI decision rules for the identification of college maladjustment: a digital computer approach. *Psychological Monographs*, 1963(a), 77, No. 14 (Whole No. 557).

———. Personality test interpretation by digital computer. *Science*, 1963(b), 139, 416–418.

———. Profile analysis revisited: a heuristic approach. *Journal of Counseling Psychology*, 1963(c), 10, 315–324. Abstracted in *American Psychologist*, 1963(c), 18, 353.

———. *Personality measurement: an introduction*. Homewood, Ill.: Dorsey Press, 1967.

———. *Clinical information processing by computer: an essay and selected readings*. New York: Holt, Rinehart and Winston, 1969.

———. Clinical information processing by computer. In Craik, K. H., Kleinmuntz, B., Rosnow, R. L., Rosenthal, R., Cheyne, J. A., and Waters, R. H. *New directions in psychology 4*. New York: Holt, Rinehart and Winston, 1970, pp. 123–210.

———. *Computers in personality assessment*. Morristown, N.J.: General Learning, 1972(a).

———. Medical information processing by computer. In Jacquez, J. (ed.), *The diagnostic process*. Springfield, Ill.: Thomas, 1972(b), pp. 45–72.

———. *Personality measurement: an introduction*. Huntington, N.Y.: Krieger, 1975.

———, **and McLean, R. S.** Diagnostic interviewing by digital computer. *Behavioral Science*, 1968, 12, 75–80.

Kleinmuntz, D. N. *The XYY syndrome and crime*. Unpublished paper, University of Chicago, 1975.

Klerman, G. L. Psychotropic drugs as therapeutic agents. In Allman, L. R., and Jaffe, D. T. (eds.), *Readings in abnormal psychology*. New York: Harper & Row, 1976, pp. 335–341.

Kline, N. S. The history of lithium usage in psychiatry. To be published as part of the Monograph Series *Modern Problems of Pharmacopsychiatry*. Basel, Switzerland: Karger (cited in Winokur et al., 1969).

Knopf, I. J. *Childhood psychopathology: a developmental approach*. Englewood Cliffs, N.J.: Prentice-Hall, 1979.

Knott, J. R., and Gottlieb, J. S. The electroencephalogram in psychopathic personality. *Psychosomatic Medicine*, 1943, 5, 139–142.

———, **Platt, E. B., Ashley, M. C., and Gottlieb, J. S.** A familial evaluation of the electroencephalogram of patients with primary behavior disorder and psychoapthic personality. *EEG and Clinical Neurophysiology*, 1953, 5, 363–370.

Koch, J. A. L. *Die psychopathischen minderwertigkeiten*. Ravensburg, Germany: Maier, 1891.

Koch, R., Baerwald, A., McDonald J., Fishler, L., and Rock, H. The child development haveling clinic project in Southern California. *Mental Retardation*, 1969, 7, 46–52.

Kockelmans, J. J. *Phenomenology: the philosophy of Edmund Husserl and its interpretation*. Garden City, N.Y.: Doubleday (Anchor Books), 1967.

Koh, S. D., and Kayton, L. Memorization of "unrelated" word strings by young nonpsychotic schizophrenics. *Journal of Abnormal Psychology*, 1974, 83, 14–22.

———, **Kayton, L., and Berry, R.** Mnemonic organization in young nonpsychotic schizophrenics. *Journal of Abnormal Psychology*, 1972, 81, 299–310.

Kohn, M. L. Rejoinder to David Mechanic. *Social Forces*, 1972(a), 50, 310–313.

———. Class, family, and schizophrenia: a formulation. *Social Forces*, 1972(b), 50, 295–304.

Kolb, L. C. *Noyes' modern clinical psychiatry*. Philadelphia: Saunders, 1968.

———. Community psychiatry. In Braceland, F. J., Freedman, D. X., Friedhoff, A. J., Kolb, L. C., Lourie, R. S., and Romano, J. (eds.), *Year book of psychiatry and applied mental health, 1976*. Chicago: Year Book Medical Publishers, 1976, pp. 355–399.

———. Community psychiatry. In Braceland, F. J., Freedman, D. X., Friedhoff, A. J., Kolb, L. C., Lourie, R. S., and Romano, J. (eds.), *Yearbook of psychiatry and applied mental health, 1977*. Chicago: Year Book Medical Publishers, 1977, pp. 365–402.

Korchin, S. J. *Modern clinical psychology: principles of intervention in the clinic and community*. New York: Basic Books, 1976.

Korman, M., and Stephens, H. Effects of training on the alcohol consummatory response in rats. *Psychological Reports*, 1960, 6, 327–331.

Kostenbaum, R., and Aisenberg R. *The psychology of death*. New York: Springer-Verlag, 1972.

Kovel, J. *A complete guide to therapy: from psychoanalysis to behavior modification*. New York: Pantheon Books, 1976.

Kraepelin, E. *Psychiatrie; ein Lehrbuch für Studierende und Ärtzte*. 3rd ed. Leipzig: Barth, 1887.

———. *Psychiatrie*. Leipzig: Barth, 1915.

———. *Manic-depressive insanity and paranoia*. Edinburgh: Livingstone, 1921.

———. *Lehrbuch*. 9th ed. Berlin: 1926.

Kraft, A. M. The therapeutic community. In Arieti, S. (ed.), *American handbook of psychiatry*, Vol. III. New York: Basic Books, 1966, pp. 542–551.

Kraft, T., and Al-Issa, I. Behavior therapy and the treatment of frigidity. *American Journal of Psychotherapy*, 1967, 21, 116–120.

———. The use of methohexitone sodium in the systematic desensitization of premature ejaculation. *British Journal of Psychiatry*, 1968, 114, 351–352.

Kramer, B. M. Day care: a phase of partial hospitalization. In Freedman, A. M., and Kaplan, H. I. (eds.), *Treating mental illness: aspects of modern therapy*. New York: Atheneum, 1972, pp. 395–399.

Kramer, M. Population changes and schizophrenia, 1970–1985. Paper presented at the Second Rochester International Conference on Schizophrenia, Rochester, N.Y., May 1976.

Krasner, L. Assessment of token economy programs in psychiatric hospitals. *Ciba Foundation symposium: the role of learning in psychotherapy*. London: Churchill, 1968.

———, **and Krasner, M.** Token economies and other planned environments. In Thoresen, C. E. (ed.), *Behavior modification in education,* 72nd Yearbook of the National Society for the Study of Education. Chicago: University of Chicago Press, 1973, pp. 351–381.

————. Personal Communication, 1978.

————, **and Ullmann, L. P.** (eds.). *Research in behavior modification.* New York: Holt, Rinehart and Winston, 1965.

Kreitman, N. The reliability of psychiatric diagnosis. *Journal of Mental Science,* 1961, 107, 876–886.

————, **Sainsbury, P., Morrissey, J., Towers, J., and Scrivener, J.** The reliability of psychiatric assessment: an analysis. *Journal of Mental Science,* 1961, 107, 887–908.

Kretschmer, E. *Physique and character.* Trans. by Sprott, W. J. H., from *Körperbau und Charakter.* 2nd ed. New York: Harcourt Brace Jovanovich, 1925.

Kübler–Ross, E. *On death and dying.* New York: Macmillan, 1970.

Kuhn, R. The treatment of depressive states with G22355 (imipramine hydrochloride). *American Journal of Psychiatry,* 1958, 115, 459–464.

Kuhn, T. S. *The structure of scientific revolutions.* 2nd ed. Chicago: University of Chicago Press, 1970.

Kupfer, D. J., Wyatt, R. J., Scott, J., and Snyder, F. Sleep disturbance in acute schizophrenic patients. *American Journal of Psychiatry,* 1970, 126, 1213–1223.

Kushner, M. The reduction of a long-standing fetish by means of aversive conditioning. In Ullmann, L. P., and Krasner, L. (eds.), *Case studies in behavior modification.* New York: Holt, Rinehart and Winston, 1965, pp. 239–242.

Lachman, S. J. *Psychosomatic disorders: a behavioristic interpretation.* New York: Wiley, 1972.

Lader, M. H., and Wing, L. Habituation of the psychogalvanic reflex in patients with anxiety states and in normal subjects. *Journal of Neurology and Psychiatry,* 1964, 27, 210–218.

Laing, R. D. *The politics of experience.* New York: Ballantine Books, 1967.

————. *The divided self: an existential study in sanity and madness.* New York: Pantheon, 1970.

————, **and Esterson, A.** *Sanity, madness and the family.* Middlesex, England: Penguin, 1970.

Lancaster, E. *The final face of Eve.* New York: McGraw-Hill, 1958.

Landis, C., and Mettler, F. A. (eds.). *Varieties of psychopathological experience.* New York: Holt, Rinehart and Winston, 1964.

Lang, P. J., Stroufe, L. A., and Hastings, J. E. Effects of feedback and instructional set on the control of cardiac rate variability. *Journal of Experimental Psychology,* 1967, 75, pp. 425–431.

Langer, E. J., and Abelson, R. P. A patient by any other name. . . : clinician group difference in labeling bias. *Journal of Consulting and Clinical Psychology,* 1974, 42, 4–9.

Lapouse, R., and Monk, M. A. An epidemiologic study of behavior characteristics in children. *American Journal of Public Health,* 1958, 48, No. 9. Reprinted in Quay, H. C.

(ed.), *Children's behavior disorders: selected readings.* New York: Van Nostrand Reinhold, 1968.

————, **Monk, M. A., and Terris, M.** The drift hypothesis and socioeconomic differentials in schizophrenia. *American Journal of Public Health,* 1956, 46, 978–986.

Lashley, K. S. Brain mechanisms and intelligence. Chicago: University of Chicago Press, 1929.

Latané, B, and Darley, J. M. Group inhibition of bystander intervention in emergencies. *Journal of Personality and Social Psychology,* 1968, 10, 215–221.

————. Bystander "apathy." *American Scientist,* 1969, 57, 244–268.

————. *The unresponsive bystander: why doesn't he help?* Englewood Cliffs, N.J.: Prentice-Hall, 1970.

Laurie, P. *Drugs,* Middlesex, England: Penguin, 1967.

Lazarus, A. A. The treatment of a sexually inadequate man. In Ullmann, L. P., and Krasner, L. (eds.), *Case studies in behavior modification.* New York: Holt, Rinehart & Winston, 1965, pp. 243–245.

————. Learning theory and the treatment of depression. *Behavioral Research and Therapy,* 1968, 6, 83–89.

————. *Behavior therapy and beyond.* New York: McGraw-Hill, 1971.

————. Has behavior therapy outlived its usefulness? *American Psychologist,* 1977, 32, 550–554.

Lazarus, R. S. *Adjustment and personality.* New York: McGraw-Hill, 1961.

————. *Psychological stress and the coping process.* New York: McGraw-Hill, 1966.

————. A cognitively oriented psychologist looks at biofeedback. *American Psychologist,* 1975, 30, 553–561.

Lee, D. *Freedom and culture.* Englewood Cliffs, N.J.: Prentice-Hall, 1959.

Lefkowitz, M. M. Short-term institutionalization for delinquent girls. *Evaluation,* 1975, 2, 22–23.

————, **Eron, L. D., Walder, L. O., and Huesmann, L. R.** Growing up to be violent. New York: Pergamon, 1977.

Leighton, A. H. *My name is legion.* New York: Basic Books, 1959.

————. A comparative study of psychiatric disorder in Nigeria and rural North America. In Plog, S. C., and Edgerton, R. B. (eds.), *Changing perspectives in mental illness.* New York: Holt, Rinehart and Winston, 1969, 179–199.

————, **Lambo, T. A., Hughes, C. C., Leighton, D. C., Murphy, J. M., and Macklin, D. B.** *Psychiatric disorder among the Yoruba.* Ithaca, N.Y.: Cornell University Press, 1963.

Leighton, D. C., Harding, J. S., Macklin, D. B., Macmillan, A. M., and Leighton, A. H. *The character of danger.* New York: Basic Books, 1963.

Lejeune, J., and Turpin, R. Chromosomal aberrations in man. *American Journal of Human Genetics,* 1961, 13, 175–184.

Lennard, H. L., Epstein, L. J., Bernstein, A., and Ransom, D. C. *Mystification and drug misuse: hazards in using psy-*

choactive drugs. San Francisco: Jossey–Bass, 1971.

———, **Epstein, L. J., and Rosenthal, M. S.** The methadone illusion. *Science,* 1972, 176, 881–884.

Lennox, W. G. The heredity of epilepsy as told by relatives and twins. *Journal of the American Medical Association,* 1951, 146, 529.

Lenz, H. Vergleichende Psychiatrie, eine Studie über die Beziehung von Kulter. *Soziologie und Psychopathologie,* Vienna: Wilhelm Maudrich Verlag, 1964.

Leonard, G. *The transformation.* New York: Dell, 1972.

Lesser, L. L., Ashenden, B. J., Debuskey, M., and Eisenberg, L. Anorexia nervosa in children. *American Journal of Orthopsychiatry,* 1960, 30, 572–580.

Lester, D., and Greenberg, L. Nutrition and the etiology of alcoholism: the effect of sucrose, saccharin and fat on the self-selection of ethyl alcohol by rats. *Quarterly Journal of Studies on Alcohol,* 1952, 13, 553.

Lester, G., and Lester, D. *Suicide: the gamble with death.* Englewood Cliffs, N.J.: Prentice-Hall, 1971.

Lever, J. Soccer: opinion of the Brazilian people. *Trans-action,* 1969, 7, 36–43.

LeVine, R. A. Behaviorism in psychological anthropology. In Wepman, J. M., and Heine, R. W. (eds.), *Concepts of personality.* Chicago: Aldine, 1963, pp. 361–384.

Levis, D. J., and Stampfl, T. G. Implosive therapy: a bridge between Pavlov and Freud? *Newsletter of the Association for Advancement of Behavior Therapy,* 1969, 4, 8–10.

Levitsky, A., and Perls, F. The rules and games of Gestalt therapy. In Fagan, J., and Shepherd, I. L. (eds.), *Gestalt therapy now: theory, techniques, applications.* New York: Harper & Row, 1970, pp. 140–149.

Levitt, E. E. Psychotherapy with children: a further evaluation. *Behavior Research and Therapy,* 1963, 2, 45–51.

———, **Persky, H. and Brady, J. P.** *Hypnotic induction of anxiety: a psychoendocrine investigation.* Springfield, Ill.: Thomas, 1964.

Levy, D. Release therapy in young children. *Psychiatry,* 1938, 1, 387–389.

Lewinsohn, P. M. A behavioral approach to depression. In Friedman, R. J., and Katz, M. M. (eds.), *The psychology of depression: contemporary theory and research.* Washington, D.C.: Winston, 1974.

———. Depression revisited: review of Becker, J. Affective disorders. *Contemporary Psychology,* 1977, 22, 603.

———, **and Libet, J.** Pleasant events, activity schedules, and depression. *Journal of Abnormal Psychology,* 1972, 79, 291–295.

———, **and Graf, M.** Pleasant activities and depression. *Journal of Consulting and Clinical Psychology,* 1973, 41, 261–268.

Lewis, N. D. C. History of the nosology and the evolution of the concepts of schizophrenia. In Hoch, P. H., and Zubin, J. (eds.), *Psychopathology of schizophrenia.* New York: Grune & Stratton, 1966, pp. 1–18.

———, **and Piotrowsky, Z. A.** Clinical diagnosis of manic-depressive psychosis. In Hoch, P., and Zubin, J. (eds.), *Depression.* New York: Grune & Stratton, 1954.

Lewontin, R. C. The fallacy of biological determinism. *The Sciences,* 1976, 16, 6–10.

Leznoff, M., and Westley, W. A. The homosexual community. In Gagnon, J. H., and Simon, W. (eds.), *Sexual deviance.* New York: Harper & Row, 1967, pp. 185–196.

Liberman, R. P. Behavioral modification of schizophrenia: a review. *Schizophrenia Bulletin,* Issue 1972, 6, 37–48.

Lichtenberg, B. On the selection and preparation of the Big Brother volunteer. In Guerney, B. G. (ed.), *Psychotherapeutic agents: new roles for nonprofessionals, parents, and teachers.* New York: Holt, Rinehart and Winston, 1969, pp. 113–120.

Liddell, H. S. The influence of experimental neuroses on respiratory function. In Abramson, H. A. (ed.), *Somatic and psychiatric treatment of asthma.* Baltimore: Williams & Wilkins, 1951, pp. 126–147.

———. *Emotional hazards in animals and man.* Springfield, Ill.: Thomas, 1956.

Liebeault, A. A. *Du sommeil et des états analogue, considérés surtout au point de vue de l'action de la morale sur le physique.* Paris: Doin, 1886.

Lieberman, M. A., Yalom, I. D., and Miles, M. B. *Encounter groups: first facts.* New York: Basic Books, 1973.

Liebert, R. M. Television and social learning: some relationships between viewing violence and behaving aggressively (overview). In Murray, J. P., Rubenstein, E. I., and Comstock, G. (eds.), *Television and social behavior.* A technical Report to the Surgeon General's Scientific Advisory Committee on Television and Social Behavior. Washington, D.C.: Government Printing Office, 1972, pp. 1–42.

———, **and Spiegler, M. D.** *Personality: an introduction to theory and research.* Homewood, Ill.: Dorsey Press, 1970.

Lihn, H., Menninger, K., and Mayman, M. Personality factors in osteoarthritis. In *Life stress and bodily disease: proceedings of the Association for Research in Nervous and Mental Diseases,* Vol. 29. Baltimore: Williams & Wilkins, 1950, pp. 744–749.

Liljefors, I., and Rahe, R. H. An identical twin study of psychosocial factors in coronary heart disease in Sweden. *Psychosomatic Medicine,* 1970, 32, 523–543.

Lindemann, E. Symptomatology and management of acute grief. *American Journal of Psychiatry,* 1944, 101, 141–148.

Lindesmith, A. R. *Addiction and opiates.* Chicago: Aldine, 1968.

Lindsley, O. R. Geriatric behavioral prosthetics. In Kastenbaum, R. (ed.), *New thoughts on old age.* New York: Springer-Verlag, 1964.

———. A reliable wrist counter for recording behavior rates. *Journal of Applied Behavior Analysis,* 1968, 1, 77–78.

Lindzey, G. *Projective techniques and cross-cultural research.* Englewood Cliffs, N.J.: Prentice-Hall, 1961.

———. Some remarks concerning incest, the incest taboo,

and psychoanalytic theory. *American Psychologist*, 1967, 22, 1051–1059.

———. Some remarks concerning incest and incest taboo. In Haddon, J. K., and Borgatta, M. L. (eds.), *Marriage and the family: a comprehensive reader*. Itasca, Ill.: Peacock, 1969, pp. 37–41.

Lingeman, R. R. *Drugs from a to z: a dictionary*. New York: McGraw-Hill, 1969.

Lipinski, E., and Lipinski, B. G. Motivational factors in psychedelic drug use by male college students. In Hormon, R. E. and Fox, A. M. (eds.), *Drug awareness*. New York: Aron, 1970.

Lippman, H. S. *Treatment of the child in emotional conflict*. New York: McGraw-Hill, 1956.

Litman, R. E. Suicide as acting out. In Shneidman, G. S., Farberow, N. L., and Litman, R. E. (eds.), *The psychology of suicide*. New York: Science House, 1970, pp. 293–304.

———, Curphey, T. J., Shneidman, E. S., Farberow, N. L., and Tabachnick, N. The psychological autopsy of equivocal deaths. In Shneidman, E. S., et al. *The psychology of suicide*. New York: Science House, 1970, pp. 486–496.

Lloyd, R. W., and Salzberg, H. C. Controlled social drinking: an alternative to abstinence as a treatment goal for some alcohol abusers. *Psychological Bulletin*, 1975, 82, 815–842.

Lobitz, W., and LoPiccolo, J. Methods in the behavioral treatment of sexual dysfunction. *Journal of Behavior Therapy and Experimental Psychiatry*, 1972, 3, 265–271.

Lolli, G., Schesler, E. and Golder, G. Choice of alcoholic beverage among 105 alcoholics in New York. *Quarterly Journal of Studies on Alcohol*, 1960, 21, 475–482.

London, P. *The modes of and morals of psychotherapy*. New York: Holt, Rinehart and Winston, 1964.

———. *Behavior control*. New York: Harper & Row, 1969.

———. Ethical problems in behavior control. In Hunt, W. A. (ed.), *Human behavior and its control*. Cambridge, Mass.: Schenkman, 1971, pp. 128–133.

Long, A. Parents' reports of undesirable behavior in children. *Child Development*, 1941, 12, 43–62.

Lorenz, K. *On aggression*. New York: Harcourt Brace Jovanovich, 1966.

Lorr, M. Measurement of the major psychotic syndromes. *Annals of the New York Academy of Science*, 1962, 93, 851–856.

———. A simplex of paranoid projection. *Journal of Consulting Psychology*, 1964, 28, 378–380.

———. A behavioral perspective od schizophrenia. *Diseases of the Nervous System*, 1968, 29, 45–52.

———. Canonical variates and second-order variates: a reply. *Journal of Consulting Psychology*, 1963, 27, 180–181.

———, Klett, C. J., McNair, D. M., and Lasky, J. J. *Inpatient Multidimensional Psychiatric Rating Scale, 1966 rev.* Palo Alto, Calif.: Consulted Psychologists Press, 1966.

———, McNair, D. M., Klett, C. J., and Lasky, J. J. Evidence of ten psychotic syndromes. *Journal of Consulting Psychology*, 1962, 26, 185–189.

Lourie, R. S. Child psychiatry. In Braceland, F. J., Freedman, D. X., Friedhoff, A. J., Kolb, L. C., Lourie, R. S., and Romano, J. (eds.), *Year book of psychiatry and applied mental health, 1976*. Chicago: Year Book Medical Publishers, 1976, pp. 91–146.

Lovaas, O. I. A behavior therapy approach to the treatment of childhood schizophrenia. In Hill, J. P. (ed.), *Minnesota symposia on child psychology*, Vol. 1. Minneapolis: University of Minnesota Press, 1967, pp. 108–159.

———, Berberich, J. D., Perloff, B. F., and Schaeffer, B. Acquisition of imitative speech in schizophrenic children. *Science*, 1966, 151, 705–707.

Luborsky, L., and Spence, D. P. Quantitative research on psychoanalytic therapy. In Bergin, A. E., and Garfield, S. L. (eds.), *Handbook of psychotherapy and behavior change: an empirical analysis*. New York: Wiley, 1971, pp. 408–433.

———, Siegal, R., and Gross, G. A. Neurotic depression and masochism. In Burton, A., and Harris, R. E. (eds.), *Clinical studies of personality*, Vol. 1. New York: Harper & Row, 1955. (Torch edition, 1966, pp. 191–212.)

Lucas, C. J., Sainsbury, P., and Collins, J. G. A social and clinical study of delusions in schizophrenia. *Journal of Mental Science*, 1962, 108, 747–758.

Lucas, G. H., Kalow, W., McColl, J. D., Griffiths, B. A., and Smith, H. W. Quantitative studies of the relationship between alcohol levels and motor vehicle accidents. In *Proceedings of the Second International Conference on Alcohol and Road Traffic*, 1953, p. 167.

Luce, G., and Peper, E. Biofeedback—mind over body, mind over mind. *The New York Times Magazine*, September 12, 1971, p. 34.

Lukianowicz, N. Survey of various aspects of transvestism in the light of our present knowledge. *Journal of Nervous and Mental Disease*, 1959, 128, 36–64.

Lundquist, G. Prognosis and course in manic-depressive psychoses. *Acta Psychiatrica Neurologica*, 1945, Supplement 35.

Luparello, T., Lyons, H. A., Bleeker, E. R., and McFadden, E. R., Jr. Influences of suggestion on airway reactivity in asthmatic subjects. In Miller, N. E., Barber, T. X., DiCara, L. V., Kamiya, J., Shapiro, D., and Stoyva, J. (eds.), *Biofeedback and self-control: 1973*. Chicago: Aldine, 1974, pp. 244–250.

Luria, A. R. *The mind of a mnemonist*. New York: Discus Books, 1969.

Lusted, L. *Introduction to medical decision making*. Springfield, Ill.: Thomas, 1968.

Lykken, D. T. A study of anxiety in the sociopathic personality. *Journal of Abnormal and Social Psychology*, 1957, 55, 6–10.

———. Neuropsychology and psychophysiology in personality research. In Borgatta, E. F., and Lambert, W. W. (eds.), *Handbook of personality theory and research.* Skokie, Ill.: Rand McNally, 1968.

Lyman, J. L. Student suicide at Oxford University. *Student Medicine,* 1961, 10, 218–234.

Lynch, J. J., Paskewitz, D. A., and Orne, M. T. Some factors in feedback control of human alpha rhythm. In DiCara, L. V., Barber, T. X., Kamiya, J., Miller, N. E., Shapiro, D., and Stoyva, J. (eds.), *Biofeedback and self-control, 1974.* Chicago: Aldine, 1975, pp. 341–350.

Maccoby, E. E., and Jacklin, C. N. Sex differences and their implications for sex roles. Paper presented at the meeting of the American Psychological Association, Washington, D.C., September 1971.

MacLean, P. D. New findings on brain functions and sociosexual behavior. In Zubin, J., and Money, R. (eds.), *Contemporary sexual behavior: critical issues in the 1970's.* Baltimore: Johns Hopkins University Press, 1973, pp. 53–74.

Maddi, S. R. The existential neurosis. *Journal of Abnormal Psychology,* 1967, 72, 311–325.

——. *Personality theories: a comparative analysis.* 2nd ed. Homewood, Ill.: Dorsey Press, 1972.

——. *Personality theories: a comparative analysis.* 3rd ed. Homewood, Ill.: Dorsey Press, 1976.

——, **and Costa, P. T.** *Humanism in personology: Allport, Maslow and Murray.* Chicago: Aldine, 1972.

Maddox, G. Activity and morale: a longitudinal study of selected subjects. *Social Forces,* 1963, 195–204.

Madsen, W. *The American alcoholic: the nature-nurture controversy in alcoholic research and therapy.* Springfield, Ill.: Thomas, 1974.

Maher, B. A. *Principles of psychopathology: an experimental approach.* New York: McGraw-Hill, 1966.

——. *Introduction to research in psychopathology.* New York: McGraw-Hill, 1970.

Mahl, G. F. Physiological changes during chronic fear. *Annals of the New York Academy of Sciences,* 1953, 56, 240–252.

Mahoney, M. J. *Cognition and behavior modification.* Cambridge, Mass.: Ballinger, 1974(a).

——. Self-reward and self-monitoring techniques for weight control. *Behavior Therapy,* 1974(b), 5, 48–57.

——. Reflections on the cognitive-learning trend in psychotherapy. *American Psychologist,* 1977, 32, 5–13.

——, **and Thoreson, C. E.** *Self-control: power to the person.* Monterey, Calif.: Brooks/Cole, 1974.

Main, T. F. The hospital as a therapeutic institution. *Bulletin of the Menninger Clinic,* 1946, 10, 66–70.

Maletzky, B. M. Behavior recording as treatment: a brief note. *Behavior Therapy,* 1974, 5, 107–111.

Malinowski, B. *The sexual life of savages in northwestern Melanesia.* Rev. ed. New York: Harvest Books, 1955.

——. *Sex and repression in savage society* (1927). New York: Harcourt Brace Jovanovich, 1961.

Maller, O. The role of sensoroverbal afferent impulses in the development of paranoid delirium. *Neurology, Psychiatry, Neurosurgery,* 1956, 1, 63.

Manded, A. Pro football fumbles the drug scandal. *Psychology Today,* June 1975.

Mann, W. E. Sexual standards and trends in Sweden. *Journal of Sex Research,* August 1967.

Marcuse, F. L. *Hypnosis: fact and fiction.* Baltimore: Penguin Books, 1959.

Margolian, S. G. Genetic and dynamic psychophysiological processes. In Deutsch, F. (ed.), *The psychosomatic concept in psychoanalysis.* New York: International Universities Press, 1953, pp. 3–36.

Marinello, M. A study of the XYY syndrome in tall men and juvenile delinquents. *Journal of American Medical Association,* 1969, 208, 321–325.

Mark, V., and Ervin, F. *Violence and the brain.* New York: Harper & Row, 1970.

Marks, J., Stanffacher, J. C., and Lyle, C. Predicting outcome in schizophrenia. *Journal of Abnormal and Social Psychology,* 1963, 66, 117–127.

Marks, P. A. An assessment of the diagnostic process in a child guidance center. *Psychological Monographs,* 1961, 75, No. 9 (Whole No. 511).

Marlatt, G. A., Demming, B., and Reid, J. B. Loss of control of drinking in alcoholics: an experimental analogue. *Journal of Abnormal Psychology,* 1973, 81, 233–241.

Marsden, G. Current analysis studies of psychotherapy: 1954 through 1968. In Bergin, A. E., and Garfield, S. L. (eds.), *Handbook of psychotherapy and behavior change: an empirical analysis.* New York: Wiley, 1971, pp. 345–407.

Martin, B. *Anxiety and neurotic disorders.* New York: Wiley, 1971.

——. *Abnormal psychology.* Glenview, Ill.: Scott, Foresman, 1973.

——. *Abnormal psychology: clinical and scientific perspective.* New York: Holt, Rinehart and Winston, 1977.

——, **and Kubly, D.** Results of treatment of enuresis by a conditioned response method. *Journal of Consulting Psychology,* 1955, 19, 71–93.

——, **and Sroufe, A.** Anxiety. In Costello, C. G. (ed.), *Symptoms of psychopathology: a handbook.* New York: Wiley, 1970.

Maslach, C., Marshall, G., and Zimbardo, P. B. Hypnotic control of peripheral skin temperature: a case report. *Psychophysiology,* 1972, 9, 600–605.

Maslow, A. H. *Toward a psychology of being.* 2nd ed. New York: Van Nostrand Reinhold, 1968.

——. *Motivation and personality.* 2nd ed. New York: Harper & Row, 1970.

——, **and Mittelmann, B.** *Principles of abnormal psychology:*

the dynamics of psychic illness. Rev. ed. New York: Harper & Row, 1951, p. 429.

Masserman, J. H. The principle of uncertainty in neurotigenesis. In Kimmel, H. D. (ed.), *Experimental psychopathology: recent research and theory.* New York: Academic Press, 1971, pp. 13–32.

Masters, R. E. L., and Houston, J. Toward an individual psychedelic psychotherapy. In Aarons, B., and Osmond, H. (eds.), *Psychedelics: the uses and implications of hallucinogenic drugs.* Cambridge, Mass.: Schenkman, 1970, pp. 325–341.

Masters, W. H., and Johnson, V. E. *Human sexual response.* Boston: Little, Brown, 1966.

———. *Human sexual inadequacy.* Boston: Little, Brown, 1970.

———. *Homosexuality in perspective.* Boston: Little, Brown, 1979.

Maurer, D. W., and Vogel, V. H. *Narcotics and narcotic addiction.* Springfield, Ill.: Thomas, 1967.

May, R., Angel, E., and Ellenberger, H. (eds.). *Existence: a new dimension in psychiatry and psychology.* New York: Touchstone, 1958.

Mayor's Committee on Marihuana. *The marihuana problem in the City of New York: sociological, medical and pharmacological studies.* Lancaster, Pa.: Cattell Press, 1944.

McBrearty, J. F., Dichter, M., Garfield, Z., and Heath, G. A behaviorally oriented treatment program for alcoholism. *Psychological Reports,* 1968, 22, 287–298.

McCarroll, J. R., and Haddon, W. Controlled study of fatal automobile accidents in New York City. *Journal of Chronic Diseases,* 1962, 15, 811–826.

McCarthy, R. G., and Douglass, E. M. *Alcohol and social responsibility—a new educational approach.* New York: Crowell, 1949.

McCary, J. J. *Sexual myths and fallacies.* New York: Van Nostrand Reinhold, 1971.

McClelland, D. C., Davis, W. N., Kalin, R., and Wanner, E. *The drinking man: alcohol and human motivation.* New York: Free Press, 1972, pp. 217–231.

McClure, C. M. Cardiac arrest through volition. *California Medicine,* 1959, 90, 440–441.

McCord, W., and Howard, J. *Life styles in the black ghetto.* New York: Norton, 1969.

———, **and McCord J.** *The psychopath: an essay on the criminal mind.* New York: Van Nostrand Reinhold, 1964.

———, **McCord, J., and Howard, A.** Familial correlates of aggression in nondelinquent male children. *Journal of Abnormal and Social Psychology,* 1961, 62, 79–93.

———, **and Zola, I.** *Origins of crime.* New York: Columbia University Press, 1959.

McDavid J. W. Immediate effects of group therapy upon response to social reinforcement among juvenile delinquents. *Journal of Consulting Psychology,* 1964, 28, 409–412.

McDonald, R. L. and Gynther, M. D. Relationship of self and

ideal-self description with sex, race, and class in Southern adolescents. *Journal of Personality and Social Psychology,* 1965, 1, 85–88.

McGhie, A., and Chapman, J. Disorders of attention and perception in early schizophrenia. *British Journal of Medical Psychology,* 1961, 34, 103–116.

McNeil, E. B. *The psychoses.* Englewood Cliffs, N.J.: Prentice-Hall, 1970.

———. *The psychology of being human.* San Francisco: Harper & Row, 1974.

———, **and Rubin, Z.** *The psychology of being human.* 2nd ed. San Francisco: Harper & Row, 1977.

McNitt, P. C., and Thornton, D. W. Depression and perceived reinforcement: a reconsideration. *Journal of Abnormal Psychology,* 1978, 87, 137–140.

Mead, M. *Coming of age in Samoa:* New York: Morrow, 1950.

Mechanic, D. Social class and schizophrenia: some requirements for a plausible theory of social influence. *Social Forces,* 1972, 50, 305–309.

Mednick, S. A. Breakdown in individuals at high risk for schizophrenia: possible predispositional perinatal factors. *Mental Hygiene,* 1970, 54, 50–63.

———, **and Schulsinger, F.** A longitudinal study of children with a high risk for schizophrenia: a preliminary report. In Vandenberg, S. (ed.), *Methods and goals in human behavior genetics.* New York: Academic Press, 1965.

Meduna, L. J. *Die Konvulsions therapie der schizophrenie.* Halle: Carl Mashold, 1937.

Meduna, L. von. General discussion of the Cardiazol therapy. *American Journal of Psychiatry,* 1938, 94, 40–50.

Meehl, P. E. Schizophrenia, catatonic form. In Burton, A., and Harris, R. E. (eds.), *Case histories in clinical and abnormal psychology.* New York: Harper & Row, 1947, pp. 72–83.

———. Some ruminations on the validation of clinical procedures. *Canadian Journal of Psychology,* 1959, 13, 103–128.

———. Schizotaxia, schizotypy, schizophrenia. *American Psychologist,* 1962, 17, 827–838.

Meichenbaum, D. H. Cognitive modification of test-anxious college students. *Journal of Consulting and Clinical Psychology,* 1972, 39, 370–380.

———. Cognitive facts in behavior modification: modifying what clients say to themselves. In Franks, C., and Wilson, T. (eds.), *Annual review of behavior therapy: theory and practice.* New York: Bruner/Mazel, 1973.

———. *Cognitive behavior modification.* Morristown, N.J.: General Learning Press, 1974.

———. *Cognitive behavior modification: an integrative approach.* New York: Plenum, 1977.

———, **and Cameron, R.** The clinical potential of modifying what clients say to themselves. In Mahoney, M. J., and Thoreson, C. E. (eds.), *Self-control: power to the person.* Monterey, Calif.: Books/Cole, 1974.

———, **and Goodman, J.** Training impulsive children to talk to themselves. *Journal of Abnormal Psychology*, 1971, 77, 115–126.

Melges, F. T., Tinklenberg, J. R., Hollister, L. E., and Gillespie, H. K. Marihuana and temporal disintegration. *Science*, 1970, 168, 1118–1120.

Mellerup, E. T., Thomsen, H. G., Ejorum, et al., Lithium, weight gain, and serum insulin in manic depressive patients. *Acta Psychiatrica Scandinavica*, 1972, 48, 332–336.

Mello, N. K. Theoretical review: a review of methods to induce alcohol addiction in animals. *Pharmacology, Biochemistry, and Behavior*, 1973, 1, 89–101.

Meltzer, H., and Stahl, S. The dopamine hypothesis of schizophrenia: a review. *Schizophrenia Bulletin*, 1976, 2, 19–76.

Meltzoff, J., and Kornreich, M. *Research in psychotherapy*. New York: Atherton, 1970.

Mendels, J. *Concepts of depression*. New York: Wiley, 1970.

———. *Psychobiology of depression*. New York: Halsted Press, 1975.

———, Secunda, S. K., and Dyson, W. L. A controlled study of the antidepressant effects of lithium carbonate. *Archives of General Psychiatry*, 1972, 26, 154–157.

Mendelson, J., and Ladou, J. Experimentally induced chronic intoxication and withdrawal in alcoholics. Part II. Psychological findings. *Quarterly Journal of Studies on Alcohol*, 1964, Supplement 2, 24.

Menaker, T. Conflict about drinking in alcoholics. Doctoral dissertation, Department of Social Relations, Harvard University, 1963. Reported in Wilkinson, R. *The prevention of drinking problems: alcohol control and cultural influence*. New York: Oxford University Press, 1970, pp. 177–180.

Menninger, K. A. *A manual for psychiatric case study*. New York: Grune & Stratton, 1952.

———. *Theory of psychoanalytic technique*. New York: Basic Books, 1958.

———. *The vital balance*. New York: Viking, 1963.

Menninger Clinic Children's Division, Menninger Foundation Staff. *Disturbed Children*. San Francisco: Jossey–Bass, 1969.

Mercer, M., and Greizman, S. Alcoholic Korsakoff psychosis. In Burton, H., and Harris, R. E. (eds.), *Case histories in clinical and abnormal psychology*. New York: Harper & Row, 1947, pp. 338–345.

Mesmer, F. A. *Schreiden über die Magnetkur an einen answärtigen Arzt*. Vienna, 1775.

Meyer, A. *Reports of the New York State Pathological Institute*. Utica, N.Y., 1904–1905.

Meyer, V., and Chesser, E. S. *Behavior therapy in clinical psychiatry*. Middlesex, England: Penguin Books, 1970.

Meyer, W. J. The psychology of aging. In Weiner, B., Runquist, W., Runquist, P. A., Raven, B. H., Meyer, W. J., Leiman, A., Kutscher, C. L., Kleinmuntz, B., and Haber, R. N., *Discovering psychology*. Palo Alto, Calif.: Science Research Associates, 1977, pp. 152–183.

Meyerowitz, J. H. Self-derogations in young retardates and special class placement, *Child Development*, 1962, 33, 443–451.

Meyers, A. W., Craighead, W. E., and Meyers, H. H. A behavioral approach to community mental health. *American Journal of Community Mental Health*, 1974, 2, 275–285.

Mezey, E., Jow, E., Slavin, R. E., and Tobon, F. Pancreatic function and intestinal absorption in chronic alcoholism. *Gastroenterology*, 1970, 59, 657–664.

Miklich, D. R. Radio telemetry in clinical psychology. *American Psychologist*, 1975, 30, 419–425.

Mikulas, W. L. *Behavior modification: an overview*. New York: Harper & Row, 1972.

Milgram, S. Behavioral study of obedience. *Journal of Abnormal and Social Psychology*, 1963, 67, 371–378.

———. Group pressure and action against a person. *Journal of Abnormal and Social Psychology*, 1964, 69, 137–143.

———. Liberating effects of group pressure. *Journal of Personality and Social Psychology*, 1965, 1, 127–134.

———. The experience of living in cities. *Science*, 1970, 167, 1461–1468.

———. *Obedience to authority*. New York: Harper & Row, 1974.

Miller, L. C., Barrett, C. L., and Hampe, I. E. Impact of application of principles of learning. In Rie, H. E. (ed.), *Perspectives in child psychopathology*. Chicago: Aldine, 1971, pp. 351–386.

———, DiCara, L. V., Solomon, H., Weiss, J. M., and Dworkin, B. Learned modifications of autonomic functions: a review of some new data. *Circulation Research*, Supplement 1, 1970, 26, 1–3; 27, 1–11. Reprinted in Barber, T. X., Dicara, L. V., Kamiya, J., Miller, N. E., Shapiro, D., and Stoyva, J. (eds.), *Biofeedback and self-control, 1970*. Chicago: Aldine, 1971, pp. 351–359.

Miller, N. E. Frustration-aggression hypothesis. *Psychological Reviews*, 1941, 48, 337–342.

———. Studies of fear as an acquired drive. *Journal of Experimental Psychology*, 1948(a), 38, 89–101.

———. Theory and experiment relating psychoanalytic displacement to stimulus response generalization, *Journal of Abnormal and Social Psychology*, 1948(b), 43, 155–178.

———. Learning of visceral and glandular responses. *Science*, 1969, 163, 434–445.

———, and Banuazizi, A. Instrumental learning by curarized rats of a specific visceral response, intestinal or cardiac. *Journal of Comparative and Physiological Psychology*, 1968, 65, 1–7.

———, and DiCara, L. V. Instrumental learning of heart rate changes in curarized rats: Shaping and specificity to discriminative stimulus. *Journal of Comparative and Physiological Psychology*, 1967, 63, 12–19.

———, and DiCara, L. V. Instrumental learning of urine formation by rats: Changes in renal blood flow. *American Journal of Physiology*, 1968, 215, 677–683.

———, **and Dollard, J.** *Social learning and imitation.* New Haven: Yale University Press, 1941.

———, **and Dworkin, B. R.** Visceral learning. In Obrist, P. A. (ed.), *Cardiovascular psychophysiology.* Chicago: Aldine, 1974.

———, **and Dworkin, B.** Visceral learning. Recent difficulties with curarized rats and significant problems for human research. In DiCara, L. V., Barber, T. X., Kamiya, J., Miller, N. E., Shapiro, D., and Stovya, J. (eds.), *Biofeedback and self-control, 1974.* Chicago: Aldine, 1975, pp. 3–103.

Miller, W. R., and Seligman, M. E. P. Depression and learned helplessness in man. *Journal of Abnormal Psychology,* 1975, 84, 228–238.

———, **Seligman, M. E. P., and Kurlander, H. M.** Learned helplessness, depression, and anxiety. *Journal of Nervous and Mental Disease,* 1975, 161, 347–357.

Mindham, R. H. S., Howland, C., and Shepherd, M. Continuation therapy with tricyclic antidepressants in depressive illness. *Lancet,* 1972, 854–855.

Mintz, E. *Marathon groups: reality and symbol.* Englewood Cliffs, N.J.: Prentice-Hall, 1971.

Mirin, S. M., Shapiro, L. M., Meyer, R. E., Pillard, R. C., and Fisher, S. Casual versus heavy use of marihuana: a redefinition of the marihuana problem. Paper presented at the 123rd Annual Meeting of the American Psychiatric Association, San Francisco, May 1970.

Mirsky, I. A. Physiologic, psychologic and social determinants in the etiology of duodenal ulcer. *American Journal of Digestive Diseases,* 1958, 3, 285–314.

Mishler, E. G., and Waxler, N. E. *Interaction in families: an experimental study of family processes and schizophrenia.* New York: Wiley, 1968.

Mittler, P. *The study of twins.* Middlesex, England: Penguin Books, 1971.

Moll, A. E. Evolution of psychiatry in general hospital and community. *Comprehensive Psychiatry,* 1963, 4, 394–408.

Money, J. *Sex errors of the body: dilemmas, education, counseling.* Baltimore: Johns Hopkins University Press, 1968.

———, Discussing sexual problems with your patients. *Practical Psychology for Physicians,* 1975, 2.

Monge, R. H. Structure of the self-concept from adolescence through old age. *Experimental Aging Research,* 1976, 2.

Montagu, A. Chromosomes and crime. *Psychology Today,* 1968, 2, 42–49.

———. *The nature of human aggression.* New York: Oxford University Press, 1976.

———. (ed.). *Man and aggression.* 2nd ed. New York: Oxford University Press, 1973.

Mora, G. History of psychiatry and psychiatric treatment. In Freedman, A. M., and Kaplan, H. I. (eds.), *Treating mental illness: aspects of modern therapy.* New York: Atheneum, 1971, pp. 3–66.

Morel, B. A. *Traité des dégénérescences physiques, intellectuelles et morales.* Paris: Baillière, 1857.

Moreno, J. L. Psychodrama. In Arieti, S. (ed.), *American handbook of psychiatry,* Vol. 2. New York: Basic Books, 1959, pp. 1375–1396.

Morgan, C. D., and Murray, H. A. A method for investigating fantasies: the Thematic Apperception Test. *Archives of Neurology and Psychiatry,* 1935, 34, 289–306.

Morgan, C. T. *Physiological psychology.* 3rd ed. New York: McGraw-Hill, 1965.

Morley, W. E. Treatment of the patient in crisis. *Western Medicine,* 1965, 3, 77–86.

Morris, D. *The naked ape.* New York: McGraw-Hill, 1968.

Mosak, H. H., and Dreikurs, R. Adlerian psychotherapy. In Corsini (ed.), *Current psychotherapies.* Itasca, Ill.: Peacock, 1973, pp. 35–83.

Mosher, D. L., and Smith, J. P. The usefulness of two scoring systems for the Bender Gestalt Test for identifying brain damage. *Journal of Consulting Psychology,* 1965, 29, 530–536.

Mosher, L. R., and Feinsilver, D. B. *Special report on schizophrenia.* Washington, D.C.: NIMH, 1970.

Mourer, S. A. A prediction of patterns of schizophrenic error resulting from semantic generalization. *Journal of Abnormal Psychology,* 1973, 81, 250–254.

Moustakas, C. (ed.). *Existential child therapy: the child's discovery of himself.* New York: Basic Books, 1966.

Mowrer, O. H. A stimulus response analysis of anxiety audits role as a reinforcing agent. *Psychological Review,* 1939, 46, 553–565.

———. An experimental analogue of "regression" with incidental observations on "reaction formation." *Journal of Abnormal and Social Psychology,* 1940, 35, 16–87.

———. *Learning theory and personality dynamics.* New York: Ronald Press, 1950.

———. *Learning theory and behavior.* New York: Wiley, 1960(a).

———. Sin, the lesser of two evils. *American Psychologist,* 1960(b), 15, 301–304.

———. Learning theory and behavior therapy. In Wolman, B. (ed.), *Handbook of clinical psychology.* New York: McGraw-Hill, 1965.

———, **and Mowrer, W. M.** Enuresis—a method for its study and treatment. *American Journal of Orthopsychiatry,* 1938, 8, 436–459.

———, **and Viek, P.** An experimental analogue of fear from a sense of helplessness. *Journal of Abnormal and Social Psychology,* 1948, 43, 193–200.

Moyer, K. E. The physiology of aggression and the implications for aggression control. In Singer, J. L. (ed.), *The control of aggression and violence.* New York: Academic Press, 1971(a).

———. *The physiology of hostility.* Chicago: Markham, 1971(b).

Mulford, H. A. Drinking and deviant drinking. U.S.A. 1963. *Quarterly Journal of Studies on Alcohol,* 1964, 25, 634–650.

Mulvihill, D. J., and Tumin, M. M. *Crimes of violence,* Vol. 12.

Staff Report to the National Commission on the Causes and Prevention of Violence. Washington, D.C.: Government Printing Office, 1969.

Munroe, R. L. *Schools of psychoanalytic thought: an exposition, critique, and attempt at integration.* New York: Dryden Press, 1955.

Murphy, J. *Homosexual liberation: a personal view.* New York: Praeger, 1971.

Murray, H. A. *Thematic Apperception Test.* Cambridge, Mass.: Harvard University Press, 1943.

———, and Harvard Psychological Clinic. *Explorations in personality.* New York: Oxford University Press, 1938.

Mussen, P. H., Conger, J. J., and Kagan, J. *Child development and personality.* 4th ed. New York: Harper & Row, 1980.

Myers, R. D. Voluntary alcohol consumption in animals: peripheral and intracerebral factors. *Psychosomatic Medicine,* 1966, 28, 484 ff.

———. Influence of stress on alcohol preference in rats. In Popham, R. E. (ed.), *Alcohol and alcoholism.* Toronto: University of Toronto Press, 1970, pp. 97–101.

———, and Veale, W. L. Alterations in volitional alcohol intake accompanying chronic intracerebral infusions of methanol, acetaldehyde, or paraldehyde. *Archives of International Pharmocodynamics and Therapy,* 1972.

Myerson, A. A review of mental disorders in urban areas. *American Journal of Psychiatry.* 1941, 96, 995–997.

Nachmani, G., and Cohen, B. D. Recall and recognition-free learning in schizophrenics. *Journal of Abnormal Psychology,* 1969, 74, 511–516.

Nagler, S. H. Erich Fromm. In Freedman, A. M., and Kaplan, H. I. (eds.), *Interpreting personality: a survey of twentieth-century views.* New York: Atheneum, 1972, pp. 193–200.

Nameche, G., Waring, M., and Ricks, D. Early indicators of outcome in schizophrenia. *Journal of Nervous and Mental Disease,* 1967, 139, pp. 232–240.

Nathan, P. E. *Cues, decisions and diagnoses.* New York: Academic Press, 1967.

———, Goldman, M. S., Lisman, S. A., and Taylor, H. A. Alcohol and alcoholics: a behavioral approach. *Transactions of the New York Academy of Science,* 1972, 34, 602–627.

———, and Harris, S. L. *Psychopathology and society.* New York: McGraw-Hill, 1975.

National Clearinghouse for Mental Health Information. *Outpatient services: a service of the community mental health center.* Public Health Service Publication No. 1578. Washington, D.C.: Government Printing Office, 1969.

National Commission on Marihuana and Drug Abuse. *Marihuana: a signal of misunderstanding.* Washington, D.C.: Government Printing Office, 1972.

The Nazi primer: official handbook for schooling Hitler youth. New York: Harper & Row, 1938.

Neale, D. H. Behavior therapy and encopresis in children. *Behavioral Research and Therapy,* 1963, 1, 139–149.

Neale, J. M., and Katahn, M. Anxiety, choice and stimulus uncertainty. *Journal of Personality,* 1968, 36, 238–245.

Neel, J. V. and Schull, W. J. *Human heredity.* Chicago: University of Chicago Press, 1954.

Neill, A. S. *Summerhill: a readical approach to child rearing.* New York: Hart, 1960.

Nelson, P. C., and Phares, E. J. Anxiety, discrepancy between need value and expectancy, and internal-external control. *Psychological Reports,* 1971, 28, 663–668.

Netter, F. H. *The CIBA collection of medical illustrations: nervous system,* Vol. 1. Newark, N.J.: CIBA Pharmaceutical Corporation, Medical Education Division, 1962.

Neubauer, P. B., and Steinert, J. Schizophrenia in adolescents. *Nervous Child,* 1952, 10, 128–134.

Neugarten, B. L. (ed.). *Middle age and aging.* Chicago: University of Chicago Press, 1968.

———, Havighurst, R. J., and Tobin, S. S. Personality and patterns of aging. In Neugarten, B. L. (ed.), *Middle age and aging.* Chicago: University of Chicago Press, 1968, pp. 173–179.

Newsweek. The deadly "angel dust." March 13, 1978.

NIAAA. *First special report to the U.S. Congress on alcohol and health from the Secretary of Health, Education, and Welfare.* Rockville, Md.: National Institute on Alcohol Abuse and Alcoholism, 1971.

———. *Second special report to the U.S. Congress on alcohol and health from the Secretary of Health, Education, and Welfare.* Rockville, Md.: National Institute on Alcohol Abuse and Alcoholism, 1974.

Nielsen, J. The XYY syndrome in a mental hospital. *British Journal of Criminology,* 1968, 8, 186–203.

———. Criminality among patients with Klinefelter's syndrome and the XYY syndrome. *British Journal of Psychiatry,* 1970, 117, 365–369.

Nikolaeva, V. V. Pathology of higher nervous activity in dogs of strong balanced type. *Pavlov Journal of Higher Nervous Activity,* 1959, 9, 620–625.

NIMH. Narcotic drug addiction. *Mental Health Monograph,* Number 2. Washington, D.C.: Government Printing Office, 1965.

———. *Alcohol and alcoholism.* Public Health Service Publication No. 1640. Washington, D.C.: Government Printing Office, 1969(a).

———. *The mental health of urban America: the urban programs of the National Institute of Mental Health.* Washington, D.C.: Government Printing Office, 1969(b).

———. Distribution of patient-care episodes in mental health facilities, 1969. *Statistical Note 58.* (Publication No. HSM 72–9012). Washington, D.C.: Government Printing Office, 1972(a).

———. *Marijuana and health: second annual report to Congress from the Secretary of Health, Education, and Welfare.* (Publication No. 72–9113.) Washington, D.C.: Government Printing Office, 1972(b).

————. *Psychiatric services in general hospitals, 1969–1970.* (Publication No. HSM 72–9139) Washington, D.C.: Government Printing Office, 1972(c).

————. *The practice of mental health consultation.* Washington, D.C.: Government Printing Office, 1975.

Nisbett, R. E. Determinants of food intake in human obesity. *Science,* 1968, 159, 1254–1255.

————. Hunger, obesity, and the ventromedial nucleus. *Psychological Review,* 1972, 79, 433–453.

Norbeck, E., Price-Williams, D., and McCord, W. M. (eds.). *The study of personality: an interdisciplinary appraisal.* New York: Holt, Rinehart and Winston, 1968.

Nowlis, D. P., and Kamiya, J. The control of electroencephalographic alpha rhythms through auditory feedback and the associated mental activity. *Psychophysiology,* 1970, 6, 476–484.

Nowlis, H. H. *Drugs on the college campus.* New York: Doubleday (Anchor Books), 1969.

Nunnally, J. C. *Popular conceptions of mental health: their development and change.* New York: Holt, Rinehart and Winston, 1961.

————. *Psychometric theory.* 2nd ed. New York: McGraw-Hill, 1978.

————. *Introduction to psychological measurement.* New York: McGraw-Hill, 1970.

Ogle, D. K. Reported in St. Petersburg *Independent,* March 29, 1967.

Oki, T. A psychological study of early childhood neuroses. In Mitsuda, H. (ed.), *Clinical genetics in psychiatry.* Tokyo: Igaku Shoin, 1967, pp. 344–359.

O'Leary, K. D., and Wilson, G. T. *Behavior therapy: application and outcome.* Englewood Cliffs, N.J.: Prentice-Hall, 1975.

————, **O'Leary, S., and Becker, W. C.** Modification of a deviant sibling interaction pattern in the home. In Guerney, B. G. (ed.), *Psychotherapeutic agents: new roles for nonprofessionals, parents, and teachers.* New York: Holt, Rinehart and Winston, 1969, pp. 408–418.

O'Leary, M. R., Donoavan, D. M., Krueger, K. J., and Cyzewski, B. Depression and perception of reinforcement: lack of differences in expectancy change among alcoholics. *Journal of Abnormal Psychology,* 1978, 87, 110–112.

Oltman, J., and Friedman, S. Parental deprivation in psychiatric conditions. *Diseases of the Nervous System,* 1967, 28, 298–303.

O'Neal, P., King, J. L., Robins, L. N., and Schaefer, J. Parental deviance and the genesis of sociopathic personality. *American Journal of Psychiatry,* 1962, 118, 1114–1123.

O'Neill, P. Self-esteem and behavior of girls with convergent and divergent cognitive abilities. Unpublished doctoral dissertation. Yale University, 1974.

Opler, M. K. *Culture, psychiatry and human values.* Springfield, Ill.: Thomas, 1956.

————. Cultural differences in mental disorders: an Italian and Irish contrast in the schizophrenias—U.S.A. In Opler, M. K. (ed.), *Cultures and mental health: cross-cultural studies.* New York: Macmillan, 1959, pp. 425–442.

Orne, M. T. The nature of hypnosis: artifact and essence. *Journal of Abnormal and Social Psychology,* 1959, 58, 277–299.

————. On the social psychology of the psychological experiment: with particular reference to demand characteristics and their implication. *American Psychologist,* 1962, 17, 776–783.

————, **and Paskewitz, D. A.** Aversive situational effects on alpha feedback training. In DiCara, L. V., Barber, T. X., Kamiya, J., Miller, N. E., Shapiro, D., and Stoyva, J. (eds.), *Biofeedback and self-control, 1974.* Chicago: Aldine, 1975, pp. 336–340.

Ornitz, E. M., and Ritvo, E. R. Perceptual inconsistency in early infantile autism. *Archives of General Psychiatry,* 1968, 18, 76–98.

OSS Assessment Staff. *Assessment of men.* New York: Holt Rinehart and Winston, 1948.

Osgood, C. E., and Luria, Z. A blind analysis of a case of multiple personality using the semantic differential. *Journal of Abnormal and Social Psychology,* 1954, 49, 579–591.

————, **Suci, G. J., and Tannenbaum, P. H.** *The measurement of meaning.* Urbana: University of Illinois Press, 1957.

Oswald, I. Induction of illusionary and hallucinatory voices with consideration of behavior therapy. *Journal of Mental Science,* 1962, 108, 196–212.

Ottenberg, P., Stein, M., Lewis, J., and Hamilton, C. Learned asthma in the guinea pig. *Psychosomatic Medicine,* 1958, 20, 395–400.

Padilla, A. M., Ruiz, R. A., and Alvarez, R. Community mental health services for the Spanish-speaking surnamed population. *American Psychologist,* 1975, 30, 892–905.

Page, J. D. *Psychopathology: the science of understanding deviance.* Chicago: Aldine, 1971.

Parad, H. J. Introduction. In Parad, H. J. (ed.), *Crisis intervention: selected readings.* New York: Family Service Association of America, 1965, pp. 1–4.

Parsons, A. Some comparative observations on ward social structure: Southern Italy, England and the United States. *Transcultural Psychiatric Research Review,* 1961, 10, 65–67.

Parsons, T. The incest taboo in relation to social structure and the socialization of the child. *British Journal of Sociology,* 1954, 2, 101.

Partridge, G. E. Current conceptions of psychopathic personality. *American Journal of Psychiatry,* 1930, 10, 53–99.

Pasamanick, B. The community care of schizophrenics. In

Williams, R. H., and Ozarin, L. D. (eds.), *Community mental health*. San Francisco: Jossey–Bass, 1968, pp. 394–415.

———, **Scarpetti, F. R., and Dinitz, S.** *Schizophrenics in the community: an experimental study in the prevention of hospitalization*. Englewood Cliffs, N.J.: Prentice-Hall, 1967.

Patterson, C. H. *Theories of counseling and psychotherapy*. 2nd ed. New York: Harper & Row, 1972.

Patterson, G. R., and Cobb, J. A dyadic analysis of "aggressive" behaviors. In Hill, J. P. (ed.), *Minnesota symposia on child psychology*, Vol. 5. Minneapolis: University of Minnesota Press, 1971, pp. 72–129.

———, **and Brodsky, G.** A behavior modification program for a child with multiple problem behaviors. In Guerney, B. G. (ed.), *Psychotherapeutic agents: new roles for nonprofessionals, parents, and teachers*. New York: Holt, Rinehart and Winston, 1969, pp. 419–442.

Patton, R. G., and Gardner, L. I. *Growth failure in maternal deprivation*. Springfield, Ill.: Thomas, 1963.

Paul, G. Physiological effects of relaxation training and hypnotic suggestion. *Journal of Abnormal Psychology*, 1969, 74, 425–437.

———, **and Shannon, D. T.** Treatment of anxiety through systematic desensitization in therapy groups. *Journal of Abnormal Psychology*, 1966, 71, 124–135.

———, **Tobias, L. L., and Holly, B. L.** Maintenance psychotropic drugs in the presence of active treatment programs: a "triple blind" withdrawal study with long-term mental patients. *Archives of General Psychiatry*, 1972, 27, 106–115.

Pavlov, I. P. *Conditioned reflexes*. London: Oxford University Press, 1927.

———. An attempt at a physiological interpretation of obsessional neuroses and paranoia. *Journal of Mental Science*, 1934, 80, 187.

Paykel, E. S. Depressive typologies and response to amitriptyline. *British Journal of Psychiatry*, 1972, 120, 147–156.

Pearlman, S. Drug use and experience in an urban college population. *American Journal of Orthopsychiatry*, 1968, 38, 503–514.

Pearson, G. H. J. *Emotional disorders of children*. New York: Norton, 1949.

Peck, H. B., Roman, M., and Kaplan, S. Community action programs in the comprehensive mental health center. In *Psychiatric Research Report 21*. Washington, D.C.: American Psychiatric Association, 1967.

Penfield, W., and Jasper, H. *Epilepsy and functional anatomy of the human brain*. Boston: Little, Brown, 1954.

Penrose, L. S. (ed.). *Recent advances in human genetics*. Boston: Little, Brown, 1961.

———. *The biology of mental defect*. 2nd ed. New York: Grune & Stratton, 1963.

Perls, F. S. Four lectures. In Fagan, J., and Shepherd, I. L. (eds.), *Gestalt therapy now: theory, techniques, applications*.

New York: Harper & Row, 1970, pp. 14–38.

———. *Gestalt therapy verbatim*. New York: Bantam Books, 1971.

———, **Hefferline, R. F., and Goodman, P.** *Gestalt therapy*. New York: Dell, 1951.

Perris, C. A study of bipolar (manic-depressive) and unipolar recurrent depressive psychoses. *Acta Psychiatrica Scandinavia*, 1966, 42, Supplement 194 (cited in Winokur et al., 1969).

Persons, R. W. Psychotherapy with sociopathic offenders: an empirical evaluation. *Journal of Clinical Psychology*, 1965, 21, 204–207.

———. Psychological and behavioral change in delinquents following psychotherapy. *Journal of Clinical Psychology*, 1966, 22, 337–340.

———, **and Pepinsky, H. B.** Convergence in psychotherapy with delinquent boys. *Journal of Counseling Psychology*, 1966, 13, 329–334.

Pervin, L. A. The need to predict and control under conditions of threat. *Journal of Personality*, 1965, 51, 570–585.

Peters, J. E., and Stern, R. M. Specificity of attitude hypotheses in psychosomatic medicine: a reexamination. *Journal of Psychosomatic Research*, 1971, 15, 129–135.

Peterson, D. R. *The clinical study of social behavior*. Englewood Cliffs, N.J.: Prentice-Hall, 1968.

———, **and London, P.** Neobehavioristic psychotherapy: quasi-hypnotic suggestion and multiple reinforcement in the treatment of a case of postinfantile dyscopresis. *Psychological Record*, 1964, 14, 469–474.

Petrie, A. Some psychological aspects of pain and the relief of suffering. *Annals of the New York Academy of Science*, 1960, 86, 13–27.

———, **McCulloch, R., and Kazdin, P.** The perceptual characteristics of juvenile delinquents. *Journal of Nervous and Mental Disease*, 1962, 134, 415–421.

Pettigrew, T. F. *A profile of the Negro American*. New York: Van Nostrand Reinhold, 1964.

Phares, E. J. *Locus of control*. Morristown, N.J.: General Learning Press, 1972.

———. *Locus of control in personality*. Morristown, N.J.: General Learning Press, 1976.

Philipp, R. J. *An experimental investigation of suggestion and relaxation in asthmatics*. Unpublished doctoral dissertation. Queens University, 1970.

———, **Wilde, G. J. S., and Day, J. H.** Suggestion and relaxation in asthmatics. *Journal of Psychosomatic Research*, 1972, 16, 193–204.

Phillips, E. L. Achievement place: token reinforcement procedures in a homestyle rehabilitation setting for "predelinquent" boys. *Journal of Applied Behavior Analysis*, 1968, 1, 213–223.

Phillips. L. Social competence, the process-reactive distinction, and the nature of mental disorder. In Hoch, P. H., and Zubin J. (eds.), *Psychopathology of schizophrenia*. New

York: Grune & Stratton, 1966, pp. 471–481.

Pichot, P., and Lamperiere, T. Analyse factorielle d'un questionnaire d'auto evaluation des symptomes depressifs. *Revue de Psychologes Appliquée*, 1966, 1, 15–25.

Pincus, J. H., and Tucker, G. J. *Behavioral neurology.* 2nd ed. New York: Oxford University Press, 1978.

Pinkney, A. *Black Americans.* Englewood Cliffs, N.J.: Prentice-Hall, 1969.

Pitts, F. N., and McClure, J. N. Lactate metabolism in anxiety neurosis. *New England Journal of Medicine,* 1967, 277, 1239–1336.

Plaut, T. F. A. *Alcohol problems.* A report to the nation by the Cooperative Commission on the Study of Alcoholism. New York: Oxford University Press, 1967.

Plog, S. C. and Edgerton, R. B. (eds.). *Changing perspectives in mental illness.* New York: Holt, Rinehart and Winston, 1969.

Pokorny, A. D. Characteristics of 44 patients who subsequently committed suicide. *A.M.A. Archives of General Psychiatry,* 1960, 2, 314–323.

———. Human violence: a comparison of homicide, aggravated assault, suicide and attempted suicide. *Journal of Criminal Law, Criminology and Police Science,* 1965, 56, 488–498.

Pollack, M., Levenstein, S., and Klein, D. F. A three-year post hospital follow-up of adolescent and adult schizophrenics. *American Journal of Orthopsychiatry,* 1968, 38, 94–109.

Pollitt, J. D. Depression and the functional shift. *Comparative Psychiatry,* 1960, 1, 381–390.

———. Suggestions for a physiological classification of depression. *British Journal of Psychiatry,* 1965, 111, 489–495.

Popham, R. E. A statistical report relating to alcoholism and the use of alcoholic beverages in Canada. *International Journal on Alcohol and Alcoholism,* 1955, 1, 5–22.

———. *Alcohol and alcoholism.* Toronto: University of Toronto Press, 1970.

Portnoy, I. The anxiety states. In Arieti, S. (ed.), *American handbook of psychiatry,* Vol. I. New York: Basic Books, 1959, pp. 307–323.

Poussaint, A. and Atkinson, C. Black youth and motivation. In Jones, R. L. (ed.), *Black psychology.* New York: Harper & Row, 1972, pp. 113–123.

Premack, A. J., and Premack, D. Teaching language to an ape. *Scientific American,* November 1972.

Prescott, J. W. Early somatosensory deprivation as an ontogenetic process in the abnormal development of the brain and behavior, *Proceedings of the 2nd Conference on Experimental Medicine and Surgery with Primates,* New York, 1969. Available from National Institute of Health, Bethesda, Md.

———. Body pleasure and the origins of violence. *The Futurist,* April 1975, 64–74.

President's Panel on Mental Retardation. A proposed program for national action to combat mental retardation. Washington, D.C.: Government Printing Office, 1962.

Prestia, C. J. (in consultation with students and personnel of Carnegie-Mellon University). A proposal for a Carnegie-Mellon University Peer Help Center. Unpublished mimeo, Carnegie-Mellon University, July 16, 1971.

Price, K. P., Tryon, W. W., and Raps, C. S. Learned helplessness and depression in a clinical population: a test of two behavioral hypotheses. *Journal of Abnormal Psychology,* 1978, 87, 113–121.

Price, R. H. *Abnormal behavior: perspectives in conflict.* New York: Holt, Rinehart and Winston, 1972.

Prichard, J. C. *A treatise on insanity.* Philadelphia: Hasswell, Barrington & Hassurd, 1835.

Prien, R. F., and Caffey, E. M. Guidelines for antipsychotic drugs. *Medical Times,* May 1976, 87–107.

———. A comparison of lithium carbonate and chlorpromazine in the treatment of excited schizo-affectives. *Archives of General Psychiatry,* 1972, 27, 182–189.

Prince, M. *The dissociation of personality.* New York: Longman, 1906.

Proshansky, H., Ittelson, W., and Rivlin, A. *Environmental psychology: man and his physical setting.* New York: Holt, Rinehart and Winston, 1970.

Provence, S., and Lipton, R. C. *Infants in institutions.* New York: International Universities Press, 1962.

Pumpian–Mindlin, E. Considerations in the selection of patients for short-term therapy. *American Journal of Psychotherapy,* 1953, 7, 641–652.

Purcell, K., Brady, K., Chai, H., Muser, J., Molk, L., Gordon, N., and Means, J. The effect of asthma in children of experimental separation from the family. *Psychosomatic Medicine,* 1969, 31, 144–164.

Puthoff, H. E., and Targ, R. A perceptual channel for information transfer over kilometer distances: historical perspective and recent research. *Proceedings of the IEEE,* 1976, 64, 329–354.

Quaade, F. On psychogenic obesity in children. III. *Acta Paediatrica,* 1953, 42, 191–205.

Quarti, C., and Renaud, J. Note préliminaire sur un nouveau traitement des constipations par réflexe conditionnel. *La Clinique,* 1962, 57, 577–583.

Rachman, S. Sexual fetishism: an experimental analogue. *Psychological Record,* 1966, 16, 293–296.

———, and Hodgson, R. J. Experimentally-induced "sexual fetishism": replication and development. *Psychological Record,* 1968, 18, 25–27.

Rado, S. The problem of melancholia. *International Journal of Psychoanalysis,* 1928, 9, 420–438.

———. Hedonic control, action-self and the depressive spell. In Hoch, P. H., and Zubin, J. (eds.), *Depression.* New York: Grune & Stratton, 1954.

Raginsky, B. B. Temporary cardiac arrest induced hypnosis. *International Journal of Clinical and Experimental Hypnosis,* 1959, 7, 53–68.

Rahe, R. H., and Holmes, T. H. Social, psychologic, and psychophysiologic aspects of inguinal hernia. *Journal of Psychosomatic Research,* 1965, 8, 487.

Rank, O. *Will therapy: an analysis of the therapeutic process in terms of relationship.* New York: Knopf, 1936.

Raphael, B. Personal communication, 1972.

Rapoport, R. Normal crises, family structure and mental health. In Parad, H. J. (ed.), *Crisis intervention: selected readings.* New York: Family Service Association of America, 1965, pp. 75–87.

Rappaport J., Chinsky, J. M., and Cowen, G. L. *Innovations in helping chronic patients: college students in a mental institution.* New York: Academic Press, 1971.

Raush, H. L., and Raush, C. L. *The halfway house movement: a search for sanity.* Englewood Cliffs, N.J.: Prentice-Hall, 1968.

Ray, O. S. *Drugs, society, and human behavior.* St. Louis: Mosby, 1972.

Razran, G. The observable unconscious and the inferable conscious in current Soviet psychophysiology: interoceptive conditioning, semantic conditioning, and the orienting reflex. *Psychological Review,* 1961, 68, 81–147.

Redlich, F. C., and Freedman, D. X. *The theory and practice of psychiatry.* New York: Basic Books, 1966.

———, **Hollingshead, A. B., Roberts, B. H., Robinson, H. A., Freedman, L. Z., and Myers, J. K.** Social structure and psychiatric disorders. *American Journal of Psychiatry,* 1953, 109, 729–734.

Redmond, D. E., Jr., Maas, J. W., Graham, C. W., and Dekirmenjiam, H. Social behavior of monkeys selectively depleted of monoaminies. *Science,* 1971, 174, 428–430.

Rees, L. The significance of parental attitudes in childhood asthma. *Journal of Psychosomatic Research,* 1963, 6, 181–190.

———. The importance of psychological, allergic and infective factors in childhood asthma. *Journal of Psychosomatic Research,* 1964, 7, 253–262.

Reich, C. *The greening of America.* New York: Random House, 1970.

Reich, W. *Selected writings.* New York: Farrar, Straus & Giroux, 1960.

———. *Character analysis.* 3rd ed. New York: Farrar, Straus & Giroux, 1970.

Reik, T. *Listening with the third ear.* New York: Farrar, Straus & Giroux, 1948.

Reinhardt, J. M. *Sex perversions and sex crimes.* Springfield, Ill.: Thomas, 1957.

Reiser, D. E. Psychosis of infancy and early childhood as manifested by children with atypical development. *New England Journal of Medicine,* 1963, 269, 790–798, 844–850.

Reiss, I. How and why America's sex standards are changing. In Gagnon, J. H., and Simon, W. (eds.), *The sexual scene.* Chicago: Aldine, 1970, pp. 43–58.

Reiss, S. Educational and psychological effects of open-space education in Oak Park, Illinois. Unpublished technical report, University of Illinois at Chicago Circle, 1974.

———, **and Dyhdalo, N.** Resistence, achievement, and open-space environments. *Journal of Educational Psychology,* 1975, 67, 506–513.

———, **Peterson, R. A., Eron, L. D., and Reiss, M. M.** *Abnormality: experimental and clinical approaches.* New York: Macmillan, 1977.

Reitan, R. M. A research program on the psychological effects of brain lesions in human beings. In Ellis, R. N. (ed.), *International review of research in mental retardation,* Vol. 1. New York: Academic Press, 1966, pp. 153–218.

Renshaw, D. C. Emotional links to coronary disease. *Practical Psychology for Physicians,* 1976, 3, 30–32.

Restak, R. The promise and peril of psychosurgery. *Saturday Review/World,* September 25, 1973.

Rhodes, W. C., and Gibbins, S. Community programming for the behaviorally deviant child. In Quay, H. C., and Werry, J. S. (eds.), *Psychopathological disorders of childhood.* New York: Wiley, 1972, pp. 348–387.

Rickels, K. Drugs in the treatment of neurotic anxiety. In Solomon, P. *Psychiatric drugs.* New York: Grune & Stratton, 1966, pp. 225–238.

Rie, H. E. (ed.), *Perspectives in child psychopathology.* Chicago: Aldine, 1971.

Rie, H. E. and Rie, E. D. (eds.), *Handbook of minimal brain dysfunction.* New York: Wiley, 1979.

Rimland, B. *Infantile autism.* Englewood Cliffs, N.J.: Prentice-Hall, 1964.

Rimm, D. C., and Somerville, J. W. *Abnormal psychology.* New York: Academic Press, 1977.

Risley, T. R., and Hart, B. Developing correspondence between the non-verbal and verbal behavior of preschool children. *Journal of Applied Behavior Analysis,* 1968, 1, 267–281.

Rizley, R. Depression and distortion in the attribution of causality. *Journal of Abnormal Psychology,* 1978, 87, 32–48.

Roach, J. L., Gursslin, O., and Hunt, R. G. Some social-psychological characteristics of a child guidance clinic caseload. *Journal of Consulting Psychology,* 1958, 22, 183–186. Reprinted in Quay, H. C. (ed.), *Children's behavior disorders: selected readings.* New York: Van Nostrand Reinhold, 1968, pp. 22–29.

Robbins, E. S., Robbins, L., Frosch, W. A., and Stern, M. College student drug use. *American Journal of Psychiatry,* 1970, 126, 1743–1751.

Robbins, J., and Robbins, J. *An analysis of human sexual inadequacy.* New York: Signet, 1970.

Robins, E. Discussion of paper by R. G. Heath. In Abramson, H. A. (ed.), *Neuropharmacology.* New York: Josiah

Macy, Jr., Foundation, 1957, p. 123.

———, Gasner, J., Kayes, J., Wilkinson, R. H., and Murphy, G. E. The communication of suicidal intent: a study of 134 consecutive cases of successful (completed) suicides. *American Journal of Psychiatry*, 1959, 115, 724–733.

Robins, L. N. *Deviant children grown up*. Baltimore: Williams & Wilkins, 1966.

Robinson, J. Occupational norms and differences in job satisfaction: a summary of survey research evidence. In Robinson, J., Athanasiou, R., and Head, K. (eds.), *Measures of occupational attrition and occupational characteristics*. Ann Arbor, Mich.: Institute for Social Research, 1969.

Rodgers, D. A., and Thiessen, D. Effects of population density on adrenal size, behavioral arousal, and alcohol preference of inbred mice. *Quarterly Journal of Studies on Alcohol*, 1964, 25, 240 ff.

Rogers, C. R. *Client-centered therapy: its current practice, implications, and theory*. Boston: Houghton Mifflin, 1951.

———. The necessary and sufficient conditions of therapeutic personality change. *Journal of Consulting Psychology*, 1957, 21, 95–103.

———. *On becoming a person: a client's view of psychotherapy*. Boston: Houghton Mifflin, 1961.

———, and Skinner, B. F. Some issues concerning the control of human behavior: a symposium. *Science*, 1956, 124, 1057–1066.

Rogler, L. H., and Hollingshead, A. B. *Trapped: families and schizophrenia*. New York: Wiley, 1965.

Rokeach, M. *The three Christs of Ypsilanti*. New York: Knopf, 1964.

Roland, J. L., and Teste, M. Le cannabisme au Maroc. *Maroc-Medical*, 1958, 387, 694–703. Also appears under Benabud, A. Psycho-pathological aspects of the cannabis situation in Morocco: statistical data for 1956. *UN Bulletin on Narcotics*, 1957, 9, 1–16.

Roman, P. M., and Rice, H. M. *Schizophrenia and the poor*. Ithaca, N.Y.: Cornell University Press, 1967.

Romano, J. Psychotherapy. In Braceland, F. J., Freedman, D. X., Friedhoff, A. J., Kolb, L. C., Lourie, R. S., and Romano, J. (eds.), *Yearbook of psychiatry and applied mental health 1977*. Chicago: Year Book Medical Publishers, 1977, pp. 233–258.

Rome, H. P., Swenson, W. M., Mataya, P., McCarthy, C. E., Pearson, J. S., and Keating, R. F. Symposium on automation techniques in personality assessment. *Proceedings of the Mayo Clinic*, 1962, 37, 61–82.

———, Mataya, P., Pearson, J. S., Swenson, W. M., and Brannick, T. L. Automatic personality assessment. In Stacy, R. W., and Waxman, B. (eds.), *Computers in biomedical research*, Vol. 1. New York: Academic Press, 1965, pp. 505–524.

Rorschach, H. *Psychodiagnostik*. Leipzig: Ernst Bircher Verlag, 1921.

Rosen, E., Fox, R. E., and Gregory, I. *Abnormal psychology*. 2nd ed. Philadelphia: Saunders, 1972.

Rosen, G. History of medical hypnosis: from animal magnetism to medical hypnosis. In Schneck, J. M. (ed.), *Hypnosis in modern medicine*. Springfield, Ill.: Thomas, 1963, pp. 3–28.

Rosen, J. *Direct analysis: selected papers*. New York: Grune & Stratton, 1953.

Rosenblatt, B. Historical perspective of treatment modes. In Rie, H. E. (ed.), *Perspectives in child psychopathology*. Chicago: Aldine, 1971, pp. 51–84.

Rosenhan, D. On the social psychology of hypnosis research. In Gordon, J. E. (ed.), *Handbook of experimental and clinical hypnosis*. New York: Macmillan, 1967, pp. 481–510.

———. On being sane in insane places. *Science*, 1973, 179, 250–258.

———. The contextual nature of psychiatric diagnosis. *Journal of Abnormal Psychology*, 1975, 84, 462–474.

———, and London, P. Therapy and remediation. In London, P., and Rosenhan, D. (eds.), *Foundations of abnormal psychology*. New York: Holt, Rinehart and Winston, 1968, pp. 557–598.

Rosenthal, D. *Genetic theory and abnormal behavior*. New York: McGraw-Hill, 1970.

———. *Genetics of psychopathology*. N.Y.: McGraw-Hill, 1971.

———. Evidence for a spectrum of schizophrenic disorders. Presented at the annual meeting of the American Psychological Association, Montreal, Canada, August 1973.

Rosenthal, R. *Experimenter effects in behavioral research*. Englewood Cliffs, N.J.: Prentice-Hall, 1966.

Ross, A. O. *Psychological disorders of children: a behavioral approach to theory, research, and therapy*. New York: McGraw-Hill, 1974.

———. Behavior therapy. In Quay, H. C., and Werry, J. S. (eds.), *Psychopathological disorders of childhood*. New York: Wiley, 1972, pp. 273–315.

Ross, F. Conrad House: a psychiatric halfway house. In Sinnett, E. R., and Sachson, A. D. (eds.), *Transitional facilities in the rehabilitation of the emotionally disturbed*. Lawrence: University of Kansas Press, 1970, pp. 83–88.

Ross, M. Suicide among physicians. *Psychiatry in Medicine*, 1971, 2, 189–197.

Rossi, J. J., and Filstead, W. J. (eds.). *The therapeutic community*. New York: Behavioral Publications, 1972.

Roth, S., and Bootzin, R. R. Effects of experimentally induced expectancies of external control: an investigation of learned helplessness. *Journal of Personality and Social Psychology*, 1974, 29, 253–264.

———, and Kubal, L. Effects of noncontingent reinforcement on tasks of differing importance: facilitation and learned helplessness. *Journal of Personality and Social Psychology*, 1975, 32, 680–691.

Rotter, J. B. *Social learning and clinical psychology*. Englewood Cliffs, N.J.: Prentice-Hall, 1954.

————. Generalized expectancies for internal vs. external control of reinforcement. *Psychological Monographs*, 1966, 80 (Whole No. 609).

————, **Chance, J. E., and Phares, E. J.** (eds.). *Applications of a social learning theory of personality*. New York: Holt, Rinehart and Winston, 1972.

Routh, K., and Robert, R. D. Minimal brain dysfunction in children: failure to find evidence for a behavioral syndrome. *Psychological Reports*, 1972, 31, 307–314.

Rubinstein, J. *The study of psychology*. Guilford, Conn.: Dushkin, 1975.

Ruitenbeek, H. M. *The new group therapies*. New York: Avon Books, 1970.

Russell, E. R., Neuringer, C., and Goldstein, G. *Assessment of brain damage: a neuropsychological key approach*. New York: Wiley, 1970.

Rutner, I. T., and Bugle C. An experimental procedure for the modification of psychotic behavior. *Journal of Consulting and Clinical Psychology*, 1969, 33, 651–653.

Rutter, M., Graham, P., and Yule, W. *A neuropsychiatric study in childhood*. London: S.I.M.P. with Heinemann Medical, 1970.

Ryan, E. D. Perceptual characteristics of vigorous people. In Brown, R. C., Jr., and Cratty, B. J. (eds.), *New perspectives of man in action*. Englewood Cliffs, N.J.: Prentice-Hall, 1969, pp. 88–101.

Sacks, J. M., and Berger, S. Group therapy techniques with hospitalized chronic schizophrenic patients. *Journal of Consulting Psychology*, 1954, 18, 297–307.

Sakel, M. A new treatment of schizophrenia. *American Journal of Psychiatry*, 1937, 93, 829.

————. *The pharmacological shock treatment of schizophrenia*. Nervous and Mental Disease Monograph Series, No. 62. New York: Nervous and Mental Diseases Publishing, 1938.

Sales, S. M. Organizational role as a risk factor in coronary disease. *Administrative Science Quarterly*, 1969, 14, 325–336.

————, **and House, J.** Job dissatisfaction as a possible risk factor in coronary heart disease. *Journal of Chronic Diseases*, 1971, 23, 861–873.

Salfield, D. F. Enuresis—with special consideration of the nocturnal encountered in children. *Zeitschrift Kinderpsychiatrie*, 1954, 21, 1–8.

Salzinger, K. *Schizophrenia: behavioral aspects*. New York: Wiley, 1973.

Sanders, D. H. Innovative environments in the community: a life for the chronic patient. *Schizophrenia Bulletin*, Issue No. 6, Fall 1972, pp. 49–59.

Sandifer, M. G., Jr., Pettus, C., and Quade, D. A study of psychiatric diagnosis. *Journal of Nervous and Mental Disease*, 1964, 139, 350–356.

Sandler, J. and Davidson, R. S. Psychopathology: an analysis of response consequences. In Kimmel, H. D. (ed.), *Experimental psychopathology: recent research and theory*. New York: Academic Press, 1971, pp. 71–93.

————. *Psychopathology: Learning theory, research, and applications*. New York: Harper & Row, 1973.

San Mateo County Department of Public Health and Welfare. "Surveillance of student drug use, 1973, San Mateo County, California."

Santostefano, S. Beyond nosology: diagnosis from the viewpoint of development. In Rie, H. E. (ed.), *Perspectives in child psychopathology*. Chicago: Aldine, 1971, 130–177.

Sarason, I. G. Verbal learning modeling and juvenile delinquency. *American Psychologist*, 1968, 23, 254–266.

————. Experimental approaches to test anxiety: attention and the uses of information. In Spielberger, C. (ed.), *Anxiety: current trends in theory and research*, Vol. II. Academic Press, 1972.

————, **Ganzer, V. J.** Concerning the medical model. *American Psychologist*, 1968, 23, 507–510.

————. Social influence techniques in clinical and community psychology. In Spielberger, C. D. (ed.), *Current topics in clinical and community psychology*. New York: Academic Press, 1969, pp. 1–66.

Sarason, S. B., Levine, M., Goldenberg, I. I., Cherlin, D. L., and Bennett, E. M. *Psychology in community settings: clinical educational, vocation, social aspects*. New York: Wiley, 1966.

Sarbin, T. R. A contribution to the study of actuarial and individual methods of prediction. *American Journal of Sociology*, 1943, 48, 593–602.

————. Contributions to role-taking theory: I. Hypnotic behavior. *Psychological Review*, 1950, 57, 255–270.

————. Hypnosis as a behavior modification technique. In Krasner, L., and Ullmann, L. P. (eds.), *Research in behavior modification*. New York: Holt, Rinehart and Winston, 1965, pp. 343–357.

Sartre, J.-P. Foreword. In Gorz, A., *The Traitor*. London: Calder, 1960, pp. 14–15.

Sarvis, M. A., Dewees, S., and Johnson, R. F. A concept of ego-oriented psychotherapy. *Psychiatry*, 1958, 22, 277–287.

Satir, V. *Conjoint family therapy*. Palo Alto, Calif.: Science and Behavior Books, 1967.

Saul, L. J., and Bernstein, C. The emotional setting of some attacks of urticaria. *Psychosomatic Medicine*, 1941, 3, 351–369.

Savage, C., Leighton, A. H., and Leighton, D. C. The problem of cross-cultural identification of psychiatric disorders. In Murphy, J. M., and Leighton, A. H. *Approaches to cross-cultural psychiatry*. Ithaca, N.Y.: Cornell University Press, 1965, pp. 21–63.

Sawrey, W. L., Conger, J. J., and Turrell, E. S. An experimental investigation of the role of psychological factors in the production of gastric ulcers in the rat. *Journal of*

Comparative Physiological Psychology. 1956, 49, 457–461.

Sayle, H. *Stress without distress.* Philadelphia: Lippincott, 1974.

Scarr, S. Genetic factors in activity motivation. *Child Development,* 1966, 37, 663–673.

———. Social introversion–extroversion as a heritable response. *Child Development,* 1969, 40, 823–832.

Scarr-Salapatek, S. Review in *American Scientist,* September-October 1975, 63, 588.

Schachter, J. Personal communication, 1973.

———, **Kerr, J., Lachin, J., Khatchaturian, Z., Williams, T., and Faer, M.** Heart rate reactivity of newborn offspring of schizophrenic parents. *Psychophysiology,* 1972, 9, 273.

Schachter, S. The interaction of cognitive and physiological determinants of emotional state. In Berkowitz, L. (ed.), *Advances in experimental social psychology,* Vol. 1. New York: Academic Press, 1964, pp. 49–80.

———. Cognitive effects on bodily functioning: studies of obesity and eating. In Glass, D. C. (ed.), *Neurophysiology and emotion.* New York: Rockefeller University Press and Russell Sage Foundation, 1967.

———. *Obesity and eating.* Science, 1968, 161, 751–756.

———. The assumption of identity and peripheralist–centralist controversies in motivation and emotion. In Arnold, M. (ed.), *Feelings and emotions.* New York: Academic Press, 1970, pp. 111–121.

———. *Emotion, obesity, and crime.* New York: Academic Press, 1971(a).

———. Some extraordinary facts about obese humans and rats. *American Psychologist,* 1971(b), 26, 129–144.

Schafer, R. *Psychoanalytic interpretation in Rorschach testing: theory and application.* New York: Grune & Stratton, 1954.

Scharfman, M. A. Psychoanalytic treatment. In Wolman, B. B., Egan, J., and Ross, A. O. (eds.), *Handbook of treatment of mental disorders in childhood and adolescence.* Englewood Cliffs, N.J.: Prentice-Hall, 1978.

Scheidlinger, S. Innovative group approaches. In Bellak, L., and Barten, H. H. (eds.), *Progress in community mental health,* Vol. 1. New York: Grune & Stratton, 1969, pp. 123–134.

Schlagenhauf, G., Tupin, J., and White, R. B. The use of lithium carbonate in the treatment of manic psychoses. *American Journal of Psychiatry,* 1966, 123, 201–207.

Schlanger, B. B. *Mental retardation.* Indianapolis: Bobbs-Merrill, 1973.

Schlesinger, A., Jr. *Violence: America in the sixties.* New York: Signet, 1968.

———. *The imperial presidency.* New York: Houghton Mifflin, 1973.

———. Can psychiatry save the republic? *Saturday Review/World.* September 7, 1974, 10–16.

Schmidt, H. O., and Fonda, C. The reliability of psychiatric diagnosis. *Journal of Abnormal and Social Psychology,* 1956, 52, 262–267.

Schneck, J. M. Hypnosis in psychiatry. In Schneck, J. M. (ed.), *Hypnosis in modern medicine.* Springfield, Ill.: Thomas, 1963, pp. 169–203.

Schneider, K. *Die psychopathischen Persönlichkeiten.* Leipzig: Deuticke, 1934.

Schofield, M. *The strange case of pot.* Middlesex, England: Penguin Books, 1971.

Schofield, W. *Psychotherapy: the purchase of friendship.* Englewood Cliffs, N.J.: Prentice-Hall, 1964.

———, **and Balian, L.** A comparative study of the personal histories of schizophrenic and nonpsychiatric patients. *Journal of Abnormal and Social Psychology,* 1959, 59, 216–225.

———, **Hathaway, S. R., Hastings, D. W., and Bell, D.** Prognostic factors in schizophrenia. *Journal of Consulting Psychology,* 1954, 18, 155–166.

Schon, N. Lithium in psychiatric therapy and prophylaxis. *Jounal of Psychiatric Research,* 1968, 6, 67–95.

Schou, M. Pharmacology and toxicology of lithium. In Elliott, H. W., George, R., and Okun, R. (eds.), *Annual review of pharmacology and toxicology.* Palo Alto, Calif.: Annual Reviews, 1976, pp. 231–243.

Schrag, P., and Divoky, D. *The myth of the hyperactive child & other means of child control.* New York: Pantheon Books, 1975.

Schrupp, M. H., and Gjerde, C. M. Teachers' attitudes toward behavior problems of children: changes over time. *Journal of Educational Psychology,* 1953, 44, 203–214.

Schuckit, M. A., Goodwin, D. W., and Winokur, G. A study of alcoholism in half siblings. *American Journal of Psychiatry,* 1972, 128, 1132–1136.

Schuham, A. The double-bind hypothesis a decade later. *Psychological Bulletin,* 1967, 68, 409–416.

Schulsinger, F. Psychopathy: heredity and environment. In Roff, M., Robins, L., and Pollack, M. (eds.), *Life history research in psychopathology,* Vol. II. Minneapolis: University of Minnesota Press, 1972, pp. 102–119.

Schwab, G. *Gods and heroes: myths and epics of ancient Greece.* New York: Pantheon Books, 1936.

Schwabb, M. R., Bralow, J. M., Brown, C. E., Holzer, C. E., and Stevenson, B. E. Sociocultural aspects of depression in medical inpatients. *Archives of General Psychiatry,* 1967, 17, 533–543.

Schwartz, A. N. Planning microenvironments for the aged. In Woodruff, D. S., and Birren, J. E. (eds.), *Aging: scientific perspectives and social issues.* New York: Van Nostrand Reinhold, 1975.

Schwartz, G. E. Biofeedback as therapy: some theoretical and practical issues. *American Psychologist,* 1973, 28, 666–673.

———, **Shapiro, D., and Tursky, B.** Learned control of cardiovascular integration in man through operant conditioning. *Psychosomatic Medicine,* 1971, 33, 57–62.

Schwartz, M. *Physiological psychology.* Englewood Cliffs, N.J.: Prentice-Hall, 1973.

Schwartz, M. D., and Errera, P. Psychiatric care in a general hospital emergency room. *Archives of General Psychiatry,* 1963, 9, 113–121.

Schwarz, B. E., Bickford, R. G., and Rasmussen, W. C. Hypnotic phenomena, including hypnotically activated seizures, studied with the electroencephalogram. *Journal of Nervous and Mental Disease,* 1955, 122, 564–574.

Schwitzgebel, R. K. A contractual model for the protection of the rights of institutionalized mental patients. *American Psychologist,* 1975, 30, 815–820.

————, and Kolb, D. A. *Changing human behavior: principles of planned intervention.* New York: McGraw-Hill, 1974.

Schwitzgebel, R. L. A new approach to reducing adolescent crime. *Federal Probation,* March 1960, 20–24.

————. Reduction of adolescent crime by a research method. *Journal of Correctional Psychiatry and Social Therapy,* 1961, 7, 212–215.

————. Delinquents with tape recorders. *New Society,* January 4, 1963, 14–16.

————. *Street-corner research: an experimental approach to the juvenile delinquent.* Cambridge, Mass.: Harvard University Press, 1964.

————. Short-term operant conditioning of adolescent offenders on socially relevant variables. *Journal of Abnormal Psychology,* 1967, 72, 134–142.

————. A belt from big brother. *Psychology Today,* April 1969, 45–65.

————, and Kolb, D. A. Inducing behavior change in adolescent delinquents. *Behavior Research and Therapy,* 1964, 1, 297–304.

————, Schwitzgebel, R. K., Pahnke, W. N., and Hurd, W. S. A program of research in behavioral electronics. *Behavioral Science,* 1964, 9, 233–238.

Scott, W. Research definitions of mental health and mental illness. *Psychological Bulletin,* 1958, 55, 1–45.

Seal, H. Crosscultural sex practices. In Kirkendall, L. A., and Whitehurst, R. N. (eds.), *The new sexual revolution.* New York: Scribner, 1971, pp. 17–31.

Sears, R. R. Experimental studies of projection: 1. attribution of traits. *Journal of Social Psychology,* 1936, 7, 151–163.

————. Transcultural variables and conceptual equivalence. In Al-Issa, I., and Dennis, W. (eds.), *Cross-cultural studies of behavior.* New York: Holt, Rinehart and Winston, 1970, pp. 164–174.

————, Maccoby, E. E., and Levin, H. *Patterns of child rearing.* New York.: Harper & Row, 1957.

————. Relation of early socialization experiences to aggression in middle childhood. *Journal of Abnormal and Social Psychology,* 1961, 63, 466–492.

Sechrest, L. Situational sampling and contrived situations in the assessment of behavior. Unpublished manuscript, Northwestern University, 1965 (cited in Webb et al., 1966).

Segovia–Riquelme, N., Hederra, A., Anex, M., Barnier, O., Figuerola–Camps, I., Campos–Hoppe, I., Jara, N., and Mardones, J. Nutritional and genetic factors in the appetite for alcohol. In Popham, R. E. (ed.), *Alcohol and alcoholism.* Toronto: University of Toronto Press, 1970, pp. 86–96.

Seiden, R. H. Campus tragedy: a study of student suicide. *Journal of Abnormal and Social Psychology,* 1966, 71, 389–399.

————. Studies of adolescent suicides. In Morris, R. J. (ed.), *Perspectives in abnormal behavior.* New York: Pergamon, 1974(a), pp. 117–143.

————. Suicide: preventable death. *Public Affairs Report,* 1974(b), 15, 1–5.

Selfridge, O. G. Pandemonium: a paradigm for learning. *Proceedings of the Symposium on Mechanization of Thought Processes.* London: H.M.S.O., 1959.

Seligman, M. E. P. *Helplessness: on depression, development, and death.* San Francisco: W. H. Freeman, 1975.

————. Comment and integration. *Journal of Abnormal Psychology,* 1978, 87, 165–179.

Selye, H. *The physiology and pathology of exposure to stress: a treatise based on the concepts of the general-adaptation syndrome and the diseases of adaptation.* Montreal: Acta, 1950.

————. *The story of the adaptation syndrome.* Montreal: Acta, 1952.

————. *The stress of life.* New York: McGraw-Hill, 1956.

————. *Stress without distress.* Philadelphia: Lippincott, 1974.

Selzer, M. L., and Vinokur, A. Life events, subjective stress, and traffic accidents. *American Journal of Psychiatry,* 1974, 131, 903–906.

Shaffer, L. F., and Shoben, E. J. *The psychology of adjustment.* Boston: Houghton Mifflin, 1956.

Shagass, C., Amadeo, M., and Overton, D. A. Eye-tracking performance in psychiatric patients. *Biological Psychiatry,* 1974, 9, 245–260.

————, Roemer, R. A., and Amadeo, M. Eye-tracking performance and engagement of attention. *Archives of General Psychiatry,* 1976, 33, 121–125.

Shanas, E., Townsend, P., Wedderburn, D., Friis, H., Millhof, D., and Stehouver, J. (eds.). *Old people in three industrial societies.* New York: Atherton, 1968.

Shapiro, A. K. Placebo effects in medicine, psychotherapy, and psychoanalysis. In Bergin, A. E., and Garfield, S. L. (eds.), *Handbook of psychotherapy and behavior change: an empirical analysis.* New York: Wiley, 1971, pp. 439–473.

Shapiro, D., Tursky, B., Gershon, E., and Stern, M. The effects of feedback and reinforcement on the control of human systolic blood pressure. *Science,* 1969, 163, 588–591.

————, and Giber, D. Meditation and psychotherapeutic effects: self-regulation strategy and altered state of consciousness. *Archives of General Psychiatry,* 1978, 35, 294–302.

———, Tursky, B., and Schwartz, G. E. Control of blood pressure in man by operant conditioning. *Circulation Research*, Supplement 1, 1970, 26, 1–27; 27, 1–32. Reprinted in Barber, T. X., DiCara, L. V., Kamiya, J., Miller, N. E., Shapiro, D., and Stoyva, J. (eds.), *Biofeedback and self-control, 1970*. Chicago: Aldine, 1971, pp. 394–399.

———, and Zifferblatt, S. M. Zen meditation and behavioral self-control: similarities, differences, and clinical applications. *American Psychologist*, 1976, 31, 519–532.

Shean, G. *Schizophrenia: an introduction to research and theory*. Cambridge, Mass.: Winthrop, 1978.

Sheard, M. H. and Flynn, J. P. Facilitation of attack behavior by stimulation of the midbrain of cats. *Brain Research*, 1967, 4, 324–333.

Shectman, F. Conventional and contemporary approaches to psychotherapy: Freud meets Skinner, Janov, and others. *American Psychologist*, 1977, 32, 197–204.

Sheehy, G. *Passages: predictable crises of adult life*. New York: Dutton, 1974.

Sheldon, W. H. *Atlas of men*. New York: Harper & Row, 1954.

Sherfey, M. J. *The nature and evolution of female sexuality*. New York: Random House (Vintage Books), 1972.

Sherman, L. J., Moseley, E. C., Ging, R., and Bookbinder, L. J. Prognosis in schizophrenia. *Archives of General Psychiatry*, 1964, 10, 123–130.

Shields, J. *Monozygotic twins: brought up apart and together*. London: Oxford University Press, 1962.

Shneidman, E. S. Content analysis of suicidal logic. In Shneidman, E. S., Farberow, N. L., and Litman, R. E. (eds.), *The psychology of suicide*. New York: Science House, 1970, pp. 73–93.

———, and Farberow, N. L. *Some facts about suicide*. Washington, D.C.: Government Printing Office, 1961.

———. The logic of suicide. In Shneidman, E. S., Farberow, N. L., and Litman, R. E. (eds.), *The psychology of suicide*. New York: Science House, 1970, pp. 68–71.

———, and Litman, R. E. (eds.). *The psychology of suicide*. New York: Science House, 1970.

———, and Mandelkorn, P. How to prevent suicide. In Shneidman, E. S., Farberow, N. L., and Litman, R. E. (eds.), *The psychology of suicide*. New York: Science House, 1970, pp. 125–143.

Shoben, E. J., Jr. Toward a concept of the normal personality. *American Psychologist*, 1957, 12, 183–189.

Shoppler, E., and Reichler, R. J. Parents as cotherapists in the treatment of psychotic children. *Journal of Autism and Childhood Schizophrenia*, 1971, 1, 87–102.

Siegel, M., Niswander, G. D., Sachse, J., and Starros, D. Taraxein, fact or artifact? *American Journal of Psychiatry*, 1959, 115, 819–820.

Sifneos, P. E. Two different kinds of psychotherapy of brief duration. *American Journal of Psychiatry*, 1967, 123, 1069–1074.

Sigg, E. B. Relationship of aggressive behavior to adrenal and gonadal function in male mice. *Proceedings of the Symposium on the Biology of Aggressive Behavior*, Milan, May 1968.

Silberberg, N. E., and Silberberg, M. C. Hyperlexia—specific word recognition skills in young children. *Exceptional Children*, 1967, 34, 41–42.

———. Case studies in hyperlexia. *Journal of School Psychology*, 1968–1969, 7, 3–7.

———. Hyperlexia: the other end of the continuum. *Journal of Special Education*, 1971, 5, 233–242.

Silverman, D. Clinical studies of criminal psychopaths. *Archives of Neurology and Psychiatry*, 1943, 50, 18.

———. EEG and the treatment of criminal psychopaths. *Journal of Criminal Psychopathology*, 1944(a), 5, 439–466.

———. The electroencephalogram of criminals. *Archives of Neurology and Psychiatry*, 1944(b), 38–42.

Simon, B., O'Leary, J. L., and Ryan, J. J. Cerebral dysrhythmic and psychopathic personalities: a study of 96 consecutive cases in a military hospital. *Archives of Neurology and Psychiatry*, 1946, 56, 677–685.

Simon, H. A., and Lea, G. Problem solving and rule induction: a unified view. In Gregg, L. W. (ed.), *Knowledge and cognition*, New York: Wiley, 1974.

Simon, R. G., and Goldstein, W. The effectiveness of group psychotherapy with chronic schizophrenics and an evaluation of different therapeutic methods. *Journal of Consulting Psychology*, 1957, 21, 317–322.

Simon, W., and Gagnon, J. H. The lesbians: a preliminary overview. In Gagnon, J. H., and Simon, W. (eds.), *Sexual deviance*. New York: Harper & Row, 1967, pp. 247–282.

Sines, J. O., Cleeland, C., and Adkins, J. The behavior of normal and stomach lesion susceptible rats in several learning situations. *Journal of Genetic Psychology*, 1963, 102, 91–94.

Singer, M. The vitality of mythical numbers. *The Public Interest*, 1971, 23, 3–9.

Singer, M. T., and Wynne, L. C. Differentiating characteristics of the parents of childhood neurotics and young adult schizophrenics. *American Journal of Psychiatry*, 1963, 120, 234–243.

Siu, R.G.H. *The tao of science: an essay on western knowledge and eastern wisdom*. Cambridge, Mass.: M.I.T. Press, 1957.

Skeels, H. M. Adult status of children with contrasting early life experiences. *Monographs of the Society for Research in Child Development*, 1966, 31, 1–65.

———, and Dye, H. B. A study of the effects of differential stimulation of mentally retarded children. *Proceedings and Addresses of the American Association of Mental Deficiency*, 1939, 44, 114–136.

Skinner, B. F. *The behavior of organisms: an experimental analysis*. Englewood Cliffs, N.J.: Prentice-Hall, 1938.

———. *Walden two*. New York: Macmillan, 1948.

——. *Science and human behavior.* New York: Macmillan, 1953.

——. *Verbal behavior.* Englewood Cliffs, N.J.: Prentice-Hall, 1957.

——. *Cumulative record.* Englewood Cliffs, N.J.: Prentice-Hall, 1961.

——. *The technology of teaching.* Englewood Cliffs, N.J.: Prentice-Hall, 1968.

——. *Contingencies of reinforcement: a theoretical analysis.* Englewood Cliffs, N.J.: Prentice-Hall, 1969.

——. *Beyond freedom and dignity.* New York: Knopf, 1971.

Slater, E. and Cowie, V. *The genetics of mental disorders.* London: Oxford University Press, 1971.

Slavson, S. R. *Freud's contribution to group psychotherapy.* In Ruitenbeek, H. M. (ed.), *Group therapy today: styles, methods and techniques.* New York: Atherton, 1969, pp. 28–36.

Slosson, E. E. A lecture experiment in hallucinations. *Psychological Review,* 1899, 6, 407–408.

Smart, R. G., and Fejer, D. Drug use among adolescents and their parents: Closing the generation gap in mood modification. *Journal of Abnormal Psychology,* 1972, 79, 153–160.

Smith, E. K. Effect of the double-bind communication on the anxiety level of normals. *Journal of Abnormal Psychology,* 1976, 85, 356–363.

Smith, J. C. Meditation as psychotherapy: a review of the literature. *Psychological Bulletin,* 1975, 82, 558–564.

——. Psychotherapeutic effects of transcendental meditation with controls for expectation of relief and daily sitting. *Journal of Consulting and Clinical Psychology,* 1976, 44, 630–637.

Smith, M. L., and Glass, G. V. Meta-analysis of psychotherapy outcome studies. *American Psychologist,* 1977, 32, 752–760.

Smith, R. E., and Sharpe, T. M. Treatment of a school phobia with implosive therapy. *Journal of Consulting and Clinical Psychology,* 1970, 35, 239–243.

——, **Sarason, I. G., and Sarason, B. R.** *Psychology: the frontiers of behavior.* New York: Harper & Row, 1978.

Smith, R. T. A comparison of socioenvironmental factors in monozygotic and dizygotic twins, testing an assumption. In Vandenberg, S. G. (ed.), *Methods and goals in human behavior.* New York: Academic Press, 1965.

Smolen, R. C. Expectancies, mood, and performance of nondepressed psychiatric inpatients on chance and skill tasks. *Journal of Abnormal Psychology,* 1978, 87, 91–101.

Snodgrass, V. Medical news. *Journal of the American Medical Association,* 1973, 225, 913–920, 1035–1045.

Snyder, S. H. *Uses of marijuana.* New York: Oxford University Press, 1971.

——. *Madness and the brain.* New York: McGraw-Hill, 1975.

Sobell, L. C., and Sobell, M. B. A self-feedback technique to monitor drinking behavior in alcoholics. *Behavior Research and Therapy,* 1973(b), 11, 237–238.

Sobell, M. B., and Sobell, L. C. Alcoholics treated by individualized behavior therapy: one-year treatment outcome. *Behavior Research and Therapy,* 1973(a), 11, 599–618.

Solari, G. Psychotherapeutic methods in alcoholism. In Popham, R. E. (ed.), *Alcohol and alcoholism.* Toronto: University of Toronto, 1970, pp. 165–169.

Solomon, P. *Psychiatric drugs.* New York: Grune & Stratton, 1966.

Solomon, R. L. Letter quoted by O. H. Mowrer, *Learning theory and the symbolic processes.* New York: Wiley, 1960, pp. 399–404.

——. Punishment. *Psychologist,* 1964, 19, 239–253.

——, **Turner, L. H., and Lessac, M. S.** Some effects of delay of punishment on resistance to temptation in dogs. *Journal of Personality and Social Psychology,* 1968, 8, 233–338.

Spanos, N. P., and Barber, T. X. "Hypnotic" experiences as inferred from subjective reports: auditory and visual hallucinations. *Journal of Experimental Research in Personality,* 1968, 3, 136–150.

——, **and Chaves, J. F.** Hypnosis research: a methodological critique of experiments generated by two alternatives. In Barber, T. X., DiCara, L. V., Kamiya, J., MIller, N. E., Shapiro, D., and Stoyva, J. (eds.), *Biofeedback and self-control, 1970.* Chicago: Aldine, 1971, pp. 168–187.

Spence, D. P. Personal communication, 1973.

——, **and Lugo, M.** The role of verbal clues in clinical listing. In Holt, R. R., and Peterfreund, E. (eds.), *Psychoanalysis and contemporary science.* New York: Macmillan, 1972, pp. 109–131.

Spence, K. W. *Behavior theory and conditioning.* New Haven: Yale University Press, 1956.

Spiegel, H. Hypnosis: an adjunct to psychotherapy. In Freedman, A. M., and Kaplin, H. I. (eds.), *Treating mental illness: aspects of modern therapy.* New York: Atheneum, 1972, pp. 169–179.

Spielberger, C. D. The effects of anxiety on complex learning and academic achievement. In Spielberger, C. D. (ed.), *Anxiety and behavior.* New York: Academic Press, 1966(a), pp. 361–398.

——. Theory and research on anxiety. In Spielberger, C. D. (ed.), *Anxiety and behavior.* New York: Academic Press, 1966(b), pp. 3–20.

Spitz, R. A. Hospitalism: an inquiry into the genesis of psychiatric conditions in early childhood. *Psychoanalytic Study of the Child,* 1945, 1, 53–74.

——. Anaclitic depression. *Psychoanalytic Study of the Child,* 1946, 2, 313–340.

——. Unhappy and fatal outcomes of emotional deprivation and stress in infancy. In Raldston, I. (ed.), *Beyond the germ theory.* New York: Health Education Council, 1954.

——, **and Wolf, K. M.** The origin of the smiling response.

Genetic Psychological Monographs, 1946, 34, 71–75.

Spitzer, R. L. More on pseudoscience and the case for psychiatric diagnosis. *Archives of General Psychiatry,* 1976, 33, 459–470.

———, **Endicott, J., Mesnikoff, A., and Cohen, G.** *Psychiatric evaluation form: diagnostic version.* Biometric Research, New York State Psychiatric Institute, 1967–1968.

Spivack, P., Haimes, P. E., and Spotts, J. Adolescent symptomatology and its measurement. *American Journal of Mental Deficiency,* 1967, 72, 74–95.

Srole, L. Urbanization and mental health: some reformulations. *American Scientist,* 1972, 60, 576–583.

———, **Langner, T. S., Michael, S. T., Opler, M. K., and Rennie, T. A. C.** *Mental health in the metropolis: the Midtown Manhattan study.* New York: McGraw-Hill, 1962.

Sroufe, L. A., and Stewart, M. A. Treating problem children with stimulant drugs. *New England Journal of Medicine,* 1973, 289, 407–414.

Stainbrook, E. The hospital as a therapeutic community. In Freedman, A. M., and Kaplan, H. I. (eds.), *Treating mental illness: aspects of modern therapy.* New York: Atheneum, 1972, pp. 385–394.

Stampfl, T. G., and Levis, D. J. Essentials of implosive therapy: a learning-theory-based psychodynamics behavior therapy. *Journal of Abnormal Psychology,* 1967, 72, 496–503.

———. Implosive therapy—a behavioral therapy? *Behavior Research and Therapy,* 1968, 6, 31–36.

Staudt, V., and Zubin, J. A biometric evaluation of the somatotherapies in schizophrenia. *Psychological Bulletin,* 1957, 56, 171–196.

Steele, B. F., and Pollock, C. B. A psychiatric study of parents who abuse infants and small children. In Helfer, R. E., and Kempe, C. H. (eds.), *The battered child.* Chicago: University of Chicago Press, 1968, pp. 103–147.

Stein, L., and Wise, C. D. Possible etiology of schizophrenia: progressive damage to the noradrenergic reward system by 6-hydroxydopamine. *Science,* 1971, 171, 1032–1036.

Stein, M. I. (ed.). *Contemporary psychotherapies.* New York: Free Press, 1961.

Steiner, C. *Games alcoholics play: the analysis of life scripts.* New York: Grove Press, 1971.

Stekel, W. *Sadism and masochism.* New York: Liveright, 1929.

———. *Sexual aberrations: the phenomenon of festishism in relation to sex.* New York: Liveright, 1930.

Stengel, E. *Suicide and attempted suicide.* Middlesex, England: Penguin, 1964.

Stephens, J., and Astrup, C. Prognosis in "process" and in "non-process" schizophrenia. *American Journal of Psychiatry,* 1963, 119, 945.

———. Treatment outcome in "process" and "non-process" schizophrenics by "A" and "B" types of therapist. *Journal of Nervous and Mental Disease,* 1965, 140, 449–456.

———, **and Mangrum, J. C.** Prognostic factors in recovered and deteriorated schizophrenics. *American Journal of Psychiatry,* 1966, 122, 1116–1121.

Sterman, M. B., Macdonald, L. R., and Stone, R. K. Biofeedback training of the sensorimotor electroencephalogram rhythm in man: effects on epilepsy. In DiCara, L. V., Barber, T. X., Kamiya, J., Miller, N. E., Shapiro, D., and Stovya, J. (eds.), *Biofeedback and self-control, 1974.* Chicago: Aldine, 1975, pp. 313–330.

Stevenson, I., and Wolpe, P. Recovery from sexual deviations through overcoming nonsexual neurotic responses. *American Journal of Psychiatry,* 1960, 116, 737–742.

Stolz, S. B., Wienckowski, L. A., and Brown, B. S. Behavior modification: a perspective on critical issues. *American Psychologist,* 1975, 30, 1027–1048.

Stone, A. A. and Stone, S. S. (eds.). *The abnormal personality through literature.* Englewood Cliffs, N.J.: Prentice-Hall, 1966, pp. 69–70. Abstracted from Gogol, N. *The diary of a madman and other stories.* Translated by A. MacAndrew. New York: New American Library, 1961.

Stone, F. B. Assessment of children's activity level. Paper presented at the 51st annual meeting of the American Orthopsychiatric Association, San Francisco, April 1974.

Stone, P. S., Dunphy, D. C., Smith, M. S., and Ogilvie, D. M. *The General Inquirer: a computer approach to content analysis.* Cambridge, Mass.: M.I.T. Press, 1966.

Storr, A. *Sexual deviation.* Middlesex, England: Penguin Books, 1964.

———. *Human aggression.* New York: Atheneum, 1968.

Straker, M. Brief psychotherapy in an outpatient clinic: evolution and evaluation. *American Journal of Psychiatry,* 1968, 124, 1219–1225.

Strange, R. E. Effects of combat stress on hospital ship psychiatric evacuees. In Bourne, P. G. (ed.), *The psychology and physiology of stress.* New York: Academic Press, 1969, pp. 75–93.

Strassberg, D. S. Relationships among locus of control, anxiety, and valued goal expectations. *Journal of Consulting and Clinical Psychology,* 1973, 41, 319.

Straub, L. R., Ripley, H. S., and Wolf, S. Disturbances of bladder function associated with emotional states. In *Life stress and bodily disease: proceedings of the Association for Research in Nervous and Mental Diseases,* Vol. 29. Baltimore: Williams & Wilkins, 1950, pp. 1019–1029.

Straus R., and Bacon, S. D. *Drinking in college.* New Haven, Conn.: Yale University Press, 1953.

Streib, G. F. Family patterns in retirement. *Journal of Social Problems,* 1958, 14, 46–60.

Strupp, H. H. *Psychotherapy and the modification of abnormal behavior.* New York: McGraw-Hill, 1971.

———, **and Bergin, A. E.** Some empirical and conceptual bases for coordinated research in psychotherapy: a critical review of issues, trends, and evidence. *International*

Journal of Psychiatry. 1969, 7, 18–90.

———, **and Hadley, S. W.** A tripartite model of mental health and therapeutic outcomes: with special reference to negative effects in psychotherapy. *American Psychologist,* 1977, 32, 187–196.

Stuart, H. C. Obesity in childhood. *Quarterly Review of Pediatrics,* 1955, 10, 131–135.

Sue, S. Community mental health services to minority groups. *American Psychologist,* 1977, 32, 616–624.

Suedfeld, P. The benefits of boredom: sensory deprivation reconsidered. *American Scientist,* January-February, 1975.

Sullivan, H. S. *Conceptions of modern psychiatry.* Washington, D.C.: W. A. White Psychiatric Association, 1946.

———. *The interpersonal theory of psychiatry.* New York: Norton, 1953.

———. *Clinical studies in psychiatry.* New York: Norton, 1956.

Sulzer, E. S. Behavior modification in adult psychiatric patients. In Ullmann, L. P., and Krasner, L. (eds.), *Case studies in behavior modification.* New York: Holt, Rinehart and Winston, 1965.

Sumner, W. G. *Folkways: a study of the sociological importance of usages, manners, customs, mores, and morals.* New York: Dover, 1906.

Sun, D. C. H., Shay, H., Olin, B., and Weiss, E. Conditioned secretory response of the stomach following repeated emotional stress in a case of duodenal ulcer. *Gastroenterology,* 1958, 35, 155–165.

Sundberg, N. D. *Assessment of persons.* Englewood Cliffs, N.J.: Prentice-Hall, 1977.

———, **and Tyler, L. E.** *Clinical psychology: an introduction to research and practice.* Englewood Cliffs, N.J.: Prentice-Hall, 1962.

———, **Tyler, L. E., and Taplin, J. R.** *Clinical psychology: expanding horizons.* 2nd ed. New York: Meredith Corp., 1973.

Sussman, M. B. Relationships of adult children with their parents in the United States. In Shanas, E., and Streib, G. F. (eds.), *Social structure and the family.* Englewood Cliffs, N.J.: Prentice-Hall, 1965.

Sutherland, E. H. *The professional thief.* Chicago: University of Chicago Press, 1937.

Swanson, D. W., Bohnert, P. J., and Smith, J. A. *The paranoid.* Boston: Little, Brown, 1970.

Swartz, J. D. and Holtzman, W. H. Group method of administration for the Holtzman Inkblot Technique. *Journal of Clinical Psychology,* 1963, 19, 433–441.

Symonds, A., and Herman, N. The patterns of schizophrenia in adolescents. *Psychiatric Quarterly,* 1957, 31, 521–530.

Szasz, T. The myth of mental illness. *American Psychologist,* 1960, 15, 113–118.

———. The psychiatric classification of behavior: a strategy of personal constraint. In Eron, L. D. (ed.), *The classification of behavior disorders.* Chicago: Aldine, 1966, pp. 123–170.

———. Science and public policy: the crime of involuntary mental hospitalization. *Medical Opinion, 2nd Review,* May 1968, pp. 25–35.

———. *The manufacture of madness: a comparative study of the Inquisition and the mental health movement.* New York: Harper & Row, 1970.

———. *The second sin.* New York: Doubleday (Anchor Books), 1973.

Tapia, F., Jekel, J., and Domke, H. R. Enuresis: an emotional symptom? *Journal of Nervous and Mental Disease,* 1960, 130, 61–66.

Targ, R., and Puthoff, H. E. Information transfer under conditions of sensory shielding. *Nature,* 1974, 252, 602–607.

Tarjan, G., and Eisenberg, I. Some thoughts on the classification of mental retardation in the United States of America. *American Journal of Psychiatry,* Supplement, 1972, 128, 14–18.

Taube, C. A. *Length of stay of discharges from general hospital psychiatric hospital inpatient units, United States, 1970–1971.* Statistical note 70. (Publication No. HSM 73–9005.) Washington, D.C.: NIMH, 1973.

———. *Readmissions to inpatient services of state and county mental hospitals 1972.* Statistical note 110. (Publication No. ADM 75–158.) Washington, D.C.: NIMH, 1974.

———. *Staffing of mental health facilities, United States, 1974.* (Publication No. ADM 76–308.) Washington, D.C.: NIMH, 1976.

Taulbee, E. S., and Wright, H. W. A psychosocial behavioral model for therapeutic intervention. In Spielberger, C. D. (ed.), *Current topics in clinical and community psychology.* New York: Academic Press, 1971, pp. 53–94.

Taylor, H. C., Jr. Life situations, emotions and gynecologic pain associated with congestion. In *Life stress and bodily diseases: proceedings of the Association for Research in Nervous and Mental Diseases,* Vol. 29. Baltimore: Williams & Wilkins, 1950, pp. 1051–1056.

Taylor, J. A. A personality scale of manifest anxiety. *Journal of Abnormal and Social Psychology,* 1953, 48, 285–290.

Teahan, J. E. Effect of group psychotherapy on academic low achievers. *International Journal of Group Psychotherapy,* 1966, 16, 78–85.

Teasdale, J. D. Effects of real and recalled success on learned helplessness and depression. *Journal of Abnormal Psychology,* 1978, 87, 155–164.

Teitelbaum, P. Sensory control of hypothalamic hyperphagia. *Journal of Comparative and Physiological Psychology,* 1955, 48, 156–163.

Telfer, M. A., Baker, D., Clark, G. R., and Richardson, C. E. Incidence of gross chromosomal errors among tall, criminal American males, *Science,* 1968, 159, 1249–1250.

Terman, L. M. *The measurement of intelligence.* Boston: Houghton Mifflin, 1916.

——, **and Merrill, M. A.** *Measuring intelligence.* Boston: Houghton Mifflin, 1960.

Terry, J., Lolli, G., and Golder, G. Choice of alcoholic beverage among 531 alcoholics in California. *Quarterly Journal of Studies on Alcohol,* 1957, 18, 417–428.

Tharp, R. G., and Wetzel, R. J. *Behavior modification in the natural environment.* New York: Academic Press, 1969.

Thigpen, C. H. and Cleckley, H. M. A case of multiple personality. *Journal of Abnormal and Social Psychology,* 1954, 49, 135–151.

——. *The three faces of Eve.* New York: McGraw-Hill, 1957.

Thomas, A., Chess, S., and Birch, H. G. *Temperament and behavior disorders in children.* New York: New York University Press, 1968.

Thomas, C. W. Psychologists, psychology, and the black community. In Spielberger, C. D. (ed.), *Current topics in clinical and community psychology.* New York: Academic Press, 1971, pp. 163–177.

Thompson, C. E. The Thompson modification of the Thematic Apperception Test. *Rorschach Research Exchange,* 1949, 13, 469–478.

Thompson, N. L., Jr., McCandless, B. R., and Strickland, B. R. Personal adjustment of male and female homosexuals and heterosexuals. *Journal of Abnormal Psychology,* 1971, 78, 237–240.

Thompson, R. F. Neuron, synapse, and brain activity. In *Readings from Scientific American.* San Francisco: W. H. Freeman, 1976, pp. 78–79.

——. *Physiological psychology.* New York: Harper & Row, 1967.

Thompson, T. History of treatment and misconceptions concerning the mentally retarded. In Thompson, T., and Grabowski, J. (eds.), *Behavior modification of the mentally retarded.* New York: Oxford University Press, 1972, pp. 3–16.

——. Colloquium delivered to the Psychology Department, University of Illinois at Chicago Circle, January 1977.

——, **and Grabowski, J.** *Behavior modification of the mentally retarded.* New York: Oxford University Press, 1972.

Thomsen, R. *Bill W.* New York: Harper & Row, 1975.

Thoreson, C. E., and Mahoney, M. J. *Behavioral self-control.* New York: Holt, Rinehart and Winston, 1974.

Thorndike, E. L. *The fundamentals of learning.* New York: Teachers College Press, 1932.

Thorndike, R. L. *Standford-Binet Intelligence Scale, form L-M, 1972 norms tables.* Boston: Houghton Mifflin, 1973.

Thorne, F. C. *Principles of personality counseling.* Brandon, Vt.: Journal of Clinical Psychology Press, 1950.

Thorpe, J. G., Schmidt, E., Brown, P. T., and Castell, D. Aversion-relief therapy: a new method for general application. *Behavior Research and Therapy,* 1964, 2, 71–82.

Tinbergen, N. *The study instinct.* London: Oxford University Press, 1951.

——. On war and peace in animal and man. *Science,* 1968, 160, 1411–1418.

Tobias, L. L., and MacDonald, M. L. Withdrawal of maintenance drugs with long-term hospitalized mental patients: a critical review. *Psychological Bulletin,* 1974, 81, 107–125.

Tobin, K., and Wicker, R. *The gay crusaders.* New York: Paperback Library, 1972.

Tolor, A., and Schulberg, H. C. *An evaluation of the Bender-Gestalt Test.* Springfield, Ill.: Thomas, 1963.

Tolstrup, K. On psychogenic obesity in children. IV. *Acta Paediatrica,* 1953, 42, 289–304.

Tomkins, S. S. *The positive affects: affect, imagery, consciousness,* Vol. 1. New York: Springer-Verlag, 1962.

——. Simulation of personality: the interrelationships between affect, memory, thinking, perception, and action. In Tomkins, S. S., and Messick, S. J. (eds.), *Computer simulation of personality.* New York: Wiley, 1963.

——, **and McCarter, R.** What and where are the primary affects? Some evidence for a theory. *Perceptual and Motor Skills,* 1964, 18, pp. 119–158.

Tooth, G. *Studies in mental illness in the Gold Coast.* Colonial Research Publication No. 6. London: H.M.S.O., 1950.

Trice, H. M. Absenteeism among high-status and low-status problem drinkers. *ILR Research,* 1958, 55, 10–13.

——. *A company program on alcoholism: a basic outline.* New York: C. D. Smithers Foundation, 1966.

——. The alcoholic employee and his supervisor: a general management problem. In Popham, R. E. (ed.), *Alcohol and alcoholism.* Toronto: University of Toronto Press, 1970, pp. 338–345.

Troll, L. E. The family of later life: a decade review. *Journal of Marriage and the Family,* 1971, 33, 263–290.

Trotter, S. Federal commission on psychosurgery. *APA Psychology Monitor,* 1976, 7, 4–5.

Truax, C. B., and Carkhuff, R. C. *Toward effective counseling and psychotherapy.* Chicago: Aldine, 1967.

——, **Schuldt, W. J., and Wargo, D. G.** Self-ideal concept congruence and improvement in group psychotherapy. *Journal of Consulting and Clinical Psychology,* 1968, 32, 47–53.

——, **Wargo, D. G., and Silber, L. D.** Effects of group psychotherapy with high accurate empathy and non-possessive warmth upon female institutionalized delinquents. *Journal of Abnormal Psychology,* 1966, 71, 267–274.

Tryon, R. C. Individual differences. In Moss, F. A. *Comparative psychology.* Rev. ed. Englewood Cliffs, N.J.: Prentice-Hall, 1942.

Tuckman, J., and Connon, H. E. Attempted suicide in adolescents. *American Journal of Psychiatry,* 1962, 119, 228–232.

Turing, A. M. Computing machinery and intelligence. *Mind,* 1950, 59, 433–460.

Turnbull, J. W. Asthma conceived as a learned response. *Journal of Psychosomatic Research,* 1962, 6, 59–70.

Tversky, A., and Kahneman, D. Judgment under uncertainty: heuristics and biases. *Science,* 1974, 185, 1124–1131.

Tyler, V. O., and Brown, G. D. The use of swift brief isolation as a group control device for institutionalized delinquents. *Behavior and Research in Therapy,* 1967, 5, 1–9.

———, and Straughan, J. H. Covert control and breathholding as techniques for the treatment of obesity. *Psychological Record,* 1970, 20, 473–478.

Ullman, A. Ethnic differences in the first drinking experience. *Social Problems,* 1960, 8, p. 48 *passim.*

Ullmann, L. P. *Institution and outcome: a comparative study of psychiatric hospitals* New York: Pergamon, 1967.

———, and Krasner, L. Introduction. In Ullmann, L. P., and Krasner, L. (eds.), *Case studies in behavior modification.* New York: Holt, Rinehart and Winston, 1965, pp. 1–63.

———. *A psychological approach to abnormal behavior.* 2nd. ed. Englewood Cliffs, N.J.: Prentice-Hall, 1975.

Urban, H., and Ford, D. H. Behavior therapy. In Freedman, A. M., and Kaplan, H. I. (eds.), *Treating mental illness: aspects of modern therapy.* New York: Atheneum, 1972, pp. 146–161.

Vaihinger, H. *The philosophy of "as if."* New York: Harcourt Brace Jovanovich, 1925.

Vaillant, G. E. Prospective prediction of schizophrenic remission. *Archives of General Psychiatry,* 1964, 11, 509–518.

———. The prediction of recovery in schizophrenia. *International Journal of Psychiatry,* 1966, 1, 617.

Valenstein, E. S. *Brain control.* New York: Wiley, 1973.

Valentine, C. W. *The normal child and some of his abnormalities.* Middlesex, England: Penguin Books, 1956.

Vandenberg, S. G., Clark, P. J., and Samuels, I. Psychophysiological reactions of twins: heritability factors in galvanic skin resistance, heartbeat, and breathing rates. *Eugenics Quarterly,* 1965, 12, 7–10.

van der Post, L. *The lost world of the Kalihari.* New York: Harcourt Brace Jovanovich, 1977.

Verville, E. *Behavior problems of children.* Philadelphia: Saunders, 1967.

Veterans Administration. *Drug treatment and society.* Washington, D.C.: Government Printing Office, 1970.

Vinokur, A., and Selzer, M. L. Desirable versus undesirable life events: their relationship to stress and mental distress. *Journal of Personality and Social Psychology,* 1975, 32, 337–392.

Voegtlin, W. L. The treatment of alcoholism by establishing a conditioned reflex. *American Journal of Medical Science,* 1940, 199, 802–809.

———, and Broz, W. R. The conditioned reflex treatment of chronic alcoholism. X. An analysis of 3,125 admissions over a period of ten and one-half years. *Annals of Internal Medicine,* 1949, 30, 580–597.

Volgyesi, F. A. "School for patients," hypnosis-therapy and psychoprophylaxis. *British Journal of Medical Hypnotism,* 1954, 5, 8–17.

Volkmar, F. R., and Greenough, W. T. Rearing complexity affects branching of dendrites in the visual cortex of the rat. *Science,* 1972, 196, 1445–1446.

Volta, A. On the electricity excited by the mere contact of conducting substances of different kinds. *Philosophical Transactions,* 1800, 90, 403–431.

Walberg, H. J., and Thomas, S. C. Open education. *American Educational Research Journal,* 1972, 9, 197–208.

Wallace, A. F. C. Cultural change and mental illness. In Plog, S. C., and Edgerton, R. B. (eds.), *Changing perspectives in mental illness.* New York: Holt, Rinehart and Winston, 1969, pp. 75–86.

Wallace, D. H., and Barbach, L. G. Preorgasmic group treatment. *Journal of Sex and Marital Therapy,* 1974, 1, 146–154.

Wallen, R. Gestalt therapy and Gestalt psychology. In Fagan, J. and Shepherd, I. L. (eds.), *Gestalt therapy now: theory, techniques, applications.* New York: Harper & Row, 1970, pp. 8–13.

Walsh, D. H. Interactive effects of alpha. In DiCara, L. V., Barber, T. X., Kamiya, J., Miller, N. E., Shapiro, D., and Stovya, J. (eds.), *Biofeedback and self-control, 1974.* Chicago: Aldine, 1975, pp. 351–359.

Wanner, E. Power and inhibition: a revision of the magical potency theory. In McClelland, D. C., Davis, W. N., Kalin, R., and Wanner, E. *The drinking man: alcohol and human motivation.* New York: Free Press, 1972, pp. 73–98.

Ward, C. H., Beck, A. T., Mendelson, M. M., Mock, J. E., and Erbaugh, J. K. The psychiatric nomenclature. *Archives of General Psychiatry,* 1962, 7, 198–205.

Ward, D. A., and Kassebaum, G. G. Lesbian liaisons. In Gagnon, J. H., and Simon, W. (eds.), *The sexual scene.* Chicago: Aldine, 1970, pp. 125–136.

Warnock, J. Insanity from hasheesh. *Journal of Mental Sciences,* 1903, 49, 96–110.

Warren, S. A. Psychological evaluation of the mentally retarded: a review of techniques. *Pediatric Clinics of North America,* 1968, 15, 953–954.

Waskow, I. E., Olsson, J. E., Salzman, C., and Katz, M. M. Psychological effects of tetrahydrocannabinol. *Archives of General Psychiatry,* 1970, 22, 97–107.

Watson, J. B. Psychology as a behaviorist views it. *Psychological Reviews,* 1913, 20, 158–177.

———. *Psychology from the standpoint of a behaviorist.* Philadelphia: Lippincott, 1924.

———. *Behaviorism.* New York: Norton, 1925.

———, and **Rayner, R.** Conditioned emotional reactions. *Journal of Experimental Psychology*, 1920, 3, 1–14.

Watson, J. D. *The double helix: a personal account of the discovery of the structure of DNA.* New York: Atheneum, 1968.

———, and **Crick, F. H. C.** Molecular structure of nucleic acids: a structure for deoxyribose nucleic acid. *Nature*, 1953, 171 (4356), 737–738.

Watson, R. I. *Psychology of the child.* 2nd ed. New York: Wiley, 1965.

Weakland, J. H. Hippies: what the scene means. In Blum, R. H., and Associates (eds.), *Society and drugs.* San Francisco: Jossey–Bass, 1969, pp. 342–372.

Webb, E. J., Campbell, D. T., Schwartz, R. D., and Sechrest, L. *Unobtrusive measures: nonreactive research in the social sciences.* Chicago: Rand McNally, 1966.

Webster's New Collegiate Dictionary. Springfield, Mass.: Merriam, 1974.

Wechsler, D. *Wechsler Intelligence Scale for Children.* New York: Psychological Corporation, 1949.

———. *WAIS Manual: Wechsler Adult Intelligence Scale.* New York: Psychological Corporation, 1955.

———, *Wechsler Preschool and Primary Scale of Intelligence (WPPSI).* New York: Psychological Corporation, 1967.

———. *Manual for the Wechsler Intelligence Scale for Children.* Rev. ed. New York: Psychological Corporation, 1974.

Wechsler, H., Kasey, E. H., Thum, D., and Demone, H. W. Alcohol level and home accidents. *Public Health Reports*, 1969, 84, 1043–1050.

Wechsler, I. *Clinical neurology.* Philadelphia: Saunders, 1963.

Weinberg, K. S. *Incest behavior.* New York: Citadel, 1955.

Weinberg, M., and Williams, C. J. *Male homosexuals: their problems and adaptations in three societies.* New York: Oxford University Press, 1974.

Weiner, B. *Theories of motivation.* Chicago: Markham, 1972.

———, and **Litman-Adizes, T.** An attributional expectancy-value analysis of learned helplessness and depression. In Garber, J., and Seligman, M. E. P. (eds.), *Human helplessness: theory and implications.* New York: Academic Press, 1978.

———, **Runquist, W., Runquist, P. A., Raven, B. H., Meyer, W. J., Leiman, A., Kutscher, C. L., Kleinmuntz, B., and Haber, R. N.** *Discovering psychology.* Palo Alto, Calif.: Science Research Associates, 1977.

Weiner, H. Diagnosis and symptomatology. In Bellak, L. (ed.), *Schizophrenia: a review of the syndrome.* New York: Logos, 1958, pp. 107–173.

Weiner, I. B. Father–daughter incest: a clinical report. *Psychiatric Quarterly*, 1962, 26, 607.

———. *Psychodiagnosis in schizophrenia.* New York: Wiley, 1966.

———. *Diagnosing schizophrenia.* New York: McGraw-Hill, 1968.

———. *Psychological disturbance in adolescence.* New York: Wiley, 1970.

Weiner, L., Becker, A., and Friedman, T. T. *Home treatment: spearhead of community psychiatry.* Pittsburgh: University of Pittsburgh Press, 1967.

Weiss, J. M. Effects of coping response on stress. *Journal of Comparative and Physiological Psychology*, 1968, 65, 251–260.

———. Somatic effects of predictable and unpredictable shock. *Psychosomatic Medicine*, 1970, 32, 397–409.

———. Effects of coping behavior in different warning signal conditions on stress pathology in rats. *Journal of Comparative and Physiological Psychology*, 1971(a), 77, 1–13.

———. Effects of punishing the coping response (conflict) on stress pathology in rats. *Journal of Comparative and Physiological Psychology*, 1971(b), 77, 14–21.

———. Effects of coping behavior with and without a feedback signal on stress pathology in rats. *Journal of Comparative and Physiological Psychology*, 1971(c), 77, 22–30.

———, **Glazen, H. I., and Pohoreckej, L. A.** Coping behavior and neurochemical changes: an alternative explanation for the original "learned helplessness" experiments. In Serban, G., and Kling, A. (eds.), *Relevance of psychopathological animal model to the human.* New York: Plenum Press, 1977.

Weissbrod, C., and Bryan, J. Film treatment as an effective fear reduction technique. *Journal of Abnormal Child Psychology*, 1973, 1, 196–201.

Weisz, J. D. The etiology of experimental gastric ulceration. *Psychosomatic Medicine*, 1957, 19, 61–73.

Weitzenhoffer, A. M. *Hypnotism: an objective study in suggestibility.* New York: Wiley, 1953.

———. *General techniques of hypnotism.* New York: Grune & Stratton, 1957.

Weizenbaum, J. ELIZA: a computer program for the study of natural language communication between man and machine. *Communications of the ACM*, 1966, 9, 36–45.

Wells, F. L., and Reusch, J. *Mental examiner's handbook.* 2nd ed. New York: Psychological Corporation, 1945.

Wender, P. H. *Minimal brain dysfunction in children.* New York: Wiley, 1971.

———, **Rosenthal, D., Kety, S. S., Schulsinger, F., and Welner, J.** Crossfostering: a research strategy for clarifying the role of genetic and experential factors in the etiology of schizophrenia. *Archives of General Psychiatry*, 1974, 30, 121–128.

Wendland, M. M. Self-concept in Southern Negro and white adolescents as related to rural-urban residence. Unpublished Ph.D. dissertation. University of North Carolina at Chapel Hill, 1967.

Werry, J. S. Organic factors in childhood psychopathology. In Quay, H. C., and Werry, J. S. (eds.), *Psychopathological disorders of childhood.* New York: Wiley, 1972, pp. 83–121.

Wertham, F. A group of benign chronic psychoses: prolonged manic excitements. *American Journal of Psychiatry*, 1929, 9, 17–78.

Westermarck, E. *Three essays on sex and marriage*. New York: Macmillan, 1934.

Wetzel, R. Use of behavioral techniques in a case of compulsive stealing. *Journal of Consulting Psychology*, 1966, 30, 367–374.

Wexler, D., Mendelson, J., Leiderman, P. H., and Solomon, P. Sensory deprivation: a technique for studying psychiatric aspects of stress. *Archives of Neurology and Psychiatry*, 1958, 79, 225–233.

Wheat, W. D. Motivational aspects of suicide during and after psychiatric treatment. *Southern Medical Journal*, 1960, 53, 273.

Wheelis, A. How people change. *Commentary*, May 1969.

White, L. *The science of culture: a study of man and civilization*. New York: Farrar, Straus & Giroux, 1949.

White, R. W., and Watt, N. F. *The abnormal personality*. 4th ed. New York: Ronald Press, 1973.

Whitkin, H. A., Mednick, S. A., Schulsinger, F., Bakkestrm, E., Christiansea, K. O., Goodenough, D. R., Hirschhorn, K., Lundstera, C., Oven, D. R., Philip, J., Rubin, D. B., and Stocking, M. Criminality in XYY and XXY men. *Science*, 1976, 193, 547–555.

Whitmont, E. C. Carl Jung. In Freedman, A. M., and Kaplan, H. I. (eds.), *Interpreting personality: a survey of twentieth-century views*. New York: Atheneum, 1972, pp. 131–143.

———, and Kaufmann, Y. Analytical psychotherapy. In Corsini, R. (ed.), *Current psychotherapies*. Itasca, Ill.: Peacock, 1973, pp. 85–117.

Whitwell, J. R. *Historical notes on psychiatry*. London: Lewis, 1936.

Whorf, B. L. *Language, thought, and reality: selected writings of Benjamin Lee Whorf* (John B. Carroll, ed.). Cambridge, Mass.: M.I.T. Press, 1956.

Wiener, D. N. Subtle and obvious keys for the MMPI. *Journal of Consulting Psychology*, 1948, 12, 164–170.

Wiessman, M. M., and Paykel, E. S. *The depressed woman: a study of social relationships*. Chicago: University of Chicago Press, 1974. Condensation appeared in *Practical Psychology for Physicians*, 1975, 2, 46–55.

Wiggins, J. Inconsistent socialization. *Psychological Reports*, 1968, 23, 303–336.

———, Renner, K. E., Clove, G. L., and Rose, R. J. *The psychology of personality*. Reading, Mass.: Addison-Wesley, 1971.

———, Wiggins, N., and Conger, J. C. Correlates of heterosexual somatic preference. *Journal of Personality and Social Psychology*, 1968, 10, 82–89.

Wiggins, N., and Wiggins, J. S. A typological analysis of male preference for female body types. *Multivariate Behavioral Research*, 1969, 5, 89–102.

Wilcoxon, L. A., Schrader, S. L., and Nelson, E. Behavioral formulations of depression. In Craighead, W. E., Kazdin, A. E., and Mahoney, M. J. (eds.), *Behavior modification:*

principles, issues, and applications. Boston: Houghton Mifflin, 1976, pp. 200–226.

Wilkinson, R. *The prevention of drinking problems: alcohol control and cultural influences*. New York: Oxford University Press, 1970.

Williams, R. J. *Alcoholism: nutritional approach*. Austin: University of Texas Press, 1959.

Williams, R. L., and Rivers, L. W. Cognitive development in black children: nonstandard English or different strokes? Unpublished manuscript, Washington University Black Studies Program, St. Louis, Missouri, 1972.

Willis, M. H., and Blaney, P. H. Three tests of the learned helplessness model of depression. *Journal of Abnormal Psychology*, 1978, 87, 131–136.

Wilsnack, S. C. Sex role identity in female alcoholism. *Journal of Abnormal Psychology*, 1973, 82, 253–261.

Wilson, E. B. *An introduction to scientific research*. New York: McGraw-Hill, 1952.

Wilson, M. S., and Meyer, E. Diagnostic consistency in a psychiatric liaison service. *American Journal of Psychiatry*, 1962, 119, 207–209.

Winick, C. Physician narcotic addicts. In Becker, H. (ed.), *The perspectives on deviance: the other side*. New York: Free Press, 1964, pp. 261–279.

Winokur, G., Clayton, P. J., and Reich, T. *Manic-depressive illness*. St. Louis: Mosby, 1969.

Wittenborn, J. R. *Wittenborn psychiatric rating scales*. Rev. ed. New York: Psychological Corporation, 1964.

Wittkower, E. D., and Dubreuil, G. Cultural factors in mental illness. In Norbeck, E., Price-Williams, D., and McCord, W. M. (eds), *The study of personality: an interdisciplinary appraisal*. New York: Holt, Rinehart and Winston, 1968, pp. 279–295.

Wittman, P., Sheldon, W. H., and Katz, C. J. A study of the relationship between constitutional variations and fundamental psychotic behavior reactions. *Journal of Nervous and Mental Diseases*, 1948, 108, 470–476.

Wolberg, L. R. *Hypnoanalysis*. New York: Grune & Stratton, 1945.

———. *The techniques of psychotherapy*. New York: Grune & Stratton, 1954.

———. *Short-term psychotherapy*. New York: Grune & Stratton, 1965.

———. *Hypnosis: is it for you?* New York: Harcourt Brace Jovanovich, 1972.

Wold, C. I. Characteristics of 26,000 Suicide Prevention Center patients. *Bulletin of Suicidology*, 1970, 6, 24–28.

Wolf, M., Risley, T., Johnston, M., Harris, F., and Allen, E. K. Application of operant conditioning procedures to the behavior problems of an autistic child: a follow-up and extension. In Guerney, B. G. (ed.), *Psychotherapeutic agents: new roles for nonprofessionals, parents, and teachers*. New York: Holt, Rinehart and Winston, 1969, 355–366.

Wolf, S. Disease as a way of life. *Perspectives in Biological*

Medicine, 1961, 4, 288–305.

———. The expectations of society. *Journal of Medical Education,* 1965, 40, 3.

———, and Glass, J. G. B. Correlation of conscious and unconscious conflicts with changes in gastric function and structure. Observations on the relations of the constituence of gastric juice to the integrity of the mucous membrane. In *Life stress and bodily disease: proceedings of the Association for Research in Nervous and Mental Diseases,* Vol. 29. Baltimore: Williams & Wilkins, 1950, pp. 665–676.

———, and Goodell, H. *Harold G. Wolff's Stress and disease.* Springfield, Ill.: Thomas, 1968.

———, and Wolff, H. G. Evidence on the genesis of peptic ulcer in man. *Journal of the American Medical Association,* 1942, 120, 670–675.

———. *Human gastric function.* New York: Oxford University Press, 1947.

Wolff, H. G. Life stress and cardiovascular disorders, *Circulation,* 1950, 1, 187–203.

Wolfgang, M. E. *Patterns in criminal homicide.* Philadelphia: University of Pennsylvania Press, 1958.

Wolman, B. B. *Children without childhood: a study of childhood schizophrenia.* New York: Grune & Stratton, 1970.

———. The rationale of child therapy. In Wolman, B. B., Egan, J., and Ross, A. O. (eds.), *Handbook of treatment of mental disorders in childhood and adolescence.* Englewood Cliffs, N.J.: Prentice-Hall, 1978(a).

———, Egan, J., and Ross, A. O. (eds.). *Handbook of treatment of mental disorders in childhood and adolescence.* Englewood Cliffs, N.J.: Prentice-Hall, 1978(b).

Wolpe, P. *Psychotherapy by reciprocal inhibition.* Stanford, Calif.: Stanford University Press, 1958.

———. The systematic desensitization treatment of neuroses. *Journal of Nervous and Mental Disease,* 1961, 112, 189–203.

———. *The practice of behavior therapy.* New York: Pergamon, 1969.

———, and Lazarus, A. A. *Behavior therapy techniques: a guide to the treatment of neuroses.* New York: Pergamon, 1966.

Woodworth, R. S. *Personal Data Sheet.* Chicago: Stoelting, 1920.

World Health Organization. The biochemistry of mental disorders. *WHO Chronicle,* 1970, 24, 6–10.

World Health Organization Expert Committee on Addiction-Producing Drugs. *World Health Organization Technical Report,* Thirteenth Report, Serial No. 273. Geneva: World Health Organization, 1964.

Wortman, C. B., and Dintzer, L. Is an attributional analysis of the learned helplessness phenomenon viable? A critique of the Abramson-Seligman-Teasdale reformulation. *Journal of Abnormal Psychology,* 1978, 87, 75–90.

Wyatt, R. J., Fram, D. H., Kupfer, D., and Snyder, F. Total prolonged drug-induced REM sleep suppression in anxious–depressed subjects. *Archives of General Psychiatry,* 1971, 24, 145–155.

———, Stern, M., Fram, D. H., Tursky, B., and Grinspoon, L. Abnormalities in skin potential fluctuations during the sleep of acute schizophrenic patients. *Psychosomatic Medicine,* 1970, 32, 301–308.

———, Termini, B. A., and Davis, J. Sleep studies: a review of the literature, 1960–1970. *Schizophrenia Bulletin,* 1971, 4, 45–66.

X, Malcolm, and Haley, A., *Autobiography of Malcolm X.* New York: Grove Press, 1965.

Yablonsky, L. *Synanon: the tunnel back.* Baltimore: Penguin Books, 1967.

Yalom, I. D. Report in *Frontiers of Psychiatry: Roche Report,* 1971, 1.

———, and Lieberman, M. A. A study of encounter group casualties. *Archives of General Psychiatry,* 1971, 25, 16–30.

Yap, P. M. *Culture-bound reactive syndromes.* Presented at the Conference on Mental Health in Asia and the Pacific, March 28–April 1, 1966, East–West Center, Honolulu, Hawaii.

Yarden, P. E., and Suranyi, I. The early development of institutionalized children of schizophrenic mothers. *Diseases of the Nervous System,* 1968, 29, 380–384.

Yates, A. J. The validity of some psychological tests of brain damage. *Psychological Bulletin,* 1954, 51, 359–379.

———. *Behavior therapy.* New York: Wiley, 1970(a).

———. Tics. In Costello, C. G. (ed.), *Symptoms of psychopathology: a handbook.* New York: Wiley, 1970(b).

———. *Theory and practice of behavior therapy.* New York: Wiley, 1975.

Young, P. T. *Motivation and emotion: a survey of the determinants of human and animal activity.* New York: Wiley, 1961.

Young, W. C., Boy, R. W., and Phoenix, C. H. Hormones and sexual behavior. *Science,* 1964, 143, 212–218.

Young, W. M., Jr. Poverty, intelligence, and life in the inner city. *Mental Retardation,* 1969, 2, 24–29.

Zahn, T. P. Psychophysiological concomitants of task performance in schizophrenia. In Keitzman, M. L., Button, S., and Zubin, J. (eds.), *Experimental approaches to psychopathology.* New York: Academic Press, 1975, pp. 109–131.

Zaslow, R., and Breger, L. A theory and treatment of autism. In Breger, L. (ed.), *Clinical-cognitive psychology: models and integrations.* Englewood Cliffs, N.J.: Prentice-Hall, 1969.

Zax, M., and Cowen, E. L. *Abnormal psychology: changing conceptions.* New York: Holt, Rinehart and Winston, 1972.

———, and Specter, G. A. *An introduction to community psychology.* New York: Wiley, 1974.

Zellweger, H., McDonald, J. W., and Abbo, G. Is LSD a

teratogen? *Lancet*, 1967, 1066–1068.

Zigler, E., and Butterfield, E. C. Motivational aspects of changes in IQ test performance of culturally deprived nursery school children. *Child Development*, 1968, 39, 1–49.

————, and Phillips, L. Psychiatric diagnosis: a critique. *Journal of Abnormal and Social Psychology*, 1961, 3, 607–618.

Zilbergeld, B. Group treatment of sexual dysfunction in men without partners. *Journal of Sex and Marital Therapy*, 1975, 1, 204–214.

Zilboorg, G., and Henry, G. W. *A history of medical psychology*. New York: Norton, 1941.

Zimbardo, P. G. *The cognitive control of motivation*. Glenview, Ill.: Scott, Foresman, 1969.

————. The human choice: individuation, reason, and order versus deindividuation, impulse and chaos. In Levine, D. (ed.), *Nebraska Symposium on Motivation, 1969*. Lincoln: University of Nebraska, 1970.

————, and Maslach, C. Internal control of complex skin temperature modification by humans. Hawthorne House Research Memorandum No. 114, Unpublished document, Stanford University, 1970.

————, and Ruch, R. L. *Psychology and life*. 9th ed. Glenview, Ill.: Scott, Foresman, 1975.

Zimmerman, E. H., and Zimmerman, J. The alteration of behavior in a special classroom situation. In Guerney, B. G. (ed.), *Psychotherapeutic agents: new roles for nonprofessionals, parents, and teachers*. New York: Holt, Rinehart

and Winston, 1969, pp. 367–370.

Zinberg, N. E. The war over marijuana. *Psychology Today*, 1976, 10, 44–52, 102–106.

————, and Kaufman, I. Cultural and personality factors associated with aging: an introduction. In Zinberg, N. E., and Kaufman, I. (eds.), *Normal psychology and the aging process*. New York: International Universities Press, 1963.

Zitrin, A., Dement, W. C., and Barchas, J. D. Brain serotonin and male sexual behavior. In Zubin, J., and Money, J. (eds.), *Contemporary sexual behavior: critical issues in the 1970's*. Baltimore: Johns Hopkins University Press, 1973, pp. 321–338.

Zubin, J. Classification of the behavior disorders. *Annual Review of Psychology*, 1967, 18, 373–406.

————, and Spring, B. Vulnerability—a new view of schizophrenia. *Journal of Abnormal Psychology*, 1977, 86, 103–126.

Zuk, G. H. Autistic distortions in parents of retarded children. *Journal of Consulting Psychology*, 1959, 23, 171–176.

Zung, W. K. Evaluating treatment methods for depressive disorders. *American Journal of Psychiatry, Supplement.* 1968, 124, 40–48.

Zussman, L., and Zussman, S. Premarital sex counseling. *Practical Psychology for Physicians*, 1976, 3.

Zwerling, I. The psychiatric day hospital. In Arieti, S. (ed.), *American handbook of psychiatry*, Vol. III. New York: Basic Books, 1966, pp. 563–576.

Name Index

Abbott, S., 348
Abraham, K., 311
Abramson, H. A., 149, 150 n., 313, 477
Ackerman, N. W., 457
Adelson, D., 554
Adler, A., 103, 138, 252, 419, 435, 481, 490–493, 514
Aguilera, D. C., 463–464, 559–560
Ahammer, I. M., 442
Ainsworth, M. D. S., 109
Albee, G. W., 6, 456, 554
Alexander, F., 149, 153, 161–162, 464
Allport, G. W., 113
Alpert, R., 210
Alstrom, C.-H., 356
Altman, D., 126
Altrocchi, J., 562
Amsel, A., 245
Anastasi, A., 42 n., 436
Anderson, F. N., 441
Ansbacher, H. L., 491–492
Aquinas, St. Thomas, 356
Ardrey, R., 388–389, 393
Argyris, C., 462
Arieti, S., 275–276, 304
Aristotle, 356, 539
Aronfreed, J., 380, 509
Arthurs, R. G. S., 376
Asclepiades, 539
Ascoush, J. C., 172
Astor, G., 359
Atkinson, J. W., 188
Atthowe, J. M., Jr., 507
Auerback, R., 212
Ausubel, D. P., 6, 206
Avis, H. H., 398
Ax, A. F., 273
Axelrod, J., 80

Ayllon, T., 252, 496, 507–508
Azrin, N. H., 57, 252, 421, 496, 507–508

Bach, G., 457, 460
Bachrach, A. J., 504
Bacon, R., 481, 541
Baer, D. M., 496
Bakan, D., 425 n.
Baldwin, J., 348
Baller, W., 423
Balthazar, E. E., 405, 410
Bandura, A., 109, 193, 234, 246 n., 252, 362, 380–381, 390, 392, 394, 497, 498 n., 509–512
Bannister, R., 88 n.
Barbach, L. G., 342–343
Barber, T. X., 170, 256
Barnes, E. J., 62
Barnett, N., 190
Barrett, C. L., 501
Bartell, G. D., 350
Barten, H. H., 463
Batchelor, I. R. C., 88 n., 185, 236, 286 n.
Bateson, G., 110–111, 120, 276–278, 391, 532
Baughman, E. E., 218, 230
Baumeister, A. A., 405, 412
Bax, M., 426
Beach, F. A., 82
Beahrs, J. O., 168 n.
Beaumont, W., 152
Beck, A. T., 29–30, 304, 306, 312, 322
Becker, H. S., 374
Becker, J., 312, 314, 317–318
Becker, W. C., 111, 379
Bednar, R. L., 468
Beers, C. W., 546, 570

Beerstecher, E., Jr., 186
Bekhterev, V. M., 105
Belknap, J. K., 473
Bellak, L., 464, 558 n.
Bem, S. L., 18–19, 127
Bender, L., 63, 65, 212, 296, 298, 378
Benson, H., 170
Berg, I. A., 48
Bergin, A. E., 461, 466, 467 n., 468
Berkowitz, W., 127, 390, 392–394
Bernal, M. E., 441, 458, 496
Bettelheim, B., 141
Bigelow, G., 412
Bijou, S. W., 55, 56, 496
Billingslea, F. Y., 63
Bindra, D., 144 n.
Binet, A., 59
Bird, C., 48
Birley, J. L. T., 270
Bischof, L. J., 246 n., 485
Bjerg, K., 322
Blachly, P. H., 202
Blake, R. R., 462
Blanchard, E. B., 522
Blaney, P. H., 312–313
Bleuler, E., 268, 275
Bleuler, M., 185
Bloch, H. S., 459
Block, J., 48
Block, J. D., 243
Bloom, B. L., 562
Blum, G. S., 101
Blum, R. H., 202, 218, 221
Bockoven, J. S., 545 n.
Boe, E. E., 468
Boelkins, R. C., 395
Bonine, W., 305
Bootzin, R. R., 193, 512
Borkovec, T. D., 56

Bower, E. M., 299
Bowlby, J., 378
Braceland, F. J., 320, 471
Brady, J. V., 154–155
Braginsky, B., 401, 548
Braginsky, D., 401, 548
Brammer, L. M., 463
Bramwell, S. T., 165
Brecher, E. M., 215
Brecher, R., 329
Bremer, A. H., 264
Brenner, J. H., 202, 212
Brill, A. A., 100
Brill, H., 4
Broca, Pierre Paul, 95
Brody, N., 467 n., 468
Broen, W. E. J., 280 n.
Bronfenbrenner, U., 119
Bronson, F. H., 124
Brooks, C. M., 157
Broverman, I. K., 18
Brown, B., 570
Brown, B. S., 549, 566
Brown, E. L., 537
Brown, F. W., 241–242
Brown, J. L., 296
Brown, N. O., 328
Bruch, H., 420
Bruner, J. S., 13
Bryan, J. H., 354, 512
Bucher, B., 412
Buchsbaum, M., 316
Buchwald, A. M., 313
Budzynski, T., 172, 520–522
Bunker, D. R., 462
Burchard, J. D., 383, 507
Burchinal, L. H., 420
Buros, O. K., 43, 436
Burt, C., 61
Buss, A. H., 17, 22, 30, 246 n., 282, 372, 380, 392
Busse, E. W., 445
Byrd, R. D., 462

Cabeen, C. W., 468
Cahalan, D., 179, 186, 188
Cain, N. N., 473
Cain, R. M., 473
Cairns, R. B., 109
Calderone, M. S., 329
Caldwell, W. F., 477
Calhoun, J. B., 124–125
Calhoun, J. F., 479
Calley, W., 391

Cameron, N., 138, 140, 289, 359, 382
Campbell, A. M. G., 215
Campbell, D. T., 34 n., 275 n.
Cannon, W. B., 83, 152
Canter, S., 76
Cantor, D. J., 348
Caplan, G., 558
Cardan, 541
Carlson, N. R., 80
Carson, R. C., 31, 110
Carter, C. O., 71 n.
Carter, J. E., 214
Carter, J. W., Jr., 554
Casey, J. F., 188
Casler, L., 119
Castaneda, C., 12
Cattell, R. B., 76
Cautela, J., 502, 514
Caveny, E. L., 31
Cerletti, U., 471
Chafetz, M. E., 179, 186, 190 n.
Chance, E., 29
Chapman, A. H., 172
Chapman, J. P., 280
Chapman, L. F., 87, 168
Chapman, L. J., 279
Christensen, D. E., 58
Christmas, J. J., 460
Chrysostom, 356
Churchill, W., 351
Ciminero, A. R., 55, 57
Clarizio, H. F., 404, 412
Clark, G. R., 72–73
Clark, K. B., 128–129, 323
Clarke, Alan, 61
Clarke, Ann, 61
Clausen, J. A., 282–284
Clayton, P. J., 309–310
Cleary, T. A., 62
Cleckley, H., 366–368, 371–373, 377–378
Clements, S. D., 427
Close, H. T., 532
Cobbs, P. M., 18, 53, 128, 290
Coffey, H. S., 459
Cohen, B. D., 279
Cohen, H. L., 383
Cohen, J., 108
Cohen, M. B., 314
Cohen, M. M., 212
Cohen, S., 206, 211
Colbert, E. G., 301
Colby, K. M., 289–290, 298
Cole, J. O., 473–474, 476

Coles, R., 53
Comfort, A., 359
Conger, J. J., 104, 109, 112, 116 n., 188, 417, 435–436
Conners, C. K., 398
Connery, R., 568
Conrad, R. W., 405
Constantine, L. L., 355
Conway, J., 61
Cook, P. E., 554
Cooper, A. J., 500
Cooper, C. C., 567
Copernicus, 481
Costello, C. G., 313
Costello, T. W., 568
Cowen, E. L., 554
Craft, M. J., 372
Craighead, W. E., 513
Craik, K., 567
Craike, W. H., 288
Crane, G. E., 398
Crichton, R., 371
Cronbach, L. J., 42 n., 48, 76 n., 436
Cropley, A. J., 322
Cruickshank, W. M., 430
Cumming, E., 444
Custance, J., 308

Dahl, H., 494
Dahlstrom, W. G., 46, 377
Daily, C. A., 41
Dally, P., 473, 477
Dalton, K., 397
Darley, J. M., 394
Darling, H. F., 382
Davenport, W., 353
Davids, A., 117, 447
Davidson, W. S. II, 397
da Vinci, L., 541
Davis, A. J., 349
Davis, J. M., 320, 474–476
Davis, K., 378
Davis, W. L., 110
Davison, G. C., 104, 292, 515
D'Elia, G., 321
DeMoor, W., 56, 501
Dekker, E., 150
Demara, F., 371
Dember, W., 188
Denner, B., 554
Descartes, R., 541
DesLauriers, A. M., 294–295
Deutsch, A., 537, 542, 544–545, 546
Deutsch, F., 149

Deutsch, J. A., 145 n.
Dimsdale, J. E., 141
Dishotsky, N. I., 212–213
Dix, D., 545, 553, 570
Dobzhansky, T., 61, 71 n.
Dohrenwend, B. P., 119, 122, 127, 249, 251, 283, 315
Dohrenwend, B. S., 119, 122, 127, 165, 249, 251, 283, 315
Dole, V. P., 224
Dollard, J., 110, 170 n., 289, 392, 496, 509
Donaldson, K., 548–549
Doniger, J., 552
Down, J. L. H., 405
Dragstedt, L. R., 153 n., 156
Dreikurs, R., 419–420, 458–459
Drew, G. C., 178
Dumont, M. P., 456
Durant, W., 353

Eaton, J. W., 250–251, 315
Edgerton, R. B., 413
Edson, L., 60
Edwards, A. L., 48
Eells, K., 219
Efron, V., 180
Egan, D. E., 314
Egan, M. H., 552
Ehrenwald, J., 242–243, 249
Ehrhardt, A. A., 397
Ehrlich, S. K., 376
Eichmann, A., 391
Einstein, A., 388
Eisenberg, L., 296, 301, 409
Ellis, A., 497, 512–513
Epstein, L. H., 58
Erickson, M. H., 278
Eriksen, C. W., 138
Erikson, E. H., 103, 252, 485–487, 490
Ernst, F., 57
Eron, L. D., 25 n., 387–389, 393, 397–398
Escher, M. C., 50
Evans, I., 497 n.
Eysenck, H. J., 31, 242–243, 246 n., 252, 304, 465–467, 468 n., 496, 497 n.

Fairweather, G. W., 468, 551, 553, 557
Fallding, H., 175
Fanon, F., 18, 53, 104, 128, 233 n.
Farber, I. E., 513, 550
Farberow, N. L., 560
Faris, R. E. L., 121, 282
Fazio, A. F., 501

Feingold, B., 427–428
Feldman, M. P., 501
Ferenczi, S., 100, 463
Ferracuti, F., 355, 356
Ferster, C. B., 55, 252, 297, 311, 496
Feshbach, S., 395
Fiedler, F. E., 468
Fine, F. B., 483
Fish, B., 273
Fiske, D. W., 41
Fixsen, D. L., 58, 383
Fleener, D. E., 109
Flowers, J. V., 58
Flynn, J. P., 395
Fontana, A. F., 457
Foreyt, J. P., 503
Fort, J., 200, 202
Fortune, R., 356
Foulds, G. A., 372
Foxx, R. M., 421
Frank, J. D., 455, 465
Frank, L. K., 49
Franklin, B., 57, 334, 544
Franklin, J. H., 53
Franks, C., 193, 194, 496, 497 n.
Freedman, A. M., 485
Freedman, D. G., 477, 509
Freedman, D. X., 473–474, 476–477, 506
Freedman, M., 348
Freeman, E. H., 150 n.
Freeman, R. D., 430
Fremming, K. H., 241
Freud, A., 378, 439
Freud, S., 48–49, 99–104, 110, 130–131, 137–138, 139, 218, 236, 252, 276, 289, 304, 311, 328, 346, 388, 439, 456, 481–484, 485, 488–490, 493, 530
Friedman, M., 163–165
Friedman, P. H., 499
Friend, D. G., 476
Fromm, E., 103, 252, 358, 386, 390, 493–494

Gage, Phineas, 90
Gagnon, J. H., 335
Galen, 539
Galileo, G., 13, 14, 541
Gallagher, C. E., 65
Galle, O. R., 127
Gantt, W. H., 245
Ganzler, S., 322
Gardner, L. I., 113–114
Gardner, W. I., 461, 466, 467 n., 512

Garfield, S. L., 513
Garmezy, N., 113, 274, 280–281
Gauron, E., 29
Gazzaniga, M. S., 95
Geer, J. H., 136, 512
Gelber, H., 424
Gellhorn, E., 152, 156
Genet, J., 348
Genovese, K., 394
Gerard, D. L., 284
Gershon, S., 320
Gibb, J. R., 462
Gillie, O., 61
Gillin, J. C., 318
Gillman, R. D., 464
Gilmer, B. v. H., 77–79
Gladfelter, W. E., 157
Glass, D. C., 162
Gliedman, L. H., 465
Goddard, H. H., 62–63
Goertzel, V., 553
Goffman, E., 27–28, 33, 549, 556
Goldenberg, H., 168, 186
Goldfried, M. R., 55, 56
Goldiamond, I., 383, 496
Goldstein, J. H., 395
Goldstein, J. W., 202, 206, 218–221
Goldstein, K., 64
Goldstein, M. L., 144 n.
Goodall, K., 496
Goodenough, E. R., 175–176
Goodwin, D. W., 186
Gorelick, M. C., 405
Gottesman, I. I., 9, 270, 272, 274, 317
Gottlieb, J. S., 376
Gottman, J. M., 55, 502–503
Gottschalk, L. A., 463–464
Gouster, M., 366
Grace, W., 166–169
Graham, D. T., 167–169
Graham, S., 334–335
Granville-Grossman, K. L., 314
Green, E., 382
Greenacre, P., 378
Greenblatt, M., 479
Greeno, J. G., 314
Gregory I, Pope, 356
Grier, W. H., 18, 53, 128, 290
Grim, P., 519–520
Grinker, R. R., Sr., 303–304
Grinspoon, L., 215
Grossman, S., 145 n.
Grosvenor, D. K., 12
Guerney, B. G., 563
Guetzkow, H. S., 84

Maurer, D. W., 201
May, R., 120, 526–527
Mead, M., 356
Mechanic, D., 282
Mednick, S. A., 273
Meduna, L. J., 470
Meehl, P. E., 31–32, 33, 265, 270, 272
Meichenbaum, D. H., 109, 497, 500, 513–514
Mello, N. K., 189
Meltzer, H., 275
Meltzoff, J., 467–468
Mendel, Gregor, 70–71
Mendels, J., 302–304, 314–315, 324
Mendelson, J., 185, 215
Menninger, K. A., 25 n., 37, 453
Mercer, M., 184
Mesmer, F. A., 517–518
Meyer, A., 366, 546
Meyer, V., 497 n., 501
Meyer, W. J., 442, 445
Meyerowitz, J. H., 410
Mezey, E., 176
Miklich, D. R., 58
Mikulas, W. L., 501, 507
Milgram, S., 8, 126, 390–391
Miller, G. A., 279
Miller, L. C., 440–441, 520
Miller, N. E., 110, 140, 170, 172, 289, 392, 496, 509, 518
Miller, W. R., 313
Mindham, R. H. S., 476
Mintz, E., 460, 462
Mirsky, I. A., 156
Mittler, P., 76–77
Moll, A. E., 557
Monge, R. H., 442
Montagu, A., 389–390
Mora, G., 537, 539, 541–542, 544
Moreno, J. L., 535–536
Morgan, C. T., 145 n.
Morishima, A., 215
Morley, W. E., 559
Morris, D., 388–389
Mosher, D. L., 63
Mosher, L. R., 274
Mourer, S. A., 279
Mouton, J. S., 462
Mowrer, O. H., 136, 246–247, 423, 496
Moyer, K. E., 376, 395, 398
Mulford, H. A., 180
Mulvihill, D. J., 387
Murphy, J., 348
Murray, H. A., 49 n., 50

Mussen, P. H., 104, 109, 112, 116 n., 417, 435–436
Myers, R. D., 188
Myerson, A., 121, 284

Nachmani, G., 279
Nagler, S. H., 493
Nameche, G., 253, 285
Nathan, P. E., 189, 471
Neale, D. H., 424
Neale, J. M., 136
Nebuchadnezzar, King, 537
Neill, A. S., 336
Nelson, P. C., 137
Netter, F. H., 92, 95, 146
Neubauer, P. B., 299
Neugarten, B. L., 444
Nielson, J., 72
Nikolaeva, V. V., 154
Nisbett, R. E., 157–159, 420
Nissenbaum, S., 334
Nixon, R. M., 214
Norbeck, E., 250
Nowlis, D. P., 172
Nowlis, H. H., 217
Nunnally, J. C., 42 n., 76 n.

Ogle, D. K., 217
O'Leary, K. D., 193, 424, 500–501, 508, 566
O'Leary, M. R., 313
Oltman, J., 378
O'Neal, P., 379
O'Neill, P., 567
Opler, M. K., 123, 250, 284
Orne, M. T., 170, 275 n.
Ornitz, E. M., 295
Osgood, C. E., 240
Oswald, I., 362

Padilla, A. M., 569
Page, J. D., 128, 318
Paracelsus, 541
Parad, H. J., 558
Parsons, A., 291
Parsons, T., 356
Partridge, G. E., 366, 378
Pasamanick, B., 557
Patterson, C. H., 382
Patterson, G. R., 425, 457, 496, 566
Patton, R. G., 113–114
Paul, G., 500, 515
Pavlov, I. P., 54, 99, 104–105, 152, 288, 496
Paykel, E. S., 476

Pearlman, S., 218
Pearson, G. H. J., 422
Peck, H. B., 460
Penrose, L. S., 70, 71 n., 405
Perls, F. S., 248, 527, 530–531, 535
Perris, C., 303, 310, 321
Persons, R. W., 382, 468
Pervin, L. A., 136
Peterson, D. R., 55, 56, 424
Petrie, A., 428
Pettigrew, T. F., 290, 323
Phares, E. J., 56–57, 110, 137
Phillips, J. F., 193, 362, 496–497, 503, 512, 516
Philipp, R. J., 151
Phillips, L., 268, 285
Pichot, P., 322
Pincus, J. H., 87, 96–97, 317–319, 446
Pinel, P., 366, 544–545, 553, 570
Pinneo, L., 89
Pitts, F. N., 244
Plaut, T. F. A., 180
Plog, S. C., 250
Pokorny, A. D., 321
Pollack, M., 300
Pollitt, J. D., 315
Postman, L., 13
Prescott, J. W., 396, 429, 431
Prestia, C. J., 561
Price, K. P., 311
Prichard, J. C., 366
Prien, R. F., 473
Prince, M., 239
Proshansky, H., 446
Provence, S., 116
Pumpian-Mindlin, E., 464
Purcell, K., 151
Puthoff, H. E., 14–15

Quaade, F., 420
Quarti, C., 424

Rachman, S., 360, 496, 497 n., 501
Rado, S., 311
Rahe, R. H., 165
Rank, O., 103
Rapoport, R., 558, 563
Raush, H. L., 552
Ray, O. S., 217 n., 473–475, 477
Razran, G., 172
Redlich, F. C., 121, 251, 278, 283, 308, 456
Redmond, D. E., Jr., 317
Rees, L., 151

Subject Index

AA. *See* Alcoholics Anonymous
Abnormality, cultural relativity and, 12
  cultural and social criteria of, 17–19
  culture-bound, 129–130
  definition of, 3, 11–24
  legal criteria of, 20
  relativity of perception and, 12
  statistical criteria of, 16–17
Abnormal psychology, definition of, 2
  other disciplines and, 7–10
Abreaction, 518
Abscess, brain damage and, 92
Acetylcholine, 80
Acquiescence, in testing, 48
Acrophobia, 233
Action-specific energy, 389
Activity groups, 459
Adaptation energy, 171
Adaptive delinquency, 374
Addiction, 197
Adlerian therapy, 458–459, 491–493
Adolescent disorders, 431–434. *See also*
  Developmental disorders
Adoptive Behavior Scale, 400–401
Adrenal gland, 83
Affective disorders, 302–327
  biological origins of, 315–318
  causes of, 311–318
  family factors model of, 314
  social and cultural influences on, 314–315
  suicide and, 320–327
  treatment of, 318–320
Age, behavior pathology and, 127–128
Aged, environment and treatment for the, 446–447. *See also* Aging
Aggression, 386–399
  anonymity and, 393

in antisocial personality, 369
benign vs. malignant, 386–387
in children, 424–425
control of, 397–398
depression and, 305
displacement and, 140
neurological model of, 395–396
obedience and, 390–391
unsocialized, 374
Aggression hypothesis, XYY syndrome and, 73
Aging, attitudes toward, 442–443
  brain damage and, 88
  problems of, 442–447
Agoraphobia, 233
Alcohol, accidents and, 178
  barbiturates and, 209
  bodily functions and, 178
  impotence and, 330
  intoxicating effect of, 176–178
  nutrition and, 176
  patterns of use of, 175
  socially approved uses of, 175–176
Alcoholics Anonymous, 192, 193, 458
Alcoholism, 175–195. *See also* Alcohol; Drinking
  attitudes of hospital personnel towards, 190
  biological causes of, 185–186
  incidence in hospitals of, 260–261
  learning models and, 188–189
  long-term effects of, 182–185
  need for power and, 188
  prealcoholic personality and, 187–188
  prevalence of, 179–182
  psychological models of, 186–189
  sociocultural models of, 189–190
  stress and, 188

subcultural differences in rate of, 123
suicide and, 185
treatment of, 190–194, 501, 503
types of, 179
Alienation, 11–12, 525
Allergenic model, of hyperactivity, 427–428
Alzheimer's disease, 88, 445
Ambisexuals, 349
Amenorrhea, 160
Amnesia, 238–239
Amniocentesis, 409
Amok, 130
Amotivational syndrome, marijuana and the, 214–215
Amphetamines, 198, 206–208
Amygdala, 395, 398
Anaclitic depression, 314
Anal character, 102
Anal stage, 102
Analytical psychology, 488–490
Androgyny, 18–19
Anogenital coitus, 346–347
Anorexia nervosa, 420, 504–507
Anoxia, 86
Antabuse, 194
Anthropology, psychology and, 8
  sexual norms studied in, 344
Antianxiety drugs, 473
Antidepressant drugs, 319, 475–476
Antihistamines, 199
Antimanic drugs, 476–477
Antisocial personality, 365–385
  causes of, 373–382
  description of, 365–373
  fugue state and, 237–238
  irresponsibility of, 371
  parental influences on, 378–380

Pathology. *See* Psychopathology
Pathology of the ghetto, 128
Patient, in psychotherapy, 455–456
PCP. *See* Phencyclidine
Pedigree studies, in genetics, 71–73
  on neuroses, 242
Pedophilia, 357
Peer Help Centers, 561–562
Pep pills, 206
Peptic ulcers, 153–157
Percodan, 198
Performance fears, sex therapy directed toward, 339
Persona, 488
Personal distress, 19
Personality, stress and, 163–165
Personality disorders, incidence in
  hospitals of, 260–261
  among the retarded, 405
Personality testing, 42–54
  projective techniques for, 49–54
  self report inventories in, 42–48
Personality types, in Freudian theory,
  102–103
Petit mal epilepsy, 96
Phallic character, 102
Phallic stage, 102
Pharmacotherapy. *See* Drug therapy
Phencyclidine, 209–210, 322
Phenobarbital, 199, 208
Phenomenology, 525
Phenothiazine, 474
Phenotype, 71 n.
Phenylketonuria, 400, 406, 409
Phobia, conditioned in "Little Albert",
  106
  displacement and, 140
  dog, 510
  insect, 501
  school, 431–432
  snake, 499–500
Phobic disorders, 233–234
Phoenix House, 223
Physical disorders, psychological factors in, 143–174
Pick's disease, 88, 445
Pituitary gland, 81–82
Placebo, 26
Placebo effect, in psychotherapy, 465
Plateau stage, of sexual response, 328
Play therapy, 439–440, 534–535
Pleasure principle, 481
Pneumococci, 92
Poisoning, brain damage and, 88–91

Polygenic inheritance, 71
Poverty, as cause of mental retardation, 408
Power needs, alcoholism and, 188
Prealcoholic personality, 187–188
Prefrontal lobotomy, 478–479
Premature birth, as cause of retardation, 407, 409
Premature ejaculation, 332–333
  impotence and, 330
  treatment of, 340–341, 500
Preorgasmic women, group treatment
  of, 342–343
Presenile dementia, 445–446
Presenile psychoses, 88
Primal therapy, 533–534
Primary process thinking, 99–101, 277
Problem behaviors, assessment of,
  55–57
Process schizophrenia, 268–269
Prognosis, psychodiagnosis and, 27
Progressive muscular relaxation, 499
Projection, 49, 140, 266, 289
Projective techniques, 49–54
  critical comment on, 53–54
Prosocial behavior, 383
Prostitution, 353–354
Protein deficiencies, retardation
  caused by, 406
Pseudocyesis, 160
Psilocybin, 199
Psychiatric Home Treatment Service,
  552
Psychiatrists, 10, 454–455
Psychoanalysis, 13, 457, 467, 481–485,
  525
  anxiety treated by, 142
  children in, 438–439
  goals of, 454
  neurosis and, 245–246
  as a science, 494
Psychoanalytic hypothesis, 160–162
Psychodiagnosis, 34–67. *See also* Classification; Diagnosis
  behavioral assessment in, 54–58
  brain damage testing in, 63–66
  intelligence testing in, 58–63
  interview in, 35–41
  observation in, 34–35
  psychological testing in, 41–66
Psychodrama, 452, 535
Psychodynamic therapy, 285, 481–495
  critical comment on, 493–494
Psychological health, 21–22

Psychological testing, 21, 41–66
  blacks and, 18
  definition of, 41
  effect of instructions in, 48
  ethical problems with, 64–66
  faking in, 47–48
  as an invasion of privacy, 64–65
  response styles in, 48
  self-knowledge in, 48
Psychologists, clinical, 10, 455
Psychology, abnormal and other
    branches of, 8
  analytical, 488–490
  cognitive, 513
  cultural anthropology and, 8
  environmental, 567
  existential, 120
  humanistic, 22, 527
  individual, 490–493
  models in, 13
  as a science of experience, 6, 525
Psychopath. *See* Antisocial personality
Psychopathology. *See also* Behavior
    pathology, Mental illness
  aggression as, 387
  aging and, 445–446
  classification and, 25–33
  definition of, 3
Psychophysiological disorders,
    143–174
  autonomic nervous system and,
    145–148
  backache as a, 152
  causative considerations on,
    160–171
  conditioning experiments on, 170
  conditioning to treat, 172–173
  gastrointestinal, 152–159
  genitourinary, 159–160
  hypnosis experiments on, 166–169
  menstrual, 160
  obesity and, 157–159
  psychoanalysis and, 160–162
  psychoses vs., 255
  respiratory, 149–152
  of the skin, 148–149
  stress and, 162–166
  treatment of, 171–173
Psychoses, categories of, 254–255
  delinquency as a symptom of,
    374–376
  incidence in hospitals of, 260–261
  incidence of, 259–262
  Korsakov's, 183–185